THE HISTORY OF
WISCONSIN

THE HISTORY OF
WISCONSIN

VOLUME IV
The Progressive Era, 1893–1914

JOHN D. BUENKER

WILLIAM FLETCHER THOMPSON
General Editor

1998
STATE HISTORICAL SOCIETY OF WISCONSIN
MADISON

Copyright © 1998 by
THE STATE HISTORICAL SOCIETY OF WISCONSIN

All rights reserved. Permission to quote or reprint passages from this volume may be obtained by writing the publisher at 816 State Street, Madison, Wisconsin 53706.

Manufactured in the United States of America by
Worzalla Publishing Company, Stevens Point, Wisconsin

Library of Congress Cataloging-in-Publication Data
(Revised for Volume VI of The History of Wisconsin)
THE HISTORY OF WISCONSIN
Includes bibliography and index.
CONTENTS: v. 1. From exploration to statehood, by Alice E. Smith. v. 2. The Civil War era, 1848–1873, by Richard N. Current. v. 3. Urbanization and industrialization, 1873–1893, by Robert C. Nesbit.
v. 4. The Progressive era, 1893–1914, by John D. Buenker.
v. 5. War, a new era, and depression, 1914–1940, by Paul W. Glad. v. 6. Continuity and change, 1940–1965, by William F. Thompson.
1. Wisconsin—History.

ISBN 0-87020-303-7

F581.H68   977.5   72-12941

PREFACE

THE YEARS 1893 through 1914 were the most momentous in Wisconsin history, so alive with the promise of constructive change that they are known to history as "the Progressive Era."

In less than a quarter-century, the Badger State reconfigured its socio-economic and demographic structure and reconstituted its polity in fundamental and permanent ways. An "industrial revolution in dairying" transformed Wisconsin's agricultural sector into America's Dairyland, enmeshing the state's farmers in a web of developing national commercial and financial systems. The sudden collapse of lumbering and grain milling forced the northwestern three-quarters of the state to reinvent its economic order. The cut-and-run strategy of the lumber barons devastated Wisconsin's majestic white pine forests, leaving behind the Cutover region, a quasi-frontier that emerged at the precise moment when Wisconsin's historian Frederick Jackson Turner was positing the disappearance of the American frontier. A passionate debate over future use of the Cutover ("Farms or forests?") permeated the state's public discourse for several decades thereafter.

The southeastern quadrant of the state likewise transformed its industrial base, shifting from one that utilized wind, water, wood, coal, iron, and steam to one that exploited structural steel, vulcanized rubber, reinforced concrete, electricity, and the internal combustion engine. Its economy inexorably emerged as an integral component of the Great Lakes manufacturing belt, characterized by the mass production of durable goods for a national market.

This economic metamorphosis greatly accelerated the development of Wisconsin's cities and contributed mightily to the emergence of a new urban form: the industrial city with a "radial center." From 1880 to 1910, the state's urban population increased four times faster than its rural population. As the primary locus of the New Industrialism, Wisconsin's cities formed a symbiotic relationship with their hinterlands, processing their raw materials, eating their foodstuffs, selling them manufactured products, and providing them with many of the amenities of modern life. The explosion of urban populations generated acute housing shortages, crises in public health and education, and alarming increases in crime and vice. Such conditions virtually mandated a massive augmentation in the volume, scope, and variety of municipal services, caused intense political conflict over their generation, financing, and distribution, and inaugurated a panoply of municipal reforms.

As Wisconsinites become more urbanized, they also become more Americanized, at least in terms of birth. Between 1890 and 1920, the percentage of American-born persons jumped from 70 to 83 per cent and that of Wisconsin-born persons from 57 to 71 per cent. Even so, the children of immigrant parents remained the largest single component of Wisconsin's population, and ethno-cultural clashes continued to divide the American-born and Wisconsin-born, every bit as much as they did the foreign-born. The acculturation and assimilation of the majority population contrasted sharply with the seemingly exotic character of its small numbers of American Indians and African Americans, and of its teeming multitudes of southern and eastern European immigrants. Most immigrants worked as semi-skilled or unskilled laborers and crowded into working-class neighborhoods abutting the factory districts of industrial cities. There they were disproportionately represented among the victims of industrial accidents and unemployment, low wages and long hours; they were also the occupants of substandard housing, the casualties of epidemics, and the host for a variety of social ills. They simultaneously augmented the forces opposed to enforced acculturation and alarmed those who regarded nativism, sumptuary laws, and various forms of discrimination as the proper response to bewildering change.

Within an amazingly short time, a technological, socio-economic, and demographic metamorphosis radically transformed the nature of work, the work force, and the workplace. The multitudes employed in the burgeoning manufacturing and service sectors soon surpassed the numbers toiling in agriculture, lumbering, and mining. The heavily capitalized, highly bureaucratized corporation, with its thousands of stockholders and employees and millions of dollars in product value, supplanted the family farm, the crossroads cheese factory or creamery, the grain or lumber mill, and the mechanical shop as Wisconsin's dominant economic unit. Within its confines, high-speed precision machinery, powered by electricity and internal combustion, displaced tens of thousands of skilled craftsmen and artisans. Machines exponentially expanded the market for laborers with no industrial experience or expertise, opening the doors for throngs of women, southern and eastern European immigrants, and young people from farms and small towns. Mass production and the assembly line "de-skilled" and fragmented industrial work, revolutionizing the structure and operation of factory and mill. Consciously or unconsciously employing the machinery of the New Industrialism as metaphor and model, businessmen, engineers, technicians, and social scientists developed systems of "scientific management" to ensure maximum efficiency, productivity, and control of the work force.

At the same time, the advent of electrical transmission, the automobile, electric trolley, telephone, mass-circulation newspapers and magazines, and motion pictures facilitated the assimilation and aggregation of great numbers of people, while drastically compressing time and space. The same logic that enrolled workers in functional, hierarchical systems for the mass production of goods and services mandated the systematic mobilization of a great percentage of the population as consumers. The benefits of mass production and mass consumption trickled down from the most advantaged to the least—not always equitably—along fault lines of wealth, income, occupation, education, race, ethnicity, gender, age, and geographical location, in a manner that reinforced, widened, and deepened existing social divisions—and created new ones.

Many Wisconsinites sought to rationalize these social fissures by invoking such doctrines as rugged individualism, natural law, laissez-faire, and Social Darwinism. Others regarded these dislocations and social divisions as destructive of traditional communities and institutions, and as contrary to the American ideals of equal opportunity and natural rights. They subjected the newly emerging order to intense criticism on moral, humanistic, and scientific grounds. A rising new class of "professionals" organized themselves, by occupation, to establish standards, to certify and discipline practitioners, to prescribe societal goals, structures, and behavior. Popularized through advertising and mass communication, the gospels of consumerism and systematization permeated nearly every aspect of Wisconsin life and helped to forge the most pervasive notion of the day: *that technological innovation, combined with the systematic application of expertise, must ultimately produce "progress."*

Impressed with the necessity of collaborative effort in the face of perplexing change, convinced of the benefits of systematic thought and action, and challenged by growing corporate power, tens of thousands of Wisconsinites recognized their need to organize or perish. The decade of the 1890's was characterized by the proliferation of trade associations, labor unions, producer and consumer co-operatives, municipal reform leagues, women's organizations, fraternal and benevolent societies, and professional associations. These and other organizations intervened purposefully in the private sector through collective bargaining, educational campaigns, moral suasion, co-operative activity, and economic pressure. They also began to do battle in the political arena for candidates and issues that might further their causes and promote "progress."

Unprecedented in intensity, scope, and volume, this organized demand for effective and continuous intervention coincided with the search by numerous intellectuals, professionals, and politicians for a middle way between state socialism and laissez-faire liberalism. Like their counterparts in western Europe and elsewhere in the United States, Wisconsin's "progressives" sought to fashion a system that would ensure every citizen's economic security and enhance every citizen's quality of life without destroying the fundamentals of democracy and capitalism.

In Wisconsin, that impetus was provided largely by four distinct, yet interactive, groups. The first was a remarkable collection of university professors and administrators, headed by Charles R. Van Hise, Richard T. Ely, and John R. Commons, who sought to harvest the fruits of higher learning for the benefit of the general public and the officers of state government. The second was a coterie of dedicated and innovative civil servants, headed by Charles McCarthy of the Legislative Reference Library, who viewed the state as a kind of efficiency expert that would allow individuals to develop to full capacity while protecting them from "the corrupting force and might of concentrated wealth." The third consisted of the advocates of a "co-operative commonwealth," chiefly the Social Democratic party and the Wisconsin Society of Equity. The fourth was a group of progressive Republican politicians, headed by Robert M. La Follette and Francis E. McGovern, who commingled personal and partisan ambitions with the concept of an activist state government, under the leadership of a charismatic governor directing an expanded and energetic executive branch that provided a wide range of social services.

Collectively and interactively, these four groups articulated and generated as public policy the most comprehensive, coherent, and celebrated version of the "middle way" ever realized in a single American state: what came to be known as "The Wisconsin Idea."

Its premise was a "commonwealth" conception of society in which there was a definable "public interest" that transcended particularistic concerns and that could best be achieved by enlightened cooperation among state government, the state university, and the private sector. Together, the government and the university were to provide the required social investment for a variety of endeavors whose immediate beneficiaries were private citizens or organizations, but which would ultimately redound to the general welfare. Increasingly, the day-to-day operations of state government became vested in appointive, apolitical, administrative commissions which applied general mandates laid down by popularly elected legislators who were in turn responsible to the educated, involved electorate posited by the Wisconsin Idea.

The various elements of the Wisconsin Idea began to cohere during the gubernatorial administrations of Robert M. La Follette (1901–1906). Elected as a "harmony" candidate in 1900, La Follette quickly achieved national recognition as a vigorous champion of the public weal against "the interests" and as a catalyst for university-government interaction. His widely publicized campaigns for equitable taxation, civil service, railroad regulation, and direct primary elections rapidly established him as a stellar light in the galaxy of national "progressivism." Beginning his long term in the United

States Senate in 1906, La Follette emerged as the leader of a feisty collection of "insurgents" pressing for Wisconsin-style measures on the national stage. He founded the National Progressive Republic League in 1911 and made his first run for president as a "progressive" in 1912. In all of these activities, and in his autobiography, La Follette never missed an opportunity to praise the achievements of his native state while continuing to exert his considerable influence for "progressive" candidates and issues back home.

Meanwhile, the Wisconsin Idea and the state's national reputation emerged more fully during the administration of La Follette's successors, James O. Davidson and Francis E. McGovern. The 1911 session of the legislature, pushed by McGovern and advised by Van Hise, Commons, and McCarthy, established a record for the enactment of substantive, forward-looking legislation rarely equaled, in or out of Wisconsin.

The Legislative Reference Library gave rise to a number of imitators in other states, trained dozens of researchers to staff them, and became a mecca for scholars and officeholders studying effective legislation. In 1912 both Theodore Roosevelt and Woodrow Wilson consulted Charles McCarthy, who also advised a number of progressive governors, helped draft the platform of the Progressive party, and in 1914 was appointed research director of the U.S. Commission on Industrial Relations.

John R. Commons, founder of the American Association for Labor Legislation and member of the Commission on Industrial Relations, helped draft labor legislation in several states, wrote and edited a cornucopia of influential books and articles, and trained countless economists for careers in academe and public service.

Charles R. Van Hise emerged as the most celebrated president of the country's most renowned public university, one that achieved national celebrity as "the university that runs a state." He, too, served on national commissions and published widely hailed books on business regulation and the conservation of national resources. Like the Legislative Reference Library, the University of Wisconsin's Extension Division became a national model.

Articles on Wisconsin's achievements in various endeavors became a staple of newspapers and periodicals nationwide, while the fateful year of 1912 witnessed the near-simultaneous publication of La Follette's *Autobiography*, McCarthy's *Wisconsin Idea*, and Frederic Howe's *Wisconsin: An Experiment in Democracy*. At the zenith of the nationwide Progressive Era, few critics disputed Wisconsin's reputation as the nation's most progressive state and the "laboratory of democracy."

Yet much of what the Progressives achieved proved to be fragile and evanescent. What had taken them nearly twenty years to construct took their rivals but two years to dismantle. Internal contradictions within the Wisconsin Idea, combined with personal and political rivalries among and between progressive Republicans and Social

Democrats, shattered the reformist coalition of the La Follette-McGovern years. The "Stalwarts" (meaning conservatives) rebounded and regained control of the Republican party. Led by Milwaukee businessman Emanuel Philipp, they stigmatized all three pillars of the Wisconsin Idea: the "progressive bill factory," the University of Wisconsin, and the expert administrative commission. In the arena of politics, they excoriated the "progressives" for their supposed radicalism, fiscal extravagance, and undemocratic elitism. Philipp's election as governor in 1914 officially marked the end of the Progressive Era.

Still, much of the Wisconsin Idea and many of its accomplishments survived for decades to come. Indeed, in Wisconsin, "progressivism" became a watchword, a touchstone, a totem of almost mythic power. Some would say progressivism lingers still—though where, how, and in what guise is a matter for pundits and scholars to debate. The ultimate test of its historical importance was best enunciated by Bob La Follette in 1912:

> If it can be shown that Wisconsin is a happier state to live in, that its institutions are more democratic, that the opportunities of all of its people are more equal, that social justice more nearly prevails, that human life is safer and sweeter, then I shall rest content in the feeling that the Progressive movement has been successful.

* * *

Over the course of more than a decade of researching and writing this book, I have benefited from the help and support of so many individuals and organizations that my all-too-faulty memory will almost certainly prove unequal to the task of recollection. For any such unintended lapses, I most humbly apologize in advance. The intellectual debt I owe to the hundreds of scholars of Wisconsin and Progressive Era history whose published work has greatly enriched my own understanding of these fields is incalculable. That is especially true of Robert S. Maxwell, Herbert F. Margulies, David P. Thelen, Roger E. Wyman, Kenneth C. Acrea, and Stanley P. Caine. Unfortunately, my only feasible method of repayment is to give them their proper attribution in the footnotes and in the essay on sources. I sincerely hope that I have done so in sufficient measure. Beyond that, however, I am especially grateful to James T. Kloppenberg and Richard L. McCormick for the recommendations that helped secure a National Endowment for the Humanities summer stipend in 1992, as well as for the intellectual stimulation provided by their published work. Nothing that I accomplish as a historian can ever repay the debt that I owe to my late mentor J. Joseph Huthmacher. My thanks also to Dave Thelen for three decades of intellectual dialogue and mutual respect, and for his pioneer role in revising the history of the Progressive Era in Wisconsin. Several historians provided special, personal assistance about specific topics; my thanks go particularly to

Virginia Crane, Derek Linton, Genevieve McBride, Anthony Orum, and Thomas Woods.

My initial involvement in this project was due primarily to the efforts and persuasive powers of two highly valued colleagues and friends. The first was Nicholas C. Burckel, my longtime collaborator, benefactor, and tennis opponent, who convinced both me and the directors of the History of Wisconsin project that I was the best available person to write Volume IV. The second was William Fletcher Thompson, former state historian, general editor of the project, and author of Volume VI, who was Nick's first convert and my valued mentor. Bill's de facto successor as general editor, Paul Hass, is at least as responsible for the finished project as I am. His ability to mold a massive and sometimes inchoate manuscript into a finished product with reasonable coherence and intellectual rigor has been masterful. That he has also been an unfailing source of encouragement and inspiration to the author with his sharp wit and keen sense of reality has been of equal value to me. To the extent that the finished product is error-free, the credit belongs primarily to Paul's alter ego, Jack Holzhueter, and his staff, especially Deborah Johnson, Ted Frantz, Reid Paul, and Kimberly S. Little. Jack has frequently been described as "a walking encyclopedia of Wisconsin history," a description that is certainly true but woefully inadequate because it neglects the many other admirable facets of his intellect and character. If their names were to appear on the title page with my own, I would have little grounds for complaint. Since I am the sole author of record, however, they are hereby absolved of any responsibility for whatever shortcomings remain.

In the best traditions of the Wisconsin Idea, the History of Wisconsin project has involved constructive collaboration among private corporations and foundations, the University of Wisconsin system, and the State Historical Society. The project's guiding light, the History of Wisconsin Advisory Committee, generously provided most of the funding that enabled me to spend a year in Madison as a visiting professor, and to engage Victor Jew and Mary Etta McClain as research assistants. The advisory committee also supplied the financial wherewithal and overall direction for the outstanding research team supplied by the University's graduate program in history and the State Historical Society. Although I came too late to the project to meet any of them in person, I am deeply appreciative of the excellent work done by Mari Jo Buhle, James Cavanaugh, Jeanne Delgado, Stanley Mallach, David Macleod, Dale Treleven, and George Roeder. I am particularly grateful to George, with an assist from Eric Lampard's *Rise of the Dairy Industry in Wisconsin*, for guiding this city boy through the mysteries of Wisconsin agriculture. Beyond that, the staffs of both the State Historical Society and the UW-Madison Memorial Library were always professional and gracious in giving me direction and access to their vast trove of materials. The University system's sabbatical program and its Institute for Research in the Humanities provided me with another stimulating year of research and writing in Madison, an opportunity that I owe primarily to David Lindberg and Paul Boyer. No words can possibly do justice to the voluntary contribution made by Joyce Follet, who provided me not only with invaluable research material and analysis on women's history, but also with vital emotional support during one of the most traumatic periods of my life.

The list of people to whom I am beholden on my own campus, the University of Wisconsin-Parkside, is legion. Former chancellor Alan E. Guskin and his staff provided me with substantial release time and summer salary support; he also acted as liaison for the project between the Madison and Parkside campuses. His chief cohort in Madison, former vice-chancellor Bernard C. Cohen, helped enormously in making smooth the rough ways of bureaucracy. My departmental colleagues provided me with stimulating intellectual discussion and criticism, proffered good-natured encouragement, and made more than the necessary allowances for my immersion in the nether world of research and writing. As has been true from my first day at Parkside, nothing could have been accomplished without the assistance rendered by our highly professional and actively helpful library staff, especially those in the interlibrary loan department and in the archives and area research center. At the risk of slighting others, I would like to extend special thanks to Judith Hamilton Pryor, Ellen Pedraza, Linda Schiesser, Debra Braun, Bruce Johnson, Linda Piele, Barbara Baruth, Marilyn Weyrauch, and Pamela Fisk for assistance above and beyond. Over the years, several of my students did vital work in bibliographical searches, note taking, and transcription of materials, most notably Cait Dallas. Elisabeth Lean, Connie Murphy, Cindy Varga Roth, Patrik Vander Velden, and Jill Makovsky all contributed their time and talent in numerous important ways. My friend and former Parkside colleague Sally McCulloch performed a first-rate copy-editing job on several chapters and mined numerous masters' theses for relevant material. But for the consummate skill and patience of Josephine McCool, this book would still consist of undecipherable handwriting on thousands of lined yellow legal pages. She lived through every minute of its gestation with me and was so exhausted by the process that she retired as our departmental secretary as soon as the final draft was typed. Her retirement has forced me to learn how to compose on a word processor. I miss her common sense, compassion, good humor, sharp wit, and friendship every time I set foot on campus.

My quintessential source of sustenance during the course of writing this book has been my ever-evolving and unconditionally loving family. My brother Robert, physical chemist extraordinaire, and his family are a constant source of connections to my roots—in both Iowa and Germany. My five adult children—Jeanne, Cathy, Eileen,

Thomas, and Joseph—are a living reminder that being their father has been both the greatest achievement and ultimate privilege of my life. My three sons-in-law—Chuck Betz, Jerry Behling, and Bruce Sigmon—have been both sons and friends. My grandchildren—Michael, John, Christopher, Jessica, Melissa, Elizabeth, and Haylee—are the joys of my life and my hope for the future. My stepson, Christian Kastman, has enriched my life in countless ways, while his brothers Ian and Tad have become good friends. Ian's children Alyssa and Lorenzo are as dear to me as if they were my own direct descendants. At the center of all this is my wife Bev, whose love and support have been indispensable to us all. She is both proud and relieved that this long journey has been completed. Without her, the trip would have been even more arduous and the destination far less rewarding.

JOHN D. BUENKER

Racine, Wisconsin

CONTRIBUTORS

THE STATE HISTORICAL SOCIETY OF WISCONSIN

THE UNIVERSITY OF WISCONSIN

WESTERN PUBLISHING COMPANY, INC.

FIRST WISCONSIN FOUNDATION, INC.

THE JOURNAL COMPANY

THE NORTHWESTERN MUTUAL LIFE INSURANCE COMPANY

PABST BREWERIES FOUNDATION

SCHLITZ FOUNDATION, INC.

APPLETON COATED FOUNDATION, INC.

APPLETON WIRE WORKS CORP.

BANTA COMPANY FOUNDATION, INC.

BERGSTROM FOUNDATION

THE FALK CORPORATION

FOX RIVER PAPER CO.

KIMBERLY-CLARK FOUNDATION, INC.

THE MARINE FOUNDATION, INC.

MARSHALL & ILSLEY BANK FOUNDATION, INC.

THILMANY PULP AND PAPER COMPANY

WISCONSIN ELECTRIC POWER COMPANY

THE JOHNSON'S WAX FUND, INC.

MILLER HIGH LIFE FOUNDATION, INC.

NEKOOSA-EDWARDS FOUNDATION INCORPORATED

WISCONSIN MICHIGAN POWER COMPANY

WISCONSIN NATURAL GAS COMPANY

WISCONSIN PUBLIC SERVICE CORPORATION

CHARLES W. WRIGHT FOUNDATION OF BADGER METER, INC.

CONTENTS

Preface		v
Contributors		xv
Note on Citations		xx
1	THE PARADOX OF PROGRESS	1
2	BECOMING AMERICA'S DAIRYLAND	25
3	INDUSTRIAL TRANSFORMATIONS	80
4	URBANISM, CRISIS, AND REFORM	126
5	NATIVES AND NEWCOMERS	179
6	REDEFINING WORK	242
7	A PASSION FOR NEWNESS AND FOR SYSTEM	303
8	EDUCATION FOR PROGRESS	360
9	ON THE EVE OF REFORM	400
10	THE ADVENT OF LA FOLLETTE	431
11	REFORM ASCENDANT	455
12	THE MOST PROGRESSIVE STATE	515
13	WISCONSIN IDEAS	569
14	DISINTEGRATION AND LEGACY	611

Appendix 665

Essay on Sources 667

Index 695

THE HISTORY OF
WISCONSIN

NOTE ON CITATIONS

SHSW   State Historical Society of Wisconsin.

UW   University of Wisconsin. (Any use of this term without a specific campus designation denotes the University of Wisconsin–Madison.)

WMH   *Wisconsin Magazine of History.*

WSA   Wisconsin State Archives.

Unless otherwise indicated, all government publications are those of the State of Wisconsin.

Unless otherwise indicated, all manuscripts, pamphlets, and government publications cited are in the collections of the State Historical Society of Wisconsin.

1

The Paradox of Progress

[1]

PROGRESS! That electrifying notion permeated virtually every aspect of Wisconsin life during the economically fateful year of 1893. Progress was the term almost universally applied to the myriad developments that had transformed the state since its admission to the Union in 1848. Progress also meant the passionately held conviction that those substantial achievements were but prologue to an even more remarkable future. Progress was both the ultimate standard against which proposed innovations in agriculture, industry, education, architecture, transportation, communication, and politics must be tested, as well as the ultimate rationale for convincing skeptics.

So ubiquitous was the notion of progress that the term was sometimes employed to justify ideas and actions that were mutually exclusive. For example, many measured progress entirely in material or quantifiable terms, while others insisted that its human, spiritual, or environmental dimensions were far more critical. Many regarded progress as inevitable and its results as sacrosanct, whatever their dislocations and inequities. Others insisted that progress was in the eye of the beholder and its results contingent and relative. Many regarded purposeful intervention by organizations or government as potentially destructive of progress. Still others regarded such intervention, commonly called "reform," as the only possibility for achieving it.

These considerable differences notwithstanding, the idea of progress became the quintessential defining notion of the years 1893 through 1914—a period known by contemporaries and historians alike as the Progressive Era.

The sense of progress that animated Wisconsin in 1893 drew its inspiration from several sources. The remarkable economic boom of the 1880's reached its zenith in 1892, causing the Milwaukee *Sentinel* to assert that "never has there been such a prosperous year." Numerous products manufactured in Wisconsin, such as agricultural implements, fanning mills, leather goods, sashes and doors, and beer, were on the verge of attaining national markets and reputations, or newly had them. Although its forests were being depleted at an alarming rate, Wisconsin was still the nation's foremost lumbering state. Barely two decades into the transition from wheat farming to dairy husbandry, Wisconsin was already relentlessly pursuing New York for the distinction of being America's Dairyland. The settlement and development of the state's "Middle North" were proceeding apace, and plans were already being laid for another frontier boom in the "New North."

The Columbian History of Education in Wisconsin, published in 1893, boasted of the remarkable network of public and private schools, from kindergarten through university, that the state had managed to erect in less than half a century. Established by the legislature in 1848, the University of Wisconsin was steadily emerging as a national leader in public higher education, with 1,300 students, numerous graduate and professional programs, and a pioneering extension or outreach program.[1]

Wisconsin's considerable sense of progress in 1893 was elevated to a state of near euphoria by its outstanding performance at the World's Columbian Exposition in Chicago. Ostensibly held to commemorate the 400th anniversary of Columbus's first expedition, the Columbian Exposition actually celebrated "American progress through time and space since 1492" and enabled the young nation and her states to define and assert their cultural identities. Built at a cost of $35 million, the exposition attracted nearly 28 million visitors during its six months' existence. Its "Great White City," designed by such architectural giants as Daniel H. Burnham, John W. Root, and Frederick Law Olmsted, Jr., and nicknamed for its distinctive white buildings and brilliant electrical illumination, set an ideal for urban planning and beautification. Its Manufactures and Liberal Arts, Machinery, Agriculture, Mining, Electricity, Transportation, Horticulture, Fisheries, Fine Arts, and Woman's buildings housed the marvels of the age. The structures raised by the forty-four states and territories and by sixty foreign countries contained the choicest fruits of their science and culture. The fair's wonders ranged from the world's largest carnival to thousands of scholarly papers and inspirational addresses delivered at the World's Congress Auxiliary.[2]

---

[1] Milwaukee *Sentinel,* January 2, 1893; Joseph H. H. Alexander, "A Short Industrial History of Wisconsin," in the *Wisconsin Blue Book, 1929,* pp. 31–49; Eric E. Lampard, *The Rise of the Dairy Industry in Wisconsin: A Study in Agricultural Change, 1820–1920* (Madison, 1963), 244–293; John William Stearns, ed., *The Columbian History of Education in Wisconsin* (Milwaukee, 1893), 9–77, 86–116, 228–321, 378–409. The Stearns volume consistently dates the university's opening to 1850, but Merle Curti and Vernon Carstensen, *The University of Wisconsin: A History, 1848–1925* (2 vols., Madison, 1949), 1: 37, 59, and 79, date the founding as 1848 and the beginning of preparatory classes as February 5, 1849.

[2] Robert W. Rydell, *All the World's a Fair: Visions of Empire at American International*

The Paradox of Progress

Despite Wisconsin's relatively brief history, and the stiff competition provided by the exposition's cosmopolitan character, the Badger State seized this opportunity to showcase its achievements. All told, 2,226 individuals and corporate bodies from Wisconsin exhibited their wares. The potential economic benefits to be derived, in the form of tourists, immigrants, investment capital, and expanded markets, inspired the State Board of World's Fair Managers to mount a major effort. The board justified the cost of Wisconsin's fisheries exhibit by expressing its confidence "that for every dollar expended by the state in making this exhibit there will be twenty dollars returned to the people of our commonwealth through this medium of advertising its fishing resources." The value of the exposition in promoting the state's natural resources, its agriculture and manufacturing, "cannot be overestimated nor too often dwelt upon."[3]

Much of the board's enthusiasm arose from Wisconsin's geographical proximity to Chicago. The fact that Big Bend in Waukesha County was only 101 miles from the fairgrounds allowed the Hygeia Mineral Springs Company of Chicago to run a 6 1/4-inch iron pipeline that carried 130,000 gallons of "pure, health-giving" water daily from springs near the village. (Water from Waukesha County was already well-known in Chicago as "Waukesha Water.") Southeastern Wisconsin's location in Chicago's hinterlands also inspired Lake Michigan steamship lines to make preparations for accommodating an anticipated 34,000 visitors a week between Milwaukee and Chicago, while the two principal Chicago-Milwaukee railroads together expanded their schedule to twenty passenger trains a day. Proximity also contributed significantly to the enormous success of Wisconsin Day on September 6, 1893, an event that reportedly attracted a crowd previously surpassed only on Illinois Day and the Fourth of July.[4]

Expositions, 1876–1916 (Chicago, 1984), 46–47 (quote); Frank A. Cassell and Marguerite E. Cassell, "Wisconsin at the World's Columbian Exposition of 1893," in the *Wisconsin Magazine of History*, 67 (Summer, 1984), 243–262, hereinafter cited as *WMH*. See also David F. Burg, *Chicago's White City of 1893* (Lexington, Kentucky, 1976), and R. Reid Badger, *The Great American Fair: The World's Columbian Exposition and American Culture* (Chicago, 1979).

[3] Cassell and Cassell, "Wisconsin at the World's Columbian Exposition," in *WMH*, 67: 258–261; Board of World's Fair Managers, *Report*, 1893, pp. 8, 18, 25–26.

[4] Cassell and Cassell, "Wisconsin at the World's Columbian Exposition," in *WMH*, 67: 247–257, 262; Michael P. McCarthy, "Should We Drink The Water?: Typhoid Fever Worries at the Columbian Exposition," *Illinois Historical Journal*, 86 (Spring, 1993), 8–10 (quote); Burg, *Chicago's White City*, 232–233; Milwaukee *Journal*, September 7, 1893; Board of World's Fair Managers, *Report*, 25–26. For an informative discussion of the symbiotic relationship between Chicago and its Wisconsin hinterlands, see William Cronon, *Nature's Metropolis: Chicago and the Great West* (New York, 1991). Spring water from the Waukesha area enjoyed a good reputation in Chicago before the fair. Hence, Waukesha Water. Paid admissions totaled 172,765 on September 6, 325,000 on July 4, and 272,000 on Illinois Day, August 4; many larger crowds than those of September 6 visited later in September and October. See Milwaukee *Sentinel*,

Thus fortuitously positioned, Wisconsin "was everywhere at Jackson Park." Parched fairgoers slaked their thirsts at the taps from which issued Waukesha County spring water or Milwaukee beer from Pabst or Schlitz. Both the thousands of electric lights that illuminated the White City and the railroad that transported visitors around its periphery were powered, in part, by engines assembled at Milwaukee's E. P. Allis Company. The Allis engines, and the agricultural equipment supplied by the J. I. Case Company and Milwaukee Harvester, were harbingers of southeastern Wisconsin's emergence as a major center for the processing of metals and the production of heavy and electrical machinery. Among the highlights of the Agriculture Building was a 2,000-square-foot pavilion containing a thousand glass jars filled with examples of Wisconsin's finest grains. The same edifice housed extensive displays of honey, wool, tobacco, and root crops—proof of the state's growing agricultural diversity. Wisconsin dairy farmers distinguished themselves as well in their displays of butter and cheese, but took few dairy cattle to Chicago for judging. Appropriately, the Board of Managers proclaimed agriculture to be "the most important exhibit" and insisted that "Wisconsin must occupy such a conspicuous position as her vast agricultural interests demand and to which her progressive farmers are entitled."[5]

Diversity also characterized the state's exhibit in the Mines and Mining Building. Though it emphasized the present, the display of lead and zinc recalled the pre-territorial and territorial eras when southwestern Wisconsin was on the nation's mining and settlement frontiers. Brownstone monoliths and iron ore exhibits advertised its new extractive bonanza near the shores of Lake Superior. The state's display in the Fisheries Building featured a 1,600-square-foot pavilion containing twenty-nine tanks filled with thirty-three different varieties of fish from the state's abundant lakes and rivers. Wisconsin's status as the leading lumber state was illustrated by its display in the Forestry Building, whose pavilion was constructed from over forty different kinds of wood. The board of managers boasted that the state's timber was "almost unequaled . . . in variety, quality, and quantity" and pledged that "the commercial character of this valuable product . . .

September 7, October 27–30, 1893, and *Halligan's Illustrated World's Fair*, 5: 25 (July, 1893), 576, and 5: 27 (September, 1893), 641.

[5] Cassell and Cassell, "Wisconsin at the World's Columbian Exposition," in *WMH*, 67: 250, 258–259 (quote); Board of World's Fair Managers, *Report*, 9–14 (quotes). For livestock exhibitors and awards, see Board of World's Fair Managers, "Final Report" (2 vols.), vol. 2, in Secretary of State, Chicago World's Fair, 1893, Records, 1891–1894, box 3, Series 282, WSA, and Hubert Howe Bancroft, *The Book of the Fair: An Historical and Descriptive Presentation of the World's Science, Art, and Industry as Viewed Through the Columbian Exposition at Chicago in 1893* (2 vols., Chicago and San Francisco, 1893), 2: 611–626, esp. 615n.

shall . . . compare favorably with the efforts that are being made by our neighboring and competitive states."[6]

The State Historical Society of Wisconsin enhanced its already considerable reputation by mounting exhibits of prehistoric copper and stone artifacts, including "the finest lot of flint arrowheads to be found," as vivid proof that the state had a long history of human habitation and technological adaptation. The Woman's Building, with its impressive display of handicrafts, reflected the Victorian era notion of separate spheres for men and women, yet also hinted strongly that technological innovation was breaking down the supposed barriers between the sexes. The emergence of what came to be called the New Woman was heralded by Frances E. Willard—reared in Rock County, Wisconsin, and the founder of the Woman's Christian Temperance Union—who proclaimed, "Woman is becoming what God intended her to be, and Christ's Gospel necessitates her being, the companion and counsellor, not the incumbrance and toy, of man."[7]

Nor did Wisconsin shrink from proclaiming its intellectual and cultural achievements. Its educational display hailed the University of Wisconsin and the state's normal, public, and private schools through photographs, diagrams, and samples of student scholarship, as well as in handsome copies of *The Columbian History of Education*. Some 500 books written by Wisconsin authors graced shelves in the Wisconsin Building, which also featured statues by Jean Miner of Madison and by Nellie Mears of Oshkosh, the latter entitled "The Genius of Wisconsin." The Fine Arts building also contained works of Wisconsin artists; the Woman's Building housed a fireplace with a terra cotta facade depicting Rip Van Winkle, constructed by Ruth Winterbotham of Eau Claire.[8]

Perhaps even more noteworthy were the contributions of individ-

---

[6] Cassell and Cassell, "Wisconsin at the World's Columbian Exposition," in *WMH*, 67: 258–260; Milwaukee *Sentinel*, September 7, 1893 (quote); Board of World's Fair Managers, *Report*, 15–18.

[7] Cassell and Cassell, "Wisconsin at the World's Columbian Exposition," in *WMH*, 67: 260; Milwaukee *Sentinel*, September 7, 1893 (quote); "Exhibit at World's Fair," in *Proceedings of the State Historical Society of Wisconsin* (74 vols., Madison, 1875–1958), 1893, pp. 65–67, hereinafter cited as *SHSW Proceedings*; Burg, *Chicago's White City*, 279; Board of World's Fair Managers, *Report*, 19–20; Jeanne Madeline Weimann, *The Fair Women* (Chicago, 1981), 487–549; Frances E. Willard, *A White Life for Two* (Chicago, 1890; microfiched reprint, *Pamphlets in American History*, 1978, no. WO610), 6. See also Reuben Gold Thwaites, "The State Historical Society of Wisconsin," in Stearns, ed., *Columbian History of Education in Wisconsin*, 395–405.

[8] Cassell and Cassell, "Wisconsin at the World's Columbian Exposition," in *WMH*, 67: 260; Weimann, *The Fair Women*, 165, 376, 391; Board of World's Fair Managers, *Report*, 18–20, 36–38; Board of World's Fair Managers, "Final Report" (vol. 2), box 3, Series 282, WSA.

ual Wisconsinites to the World's Congress Auxiliary, a gathering of "leaders of human progress" achieved in hundreds of subject areas to explore "practical means by which further progress might be made and the prosperity and peace of the world advanced." In the august company of nearly 4,000 scholars from almost a hundred nations, several Wisconsinites played a prominent role. Probably the most memorable paper of all—though few recognized it at the time—was "The Significance of the Frontier in American History," rendered by young Frederick Jackson Turner of the University of Wisconsin. Drawing upon his boyhood in Portage, as well as considerable research, Professor Turner posited that "the existence of an area of free land, its continuous recession, and the advance of American settlement westward, explain American development." The frontier experience, he said in his paper, promoted political and social democracy and developed such distinctive national traits as inquisitiveness, practicality, inventiveness, restlessness, and exuberance. At least two generations of American historians would devote themselves to elaborating or refuting what came to be called Turner's Frontier Thesis.[9]

Scarcely less influential were the contributions of Richard T. Ely, cofounder of the reformist American Economic Association and recently appointed head of the university's School of Economics, Political Science, and History. As one of the nation's earliest and most articulate exponents of the Social Gospel, which applied Christian principles to social and economic questions, Ely contended that "social solidarity" was the essence of Christianity. He scored those who ignored the growing inequality of America's socio-economic order and pleaded for "private frugality and generous public expenditures." He questioned the sincerity and integrity of those who offered "long prayers" and performed rituals, while "neglect[ing] widows and orphans in need." A nation that consistently exalted property over human rights, Ely argued, must be confronted by a Christianity that embodies "a mighty transformation and turning of things upside down."[10]

Equally illustrative of Wisconsin's growing intellectual prowess were the contributions of John R. Commons and Hamlin Garland to the World's Congress Auxiliary. Commons, who in 1904 would join Ely on the faculty in Madison, lectured on the rights of working people,

[9] Burg, *Chicago's White City*, 235–285, esp. 236–238 (quotes); Martin Ridge, ed., *Frederick Jackson Turner: Wisconsin's Historian of the Frontier* (Madison, 1986), 7–12, 26 (quote); Richard Hofstadter, *The Progressive Historians: Turner, Beard, Parrington* (New York, 1968), 47–80.

[10] Richard T. Ely, "Christianity as a Social Force," esp. pp. 10, 11, 14, 20, in box 2, folder 3, the Richard T. Ely Papers; Burg, *Chicago's White City*, 271–272; Benjamin G. Rader, *The Academic Mind and Reform: The Influence of Richard T. Ely in American Life* (Lexington, Kentucky, 1966), 28–105.

a subject on which he was already attaining national prominence. Garland, a novelist born in West Salem (La Crosse County) in 1860, addressed the Congress on "Local Color in Fiction" and joined several nationally prominent thinkers in discussing profit sharing, the single tax, and the public ownership of utilities.

Largely unnoticed at the time were the World's Fair activities of a young apprentice architect with roots in Richland, Iowa, and Dane counties, Frank Lloyd Wright. Having worked for Louis H. Sullivan, who designed the Transportation Building, Wright is believed to have made frequent trips to Jackson Park both before and after the fair. High on his list of memorable sights was the Japanese Building, especially its half-sized facsimile of the eleventh-century temple of Ho-o-den; and though Wright himself never acknowledged it, many scholars have insisted upon the Japanese influence in his work.[11]

Capping Wisconsin's contributions to the Columbian Exposition were its state building and its "day." The building was designed as a "day home to those people who visit the fair" and was equipped with "every convenience." The three-story edifice contained 14,000 square feet of space, was constructed of Wisconsin materials, and could have been one of the mansions on Milwaukee's Prospect Avenue. The Building's finest hour came on Wisconsin Day (September 6), when it played host to thousands of visitors and dignitaries who crammed inside to view the mounted remains of Old Abe, famed mascot of the Eighth Wisconsin Infantry during the Civil War. (The bird had died in 1881 but remained a celebrity.) A representation of Old Abe was featured in the evening fireworks display, as was the state motto: "Forward!" The *Sentinel* proudly proclaimed, "It looked like Milwaukee on State street to-night."[12]

Undoubtedly the best gauge of Wisconsin's status and future prospects was the impressive number of awards won by its exhibitors in a wide variety of fields. Wisconsin claimed 1,067 medals and certificates, about 4.5 per cent of the 23,757 awarded at the Fair. Of these, 446 were earned by its grains and cereals displays—one-sixth of the total in those departments, convincing evidence that husbandry was still the state's main economic pursuit. Dairy farmers' displays of cheese and butter finished a respectable second, with 336. The next largest share of Wisconsin's prizes was won by the state's burgeoning

---

[11] Cassell and Cassell, "Wisconsin at the World's Columbian Exposition," 261, in *WMH*, 67: 261; Badger, *Great American Fair*, 100; Grant Carpenter Manson, *Frank Lloyd Wright to 1910: The First Golden Age* (New York, 1958), 33–38.

[12] Cassell and Cassell, "Wisconsin at the World's Columbian Exposition," in *WMH*, 67: 248–249, 256–257, 260; Milwaukee *Sentinel*, September 6 (quote), 7, 1893; Board of World's Fair Managers, *Report*, 3–6 (quotes). On Wisconsin's celebrated eagle, see Richard H. Zeitlin, *Old Abe the War Eagle: A True Story of the Civil War and Reconstruction* (Madison, 1986).

industries, even though Milwaukee Harvester refused to participate in the field testing of farm machinery. That controversy was mild, however, compared to the "battle of the beers" between Pabst of Milwaukee and Anheuser-Busch of St. Louis. A margin of less than 1 per cent in special jury scoring allowed Pabst to nickname its product "Blue Ribbon" and ever after proclaim the slogan "Selected as America's Best in 1893." Wisconsin also garnered a sufficient cache of awards in education, literature, and "woman's work" to buttress its claim to intellectual and esthetic respectability.[13]

But the long-term significance of the Columbian Exposition for Wisconsin lay not in certificates and medals, nor in a transient "day," or a temporary building, or even in its symbolic paean to progress. It rested instead upon the role that the World's Fair played as a forum for several men who would soon help to earn the state its national reputation for "progressivism." Professor Ely returned to the University of Wisconsin campus where he built his school into a nationally renowned center for the application of social science in the service of socio-economic and political reform. His precedent-setting 1894 trial for economic heresy resulted in a celebrated affirmation of academic freedom when the Board of Regents committed the university to "ever encourage that continual and fearless sifting and winnowing by which alone the truth can be found." Ely had already helped establish much of the ideological climate for progressive reform and continued to train a veritable host of activist political economists. He also served as an informal adviser to Robert M. La Follette, who reportedly credited the economist with being his teacher. Ely became the chief intellectual progenitor of the "Wisconsin Idea," whereby the state government, the university, and the people of the state worked together towards progress. After John R. Commons joined his former mentor on the Madison campus, he quickly surpassed Ely as the foremost exponent of the new or institutional economics, virtually inventing the study of labor economics. As scholar, teacher, political consultant, and author of labor legislation, Commons became the most influential progressive political economist of his time and the foremost champion of the assault on laissez-faire economics. Instrumental in founding the American Association for Labor Legislation and head of the U.S. Commission on Industrial

---

[13] Board of World's Fair Managers, "Final Report," 1: 20–28, box 3, Series 282, WSA; Milwaukee *Journal*, October 26–30, November 3, 1893; Cassell and Cassell, "Wisconsin at the World's Columbian Exposition," in *WMH*, 67: 258–260; Bancroft, *Book of the Fair*, 2: 964; Lampard, *Rise of the Dairy Industry*, 178–180; Thomas C. Cochran, *The Pabst Brewing Company: The History of an American Business* (New York, 1948), 137–138.

Relations, Commons helped draft much of the landmark legislation that earned Wisconsin its progressive reputation.[14]

Likewise, Frederick Jackson Turner soon emerged as one of the leading progressive historians who interpreted the nation's development in terms of a continuing struggle between ordinary people and vested interests over the progress of socio-economic and political democracy. Turner faced historians inward in their search for the roots of modern America, and he influenced scholars to utilize their findings on behalf of public service and reform. A confidant of La Follette and a driving force behind the university's extension work, Turner also recommended the appointment in 1901 of his student, Charles McCarthy, as director of what soon became the Legislative Reference Library. Ely, Commons, and McCarthy were all frequent participants in the Saturday Lunch Club, an informal gathering of faculty members and state government officials established by La Follette. Frank Lloyd Wright, who had studied briefly at the university, went on to become the nation's most celebrated architect; he pioneered "organic" architecture imbued with the spirit of man and possessing the capability to reshape American civilization. Wright regarded his work as an expression of the democratic impulse and believed wholeheartedly in the power of architecture to effect social reform, especially through the decentralization of congested cities.[15]

[2]

Even as so many Wisconsinites basked in the warm glow of the Chicago exposition and dreamed of an even brighter future, many others were forced to confront the harsh reality. For progress had a darker side, especially in a culture whose operational values were those of

---

[14] Rader, *The Academic Mind and Reform*, 106–191, esp. 130–131; Curti and Carstensen, *University of Wisconsin*, 1: 508–527 (525, quote); Richard T. Ely, *Ground Under Our Feet: An Autobiography* (New York, 1938), 121–233; Charles McCarthy, *The Wisconsin Idea* (New York, 1912), 27–30; Lafayette G. Harter, Jr., *John R. Commons: His Assault on Laissez-Faire* (Corvallis, Oregon, 1962), 69–256; John R. Commons, *Myself: The Autobiography of John R. Commons* (Madison, 1964), 95–189.

[15] Ridge, ed., *Frederick Jackson Turner*, 1–2; Hofstadter, *The Progressive Historians*, xi–xiii, 47–164, 437–466; Ray Allen Billington, *Frederick Jackson Turner: Historian, Scholar, Teacher* (New York, 1973), 472–497; Marion Casey, *Charles McCarthy: Librarianship and Reform* (Chicago, 1981), 21–24, 28–30; Robert M. La Follette, *La Follette's Autobiography: A Personal Narrative of Political Experiences* (Madison, 1913; reprinted, Madison, 1960), 15; Manson, *Frank Lloyd Wright to 1910*, pp. 99–213; Norris Kelly Smith, *Frank Lloyd Wright: A Study in Architectural Content* (Englewood Cliffs, New Jersey, 1966), 19–47; Robert C. Twombly, *Frank Lloyd Wright: His Life and His Architecture* (New York, 1979), 58–118.

rugged individualism, unbridled competition, classical economics, and laissez-faire liberalism. Progress was clearly not all of a piece, and it exacted a heavy toll on those with little or no capital, skills, education, or organization.

"The exposition came," observed the Milwaukee *Journal* in October of 1893, "during a time of depression such as the country has not witnessed for twenty years." The general public was "not in shape to do good service by the fair, their finances being badly out of plumb," and attendance would have been at least twice as high if the exposition had been held the previous year. As late as April 18, 1893, the Milwaukee *Sentinel* exulted that "it is generally conceded that the country is prosperous, that wages were never better, nor the demand for work on the part of employers." By the time of its year-end issue, however, the newspaper agonized that "the new year now opens after a period of depression such as has never before been known here" and that "the decrease in 1893 practically equals all of the gain made during the two previous years."[16]

In Wisconsin, as in the nation as a whole, the depression of 1893–1897 began with the collapse of its overextended financial system. On May 12, there was a run on the Plankinton Bank of Milwaukee during which depositors withdrew a record $72,000. The panic was precipitated by the failure of the Frank A. Lappen Furniture Company, a local business to which the bank had lent $267,000. An even more serious run during the next four days cost the bank more than $100,000, reducing its cash reserves to $148,000. When vice-president William Plankinton ordered the bank's doors closed just five minutes after they opened on June 1, the institution's assets had dwindled to a paltry $7,300. The *Sentinel* blamed the bank's failure on the excessive amounts of money lent to Lappen and a few other large borrowers and claimed that it came as a complete surprise to the city's business community.[17]

The Plankinton failure initiated a chain reaction that claimed nearly one-quarter of the state's 119 banks by the end of 1893. The nationwide bank disaster of mid-July destroyed four more Milwaukee institutions, including the Wisconsin Marine and Fire Insurance Company Bank, "the oldest and largest banking institution in the state, a bank that had weathered all financial storms for half a century." Treasurer John Hunner advised all Milwaukee banks to close their doors, to show Milwaukeeans "how hard it is to get along without the banks." That same month banks failed in Manitowoc, Chip-

---

[16] Milwaukee *Journal*, October 28, 1893; Milwaukee *Sentinel*, April 18, December 31, 1893.

[17] Milwaukee *Sentinel*, May 13, 17, June 2, 1893; Theodore A. Andersen, *A Century of Banking in Wisconsin* (Madison, 1954), 75–80.

pewa Falls, Port Washington, Sparta, Portage, Tomah, Washburn, Shell Lake, and Prescott. The aftershock eventually claimed banks in La Crosse and Superior. This virtual collapse of the state's financial structure, though temporary, evoked demands from most sectors of society for government regulation of the banking system, and plunged Wisconsin into a severe downward spiral of business and personal bankruptcies, plant shutdowns, layoffs, wage cuts, and reductions in working hours.[18]

So precipitous was the downhill slide, and so persistent the malaise, that 1892 figures of economic performance were not matched again until the new century dawned. Despite its prosperous beginning and a substantial recovery of about one-third between 1897 and 1899, the entire decade yielded a net decline in manufacturing. Based upon its survey of about 65 per cent of the state's productive capacity, the Wisconsin Bureau of Labor and Industrial Statistics reported a 30 per cent decline in capital investment and a one-third drop in the value of manufactured products between 1890 and 1896. The total number of persons employed in manufacturing fell 20 per cent between 1892 and 1895, with thousands more suffering from cuts in hours or wages. Employment among skilled workers declined by nearly one-quarter. Total wages, which had increased by more than one-third between 1888 and 1892, were nearly halved by 1896 and recovered only to about two-thirds of the 1892 figure by the end of the decade. The average annual wage in Wisconsin declined from $426 in 1892 to $376 in 1894, and climbed only to $418 by 1897. The percentage of wage earners receiving over $4.00 a day declined from 2.29 to 0.86 between 1891 and 1897, while the proportion of those making less than $1.50 a day jumped from 45 to 57 per cent. The bureau attributed this loss to the general business depression and to the greater growth in industries employing women and children than in those employing skilled males. Despite the steady recovery after 1897, the bureau concluded that by the end of 1899, "the level of 1892 had not been attained."[19]

The situation was especially severe in the state's industrial cities. Estimates of unemployment in Milwaukee ranged from a police census of 11,200 out-of-work men in December, 1893, to the typographer's union figure of 35,000 during that winter. Most calculations varied between 35 and 40 per cent of the work force. Even the E. P.

---

[18] Milwaukee *Sentinel,* July 23, 26 (quote), September 24, and October 18, 1893; David P. Thelen, *The New Citizenship: Origins of Progressivism in Wisconsin, 1885–1900* (Columbia, Missouri, 1972), 57; Andersen, *A Century of Banking,* 80–83; David V. Mollenhoff, *Madison: A History of the Formative Years* (Dubuque, 1982), 171.

[19] Bureau of Labor and Industrial Statistics, *Biennial Report,* 1899–1900, xii, 214–215, 222–223, 231–242 (quote).

Allis Company, whose employees considered it both solvent and humane, laid off 300 workers and cut wages for the remainder by 10 per cent. By late August, the Bay View rolling mills reportedly had laid off over one-half of their labor force, and wages in Milwaukee's lumberyards had fallen below $1.00 a day. "For the first time since 1886," the *Sentinel* reported, "Milwaukee was yesterday the scene of a riotous demonstration on the part of unemployed labor."

By April, the combination of unemployment and wage and hours reductions in manufacturing had shrunk the average Wisconsinite's annual income by 20 per cent. A survey of forty-eight manufacturing establishments found that employment and product value had declined by nearly one-third, and wages by almost 45 per cent, between June 1, 1893, and May 31, 1894. The number of families on the Milwaukee County poor list jumped from an average of 681 between 1887 and 1892 to a high of 3,430 by January, 1894. On December 13, 1893, the Milwaukee *Sentinel* observed that at least 13,000 persons were destitute, placing a burden on the nearly empty county treasury of about $10,000 per month. All told, during 1893, the county dispensed relief to 14,975 persons constituting 4,006 families, at a total cost of $73,318, up nearly $40,000 from the previous year. And in 1894, relief expenditures soared to $110,000.[20]

A conservative estimate put unemployment in La Crosse at over one-half the city's work force during the winter of 1893, a figure approximated by both Sheboygan and Beloit. The situation was much the same in the mills of the Fox and Wisconsin river valleys, the logging camps of the north woods, and the mining ranges of the Lake Superior region. In Madison, the Gisholt Machine Company laid off half its workers in June of 1893, while Fuller and Johnson, the city's largest employer, was closed entirely from August through October. The railroads discharged many employees and the Chicago, Milwaukee and St. Paul Railway Company cut wages by 10 per cent. Bank loan levels dropped nearly 30 per cent between 1893 and 1894; new construction declined so drastically that the city's newspapers dispensed with their annual year-end construction summaries.[21]

In Racine, local newspapers were in substantial agreement that 1893 had been a disastrous year. A prominent civic leader informed his audience that the city had 3,000 unemployed out of a possible work force of about 6,000, and a daily wage loss of $5,500. He con-

---

[20] Carlos C. Closson, Jr., "The Unemployed in American Cities," part 1, in the *Quarterly Journal of Economics*, 8 (January, 1894), 168–217; Thelen, *New Citizenship*, 58–60; Milwaukee *Sentinel*, April 2, August 2, 19, 23 (quote), October 4, 23, November 11, and December 4, 1894.

[21] Thelen, *New Citizenship*, 59–60; Milwaukee *Sentinel*, June 19, August 15, November 10, 1893, and November 4, 1894; Mollenhoff, *Madison*, 171.

cluded that never in Racine's fifty-year history had there been such widespread destitution. In October, 1894, the Racine *Daily Journal* set the number of idle workers at 2,000, with many others working three-day weeks or reduced hours, and lamented that there was not a "wheel turning in half of the largest factories." Even the rapidly growing industrial city of Kenosha was adversely affected. In August, 1893, the Bain Wagon and Chicago Brass companies closed their doors indefinitely, idling 500 workers. The city's newspapers warned Kenoshans to save their money, form coal and flour clubs, and leave their savings in banks where they could be lent out to merchants and manufacturers to "allow them to run their factories and business houses, keeping the men, boys and girls employed." Despite these pleas, one Kenosha bank failed in August, 1895, and another barely survived a run by paying out more than $300,000 in a single morning.[22]

Farm prices hit all-time lows in 1895–1896, though primarily as the continuation of a long downward spiral. Compared to the years 1870–1875, the value of the state's seven leading crops—wheat, corn, oats, barley, buckwheat, and potatoes—was 36 per cent lower by 1895. However, these declines were somewhat offset because Wisconsin's agriculture was so diversified and in a state of transition. Dairy farming was clearly on the upswing during the 1890's and Wisconsin agriculture was no longer tied to the fluctuating prices of grain staples. Many farmers were forced to accept payment in trade and could not afford to buy proper winter clothing. The *Wood County Reporter* concluded that, in thirty-five years in the Stevens Point-Grand Rapids (later Wisconsin Rapids) area, "never before have we noticed the results of hard times and poverty as we have noticed in this year." And while the amount of acreage under cultivation in Wisconsin declined in the first half of the 1890's, the number of people engaged in agriculture actually increased. Even so, the Bureau of Labor and Industrial Statistics obliquely concluded that there "are reasons for believing, however, that during the last three years the farmers have not suffered more disappointments than those engaged in other occupations."[23]

One index of unemployment during the depression was the substantial number of tramps who roamed Wisconsin and other states

---

[22] Kathy McVicker, ". . . Who Would Otherwise Have Suffered: Charity and Poor Relief in Racine, Wisconsin During the Depression of 1893" (unpublished seminar paper, May 29, 1984, in the Area Research Center, University of Wisconsin-Parkside, Kenosha), 1–2, 21; Kenosha *Union*, August 3, 1893; Racine *Daily Journal*, January 2, 5, 16, October 27, 1894, April 25, July 10, 22, 1895, August 29, 1896, and June 22, 1897.

[23] Bureau of Labor and Industrial Statistics, *Biennial Report*, 1895–1896, pp. 137–140. The *Wood County Reporter* (Grand Rapids [later Wisconsin Rapids]), February 7, 1895, as quoted in Thelen, *New Citizenship*, 59–60.

in search of food, lodging, and work. Several Wisconsin cities and villages allowed them to sleep in their jails or established municipal lodging houses where they could earn their keep through manual labor. But many more fortunate citizens viewed their presence with alarm and disdain, as when an "army" of some fifty transients reportedly terrorized residents of Racine's Junction section, stealing chickens from a nearby barn and meat from adjacent stores. The *Badger State Banner* in Black River Falls reported that "tramps were never so numerous here as for the past week or two," and that rebuffed tramps in Winnebago County had slit the throats of three cows. In June, 1894, five tramps reportedly held up a Beloit store at gunpoint, "finally having a free-for-all fight over the division of the spoils."[24]

The depression's length and severity eventually caused a great many Wisconsinites to reconsider their conceptions of progress. The impressive economic boom of the 1880's, in conjunction with the technological advances that undergirded it, had improved the quality of life for much of the citizenry. But large numbers failed to share in these benefits, and some even lost ground because standards for the good life escalated appreciably. As long as society persisted in interpreting economic and class differences as a byproduct of competition among individuals under conditions of equal opportunity, many found it easy to believe that prosperity was the legitimate, even the inevitable, reward earned by those who possessed ability, virtue, and ambition. *Ipso facto*, these same persons saw poverty as the natural and well-deserved fate of those who were deficient in any or all of these admirable qualities.[25]

The majority of Americans tended to believe that America was in fact a land of abundant and equal opportunity that equitably produced widely diverging degrees of prosperity and security. This dominant mind-set posited society as a loosely structured aggregation of autonomous individuals, constantly competing for finite resources and benefits in a marketplace governed by a canon of immutable natural laws. These natural laws included the law of supply and demand, which regulated both prices and fluctuations in the level of economic activity; the law of diminishing returns, which constrained businesses from producing for marginal consumers or hiring marginal workers; the iron law of wages, which lauded low pay as the best

---

[24] Michael Lesy, *Wisconsin Death Trip* (New York, 1973), unpaginated; see the 1893 (leaves 1 and 3) and 1894 sections (leaf 4). See also Paul T. Ringenbach, *Tramps and Reformers, 1873–1916: The Discovery of Unemployment in New York* (Westport, Connecticut, 1973), esp. pages vi and 36–81.

[25] See, for example, the discussions in Harter, *John R. Commons*, 25–44; Rader, *Academic Mind and Reform*, 30–45; and Thelen, *New Citizenship*, 9–32.

guarantor of high employment and condemned both collective bargaining and labor legislation; and the Malthusian law of population, which warned that the proliferation of offspring among the lower socio-economic classes would continue to outstrip even the most spectacular increases in resources and benefits. Many believed that intervention, whether by organized interest groups or government agencies, into the operation of these natural laws ran the risk of spreading economic disaster to more fortunate members of society. Within this closed universe, the general welfare consisted only of the greatest good for the greatest number, while the public interest was nothing more nor less than the sum total of individual successes and failures.[26]

For many Wisconsinites, the regimen imposed by these commonly held beliefs was augmented by two complementary doctrines which came to be called Social Darwinism and the Gospel of Wealth. The former insisted that individual human beings were destined to compete for limited resources in a brutal struggle for survival of the fittest. Any attempt to interfere in this process, either by constraining the fit or by aiding the unfit, squandered scarce resources and threatened widespread devastation. On the other hand, for those who preferred a more theological justification, the Gospel of Wealth utilized the Calvinist doctrine of predestination to contend that the affluent and the poor were analogous to the elect and the damned. The test was not piety or right behavior, but rather the achievement of material success. Both taxing or regulating the affluent and aiding the less fortunate were tantamount to flouting God's grand design for salvation. More sensitive (or squeamish) devotees of the Gospel of Wealth professed the stewardship doctrine, which enjoined the affluent to dispense charity to "the worthy poor."[27]

In such a world view, depressions were merely brief detours in the inexorable march of progress: automatic, periodic corrections necessary to purge a self-regulating system of marginal or aberrant elements. Depressions also served to impose discipline upon those individuals and businesses that violated natural laws. The most widely accepted remedy was rigorous retrenchment by government, business, and consumers, until natural economic laws began to stimulate new investment, production, employment, and consumption. Ac-

---

[26] Eric F. Goldman, *Rendezvous with Destiny: A History of Modern American Reform* (New York, 1953), 85–93.

[27] Richard Hofstadter, *Social Darwinism in American Thought* (revised ed., New York, 1959), 3–12, 31–66; Irvin G. Wyllie, *The Self-Made Man in America: The Myth of Rags to Riches* (New Brunswick, New Jersey, 1954), 116–132; Goldman, *Rendezvous with Destiny*, 87–93; Daniel Seely Gregory, *Christian Ethics: Or, the True Moral Manhood and Life of Duty; a Text-Book* (Philadelphia, 1875).

cordingly, many well-established Wisconsinites were at great pains to assert the temporary, relatively mild, and ultimately positive character of the depression of 1893–1897, and to fix the blame for the disaster squarely upon errant individuals and institutions.[28]

Thus, despite occasional, grudging admission of the depths of economic disaster, the Milwaukee *Sentinel* continued to assert that no one went hungry, that business failures were fewer in Milwaukee than in other major industrial cities, and that the city's unemployment picture was no darker than that elsewhere. Superior's *Evening Telegram* maintained that the city remained comparatively well-off. In his 1895 message to the legislature, Governor William H. Upham (1895– 1897), a Marshfield manufacturer and businessman, proclaimed that Wisconsin "has suffered less, perhaps, than many others," and that it had been "singularly free from those manifestations of lawlessness which have brought discredit upon several states." His successor, Edward Scofield (1897–1901)—from Oconto, and also a businessman—likewise assured the legislature that "Wisconsin has not suffered greatly" in relation to other states, though he acknowledged the high rate of business failures and unemployment. Even the Bureau of Labor and Industrial Statistics, while continuing to paint a grim statistical picture of the state's economic conditions, concluded that "there are also reasons to believe that it suffered less from the crisis than many other states," contending that the cheap lands of Wisconsin's heavily logged northern counties, known as the Cutover, had absorbed many urban refugees and attracted many recent immigrants.[29]

Chief among the culprits whose machinations had visited the wrath of the natural laws upon Wisconsin were individual bankers, businessmen, politicians, labor "agitators" and "radicals." High on the list of malefactors was Frank Lappen of Milwaukee, who not only borrowed enough money to bankrupt the Plankinton bank but also induced his employees, saloonkeepers, and "disreputable women" to remove their money from solvent institutions. When Lappen disappeared, the Milwaukee press religiously reported on his supposed

---

[28] Samuel Rezneck, *Business Depressions and Financial Panics: Essays in American Business and Economic History* (revised ed., New York, 1968), 3–20, 175–186; Douglas W. Steeples, "The Panic of 1893: Contemporary Reflections and Reactions," *Mid-America: An Historical Review*, 47 (July, 1965), 155–175; Rendig Fels, *American Business Cycles, 1865–1897* (Chapel Hill, 1959; reprinted, Westport, Connecticut, 1973), 184– 185.

[29] Milwaukee *Sentinel*, May 19, July 28, September 19, 1893, and February 25, 1894; Superior *Evening Telegram*, August 2, 25, 1893; William H. Upham, *Governor's Message*, doc. 1, pp. 1, 12–13, in *Wisconsin Public Documents*, 1893–1894, vol. 1; Edward Scofield, *Governor's Message*, doc. 1, p. 1, in *Wisconsin Public Documents*, 1895–1896, vol. 1; Bureau of Labor and Industrial Statistics, *Biennial Report*, 1899–1900, xiii.

whereabouts, as well as that of other renegade capitalists. The Plankinton bank's president, Frederick T. Day, also fled the city and was eventually apprehended in Tennessee where, because "his nervous system was in a more deplorable state than when he left Milwaukee," he was placed in a sanitarium. The failure of Milwaukee's South Side Savings Bank was charged primarily to the misadventures of cashier John B. Koetting, who fled with "more or less of the funds," and to president Gustave C. Trumpff, who "left town to avoid possible arrest and what he regarded as anonymous annoyances from unfortunate depositors and sheriff's deputies." Trumpff finally was apprehended in Mexico.[30]

In early November, 1893, a grand jury, composed largely of farmers, saloonkeepers, workers, and small businessmen, and chaired by Henry Smith, co-founder of Milwaukee's Peoples Party, indicted Day, Koetting, William Plankinton, and several other bank officers. The jury also made recommendations for state regulation of lending institutions. Even so, the *Sentinel* disparaged the jury's findings because of its members' humble origins in contrast to the successful businessmen who stood before them. One irate victim of the Plankinton fiasco included Governor George Peck (1891–1895) on his list of villains because the chief executive had announced, from the bank's steps, that the institution "was just as solid as the Rock Of Ages." Residents of West Superior were both appalled and fascinated by revelations that Francis H. Weeks, president and treasurer of both the Land and River Improvement Company and the West Superior Iron and Steel Company, had absconded with over $100,000 and fled to Cuba. When banks at Shell Lake, Washburn, and Prescott all failed on the same day, the disaster was blamed on A. C. Probert, "Washburn's foremost and most enterprising citizen" who "seemed to have lots of money and flew high," but who now had "not a friend in the town."[31]

As the frustrated working class became more militant and its leaders more vocal in demands for relief and reform, many middle- and upper-class Wisconsinites blamed the economic malaise on what they saw as the moral deficiencies and radicalism of the lower socio-economic orders. Industrial workers, they declared, were lazy and unwilling to accept necessary layoffs, wage cuts, and reduced hours.

---

[30] Thelen, *New Citizenship*, 63–64; Milwaukee *Sentinel*, May 13, 14, June 9 (quote), 27 (quote), July 12, 16, 19, 26, 30 (quote), August 2 (quote), 19, and September 10, 1893.

[31] Milwaukee *Sentinel*, July 19 (quote), 26 (quote), November 3, 1893; Milwaukee *Journal*, November 1, 1893. The irate victim may have confused Governor Peck with Milwaukee mayor Peter J. Somers who in May said from the bank steps that it "was as solid as the rock of Gibraltar." *Milwaukee Sentinel*, May 14, 1893.

They produced too many children, and they drowned their sorrows in alcohol. The Milwaukee *Sentinel*, an advocate of the business and industrial managers, solemnly preached that self-respecting unemployed men carried themselves "philosophically and calmly," had "no sympathy with the rioters or looters," rejected "the specious arguments of the labor agitators," and were always willing to work for the prevailing wage. Decrying the rising demand for public works projects, the Janesville *Recorder* charged that "the fellows who howl the loudest for work don't like to shovel." Native-born Wisconsinites quickly pointed out that many of the most culpable were recent immigrants whose willingness to accept lower standards, even during prosperous times, was injurious to the status of the working class. Even those who professed sympathy for the needy were careful to distinguish between those who were "deserving" and those who were seeking a free ride. Demands to "weed out the unworthy among those who are accepting charity" were commonplace, as were complaints that local politicians, especially in ethnic neighborhoods, rapidly reinstated large numbers of their excised constituents. Fearing the creation of a permanent class of paupers, many proposed that all able-bodied adults be required to work for their sustenance. "Honest workingmen are slow to accept charity," the *Sentinel* acknowledged, "but when once their names are on the poor lists, they are equally slow to conclude, even after becoming more self-supporting, they can care for their families without assistance."[32]

Demonstrations, strikes, and other manifestations of working-class militancy were invariably blamed on ignorance and gullibility, labor agitators, and political radicals. Labor leaders were advised to teach frugality and self-control instead of hatred of employers. Much of the initial empathy of more comfortable Wisconsinites toward the less fortunate turned increasingly to fear and loathing, as the latter organized into "armies" and unions struck to protest reductions in wages or hours. Increasing support for unions, for populists and socialists was interpreted by many as the harbinger of revolution.[33]

Nor could some resist the temptation to play partisan politics with the depression. Democrats blamed Republican policies of tight money and tariff protection; Republicans stigmatized Democratic doctrines

---

[32] Milwaukee *Sentinel*, August 19 (quote), 25, 1893, February 4, April 26 (quote), 27, August 19, 21, September 3, 6, and October 4, 5, 6, 1894.

[33] Steeples, "The Panic of 1893," *Mid-America*, 47: 169–173; Milwaukee *Sentinel*, September 13, 1894. For discussions of the growing apprehension that gripped more established Americans during the depression, see Nell Irvin Painter, *Standing at Armageddon: The United States, 1877–1919* (New York, 1987), xii, xxxvii–xliv, 110–140; John Whiteclay Chambers II, *The Tyranny of Change: America in the Progressive Era, 1900–1917* (New York, 1980), 1–104; and Stanley P. Caine, "The Origins of Progressivism," in Lewis L. Gould, ed., *The Progressive Era* (Syracuse, 1974), 11–34.

of currency expansion and tariff for revenue only. In Milwaukee, two prominent Republicans toured the city in a dilapidated "hard-times hack," charging outgoing Democrats with responsibility for their plight, while the Kenosha *Telegraph-Courier* castigated "the economic logic of the Democratic party when applied in practice." As a candidate for governor, William H. Upham said in 1893 that Republican prosperity had built Milwaukee, but "when the Democrats came into power they put a stop to the development of Milwaukee as surely as the ashes of Vesuvius covered Herculaneum and Pompeii." The *Sentinel* promised readers "almost instant relief" if the Sherman Act of 1890 were repealed, thus ending the act's mandated monthly purchase by the federal government of 4.5 million ounces of silver bullion for coinage into dollars. Newspapers in Sheboygan and Grand (Wisconsin) Rapids contended that "all that is needed now to assure us prosperous times is to let the tariff alone."[34]

Yet even though a substantial number of solid Wisconsinites continued to profess their faith in laissez-faire economics, many others began to urge the necessity for organization, intervention, and collaboration by various public and private agencies. By the onset of the new century, that necessity, together with the corollary that government was the most efficacious instrument for the promotion of universal prosperity and security, would become a central tenet of progressivism. Growing empathy for the have-nots, and fear of revolution from below, prompted many to view the plight of the unemployed and destitute in less judgmental terms and to listen to demands for amelioration.

Drastic declines in tax revenues and charitable giving, combined with the loss of substantial public and private funds in bankruptcies and bank failures, severely depleted the resources required to sustain even the "worthy poor." The Superior school system suffered a loss of $34,000 due to bank failures. The municipal governments of Milwaukee and Oshkosh had to beg and borrow to render rudimentary services. In Racine, a 50 per cent unemployment rate among industrial workers and threefold increase in the number of registered tramps motivated more established citizens to form the Racine Relief Association to co-ordinate a hodgepodge of relief efforts by ethnic and employee benefit societies, labor unions, churches, private charities, women's and temperance associations, and public agencies. Devoted to "scientific charity," the new association sponsored public works projects, workhouses, a garden plan that made vacant land available for cultivation, and a women's exchange that allowed mothers to work for income in their homes. Speaking to University of

[34] Milwaukee *Sentinel*, August 25, 1893 (quote), October 9, 21, 23 (quote), 1894; Kenosha *Telegraph-Courier*, May 6, 1894; Thelen, *New Citizenship*, 60 (quote).

Wisconsin graduates in June, 1894, president Charles Kendall Adams warned that there existed "everywhere in the country symptoms of social and political discontent." He went on to say that many Wisconsinites were raising "questions that are connected with the very foundations of society and have to do with the most elemental principles of human liberty and modern civilization."[35]

Much of the intellectual underpinning for this discontent and questioning was provided by the emerging social sciences and Social Gospel. The former abandoned the concept of a closed socio-economic system, governed by immutable natural laws, in favor of the empirical method of examining socio-economic institutions as they actually evolved and functioned. This involved gathering as much concrete data as possible, then analyzing and interpreting this material in an objective and dispassionate manner, and allowing conclusions to emerge from the evidence. Such exercises generally buttressed the impression that the existing order had arisen out of purposeful management and manipulation by aggressive, intelligent financiers, entrepreneurs, corporate executives, and politicians. The Social Gospel rejected both material prosperity and personal piety as the measure of sanctity, instead judging individuals using the criteria of concern for the human condition and tangible aid to fellow human beings.

The precepts of the social sciences and the Social Gospel were synthesized by Richard T. Ely. He both asserted the hypocrisy of those who exuded personal piety and social indifference, and challenged comfortable Wisconsinites to prove their Christianity by combating social and economic evils. Calling for large-scale government intervention into the socio-economic order, Ely warned that any nation that failed to promote justice and equity might come to deserve the punishment of violent revolution. Although gradually Ely became more circumspect in his advocacy and activism, John R. Commons, Charles McCarthy, Frederick Jackson Turner, the sociologist Edward A. Ross, and other university social scientists soon produced even more rigorous and systematic critiques of the existing order. They called for even more extensive and persistent government intervention.[36]

---

[35] Thelen, *New Citizenship*, 55–58; Milwaukee *Sentinel*, February 6, July 29, December 13, 1893, June 18 (quote), July 23, August 21, 1894; Superior *Evening Telegram*, February 22, 1897; McVicker, ". . . Who Would Otherwise Have Suffered," 16–81. See also the minutes of the Racine Relief Association, 1883–1898, in the Eugene W. Leach Papers, box 7, University of Wisconsin-Parkside, Area Research Center.

[36] Goldman, *Rendezvous with Destiny*, 85–207; Rader, *Academic Mind and Reform*, 28–105; Harter, *John R. Commons*, 25–44; Ronald C. White, Jr., and C. Howard Hopkins, *The Social Gospel: Religion and Reform in Changing America* (Philadelphia, 1976), 129–198. For a recent interpretation, see Susan Curtis, *A Consuming Faith: The Social Gospel*

The tenets of this new dispensation were disseminated among scholars, students, and government officials, as well as to the general public, through a variety of media. As many as 50,000 Wisconsinites participated in courses taught by the newly organized University of Wisconsin Extension Division during the depression years. The lecture series for the winter of 1893–1894 included talks by Ely on "Socialism and the Distribution of Wealth," by Turner on "United States Politics" and the "Colonization of the United States," and by home economist Helen Campbell on "Woman's Place in the Social Economy." University-sponsored extension centers sprang up in most of the state's cities and in many rural areas, offering up to 100 courses during the 1895–1896 session. Their audiences consisted of the members of women's clubs, labor unions, business and professional associations, and farmers' organizations. In 1895 a delegate to the state meeting of the Grange endorsed the importance of such contacts, saying, "When the body politic is diseased we must look to men who have made a life study of the science of government. Our modern political economist can learn [sic] us much we must learn." Numerous newspapers either embraced elements of the new critique of society or paid unintended homage to their popularity by fiercely disputing its tenets.[37]

Especially after 1893, a variety of existing organizations established discussion and study groups to investigate current issues; and new organizations, many of which included people from diverse walks of life, were formed expressly to examine social questions, exchange points of view, and seek common ground as consumers, taxpayers, or citizens. The Wisconsin State Federation of Labor was founded in June, 1893, to co-ordinate union locals and lobby for statewide legislation. Women's clubs gradually turned from discussion of classical literature and domestic concerns to "municipal housekeeping" and socio-economic reform, organizing as the Wisconsin State Federation of Women's Clubs in 1897. That same year, a combination of intellectuals and trade unionists in Milwaukee formed Branch One of the Social Democratic Party of America, dedicated to fostering a cooperative commonwealth through ameliorative legislation and political action. The Wisconsin Dairymen's Association increasingly looked to state government and the university's College of Agriculture to regulate and inform their industry. Various professional associations began to lobby for state intervention in education, social work, and public health. Milwaukee businessmen and lawyers debated the mer-

---

and Modern American Life (New Studies in American Intellectual and Cultural History series, Baltimore, 1991).

[37] The quotes appear in Thelen, New Citizenship, 67–72; Milwaukee Sentinel, October 25, 1893.

its of socialism with Social Democratic leader Victor Berger at the Liberal Club, while banker John Johnston of Milwaukee joined Populists, Socialists, and Social Gospel clergymen in an appeal for "men to help create the new society [where] class privileges will be abolished because all will belong to the human family."[38]

So popular were this emerging progressivism's tenets that even the staunchest defenders of the established order found it necessary to modify their positions. *Sentinel* editor Horace Rublee conceded, in August, 1894, "The extension of government management into other fields, is a question to be decided, not in accordance with theory, or any immutable principle, but with regard to circumstances." The following January, Governor Upham instructed the legislature not only to pass laws attracting investment capital but also measures safeguarding the interests of all classes of citizens, ensuring labor its "just and fair recompense," and dealing with changing industrial conditions. His successor, Governor Scofield, expressed alarm that, in the absence of state regulation, "great aggregations of capital may be tempted to exercise that power outside of its legitimate province." The Bureau of Labor and Industrial Statistics steadily evolved from a purely data-gathering agency to an influential advocate of state activism in factory health and safety, the wages and hours of labor, unemployment relief, and child and women's labor.[39]

Nowhere was the dramatic paradox between the opulence of the World's Columbian Exposition and the devastation of the depression of 1893 captured more vividly than in the writings of Wisconsin-born journalist Ray Stannard Baker, in whose life it became a pivotal event. In 1892, fresh from a nearly idyllic boyhood in St. Croix Falls and an education at the University of Michigan, Baker went to work for the Chicago *News Record*. He was perfectly situated to observe "the bright banners, the music, and the tinsel of the World's Fair, gorgeous as they were," but his delight in the pageantry dissipated. He wrote that he was appalled by the "dizzying haste" with which it gave way to "another pageant, sombre and threatening. . . . It was marked by unprecedented extremes of poverty, unemployment, unrest." He was amazed at the spectacle of such enormous "human downfall after

---

[38] Thelen, *New Citizenship*, 68–77 (quote, 71), 156–175; Robert W. Ozanne, *The Labor Movement in Wisconsin: A History* (Madison, 1984), 34–45; Marvin Wachman, *History of the Social-Democratic Party of Milwaukee, 1897–1910* (Urbana, 1945); Genevieve G. McBride, *On Wisconsin Women: Working for Their Rights from Settlement to Suffrage* (Madison, 1993), 134–200; Lampard, *Rise of the Dairy Industry*, 245–247, 333–351.

[39] Thelen, *New Citizenship*, 73, 81 (quotes); Milwaukee *Sentinel*, August 25, 1894; William H. Upham, *Governor's Message*, doc. 1, pp. 1, 12–13, in *Wisconsin Public Documents*, 1893–1894, vol. 1; Bureau of Labor and Industrial Statistics, *Biennial Report*, 1903–1904, pp. 122–154, 500–539, and *Biennial Report*, 1895–1896, pp. 287–300, 317–336.

the magnificence and prodigality of the World's Fair which had so recently closed its doors!"

In the spring of 1894 his paper assigned him to cover the march of Coxey's Army of unemployed from Massillon, Ohio, to Washington, D.C., and its demand for massive public works projects. Baker was converted to the understanding "that there could have been no such demonstration in a civilized country unless there was profound and deep-seated distress, disorganization, unrest, unhappiness behind it—and that the public would not be cheering the army and feeding it voluntarily without a recognition, however vague, that the conditions in the country warranted some such explosion."

Transformed largely by the stark nature of that paradox, Baker went on to become a celebrated journalist and "muckraker," exposing and decrying before a wide audience the harsh inequities of life in a "progressive" society, especially the pervasive discrimination based upon race.[40]

For many Wisconsinites, then, 1893 was a year in which the paradox of progress was revealed in all its complexity. The state's performance at the World's Fair testified not only to its considerable achievements, but also to its passionate conviction that even greater accomplishments were yet to come. That interpretation, however, obscured the fact that rapid technological and economic "progress" did not automatically benefit everyone, and actually exacerbated many socio-economic inequities. The panic of 1893 and the prolonged and severe economic depression which continued into 1897 starkly revealed many of the societal dislocations and inequities that were easily ignored during periods of growth. What was more, the depression transmitted them to large numbers of Wisconsinites who thought themselves prosperous and successful. Problems easily rationalized during good times demanded more thorough examination now that they touched a significant portion of mainstream society. And such problems did not disappear with the return of general prosperity.

Many prominent Wisconsinites—principally the bankers and industrialists, the manufacturers and upper-echelon managers who had long ruled business and politics—continued to regard these phenomena as the inevitable, and ultimately beneficial, price of "progress." But others—an odd but potent mixture of middle-class intellectuals and new-style academics, of populists and socialists, ideologues and utopians, political mavericks and ordinary men and women of conscience—came to regard "progress" as subjective, rela-

---

[40] Ray Stannard Baker, *American Chronicle: The Autobiography of Ray Stannard Baker* (New York, 1945), 1–25 (quotes, 1, 2, 19); Carolyn Wedin Sylvander, "Fame and Obscurity: The Baker Brothers of St. Croix Falls," in *WMH*, 69 (Spring, 1986), 171–186.

tive, and contingent. To them, "progress" was more a product of conscious human definition and manipulation than of Darwinian mechanics. Progress did not seem inevitable, any more than it seemed universally beneficial.

So persuaded, they determined to organize, to intervene purposefully in the operations of the socio-economic order, to build reform coalitions across seemingly impermeable lines of class, ethnicity, religion, and locale, and to make numerous demands for redress upon municipal and state government. Whatever their differences, they shared at least one common goal: they would be heard.

2

Becoming America's Dairyland

[1]

"THE period after 1900 and preceding the World War," observed Wisconsin agricultural statistician Walter H. Ebling in 1935, "was one of progress, stability, and prosperity. It may be looked upon as a 'golden age' of agriculture. . . ." Those were also the years when an "industrial revolution in dairying" and "the Wisconsin Idea in dairying" enabled the state to survive the collapse of wheat farming by promoting the transition to dairy husbandry. So complete was this metamorphosis by 1914 that Wisconsin outstripped any other single state in milk production and the making of butter and cheese. So successful were the collaborative efforts of dairy farmers, the University of Wisconsin's College of Agriculture, and state government that they established a powerful precedent for similar co-operative endeavors involving private interest groups, the university, and the state. By 1914, Wisconsin unquestionably had emerged as "America's Dairyland," although a healthy admixture of specialty crops, livestock raising, and vegetable canning prevented the state from becoming a dairy monolith.[1]

This golden age was characterized by significant expansion of Wisconsin's agricultural domain, especially in the northern two-thirds of the state. Whereas only about 48 per cent of the state's land was in farms in 1890, more than 60 per cent was farmed by 1914. Total farm acreage increased by nearly one-third, and the number of farms grew from 146,409 in 1890 to 189,295 in 1920. The ratio of improved land to total area was nearly twice that of the U.S. average, although less than half that of Iowa and Illinois—principally because more than 40 per cent of Wisconsin was still forested. The number of Wisconsin

[1] Walter H. Ebling, "The Situation in Agriculture," in the *Wisconsin Blue Book, 1935*, p. 45; Eric E. Lampard, *The Rise of the Dairy Industry in Wisconsin: A Study in Agricultural Change, 1820–1920* (Madison, 1963), 244–293, 333–351.

farms increased 29 per cent between 1890 and 1920, compared to the U.S. rate of 41 per cent, while the amount of cultivated land grew one-third, compared to the national figure of 53 per cent. Even so, the amount of state land in cultivation was larger than the entire area of many eastern states and of several European countries.[2]

The most impressive gains came in the central Wisconsin and Middle North counties. Between 1890 and 1920, Marathon jumped from nineteenth to second place among Wisconsin counties in percentage of acreage in cultivation; Clark, from thirty-eighth to fifth; Barron, from forty-fifth to ninth. These eleven counties became increasingly agricultural as the lumbering frontier receded, leaving the Cutover in its wake. During the lumber era, many settlers farmed during the summer months and logged during the winter. Logging camps served as the principal market for farm products. Some prospective farmers sold or leased cutting rights to lumber companies; others cut the trees themselves and sold logs to the logging companies or sawmills.

The belief—or the illusion—that "the plow follows the saw" became part of the era's conventional wisdom. This conversion from lumber to agriculture was especially successful in the Middle North, where the heavy soil produced significant crop yields, and where burgeoning urban markets replaced those lost by the loggers' exodus. The lighter, sandier soil and interspersed marshlands of Jackson, Juneau, and Adams counties were somewhat less conducive to agriculture, except for the production of cranberries and other fruit crops. By 1914, half of the Middle North's area was devoted to agriculture, and the crossroads cheese factory and the capacious dairy barn quickly became dominant features of the landscape. This success emboldened many Wisconsinites to expand the agricultural frontier into the eighteen northernmost counties.[3]

Between 1898 and 1904, Wisconsin ranked first among the nation's lumbering states, cutting over 3 billion board feet a year, much of it valuable white pine. (A board foot is a standard measure of wood, one foot square by one inch thick.) At that frantic pace, the forests rapidly receded, adding greatly to the Cutover's total area. By 1914, the timber yield had fallen below 1 billion board feet, dropping Wisconsin to tenth among the lumber-producing states and triggering a massive effort to reorient the region's economy. Railroad, lumber,

---

[2] Walter H. Ebling et al., *A Century of Wisconsin Agriculture, 1848–1948*, Department of Agriculture, Crop and Livestock Reporting Service, *Bulletin*, no. 290 (1948), 135; Walter H. Ebling, comp., *Wisconsin Agriculture in Mid-Century*, Department of Agriculture, Crop and Livestock Reporting Service, *Bulletin*, no. 325 (1954), 2–4, 53; "The Industries of Wisconsin," in the *Wisconsin Blue Book, 1915*, p. 2.

[3] Ebling et al., *A Century of Wisconsin Agriculture*, 11–13; Ebling, comp., *Agriculture in Mid-Century*, 4; "Industries of Wisconsin," *Wisconsin Blue Book, 1915*, p. 2.

and land companies, with significant help from the College of Agriculture and the Wisconsin Board of Immigration, mounted an all-out effort to attract agricultural settlers. Farmers, it was widely believed, would revivify the Cutover. As late as 1900, for example, only 49,000 of Lincoln County's 575,000 acres were devoted to farming. Railroad, lumber, and land companies retained ownership to all the rest, save for the 35,000 acres held by federal, state, and county governments. The thin layer of arable soil was soon exhausted, causing crop yields to plummet. The steady disappearance of lumber camps deprived farmers of both the opportunity for supplemental employment and their major produce market. Unable to sell large tracts of land once the timber had been harvested, lumber companies and railroads allowed much of their holdings to become tax-delinquent, increasing the burden on farmers and villagers who were already struggling. By 1914, only about one-fourth of the Cutover was being farmed, and not one of the eighteen northernmost counties had even half its land in farms.[4]

At the other extreme lay the state's southern and eastern counties, where a much more productive agricultural domain was shrinking steadily. During the generally expansionist 1890's, Ozaukee, Dodge, Manitowoc, and Kewaunee were the only counties to experience even small declines in farm acreage. Between 1900 and 1910, however, thirty-six southern and eastern counties suffered a loss of agricultural land; Milwaukee, Adams, Waukesha, Juneau, and Green Lake counties each lost over a hundred farms in the next decade. Much of the existing farmland in Milwaukee County was absorbed by the city's expansion and the creation of industrial suburbs. Annexation of existing farmland by such emerging industrial cities as Racine, Kenosha, Janesville, and Beloit proceeded apace. Virtually no underdeveloped farmland remained in the southern third of the state. There, land of any quality was simply too expensive for aspiring farmers, who instead began flocking to the Cutover.[5]

The average Wisconsin farm in 1914 was just under 120 acres—less than the national average of 140 acres and only slightly larger than it had been in 1860. Smaller farms predominated in the rich, level country near Lake Michigan, while larger ones prevailed in the rolling hills of the southwest, in the west-central marshland, and near Lake Superior. The typical Wisconsin farm was owned and operated

---

[4] Ebling et al., *A Century of Wisconsin Agriculture*, 11–13; Ralph Storm, "A Social and Cultural History of Lincoln County, 1847–1920" (master's thesis, University of Wisconsin, 1965), 103; "Industries in Wisconsin," *Wisconsin Blue Book, 1915*, p. 2.

[5] Ebling et al., *A Century of Wisconsin Agriculture*, 13–14. Despite this exodus, nearly 90 per cent of the land in most southern and eastern counties remained in farms in 1914.

by its occupant. The tenancy rate rose from 11 to 14 per cent between 1890 and 1920, but remained less than half the national average, thanks to relatively small farm size, moderately priced land, and the dearth of speculation. The labor-intensity of livestock husbandry made it unconducive to large farms or tenancy, and many Wisconsin farmers placed a high value upon ownership, even if that entailed a substantial mortgage. "There is no risk, whatever, in going in debt for a farm or for well bred stock," the *Wisconsin Farmer* advised in 1898, "for with industry and a fixed determination to surmount every obstacle, success is as sure to follow as is the sun to rise tomorrow." Almost 52 per cent of Wisconsin farmers chose mortgaged ownership in 1910, substantially above the national figure of one-third and nearly four times the state's tenancy rate.[6]

The years from 1893 to 1914 were generally prosperous for Wisconsin farmers, and the last five probably deserved their designation as a golden age. Federal agricultural officials later selected 1910 to 1914 as the base years on which to build performance indices and to generate definitions of "parity," since wartime inflation did not affect the period. If anything, Wisconsin probably outperformed national norms between 1893 and 1914, because of the explosive growth of dairying, which proved as stable and profitable an agricultural pursuit as any ever devised. One measure of the period's prosperity was the significant rise in the value of Wisconsin farm real estate. Even in the depression-ridden 1890's, the value of farmland and buildings increased by nearly 40 per cent; during the next decade, it appreciated by a staggering 75 per cent. In many northern counties, the value of farm real estate was anywhere from three to five times greater in 1910 than it had been in 1900. Its value equalled the national debt and represented about half the cost of constructing the Panama Canal, ranking it tenth among the several states.[7]

---

[6] Eighty-acre farms predominated because land sales and grants were generally made in multiples of forty acres and because eighty acres were considered the maximum that could be cleared and worked by a single family using horses or oxen. Ebling, comp., *Agriculture in Mid-Century*, 4–5; Ebling et al., *A Century of Wisconsin Agriculture*, 23–26; Vernon Castle Johnson, "Large Farms in Wisconsin" (master's thesis, University of Wisconsin, 1951), 12–13; Benjamin H. Hibbard and Guy A. Peterson, *How Wisconsin Farmers Become Farm Owners*, UW Agricultural Experiment Station, *Bulletin*, no. 402 (1928), 8–9, 14, 15–24, 31; John Cownie, "To Buy or Rent a Farm?" *Wisconsin Farmer*, December 29, 1898, p. 2 (quote); Benjamin H. Hibbard and John D. Black, *Farm Leasing Systems in Wisconsin*, UW Agricultural Experiment Station, *Bulletin*, no. 47 (1920), 1–3, 10, 58–60; Charles J. Galpin and Emily F. Hoag, *Farm Tenancy: An Analysis of the Occupancy of 500 Farms*, UW Agricultural Experiment Station, *Research Bulletin*, no. 44 (1919), 8–9, 16–18; John Lee Coulter, *The Problem of Rural Credit or Farm Finance in the United States*, State Board of Agriculture, *Bulletin*, no. 1 (1913), 12–13.

[7] Ebling et al., *A Century of Wisconsin Agriculture*, 25.

The fact that more than half of Wisconsin's farms were mortgaged offset these achievements. The amount of agricultural mortgage debt increased by nearly three-fifths between 1910 and 1915, due largely to the opening of marginal farmsteads in the northern third of the state. Even in prosperous Dane County, about two-thirds of 1914 farms were mortgaged at an average of 38 per cent of their value, for a five-year period, at 5 per cent interest. In the Middle North county of Rusk, an even larger proportion of farms were either mortgaged, at an average interest rate of 7 per cent, or bought on contract at about 6 per cent. The cost of mortgage payments, plus interest, was largely responsible for a decline in net farm income of nearly 25 per cent during the "golden years" of 1909–1914. Even so, gains in real estate value were both real and significant, especially for those farmers in the southern two-thirds of Wisconsin.[8]

Prosperity was even more evident in the burgeoning value of the state's livestock, crops, and animal products. As early as 1905, Wisconsin led all states that had large areas of undeveloped agricultural lands in both production and earnings per acre. In earnings per acre, the state was in the same league as Ohio, Indiana, Illinois, and Missouri, and ahead of Kansas, Nebraska, Minnesota, and the Dakotas. It exceeded the national average in corn, wheat, oats, barley, and flax, equalled it in hay, and fell below the norm only in potatoes, rye, and buckwheat. Wisconsin ranked first in the value of milk cows, fourth in sheep, sixth in other cattle, and seventh in swine. In production per acre, it ranked first in wheat and barley, second in potatoes, and fourth in corn and buckwheat. Ten years later, the value of the state's farm products still exceeded that of its manufactured goods, less the cost of raw materials.[9]

During the first decade of the new century, the value of Wisconsin's barley harvest more than doubled, that of its oats and potatoes approximately tripled, and that of its corn, rye, and hay jumped 400 per cent. In nearly every major crop, there was a steady increase in value between 1895 and 1910, followed by a sizable leap during the next five years. Corn rose from $10 million in 1895 to $25 million in

---

[8] Chien Chung Wan, "Consolidated Balance Sheet and Income Statement of Wisconsin Agriculture Since 1910" (doctoral dissertation, University of Wisconsin, 1950), 30–32; Benjamin H. Hibbard, unattributed clipping of April 16, 1914, talk about farm credit in Wisconsin at the National Conference on Marketing and Farm Credits, Chicago, 1914, in the LRB.

[9] Bureau of Labor and Industrial Statistics, *Biennial Report*, 1905–1906, pp. 374–378; Secretary of State, *Tabular Statements of the Census Enumeration and the Agricultural, Mineral and Manufacturing Interests of the State of Wisconsin*, 1895, vol. 1, pp. 817–818; Secretary of State, *Tabular Statements of the Census Enumeration and the Agricultural, Dairying and Manufacturing Interests of the State of Wisconsin*, 1905, vol. 1, part 2, pp. 358–360, 398–404.

1909, and to $46 million by 1915. The most spectacular increases came in dairy products, where the number of milk cows in the state doubled and their value per head increased nearly two-thirds. By 1914, the value of the state's butter output reached over $34 million while that of its cheese exceeded $28 million. Despite these striking gains, Wisconsin dropped from seventh to tenth place nationally in the total value of its agricultural products.[10]

Whether these increases in value translated into substantial gains in farm income is difficult to determine. Farm income included proceeds from the sale of livestock, crops, and animal products, appreciation of the value of land, buildings, livestock, and implements, as well as "home consumption" (meaning the worth of crops grown for feed). Property taxes, mortgage payments (including interest rates of 6 to 10 per cent), various expenses of doing business (the farmer's business costs), and "farm maintenance" (the prices paid for commodities consumed by the household) all reduced income. As agriculture became more specialized, farmers increasingly became consumers of goods that they had formerly produced. While prices received for foodstuffs were increasingly subject to the vagaries of national markets, expenses for the necessities and amenities of life were inflated by the ability of corporations to manipulate supply and demand, and by tariff protection.[11]

The period from 1897 to 1915 was generally marked by rising, though fluctuating, prices. Even though Wisconsin farmers sometimes earned less than the national averages, significantly lower production costs offset this ranking. For example, in 1914, Jefferson County farmers received only $1,566 for their products, compared to $1,750 for those in Middlesex County, Massachusetts; but the Wisconsin farmers' cost of doing business was only one-third that of their eastern competitors. That same year, a U.S. Department of Agriculture survey of sixty southern Wisconsin farmers found that although only seven realized a return on their labor of $500 or more, "more than half the farmers made labor incomes which when combined with what the farm furnished the family gave them enough to get ahead financially each year." "Even when he receives small pay for his labor," the survey concluded, a farmer's "disposable income may be comparatively large."[12]

---

[10] *Wisconsin Blue Book, 1915*, p. 139; *State Census*, 1895, vol. 1, pp. 1022–1025; *State Census*, 1905, vol. 1, part 2, pp. 358–360, 398–404; *Fourteenth Census of the United States, 1920: Manufactures, Volume IX*, 1624.

[11] B. G. Packer, "Why Wisconsin Leads in Dairying. No. VI: Economy in Production," *Wisconsin Agriculturist*, September 2, 1915, p. 9; Thornton L. Smith, "The Farmer's Labor Income: Survey in Wisconsin Reveals Interesting Facts," *ibid.*, December 27, 1919, pp. 13, 25.

[12] Packer, "Why Wisconsin Leads in Dairying," *Wisconsin Agriculturist*, September 2, 1915, p. 9; Smith, "Farmer's Labor Income," *ibid.*, December 27, 1919, p. 25 (quote).

Sales figures for that era cast substantial doubt upon the survey's rosy conclusion. Although gross farm receipts from average annual sales jumped an astronomical 130 per cent between 1910 and 1920, increases in farm expenses and war-generated inflation compensated for the gains. Between 1893 and 1915, escalating out-of-pocket costs rocked farmers. Property taxes leaped from fourteen to forty-nine cents per acre; the wages of hired help soared 50 per cent. Farm income, corrected for inflation, may actually have declined during agriculture's "golden age": cash receipts from commodities plummeted from $223 million in 1909 to $208 million by 1914; net farm income declined from $207 million to $158 million. Although Wisconsin farmers in general had less cash income than did their village or urban cousins, their non-cash advantages, such as self-sufficient food production, enabled many on the farm to maintain a comparable standard of living.[13]

Farm spokesmen were ambivalent about the degree of prosperity. While acknowledging that a severe and protracted drought had caused problems in 1895, the president of the Wisconsin State Agricultural Society still rejoiced that "never in the state's history has the farmer been so magnificently rewarded with an abundant harvest as during the year just closed." The following year, *Hoard's Dairyman*, the nationally important newspaper published in Ft. Atkinson, boasted, "There never before was a time when a dollar paid for cow food and fed to a good dairy cow would buy so much of the necessaries of life as during the past year." But it admitted, "Notwithstanding all these things, there is more grumbling than ever before and more saying that 'dairying don't pay.' " As 1898 drew to a close, the *Wisconsin Farmer*, published in Madison, said that it was imperative "to recognize the truth that the departing year has been a kindly one to the country and to the farmers who are its bone and sinew."[14]

By contrast, the State Board of Agriculture pronounced the 1901 drought "the most serious the state has ever known," especially in the southern third of the state, where the crop yield was half the usual and where "a great deal of money has already been paid out for feed-stuffs." Although the board considered 1902 a year when "[t]he yield of most crops has been above the average, while prices have been satisfactory," it pronounced 1903 below the norm, except for grass and hay. It considered 1906 to be a good crop year, 1907 a

---

[13] "Farm Income in Wisconsin," *Farm Bureau News*, October, 1923, LRB clipping; Walter H. Ebling and Emery C. Wilcox, *Wisconsin Farm Prices, Production, and Income*, Department of Agriculture, *Bulletin*, no. 249 (1944), 102–103, 110–111, 142–145; Wan, "Consolidated Balance Sheet," 40–42, 62–63, 74.

[14] S. D. Hubbard, "Annual Address," in the *Transactions of the Wisconsin State Agricultural Society* (1896), 120–123; "Prospects for Dairymen," *Hoard's Dairyman*, April 23, 1897, p. 186; "The New Year," *Wisconsin Farmer*, December 29, 1898, p. 817.

bad one, and 1910 an adequate year, despite "extremely unfavorable weather conditions, that at times, threatened disastrous results." The board's secretary lauded 1913 as a year in which "never in the history of the State have crops been more abundant nor prices as a rule, better." But when the U.S. Country Life Commission surveyed the nation's farmers in 1908, Wisconsinites joined those in Missouri and North Dakota, as well as those in the American South and West, in doubting that they received a fair return.[15]

Because of these enormous variations, generalizing about the state of agriculture and the level of farm prosperity in Progressive Era Wisconsin is extremely hazardous. Technological innovation and expert knowledge flowed from southeast to northwest; completely rural areas lagged behind those near larger cities; and amenities were everywhere distributed according to socio-economic status. By 1870, Trempealeau County exhibited the "same top heavy distribution of total property" as did similar areas in New England, while residents of Lincoln County by 1900 "freely admitted that there were social classes in the county." The more thoroughly rural the county, the lower its income and educational level. And most New North counties fell below state economic norms. Electricity, running water, and telephones were becoming commonplace on farms in the southern third of the state by 1914, but they remained almost nonexistent in the northern third. By 1910, the total value of farmland, buildings, implements, and machinery in the southern third stood at $605 million, compared to $480 million in the Middle North and only $170 million in the New North. Individually, according to rural sociologist Charles J. Galpin, farmers ranged from "the machine-farmer–new cerebral type," who embraced every technological and educational advance, to the "hoe-farmer–primitive muscular type," who persisted in the old methods, either out of stubbornness, isolation, or deprivation.[16]

Farms in the southern third of the state tended to be modern, comfortable, and prosperous. A Norwegian-born supervisor for the

---

[15] Clayton Ellsworth, "Theodore Roosevelt's Country Life Commission," *Agricultural History*, 34 (October, 1960), 165; State Board of Agriculture, *Annual Report*, 1902, pp. 307, 373–375; 1903, p. 363; 1904, pp. 350–351; 1907, pp. 452–454; 1911, pp. 452–454; 1914, p. 5.

[16] Zahava Fuchs and Douglas G. Marshall, *The Socioeconomic Composition of Wisconsin's Population, 1900–1960*, UW Department of Rural Sociology, *Population Series*, no. 12 (1968), 116–117; John H. Kolb, *Rural Primary Groups: A Study of Agricultural Neighborhoods*, UW Agricultural Experiment Station, *Research Bulletin*, no. 51 (1921), 56–64; Merle Curti, *The Making of an American Community: A Case Study of Democracy in a Frontier Community* (Stanford, California, 1959), 112–114, 442–448 (quote); Storm, "Social and Cultural History of Lincoln County," 142–143 (quote), 154–160; Charles J. Galpin, *Rural Life* (New York, 1922), 31–51 (quotes).

University Experiment Station painted a glowing picture of dairy farms in Waukesha and Jefferson counties in 1911, noting that "a farmer in this country can afford to have a comfortable house and even an automobile at his disposal," and that Wisconsin agriculture was certainly a "paying business." Particularly impressive was the farmstead of a "young German about thirty years old" who cultivated 175 acres of good land near Oconomowoc. A graduate of the University of Wisconsin's College of Agriculture's short course, he had bought his spread for $20,000 at 6 per cent interest, on notes endorsed by his father and father-in-law. After a $1,000 mortgage payment, stock additions, and farm improvements, the young farmer still realized a yearly profit of $3,000 on the sale of calves, hogs, barley, eggs, and cream. "You have to apply science and business system in your work and then go in for the pure bred cattle," he said, confiding that he kept "nothing but pure bred Holstein cattle, most of which are in the Advanced Registry with high records."

Generalizing from the southeastern corner of the state, the Kenosha automobile manufacturer Thomas B. Jeffery rhapsodized that "the mortgage has gone from the middle western farm, and to take its place there is the telephone, the heating system, the water supply, improved farm machinery and the automobile." In a similar vein, a Kenosha County schoolteacher, M. Oveda Crane, predicted, "The farm home of tomorrow will be a modern up-to-date city residence placed in the pure, wholesome air of the country, with the city brought to its back door by auto, bus, train and truck and–perhaps– airplane." When the College of Agriculture gave its first prizes for the best farm homes in 1914, most of the eight winners lived in the southern part of the state, subscribed to the principles of agricultural and domestic science, and enjoyed running water, electricity, automobiles, telephones, typewriters, safes, and letter files.[17]

Much farther down the economic and technological ladder in the early 1900's was the Waushara County potato farm of John Coombes. Each spring, he and his team of horses, Duke and Queenie, plowed and disked ten acres of Middle North sandy soil before employing a horse-drawn wooden marker to create a giant checkerboard of evenly spaced rows, thirty-six inches apart. With bags over their shoulders, John and his son Weston slowly walked each row, dropping pieces of seed potatoes, laboriously cut by his wife and children, every few inches. They then shoved the chunks into the ground with a hand-

---

[17] E. Figved, "Visit to Some Wisconsin Dairy Farms," *Hoard's Dairyman*, May 5, 1911, p. 482 (quote); Thomas B. Jeffery, *Motor World*, 20 (April 8, 1909), 68; Joseph M. Schafer, *Four Wisconsin Counties: Prairie and Forest* (Madison, 1927), 288–291 (quote); Nellie Kedzie Jones, "Homes That Score High: What Wisconsin Found Out About Her Farmhouses," *Country Gentleman*, October 10, 1914, pp. 1697–1698.

held potato planter and dragged one foot, usually the right, to cover each hole. Throughout the hot, dry summer months, Coombes carefully cultivated the tiny seedlings, battling crows, ragweed, drought, and potato bugs. During late September, he walked backward down each row, digging with a six-tined fork to unearth the large red potatoes. His children followed, filling pails with potatoes which they dumped into wooden, bushel-sized boxes. The digging season could last into late October, when falling temperatures made it difficult and painful to harvest the crop by hand. Each time they accumulated fifty bushels, the Coombeses loaded them onto a horse-drawn wagon and trundled off to the village of Wild Rose to sell them. There potato buyers bid on each wagonload, storing their purchases in warehouses near the railroad track where they awaited shipment to Chicago. At thirty-five cents a bushel, an entire wagonload of potatoes might fetch John Coombes as much as $17.50. After selling enough potatoes to pay his seed, grocery, and farm equipment bills, Coombes buried the remainder of his crop in pits covered with soil and horse manure, to be dug up later when the price had risen upwards of a dollar a bushel—provided the potatoes had not frozen and spoiled in the meantime.[18]

For those who tilled the marginal soil of the New North, the issue was usually survival rather than prosperity; nature was far more often an unyielding adversary than a bounteous partner. Before the Cutover farmer could even begin to do battle with the poor soil and abbreviated growing season, he first had to clear the land of stumps and rocks. Even after three and a half years in the Wisconsin or Chippewa valleys in the late 1910's, the average settler had managed to clear only seven acres, was cultivating an additional ten dotted with tree trunks, and had over fifty acres still covered with brush and stumps. By that point, he owned two or three cows, a heifer, a calf, twenty-five chickens, and a horse, as well as $1,000 worth of buildings and $115 more of machinery. His total equity averaged $2,500, although he could probably find no actual buyer who would pay such a price. Such a bounty was "not exactly the fulfillment of the average American's dream." Land values in 1910 averaged only $5.10 per acre in Burnett County and $19.57 in Clark, compared to $42.57 in Winnebago County and $48.26 in Walworth. The correspondence files of Cutover land companies were filled with penciled letters pleading for a stay in payments or an advance against property values with which to pay taxes or clear additional land. Together, they constituted a catalog of misfortunes which included crop failures, tornadoes, drought, fires, death, sickness, and accidents to man and beast.[19]

[18] Jerold W. Apps, *The Land Still Lives* (Madison, 1970), 84–90.
[19] Arlan Helgeson, *Farms in the Cutover: Agricultural Settlement in Northern Wisconsin*

Gaining an accurate fix on the condition of Wisconsin agriculture is also complicated by the deep-seated ambiguity which prevailed over whether farming was, or should be, a unique way of life or a business like any other. The organizers of the first Wisconsin Country Life Conference in 1911, for example, asserted that a "community life" that "will stimulate mental activity to amply satisfy the social aspirations of the countryman and his family" was an essential for a "contented and intelligent rural population." At the same time, the organizers acknowledged, "The success of the farm as a business enterprise is of prime importance." Wisconsin author Ben Logan, whose own roots extended back to the generation influenced by the Country Life Movement, proclaims the tiller of the soil "a partner with its moods, secrets, and seasons," and, in the words of one Native American leader, at one with "the corn, the rabbit, the sun, the rain, and the deer." Those of Logan's era portrayed a world in which "neighbor relied upon neighbor" for treating illnesses, delivering babies, sharing costly equipment, exchanging labor at planting or harvesting time, and grading roads. They stressed the frequency of communal "bees" for building, quilting, husking, and fueling. In Trempealeau County, as in other rural areas, the harshness of life was supposedly ameliorated by a social creed which stressed "mutual helpfulness and voluntary association for common ends," as well as concern for the unfortunate, social equality, and tolerance.[20]

Concrete proposals to improve the quality of rural life, however, overwhelmingly reflected the conviction that improved technology, business organization and systems, formal education, and greater efficiency and expertise were the keys to progress. Country Life Conferences and agricultural publications abounded with prescriptions

---

(Madison, 1962), 53–65 (quote); Paul William Icke, "The Northern Lakes Region of Wisconsin: A Study in Cultural Geography" (doctoral dissertation, University of Wisconsin, 1934), 2–22; Lucile Kane, "Settling the Wisconsin Cutovers," in *WMH*, 40 (Winter, 1956–1957), 97–98; James I. Clark, *Farming the Cutover: The Settlement of Northern Wisconsin* (Madison, 1956), 3–13; Vernon R. Carstensen, *Farms or Forests* (Madison, 1958), 47–74; Storm, "Social and Cultural History of Lincoln County," 92–104.

[20] William L. Bowers, *The Country Life Movement in America, 1900–1920* (Port Washington, New York, 1974), 3–29, 62–85, 128–134; Brian W. Beltman, "Rural Renaissance in an Urban Age: The Country Life Movement in Wisconsin, 1895–1918" (doctoral dissertation, University of Wisconsin, 1974), 1–8, 22–39, 57–102, 401–414; "The Call for the Conference," UW College of Agriculture, Wisconsin Country Life Conference, *Bulletin*, no. 1 (1911), 5 (quotes); Ben Logan, *The Land Remembers: The Story of a Farm and Its People* (New York, 1975), 5–6 (quotes), 275–278; Josie Churchill, *Dirt Roads*, (La Crosse, 1981), 7, 13, 19–23 (quote), 27–30, 45, 55, 83, 93, 103; Curti, *Making of an American Community*, 114–120, 138–139 (quote); Edmund de S. Brunner and John H. Kolb, *Rural Social Trends* (New York, 1933), 59–62; John H. Kolb, *Emerging Rural Communities: Group Relations in Rural Society, a Review of Wisconsin Research in Action* (Madison, 1959), 5–9.

for more systematic planning of the farmstead and with tips for modernizing an old farm house. They advocated the installation of the "modern conveniences enjoyed by our friends in the city," and insisted that "it is as a business proposition that the telephone stands out as a necessity on the farm." In fact, it was more than a business proposition. Wisconsin's Nellie Kedzie Jones, a noted home economist and the gentlewoman columnist for *The Country Gentleman*, wrote in the 1910's, "Visiting on the party line is permissible. I believe in it as a great socializer. . . . In the country the function of the telephone is even more social than commercial." Experts frequently urged farmers to emulate the railroads and corporations in establishing a community of interests. Despite some initial doubts, agricultural spokesmen also generally supported rural free delivery of mail, the Good Roads Movement, and the automobile as devices that would help conserve their way of life.[21]

Regardless of whether they stressed farming as a business or as a way of life, those associated with it generally agreed about the isolation and drudgery of rural life. Josie Churchill wrote that she did not miss the modern conveniences growing up in rural Vernon County. She first learned of the sinking of the *Titanic* from an itinerant peddler in September, 1912, five months after the tragedy. Similarly, while trapped in their Rock County farmhouse for three days during a blizzard, the characters in Sterling North's *Plowing On Sunday* entertain themselves by using the 1914 Sears Roebuck catalog, "living in the romantic world . . . where they were all rich as kings, where every woman wore a beautiful new dress and every man was handsome and stylish, where there were bon bons and books and beautiful buggies."

"Isolation of rural life," observed sociologist Charles Galpin, "is a much heralded truism" because in the 1910's and early 1920's farmers everywhere inhabited a "peculiar residential environment." These environments differed "not only from the habitat of the urban dweller, but also in some important respects from that of the European or Asiatic countryman." The greatest deficiency of rural life, he believed, was "a restricted contact with a human mind," remediable only through "human contacts, more human contacts, and still more human contacts." Even the most sympathetic advocates of this

---

[21] George Wylie, "Telephones in Farm Homes," State Board of Agriculture, *Annual Report*, 1902, pp. 255–263 (quote); Mrs. F. F. Showers, "Modernizing an Old Farm House," UW College of Agriculture, Wisconsin Country Life Conference, *Bulletin*, no. 3 (1913), 25–33 (quote); Jeanne Hunnicutt Delgado, ed., "Nellie Kedzie Jones's Advice to Farm Women: Letters from Wisconsin, 1912–1916," in *WMH*, 57 (Autumn, 1973), 24 (quote); Ballard Campbell, "The Good Roads Movement in Wisconsin, 1890–1911," in *WMH*, 49 (Summer, 1966), 273–293.

way of life acknowledged that babies and mothers often died in childbirth and that rural people frequently succumbed to illnesses easily treatable in more populous areas. Medicine was all too often practiced by quacks, such as the "wise" woman who asks the local druggist for "medicines of different taste and color, bitter, sour and sweet; also different kinds of powders; large and small pills; and also syrup for the children."[22]

Doing laundry during winter required pumping water outside from an often-frozen pump, carrying it inside to the cook stove for heating, and hanging the wash on ice-encrusted lines. Nellie Kedzie Jones mixed descriptions of female hardships with recommendations for amelioration. "It is heart breaking," she wrote, "to see the way some farm women, who have neither store room nor ice box, must climb up and down cellar stairs, with one or both hands loaded." She reminded her readers that "the housewife's day begins yesterday though a man's day begins shortly before breakfast." Professor Galpin argued that hard work and strain "brings upon the farm woman a more or less chronic state of fatigue," while their souls risked "perpetual eclipse, partial or entire." He noted, "It is a matter of gossip that there is a growing reluctance on the part of the farm-bred girl to marry the young hoe-farmer and repeat the experience of isolation and drudgery endured by her mother." Even during the 1920's, farm women around the country still labored an average of sixty-three hours a week.[23]

Isolation and drudgery were the two most frequently cited causes for the most disturbing rural problem of the age: the inexorable movement of young people from farm to city. This rural drain permeated agricultural discourse from the 1880's onward. In 1896, the University of Wisconsin's Agricultural Experiment Station director warned that so many capable young people were moving to the city that "in some sections of our country a residue is left upon the farm not worthy of the name of farmers." A correspondent to *Hoard's Dairyman* contended that "most of the farmers . . . despise their business" and have "no class pride or class spirit," while another said that many farm parents believed that steering their offspring into another occupation "raised them one notch in the standard of honorable

---

[22] Churchill, *Dirt Roads*, 75–76; Sterling North, *Plowing On Sunday* (New York, 1934), 225–238 (quote); Galpin, *Rural Life*, 15–16, 57 (quotes); Milo K. Swanton, "Cherishing the Past—Improving the Future," address before the American Country Life Association, September 5, 1950, p. 10, in box 1, folder 32, Wisconsin Federation of Cooperatives Records.

[23] *Wisconsin Agriculturist*, February 5, 1903, p. 13; *ibid.*, July 9, 1914, p. 20; Churchill, *Dirt Roads*, 21–26, 75–76; North, *Plowing On Sunday*, 225–231; Delgado, ed., "Nellie Kedzie Jones's Advice," in *WMH*, 57: 9, 13; Galpin, *Rural Life*, 101–118 (quotes on 105 and 118); Brunner and Kolb, *Rural Social Trends*, 62–66.

living." The agricultural press responded to this crisis with a barrage of articles that condemned urban life and called for the improvement of rural working and living conditions. The same concerns inspired the Country Life Movement, whose proponents included agricultural college faculty, government agricultural bureaucrats, leaders of agrarian organizations, agricultural journalists, businessmen with an economic stake in rural productivity and markets, and urban professionals infused with altruistic or nostalgic conceptions of farming as a way of life. Nearly all of their deliberations and prescriptions mixed paeans for preserving farming as a unique and superior way of life with specific proposals to integrate agriculture ever more completely into modern, urban, industrial life.[24]

In the long run, all such efforts to preserve farming as a hallowed enterprise were doomed to fail. Formulas for improving the quality of rural life were largely irrelevant to most farmers in the Cutover who were immersed in a quotidian struggle for survival, and who lacked the necessary financial resources. Even prosperous farmers in the southern counties who embraced the "modernize to preserve" slogan found themselves trapped in its inherent contradiction. The adoption of modern technology, organization, and expertise inevitably enlarged the size of the sphere in which farm residents moved and contributed to citifying rural life. Where modernizing methods were adopted, institutions became less distinctively rural; where they were not implemented, rural institutions grew further obsolete. Everything that was done to enhance agriculture as a business enterprise progressively undermined its status as a unique way of life.[25]

[2]

While not everyone agreed on the degree of growth and prosperity attained during Wisconsin's "golden age of agriculture," there was a universal consensus that most gains occurred because of the conversion from wheat growing to dairying and specialty crops. This transition was primarily an ingenious and pragmatic response to the

---

[24] Ransom A. Moore, "Agricultural Education," in the *Transactions of the Wisconsin State Agricultural Society* (1896), 99–101 (quote); letter from H.C.R., Oneida, New York, "He Thinks We Have a Difficult Task," *Hoard's Dairyman*, September 18, 1903, p. 717 (quote); letter from Eva Lehman, *ibid.*, April 30, 1909, p. 439 (quote); Bowers, *Country Life Movement*, 3–29, 62–85; Beltman, "Rural Renaissance," 22–39, 57–102; Harold T. Christensen, "Population Pressure Among Wisconsin Farmers" (doctoral dissertation, University of Wisconsin, 1941), 7–10; Robert R. Polk, "A Geographical Analysis of Population Change in the Hill Land of Western Wisconsin, 1870–1950" (doctoral dissertation, University of Wisconsin, 1964), 126–266.

[25] Bowers, *Country Life Movement*, 128–134; Beltman, "Rural Renaissance," 401–414.

pressing need for a type of agriculture suited to the state's climate, geography, and population. It was guided and motivated by a group of dedicated enthusiasts who pioneered new production and marketing methods and engaged in an ambitious and rigorous program of self-regulation. It gave rise to such energetic organizations as the Wisconsin Dairymen's Association, which sought to pursue their members' self-interest through economic and political action. These, in turn, formed a mutually beneficial relationship with the University of Wisconsin's emerging College of Agriculture, and convinced state politicians and bureaucrats to engage in an unprecedented program for the promotion and regulation of agriculture.

Wisconsin's decline from preeminence in wheat growing began in the 1870's and accelerated rapidly. By 1910, only 0.7 per cent of cropland was planted in wheat, and the yield had declined from 27 million bushels in 1860 to 3.2 million. Much of this decline was due to the opening of the Great Plains, combined with the increase in land values in southern Wisconsin. By 1907, the only remaining wheat-intensive regions consisted of two small areas in the neighborhood of Green Bay and Lake Winnebago in the east and near the Mississippi River to the west. Wisconsin farmers badly needed a type of agriculture that would guarantee both a greater return per acre and a more stable and predictable income, and one that would replenish the rapidly deteriorating soil.[26]

The gradual demise of wheat growing in the last decades of the nineteenth century was matched by a corresponding decline in wool. In 1885, the state boasted nearly 1.5 million sheep, producing over 6 million pounds of wool valued at $1.3 million. Ten years later, the number of sheep and the amount of wool produced had declined by only 7 per cent, but its value had been virtually halved. The opening of new grazing lands in the West signaled a steady decline in prices that soon made wool production unprofitable compared to the income from supplying meat and dairy products to Wisconsin's growing cities and areas beyond. By the turn of the century, Wisconsin's sheep population had declined to about 1 million; by 1922 it was but 300,000.[27]

The search for an alternative to wheat and wool had begun during the 1860's, when some of the state's more enterprising farmers took advantage of Civil War-induced prosperity to experiment with hops,

---

[26] Harry S. Perloff et al., *Regions, Resources, and Economic Growth* (Lincoln, Nebraska, 1960), 197–202; John G. Thompson, *The Rise and Decline of the Wheat Growing Industry in Wisconsin* (Madison, 1909), 91–102; "Industries of Wisconsin," *Wisconsin Blue Book, 1915*, p. 27; Ebling et al., *A Century of Wisconsin Agriculture*, 11.

[27] Ebling, comp., *Agriculture in Mid-Century*, 41; *State Census*, 1895, vol. 1, pp. 1011–1016.

flax, tobacco, and sorghum. During the postwar recession, when such diversification proved unprofitable, many turned to sheep raising. Others, particularly in the extreme southern tier of counties, emulated the corn, hog, and beef combinations of their northern Illinois neighbors.

Still other Wisconsin farmers turned to dairy husbandry and related pursuits primarily because they met the desired criteria better than any conceivable alternative. The state's cool summers, its long, cold winters, and adequate rainfall concentrated in the spring and summer were ideal for the grass and forage crops necessary to support a large livestock population. Planting land in grasses and forage crops also restored much of the fertility depleted by cereal grain agriculture. The relatively short growing season and marginal soil that characterized the northern two-thirds of the state were more conducive to dairying than to grain culture. The rugged hills and creek bottoms of the western counties, and the swampy glacial swales of the eastern counties, all generally unfit for cropland, were well suited to grazing. Dairying could also be combined with other agricultures in different sections of the state, such as corn and hog raising in the southwest, tobacco growing in the south-central counties, and the growing of market and canning vegetables in the eastern counties. Dairy prices were much more stable and predictable than were grain prices, and more susceptible to management by boards of trade. Moreover, dairy prices were more dependent upon product quality, and were sustained by a seemingly insatiable market in nearby cities. Dairy farm income, unlike the once-a-year payoff of grain, could be spread fairly evenly over the entire year, provided the cows' lactation period could be extended through the winter months.[28]

Finally, Wisconsin was inhabited by large numbers of people with previous experience in dairy husbandry and processing. Foremost among these were the Yankees from New England, and the Yorkers from upstate New York, which from 1893 to the early 1910's remained the nation's leading dairy state. Nearly as crucial were the immigrants from Germany, Norway, and Switzerland who, together with the eastern immigrants, constituted a sizable majority of the state's farm population.[29]

The U.S. Census Bureau defined a dairy farm as one in which dairy products accounted for at least 40 per cent of the farm's income, or in which 40 per cent of the crops were used as livestock feed. A milch cow was any cow or heifer, at least two years old, kept primarily for

---

[28] Perloff et al., *Regions, Resources, and Economic Growth*, 198–200; Ebling et al., *A Century of Wisconsin Agriculture*, 10–12.
[29] "Industries of Wisconsin," *Wisconsin Blue Book, 1915*, p. 27.

milk production. By those definitions, only 17.4 per cent of the state's farmers were considered "dairy" in 1899, although over 90 per cent kept at least some milk cows. Even so, as early as 1901, a member of the State Board of Agriculture boasted to its annual convention that "the words Wisconsin and dairying are almost synonymous." In 1909, about 93 per cent of Wisconsin farms kept dairy cows and over 40 per cent of those sold milk or cream. The number of milk cows doubled between 1890 and 1912; their value increased even more. They accounted for about 40 per cent of the state's cattle population in 1890, and nearly two-thirds of its almost 3 million cattle by 1919.[30]

Butter production nearly doubled between 1890 and 1912, and its value tripled. Cheese production rose by nearly 500 per cent, while its value increased by over 800 per cent. In 1889, Wisconsin produced about 8 per cent of the nation's creamery butter, placing it fifth among the states. By 1909, it had risen to first place, accounting for almost 17 per cent of the country's total. During the same period, Wisconsin leaped to first place in factory cheese, going from 22.6 per cent to 47.6 per cent. Ten years later, its share had jumped to over 63 per cent, nearly double that of second-place New York, whose cows produced nearly as much raw milk as Wisconsin's. Although Wisconsin had but one milk condensery in 1889, and did not build its second until 1905, it produced nearly a quarter of the nation's condensed and evaporated milk by the end of World War I. During the first decade of the twentieth century alone, Wisconsin's total dairy output increased by 190 per cent, compared to 93 per cent for Pennsylvania and nearly 85 per cent for New York. Sixth in the nation in total milk production in 1899, the state had attained first place by 1912, accounting for 15 per cent of the whole. Within the state, dairying jumped from seventh place in the value of its manufactured products to third by 1910; by 1920 it ranked first, nearly doubling the worth of meat packing, its closest competitor. In 1912, Dairy and Food Commissioner John Q. Emery proudly proclaimed, "In . . . her dairy products, Wisconsin now ranks first in the Union."[31]

The pace and magnitude of Wisconsin's conversion to dairy husbandry and related agricultural pursuits was phenomenal. The transition began in the 1870's, had already reached a significant stage of

---

[30] Ebling, comp., *Agriculture in Mid-Century*, 46–53; "Industries of Wisconsin," *Wisconsin Blue Book, 1915*, pp. 111–119; *State Census*, 1895, vol. 1, pp. 817, 849, 1022, 1025; Lampard, *Rise of the Dairy Industry*, 267, 276–279; John W. Thomas, "The Relation of the State Board of Agriculture to the Dairy Industry," State Board of Agriculture, *Annual Report*, 1901, p. 312; *Thirteenth Census of the United States, 1910: Agriculture, Volume VII*, 905.

[31] Ebling, comp., *Agriculture in Mid-Century*, 48–53; Lampard, *Rise of the Dairy Industry*, 278–279; Dairy and Food Commissioner, *Biennial Report*, 1912, p. 6.

evolution by 1893, then took a brief hiatus during the depression years. Afterwards, dairying enjoyed nearly three decades of uninterrupted growth.

The dramatic transition to dairy farming also significantly changed the sources of farm income. Whereas the sale of crops had been the major component of farm income in the heyday of wheat and wool, it dropped to a mere 23 per cent by 1915. By contrast, livestock and livestock products grew from 65 per cent in 1899 to 77 per cent in 1915. Milk and milk products, which had constituted only 23 per cent of farm income in 1899, climbed to 38 per cent by 1915.[32]

Apart from cash crops and milk products, by 1914 state farmers' income derived primarily from the sale of cattle and hogs by 1914. While the number of milk cows had risen from 770,000 to 1,626,000 between 1893 and 1914, other cattle jumped from only 811,000 to 1,200,000, more than reversing the relative proportions of earlier years. Still, 15 per cent of farm income in 1914 came from cattle for slaughter. Close behind cattle were hogs, which constituted about 14 per cent of farm income in 1915. The number of hogs doubled to one million between 1870 and 1900, and nearly doubled again during the next two decades. Their total value more than doubled between 1893 and 1915. Raising swine for national markets steadily displaced their use for home and local consumption, especially in the southern third of the state. Their rapid proliferation between 1890 and 1920 was due largely to the surging demand for pork in urban Chicago and Milwaukee markets.[33]

Another 5 per cent of farm income in 1914 came from selling eggs and chickens, a sideline that flourished in dairy areas. Although not a great source of income, horses and mules were invaluable as work animals in an era when the internal combustion engine was only on the verge of transforming production. As late as 1908, according to farm leader Milo Swanton, "a fellow in a nearby town who was experimenting with a gas powered plow was considered a freak." The state's horse population peaked at 730,000 in 1915. Nearly 95 per cent of Wisconsin farmers owned at least one horse, and the state averaged nearly four per farm.[34]

Closely related to the increase in livestock was the growing preponderance of feed over cash crops. By 1914, Wisconsinites planted

---

[32] Ebling, comp., *Agriculture in Mid-Century*, 58–60; Ebling et al., *A Century of Wisconsin Agriculture*, 116; "Crop Report for 1915–16," *Wisconsin Blue Book, 1917*, p. 430.

[33] Ebling, comp., *Agriculture in Mid-Century*, 37–43; *State Census*, 1895, vol. 1, pp. 1022–1026; Ebling et al., *A Century of Wisconsin Agriculture*, 26–27.

[34] Ebling et al., *A Century of Wisconsin Agriculture*, 26–27; *State Census*, 1895, vol. 1, pp. 1022–1026; Swanton, "Cherishing the Past," p. 10, in the Wisconsin Federation of Cooperatives Records.

nearly 80 per cent of their cultivated land in corn, oats, and hay, primarily because agricultural scientists had discovered that silo storage was the most efficient and economical method of guaranteeing winter feed. Prior to the 1880's, corn had been grown in the southern and southwestern counties primarily for grain. As dairying and livestock production increased, the cornbelt steadily expanded to embrace most of the southern third of the state. Corn acreage nearly doubled between 1895 and 1915, total production rose about one-third, and the crop's value almost quadrupled.[35]

The rise of dairying also coincided with significant expansion of oats. Between 1870 and 1900, oats acreage increased nearly fourfold, peaking at 2.38 million acres in 1902, mostly in the southern two-thirds of the state. In 1914, it still stood at over 2.2 million acres, producing nearly 134 million bushels with a value of nearly $45 million—increases of 300 and 400 per cent respectively. The oats area tended to correspond very closely with the pattern of livestock and poultry raising.

Almost as spectacular was the increased production of "tame hay," especially timothy, clover, and alfalfa. As early as 1903, William D. Hoard warned that farmers who stopped growing alfalfa had made a "fatal mistake" in not persevering. By 1914, however, farmers planted less than 70,000 acres in alfalfa, compared to the some 3 million acres of clover and timothy, nearly three times the hay acreage in 1880. This enormous increase in hay production was owing to its utility as a feed crop and from its power to prevent erosion and replenish fertility of the soil.[36]

Beyond dairying and livestock raising, and the feed crops that supported them, Wisconsin agriculture consisted largely of specialty crops grown expressly for market. Chief among these were wheat, barley, potatoes, tobacco, rye, cranberries and other fruits, and various vegetables grown either for processing or for urban marketplaces. Corn and oats gradually displaced wheat and barley as the leading feed crops, although barley continued to expand because of increased demands by breweries. Between 1895 and 1914, barley acreage nearly doubled, as did its yield in bushels, and the crop's value almost tripled. Its greatest concentration was from Lake Winnebago to the Door County peninsula.

---

[35] George McKerrow, president, remarks, in "Proceedings," State Board of Agriculture, *Annual Report*, 1909, pp. 363–366; "Crop Report for 1915–1916," *Wisconsin Blue Book, 1917*, p. 430; Ebling, comp., *Agriculture in Mid-Century*, 24–29; Ebling et al., *A Century of Wisconsin Agriculture*, 26–27.

[36] *State Census*, 1895, vol. 1, p. 1023; "Crop Report for 1915–16," *Wisconsin Blue Book, 1917*, p. 430; William D. Hoard, remarks, State Board of Agriculture, *Annual Report*, 1903, p. 227; Ebling, comp., *Agriculture in Mid-Century*, 28–29.

Foremost among cash crops was potatoes. During the 1890's, expanding urban markets led farmers, especially in the central part of the state, to grow them commercially. By the turn of the century, farms in Portage, Waupaca, Waukesha, and Adams counties produced nearly one-third of Wisconsin's potatoes, while production was increasing significantly in Langlade and Barron counties. Even though only about 1 per cent of the state's farmland was planted in potatoes, they became the leading cash crop by 1910, having been promoted by the same university, governmental, and private coalition as dairying. Seventh in the United States in potato production in 1889, Wisconsin held third place from 1899 to 1929.

Growing urban demand for special grains generated a modest increase in rye, while its escalating use as a feed crop, and as a source of "green manure," added impetus. Rye acreage increased by 250 per cent between 1885 and 1915; the yield quadrupled and the value grew nearly sevenfold. Production was concentrated primarily in the sandy central region, especially in Marquette, Adams, Waukesha and Portage counties.[37]

Tobacco, a Wisconsin cash crop since the 1850's, expanded significantly beginning in the 1880's in response to the cigar-making industry in cities and towns around the state and nationally. The original center of tobacco growing was in southern Dane County, with a significant spillover into neighboring Rock, Jefferson, and Columbia counties and a strong association with Norwegian-American farmers. In the early twentieth century, farmers began to grow a new strain, Type 55 tobacco, north and west of the Wisconsin River, chiefly in Crawford and Vernon counties. The depression of the 1890's caused a temporary decline in tobacco production, but by 1900 some 7,000 farmers were producing 45.5 million pounds valued at about $3 million. An increasing amount was exported to other states for use as cigar binders or fillers, or as scrap for chewing tobacco. As early as 1903, the state legislature began allocating money to improve product quality, causing tobacco's value to double over the next two decades.[38]

Although cranberries had been grown commercially in the marshes of the Wisconsin River Valley and around Berlin since the

---

[37] *State Census*, 1895, vol. 1, pp. 1023–1025; Ebling et al., *A Century of Wisconsin Agriculture*, 27–29; Ebling, comp., *Agriculture in Mid-Century*, 31–32; "Crop Report for 1915–16," *Wisconsin Blue Book, 1917*, p. 430.

[38] Ebling et al., *A Century of Wisconsin Agriculture*, 29; *State Census*, 1895, vol. 1, pp. 1024–1025; "Crop Report for 1915–16," *Wisconsin Blue Book, 1917*, p. 430; Henry Larzelere, "The A.A.A. and the Marketing of Wisconsin Tobacco" (doctoral dissertation, University of Wisconsin, 1938), 29–30; Emil P. Sandsten, *Report on Tobacco Investigations in Wisconsin for 1903 and 1904*, UW Agricultural Experiment Station, *Bulletin*, no. 124 (1905), 3.

1860's, a nearly fatal combination of drought, frost, and fire forced a serious reorientation in the 1890's. Growers leveled ridges and knolls, better prepared the ground, and seeded many burned-over marshes with better plants. To solve the perennial water problem, they dredged long ditches and installed systems of gates for regulating water levels in the bogs. They also experimented with various strains of cranberries and developed effective insect controls. In 1906, growers in the Wisconsin Rapids area organized into the Wisconsin Cranberry Sales Company, which soon grew into the leading marketing co-operative in the state. By 1914, Wisconsin had risen to third place nationally in cranberry production (33,000 barrels) behind Massachusetts (471,000 barrels) and New Jersey (160,000 barrels).[39]

Rounding out Wisconsin's specialty or commercial crops was a variety of fruits and vegetables, both as fresh produce and for processing. Apple orchards flourished in Door, Ozaukee, Milwaukee, Crawford, and Bayfield counties, in the Fox River and Kickapoo River valleys, and the Galesville area of Trempealeau County. Even though apple growing was passing rapidly into the hands of commercial specialists by 1914, small orchards remained the norm, producing for farm and home consumption and for local markets. Sour cherries also were cultivated on the Door County peninsula, where frost damage posed comparatively little threat. Strawberry production was scattered throughout the state, but the greatest concentrations were in Jackson, Monroe, La Crosse, and Bayfield counties.[40]

Vegetables, too, were well established by 1914, chiefly green peas, sweet corn, cucumbers, snap beans, lima beans, beets, cabbage, carrots, tomatoes, and onions, grown either for sale in urban marketplaces or for commercial canning. These crops were principally cultivated in the southeastern quarter of the state, and secondarily in the central and northeastern sections. Cabbage, grown principally in Brown and Outagamie counties and in the Milwaukee-Racine-Kenosha area, was sold fresh or made into sauerkraut. Cucumbers, raised especially for pickles, were grown in the central and northeastern sections.

The remaining vegetables were raised primarily for commercial canning. As late as 1894, there were only two canning factories in the entire state. By 1900, the number had risen to twenty-eight, about

---

[39] Vere E. Bufton, *Cranberries of Wisconsin*, State Department of Agriculture, Federal-State Crop Reporting Service, *Special Bulletin*, no. 70 (1957), 18–19; Neil E. Stevens and Jean Nash, "The Development of Cranberry Growing in Wisconsin," in *WMH*, 27 (March, 1944), 276–294.

[40] Ebling et al., *A Century of Wisconsin Agriculture*, 51; Frederick O. Cranefield, "Farm Orchards Again, Or Yet," *Wisconsin Horticulture*, 6 (November, 1915), 234.

half of which specialized in sweet peas. The industry was aided by the university's Agricultural Experiment Station, which dissuaded pea canneries from growing large crops on their own fields because repeated use led to crop disease. By 1914, Wisconsin was well on its way to becoming the nation's leading vegetable-processing state.[41]

Beyond these commercial crops, Wisconsin farmers dabbled in a handful of others. Sugar beets gained popularity early in the century and, by 1915, the state was producing nearly 125 tons of them, at a value of almost $750,000. Buckwheat had been grown in the state at least since 1850, mostly for flour. Flax, hemp fiber, and sorghum also played minor roles, while some northern counties produced significant quantities of maple syrup and sugar. Specialty crops soared so quickly that a speaker at the 1910 State Board of Agriculture convention noted that "in many localities in southern Wisconsin, with a large number of farmers the pendulum has swung back from grass and live stock growing to cash crops, such as tobacco, sugar-beets, cabbage, and other vegetable crops with fair success." Even he, however, warned that most farmers "must necessarily keep live stock of some kind to convert all the roughage and grains into a finished product in order to maintain the fertility of the land, or it will lead to an impoverished soil as sure as night follows day." Wisconsin agriculture, while well diversified, was firmly centered on dairy husbandry.[42]

The dairy revolution in Wisconsin was well underway by 1893. It originated during the Civil War era with an unlikely cadre of "revolutionaries"—especially transplanted dairymen from upstate New York, Vermont, and New Hampshire, led by Hiram Smith, Stephen Favill, and William Dempster Hoard. Convinced that dairying alone could answer Wisconsin's need for an agriculture that would yield a greater return per acre while replenishing the wheat-exhausted soil, they preached their gospel with religious fervor. Smith, the member of the Board of Regents most supportive of the new College of Agriculture, publicly denounced the conversion to mixed farming a "snare and a delusion." Hoard, of Fort Atkinson, became the national spokesman for the state's dairy interests, both as editor of the

---

[41] Ebling, comp., *Wisconsin Agriculture in Mid-Century*, 35–36; Fred A. Stare, *The Story of Wisconsin's Great Canning Industry* (Baltimore, 1949), 14, 39, 59, 78; Lawrence A. Rens, "The Wisconsin Processed Vegetable Industry" (doctoral dissertation, University of Wisconsin, 1964), 26–30; Fred R. Jones and Maurice B. Linford, *Pea Disease Survey in Wisconsin*, UW Agricultural Experiment Station, Research Bulletin, no. 64 (1925), 1.

[42] "Crop Report for 1915–16," *Wisconsin Blue Book, 1917*, p. 430; Ebling et al., *A Century of Wisconsin Agriculture*, 47; R. E. Roberts, "Profitable Farming in Southern Wisconsin," State Board of Agriculture, *Annual Report*, 1910, p. 345 (quote); A. F. Postel, "The Beet Sugar Industry," *ibid.*, 1902, pp. 211–216.

Jefferson County Union and *Hoard's Dairyman*, and as governor from 1889 to 1891. "To him who loveth the cow," Hoard promised in one of his celebrated aphorisms, "to him shall all other things be added—feed, ensilage, butter, more grasses, more prosperity, happier homes, and greater wealth." All of these dairy advocates were at great pains to disassociate themselves from the politicized programs of the Grangers, the Populists, and the various alliances which urged government intervention to punish the farmer's enemies, such as railroads, banks, and grain elevators, and to advance the cause of agrarians as a class. Instead, they urged farmers to accept the "realities" of the American economic system and to enhance their place in it through discipline, frugality, piety, co-operative effort, and obedience to the "inevitable natural and progressive laws of . . . science."[43]

[3]

Founded in 1872, the Wisconsin Dairymen's Association (WDA) quickly became the institutional embodiment of the dairy revolution. The association initially focused on the feeding and breeding of dairy cattle in order to increase the volume of milk at the lowest possible cost. This meant developing more balanced crops and extending cows' lactation through the barren months of the breeding cycle, normally the winter months. Fortunately, the crops that provided the best cattle feed flourished in Wisconsin's soil and climate. After much experiment, dairy farmers adopted the German concept of the "balanced dairy ration," which combined various foods in proportions that maximized the milk flow. Calculating the particular nutritive ratio of carbohydrates, fats, and proteins impelled dairy farmers to familiarize themselves with the findings of science. They extended milk yields through the winter largely by feeding ensilage: green fodder stored in airtight silos until needed. Although the first above-ground silos in Wisconsin were erected in the early 1880's, and despite Hoard's insistence that silage made it possible to keep three cows at the cost of feeding one over the winter, the practice made slow headway. As late as 1904, the university's experiment station counted only 716 silos in the entire state. But by 1915, the number had soared to 58,992, or one for every three farms.

The improvement of dairy breeds consumed an equal amount of the WDA's time and effort. Hoard had long and vigorously crusaded to demonstrate the superiority of the single-purpose dairy cow over the dual-purpose animal which was kept for both milk and meat. His

---

[43] Lampard, *Rise of the Dairy Industry*, 83–89, 336–340 (quote); George William Rankin, *William Dempster Hoard* (Fort Atkinson, 1925), 180 (quote).

Dairy Temperament of Cows, published in Boston in 1891, soon became the bible of the "cows for milk only" movement, a cause aided by declining beef prices after 1890. Dairy farmers began turning to the Jersey, Guernsey, and Holstein breeds as the best producers. Holsteins constituted about half the state's dairy cattle by 1914, predominating in all market areas and in most cheese and condensery belts in the southern counties. Guernseys quickly became the leading breed in the northern and western sections, especially in butter-making areas. Jerseys were also found primarily in butter regions, but their numbers declined steadily after 1900.

Beginning in 1899, the WDA, the College of Agriculture, and a variety of breeders' associations sponsored public testing and open competition, plus intensive programs to eradicate hoof-and-mouth disease, milk fever, bovine abortion, and bovine tuberculosis. But most farmers demonstrated their reluctance to participate. Even so, improvements in breeds were every bit as impressive as those in feed, at least in the long run.[44]

Equally crucial were WDA efforts to promote and market dairy products. The association's initial purpose, according to Stephen Favill, was "establishing a market and have the buyers come to us" since "the producers of butter and cheese were at the mercy of a disorganized market, or at least what organization existed was against rather than for them." Hoard soon secured a significant reduction in freight charges from the Star Union Company of Chicago, improving the competitive edge which the state already enjoyed over eastern dairymen due to lower land and feed costs. Wisconsin dairy farmers were soon working to help fill the more than 3,000 refrigerated freight cars which regularly transported products from Chicago to the East Coast. The WDA established a board of trade at Watertown to serve as a clearinghouse for information about various markets and to freeze out cheese dealers who functioned as acquisitive middlemen. A second board of trade was organized at Sheboygan Falls, primarily to develop a close connection for shipment to Great Britain.

Although dealers soon found ways to frustrate board of trade efforts, the board performed an invaluable educational function in apprising dairy farmers of technological innovations and processes. It also supported county fairs and other dairy-product exhibitions, sponsored demonstrations by cheese-making experts, and adopted rules for the care of milk, the conduct of factories, the settlement of weight disputes, the enforcement of tests, and the punishment of members judged guilty of adulteration. Like all professional associa-

---

[44] Lampard, *Rise of the Dairy Industry*, 125–138, 169–182.

tions, the WDA was determined to drive marginal operators out of business. Its attempts to establish butter boards of trade were much less successful, although Wisconsin producers benefited from the efforts of the Elgin, Illinois, board to establish standards and prices for the Upper Midwest. By the late 1890's, the need became much less critical, since most butter was sold on contract and the commission system virtually disappeared.[45]

WDA efforts to promote Wisconsin's products in domestic and foreign markets also led it to participate in international expositions. Even before 1890, Wisconsin dairy products had won awards at shows in Chicago, New York, Milwaukee, and New Orleans. Despite controversy over testing standards at the World's Columbian Exposition of 1893, Wisconsin dairy farmers more than held their own. WDA members also earned recognition at the Pan-American Exposition in Buffalo in 1901 and the Louisiana Purchase Exposition in St. Louis in 1904. At St. Louis, the state dairy exhibit did not win any grand prizes, but the university's dairy education programs won three awards, and a state cow won what was billed as the "greatest dairy cow test of modern times."[46]

As important as these accomplishments were, they paled in comparison to the WDA's two major contributions: the application of the principles and methods of the industrial revolution to dairying, and the creation of an ongoing collaborative effort among dairymen, the state university, and state government. The former began with the importation from upstate New York of the system of "associated dairying," meaning that milk processing was gradually transferred from the farmstead to the cheese factory, the creamery, and the condensery. In that way, the skills of a single cheese maker or butter maker could be placed at the service of numerous dairy farmers, enabling them to concentrate on producing as much high-quality milk as possible. Technical skills, efficiency, and economies of scale would translate to higher prices. Dealers generally preferred to buy from one or two factories or creameries of known quality than to travel from farm to farm, and they were willing to pay a higher price for this convenience and certainty. Dairy factories also benefited from economies of scale, especially when purchasing equipment and materials. The factory system freed thousands of dairy farmers, and their wives, from

---

[45] *Ibid.*, 125–138.
[46] *Ibid.*, 138–141, 178–186; "Wisconsin Prizes Drawn at the Louisiana Purchase Exposition Held at St. Louis in 1904," Bureau of Labor and Industrial Statistics, *Biennial Report*, 1905–1906, pp. 865–866; Marilyn Grant, "Wisconsin at the Louisiana Purchase Exposition of 1904," in *WMH*, 65 (Summer, 1982), 289–297 (quote); David W. Curtis, "Wisconsin Dairy Exhibit at the Columbian Exposition," in the *Transactions of the State Agricultural Society* (1893), 403–406.

the time, energy, and anxiety associated with manufacturing and marketing, allowing them to focus upon livestock husbandry and farm management.[47]

Conversion to the factory system presented a number of obstacles that were overcome only by the persistent efforts of dairymen, agricultural experts, and politicians. Notoriously poor rural roads made transporting milk from farm to factory hazardous and tedious. Highly individualistic farmers, used to working at their own pace and constrained only by the weather, had a difficult time adjusting to the schedule and rhythm of "the system." Factory managers demanded standards of quality and cleanliness that forced grudging changes in farm practice and caused many dairymen to grumble. Efforts to exclude milk producers who failed to meet these standards frequently provoked bitter squabbles. So did disputes over prices. Invention in 1890 of an accurate, efficient, and cheap method of measuring milk quality by University of Wisconsin chemist Stephen M. Babcock helped end disagreements. Before, many farmers watered their milk and sought to sneak it through during times of peak operation. Most factories operated only eight or nine months out of the year, so farmers who managed their cows to obtain year-round milk production still had to make their own butter or cheese periodically. In the long run, most of these problems proved solvable, since the advantages of associated dairying so clearly outweighed its disadvantages.[48]

The majority of Wisconsin's dairymen strongly resisted this revolution. They resented the disruption of their modes of production and their loss of independence. "If cows could talk," Hoard observed sarcastically, "they would be heard all over this country calling for an improved breed of dairyman." Nearly ten years after the invention of the Babcock milk tester, *Hoard's Dairyman* found that only twenty-one of 2,837 creamery patrons surveyed owned one. As late as 1910–1912, John Q. Emery, the state dairy and food commissioner, wrote disturbing "pen pictures" describing conditions in some Wisconsin dairy barns, cheese factories, and creameries. He portrayed some barns as dark, unventilated, and filthy, with "air so charged with impurities and strong odors as to be stifling," air which "adheres to the streams of milk and is carried beneath the surface of the milk in the pail and rises in minute bubbles." The milker, he lamented, frequently "has dung beneath him, behind him, in front of him and above him and manipulates a filthy surface above the milk pail." Many pre-inspection cheese factories had "faulty systems of whey and

---

[47] Lampard, *Rise of the Dairy Industry*, 91–98.
[48] *Ibid.*, 98–100; "Need of Dairy Education in Wisconsin," *Hoard's Dairyman*, May 27, 1898, p. 320.

sewage disposal," while the typical creamery was filthy, malodorous, and fly-infested, its rotten floors leaking sewage. Gradually the impersonal dictates of specialization, expertise, standardization, and concentration forced farmers to adapt. Slowly, and often grudgingly, they incorporated WDA standards in feeding, breeding, sanitation, and scheduling. These, in turn, resulted in a ninefold increase in the volume of milk produced in the United States between 1870 and 1900. By 1910, Wisconsin was the source of more than 15 per cent of the approximately 20 billion pounds produced annually. The total number of cheese factories, creameries, and condenseries grew from 966 in 1890 to 2,630 in 1910.[49]

Associated dairying first proved its worth in cheese making, whose complicated nature put a premium on expertise and consolidation. In 1870, nearly half the state's cheese was still produced on the farm; by 1900 the figure had dwindled to 2 per cent. The number of cheese factories grew from 1,337 in 1895 to 2,541 in 1915, and their production leaped from 52,481,000 to 234,929,037 pounds.[50]

Cheese making's complex chemical process required precise temperature controls. These were nearly impossible to achieve on the individual farm, especially when "cold curing" mandated temperatures as low as 25° to 30° Fahrenheit. In the late 1880's and early 1890's, Wisconsin cheese makers sold "filled cheese," an inferior product made with skim milk and non-milk fats, thus damaging the state's reputation. The scandal mandated quality in subsequent production, as did competition from meat packers who entered the cheese-distribution business. The introduction of many new varieties of "foreign" cheese, and the development of "processed" cheese (a blending of several cheeses) in 1904, also accelerated factory production. This irresistible trend received great impetus from the Wisconsin Cheese Makers Association, founded in 1893.

Between 1905 and 1915, some 845 new cheese factories opened, the bulk of them in the north-central and northwestern counties. It was the heyday of the crossroads cheese factory, small operations within easy distance of farms. But the trend towards fewer, larger establishments with greatly augmented output was already well under way in the southern third of the state. In Dodge County, the number of cheese factories declined by almost one-fourth between 1895 and 1905, but production increased by 122 per cent. Less evident was the gradual trend towards cheese distribution by meat packers and food-

---

[49] Lampard, *Rise of the Dairy Industry*, 196–197, 276, 453; Rankin, *Hoard*, 180; John Q. Emery, Dairy and Food Commissioner, *Biennial Report*, 1910–1912, p. 18.

[50] Lampard, *Rise of the Dairy Industry*, 283–287, 454; *State Census*, 1895, vol. 1, p. 849; "The Dairy Industry," *Wisconsin Blue Book, 1917*, pp. 420–421.

processing companies that would eventually put hundreds of independent cheese factories out of business.[51]

The trend towards making butter in factories proceeded more slowly but its eventual impact was even greater. In 1889, 76.7 per cent of all Wisconsin butter was still produced on the farm; by 1909, the percentage had dropped to 20.5. Wisconsin led the nation in converting from farm to creamery production, since 43 per cent of U.S. butter in 1919 was still produced domestically. The state rose from fifth to first place in creamery butter production between 1889 and 1909. The number of creameries increased from 753 in 1895 to 1,005, the peak number, in 1910. After that, the number declined steadily, as creameries' size and productivity continued to increase. Newer, smaller creameries proliferated in the northern two-thirds of the state, while fewer, larger, more productive plants dominated in the southern third, due to the conversion of many smaller creameries to skimming stations, which collected, separated, and pasteurized milk and supplied it to manufacturing plants. When these declined after 1905, as use of hand-cranked separators spread, the trend turned towards large, centralized plants. Creameries used substantially more milk than cheese factories and were capitalized at three to four times as much. By 1914, each cow supplying a creamery with milk had to produce 5,000 pounds annually to permit efficient operation—double that needed for cheese factories. "In this business as in many other lines," observed Harry L. Russell in 1905, "consolidation of interests is taking place."[52]

The industrial revolution in dairying also entailed greater fluid and condensed milk production. In 1900, more than 80 per cent of Wisconsin's milk still went into butter and cheese, but demographic and nutritional developments to use milk in other ways had already begun. Two decades later, condenseries bought about 15 per cent, while urban markets consumed another 10 per cent. About 39 per cent went to creamery butter and the remaining 35 per cent to cheese. Rapid population growth, urbanization, and increased human consumption of fluid milk combined to increase demand. Consequently, milk prices rose, motivating many dairy farmers to earmark their product for burgeoning Midwest cities. Development of glass delivery

---

[51] Lampard, *Rise of the Dairy Industry*, 215–227, 276–289; Ebling et al., *A Century of Wisconsin Agriculture*, 70–71; Bernard O. J. Linnevold, "The Wisconsin Cheese Industry and Government" (doctoral dissertation, University of Wisconsin, 1949), 155–168.

[52] Marvin A. Schaars, "The Butter Industry of Wisconsin" (doctoral dissertation, University of Wisconsin, 1932), 13; *Wisconsin Butter, Production, Marketing, Disposition*, Department of Agriculture, *Special Bulletin*, no. 73 (1958), 27–32; Ebling et al., *A Century of Wisconsin Agriculture*, 70; Lampard, *Rise of the Dairy Industry*, 212–215, 276–280 (quote).

jars in the 1880's and of improved milk-cooling apparatus in the 1890's lowered handling costs and increased appeal to urban consumers. So did the invention of the automatic bottler, the rotary filler, and the mechanized capper in the early twentieth century.

The opportunities for consumption in the cities were paralleled by regulatory problems. Scientific research in the late nineteenth century identified bacteria in milk as a major cause of typhoid, diphtheria, scarlet fever, and tuberculosis. Pushed by the scientific, medical, and social work communities, urban administrators and legislators mandated ever more stringent regulation of fluid milk, culminating in a universal pasteurization requirement. Milwaukee led nationally in this movement, but only after a major struggle with recalcitrant milk producers that resulted in boycotts and other actions. The city's Medical Milk Commission certified between 1,000 and 2,000 quarts a day, which sold for as much as fifteen cents a quart, with farmers receiving about nine cents. Uncertified milk was still available at a lower price for those whose incomes demanded it. In other Wisconsin cities, the results were decidedly uneven, despite growing efforts at state regulation by the Dairy and Food Commission. In 1916, the percentage of pasteurized milk ranged from about 75 in Green Bay to 50 in Beloit to 20 in Eau Claire to a mere 8.6 per cent in Oshkosh.[53]

Even more a harbinger for dairying's growth than fluid milk consumption was the trend towards condensed milk. The first condensery in the state was established in Monroe in 1889, a subsidiary of the New York company owned by Gail Borden, inventor of the "vacuum" process and namesake of the giant milk concern. In only its second year of operation, the Monroe plant daily handled about 25,000 pounds of milk, produced by 1,000 cows, and hauled by team and rail from a radius of fifteen miles. It was another fifteen years before a second condensery was established. It appeared in Racine County, built by a British immigrant, William Horlick, another household name. The necessity for substantial capital, restrictive patents, and the costs and vagaries of transportation guaranteed that condenseries were large-scale operations. These considerations also limited their development to long-established dairy regions, as did the widely held opinion that "the establishment of a great condensery means a step backward for a thriving, booming dairy community." Between 1905 and 1910, seventeen additional plants were opened, nearly all of them near the southeastern Wisconsin market zone. By 1917, the number reached thirty-three. These plants made nearly one-quarter of the nation's condensed milk. They were as far north as Clark County and as far west as La Crosse. Condenseries were the ultimate

[53] Lampard, *Rise of the Dairy Industry*, 227–237; Judith Walzer Leavitt, *The Healthiest City: Milwaukee and the Politics of Health Reform* (Princeton, 1982), 156–189.

in mechanized dairying. From the time the milk was poured into a vacuum pan until it was injected into cans that were "automatically sealed, labeled, wrapped, lithographed, and cased by machine," dairy historian Eric Lampard has observed, "the condensery product was exposed to neither hand nor air."[54]

Inexorable regional specialization also indicated the impact of industrialization upon dairying. During the late nineteenth century, many plants and regions fluctuated between butter and cheese, depending on market conditions. Goods that are perishable, bulky, and of high value tend to be produced in close proximity to their prime markets. Fluid milk zones concentrated around larger cities in Wisconsin, Minnesota, Illinois, and Iowa. Just beyond them lay the condensery regions. Most dairy farms lay beyond these two zones, forming a variety of cheese or butter regions. Cheese making flourished where farm enterprises produced higher quality milk and competed relatively little. Butter predominated where milk had less value and where farm enterprises combined dairying and corn, beef, or hog production. Both cheese and butter followed the general pattern of Wisconsin agriculture, originating in the south and east and progressing steadily north and west. Perhaps the oldest cheese region centered in Dodge County and specialized in brick, Muenster, and other foreign types. Next oldest was the eastern lakeshore, north of Milwaukee, which specialized in American cheese and included Sheboygan, Fond du Lac, Manitowoc, and Kewaunee counties. Last to develop was the mixed American and foreign cheese region in Barron, Polk, Dunn, and St. Croix counties.[55]

The industrialization of butter making developed more slowly than that of cheese. It accelerated most rapidly in the 1890's, the "creamery decade," when Wisconsin's cheese reputation declined and butter-making mechanization improved, prompting many dairymen to switch from cheese to butter. Widespread use of hand separators to divide their products between market milk and creameries led to a 340 per cent increase in butter production in ten years. The production of milk for creameries required less attention and was more compatible with other forms of agriculture, particularly corn and livestock raising.

The adoption of the centrifugal separator, the power churn, and

[54] "A Step Backward," *Wisconsin Farmer*, December 15, 1910 (quote); Thomas R. Pirtle, *History of the Dairy Industry* (Chicago, 1926), 121; Lampard, *Rise of the Dairy Industry*, 237–242 (quote); *Wisconsin Farmer*, December 15, 1910, p. 1144.

[55] Loyal Durand, Jr., "The Cheese Manufacturing Regions of Wisconsin, 1850–1950," in the *Transactions of the Wisconsin Academy of Sciences, Arts and Letters*, 42 (1953), 109–130; Gordon R. Lewthwaite, "The Regionalization of Butter and Cheese Production in Wisconsin" (doctoral dissertation, University of Wisconsin, 1956), 30–35, 62–91.

the milk fat tester moved more rapidly and on a larger scale in creameries than mechanization in cheese factories. Butter production was more conducive to large-scale enterprise and to corporate and cooperative organization. It spread most rapidly in western Wisconsin, north of Vernon and west of Sauk and Juneau counties, where it formed a vital part of a tri-state butter district with eastern Iowa and Minnesota. Another zone ran northwestward through Rock, Dane, and Columbia counties, northeastward through Portage and Waupaca counties to Lake Winnebago, and westward into the central sandy plain. Butter zones also formed in the southeast, near urban milk sheds and condenseries, in the southwestern corn belt, and in Langlade, Shawano, and Brown counties. The predominance of small, scattered dairy farms in the central plain and Cutover obviated formation of cheese regions and facilitated the sale of cream for butter making. Fluid milk for markets fetched about $120 per cow annually; for condenseries, $86; for butter and cheese production, $70. Accordingly, fluid and condensery sales predominated in the state's most populous areas.[56]

Adoption of machinery, too, demonstrated the impact of industrialization on farming. In the 1890's, horse-drawn corn pickers, mowers, corn binders, and silo fillers had become common; belts running off stationary engines pumped water, ran cream separators, and drove a wide variety of farm machines. Such advances became even more common, and in the 1910's, machinery's share of total value of farm property jumped from 4 per cent at the beginning of the decade to 7 per cent at the end. Several hundred Wisconsin farmers already employed milking machines, although adoption spread relatively slowly. The use of commercial fertilizer increased 250 per cent between 1910 and 1915. The demand for professionally trained agricultural experts and for College of Agriculture publications increased substantially. By 1915, a University of Wisconsin agricultural engineer could conclude, "Enough tractors have been tried to demonstrate their practicality" and that "the application of mechanical power will be fully as important a step in our agricultural progress as any yet made." And by the early 1920's, the Farm Bureau *News* proclaimed, "Agriculture in Wisconsin [is] representative of an advanced stage of the industry in which most of the crop production is consumed on the farm where grown in the production of livestock and their products." In thirty years, the transition was virtually complete.[57]

---

[56] Lewthwaite, "Regionalization of Butter and Cheese Production," 7–9, 61–62, 90–93, 131–132, 185–189, 266–269; Wan, "Consolidated Balance Sheet," 6–7; Lampard, *Rise of the Dairy Industry*, 266–267.

[57] F. M. White, "The Tractor Is Here," *Wisconsin Country Magazine*, October, 1915, pp. 12–13 (quote), 16, 36; Ebling et al., *A Century of Wisconsin Agriculture*, 62, 79; "The

Other aspects of the industrial revolution in agriculture were mandates to disseminate a considerable body of scientific and technological knowledge in a systematic and sustained fashion, and to enforce reasonably uniform standards of sanitation and quality. The Wisconsin Dairymen's Association made great initial strides in both areas, with increasing help from the College of Agriculture for the former and from state government for the latter. This assistance was remarkable, considering that Wisconsin farmers committed themselves fiercely to private enterprise and sound business practices, that they openly expressed contempt for "book farming," and that they appeared to be instinctively hostile towards government "interference." Although the WDA deserved most of the credit for this reorientation, the filled-cheese crisis of the 1890's and the oleomargarine threat posed to butter makers lightened the association's task. The WDA also convinced a sufficient number of Wisconsinites that measures so obviously in the self-interest of dairymen actually would benefit the entire state. Thus the association unwittingly pioneered a rationale and a process that others could use as a precedent. Together, the dairymen, the College of Agriculture, and state government erected what they called a "great edifice of dairy education and regulation."[58]

[4]

Dairymen themselves deserve much of the credit for the educational half of the edifice. In 1906, on the eve of his retirement as the first dean of the College of Agriculture, William A. Henry acknowledged, "The Wisconsin State Dairymen's Association is the true parent of the Wisconsin College of Agriculture of today." During its crucial formative years, the WDA functioned as mediator, aiding farmers to overcome their bias against agricultural education, while pushing the college to meet dairymen's practical needs. Many of the association's initiatives in teaching, testing, and demonstration served as models for the college; and many of the college's research breakthroughs came because of association requests.[59]

If the College of Agriculture was the offspring of the WDA, then the University of Wisconsin was the college's reluctant adoptive parent. Initiatives in the late 1800's to launch a separate agricultural

---

Automobile and the Farmer," *Hoard's Dairyman*, July 28, 1911; "Farm Income in Wisconsin," *Wisconsin Farm Bureau News*, October, 1923.

[58] Lampard, *Rise of the Dairy Industry*, xi–xii (quote), 337–344.

[59] Wilbur H. Glover, *Farm and College: The College of Agriculture of the University of Wisconsin, A History* (Madison, 1952), 86–87.

college met with opposition from the university establishment, which feared incorporation into the university would compromise the campus's reputation, create competition for state funding, and proliferate much maligned "vocational" courses. Despite lobbying by the state agricultural society, the appointment of dairyman Hiram Smith to the Board of Regents in 1878, the subsequent establishment of a one-professor department of agriculture, and the founding of a demonstration farm, the 1885 legislature killed a bill providing for a separate agricultural institution. Farm groups became aroused, and to placate them the regents expanded the department of agriculture's mission to encompass farmer institutes, both "long" (four-year) and "short" (two twelve-week terms in successive winters) courses of study, and the conversion of the demonstration farm to an experimental research station. In 1891, the university established its own College of Agriculture, with William A. Henry as its first dean.[60]

Agrarian regents, lawmakers, Governor William D. Hoard (1889–1891), and the WDA all contributed to conceiving the college. However, its first two deans, William A. Henry and Harry L. Russell, played the critical roles of midwife and wet nurse. Primary credit belongs to them for its success as transformer of Wisconsin's agricultural system. Henry's insistence that basic research remain at the core of the college's identity, his courting of grassroots support from farmers, his penchant for practical applications of research findings, his development of institutes, short courses, and extension programs, as well as his performance as a master lobbyist for legislation and funding— all were absolutely crucial. His tenure produced eight major buildings, enrollment increases from three to forty-six in the long course and from forty-five to 390 in the short course, and the establishment of eight new departments. By 1907, the combined annual appropriations for the college and the experimental station exceeded $200,000. The physical and emotional costs of those achievements were high, however. Henry successfully weathered charges of financial mismanagement and dictatorial methods, but resigned in 1907. A few critics applauded "the Dean of Deans'" comeuppance, but most joined with Hoard, university president Charles R. Van Hise, and Congressman Henry C. Adams in praising Henry. The Board of Regents enthusiastically adopted Hoard's resolution: "We feel that the people of Wisconsin as a whole are under great obligation to Professor Henry for much of the advancement and prosperity which has come to the state in the last quarter of a century."[61]

[60] *Ibid.*, 89–107, 133–136.
[61] *Ibid.*, 133–148 (quote); Merle Curti and Vernon Carstensen, *The University of Wisconsin: A History, 1848–1925* (2 vols., Madison, 1949), 1: 398–412, 2: 376–380; Madison *Capital Times*, August 2, 1927; William A. Henry, letter to students, 1894, box 1,

Nor did Henry's partial fall from grace adversely affect the college's fortunes. In 1907, Harry L. Russell firmly assumed the deanship. He was a bacteriologist who had already achieved significant fame by campaigning against bovine tuberculosis, and by collaborating in development of cold-curing processes for cheese. Under Russell, enrollment in the long course increased to 616 by 1914; in the short course, to 464. The number of graduate students increased from fourteen to 114; the college added new departments of agricultural journalism, home economics, poultry husbandry, agricultural and extension education, entomology, plant pathology, and experimental breeding (genetics). By 1915, the agricultural complex included a stock pavilion, a new horticulture hall, an agricultural chemistry building, and a new wing for the soils building. Russell also greatly expanded the college's role in the university's extension service and initiated co-operative research projects with several food-processing companies. Perhaps most importantly, Russell presided in 1907 over the development of a new curriculum which allowed long-course students to substitute courses in agronomy, animal husbandry, horticulture, and agricultural bacteriology and chemistry for the general science courses usually required of freshmen and sophomores.[62]

Notwithstanding these considerable successes, Russell's early deanship was frequently stormy. Russell lacked Henry's common touch, though he was similarly dedicated and energetic. His approach to the legislature was "to contact the few key men who really ran things there," which smacked of conspiracy to his detractors. Russell and the college came under attack from the leaders of the Society of Equity, a militant organization of less prosperous farmers, and from a group of progressives led by Charles McCarthy and Governor Francis E. McGovern (1911–1915). They jointly criticized Russell and the college for emphasizing production to the detriment of marketing, for advocating education over government intervention as a solution to farmers' problems, and for stressing sound business practices rather than fostering co-operative initiatives in production, marketing, and purchasing. Their critics kept Russell and the college on the defensive, especially when the newly created Board of Public Affairs

---

Edward H. Farrington Papers; James G. Moore, "Some Recorded Facts Relative to the Development of Agriculture in the University of Wisconsin," 1955, pp. 52–58, in folder 7, department file, agriculture series 9, University of Wisconsin Archives.

[62] Curti and Carstensen, *University of Wisconsin*, 2: 406–407; Glover, *Farm and College*, 269–280. See also Edward H. Beardsley, *Harry L. Russell and Agricultural Science in Wisconsin* (Madison, 1969), also published in part in *WMH*, "The Making of a Scientist: Harry L. Russell in Europe," 49 (Autumn, 1965), 3–15, and "An Industry Revitalized: Harry Russell, Stephen Babcock, and the Cold Curing of Cheese," 49 (Winter, 1965–1966), 122–137.

launched an investigation of the university. Although the investigation's findings were not as damaging as first predicted, and although Governor Emanuel Philipp (1915–1921) protected the institution, Philipp's commitment to budget cutting and fiscal responsibility restricted the college's discretion. Nevertheless, by 1915 the college had firmly established itself as important, both within the university and throughout the state.[63]

An overview of its major accomplishments in teaching, research, and extension work conveys a sense of their magnitude and diversity. The relative concentration given each is reflected in the 1912–1913 budget, which allocated $65,000 to research, $81,000 to teaching, and $83,000 to extension. From the university's perspective, the college's four-year long course, and the graduate program that emerged out of it, were the crux of its curriculum. But some university faculty members denigrated this curriculum as mere vocational education, and some farmers called it impractical. Indeed, the long course enrolled only eighteen students by 1901 and 146 by 1907; the graduate school attracted only thirteen by 1907. Although the 1907 curriculum revision legitimized "the educative value of practical work under professors of scientific competence," many non-agricultural faculty remained skeptical or even hostile. Nevertheless, the revision significantly increased the attractiveness of a college education to farmers' sons whose vocational interests served as a focus for solid grounding in academic disciplines. It was primarily from the ranks of long-course graduates that the state recruited its station scientists, its teachers of agriculture, its county agents, farm managers, and agricultural technicians.[64]

From the farmer's viewpoint, the farmers' institutes and the two-winter short courses were the heart of the college's teaching program, largely because they were both almost entirely practical. Even so, early institute teachers felt that, although farmers were generally receptive, "many were indifferent, some sneered, and a few thought it amusing to create disturbances." One farmer-correspondent admitted to having been "somewhat prejudiced" that the institutes would be conducted "by scientists, with a general lack of common sense and natural ability." But the same man later confessed, "I was happily disappointed, for practical men came to the front," dealing with such everyday subjects as butter, potatoes, hogs, and gardens.

As early as 1887, there were eighty-one institutes serving 50,000 farmers. The format consisted of descriptions by local farmers of

---

[63] Glover, *Farm and College*, 281; Curti and Carstensen, *University of Wisconsin*, 2: 406–407 (quote).

[64] *Capital Times*, August 2, 1927; Curti and Carstensen, *University of Wisconsin*, 2: 399–403; Glover, *Farm and College*, 240–243 (quote).

their personal experiences in farming methods, followed by general discussion and questions from the audience. The institutes were held in communities sufficiently interested to provide both speakers and partial financing, and were aimed at drawing farmers from a fifteen-mile radius. The Farmers' Institute published a bulletin to disseminate insights throughout the state. The institutes' avowed purpose "was to communicate to farmers the scientific experiments and findings of the Wisconsin Agricultural Experiment Station and the best practices of real dirt farmers." As farmers moved northward, institutes followed them with programs designed for the peculiar problems of the Cutover. In 1914, the college held its first institute on the Menominee Indian Reservation for Native Americans who were either farmers or becoming farmers. Still, institutes barely survived a serious attempt to abolish them in the 1911 legislature and, two years later, were brought directly under the control of a College of Agriculture committee.[65]

Equally successful, over time, were the short course and the dairy course, a single-year, twelve-week course begun in 1890. The short course attracted only seventeen students in 1891; the first dairy course session enrolled seventy. It featured practical training for makers of butter and cheese, stressing the value of sanitation. Within years, creameries and cheese factories were competing for its graduates, and observers praised both the cleanliness of these establishments and the quality and value of their products. *Hoard's Dairyman* asserted that "if every cheesemaker in Wisconsin could have the benefit of even one term in the Dairy School the value of the state's cheese product would be increased 15 to 25 per cent." By 1901, the dairy course had graduated 1,142 men; the annual enrollment fluctuated between ninety and 169. Its success stimulated interest in the more general short course, which soon outdistanced it. In its 1910–1911 session, short course enrollment peaked at 473.

Much of this success was due to the energy of its director, Ransom A. Moore, who toured Dane County on a bicycle, took exhibits to county fairs, and generally advertised the course to anyone within his reach. It was out of Moore's short course that the Agricultural Experiment Station was born in 1883. Aided by scholarship money provided by Milwaukee banker John L. Mitchell beginning in 1891, Moore expanded the course to two consecutive winter terms in 1893.

[65] Glover, *Farm and College*, 149–159 (quotes); Robin Hood, "The Progress of our Farmers' Institutes," *Wisconsin Country Magazine*, April, 1916, pp. 332–333; E. L. Luther, "Institutes Still Aiding Wisconsin," *Wisconsin Agriculturist*, April 3, 1926 (quote); E. L. Luther to Henry C. Gignilliot, May 15, 1937, box 1, E. L. Luther Papers; J. F. Wojta, "Indian Farm Institutes in Wisconsin," in *WMH*, 29 (June, 1946), 423–424; Madison *Democrat*, April 8, 1911.

There were no entrance requirements save a common school education, and even that was waived for those "who are by age and experience fitted for the work." Many of the early students were barely literate in English. Although the faculty constantly strove to expand the curriculum, increase its academic rigor, and extend the length of the term, the short course remained primarily a vehicle for training young men who would return to the farm. By 1897, the number of requests to hire its graduates exceeded the available supply.

Faculty members complained that teaching left them little research time, and students griped that professors were more interested in research than in teaching. But the short course prospered in the new century. Its students eventually were exposed to new specializations: economics, agronomy, mechanics, engineering, physics, journalism, and livestock breeding and judging. The annual term was increased to fourteen weeks in 1896 and to fifteen some twenty years later; academic requirements were gradually tightened. By 1911, formal graduation exercises were introduced and the first woman was certified, even though the embarrassed faculty excused her from the course in animal husbandry. That same year, *Wisconsin Country Magazine* proclaimed that "so rapidly has the short course advanced in importance and in popularity that it is now one of the most potent factors in agricultural education."[66]

The ongoing dispute over teaching versus research and pure versus applied research, primarily through the Agricultural Experiment Station, led the college to make empirical contributions of at least equal magnitude to its educational achievements. College spokesmen always insisted that these presumed conflicts were really false dichotomies, since (as they said) teaching and pure and applied research were reinforcing aspects of the same process of advancing a general understanding of agricultural science. Practical advances, according to Dean Russell's annual report in 1915, could be made only when researchers comprehended the universal scientific principles involved. Consequently, he argued, it was "imperative that an Experiment Station devoted to the improvement of plant and animal life along economic lines should give large place to a consideration of these problems that are of such fundamental, and, at the same time, practical importance." In practice, conflicts between pure and applied research were inevitable, as the need to justify work by practical, and even monetary, standards sometimes necessitated shortcuts that undermined long-term, scientifically controlled investigations. Its impressive success, Russell contended, was due largely to the staff's ability to involve farmers in setting the research agenda and in applying

[66] Glover, *Farm and College*, 96–97, 228–238.

the results, as well as to the staff's astuteness in justifying the empirical in terms of the experimental.[67]

Easily the college's most renowned research accomplishment was Stephen Babcock's development in 1890 of a relatively efficient and economical test for determining milk's butterfat content. By adding a small amount of sulphuric acid just before the milk was whirled in a centrifuge, Babcock was able to separate the butterfat that rose to the neck of the bottle, where it could be measured easily. The Babcock test provided a nearly infallible, and easily replicable, method of determining the quality of milk, thereby setting fair prices. Honest farmers, said *Hoard's Dairyman*, hailed the Babcock test as "the most practical and God-like umpire ever given to man to divide money arising from the sale of products manufactured from pooled milk, whether put into butter or cheese." It was estimated that the Babcock test saved as much as 0.2 per cent of the fat that previously had been lost, and the U.S. Department of Agriculture claimed that it saved Wisconsin dairymen $800,000 a year—more than twice the budget of the entire University of Wisconsin.

Perhaps even more remarkable was Babcock's altruistic refusal to patent the process, a decision that allowed farmers to use it merely for the cost of the equipment. Working with Russell and other bacteriologists, Babcock helped develop more efficient means of extracting cream from milk and design the first American apparatus for thorough pasteurization. In 1897, Babcock and Russell isolated galactose, the enzyme that exerts a digestive action on milk protein and, in 1908, developed a simple test that established the relation of casein to fat in milk and of fat to cheese quality. By the turn of the century their curd test for detecting tainted milk was saving cheese makers an estimated $100,000 to $200,000 a year. In another breakthrough, upon discovering that producing cheese at the temperatures that prevailed in cold-storage plants and grocery store coolers was safer, Babcock and Russell perfected a revolutionary cold-curing process.[68]

Perhaps the most sensational and controversial episode at the experiment station involved Russell's experiments with bovine tuberculosis. In 1893, applying a test for tubercle bacillus he learned from German researchers, Russell discovered that two of the station's cows were infected. He validated his findings at autopsies. When he tested

---

[67] Harry L. Russell, *Work Done by the Experiment Station in 1915*, UW Agricultural Experiment Station, *Bulletin*, no. 268 (1916), 3; Curti and Carstensen, *University of Wisconsin*, 2: 380–384; Glover, *Farm and College*, 112–132.

[68] Lampard, *Rise of the Dairy Industry*, 199–204; Curti and Carstensen, *University of Wisconsin*, 2: 387–392 (quote); "Paying for Milk by Test for Fat to Make Cheese," *Hoard's Dairyman*, January 1, 1892, p. 1905 (quote); Stephen M. Babcock and Harry L. Russell, *The Cheese Industry: Its Development and Possibilities in Wisconsin*, UW Agricultural Experiment Station, *Bulletin*, no. 60 (1897), 3–18.

the remainder of the herd, he found that twenty-five of twenty-eight animals were infected. Before a shocked and angry audience of several hundred farmers, Russell had the infected cows slaughtered and displayed their diseased lungs as evidence. Although many dairy farmers remained hostile or indifferent, Russell and his students persevered in perfecting and applying the tuberculosis test. They proved that about 15 per cent of the cows tested over the next two decades were tubercular. Russell received immense aid and support from William D. Hoard, who crusaded for the test in his *Dairyman* and resolutely destroyed infected cows from his own valuable herd. Their combined efforts did not achieve complete success until the late 1930's, but Russell and Hoard clearly prepared the way.

Tuberculin testing was but one aspect of an extensive effort to rate cows to improve the quantity and quality of their milk. With the help of various breeder associations, the College of Agriculture began official testing in 1899, examining nearly 3,000 cows during the first decade. After 1909, a number of co-operative herd improvement associations augmented these efforts. Farmer inertia slowed progress, but even so by 1915 thirty-nine associations had formed and were testing 19,000 cows annually. The college's experiments proved that a cow yielding 300 pounds of butterfat brought the farmer five times the annual profit of a cow producing 200 pounds. As the authors of a popular Wisconsin feed manual put it, "[T]he first cow is worth more to the dairyman than five of the second."[69]

Just as substantive was the experiment station's role in improving crops for feed and market. Agricultural engineers and physicists designed the cylindrical silo and made great advances in enhancing soil quality through irrigation and mineral replenishment. Station horticulturalists enhanced the quality of fruits and vegetables, and made strides against pests and disease. Henry, Russell, Babcock, and others helped develop more nutritious silage and a practical feeding ration. Henry's monumental *Feeds and Feeding* (1898) demonstrated that protein acts as the crucial variable in animal diet, and that diet determines milk quality. Refinements of Henry's work revolutionized feeding practices and crop selection, and paved the way for later discoveries in human nutrition.[70]

Less obviously related to practical farming were the college's pioneering steps in the agricultural social sciences, beginning in 1909 with the creation of the agricultural economics department under

---

[69] Lampard, *Rise of the Dairy Industry*, 180–190 (quote); Glover, *Farm and College*, 126–128; Gail D. Bremer, "The Wisconsin Idea and the Public Health Movement, 1890–1915" (master's thesis, University of Wisconsin, 1963.)

[70] Lampard, *Rise of the Dairy Industry*, 162–169; Curti and Carstensen, *University of Wisconsin*, 2: 386–387; Glover, *Farm and College*, 112–118.

WISCONSIN IN 1908

Henry C. Taylor. The Wisconsin Dairymen's Association viewed the new department as a logical outgrowth of its own efforts to promote sound business management practices among farmers. Taylor's *An Introduction to the Study of Agricultural Economics* (1905) quickly became a classic, and its author was widely regarded as the father of agricultural economics. He was a student of Frederick Jackson Turner, and he credited his professor with instilling in him a historical approach to his field. Pushed by Charles McCarthy and the Society of Equity, Taylor and others in his department critiqued the prevailing pricing system and advocated co-operative marketing by marginal farmers— actions which disenchanted Hoard and the WDA. The birth of the Country Life Movement and growing concern over the drift of farm boys to the city fostered development of rural sociology within the economics department. Rural sociology's leading practitioner, Charles J. Galpin, joined the faculty in 1912. Using Walworth County as his laboratory, he quickly gained nationwide recognition for *The Social Anatomy of an Agricultural Community* (1915), which introduced the concept of farm-village communities defined by church, school, press, and business connections. Galpin organized Country Life conferences in Wisconsin and published his findings in *Rural Life* (1918).[71]

[5]

With research and teaching in full flower, the college turned more and more towards agricultural extension, which had its origins in the farmers' institutes and in the bulletin publications of the experiment station. By 1907, it had published 141 bulletins in editions of about 20,000. Extension's evolution was greatly facilitated by the example of the Agricultural Experiment Association, which coordinated crop improvement projects statewide. It founded co-operative activities with the state's high schools and sponsored a railroad train that toured the state to promote crop improvement. Based partly on that model, the university, unlike other state universities, made extension work an outgrowth of existing departmental activities rather than a separate entity. When the university revitalized its extension division in 1907, the college had sufficient experience, achievements, and influence to establish Agricultural College Extension as its own coordinate. "Ag Extension's" major purpose was to administer the already ongoing teaching and demonstration work of college departments. Along the way it initiated new programs in conjunction with rural public schools and various business organizations. During the 1912–1913 academic year, Dean Russell estimated that these extension programs reached 228,000 people. Innovatively and significantly,

---

[71] Glover, *Farm and College*, 328–339; Marvin A. Schaars, *The Story of the Department of Agricultural Economics, 1909–1972* (mimeographed, Madison, 1972); Charles J. Galpin, *My Drift into Rural Sociology* (Baton Rouge, 1938), 29–33; Everett E. Edwards, "Agricultural History and the Department of Agriculture," *Agricultural History*, 16 (July, 1942), 129–136. It was Oscar C. Stine, a student of Turner and Taylor, who in 1916 instituted historical studies in the U.S. Department of Agriculture.

the college led nationally in introducing the county agent program. Agents functioned both as teachers and educational middlemen. The first was appointed in Oneida County in 1912; eleven additional men, all in the northern half of the state, were in place by 1915. It soon became evident that farm visits and direct demonstrations were the agents' most effective and popular jobs. Automobiles early became standard equipment for them. Southern counties were slower to follow suit, until passage of a 1913 law granted county boards authority to hire agents. The Smith-Lever Act, passed by Congress in 1914, also facilitated the program's expansion. The act granted federal funds for agricultural extension in return for a virtual end to the formal teaching activities of county agents. Despite occasional conflict with the University Extension Division, the Extension Service of the College of Agriculture flourished.[72]

By 1914, the mutually beneficial collaboration of the Wisconsin Dairymen's Association, and its spinoff organizations, with the College of Agriculture had persisted for more than a quarter-century. A decade later, Theodore Kronshage, the president of the Board of Regents, enumerated twelve services that the college had performed for the state's farmers, most of which had been accomplished by 1914. Chief among these were silos, seven renowned dairy tests, pedigreed seeds, alfalfa, soil surveys, and the eradication of bovine tuberculosis and various plant diseases. In celebrating them, Kronshage emphasized their economic value. The state's farmers and editors did the same. The *Wisconsin Farmer* observed that "the only kind of farming worth talking about is that which pays dividends" and lauded the College's programs as a forum where "science and practicality meet at every turn in the road." Similarly, the *Wisconsin Agriculturist* supported college courses because those who participated "make more money" and "grant to the College of Agriculture the credit for their material success." Even the New York *Evening Post* in 1910 saw fit to tout the university's achievements: "The entire financial returns each year to that state from the university agricultural investigations and teaching alone are simply incalculable, but enough measurable concrete cases are known to show that this department alone returns to the state each year ten to twenty times the entire amount spent on the whole university."[73]

---

[72] Harry L. Russell, *New Facts in Farm Science*, UW Agricultural Experiment Station director, *Annual Report*, 1922–1923, *Bulletin*, no. 362 (1924), 10–11; Glover, *Farm and College*, 202–227; Andrew W. Hopkins, "Where the County Agent Came From: Source of a Farm Institution Which Has Spread Over the World," *Wisconsin Agriculturist*, January 7, 1922, p. 7. See also Elwood R. McIntyre, *Fifty Years of Cooperative Extension in Wisconsin, 1912–1962*, UW College of Agriculture, Extension Service, *Circular*, no. 602 (1962).

[73] Theodore Kronshage, Jr., "What University Does For Farmers," *UW Press Bulletin*,

Besides cementing its alliance with the College of Agriculture, the WDA looked increasingly to state and federal government for funding and regulation. Just as agriculture's growing complexity persuaded most farmers to accept "book farming," so too did a modernizing industrial economy force them to modify opposition to government intervention. The WDA's abiding *concern* was to advance associated dairying; its basic *credo* maintained that quality and efficiency paid off in cold, hard cash. It emphasized that hard work, businesslike operation, and expert knowledge—not government policy—best guaranteed prosperity. Education and regulation were the proper functions of private organizations such as the WDA; farmers should ask government to intervene only in the direst emergency, lest government subvert the benefits of natural competition. The magnitude and complexity of these self-assigned tasks encouraged dairy leaders to modify their outlook, realizing that other segments of the economy, chiefly businessmen, were seeking government favors.[74]

In 1888, the WDA demanded the creation of the position of dairy commissioner "whose duty it shall be to ferret out and prosecute all adulterations of butter and cheese." At the next WDA annual meeting, the delegates called for a comprehensive program of dairy and food legislation. Meanwhile, Hoard managed to secure the Republican gubernatorial nomination and in 1888 was elected, at least in part because of his designation as "the cow candidate." In response to a message from Hoard, the legislature did indeed establish the office of dairy and food commissioner, empowering the commissioner to enforce all laws respecting food, drink, or drugs, and to prosecute anyone selling adulterated or counterfeit articles. The state dairy commissioner and the staff did their best, but the second commissioner, Henry C. Adams, continued to complain that the making of filled cheese between 1889 to 1895 demoralized the state's cheese industry. Only a wholesale shift to butter production saved the dairy industry from devastation.

A handful of successful prosecutions under the new law, coupled with the farmers' institutes and the inauguration of the dairy course, had already improved the situation by 1895. So did the newly created (1893) Wisconsin Cheese Makers Association, which established local protective associations to compel use of the Babcock test. Even so, dairy organizations tacitly admitted their efforts' inadequacy by suc-

---

April 15, 1925, clipping in LRB; *Wisconsin Farmer*, April 16, 1914, p. 461 (quote); "The Farmers' Course," *Wisconsin Agriculturist*, February 22, 1912; Charles H. Everett, "Millions For Agriculture," *ibid.*, April 24, May 4, June 12, July 10, and August 7, 28, 1926; New York *Evening Post* article in Milwaukee *Sentinel*, March 8, 1910, clipping in LRB.
[74] Lampard, *Rise of the Dairy Industry*, 246–266, 344–345.

cessfully lobbying for a state law prohibiting the manufacture and sale of cheese made from skim milk—the basis of filled cheese. Passage of a federal law branding and taxing filled cheese the following year reinforced the Wisconsin statute. Although the dairy commissioner's office claimed total victory over adulterated cheese by the end of the decade, the fight actually continued for many more years. Not until 1912 could commissioner John Q. Emery, commanding a staff of thirty experts, assert that his department "has not found a pound of 'filled cheese' manufactured or sold in Wisconsin during the past ten years." He also boasted that the state "is now producing in great variety and in quality unexcelled anywhere, upwards of 164,000,000 pounds of cheese annually for which, including by-products, the producers are receiving upwards of $24,000,000."[75]

The dairymen's triumph over oleomargarine was to prove both more arduous and lengthy than the filled cheese struggle, primarily because the butter substitute was manufactured by large corporations whose political clout at least equalled that of the dairy associations. Since some margarine was actually superior to the low-quality butter produced on individual farms ("western grease"), it was also difficult to make much headway until the switch to creamery production justified the industry's claim to superior quality.

The WDA successfully lobbied for a butter labeling law as early as 1881. Over the next three sessions, the legislature enacted laws that virtually prohibited the use of animal fats and oils in dairy manufacture, including the cheese labeling law of 1887. That law dictated that cheese labels had to include the name of the manufacturer, the place of origin, and the quality of milk used. Still, the dairy commissioner estimated oleo's annual sales at 4 to 5 million pounds by 1890—equivalent to the butter product of 30,000 cows. The cost, he charged, not only impoverished farmers but amounted to a "tribute" of $1 million a year from Wisconsin consumers, exacted by Chicago meat-packers, who sold much of the oleo. Following the commissioner's reasoning, the 1891 legislature required exact labeling of oleomargarine and forbade the use of what it termed "imitation butter" by state institutions. In 1895, it outlawed oleomargarine made in "imitation of yellow butter." Ironically, many farmers purchased oleo for their own tables during the depression of 1893–1897, while lobbying against purchase of the cheaper spread by financially strapped urban consumers. Wisconsin farmers tended to be frugal, even if it meant being inconsistent.[76]

At the same time, the WDA and its offshoots joined other dairy organizations to seek a national ban on oleomargarine. In 1896, Con-

[75] Ibid., 249–257.
[76] Ibid., 257–261.

gress prohibited selling oleo in quantities of less than ten pounds and imposed a small tax on its manufacturers, who largely evaded the law by repacking the product after shipment or by mixing it with butter. While the 1895 statute indeed reduced oleo sales in the state, dairy commissioner Henry C. Adams charged that Chicago meat-packers flouted the law by shipping oleo directly to consumers, a ruse that permitted the sale of 1.7 million pounds in 1899 alone. He also estimated that, despite state laws and the lobbying of the National Dairy Union (NDU), about 107 million pounds of oleo had been produced that year. Hoard and Adams spent several months lobbying for the NDU in Washington in 1902; then Adams resigned as commissioner in order to run for Congress. He won, and in Congress quickly managed the passage of laws imposing a tax on colored and uncolored oleo, made both subject to regulation by the state in which they were purchased, and levied a series of license fees and taxes on manufacturers, wholesalers, and retail dealers.

But the general rise in butter prices after 1905 increased the demand for oleo. Oleo manufacturers responded with a number of ingenious devices to get around the new laws, too. The federal pure food and drug laws of 1906 also forced oleo sellers to improve their product, undermining one of the butter maker's most potent arguments. The Wisconsin Supreme Court and researchers at the Agricultural Experiment Station rescued butter's cause. In *State v. Meyer and Nowack* 1908, brought by commissioner Emery, the court held that any attempt to alter the color of oleo, regardless of the ingredient used, violated state law. Two years later, Emery proclaimed that enforcement of the oleo law by his office had saved consumers "five and one-half times the cost of maintaining the dairy and food department for that year." For their part, researchers produced solid evidence that butterfat is a major source of vitamins A and B and therefore healthful. Although oleo's lower price continued to attract many consumers, the prosperity of the butter industry was ensured through co-operation by representatives of the standard triumvirate—dairymen, the university, and the state.[77]

[6]

The WDA and its affiliates lobbied for other government aids to agriculture as well, including the transformation of the State Agricultural Society into the State Board of Agriculture in 1897. Even this was not an end, for in 1915 the Wisconsin Dairymen's Association and other farm organizations successfully pushed for the formation

[77] *Ibid.*, 261–266.

of a State *Department* of Agriculture which subsumed all of the state's agricultural programs, save for those of the dairy and food commissioner. Transportation, too, figured into the dairy story. Many farmers originally opposed a turn-of-the-century movement to improve the state's roads because they feared urban invasion. But the growing need for safe and speedy transit to creameries, cheese factories, condenseries, and markets eventually convinced them otherwise. By 1903 the WDA, the Grange, the state's agriculture board, and countless farmers' institutes declared in favor of state aid for road building. Although generally not among the original supporters of railroad regulation in the later nineteenth century, most agricultural organizations had joined that movement by 1905. As for rural education, the WDA and its allies, including the Country Life Conference, led reform efforts. *Hoard's Dairyman* initiated the campaign in the early 1890's, and it gathered strength thereafter. The WDA and its affiliates charged that education in the legendary one-room schoolhouse did not in fact prepare young people for the complexities of modern farming, or for the various programs of the College of Agriculture. The groups also pushed for school consolidation, teacher education institutions in the counties, agricultural courses in public school curricula, and special county-level agricultural schools that offered a mixture of vocational and academic courses.[78]

At the national level, the WDA and its allies joined other dairymen to lobby for federal oleomargarine and pure food and drug laws. As a congressman, Henry C. Adams wrote a 1906 law which provided increased federal funding to agricultural experiment stations. The WDA groups also advocated Rural Free Delivery in 1897, postal savings banks in 1910, and the parcel post system in 1913. *Hoard's* and other agricultural voices joined to call for more railroad supervision by the Interstate Commerce Commission. Dairy farmers also backed the Smith-Lever Act of 1914 (which allocated federal money for state extension work). In educational endeavors generally, friends from the College of Agriculture strongly supported all farmer organizations.[79]

But these demands for government intervention bore definite limits. Most WDA political activities fell more properly into the category

---

[78] "He Thinks the Dairyman Too Scientific," *Hoard's Dairyman*, February 22, 1895, p. 2; Ann M. Keppel and James I. Clark, "James H. Stout and the Menomonie Schools," in *WMH*, 42 (Spring, 1959), 207–208; J. C. Brockert, "The Consolidated Country School," UW College of Agriculture, Wisconsin Country Life Conference, *Bulletin*, no. 2 (1912), 67–68; Campbell, "The Good Roads Movement," in *WMH*, 49: 273–293; Stanley P. Caine, *The Myth of A Progressive Reform: Railroad Regulation in Wisconsin, 1903–1910* (Madison, 1970), 98–105.

[79] Untitled editorial, *Hoard's Dairyman*, December 1, 1905, p. 1096; Howard Murray Jones to Ada Jones, January 7, 1913, in the Howard Murray Jones Papers.

of lobbying than into politics. The association refused to join with more radical agrarian groups, which demanded alterations in the capitalist system or direct aid to the disadvantaged or unsuccessful. The dairymen did believe that limited governmental intervention could serve to establish conditions under which the natural laws of economics could operate freely, but they were careful not to allow such minor deviations to compromise what Adams called "its plain business principles." At most, the WDA wanted the state to supply experts with knowledge that would help individuals upgrade their producer skills, and it wanted the state to enforce quality standards that would eliminate marginal operators. Its model was "the nightwatchman state," in which government intervened only when threats appeared to normally beneficial competition. The WDA generally ignored or opposed political issues that did not directly affect dairying, or that addressed the concerns of those presumed antagonistic to dairymen, such as industrial workers, consumers, or marginal farmers. Originally allied with progressive politicians who courted its support, the WDA gradually distanced itself from progressive politicians when its erstwhile champions cultivated other constituencies.

Over time, the College of Agriculture gradually usurped the association's teaching function, while the Dairy and Food Commissioner's office and the State Board of Agriculture took over regulatory work, and became more concerned with the broader public interest. The very success of the WDA fostered functionally and regionally specialized divisions within its own ranks that made government the only arbiter capable of adjudicating conflicting demands, as well as those of consumers, experts, and the general public. New agricultural organizations, with agendas different from, and even hostile towards, those of the WDA and its offshoots further eroded its hegemony. The association's once-compelling slogan, "What's good for the dairy is good for Wisconsin," failed to convince dissenters.[80]

Ironically, the success of a project modeled on collaboration among the state university, the dairymen, and state government seriously undermined the WDA's status as an agricultural spokesman, as well as its mutually beneficial coalition with progressive politicians: the promotion of agriculture in the Cutover.

[7]

Initially, railroads, lumber companies, and land developers pushed resettlement in the logged-over northern reaches of the state. Faced with declining business and revenues as the lumber industry re-

[80] Lampard, *Rise of the Dairy Industry*, 344–347.

treated, the Wisconsin Central and other railroads stepped up efforts to attract settlers by advertising both in the U.S. and abroad, and by employing land agents who worked on commission. For their part, the lumber companies had four alternatives: hold their lands in anticipation of rising prices, allow them to be attached by counties for nonpayment of taxes, sell them to land speculators, or get into the land-promotion business themselves. Some preferred to discourage settlement "so long as we have standing pine of any considerable quantities in a county," on the grounds that increasing demands for public services would cause higher taxes. Others sought to encourage settlers who farmed in the summer and worked as loggers in the winter or to develop wood-based industries. Land speculation in the Cutover boomed for both individual and corporate entrepreneurs.

By far the most flamboyant and ambitious entrepreneur was Milwaukee's James L. "Stumpland" Gates, who boasted that he had sold 456,000 acres for over $2 million between 1898 and 1902. (So well known was Gates that in 1901 the legislature bestowed his name on a new northern county, only to change it in 1905 to Rusk for Governor Jeremiah Rusk.) Less extravagant but no less important were the efforts of such combinations as the Wisconsin Colonization Company, the American Immigration Company, the Wisconsin Development Association, the Wisconsin Advancement Association, and the Northern Wisconsin Farmers Association. Most of these were coalitions of lumbermen, railroads, bankers, real estate speculators, and businessmen-boosters in northern communities. The state's newspapers and agricultural periodicals also avidly promoted the wonders of the Cutover. Typical was the claim in *Hoard's Dairyman* that "the hum of the cream separator has taken the place of the buzz saw, and the plow and mower that of the lumber shed."[81]

Until the early twentieth century, most promoters concentrated on attracting individual settlers through advertising. Newspapers, brochures, and land agents boasted of the unparalleled opportunities guaranteed by economic development. They appealed primarily to discontented urban factory workers and immigrants, printing their literature in German, Polish, Norwegian, and other languages. Their exaggerated claims and hard-sell techniques induced thousands to stake their economic futures on tenuous homestead farms. As reality

---

[81] Arlan Helgeson, "Nineteenth Century Land Colonization in Northern Wisconsin," in *WMH*, 36 (Winter, 1952–1953), 115–121; Helgeson, *Farms in the Cutover*, 1–24 (quote), 41–52; *Hoard's Dairyman*, November 1, 1907, p. 1012 (quote); "How U.W. Aids State Farmers," Milwaukee *Journal*, June 20, 1915, clipping in LRB; State Board of Agriculture, *Annual Report*, 1901, p. 326; *ibid.*, 1906, p. 121; *ibid.*, 1911, pp. 26–28; Department of Agriculture, *Biennial Report*, 1915–1916, pp. 2–60; *Wisconsin Farmer*, February 1, 1900, p. 77; Lucile Kane, "Selling Cut-Over Lands in Wisconsin," *Business History Review*, 28 (September, 1954), 236–247.

set in, promoters were forced to tone down their rhetoric and to provide solutions for some of the problems that plagued earlier arrivals. Many promoters recognized the need to bring together capital, settlers, and agricultural knowledge in a joint enterprise, and to sponsor carefully supervised colonies with a reasonably high level of public services: townsites with schools, churches, and stores; affordable mortgages; and techniques and devices to clear stumpland and produce thriving crops and livestock. The Northern Wisconsin Farmers Association, formed by businessmen in Douglas, Bayfield, Ashland, and Iron counties, sponsored a "Grasslands" railroad car, which contained agricultural exhibits. Co-operating railroads pulled it through Wisconsin, Illinois, Iowa, and Minnesota. Other associations worked with local banks on long-term financing, focused on improving dairy and farm methods, and formed land-clearing organizations. They also lobbied for state aid to northern settlement.[82]

Cutover development had been a joint private-public enterprise from the outset. Beginning in 1853, the various incarnations of a state immigration board had advertised northern Wisconsin as ideal for foreign-born settlers. A later board worked closely with the Wisconsin Central Railroad and followed the same strategy, until anti-immigrant sentiment dictated its abolition in 1887. Eight years later, an Ashland County lumberman introduced a successful bill to reconstitute the board. Governor William Upham (1895–1897), also a lumberman, appointed no one to the board who lived south of Portage County, and he and its secretary toured cities in the East to advertise the Cutover and create ties with European immigration agencies. In 1895, the Wisconsin legislature supported publication of 500,000 copies of *Northern Wisconsin: A Hand-Book for the Homeseeker*, written by William A. Henry, dean of the College of Agriculture. The illustrations in the book implied that giant cabbages and other farm produce would spring out of the fertile soil of the Cutover. Between 1895 and 1897, the new board issued some 60,000 pamphlets and booklets in German, English, and Norwegian, borrowing heavily from Henry's work. It also helped found local immigration boards, corresponded with potential settlers, and worked closely with private land agents. Although the legislature abolished the board in 1905, that same year it authorized county boards to spend up to $1,000 annually to attract settlers. Reinstated in 1907, largely at the urging of the privately funded Wisconsin Immigration and Development Association, the immigration board emphasized attracting only potentially successful settlers. From 1911 on, the board interviewed would-be settlers individually, warned them of the dangers of land fraud and the diffi-

---

[82] Helgeson, *Farms in the Cutover*, 53–81.

culties of farming the Cutover, and provided them with appropriate publications. In short, the board evolved from an intermediary between sellers and buyers to an agency primarily concerned with settlers' welfare. It also continued to advertise the agricultural promise of the Cutover through newspapers, periodicals, county and state fairs, and a special train featuring Wisconsin products. After 1915, work continued under the name of the Division of Immigration in the newly established Department of Agriculture.[83]

Co-operation by the College to settle the Cutover dated from the publication of Henry's handbook. He wrote it partly as "an instrument in removing the great ignorance and even prejudice which prevails in the southern half of our own state concerning the agricultural possibilities of northern Wisconsin." He cautioned, "let it be distinctly understood that clearing up a farm in a wooded country is an undertaking requiring much hard labor extending over a period of years." But in the end settlers could have a comfortable home with plenty of fuel and an abundant supply of good water. The handbook also provided settlers with practical and scientific information about topography, soil, and climate, prices of available lands, and types of crops, with emphasis on swine, sheep, potatoes, fruit, and dairying. Various business and promotional associations snapped up and broadcast the handbook. Henry followed up with reprints of enthusiastic settlers' letters in Cutover newspapers.

There can be little doubt that Henry and the College of Agriculture bore a sizable share of the responsibility for inducing unreasonable expectations among those least able to afford disillusionment. Henry's successor as dean, Harry L. Russell, took a somewhat more realistic approach, based upon strong evidence of the problems involved; but he, too, remained basically optimistic. At his direction, the College devised methods (including acids and dynamite) to clear stumps and brush, developed crops suitable for the northern soil and climate, and studied alternative credit sources and methods. The College also established several Cutover branch experiment stations and demonstration farms, published numerous technical bulletins for existing and prospective settlers, and helped place county agricultural agents there.[84]

Between 1900 and 1920, roughly 20,000 new farms, encompassing almost 2 million acres, were established in the state's twenty-four northernmost counties. During the same period, nearly a million

---

[83] *Ibid.*, 25–40, 67–118; Department of Agriculture, *Biennial Report*, 1915–1916, pp. 2–3; Glover, *Farm and College*, 202–227.

[84] William A. Henry, *Northern Wisconsin: A Hand-Book for the Homeseeker* (Madison, 1896), 6, 162; Helgeson, *Farms in the Cutover*, 97–118; Glover, *Farm and College*, 202–227.

acres were cleared of brush and stumps. The population of the twenty-nine counties of the New North grew by 140,000, and by 1920 they were home to almost 27 per cent of the state's citizens.

Yet this twenty-year resettlement story had a somber ending. To be sure, individual counties—among them Shawano, Vilas, and Marathon—achieved success. But overall, the results failed to meet expectations. Most of the successes came in the Old North and on the southern fringes of the New. In the upper seventeen of the northernmost twenty-four counties, less than 7 per cent of the land had been improved by 1920. The bulk of the population gains in the twenty-four counties came primarily in cities and lumber camps: slightly over 300,000 people between 1890 and 1920. This figure was nearly matched by an increase of 252,679 in Milwaukee alone. By the onset of the Great Depression, the New North was widely regarded as "the land of 10,000 failures" and as "Wisconsin's Appalachia." Its future lay in abandoning agriculture in favor of recreation, tourism, and wood-related manufacturing. Settlement proved only a marginal success, and for thousands of individuals it proved a disaster.[85]

The reasons were not difficult to comprehend. In the competition for pioneers, northern Wisconsin lost out to Canada, just as it had been outstripped earlier by the Great Plains. Rural areas trailed the Cutover's own rapidly growing cities, which offered a relatively higher living standard, more work choices, and measurably less hardship. The inexorable trend towards agricultural overproduction elsewhere also rendered marginal farmsteads obsolete. Reclaiming the Cutover for recreation and reforestation created competition to farming that ultimately proved irresistible. The rapacity of many lumber companies and land speculators clouded their better judgment, as did the naivete and overconfidence of various "experts"—meaning, principally, public officials and academics. They grossly underestimated the obstacles to agriculture posed by soil, topography, and climate. The short-term indications of agricultural progress in the late 1890's and during World War I came unstuck during the 1920's.[86]

Perhaps the most immediate effect of Cutover settlement was the creation in the Old North and parts of the New North of a new class of moderately successful farmers whose demands and interests varied from those of established dairymen. Eventually, they found an effec-

---

[85] Helgeson, *Farms in the Cutover*, 105–117; Loyal Durand, Jr., "The West Shawano Upland of Wisconsin: A Study of Regional Development Basic to the Problem of Part of the Great Lakes Cut-Over Region," Association of American Geographers, *Annals*, 34 (September, 1944), 135–163; Edmund C. Espeseth, "Lodestar in the Northland," in *WMH*, 36 (Autumn, 1952), 23–27, 56; Robert C. Nesbit, *Wisconsin: A History* (2nd ed., by William F. Thompson, Madison, 1989), 469–472.

[86] Helgeson, *Farms in the Cutover*, 112–117.

tive spokesman in the American Society of Equity and a powerful champion in Charles McCarthy, the progressive librarian, educator, and first director of the Legislative Reference Library.

The American Society of Equity was the brainchild of Indiana farm editor James A. Everitt, who in 1902 urged wheat farmers to organize and withhold their crops from market in order to raise prices, taking credit for the favorable outcome. Although Everitt soon lost control, the organization spread rapidly, especially in grain and tobacco belts. Adherents explicitly rejected agriculture as a "way of life." They viewed it as a business enterprise operating within the framework of modern industrial capitalism, and urged farmers to emulate corporations and labor unions; they advocated direct government intervention and organized action to raise return by controlling the supply. While railing against the "monopolists" and "middle-men" whom Equity believed appropriated the farmer's profits, the organization urged the creation of an agricultural monopoly that would outmuscle all its enemies. Equity stopped short of asking government for administered parity. But it did advocate government sponsorship of co-operative marketing and intervention into the credit system. It also sanctioned limited co-operation with labor unionists on special issues of mutual self-interest, as well as pragmatic political coalition with socialists, prohibitionists, woman suffragists, and others with compatible agendas.[87]

The Wisconsin Society of Equity (WSE) was founded officially in 1906 and a year later claimed more than 10,000 members. It originated in the tobacco and wheat counties along the Mississippi River and spread over the northern two-thirds of the state. It began publication in 1908 of the *Wisconsin Equity News* and opened its pages to members, one of whom pronounced that only "Indians, Idiots, and Farmers" remained unorganized in the modern world. The trend towards farm tenancy and mortgaged indebtedness, plus the leveling of dairy prices after 1912, spurred the WSE's growth. Early efforts on its part to control production of wool, potatoes, wheat, and tobacco were largely unsuccessful. But its co-operative grain elevators and warehouses won over many. It attracted less affluent dairy farmers by gradually amalgamating with the co-operative movement, and was instrumental in market milk producers' efforts to resist regulation of prices and quality.

By 1915, an estimated 36 per cent of the state's cheese factories and 45 per cent of its creameries were co-operatively organized. The

---

[87] Robert H. Bahmer, "The American Society of Equity," in *Agricultural History*, 14 (April, 1940), 33–63; Theodore Saloutos, "The Wisconsin Society of Equity," *ibid.*, 14 (April, 1940), 81–95; Walter H. Ebling, "Recent Farmer Movements in Wisconsin" (master's thesis, University of Wisconsin, 1925), 27–42.

WSE also organized co-operative livestock associations and meatpacking plants. Its most ambitious schemes—the Industrial Co-operative Union and the American Co-operative Association—ended in failure, but the Equity Home Market, established in Milwaukee's Gimbel Brothers department store, did an estimated $2.5 million worth of business in 1920. By that same year, some 400 purchasing and selling associations in the state bore the name "Equity." Politically, the WSE joined hands with the Social Democrats and the Wisconsin State Federation of Labor on many issues, including co-operative legislation, workers' compensation, and government ownership of utilities. It characterized farmers who refused to join the organization as "hogs."[88]

Not surprisingly, the WSE soon became embroiled in an acrimonious relationship with both the Wisconsin Dairymen's Association and the College of Agriculture. Equity spokesmen were denounced both for their persistent focus on improving production in the face of market surpluses, for their acceptance of the inequities in the existing pricing and credit systems, and for their indifference or hostility towards co-operative marketing. Greater production was self-defeating, said another Equity paper, unless farmers also trained themselves in co-operative marketing, grading, packaging, and advertising. The *Equity News* kept up a steady barrage against both the WDA and the college, accusing it of luring young men away from the farm. Its members were among those whom progressive analyst Frederic C. Howe had in mind when he observed that "to the average farmer the state univeristy is a cold-storage institution of dead languages and useless learning which costs several million bushels of wheat each year."[89]

Although the WDA and the college were not totally opposed to co-operative marketing, price manipulation, and modern selling techniques, farm leaders generally preached that "education rather than government was the farmer's hope." William D. Hoard was leery of growing farmer radicalism and reasserted his faith "in the renovating power of sound knowledge and the stimulating effect of broader intelligence." In response to a disparaging letter from an Equity official, Hoard defended his record in supporting dairy and cow-testing co-operatives; but acknowledged that "we have perhaps not emphasized the importance of cooperation among farmers as much as we

---

[88] Lampard, *Rise of the Dairy Industry*, 347–349; Julia A. Roberts, "Farm Organizations and Labor in Wisconsin" (master's thesis, University of Wisconsin, 1946), 20–22; "The American Society of Equity: Its Objects, Plans, and Accomplishments, Economically Considered," *Wisconsin Equity News*, April 10, 1911, p. 2 (quote).

[89] Saloutos, "The Wisconsin Society of Equity," 84–86; *Lake Superior Farmer* (Ashland), December 13, 1913, clipping in LRB; Schaars, "Story of the Department of Agricultural Economics," 16–17, 42–47; Frederic C. Howe, *Wisconsin: An Experiment in Democracy* (New York, 1912), 164.

have some other things" and that "farmers as a class have been independent and have not felt the necessity of acting together." For his part, Dean Russell scored the WSE for "labor union methods" and flirtation with radical politics. He frequently expressed the unwillingness of the college to become an agent of the co-operative movement, even though he permitted the department of agricultural economics to conduct research and develop courses on marketing and co-operation.[90]

The WSE soon found its own pipeline to the establishment in the person of Charles McCarthy, a formidable intellectual and activist in his own right and also a confidant of both Governor Francis McGovern (1911–1915) and Charles R. Van Hise, president of the university. McCarthy had grown up in a Massachusetts mill town and had virtually no exposure to agriculture before coming to Wisconsin as a graduate student, but he became increasingly interested in the topic through his involvement in national progressive politics. Participation in the Country Life Movement introduced him to a wide range of rural concerns, and he became acquainted with Sir Horace Plunkett, a renowned Irish agrarian reformer, and with Gifford Pinchot, Theodore Roosevelt's reigning agricultural expert. Plunkett, Pinchot, and McCarthy became founding members of the Agricultural Organization Society, dedicated to the formation of marketing and consumer co-operatives. Through these contacts, and through his correspondence with state assemblyman Henry Krumrey and WSE president D. O. Mahoney, McCarthy became an influential advocate of legislation facilitating co-operatives, regulating credit arrangements, improving rural education, and establishing schools of domestic and agricultural science. More visionary than the leaders of Equity, McCarthy regarded co-operatives as the vanguard of fundamental socio-economic change that would provide significant redistribution of income, create new sources of capital, alter the relationship between producer and consumer, and develop new mechanisms for economic decision-making.

Francis McGovern said that co-operative marketing would make farming profitable enough to stem the flow of young men to the city; Charles Van Hise claimed it would save consumers millions of dollars per year—dollars skimmed by food wholesalers and retailers whose profit margins sometimes ran as high as 250 per cent. Before the outbreak of war in 1914, the practical farmers of the WSE and the agrarian social reformers led by Charles McCarthy had achieved sufficient political clout to translate their vision of a co-operative com-

---

[90] Lampard, *Rise of the Dairy Industry*, 347–349 (quotes); Glover, *Farm and College*, 332–333; *Hoard's Dairyman*, February 25, 1910, p. 131 (quote).

monwealth and an agricultural service state into concrete legislation.[91]

By 1914, then, Wisconsin had successfully completed the transition from cereal grain agriculture to dairying with a healthy admixture of specialty crops. It had emerged as the nation's premier dairy state, and it led not only in production but also in ideas. This transformation had been accomplished largely through the pragmatic and mutually beneficial workings of a coalition of dairymen, the state university, and a state government controlled by progressive (or sympathetic) Republicans. Together they had forged a framework of education and regulation that served as a prototype of what came to be called the Wisconsin Idea. But the mixed success of this coalition in opening marginal agricultural lands in the Cutover had produced a new class of less affluent farmers who now agitated for radically new forms of intervention and aid. This conflict shook the original coalition to its very foundation, but it also created new alignments involving other segments of society, and it laid the groundwork for the establishment of an agricultural service state. It was a process that was to be repeated, with variations, by other groups of people in other Wisconsin arenas.

[91] *Lake Superior Farmer*, February 14, 1914; James H. Vint, "Dept. of Markets, Its Work to Bring Farmers Together," *Wisconsin State Journal*, April 1, 1928 (state government special section); Theodore Saloutos and John D. Hicks, *Agricultural Discontent in the Middle West, 1900–1939* (Madison, 1951), 62; Charles McCarthy to Horace Plunkett, August 17, 1912, box 3, folder 8, and Gifford Pinchot to Henry S. Pritchett, May 6, 1913, box 4, folder 7, in the Charles McCarthy Papers.

3

Industrial Transformations

[1]

EVEN as Wisconsin was becoming America's Dairyland, it was just as busily transforming its manufacturing base, thereby enhancing its position among America's major industrial states. Indeed, manufacturing grew three times faster than farming, in both product value and work force, during the state's "golden age of agriculture." Indicators of this growth are stunning. Between 1889 and 1914, the number of manufacturing workers rose by 75 per cent; their wages and salaries tripled; total capital invested jumped 206 per cent; the cost of materials, 180 per cent; product value, 120 per cent; and value added by manufacturing, 170 per cent, placing Wisconsin ninth among the forty-eight states.

In those same years, Wisconsin's industrial growth equaled or surpassed national averages in every category except capital invested. By 1914, it ranked first among the states in dairy processing; second (to Illinois) in agricultural implements; third in lumber and timber products, leather tanning, and brewing; and fourth in iron and steel fabrication, foundry and machine shop products, engines and motors, heavy-duty construction and excavation machinery, railroad equipment, and automobiles. In product value, it ranked eighth in 1910 and tenth in 1914, despite being thirteenth in population and twenty-second in population density.[1]

The roots of industrialization extended back to the years before the Civil War. By then, Wisconsin was already processing the yield of its wheat farms, pine forests, and iron mines, and it was forging the tools essential to those tasks. Between 1860 and 1890, the state

---

[1] *Eleventh Census of the United States, 1890: Manufacturing Industries, Volume VI, Part 1, Totals for States and Territories,* 7–8, 628–634; *Census of Manufactures, 1914: Volume I, Reports by States with Statistics for Principal Cities and Metropolitan Districts,* 1629–1641, 1654–1655.

jumped from eighteenth to tenth nationally in product value. Flour milling and lumbering led the trend, both with beginnings in settlement necessities. All of the other eighteen leading manufacturing enterprises in the 1880's had similar beginnings, or else in the state's undeveloped natural resources. The small-scale mill, shop, or foundry reigned supreme, being primarily owned and operated by skilled craftsmen and producing mainly for a local or regional market.[2]

Over the next quarter-century, manufacturers, workers, and consumers confronted twin challenges that demanded that Wisconsin reinvent its industrial system. On the one hand, the decline of flour milling and lumbering threatened to destroy the economy of the northern two-thirds of the state unless business and political leaders there could discover new enterprises to make profitable use of the region's resources: water, wood, iron ore, entrepreneurship, a disciplined work force, and a manufacturing infrastructure. On the other hand, the so-called "neotechnic revolution" of the late nineteenth century rapidly displaced the water and steam, coal and iron that had sustained manufacturing activities for half a century. The fruits of this new technology—steel and other lighter, more flexible metals, vulcanized rubber, petroleum products, electrical power, and the internal combustion engine—permitted the construction and operation of high-speed machines capable of producing a seemingly endless supply of goods.[3]

Wisconsin industrialists and financiers seized the opportunity and designed the highly capitalized, large-scale, complex organizations that defined and heralded the emergence of "big business." Their new corporations transformed the nature of work and the workplace, facilitated mass production and the assembly line, and pursued national and international markets through innovative strategies and techniques. They so changed manufacturing by 1910 that in proportion to population Wisconsin was ahead of all states west of Ohio in value of manufactured product.[4]

---

[2] Joseph H. H. Alexander, "A Short Industrial History of Wisconsin," in the *Wisconsin Blue Book, 1929*, pp. 34–36; Margaret Walsh, *The Manufacturing Frontier: Pioneer Industry in Antebellum Wisconsin, 1830–1860* (Madison, 1972), 1–36; Wilbur R. Voigt, "A Survey of Manufacturing in Wisconsin" (master's thesis, University of Wisconsin, 1938), vii–ix; *Eleventh Census of the United States, 1890: Manufacturing Industries, Volume VI, Part 1, Totals for States and Territories*, 7, 628–634.

[3] Alexander, "Industrial History of Wisconsin," in the *Wisconsin Blue Book, 1929*, pp. 36–39; Harvey S. Perloff et al., *Regions, Resources, and Economic Growth* (Baltimore, 1960), 160–162; Eric E. Lampard, *Industrial Revolution: Interpretations and Perspectives* (Washington, 1968), 11–36; Lewis Mumford, *The Culture of Cities* (New York, 1938), 495–496.

[4] "The Industries of Wisconsin," in the *Wisconsin Blue Book, 1915*, p. 34. On the rise of big business in this era, see Glenn Porter, *The Rise of Big Business, 1860–1910*

Manufacturing, agriculture, and extractive industries have always enjoyed a symbiotic relationship in Wisconsin. Its first dominant industrial enterprise—flour and grist milling—rose and fell with the wheat boom of the mid-nineteenth century. Its second—logging and lumber milling—had the same connection to soil and climate. The state's trees, and iron ore from the mines of Dodge and Sauk counties, supplied the raw materials for manufacturing flour and sawmilling machinery and agricultural implements. The state's 15,000 lakes and 32,000 miles of rivers and streams provided the power for operating machinery, as well as a phenomenal transportation network.[5]

The flour mill and the sawmill emerged contemporaneously in Wisconsin, but the latter enjoyed a longer life span and made a greater impact. Lumbering blossomed after the Civil War and grew into the leading industry, surpassing flour milling during the 1880's. Lumbering concentrated on white pine, which made wonderful straight-grained and lightweight lumber, and which, unlike hardwoods, could be floated to the mill. The river systems bore logs first to the mill, then lumber and its byproducts to Lake Michigan and the East, or down the Mississippi River and the West. Wisconsin timber helped to satiate the need of the Midwest and the Great Plains for construction materials. The value of the state's lumber products more than tripled during the 1880's, catapulting the industry into first place for upwards of two decades. By the 1890's, Wisconsin had emerged as the nation's leading lumber state, and it held that distinction until 1904. In 1897, lumbering constituted nearly one-quarter of the state's investment capital and manufacturing work force. At the turn of the century, 1,033 sawmills still generated products worth more than double the products of lumbering's closest competitors: flour milling, foundry and machine shops, dairy processing, leather tanning, and brewing.[6]

In 1890, flour milling and lumbering together generated more than one-third of Wisconsin's product value, but flour had fallen

---

(Arlington Heights, Illinois, 1973), and Alfred D. Chandler, Jr., *The Visible Hand: The Managerial Revolution in American Business* (Cambridge, 1977), 209–376.

[5] Walsh, *The Manufacturing Frontier*, 221–229; Alexander, "Industrial History of Wisconsin," in the *Wisconsin Blue Book, 1929*, pp. 34–42.

[6] Robert F. Fries, *Empire In Pine: The Story of Lumbering in Wisconsin, 1830–1900* (Madison, 1951), 3–8, 18–21, 103; Alexander, "Industrial History of Wisconsin," in the *Wisconsin Blue Book, 1929*, pp. 36–42. William F. Raney, *Wisconsin: A Story of Progress* (Appleton, 1963), 199–206, divides the state into seven lumbering districts, but asserts that the earliest, a triangle formed by Door and Ozaukee counties and Lakes Michigan and Winnebago, was exhausted by 1875. For a contemporary account of lumbering, see George W. Hotchkiss, *History of the Lumber and Forest Industry of the Northwest* (Chicago, 1898), 380–523.

from 22 per cent in 1880 to 10 per cent. Flour and grist milling had been the foremost industry from territorial days, making up 40 per cent of product value on the eve of the Civil War. It flourished wherever there was sufficient water power to turn a wheel. Milling on a larger scale was practiced in Janesville, Milwaukee, the Fox River Valley, La Crosse, and, eventually, Superior. But after the war, as the wheat belt advanced towards Minnesota and the Dakotas, Wisconsin millers began to import grain from the Great Plains. They steadily lost ground to Minneapolis, which profited from lower transportation costs and from early adoption of improved milling processes. By the 1880's, most Wisconsin cities, villages, and towns were searching for alternative enterprises. In the 1860's, the twin cities of Neenah and Menasha had made a concerted effort to expand their mills and overtake Milwaukee in flour-milling. By 1870, they had fifteen mills and were turning out products worth $1 million, second only to Milwaukee. But with the rise of milling in the Twin Cities of Minnesota, the Neenah-Menasha dream swiftly turned to ashes. By 1883 the industry was in the doldrums; by 1908 neither city had a single flour mill.[7]

Meanwhile, technology and organizational innovation, soaring profits, and westward expansion had converted the colorful first generation of lumbermen into "lumber barons" who dominated the economic, social, and political life of the Chippewa and Wisconsin river valleys and wielded power and influence in Madison, the Twin Cities, St. Louis, and Washington. The substitution of steam for water power handsomely augmented productivity. The extension of railroad lines into northern and western Wisconsin and across the Great Plains shrank the time and distance between producers and consumers, especially in the trans-Mississippi West, which had a nearly bottomless appetite for Great Lakes lumber. Lumber companies of course wanted to take maximum advantage of these opportunities, and accordingly required greater capital. So they incorporated and sold stock. By 1896, 100 of Wisconsin's 168 lumber companies were corporations. Of these, the largest was the Knapp, Stout & Co. Lumber Company of Menomonie (Dunn County), which employed an average of 2,000 men and had a daily sawing capacity of 750,000 board feet of lumber. In 1897, Knapp, Stout and the Northwestern Lumber Company of Eau Claire each produced about 80 million board feet, while the Chippewa Lumber and Boom Company of Chippewa Falls turned out 48 million. These corporations controlled every stage of the manufacturing process, from cutting timber to retailing lumber.

[7]Alexander, "Industrial History of Wisconsin," in the *Wisconsin Blue Book, 1929*, pp. 34–39; Charles N. Glaab and Lawrence H. Larsen, *Factories in the Valley: Neenah-Menasha, 1870–1915* (Madison, 1969), 48–77.

In 1891 and 1892, the Northwestern Lumber Company alone sent 5,200 carloads of lumber to twenty-three states and territories.[8]

Intent upon controlling production and managing prices in a highly competitive and risky enterprise, Wisconsin's principal lumbermen formed associations or syndicates. One of the most ambitious was the Mississippi Valley Lumberman's Association, formed in 1891, whose primary goal was to fix prices. The following year, after having been acquitted of antitrust charges, the association expanded to include producers of more than 4 billion board feet of lumber annually. By 1895, it co-ordinated efforts of seventy member companies, thirteen sympathetic producers, and the twenty-five members of the Wisconsin Valley Lumbermen's Association. By 1905, the association controlled 90 per cent of white pine production in Wisconsin and Minnesota and processed over half the white pine lumber sold in the entire nation. Equally powerful was the Mississippi River Logging Company, brainchild of Frederick Weyerhaeuser, the nation's leading lumber magnate. By 1892, his organization controlled 75 per cent of all the sawmilling investment between Winona, Minnesota, and St. Louis, Missouri—including most operations in the pine-rich Chippewa River Valley.[9]

High transportation costs, seasonal operation, substantial fire losses, uncertain climate, and a nomadic, volatile labor force all constrained lumbering profits. Even so, Weyerhaeuser and dozens of other lumber barons built substantial fortunes. Some invested their riches in the fine arts and the New York stock market; others purchased timberland in the West and South against the inevitable demise of Wisconsin's pineries. Still others bought substantial tracts in the Cutover, anticipating settlement by aspiring farmers. Many of the most successful diversified in other lines of business. Orrin H. Ingram of Eau Claire, president of the Empire Lumber Company, was an officeholder or director of a half-dozen other lumber companies, an investor in midwestern, southern, and Pacific Coast forests, president of both the Eau Claire National Bank and the city's privately owned water works, treasurer of the Canadian Anthracite Coal Company, and part owner of Florida orange groves, a Texas rice plantation, and an Arizona copper mine. Similarly, Philetus Sawyer of Oshkosh and Isaac Stephenson of Marinette owned hundreds of thousands of acres of timberland; besides possessing wealth and power, both eventually held seats in the United States Senate.[10]

---

[8] Fries, *Empire in Pine*, 84–140; A. R. Reynolds, *The Daniel Shaw Lumber Company: A Case Study of the Wisconsin Lumbering Frontier* (New York, 1957), 154.

[9] Fries, *Empire in Pine*, 141–160.

[10] *Ibid.*, 138–139, 174; Randall Rohe, *Survival of the Fittest: A Centennial History of the Jones Lumber Corporation* (Wisconsin Rapids, 1993), 11–32; Charles E. Twining, *Down-*

But Wisconsin's pine forest would not last forever. In 1892, lumber production peaked at 4 billion board feet, more than triple what it had been two decades earlier. Only five years later, Filibert Roth, a German-born special forestry agent of the U.S. Department of Agriculture who conducted a prophetic and now famous survey of Wisconsin forests, warned that, of the original stand of 130 billion feet of pine, only about 17 billion remained. Combined with 12 billion feet of hemlock and 16 billion feet of various hardwoods, that left a balance of but 45 billion feet in a state that was cutting 3 to 4 billion feet a year. The industry accounted for one-sixth of the state's taxable property, paid over $15 million annually in wages to more than 55,000 persons, mostly men, and generated products worth more than one-third that of agriculture. In calm, measured phrases, Roth predicted its end: "[C]utting will go on without regard to the end, and its rate depends merely on considerations of market conditions and facilities for handling timber, so that the end of the greater part of pine lumbering is likely to be quite sudden, and its effect correspondingly severe." Roth's predictions proved true. By the turn of the century, when Wisconsin still ranked first among lumber states, lumber output had declined by more than 5 per cent over the previous decade. The state retained its lofty perch until 1904, then fell to seventh place in 1910 and to thirteenth by 1920. Even though by 1900 most counties had already had their lumbering day, in 1910 it still remained Wisconsin's leading industry, and the 1910 product value remained the same as 1900's. Meanwhile, foundry and machine shop products, dairy processing, and leather tanning had more than doubled.[11]

The last log drive on the Black River took place in 1897, on the Chippewa in 1910, and on the St. Croix in 1914. The Empire Lumber Company closed operations at Eau Claire in 1898, going out of business altogether in 1909. In Chippewa Falls, Weyerhaeuser's "largest mill in the world," with a capacity of 2 million board feet a week, sawed its last lumber in 1911. Between 1900 and 1905, nearly all of the companies involved in the Mississippi and Chippewa river associations ceased operations in Wisconsin. The Mississippi River Logging Company dissolved in 1909. At noon on October 25, 1912, the Daniel Shaw Lumber Company, after fifty-five years of continuous lumbering in the Chippewa Valley, sawed its last log.[12]

---

river: *Orrin H. Ingram and the Empire Lumber Company* (Madison, 1975), 279–281; Rohe, *Survival of the Fittest*, 11–20. By 1913, ten persons owned 24 per cent of all the standing timber in Wisconsin; ninety-six persons held 75 per cent.

[11] Fries, *Empire in Pine*, 239–244; Filibert Roth, *On the Forestry Conditions of Northern Wisconsin*, Geological and Natural History Survey, *Bulletin*, no. 1 (1898), 42–55; Forestry Commission, *Report*, 1898, pp. 15–16.

[12] Alexander, "Industrial History of Wisconsin," in the *Wisconsin Blue Book, 1929*, pp. 39–41; Howard R. Klueter and James J. Lorence, *Woodlot and Ballot Box: Marathon*

The demise of lumbering was greatly accelerated by forest fires and wasteful operations. As many as 1 billion board feet were wasted between 1872 and 1905 simply through the use of muley and circular saws instead of band saws; logging crews consistently left behind high stumps and wasted timber while cutting it into logs. They frequently removed young timber in constructing roads and camps, or sacrificed it in the scramble to cut mature trees. Wherever they departed, they left the landscape choked with the "slashings" that all too often led to fires. In 1905 alone, 1,435 forest fires in thirty-two counties laid waste to more than a million acres.[13]

The virtual destruction of the state's second most valuable natural resource in just over fifty years provoked a decades-long debate about how to reinvigorate the economy of the northern two-thirds of the state. On one side were arrayed the lumbermen, the railroads, regional bankers and boosters, and the university's College of Agriculture, each of which had a stake in promoting agricultural resettlement of the Cutover. On the other side stood foresters, scientists, public servants, and a growing band of politicians who had been sensitized to the notion of conservation and reforestation.[14]

Somewhat less visible were those northern businessmen and politicians who regarded a new manufacturing base as more vital than either agriculture or reforestation. They suggested two broad strategies. One would have abandoned lumbering in favor of processing other raw materials into manufactured products—for example aluminum cookware or canned vegetables—viable mostly in the southern half of the state. The other would have shifted from pine lumbering to hemlock, hardwoods, and other lesser species for making many wood-based products—such as furniture or pulp for papermaking—viable in the north as well as the south.[15]

County in the Twentieth Century (Wausau, 1977), 37–68; Fred W. Kohlmeyer, *Timber Roots: The Laird, Norton Story, 1855–1905* (Winona, Minnesota, 1972), 311–312; Twining, *Downriver*, 273–277; Reynolds, *Daniel Shaw Lumber Company*, 149–152; Raney, *Wisconsin*, 208–209.

[13] Fries, *Empire In Pine*, 245–246.

[14] Roth, *Forestry Conditions of Northern Wisconsin*, 44; Fries, *Empire in Pine*, 172–178, 246–252; Vernon R. Carstensen, *Farms or Forests: Evolution of a State Land Policy for Northern Wisconsin, 1850–1932* (Madison, 1958), 19–85; J. Willard Hurst, *Law and Economic Growth: The Legal History of the Lumber Industry in Wisconsin, 1836–1915* (Cambridge, 1964), 592–596.

[15] Ironically, the latter strategy ultimately required importing the wood that had existed in such abundance only decades before. See Klueter and Lorence, *Woodlot and Ballot Box*, 47–49, 92–95; Steven B. Karges, "David Clark Everest and Marathon Paper Mills Company: A Study of a Wisconsin Entrepreneur, 1909–1931" (doctoral dissertation, University of Wisconsin, 1968), 48–75; James B. Smith, "The Movements for Diversified Industry in Eau Claire, Wisconsin, 1879–1907: Boosterism and Urban

Manufacture of aluminum novelty items and cookware was one of these new, non-wood industries. The discovery in 1886 of an electrochemical process for producing aluminum coincided with the decline of lumbering in northeastern Wisconsin. The industry began when Joseph Koenig, an immigrant jack-of-all-trades, became inspired by a German exhibit at the 1893 World's Columbian Exposition and founded the Aluminum Goods Manufacturing Company in Two Rivers, on the Lake Michigan shore. He operated out of a small room in another factory and produced combs, trays, bicycle guards, fobs, cigar cases, mustache cups, salt and pepper shakers, ash trays, and penny pieces. Dissident Koenig employees later helped found two competing firms: Manitowoc Aluminum in 1898 and the Aluminum Sign Company of Two Rivers (later the Leyse Aluminum Corporation) in 1903. In 1908, Keonig's firm and Manitowoc Aluminum merged with a New Jersey manufacturer to form the Aluminum Goods Manufacturing Company (Mirro), with one-third of its capital supplied by the Aluminum Company of America (Alcoa) of Pittsburgh. After a financial panic in 1907, the entire aluminum industry shifted from novelties to cookware. Between 1900 and 1919, as housewives learned to prefer light aluminum utensils, despite their higher cost, aluminum's share of the national cookware industry leaped from 5 to 20 per cent. In 1911, a fourth company, the West Bend Aluminum Company, began making fifteen different kinds of utensils, and soon was selling nearly half of them to Sears, Roebuck and Company. Four years later, Mirro also entered the cookware business, selling mostly to jobbers, chain stores, and mail-order houses. By 1920, northeastern Wisconsin rivaled Pittsburgh as a center of the aluminum cookware industry.[16]

As for vegetable canning (in steel, not aluminum, cans), the first successful pea-canning factory was established at Manitowoc in 1889 by Albert Landreth, a representative of a Pennsylvania seed company. Landreth's company canned the yield of only seventy-five acres in 1889; by 1907, it canned the yield of a thousand acres. In 1890, the company built a branch plant in Sheboygan, the same year that William Larsen opened a cannery in Green Bay. Five years later, the owners of a declining lumber mill started the Reynolds Preserving Company in Sturgeon Bay. At the turn of the century, twenty-one

---

Development Strategy in a Declining Lumber Town'' (master's thesis, University of Wisconsin, 1967), 117–173.

[16] James M. Rock, "A Growth Industry: The Wisconsin Aluminum Cookware Industry, 1893–1920," in *WMH*, 55 (Winter, 1971–1972), 86–99; Robert T. Hilton, "Men of Metal: A History of the Foundry Industry in Wisconsin" (master's thesis, University of Wisconsin, 1952), 77–82.

canning factories operated in the state, most of them in the corridor between Sheboygan and Door County. The following year saw canneries open in Eau Claire, New Holstein, Sawyer, Reedsburg, Winneconne, Chippewa Falls, Appleton, Kewaunee, and Columbus. During peak times in 1904, the Larsen cannery alone packed nearly 4 million cans of peas and employed over a thousand people. In 1907, Wisconsin packed 1.5 million cases of peas, more than one-fourth the U.S. total. Eight years later, the figures had soared to 3.5 million cases, representing one-third of the national total, and the state ranked eighth in corn canning. Representatives of several leading firms formed the Wisconsin Canners Association in order to curb overcanning of peas. By 1913, the association represented forty-nine canning companies and in 1916 incorporated as the Wisconsin Pea Packers' Association. This group divided the state into seven zones, to enforce production standards and cost accounting.[17]

For the most part, non-wood manufacturing in the northern two-thirds of Wisconsin was characterized by diversity and small and medium-sized enterprises. Eau Claire, Wausau, and Neenah all developed boot-and-shoe factories. Menasha expanded its woolen mill in the 1890's. The Horn and Blum Company, manufacturers of overalls, jackets, shirts, and durable clothing for lumbermen, opened in Eau Claire in 1911. Oshkosh, earlier known as "Sawdust City," began to gain attention for making clothing. Superior joined Manitowoc and Two Rivers in shipbuilding. Wausau, Neenah, Eau Claire, and Superior increasingly involved themselves in the foundry and machine-tool business, turning out iron castings, plows, kettles, stoves, sawmills, and engines. The Sheboygan-Kohler area became a plumbing supply center. Reorganized and relocated to a specially designed "garden village" bearing its name, the Kohler Company's sales grew from $175,000 to over $2 million between 1900 and 1914. It set up branch offices in several American cities and in London, and the value of its manufacturing plant increased nearly six times between 1905 and 1915. Breweries in Menasha, Stevens Point, La Crosse, Wausau, Superior, Eau Claire, and Sheboygan served growing local and regional markets. Smaller cheese factories, creameries, and meatpacking plants proliferated in the New North and Middle North, reflecting Cutover agricultural settlement. In the farthest north, Superior handled grain from Minnesota and the Dakotas and seriously challenged Milwaukee as the state's leading center of flour milling and wheat shipping.[18]

---

[17] Fred A. Stare, *The Story of Wisconsin's Great Canning Industry* (Baltimore, 1949), 26–83, 195–198, 262–268, 460–479, 537–541.
[18] Glaab and Larsen, *Factories in the Valley*, 165–166; Klueter and Lorence, *Woodlot and Ballot Box*, 105, 115–116; William F. Bailey, ed., *History of Eau Claire County, Wis-*

However impressive this diversification, the post-lumbering economy in fact was based primarily on less exalted species of timber than white pine, which by 1910 accounted for only about one-ninth of the wood Wisconsin manufacturers used. Spruce and hemlock constituted nearly one-third; western pine, basswood, and birch totaled almost one-quarter. Just under half the wooden raw materials used by the state's manufacturers were imported, including nearly 30 per cent of the white pine. Twenty-five industries utilized wood as a significant raw material in 1910, although several—makers of beehives, handles, musical instruments, toys, cigar boxes, and caskets—were of negligible importance. Metal was rapidly replacing wood as the major construction material in agricultural implements, ships, vehicles, and refrigerators. Of significantly greater importance were woodenware (constituting 7 per cent of the total wood used), furniture and chairs (10 per cent), boxes (13 per cent), and sashes, doors, blinds, and interior and exterior finish (19 per cent).[19]

Woodenware products included tubs, pails, buckets, churns, barrels, staves, broom handles, clothes pins, and cheese boxes. By 1910, the state had thirty-seven woodenware factories, concentrated in and around Sheboygan and in the Fox River Valley. The Menasha Wooden Ware Company, that city's largest employer, called itself the "largest woodenware plant on earth." Begun in 1852 as a shop with a single lathe, Wooden Ware was selling $1.5 million worth of items by 1915, processing 6,000 carloads of raw material, and producing 50,000 pieces a day. It utilized over 150,000 acres of timberland annually, occupied more than a hundred acres of manufacturing space, and sold its wares all over the eastern half of the country. So prosperous was Menasha Wooden Ware that it paid a 40 per cent dividend during the depression year of 1897. Nearly as successful was the Menasha Wood Split Pulley Company, begun in 1892 by Publius V. Lawson, Jr., on his father's wagon wheel and agricultural implement business. Lawson constructed a new factory and by 1915 was making every wooden part essential to papermaking, the area's dominant industry.[20]

---

consin, Past and Present: Including an Account of the Cities, Towns and Villages of the County (Chicago, 1914), 474–488; Richard McLeod, "The Development of Superior, Wisconsin, As a Western Transportation Center," *Journal of the West*, 13 (July, 1974), 20–24; J. E. Leberman, *One Hundred Years of Sheboygan, 1846–1946* (Sheboygan, 1946), n.p.; Trudi J. Eblen, "A History of the Kohler Company of Kohler, Wisconsin, 1871–1914" (master's thesis, University of Wisconsin, 1965), 30–85.

[19] Franklin H. Smith, *A Study of the Wisconsin Wood-Using Industries* (Madison, 1910), 9–15. According to Klueter and Lorence, *Woodlot and Ballot Box*, p. 83, by 1912, "much of northern Wisconsin had partially completed the transformation of its industrial profile . . . [to] manufacturing concerns which used wood as their chief raw material."

[20] Smith, *Wisconsin Wood-Using Industries*, 12, 42, 56; Glaab and Larsen, *Factories in*

The major manufacturers of furniture, chairs, and bedding were located on or near the Lake Michigan shore. Milwaukee was an important furniture producer, but the industry's center of gravity shifted in the 1890's and 1900's northward to Fond du Lac, Oshkosh, Sheboygan, Plymouth, and Green Bay, with Sheboygan having eight furniture factories and Plymouth three by 1910. The chair factories in Sheboygan and Sheboygan Falls earned them the nickname the "Chair City." Eau Claire, Oshkosh, and Marshfield joined Milwaukee and Kenosha as the state's leading manufacturers of bedding. Marshfield, Richland Center, Sheboygan, and Wausau also challenged Milwaukee in excelsior, the wooden "wool" used for stuffing and packing. Wausau opened one excelsior plant in 1892 and another in 1898, principally for Chicago manufacturers.[21]

Both the excelsior and the burgeoning box-making industries acquired most of their raw materials from Wisconsin forests—poplar and basswood for excelsior, and white pine, hemlock, and birch for boxes. Although Janesville and Milwaukee continued to be important box-manufacturing cities, Appleton, Eau Claire, Green Bay, La Crosse, Stevens Point, and Wausau all made strides in the same direction by the 1890's. In Wausau in the late 1880's, for example, three Chicagoans purchased a planing mill and converted it into a box factory. By the onset of World War I, the plant covered five acres, employed over a hundred workers, and made everything from soap boxes to piano crates. It allegedly produced enough boxes in a single year to build a sidewalk from Wausau to New York City.[22]

The most direct and enduring survival of lumbering's heyday was the nearly 20 per cent of wood-based manufacturing devoted to sashes, doors, blinds, and interior and exterior finish. They required high-grade lumber—over $5 million worth, four times more than used for chairs or furniture, three times more than for box making. Sash, door, and blind factories proliferated all over the northern two-thirds of the state in the 1890's, especially in Appleton, Chippewa Falls, Eau Claire, Fond du Lac, Oshkosh, La Crosse, Marinette, Stevens Point, and Wausau.[23]

As important as these various undertakings were to the restructuring of the Cutover's economy, they paled beside pulp and paper in-

---

the Valley, 166–187; Alice E. Smith, *Millstone and Saw: The Origins of Neenah-Menasha* (Madison, 1966), 68.

[21] Smith, *Wisconsin Wood-Using Industries*, 12, 20–23, 26–28, 46–50; Leberman, *One Hundred Years of Sheboygan*; Bailey, ed., *History of Eau Claire County*, 479–486; Klueter and Lorence, *Woodlot and Ballot Box*, 89.

[22] Smith, *Wisconsin Wood-Using Industries*, 12, 20–21, 46–47; Klueter and Lorence, *Woodlot and Ballot Box*, 85–88; Bailey, ed., *History of Eau Claire County*, 479–480.

[23] Smith, *Wisconsin Wood-Using Industries*, 12, 34–35, 51–52; Klueter and Lorence, *Woodlot and Ballot Box*, 83–85.

dustries. In less than two decades, papermaking came to define the post-lumbering economy in much of the state, even though its origins had little or nothing to do with lumbering's decline. Wisconsin papermaking originated in Milwaukee and Beloit in the late 1840's, where there were plenty of the rags from which paper was then made. For the next quarter-century, it remained confined to the most heavily populated, southeastern part of the state, where the printing industry concentrated. Paper mills had to be located on fast-flowing streams, both for power and the substantial amounts of water required to make paper. (While flowing water supplied only 22 per cent of manufacturing power in the United States in 1890, it generated 69 per cent of that in papermaking.) Some mills also used rivers for transportation, especially in the Fox Valley. Wisconsin's paper industry advanced northward, took over lumber and flour mills and their sites, and harnessed previously undeveloped water sources.[24]

Wisconsin's modern papermaking industry began in the Fox River Valley in the 1870's in response to three distinct developments. The first was the virtual exhaustion of good timber in the state's first important hardwood lumbering region—the area between Ozaukee and Door counties, east of Lake Winnebago. The second was the collapse of wheat farming, with its devastating impact upon flour milling. These concurrent collapses temporarily jolted the area's economic life, but left it with ambitious entrepreneurs, investment capital, a skilled and disciplined work force, vacant mills, and unused waterpower sites. Third was technological innovations in the manufacture of paper—the substitution of wood pulp for rags and straw, the supplanting of waterpower by steam, and the invention of various electrochemical processes and machinery for converting pulp into paper. Wood pulp made up less than 4 per cent of the raw materials used in papermaking in 1879, but 52 per cent by the end of the century. Steam made up only 31 per cent of total power used in the paper industry in 1890, but 44 per cent by 1919, a trend accelerated by the advent of the steam turbine around 1905.[25]

These changes in raw materials and power sources were matched by innovations in machinery and production. By 1870, only eight paper mills in the entire country used the wood pulp or "ground-

---

[24] Maurice L. Branch, "The Paper Industry in the Lake States Region, 1837–1947" (doctoral dissertation, University of Wisconsin, 1954), 15–25; Howard Publishing Company, *1848–1948: A History of the Wisconsin Paper Industry* (Chicago, 1948), 3–7.

[25] Raney, *Wisconsin*, 199–201; Howard Publishing Company, *History of the Wisconsin Paper Industry*, 7–10; Branch, "The Paper Industry," 29–58; Glaab and Larsen, *Factories in the Valley*, 64–108. Wisconsin and Great Lakes states papermakers were slower to convert to steam because of the region's outstanding waterpowers. In 1919, they still relied on water for 61 per cent of their power needs, compared to 56 per cent for the entire United States.

wood" process. The first Wisconsin groundwood mill opened in Appleton in the late 1870's. The discovery of the sulfate or kraft process, in which the groundwood was cooked in a solution of caustic soda and sodium sulfite, significantly improved product quality in the 1880's. The replacement of the Hollander machine—essentially a huge oval tub agitated by wooden beaters—with continuous-process Fourdrinier and cylinder machines considerably increased papermaking capacity and speed. Originally a handicraft in which skilled workers employed the "feel-it, taste-it, smell-it" method, papermaking evolved into controlled mechanical and chemical methods applied to the fibers which formed the basis of paper.[26]

Between 1860 and 1890 in Wisconsin, papermaking was still largely a handicraft confined to the Fox Valley. Even so, the worth of the paper in the state's economy increased twenty-two times in those years. Paper and wood pulp moved from eighteenth to twelfth place among the state's industries between 1880 and 1890, while their value jumped from $1.3 to $4.5 million. In the early 1890's, nearly two-thirds of Wisconsin's paper mills were in the Fox Valley. They annually produced over 260 million pounds of paper valued at more than $9 million, and employed 2,596 workers with a payroll of more than $1 million.[27]

The new papermaking processes and machines cemented wood as paper's primary raw material. These developments assured an expanding market for cheaper lumber at the very time that Cutover lumbermen were seeking a replacement business, a profitable market for their remaining timber (much of it of lesser quality), and enterprises in which to invest their surplus capital. Accordingly, Fox Valley industrialists, lumbermen, and Milwaukee and Chicago investors launched paper and pulp undertakings in the Wisconsin and Chippewa valleys. The first mill in the Wisconsin Valley opened in 1888, just a few miles south of Grand (Wisconsin) Rapids, six years after the Eau Claire Pulp and Paper Company began in the Chippewa Valley.[28]

By 1914, paper and pulp manufacturing was the major industry in the Fox, Wisconsin, and Chippewa valleys. Two-thirds of the raw material the factories used was wood. Wood pulp saved the day and

---

[26] Howard Publishing Company, *History of the Wisconsin Paper Industry*, 17, 62; Glaab and Larsen, *Factories in the Valley*, 80–84; Norman B. Wilkinson, *Papermaking in America* (Greenville, Delaware, 1975), 36–48.

[27] Branch, "The Paper Industry," 23; Glaab and Larsen, *Factories in the Valley*, 118–125 (quote), 285; Alexander, "Industrial History of Wisconsin," *Wisconsin Blue Book, 1929*, pp. 36–39.

[28] Howard Publishing Company, *History of the Wisconsin Paper Industry*, 10–32; Glaab and Larsen, *Factories in the Valley*, 121–126; Klueter and Lorence, *Woodlot and Ballot Box*, 90–104.

guaranteed continuing prosperity in many communities that had faced devastation when lumbering declined. In Marathon County, papermaking revitalized the sagging economy and helped both to preserve and to create other institutions and industries. By 1900, paper and wood-pulp manufacturing had become the eighth most lucrative industry in Wisconsin, with a product valued at nearly $11 million. Twenty years later, it still occupied the eighth position, with a product valued at almost eight times as much.[29]

The earliest successful transformation occurred in the Fox Valley, even before the collapse of flour milling and lumbering. The region's most lucrative paper firm, Kimberly, Clark & Company, was founded in 1872 by four homegrown partners from diverse business backgrounds with no previous experience in papermaking. From then until the depression of the 1890's, Kimberly, Clark founded paper mills throughout the Fox Valley, leading the way in forming a prosperous, urban-industrial crescent of the seven "Fox Cities," Appleton, Neenah, Menasha, Little Chute, Kaukauna, Combined Locks, and Kimberly. By that point, papermaking also had taken off in the Green Bay-De Pere area. In its first twenty-five years, Kimberly, Clark multiplied a $30,000 investment into a business worth more than $3 million. By 1895, Brown, Outagamie, and Winnebago counties accounted for five-sixths of Wisconsin's paper production. Led by the Fox Valley enterprises, Wisconsin leaped to fifth among papermaking states at the turn of the century, turning out 8 per cent of the nation's paper.[30]

Between 1900 and 1915, Kimberly, Clark & Company and the other Fox Valley papermakers integrated themselves into the national economy. They expanded their product lines to include specialty papers, and they restructured their distribution networks, seeking new markets. As the state's forests receded, Fox Valley papermakers invested in Wisconsin and Chippewa valley trees and mills. By 1915, many produced significantly more paper in their "colonial" mills than at home. To ensure control over the Fox Valley's waterpowers, and to lobby for river and dam projects, several organized the Neenah and Menasha Water Power Company. And to protect themselves against incursions by eastern and foreign investors, papermakers formed trade associations such as the Wisconsin Paper Manufacturers Asso-

---

[29] Howard Publishing Company, *History of the Wisconsin Paper Industry*, 24, 40 (quote); Klueter and Lorence, *Woodlot and Ballot Box*, 104–120; Smith, *Wisconsin Wood-Using Industries*, 12; Alexander, "Industrial History of Wisconsin," in the *Wisconsin Blue Book, 1929*, pp. 39–41.

[30] Glaab and Larsen, *Factories in the Valley*, 78–126, 258–260; Branch, "The Paper Industry," 29–39 (quotes); Howard Publishing Company, *History of the Wisconsin Paper Industry*, 8–30.

ciation and the Northwestern Paper and Pulp Manufacturers' Association. These associations sought to regulate production, allocate markets, and fix prices through pooling arrangements, such as the General Paper Co., which was dissolved by a federal antitrust suit in 1906. They unified paper manufacturers in labor relations, enabling them to resist unionization, and they aided in the founding of the Institute of Paper Chemistry at Appleton, a degree-granting graduate school and research facility affiliated with Lawrence University.

Non-paper, wood-based industries formed separate associations. Menasha's woodenware companies belonged to the Midwestern Wooden Ware Association. It similarly engaged in price fixing, standardization of products, co-option of competitors, imposition of retail prices, and allocation of contracts, in the hope of increasing profits and combating eastern competition.[31]

Although Fox Valley paper manufacturers helped lead Wisconsin Valley development, indigenous businessmen played the larger roles. They were chiefly lumbermen who owned sizable tracts and had surplus investment capital. Their earliest effort, the Wisconsin Valley Advancement Association (1899), proposed a 150-mile interurban electric railway along the upper river between Port Edwards in Wood County and Eagle River in Vilas County. The electric generators for running the railway also were to supply heat and light "for a community of a million souls" and for manufacturing and quarrying. The association's literature stressed that the death of "King Pine" provided an opportunity to free the Wisconsin Valley from subservience to lumbering, proving itself "the natural location for paper mills, wood pulp mills, sulphite mills, tanneries and hardwood manufacturers."

The association expired in 1903 for lack of funds and leadership. But it inspired similar organizations and efforts, especially those of the Wausau Group, also composed primarily of lumbermen who wanted to make themselves richer and the region more profitable. The group's first project was the $400,000 Wausau Paper Mills complex in 1900. Second was the Wausau Sulphate Fibre Company, an achievement that reversed a serious population decline in the village of Mosinee. Its foremost venture was the Marathon Paper Mills Company with a mill on the waterpower site at Rothschild, just south of Wausau. There the group built a 450-foot dam across the Wisconsin River, creating a lake that would "make Wausau one of the most attractive summer resorts in the state" and, not incidentally, would supply water for a $750,000 factory employing 350 workers.[32]

---

[31] Glaab and Larsen, *Factories in the Valley*, 258–280.
[32] Klueter and Lorence, *Woodlot and Ballot Box*, 68–99 (quotes); Karges, "David Clark Everest," 48–75.

Marathon began production late in 1910, operating at a loss for three years because of floods and other disasters. Switching to wrapping and other specialty papers, it earned a net profit of over $100,000 in 1915. The company's development of bleached lined board for butter cartons revolutionized the food packaging industry in 1916 and motivated the spread of paper manufacturing throughout the Wisconsin River Valley. Utilizing profits from lumbering and papermaking, members of the Wausau Group expanded into other enterprises. In 1914, they financed the Marathon Electric Manufacturing Company and the Wausau Abrasive Company, which used quartzite from nearby Rib Mountain to make sandpaper. They later underwrote much of the expense of developing Masonite hardboard. The Wausau Group's members also constituted, de facto, an interlocking directorate of Wausau's financial institutions and most of its public utilities. Their most ambitious and long-lived enterprise was the Employers Mutual Liability Insurance Company (1911), formed in response to Wisconsin's landmark workers' compensation law adopted the same year. So successful was the Wausau Group's effort to create a post-lumbering economy that the share of total manufacturing capital invested in non-wood enterprises in Marathon County rose from 22 per cent in 1900 to 40 per cent by 1920.[33]

Eau Claire's equivalent of the Wausau Group was the Commercial Association. Founded in 1896, the association initially operated on the assumption that agriculture would supplant lumbering, so it focused on encouraging farm trade, improving transportation arteries with rural hinterlands, and establishing agricultural processing industries. For a time, it functioned as the Northern Wisconsin Immigration and Improvement Association, trying to entice agricultural settlers. Internally, the Commercial Association created committees on municipal affairs, legislation, industrial sites, streets and highways, and transportation and freight rates. It offered rebates and other incentives in unsuccessful efforts to attract a sugar beet factory and a cotton mill. In 1899, as a first step in promoting industry, the Eau Claire city council enacted an ordinance exempting factories from municipal taxation, an initiative which led to the establishment of the Lange Canning Company. Following a policy of cautious industrial promotion, the Commercial Association attracted a bedding factory, a shoe factory, the Northwestern Steel & Iron Works, and the John H. Kaiser Lumber Company, a box and hardwood lumbering concern. The Dells Paper & Pulp Company, an offshoot of the Empire Lumber Company, became the city's largest single manufacturer.

[33] Klueter and Lorence, *Woodlot and Ballot Box*, 99–119; Karges, "David Clark Everest," 76–127; John G. Gregory, ed., *West Central Wisconsin: A History* (4 vols., Indianapolis, 1933), 2: 638–640.

Once known as "Sawdust City," as were several other Wisconsin communities, by 1914 Eau Claire had developed a reasonably diversified manufacturing base.[34]

La Crosse, another "sawdust city," had ten sawmills which annually cut over 135 million board feet of lumber in the early 1880's. It also was home to three flour mills, a tannery, five breweries, three pork-packing plants, and manufacturers of agricultural implements, boilers, heavy machinery, wagons, barrels, and furniture. It later added a rubber plant, a gauge and equipment company, a garment factory, and a manufacturer of heating equipment. Stevens Point, with several waterpowers on the Wisconsin River, switched from lumbering to paper and pulp manufacturing and furniture construction in the early part of the new century.

Oshkosh, yet another "sawdust city," responded to the decline of basic lumbering in the 1870's by advancing to "finer and ever finer [wood-milling] processes." By the end of the century, Oshkosh was known as "the world's emporium for sash, doors, and blinds, the country's greatest producer of matches, and one of the greatest wagon and carriage factory centers in the United States." Its largest concern, the Paine Lumber Company, emerged as one of the country's leading door manufacturers. Fond du Lac, blessed with eight railroads and with status as the commercial center for the rich agricultural region south of Lake Winnebago, prospered because of quarrying and lime, tanning, ice harvesting for household and commercial use in Milwaukee and Chicago, and various heavy industries. Green Bay, still a thriving river and lake port in the early twentieth century, became home to almost a hundred small-scale factories. The percentage of its population engaged in manufacturing almost doubled in the 1890's.[35]

[2]

The adaptation from lumber to diversified industries in the Fox, Wisconsin, and Chippewa valleys actually pales in comparison to events

---

[34] Smith, "The Movements for Diversified Industry," 116–173; Bailey, ed., *History of Eau Claire County*, 474–488; Lois Barland, *Sawdust City: A History of Eau Claire, Wisconsin from Earliest Times to 1910* (Stevens Point, 1960), 118–120; Gregory, ed., *West Central Wisconsin*, 1: 232–235, 388–395, 2: 535–559, 627–629; J. Rogers Hollingsworth and Ellen J. Hollingsworth, *Dimensions in Urban History: Historical and Social Science Perspectives on Middle-Size American Cities* (Madison, 1979), 59–65.

[35] Gregory, ed., *West Central Wisconsin*, 2: 611–615, 644–648; Glaab and Larsen, *Factories in the Valley*, 276–277; Joseph Schafer, *The Winnebago-Horicon Basin: A Type Study in Western History* (Madison, 1937), 278–284, 290–297 (quote); Hollingsworth and Hollingsworth, *Dimensions in Urban History*, 97–101.

in the southeastern corner of the state, which had always benefited from its strategic transportation location on Lake Michigan. Manufacturing had been firmly established there for several decades. During the territorial period and early statehood, manufacturing had been limited mostly to the processing of nearby raw materials for local markets: grinding wheat into flour, sawing logs into boards, smelting iron ore, or tanning hides. Then raw materials dwindled, transportation and technology improved, and capital increased. The southeast accordingly progressed into more complex and sophisticated stages: finishing wood into sashes, doors, furniture, woodenware, and paper; forging iron into agricultural implements, wagon wheels, railroad ties, boilers, and machine tools; transforming grain into bread and beer and leather into boots, shoes, coats, and gloves. By the 1870's, southeasterners were building the saw mills, flour mills, papermaking machinery, lathes, and foundry equipment used by other Wisconsinites in earlier stages of industrial evolution. Markets formerly concentrated in the southeast spread statewide and regionally, the area's factories and work forces grew, and processes became more mechanized and complicated. By the 1890's, southeastern Wisconsin's industrial complex rivaled that of most eastern states.[36]

At that time, industrialization was undergoing even further transformation with new technologies and new processes connected with the neotechnic revolution, which spawned new industries, substantially transformed existing ones, and consigned others to oblivion. Giant corporations and factories, highly mechanized mass production, specialized organization, and elaborate nationwide marketing systems appeared—the "new industrialism." The pair—the neotechnic revolution and the new industrialism—made their greatest initial impact upon already heavily industrialized and urbanized areas like those in southeastern Wisconsin. It emerged as an integral component of the Great Lakes metal and machinery belt that connected Buffalo, Cleveland, Detroit, Chicago, Milwaukee, and Duluth-Superior.[37]

Wisconsin's railroad system reinforced and multiplied the Lake Michigan connections which made Milwaukee the linchpin of Chicago's links to Lake Superior and the Twin Cities in Minnesota. Farther west in Wisconsin, railroad lines linked Dane, Rock, Jefferson,

---

[36] Walsh, *The Manufacturing Frontier*, 210–220; Ray H. Whitbeck, *The Geography and Industries of Wisconsin* (Madison, 1913), 59–90, and Whitbeck's *The Geography and Economic Development of Southeastern Wisconsin*, in Wisconsin Geological and Natural History Survey, *Bulletin*, no. 58 (Madison, 1921), 30–40, 82–94, 161–170, 199–211.

[37] Mumford, *Culture of Cities*, 495–496; Peter George, *The Emergence of Industrial America: Strategic Factors in American Economic Growth Since 1870* (Albany, 1982), 32–54; Perloff et al., *Regions, Resources, and Economic Growth*, 160–162; Eric E. Lampard, *Industrial Revolution: Interpretations and Perspectives* (Washington, 1968), 11–36.

and Walworth counties with Chicago by way of Rockford, Illinois, making good use of the Rock River Valley. The region's rich agricultural bounty needed processing, while the state's forests provided a seemingly unlimited supply of construction materials. Nearby Dodge and Sauk counties contained enough iron ore to satisfy metal-working industries for several decades. Later, shipping and rail connections to the Lake Superior iron ranges, which yielded three-quarters of the nation's output, guaranteed the metal supply. By 1910, Wisconsin ranked fifth in mining iron ore. (Neighboring Minnesota and Michigan ranked first and second.) Wisconsin's smelting needs were met partly by domestic charcoal, and partly by coal and coke from eastern states, used only in port cities because of transportation costs. Thus it was that southeastern Wisconsin, which was first settled and most densely populated, continued to provide a solid and expanding base for industry and manufacturing of all kinds.[38]

Two amazing new power sources, electricity and the gasoline engine, propelled the neotechnic revolution. Wisconsin manufacturers had always relied heavily upon water to drive machinery, and waterwheels still supplied over one-third of the state's mechanical power in 1889. Steam generated nearly all the rest, as it had since the 1850's. By 1915, 38 per cent of the power used by Wisconsin industry came from electricity, 20 per cent from waterpower, and 40 per cent from steam engines and turbines. The trend towards electricity as the dominant power source was firmly established.[39]

Electricity was introduced in Wisconsin in the 1880's, and its advantages over water and steam power had become increasingly apparent during the 1890's: it was relatively clean and quiet, required minimal maintenance and supervision, and could be transmitted over long distances economically, freeing factories from having to locate near flowing water. Electric power was especially suited to running small motors, it could be turned on or off instantly, and could be rented cheaply from a central power station or generated by a company-owned dynamo. By 1907, Wisconsin had 193 electric power plants, thirty-one of which ran on water power, ninety-six on steam, and twenty-four on some combination of both.[40]

---

[38] Walsh, *The Manufacturing Frontier*, vii–xi, 20–36; Whitbeck, *Economic Development of Southeastern Wisconsin*, 24–211, and *Geography and Industries of Wisconsin*, 5–8, 8–17, 59–82.

[39] Whitbeck, *Geography and Industries of Wisconsin*, 73–76; George, *Emergence of Industrial America*, 49–51; Courtney R. Hall, *History of American Industrial Science* (New York, 1972), 157–165; *Census of Manufactures, 1914: Volume I, Reports by States with Statistics for Principal Cities and Metropolitan Districts*, 491–494.

[40] "Industries of Wisconsin," in the *Wisconsin Blue Book, 1915*, 39–40; *Fourteenth Census of the United States, 1920: Manufactures, 1919, Reports for States with Statistics for Principal Cities*, 1626; David E. Nye, *Electrifying America: Social Meanings of a New Tech-*

Electricity spawned a new industry in Wisconsin, the manufacturing of electrical machinery, and it transformed another, the laundry business, which switched from hand work to various forms of power. In 1889, the entire electrical machinery, apparatus, and supplies industry consisted of three plants employing fifteen people, with a product value of $38,870. Twenty-five years later, there were twenty-nine factories employing over 2,000 people, with a product value of over $5 million. During the same period, the number of power laundries leaped from zero to 150.[41]

The internal combustion engine had a lesser impact on manufacturing than electricity. As late as 1914, gasoline engines provided only about 4 per cent of the state's total manufacturing power. Ironically, the making of internal combustion machines (for automobiles, trucks, motorcycles, etc.) and their parts and supplies was becoming one of southeastern Wisconsin's most important industries. The automobile epitomized the neotechnic revolution. Within a decade of its founding, the industry became a prototype of mass production, the assembly line, complex industrial organization, and mass marketing and financing techniques—the consummate "big business" of the new industrial era. Auto making centered in the Great Lakes region, which contained most of the nation's iron deposits, possessed a huge labor force already skilled in metallurgy, engines, and vehicles because of the area's primacy in agricultural implements and wagons, and was well-connected by water and rail with petroleum-producing states. By 1914, Michigan produced 63 per cent of all U.S. automobiles, Ohio 13 per cent, and Wisconsin hoped vainly to catch up.[42]

Automobile manufacturing in the state dates to as early as 1871, but began in earnest in the early 1890's when Gottfried Schloemer, a Milwaukee mechanic and cooper, aided by blacksmith Frank Toepler, successfully built and operated a one-cylinder, two-speed "motor wagon" capable of making twelve miles an hour. Capital materialized slowly. Nevertheless, during the next decade at least ten companies—mostly in Milwaukee, Racine, Oshkosh, and Appleton—engaged in

---

nology, 1880–1940 (Cambridge, 1990), ix–xi, 381–391; Thomas P. Hughes, *Networks of Power: Electrification in Western Society, 1880–1930* (Baltimore, 1983), 1–46.

[41] *Eleventh Census of the United States, 1890: Manufacturing Industries, Volume VI, Part 1, Totals for States and Territories*, 630–641; *Census of Manufactures, 1914: Volume I, Reports by States with Statistics for Principal Cities and Metropolitan Districts*, 1630, 1646; *Fourteenth Census of the United States, 1920: Manufactures, 1919, Reports for States, with Statistics for Principal Cities*, 1612.

[42] *Fourteenth Census of the United States, 1920: Manufactures, 1919, Reports for States with Statistics for Principal Cities*, 1626; Forrest McDonald, *Let There Be Light: The Electric Utility Industry in Wisconsin, 1881–1955* (Madison, 1957), 99; Frank J. Coppa and Richard Hammond, *Technology in the Twentieth Century* (Dubuque, 1983), 89–94; John B. Rae, *American Automobiles* (Chicago, 1965), 28–30.

auto manufacturing at least briefly. An English-born bicycle manufacturer, Thomas B. Jeffery, successfully produced the first Rambler in Kenosha in 1902, the year after the first Oldsmobile and the year before the first Ford. In its initial decade, the Jeffery Company manufactured over 56,000 automobiles. In Racine, the Mitchell & Lewis Wagon Works and the J. I. Case Threshing Machine Company both branched out into auto making, while fifty different automobile manufacturers set up shop in Milwaukee before World War I. Nonexistent at the end of the nineteenth century, the industry vaulted to thirteenth place among Wisconsin manufacturing endeavors by 1910, with a product worth more than $11 million. Four years later, it climbed to eleventh place, with forty-three factories, nearly 5,000 workers, and 53,160 automobiles worth $18 million. (This constituted just under 10 per cent of the total manufactured nationally.)[43]

Besides being responsible for creating the auto industry, the internal combustion engine prompted the formation of such Milwaukee firms as the Briggs and Stratton Corporation, Seaman Body Corporation, and Harley-Davidson Motor Company. Harley-Davidson made forty-nine motorcycles in 1906, many of them purchased by rural mail carriers. Incorporated in 1907, the company gained national celebrity when one of its cycles won an endurance run in New York. In 1912, 1,000 workers made 11,000 Harleys; in 1914, a peak of 71,000. Successful auto-related manufacturers elsewhere in Wisconsin included the Four Wheel Drive Auto Company in tiny Clintonville (Waupaca County) and, in Racine, a number of spinoffs.[44]

The chief construction material for the new industrialism was steel. Significantly lighter, stronger, and more flexible than iron, steel provided the essential metal for massive, high-speed precision machinery, high-rise construction, and modern transportation and communications. Steelmaking evolved in the late nineteenth century out of continuous improvements in the superheating of ores to make metal. Steel production totaled a mere 11,000 tons in 1860, compared to 1 million tons of iron. Then came the Bessemer process by which air was pneumatically forced through a bath of molten iron in a pear-shaped vessel. It increased U.S. steel production to 1.2 million

[43] Terry D. Potts, "The Automobile Industry in Wisconsin, 1895–1915" (1973), unpublished research report, in the SHSW; Alexander, "Industrial History of Wisconsin," 41; *Census of Manufactures, 1914: Volume I, Reports by States with Statistics for Principal Cities and Metropolitan Districts*, 1630; Thomas J. Noer, "Charles W. Nash: Self-Made Man," in Nicholas C. Burckel and John A. Neuenschwander, eds., *Kenosha Retrospective: A Biographical Approach* (Kenosha, 1981), 118–121; *Fourteenth Census of the United States, 1920: Manufactures, 1919, Reports for States, with Statistics for Principal Cities*, 1612.

[44] Harry V. Sucher, *Harley-Davidson: The Milwaukee Marvel* (Newbury Park, California, 1985), 20–30; Richard H. Keehn, "Industry and Business," in Nicholas C. Burckel, ed., *Racine: Growth and Change in a Wisconsin County* (Racine, 1977), 294–295.

tons in 1880, most of which was used to replace iron railway rails with steel. The steel revolution continued in the 1890's with the discovery of the world's largest deposit of easily mined iron ore near the shores of Lake Superior. This discovery coincided with the widespread adoption of the open-hearth process, which allowed large quantities of scrap metal to be mixed with relatively small amounts of molten pig iron. Although the open-hearth process took twenty times longer, it produced ten times as much steel, and that steel was of significantly greater tensile strength. Between 1895 and 1900, the amount of steel produced by the open-hearth process tripled, to nearly 4 million tons a year.[45]

In Wisconsin, blast furnaces and rolling mills had been part of the scene since statehood, consolidated around Bay View just southeast of Milwaukee. In 1889, the state had twelve iron and steel plants which employed just under 2,000 workers and turned out nearly $7 million worth of metal. By 1914, its iron and steel works, rolling mills, and blast furnaces produced almost $10 million worth of steel, representing about 1.5 per cent of Wisconsin's manufacturing product, even though the industry fell from eighth to eighteenth place in the interim.

Brass, bronze, and copper production also made significant strides, from an 1889 base of five mills employing less than 200 people and a product valued at only $370,451, to 1914 figures of thirty mills, 1,222 workers, and $5.5 million dollars worth of product. Copper, tin, and sheet-iron production, virtually nonexistent in 1889, accounted for 1.5 per cent of Wisconsin's total product value by 1914, with 111 factories, almost 3,500 workers, and a product worth over $10 million. All told, basic metals processing occupied 3.5 per cent of Wisconsin's work force by 1914, and constituted nearly 5 per cent of its product value and 3 per cent of its value added by manufacturing.[46]

Steel had its most immediate effect on foundries and machine shops, one of southeastern Wisconsin's oldest and most valuable in-

---

[45] Victor S. Clark, *History of Manufactures in the United States* (3 vols., New York, 1929; reprinted, New York, 1949), 3: 17–22, 34–36, 45–47, 54–71, 84–86; Whitbeck, *Geography and Economic Development of Southeastern Wisconsin*, 111–116; William T. Hogan, *Economic History of the Iron and Steel Industry in the United States* (5 vols., Lexington, Massachusetts, 1971), vol. 1, *passim*; W. David Lewis, *Iron and Steel in America* (Greenville, Delaware, 1976), 35–54. By 1913, according to economic geographer Ray Hughes Whitbeck, nearly half of Wisconsin's metal-working plants were in Milwaukee and about 80 per cent were in the state's southeast quarter. See his *Geography and Industries of Wisconsin*, 65–71.

[46] Bernhard C. Korn, "Eber Brock Ward: Pathfinder of American Industry" (doctoral dissertation, Marquette University, 1942), 178–198; Whitbeck, *Economic Development of Southeastern Wisconsin*, 111–118; Alexander, "Industrial History of Wisconsin," in the *Wisconsin Blue Book, 1929*, pp. 34–38; Bayrd Still, *Milwaukee: The History of a City* (Madison, 1948), 335–337.

dustries. In the 1880's, numerous well-trained immigrants from Germany, Scotland, and Slavic countries readily found employment in them. They turned out an amazing variety of metal goods for consumers and adopted mass-production machinery and methods. These goods and machines required steel castings that were increasingly complex, durable, specialized, and precise. New devices—the molding machine, ventilated tumbling barrel, sand blaster, and hinged-bottom cupola, all developed in the 1880's—transformed the proverbial "wood butcher's shanty" into a "mechanized precision tool gallery" that demanded tolerances of .015 instead of .25 inches. Milwaukee foundries adopted the crucible method of melting steel and designed what came to be known as the Milwaukee furnace, enabling them to melt steel in the small quantities that local shops needed.

Foundries increasingly separated themselves into "captive shops" and "jobbers." The former engaged almost exclusively in casting the few standardized parts used in agricultural implements, automobiles, and heavy machinery. The jobbers, conversely, produced small, individual batches of a wide assortment of custom castings. Unable to standardize, mechanize, expand, or innovate to any great extent, the jobbing foundries lived precariously, dependent upon making items that the larger, captive shops ignored.

Meanwhile, Wisconsin foundrymen embraced the organizational and operational methods of big business. Incorporation and consolidation into holding companies yielded undreamed-of expansion capital, allowing the new combines to manipulate production, pricing, and distribution. Producers wanted to curb cutthroat competition that tended to lower prices, and to share the trade secrets that allowed some foundries to prosper at others' expense. Several joined the regional Western Foundrymen's Association in the 1890's and later the national American Foundrymen's Association (AFA). In 1903, the AFA held its annual meeting in Milwaukee, a typical American foundry center. The gathering resulted in formation of the Milwaukee Foremen's Association, which included foremen from twenty-eight iron, four steel, and several brass foundries. These associations directed and disseminated technological research, set casting standards, established testing and grading methods for molding material, and pioneered practices for prolonging the longevity and broadening the application of cast articles. They also encouraged cost-analysis systems for pricing products, warning members that they should "count that day lost, whose low descending sun . . . shows prices shot to hell, and business done for fun."[47]

---

[47] Hilton, "Men of Metal," 54–63, quoting the *Foundry*, 41 (March, 1913), 20.

Milwaukee, the chief locus of Wisconsin's foundry and machine-shop industry from its inception, greatly augmented its hegemony between 1880 and 1913, rising to national prominence. In 1892, Milwaukee had only twenty iron foundries, annually making 95,000 tons of goods. A decade later, it had thirty-three iron, eight steel, and twelve brass foundries, and was recognized as one of the leading foundry centers in the world. Some of the nation's heaviest iron castings came from Milwaukee, which led America in the value of its engine castings.[48]

Foundries in other Wisconsin cities joined the prosperity. In Racine, Belle City Malleable Iron Company constructed a 112,000-square-foot facility with the latest in automated equipment in 1899. The city also had several other large foundries, including two subsidiaries of the J. I. Case Threshing Machine Company and the Lakeside Malleable Company (1903). By 1912, its twelve foundries ranked Racine thirtieth among the country's foundry seats. Other Wisconsin cities with expanding foundry industries in the period were Kenosha, Sheboygan and Kohler, Manitowoc, Beloit, Janesville, Madison, Beaver Dam, Stevens Point, Oshkosh, Green Bay, La Crosse, Superior, and Ashland, many of which had specialized industries requiring foundry work.

Foundry and machine-shop products became Wisconsin's fastest-growing industry. In 1880, the state's sixty-four foundries yielded less than $2.5 million in products. Sixty made mostly gray iron castings. By 1912, Wisconsin possessed 185 gray iron, twenty malleable iron, thirty-seven brass, twenty-two steel, and sixty-four aluminum foundries—a total of 246, ranking it eighth in the nation.[49]

The interrelationship between foundries and the agricultural implement manufacturers helped Wisconsin's foundry industry grow. Like foundries, the implement business transformed itself during this era of the new industrialism, through the adoption of internal combustion, fabricated metals, and electric power. At the era's outset in the 1880's, skilled craftsmen in wood, iron, and steam made the implements. They adapted or were soon replaced. For example, in 1897, Racine's J. I. Case replaced its popular cast-iron traction engine, used to power both plows and threshing machines, with all-steel models. Seven years later, it produced the first completely steel threshing machine, which competitors hastily copied. For all-steel plows, however, Case bought out a firm in 1919, and began to manufacture its first ones. Case's reputation from 1889 to 1914 depended largely upon

---

[48] *Ibid.*, 63–75.
[49] *Ibid.*, 75–79, 82–95; Eblen, "A History of the Kohler Company," 30–76; Alexander, "Industrial History of Wisconsin," in the *Wisconsin Blue Book, 1929*, pp. 35–38; Whitbeck, *Economic Development of Southeastern Wisconsin*, 112–116.

farm steam engines, of which it made more than any other manufacturer in the world. The period was the heyday of steam threshing. In its midst, in 1892, Case also built the nation's first gasoline tractor. It was another twenty years, however, before the company actually placed them on the market, a decade after two University of Wisconsin graduates unveiled the first successful gasoline traction engine—dubbed a "tractor" for short. By 1905, U.S. tractor manufacturers were making 600 a year; by 1914, 14,500; by 1917, almost 90,000. Case introduced gasoline-powered tractors in 1911, the same year its sales of steam traction engines reached a peak of 2,321 and Milwaukee Harvester and Allis-Chalmers also began making them. Led by Case and Harvester, Wisconsin's farm implement industry virtually quadrupled in product value and value added by manufacturing between 1889 and 1914. Modern farm machinery was turned out by modern industrial machinery, and Wisconsin continued to rank second only to Illinois in output.[50]

Also quadrupling its value was another industry: railroad shop construction and repair. It, too, depended upon innovations in power and metals technology. Construction of refrigerator cars, to meet the demand of the meat-packing, brewing, and dairy industries, constituted a large fraction of this growth. When Edward P. Allis died in 1889, his company's Milwaukee plant covered twenty acres, employed 1,500, and turned out more milling equipment and large steam engines than any other manufacturer in the country. By 1904, the newly formed Allis-Chalmers combine was also producing giant electric, gasoline, and hydroelectric turbine engines, as well as mining machinery. Soon Allis-Chalmers itself was building steam and hydroelectric turbines. Its new West Allis works was capable of employing 10,000 men and of producing up to $30 million worth of heavy machinery a year.[51]

For giant excavating machinery, the Bucyrus-Erie Company of South Milwaukee set national standards. It switched in the 1890's to

---

[50] Stewart H. Holbrook, *Machines of Plenty: Chronicle of an Innovator in Construction and Agricultural Equipment* (New York, 1955), 165–187; Michael S. Holmes, *J. I. Case: The First 150 Years* (Racine, 1992), 23–45; Charles H. Wendel, *150 Years of J.I. Case* (Sarasota, 1991), 10–25; James I. Clark, *Farm Machinery in Wisconsin* (Madison, 1956), 3–19; Reynold M. Wik, *Steam Power on the American Farm* (Philadelphia, 1953), 100–108, 202–207; J. I. Case Company, *Serving Farmers Since 1842* (Racine, 1948), 29–37. The two university graduates were Charles W. Hart and Charles H. Parr.

[51] Barbara Marsh, *A Corporate Tragedy: The Agony of International Harvester Company* (Garden City, New York, 1985), 35–48; *Eleventh Census of the United States, 1890, Manufacturing Industries, Volume VI, Part 1, Totals for States and Territories*, 628–629; *Census of Manufactures, 1914: Volume I, Reports by States with Statistics for Principal Cities and Metropolitan Districts*, 1630; Walter Geist, *"Allis-Chalmers": A Brief History of 103 Years of Production* (New York, 1950), 9–16; Walter F. Peterson, *An Industrial Heritage: Allis-Chalmers Corporation* (Milwaukee, 1978), 84–167.

cast-steel and variable-speed electric motors. In 1905, it manufactured a fleet of electric dredges for irrigation projects in India. It also developed several special alloy steels used in machines digging the Panama Canal, enhancing the company's reputation. By 1911, Bucyrus introduced its first gasoline-powered machinery, although steam remained the paramount power source.[52]

Tanning, brewing, meat-packing, and the shoe and clothing industries in southeastern Wisconsin also benefited from the new power sources and precision machinery. In 1890, leather tanning was the state's fourth-leading industry and Milwaukee was its center. Over the next two decades, tanning's product value quadrupled, moving Wisconsin into second place behind Pennsylvania among states in 1909 and Milwaukee into second place behind Philadelphia among cities. (For plain leather, it led internationally in 1890.) Pfister and Vogel, Milwaukee's largest operation, expanded to five plants by the early twentieth century and established marketing branches in Boston, New York, and overseas. Kenosha touted its Allen Tannery as the largest single operation in the world by 1915, while Racine's Eisendrath and Fond du Lac's Rueping tanneries also enjoyed nationwide reputations. Trusts such as the United States Leather Company and the American Hide and Leather Company acquired some Wisconsin tanneries, but the major ones remained under local control.[53]

Brewing, too, experienced tremendous growth, although the specter of prohibition constantly threatened its prosperity. Annual output jumped from 150,000 barrels in 1871 to nearly 4 million by 1910. Between 1889 and 1914, technological innovations—including a new apparatus to produce yeast culture, electric grain elevators, grain soaking tanks, refrigeration in processing, storage and shipping, underground vats for storing and aging, and mechanical bottle washers—helped to triple the value of the product. These advances stimulated investment and market expansion, aided by new advertising and promotion techniques that included networks of brewery-owned saloons. They also created a variety of subsidiary industries: malting, cooperage, ice harvesting, refrigeration, brewery machinery, saloon furnishings, and cartage equipment. Between 1880 and 1910, brewing's product value quintupled, reaching 6 per cent of the state's

---

[52] Harold F. Williamson and Kenneth H. Myers II, *Designed for Digging: The First 75 Years of Bucyrus-Erie Company* (Evanston, 1955), 55–132.

[53] Charles E. Schefft, "The Tanning Industry in Wisconsin: A History of Its Frontier Origins and Its Development" (master's thesis, University of Wisconsin, 1938), 53–80; *Eleventh Census of the United States, 1890: Manufacturing Industries, Volume VI, Part 1, Totals for States and Territories*, 630–631; *Census of Manufactures, 1914: Volume 2, Reports for Selected Industries and Detail Statistics for Industries, by States*, 673–674, 1630–1632; Wisconsin, *Gazetteer and Business Directory*, 1915–1916, p. 339; Whitbeck, *Economic Development of Southeastern Wisconsin*, 106–111.

total. In 1914, Wisconsin ranked third behind New York and Pennsylvania among the country's brewing states, with 9 per cent of the total, and second to New York among its malt-producing states, with 32 per cent.[54]

Applying electric power to the slaughtering and dressing process, and the refrigeration of plants and railroad cars made the difference in meat-packing. Milwaukee sits on the northern boundary of the corn-hogs belt, and had been an important center for the processing and shipping of pork since the early 1850's. By 1890, meat-packing ranked sixth in the state with $8 million in products. Cudahy, Plankinton, and Layton, all of Milwaukee, were household names nationally. Over the next quarter-century, the number of meat-packing workers more than doubled, while the value of their output nearly quadrupled. They made up only 1 per cent of the state's work force but turned out 5 per cent of its product value. Pork amounted to about 60 per cent of that total in 1914. Between 1895 and 1910, there were five different years in which at least a million hogs were slaughtered in Milwaukee and suburban Cudahy. Using electrical power to run high-speed machinery also revamped the hosiery and knit goods, men's clothing, and boot and shoe industries. In each case, the value of the industry's product grew at least three times faster than its work force, due to mechanization and mass production. By 1914, these three industries combined accounted for 5 per cent of Wisconsin's product value.[55]

The new industrialism affected Milwaukee and its immediate environs more than any other area in Wisconsin. Milwaukee—known far and wide as the Cream City for its distinctive cream-brick buildings—experienced a 125 per cent increase in product value during the 1880's, accounting for almost 40 per cent of the state's total product in 1890. Its workers produced nine-tenths of Wisconsin's men's clothing and packaged meat, three-fourths of its tanned leather, and two-thirds of its foundry and machine-shop products. Tanneries, warehouses, ice houses, lumber and coal yards, meat-packing plants,

---

[54] Thomas C. Cochran, *The Pabst Brewing Company: The History of an American Business* (New York, 1948), 102–128, 199–202; Stanley Baron, *Brewed in America: A History of Beer and Ale in the United States* (New York, 1972), 257–273, 295–310; Still, *Milwaukee*, 329–333; Whitbeck, *Economic Development of Southeastern Wisconsin*, 101–103; *Eleventh Census of the United States, 1890: Manufacturing Industries, Volume VI, Part 1, Totals for States and Territories*, 632–633; *Census of Manufactures, 1914: Volume I, Reports by States with Statistics for Principal Cities and Metropolitan Districts*, 1630–1632.

[55] Whitbeck, *Economic Development of Southeastern Wisconsin*, 103–106; Porter, *The Rise of Big Business*, 47–50; *Eleventh Census of the United States, 1890: Manufacturing Industries, Volume VI, Part 1, Totals for States and Territories*, 628–635; *Census of Manufactures, 1914: Volume I, Reports by States with Statistics for Principal Cities and Metropolitan Districts*, 1630–1648.

Industrial Transformations 107

and railroad yards commanded the valleys of the Menomonee and Milwaukee rivers. The Allis Reliance Works occupied an entire city block. In Bay View, there were railroad shops, brickyards, machine shops, rolling mills and foundries, branch plants of Allis Reliance, and the Schlitz and Pabst breweries. The city's brewers, tanners, meatpackers, millers, and machinists competed nationally; Allis and a few others ventured into international business.

Almost 60 per cent of Milwaukee's nearly 3,000 manufacturing establishments were small-scale shops. As for the workers, 41 per cent in 1891 labored in six industries: cigars; boots and shoes; iron, steel, and heavy machinery; tanning; brewing; and railroad shops. Allis, the Bay View Iron Works, and the Chicago, Milwaukee, and St. Paul Railway Company regularly employed between 1,000 and 1,800 workers, while the Cudahy and Plankinton meat-packing plants hired as many as 1,200 during peak seasons. In the 1880's, the value of Milwaukee products increased by $54 million, a figure $14 million larger than their entire worth at the beginning of the decade.[56]

The depression of 1893–1897 so devastated Milwaukee that its economic growth during that entire decade was only half what it had been in the 1880's. Then the first ten years of the new century brought Milwaukee its greatest industrial spurt: nearly 90 per cent compared to 80 per cent for the entire United States. By 1910, the city's manufacturers had increased their aggregate product value by $98 million, from a 1900 base of $110 million. Boot and shoe production increased twice as fast as it had during the previous sixty years; hosiery and knit goods jumped 175 per cent; leather gloves and mittens, 500 per cent. Electrical machinery and supplies grew by 440 per cent; sheet metal products, 300; confectionery goods and boots and shoes, 200; tanned leather, 170; stoves and furnaces, 110; and leather goods and lumber and timber products, 100 per cent. Between 1880 and 1910, the per capita value of Milwaukee's manufactured products rose from $165 to $550, while the city's population merely doubled.[57]

Although not in the same league with Chicago as a manufacturing center, Milwaukee held its own among other Great Lakes giants by 1914. It competed with Detroit, Cleveland, and Buffalo with products valued at $224 million; it was the country's tenth-leading industrial

[56] Whitbeck, *Economic Development of Southeastern Wisconsin*, 87–91; *Eleventh Census of the United States, 1890: Report on Manufacturing, Part I, Totals for States and Industries*, 628–636; Alexander, "Industrial History of Wisconsin," in the *Wisconsin Blue Book, 1929*, pp. 34–36; Gerd Korman, *Industrialization, Immigrants, and Americanizers: The View from Milwaukee, 1866–1921* (Madison, 1967), 17–21.

[57] Whitbeck, *Geography and Economic Development of Southeastern Wisconsin*, 90–93. For an overview of Milwaukee's industrial development between 1870 and 1910, see Still, *Milwaukee*, 321–355.

center; and it ranked third behind Detroit and Cleveland in the proportion of its work force engaged in manufacturing (just under 60 per cent). Milwaukee factories made 90 per cent of the state's steel and rolling-mill products, paint and varnish, fur, millinery, and lace goods; two-thirds of its beer and boots and shoes; and three-fourths of its electrical machinery. It manufactured 60 per cent of the men's clothing and tobacco products and 55 per cent of the hosiery and knit goods, tanned leather, printed and published books, and baked goods. Milwaukee packed half Wisconsin's meat and generated one-third of its malt and foundry and machine-shop products. In metals-based industries, Milwaukee was Wisconsin's leading producer of everything except farm implements, automobiles, carriages and wagons, and brass and copper.[58]

Iron and steel formed the base upon which Milwaukee expanded. By the outbreak of World War I, it ranked behind only Pittsburgh, Cleveland, and Detroit in the number of workers in iron and steel fabrication. Milwaukee's blast furnaces, rolling mills, foundries, and machine shops yielded almost $26 million worth of metal products in 1914. By 1920, its industries related to iron and steel exceeded 200 plants, several of them employing more than a thousand workers, with an annual product value of over $150 million.[59]

The emergence of several mammoth enterprises highlighted the city's new industrialism. Assembly-line production prompted construction of numerous plants covering one or more city blocks, quickly absorbing nearly all available land. Massive, highly mechanized factories clogged the Menomonee and Kinnickinnic river valleys and transformed Milwaukee from a city known for its commercial port to one known for its industries.

Space requirements and the rising cost of inner-city real estate pushed many manufacturers to surrounding suburbs. West Allis literally grew up around the immense Allis-Chalmers complex, the largest single plant in Wisconsin. It also became home to two dozen other plants, most of which made iron and steel products and machinery. South Milwaukee, founded in 1891, was home to ten different metals processing plants, headed by the Bucyrus Steam Shovel and Dredge Company, which relocated from Ohio. The suburb of Cudahy was established as a company town in 1891 by former associates of the

---

[58] Whitbeck, *Economic Development of Southeastern Wisconsin*, 93–94; Still, *Milwaukee*, 321–326; Korman, *Industrialization, Immigrants, and Americanizers*, 79–80; *Census of Manufactures, 1914: Volume I, Reports by States with Statistics for Principal Cities and Metropolitan Districts*, 1644.

[59] Whitbeck, *Economic Development of Southeastern Wisconsin*, 92–115; Hilton, "Men of Metal," 63–75; *Census of Manufactures, 1914: Volume I, Reports by States with Statistics for Principal Cities and Metropolitan Districts*, 1644; Still, *Milwaukee*, 335–340.

Plankinton and Armour meat-packing firm. Producers of rubber products, mining machinery, drop forgings, and gloves and mittens also built factories there. North Milwaukee, founded in 1897, grew to a manufacturing suburb of 3,000 in two decades. West Milwaukee, incorporated as a village in 1906, was the site of the Pawling and Harnischfeger Company, the world's foremost manufacturer of electric motor-driven cranes. Governmental boundaries notwithstanding, Milwaukee County evolved within twenty-five years into a functional manufacturing entity, linked by sinews of steel.[60]

Of all the county's major manufacturing firms, none epitomized the new industrialism better than E. P. Allis and Company. By 1889, the Reliance Works occupied a complex more than a block wide and four blocks long, employed almost 1,500 workers, and produced $3 million worth of machinery a year. Reorganized the following year, the company weathered the depression of 1893–1897 and almost doubled its output of engines during the decade, making it the nation's largest steam engine manufacturer. Allis's ever larger and more powerful engines and generators gained national celebrity as it supplied them to the Narragansett Electric Light Company of Providence and the New York City Railway Company. Its 3,000-horsepower Reynolds-Corliss engine was the "Pride of Machinery Hall" at the World's Columbian Exposition of 1893.[61]

By 1904, Allis-Chalmers boasted it could make or furnish equipment for almost any plant. Its combined West Allis, Reliance, and South Side works gave Allis-Chalmers one of the world's most extensive and modern foundry complexes. In 1905, the corporation built the first "Manhattan" Corliss engine for the New York City subway system, ultimately supplying the project with twenty-four identical machines. By 1908, new products like these constituted almost two-thirds of company sales. Five years later, it owned, controlled, or had applications pending for 1,030 domestic and a hundred foreign patents, nearly all for high-powered machinery.[62]

---

[60] Roger D. Simon, "The Expansion of an Industrial City: Milwaukee, 1880–1910" (doctoral dissertation, University of Wisconsin, 1971), 62–76; Whitbeck, *Economic Development of Southeastern Wisconsin*, 118–120; Frederick I. Olson, "City Expansion and Suburban Spread: Settlements and Governments in Milwaukee County," in Ralph M. Aderman, ed., *Trading Post to Metropolis: Milwaukee County's First 150 Years* (Milwaukee, 1987), 21–55; Korman, *Industrialization, Immigrants, and Americanizers*, 18, 31, 47–48, 69–70.

[61] Still, *Milwaukee*, 321–326; Peterson, *An Industrial Heritage*, 57–63, 89–95; Hilton, "Men of Metal," 65–66.

[62] Hilton, "Men of Metal," 66–68; Peterson, *An Industrial Heritage*, 101–142. See also Walter F. Peterson, "Allis-Chalmers: A Representative Wisconsin Industry," in the *Transactions of the Wisconsin Academy of Sciences, Arts and Letters*, 54, Part A (1965), 67–75; Korman, *Industrialization, Immigrants, and Americanizers*, 37–40; and Stephen

Despite this remarkable expansion, Allis-Chalmers was weakened by infighting between Milwaukeeans and eastern investors which plunged the company into receivership in 1912. The resultant restructuring led to the formation of the Allis-Chalmers Company, headed by Otto H. Falk. He remained in charge until his death in 1940. Falk streamlined and integrated operations, and, aided by World War I needs, set Allis-Chalmers on a twenty-year course of growth and profits.[63]

The company's dramatic expansion was roughly paralleled by that of other Milwaukee-area foundries and machine shops. The Filer & Stowell Company, for example, originated as a sawmill maker, then evolved by the 1880's into a maker of steam engines and water works, including those for New York City and Milwaukee's own Jones Island pumping station. In 1902, new owners doubled plant capacity by erecting an 88,000-square-foot foundry on the city's south side, complete with electric cranes and thirty-ton trolleys. In 1906, they constructed another, almost as large. Filer & Stowell could turn out a thirty-five-ton Corliss engine or a seventy-ton flywheel. These improvements occurred after John M. Stowell sold out to two of his employees. But Stowell stayed in the business. In 1896, he bought the Moore Manufacturing and Foundry Company, erected a modern malleable-iron foundry with twice the capacity of Filer & Stowell, installed a system of specially designed molding machines, and developed techniques for daily control testing.[64]

Especially spectacular was the rise of the Falk Corporation, begun in 1892 in a small frame shanty on the south side Menomonee swamp by Otto Falk's brother Herman. He had discovered a new steel cast-welding process, ideal for street railway equipment. He built a foundry containing an open-hearth furnace with a fifty-ton daily capacity. Falk became a jobber and soon owned the country's largest acid open-hearth shop, with almost 295,000 square feet of floor space. In 1907, only fifteen years from its beginnings, the Falk Company had become the nation's largest steel foundry. (Milwaukee's George H. Smith Steel Casting Company was second.) All told, Milwaukee's eight steel foundries, the only ones in the state, produced 19,000 tons of steel castings a year, of which Falk made nearly 13,000.[65]

Modernization and consolidation also profoundly affected Milwaukee Harvester, the city's major manufacturer of farm implements. In 1901, Milwaukee Harvester constructed a new 40,000-square-foot

---

Meyer, "Technology and the Workplace: Skilled and Production Workers at Allis-Chalmers, 1900–1941," *Technology and Culture*, 29 (October, 1988), 839–864.

[63] Peterson, *An Industrial Heritage*, 149–182.
[64] Hilton, "Men of Metal," 68–70.
[65] *Ibid.*, 70–75. Most noteworthily, he virtually eliminated the need for skilled labor.

foundry, complete with a labor-saving overhead trolley system and the latest in lighting, ventilation, and materials routing. The following year, Harvester merged with McCormick and Deering of Chicago and two other firms to form the International Harvester Company of America, producer of 88 per cent of the nation's harvesting machines with assets of $110 million. The Milwaukee firm became a division of this integrated operation that owned many businesses. Its new board of directors included partners in J. P. Morgan's operations, as well as Elbert Henry Gary, chairman of U.S. Steel; part of its financing was supplied by John D. Rockefeller. Over the next decade, Harvester acquired several competitors, doubled its sales, increased its profits eightfold, and broadened its product line to include tractors, trucks, and gasoline engines. It also fashioned a network of farm machinery factories in Canada, Sweden, France, Germany, and Russia. By 1910, Harvester ranked fourth in size nationally to U.S. Steel, Standard Oil, and American Tobacco. During the war, its Milwaukee affiliate doubled its work force to almost 6,000.[66]

The growth of the Bucyrus Steam Shovel and Dredge Company provides another impressive example of dynamic expansion. It moved to South Milwaukee in 1893 and filed bankruptcy by early 1895. Bankruptcy persuaded the company's new management to concentrate on special-purpose excavating machines, especially hydraulic and placer dredges, forty-and-fifty-ton shovels, and their replacement parts. Between 1895 and 1901, Bucyrus produced 251 shovels, most of which were purchased by railroads, railroad contractors, and Lake Superior iron mine operators. In the same period, its output, work force, and annual payroll almost tripled. Over the next nine years, Bucyrus spent $1.5 million on plant expansion and maintenance, pioneered full-revolving shovels, back-acting excavators, and self-laying or "caterpillar" tracks, while experimenting with steam and electrical power. Annual sales reached a million dollars in 1902 and doubled over the next decade. Reorganized as the Bucyrus Company in 1911, it was capitalized at $10 million.[67]

Milwaukee's new industrial giants worked mostly in metals and machinery, but they also emerged in tanning, meat-packing, and brewing. The leading tannery was the Pfister and Vogel Tanning Company, which achieved leadership between the 1870's and 1890's. As early as 1891, when Milwaukee tanneries produced more than 600,000 hides valued at just over $8 million, Pfister and Vogel turned out 4,000 daily; its annual output stood at $3 million. Between 1880 and 1909, the

---

[66] *Ibid.*, 70–71; Marsh, *A Corporate Tragedy*, 35–48; Korman, *Industrialization, Immigrants, and Americanizers*, 79.

[67] Williamson and Myers, *Designed for Digging*, 45–111; Still, *Milwaukee*, 340–500; Korman, *Industrialization, Immigrants, and Americanizers*, 48, 70.

annual worth of Milwaukee's tanned leather leaped from $2 million to $27 million. This rapid expansion stimulated the city's footwear, glove, and mitten production.[68]

The meat-packing industry specialized in salt pork, bacon, ham, lard, and sausage. The Cudahy Brothers Company gradually dominated its three nearest competitors: the Plankinton, Layton, and Bodden corporations. Cudahy bought out Plankinton in 1888, and in 1893 moved to its new company town. A quarter-century later, the huge plant was slaughtering and dressing a million animals a year. However, John Plankinton did not leave the business; in 1894, he renovated Cudahy's old facilities and soon became the city's second-leading packer.

Brewing supported nearly a dozen different manufacturers in 1889. Over time, the dozen yielded control to Pabst, Schlitz, and Miller, the "Big Three." By 1914, the city's breweries had more than doubled production to more than 4 million barrels annually. Pabst and Schlitz battled for national supremacy; Miller remained largely an also-ran. By 1892, Pabst passed the $10 million mark in capitalization, and 1 million barrels in production. From then until 1902, its Blue Ribbon brand was America's largest seller, and it owned the country's largest bottling plant and its first underground pipeline from cellar to bottling house. Its success derived from an unprecedented promotional campaign that included fashionable restaurants and "palm gardens" in Chicago, San Francisco, Minneapolis, and New York, but more so to the universal display of its slogan: "Milwaukee beer is famous—Pabst has made it so."[69]

Pabst soon lost its status as the nation's number-one beer to Schlitz, whose capitalization soared from $200,000 to $12 million between 1874 and 1903. Schlitz emulated Pabst in nationwide distribution and sales promotion, awarding 3,600 bottles to Admiral George Dewey and his men for their 1898 victory over the Spanish in the Battle of Manila Bay. When Pabst claimed that Robert E. Peary found a bottle of Blue Ribbon near the North Pole, Schlitz countered that its beer had gone to Africa with Theodore Roosevelt. So fierce was this competition that in 1898 they battled in court over their slogans' similarity. Pabst lost and reluctantly conceded Schlitz's right to boast: "The beer that made Milwaukee famous."[70]

---

[68] Still, *Milwaukee*, 334–335; Schefft, "The Tanning Industry," 64–71; Korman, *Industrialization, Immigrants, and Americanizers*, 21, 34, 181; Whitbeck, *Economic Development of Southeastern Wisconsin*, 109–111.

[69] Still, *Milwaukee*, 329–334; Whitbeck, *Geography and Industries of Southeastern Wisconsin*, 101–106; Cochran, *The Pabst Brewing Company*, 70–238.

[70] Still, *Milwaukee*, 330–333; Whitbeck, *Economic Development of Southeastern Wisconsin*, 102–103.

[3]

Two other southeastern cities, Racine and Kenosha, played satellite industrial roles to Chicago and Milwaukee. Racine, self-styled the Belle City, had achieved national prominence by the 1880's for threshing machines, wagons, and fanning mills, and it had built solid foundations in the foundry and machine shop, tanning, sash and door, luggage, and footwear industries. By 1890, the city turned out products valued at $8.5 million, and, despite the depression of 1893–1897, its manufacturing output rose by nearly half during the decade. It generated only 3.5 per cent of the state's manufacturing product value in 1900, but that was sufficient to rank it third among the nation's cities in agricultural implements and fourth in carriages and wagons, thanks to the J. I. Case Threshing Machine Company and the Mitchell & Lewis Wagon Works. In 1900, Racine's 190 factories employed some 5,000 workers. Fifteen years later, its capital investment had quadrupled, the labor force stood at 13,000, and product value had increased more than threefold to over $43 million.[71]

The rapid ascendancy of automobiles and their parts, electric and gas motors, iron and steel fabrication, and foundry and machine-shop products sparked this growth, while wagon, sash and door, fanning mill, and tanning industries declined. Two wagon makers, Racine Wagon & Carriage Company and Fish Brothers Wagon Works, both closed their doors before World War I; another, Mitchell & Lewis, merged with a local bicycle manufacturer, became Mitchell-Lewis Motor Car Company, and made automobiles. By adopting new high-speed precision machinery, the footwear and luggage industries grew nicely without increasing their work forces appreciably. Racine's dozen foundries expanded and modernized. The emergence of Hamilton Beach, Racine Electric, and the Dumore Company in the early 1910's established the city as a major manufacturer of fractional electric motors. Johnson's Wax, Horlick Malted Milk, and the Western Publishing Company also entered the national scene.

As the automobile industry boomed, Mitchell-Lewis achieved spectacular, though short-lived, success and became the city's largest employer between 1911 and 1915. Pierce-Racine, Case, and smaller manufacturers also got involved in automobiles and their parts, making them the city's third-largest industry, employing 1,500 people and turning out almost $6 million worth of product annually by 1919. Subsidiary industries included Walker Manufacturing (mufflers and jacks), Modine Manufacturing (radiators), Twin Disc Clutch, Racine

[71] Whitbeck, *Economic Development of Southeastern Wisconsin*, 162–173; Keehn, "Industry and Business," in Burckel, ed., *Racine*, 287–295; Hilton, "Men of Metal," 76–77.

Manufacturing (auto bodies), and two tire firms, Racine Auto and the Racine Rubber Company.[72]

These industries' impressive expansion and modernization were paced by the technological and organizational innovations of the J. I. Case Company, which had been Racine's defining industry since the 1840's. Case increased its capitalization from $2 million to $40 million between 1904 and 1912. Known initially for its threshing machines, Case diversified into traction engines, steam rollers, rock crushers, ensilage cutters, gang plows, tractors, and automobiles. Its new South Works, completed in 1913 and located on the lakeshore just south of the city limits, covered 114 acres and had a capacity of 30,000 tractors a year. By the end of World War I, Case's Main and South works together occupied 140 acres, employed 4,500 workers, and generated annual sales in excess of $30 million. Its vast marketing organization included eighty branch outlets: sixty-six in thirty American states, seven in Canada, and one each in Russia, France, Mexico, Argentina, Chile, and Brazil. Its extensive sales promotion and advertising operation featured railroad trains, called Case Specials, that carried threshing machines all over the Midwest, complete with a steam calliope to attract crowds. Competition prizes enhanced its reputation; between 1901 and 1913, for example, Case tractors won the most gold medals at the prestigious Winnipeg plowing contest.[73]

As Racine solidified its second-place manufacturing position in Wisconsin by altering its product base, Kenosha leaped to third place. It did not merely adapt; it reinvented its industrial system. The transformation began in 1886 when the Chicago Brass Company moved to Kenosha. In 1890, Kenosha was essentially a village of 6,500. Still, the Bain Wagon Company (founded in 1852) annually made 12,000 wagons, and the Allen tannery (1856) handled 200,000 sides of leather. During the depressed 1890's, the city's work force and product value both tripled, from 1,000 to 3,000 and $2.5 million to $7.5 million, making it Wisconsin's sixth-largest manufacturing center. In the decade of the 1900's, Kenosha's work force more than doubled. Its product value similarly increased, by 220 per cent, moving the city into third place. Altogether, between 1899 and 1919, the city's work force quadrupled, and its total product value grew by almost 600 per cent.

The auto industry, the Allen Tannery, the Simmons Mattress Company, and brass and clothing industries set the pace in Kenosha, led

---

[72] Whitbeck, *Economic Development of Southeastern Wisconsin*, 166–173; Keehn, "Industry and Business," in Burckel, ed., *Racine*, 290–295.

[73] Whitbeck, *Economic Development of Southeastern Wisconsin*, 173–175; Keehn, "Industry and Business," in Burckel, ed., *Racine*, 291–295; Holmes, *J. I. Case*, 25–45; Holbrook, *Machines of Plenty*, 108–120.

by Rambler automobiles. In 1902, the Jeffery Company, makers of Rambler bicycles, produced its first automobile, inaugurating what was to become the city's dominant business. By 1910, the company employed about a thousand workers and was turning out 2,273 automobiles and trucks a year. In 1914, production had surged to 13,513 before slumping by more than half over the next two years and placing Jeffery's heirs in dire financial straits. In July, 1916, they sold the company to Charles W. Nash, former president of General Motors, for $5 million. The new Nash corporation prospered immediately. It benefited from World War I government contracts, expanding to over 4,000 workers by 1920 and producing 35,000 automobiles and 3,700 trucks worth more than $57 million.[74]

Subsidiary to the Milwaukee-Racine-Kenosha industrial complex were the lakeshore manufacturing centers of Sheboygan, Manitowoc, and Marinette. Sheboygan trailed only the three southeastern counties in size of work force and product value, employing 60 per cent of its workers in manufacturing. It was a national center for plumbing supplies, furniture, and refrigerators, and it also made woodenware, ranging from beehives to pianos, as well as footwear, gloves, and clothing. Sheboygan also had Wisconsin's largest coal and salt docks.

Manitowoc (with neighboring Two Rivers) was the state's leading malt manufacturer, a pioneer in aluminum cookware, and Wisconsin's largest shipyard. Marinette, located at the confluence of the Menominee River and Green Bay on the Michigan state line, built upon its proximity to both forests and iron ore deposits. Its chief industry remained the processing of lumber and timber products, supplemented by a paper and wood-pulp plant and other wood-related businesses.[75]

The impact of the new industrialism on the Rock River Valley differed mostly in scale. The cities along the Rock and its tributaries, too, were industrialized, including such small places as Beaver Dam, Watertown, and Fort Atkinson, as well as Beloit, Janesville, and Madison. The valley itself formed a natural thoroughfare for railroad lines which linked it to Chicago and Rockford, the second-largest city in Illinois.

Beloit, on the Illinois border, had the valley's largest establishment by 1890: the Fairbanks, Morse and Company, founded in the 1830's,

---

[74] Whitbeck, *Economic Development of Southeastern Wisconsin*, 201–207; Noer, "Charles W. Nash," in Burckel and Neuenschwander, eds., *Kenosha*, 118–120; Keehn, "Industry and Business," in Burckel, ed., *Racine*, 174–185.

[75] *Census of Manufactures, 1914: Volume I, Reports by States with Statistics for Principal Cities and Metropolitan Districts*, 1640–1655; *Thirteenth Census of the United States, 1910, Occupational Statistics*, 269–273; *State Gazetteer and Business Directory*, 1915–1916, pp. 481–489, 1027–1028.

which made iron and steel products. The Beloit Iron Works, begun in the 1860's, turned out papermaking machinery for Fox Valley, Indiana, and Michigan mills, and achieved an international reputation for efficiency and quality. The Berlin Iron Works, which relocated from Green Lake County in 1893, manufactured woodworking tools and machinery for markets in Europe, Asia, and Africa as well as the United States. It employed 1,500 workers prior to the decline of midwestern lumbering.

Fairbanks, Morse—the result of an 1893 merger—manufactured steam and gas engines and power-transmission machinery. Between 1895 and 1911, it expanded its line to include tractors, mining engines, outboard motors, pneumatic hammers, and fiber-chopping machines. Constantly enlarging and modernizing its Beloit facilities, the company installed a three-motor crane that rivaled those at Allis-Chalmers, mechanizing virtually the entire materials-handling process.[76]

Janesville, just a few miles upriver from Beloit, was the only Rock River city to benefit substantially from its waterpower. Factories there made agricultural implements and machine tools. And its proximity to the tobacco fields of Rock and Dane counties led to the formation of cigar and cigarette companies. The Parker fountain pen company began in the 1880's and later earned Janesville a national and international reputation. The making of plows, threshers, reapers and other farm implements prepared it for a later role in automobile manufacturing. The city also had cotton and woolen mills which hired the highest percentage of women in the local work force.[77]

Madison, on the Yahara tributary of the Rock River, was not primarily a manufacturing center, but by 1893 it was already home to the Fuller and Johnson agricultural implement works and the Gisholt Machine Tool Company. Smaller companies made corsets, bicycles, cigars, beer, flour, soap, lumber, printing presses, socks and underwear, telephones, and harnesses. The city also was a regional railroad center whose yards and shops (the city's largest employer) stimulated local foundries and machine shops. Opposition by many of Madison's most prominent citizens retarded industrial development. They feared an adverse impact upon the atmosphere of state government and the university, but reached what came to be called "the Madison compromise," an informal agreement that limited manufacturing to

[76] John W. Alexander, "Geography of Manufacturing in the Rock River Valley" (doctoral dissertation, University of Wisconsin, 1949), 3–14, 43–54, 135–141, 161–191, 197–200; Hilton, "Men of Metal," 82–90; *State Gazetteer and Business Directory*, 1915–1916, pp. 180–181.

[77] Hollingsworth and Hollingsworth, *Dimensions in Urban History*, 78–83; *State Gazetteer and Business Directory*, 1915–1916, pp. 377–378; Hilton, "Men of Metal," 90–91.

"high grade factories" employing skilled workers, reduced air and noise pollution, and restricted new plants to the city's east side. Between 1900 and 1920, the industrial work force and the value of the city's output increased five times faster than its overall population. Fuller and Johnson passed the million-dollar mark in sales early in the century, establishing outlets in Europe, South America, and Australia. Similarly, after winning a gold medal for the quality of its lathes at the 1900 Paris World's Fair, the Gisholt company greatly expanded its facilities and its distribution network.

In Beaver Dam (Dodge County), local businessmen began the Malleable Iron Range Company in 1901. Plant capacity doubled in 1913 and the labor force increased to 500. Another industry, the Beaver Dam Malleable Iron Company, grew similarly. It constructed a fireproof foundry building in 1900, equipping it with three air furnaces, several pneumatic cranes, and numerous other technological innovations.[78]

Three hundred miles northwest of the Rock River Valley, the new industrialism boomed in Douglas and Ashland counties, mostly because of planning and underwriting by eastern capitalists. The transformation was truly dramatic. Superior's population soared from 12,000 to 40,000 between 1890 and 1910. Ashland County had only 1,559 residents in 1880; by 1887, the year the City of Ashland incorporated, the city alone had 11,594. Superior, founded in the 1850's, languished until the 1880's, when the Northern Pacific Railroad began to develop West Superior.

James J. Hill, the railroad's president, emerged as Superior's most powerful promoter and largest employer by the turn of the century. He made it the entrepôt for transshipping bulky goods between the Midwest and the Great Plains. In 1900, he built the world's biggest grain elevator there, and Superior suddenly became the second-largest primary wheat market in the country, trailing only Minneapolis. Hill also shipped iron ore eastward from the nearby Mesabi Range in Minnesota, constructing the world's largest ore dock in 1899 and operating a fleet of steel freighters between Buffalo and Superior. He was soon challenged by John D. Rockefeller, who also was interested in transshipment—for his petroleum and ore products.

Rockefeller opened the West Superior Iron & Steel Company and the American Steel Barge Company, maker of the "whaleback" ore freighters—football-shaped vessels that carried their cargoes largely below the waterline. Both Hill and Rockefeller envisioned Superior

---

[78] David V. Mollenhoff, *Madison: A History of the Formative Years* (Dubuque, 1982), 181–192, 264–276; *State Gazetteer and Business Directory*, 1915–1916, pp. 451–452; Larson, *John A. Johnson*, 128–205; Hilton, "Men of Metal," 90–91; Hollingsworth and Hollingsworth, *Dimensions in Urban History*, 78–83.

as a gateway to the Pacific ports and thence to Asia, motivating Rockefeller to construct a petroleum depot for products from his Standard Oil refinery in Whiting, Indiana. Besides these port facilities, by 1910 Superior also had nine coal docks, including the world's largest. Easterners owned virtually all of these enterprises or otherwise they were subsidiaries of nationwide corporations run by "outsiders."[79]

Local businessmen and real estate brokers also played roles in achieving growth. They organized clubs and associations and engaged in promotional efforts from the 1890's forward. The Chamber of Commerce, the Manufacturers', Shippers' and Jobbers' Association, and the Lake Superior Agricultural, Industrial, and Fine Arts Society sought to increase manufacturing through civic advertising. These boosters confidently expected that Superior would become Wisconsin's second city after Milwaukee. They worked for and subsidized flour mills, the American Steel Barge Company, the West Superior Iron and Steel Company, various lumber mills, and other manufacturing establishments. By 1895, Superior's manufacturing plants were worth nearly $7 million and 2,500 persons worked in them; the docks, railroads, and building trades employed another 3,000.[80]

[4]

To achieve these local success stories required far greater capital, and a much larger and more specialized work force, than most individual proprietors or partnerships could command. The neotechnic revolution was made possible by employing the strategy of legally incorporating companies as a means of organizing them. Corporations raised huge sums of capital through the sale of stock while guaranteeing investors limited financial and legal liability. Nationally, between 1904 and 1914, corporations increased their control over nearly every kind of manufacturing, ultimately accounting for more than 80 per cent of the nation's work force and product value, despite constituting only 28 per cent of its manufacturing firms.[81]

---

[79] McLeod, "The Development of Superior," 18–14; Helen M. Wolner, "The History of Superior, Wisconsin to 1900" (master's thesis, University of Wisconsin, 1939), 113–148; Kendall A. Birr, "Social Ideas of Superior Business Men, 1880–1898" (master's thesis, University of Wisconsin, 1948), 16–28.

[80] Birr, "Social Ideas of Superior Business Men," 108–160; Wolner, "History of Superior," 129–147.

[81] *Thirteenth Census of the United States, 1910: Census of Manufactures, 1914: Volume I,* 374, 390–391; Porter, *The Rise of Big Business,* 9–24; Mansel G. Blackford and K. Austin Kerr, *Business Enterprise in American History* (Boston, 1986), 163–164; Chandler, *The Visible Hand,* 285–314, 484–497.

Wisconsin corporations followed suit. They controlled 28 per cent of industrial firms by 1914, and about 90 per cent of the work force, product value, and value added by manufacturing. In Milwaukee the figures were even higher: 36 per cent of firms, and 90 per cent of employees and product value. In Kenosha, those figures were 33 and 97 per cent; in Racine, 50 and 95 per cent. Even though corporations were a numerical majority in only seven of Wisconsin's fifteen most important industries in 1914, they dominated the work force and product value of every one except dairy processing. Wisconsin's fifteen largest corporations each employed over 1,000 people, a total of 14 per cent of manufacturing workers. The average number of workers employed by Wisconsin manufacturing firms rose from thirteen to twenty-one between 1890 and 1914, but that figure increased to sixty-nine for corporations, and to 155 for companies generating over $100,000 worth of product.[82]

Barely 1 per cent of Wisconsin's manufacturing firms generated over $1 million by 1914. Even so, that 1 per cent employed one-third of the work force and turned out 44 per cent of product value and value added by manufacturing. The 11 per cent of companies doing over $100,000 worth of business accounted for at least 80 per cent in all three categories. Only 2.4 per cent of Milwaukee's manufacturers turned out a product worth over $1 million, but they employed about half the workers and produced three-fifths of total value. More than half Milwaukee's industrial workers labored in plants with over 250 employees, and one worker in five, for the seven local corporations employing over 1,000 people. Federal census compilers merely stated the obvious when they concluded that there was a clear trend in Wisconsin "for manufacturing to become concentrated in large establishments between 1904 and 1914." Ray Hughes Whitbeck, an economic geographer, agreed in 1913 that "the tendency of the age is . . . toward concentration whenever profits may thereby be increased."[83]

Seeking ever-increasing leverage over production, marketing, prices, and profits, Wisconsin corporations pursued both vertical and horizontal integration. Vertical integration meant internal consolidation of all activities, from the harvesting of raw materials to the selling and servicing of the ultimate consumer. For vertically inte-

---

[82] *Thirteenth Census of the United States, 1910: Census of Manufactures, 1914: Volume I*, 1339–1342; *Thirteenth Census of the United States, 1910: Abstract of the Census of Manufactures, 1914*, pp. 1629, 1641–1642; Edgar Z. Palmer, *The Prewar Industrial Pattern of Wisconsin*, UW Wisconsin Commerce Studies, vol. 1, no. 1 (Madison, 1947), 91–95; Korman, *Industrialization, Immigrants, and Americanizers*, 79–80.

[83] Korman, *Industrialization, Immigrants, and Americanizers*, 79; *Census of Manufactures, 1914: Volume I, Reports by States with Statistics for Principal Cities and Metropolitan Districts*, 1339–1342; Whitbeck, *Geography and Industries of Wisconsin*, 67.

grated firms, manufacturing a "full product line," establishing networks of regional, national, and international branches, and expanding operations into various extractive, transport, and marketing industries became standard practice. Wisconsin meat-packers, for example, took advantage of railway refrigeration and telecommunications to manage their own sales outlets in eastern cities. Manufacturers of automobiles practiced "forward" integration from the outset to ensure proper introduction, sales, and service of their totally new product; they also soon perceived the benefits of "backward" integration into the foundry and auto-parts industries. Manufacturers of agricultural implements, sewing machines, heavy industrial apparatus, and office equipment increasingly marketed their own products, because of the need for trained demonstrators, expert service, and consumer credit.[84]

Horizontal integration, on the other hand, involved the efforts of two or more corporations in the same industry to combat competition through pooling agreements, mergers, holding companies, trade associations, and what were commonly called "trusts." The astonishing increase in productivity generated by the new industrialism led to large surpluses in many industries, inducing price wars that tended to drive down consumer prices. (Indeed, between 1886 and 1890 the U.S. wholesale price index declined by 50 per cent.) To stem this downward trend, manufacturers experimented with combinations to fix prices, regulate production quotas, and allocate markets. Many newer industries, able to realize significant economies of scale through product standardization, worked through loose federations or holding companies. Many others participated in a wave of mergers between 1894 and 1905, during which more than 3,000 firms, which were capitalized at over $6 billion, amalgamated into several hundred super-corporations—among them United States Steel, International Harvester, and Allis-Chalmers.[85]

Inspired by such models, most Wisconsin manufacturers also sought to expand, using a blend of vertical and horizontal integration. In Milwaukee, the iron and steel works at Bay View, for example, became amalgamated step by step into the country's largest metals combine. The process began with their absorption by the North Chicago Rolling Mill Company in 1876. Thirteen years later, North Chicago merged with Joliet Steel to form Illinois Steel. Then, in 1898, Illinois Steel became part of J. P. Morgan's Federal Steel. Three years

---

[84] Porter, *The Rise of Big Business*, 43–54; Chandler, *The Visible Hand*, 287–314, 345–374; Peterson, *An Industrial Heritage*, 101–145; Holmes, *J. I. Case*, 42–48.

[85] Porter, *The Rise of Big Business*, 54–84; Chandler, *The Visible Hand*, 315–344; Blackford and Kerr, *Business Enterprise*, 174–179; Korman, *Industrialization, Immigrants, and Americanizers*, 78–80.

later, Federal Steel participated in the merger that produced United States Steel, a colossus that produced 65 per cent of the nation's steel. The E. P. Allis Company, a Milwaukee giant since the 1850's, merged in 1901 with Chicago and Pennsylvania manufacturers of heavy machinery and engines to form the Allis-Chalmers Corporation. The resulting combine employed 5,000 workers in five plants around the country, had offices in ten U.S. cities and overseas, and annually did over $10 million in business. It boasted a combined floor space of 3 million square feet on 175 acres of land. A year later, Milwaukee Harvester became part of the International Harvester combine. In 1911, the Bucyrus Company of South Milwaukee merged with Indiana's Vulcan Steam Shovel Company and the Atlantic Equipment Company, another Morgan affiliate, to form an organization capitalized at $10 million. And so it went with one firm after another in the first decades of the new century.[86]

As Wisconsin corporations grew stronger and yet dwindled in number, and as their connections with larger combines increased, regional and national trade associations multiplied and advanced in importance. Manufacturers of lumber, food, paper, and all manner of other goods protected their interests and enlarged their influence by leaguing together. For example, the American Foundrymen's Association, with affiliates in Milwaukee, Racine, and Beloit, directed and sponsored research in metals technology, then disseminated the results through its trade journal. It developed an industry-wide pricing system for castings, and railed against small competitors and outsiders. Its research arm, the American Society for Testing Materials, enforced standards nationally and acted as a watchdog. The association presented a united front against organized labor, pressed for advantageous railroad, tax, and insurance rates, and lobbied in Madison on relevant issues, from workers' compensation to industrial education. After 1900, a national coalition, the National Metal Trades Association, provided foundrymen with a vehicle to defend the open shop and to fend off unions and reformers.[87]

Because it quickly became obvious that concerted political action paid benefits, manufacturers and businessmen founded local and state trade associations around the turn of the century. The Wisconsin Manufacturers' Association was formed in 1901 by representatives of over seventy industrial companies in twenty-six cities. Its leaders

---

[86] Korman, *Industrialization, Immigrants, and Americanizers*, 78–80; Still, *Milwaukee*, 337–340; Peterson, *An Industrial Heritage*, 101–145; Williamson and Myers, *Designed for Digging*, 48–118; Marsh, *A Corporate Tragedy*, 35–48; W. O. Hotchkiss, "Geography and Industries of Wisconsin," in the *Wisconsin Blue Book, 1925*, pp. 40–42.

[87] Hilton, "Men of Metal," 56–60, 110–124; Korman, *Industrialization, Immigrants, and Americanizers*, 80, 176.

came from larger industries all over the state. Legislative proposals to increase the tax on railroad property and to regulate service and rates provided the immediate impetus to organize. The association lobbied vigorously against such regulatory and taxation measures, and worked to defeat or modify labor and welfare legislation. It supported industrial education, both in public schools and factories, so long as manufacturers themselves could design and supervise their operation. And it fought income taxation, which was bruited about by Wisconsin progressives from the 1890's onward.

The Wisconsin Bankers' Association (WBA), founded in the late 1850's as a kind of gentleman's club, involved itself in politics during the 1893–1897 depression, when the high rate of bank failures demonstrated the inadequacy of self-regulation. The WBA lobbied to create the office of state bank examiner and for stricter regulation of private and marginally solvent banks. At its 1902 convention, one delegate boasted that "you will not find one single act affecting banks which passed where the banks were not the authors of the act and desired its passage." The WBA also campaigned against deposit insurance, branch banking, and bank taxation. Like many other similar associations, it consistently attacked both organized labor and socialism.[88]

The Milwaukee Chamber of Commerce, an outgrowth of the Grain Exchange, became the primary advocate of the city's commercial interests. In 1897, it successfully petitioned the Interstate Commerce Commission to grant Milwaukee railroad shipping rates comparable to those awarded Chicago and Minneapolis. Its spokesmen broke ranks with the state's manufacturers by favoring state rather than federal rate regulation, but characteristically joined with them in denouncing income taxation, organized labor, and socialism. The chief advocate of Milwaukee's prodigious industrial interests was the Merchants' and Manufacturers' Association of Milwaukee (MMAM), founded in 1894. Originally interested in civic affairs and in securing favorable transportation and insurance rates for city businesses, the MMAM evolved into an implacable foe of the "closed" or union shop and into a highly effective lobbyist, through representatives of the city's biggest manufacturers. The MMAM exerted formidable pres-

---

[88] Stanley P. Caine, *The Myth of a Progressive Reform: Railroad Regulation in Wisconsin, 1903–1910* (Madison, 1970), 30–36, 78, 112; W. Elliot Brownlee, Jr., *Progressivism and Economic Growth: The Wisconsin Income Tax, 1911–1929* (Port Washington, New York, 1974), 41–87; Herbert F. Margulies, *The Decline of the Progressive Movement in Wisconsin, 1890–1920* (Madison, 1968), 136–140; Industrial Commission, *Biennial Report*, 1912–1914, pp. 3–11; Theodore A. Andersen, *A Century of Banking in Wisconsin* (Madison, 1954), 85–101; Wisconsin Bankers' Association, *Proceedings*, 1895, n.p.; 1896, pp. 13–14, 100–101; 1897, pp. 24, 85–87; 1898, pp. 60–61; 1902, pp. 38–45, 76 (quote); 1906, pp. 31–33; 1912, p. 131.

sure—usually negative—on laws or proposed legislation affecting industrial education and apprenticeship, workers' compensation for industrial accidents, factory health and safety, minimum wages, and maximum hours. It espoused charity for the "worthy poor," eulogized the "yeoman farmer" and the "self-made man," and insisted that the welfare of the working class should be entrusted to employers, rather than to unions or state government.[89]

Expansion and consolidation also transformed Wisconsin's railroads—the state's first truly big business and the network that linked the various elements of the new industrialism. Railroads readily assimilated the new technology of steel, electricity, and gasoline, which resulted in faster, more powerful engines pulling longer, heavier trains. Between 1880 and 1915, total track mileage in Wisconsin grew from 3,120 to 7,550, completing a system that connected all parts of the state from the manufacturing centers of the southeast to the north and northwest. Three railroad complexes owned or controlled more than four-fifths of that trackage: the North Western and Omaha lines together, 2,951 miles (39 per cent); the Milwaukee Road, 1,805 miles (24 per cent); and the Soo Line, which included the old Wisconsin Central tracks, 1,395 miles (18 per cent). The 1914 railroad picture resulted from a half century of consolidation and more than 100 smaller lines, many of which had been financed originally by local investors and local, state, and federal governments. Grants of public land to the railroads totaled nearly 3 million acres, representing roughly one-twelfth of Wisconsin's land mass. Sales of this land by the railroads provided much of the necessary capital to build them, a circumstance which railroad men did not regard as welfare or state socialism.[90]

---

[89] Hilton, "Men of Metal," 111–124; Korman, *Industrialization, Immigrants, and Americanizers*, 124–130, 177–184; Margulies, *The Decline of the Progressive Movement*, 195; Robert S. Maxwell, *La Follette and the Rise of the Progressives in Wisconsin* (Madison, 1956), 157–158; Merchants' and Manufacturers' Association of Milwaukee, *Bulletin*, May, 1906, p. 14; November, 1906, pp. 24–26; February 1, 1909, pp. 16–17; April, 1909, p. 15; December, 1909, p. 8; April–May, 1910, pp. 14–16; December, 1910, p. 12; February, 1911, pp. 19–20; March, 1911, p. 15; May, 1911, p. 14; October 6, 1911, p. 10; February, 1912, p. 8; April, 1912, p. 9; October, 1913, p. 15; February 1, 1915, p. 21; Minutes, Board of Directors, vol. 14, July 22, 1907, December 17, 1908; vol. 16, January 14 and September 5, 1896, February 9, 1897, August 8, September 13, 17, and November 14, 1899, all in the Milwaukee Grain Exchange Records, 1849–1976, Milwaukee Area Research Center.

[90] Caine, *The Myth of a Progressive Reform*, 3–6; James P. Kaysen, comp., *The Railroads of Wisconsin, 1827–1937* (Boston, 1937), 4–6, 8–13, 20–26, 53–55, 64–67; Roy L. Martin, *History of the Wisconsin Central* (Boston, 1941), 98–144; William F. Raney, "The Building of Wisconsin Railroads," in *WMH*, 19 (June, 1936), 387–403; "Railroad Mileage in Wisconsin," *Wisconsin Blue Book, 1913*, pp. 562–563; Railroad Commission, *Annual Report*, 1915, pp. 854–855.

From their inception, Wisconsin's railroads had been involved in state politics, and by the late 1800's had evolved into what was virtually a government within the government. Between 1850 and 1890, railroad companies acquired the status of a semi-autonomous agent of public policy which parceled out favors, defined spheres of interest, and, in effect, set its own rules for the development and governance of Wisconsin. They had a diverse political constituency which depended on them: a battalion of lobbyists, regiments of lawyers, and an army of politicians, all eager to curry favor. The Wisconsin constitution prohibited the state from incurring bonded indebtedness to finance public works, and legislators were loath to exercise their powers to tax. So they continually enticed railroad entrepreneurs with the prospect of untrammeled profit.[91]

The railroads had forged a natural partnership with the lumbering industry that redounded to their mutual advantage. The lumber companies acquired huge surplus tracts of timber from the railroad's land grants, and they invested their profits in railroad construction and operation. Both lumbermen and railroad men profited from land speculation and from shipping, wholesaling, and retailing of lumber products; both opposed state regulation and taxation. Lumbermen virtually controlled politics in the northern part of the state; opposition newspapers, with some truth, referred to certain counties as the property of lumber companies. In some towns, lumber barons controlled newspapers and banks, rigged elections, and routinely bought public officials. Many eventually became officeholders themselves, discovering (as Marinette baron Isaac Stephenson recounted) that "[f]rom the building of roads, the carrying out of public improvements, and the regulation of general affairs as manager of the mill, it was but a short step to membership on the county board"— or even the United States Senate, where Stephenson served from 1907 to 1915. The duties of public service Stephenson accepted as "a matter of course, as I would have done them whether I had held office or not." Lumbermen kept in close touch with their state representatives, hired and financed the activities of lobbyists, and lobbied personally in Madison.

Railroad and lumber magnates were at the zenith of their power in the 1890's, and while they were soon to be displaced and overshadowed by new manufacturing corporations and utility companies, they still possessed, and had grown used to wielding, near-absolute power in the political arena. When thwarted, they took it hard, as when Congressman William Thompson Price of Black River Falls

---

[91] Caine, *The Myth of a Progressive Reform*, 3–6; Robert S. Hunt, *Law and Locomotives: The Impact of the Railroad on Wisconsin Law in the Nineteenth Century* (Madison, 1958), 32–43, 167–175; Margulies, *The Decline of the Progressive Movement*, 47.

apologized for his relative ineffectiveness in Washington. Price was a railroad and lumbering man who had served in both the state assembly and senate. Washington flummoxed him. About Congress, he wrote home, "This is *not* so easy a place to get what one wants as is the Wisconsin legislature."[92]

Perhaps Congressman Price, a minor cog in Wisconsin's business-dominated political machine, sensed the winds of change blowing in both Madison and Washington. Perhaps he understood that the escalating demands for a variety of socio-economic "reforms" signaled the formation of widespread and increasingly effective opposition to the hegemony of the business coalition that had dominated the public arena since the Civil War. A growing number of Wisconsinites were advocating a wide variety of measures designed to curtail corporate influence in politics and government. Many others were pressing for ways to cope with the rise of big business, whether by public ownership, government regulation, or outright "trust-busting." Some were demanding alterations in the tax system that would end corporate tax-dodging and promote "tax equity." Others, alarmed by the impact of industrialization on Wisconsin's forests, waters, and air, were demanding state government leadership in the conservation and revitalization of natural resources.

Yet even had Congressman Price possessed some inkling of the pressure that was building, it seems certain that neither he, nor anyone else in Wisconsin, could have foreseen the magnitude, the fury, or the duration of the Progressive storm that was soon to break.

---

[92] Fries, *Empire in Pine*, 221–227 (quote); Caine, *Myth of a Progressive Reform*, 5–6; Hurst, *Law and Economic Growth*, 9–12, 47–92; Isaac Stephenson, *Recollections of a Long Life, 1829–1915* (Chicago, 1915), 150, 190 (quote).

4

Urbanism, Crisis, and Reform

[1]

SPEAKING in Boston in December of 1889, Richard T. Ely proclaimed, "Every new good road, every new canal, every new railway, every new invention, every economic improvement, in short, nearly all industrial progress centralizes the population in cities." With these words, the future University of Wisconsin economist effectively portrayed the demographic trend that was already dominating Wisconsin, and the entire country, and would continue to do so throughout the next three decades.[1]

The new industrialism was transforming Wisconsin's social order as well as its economic life, drawing larger and larger numbers of people to the state's cities. Proliferation of industry near waterfronts and railroad lines, combined with innovations in construction and mass transportation, were causing both inner-city congestion and urban sprawl. People accordingly segregated themselves and were being segregated along socio-economic and ethno-cultural lines. The mobility and instability of city life accelerated dizzyingly. Demands for municipal services escalated, then gave rise to conflicts over how, by whom, where, and in what order they would be delivered and paid for. Scores of municipal reform movements—differing widely in composition, motivation, program, and effectiveness—swept Wisconsin cities and inundated the legislature. Cities exerted a gravitational pull upon their hinterlands, becoming concentrated centers of specialized activity for and within larger and evolving metropolitan areas. The larger and more articulated the city, the wider its range of influence and the stronger its attractive power.

Cities in close proximity to one another—such as Beloit and Janes-

---

[1] Richard T. Ely, *The Needs of the City: An Address Delivered Before the Boston Conference of the Evangelical Alliance, December 4, 1889* (n.p., n.d.), p. 7, in box 7, folder 6D, Richard T. Ely Papers.

ville, Racine and Kenosha, Appleton and Oshkosh—vied for control of the hinterlands that divided them. By 1920, this process had blurred much of the distinction between "urban" and "rural," forging an ecological continuum that still urbanizes most of the state, as well as linking Wisconsin with an evolving regional and national network that just as continuously urbanizes the entire United States.[2]

Throughout the nineteenth century, Wisconsin was consistently more industrialized yet less urbanized than the nation as a whole. But in the long run, these two processes operated symbiotically: industry's growth in size and importance generated geographical concentrations of workers, consumers, and service providers; the urban infrastructure and services needed by these concentrated populations stimulated industry.[3]

In 1890, about one-third of Wisconsin's citizens lived in what the federal census bureau termed "urban places" of 2,500 or more; the national figure was 35 per cent. However, almost 42 per cent resided in the state's 206 officially incorporated cities and villages, many of which had fewer than 2,500 residents. Both federal and state calculations were somewhat arbitrary and political. But the state's numbers probably distinguished more precisely between persons engaged in agricultural and nonagricultural occupations. By the state's measure, over 38 per cent of her citizens lived in 108 "cities," ranging from Buffalo County's tiny Buffalo with its 223 residents, to Milwaukee's 204,468. Wisconsin's second-largest city was La Crosse, with just over 25,000 residents, followed by Oshkosh (22,836) and Racine (21,014). Only seven other cities had populations over 10,000, not including Green Bay, whose twin-city status with Fort Howard finally ended in 1895 when the two merged. Fourteen more exceeded 5,000. In only ten counties did urban residents outnumber rural. Milwaukee County and Douglas County (with Superior) hovered around the 90 per cent mark. Winnebago (Oshkosh), Lincoln (Merrill and Tomahawk), La Crosse, Eau Claire, and Racine counties surpassed 65 per cent. Milwaukee County had 1,447 persons per square mile; Racine, 141; Winnebago, 106; and Sheboygan, 99. Only fifteen other coun-

---

[2] See, for example, William Cronon, *Nature's Metropolis: Chicago and the Great West* (New York, 1991), 5–19, 371–385; Roger D. Simon, "The City-Building Process: Housing and Services in New Milwaukee Neighborhoods, 1880–1910," in the *Transactions of the American Philosophical Society*, vol. 68, pt. 5, (Philadelphia, 1978), 5–8, 10–25, 53–71; David R. Goldfield and Blaine A. Brownell, *Urban America: From Downtown to No Town* (Boston, 1990), 1–9, 178–233; and Michael P. Conzen, *Frontier Farming in an Urban Shadow: The Influence of Madison's Proximity on the Agricultural Development of Blooming Grove, Wisconsin* (Madison, 1971).

[3] Guy-Harold Smith, "The Settlement and the Distribution of the Population of Wisconsin," in the *Transactions of the Wisconsin Academy of Sciences, Arts and Letters*, 24 (1929), 83–95.

ties, nearly all in the state's southeastern quadrant, had as many as fifty people per square mile.

Wisconsin had ninety-eight "villages," which ran the gamut from the Juneau County communities of Camp Douglas, with 225 people, to Necedah, with 1,708. Statewide, villages contained only 3 per cent of the population, and but 7 per cent of its total in officially incorporated communities.[4]

All of Wisconsin's urban places in the early 1890's were essentially "walking cities," meaning that in thirty minutes most residents could reach their centers on foot from almost any point within their legal boundaries. As late as 1891, even Milwaukee encompassed only seventeen square miles—less than half the size of a township. About one-third of its population lived within a mile of Third Street and Wisconsin Avenue; only about 17 per cent lived as far as three miles away. Madison (population 13,426 in 1890) occupied a mere 4.7 square miles between 1880 and 1900. The western city limits of Racine and Kenosha were only two miles from Lake Michigan, and their shorelines extended less than three miles north and south. Each city's central business district had emerged out of the original townsite plat. These downtowns contained virtually all of the necessities and amenities, including government offices, businesses, financial institutions, factories, warehouses, transportation terminals, churches, schools, theaters, restaurants, and hotels, all of which competed for precious space. They formed a crazy-quilt pattern on the landscape, an "offensive stew of factories, furnaces, and warehouses jumbled across a tangle of streets, alleys, canals and railroads."

Even those residents whose resources permitted them to live anywhere generally preferred to reside within a brisk walk, or a pleasant carriage ride, from these beehives of activity. Everyone else, from the upper middle class to the indigent, lived cheek by jowl in the potpourri of dwellings in and around the city's core. People from all social classes, occupations, and ethnic groups could scarcely avoid crossing each others' paths and attracting each others' attention.[5]

---

[4] *Eleventh Census of the United States, 1890: Compendium, Part I, Population*, 357–367; "Population of Wisconsin," in the *Wisconsin Blue Book, 1901*, pp. 455–498; Smith, "Settlement and Distribution," *Transactions of the Wisconsin Academy*, 24: 95–96.

[5] Simon, "City-Building Process," *Transactions of the American Philosophical Society*, 68: 11; Bayrd Still, *Milwaukee: The History of a City* (Madison, 1948; reprinted, 1965), 380–381, 595–598; David V. Mollenhoff, *Madison: A History of the Formative Years* (Dubuque, 1982), 195–201; Racine Department of Traffic and Lighting, *Annexation Map: The Growth of Racine, 1962*, no. 215, at the University of Wisconsin-Parkside Area Research Center, Kenosha; Harland K. Bartholomew and Kenosha City Planning Department, map no. 138, *Growth of the City in Area, 1925*, at the University of Wisconsin-Parkside Area Research Center, Kenosha. The characterization of the working city as an "of-

The level of municipal services in Wisconsin and elsewhere in 1890 ranged from nonexistent to barely adequate. They were in a constant state of improvement from the 1880's forward and had been almost wholly transformed by about 1915. In 1890, most streets, especially those outside the central business districts, were unpaved—41 per cent in Milwaukee, 88 per cent in La Crosse, 93 per cent in Oshkosh, and 96 per cent in Racine. Paving consisted of wooden or stone blocks, bricks, broken stone, gravel, and forms of asphalt. Sidewalks were generally made of wooden planks, except in certain downtown areas, where they might be brick, macadam, or another form of asphalt. Wisconsin cities over 10,000 population drew their water mostly from rivers and lakes; only Appleton, Fond du Lac, Madison, and Janesville had central artesian wells, and only Milwaukee, Sheboygan, and La Crosse had city-owned systems. Gas works were all privately owned and operated; city governments purchased the energy to illuminate their street lamps, mostly using electric arc lamps, but also gas, oil, and "vapor." Electric street lighting had appeared in the 1880's and was quickly coming to dominate. Customer rates varied widely, and service deteriorated during periods of peak use.

Cities were beginning to build government buildings, and by 1890, six of Wisconsin's eleven 10,000-plus communities had city halls (only three had had them in 1880). Public sewers, too, were becoming more common. Only Janesville had none in 1890, and it continued to lag in 1900 with less than two miles of sewer line. But the availability of sewers did not mean that households or institutions employed them. Wastes from toilets, laundries, kitchens, and factories still were haphazardly disposed of in privy vaults or cesspools. Outside Milwaukee, which employed 300 garbage collectors by 1903, householders or private contractors usually removed garbage, ashes, and dead animals. Municipal governments had assumed responsibility for street cleaning and public health, but their efforts were usually minimal and enforcement of regulations was sporadic. Almost no cities except Milwaukee had refuges or hospitals for persons with communicable or contagious conditions. Vaccinations were largely voluntary and at personal expense, and quarantining was the most common measure to prevent epidemics. Only fire and police protection and education were clearly municipal responsibilities, and even these seldom kept up with escalating needs.[6]

---

fensive stew" is that of urban historian Joseph Arnold, quoted in Raymond A. Mohl, *The New City: Urban America in the Industrial Age, 1860–1920* (Arlington Heights, Illinois, 1985), 28–29.

[6] *Eleventh Census of the United States, 1890: Report on the Social Statistics of Cities*, 22–23, 29–30, and tables 63–70; Mollenhoff, *Madison*, 134–135; *Tenth Census of the United*

The level of municipal services in Milwaukee was appreciably higher than in the state's other cities, but they were still in the early stages of development. By 1888, the police and fire departments were of sufficient size and professionalism, and supplied with enough modern equipment, to meet the city's needs. In 1889, it had 220 miles of improved streets; in 1890, the total had risen to 249; by 1903, to 397, an indication of the constantly changing urban picture. Even with 165 miles of sewers, built at a cost of over $2 million by 1888, concerns about pollution of the water supply fueled agitation for additional construction, and 357 miles of sewers were in place by 1903. The high cost of electric lighting, supplied by private contractors, was also becoming a political issue.

Although educational expenditures had increased sixfold in the 1870's and 1880's, the city's thirty-seven schools were still overcrowded. Its board of health, begun in the late 1860's, could not cope with serious public health problems when they arose. The public library and the public museum had become city responsibilities in 1878 and 1882, respectively. A park commission had been established in 1889, with a $100,000 appropriation to get things going. Though more advanced than other Wisconsin cities in municipal services in 1890, Milwaukee still was merely at a halfway point in its development of social responsibility.[7]

The tendency towards residential dispersion that was arising in the state's centralized "walking" cities during the 1890's stemmed from the push of industrialization, in combination with the pull of improved mass transit. The new industrialism's machines required ever-larger factories and warehouses, built near water and rail transportation. Profits from industrial land eclipsed other real estate returns, inducing landowners to convert as much urban space as they could to industrial use. The industrial city steadily displaced its commercial predecessor, which had been a relatively desirable place to live. But intensifying noise, congestion, and environmental pollution rendered the central city increasingly unpleasant. Those who could afford it created elite enclaves on the city fringes. Housing for factory workers began filling up the residential space within walking distance of the factory and warehouse districts. An expanding middle class of

---

States, 1880: Report on the Social Statistics of Cities, Part II, the Southern and the Western States, 641–686; Lawrence H. Larsen, "Urban Services in Gilded Age Wisconsin," in *WMH*, 71 (Winter, 1987–1988), 83–114.

[7] *Tenth Census of the United States, 1880: Report on the Social Statistics of Cities, Part II, the Southern and the Western States*, 660–677; Still, *Milwaukee*, 356–395; Larsen, "Urban Services," in *WMH*, 71: 83–114; Roger D. Simon, "The Expansion of an Industrial City: Milwaukee, 1880–1910" (doctoral dissertation, University of Wisconsin, 1971), 105–121.

skilled craftsmen and white-collar managers, professionals, and clerks gravitated to neighborhoods between the two extremes.[8]

Retreat from the industrial city's core depended primarily on transportation technology. Initially, slow and unreliable horse-drawn omnibuses were all that was available. Then horses or mules pulled somewhat larger passenger vehicles over fixed tracks along major urban streets—a railway system. These "horse cars" carried more passengers, provided a more comfortable ride, traveled at speeds of up to eight miles per hour, and cost a nickel to ride. They gave rise to commuting, enabling riders to live farther than before from their places of employment. By 1882, Milwaukee had three privately owned street railway companies which together had thirty-three miles of track, 610 horses, 200 workers, and carried 4 million passengers annually.[9]

Large-scale dispersion of city housing occurred with the introduction of electric trolleys and railways. Trolleys more than doubled practical commuting distances. They could carry greater numbers of passengers at speeds of up to thirty miles per hour, at fares equal to, and sometimes less than, that of their horse-drawn predecessors'. Milwaukee's first electric trolley ran down Wells Street on April 3, 1890. Some feared that electricity was dangerous, but by September of 1891, a correspondent to the Milwaukee *Journal* thanked "divine providence" for "electricity as a mode of transit" because it allowed one to "slide through the city like a grease[d] pig through a lasso, . . . and return to your starting point in less than an hour."[10]

In Wisconsin cities, as elsewhere, electric trolley systems became "urban sculptors," changing the standard notions of how cities could look and where people could live. They expedited creation of residential sectors several miles from a city's center, each of which could encompass approximately four blocks on either side of a right-of-way or beyond a line's terminus. Streetcars effectively quadrupled a city's potential area, providing residents of new neighborhoods with cheap and quick access to the amenities that continued to lie almost entirely

---

[8] Simon, "The Expansion of an Industrial City," 62–89; Goldfield and Brownell, *Urban America*, 185–204; Mohl, *The New City*, 53–66; Still, *Milwaukee*, 379–381; Mollenhoff, *Madison*, 264–276.

[9] *Tenth Census of the United States, 1880: Report on the Social Statistics of Cities, Part II, the Southern and the Western States*, 651, 657, 667, 684; Still, *Milwaukee*, 248–249, 368, 370; Mollenhoff, *Madison*, 60, 135, 201–202, 215–216; Clay McShane, *Technology and Reform: Street Railways and the Growth of Milwaukee, 1887–1900* (Madison, 1974), 4, 7–11, 19, 23, 52–78, 84, 103, 113; Mohl, *The New City*, 29–33; Joseph M. Canfield, *TM: The Milwaukee Electric Railway & Light Company* (Chicago, 1972), 13–25.

[10] Still, *Milwaukee*, 369–379 (quote); McShane, *Technology and Reform*, 1–39, 65–83; Canfield, *TM*, 17–21.

within the city's nucleus. They also linked city centers more efficiently with outlying communities; visitors from these areas, too, could take the trolleys downtown once they reached the outskirts. Trolleys quickly evolved into electric interurban railway systems which connected strings of communities, like those around the southern end of Lake Michigan, a system which considerably broadened residential options in southeastern Wisconsin.[11]

In Madison, the electric trolley made its debut on October 1, 1892. By 1897, Madison traction lines had put 1,815 acres of new residential land within a fifteen-minute ride of the Capitol Square for just ten cents a day. And by 1901, about 3,000 riders made the trek downtown daily, where businesses occupied all the land around the square and the streets connecting the North Western depot with the university and the capitol building. Property values along the streetcar lines rose as much as 45 per cent, deflating expectations that some outlying lots might be used for low-cost housing. Between 1900 and 1920, some 10,000 building lots were developed outside Madison's core, and nearly 1,100 acres were added to its tax rolls.[12]

In Milwaukee, topography and patterns of economic development frustrated the Milwaukee *Sentinel*'s optimism about electric traction. Wrote the *Sentinel*, "This makes it possible for all classes of people to live far away from the close quarters, bad air, smoke and bustle of the business part." The confluence of the Milwaukee, Menomonee, and Kinnikinnic rivers divided the city into three distinct sections, a division reinforced by the placement of railroad yards, warehouses, and manufacturing plants. Although the central business district remained the commercial hub, its primacy was offset by the development of industrial zones in Bay View, the Menomonee Valley, and the northern banks of the Milwaukee River, as well as by new secondary commercial districts along Fond du Lac Avenue on the west side, North Avenue on the northeast side, and Lincoln Avenue on the south side. Each of these three districts was virtually self-contained, reducing the importance of the central district to those who lived in them. Thus housing could be expanded significant distances from the city's center without making residents reliant upon mass transit.

Accordingly, electric trolley lines concentrated on moving people from middle-class residential areas, not working-class, to and from the central business district. There was no direct service from outly-

---

[11] Mohl, *The New City*, 34–40; Simon, "The Expansion of an Industrial City," 122–162. The classic study of the impact of mass transit upon urban expansion and congestion is Sam Bass Warner, Jr., *Streetcar Suburbs: The Process of Growth in Boston, 1870–1900* (Cambridge, 1962).

[12] Mollenhoff, *Madison*, 201–204, 216–217, 273, 358–359; Warner, *Streetcar Suburbs*, 46–66.

ing locations to the industrial Menomonee Valley and Bay View areas, and there were no crosstown lines except on North Avenue. Also, the fares were too high for most unskilled and semiskilled laborers. Working-class connections to downtown were further weakened by several new industrial suburbs established between 1892 and 1906, including Cudahy, West Allis, and North, West, and South Milwaukee. Most either provided working-class housing or were only a brief trolley ride from the residential south side's commercial district—in the opposite direction from downtown Milwaukee. As a result, by 1902 Milwaukee ranked third in the nation in population density, fifteenth in persons per dwelling, and twenty-first in streetcar rides per inhabitant.[13]

In Racine, mass transit mileage almost doubled between 1883 and 1919, an index to development. Electrified in 1892, the transit system soon became part of a holding company controlled by The Milwaukee Electric Railway and Light Co. (TMER&L), the most significant utility in the state. Construction of north-side lines led to annexation of almost ninety square blocks in 1911. New trolley service to the west, combined with the start of the North Shore electric commuter railway between Milwaukee and Chicago, made West Racine development possible. It was a middle-class residential and secondary commercial area annexed to the city in 1911 and 1918. To the south, extension of trolley service and the construction of the J. I. Case South Works spurred working- and middle-class enclaves and other annexations.

In Kenosha, trolley service developed concurrently with the city, whose land area tripled between 1894 and 1918. Mass transit efforts dated from 1896, but did not materialize until 1903. By 1912, the company had become a subsidiary of another TMER&L component, the Wisconsin Gas and Electric Company. Its branch trolley lines extended nearly thirty blocks west, to the rapidly expanding Jeffery-Nash automobile manufacturing compound, and some twenty blocks south, passed the brass factory complex.[14]

---

[13] Still, *Milwaukee*, 340, 370, 378–381; Simon, "City-Building Process," *Transactions of the American Philosophical Society*, 68: 10–15; McShane, *Technology and Reform*, 65–83; Milwaukee *Sentinel*, November 1, 1891; Arnold Fleischmann, "The Territorial Expansion of Milwaukee: Historical Lessons for Contemporary Urban Policy and Research," in the *Journal of Urban History*, 14 (February, 1988), 148–150.

[14] "Map of the City of Racine," in Hennessey & Co., *Plat Book of Racine and Kenosha Counties, Wisconsin* (Delavan, 1908), 48–61, 68–77; Canfield, *TM*, 118–130, 133, 140. The discussion of Racine and Kenosha is based partly on information contained in two unpublished seminar papers in the Area Research Center of the University of Wisconsin-Parkside: Barbara Schwaiger, "The History of Streetcars in Kenosha and Racine" (1977), and Patricia A. McGray, "The History of Streetcars in Racine, Wisconsin" (1987).

But even as Wisconsin's largest cities were adapting to the electric trolley, a more powerful urban sculptor confronted them: the automobile. The new "horseless carriage" redefined notions of space and time in the first decade of the twentieth century, just as trolleys had ten years before. Not bound to tracks or overhead electrical wires, the automobile extended residential commuting distances by several miles, helping to fill the residential interstices between trolley lines. Automobiles made their first appearance on Milwaukee streets in the late 1880's; by 1913 there were already 3,608. As was the case elsewhere, automobiles were owned primarily by the affluent. The Madison experience was typical. The first automobile, powered by steam, "snorted" along its streets "as though it was a wild animal escaped from the jungle" in 1900; three years later the city still had only eight. By 1916 there were more autos than horses in the city, and one household in eight possessed the new contraption. This proliferation made subdivisions possible as much as five miles from the Capitol Square and three miles from the nearest trolley line. By 1912, their developers introduced twenty passenger motor buses, which charged double the fare of streetcars.[15]

[2]

These transportation revolutions unleashed both centrifugal and centripetal forces. They gave rise to annexations in developing sectors and to scattered secondary commercial districts. They sorted out urban land use into industrial, commercial, residential, storage, transportation, and governmental areas, lending impetus to demands for zoning and planning. They segregated residential areas along socioeconomic and ethno-cultural lines, according to a complex calculus of housing and transportation costs, group enclaving, discriminatory practices, and personal choice. They heightened mobility and instability, as people moved in and out of, and around within, the city. Innovations in construction technology stepped up congestion in central business districts. Before the late 1880's, existing materials kept buildings under ten stories in height. Then came steel, poured concrete reinforced with steel rods, and electric elevators. Steel beams, rivets, and reinforced concrete subfloors made possible taller, sturdier, and lighter buildings with more interior space and more windows. Electric-powered elevators and lighting systems made the

---

[15] Mollenhoff, *Madison*, 359–368; Still, *Milwaukee*, 553; McShane, *Technology and Reform*, 36–37.

new skyscrapers practical. Wisconsin cities received such buildings relatively late, but neighboring Chicago set the pace nationally.[16]

These transportation and construction innovations were adopted largely through realtors, developers, transit companies, and politicians, all of whom had a vested interest in urban expansion. Transportation connections raised property values; population dispersion and aggregation profited transit companies. Promoters and developers sponsored excursions to recreation and amusement parks to increase ridership, while traction companies designed fare schedules to benefit residents of new developments. Politicians, developers, transit companies, and financial institutions shared a common interest in long-term franchises, minimal regulation, increased property values, rising transportation revenues, and "watered" stock.

In Milwaukee, the Chamber of Commerce, the Merchants' and Manufacturers' Association, the Citizens' Business League, and similar organizations constantly stimulated expansion. They sponsored annual industrial expositions, led promotional junkets, established an information bureau, and founded an advisory committee on commercial and general welfare. That committee evolved into the Association for the Advancement of Milwaukee, which worked to attract manufacturers, using incentives like low rent, free building sites, and subscription of capital.[17]

By contrast, Madison restrained industrial promotion because many influential citizens wanted the city to retain its identity as a university town and the capital. Many, but not all. In 1900, a *Wisconsin State Journal* editorial, "Wake up, Madison, wake up," inspired proindustry boosters to form an association that attracted an estimated 75,000 visitors in 1900. The following year, boosters organized the Forty Thousand Club, whose goal was to more than double Madison's population to 40,000 by 1910. Although it fell short by 15,000 persons, the club secured a significant amount of industry. Its successor, the Board of Commerce, engineered the "Madison Compromise," in which opponents of industrial development acquiesced. It limited factories to the east side (the university occupied the west side) and

---

[16] Alan I. Marcus and Howard P. Segal, *Technology in America: A Brief History* (San Diego, 1989), 181–185; Kenneth T. Jackson, "The Impact of Technological Change on Urban Form," in Joel Colton and Stuart Bruchey, eds., *Technology, the Economy, and Society: The American Experience* (New York, 1987), 150–161; Mohl, *The New City*, 27–52.

[17] Roy Lubove, "The Urbanization Process: An Approach to Historical Research," in the American Institute of Planners, *Journal*, 33 (January, 1967), 33–39; McShane, *Technology and Reform*, 31–39; Mohl, *The New City*, 67–73; Still, *Milwaukee*, 345–355; Eric H. Monkkonen, *America Becomes Urban: The Development of U.S. Cities and Towns, 1780–1980* (Berkeley, 1988), 69–88.

attracted only skilled workers. Thus manufacturing gradually challenged the university and state government as the city's primary economic assets.

Industrial boosters in Appleton, Menasha, and Neenah had hoped for a single industrial metropolis in the Fox River Valley—what they hoped would be a "Pittsburgh of the west." Their dream did not materialize, but they continued to push for a manufacturing region in the midst of the area's naturally beautiful setting. Farther west, the Wisconsin Valley Advancement Association sought to adapt to the end of the lumber era by attracting capital and labor to develop a six-county multi-faceted economy of national significance along the Wisconsin River in the center of the state. Newspapers in the Fox and Upper Wisconsin River valleys, as well as those in Racine and Kenosha, consistently promoted industrial development.[18]

Urban spatial expansion between 1890 and 1920 actually was exceeded by population growth, which increased nearly twice as rapidly as that of the nation as a whole, and four times as fast as in the state's rural areas. The percentage of people living in census-defined urban places rose from 33 to 47, and the number of such places jumped from forty-seven to eighty-two. The total of incorporated cities advanced from 108 to 136, while their population share increased from 38 to 50 per cent. The number of cities with over 25,000 residents increased from two to nine; the number of those with more than 10,000, from eight to twenty-one. The dominant city, Milwaukee, had 204,468 residents in 1890 and 457,147 in 1920—about 17 per cent of the state's population. It was then the thirteenth most populous city in the country.

During the same period, Racine jumped from 21,014 to 58,593; Madison, from 13,426 to 38,378; Kenosha, from 6,532 to 40,472; Green Bay, from 13,821 (including Fort Howard) to 31,017; and Sheboygan, from 16,359 to 30,955. Beloit more than tripled; Fond du Lac, Janesville, Manitowoc, Wausau and Waukesha nearly doubled. Superior exploded from 11,983 to 40,384 between 1890 and 1910, only to suffer a slight loss by 1920. Of the state's twenty-one largest cities, only Oshkosh, La Crosse, Eau Claire, Stevens Point, and Appleton failed to come close to doubling their populations.[19]

---

[18] Mollenhoff, *Madison*, 251–294; Charles N. Glaab and Lawrence H. Larsen, *Factories in the Valley: Neenah-Menasha, 1870–1915* (Madison, 1969), 278–280; Howard R. Klueter and James J. Lorence, *Woodlot and Ballot Box: Marathon County in the Twentieth Century* (Madison, 1977), 69–83. See also the Racine *Daily Times*, March 3, 22, 28, 29, April 28, and December 23, 1910; Kenosha *Telegraph-Courier*, March 16, 1893; and Albert H. Sanford and H. J. Hirschheimer, *A History of La Crosse, Wisconsin, 1841–1900* (La Crosse, 1951), 213–214.

[19] *Fourteenth Census of the United States, 1920: Composition and Characteristics of the Population by States, Volume III*, 137–138; *Seventeenth Census of the United States, 1950: Char-*

Most urban growth occurred where the new industrialism had had its greatest effect. The largest increase occurred in the three southeastern counties—Kenosha, Racine, and Milwaukee—which constituted the northwest outpost of the Great Lakes industrial belt. By 1900, these counties were home to one Wisconsin resident in five; by 1920, one in four. In a state which was not quite one-half urban by 1920, Milwaukee County was 95 per cent urban, Racine, 78, and Kenosha, 76. Population density told a similar story: 47.6 people per square mile statewide; 2,296 in Milwaukee; 244 in Racine; and 182 in Kenosha. The next most heavily urbanized section included the Fox Valley counties of Fond du Lac, Winnebago, Outagamie, Calumet, and Brown, together with the Lake Michigan counties of Sheboygan, Manitowoc, and Kewaunee. In 1920, these eight contained about 15 per cent of Wisconsin's total population. Away from the Lake Michigan shoreline, there were only five other substantial urban counties: Dane (Madison), Rock (Beloit and Janesville), La Crosse, Eau Claire, and Douglas (Superior). But they lacked the population concentrations of the Lake Michigan and Fox Valley regions.[20]

"Natural increase," meaning a favorable ratio of live births to deaths, accounted for some urban growth and can be attributed to improvements in water supplies and public health. But primarily cities grew because of migration from farms and villages in both America and Europe to America's industrializing cities. For every city boy who moved to the country, twenty farm boys moved to the city. Although promotion of agricultural settlement in the Cutover somewhat skewed Wisconsin's rural-to-urban flow, the decline of the farm population in the southern half of the state was dramatic. Of the twenty-nine counties that lost rural population between 1900 and 1910, all but five lay south of a line between Green Bay and La Crosse. By contrast, the rural populations of Sawyer, Price, and Forest counties in the north increased by more than one-half, while eleven other northern counties grew by more than one-quarter. Wisconsin's rural population declined from 67 to 53 per cent of the total between 1890 and 1920, and the share of those actually living on farms fell from 57 to 35 per cent. Even though the state's rural population increased by more than 156,000, its urban counterpart leaped ahead by more than 682,000.[21]

---

acteristics of the Population, Volume II, part 49, Wisconsin, 2–10; "Cities of Wisconsin by Classes," in the *Wisconsin Blue Book, 1921*, pp. 494–502.

[20] "Population of Wisconsin," in the *Wisconsin Blue Book, 1901*, pp. 455–498; "Population of Wisconsin by Counties," in the *Wisconsin Blue Book, 1911*, pp. 49–50, 100–109; "Cities of Wisconsin by Classes," in the *Wisconsin Blue Book, 1921*, pp. 441–491.

[21] Mohl, *The New City*, 18–21; Edgar Z. Palmer, *The Prewar Industrial Pattern of Wisconsin*, University of Wisconsin Bureau of Business Research and Service, *Wisconsin Commerce Studies*, vol. 1, no. 1 (Madison, 1947), 32–34.

This rural-to-urban flow generally followed what scholars call the push-pull model of migration. For rural Wisconsinites, push factors were largely economic and related to agriculture. Wisconsin farmers, like Great Plains grain producers, were forced to sell in a rapidly expanding, competitive market, and to buy in an ever more protected and managed one. Increased productivity through mechanization drove down prices and undercut the need for labor. Adapting to mechanized, commercialized agriculture increased farmers' dependence upon creditors, implement dealers, middlemen, and railroads. Dairy farmers, however, had some advantages over grain farmers. They were linked directly to the Midwest's expanding cities by the organization, agenda, and power of the Dairymen's Association and the Society of Equity, by the popularity of agricultural co-operatives, and by the "safety valve" of Cutover settlement, which was pulling city dwellers into the countryside. But there were push factors related to dairying, too. It required more capital and education than many farmers had. And Cutover development brought millions of acres of marginal land into play, exacerbated agricultural surpluses, and inflated farm failures and foreclosures. Finally, the industrializing of dairying reduced the need for agricultural labor and caused rural unemployment.[22]

There were social push factors as well. The size of farms, the distances between them, vagaries of weather, and primitive transportation and communication systems made loneliness and isolation commonplace. Long, hard hours of physical labor took a toll on families, especially on women, who were usually the last to benefit from labor-saving technology.[23]

These economic and social considerations helped push people off farms, while cities pulled them in their direction for equally compelling reasons, usually associated with economic welfare. Industrialism was generating a plethora of manufacturing and service jobs which required little or no experience or training. They inspired in migrants a vision of relative advantage, despite the jobs' long hours, hazardous and monotonous conditions, low wages, and diminished job security. According to a survey conducted in 1895 by the state's Bureau of Labor and Industrial Statistics (BLIS), almost 75 per cent of unmarried farm laborers yearned for city life, and only 20 per cent wanted to farm throughout their lives. Many were lured by the prom-

---

[22] Samuel P. Hays, *The Response to Industrialism, 1885–1914* (Chicago, 1957), 27–32; Mohl, *The New City*, 18–21; Marcus and Segal, *Technology in America*, 187–194; Eric E. Lampard, *The Rise of the Dairy Industry in Wisconsin: A Study in Agricultural Change, 1820–1920* (Madison, 1963), 333–351.

[23] For a fictional example of a woman's attitude about farming, see Hamlin Garland, *Main-Travelled Roads* (New York, 1899), esp. p. 79.

ise of labor-saving appliances, improved educational, recreational, and entertainment opportunities, and by the bright lights and excitement free from the social constraints of rural life.[24]

The dangers posed by "rural drain" became a standard theme of agricultural discourse by the 1880's. Experts deplored the loss of the best prospective farmers to the cities. But eventually they came to see some advantages to urban amenities to migration itself. It relieved population pressures on the countryside, while the automobile, the telephone, rural free postal delivery, mail-order catalogs, the phonograph, rural electrification, and home appliances closed the gap between farm and city. These conveniences helped to stanch the rural drain. So did the Country Life Movement, rural school consolidation, and agricultural extension work, though some of these did not have much impact until after World War I. In the meantime, both the exodus of young people and the concern about it continued, as did urban-rural rivalry. This rivalry remained a social and political fact of life, especially among rural and small-town legislators, who fought a bitter rear-guard action against the blandishments of urban civilization.[25]

Foreign immigration, especially from southern and eastern Europe to southeastern Wisconsin, also bolstered urban population. These newcomers came to fill the demand for minimally skilled workers in industrial cities. Despite their high numbers, the percentage of foreign-born and their immediate offspring in Wisconsin actually declined from 75 to 61 per cent between 1890 and 1920. Germans, Scandinavians, and Britons continued to constitute nearly one-half of Wisconsin's immigrants by 1920, but recently arrived Poles, Austrians, Hungarians, Czechs, Slovaks, Russians, Serbs, Lithuanians, Greeks, Italians, and Eastern European Jews made up well over one-quarter. A significant minority of immigrants settled in the Cutover; the majority flocked to the industrial southeast. In Wisconsin's eight largest cities in 1910, first- and second-generation immigrants accounted for almost 77 per cent of the inhabitants.[26]

Besides being more ethnically diverse, Wisconsin's industrial cities were also far more segmented, fragmented, and stratified than their smaller counterparts. Geographical dispersion fostered increasing so-

---

[24] Bureau of Labor and Industrial Statistics, *Biennial Report*, 1895–1896, p. 108; *Hoard's Dairyman*, January 6, 1893, p. 2771, advertisement.

[25] Ransom A. Moore, "Agricultural Education," in the *Transactions of the Wisconsin State Agricultural Society* (1896), 99–101. See also Chapter 2.

[26] *Thirteenth Census of the United States, 1910*, Volume II, p. 1082; *Fourteenth Census of the United States, 1920: Composition and Characteristics of the Population by States*, Volume III, p. 1118; Still, *Milwaukee*, 574–575; John D. Buenker, "The Immigrant Heritage," in Nicholas C. Burckel, ed., *Racine: Growth and Change in a Wisconsin County* (Racine, 1977), 70–74, and "Immigration and Ethnic Groups," in John A. Neuenschwander, ed., *Kenosha County in the Twentieth Century* (Kenosha, 1976), 1–6. See also Chapter 5.

cial and ethnic differentiation of residential areas, although central business districts remained a common denominator. The cold, hard statistics of population and residential density, housing-stock quality, property values, and crime, disease, mortality, and delinquency both exposed and masked widely varying standards of life and diverse modes of living, working, playing, and thinking.

In Milwaukee, this fragmentation produced highly distinctive zones. Industry, and new immigrants, concentrated in the south and southwest sides where decentralization had resulted in relatively cheap land for single-family and duplex housing. The area north of the Menomonee River Valley and west of the Milwaukee River was the home of middle-class artisans, skilled workers, shopkeepers, and clerical workers, mostly of northwestern European ancestry. Milwaukee's upper east side, the area directly west of downtown, and the lakeshore just south of the central business district were elite residential sections. Compared to the typical industrial metropolis of the Northeast and Midwest, Milwaukee was spatially more compact, ethnically and occupationally more homogeneous, and less dependent upon mass transportation. Yet it was just as socially diverse as others. In his thinly disguised depiction of upper-middle-class life in Milwaukee at the turn of the century, novelist Charles K. Lush observed that "a city is made up of circles, or groups, great and small, divisions and sub-divisions, the members of which have apparently little in common, whose mode of life is dissimilar, and who really know as little of each other as do Hottentots and Esquimaux."[27]

In Racine, the twisting Root River divided the city into three parts: a central business district just south of the river's estuary; a working- and middle-class district to the north; and a commercial and light manufacturing district to the west, which gave way to a largely middle-

---

[27] *Thirteenth Census of the United States, 1910, Volume III*, pp. 1075–1077; Still, *Milwaukee*, 340, 378–381, 427–430, 595–599; Simon, "The Expansion of an Industrial City," 35–47, 76–121, 298–302; Roger D. Simon, "Housing and Services in an Immigrant Neighborhood: Milwaukee's Ward 14," in the *Journal of Urban History*, 2 (August, 1976), 437–440; McShane, *Technology and Reform*, 42–44, 82–90; Randy Garber, ed., *Built in Milwaukee: An Architectural View of the City* (Milwaukee, 1981), 17–21; Frank P. Zeidler, "Milwaukee's South Side: A Historical Look," in *Milwaukee History*, 8 (Summer–Autumn, 1985), 68–80; Frederick I. Olson, "City Expansion and Urban Sprawl," in Ralph M. Aderman, ed., *From Trading Post to Metropolis: Milwaukee County's First 150 Years* (Milwaukee, 1987), 1–90, 32–47; Fleischmann, "The Territorial Expansion of Milwaukee," *Journal of Urban History*, 14: 149–151; Henry J. Schmandt, John C. Goldbach, and Donald B. Vogel, *Milwaukee: A Contemporary Urban Profile* (New York, 1971), 2–4, 21–22, 223–224; Charles D. Goff, "The Politics of Governmental Integration in Metropolitan Milwaukee" (doctoral dissertation, Northwestern University, 1952), 20–28, 82–86; Howard A. Botts, "Commercial Structure and Ethnic Residential Patterns in the Shaping of Milwaukee: 1880–1900" (doctoral dissertation, University of Wisconsin, 1985), 189–203; Charles K. Lush, *The Autocrats* (New York, 1901).

class residential area. The Chicago and North Western rail lines ran north–south about a mile west of the lakefront, isolating the central business district, the major secondary commercial district, and the southeastern residential area. Racine's considerable industrial complex began at the southeast lakeshore, in the town of Mt. Pleasant, and paralleled the railroad tracks to the northern city limits. Ethnocultural differences among Yankees and northwestern and southeastern Europeans exacerbated economic segregation of the various residential neighborhoods.[28]

Kenosha's contours largely resulted from conscious design—relatively unusual for the time in Wisconsin and elsewhere. The central business district and the lakefront residential area originally were separated from the less prosperous north side by Pike Creek, which flowed into Lake Michigan. The residents of the southeast section also isolated themselves by constructing an extensive cemetery and park on the section's western fringe. The city was further divided by three railroad lines that came from the south and southwest and ran northward towards Racine. Kenosha's five substantial manufacturing districts roughly paralleled these lines. Its growing and heavily immigrant working class generally lived in single-family dwellings and duplexes interspersed among the manufacturing districts on the west side, whose housing and public services ranged from fair to poor. High rates of crime, disease, and mortality plagued it as well. The west side was, literally and figuratively, the wrong side of the tracks. In between these extremes were middle-class neighborhoods, mostly occupied by skilled and white-collar workers of northwestern European ancestry.[29]

Madison felt the impact of industrialization less than Milwaukee, Racine, and Kenosha, owing to its deliberate decision to segregate factories. This led to obvious class and status divisions in neighborhoods. The industrial east side became home to both factories and their workers. The west side remained largely unaffected by the city's

[28] Susan E. Karr, *Architectural and Historical Survey of the City of Racine* (Racine, 1979), 3–52; Buenker, "Immigrant Heritage," in Burckel, ed., *Racine*, 85–95; Robert R. Alford and Harry M. Scoble, *Bureaucracy and Participation: Political Culture in Four Wisconsin Cities* (Chicago, 1969), 80–85. The two-volume, 1,141-page *Racine, Belle City of the Lakes, and Racine County, Wisconsin: A Record of Settlement, Organization, Progress and Achievement* (Chicago, 1916), edited by Fanny S. Stone, makes no mention either of southern and eastern European immigrants or of industrial workers.

[29] Barbara M. Duncan, "Kenosha, Wisconsin: A Study in Urban Choreography" (master's thesis, University of Chicago, 1935), 34–91; Buenker "Immigration and Ethnic Groups," in Neuenschwander, ed., *Kenosha County*, 11–16; Alford and Scoble, *Bureaucracy and Participation*, 59–64. Frank H. Lyman, ed., *The City of Kenosha and Kenosha County, Wisconsin: A Record of Settlement, Organization, Progress, and Achievement* (Chicago, 1916), a work of 1,110 pages, concentrates on the "founding fathers" and ignores close to one-half the city's population.

industrial boom, except insofar as it enhanced property values and the standard of living. So successful was the Madison Compromise that manufacturing became the single largest sector of the city's economy by 1914. Between 1910 and 1920, factory employment and output grew five times faster than the population, the east side growing by 70 per cent, compared to 44 per cent for the west side. Increasingly, the east side came to resemble Milwaukee's south side or Kenosha's railroad district, with working-class cottages and duplexes nestled among factories and railroad tracks. The west side of Madison, on the other hand, aided and abetted by the rapid growth of state government and the state university, came to rival Milwaukee's upper east side, though on a much smaller scale. They were among the most desirable residential areas in the entire state. For many residents of Madison's west side, the east side might as well have been on another planet, though handsome lakeshore neighborhoods and suburbs dotted both the east and the west sides.[30]

A similar mixture of expansion, congestion, and segmentation transformed Wisconsin's other industrial cities. So growth-oriented and competitive were they that, at various points between 1890 and 1915, La Crosse, Eau Claire, Superior, Oshkosh, Racine, and Madison all claimed to be Wisconsin's second city. The rapid decline of the lumber industry after 1880 served to reorient several municipal economies towards other manufacturing endeavors. Green Bay's substantial growth dated from 1895, when the first paper mill was opened. By 1915, the city was ethnically diverse and firmly blue-collar, with a high rate of home ownership. In Oshkosh, industrial expansion along the Fox River divided north and south. The northern part contained the central business district and most middle-class neighborhoods; the southern housed the vast majority of laborers and small merchants. The city's street names did not even match up on opposite sides of the river. Similarly, in Eau Claire, two separate communities emerged while it was making the transition from lumbering to a diversified manufacturing economy. One was predominantly working-class of German and Norwegian ancestry; the other was a smaller commercial-proprietor-professional community which dwelt apart. In La Crosse, as in Oshkosh with the Fox River, the La Crosse River permitted a division that separated people along class and ethnic lines, north and south.[31]

---

[30] Mollenhoff, *Madison*, 234–238, 251–271; Alford and Scoble, *Bureaucracy and Participation*, 96–104.

[31] "The Industries of Wisconsin," in the *Wisconsin Blue Book, 1915*, p. 11; David P. Thelen, *The New Citizenship: Origins of Progressivism in Wisconsin, 1885–1900* (Columbia, Missouri, 1972), 132–135; Alford and Scoble, *Bureaucracy and Participation*, 37–45; J. Rogers Hollingsworth and Ellen Jane Hollingsworth, *Dimensions in Urban History:*

Such class-division tendencies were even more pronounced in the northwestern boom towns of Ashland and Superior on Lake Superior. Situated on both Chequamegon Bay and four major rail lines, Ashland manifested boundless need for workers by the 1890's. Immigrants and transient workers alike could find both seasonal and sustained employment in Ashland area logging camps, sawmills, docks, railroads, and ships. Its railroad tracks and ravines formed effective dividers among residential, commercial, and industrial districts. Incorporated the same year as Ashland (1887), Superior had mushroomed into a city of 35,000 people by 1893. The city was divided into several sections by bays and rivers. Superior sectioned itself by railroad tracks, speculative developments, and manufacturing plants. The east end on the lake was settled first, and remained the city's finest residential area for several decades. The construction of iron and coal docks southeast of the Nemadji River and new steel mills and coal docks in West Superior in the 1890's created major working-class residential areas. By 1910, elevators, mills, ore docks, and coal yards lined its waterfront.[32]

A need for improved municipal services developed simultaneously with the urban population boom. "Property owners were anxious for improvement," the Appleton *Weekly Post* wrote in 1891. "They wanted pavement, they wanted water, they wanted sewers. If more conservative men tried to prevent this breakneck rush for public improvement and municipal bankruptcy, they were at once accused of being obstructionists. . . ." In Milwaukee, the residents of new outlying neighborhoods led the chorus. But the litany grew everywhere, despite the well-earned reputation for frugality enjoyed by Wisconsin cities, and regardless of the depression.

As late as the 1880's, per capita indebtedness ranged from $9.43

Historical and Social Science Perspectives on Middle-Size American Cities (Madison, 1979), 59–67, 97–103; City of Green Bay Redevelopment Authority, Intensive Resource Survey, *Final Report* (Milwaukee, 1988), 14–51, 178; Betsy Foley, *Green Bay: Gateway to the Great Waterway* (Woodland Hills, California, 1983), 66–69; City of Oshkosh, Intensive Historic Resource Survey, *Final Report* (n.p., 1981), 161–166; William and Clara Dawes, *History of Oshkosh* (Oshkosh, 1938), 43–49; Clinton F. Karstaedt, ed., *Oshkosh: One Hundred Years A City, 1853–1953* (Oshkosh, 1953), 205–255; Mary Taylor, comp., City of Eau Claire, Intensive Historic/Architectural Survey, *Final Report*, (n.p., 1983), 27–33; James B. Smith, "The Movements for Diversified Industry in Eau Claire, Wisconsin, 1897–1907: Boosterism and Urban Development Strategy in a Declining Lumber Town" (master's thesis, University of Wisconsin, 1967), 1–5, 174–183; Joan M. Rausch and Richard Zeitlin, comps., City of La Crosse, Intensive Historical-Architectural Survey, *Final Report* (1984), 19–27, 216–242.

[32] Steve Sennott, comp., City of Ashland, Historic-Architectural Intensive Survey, *Report* (n.p., 1983), 21–27, 60–63; J. M. Dodd, "Ashland Then And Now," in *WMH*, 28 (December, 1944), 188–197; Paul R. Lusignan, comp., Superior Intensive Survey, *Report* (n.p., 1983), 5–14, 82–95.

for Oshkosh to $18.69 for Milwaukee, while comparable Ohio cities stood between $20.07 and $86.20. Milwaukee's net indebtedness was only one-fifth that of Chicago's and one-tenth that of Cincinnati's. Change soon occurred. Between 1889 and 1899, the bonded indebtedness of Wisconsin's local governments nearly doubled. In a single two-year period, Milwaukee spent over a million dollars to purchase and improve public park lands, while Superior issued $65,000 in tax certificates to construct a new state normal school. By 1895, the depression had forced three-fourths of Wisconsin's urbanized counties to scale back improvements. But the public demanded them anyway.[33]

[3]

Nowhere did the quantity and quality of municipal services prove equal to these demands, virtually guaranteeing a sense of impending crisis in Wisconsin's cities. Urban fiscal problems were worsened by the residual control exercised over municipal affairs by the state legislature, even after passage of a general incorporation law in 1892. Despite complaints by municipal leaders, lawmakers still arrogated to themselves the power to determine local tax rates, to collect levies on corporations, to determine administrative rules for law enforcement, poor relief, and other vital services, and to make some important policy decisions.

As Wisconsin's only city of the "first class" (a statutory definition, requiring a population of more than 150,000), Milwaukee continually had been the object of special legislation. This prompted Mayor William J. Rauschenberger to charge in 1896 that the municipality had "grown to be too large a city to be hampered by state laws passed without the knowledge and consent of her common council and citizens." The power to get things done in Milwaukee typically was divided among the legislature, the county board of supervisors, the mayor, the city council, and a variety of quasi-independent, special-purpose boards and commissions which dealt with such diverse areas as parks and recreation, sanitation, public health, water, police and fire protection, education, and the civil service. In Madison, as late as 1892 the city attorney still found it necessary to draft three amendments to the city's special incorporation charter, entreating the legislature to permit the city to sprinkle its streets, issue bonds for street repairs, and acquire its own lighting plant. Gaining home rule and

---

[33] Appleton *Weekly Post*, February 19, 1891, as quoted in Thelen, *New Citizenship*, p. 135; *ibid.*, 133–138; Larsen, "Urban Services," in *WMH*, 71: 84–89.

achieving governmental co-ordination became urgent in the 1890's for Wisconsin's industrial cities.[34]

A popularly held notion called "privatism" also restricted cities' control over their destinies. Privatism meant that a city had to offer each citizen a chance to prosper, as under the rules of laissez-faire economics. Municipal governments typically built their infrastructures and produced necessary services by granting franchises, land grants, and tax incentives to private individuals and corporations who hoped to make a profit. Decisions to extend and finance such basic services as water, sewers, and streets typically were shared by city government and the affected property owners, who were assessed for part of the cost and could petition to accelerate or delay the work. Utilities such as electricity and streetcars usually arranged for higher rates of profit for services in less affluent neighborhoods, since fewer people would subscribe.[35]

The American conviction and long-standing expectation that voluntary associations provide social services reinforced privatism. By combining their individual resources, some people with common ethnic, religious, occupational, residential, or other ties could provide each other with some protection against industrial accident, illness, old age, unemployment, or the death of a breadwinner. Those unable to belong to these mutual benefit organizations were forced to depend mostly upon private charities that generally maintained stringent eligibility requirements. Only when conditions reached crisis proportions, as during the depression of 1893–1897, did calls for government intervention and public relief gain a serious hearing. Even then, the resulting measures usually were regarded as temporary.[36]

These formidable governmental and cultural constraints on cities fostered "machine politics." In the late nineteenth century, the term

---

[34] Thelen, *New Citizenship*, 132–135; Still, *Milwaukee*, 377–378 (quote); Mollenhoff, *Madison*, 227; James R. Donoghue, "The Local Government System of Wisconsin," in the *Wisconsin Blue Book, 1968*, pp. 108–126.

[35] The classic statement of "privatism" is by Sam Bass Warner, Jr., in *The Private City: Philadelphia in Three Periods of Its Growth* (Philadelphia, 1968), ix–xii, 3–23, 201–223, and in his book *Streetcar Suburbs*, 1–14, 153–168. The "release of energy" principle and its consequences are developed by James Willard Hurst in *Law and the Conditions of Freedom in the Nineteenth Century United States* (Madison, 1956), 3–70. See also Monkkonen, *America Becomes Urban*, 3–7, 131–157; Mohl, *The New City*, 147–185, 177–179; and Hollingsworth and Hollingsworth, *Dimensions in Urban History*, 118.

[36] John A. Fleckner, "Poverty and Relief in Nineteenth-Century Janesville," in *WMH*, 61 (Summer, 1978), 279–299; Kathy McVicker, "... Who Would Otherwise Have Suffered: Charity and Poor Relief in Racine, Wisconsin During the Depression of 1893" (unpublished seminar paper, May 29, 1984, in the Area Research Center, University of Wisconsin-Parkside, Kenosha), 16–49; Mollenhoff, *Madison*, 239–242.

meant something different than it does in the late twentieth century. It was not an altogether negative metaphor for the machine-like methods by which local political party organizations manufactured elections and legislation, thereby delivering "the goods." In exchange, organization politicians solicited the fuel—the votes, money, and private-sector jobs for themselves and their constituents—to run the machine. The chain of command and lines of communication among party officials, officeholders, service providers, and all their varied constituents constituted the closest thing to public service policy. Except for education and police and fire protection, private entrepreneurs generally met cities' needs. They operated under contracts and franchises negotiated with politicians. And the politicians typically approved franchises that were long on insider benefits and short on public responsibility. Politicians often sweetened the entrepreneurs' pie with subsidies, land grants, and tax breaks. Numbers of wealthy and powerful Milwaukee politicians enjoyed intimate working relationships with the city's quasi-public corporations, either as stockholders, corporate board members, or lobbyists.[37]

With so much opportunity and so little accountability, businessmen and politicians occasionally strayed beyond "honest graft." In 1904, a Milwaukee grand jury returned fifty indictments against pavement suppliers and contractors who had charged the city $2.30 a yard for materials that cost other cities $1.56. It also indicted former aldermen: one for accepting a $3,000 bribe from TMER&L, and another for taking money to secure licenses for illicit gambling houses. During the 1904 mayoral campaign, Victor L. Berger, the Socialist newspaper editor who was running for mayor, sarcastically praised Mayor David S. Rose for being able to "save $150,000 out of a salary of $4,000 a year." The following year, Milwaukee district attorney Francis E. McGovern (who would later become governor) indicted eighteen county supervisors, several fire department officials, Republican party boss Charles Pfister, and common council president Cornelius Corcoran. Attempts to indict Mayor Rose for assessing officials for "contributions" to his re-election campaign failed, but barely. Rose, the colorful, five-time mayor whose nickname was "All-the-time Rosy," was widely suspected of accepting protection payments from proprietors of the saloons, brothels, and gambling houses which had

---

[37] Still, *Milwaukee*, 305–316, 374–389; Thelen, *New Citizenship*, 223–289; McShane, *Technology and Reform*, 84–105; Mollenhoff, *Madison*, 204–227. The classic statement on the operation of "honest graft" is William L. Riordon, *Plunkitt of Tammany Hall: A Series of Very Plain Talks on Very Practical Politics*, Terrence J. McDonald, ed. (New York, 1963), vii–xxii, 3–6, 29–32, 54–56, 61–64.

earned Milwaukee its turn-of-the-century reputation as a wide-open town.[38]

In Madison during the same period, Democratic aldermen reaped personal and political gain from franchises, periodic raids on the city treasury, and a "live-and-let-live" policy towards gambling, prostitutes, and saloons. Half of Madison's saloons were equipped with back-room stalls for prostitution. The city had 100 saloons, and their number was growing faster proportionately than the population. A joint legislative investigative commission reported in 1914 that the capital ranked third behind only Milwaukee and La Crosse in the number of "immoral places." The Civic Union and the Madison Temperance Board responded to charges that the council and the police were protecting commercialized vice with a crusade to create the "city virtuous" at a time when Madison's appearance was being transformed into a model "city beautiful."[39]

In Milwaukee, the same ingredients resulted in an open town, especially during the Rose mayoralty from 1898 to 1910. Saloons and beer gardens, ranging from the respectable to the disreputable, were everywhere. Dens for poker, faro, and roulette existed over or behind numerous bars and restaurants. Affluent Milwaukeeans, and an army of out-of-towners, frequented River Street, a compact, high-class redlight district. For fifty cents, potential clients could purchase *The Sporting and Club House Guide to Milwaukee*, which advertised only "the best and reliable places where one can go in perfect safety." Mayor Rose actually advocated making Milwaukee an open town, and he opposed prohibition—a popular stand in the nation's beer capital.[40]

Although vice was a problem for Wisconsin cities, housing shortages affected relatively more people. Milwaukee, Sheboygan, and Superior consistently exceeded the national urban average for number of people per dwelling between 1890 and 1910. In the rest of the state things were not as bad, mostly because of a high incidence of home ownership, and of single-family dwellings. In its report for 1895–1896, the Bureau of Labor and Industrial Statistics (BLIS) asserted that 78 per cent of the money lent by urban savings and loan associations went to wage-earners, whose principal goal was to own a

---

[38] Still, *Milwaukee*, 305–316 (quote), 374–389; David G. Ondercin, "Corruption, Conspiracy, and Reform in Milwaukee, 1901–1909," in the Milwaukee County Historical Society, *Historical Messenger*, 26 (December, 1970), 112–117; Duane Mowry, "The Reign of Graft in Milwaukee," in *The Arena*, 34 (December, 1905), 589–593.

[39] Mollenhoff, *Madison*, 311–316.

[40] Robert W. Wells, *This Is Milwaukee* (Garden City, New York, 1970), 136–142; Still, *Milwaukee*, 357–358; Kathleen M. Carlin, "Chief Janssen and the 'Thirty-three Year War,' Law Enforcement in an Urban Society: The Concepts of Police Chief Janssen" (master's thesis, University of Wisconsin-Milwaukee, 1961), 3–102.

home outright, not mortgaged. Many were able to realize that goal only by purchasing cheaply built houses on narrow lots, by taking in boarders or lodgers, and by postponing improvements and municipal services until they had paid off their mortgages. Nearly half Wisconsin's urban residents were renters. In Milwaukee, the figure approached two-thirds among the working-class immigrant families who inhabited the southwest side's Fourteenth Ward. In 1904, the typical frame cottage there resembled "a stable where the family herds together like cattle." Some developers and homeowners crammed additional housing in the rear of lots to realize more income, thus worsening physical congestion without affecting the ratio of people per dwelling.[41]

Summarizing an intensive survey in 1906, BLIS concluded that Milwaukee suffered every kind of unsatisfactory housing condition to some extent. The survey found no distinct tenement district in the city, but it did have a profusion of cheap, overcrowded, and unsanitary lodging and boardinghouses in eight working-class, immigrant districts where single men and young families predominated. For example, nearly thirty men slept in basements in the largely Italian Third Ward, and seventeen people were jammed into eight rooms in a boardinghouse run by Hungarian immigrants. Inspectors found defective plumbing and filthy rooms and beds in nearly every building. Most lacked bathrooms, fire escapes, garbage disposal, and adequate heating, lighting, ventilation, sanitation, and safe places for children to play. Disease, especially tuberculosis, was rampant.[42]

In 1909–1910, BLIS found housing conditions in Superior, Racine, La Crosse, Oshkosh, and Eau Claire that differed only in degree from Milwaukee's. Superior's "bowery" had numerous three-story, wood-frame tenements and lodging houses with poor light and air, and no bathrooms or clothes closets. Investigators declared the West Hotel dangerous "to life, health and morals," and characterized its lodgers as "wrecks of humanity, drifted in from the lakes." They judged housing in La Crosse to be somewhat better, although they still discovered very unsanitary conditions in certain Assyrian, Jewish, and Polish

---

[41] *Thirteenth Census of the United States, 1910: Abstract, Statistics of Population, Agriculture, Manufactures, and Mining*, 259–262; Bureau of Labor and Industrial Statistics, *Biennial Report*, 1895–1896, pp. 506–513; Milwaukee *Sentinel*, March 19, 1904; Simon, "Housing and Services," in *Journal of Urban History*, 2: 435–458. For a contemporary analysis of the problem by an assistant factory inspector for the BLIS, see Odessa Kunz, "The Housing Problem in Wisconsin," in *Charities and The Commons*, 18 (September, 1907), 251–255.

[42] Bureau of Labor and Industrial Statistics, *Biennial Report*, 1905–1906, pp. 288–334; Still, *Milwaukee*, 389–390; Carl D. Thompson, "The Housing Awakening II: Socialists and Slums—Milwaukee," in *The Survey*, 25 (October, 1910–March, 1911), 367–370.

neighborhoods, and in "Hunger Point" along the river at the south end of town. Racine was pronounced "one of the cleanest cities visited," presumably because most of the cottages near the factory district were owner-occupied. But a significant number of flats and tenements had inadequate sanitation. Oshkosh's housing ranked just below La Crosse and Racine. Eau Claire suffered from a housing shortage and inadequate sanitation, exacerbated by residents' keeping horses, cattle, and chickens in the most congested districts. BLIS concluded that Wisconsin should extend housing regulations, especially measures dealing with sanitation, to all municipalities with more than 10,000 residents.[43]

Even Madison, which touted itself as a city of beautiful homes, had slums, especially in "the Latin Quarter"—a hodgepodge of rooming houses, fraternities, and sororities adjoining the university—and in the eighty-acre Greenbush addition (known as "The Bush"). Latin Quarter landlords exploited students. One rented a single rooming house with no indoor plumbing to seventeen men; another rented a house with a single bathtub to twenty-two women. The Bush consisted primarily of former marshland that had been filled with household refuse and building debris, then was built up with cheap housing, inhabited largely by Italian and Jewish immigrants and the city's minuscule Negro population.* In 1910, an investigation found that over one-third of the homes in the Bush had no water connections; nearly all were overcrowded and unsanitary. Six years later, an international housing authority stunned Madisonians by remarking of the Bush, "Why you've got as bad a slum as any city in the country." He said the fire dangers in the cheaply built rooming houses, flats, and apartments—typically without fire exits—were the worst in the state.[44]

These miserable working-class housing conditions in Wisconsin industrial cities contributed mightily to an even more widespread urban crisis: poor public health. Overcrowded and unsanitary housing helped spread infectious diseases, which were responsible for nearly 60 per cent of Milwaukee's deaths between 1880 and 1910. Tuber-

---

*EDITOR'S NOTE: The policy was established with the first volume in this series to refer to groups in Wisconsin society by those names which were most commonly used *at the time*. The term "Negro" was used between 1893 and 1914.

[43] Bureau of Labor and Industrial Statistics, *Biennial Report*, 1909–1910, pp. 1–66; Elizabeth Krimmel, "The History and Development of the Central Association of Racine, Wisconsin from 1910 to 1930" (unpublished research paper, 1985, in the Area Research Center, University of Wisconsin-Parkside, Kenosha), 27–34; Kathy McVicker, "The Hull House of Racine: The Central Association, 1910 to 1920" (unpublished seminar paper, 1985, in the Area Research Center, University of Wisconsin-Parkside, Kenosha), 19–23.

[44] Mollenhoff, *Madison*, 352–360; Duncan, "Kenosha," 16–25, 70–90.

culosis, diphtheria, and other diseases particularly affected children under five years of age, whose mortality rate was almost three times the city average. Infectious diseases most affected wards inhabited primarily by working-class immigrants, who had the highest ratio of persons per dwelling. An 1893 diphtheria epidemic demoralized local physicians because they could not contend with the housing conditions that caused the epidemic.[45]

But hazards to public health were not limited to the poorest residential sections. Unregulated growth had resulted in miles of unpaved streets which were saturated with animal droppings and littered with garbage, insufficient and contaminated water supplies, noxious (and often toxic) privy vaults, stagnant pools of water, open sewers, industrial smoke, and an all-pervasive stench. Dead horses sometimes lay in streets and alleys for days, attracting insects and carnivorous animals. This foul agglomeration sometimes rendered Milwaukee streets impassable. Health officials reported that Green Bay, Sheboygan, and Madison were no better.[46]

City water frequently came from wells contaminated by privies and refuse piles, or from rivers and lakes polluted by street runoff and industrial, household, and human wastes. Drinking water sources were routinely located downstream from sewage outlets. In 1879, the *Evening Wisconsin* charged that Milwaukeeans drank "a decoction of uncertain proportions of Milwaukee river, Milwaukee sewage, Menomonee Marsh, slaughterhouses, breweries, and tanneries." A *Daily News* reporter warned the same year, "There is death in our drink." By the 1890's, improvements had occurred but dangers abounded nonetheless. Food purveyors rarely concerned themselves with sanitary conditions. Perishable items often stood unprotected and unrefrigerated for weeks. Milk was generally sold on the streets by vendors, some of whom dipped it out of open containers into their customers' buckets.[47]

The public health crisis was aggravated by ignorance, fear, and unimproved institutional facilities and methods. The "miasma theory" provides a good example of ingrained foolishness. It held that dirt

---

[45] Judith W. Leavitt, "Health in Urban Wisconsin: From Bad to Better," in Ronald L. Numbers and Judith W. Leavitt, eds., *Wisconsin Medicine: Historical Perspectives* (Madison, 1981), 155–176; Judith W. Leavitt, *The Healthiest City: Milwaukee and the Politics of Health Reform* (Princeton, 1982; reprinted, 1996), 10–41.

[46] Milwaukee *Sentinel*, January 27, 28, 30, and February 2, 28, 1892; Leavitt, "Health in Urban Wisconsin," in Numbers and Leavitt, eds., *Wisconsin Medicine*, 156–164; Leavitt, *Healthiest City*, 22–41, 122–124; Still, *Milwaukee*, 362–365; Thelen, *New Citizenship*, 236–239; Mollenhoff, *Madison*, 207–210, 219–227.

[47] Leavitt, "Health in Urban Wisconsin," in Numbers and Leavitt, eds., *Wisconsin Medicine*, 161–168 (quotes); Leavitt, *Healthiest City*, 156–189; Mollenhoff, *Madison*, 385–386.

and decaying organic matter poisoned the atmosphere, and that this infected air transmitted disease. This theory, wrong or no, motivated improvements in sanitation, though it did little to eliminate the root cause of epidemics: germs. On the other hand, gradual acceptance of the "germ theory"—that bacteria propagated diseases and that immunizations with antitoxins helped prevent them—led to progress. Even then, such organizations as the Milwaukee Anti-Vaccination Society, composed largely of the city's two dominant ethnic groups, Germans and Poles, mobilized resistance to compulsory vaccination for smallpox and other diseases. Their opposition caused some political leaders to reject mandatory inoculation; it also resulted in the firing of the Milwaukee health commissioner for his advocacy of vaccination during a smallpox epidemic in 1894. Opposition by property owners and taxpayers also undermined effective control over water and sewage systems and garbage collection. The objection of milk producers and vendors to government regulation, especially testing for tuberculosis, caused the health commissioner to bemoan in 1900, "So much needs to be done that the outlook seems rather hopeless."[48]

Oddly, this public health crisis was especially acute in Madison, which prided itself on its gracious life style. University of Wisconsin scientists, physicians, and local newspaper reporters demonstrated that contaminated milk was a major cause of tuberculosis, scarlet fever, and diphtheria, and that the practice of adding formaldehyde and other preservatives to milk caused numerous illnesses and fatalities. In 1907, an inspection of the city's most respectable butcher shops, grocery stores, bakeries, and restaurants by the board of health found dead mice lying in front of ice boxes, blood-soaked floors, maggots, rotting meat and vegetables stored in flooded cellars, filthy equipment, and predictably horrible odors. Until the late 1800's, garbage collection was left up to individuals. Ten tons of horse droppings a day in stables and streets produced millions of disease-carrying flies. In 1910, water from a bubbler on the university campus was found to be contaminated by raw sewage dumped into Lake Mendota by the state mental hospital. Summer weeds and scum in Lake Monona, fed by improperly treated sewage, became so dense that power boats could not plow through it. Uniquely troublesome were Madison's many marshes, popular dumping places for dead animals and garbage, and breeding places for communicable diseases. Ironically, as late as the 1890's, Madison did not have a public hospital.[49]

The sense of crisis in Wisconsin's expanding cities was greatly

[48] Leavitt, *Healthiest City*, 44–45, 70–72, 94–121, 156–189, 243–245; Mollenhoff, *Madison*, 384–385.
[49] Mollenhoff, *Madison*, 385–407.

heightened by mounting consumer dissatisfaction with the performance of the quasi-public corporations, or "public utilities," that had been enfranchised to provide gas, electricity, water, mass transit, and telephone service. Five Wisconsin cities experienced major battles with utility companies between 1887 and 1892; nineteen waged them during 1899 alone. Municipal and state authorities typically relied upon competition among service providers to guarantee acceptable levels of quality and rates. Larger cities would license two or more companies to provide the same service to different areas, on the theory that unsatisfactory performance could be improved by granting a competing franchise. Then came the depression of 1893–1897, which accelerated a tendency towards monopoly, shaking out most of the marginal companies and allowing the strongest to combine. By the end of the century, one or two consolidated utility companies served a city and often a region.[50]

Municipal enthusiasm over consolidation was generally short-lived. Most mergers were financed by watered stock, forcing conglomerates to realize extremely high earnings in order to meet operating costs and satisfy stockholders. But the depression reduced revenues and precluded additional borrowing. In turn, the companies responded by raising rates and fares or decreasing service; many went so far as to raise rent paid by city governments for fire hydrants, light poles, and so forth, at a time when tax revenues had declined drastically. These circumstances discouraged enfranchisement of city-wide, multiservice competitors.[51]

Clashes between city government and privately owned utilities quickly became epidemic. Superior, Fond du Lac, Ashland, and Waukesha feuded with their water utilities; Grand Rapids, South Milwaukee, Appleton, Oshkosh, Superior, and Stevens Point, with their electric power companies; Racine, Sheboygan, Neenah, Appleton, and Ashland, with their street railway companies. Some cities resorted to laying their own track, or cutting down utility poles, when corporations defied municipal will. Most preferred to fight their battles in court, or in the political arena. Milwaukee engaged in a six-year war with enfranchised garbage collectors; struggles with TMER&L were a political staple for nearly a decade. La Crosse's frustration with the Wisconsin Telephone Company eventually led to a lawsuit in which a locally owned utility took over. These conflicts typically revolved around inadequate service and excessive rates, defiance of city orders, tax avoidance, and corporate corruption of the political system. But city councils and angry consumers did not always have their way. The Oshkosh Electric Light and Power Company responded to criti-

[50] Thelen, *New Citizenship*, 221–226; McShane, *Technology and Reform*, 65–82.
[51] Thelen, *New Citizenship*, 226–229.

Urbanism, Crisis, and Reform   153

cism of proposed rate increases by turning out most of the lights in town.⁵²

The most spectacular utility crises occurred in Superior, Madison, and Milwaukee. Superior jousted with the water, light, and power company over water quality, taxation, and rates, and with its street railway utility over free transfers. In 1897, the municipality won some victories over water rates; then a typhoid epidemic proved that water quality was still a serious problem. The city refused to pay its hydrant rentals and sought to annul the company's charter. At last, the utility agreed to pay its taxes, reduce rates, and build a filtration plant. Superior also struggled for over two years over street light rates. At one point the company turned off the city's lights, but ultimately agreed to lower rates—though only after the city threatened to purchase illumination from a gas company.⁵³

In Madison, conflicts developed over telephone, streetcar, electric, and water service, sewage disposal, and public health. Nearly a decade of turmoil resulted in the Madison Gas, Light and Coke Company's gaining control of the sole electric franchise in 1892. Within four years, complaints about quality and costs inspired proposals for municipal ownership. Purchase of the gas, electric, and street railway franchises by a New York-based company obviated municipal operation.⁵⁴

Milwaukee had owned and operated its own waterworks since the 1870's, but the ensuing population explosion had put great strains on its capacity and quality. Three decades of debate followed, from the 1890's into the 1920's. Efforts to enfranchise garbage disposal firms also dated to the 1870's, but the situation became critical during the 1890's. Surrounding communities refused to allow contractors to cross their land en route to a dump site, so most ferried garbage on barges down the rivers and either dumped it in Lake Michigan or burned it. Politics also entered in. In 1891, the Democratic-controlled city council awarded the franchise to a combine of ward heelers and campaign contributors. A few years later, triumphant Republicans transferred the entitlement to an outfit composed of their cronies. And so it went until the end of the century.⁵⁵

The conflicts over water treatment and garbage disposal were modest compared to those surrounding TMER&L. Combining rails and power into one corporation became commonplace during the 1890's,

---

⁵²*Ibid.*, 229–239; Still, *Milwaukee*, 365–375; Sanford and Hirschheimer, *La Crosse*, 186–190.
⁵³Thelen, *New Citizenship*, 193–201.
⁵⁴Mollenhoff, *Madison*, 201–220, 307–311, 384–397.
⁵⁵Still, *Milwaukee*, 362–365, 545–546; Thelen, *New Citizenship*, 236–239; Leavitt, *Healthiest City*, 122–155.

with Milwaukee being first. The logic was that transit companies wanted a controllable power source and electric companies desired a daytime use for electricity. Electrification of Milwaukee's four trolley systems in the early 1890's led to a merger, which also included two power suppliers. The new combine sold the bulk of its stock to a New York holding company, and the result was the nation's first transportation-electric power monopoly. To mend its local political fences, the syndicate appointed Republican state chairman Henry Clay Payne president of the new company and his Democratic counterpart, Edward C. Wall, vice-president. The new combine had $14 million in outstanding stock, far exceeding its actual worth, and the depression subsequently drove it into receivership. Before resorting to bankruptcy, however, the company severely damaged its community standing by raising streetcar fares and abolishing quantity discounts to working-class riders.[56]

On August 2, 1894, the Milwaukee council declared war on the street railway company. It called for either municipal ownership or enfranchisement of a competing company. After nearly two years of unraveling the financial and legal tangles, TMER&L was born in January, 1896, with Payne as vice-president, New York corporation lawyer William N. Cromwell as president, and New York utility veteran John I. Beggs as general manager. Under their management, the company expanded its influence as far south as Racine and Kenosha, and as far west as Waukesha.[57]

Even before Beggs's arrival, TMER&L further eroded its popular support by its handling of a strike called that May by the Amalgamated Street Railway Employees over union recognition and a pay increase of a penny an hour. The company barricaded its property and imported strikebreakers, incensing Milwaukeeans, some of whom sported signs and buttons proclaiming "I'll Walk, Will You?" and "To Ride Gives Me a Payne." The common council entreated TMER&L to rescind the fare increase and recognize the union, and the utility company was the major issue of the city elections of 1898 and 1900. Despite such formidable opposition, however, TMER&L broke both the strike and the union.[58]

TMER&L also precipitated a serious conflict over electric power. Between 1881 and 1894, quasi-public corporations had Milwaukee's

---

[56] Still, *Milwaukee*, 368–375; Thelen, *New Citizenship*, 250–276; McShane, *Technology and Reform*, 78–135; Canfield, *TM*, 3–30; Forrest McDonald, "Street Cars and Politics in Milwaukee, 1896–1901, Part I," in *WMH*, 39 (Spring, 1956), 166–169.

[57] John A. Butler, "Street Railway Problems in Milwaukee," in *Municipal Affairs*, 4 (March, 1900), 212–218.

[58] Still, *Milwaukee*, 368–375; Thelen, *New Citizenship*, 262–289; McShane, *Technology and Reform*, 106–131; Butler, "Street Railway Problems," in *Municipal Affairs*, 4: 213–218; McDonald, "Streetcars and Politics," in *WMH*, 39: 169–212, 253–273.

electricity franchise, although a proposal for a municipal lighting plant came before the board of public works in 1890. The argument for municipal control was that Milwaukee paid more than twice as much per street light than Chicago, and Chicago had a city-owned utility. The movement for municipal ownership did not abate after TMER&L entered the scene, since the public was dissatisfied with both its transportation and electric services. Support for a municipal lighting facility escalated. In 1904, voters passed a referendum to that effect, authorizing a bond issue. When the company's electric power franchise expired the following year, it offered to reduce its rates to match Chicago's; but the council refused, preferring to issue construction bonds. Taking its case to the Wisconsin Supreme Court, TMER&L succeeded in overturning the council's action. But civic reform groups and their political allies, including the Socialists, continued to use the threat of a municipal plant to force lower rates and better service.[59]

Across Wisconsin, mounting dissatisfaction with franchised utilities produced three alternative solutions, each designed to make utilities more accountable. First was government ownership and operation. Many newspapers, mayors, and civic and political organizations advocated it, and between 1896 and 1900, Oconomowoc, Wausau, Janesville, Whitewater, Sheboygan, Berlin, River Falls, and Plymouth established municipal waterworks or lighting plants. Milwaukee circumvented an unfavorable ruling by the state supreme court and built a municipal garbage incinerator by 1903. Madison earned a national reputation for "municipal socialism." It tried, but failed, to achieve public ownership of gas and electric utilities, and constantly attacked the privately owned trolley system (whose principal owner was aloof and unpopular). The municipality did gain ownership of the sewer system in 1902. Complaints about municipal utilities' rates and services continued, but most Wisconsinites seemed to concur with the Milwaukee Municipal League that public waterworks did a much better job than private ones.[60]

The second and less common solution was the consumer co-operative. Most noteworthy was the Wisconsin Valley Plan, which originated in Wausau, Grand Rapids, Merrill, and Marshfield as part of a revolt against the Wisconsin Telephone Company. Begun in the 1890's, the Valley Plan eventually resulted in more than one hundred local co-operatives. Fond du Lac, Grand Rapids, and Wausau also experimented with electrical co-operatives at the end of the century.

[59] Still, *Milwaukee*, 365–368; Thelen, *New Citizenship*, 284–289.
[60] Still, *Milwaukee*, 368–376; Mollenhoff, *Madison*, 307–311, 388–396; Thelen, *New Citizenship*, 239–242, 270–287; Leavitt, *Healthiest City*, 122–155; McShane, *Technology and Reform*, 106–135.

For the most part, municipal ownership and consumer co-operatives enjoyed their greatest success in smaller cities, and especially in the areas of water, telephone, electricity, and garbage disposal.

The third solution was to seek redress in the legislature. The Milwaukee Municipal League and the League of Wisconsin Municipalities lobbied for the power to submit utility franchises to popular referenda, for greater latitude in framing franchise regulations, for the right to provide certain municipal services, and for greater leverage in taxing quasi-public corporations. Such efforts fueled a vigorous debate over what role state government ought to play in the movement towards more public involvement in providing basic municipal services.[61]

Explosive urban growth also put pressure on other municipal services, such as schools, police and fire protection, and poor relief. Between 1889 and 1904, at a cost of more than $2 million, Milwaukee built thirty-one new schools, constructed ten additions to existing ones, purchased twenty-three new sites, and added numerous temporary barracks and mobile classrooms. School expenditures increased nearly twice as fast as the population, despite the facts that nearly half the city's children did not attend any school, and large numbers attended parochial schools. Between 1910 and 1920, public school enrollments jumped 48 per cent, more than double the city's population increase. The school system also began night schools and summer sessions; classes for the deaf, blind, anemic, and speech defective; adult education; vocational and technical schools; free textbooks; and school lunches.[62]

Milwaukee's police department grew at a significantly slower pace, with ambivalent results. Police chief John T. Janssen ruled the department with an iron hand from 1888 to 1912. He did much to improve the force's discipline and efficiency, virtually eliminated organized crime (especially the protection racket), and oversaw the doubling of per capita police expenditures between 1888 and 1910. However, his tolerance of gambling, prostitution, and similar diversions contributed to Milwaukee's reputation as a wide-open city. This paradox disturbed many clergymen, club women, and civic reformers. (It also made Milwaukee highly attractive to conventioneers, working-class males, and Chicago "sports.") Then the Social Demo-

---

[61] Thelen, *New Citizenship*, 239–248; David Nord, "The Experts Versus the Experts: Conflicting Philosophies of Municipal Utility Regulation in the Progressive Era," in *WMH*, 58 (Spring, 1975), 219–236.

[62] Still, *Milwaukee*, 359–360, 414–416; Laurence M. Larson, *A Financial and Administrative History of Milwaukee* (Madison, 1908), 150–152; John A. Butler, "Milwaukee: Gas and Electric Light Service," in *Annals of the American Academy of Political and Social Science*, 27 (January, 1906), 213–215.

cratic administration of Mayor Emil Seidel closed down the middle-class vice district on River Street in 1911, and Milwaukee finally became a model of rectitude.[63]

Fire protection followed a similar pattern. Bad fires in the 1890's had prompted the city government to expand the fire-fighting force and to purchase new equipment, expanding the budget by 60 per cent between 1888 and 1910. But the council proved painfully slow in enacting and enforcing an effective inspection code, until the advent of the Social Democrats under Seidel.[64]

Statewide, pressures for poor relief varied according to business cycles. The depression of 1893–1897 and less drastic downturns of 1907–1909 and 1914–1915 all swelled the ranks of the indigent and accelerated calls for more comprehensive and effective programs and more stringent standards for measuring "need" and "worth." Wisconsin cities responded by relying primarily upon churches, fraternal and benevolent associations, charitable institutions, and settlement houses. In Janesville, these concerns resulted in Associated Charities, an affiliate of the National Conference of Charities and Corrections. It aimed "to discover and relieve the worthy poor, to discover mendicancy, expose imposture, and diminish pauperism." Similarly, in Racine, there were the Relief Association, organized in the 1890's, and the Central Association, organized in 1910, which gradually adopted a settlement house approach, meaning that "social workers" lived and worked in the city's poorer districts and did not confine themselves to paying visits to the needy. During the 1890's, Milwaukee, Superior, Sheboygan, La Crosse, and Eau Claire all established affiliates of Associated Charities; Madison and Milwaukee established settlements. Public, tax-supported relief programs remained small and sparsely funded. They ranged from "outdoor relief," provided to persons in their residences by the city or county, to "indoor relief," bestowed in what were variously called "tramp," "poor," or "work" houses.[65]

An often overlooked but lasting urban legacy has come down to

---

[63] Still, *Milwaukee*, 357–358; Larson, *A Financial and Administrative History*, 140.
[64] Still, *Milwaukee*, 358–359; Larson, *Financial and Administrative History*, 140.
[65] Fleckner, "Poverty and Relief in Janesville," in *WMH*, 61: 291–298 (quote); McVicker, ". . . Who Would Otherwise Have Suffered," 16–79; Thelen, *New Citizenship*, 113–129; Mollenhoff, *Madison*, 408; and Steven M. Avella, "Health, Hospitals, and Welfare: Human Services in Milwaukee County," in Ralph M. Aderman, ed., *Trading Post to Metropolis: Milwaukee County's First 150 Years* (Milwaukee, 1987), 216–229; Ruth Harman and Charlotte LeKachman, "The 'Jacobs' House,'" in *WMH*, 16 (March, 1933), 252–273; Ann S. Waligorski, "Social Action and Women: The Experience of Lizzie Black Kander" (master's thesis, University of Wisconsin, 1970), 43–62, 82–105.

the present from this era. The services, institutions, infrastructure, and appearances created then remained largely in place almost everywhere until well after World War II and even into the 1990's. Wisconsin cities took their shape out of the tumult which churned a century ago.

[4]

Each crisis in municipal services produced its own reform movement, usually multifaceted in membership, motivation, goals, and methods. And each reform movement involved some remedies that were essentially private and voluntary, some that called for government involvement. None met with complete success, but most did ameliorate harsh conditions. Urban housing reform received special attention, mostly aimed at fulfilling the American dream of home ownership. In Madison, newspaper editors, professors, club women, and BLIS officials joined together to reveal miserable housing conditions and to push the city council in 1910 into adopting a building permit system and a construction code. The new code authorized a full-time inspector who could halt construction, demand repairs, and condemn property. During his first tour, the inspector ordered 200 landlords to add newly required fire escapes.[66]

In Milwaukee, social settlement workers, health officials, politicians, the South Side Women's club, the North Side Civic League, and the City Club tackled the housing problem together. Most threw their efforts behind playgrounds, parks, and social centers as temporary retreats for those who lived in wretched conditions. An ordinance regulating new housing finally passed in 1906, but enforcement was weak and a state law superseded it. In 1910, the incoming Socialist administration made inspection tours of Polish, Italian, and Jewish neighborhoods and came up with a broad remedial program. It included cleaning up garbage and sewage in slums, city planning, extending mass transit, and experiments in municipal housing. The Socialists proposed buying a million dollars' worth of real estate on the city's periphery, constructing low-cost working-class dwellings on it, then connecting it to the central business district by a municipally run streetcar line. The Socialists' defeat in 1912 doomed the plan, although opposition by developers and contractors probably would have killed it had the Socialists won.[67]

---

[66] Mollenhoff, *Madison*, 353–359.
[67] Still, *Milwaukee*, 389–390; Thompson, "Socialists and Slums—Milwaukee," in *The Survey*, 25: 367–376; Lawrence M. Friedman and Michael J. Spector, "Tenement House Legislation in Wisconsin: Reform and Reaction," in the *American Journal of Legal History*, 9 (January, 1965), 41–63.

Public health improvement was more successful in Milwaukee. In just under twenty-five years, an ambitious coalition of private associations and public officials transformed it from a city with the usual number of health problems to one vying to be called the nation's healthiest. A host of community health and welfare organizations played a critical intermediary role between city government and the public to achieve the transformation. The city's health department, through a succession of activist commissioners, broadened government's responsibility and authority. New medical knowledge and the Social Democratic administration helped this alliance revolutionize prevention and control of infectious diseases, sanitation standards, and regulation of foods. The outcome was that between 1892 and 1920 Milwaukee's mortality rate was slashed nearly in half.[68]

Advancement occurred even during Mayor Rose's administration. One of his health commissioners, Dr. F. M. Schulz, was appointed over objections that he was unqualified. Indeed, Schulz ignored civil service regulations and had a penchant for self-promotion. Nevertheless, he expanded the public health staff and laboratory, began public school inspections and regulation of exposed food, oversaw the openings of a new isolation hospital and the municipal garbage-incineration plant, and lobbied for an anti-spitting ordinance. His immediate successors continued in the same vein.[69]

Madison rivaled Milwaukee in trying to become "the city healthful." Energetic women's organizations and University of Wisconsin scientists spearheaded the work, which was notable for an effort to eliminate harmful microorganisms, especially tuberculosis bacteria, from its milk supply. In 1907, the board of health inveighed against unsanitary butcher shops, grocery stores, bakeries, and restaurants. In 1909–1910, the Women's Club waged war against the house fly. Revelations about the impurity of the city's drinking water helped university scientists and the board of health in a decades-long campaign for sewage disposal and treatment. The Women's Club and political scientist and city alderman Samuel Sparling championed the collection and disposal of garbage. In 1912, a team of physicians and visiting nurses backed a school hygiene drive which included sanitary drinking fountains, lavatories, inoculations, physical examinations, and preventive education. Members of the Madison Literary Club inaugurated a private-public coalition that culminated in the opening of three hospitals between 1903 and 1911.[70]

In Madison and several other cities, single-issue efforts to ameliorate one or another of the harshest realities of urban industrial life merged into broad-based municipal reform movements. Solutions

---

[68] Leavitt, *Healthiest City*, 42–75, 190–264; Still, *Milwaukee*, 555–561.
[69] Leavitt, *Healthiest City*, 42–75, 97–120, 141–155, 174–189, 214–227, 268–271.
[70] Mollenhoff, *Madison*, 384–405.

varied, and often incorporated private-sector efforts, but most reformers recognized that only city government possessed the necessary authority and resources to make and enforce changes. Reformers joined the political process as campaigners, contributors, lobbyists, advisors or officeholders, greatly expanding political discourse and enlarging the scope of government.[71]

Reform methods and outcomes differed greatly from city to city. In Ashland, preoccupation with fiscal retrenchment, nonpartisan political approaches, and anti-vice crusades dominated reform efforts. The Civic Federation, founded in 1895, was governed by the Committee of Forty-Five, which included laborers, women citizens, and clerks, as well as the usual businessmen and professionals. It stressed enforcement of moralistic blue laws, nonpartisan local elections, tax relief, and governance by "the best men." When Mayor C. M. Everett McClintock blatantly dispensed patronage, ignored abuses by the water utility company, and failed to prosecute tax dodgers, the federation initiated impeachment proceedings. They failed. The federation worked particularly for lower taxes, regarded high taxes as a way for government to seize private property, and blamed high taxes on extravagant city and county spending. It was instrumental in the election of a five-term mayor, Thomas Bardon, a well-to-do businessman. He cut budgets through reducing services and laying off employees; and he courted support through stricter regulation of the water utility and promises of tax equalization and a municipal waterworks, pledges he failed to fulfill.[72]

In Superior, a dizzying political scenario played out between 1894 and 1900. In 1894, the Taxpayers' League helped elect Frank A. Woodward (president of the local chamber of commerce) mayor. Woodward cut taxes by almost one-third, pushed for local civil service, and ignored public demands to regulate the Superior Light and Power Company. In 1895, working-class voters successfully ousted Woodward and elected an Episcopal priest and populist Democrat, Charles S. Starkweather. He refused to enforce Superior's blue laws and was consequently impeached, largely at the urging of the elitist Civic Federation and the Good Government Club. A more broadly based activist coalition within the Republican party succeeded this alliance, and it abandoned retrenchment, civil service, antivice crusades, and nonpartisanship in favor of city-owned utilities. The coalition succeeded in electing Martin Pattison, who forced both the street railway and the water, power, and light utility company to make

---

[71] Holli, "Urban Reform," in Gould, ed., *The Progressive Era*, 133–151; Mohl, *New City*, 108–138; Michael H. Ebner and Eugene M. Tobin, eds., *The Age of Urban Reform: New Perspectives on the Progressive Era* (Port Washington, New York, 1977).
[72] Thelen, *New Citizenship*, 176–184.

concessions. When the utility companies managed to deny Pattison renomination, progressive Republicans joined with Populists and Democrats to elect Starkweather to another term on a municipal ownership platform. Starkweather then confounded many of his supporters by vetoing an annulment of the utility company's franchise during a typhoid epidemic in which the company was implicated. Finally reform Republicans and Democrats, along with most Populists, rallied behind Hervey Dietrich, an attorney. He won by promising to tame utility companies, which he did by gaining control over the water utility and annuling, in 1900, the street railway company's franchise.[73]

In Madison, municipal reform frequently blurred the lines between private and public, state and local, expertise and democracy, elitism and populism. University faculty members and state government officials—and their wives, sisters, and daughters—exerted disproportionate influence on governance, often enforcing as public servants what they advocated as private citizens. Their efforts sometimes complemented those of the city's businessmen and professionals, whose first priority was economy. Several women's organizations were especially influential. In 1910 Madison became the national focal point for the Civic Center movement, which used public schools as forums for discussion of public issues and as laboratories for experimenting with solutions. Its founder, Edward J. Ward, was enticed to the University of Wisconsin from Rochester, New York.[74]

Madison reformers headed statewide crusades to implement the state's Corrupt Practices Act of 1911, the Non-Partisan Act of 1912, and the Uniform Municipal Accounting Act of 1911. The first attempted to prohibit local politicians from attracting voters to the polls with free beer, cigars, and transportation. The second sought to separate local politics from state and national, making local politics nonpartisan, thus eliminating the time-honored ethno-cultural, partisan appeals to working-class voters. The third permitted Madison to hire an expert from the state tax commission, who divided expenditures into functional categories, held department heads accountable, and required frequent, consistent, and comparable disclosure.[75]

Such reforms held little attraction for the city's lower social orders. The working class believed that they benefited from increased government spending. They responded positively to the personalized politics of ward bosses and ethno-cultural and partisan appeals, and regarded political activities as a vital part of their social lives. Struc-

---

[73] *Ibid.*, 185–201.
[74] Mollenhoff, *Madison*, 295–303.
[75] *Ibid.*, 228, 305–307, 407–408; *Wisconsin State Journal*, March 25, 1896. The *Journal* urged voters to approve the commission government.

tural reform also troubled some middle-class Madisonians, who feared alienating the working class. Many social reformers embraced Ward's civic center movement, in which the public used schools during off hours for debating, literary, artistic, social, and athletic activities. Their efforts resulted in neighborhood associations in each of the city's ten wards, and in Neighborhood House, a social settlement based upon Chicago's Hull House.[76]

Tension between efficiency and democracy surfaced in a 1912 referendum on the commission form of government. It polarized the Madison electorate, largely along socio-economic and ethno-cultural lines, with the most vocal opposition emanating from German-Americans. Opponents won by 55 per cent, opting for personalized, tolerant, and compassionate machine politics over efficiency, expertise, and professionalism. The same basic tension affected attitudes towards the famed progressive reforms of direct primary elections, initiative, referendum, and recall. Each was usually proposed as a way to give power to the citizenry, but many activists were highly skeptical, charging that these reforms would benefit already advantaged Madisonians. Legislative enactment of the nonpartisan local election law produced the same division, and led to the establishment of a Madison chapter of the Municipal Voters League, composed almost entirely of persons from the middle and upper classes.[77]

Ethno-cultural and class divisions also permeated the movement to make Madison "the city virtuous" by curtailing alcohol, gambling, and prostitution. The ward-based city council preferred leniency towards saloons but not towards vice, and it generally backed Republican mayors. In 1904, during the mayoralty of Dexter Curtis, gambling and prostitution were virtually eliminated, and a referendum to raise liquor license fees barely failed. Madison's Prohibition party debuted in 1912; it and related organizations endorsed civil service, the commission form of government, and public ownership of utilities. Arrayed against prohibitionists and law-and-order Republicans were local Democrats and the city's saloon organization. Although pro-alcohol "wets" managed to win most elections and referenda, they did so by ever decreasing margins, and only by making major concessions.

In self-conscious Madison, municipal reform also was characterized by attempts to achieve "the city beautiful" and "the city functional." Beginning in the 1890's, the Madison Park and Pleasure Drive Association under John M. Olin launched an ongoing crusade for numerous parks and the Yahara River Parkway, built with private donations but maintained with tax dollars. The passage of a one-half-

[76] Mollenhoff, *Madison*, 407–408.
[77] *Ibid.*, 304–307.

mill park tax in 1908 and proposals for new parks vexed some property owners, but were sustained by the voters. Madison's success in creating a park system and landscape amenities attracted favorable national attention, and libraries around the country collected the Park and Pleasure Drive Association's reports.[78]

Olin also lured to Madison a nationally renowned urban planner, John M. Nolen, one of the leading architects of the "city functional" movement. His comprehensive 1911 plan, *Madison: A Model City*, suggested ways to make the city humane, convenient, efficient, and beautiful, through a combination of housing, recreation, transportation, and land use controls. The city's business elite stymied adoption of the plan's seventeen key recommendations. Nolen later contributed to city planning in Milwaukee, La Crosse, Janesville, and Kenosha.[79]

Finally, Madison municipal reform owed a great deal to numbers of well-educated, economically secure women committed to civic involvement. The Women's Club concentrated on "municipal housekeeping," which included education, health, housing, esthetics, morals, recreation, and charity. Women's organizations succeeded in implementing or improving garbage collection, milk inspection, pest control, the first hospital, anti-litter crusades, a free dental clinic, and experiments in low-cost housing.[80]

[5]

In Milwaukee, in contrast to Madison's emphasis on principles and a sedate intellectual approach, municipal reform was highly politicized. Both major parties were part of symbiotic business-government relationships, personified by Republicans Henry Clay Payne and Charles F. Pfister and Democrats Edward C. Wall and John Mitchell. The system guaranteed that public utilities, contractors, and other businesses benefited from franchises, minimal taxation, and regulation. The ethno-cultural partisan politics which lay at the core of the system emphasized prohibition, foreign-language instruction, and Sunday observance. Parties took care to select candidates and officeholders from specific ethnic groups. The Democratic party appealed primarily to Catholic ethnic groups; the Republicans, to non-Lutheran Protestants. German Lutherans frequently held the electoral balance. Important socio-economic reform issues often took second place to ethnic recognition, to the struggle between morality and advocates of personal liberty (who tended to tolerate the wide-open

---

[78] *Ibid.*, 311–320, 324–341.
[79] *Ibid.*, 324–369.
[80] *Ibid.*, 369–384.

city), and to ethnic issues like foreign-language instruction and anti-Catholicism.[81]

The fires of reform were sparked by the depression and by indignation against public utilities and their political allies. Eventually, the various streams of discontent channeled into two distinct, but often interactive, movements. One was a middle-class reform movement operated through nonpartisan civic organizations like the Milwaukee Municipal League (MML), which was an affiliate of the National Municipal League, founded in 1893, and the Voters League, founded in 1904. MML members consisted of leading businessmen and professionals who concerned themselves with civil service, retrenchment, and tax reduction. The MML battled the "system" in Milwaukee and backed Republican candidates who promised to apply business methods to government. It lobbied successfully for civil service and corrupt practices legislation and became perhaps the most influential reform organization in the state by 1897. Its techniques of distributing pamphlets, holding mass meetings and public forums, and using newspapers revolutionized Milwaukee politics.[82]

From 1896 on, the MML focused on tax equity, reforming parties' nominating mechanisms, and regulating public utilities. It played a crucial role in the struggles against TMER&L and other utilities, the brazen Rose administration, and nefarious elements in the common council.

The Voters League often aided the MML. The League established organizations in selected wards to campaign against "unsavory" aldermen; it allied with the progressive wing of the Republican party by 1896; and it helped in 1898 to form the Republican Club of Milwaukee County, which soon became the political vehicle of Francis E. McGovern. It also affected the Democratic party by leading a 1906 middle-class revolt within the party against the excesses of the Rose administration.

Although working-class politics in Milwaukee dated back at least to 1848, it was the Bay View massacre of May 4, 1886, in which five workers demonstrating for an eight-hour day were killed by the state militia, that truly galvanized it. Labor organizations which even before Bay View had backed a series of unsuccessful working-class po-

---

[81] Still, *Milwaukee*, 279–320; Roger E. Wyman, "Voting Behavior in the Progressive Era: Wisconsin as a Case Study" (doctoral dissertation, University of Wisconsin, 1970), 26–162; Sarah C. Ettenheim, *How Milwaukee Voted, 1848–1968* (Milwaukee, 1970), 2–20; Bernard E. Fuller, "Voting Patterns in Milwaukee, 1896–1920: A Study with Special Emphasis on the Working Class of the City" (master's thesis, University of Wisconsin-Milwaukee, 1973), 20–78.

[82] Still, *Milwaukee*, 299–302, 307, 310, 373, 378; Thelen, *New Citizenship*, 158–75, 202–22; Herbert F. Margulies, *The Decline of the Progressive Movement in Wisconsin, 1890–1920* (Madison, 1968), 106–123, 137–138, 148–152.

litical parties, helped form the nucleus of the very successful Social Democratic Party (SDP) in the city and state. A critical election took place in 1896, when Milwaukee labor backed Populist Henry Smith for mayor, although Smith received only about one-fifth of the vote.[83]

Just two years later, the Social Democratic Party made its debut; its mayoral candidate received only 5 per cent of the vote. Yet, within a dozen years, this new party engineered a victory that made Milwaukee the largest Socialist-run city in the country. Much of the credit belonged to Victor L. Berger, an Austrian-born intellectual and editor who came to Milwaukee in 1892. Berger vigorously supported organized labor's candidates in his newspaper, *Vorwärts*. He also allied with "Yankee" reformer Frederic Heath, a co-founder of the Milwaukee Ethical Society. In 1897, he and Heath joined with Eugene Debs, president of the American Railway Union, in organizing the Social Democracy of America. The Milwaukee group formed "Branch One," a distinction it kept even after Debs changed the name of the national organization to the Socialist Party of America in 1901.[84]

The SDP's electoral strongholds were on the Germanic northwest side, whose residents had already imbibed socialist philosophy. It took a decade to make inroads among Poles and other predominantly Catholic working-class ethnics. The party extended its appeal to the middle class by championing honest, efficient government, in contrast to that of business-oriented Republicans and corrupt Democrats. Equally crucial were the party's close ties to the Milwaukee's Federated Trades Council and the Wisconsin State Federation of Labor, both of which were dominated by Socialists for more than twenty years.[85]

The SDP employed the model of Europe's highly centralized and disciplined socialist parties, with precinct organizers, official membership, dues, multilingual flyers and orators, lectures, concerts, ba-

---

[83] Still, *Milwaukee*, 284–302; Wyman, "Voting Behavior in the Progressive Era," 163–211; Sally M. Miller, *Victor Berger and the Promise of Constructive Socialism, 1910–1920* (Westport, Connecticut, 1973), 17–44; Robert M. Rice, "The Populist Party in Milwaukee" (master's thesis, University of Wisconsin-Milwaukee, 1967), 190–203; J. Martin Klotsche, "The 'United Front' Populists," in *WMH*, 20 (June, 1937), 375–389; Leon Fink, *Workingmen's Democracy: The Knights of Labor and American Politics* (Urbana, 1983), 202–212, 221–230; Robert C. Nesbit, *History of Wisconsin. Volume III: Urbanization and Industrialization, 1873–1893* (Madison, 1985), 390–414.

[84] Marvin Wachman, *History of the Social-Democratic Party of Milwaukee, 1897–1910* (Urbana, 1945), 30–40; Frederick I. Olson, "The Milwaukee Socialists, 1897–1941" (doctoral dissertation, Harvard University, 1952), 41–84; Edward J. Muzik, "Victor L. Berger: A Biography" (doctoral dissertation, Northwestern University, 1960), 131–137, 175–179.

[85] Although the majority of Socialist voters were German, the majority of Germans supported either of the two major parties, at least until 1910. See Fuller, "Voting Patterns in Milwaukee," 83–143.

zaars, and women's branches, and newspapers (the English-language *Herald* and *Leader*, the German-language *Vorwärts* or "Forward," and the Polish-language *Naprzod*, also "Forward"). The SDP advocated constitutional processes, favored incremental progress instead of revolution, unemployment and worker's compensation, health and safety legislation, workers' pensions, municipal ownership of public utilities, public markets, good government, equitable taxation, business regulation, and protection of workers' rights and welfare. Some of these goals it shared with the two major parties. To achieve them, it downplayed its more doctrinaire socialistic demands and concentrated on the rest. In its 1910 platform, the SDP promised municipal ownership and management of a variety of public services, free schoolbooks, lunches, and concerts, tax reform, an eight-hour day and a union wage for city employees, the use of schools as social centers, charter reform, parks and playgrounds, and electoral redistricting. In general it taught other parties the need to widen their concept of urban services.[86]

Between the middle of the 1890's and 1915, Milwaukee's reform movements—the "elitist" and the "populist"—operated in separate streams, converged for a time, and ultimately diverged. The Milwaukee Municipal League came into being because of concerns over rising taxes and political corruption. Its campaign for a nonpartisan civil service commission eventually removed 1,300 positions from the patronage system. The Populists demanded municipal ownership of the electric utility and the enfranchisement of a competing transit company; the MML wanted the city to purchase utility franchises in order to lower taxes. Aroused by a utility tax reduction act and by a tragic streetcar accident of February, 1895, Populists again demanded a competing company and a four-cent fare, while the MML came out for municipal ownership, with compensation to the company, and repeal of the tax law. In the 1896 mayoral election, the MML supported victorious progressive Republican William J. Rauschenberger, who vacillated between enfranchising a competitor and municipal ownership. A focus on public utility issues during Rauschenberger's two years in office energized a coalition that included people from both municipal reform streams, all political parties, and a variety of ethnic societies and socio-economic organizations. It was a coalition that persisted for nearly two decades.[87]

---

[86] Miller, *Victor Berger*, 33–39; Wachman, *History of the Social-Democratic Party*, 77–81; Olson, "Milwaukee Socialists"; Muzik, "Victor L. Berger," 137–149; Roderick Nash, "Victor L. Berger: Making Marx Respectable," in *WMH*, 47 (Summer, 1964), 301–308; Joseph A. Gasperetti, "The 1910 Social-Democratic Mayoral Campaign in Milwaukee" (doctoral dissertation, University of Wisconsin-Milwaukee, 1970), 73–139.

[87] Thelen, *New Citizenship*, 156–175, 252–267; McShane, *Technology and Reform*, 84–122; Still, *Milwaukee*, 299–309.

In 1898, Henry Clay Payne confounded the MML and the progressive Republicans by denying the mayoral nomination to Henry J. Baumgaertner and instead giving it to William Gueder. Populists and Democrats countered by jointly nominating David Rose on a platform promising municipal ownership of public transit—an unresolved issue from the previous administration. Rose defeated Gueder by 8,000 votes. (The SDP candidate received only 2,441 votes.) Municipal ownership seemed a certainty because Rose was mayor and the so-called "Popocrats" were but one vote shy of a two-thirds majority in the council. (Some municipal ownership did come about when Rose signed a garbage plant ordinance; legal maneuvers delayed completion until 1903.) Federal judge William H. Seaman complicated the streetcar question by invalidating an 1896 four-cent fare ordinance, only to have the Popocrat council repass the measure.[88]

In February of 1899, Rose touched off a political firestorm by negotiating a compromise ordinance which would have given TMER&L a twenty-year franchise renewal and a five-cent fare, in exchange for a yearly payment. The resulting protest had the odd effect of uniting Populists and Socialists with the MML and the Merchants and Manufacturers Association. Rose and Payne were forced to work out another compromise ordinance, providing for a four-cent fare during rush hour, in exchange for a grant of immunity until 1934. The action generated the largest and most broadly based protest to date. Despite eleven injunctions and a $100,000 libel suit filed by Payne against the *Sentinel*, the council passed the ordinance, which Rose signed on January 2, 1900. Eighteen of the twenty-five pro-compromise aldermen went down to defeat in the next election. But Mayor Rose, wily and resourceful, won again, relying on ethno-cultural appeals and thinly veiled support of the city's wide-open status.[89]

Socialists continued to campaign for municipal ownership after 1900, but middle-class reformers turned their attention elsewhere—to issues provided by the Rose administration: MML-backed civil service, which Rose called hypocritical, and corruption, which got the most attention. Rose ran what was probably the most graft-ridden administration in the city's history. To counteract criticism, he appealed to Catholic voters' parochial interests. The chief actor in exposing Rose was Francis McGovern, assistant district attorney from 1901 to 1905 and district attorney from 1905 to 1909. In December, 1903, his office called for a grand jury to investigate charges of corruption in the Milwaukee County House of Correction. By the end of January, 1904, the jury had brought in sixty-nine indictments

---

[88] Thelen, *New Citizenship*, 270–289; McShane, *Technology and Reform*, 123–130; Still, *Milwaukee*, 307–309, 373–376.

[89] The *Wisconsin State Journal*, February 27, 1900, observed ironically that Milwaukee might be run by a council behind bars.

against twenty-four employees. In March, 1904, another grand jury returned fifty more indictments, most of them against the so-called "Asphalt Ring," whose members had profited from paving contracts.[90]

The scandal prompted formation of the Voters' League, and the 1904 mayoral nomination of progressive Republican Guy Goff. Victor Berger ran against Goff and Rose. Rose won by nearly 6,000 votes over Goff, and Berger received only 2,500. But Francis McGovern was elected district attorney.

McGovern quickly indicted eighteen current or former county supervisors. In July, 1905, he indicted fourteen more, including the fire chief and other fire officials. He reached into elite ranks by naming Charles Pfister for his role in a rendering company bribery scandal. Before it was finished on September 30, 1905, the grand jury barely failed to indict Rose for requiring officeholders to contribute to his reelection. Despite all this, McGovern and progressive Republicans proposed no important local reforms. Instead, they turned to state and national politics, relinquishing the municipal field to the Social Democrats after 1906.[91]

The graft trials helped subdue Mayor Rose temporarily in 1906. The trials' chief beneficiary was a neophyte with no reform agenda: Sherburn M. Becker, twenty-nine, the politically inexperienced son of a prominent Milwaukee financier. He received the Republican nomination for mayor in 1906. Becker hired a public relations agent and organized "betterment clubs" for young men. When Rose accused him of being born with a silver spoon in his mouth, Becker countered that the mayor had been born with a tin horn in *his* mouth and had been tooting it ever since. Becker upset Rose by 1,500 votes, while Socialist William A. Arnold received 28 per cent.[92]

As the "boy mayor," Becker toured the eastern half of the United States in his carmine-colored Pope-Toledo automobile, nicknamed the "Red Devil." Becker's two-year term was characterized by colorful antics and virtually nothing of substance, paving the way for Rose's re-election to his fifth term in 1908. Rose's closest competition came from Social Democrat Emil Seidel, who polled just over one-third of the vote.

As it proved, this was David Rose's last fling. In April, 1910, the SDP

---

[90] Still, *Milwaukee*, 308–312, 361; Ondercin, "Corruption, Conspiracy and Reform," in *Historical Messenger*, 26: 112–117; Mowry, "The Reign of Graft in Milwaukee," in *The Arena*, 34: 589–593.

[91] Still, *Milwaukee*, 312–316; Ondercin, "Corruption, Conspiracy and Reform," in *Historical Messenger*, 26: 117–122.

[92] Still, *Milwaukee*, 312–316; Milwaukee *Journal*, December 10, 1929, February 6, 1949.

Urbanism, Crisis, and Reform 169

swept to victory. Emil Seidel polled 27,608 mayoral votes, to 20,530 for Democrat Vincenz J. Schoenecker and 11,346 for conservative Republican J. M. Beffel. The progressive Republicans were totally preoccupied with state politics, especially with Francis McGovern's successful campaign for governor. The triumphant Socialists also elected twenty-three of thirty aldermen, a majority of the county board, and a quarter of the school board; and they captured all the major city offices. That November, Victor Berger was elected to represent the city's northwest side in Congress.[93]

[6]

These electoral victories focused national attention on Milwaukee's Socialists. Locally they signified growing acceptance by middle- and upper-middle-class voters of the party and its pledges of good government; they also had been impressed by the exemplary behavior of those Socialists who held public office before 1910. The Socialists downplayed their ideological differences with mainstream reformers, stressing measures that would leave private property largely intact. Indeed, the SDP's 1910 platform differed little from that of the Democrats and progressive Republicans, although its support came principally from working-class wards. Their biggest gains after 1908 were in districts dominated by unskilled workers of Polish ancestry and other recent immigrants, largely of Catholic backgrounds. The Socialist triumph was a blend of organized labor, converts from the ranks of unskilled, recent immigrant workers, middle-class voters revolted by the corruption of both major parties, Socialist officeholders and their good reputations, and a lot of hard grass-roots campaigning. Victor Berger brilliantly orchestrated the entire operation, combining the precinct-level organization and discipline of the old politics with the systematic techniques of the new.[94]

Once in office, Milwaukee's Socialists expanded municipal services and instituted reforms. They abolished public drinking cups, installed public toilets, rubber garbage cans, and wastepaper boxes, and began flushing the streets regularly. A pilot child welfare "station" decreased infant mortality in the Fourteenth Ward by 50 per cent.

---

[93] Fuller, "Voting Patterns in Milwaukee," 83–143; Ettenheim, *How Milwaukee Voted*, 33–50, 84–88, 102–104, 124; Still, *Milwaukee*, 304–320; Miller, *Victor Berger*, 37–39; Wachman, *History of the Social Democratic Party*, 67–76; Olson, "Milwaukee Socialists," 129–150; Gasperetti, "The 1910 Social-Democratic Mayoral Campaign," 109–112.

[94] Still, *Milwaukee*, 316–320; Miller, *Victor Berger*, 69–73; Wachman, *History of the Social-Democratic Party*, 71–76; Olson, "Milwaukee Socialists," 150–170; Fuller, "Voting Patterns in Milwaukee," 200–203; Gasperetti, "1910 Social-Democratic Mayoral Campaign," 110–137.

Unable to abolish the contract system of street improvements because they lacked a three-fourths majority in the council, Socialist aldermen created the post of street commissioner, cut the cost of paving by nearly 80 per cent, increased competition among contractors, and provided penalties for contract default. They also passed eight streetcar ordinances that regulated speed, expanded facilities during rush hours, and provided for the inspection and cleaning of cars. Allied with organized labor, Emil Seidel's administration set a minimum wage and a union scale for city employees and established a joint labor-industry-government committee on unemployment. Seidel and his city attorney, Daniel W. Hoan, expanded the public concert program, used the public schools as social centers, and attempted to close the rowdiest saloons and gambling dens. Socialists created commissions to oversee land, housing, the harbor, and city planning. The city building inspector stringently enforced the building codes. As city attorney, Hoan gained $13 million worth of concessions from public utility companies, and succeeded in reducing gas, light, streetcar, and telephone rates.[95]

The Seidel administration outdid middle-class reformers by hiring the university's labor economist, John R. Commons, for advice about internal government efficiency and economy. The professor later marveled that his cohorts—mostly mechanics and trade unionists—were more capable and rational than their British counterparts. Even critics of the Socialists admitted that they had improved the quantity and quality of municipal services without significantly raising per capita expenditures.

What Milwaukee's Social Democrats failed at most notably was socialism. Municipal ownership of major utilities, except for water and garbage disposal, was thwarted by long-term franchises and legal limits on indebtedness. Charter restrictions and an unbeatable non-Socialist majority in the council prevented a municipal commodities market, co-operative housing, and municipal plumbing, lodging, icehouses, and slaughterhouses. The survival of Rose appointees in key positions also hampered Seidel. (They were protected by the very civil service system that Rose had so abhorred.) The Socialists were also fiscally conservative, which pleased homeowners and lending institutions. Socialists feared arousing middle- and upper-class opposi-

---

[95] Still, *Milwaukee*, 515–519; Douglas E. Booth, "Municipal Socialists and City Government Reform: The Milwaukee Experience, 1910–1940," in the *Journal of Urban History*, 12 (November, 1985), 52–70; Olson, "Milwaukee Socialists, 171–217; Robert C. Reinders, "The Early Career of Daniel W. Hoan: A Study of Socialism in the Progressive Era" (master's thesis, Notre Dame University, 1948), 49–83; Floyd Stackowski, "The Political Career of Daniel Webster Hoan" (doctoral dissertation, Northwestern University, 1966), 31–49.

Urbanism, Crisis, and Reform   171

tion with high property taxes, nor did they want to see bankers and financiers realize high profits on municipal bonds. Nor was Seidel infallible. Although he generally appointed qualified people to office, regardless of party, he also rewarded some inexperienced Social Democrats, leading to charges of partisanship and incompetence. Other Milwaukeeans complained about the growing cost of government services and the activities of new tax examiners. Finally, the 1911 legislature prevented the city from eliminating the contract system for street paving.[96]

In a sense, the Socialists were the victims of their own success. Their achievements mitigated Milwaukee's urban crisis, satisfying many who had voted for them. Once the crisis was overcome and the rascals thrown out, enough of those voters returned to major party rule, not giving the Socialists enough time and power to fully impose their ideology on the city. "Nonpartisan government" gradually replaced "good government" as a slogan among many middle-class reformers; but this was really a euphemism for ridding the city of Socialist "radicalism." Upper-middle-class institutions and the Milwaukee *Journal* made nonpartisanship their rallying cry for those of high character. Just a few days after the 1910 election, the *Journal* prophesied that in 1912 Republicans and Democrats would have to unite in order to beat the SDP. Both parties introduced a nonpartisan local election law in the 1911 legislature, but a coalition of Social Democrats and McGovern Republicans defeated it.[97]

In 1912, Milwaukee Republicans and Democrats united behind Gerhard Bading, whom Seidel had removed as health commissioner. Berger's *Leader* complained that the Bading forces were "fusing everybody crooked with everybody ignorant," and that nonpartisanship really meant " 'all-partisan' against the Socialists." Even though Seidel received 3,000 more votes than he had two years earlier, his share dropped from 47 to 40.6 per cent. Bading received virtually all of the balance. The fusion ticket fashioned a fifteen-seat margin on the common council, and Daniel Hoan was the only Socialist to retain office.[98]

Just one month later, the legislature enacted a nonpartisan local election law, which Governor McGovern signed despite his personal opposition. Running as a nonpartisan in 1914, Mayor Bading stressed

[96] Still, *Milwaukee*, 518–520; Booth, "Municipal Socialists," in *Journal of Urban History*, 12: 65–70; Olson, "The Milwaukee Socialists," 218–274.
[97] Still, *Milwaukee*, 519–521; Milwaukee *Journal*, April 6, 1910; Fuller, "Voting Patterns in Milwaukee," 148–159; Margulies, *Decline of Progressive Movement*, 156.
[98] Still, *Milwaukee*, 520–522 (quote); Fuller, "Voting Patterns in Milwaukee," 159–165; Reinders, "The Early Career of Daniel W. Hoan," 96–101; Margulies, *Decline of Progressive Movement*, 156; Stackowski, "The Political Career of Daniel Webster Hoan," 45–60.

administrative efficiency, civil service, durable paving, pure drinking water, scientific sewage treatment, child welfare, home rule, and privately supported administrative research. Seidel attacked nonpartisanship, insisting that without parties no poor man could be elected. Socialists accused Bading of extravagance and of concentrating authority in the hands of wealthy commissioners. They pledged to continue to seek municipal ownership of utilities, including street railroads, believing transit profits would lower taxes. Although Seidel did get more votes in 1914 (43.5 per cent), Bading was reelected. Only Hoan again upheld the honor of the SDP.[99]

One major outcome of municipal reform between 1893 and 1914 was a tremendous expansion of city government in size, scope, and budget, and in public services. Milwaukee added over a hundred new functions, ranging from public health agencies to specialized libraries, from free employment bureaus to traffic control. During the 1890's, it established a public library and museum, its first public bath and swimming pool, and a park complex that included a zoo and concert facilities. In 1907 alone, the city instituted teachers' pensions, municipal rubbish collection, a technical high school, supervised playgrounds, an auditorium, a tuberculosis hospital, and a fingerprint system for identifying criminals. Five years later, it added centralized voter registration, child welfare stations, continuing and adult education, and chemical testing of the city's water and pavement.[100]

The educational system undertook innovations in vocational, extension, and night instruction. Its operational costs quadrupled and its per pupil expenditures doubled between 1890 and 1920. During the same period, per capita police spending increased by 150 per cent, firefighting by 95 per cent, public health and parks by 200 per cent, and the construction and maintenance of bridges and public buildings by 135 per cent. Between 1900 and 1910, Milwaukee spent nearly $1 million on newly perfected concrete and asphalt paving. Between 1889 and 1906, the city's bonded indebtedness increased from just under $3 million to $5.7 million. From the Dickensian 1880's, Milwaukee had emerged a near model of civic consciousness.

Madison established nearly all of its public services between 1880 and 1900. Between 1900 and 1920, it significantly expanded government's scope and influence and the role of expert professional guid-

---

[99] Still, *Milwaukee*, 522–523; Reinders, "The Early Career of Daniel W. Hoan," 96–105; Fuller, "Voting Patterns in Milwaukee," 165–168; Olson, "Milwaukee Socialists," 275–332.

[100] Still, *Milwaukee*, 356–395, 582–588; Larson, *Financial and Administrative History*, 135–157; Holli, "Urban Reform," in Gould, ed., *The Progressive Era*, 148–151. Holli argues persuasively that escalating demands upon municipal services led to higher expenditures, regardless of the structure or ideology of city government.

ance. By 1920, according to historian David Mollenhoff, Madisonians "had abandoned the stand pat get-out-of-the-way-do-little concept of local government for the interventionist progressive model." Racine also greatly expanded municipal services between 1890 and 1920, establishing a professional police department, paving principal streets, building parks, and offering residential water and electrical service, garbage collection, and sewage disposal. Kenosha responded to its population explosion with a pavement program (1892), city engineer (1893), board of health and municipal water system (1895), garbage collection (1901), franchised streetcars (1902), and new sewer system (1910). Janesville, Eau Claire, Green Bay, La Crosse, and Neenah-Menasha followed suit.[101]

These municipal reforms made demands, often conflicting, on state government. Because the legislature exercised control over municipal affairs, urbanites of various political persuasions generally united under the rubric of "home rule," which in turn led them to want state government to intervene on behalf of a variety of controversial causes. Lawmakers often found themselves caught in a crossfire between competing urban interest groups. Losers in municipal battles turned to state government to gain leverage. Besieged utility companies sometimes lobbied for state regulation to ward off municipal ownership. Utilities like TMER&L and the Wisconsin Telephone Company held franchises in several cities, so their reform-minded clients regarded state government as the only agency with sufficient scope and power to regulate or tax them. Common problems led cities to form umbrella organizations like the League of Wisconsin Municipalities, and to seek statewide solutions.[102]

Urban lobbyists and initiatives from Madison and Milwaukee played important roles in the adoption of the general municipal incorporation law of 1892. Then, in 1893, Madison mayor William H. Rogers organized a meeting of chief executives from eighteen Wisconsin cities (not including Milwaukee) to discuss the new law's inadequacies. The mayors elected Rogers chairman and moved to seek

[101] Mollenhoff, *Madison*, 205–227, 295–303, 408–411, 436 (quote); William J. Murin, "Politics and Government, 1836–1920," in Nicholas C. Burckel, ed., *Racine: Growth and Change in a Wisconsin County* (Racine, 1977), 222–226; Racine, Common Council, *Proceedings*, May 31, 1893, December 2, 1913, pp. 304–309; Racine, Treasurer, *Report*, 1893, pp. 16–19; Racine, Common Council, *Budget*, 1914; Steven C. Hansen et al., *History of the Racine Fire Department: 150 Years of Fire Protection in Racine, Wisconsin* (Dallas, 1992), 55–80; Keith Bosman, "Evolution of City Services in Kenosha, Wisconsin, 1850–1920," unpublished research paper, May, 1994, at the University of Wisconsin-Parkside Area Research Center, Kenosha, pp. 8–12; Hollingsworth and Hollingsworth, *Dimensions in Urban History*, 113–117; Glaab and Larsen, *Factories in the Valley*, 216–219, 277–280.
[102] Thelen, *New Citizenship*, 244–249; Nord, "Experts Versus the Experts," in *WMH*, 58: 222–231.

several new powers for cities of the second and third class. The following year, the MML organized an intercity campaign to extend civil service and corrupt practices legislation. Leading figures in forty-two cities responded, and MML chapters resulted in Ashland, Superior, Beloit, Racine, Madison, Appleton, La Crosse, and other cities.[103]

Four years later, the MML sponsored a meeting of eleven mayors and other state officials. This evolved into the League of Wisconsin Municipalities (LWM), which began a statewide information clearinghouse. In 1899, at the second conference, twenty-seven mayors endorsed the MML's model city charter, which included utility regulation and home-rule provisions. The conference also appointed a committee to manage its legislative agenda. During the 1899 legislative session, these lobbyists pushed for limiting utility franchises to twenty-one years, mandating them to file financial statements, requiring referenda on franchise extensions or municipal ownership proposals, and eliminating the municipal debt limit for investment in municipal ownership. The LWM also pressed for the registration of utility lobbyists and for required referenda on franchise extensions, increased taxation of utility companies, and the banning of free railway passes for public officials. The following year, LWM founded a magazine called *Municipality*. At the National Municipal League's 1900 Good City Government Conference in Milwaukee, its secretary roundly praised Wisconsin as the place "where the chosen officials of the cities show an intelligent and generous disposition to co-operate with public spirited citizens," and declared that Wisconsin held great promise for passage of the league's urban agenda.[104]

Following LWM's lead, Wisconsin's urban reformers escalated their involvement in statewide politics. Their most urgent popular demand was for home rule. The general incorporation act of 1892 required that statutes apply uniformly to all cities of the same class, but this still left Milwaukee and the handful of cities of the second class vulnerable to special legislation. The law also let the legislature continue to determine policy, set local tax rates, collect corporate taxes, and oversee law enforcement, poor relief, and other municipal services. Urban lobbying began to succeed after 1900. In 1907, the legislature granted Milwaukee permission to call a convention to draft a comprehensive home-rule charter, much to the delight of progressive Republicans and Social Democrats. Twenty-eight separate civic and commercial associations united in the Milwaukee Federation of Civic

[103] Mollenhoff, *Madison*, 227; Thelen, *New Citizenship*, 244–249; Nord, "Experts versus the Experts," in *WMH*, 58: 222–228.
[104] Thelen, *New Citizenship*, 245–248. The NML also designated Wisconsin its pilot state for enactment of its model city charter.

Societies endorsed the convention. Only the Wisconsin Chamber of Commerce did not.[105]

Mayor Rose headed the opposition. He branded the convention as an SDP attempt to turn its ideology into law, denied the gathering the use of city hall because it had no legal standing as an organization, and persuaded the city council's finance committee to deny it funding. Rose was joined by most of the city's liquor and vice merchants, and by the major utility companies, all of whom feared stronger local government. Despite such formidable opposition, the convention met and adopted a home-rule charter; but the 1909 legislature failed to approve it. Undaunted, advocates pressed for a home-rule constitutional amendment.

Lacking home rule, many municipal reformers sought the potential benefits of intervention by state government. They continued to propose amendments to the electoral process and ways to modernize administration. Nonpartisan municipal elections and the commission form of government, as a means to combat both urban political machines and the Social Democrats, remained favorites. The LWM initially supported retention of caucuses for selecting delegates to party conventions, provided that caucus participants voted secretly in booths. By 1898, that stand motivated the LWM to campaign for direct primary elections, a position shared with MML. Many reformers also campaigned strongly for initiative, referendum, and recall— means by which the electorate could directly intervene in the legislative process.[106]

As for modernizing administration, municipalities advocated tax reform, especially after 1895. Faced with demands for public services and incensed by tax evasion and tax delinquency, urban activists petitioned the legislature to redistribute tax burdens according to citizens' ability to pay, to equalize the general property tax, and to tax intangible personal property like stocks, bonds, and securities more heavily. City officials and reformers also endorsed establishing an investigative state tax commission.[107]

The MML and its allies also lobbied hard for more equitable and efficient taxation of railroads and public utility companies. Two circumstances spurred them. First, the railroads' contribution to total state revenues declined from 72 to 47 per cent between 1892 and 1897; second, the 1895 legislature brought other public utilities under the license fee umbrella. Accordingly, the MML headed the fight

---

[105] Still, *Milwaukee*, 377–378; Thelen, *New Citizenship*, 244–246, 288, 304–306, 312; Donoghue, "Local Government System," in *Wisconsin Blue Book, 1968*, pp. 108–110.
[106] Thelen, *New Citizenship*, 141–149, 213–218, 291–312; Still, *Milwaukee*, 520–522.
[107] Thelen, *New Citizenship*, 204–208.

to restore *ad valorem* taxes on corporate property; and city officials and taxpayer groups pressed for the repeal of the 1895 license fee system for public utilities, the trebling of existing license fee taxes, prevention of the inclusion of city water companies under the license fee umbrella, and the removal of sleeping car, freight line, and equipment companies from the same protection. In 1899, they lobbied for a significant increase in the license fee taxes paid by the state's insurance companies.[108]

Municipal reformers led, too, in the fight to regulate public utility companies, although many preferred municipal ownership. In the late 1890's, the MML, its affiliates, and various urban newspaper editors began advocating public ownership of utilities. Related crusades sprang up in nearly every Wisconsin city, and almost every local political party pledged to "municipalize" at least one utility. However, many urban reformers apparently viewed municipal ownership as merely a weapon with which to coerce private utility companies, either to make concessions in rates and service or to accept more regulation. Other reformers were seemingly daunted by the legal and financial problems inherent in ownership and operation. The strength of the municipal ownership movement eventually persuaded many utility companies to embrace regulation by a state commission, either as the lesser of two evils or because they had learned from experience that they could exercise influence over regulatory bodies.[109]

By 1907, many urban reformers contented themselves with granting municipalities the authority to construct, purchase, own, and operate all utilities, except telephones and streetcars, and to enjoin private corporations to surrender their properties for "just compensation." By 1914, municipal utility reformers were divided among themselves over the intent and efficacy of state regulation, with a significant number stigmatizing it as a ploy to frustrate municipal ownership.[110]

Urban-state rivalry also hampered efforts at comprehensive housing reform. Milwaukee's local ordinance regulating new multi-unit

[108] *Ibid.*, 208–211.

[109] *Ibid.*, 244–249; Nord, "Experts Versus the Experts," in *WMH*, 58: 228–234; Charles J. McNally, "The History of Public Utility Legislation in Wisconsin" (master's thesis, Marquette University, 1935), 1–42.

[110] John R. Commons, "The Wisconsin Public-Utilities Law," in *The American Review of Reviews*, 36 (July–December, 1907), 221–224; B. H. Meyer, "The Wisconsin Public Utilities Law," in the Pittsburgh Conference for Good City Government of the National Municipal League, *Proceedings*, 1908, pp. 257–268; McNally, "History of Public Utility Legislation," 42–45; Stiles P. Jones, "State Versus Local Regulation," in the American Academy of Political and Social Science, *The Annals*, 53 (May, 1914), 94–107; G. C. Mathews, "The Truth About State Regulation of Utilities in Wisconsin," in *The Annals*, 54 (July, 1914), 303–320; Nord, "Experts Versus the Experts," in *WMH*, 58: 234–236.

construction was overridden by the state tenement law of 1907, which made the Bureau of Labor and Industrial Statistics a state watchdog. Milwaukee officials, realtors, and contractors objected vigorously. The Social Democrats belatedly leaped to the measure's defense. Then the state supreme court invalidated the law in 1908 (partly on the grounds that it was unreasonable to apply the same standards to metropolitan and non-metropolitan areas). The Republicans responded by suggesting a new law that would protect "home life" in cities. In 1909, Milwaukee realtors backed a successful bill that limited state inspection and enforcement to only the largest cities and multiple family housing.[111]

Between 1900 and 1920, advocates of poor relief and public health reform demanded state government intervention. The Wisconsin Conference of Charities and Corrections, the umbrella organization for the state's social workers, sought state action on behalf of child and women's labor, education, housing, recreation, and public health. University Extension sponsored an institute in 1911 that revitalized the organization. After that, it pushed for mothers' pensions, juvenile courts, and a state industrial commission.[112]

Through the *Wisconsin Medical Journal*, its official organ, the State Medical Society lobbied for mandatory smallpox vaccinations, stronger local health boards, disinfection of homes where tuberculosis sufferers lived, regulation of child labor and tenement housing, compulsory examination of schoolchildren, "eugenic" sterilization of the "insane, idiots, imbeciles, sexual perverts, defectives, epileptics, rapists and criminals," and for state inspection of water and milk. It joined the College of Agriculture in 1911 to campaign for government aid in fighting tuberculosis.[113]

Beginning in the 1890's, Wisconsin's rapidly expanding cities were beset by a mounting sense of crisis—in governance, revenue, health, housing, environment, and the provision of seemingly countless services. This crisis mentality energized several urban reform movements representing people from government, universities, profes-

---

[111] Friedman and Spector, "Tenement House Legislation," in *American Journal of Legal History*, 9: 53–63.

[112] Harman and LeKachman, "The 'Jacobs' House,' " in *WMH*, 16: 273–281; Mark H. Leff, "Consensus for Reform: The Mothers' Pension Movement in the Progressive Era," in *Social Science Review*, 47 (September, 1973), 397–417; Wisconsin Conference of Charities and Corrections, *Proceedings*, 1893, pp. 5–9; 1913, p. 120; 1914, p. 9; 1915, pp. 12–13; Virgil E. Long, "State Supervision and Control of Welfare Agencies and Institutions in Wisconsin: Processes and Structures" (doctoral dissertation, University of Wisconsin, 1914), 253–255; "Social Center Work in Milwaukee," in *Charities and the Commons*, 21 (October, 1908–April, 1909), 441.

[113] "What the 1907 Legislature Has Done," in *The Wisconsin Medical Journal*, 6 (July, 1907–May, 1908), 93.

sional organizations, and urban-based interest groups. They differed widely in their diagnoses of and prescriptions for urban malaise; but most eventually agreed that no truly effective solutions were possible without purposefully restructuring and expanding municipal government. The effort to bring about that transformation turned Wisconsin cities into municipal reform battlegrounds by the end of the decade and created many conflicts, some of which persisted throughout the remainder of the Progressive Era.

At the same time, most of these same activists were forced to concede that many of the state's urban problems were so widespread and complex as to defy solution by municipal government alone. So they expanded their theater of operations to the state capital, where they lobbied for both increased home rule and governmental oversight of urban development. Persistent and persuasive, they soon added their voices to a swelling chorus of those who advocated a vastly expanded role for state government.

5

Natives and Newcomers

[1]

THE people of Wisconsin—like people everywhere, in all times—were from the beginning a volatile mixture of natives and newcomers; but rarely more so than between 1893 and 1914. As early as 1853, one slightly hyperbolic publicist had proclaimed that the infant state's population, like that of the new nation, consisted "of heterogeneous masses collected together from every quarter of the globe" who would "jar for a moment, like different metals in the furnace," before amalgamating into "the most perfect race of men that has ever appeared on earth." As it turned out, the jarring phase proved to be of far longer duration.[1]

The original Wisconsinites were Native Americans, who by the 1820's had consolidated themselves into four principal groups: the Chippewa, a mixed group of Chippewa and Ottawa and Potawatomi, the Menominee, and the Winnebago. A few members of the Sioux and other tribes still were living along the borders, and "newcomers" from several eastern tribes were moving in, all part of a fluid situation that had existed among Great Lakes Native Americans and new European immigrants for at least two centuries. Between 1829 and 1848, these four principal tribes ceded most of their domain to the United States. Drastically diminished in numbers, land, and resources, their descendants lived largely on reservations in the northern half of the state. By 1890, Wisconsin's Native American population had declined to 6,095 "reservation Indians" and 3,835 "civilized Indians"—meaning those who did not live on reservations, including everyone from "traditionals" to persons who had attempted to join the American mainstream.

At the point when territorial status was achieved in 1836, the picture had already become more complex. During the fur-trade era, from the late 1600's to the 1830's, a small contingent of French-Canadians had settled in Wisconsin, many of them of mixed French

[1] John Gregory, *Industrial Resources of Wisconsin* (Milwaukee, 1855), 12–13 (quotes), 22–25.

and Indian ancestry. The southwestern lead-mining region, which flourished during the early nineteenth century, attracted a few thousand migrants, most from the American border states, especially Missouri, and some directly from Cornwall and Wales.[2]

Indian land cessions and Wisconsin's attainment of territorial status (1836) and statehood (1848) attracted two substantial migration streams. Their interaction defined much of the state's ethno-cultural identity. The first consisted of "Yankees" from New England, New York, Pennsylvania, and Ohio. Endowed with capital and skills, well-versed in pioneering and the workings of federal land laws, and experienced in government and politics, Yankees quickly seized control of Wisconsin's socio-economic engine. Fiercely pietistic, they soon established a functional moral community and set about their mission of "saving" others. Deeply committed to formal education and universal literacy, they used the public school to inculcate moral and civic virtue. Prizing direct personal participation in both church and government, they designed a polity that demanded continuous, informed involvement from the grass roots up. Although they were soon a numerical minority in the new state, Yankees continued to exercise a pervasive influence upon its private and public cultures through several generations. Looking backward from the close of the nineteenth century, the Maine-born journalist, politician, and historian Ellis B. Usher astutely observed that Wisconsin, for all its ethnic diversity, was still "distinctively American . . . in its educational impulse and its progress." "Wisconsin institutions," he continued, "have been dominated by Americans of the Puritan seed from the beginning."[3]

The second migration stream flowed from northern and western Europe, lured by the state and nation's economic promise and ready acceptance of newcomers. The state constitution of 1848 granted suffrage to any foreign-born adult male who resided in Wisconsin for a year and officially declared his intention to become a citizen. By 1860, the number of immigrants and their children approximately equaled

---

[2] Alice E. Smith, *The History of Wisconsin. Volume I: From Exploration to Statehood* (Madison, 1973), 13–15, 122–161; Nancy O. Lurie, *Wisconsin Indians* (Madison, 1980; reprinted, 1987); Robert C. Nesbit, *Wisconsin: A History* (2nd ed., by William F. Thompson, Madison, 1989), 89–132. The most comprehensive study of Wisconsin Indians is Robert E. Bieder, *Native American Communities in Wisconsin, 1600–1960: A Study of Tradition and Change* (Madison, 1995). In keeping with the *History of Wisconsin* series policy to use the historic names of ethnic groups current during the periods covered by each volume, the name "Winnebago" for what its members now call the Ho-Chunk tribe will be used in this volume.

[3] Smith, *From Exploration to Statehood*, 162–198, 464–498; Ellis B. Usher, "Puritan Influence in Wisconsin," in *SHSW Proceedings*, 1898, p. 127; Nesbit and Thompson, *Wisconsin*, 91–105; Richard N. Current, *Wisconsin: A Bicentennial History* (New York, 1977), 39–40.

the total population of those who were American-born of American-born parents. By 1890, three-fourths of all Wisconsinites were either immigrants or the children of foreign-born parents.[4]

Far and away the largest component of this immigrant stream was Germanic, from the various independent German states as well as Austria, Switzerland, and Luxemburg. By 1890, Germans alone constituted half the foreign-born population and about half of the American-born children of immigrant parents, making them at least one-third of Wisconsin's total population. They concentrated in the southern and eastern counties, providing an effective counterpoint to Yankee culture and earning Wisconsin its well-known (though oversimplified) reputation as a "German state." Close behind came the Scandinavian stream of Norwegians, Danes, Swedes, Finns, and even Icelanders, who had generally settled in northern and western Wisconsin, with Dane County as the most significant location in the U.S. for Norwegians. Slightly less numerous were arrivals from the British Isles: English, Scots, Welsh, and Irish. Except for the Catholic Irish, British immigrants soon blended with Yankee society and culture, as did English-speaking newcomers from Canada. Then came Poles, who because of European boundaries and census bureau dicta were mostly counted among the Russians, Austrians, Germans, and "others." Much smaller contingents of Dutch, Belgian, and French immigrants added to the state's overwhelming northwestern European flavor. A relative trickle from Bohemia, Italy, and Greece added a southern and eastern European flavor.[5]

Throughout the nineteenth century, these "different metals in the furnace" continued to "jar" rather than blend. Conflicts arose over using alcohol, properly observing Sunday, retaining foreign languages and customs, and the educational system. Each of these ethnocultural issues penetrated Wisconsinites' self-esteem and frequently caused moral struggles.

Ostensibly contests between Yankee and Teutonic views of life, these conflicts most frequently divided along religious lines that were often more complex than mere ethnic divisions. The predominant Yankee values of temperance, Sabbataranism, personal salvation, and the need to enforce individual morality were firmly rooted in a pietistic or evangelical outlook. These values were generally shared by most Scandinavian and British immigrants, by certain German Prot-

---

[4] Nesbit and Thompson, *Wisconsin*, 142–162; Richard N. Current, *The History of Wisconsin. Volume II: The Civil War Era, 1848–1873* (Madison, 1976), 42–83; La Vern J. Rippley, *The Immigrant Experience in Wisconsin* (Boston, 1985), 1–27; *Eleventh Census of the United States, 1890: Report on Population, Part 1*, pp. 606–609, 684–703.

[5] Current, *Wisconsin: A Bicentennial History*, 34–66; Current, *Civil War Era*, 42–83; Rippley, *Immigrant Experience*, 1–58.

estants and Freethinkers, and by pietist-evangelical Dutch and Swiss newcomers. They were opposed by those with a liturgical or ritualist orientation that stressed "right belief," prescribed practices, hierarchical organization, and a communal religious orientation. That world view united Roman Catholics—whether German, Irish, Belgian, Dutch, Polish, Czech, or Swiss—and the occasional Episcopalian, Jew, or Freethinker. Sometimes it also encompassed sizable numbers of German Lutherans, who generally played a wild-card role in ethno-cultural disputes, depending upon which side of their outlook the issue energized.[6]

In 1890, Wisconsin maintained a delicate balance between natives and newcomers, between pietists and ritualists. In addition to the 9,930 Indians and the vast majority of the 2,444 Negroes identified in the census, nearly 70 per cent of the state's white population had been born in the United States. Almost 57 per cent had originated in the state itself, an indication that Wisconsin had nearly concluded its pioneer phase. Yet among states with over 1 million residents, Wisconsin was second only to Minnesota in its proportion of immigrants and their children. Combined, these two accounted for nearly 74 per cent of the state's population, meaning that only 26 per cent of the total had two American-born parents. Whether natives or newcomers dominated depended entirely upon how one interpreted the 43 per cent who were the American-born children of foreign-born parents. This was a category in which Wisconsin led among million-plus states: 726,835 children out of a total population of 1,693,330. These were distributed along a continuum, with those who were thoroughly acculturated and assimilated at one extreme, and those who remained as "old country" as their parents at the other.[7]

In 1890, about one-half of Wisconsin's 519,199 immigrants were natives of Germany; nearly one-fifth, natives of Norway, Sweden, or Denmark; another one-fifth, natives of Great Britain, Canada, or Ireland. For their American-born children, the figures were about the same: German-Americans, just over half the total; Scandinavian, 11 per cent; Irish, 11 per cent; British, 8 per cent; and Canadian, 6 per cent.[8]

Religious divisions that cut across ethnic lines complicated matters. Approximately 45 per cent of Wisconsin's churchgoers were Roman Catholics, at least half of whom were Germans or German-speakers who frequently were at odds with their Irish, Czech, Polish, Belgian, Dutch, or French co-religionists. Just under one-fourth of all church-

---

[6] Current, *Wisconsin: A Bicentennial History*, 39–54; Current, *Civil War Era*, 117–155; Rippley, *Immigrant Experience*, 28–58.
[7] *Eleventh Census of the United States, 1890: Report on Population, Part 1*, pp. 486–487.
[8] *Ibid.*, 606–609, 667–668, 686–687.

goers professed mainline Yankee religions: Methodists, Congregationalists, Episcopalians, Baptists, Presbyterians, or Unitarians. Occupying the middle ground were the nearly 30 per cent who belonged to immigrant Protestant churches, the overwhelming majority of whom were affiliated with one of several Lutheran synods. While virtually all Catholics were "ritualists," and nearly all communicants of Yankee churches were "pietists," the Lutherans were more difficult to categorize and frequently considered themselves both. Although most were anti-Catholic, German Lutherans frequently coalesced with German Catholics to oppose prohibition and blue laws.[9]

During the early 1890's, this volatile mix generated bitter ethno-cultural conflicts. The battle lines generally pitted Yankees, Scandinavians, and other advocates of "right behavior" against German, Irish, Polish, and Bohemian Catholics, and other proponents of "right belief." In general, pietists sought to use state and local government to ensure right behavior, ritualists regarded such questions as matters of private conscience, informed by church doctrine. Because they reflected each person's sense of identity and self-esteem, such conflicts often became more fierce than struggles over economic competition or politics. Religious upbringing was the major determinant of political affiliation, so ethno-cultural issues frequently became partisan, reinforcing or realigning standard divisions. As the ranks of the ritualists increased, through both immigration and procreation, pietists felt evermore constrained to "save" them. By the 1890's, Yankee and European-stock pietists had united under the aegis of the Republican party; ritualists, along with some social dissidents, under that of the Democratic party.[10]

The most celebrated ethno-cultural conflict of the time—and perhaps in all of Wisconsin history—erupted over the Bennett Law (1889), which required that all Wisconsin schools, public and parochial, teach certain subjects only in the English language. Named for its legislative sponsor, the Bennett Law touched off a furious reaction among German Catholics and Lutherans. They viewed the law as an attack not only on their parochial schools but also on their language and culture. The Democrats astutely made repeal of the Bennett Law the primary plank in their 1890 platform and swept the Republicans out of office. Almost simultaneously, Humphrey J. Desmond, editor

---

[9] *Eleventh Census of the United States, 1890: Report on Statistics of Churches*, 38–43, 87; Nesbit and Thompson, *Wisconsin*, 346; Richard J. Jensen, *The Winning of the Midwest: Social and Political Conflict, 1888–1896* (Chicago, 1971), 58–88; Paul Kleppner, *The Cross of Culture: A Social Analysis of Midwestern Politics, 1850–1900* (New York, 1970), 35–91.

[10] Jensen, *Winning of the Midwest*, 123–148; Kleppner, *Cross of Culture*, 316–375; Roger E. Wyman, "Voting Behavior in the Progressive Era: Wisconsin as a Case Study" (doctoral dissertation, University of Wisconsin, 1970), 24–70.

of the *Catholic Citizen*, which circulated statewide, mounted a legal challenge against compulsory reading from the King James version of the Bible as a moral textbook in the state's public schools. A lawsuit ensued in Edgerton; the resultant case ignited bitter ethno-religious conflict, earned national notoriety, and culminated in a landmark decision by the Wisconsin Supreme Court that upheld the Catholic position, outlawing all Bible reading in the public schools.[11]

The Bennett Law and the Edgerton Bible Case contributed very heavily to the formation of the Wisconsin chapter of the American Protective Association (APA), an organization dedicated to saving the United States from what members viewed as conspiracies fomented by Catholic immigrants in league with the Pope and the Vatican. By 1894, Wisconsin had some 100 local chapters and 177,000 members, and was the APA's largest statewide affiliate. (Milwaukee alone had twenty councils.) Opposition to Catholic influence united pietists, evangelical Lutherans, freethinkers, and anticlericals throughout the state—a curious amalgam of the fervently churched and the militantly unchurched. The APA's chief outlet was the Milwaukee-based *Wisconsin Patriot*, published between 1894 and 1898. (Kenosha and Portage each had smaller papers.) The *Patriot* routinely warned of the "plot" by the Roman Catholic church to "take over" the United States. One of the principal "plots" was the successful effort to place a statue of Father Jacques Marquette, the French Jesuit explorer, as one of Wisconsin's two permanent statues in the U.S. Capitol. It touched off an ugly debate between the APA on the one hand and Catholics and more tolerant Protestants on the other.[12]

Although they usually stopped short of endorsing the APA, several leading Protestant publications called for public restrictions on Cath-

---

[11] Robert C. Nesbit, *The History of Wisconsin. Volume III: Urbanization and Industrialization, 1873–1893* (Madison, 1985), 605–612; Wyman, "Voting Behavior in the Progressive Era," 170–114; Robert J. Ulrich, "The Bennett Law of 1889: Education and Politics in Wisconsin" (doctoral dissertation, University of Wisconsin, 1965); William F. Whyte, "The Bennett Law Campaign in Wisconsin," in *WMH*, 10 (June, 1927), 363–390; Janet C. Wegner, "The Bennett Law Controversy in Wisconsin, 1889–1891: A Study of the Problem of 'Americanization' in the Immigrant Church and Its Relation to the History of Church and State in the United States" (master's thesis, Brown University, 1966).

[12] The statue is no longer in the U.S. Capitol's Statuary Hall itself, where each state now is limited to one. A statue of Robert M. La Follette, Sr., is there today. Donald L. Kinzer, *An Episode in Anti-Catholicism: The American Protective Association* (Seattle, 1964), 64–67, 91, 115–118, 151–154, 179–180, 258–260; K. Gerald Marsden, "Patriotic Societies and American Labor: The American Protective Association in Wisconsin," *WMH*, 41 (Summer, 1958), 287–294; E. David Cronon, "Father Marquette Goes to Washington: The Marquette Statue Controversy," in *WMH*, 56 (Summer, 1973), 266–283; Harry H. Heming, *The Catholic Church in Wisconsin: A History of the Catholic Church in Wisconsin from the Earliest Time to the Present Day* (Milwaukee, 1895), 278–279.

olic immigration, and for the private conversion and Americanization of those who had already arrived. Some Yankee denominations also expressed occasional hostility towards Lutheran immigrants. The 1886 Wisconsin Baptist convention charged that immigration fueled both the "Romish church" and "Socialism," and characterized socialism as "fiendish work." William Walter Webb, the Episcopal bishop of Milwaukee, reminded his own clergymen that "sometimes we are spoken of as 'Apostles to the Genteels,' " and he urged them to reach out to working-class people, Germans, and Scandinavians.[13]

Few issues vexed Protestant churches more than Sunday and temperance laws. Operating through such organizations as the Wisconsin Sunday Rest Day Association, Christian Endeavor, and the Epworth League, clergymen and laity alike opposed the efforts of organizations such as the Personal Liberty League to repeal Sunday blue laws. Sabbatarians coordinated and publicized these efforts through publications like the *Lord's Day Papers*. Congregationalist conventions condemned Sunday activities—baseball games, theatrical performances, saloon visits, business meetings, and day excursions. The Epworth League of the Methodist church urged members to put Christianity into politics and condemned sales of beer at the state fair, riding bicycles on Sunday, and even Sunday travel by state militiamen to encampment.[14]

This ethno-cultural furor among natives and newcomers gradually ebbed, as the depression of 1893–1897 and Progressive Era reformers pushed socio-economic and political questions to the fore. The disavowal of APA support by the national Republican party during the 1896 campaign helped kill the APA. However, similar antagonisms lurked just below the surface, poised to spring up under pressures from three different "metals" being added to Wisconsin's "furnace": Indians who lost their reservations by a federal law which permitted them to subdivide and sell their lands, thus forcing them to attempt to acculturate; immigrants from southern and eastern Europe; and Negroes who had begun migrating from the rural South to south-

---

[13] Wisconsin Baptist Convention, *Minutes*, 1886, p. 21; H. A. Miner, "Report on the Work of Our Churches," in Congregational Convention of Wisconsin, *Minutes*, 1897, pp. 13, 35–37; Superior *Evening Telegram*, July 2, 1894; Wisconsin State Epworth League of the Methodist Episcopal Church, *Proceedings*, 1897, p. 5, 1898, pp. 13, 75–76, and 1899, p. 25; William Walter Webb, "The Call to the Ministry," in *The Church Times*, 19 (no. 5, 1909), 78.

[14] *Lord's Day Papers*, 26 ([September, 1896]), 1–4, 31 ([February, 1897]), 1–2, and no. 74 ([August, 1900]), 1–4; A. McK., "Reaching the Masses," in *Our Church Life*, 1 (September, 1895), 157; Pilgrim, "Milwaukee Letter," in *Our Church Life*, 9 (December, 1902), 10; "Labor Day," in *Wisconsin Congregational Church Life*, 18 (September, 1911), 1; S. H. Anderson, "Report of Department Conference on Literary Work," Wisconsin State Epworth League of the Methodist Episcopal Church, *Proceedings*, 1895, p. 49.

eastern Wisconsin's industrial cities. Together, they touched off another round in the ongoing debate over what constituted an American.

Clearly, many Wisconsinites doubted whether American Indians, southeastern Europeans, and black migrants could internalize the values of Yankees and northwestern Europeans sufficiently to justify their assimilation. Whites denied assimilation even to acculturated people of color, and whites constituted over 99 per cent of the state's population between 1890 and 1950, let alone 1920.[15]

Between 1890 and 1920, Wisconsin's population grew by more than three-fifths, and the native-born element increased its predominance. The reported Indian population jumped to 10,142 by 1910, then fell to an all-time low of 9,611 in 1920. The state's Negro population swelled by over 80 per cent, although Negroes still numbered a mere 5,201 by 1920. For whites, the native-born proportion grew from 70 per cent to 82 per cent. In that group, the portion whose parents had been born in the United States went from 26 to 41 per cent; and in that group, the percentage of those born in Wisconsin went from 57 to 71 per cent. By 1920, one-quarter of those born in the state had migrated to other states. Wisconsin was a net loser in interstate migration during the Progressive Era, with out-migrants averaging between 22 and 25 per cent, and in-migrants, from 11 to 13 per cent. The largest single segment of the state's population, 42 per cent, continued to be the American-born children of immigrant or mixed parentage, consisting mostly of the children of northwestern European immigrants.

At the same time, the proportion of foreign-born Wisconsinites declined from nearly 31 per cent to slightly over 17 per cent during the most prolific period of immigration in American history. (Nearly a million immigrants a year were pouring into the United States between 1897 and 1914.) But the number of foreign-born Wisconsinites declined from 519,199 to 460,485, due partly to natural attrition but mostly to a drop in emigration from northwestern Europe. Even so, by 1920 Wisconsin still had the seventh-largest foreign-stock population in the country, more than 58 per cent of German ancestry, and 15 per cent of Scandinavian.[16]

The status of Native Americans in the state was made particularly

---

[15] Wyman, "Voting Behavior in the Progressive Era," 115–162; Jensen, *Winning of the Midwest*, 159–169; Kleppner, *Cross of Culture*, 369–375; David L. Brye, *Wisconsin Voting Patterns in the Twentieth Century, 1900–1950* (New York, 1979), 163–224; Rippley, *Immigrant Experience*, 43–59.

[16] *Eleventh Census of the United States, 1890: Report on Statistics of Churches*, 684–689; *Fourteenth Census of the United States, 1920: Population, Volume 2, General Report and Analytical Tables*, 902–905.

shaky in 1887 when the president signed the Dawes General Allotment Act. The Dawes Act reversed sixty years of "removal and reservation" policy in favor of one which ultimately forced acculturation of the nation's Indians. It permitted tribes to allot "in severalty" their reservation lands among tribal members. Each family would receive 160 acres; each single adult or orphaned child, eighty acres; all other single persons under eighteen years of age, forty acres. Allotted land was to be held in trust for twenty-five years, before becoming the private property of individuals. Then they were free to sell it under state or territorial laws. Those Indians who had "voluntarily taken up residence separate and apart from any tribe of Indians therein" and "adopted the habits of civilized life" might become citizens. Any reservation lands remaining after allotment would be sold to the general public under federal land laws, with the proceeds to be held in trust for tribes as a whole.[17]

The stated purpose of the Dawes Act was to turn Indians into self-sufficient farmers who would be devoted to normative American ideals of private property, free enterprise, and social mobility. Its most obvious result, however, was to decrease the amount of land held by Indians from 139 million acres in 1887 to 78 million by 1900.[18]

The Dawes Act eventually cost Wisconsin's Indians half their remaining land. By 1895, the Chippewa had allotted over one-third of their land; by 1910, almost three-quarters. By the early 1930's, the Oneida retained less than 1,000 acres of their original 65,000; the Stockbridge-Munsee, virtually nothing of their 44,000 acres. The Winnebago, who had been granted homesteads under an 1884 congressional act, lost most of them through tax default, sale, or excessive subdivision among family members. They survived by hunting, trap-

---

[17] Wilcomb E. Washburn, comp., *The American Indian and the United States: A Documentary History* (4 vols., New York, 1973), 3: 2188–2192; Delos S. Otis, *The Dawes Act and the Allotment of Indian Lands*, ed. Francis Paul Prucha (Norman, 1973); Vine Deloria, Jr., and Clifford M. Lytle, *American Indians, American Justice* (Austin, 1983), 8–12.

[18] Necah Furman, "Seedtime for Indian Reform: An Evaluation of the Administration of Commissioner Francis Elbington Leupp," in *Red River Historical Review*, 2 (Winter, 1975), 495–517; David R. Wrone, "Indian Treaties and the Democratic Idea," in *WMH*, 70 (Winter, 1986–1987), 83–101; Wilcomb E. Washburn, *Red Man's Land/White Man's Law: A Study of the Past and Present Status of the American Indian* (New York, 1971), 145; John F. Berens, "Old Campaigners, New Realities: Indian Policy Reform in the Progressive Era, 1900–1912," in *Mid-America*, 59 (January, 1977) 51–64; Henry E. Fritz, *The Movement for Indian Assimilation, 1860–1890* (Philadelphia, 1963; reprinted, Westport, Connecticut, 1981), 135–122; Robert W. Mardock, *The Reformers and the American Indian* (Columbia, Missouri, 1971), 67–210; Frederick E. Hoxie, *A Final Promise: The Campaign to Assimilate the Indian, 1880–1920* (Lincoln, Nebraska, 1984), 1–77; Christine Bolt, *American Indian Policy and American Reform: Case Studies of the Campaign to Assimilate the American Indians* (London, 1987), 71–102.

ping, and fishing, occasionally working for wages, and selling handicrafts. The Potawatomi, officially landless since 1838, were so destitute that they were granted some 14,000 acres by a 1913 special act of Congress. Only the Menominee were able to keep their tribal lands largely intact, due to tribal cohesion, success at lumbering, and some luck (they actually voted to allot their lands but the government failed to follow through).[19]

The Menominee had begun logging on a modest scale in the 1870's and built a water-powered sawmill in 1886. Three years later, the government gave them permission to log and market "dead and down" timber. In 1890, Congress permitted them to cut up to 20 million board feet of green timber annually, financed by a repayable cash loan of $75,000, with the revenue to be held in trust at 5 per cent interest. During the first year alone, the Menominee realized $232,262 in lumber sales and repaid almost all of the loan. Over the next two decades, they managed to cut over 300 million board feet, enough to pay the costs of maintaining the reservation, while providing a small per-capita payment to tribal members. In 1908, after a tornado destroyed 20 to 30 million feet of timber, Congress allowed the tribe to construct a new sawmill and to market their lumber under BIA supervision. (Before this legislation, lumbermen from Oshkosh and Oconto had purchased Menominee-cut logs at a fixed price.) Despite difficulties, the mill eventually opened and the village of Neopit grew up around it. Selling finished lumber directly yielded appreciably more money for the tribe and provided employment for hundreds of individual Menominee.[20]

---

[19] Lurie, *Wisconsin Indians*, 24–25; Nancy O. Lurie and Helen M. Miller, *Historical Background of the Winnebago People* (n.p., 1965), 1–2; Robert E. Ritzenthaler, "The Oneida Indians of Wisconsin," in the *Bulletin of the Public Museum of the City of Milwaukee*, 19 (November, 1950), 12–15; Nancy O. Lurie, "The Winnebago Indians: A Study in Cultural Change" (doctoral dissertation, Northwestern University, 1952), 252–258; Wrone, "Indian Treaties," in *WMH*, 70: 101; Jay P. Kinney, *A Continent Lost—A Civilization Won: Indian Land Tenure in America* (New York, 1975), 187–246; Patricia K. Ourada, *The Menominee Indians: A History* (Norman, 1979), 179–182; Edmund J. Danziger, Jr., *The Chippewas of Lake Superior* (Norman, 1978), 97–112; U.S. Senate, Committee on Indian Affairs, *Condition of Indian Affairs in Wisconsin*, 61 Cong., 1 sess. (1910), 825; Spicer, "American Indians," in *Harvard Encyclopedia of American Ethnic Groups*, 75–78; Publius V. Lawson, "The Potawatomi," in *The Wisconsin Archeologist*, 19 (April 1920), 106–108; Robert E. Ritzenthaler, "The Potawatomi Indians of Wisconsin," in the *Bulletin of the Public Museum of the City of Milwaukee*, 19 (January, 1953), 99–112.

[20] Jay P. Kinney, *Indian Forest and Range: A History of the Administration and Conservation of the Redman's Heritage* (Washington, 1950), 4–121; Kinney, *A Continent Lost*, 246–285; Spicer, "American Indians," in *Harvard Encyclopedia*, 75–6; Ourada, *Menominee Indians*, 146–156, 170–175; Felix M. Keesing, *The Menomini Indians of Wisconsin: A Study of Three Centuries of Cultural Contact and Change* (Philadelphia, 1939; reprinted,

Earlier lumbering efforts by the Chippewa produced relatively poorer results. In 1882, the Department of the Interior granted them permission to cut and sell timber under BIA supervision. Lacking knowledge, experience, and capital, the Chippewa contracted with Euro-American lumbermen, the lumbermen realized most of the profit. Seeking to minimize risk, the BIA began to regulate the price of mature timber, guarantee the participation of reliable and bonded contractors, and supervise the operation of the lumber camps. In 1888 alone, the Chippewa executed 731 contracts which resulted in the cutting of almost 200 million board feet, at prices ranging from $4.75 to $7.00 a thousand board feet. As late as 1914, the Chippewa earned nearly $35,000 in lumber-industry wages; at Lac du Flambeau in 1912–1913, the tribe received nearly $120,000 for over 23 million board feet.[21]

Unfortunately, lumbering operations failed to ensure either prosperity or equity to the Menominee or the Chippewa. In 1896, the Indian agent at Keshena on the Menominee reservation charged that members of a white lumber company pool kept log prices low by not bidding against each other. Lumber contractors were also charged with overstaffing, padding expenses, and racial discrimination in hiring and wages. During the 1908–1909 logging season, for example, the 7,380 white employees received over $200,000 in wages, while the 3,533 Indian workers realized just under $70,000. Unauthorized lumber crews regularly stripped reservation lands of timber, and large numbers of whites and persons of mixed blood fraudulently claimed Chippewa ancestry. Because Indian agents concluded that many Chippewa spent their lumber incomes profligately, they began to deposit their wages in interest-bearing accounts, doling them out jealously. The Chippewa protested, but the United States Supreme Court in 1907 upheld the practice. The Menominee were generally satisfied with federal policy, but had complaints about Euro-American contractors. The Chippewa depended almost entirely on lumbering for their income, and were left nearly destitute whenever the government, or the weather, forced them to suspend operations.[22]

New York, 1971, and Madison, 1987), 170–187, 224–231; George D. Spindler, *Sociocultural and Psychological Processes in Menomini Acculturation* (Berkeley, 1955), 36–37, 51–53; Bieder, *Native American Communities*, 156–164.

[21] Danziger, *Chippewas of Lake Superior*, 100–115; U.S. Senate, Committee on Indian Affairs, *Condition of Indian Affairs in Wisconsin*, 61 Cong., 1 sess. (1910), 826–829, 911, 933–934; Robert E. Ritzenthaler, "Chippewa Preoccupation with Health," in the *Bulletin of the Public Museum of the City of Milwaukee*, 19 (June, 1953), 224–228; Bieder, *Native American Communities*, 166–170.

[22] Danziger, *Chippewas of Lake Superior*, 103–121; Ourada, *Menominee Indians*, 171–172; Kinney, *Indian Forest and Range*, 30–121; U.S. Senate, Committee on Indian

For most Indians, the campaign to make them economically self-sufficient was a patent failure. Even the minority who managed to retain their allotments fought overwhelming odds to become successful farmers. Except for the Oneida reservation in Brown and Outagamie counties, Wisconsin's reservations were in the north, where soil and climate were not conducive to most forms of agriculture (as thousands of white settlers also learned to their despair). Indians generally lacked the capital, expertise, and experience necessary to prosper as northern dairy farmers. Even those who participated in the University of Wisconsin extension programs and farmers' institutes, or the BIA's agricultural fairs, enjoyed only modest, often temporary, success. Male Indians considered farming "women's work." Some insisted that the government have land cleared for them and supply provisions until they could produce a crop. By the mid-1890's, the Chippewa had less than 3,000 acres under cultivation, and only 15 per cent of the tribe engaged in agriculture. Women, children, and the elderly did most of the cultivating. Adult males usually worked in lumber camps, wood-related industries, on the docks, or as deckhands. Many Winnebago planted small gardens, but the tribe's main livelihood came from migrant harvesting, supplemented by occasional wage work in mills, factories, or on roads, and by selling baskets and handicrafts. Figures from 1915 suggest that the nearly 2,000 gainfully employed Wisconsin Indians averaged less than $80 a year in wages, although those who worked for the federal government averaged $383.[23]

Inseparably intertwined with allotment was a campaign to "civilize" Native Americans through speaking English, joining a Christian church, adopting American grooming and fashion styles, eschewing liquor and gambling, practicing American sexual mores, and manifesting a Euro-American work ethic. This crusade sought strict enforcement of these values on and off the reservation and instituted compulsory moral, patriotic, and academically based vocational education. All over the country, the federal government and various religious groups established day schools and boarding schools for Indian children, both to educate them and to encourage assimilation. Some lived in exile at the boarding schools for years at a time.

Despite differences in emphasis, these various boarding, federal

---

Affairs, *Condition of Indian Affairs in Wisconsin*, 61 Cong., 1 sess. (1910), 65, 826–829, 911–916; U.S. Commissioner of Indian Affairs, *Annual Report*, 1896, pp. 52–54, 323–330.

[23] Danziger, *Chippewas of Lake Superior*, 95–117; Lurie and Miller, *Historical Background of the Winnebago*, 1–3; J. F. Wojta, "Indian Farm Institutes in Wisconsin," in *WMH*, 29 (June, 1946), 423–427; U.S. Commissioner of Indian Affairs, *Annual Report*, 1915, p. 136.

day, and religious schools substantially agreed that the primary purpose of Native American education was to produce a new generation which would speak English, live in nuclear family groups, and observe Victorian mores—sobriety, industriousness, and self-sufficiency. Church and school acted as mutually reinforcing instruments of acculturation.

In 1895, Wisconsin had six government-run reservation day schools, three government boarding schools, four contract boarding schools, and two contract day schools, accommodating a total of 1,415 Indian students. In 1915, there were nine boarding and six day schools, four of which were Catholic and one each Episcopalian, Lutheran, and Seventh Day Adventist, with a capacity of nearly 2,800. The primary subjects, besides English and citizenship, were vocational, including agriculture, stock-raising, carpentry, and domestic science. By design, only the academically brightest were prepared for college. In 1905, the Wisconsin legislature extended the state's compulsory school-attendance law to reservation schools. The praises of the system's advocates, as well as the criticisms of its detractors, testified to the schools' effectiveness in alienating young Indians from their roots and traditions.[24]

This policy of assimilation, coupled with the generally antagonistic nature of reservation life to traditional Native American ways, took a heavy toll on Wisconsin's Indians. In 1893, their numbers consisted of 3,075 Chippewa, 1,806 Oneida, 1,286 Menominee, 903 Winnebago, 280 Potawatomi, and 142 Stockbridge-Munsee. (Those proportions remained much the same in 1914.) Nearly all of the Oneida, Menominee, and Stockbridge-Munsee lived on reservations administered by the Green Bay Agency of the Bureau of Indian Affairs (BIA). Most of the Chippewa lived on the Red Cliff, Bad River, Lac du Flambeau, and Lac Court Oreilles reservations overseen by the La Pointe Agency; two bands—the Mole Lake and St. Croix—had no reservations. This arrangement placed the Oneida primarily in Outagamie and Brown counties, the Stockbridge-Munsee in Shawano and Marathon, and the Chippewa in Bayfield, Ashland, Sawyer, Iron, Vilas, Oneida, Forest, Polk, Barron, and Burnett counties. The Potawatomi had no reservation and resided primarily in Forest and Mar-

---

[24] Berens, "Old Campaigners, New Realities," in *Mid-America*, 59: 56–64; Furman, "Seedtime for Indian Reform," in *Red River Valley Historical Review*, 2: 508–513; Wrone, "Indian Treaties," in *WMH*, 70: 101–102; Spicer, "American Indians," in *Harvard Encyclopedia of American Ethnic Groups*, 74–78; Clyde A. Morley, "A General Survey of the Schooling Provided for the American Indian Throughout Our Country's History with Special Study of Conditions in Wisconsin" (master's thesis, University of Wisconsin, 1927); M. Carolissa Levi, *Chippewa Indians of Yesterday and Today* (New York, 1956), 68–80; U.S. Commissioner of Indian Affairs, *Annual Report*, 1900, p. 656, and 1912, pp. 94, 159.

inette counties, while the Winnebago, also without a reservation, were scattered among Wood, Clark, Jackson, Monroe, Juneau, and La Crosse counties. Most Indians, even those who lived off the reservation, remained resolutely rural (and poor) during an urbanizing era. At the turn of the century, only 439 out of 8,372 Indians lived in urban places; twenty years later, 223 out of 9,611 lived in Wisconsin's nine largest cities. On this point, at least, the Native American desire to live in harmony with nature coincided with the aims of the federal government.[25]

The Indians' new sedentary life occasioned an alarming increase in smallpox, tuberculosis, trachoma, venereal disease, and alcoholism. Inadequate diet, unsanitary living conditions, and overcrowded housing caused poor health, which was exacerbated by Indians' reluctance to be vaccinated, quarantined, or medicated. The infant mortality rate was as high as that in large cities. Quarantines and vaccinations significantly reduced smallpox after 1900, but tuberculosis remained a problem. In 1903, when tuberculosis infected one in sixty U.S. citizens, the ratio among Wisconsin's Chippewa was one in twenty. In 1915, on the Bad River reservation, a physician discovered 130 cases among 808 residents. Statewide, there were 464 cases of tuberculosis and 195 of trachoma among the 3,159 Native Americans examined that year. An estimated one-fifth of all Chippewa children died from the effects of hereditary syphilis before the age of six months. The BIA worked to improve living conditions and medical services, but inadequate facilities and overworked, underpaid, and inferior health-care personnel stymied everyone.[26]

Alcoholism ran as high as 90 per cent among the Bad River Chippewa in 1914 and was considered by the BIA superintendent to be the tribe's worst problem. Indians could reach nearby Ashland and its fifty-three saloons by train. Liquor was not allowed on reservations but was smuggled in by both whites and Indians. To combat the problem, federal authorities created Indian police and courts, but the task was too formidable. Indians arrested and convicted of liquor trafficking were often considered heroes and social benefactors by their

[25] Nancy O. Lurie, "Wisconsin: A National Laboratory for North American Indian Studies," in *WMH*, 53 (Autumn, 1969), 3, 15, 24–25; *Eleventh Census of the United States, 1890: Report on Population, Part 1*, pp. 396, 401, 965; *Twelfth Census of the United States, 1900: Population, Part 1*, pp. 488, 492, 563–564; *Fourteenth Census of the United States, 1920: Population, Volume III, Composition and Characteristics of the Population by States*, pp. 1121, 1140; *House Documents*, 54th Cong., 1 sess., no. 5 (serial 3382), *Report of the Secretary of the Interior* (vol. 2 of 5).

[26] Danziger, *Chippewas of Lake Superior*, 104–105, 119–121; Ourada, *Menominee Indians*, 141–142; U.S. Commissioner of Indian Affairs, *Annual Report*, 1893, pp. 344–345, 1901, p. 407, 1903, pp. 351–352, 1913, p. 144, 1915, p. 140.

peers, despite the fact that many had signed total abstinence pledges.²⁷

The BIA and most white Wisconsinites interpreted the prevalence of disease and drunkenness as measures of the Indians' uncivilized character, thereby underscoring the need for forced acculturation. On the other hand, Indians, and a few of their supporters, believed that these dysfunctions actually resulted from those very policies. The BIA viewed as positive signs the allotment of reservation land, the switch to farming, lumbering, participation in mainstream economic life, wearing "citizen clothing," short hair, the ability to read and speak English, membership in a Christian church, and living in log or frame houses. In 1912, the bureau claimed that, of the state's 9,816 Indians, 5,569 were professed Christians, 5,673 spoke English, 3,780 could read and write English, 9,210 wore modern attire, 2,918 worked for a wage, and 5,652 had become U.S. citizens. By the eve of the First World War, the bureau's policies—however harsh and short-sighted they may have been—seemed to have borne fruit.²⁸

The BIA put together impressive statistics to prove that its "civilizing" policies had succeeded. Nonetheless, many Indians practiced selective acculturation, and many others remained suspended uneasily between two worlds. School truancy was common, despite compulsory education laws. Many Indian parents apparently sent their children to school primarily so that they could receive warm clothing and nourishing food in the winter. The illiteracy rate among Indians was one-third in 1910 and one-fifth in 1920; for those over age twenty, it was 46 and 27 per cent, respectively.

Wisconsin's Indians were endlessly adaptable. They learned to manipulate white culture to obtain economic benefits. Similarly, they mixed the religious beliefs and practices of Christianity with native traditions, and often modified only surface behavior. Some bands exhibited open hostility towards missionaries; others revived or adopted competing spiritual systems. Many Wisconsin Indians practiced derivations of Dream, Ghost, or Drum Dance cultures, which had originated among the Plains Indians, as a means of resisting

---

²⁷ Danziger, *Chippewas of Lake Superior*, 121–123; Lurie, *Wisconsin Indians*, 23–24; U.S. Commissioner of Indian Affairs, *Annual Report*, 1906, p. 38, 1915, pp. 13, 170; Ourada, *Menominee Indians*, 152–153; Heming, *Catholic Church in Wisconsin*, 666–667.

²⁸ Danziger, *Chippewas of Lake Superior*, 92–109; Lurie, *Wisconsin Indians*, 23–24; Willard H. Titus, "Observations on the Menominee Indians," in *WMH*, 14 (September–December, 1930), 94–96; Ritzenthaler, "Oneida Indians of Wisconsin," *Bulletin of the Public Museum of the City of Milwaukee*, 19: 12–14; George W. Thatcher, "The Winnebago Indians, 1827–1932" (master's thesis, University of Wisconsin, 1935), 203–208; U.S. Commissioner of Indian Affairs, *Annual Report*, 1900, p. 656, 1912, pp. 94, 159; Keesing, *Menomini Indians of Wisconsin*, 220–228.

Euro-American domination. Others joined "peyote cults" which used the hallucinatory drug mescal in a mystical rite. The Menominee split between the Catholics of Neopit and the "pagans" of Zoar. The Chippewa divided between "progressives" and "vagabonds." Individuals ran the gamut from almost totally acculturated to native-oriented Dream Dancers or peyote users. But even fully acculturated Indians experienced racial intolerance. Their skin color did not vanish when they adopted white clothing and folkways, and many ended up both alienated and isolated. Like their brethren throughout the country, Wisconsin's Indians endured a precarious existence as "wards of Washington" and "people of two worlds."[29]

[2]

Black Americans perplexed Wisconsinites, particularly in the industrial cities of the southeast where they concentrated. Their situation differed in important ways from that of Native Americans. While Euro-Americans coveted American Indian lands, they had little or no use for Negroes, who possessed little of "value." Indians were given at least some hope of eventual salvation, provided they gave up their tribal ways and made a concerted effort to become acculturated; but in general Negroes were extended no such invitation. The federal government forced Indians into formal education; but government at all levels was generally either hostile or indifferent towards the schooling of Negroes. Native Americans kept their determination to retain a separate identity, culture, and habitat; Negro Americans usually pursued racial integration, justice, equity, and full participation in the life of the state. But to no avail. Plainly put, the white people of Wisconsin preferred to keep black people segregated.[30]

White Wisconsinites widely regarded Negroes as newcomers in the early twentieth century, but they had been an integral, albeit minuscule, segment of the population since territorial days. In 1910, cen-

---

[29] Spindler, *Sociocultural and Psychological Processes*, 43, 61–81; Lurie, "Winnebago Indians," 261–269; Keesing, *Menomini Indians of Wisconsin*, 179–181; Ourada, *Menominee Indians*, 149–150; Danziger, *Chippewas of Lake Superior*, 107–109; *Fourteenth Census of the United States, 1920: Population, Volume III, Composition and Characteristics of the Population by States*, 1121, 1140; William H. Hodge, "The Indians of Wisconsin," *Wisconsin Blue Book, 1975*, pp. 117–123; Bieder, *Native American Communities*, 170–177.

[30] For perceptive discussions of acculturation and assimilation of ethnic groups, see Milton M. Gordon, *Assimilation in American Life: The Role of Race, Religion and National Origins* (New York, 1964), 60–83, 233–265; and the following essays in the *Harvard Encyclopedia of American Ethnic Groups*: Harold J. Abramson, "Assimilation and Pluralism," 150–160, George M. Fredrickson and Dale T. Knobel, "Prejudice and Discrimination, History of," 829–847, and Nathan Glazer and Reed Ueda, "Prejudice and Discrimination, Policy Against," 847–858.

sus enumerators counted a mere 2,900 blacks in the state—probably an understatement. By 1920, the population increased by nearly 80 per cent to 5,201, or 0.2 per cent of the total. Nearly all had been born in the United States; nearly one in four, in Wisconsin. The vast majority had migrated, either from such border states as Kentucky, Tennessee, Virginia, or Missouri, from nearby Illinois, Ohio, Michigan, or Indiana, or from the Deep South. These last, especially, were the vanguard of what came to be called the Great Migration, which between 1915 and 1960 brought nearly 5 million southern blacks to the cities of the North.[31]

Segregation, racism, and devastation of southern agriculture wrought by share-cropping, the boll weevil, and floods pushed Negro migrants northward. Greater economic and educational opportunities and political participation pulled them. Wisconsin's northerly location rendered it less attractive than other Great Lakes states, but the cities in its industrial southeast nevertheless exercised a considerable attraction. Prior to the 1890's, the state's small Negro population had been fairly evenly divided between urban and rural areas. (Wisconsin had 2,444 Negroes in 1890, 2,542 in 1900, 2,900 in 1910, and 5,201 in 1920.) Some of the oldest Negro settlements were in rural settings: Cheyenne Valley near Hillsboro in Vernon County, Pleasant Ridge between Beetown and Lancaster in Grant County, Fox Lake in Dodge County, and in a few locations in Racine and Walworth counties.[32]

By the turn of the century, however, nearly three-fourths lived in urban places, almost two-thirds in the ten largest cities. Twenty years later, 70 per cent lived in Beloit, Racine, Madison, Kenosha, or Milwaukee; 40 per cent in Milwaukee alone. More than half Wisconsin's black population, in both 1910 and 1920, were in their most produc-

---

[31] *Eleventh Census of the United States, 1890: Report on Population, Part 1*, 397, 400; *Twelfth Census of the United States, 1900: Population, Part 1*, cxiii–cxxiv, 486, 702–705; *Fourteenth Census of the United States, 1920: Population, Volume II, General Report and Analytical Tables*, 31–41, 54, 82–88, 92–95; Joe William Trotter, Jr., *Black Milwaukee: The Making of an Industrial Proletariat, 1915–1945* (Urbana, 1985), 8–9, 44–47.

[32] Zachary L. Cooper, *Black Settlers in Rural Wisconsin* (Madison, 1977), 5–26; Trotter, *Black Milwaukee*, 8, 45; Thomas R. Buchanan, "Black Milwaukee, 1890–1915" (master's thesis, University of Wisconsin-Milwaukee, 1974), 1–14; Thomas C. McCormick and Richard A. Hornseth, "The Negro in Madison, Wisconsin," in *American Sociological Review*, 12 (October, 1947), 519–525; Velma F. Bell, "The Negro in Beloit and Madison, Wisconsin" (master's thesis, University of Wisconsin, 1933), 11–53; John D. Buenker, "The Immigrant Heritage," in Nicholas C. Burckel, ed., *Racine: Growth and Change in a Wisconsin County* (Racine, 1977), 73–79; Racine *Journal Times*, May 13, 1984; Jonathan W. Zophy, "Invisible People: Blacks and Mexican-Americans," in John A. Neuenschwander, ed., *Kenosha County in the Twentieth Century: A Topical History* (Kenosha, 1976), 51–54. Census population schedules and published breakdowns of them, plus scattered local histories, document minorities in various rural areas.

tive years, with 80 per cent being under forty-five years old. Men had outnumbered women by a significant amount in 1900. Then the growing demand for domestic labor, and the desire for family life, produced an almost even gender ratio by 1920. Both men and women newcomers worked as laborers.[33]

Negroes were generally relegated to marginal residential areas in every city, although true "ghettos" had not yet developed. In Milwaukee, most lived on the east side, then the community moved west of the Milwaukee River, the result of their economic status and clashes with Irish and Italian residents. By 1910, 84 per cent lived in five of the city's twenty-three wards, principally in a thirty-five-block area just west of the river. The residential segregation of blacks from American-born whites, as measured by an "index of dissimilarity," increased from 46.6 to 66.7 between 1890 and 1910, putting Milwaukee at about the same level as Chicago, and higher than several other northern cities. At the same time, the index compared to the foreign-born decreased slightly, highlighting the competition for lower-grade housing among Negroes, Italians, Jews, and Greeks. Expansion to the north and west was the only real option because of the central business district to the south, and the Milwaukee River and the Third Street shopping district to the east. Negroes made up less than 3 per cent of Milwaukee's total population, even in the near west side wards. A few prominent individuals, generally railroad employees, lived outside the main concentration.

Elsewhere in Wisconsin, the story was much the same. In 1920, Racine's 294 blacks lived along Grand Avenue, south of the main business district, where they competed with eastern European immigrants for housing. Madison's 259 blacks established three enclaves: on the east side along East Dayton Street, on the west side along West Washington Avenue, and in the Greenbush area, where they vied with Italian and Jewish immigrants. Blacks in Kenosha (101) and Beloit (834) generally occupied the fringes of the factory district, along with working-class southern and eastern Europeans.[34]

Ghettoized or not, Wisconsin's Negroes endured living conditions as bad as those in any cities in the land. In Milwaukee, they took over a German and Jewish area whose residents were moving to new sub-

---

[33] *Twelfth Census of the United States, 1900: Population, Part 1*, pp. 563–564, 607–608, 645–646, 683–684; *Fourteenth Census of the United States, 1920: Population, Volume III, Composition and Characteristics of the Population by States*, 1118–1135.

[34] Trotter, *Black Milwaukee*, 21–25; Buchanan, "Black Milwaukee," 7–8; Buenker, "Immigrant Heritage," in Burckel, ed., *Racine*, 91–94; Zophy, "Invisible People," in Neuenschwander, ed., *Kenosha*, 52–53; Bell, "Negro in Beloit and Madison," 44–53; David V. Mollenhoff, *Madison: A History of the Formative Years* (Dubuque, 1982), 426–427.

divisions on the northwest side. The dwellings had been among those judged worst by governmental boards and commissions: old, dilapidated, with basement rooms and inadequate and unsanitary facilities. The Milwaukee health commissioner reported that 26.5 per cent of deaths from acute diseases between 1911 and 1915 occurred among the 12 per cent of the city's population crammed into its worst residential areas. Most blacks rented, in a city that prided itself on home ownership. The 1905 state census listed almost 30 per cent of Negroes as lodgers or boarders, and many others lived in their place of employment. Even when they made sufficient income to afford better housing, they had trouble finding any beyond their declining district. "Men will not rent to decent, respectable Negroes a house," *Wisconsin Weekly Advocate* editor Richard B. Montgomery charged, "even though the latter are in a position to pay with equal regularity as much rental as any other class of whites."[35]

Milwaukee's largest Negro enclave abutted the red-light district and what was known locally as the "Bad Lands." In Beloit, many lived in flimsy structures owned by Fairbanks, Morse and Company near the railroad tracks. In Madison, many rented homes without indoor plumbing. In Kenosha, black residents complained that they "couldn't rent a house from the foreign speaking or from some of the early settlers."[36]

Despite industrial expansion, Negroes had a harder time finding suitable employment than housing. They were largely relegated to ill-paid domestic, personal service, and day laboring jobs; nationwide, over two-thirds of the black work force were porters, waiters, servants, cooks, and common laborers in 1880. Twenty years later, that percentage had changed little, except for a significant increase in female domestics. Black men were hired as common laborers on construction projects because of their supposed "ability to endure heat." More frequently they worked in hotels, resorts, and recreation centers, in the homes of white families, on railroads, and in other domestic and personal service jobs. Wages ranged from four to six dollars a week for women, and slightly more for men—lower even than the wages paid unskilled white factory workers. Demand for black women domestics was so great after 1890 that Milwaukee's *Wisconsin Afro-American* and the *Wisconsin Weekly Advocate* regularly printed advertisements aimed at potential migrants from the South. Black males actually began to lose ground, as when employers such as the Plankinton House and Gimbel Brothers Department Store replaced them

[35] Trotter, *Black Milwaukee*, 21–25; Buchanan, "Black Milwaukee," 14–57.
[36] Trotter, *Black Milwaukee*, 24; Zophy, "Invisible People," in Neuenschwander, ed., *Kenosha*, 53–54; Bell, "Negro in Beloit and Madison," 34–53.

with white immigrants, on the grounds that Negroes "did not tend to business."[37]

Eleven per cent of males and 12 per cent of females in 1900 worked mostly as unskilled laborers. They secured their positions either through personal contacts with whites or as strikebreakers; they rarely found permanent employment. Those who did land skilled or semi-skilled jobs were predominantly lighter-skinned and better-educated, and had strong ties to the white community. Negro women were almost completely relegated to the basement of Milwaukee's economy. Some 68 per cent worked in domestic and personal service in 1900, compared to 15 per cent of all males and 33 per cent of all female workers.

Milwaukee's blacks were also generally worse off than their counterparts in other northern cities, although the gap was closing. After 1900, the tremendous influx of immigrants glutted the market for unskilled labor, and racism among industrialists and labor unions denied work to non-white laborers. Black labor organizations yielded some gains, but these proved transitory because they threatened white employers and unions. The same general pattern characterized employment in Racine, Kenosha, Madison, and Beloit.[38]

Despite all the obstacles, a small number of Wisconsin Negroes did become small businessmen and professionals. The 1900 census listed nineteen black men and four women as proprietors of small businesses in Milwaukee, chiefly barbers and saloonkeepers. Ten years later, an informal census discovered twenty-six men and fourteen women so engaged, and black business investment had increased from $60,000 to $200,000 between 1895 and 1908. Many Negro businessmen experienced discrimination and harassment. Some accordingly used white people as business "fronts." Some businesses, especially those run by light-skinned Negroes, served a predominantly white or integrated clientele. Mostly, black businesses served black customers.[39]

The education picture was a little brighter. By 1910, 65 per cent of the Negro population between the ages of five and twenty years attended school, compared to 64 per cent for the entire state and 41 per cent for the foreign-born. Males in that age bracket attended school with almost exactly the same frequency as all males statewide, and more than twice as much as foreign-born males. Black females lagged behind the statewide average but still were far ahead of for-

---

[37] Trotter, *Black Milwaukee*, 9–13.

[38] *Ibid.*, 13–19; Buenker, "The Immigrant Heritage," in Burckel, ed., *Racine*, 84–85; Zophy, "Invisible People," in Neuenschwander, ed., *Kenosha*, 53–54; Bell, "Negro in Beloit and Madison," 26–49; Mollenhoff, *Madison*, 426–427.

[39] Trotter, *Black Milwaukee*, 19–21; Buchanan, "Black Milwaukee," 24–53.

eign-born women. Ten years later, the relative proportions remained about the same, although black women were closing the gap on females statewide.[40]

Nor were Wisconsin Negroes particularly disadvantaged by illiteracy. Only 4.5 per cent were illiterate in 1910, compared to 8.7 per cent of the foreign-born and 3.2 per cent of the population statewide. By 1920, those figures stood at 4.1, 8.4, and 2.4 per cent, respectively. Except for offenses linked to vice and gambling, there was no indication that Negroes were significantly less law-abiding. In Kenosha, for example, only twenty-seven of the 3,359 persons arrested in 1918 were listed as "colored"—far less than the proportion of southern and eastern European immigrants. In short, there was little hard evidence on which to build a perception that Wisconsin's Negro population was either inferior or disruptive.[41]

Nevertheless, race relations continued to deteriorate from the 1890's on, despite an 1890 ruling by a state circuit court that theaters and other forms of public amusement could not deny equal access. Pressed by the Milwaukee branch of the national Afro-American League, the state legislature passed a watered-down civil rights act stipulating penalties of $100 to $500 and six months in jail. Because the courts enforced only the minimum penalty, public discrimination continued to escalate. For example, John J. Miles, a Milwaukee black businessman, successfully brought suit against the Schlitz Palm Garden for refusing him service, but he received only a five-dollar judgment. In 1906, blacks and whites both protested the staging at the Davidson Theater of the play *The Klansman* by Thomas Dixon, the forerunner of the movie *The Birth of a Nation*. Harassment of interracial couples, married or otherwise, was commonplace. Bills outlawing miscegenation were introduced in the state legislature in 1901, 1903, and 1913, and were thwarted only by a coalition of Negro leaders and sympathetic whites. One white woman was sent to an asylum when she attempted to marry a black man.[42]

---

[40] *Thirteenth Census of the United States, 1910: Population, Volume III, Reports by States, with Statistics for Counties, Cities, and Other Civil Divisions*, 1092–1099; *Fourteenth Census of the United States, 1920: Population, Volume III, Composition and Characteristics of the Population by States*, 1118–1120; Trotter, *Black Milwaukee*, 24–28, 72; Buchanan, "Black Milwaukee," 60–94.

[41] *Thirteenth Census of the United States, 1910: Population, Volume III, Reports by States, with Statistics for Counties, Cities, and Other Civil Divisions*, 1092–1099; *Fourteenth Census of the United States, 1920: Population, Volume III, Composition and Characteristics of the Population by States*, 1120; Zophy, "Invisible People," in Neuenschwander, ed., *Kenosha*, 53–54; Bell, "Negro in Beloit and Madison," 72–75.

[42] Trotter, *Black Milwaukee*, 25–30; Buchanan, "Black Milwaukee," 54–95. For an enlightening discussion of the racial views of one of the state's most prominent Republican politicians, see James R. Parker, "Paternalism and Racism: Senator John

Milwaukee's Negroes organized effectively in two ways. First they used the integrationist and protest goals of longtime Negro residents, often persons of mixed racial composition, who frequently depended on white patronage and who saw black institutions as temporary expedients to achieve integration. They also used techniques promoted by the new elite and personified by *Weekly Advocate* editor Montgomery. This group advocated a version of Booker T. Washington's credo of self-help, racial pride, and solidarity, answering discrimination, not with protest, but with strategies to build a separate institutional life. Montgomery sometimes rationalized discrimination, such as the refusal of the General Federation of Women's Clubs to allow blacks to participate, by arguing that Negro women should "be content to remain by themselves and toil for the uplift of their race." In response, the old elite denounced both the women's group and Montgomery. The two factions also clashed over Montgomery's plans to construct an industrial school for Negroes in northern Wisconsin, and to have Booker T. Washington speak in Milwaukee in 1902.

The growing black working class—an amalgam of migrants from border, midwestern, and southern states—allied with neither side. Montgomery and his followers frequently blamed the influx for the deteriorating racial climate, calling the newcomers "a floating, shiftless and depraved element." "[W]e would impress upon our Southern brethren and sisters to locate in smaller towns and villages where they will not be subjected to the same [urban] temptations."[43]

By 1914, Wisconsin's Negroes had succeeded in developing a network of social institutions. The most important and long-lasting of these was the church, which in Milwaukee traced its roots to 1869 and the founding of St. Mark's African Methodist Episcopal Church. It had over one hundred members by 1914 and merged the old elite with more affluent representatives of the working class. Seminary-trained ministers presided over its activities. Calvary Baptist, founded late in the century, absorbed many of the incoming Southern migrants. Catholics responded with St. Benedict the Moor Mission and School of the Capuchin order, which became a separate parish in 1909. Meanwhile, white churches grew more inhospitable to integrated congregations. For example, St. Gall's Catholic Church had had a Negro contingent which dwindled from about 100 to less than five between 1895 and 1911; and the Wisconsin Baptist Convention refused financial aid to Calvary.[44]

In Racine, the black Methodist and Baptist churches dated from

---

C. Spooner and American Minorities, 1897–1907," in *WMH*, 57 (Spring, 1974), 195–200.
[43] Trotter, *Black Milwaukee*, 29–31.
[44] *Ibid.*, 31; Buchanan, "Black Milwaukee," 119–135.

the Civil war era; later two Episcopal congregations served black parishioners. In Madison, John Turner, a talented but illiterate former slave, founded the Free African Methodist Church in 1902. Later, under Jesse Woods, who had a degree from Beloit College and had edited the *Afro-American Review*, the church was Madison's center of black community life for many years. Racine and Beloit had similarly successful churches.[45]

Second in influence to churches were newspapers, which had enticed southern Negroes to migrate and which played roles in politics and in the fight against discrimination. The first in Wisconsin was the weekly *Wisconsin Afro-American*, founded in 1892; but it lasted only a year. Five years later, Montgomery began the *Wisconsin Weekly Advocate*. After eighteen years, it moved to Minneapolis, retitled the *National Advocate*. Between 1906 and 1916, the *Wisconsin Weekly Defender* was published in Milwaukee, founded by a coal dealer and an itinerant minister.

The black press, in Milwaukee as elsewhere, served as a virtual employment agency, publishing advertisements (including work for strikebreakers), and making job arrangements. The *Afro-American* published an appeal "To Our Southern Readers," urging anyone seeking domestic employment, "no matter where your home is, [to] write to us, at this office, [and] we will make for you all arrangements." The *Advocate* established the Colored Helping Hand Intelligence Office to facilitate domestic employment. The papers relied on white support for capital, advertisements, and contributions, but they catered to black readers with stories about race conditions which the mainstream press ignored. The *Advocate* reflected its editor's adherence to the self-help doctrine, and sometimes downplayed discrimination. The *Afro-American* and the *Defender* expressed demands for racial equality and urged readers to exercise their full civil and political rights.

Lodges and fraternal organizations were also important social institutions in the Negro community, providing members with protective insurance and social outlets. Probably the oldest in Milwaukee was the Prince Hall Masonic Widows Son Lodge, Number 25, founded in 1891. It was followed the next year by the Knights of Pythias, and in 1903 by a branch of the United Order of Odd Fellows. Two years later, there were eight fraternal organizations in the city, most of them made up of the old elite. Social and service clubs, literary societies, self-improvement associations, and women's clubs, such as the Silver Leaf Charity Club, the Woman's Improvement Club, the Phillis Wheatley Club (one of many groups nationally named

[45]Buenker, "Immigrant Heritage," in Burckel, ed., *Racine*, 100; Bell, "Negro in Beloit and Madison," 54–63; Mollenhoff, *Madison*, 426.

after the famous black slave poet of eighteenth-century Boston), and the Cream City Social and Literary Society were Negro counterparts to white organizations of the day. Women's clubs raised funds for charity through socials, balls, picnics, and the like.[46]

In Racine, the African Methodist Episcopal Church Literary Society, the Phillis Wheatley Civic Club, the Elks, the Odd Fellows, and the Masons all antedated the First World War. In Kenosha, Negroes founded the Lincoln Civic League in 1917. In Madison in 1904, they established the Prince Hall Masonic Lodge and later a number of small self-help groups, such as the Book Lovers Club. In Beloit, the most important black organizations were the W. B. Kennedy Lodge of the Masonic Order and the Rebecca Chapter of the Eastern Star.[47]

Negroes had an especially difficult time breaking into such mainstream institutions as labor unions and political parties. The Wisconsin State Federation of Labor and the Milwaukee Federated Trades Council organized only skilled workers, and were dominated by whites, so Negroes had virtually no chance to affiliate. Their occasional role as strikebreakers gave unions an additional reason for drawing the color line. In politics, Negroes generally had to content themselves with crumbs of patronage and professions of belief in racial equality, stingily doled out by the Republican party. "I always voted the Republican ticket—in them days, you know, that was the colored man's hobby because they wanted to give Abraham Lincoln credit for what he'd done for the black people," an old-time Racine resident later recalled. "And anytime that you saw or heard of a person, Negro, voting the Democratic ticket he was throwed out of society." (Even so, the only known black officeholder in nineteenth-century Racine was coroner Peter Thomas, a Democrat.)

In Milwaukee, the major black politician was Lucien H. Palmer, a businessman who arrived from Alabama in 1878 and was appointed to minor federal offices in the 1890's and after. In 1906, Palmer became the first Negro elected to the Wisconsin legislature—apparently because many voters mistook him for a prominent white resident of the same district. Otherwise, Milwaukee's blacks lacked the economic resources and the population to carry a ward or even a district. They were largely taken for granted by Republicans and ignored by Democrats and Socialists. It was not until after World War II that Wisconsin's black population truly began to "count" politically.[48]

[46] Trotter, *Black Milwaukee*, 12–15, 21–31; Buchanan, "Black Milwaukee," 95–110.
[47] Buenker, "Immigrant Heritage," in Burckel, ed., *Racine*, 112–113; Zophy, "Invisible People," in Neuenschwander, ed., *Kenosha*, 53; Bell, "Negro in Beloit and Madison," 64–71; Mollenhoff, *Madison*, 427.
[48] Trotter, *Black Milwaukee*, 25–28; Zophy, "Invisible People," in Neuenschwander,

[3]

The most immediate challenge to Wisconsin's ethno-cultural balance came from southern and eastern European immigrants, who constituted only 4 per cent of the state's foreign-born population in 1890. By 1920, the figure was nearly one-third. Most had arrived in a rush between 1900 and 1914. The Polish segment of the foreign-born population increased from 6 to 11 per cent between 1900 and 1920; the Russian and Lithuanian, from 1 to 5 per cent; and the Italian, Hungarian, and Finnish, from virtually nothing to 2 per cent each. Grouped by first language, Wisconsin had 8 per cent of the country's Czechs and Slovaks, 6 per cent of its Poles, 5 per cent of its Finns and Slovenians, and 3 per cent of its Serbs and Croats.[49]

Poles made the largest gains. By 1920, they surpassed Norwegians as Wisconsin's second-largest immigrant group. Though figures are hard to calculate, there were at least 17,660 Poles in the state by 1890 and 31,789 by 1900, mostly from the German provinces of West Prussia and Posen. (By the late 1880's, enough Poles lived in Milwaukee alone to support a daily newspaper.) Ten years later, their number had increased to 51,000, with most of the new arrivals coming from Russia or Austrian Galicia. By 1920, Polish-speaking immigrants numbered 52,121, or 11 per cent of the state's foreign-born.

Close behind were other Slavic peoples. First among them were the Czechs (Bohemians) and Slovaks, who shared a similar language and (after 1918) the same country of origin, but little else. Czechs began arriving in Wisconsin in the 1850's and totaled nearly 12,000 by 1890; twenty years later, the number had risen to 16,301, a peak that declined slightly afterwards. Because Slovakia was part of Hungary, it was difficult to identify Slovaks until the U.S. Census Bureau adopted a mother-tongue classification in 1910. By then, there were 3,408 Slovak speakers, a number that nearly doubled over the next decade. These western Slavs were joined by a contingent of southern Slavs, chiefly from what became "Jugoslavia" after 1918. By 1910, almost 4,300 immigrants claimed Slovenian as their mother tongue, and another 3,188 listed Serbo-Croatian. Ten years later, those figures had climbed to 5,559 and 4,888, respectively.

---

ed., *Kenosha*, 60–70; Buenker, "Immigrant Heritage," in Burckel, ed., *Racine*, 120; Angela Howard Zophy,"UAW Local 72: Assertive Union," in Nicholas C. Burckel and John A. Neuenschwander, eds., *Kenosha Retrospective: A Biographical Approach* (Kenosha, 1981), 316.

[49] *Thirteenth Census of the United States, 1910: Population, Volume I, General Report and Analysis*, 808, 812, 832–837; *Fourteenth Census of the United States, 1920: Population, Volume II, General Report and Analytical Tables*, 697–699, 700–701, 714–715, 727, 782–783, 988–989; Leonard Dinnerstein and David M. Reimers, *Ethnic Americans: A History of Immigration and Assimilation* (New York, 1975), 36–39.

More difficult to sort out were the 21,447 immigrants who in 1920 claimed Russia as their homeland. They included Russians, Ukrainians, Poles, Lithuanians, Estonians, Finns, Armenians, and Rumanians. The Russian Empire also ruled several million Jews, representing 6 per cent of its total population and nearly two-thirds of European Jewry. By 1910, there were 8,361 foreign-born Wisconsinites who claimed Hebrew or Yiddish as their mother tongue, and almost 10,000 by 1920. Milwaukee was home to 7,000 Jews by 1895, about 40 per cent from Russia. Fifteen years later the city had 7,757 Yiddish speakers—from all over Europe and a smattering from America.[50]

Between 1890 and 1910, the number of Wisconsinites born in Austria nearly doubled, from 16,855 to 33,646. They included thousands of Slavs, whose "country of origin" changed with the boundary shifts occasioned by the World War's outcome. By 1920, only 19,641 Wisconsinites claimed Austria as their land of birth. Although the state's Hungarian-born population swelled from 486 to over 10,000 between 1890 and 1920, less than half listed Magyar as their mother tongue; the remainder were Jews, Austrians, Slovaks, Ukrainians, Rumanians, Slovenians, and Croatians. Wisconsin's Lithuanian population jumped from 2,907 in 1910 to 4,642 in 1920. Between 1908 and 1920, the Finnish-born population soared from 2,198 to 6,757, about 800 of whom spoke Swedish, Estonian, or Russian. Another 970 immigrants came from Rumania by 1920, but only 411 spoke Rumanian; the rest were Jews, Austrians, Hungarians, Russians, or South Slavs. An almost equal number of Armenians had fled Turkish pogroms and ended up in southeastern Wisconsin by 1920. They were joined by nearly 600 "Syrians" and a handful of Palestinians and Turks. Greeks (4,000) and Italians (10,000) were more numerous by 1920; most of the Italians came from the southern provinces and Sicily. Between 1890 and 1920, the state's Italian-born population jumped from 1,123 to 11,188.

The Wisconsin-born children of these immigrants often retained their parents' language. By 1920, nearly 100,000 claimed Polish as their native language; 31,000, Czech; 11,445, Italian; 7,768, Yiddish or Hebrew; 6,817, Finnish; 5,591, Slovak; 3,433, Russian; 2,936, Lithuanian; 2,836, Magyar; and over 1,000, Greek. Counting immigrants and their children, there were over 150,000 Polish-speaking Wisconsinites in 1920, representing almost 10 per cent of the state's first- and second-generation immigrant population. Only the Germans outnumbered them. In addition, there were 46,425 speakers of

---

[50] *Thirteenth Census of the United States, 1910: Population, Volume I, General Report and Analysis*, 801, 808, 836–837, 998–1006; *Fourteenth Census of the United States, 1920: Population, Volume II, General Report and Analytical Tables*, 687–689, 697–699, 714, 727, 967–969, 995; Dinnerstein and Reimers, *Ethnic Americans*, 36–39.

Czech, 22,763 of Italian, 11,792 of Slovak, 8,111 of Russian, 9,765 of Slovenian, 6,853 of Serbo-Croatian, 4,765 of Greek, 7,578 of Lithuanian, 7,338 of Magyar, and 17,676 of Hebrew or Yiddish. Together, they constituted almost 20 per cent of Wisconsin's foreign-stock population, which itself was about 60 per cent of the state's total population. Thus, within a single generation, southern and eastern European immigrants and their children had become a substantial part of Wisconsin's people.[51]

Personal contacts accounted for most immigration. Earlier arrivals from the same family or village sent word back home about opportunities in Wisconsin to acquire land and jobs, attracting yet more newcomers in a pattern called "chain migration." State government, private industry, and ethnic organizations also got the word out. The state government revived its immigration bureau in 1895 after an eight-year hiatus. The revival was part of lumberman-governor William H. Upham's plan to promote settlement in the Cutover. Upham and the bureau secretary toured eastern cities, established contacts with European immigration agencies, and circulated foreign-language editions of promotional literature. Abolished again in 1901, the board was reinstated six years later, largely at the urging of a private group, the Wisconsin Immigration and Development Association. After 1915, the work was assumed by the Division of Immigration, a part of the newly constituted State Department of Agriculture.[52]

Beginning in the 1890's, the business community formed numerous private organizations to entice settlers. They used foreign-language newspaper advertising, brochures, and land agents to appeal to recent immigrants. They also offered long-term financing and, in the Cutover, organized land-clearing expeditions. In the 1870's the Wisconsin Central Railroad recruited Poles for Portage County settlement; in 1909 a Chicago insurance company offered to buy eighty acres of land for anyone who would settle near Eagle River in Vilas County. Many private employers skirted the federal prohibition against importing contract laborers by negotiating with agents to find them. Several Wisconsin corporations targeted immigrant labor in

[51] *Thirteenth Census of the United States, 1910: Population, Volume I, General Report and Analysis*, 836–837, 894–895, 919, 929, 998–1006; *Fourteenth Census of the United States, 1920: Population, Volume II, General Report and Analytical Tables*, 687–689, 697–699, 714, 727, 902–905, 967–969, 982–989, 995; Richard M. Bernard, *The Melting Pot and the Altar: Marital Assimilation in Early Twentieth-Century Wisconsin* (Minneapolis, 1980), 23–30.

[52] Rippley, *Immigrant Experience*, 79–84; "State Board of Immigration," in the *Wisconsin Blue Book, 1915*, p. 380; Arlan Helgeson, *Farms in the Cutover: Agricultural Settlement in Northern Wisconsin* (Madison, 1962), 1–24; Lucile Kane, "Selling Cut-Over Lands in Wisconsin," in *The Business History Review*, 28 (September, 1954), 236–247.

New York and Chicago. Even so, the vast majority of southern and eastern European immigrants came because they had heard from relatives or neighbors who provided information, financial aid, and housing and employment opportunities.[53]

Census statistics tell where eastern and southern Europeans settled. In 1910, when the state was only 43 per cent urban, 85 per cent of its Greeks, 81 per cent of its Hungarians and Slovaks, and 67 per cent of its Poles and Russians lived in urban places, generally in southeastern industrial cities. Only the Finns were predominantly rural. Ten years later, when the entire state was still less than half urban, Greeks, Rumanians, Lithuanians, Italians, South Slavs, Hungarians, and Russian-born Jews all exceeded the three-quarter mark as city dwellers. Only Czechs and Austrians were evenly distributed between urban and rural.[54]

Poles, the largest contingent in this group, were the most dispersed. Half lived in Milwaukee or adjacent Cudahy, South Milwaukee, or West Allis. Outside the Milwaukee area, Poles lived in every county except Pepin, with concentrations in industrial counties (Kenosha, Racine, Brown, Winnebago, and Marinette—where most lived in cities) and Cutover counties (Portage, Marathon, Oconto, Douglas, Clark, and Taylor—where they divided between villages and the country). Exceptions were found in Portage and Marathon counties, and especially in Trempealeau County, where Silesian Poles farmed around Arcadia and Independence.[55]

Northwest of Green Bay were the rural settlements of Krakow, Sobieski, Pulaski, and Hofa Park. Land agents for the Polish Industrial Association energetically recruited immigrants to Crivitz in Marinette County, from among Chicago and Milwaukee Poles. Douglas, Taylor, Bayfield, Barron, Iron, Price, Sawyer, and Rusk counties had rural Polish enclaves.[56]

---

[53] Helgeson, *Farms in the Cutover*, 41–52; Kane, "Selling Cut-Over Lands," *Business History Review*, 28: 242–247; Gerd Korman, *Industrialization, Immigrants, and Americanizers: The View From Milwaukee, 1886–1921* (Madison, 1967), 25–28; John S. MacDonald and Leatrice D. MacDonald, "Chain Migration, Ethnic Neighborhood Formation and Social Networks," in *The Milbank Memorial Fund Quarterly*, 42 (January, 1964), 82–97; Golda Meir, *My Life* (London, 1975), 21–29.

[54] *Thirteenth Census of the United States, 1910: Population, Volume I, General Report and Analysis*, 841; *Fourteenth Census of the United States, 1920: Population, Volume II, General Report and Analytical Tables*, 769–702; John I. Kolehmainen and George W. Hill, *Haven in the Woods: The Story of the Finns in Wisconsin* (Madison, 1951; reprinted, 1965), 3–26.

[55] *Fourteenth Census of the United States, 1920: Population, Volume III, Composition and Characteristics of the Population by States*, 1135–1136; Rippley, *Immigrant Experience*, 83–88; Bernard, *Melting Pot and Altar*, 19–21; Albert Hart Sanford, "Polish People of Portage County," in *SHSW Proceedings*, 1907, pp. 259–278.

[56] Ladislas J. Siekaniec, "The Poles of Upper North Wisconsin," in *WMH*, 39 (Spring, 1956), 195–198; Richard H. Zeitlin, "White Eagles in the North Woods,

Urban-rural division appeared among Czechs and Slovaks, too. Those who arrived before the 1890's settled in rural areas, either in the southeastern counties of Milwaukee, Racine, Kenosha, Winnebago, Manitowoc, and Kewaunee, or in the southwestern counties of Crawford, Grant, Richland, and Vernon. Later arrivals, predominantly Slovaks, congregated primarily in the southeast industrial cities or the Cutover counties. In seven of the state's nine largest cities, Czechs outnumbered Slovaks two to one; the exceptions were Kenosha and Superior. By 1920, all but 2 per cent of Kenosha County's Czechoslovakians (two-thirds of them Slovak) lived in the city; so did nearly 80 per cent in Racine County, and 78 per cent in Milwaukee and La Crosse counties. The figures were reversed in Manitowoc County and the Cutover. Overall, the Czechoslovakian population was almost evenly divided between urban and rural, with Slovaks more concentrated in industrial cities.[57]

By contrast, the state's Serbian, Croatian, and Slovenian immigrants were almost entirely urban. About 80 per cent settled in Milwaukee, Sheboygan, Kenosha, or Racine counties, although handfuls of South Slavs lived in every county except Buffalo. Only Clark County, with about 300, had any appreciable rural concentration.[58]

That same affinity for the urban southeast was evident among other southern and eastern European immigrants. Early north Italian settlements in rural Vernon (Genoa), Barron (Cumberland), Fond du Lac (Campbellsport), and Marinette (Pound and Coleman) counties. The southern Italians came after 1895 and settled in the southeast. By 1920, over three-fourths lived in Milwaukee, Kenosha, Racine, Dane, Rock, or Waukesha counties. Nearly all of Madison's Italians, and about two-thirds of Milwaukee's, were Sicilian, while those in Racine and Kenosha were usually from Calabria. Italians also lived in the mining and lumbering counties of Barron, Washburn, Florence, and especially Iron, which had an Italian population of 856 in 1920, while the other northern counties were about 5 per cent Italian.

Over 70 per cent of Hungarian-born newcomers resided in Mil-

Polish Immigration to Rural Wisconsin, 1857–1900," in *The Polish Review*, 25 (March, 1980), 69–92; Harriet Pawlowska, "Gamroth the Strong," in *Polish-American Studies*, 5 (July–December, 1948), 104–107.

[57] *Fourteenth Census of the United States, 1920: Population, Volume II, General Report and Analytical Tables*, 1036–1037; *Fourteenth Census of the United States, 1920: Population, Volume III, Composition and Characteristics of the Population by States*, 1135–1136; Karel D. Bicha, "The Czechs in Wisconsin History," in *WMH*, 53 (Spring, 1970), 194–198; Bernard, *Melting Pot and Altar*, 21–22.

[58] *Fourteenth Census of the United States, 1920: Population, Volume II, General Report and Analytical Tables*, 1036–1037; *Fourteenth Census of the United States, 1920: Population, Volume III, Composition and Characteristics of the Population by States*, 1135–1136; Marie Prisland, "The Slovenians, Most Recent American Immigrants," in *WMH*, 33 (March, 1950), 265–280; Charles A. Ward, "The Serbian and Croatian Communities in Milwaukee," in *General Linguistics*, 16 (Summer/Fall, 1976), 151–157.

waukee and Racine counties, with sizable concentrations in Dodge, Kenosha, Waukesha, and Winnebago counties. Elsewhere, only Marathon and Marinette counties contained as many as one hundred Hungarians.

Just over half of Wisconsin's Greek immigrants lived in Milwaukee County, and one-third divided themselves among Racine, Sheboygan, Rock, Fond du Lac, and Kenosha counties. Outside the southeast, only Superior had an appreciable colony. As for Lithuanians, nearly eight in ten lived in Kenosha, Racine, Milwaukee, Sheboygan, or Rock counties. In the northern two-thirds of the state, only Clark, Ashland, and Douglas counties had as many as fifty, and twenty-five counties had not a single Lithuanian immigrant. Virtually all of the few hundreds of immigrant Armenians, Rumanians, Bulgarians, and Syrians settled in the southeast.[59]

At the opposite end of the spectrum were Swedish and Finnish immigrants, who markedly preferred the northern third of the state. Nearly 80 per cent of the Finns settled in Douglas, Iron, Bayfield, Ashland, Price, Vilas, or Clark counties. More than two-thirds lived in rural areas, and less than 7 per cent lived in Milwaukee, Kenosha, or Racine. Virtually no Finns chose the southwestern part of the state.

A similar pattern distinguished Swedish immigrants, who had come mainly from western Finland. Nearly 45 per cent lived in Douglas, Burnett, Polk, Bayfield, Ashland, Price, and Barron counties; several thousand more settled throughout the rest of the Cutover. Marinette, on the border between the Cutover and the Michigan lakeshore, had 1,116 Swedes. Eau Claire, Dunn, Pepin, and St. Croix counties on the state's western edge were home to a total of 1,375. Nearly two-thirds of Swedish immigrants lived in rural areas, but sizable numbers pursued skilled trades in Superior, Milwaukee, Kenosha, Ashland, and Racine.[60]

Plotting the settlement patterns of Wisconsin's 19,641 Austrians and 21,447 Russians is complicated by the division between Jews and Gentiles. An appreciable number of immigrants from Hungary, Po-

---

[59] *Fourteenth Census of the United States, 1920: Population, Volume III, Composition and Characteristics of the Population by States*, 1135–1136; Bernard, *Melting Pot and Altar*, 23–24; Theodore Saloutos, "The Greeks of Milwaukee," in *WMH*, 53 (Spring, 1970), 175–181; St. Casimir's Church, *Golden Jubilee, 1913–1963* (Racine, 1963); Dorothy Mitchell, "Lithuanian Immigrants to Kenosha" (unpublished seminar paper, 1981, in the Area Research Center, University of Wisconsin-Parkside, Kenosha).

[60] *Fourteenth Census of the United States, 1920: Population, Volume II, General Report and Analytical Tables*, 769–770; *Fourteenth Census of the United States, 1920: Population, Volume III, Composition and Characteristics of the Population by States*, 1135–1136; Kolehmainen and Hill, *Haven in the Woods*, 27–69; Rippley, *Immigrant Experience*, 76–79. See also Mark Knipping, *Finns in Wisconsin* (Madison, 1977), 11–19; Guy-Harold Smith, "Notes on the Distribution of the Foreign-Born Scandinavians in Wisconsin in 1905," in *WMH*, 14 (June, 1931), 419–436.

land, Lithuania, Czechoslovakia, and Rumania were Jewish, but they at most constituted a significant minority. Russian Jews, however, constituted a substantial majority of Russian immigration to Wisconsin. Some Austrians were Jewish, of course, but more were Gentiles and Catholics. Austrians lived in every county of the state, 37 per cent lived in Milwaukee alone, and just over one-half in the state's nine most urbanized counties. Roughly eight in ten Austrians resided in those counties' major cities.

Over three-fourths of the Russian immigrants settled in the urbanized counties of Milwaukee, Sheboygan, Kenosha, Racine, Winnebago, Douglas, Dane, Fond du Lac, Marinette, and Manitowoc; and about 88 per cent of them lived in those counties' principal cities. Over one-third, nearly all Jewish, lived in Milwaukee. As for non-Jews, only Kenosha and Milwaukee, among the state's major cities, had notable populations. The 800 Russians in Lincoln, Barron, and Clark counties were mostly Gentiles as well.[61]

By 1920, the county-by-county proportions of foreign-born population were highest in the far or "new" north, and in the industrialized counties along Lake Michigan; the statewide average was 17.5 per cent. The New North contained nine of the thirteen counties whose populations were over 20 per cent foreign-born in 1920, and all but Washburn and Langlade exceeded 15 per cent. In nearly all cases, the dominant immigrant groups were Swedes, Finns, and Norwegians, with sizable admixtures of Canadians and Germans.

In the thirty-two counties of the more-established Middle North, the proportion of foreign-born was generally between 10 and 20 per cent, with only Taylor County exceeding that figure. The dominant immigrant groups remained German in the eastern counties; Norwegian in the western ones. Poles comprised the next most numerous contingent.

The seven southwestern counties generally had the lowest proportion of foreign-born in the state, and the vast majority of people were of northwestern European extraction. The same was true for the six south-central counties, except for small enclaves of Italians, Greeks, and Lithuanians in Rock County, and of Italians, Russian Jews, and Hungarians in Dane. Even in the southeastern counties of Washington, Ozaukee, Waukesha, and Walworth, the foreign-born population generally hovered between 10 and 15 per cent, mostly of German or other northwestern European origins. By contrast, approximately

---

[61] *Fourteenth Census of the United States, 1920: Population, Volume II, General Report and Analytical Tables*, 769–770, 1036–1037; *Fourteenth Census of the United States, 1920: Population, Volume III, Composition and Characteristics of the Population by States*, 1135–1136; Rippley, *Immigrant Experience*, 88; Bernard, *Melting Pot and Altar*, 23–30; Michael J. Anuta, *East Prussians From Russia* (Menominee, Michigan, 1979), 104–165.

one person in four was foreign-born in Kenosha, Racine, and Milwaukee counties, with southern and eastern Europeans comprising about half the total.[62]

Germans still constituted over one-third of Milwaukee County's foreign-born residents by 1920; more than one-fifth were Polish, while another one-fourth emanated from Russia, Austria, Hungary, Czechoslovakia, or Yugoslavia. Over 4,000 Italians, 1,940 Greeks, 480 Lithuanians, and a few hundred Armenians and Finns enriched the mosaic. All told, just over 52 per cent of Milwaukee County's immigrants were from southern and eastern Europe.[63]

It would be difficult to exaggerate the degree to which immigrants from southern and eastern Europe gravitated to heavily urban and industrialized Wisconsin. More than 70 per cent of Kenosha's foreign-born population in 1920 had arrived after 1900, as had more than half of those in the cities of Racine, Sheboygan, and Milwaukee. Fifty-five per cent of Hungarian immigrants, and nearly all Armenians, lived in Milwaukee and Racine. Fifty-six per cent of Lithuanians lived in Kenosha, Racine, and Milwaukee; 62 per cent of Greeks in Milwaukee, Racine, and Sheboygan. Seven of ten South Slavs lived in Milwaukee, West Allis, Sheboygan, and Kenosha, and the same share of Italians in Milwaukee, Kenosha, Racine, Madison, Beloit, and Waukesha. Six-tenths of the Russian-born lived in Milwaukee, Sheboygan, Kenosha, Racine, Stevens Point, Superior, or West Allis.[64]

Within Wisconsin's cities, settlement patterns were conditioned by an interplay of forces, some voluntary, some not. Chain migration meant that newcomers usually had arranged housing beforehand. Single males were inclined to live in boardinghouses owned by relatives or friends, an arrangement that provided income for landlords, household services for lodgers, and fellowship for all concerned. Even when they were able to move out of their initial accommoda-

---

[62] *Fourteenth Census of the United States, 1920: Population, Volume II, General Report and Analytical Tables*, 769–770; *Fourteenth Census of the United States, 1920: Population, Volume III, Composition and Characteristics of the Population by States*, 1135–1136; Mollenhoff, *Madison*, 423–426; Buenker, "Immigrant Heritage," in Burckel, ed., *Racine*, 71–73; Buenker, "Immigration and Ethnic Groups," in Neuenschwander, ed., *Kenosha*, 1–44.

[63] *Fourteenth Census of the United States, 1920: Population, Volume III, Composition and Characteristics of the Population by States*, 1135–1136; Still, *Milwaukee*, 267–268; Korman, *Industrialization, Immigrants, and Americanizers*, 22, 27, 44–51. See also Justin B. Galford, "The Foreign Born and Urban Growth in the Great Lakes, 1850–1950: A Study of Chicago, Cleveland, Detroit, and Milwaukee" (doctoral dissertation, New York University, 1957), 245–290.

[64] *Fourteenth Census of the United States, 1920: Population, Volume II, General Report and Analytical Tables*, 769–772, 788, 791–794, 797; *Fourteenth Census of the United States, 1920: Population, Volume III, Composition and Characteristics of the Population by States*, 1121, 1135–1136.

tions, immigrants associated with "their own kind." But by the late nineteenth century their ability to carve out new enclaves was severely constrained by a combination of topography, the built environment, economic necessity, and existing settlement patterns.[65]

In Kenosha, newcomers found that Yankees and northwestern Europeans had preempted the better residential areas. Clusters of working-class boardinghouses, duplexes, and cottages in the west-side factory district were largely cut off from the lakefront by natural and man-made barriers. Italians, Poles, Lithuanians, Slovaks, and Russians soon founded distinct enclaves on the west and northwest sides, near "the motors," the brass factories, and foundries. The less numerous groups—Greeks, Hungarians, Finns, Slovenians, Serbians, and Armenians—squeezed in among them. Nearly two decades after the massive immigration of 1900 to 1915, the northern and western sections of the city were crowded with Germans, Italians, Poles, Russians, and immigrants from southeastern Europe. American-born citizens were virtually the only residents in the more affluent southeast section.[66]

Racine's more gradual growth and the continuing influx of northwestern Europeans produced a slightly different pattern. The city was already a patchwork of ethno-cultural and socio-economic enclaves by the 1890's, being divided into three sections by the meandering Root River. Recent immigrants generally located in the "investment zone," meaning neighborhoods of working-class cottages and duplexes left behind when established residents "moved up." Italians primarily settled in Northside, near the railroad tracks and foundries, or in Lakeside, close to the Case Company's south works. Eastern Europeans picked the area south of the main business district, west of the exclusive lakeshore residential district, and around the "industrial junction." Poles selected the Fourteenth Ward on the south side, which was over 40 per cent Polish by 1920. Lithuanians, Hungarians, and Slovaks chose Lakeside and Northside. Russian Jews,

---

[65] Howard P. Chudacoff, *Mobile Americans: Residential and Social Mobility in Omaha, 1880–1920* (New York, 1972), 33–34, 63–83; Humbert S. Nelli, *Italians in Chicago, 1880–1930: A Study in Ethnic Mobility* (New York, 1970), 22–55; Howard A. Botts, "Commercial Structure and Ethnic Residential Patterns in the Shaping of Milwaukee, 1880–1900" (doctoral dissertation, University of Wisconsin, 1985), 3–58. See also *Reports of the Immigration Commission, Volume I: Abstracts*, 1911 (serial 5865).

[66] Buenker, "Immigration and Ethnic Groups," in Neuenschwander, ed., *Kenosha*, 12–15; Barbara M. Duncan, "Kenosha, Wisconsin: A Study in Urban Choreography" (master's thesis, University of Chicago, 1935), 15–20; Virginia Mattes, "Immigration in American Life: A Study of Kenosha County in the Late 19th and Early 20th Centuries with a Focus on Wards 1, 2, and 5 in the Year 1910" (unpublished seminar paper, 1989, in the Area Research Center, University of Wisconsin-Parkside, Kenosha).

Greeks, and Armenians settled in and around downtown, frequently living above, behind, or next door to their small shops.[67]

Much the same circumstances prevailed in Milwaukee. Newcomers there found cheap, hastily constructed housing between the Menomonee Valley, West Allis, and Bay View. Italians located chiefly in the southeast Third Ward in houses left behind by upwardly mobile Irish. Russian Jews, Czechs, and Slovaks located in the wards just northwest of the central business district; Hungarians and Austrians located nearby, or in the lakefront Fifth Ward. Poles dominated most of the south side, especially the southwest corner, and westward along Lincoln and Greenfield avenues to West Allis. A smaller colony of 2,000 Poles grew up northwest of the Menomonee River, while about 3,000 Kashubian Poles from the Baltic Coast lived on Jones Island.[68]

Wherever the latecomers from southern and eastern Europe settled, they had to make do with substandard housing and living conditions, whether it was Jones Island in Milwaukee, the Bush in Madison, the bowery in Superior, or Hunger Point in La Crosse. Here dwelled the unskilled, the non-English-speaking, the despised "other" whose name was Greek or Pole, Slovak or Hungarian, Lithuanian or Jew. Contemporary observers noted ruefully how these newcomers sought out the darkest and most demoralizing areas and seemingly became accustomed to them, the relative lack of air and sunlight, and lack of interior ventilation.[69]

The new immigrants paid a price for what some seemed to feel was

---

[67] *Fourteenth Census of the United States, 1920: Population, Volume III, Composition and Characteristics of the Population by States*, 1139; Buenker, "The Immigrant Heritage," in Burckel, ed., *Racine*, 90–91; Christian D. Nokkentved, "Danes, Denmark and Racine, 1837–1924: A Study of Danish and Overseas Migration" (doctoral dissertation, University of Chicago, 1984), 77–130.

[68] *Fourteenth Census of the United States, 1920: Population, Volume III, Composition and Characteristics of the Population by States*, 1137–1138; Still, *Milwaukee*, 269–278; Korman, *Industrialization, Immigrants, and Americanizers*, 46–48; Swichkow and Gartner, *Jews of Milwaukee*, 155–168; Botts, "Commercial Structure and Ethnic Residential Patterns," 124–174; *Senate Documents*, 61 Cong., 3 sess., vols. 7 and 8, no. 747 (serials 5865, 5866), *Reports of the Immigration Commission. Abstracts of Reports of the Immigration Commission with Conclusions and Recommendations and Views of the Minority* (2 vols., 1911; reprinted, New York, 1970); Roger D. Simon, "The Expansion of an Industrial City: Milwaukee, 1880–1910" (doctoral dissertation, University of Wisconsin, 1971), 90–105.

[69] For housing conditions, see reports on cities in Bureau of Labor and Industrial Statistics, *Biennial Report*, 1908–1909, pp. 1–66; Duncan, *Kenosha*, 16–25, 70–90; Elizabeth Krimmel, "The History and Development of the Central Association of Racine, Wisconsin for 1910 to 1930" (unpublished research paper, 1985, in the Area Research Center, University of Wisconsin-Parkside, Kenosha), 27–34; Mollenhoff, *Madison*, 352–360; and Kathy McVicker, "The Hull House of Racine: The Central Association, 1910–1920" (unpublished seminar paper, 1985, in the Area Research Center, University of Wisconsin-Parkside, Kenosha), 19–22.

their refusal to be clean and prosperous. In Milwaukee (and likely in other cities as well), the highest mortality rates correlated with the most densely populated immigrant neighborhoods, though other factors were certainly implicated as well. Health officers' accounts and newspaper stories supported the popular impression that infectious diseases flourished "among a class whose antipathy to soap and water and other requisites of decency was proverbial." Epidemics hit hardest in German and Polish wards. In Kenosha, too, the city health department found that contagious diseases were more prevalent on the working-class west side.[70]

Nor did southern and eastern European immigrants fare much better occupationally. Those in the Cutover generally eked out a tenuous livelihood from farming, lumbering, or mining combined with off-season and odd jobs. In the cities, newcomers usually toiled in the factories, foundries, and mills. By 1910, immigrants were 22 per cent of the state's population and 31 per cent of its work force. Over 98 per cent of foreign-born males over ten years of age had jobs, compared to just over three-fourths of the general population. Immigrants held over 50 per cent of the jobs in mines, over 40 per cent of those in factories, and about one-third of those in agriculture, lumbering, transportation, and public and domestic service. Male immigrants and their sons made up 80 per cent of the manufacturing work force and 70 per cent in trade and transportation. Immigrant women were more apt to toil in their own homes, while their daughters worked in either manufacturing or domestic service.[71]

Investigating Milwaukee in 1910, the U.S. Immigration Commission determined that the bulk of the city's Polish and Italian immigrants worked as day laborers, street railway track layers, or dockhands. In a sample of 551 male immigrants, the study found that 60 per cent of Italians and 52 per cent of Poles were laborers, while over half the Russian Jews and a quarter of the Italians were either peddlers or shopkeepers. In another sample of 1,367 workers, it discovered that anywhere from two-thirds to three-fourths of Czechs, Germans, and Poles, and 55 per cent of Armenians, were engaged in manufacturing and mechanical pursuits, while half the Jews were in trade. The 362 Italian males were almost evenly divided among manufacturing, trade, general labor, and transportation. Daughters of im-

---

[70] Judith W. Leavitt, *The Healthiest City: Milwaukee and the Politics of Health Reform* (Princeton, 1982; reprinted, Madison, 1996), 22–41 (quote); Buenker, "Immigration and Ethnic Groups," in Neuenschwander, ed., *Kenosha*, 13–14; Meir, *My Life*, 37.

[71] *Thirteenth Census of the United States, 1910: Occupation Statistics, Volume IV*, 138–151, 531–533; *Thirteenth Census of the United States, 1910: Population: Reports by States, with Statistics for Counties, Cities, and other Civil Divisions*, 1075–1076; Bernard, *Melting Pot and Altar*, 34–41.

migrant parents were four times as likely as their mothers to work in manufacturing, and both generations were heavily involved in domestic service.[72]

Southern and eastern Europeans augmented or supplanted northwestern Europeans as "cheap labor" in Milwaukee. Eighteen different nationalities—chiefly Poles, Russians, Italians, Croatians, Slovaks, and Lithuanians—toiled in its tanneries. Slovaks also worked in foundries, breweries, and saloons, or served as steamship or travel agents. Hungarians were usually factory workers or boardinghouse operators. Greeks largely engaged in factory work and monopolized the shoe-shine business. Italians frequently labored in foundries, coal yards, docks, or on street crews and railroad gangs; others ran grocery stores, saloons, or wholesale fruit outlets. By 1909, the vast majority of Poles still worked in foundries, steel mills, and machine shops, though some had become small businessmen.[73]

Immigrants typically entered the work force as unskilled seasonal workers, digging sewers and ditches, carrying hods of bricks, or cutting ice; then they would rise to unskilled or semiskilled jobs in mills, tanneries, foundries, and factories. Within the factory, a stereotypical pecking order affected those from central, eastern, and southern Europe. Native-born Wisconsinites, mainly of northern European extraction, contradictorily could regard the newer immigrants as plodding and industrious, socially inferior, willing to work in undesirable occupations, ignorant and easily misled by labor and political agitators, and generally unsuited to discipline and efficiency. By the 1890's, stereotyping labeled Germans as sober, industrious, thrifty, productive, and frugal. Poles were considered unstable, given to quarreling and pilfering, and "Popish." Italians were stigmatized as untidy, ignorant, easily duped by labor and political agitators, and volatile if not downright violent. Hungarians were regarded as honest and industrious, but also as uncleanly and transient. Greeks were dismissed as more unstable than Italians or Hungarians, and less sober and industrious than Italians or Jews. The stereotyping of eastern European Jews naturally ran towards anti-Semitism.[74]

---

[72] *Senate* Documents, 61 Cong., 3 sess., vols. 7 and 8, no. 747 (serials 5865, 5866), *Reports of the Immigration Commission*, I: 285–366, 723–772. The report demonstrates that across the nation southern and eastern European immigrants and their children were primarily unskilled or semi-skilled workers.

[73] Korman, *Industrialization, Immigrants, and Americanizers*, 46–47; Still, *Milwaukee*, 273–277; Bernard, *Altar and Melting Pot*, 20–21; Saloutos, "The Greeks of Milwaukee," in *WMH*, 53: 175–193; Botts, "Commercial Structure and Ethnic Residential Patterns," 84–118, 175–176; Simon, "Expansion of an Industrial City," 90–105.

[74] Korman, *Industrialization, Immigrants, and Americanizers*, 41–46; George La Piana, *The Italians in Milwaukee, Wisconsin: General Survey* (Milwaukee, 1915; reprinted, San Francisco, 1970), 5–6; Alberto C. Meloni, "Italy Invades the Bloody Third–Milwaukee

The Milwaukee knitting industry allegedly preferred German and Polish women, because of a presumed aptitude. The meat-packer Patrick Cudahy refused to hire Greeks because he believed they fought with knives. An ice manufacturer informed the Milwaukee *Journal* that Swedes and "Polacks" were the best workers, even though they were unreliable and probably tramps at heart. Railroad bosses resignedly hired Greeks, Italians, Bulgarians, Austrians, and Hungarians as common laborers, but believed that "hoboes" were better, and could do four or five times more work than a similar gang of Greeks or Bulgarians. The Pabst brewery favored Germans but did hire Polish women for unskilled, low-wage jobs in the bottling house.

Many factories relied upon assistant foremen or straw bosses of southern and eastern European ancestry as recruiters. The chipping room of the International Harvester foundry, where rough edges were removed from castings, was virtually an Italian preserve for many years because of the activities of one "padrone," while a Scottish-born foundry foreman at Harvester hired Poles because his own countrymen tended to expect too much of him. Whatever their ancestry or skill levels, workers were usually admonished to keep ethnic conflicts off the shop floor and were punished for violating that injunction. Foremen regularly employed ethnic slurs to motivate and reprimand.[75]

Alone among Milwaukee's larger immigrant groups, Jews avoided factory work. Newer Jewish immigrants generally spoke no English, had no factory experience, refused to work on Saturdays and high holy days, preferred to work for other Jews, and were victims of pervasive anti-Semitism—all of which tended to exclude them from work in heavy industry. Quite a few worked as laborers, tinsmiths, or painters; a substantial majority were peddlers, junk dealers, butchers, clothiers, grocers, shoe repairmen, restaurateurs, and shopkeepers. A survey made in 1910 estimated that among 7,500 immigrant Jews, 500 households were supported by peddling, about 300 by common labor, and 100 by shopkeeping—totals that accounted for two-thirds of the Jewish population.[76]

For Wisconsin Jews, the pre-World War I era was the golden age of street peddling and Milwaukee was its golden land. Petty trade was frequently a steppingstone to retail or wholesale business. Artisans or their children could become manufacturers; scrap-metal collectors entered the iron business or plumbing and heating. Many Jewish

---

Italians, 1900–1910," in Milwaukee County Historical Society, *Historical Messenger*, 25 (March, 1969), 34–46.

[75] Korman, *Industrialization, Immigrants, and Americanizers*, 42–46, 64–67; Still, *Milwaukee*, 273–277.

[76] Swichkow and Gartner, *Jews of Milwaukee*, 160–166.

metal or leather workers turned to peddling during depressions. Jewish unions and trade associations soon proliferated. The city's Jewish quarter abounded with shops and services, and some residents became professionals—physicians, attorneys, opticians, and dentists.[77]

In Madison, Jewish immigrants typically engaged in street sales and collected rags and junk. Italians worked as ditch diggers, quarry workers, railroad hands, and hod carriers. As late as 1915, only 15 per cent of Italian workers were considered skilled. "On the same street with fine stores that cater to metropolitan trade," observed a later historian about Italian neighborhoods in general, "are little hole-in-the-wall places where a few vegetables, cans of tomato paste and bottles of olive oil give evidence of a shopkeeper." By 1920, Jews and Italians constituted nearly 30 per cent of Madison's work force. In Kenosha, newcomers quickly dominated the unskilled work force, pushing German, Scandinavian, Irish, and British workers up the occupational ladder. As late as the 1930's in Kenosha, seven of ten Italian males out of 559 sampled listed their occupations as laborers or unskilled workers; only one in five was skilled. Nearly 65 per cent of women were housewives, although many ran boardinghouses for single male workers.[78]

In Racine, the same conditions prevailed. A large percentage of Italian immigrants worked at J. I. Case or in Northside foundries. Others built roads and buildings, toiled in agriculture and on the lower rungs of industry. The earliest Polish immigrants to Racine were cabinetmakers specifically recruited for their skills. Later, a 1929 survey of 500 Polish workers revealed that almost half were molders, machinists, or laborers, while 38 per cent were assemblers, clerks, foremen, or city government workers. The same was generally true of the city's Hungarians, Slovaks, Lithuanians, Greeks, and Armenians. Only Russian Jewish newcomers largely eschewed factory work and became fruit peddlers or junk dealers, scissors grinders, umbrella menders, or proprietors of second-hand stores. "Like 'Fiddler on the Roof'," a prominent Racine Jew later recalled, "the first Jewish settlers had horses and wagons and five or six children."[79]

---

[77] A vivid description of work and life in Milwaukee's Jewish community between 1905 and 1920 appears in the transcription of an interview with Robert A. Hess, February 3, 1965, SC 1005.

[78] Mollenhoff, *Madison*, 196, 245–246; Fred L. Holmes, *Old World Wisconsin: Around Europe in the Badger State* (Eau Claire, 1944), 321–336 (quote); Buenker, "Immigration and Ethnic Groups," in Neuenschwander, ed., *Kenosha*, 8–11; John D. Buenker, "Reconstructing Kenosha's Italian-American Community: A Research Model," paper delivered to the American Italian Historical Association, Chicago, November 15, 1987, in the author's files.

[79] Buenker, "The Immigrant Heritage," in Burckel, ed., *Racine*, 79–84.

Although Finns and Swedes usually avoided industrial occupations, they did not do so altogether. Swedes held skilled jobs in the southeast lakeshore cities and in Superior. Finns labored in the foundries, mills, and tanneries of Milwaukee, West Allis, Racine, and Kenosha, as well as in the shipyards, docks, and railroads of Superior, and Ashland; some joined Norwegians, Danes, and Poles as Great Lakes fishermen. Most Finns settled in the rural areas of the New North, especially the counties bordering Lake Superior, where they eked out a living on farms of forty or eighty acres, some of them building distinctive log structures, including saunas. Most supplemented their marginal farm income with employment in logging camps, sawmills, and iron mines. Whether in the mines of the Cutover or the factories of the southeast, Finns became labor activists, frequently affiliating with radical organizations like the Industrial Workers of the World (IWW) or the Socialist party.[80]

For immigrant workers, adjustment to the new world began with the search for a steady job. Chain migration often provided newcomers with initial employment, but these jobs were commonly temporary, seasonal, or transitional. Labor agents, land companies, railroads, and other employers in New York, Chicago, and other large cities recruited some immigrants. In Racine and Kenosha, labor agents were known as "head hunters" and received three dollars for each successful recruitment. To hold their jobs, workers often had to resort to "basketeering"—meaning that they provided foremen or bosses with gifts of fruit, vegetables, wine, or money. Saloonkeepers and ward politicians secured jobs in exchange for patronage and votes. Ethnic fraternal and benevolent societies also helped newcomers find work, as did the Young Men's Christian Association, Associated Charities, and settlement houses.[81]

In times of depression or economic crisis, civic leaders established temporary centers where workers gathered for day jobs. Newspapers, both mainstream and foreign-language, carried employment notices and job tips, frequently geared towards skilled and semiskilled workers. Some shops in the Milwaukee area acquired reputations for hiring within ethnic groups. Both Cudahy and E. P. Allis seem to have opted for Poles. In Racine, both J. I. Case and the Mitchell Wagon Works reportedly sought Danes, while Czechs could always find employment in the trunk and luggage industry through Martin M. Se-

---

[80] Kolehmainen and Hill, *Haven in the Woods*, 46–69, 118–135; Rippley, *Immigrant Experience*, 78–79.

[81] William M. Leiserson, *Adjusting Immigrant and Industry* (New York, 1969), 28–48; Korman, *Industrialization, Immigrants, and Americanizers*, 28–37; Rippley, *Immigrant Experience*, 84–86.

cor, himself a Bohemian immigrant. Besides these informal networks, private employment agencies specialized in placing unskilled immigrants in lumber camps, railroad gangs, and construction crews.

[4]

Once immigrant workers secured steady employment, they still had to contend with difficult and dangerous working conditions. In 1908, the average immigrant worker in Milwaukee earned $453 a year, at a time when the income necessary for a family of five was calculated to be about $700. To make ends meet, women and children had to work. Wives and daughters ran boardinghouses, did "homework" (meaning piecework) for the clothing industry, or worked in factories or shops. Boys hawked newspapers, shined shoes, or served as delivery boys. When old enough, boys and girls took jobs in factories, mills, or foundries. By pooling their returns, the typical immigrant family in Milwaukee could increase its average income to about $650 a year—still short of the minimum standards for diet, health, and general welfare. In 1916, the Racine *Labor Advocate* estimated that most of the city's unskilled workers failed to meet the federal government's income standard of $16.50 per week, or $858 annually, for a family of six.[82]

The typical industrial work week ran ten to twelve hours a day, six days a week, leaving little free time except on Sunday. Generally untrammeled by labor unions, public opinion, or government regulations, employers usually provided just enough concern for health and safety to ensure productivity and profit. Occupational injuries, illnesses, and death were commonplace; immigrant workers had little recourse except litigation, in a court system which they did not understand, and which was frequently hostile. Loss of the breadwinner usually condemned a family to abject poverty or life on the dole.[83]

Southern and eastern Europeans endured isolation in other ways as well. Since many planned to return home and not stay in America, they were slow to become American citizens. In West Allis, Kenosha, Sheboygan, Racine, Beloit, Waukesha, Milwaukee and Manitowoc,

---

[82] Swichkow and Gartner, *Jews of Milwaukee*, 165–166; Isaac A. Hourwich, *Immigration and Labor: The Economic Aspects of European Immigration to the United States* (New York, 1912; reprinted, 1969), 5–34, 284–352; Leiserson, *Adjusting Immigrant and Industry*, 104–148; Korman, *Industrialization, Immigrants, and Americanizers*, 51–60; John Higham, *Strangers in the Land: Patterns of American Nativism, 1860–1925* (New Brunswick, New Jersey, 1955; 2nd ed., 1988), 71–72, 112, 163, 305–306, 321.

[83] Italian-American railroad workers periodically engaged in disputes with both employers and white workers. See the Milwaukee *Sentinel*, January 15, 1893, and the *Wisconsin State Journal*, June 7, 1906.

where southern and eastern Europeans were numerous, naturalization rates ranged from 41 to 54 per cent. In Appleton, Ashland, Marinette, and Wausau, where northwestern Europeans predominated, they approached three-fourths. In the eleven Milwaukee wards inhabited primarily by newcomers from southeastern Europe, naturalization rates fell below one-half; on the heavily Germanic northwest side, rates generally exceeded two-thirds. In Racine, nearly two-thirds of the immigrants in the heavily Scandinavian Eighth Ward had become citizens by 1920, compared to less than one-third in the largely eastern European Fourteenth Ward. Whatever the locale or ethnic mix, naturalization rates for woman exceeded that for men, because married women automatically become citizens when their husbands did, and because single males were the least likely group to become citizens.

Regardless of citizenship status, immigrants were three-and-a-half times more likely to suffer from illiteracy, or more than twice the rate among Negroes. Even among the foreign-born, the illiteracy rate was significantly higher in southern and eastern European areas. Illiteracy among immigrants exceeded the statewide average in thirteen of Wisconsin's twenty-one largest cities. Virtually everywhere and in almost every age bracket, foreign-born women were slightly more inclined towards illiteracy, probably because they were not under the same pressure as men to function in the wider society.

Nor had recent immigrants and their children fully closed the gap in formal education. By 1910, 64 per cent of all Wisconsinites between the age of five and twenty attended school. Among immigrants, the rate was only 41 per cent; their children, however, matched the state average. Ten years later, the percentage among foreign-born had jumped to one-half; their children remained steadily average. At ages five and six immigrant children were likely to be in school; then they dropped out in large numbers after age thirteen. Slightly less than 30 per cent finished high school, even as late as 1920, compared to 38 per cent of second-generation children and 47 per cent of the children of American-born parents. Ironically, because immigrant children found it easier to obtain employment than Negro children, they frequently left school at a more tender age to help support their families. In the long run, urban residence meant extended education for immigrants, because larger cities had more stringent attendance laws and enforced them rigorously.[84]

Charges of inherent inferiority made by ordinary Americans and by leading social reformers added to the burden borne by southern and eastern Europeans. Academics and racialists reached a consensus

---

[84] *Fourteenth Census of the United States, 1920: Population, Volume III, Composition and Characteristics of the Population by States*, 1118, 1120, 1124, 1131–1132, 1137–1139.

that newcomers displaced native-born workers, retarded unionization, and kept wages, hours, and conditions of labor at the subsistence level. Newcomers were held responsible for the very living and working conditions under which they suffered, as well as for pauperism, crime, vice, and insanity. The Milwaukee *Sunday Telegraph* called Polish strikers in 1886 "the dregs, the scum, the filth and the sewers of the old country." But the press was not alone in slurring the new immigrants. Edward A. Ross, a noted reform-minded sociologist at the University of Wisconsin, stigmatized southern and eastern European immigrants as those who "belong in skins, in wattled huts at the close of the Great Ice Age. These oxlike men are descendants of those who always stayed behind." Ross scored them for their lack of mental acumen, for being excitable and impulsive, for being morally inferior, and for impeding the nation's social progress. Similarly, the university's economist and labor historian John R. Commons, like his colleague a respected "progressive" intellectual, insisted that no matter how much adaptation the newcomers made to American life, "underneath all these changes they may continue the physical, mental, and moral capacities and incapacities which determine the real character of their religion, government, industry, and literature." Ross and Commons contributed significantly to the intellectual justification for congressional restriction of immigration from southern and eastern Europe.[85]

Despite such denunciations and socio-economic obstacles, Wisconsin's newest immigrants painstakingly and painfully adapted. In part, they modified such Old World institutions as mutual-aid societies, agricultural co-operatives, craft guilds, and labor unions to Wisconsin conditions. In part, they borrowed models pioneered by Yankees and earlier immigrants from northwestern Europe. In part, they developed new institutions, more appropriate to modern, urban, industrial society. In the end, they constructed complex associational networks that enriched the state. In so doing, they enabled their members to confront the paradox of change by conserving portions of their past.[86]

---

[85] The *Sunday Telegraph* statement is quoted in Robert W. Ozanne, *The Labor Movement in Wisconsin: A History* (Madison, 1984), 12. See also John R. Commons, *Races and Immigrants in America* (New York, 1907; reprinted, 1967), 1–21 (quote), 63–106, 135–178, 198–238; Edward A. Ross, *The Old World in the New: The Significance of Past and Present Immigration to the American People* (New York, 1914); Higham, *Strangers in the Land*, 131–193; Oscar Handlin, *Race and Nationality in American Life* (Boston, 1948), 74–110; and Alan M. Kraut, *The Huddled Masses: The Immigrant in American Society, 1880–1921* (Arlington Heights, Illinois, 1982), 148–178.

[86] Richard N. Current, "The 'New Ethnicity' and American History: Wisconsin as a Test Case," in *The History Teacher*, 15 (November, 1981), 43–55; Harold A. Pedersen,

Of all immigrant institutions, none proved more enduring or crucial than the family. In nearly all southern and eastern European countries, the nuclear family was the principal tool for organizing how lives were led, determining patterns for socialization, and distributing land and other resources. The key was co-operation in a system which bound members by reciprocal duties, obligations, and privileges. The family pooled its limited resources; individuals muted aspirations in the common interest. Parents decided careers and marriage partners, determined whether children should work or attend school, and provided job training. Family leaders decided the order of emigration and arranged for passage, employment, and housing. Immigrant streams were comprised both of young adults and "middling people" (who generally had experienced neither poverty nor power and wealth). The urban industrial environment in which they became immersed provided little public assistance, promoted mutual aid, and forced many in each family to earn wages. Thus the immigration experience increased the importance of family as the basic socio-economic unit.[87]

Young immigrant men who decided to remain in Wisconsin generally married quickly, which provided companionship, and improved financial and decision-making resources. Marrying someone from a common ethnic and religious background enhanced the likelihood of those gains, and most did in fact marry among their own kind: 86 per cent of German immigrants, 80 per cent of their offspring, and nearly as high a proportion of Poles and Russians. They welcomed children as a source of pride, as a guarantee of security in old age, a slice of immortality, and a household economic benefit. If children were too young to work, or after they had grown up and moved out, families frequently took in boarders to supplement income. However, the nuclear family with working children was the prevailing model—an assumption that affected decisions about school, work, and marriage. Unmarried women typically worked outside the home. A married woman with children generally managed the household, functioning as confidant, co-worker, advisor, comptroller, and socializer of children, unless economic necessity dictated otherwise. When individual aspirations clashed with familial imperatives, the transition from the Old World to Wisconsin could produce frustrated ambitions, sibling rivalry, and intergenerational estrange-

---

"Acculturation Among Danish and Polish Ethnic Groups in Wisconsin" (doctoral dissertation, University of Wisconsin, 1949), 168–195.

[87] Bernard, *Melting Pot and Altar*, 117–124; Kraut, *Huddled Masses*, 31, 101–108; Tamara K. Hareven and John Modell, "Family Patterns," in *Harvard Encyclopedia of American Ethnic Groups*, 345–384.

ment. Still, the family household generally remained paramount for immigrants entering the American industrial-urban economy.[88]

Nearly as central was the ethnic neighborhood, which stood somewhere between a melting pot and a homogeneous ghetto. Inner-city neighborhoods generally accommodated clusters of different groups, although one usually predominated, identifying an area as "Little Italy," "Polonia," or "Greektown." Chain migration all but guaranteed that kin and acquaintances from the same village or region occupied the same or adjoining blocks. There was in Milwaukee a block on Pulaski Street that contained ninety first- and second-generation Polish, one Irish, and three German households. At the other extreme was a block on State Street that contained twenty-nine German-headed households, three Irish, and one each of Czech, Greek, Russian-Jewish, Polish, Scottish, Slovak, and Syrian. Neighborhoods earned their ethnic designations through the clumps of businesses, churches, and clubs which focused on a particular ethnic clientele. Immigrant merchants and professionals catered to co-ethnic customers and clients. In those enclaves Wisconsin's immigrants found familiar faces, language, folkways, food, and the rhythm and texture of life that gave them a sense of security and belonging. Ethnic enclaves also served as "incubators" from which immigrants and their offspring could sally forth to interact with other groups and mainstream America.[89]

The enclave's nucleus was usually a church or synagogue, transplanted intact from abroad, even though the new environment soon forced alterations. Nearly 80 per cent of religious Wisconsinites were either Catholic or Lutheran in 1916—both of them immigrant denominations. Religion served as a vehicle for transmitting language and customs. Co-religionists in the old country frequently provided financial aid, art, and clergy. Besides spiritual needs, churches filled social and recreational needs with dances, socials, athletics, and organizations. Families centered their social and recreational lives around the church calendar; holy days were the highlights of the year. The church also helped new arrivals find jobs and housing, counseled families, aided the needy, and cared for the sick. Priests, ministers, and rabbis were frequently among the leaders of an immigrant community, especially in its formative stages. Constructing a place of worship was generally among the first orders of business for any immi-

---

[88] John Bodnar, *The Transplanted: A History of Immigrants in Urban America* (Bloomington, Indiana, 1985), 57–84.

[89] Botts, "Commercial Structure and Ethnic Residential Patterns," 3–18; *Senate Documents*, 61 Cong., 3 sess., vols. 7 and 8, no. 747 (serials 5865, 5866), *Reports of the Immigration Commission*, I. See also the discussion in Kraut, *Huddled Masses*, 115–122, and Chudacoff, *Mobile Americans*, 63–73.

grant group, despite the economic sacrifice. Frequently men and boys built much of the structure with their own heavy labor, while women and girls helped out with lighter labor and with food, drink, and encouragement.[90]

Harmony did not always prevail. Discord and disunion frequently rent immigrant churches. Clerics found their authority challenged by activist laymen, secular leaders, and working-class organizers. Americanizers and traditionalists fought over dogma and liturgy, and some Protestant churches picked up new members by proselytizing among the disgruntled newcomers. Splits among orthodox, conservative, and reform Jews divided their congregations, while the largely Irish and German Catholic church of Wisconsin frequently proved hostile to demands by Polish, Italian, and Lithuanian co-religionists for ethnic parishes, compatible clergy, their own language of worship, and observance of national and regional devotions. The inevitable generation gap also affected churches negatively, as second- and third-generation immigrants questioned the faith of their fathers.[91]

In addition to Catholicism, Lutheranism, and Judaism, new immigrants brought other religions that were decidedly unfamiliar— among them Eastern Orthodox Christianity, Orthodox Judaism, Armenian Apostolicism, and Coptic Catholicism. The largest portion of the newcomers were Roman Catholic, although their practices varied sometimes from the Irish and German. Lithuanians, Poles, Slovaks, Austrians, Slovenes, Croatians, Ukrainians, Syrians, Rumanians, Italians, and most Hungarians and Czechs were adherents of that same tradition. National Orthodox churches prevailed among Greeks, Serbians, Bulgarians, Ukrainians, Albanians, and non-Jewish Russians. Lutherans predominated among Swedes and Finns; smaller numbers appeared among several northeastern European peoples. Most of Wisconsin's Russian immigrants were Orthodox Jews, as were significant minorities of Poles, Lithuanians, Austrians, Czechs, Hungarians, and Rumanians. Between 1890 and 1916, the number of Roman Catholics in Wisconsin doubled, from 293,134 to 594,836, representing one-quarter of the state's total population, and just over half of those affiliated with one religious body or another. From 1902 to 1916, nearly two-thirds of them lived in the southeastern quarter of

---

[90] Jay P. Dolan, *The American Catholic Experience: A History from Colonial Times to the Present* (Garden City, New York, 1985), 147–220; Nathan Glazer, *American Judaism* (Chicago, 1957; reprinted, 1972), 43–78; Kraut, *Huddled Masses*, 119–124; Oscar Handlin, *The Uprooted* (Boston, 1951; 2nd enlarged ed., 1973), 105–128.

[91] John Gurda, "The Church and the Neighborhood," in *Milwaukee Catholicism: Essays on Church and Society*, ed. Steven M. Avella (Milwaukee, 1991), 8–25; Anthony J. Kuzniewski, *Faith and Fatherland: The Polish Church War in Wisconsin, 1896–1918* (Notre Dame, 1980), 36–89, and Donald Pienkos, "Politics, Religion, and Change in Polish Milwaukee, 1900–1930," in *WMH*, 61 (Spring, 1978), 193–204.

the state. Outside the southeast, Catholics could be found in significant numbers in heavily Polish Marathon, Portage, and Wood counties, Douglas and Ashland on Lake Superior, Grant in the southwest corner, and in the western counties of Eau Claire, Trempealeau, Chippewa, and La Crosse.[92]

Almost 30 per cent of the state's churchgoing population affiliated with one of the many different Lutheran synods, the number changing regularly from 1890 to 1926, when censuses were taken. Membership corresponded closely with the distribution of German and Scandinavian settlement. Wisconsin's entire Serbian Orthodox population was in Milwaukee, as were most of its Greek Orthodox Christians. Nearly three-fourths of the members of Jewish congregations resided in Milwaukee County. By 1916, Wisconsin had 2,516 foreign-language church organizations, with 808,518 members speaking twenty-six separate languages. Nearly 70 per cent of the state's churchgoers still worshiped in a foreign language on the eve of World War I.

Southern and eastern Europeans had a great impact on the Catholic church. Polish, Italian, and other recently arrived Catholics demanded their own priests and parishes, devotions, and languages. The mostly German hierarchy was reluctant to make concessions, but did create numerous de facto national parishes. The Lutherans—predominantly German, Norwegian, and Danish up until the 1880's—were augmented by Swedes, Finns, Icelanders, Lithuanians, Latvians, Estonians, and Slovaks. Finns split into three new synods which frequently warred with one another. Some traditional American Protestant sects such as the Baptists and Congregationalists established missions and conducted revival meetings among the newcomers from Europe, much as they did in foreign missions. Orthodox churches made their first appearances in the early twentieth century, chiefly in major industrial cities, but also in such rural settings as Clayton (Polk County), Cornucopia (Bayfield County), Huron (Chippewa County), and Lublin (Taylor County). Beginning with St. Stanislaus in the late 1860's, Polish Catholics established twenty parishes in greater Milwaukee. Polish parishes also sprang up in Racine, Kenosha, Superior, Ashland, Stevens Point, and Green Bay, and in such rural counties as Portage, Trempealeau, Shawano, and Oconto. Sev-

---

[92] U.S. Bureau of the Census, *Religious Bodies, 1916, Part 1: Summary and General Tables*, 86, 109, 125, 327–328; Roman Catholic Archdiocese of Milwaukee, *Census Report*, 1902, file 72, Archives of the Milwaukee Archdiocese; Rippley, *Immigrant Experience*, 43–44, 74–91. In 1896 there were 172 German, 113 Irish, forty-one French, twenty-nine Polish, thirteen Czech, seven Dutch, four Italian, two Belgian, and one Swiss Catholic churches in Wisconsin.

eral thousand Wisconsin Poles also joined the schismatic Polish National Catholic Church.[93]

Milwaukee's religious diversity was enhanced by Czech, Slovak, Italian, Hungarian, and Slovenian-Croatian Catholic parishes; by Greek, Serbian, Ukrainian, and Russian Orthodox churches; a Hungarian Reformed church; and three eastern European Orthodox Jewish synagogues. Between 1900 and 1920, Kenosha acquired Italian, Polish, Slovak, and Lithuanian Catholic parishes, two Jewish synagogues, and Russian Orthodox, Slovak Lutheran, and Italian Baptist and Evangelical churches. Racine immigrants founded Italian, Hungarian, Lithuanian, Polish, Slovak, and Czech Catholic parishes, an Orthodox Jewish synagogue, and Greek and Serbian Orthodox, Armenian Apostolic, Slovak Lutheran and Baptist, Italian Baptist and Evangelical, and Hungarian Evangelical and Reformed churches.[94]

As the Edgerton Bible Case and the Bennett Law uproar clearly indicated, education meant much to immigrants and their offspring, arousing both anxiety and controversy. Many immigrants rightly valued formal education as an avenue of social mobility. Many also believed education could reinforce family and church in preserving languages and inculcating traditions and religious values. Wisconsin's public schools enabled social mobility, but they were seriously deficient in achieving ethnic and religious goals. Many native-born Wisconsinites viewed public schools as valuable instruments of Americanization and "Protestantization," and schoolteachers often regarded it as their solemn duty to strip away the last vestiges of "foreignness," even if that meant alienating students from their families and compatriots. Non-Lutheran Protestant families generally found public school basically compatible, contenting themselves with Sunday schools for religious instruction, and sometimes for language and culture instruction. Most Catholics and German Lutherans, however, believed that only parochial schools would preserve culture among the young and prevent their estrangement.[95]

---

[93] Holmes, *Old World Wisconsin*, 235–354; Swichkow and Gartner, *Jews of Milwaukee*, 192–207; Gurda, "Church and Neighborhood," in Avella, ed., *Milwaukee Catholicism*, 8–25; Siekaniec, "Poles of Upper Northern Wisconsin," 196–198; Zeitlin, "White Eagles in the North Woods," in *Polish Review*, 76–77, 91–92; Thaddeus Borun, comp., *We, The Milwaukee Poles: A History of Milwaukeeans of Polish Descent and a Record of Their Contributions to the Greatness of Milwaukee* (Milwaukee, 1946), 3–40; Sanford, "Polish People of Portage County," in *SHSW Proceedings*, 1907, pp. 267–276; Kolehmainen and Hill, *Haven in the Woods*, 106–113.

[94] Still, *Milwaukee*, 269–278; Buenker, "Immigration and Ethnic Groups," in Neuenschwander, ed., *Kenosha*, 18–19; Buenker, "Immigrant Heritage," in Burckel, ed., *Racine*, 99–100.

[95] Jensen, *Winning of the Midwest*, 58–88; Kleppner, *Cross of Culture*, 77–79, 112–117, 167–174.

By 1893, the Catholic church in Wisconsin counted 239 parochial schools with 44,669 pupils, while nine Lutheran synods at the time claimed nearly 20,000 students in about the same number of schools. German Lutheran synods ran most of these; Scandinavians generally favored public school instruction, supplemented by weekend Sunday schools and catechism classes and "bible schools." Milwaukee's German Jews experimented with parochial and afternoon schools, but generally settled for Sabbath schools, where children studied the Old Testament. (Wisconsin Jewish leaders joined Catholics and German Lutherans in applauding the supreme court's decision in the Edgerton Bible Case; but unlike Catholics and Lutherans, supported the Bennett Law because it did not infringe on personal liberty.) For the most part, southern and eastern European Catholics were as devoted to parochial schools as German Catholics. (Irish Catholics had fewer schools than Germans.) Still, there were some tensions. A Polish-American later recalled his education at St. Stanislaus School in Racine where he studied "Polish language, Polish literature, Polish math—if you can figure that out—and Polish religion. There'd be half an hour of lessons in English." In Milwaukee, a lay-dominated Education Society split the Polish Catholic community. The Society wanted to make the public schools more attractive to Catholics and drew condemnation from the clergy. Moreover, the public schools partially undercut parochial schools by offering classes in German, Polish, Italian, and Greek.[96]

Nor were Catholic newcomers the only ones who developed their own schools. Orthodox Christians established ethnic-folk schools, where children studied language, religion, and history after the public school day. Danes imported folk schools from the old country, blending vocational, scientific, cultural, and citizenship courses. (The University of Wisconsin modeled its popular "short course" on such folk schools.) Finnish Socialists supplemented public education with instruction in the history of labor, heightening class consciousness. Racine County Czechs operated a weekend school that taught language and culture.[97]

Closely allied with church and school as preserver of language and culture was the foreign-language press. It kept immigrant communities abreast of old country developments neglected by the main-

---

[96] Heming, *Catholic Church in Wisconsin*, 292–294; Buenker, "The Immigrant Heritage," in Burckel, ed., *Racine*, 101–102; Kraut, *Huddled Masses*, 133–141; Swichkow and Gartner, *Jews of Milwaukee*, 51–52, 66, 93, 110, 131–132, 245, 257–260, Kuzniewski, *Faith and Fatherland*, 36–39.

[97] Saloutos, "Greeks of Milwaukee," in *WMH*, 53: 187–188; Holmes, *Old World Wisconsin*, 313–318; Kolehmainen and Hill, *Haven in the Woods*, 75–83, 110–112; Buenker, "The Immigrant Heritage," in Burckel, ed., *Racine*, 102.

stream press, interpreted American events from an ethnic perspective, influenced voting behavior, covered news of local enclaves, and served as an incubator for writers. It also helped keep the native tongues alive, although most newspapers and journals eventually had to resort to bilingual, and even English-language, editions. Germans and Norwegians founded the state's first foreign-language newspapers. More than 150 German-language newspapers were published in Wisconsin at one time or another. By 1884, the combined circulation of Milwaukee's three most widely read German papers was double that of the *Sentinel, Journal*, and *Evening Wisconsin* combined. Norwegians were a distant second with twenty-eight papers, but some, such as *Amerika* (Madison, 1899–1922), and *Tidende* (Superior, 1893–1962) survived into the twentieth century. The four Swedish papers in Superior and Marinette also existed into the 1900's, as did Racine's Danish *Folkets Avis* (1876–1919) and Superior's Finnish *Tyomies-Eteenpain* (1903 forward). Czech newspapers were published in Milwaukee, Racine, La Crosse, and Kewaunee for almost seventy years. Milwaukee's *Kuryer Polski* appeared from 1888 into the 1950's. As the *Kuryer* grew more critical of the Catholic church, the church sponsored the *Nowiny Polski* in 1895. The two papers kept up a spirited rivalry into the 1940's. Of the remaining southern and eastern European immigrant groups, only the Slovenians, Hungarians, Italians, and Jews published their own newspapers, usually briefly—an indication of the difficulties connected with small newspaper operations. The rising cost of publication, and the growing consolidation of the newspaper industry, forced most groups to rely upon the ethnic papers published in major metropolitan areas.[98]

In addition to churches, schools, and newspapers, Wisconsin's immigrant groups also constructed a complex network of fraternal, benevolent, and cultural societies, much like their American and European counterparts. A reasonable initiation fee and modest weekly or monthly dues would entitle members to benefits like sickness, accident, and death insurance, pensions, or a decent burial. Many associations also aided newcomers with housing and employment; they protected "greenhorns" from exploitation; provided food and cloth-

---

[98] Robert E. Park, *The Immigrant Press and its Control* (New York, 1922), 3–13, 89–149, 251–356; Carl Wittke, *The German-Language Press in America* (New York, 1957), 1–8; Arlow William Andersen, *The Immigrant Takes His Stand: The Norwegian-American Press and Public Affairs, 1847–1872* (Northfield, Minnesota, 1953), 3–9, 153–60; Mordecai Soltes, *The Yiddish Press: An Americanizing Agency* (New York, 1969), 174–181; Lubomyr R. and Anna T. Wynar, *Encyclopedic Directory of Ethnic Newspapers and Periodicals in the United States* (Littleton, Colorado, 1976), 14–27; Donald E. Oehlerts, comp., *Guide to Wisconsin Newspapers, 1833–1957* (Madison, 1958), *passim*; Still, *Milwaukee*, 264–278; Rippley, *Immigrant Experience*, 30–93; Kolehmainen and Hill, *Haven in the Woods*, 121–129.

ing to victims of fires or other natural disasters; and protested against prejudice and discrimination. Literary societies collected foreign-language books, sponsored lectures and discussions, and published newsletters or periodicals. Theatrical, musical, and dance associations presented traditional performance fare, helping preserve identity, language, and culture, teaching younger people traditions, and served as an outlet for talent. German Turners, Polish Falcons, or Czech and Slovak Sokols did the same for the athletically inclined, often branching out into American sports. The church sponsored many immigrant organizations—rosary and temperance societies, mission clubs, groups for men, women, and children, and self-help and outreach organizations. Whatever their functions, all these societies provided companionship, an opportunity to reminisce about the old country, to commiserate about the new, all in the native tongue, sweetened by familiar food and drink—a haven from the world of work and struggle, the chance to enjoy again the ancient rituals and ceremonies.[99]

The newcomers from southern and eastern Europe benefited from the example of those who had preceded them in forming their societies. Norwegian, Danish, Irish, Welsh, Scottish, and other national societies dotted Wisconsin by the middle 1890's. Some of them, like the Sons of Norway, founded in 1895, were very new. But no other Wisconsin groups could begin to compete with German-America in the diversity of its associational life. Turners, Bunds, vereins, and a vast array of musical, dramatic, literary, cultural, and benevolent societies contributed to Wisconsin's renown as "the most German state in the union" and to Milwaukee's reputation as "the German Athens." The Germania Association, the Stadt Theatre, and several German musical groups dominated the city's cultural life. In 1890, over 12,000 Germans, representing every organization in the city, marched in the German Day parade. In 1895 German-Americans held the most prominent places in the celebration of Milwaukee's semi-centennial. As late as 1910, observed the Wisconsin novelist and playwright Zona Gale, the city still had a "foreign flavor of a yet genuinely American viand" with something of "Nuremberg and Strassburg and Heidelberg in its veins." By that time, however, German cultural hegemony was already on the wane, the result of the decline in Teutonic immigration and the admixture of southern and eastern European institutions and culture. The catastrophe of the Great War simply put an end to an ideal that was already shopworn and fading.[100]

---

[99] Kraut, *Huddled Masses*, 130–133; Handlin, *Uprooted*, 170–200; Buenker, "The Immigrant Heritage," in Burckel, ed., *Racine*, 102–112; Buenker, "Immigration and Ethnic Groups," in Neuenschwander, ed., *Kenosha*, 20–28; Still, *Milwaukee*, 259–278.
[100] Buenker, "The Immigrant Heritage," in Burckel, ed., *Racine*, 102–109; "Immi-

Only the Poles approached the Germans in the variety and complexity of their institutional life, although the tension between ethnicity and religion generated conflict. By 1890, Michael Kruszka, charismatic editor of the *Kuryer Polski*, petitioned the city for Polish-language teaching and translators in the public schools, bilingual publication of official notices, and Polish publications for the public library. Writing in *Cosmopolitan* the following year, Milwaukee's soldier-author Charles King sneeringly observed that on the city's southwest fringes "you read no names but those that end with a sneeze." Five years later, fifty-five Polish societies existed in Milwaukee, most of them connected with a church or consisting of immigrants from a particular village.

The membership trend was towards either the Polish National Alliance (PNA), which stressed Polish ethnicity and patriotism, or the Polish Roman Catholic Union (PRCU), which insisted on the centrality of Catholicism to Polish-American identity. The chief divisions were public versus parochial schools, and lay versus clerical leadership of the Catholic church. The split intensified when Kruszka and the PNA lodges formed the Polish Educational Society, dedicated to improving young Poles in public schools. The division became formalized in 1905 when the PNA aggregated local societies and held a council. The first PRCU council occurred two years later. It was complicated further by the secession of 4,000 Milwaukeeans from the Chicago-dominated PRCU to form the Polish Organization of America, a mutual benefit society. By 1910, Milwaukee had 100 Polish societies, three Polish public libraries, five Polish-language newspapers, a Falcon's Nest, and all the many churches and schools. Racine Poles also affiliated with the PNA in 1905, established a Falcon's Nest, formed a Polish veterans' society, and built Polish Hall on the city's southeast side. In Kenosha their compatriots founded several mutual-aid societies, established a Falcon's Nest and a veterans' society, and built Polonia Hall.[101]

---

gration and Ethnic Groups," in Neuenschwander, ed., *Kenosha*, 20–25; Still, *Milwaukee*, 259–267; James M. Bergquist, "German-American in the 1890s: Illusions and Realities," in E. Allen McCormick, ed., *Germans in America: Aspects of German-American Relations in the Nineteenth Century* (New York, 1983), 1–14; Frederick Luebke, "The Social Bases of German-American Cultural Chauvinism, 1870–1914," in Werner Braatz, ed., *Transactions of the Conference Group for Social and Administrative History* (Oshkosh, 1971), 14–26; Zona Gale, "Milwaukee," in *Good Housekeeping*, March, 1910, pp. 317–325; Kathleen N. Conzen, *Immigrant Milwaukee, 1830–1860: Accommodation and Community in a Frontier City* (Cambridge, 1976), 154–191.

[101] Still, *Milwaukee*, 268–273; Borun, *We The Milwaukee Poles*, 167–203; Kuzniewski, "Milwaukee Poles," 18–22; Kuzniewski, *Faith and Fatherland*, 23–51; Buenker, "The Immigrant Heritage," in Burckel, ed., *Racine*, 109–110; Buenker, "Immigration and Ethnic Groups," in Neuenschwander, ed., *Kenosha*, 26; Charles King, "The Cream City," in *Cosmopolitan*, March, 1891, pp. 554–556; Boleslaus E. Goral, in Jerome A.

Similarly, the Czech community divided over religion, causing fraternal societies to proliferate. The mid-nineteenth-century Czech adherents to Freethought, who populated Milwaukee and Racine, transplanted *Slovanska Lipa*, an organization dedicated to non-religious brotherhood and theological liberalism, and which sponsored newspapers and literary magazines, language schools, burial societies, and theatrical organizations. In the 1880's, *Slovanska* became more involved in the Sokol gymnastics movement, and its fraternal and benefit functions were gradually assumed by the Czech-Slavic Benevolent Society. Czech Catholics were slower to organize, but eventually they established parish-oriented fraternal and benevolent societies affiliated with either the First Bohemian Catholic Central Union or its offshoot, the Czech Roman Catholic Union in the State of Wisconsin. The predominantly Catholic Slovaks organized parish-level benevolent societies which affiliated with the national bodies. The small minority of Slovak Lutherans generally identified with the nationalistic societies.[102]

By 1912 Milwaukee had four Serbian fraternal organizations. It later added a Sokol, a chapter of the Serbo-American Defense League, a singing group, and a theatrical society. Croatians established lodges of both the Croatian Fraternal Union and the Croatian Catholic Union, a dance group, an orchestra, several women's and cultural organizations, and a variety of church groups. In Sheboygan in 1901, Slovenians founded the state's first sick benefit society for their ethnic group, and Milwaukee followed in 1903. As their benevolent and fraternal lodges multiplied, most affiliated with either the Slovenian Catholic Union or the South Slavic Benevolent Union, the latter founded in Milwaukee in 1908. By 1907, Milwaukee had three Greek fraternal, benefit, and mutual-aid societies—one for each region of Greece from which immigrants originated. They also had numerous coffeehouses which became social centers for adult males. Sicilian immigrants to Milwaukee and Calabrian immigrants to Kenosha and Racine formed several mutual-benefit secret societies of fifty to a hundred members, each from the same village or province and named after a local patron saint. Eventually, most combined into

---

Watrous, ed., *Memoirs of Milwaukee County: From the Earliest Historical Times Down to the Present, Including a Genealogical and Biographical Record of Representative Families in Milwaukee County* (2 vols., Madison, 1909), 1: 619–631; Bodnar, *The Transplanted*, 157–161; Donald E. Pienkos, *PNA: A Centennial History of the Polish National Alliance of the United States of North America* (New York, 1984), 3–34, 67–98. See also the Polish Church War collection in the Archdiocese of Milwaukee Archives, St. Francis.

[102] Bicha, "The Czechs in Wisconsin History," in *WMH*, 53: 199–203; Buenker, "The Immigrant Heritage," in Burckel, ed., *Racine*, 109–112; Still, *Milwaukee*, 273–277.

a city-wide Italian-American organization affiliated with the Order of the Sons of Italy.[103]

Although numerically far fewer than either the Germans or the Poles, Wisconsin's Jews still rivaled them in institutions. Jewish tradition mandated "charity conceived as justice," and Jews reinforced that tradition with involvement in trade unionism, socialism, and Zionism. Many established German Jews initially were hostile to newcomers, but anti-Semitism from without soon broke down those barriers. The inpouring of needy southern and eastern Europeans revitalized and transformed Jewish charity in Milwaukee and other cities. Prior to the depression of 1893, Jewish organizations dispensed charity on an ad hoc basis. The Hebrew Association's efforts fell short during the 1893 depression, so the community founded Federated Jewish Charities in 1902, switching the emphasis from emergency aid to systematic social service. At the same time, several women's organizations coalesced to form the Milwaukee Jewish Settlement, whose Abraham Lincoln House played host to myriad cultural, athletic, literary, musical, political, and religious groups. The Settlement's renowned "lady bountiful," Elizabeth Black Kander, raised over $50,000 to build the Jewish Community Center through sales of her *Settlement Cook Book*, first published in 1901. The Milwaukee Jewish Community also built Mount Sinai Hospital, the Home for the Aged, the Jewish Children's Home, and the Hebrew Free Loan Association. Although Zionists, Socialists, and trade unionists frequently disputed among themselves, all dispensed benefits to their members, raising the entire community's political and social consciousness.[104]

Unique among the social organizations of Wisconsin's newer immigrants were those of the Finns who settled in the New North. The fierce evangelical Lutheranism of the one-third who attended church expressed itself in temperance societies bearing such inspirational names as Hope of Our Fathers, Life, Light, and Hero. Besides crusading against liquor, they also provided illness and funeral benefits, sponsored dramatic and choral groups, founded banks and debating clubs, established libraries and reading rooms, and catered to rec-

---

[103] Still, *Milwaukee*, 273–277; Ward, "Serbian and Croatian Communities," in *General Linguistics*, 16: 151–152, 156; Prisland, "Slovenians," in *WMH*, 33: 273–274; Saloutos, "Greeks of Milwaukee," in *WMH*, 53: 182–185; Meloni, "Italy invades the Bloody Third," in *Historical Messenger*, 25: 40; Frank G. Paras, "The Assimilation of the Greek Population of Milwaukee" (masters' thesis, Marquette University, 1945).

[104] Mordecai M. Kaplan, *Judaism as a Civilization: Toward a Reconstruction of American-Jewish Life* (New York, 1967), 472–478; Swichkow and Gartner, *Jews of Milwaukee*, 215–256; Still, *Milwaukee*, 277–278; Buenker, "The Immigrant Heritage," in Burckel, ed., *Racine*, 111–112; Buenker, "Immigration and Ethnic Groups," in Neuenschwander, *Kenosha*, 27–28. Kander's cookbook had appeared in thirty editions by 1951.

reational needs through folk games, dancing, and festivals. In many places, the Finnish Temperance Hall was the community's social, cultural, and welfare center. Equally zealous and fraternal were the secular organizations formed by the thousands of Finns who worked in mines, quarries, lumber mills, and factories, or on docks and ships. They found fellowship, culture, and welfare in Imatra societies, which evolved into socialist workingmen's associations devoted to various messages of socialism, communism, or syndicalism. Beginning with four societies of 120 members in 1906, by 1911 the workingmen's associations numbered sixteen with 537 members, including 148 women. Organizers from the Communist and Socialist parties and the Industrial Workers of the World moved among them, but members also enjoyed songs, recitations, games, dancing, plays, libraries, study clubs, debates, sewing circles, and gymnastic exhibitions. Closely connected to the workingmen's associations were the consumer co-operatives that popped up all over the New North.[105]

The particular mix of natives and newcomers in Progressive Era Wisconsin heightened ethno-cultural tensions and added a critical dimension to demands that state government intervene in them. That was least true for Native Americans, since the state exercised little jurisdiction over them, and because their numbers were small and concentrated in isolated areas. It was most true for immigrants from southern and eastern Europe, who contributed substantially to the growth of the state's most rapidly expanding areas.

The huge influx of newer immigrants, together with the minuscule numbers of Negroes, were central to Wisconsin's socio-economic problems. Many Wisconsinites regarded these newcomers as victims of an array of problems: unsafe and unsanitary living and working conditions, inadequate income, chronic disease and epidemics, illiteracy, crime, alcohol abuse, and more. Another sizable segment charged that these newcomers, by reason of their biological or cultural "inferiority," were themselves the major cause of these same problems. As the new century dawned, Wisconsin society contained a volatile mix of compassion and condescension, fear and hostility towards recent immigrants and black migrants. At the same time, the state was becoming a forum for new ideas and a laboratory for new remedies in the areas of workmen's compensation, industrial health and safety standards, wages and hours legislation, housing and public health codes, the regulation of child and female labor, educational

---

[105] Kolehmainen and Hill, *Haven in the Woods*, 113–160; Knipping, *Finns in Wisconsin*, 32–38; John I. Kolehmainen, "The Finns of Wisconsin," in *WMH*, 27 (June, 1944), 396–399.

reform, mothers' pensions, and crusades against prostitution, gambling, pornography, and alcohol.[106]

[5]

Reports by both state and federal agencies documented arguments for government intervention, and they invariably focused on southern and eastern European immigrants as worst-case examples. So did professionals and social scientists, public and industrial health officials, and reform organizations. Many of their reports cited Milwaukee's Fourteenth Ward—the center of the Polish district with other southeastern European groups mixed in—as the worst of the worst. In 1905, the ward had the poorest housing conditions, the most child laborers and people doing piecework at home, the worst health record, and the most arrests and juvenile offenders. It also had twice as many families on the poor list as any other ward and 43 per cent of the city's smallpox cases and one-third of its infant deaths. By itself, the Fourteenth Ward served as a powerful argument for corrective legislation, vocational and night schools, social centers, and public playgrounds.[107]

Typical of many would-be reformers was Professor John R. Commons of the University of Wisconsin, author of landmark labor and welfare legislation, co-founder of the American Association for Labor Legislation, charter member of the state's industrial commission and the U.S. Commission on Industrial Relations, and an acknowledged opponent of laissez-faire capitalism. He believed that social justice required a judicious blend of unionized collective bargaining and "coercive legislation," and he argued that unregulated immigration prevented the United States from realizing stable employment—"the first important task of business and the nation." Southeastern Europeans and Negroes, he said, were "America's convenient reserve army of the unemployed." They also comprised the chief constituency for a "revolutionary unionism" which would compel the nation "to help the capitalists maintain their dictatorship." Commons pas-

---

[106] For varying interpretations of the origins of Progressive Era labor and welfare legislation, see Paul Boyer, *Urban Masses and Moral Order in America, 1820–1920* (Cambridge, 1978); Nell Irvin Painter, *Standing at Armageddon: The United States, 1877–1919* (New York, 1987); Robert H. Wiebe, *The Search for Order, 1877–1920* (New York, 1967); John D. Buenker, *Urban Liberalism and Progressive Reform* (New York, 1973); and Thelen, *New Citizenship*.

[107] Bernard E. Fuller, "Voting Patterns in Milwaukee, 1896–1920: A Study with Special Emphasis on the Working Class of the City" (master's thesis, University of Wisconsin-Milwaukee, 1973), 20–68.

sionately advocated legal restrictions on immigration and the deliberate Americanization of newcomers, so that "those on the ground have time to get experience and training in self-government." Without such strictures, he feared, "older" Americans would denounce immigrants as "foreigners, aliens, un-American, led on by anarchists and revolutionists, and [would] reach for our guns."

Commons' colleague at the university, the sociologist Edward A. Ross, an equally avid reformer, contended that current immigration "alters the distribution of the national dividend to the hurt of wage-earners, and to the advantage of those who live from interest, dividends, profits, rentals, commissions, fees, and salaries." The effect of "low-standard immigrants" on "high-standard native workers" was "shown by the fact that from 1889 to 1916, a period of wonderful advance, the workers in American manufacturing industries made no gain in real wages." Ross pronounced restriction of southern and eastern European immigration "a democratic policy put through in the teeth of capitalists yearning for cheap foreign labor," and "a triumph of the common people and far-sighted idealists against the alliance of employers and sentimentalists."[108]

That southern and eastern European immigration was a central issue in the debate over social-welfare legislation was further affirmed in 1914 by a future University of Wisconsin philosopher, Horace M. Kallen. Kallen himself was an immigrant of Russian Jewish extraction, and he took issue with Ross's 1914 book, *The Old World in the New*, which attacked most recent immigrant groups. Kallen argued that "the external dangers of immigration are in the greed of the capitalist and the indifference of the government. The proper restriction of immigration can naturally succeed [in improving the lot of the lower classes] only with the restriction of the entrepreneur's greed, which is its cause, and the abolition of his control on government by which he works his effects." In the "haste to accumulate wealth," Kallen said, "considerations of human quality have been neglected and forgotten, the action of government has been remedial rather than constructive. . . ." If the state would instead fulfill its function to liberate and protect human capacity, Kallen said, immigrants from southern and eastern Europe would make rapid progress as workers and citizens.[109]

To the extent that they were able, Wisconsin's newcomers supported efforts to improve socio-economic conditions. Their fraternal and benevolent associations provided direct assistance and func-

---

[108] Commons, *Races and Immigrants*, xviii, xxii, xxvi; Edward Alsworth Ross, *Standing Room Only?* (New York, 1927; reprinted, 1977), 314–315, 319, 339.

[109] Horace M. Kallen, *Culture and Democracy in the United States: Studies in the Group Psychology of the American Peoples* (New York, 1924), 91–92, 116–117.

tioned as conduits to mainstream institutions like labor unions and political parties. In Milwaukee, the Knights of Labor and the Central Labor Union began to admit Polish laborers in 1895; indeed, with 1,600 members, the Knights' Polish assembly was the city's largest. Polish Knights formed the vanguard of the eight-hour-day demonstrations that culminated in the Bay View Massacre of May, 1886. Its members bore the brunt of both public hysteria and militia bullets, which left five persons dead. The Bay View riot effectively destroyed the Knights and the Central Labor Union, and temporarily frustrated efforts to promote an industrial unionism that would unite skilled and unskilled workers, regardless of national origin or race. The existing trade unions enrolled only skilled craftsmen, relied almost exclusively upon collective bargaining, and consisted almost entirely of first- and second-generation northwestern Europeans, who generally regarded southern European immigrants and Negroes as tools of corporations. Trade unionists resented both new immigrants and Negroes because they often worked as strikebreakers and accepted lower wages, longer hours, and more hazardous conditions. The trade unionists' new national organization, the American Federation of Labor (AFL), formed in 1886, opposed accepting low-skilled newcomers into membership, drew the color line against black workers, and lobbied for restrictions on immigration from southeastern Europe and Asia. In this the AFL eventually received support from Professor Commons, who was probably academe's most well-known champion of trade unionism.

Although affiliated with the AFL, the Milwaukee Federated Trades Council (MFTC) and the Wisconsin State Federation of Labor (WSFL), formed in 1893, also relied upon the traditions of the Knights and the Central Labor Union. They had a symbiotic relationship, too, with the Social Democratic Party (SDP), which believed in a proletarian solidarity that transcended skills and ethnic and racial differences. Many SDP leaders challenged the AFL over industrial unionism, political action, and socialist ideology, and were alarmed by the inroads made by the radical IWW, which advocated "one big union" and the general strike. On the other hand, the MFTC and the WSFL were dominated by Germans and other northwestern Europeans who were members of skilled elites. They harbored prejudices against the newcomers, and despised them as pawns in a capitalist conspiracy to destroy organized labor and reduce all wage earners to near peonage. Wisconsin's trade unionists were constantly torn between the impulse to mobilize the mass of newcomers into a mighty proletarian movement and the impulse to send them all back where they came from.

In 1905, the MFTC appropriated $5 a month to hire a Polish unionist for its efforts among Polish workers. Two years later, it requested each council delegate to recruit Polish-speaking members for an organizational drive. That same year, the WSFL proclaimed the need to unionize Poles and endorsed the Chicago daily newspaper *Dziennik Ludowy* as an educational medium. The newspaper accordingly increased Milwaukee and Wisconsin labor coverage. But most local unions proved highly reluctant to admit Polish or other southeastern European members; success in that area did not come until the rise of industrial unionism in the 1930's. Outside Milwaukee, southeastern Europeans experienced similar rebuffs. Polish and Bohemian workers joined Germans during a general woodworkers' strike at Oshkosh in 1898, but still were not accepted. Italian and Finnish immigrants in the mining and lumbering regions promoted militant unionization and embraced the IWW, an unusual circumstance in the state.[110]

Newcomers' efforts in politics were somewhat more productive. The massive migrations of the nineteenth century had solidly implanted ethno-cultural partisan politics in the state. Yankees, Scandinavians, British, European and northwestern European Protestants in general had come to dominate the Republican party; the Irish, Poles, and other Catholic immigrant groups, the Democratic party. Common issues—temperance, Sunday observance, foreign-language instruction and bible reading in the schools, and immigration restriction—held these two coalitions together, divided them, and usually overshadowed economic or ideological questions. German Lutherans held the swing vote. The state's small black population voted Republican but played no significant role in party politics. The Fifteenth Amendment to the U.S. Constitution enfranchised adult Negro males in 1870, and the Republican-dominated Wisconsin legislature rewarded their solidarity in 1895 by passing the state's civil rights act. Later it defeated bills that would have prohibited interracial marriage.[111]

The earliest Slavic immigrants—Poles and Czechs—got involved in politics during the Civil War era, generally as Democrats. Both groups, angered by the Bennett Law, were key in the Democratic victories of 1890 and 1892. Polish and Irish Catholics were equally devoted to the Democratic party, regarding it as an extension of their religion. Polish priests regularly marshaled voters on election day, delivered partisan sermons, announced donations from prominent Democrats on the Sunday before election day, and let Democratic politicians use schools and pulpits for rallies. (In 1893, one Polish

---

[110] Thomas W. Gavett, *Development of the Labor Movement in Milwaukee* (Madison, 1965), 35–115; Ozanne, *Labor Movement in Wisconsin*, 6–22.

[111] Wyman, "Voting Behavior in the Progressive Era," 24–114; Rippley, *Immigrant Experience*, 74–90; Brye, *Wisconsin Voting Patterns*, 163–210.

cleric declaimed that any Pole who failed to vote for the Democrats was not a good Catholic!) Of course not all Catholics approved. The *Catholic Citizen* and *Kuryer Polski* denounced clerical interference in Milwaukee elections. From the 1890's onward, the Democrats consistently heeded Polish concerns and demands and fielded Polish candidates for city and county office. The city comptroller's office became, in effect, a Polish fiefdom for nearly four decades. With a few rural exceptions in Clark, Rusk, and Shawano counties, Poles constituted a Democratic bloc. However, the Democrats knew that Polish loyalty was largely ethno-cultural, so they rarely sponsored measures to benefit Polish workers or citizens. Neither did the Republicans, who usually conceded the Polish vote.

The Czechs' Democratic proclivities were less pronounced. Divided in religion and lacking the Poles' urban concentration, Czech voters periodically flirted with the Republicans. Freethought advocates supported the party, Lincoln, and the Union during the Civil War and Reconstruction, then turned to the Democrats over the liquor question. Their most prominent leader, Karel Jonas of Racine, led the switch, rising through the Democratic ranks to become lieutenant-governor in 1891. The Bennett Law controversy bound most Czechs more firmly to the Democrats who nominated John Karel for governor in 1912 and 1914, ensuring Czech fealty virtually forever.[112]

The remaining southeastern European groups did not arrive in substantial numbers until the 1890's. Most were unattached males, many of whom planned to return to their homelands. Many were illiterate, slow to learn English, and reluctant to become naturalized citizens. In 1908 Wisconsin voters amended the constitution to encourage naturalization. The new law disfranchised immigrants who did not become full-fledged citizens. (Previously they could vote if they had obtained "first papers," declaring their intention to become citizens.) The amendment was inspired by antipathy among earlier residents who resented and perhaps feared the inpouring of eastern and southern Europeans with their queer ideas about religion and politics. Male immigrants could vote only if they had taken out their first papers before December 1, 1908; they had to become U.S. citizens by December 1, 1912, or lose their voting privileges entirely. The electorate approved the amendment overwhelmingly on November 3, 1908, by a margin of 88,576 to 36,773. It failed to carry only Calumet and Shawano counties, and encountered serious opposition in only six others: Dane, Manitowoc, Marathon, Outagamie, Ozaukee, and Sheboygan.[113]

---

[112] Wyman, "Voting Behavior in the Progressive Era," 702–723.
[113] Fuller, "Voting Patterns in Milwaukee," 66–70; "Constitution of the State of Wisconsin, Article III, Suffrage," in the *Wisconsin Blue Book, 1909,* pp. 23–24.

The amended suffrage article in the constitution granted the right to vote to "every male person of the age of twenty-one years or upwards," provided that he was an American citizen and had resided in the state for one year. It enfranchised "persons of Indian blood" who had been declared citizens by act of Congress, and "civilized persons of Indian descent not members of any tribe." (Reservation and tribal Native Americans remained non-citizens and therefore non-voters.)[114]

The ultimate ethno-cultural conflict of the period occurred over the liquor question—meaning, at the outset, temperance; in the end, prohibition. Prohibition's proponents had diverse origins, motives, and goals—some even mutually contradictory. They generally came from old-stock, middle- and upper-middle-class evangelical Protestant and northwestern European backgrounds, and they principally targeted the working class and those on the lowest rungs of the socio-economic ladder—among them Negroes and Indians, but especially European immigrants. In Wisconsin, the temperance battles generally pitted Yankees, Scandinavians, Britons, and other evangelical Protestants against the Germans, Irish, Poles, Czechs, and other Catholic ethnic groups. After 1900, southern and eastern European immigrants tipped the balance against prohibition and heightened its advocates' efforts.

Prohibition was a ticking bomb in Wisconsin, especially for those who sought to enlarge socio-economic or ideological divisions. The Democrats alone had the luxury of being able to oppose prohibition outright, and they brought together a coalition of wet ethnic groups on the issue. The other parties found it attractive and easier to maintain silence on the subject. Conservative or Stalwart Republicans had close connections to the brewing and liquor interests and relied on German Lutheran voters, but they also needed Yankee, British, and Scandinavian support, so they were in a serious bind. Progressive Republicans avoided the issue "like a dread disease," even though many of their Scandinavian followers were ardent prohibitionists. Socialist theory favored eliminating all "opiates of the masses," but the SDP was heavily German and courted new immigrants from eastern Europe—persons who opposed prohibition, thus putting the SDP in a similar bind.[115]

---

[114] The amended Article III appears in "Constitution of the State of Wisconsin, Article III, Suffrage," in the *Wisconsin Blue Book, 1909*, pp. 23–24; Trotter, *Black Milwaukee*, 25–27; Buchanan, "Black Milwaukee," 60–94.

[115] Wyman, "Voting Behavior in the Progressive Era," 335–337; Herbert F. Margulies, *The Decline of the Progressive Movement in Wisconsin, 1890–1920* (Madison, 1968), 80, 98, 106, 129, 166, 190–191; Danziger, *Chippewas of Lake Superior*, 108–109, 121–123. The best study of prohibition and ethnicity is James H. Timberlake, *Prohibition and the Progressive Movement, 1900–1920* (Cambridge, 1966).

Since silence reigned politically, prohibitionists tried to dry up the state piecemeal by introducing referenda locally on high license fees or no licensing altogether, and by pressing the legislature for a county-option law. The drys made good headway. By the spring of 1908, a Methodist periodical reported that there were 789 dry towns, villages, and cities in Wisconsin, with another eighty-one estimated to put referenda on the ballot. The Methodists claimed, too, that twenty-five of the state's seventy-one counties would vote dry if given the chance. In 1910, wets and drys forced a virtual referendum on the county-option law by demanding that legislative candidates take a stand on it, one way or the other. This tactic affected primary elections and probably cost progressive Republicans a few legislative seats. Prohibition continued to gain momentum during the next decade, but wet forces were able to prevent either statewide or county-option laws. It took wartime prohibition and the subsequent nationwide debate over the Eighteenth Amendment to bring the issue to a head in 1919.

The new immigration also revived another perennial of ethnocultural politics: anti-Catholicism. The influx of tens of thousands of new Catholics between 1890 and 1910 intensified the kinds of fears and prejudices that had earlier given rise to the American Protective Association and *The Wisconsin Patriot*. After 1910, there were concerns about a Catholic "takeover" and "papist" candidates for statewide office. Similar developments in other states seemed to confirm the existence of a nationwide Catholic plot, and soaring birth rates among Catholics seemed to guarantee Rome's eventual triumph.

Anti-Catholicism exploded with vehemence in 1914, when Lieutenant-governor Thomas Morris, a Catholic, entered the Republican primary as a candidate for the U.S. Senate. Anti-Catholic organizations such as the American Federation of Voters and the Guardians of Liberty (which soon claimed 150,000 adherents) sprang up overnight. Morris suffered significant losses among Scandinavian voters who had supported him before, and he lost the primary. The election symbolized the bigotry and rancor behind many ethno-cultural issues, and they did not go away after 1914. The furor over growing Catholic political strength continued to poison Wisconsin elections in the 1920's.[116]

Public concern over the escalating numbers of southern and eastern Europeans, Negroes, and Indians also gave impetus to the eu-

---

[116] Wyman, "Voting Behavior in the Progressive Era," 335–340; Margulies, *Decline of the Progressive Movement*, 159–162, 232–247. For a detailed discussion of prohibition, see Peter R. Weisensel, "The Wisconsin Temperance Crusade to 1919" (master's thesis, University of Wisconsin, 1965). For the political effect of the 1914 anti-Catholic campaign, see Chapter 14.

genics movement. Edward A. Ross and other academic elitists supplied the intellectual underpinnings; social workers, reformers, educators, and physicians carried the banner. They attributed poverty and other social deficiencies to the inherent biological inferiority of immigrant peoples. Among other remedies, they proposed the institutionalization of "defectives," stringent regulation of marriage, and, above all, enforced sterilization. This movement against what was termed "racial degeneracy" gathered momentum in 1907, supported even by Charles R. Van Hise, president of the University of Wisconsin and himself an avowed "progressive." In 1911, the head of the State Medical Society warned that "the hereditary tendency of these classes (insane, idiots, imbeciles, sexual perverts, defectives, epileptics, rapists, criminals) to reproduce their kind is unquestioned." Inspired by the slogan, "Sterilization or racial disaster," the legislature in 1913 enacted a law authorizing the sterilization of inmates in the state's mental and penal institutions. Many "progressive-minded" citizens completely approved. In the years to come, this reform, perhaps more than any other of the Progressive era, would be one to reflect upon and possibly regret.[117]

By 1914, Wisconsin's population of approximately 2.5 million people had achieved an ethnic mix that was to persist for more than half a century. Substantial numbers of southern and eastern Europeans, and a much smaller contingent of Negroes who had emigrated from elsewhere in the nation, had begun to contribute to the state's economy and society, to its culture and polity. Their presence buttressed Wisconsin's claim as a haven for "heterogeneous masses collected together from every corner of the globe." However, these newcomers, together with the descendants of Wisconsin's original peoples and earlier settlers, also endured far more than their fair share of jarring, "like different metals in the furnace," in their efforts to become full members of what all hoped would become "the most perfect race of men that has ever appeared on earth." To forge a cohesive community out of diverse ethno-cultural ingredients has been a persistent challenge throughout history—the world's, the nation's, and Wisconsin's. Having failed to forge such a community by the early 1890's with its initial mix of Native Americans, Yankees, and immigrants from northwestern Europe, Wisconsin was in no position to

---

[117] Rudolph J. Vecoli, "Sterilization: A Progressive Measure?" in *WMH*, 43 (Spring, 1960), 191–201 (quote); George B. Mangold, "State Care of Defectives," in Wisconsin Conference of Charities and Corrections, *Proceedings*, 1911, pp. 41–50; Editorial Comment, "The Eugenic Marriage Bill," in *Wisconsin Medical Journal*, 12 (June, 1913–May, 1914), 237–239. The state's total population was 2,333,860 in 1910 and 2,632,067 in 1920. See *Fourteenth Census of the United States, 1920: Population, Volume III, Composition and Characteristics of the Population by States*, 1118.

integrate the new ethnic groups which arrived during ensuing decades. Beset by bewildering technological, economic, and demographic change, the groups confronted each other across ethnic, racial, religious, and cultural chasms, fiercely disputing the sense of identity and self-worth of those deemed "different" or "alien." As the twentieth century dawned, a growing segment of Wisconsin's various peoples had come to regard the political system as one of the few patches of common ground accessible to them, and state government as the most responsive, equitable, and effective mechanism for redressing their grievances.

6

Redefining Work

[1]

NO MATTER how fast its population grew, Wisconsin's work force grew even faster. At the beginning of the 1890's, 46 per cent of eligible Wisconsinites worked for pay, ranking it thirty-ninth among the total of forty-nine states, territories, and the District of Columbia. Nearly 86 per cent of that labor force was male; just over three-quarters of eligible males were employed, as compared to 14 per cent of females. Between 1890 and 1920, the state's population increased by 56 per cent; the number of workers, by 74 per cent. And by 1920, almost half of all Wisconsinites over ten years of age were "gainfully employed," a figure that omitted hundreds of thousands of women who labored without compensation on farms and in homes.[1]

Males toiled for a livelihood in overwhelming numbers in 1890, whatever their marital status. However, 84 per cent of working women were single, while another 12 per cent were widowed or divorced. Nearly 30 per cent of single women and widows, and almost half of divorcees, were employed, compared to less than 5 per cent of wives. Single women were only half as likely as single males to support themselves or to contribute to the family kitty. Obviously, married women sought outside employment only under unusual conditions—as in family businesses, having to support invalid spouses or family members, continuing to work after marriage (often a late marriage), and the like.[2]

The largest segment of the work force—some 43 per cent—was

---

[1] *Eleventh Census of the United States, 1890: Special Census Report on Occupations of the Population of the United States,* 76–77; *Eleventh Census of the United States, 1890: Population, Progress of the Nation,* Part 2, p. 100; *Tenth Census of the United States, 1880: Compendium,* Part 2, p. 1358; *Fourteenth Census of the United States, 1920: Population, Occupation Statistics,* Volume IV, 44–45. I have generally relied upon the occupational data in the U.S. Census because the Wisconsin Bureau of Labor and Industrial Statistics primarily depended upon voluntary compliance of employers for its information.

[2] *Eleventh Census of the United States, 1890: Special Census Report on Occupations of the Population of the United States,* 22, 94–99; *Eleventh Census of the United States, 1890: Population, Progress of the Nation,* Part 1, p. 829; *ibid.,* Part 2, p. 100.

engaged in agriculture and extractive industries, although both were already declining. Pointing to the future were the 23 per cent who worked in manufacturing and mechanical jobs, and the 12 per cent in trade and transportation. On the bottom rung of the occupational ladder, in both status and income, was the nearly 20 per cent in domestic and personal service. The most elite workers were the 4 per cent classified as professionals. Working women were concentrated in a small number of low-paid and poorly regarded occupations, nearly half in domestic and personal service, and just over one-quarter in low-level manufacturing jobs. Among women classified as "professionals," an inordinate number taught school or music. Those in the trade and transportation industries were nearly all clerks, copyists, sales personnel, or bookkeepers.[3]

A total of 236,168 men worked in extractive industries in 1890, two-thirds as farmers and one-fourth as farm laborers. The balance were lumbermen or miners. Nearly three-fourths of the 73,196 men in domestic and personal service were common laborers. Of the 63,830 men in trade and transportation, well over half were retail merchants, clerks, agents, bookkeepers, druggists, grocers, salesmen, commercial travelers, or telephone operators. Another 30 per cent were railroad employees, locomotive engineers or firemen, or teamsters. There were 108,490 men in manufacturing and mechanical occupations; of these, nearly eight in ten were skilled.[4]

By contrast, virtually no women worked in the skilled crafts. Over 86 per cent of women in domestic and personal service were servants. In manufacturing, women had 16 per cent of the jobs, but almost none in the skilled crafts. There were only seventeen female foundry and machine shop operatives in Wisconsin in 1890 out of 5,304 total. There was but one female iron and steel worker out of 1,920. There were no female butchers or machinists, and only a handful of female blacksmiths or carpenters. Some may have done this kind of work informally in connection with family operations, but they were not counted in census schedules. Women concentrated in the textile industry, where they had one-third of the jobs. Among tailors, milliners, seamstresses, and hosiery workers, they outnumbered men by 25 to 1.[5]

---

[3] *Eleventh Census of the United States, 1890: Special Census Report on Occupations of the Population of the United States*, 30–37.

[4] *Ibid.*, pp. 52–63; *Eleventh Census of the United States, 1890: Manufacturing Industries: Totals for States and Industries, Part 1*, pp. 628–637.

[5] *Eleventh Census of the United States, 1890: Special Census Report on Occupations of the Population of the United States*, 52–63; *Eleventh Census of the United States, 1890: Manufacturing Industries: Totals for States and Industries, Part 1*, pp. 88–89, 628–637. The 1890 census schedules did not distinguish between skilled and unskilled workers. The 104,621 "operatives, skilled and unskilled," constituted nearly 80 per cent of the

The manufacturing work force was as widely dispersed geographically as factories themselves. One-third labored in Milwaukee County; only Winnebago, Chippewa, Racine, and La Crosse counties had as much as 3 per cent each of the state's factory workers. Marathon, Marinette, Eau Claire, Outagamie, and Fond du Lac counties had about 2 per cent each; Rock, Douglas, Oconto, Wood, St. Croix, and Sheboygan counties had about 1 per cent each. Even Kenosha County, on the verge of its urban-industrial explosion, ranked seventeenth with about 1 per cent. Except for the sparsely populated counties of the New North, and the monolithically agricultural southwest region, nearly every other county had at least 500 manufacturing employees.

The typical Wisconsin workplace employed thirteen persons. On average, the crossroads cheese factory or creamery might employ two; the flour mill, five; and the carriage and wagon shop, seven. Moving up the scale, the average lumber mill employed thirty-eight persons; the foundry or machine shop, thirty-four; the brewery, thirty. Agricultural implement shops averaged fifty-one employees; paper mills, eighty-five; tanneries, ninety-two. Railroad shops typically employed a hundred workers; women's clothing factories, 120. At the upper end in 1890, the state's three giant iron and steel works, with average work forces of 640, foreshadowed the future.[6]

Immigrants made up only 31 per cent of the state's population in 1890, but they represented 46 per cent of its work force. Foreign-born men were a third of the male population and nearly half of the male work force; immigrant women constituted about 30 per cent of both. Nearly 88 per cent of immigrant males aged ten or older were gainfully employed, compared to only 11 per cent of immigrant women. The children of immigrants constituted one-third of the work force, and nearly one-half of all female workers. Almost 50 per cent of all immigrant workers were German; 20 per cent were Scandinavian; and 20 per cent, either British, Irish, or Canadian. Except for contingents of Bohemians, Poles, and Italians, the remainder came from northern Europe.[7]

In 1895, two-thirds of Wisconsin's unskilled workers were foreign-born, either Germans or Scandinavians. Nearly two-thirds of all unskilled workers in Wisconsin's thirteen leading industrial cities were

---

total work force in manufacturing and mechanical pursuits, along with clerks. My discussion is intended to demonstrate that the vast majority of operatives was skilled.

[6] *Eleventh Census of the United States, 1890: Manufacturing Industries: Totals for States and Industries, Part 1*, pp. 628–637; *Eleventh Census of the United States, 1890: Statistics of Cities, Part 2*, pp. 278–485.

[7] *Eleventh Census of the United States, 1890: Population: Progress of the Nation, Part 1*, pp. 395–396, 486–487, 606–609, 686–693; *Eleventh Census of the United States, 1890: Special Census Report on Occupations of the Population of the United States*, 64–69, 112–113, 120–121.

immigrants, compared to about one-third of machinists, machine hands, or woodworkers. And in the work force generally in the early 1890's, 80 per cent were immigrants and their offspring, especially males of northwestern European origins. Roughly one-half of Neenah-Menasha's manufacturing labor force in the 1890's was born in the United States, though many of these were children of immigrant parents. The rest were mostly German, Scandinavian, or Polish. The mixture produced a babel of tongues in the factories and ethnic tensions in the twin communities. Sixty per cent of Racine's foreign-born workers made their living in manufacturing. Irish and Welsh immigrants worked on Racine's railroads and docks; Norwegians worked as farmers or sailors; and Englishmen and Scotsmen formed an elite of mechanics, woodworkers, carpenters, and masons. The city's wagon and farm implement shops recruited Danish- and German-born workers; "Vitchell Vagon Vorks" were supposedly the first three English words mastered by Danish newcomers. Germans dominated virtually every craft in Wisconsin during the 1890's, leavened by a mixture of British, Irish, Scandinavian, and American-born co-workers.[8]

In Janesville, the occupational breakdown varied. Iron workers, mechanics, carpenters, and painters were largely American-born; gunsmiths, weavers, shoemakers, and tinsmiths were immigrants. More than 90 per cent of British immigrants in Janesville were skilled craftsmen, while the majority of Irish were common laborers. In Milwaukee there was a distinct pecking order. Native-born Americans held management and supervisory positions, northwestern European immigrants worked in skilled middle-range occupations, and southern and eastern newcomers landed at the unskilled bottom. The lumber mills of Oshkosh were operated primarily by German, Polish, and Bohemian immigrants. In Madison, Norwegian, British, and German mechanics and craftsmen predominated in the metal industries.[9]

---

[8] *Eleventh Census of the United States, 1890: Compendium, Part 3*, pp. 520–531, 540–541; Bureau of Labor and Industrial Statistics, *Biennial Report*, 1895–1896, pp. 178–295; Charles N. Glaab and Lawrence H. Larsen, *Factories in the Valley: Neenah-Menasha, 1870–1915* (Madison, 1969), 221; John D. Buenker, "The Immigrant Heritage," in Nicholas C. Burckel, ed., *Racine: Growth and Change in a Wisconsin County* (Racine, 1977), 80–81; U.S. Department of the Interior, *Report on the Social Statistics of Cities: The Southern and the Western States, 1887, Part 2*, p. 683; R. David Weber, "Socioeconomic Change in Racine, 1850–1880," in *Journal of the West*, 13 (July, 1974), 98–108.

[9] Edward M. Lang, Jr., "The Common Man: Janesville, Wisconsin, 1870 to 1900" (master's thesis, University of Wisconsin, 1968), 56; Wisconsin State Federation of Labor, *Directory*, 1899–1900, pp. 17–143; Gerd Korman, *Industrialization, Immigrants, and Americanizers: The View from Milwaukee, 1866–1921* (Madison, 1967), 41–53, 195–292; Robert W. Ozanne, *The Labor Movement in Wisconsin: A History* (Madison, 1984), 11–22; David V. Mollenhoff, *Madison: A History of the Formative Years* (Dubuque, 1982), 190–196, 234–236, 267–271.

From the 1890's to 1920, Wisconsin's labor force multiplied by almost two-thirds, nearly reaching the 1 million mark by the end of World War I. However, even with nearly 49 per cent of all eligible Wisconsinites gainfully employed, the state still lagged three percentage points behind the national norm. Immigration had of course provided a sizable portion of the increase, especially newcomers from southern and eastern Europe. But a rise in women workers also assisted. Women working outside the home rose in number by more than one-third, making them almost one-fifth of the work force. Only among Negroes did a significant portion of women—almost one-fourth—have jobs outside the household. For the overwhelming majority of women, marriage removed them from the official work force and into the world of unpaid domestic labor.[10]

By far the most striking employment change between 1890 and 1920 was a dramatic drop in agricultural, lumbering, and domestic service jobs, and corresponding increases in manufacturing and clerical jobs. The new industrialism pushed manufacturing employment relentlessly upward until its share of all employment reached 34 per cent by 1919. Clerical occupations rose so dramatically that the Census Bureau designated them a separate category in 1910. Clerks represented about 4 per cent of Wisconsin's labor force in 1910; this number had almost doubled by 1920. By the eve of World War I, manufacturing employment, and the jobs that complemented it, had attained an irresistible momentum.[11]

However, the impressive growth and reorganization of the state's work force did little to alter gender differences in the workplace. The proportion of women in manufacturing and agriculture held steady at about one-third between 1910 and 1920, even as manufacturing expanded and agriculture declined in importance. Teachers, domestics, nurses, clerks, bookkeepers, cashiers, and office workers still accounted for six of every ten female employees.[12]

The trend towards segregation by gender and what has come to be called the "de-skilling" of labor were especially apparent in specific

---

[10] *Eleventh Census of the United States, 1890: Special Census Report on Occupations of the Population of the United States*, 22, 30–37, 94–99; *Twelfth Census of the United States, 1900: Special Report on Occupations*, lxvii, 154–155; *Thirteenth Census of the United States, 1910: Occupation Statistics*, Volume IV, 34–35, 139, 531–532; *Fourteenth Census of the United States, 1920: Population, Occupation Statistics*, Volume IV, 44–55, 518, 593–595, 741–744, 1042–1045; *Sixteenth Census of the United States, 1940: Population: Comparative Occupation Statistics, 1870–1940*, pp. 93, 100, 142; U.S. Bureau of the Census, *Historical Statistics of the United States: Colonial Times to 1970, Part 1*, pp. 126–128.

[11] *Eleventh Census of the United States, 1890: Special Census Report on Occupations of the Population of the United States*, 30–37; *Thirteenth Census of the United States, 1910: Occupation Statistics*, Volume IV, 138–151; *Fourteenth Census of the United States, 1920: Population, Occupation Statistics*, Volume IV, 44–55.

[12] *Ibid.*, 44–45, 797–798, 1042–1045.

occupations and industries. The proportion of farm laborers rose by 30 per cent among men and 300 per cent among women from 1890 to 1920. By 1919, of 45,466 women employed in manufacturing, 15 per cent were laborers and 61 per cent were semiskilled operators, most of whom ran new high-speed precision machines. More than half of all male transportation workers held skilled positions on railroads and street railways; more than nine-tenths of the women in the transportation industries were in fact telephone operators. Almost two-thirds of men working in trade were retail dealers, salesmen, delivery men, or store clerks; eight of every ten women engaged in trade were sales personnel or store clerks, and but one in ten was a retail dealer. Women still outnumbered men in the professions, but the figures were deceptive because 85 per cent of all teachers and 98 per cent of all nurses were women. The same general pattern prevailed in domestic service, a declining industry where women outnumbered men two to one, and in clerical work, a rapidly growing area in which women were fast approaching numerical parity with men.[13]

The reconstitution of the work force and the segregation of the sexes was nowhere more apparent than in manufacturing, whose emergence as the state's chief employment sector changed momentously the way Wisconsinites earned a living. In the early 1890's, nearly 80 per cent of the state's male workers had been skilled craftsmen. By 1919, almost half were laborers or semiskilled operatives, 83 per cent of all manufacturing employees were wage earners, and another 15 per cent were salaried personnel. Between 1899 and 1919, the number of wage earners increased by almost 92 per cent, while salaried employees grew by an incredible 340 per cent. Over the same span, the number of proprietors and members of firms steadily declined, reflecting the triumph of the corporation over other forms of business organization.

The switch to unskilled and semiskilled labor was the most important employment development of the new industrialism, but men and women experienced the switch very differently. By 1920, just under one-half of all male and over three-fourths of all female manufacturing workers fell into the two lowest job classifications. Women made their greatest inroads as semiskilled operatives, which required neither physical strength nor craft skills. One-fifth of all woman laborers, and over half of all female semiskilled operatives, had jobs in the clothing, textile, and shoemaking industries. Many ran "smart" ma-

---

[13] *Thirteenth Census of the United States, 1910: Occupation Statistics, Volume IV*, 531–533; *Fourteenth Census of the United States, 1920: Occupations*, 111–119, 1044–1045; *Eleventh Census of the United States, 1890: Special Census Report on Occupations of the Population of the United States*, 30–37; *Fourteenth Census of the United States, 1920: Manufactures, Reports for States, with Statistics for Principal Cities*, 1610.

chines. The metals, lumber, and furniture industries employed nearly two-thirds of all male laborers, but only 4 per cent of the women, and 44 per cent of all semiskilled men, but only 11 per cent of the semiskilled women. In no single industry did female laborers outnumber males. Semiskilled women predominated only in the clothing, textile, tobacco, and publishing industries.[14]

By 1920, six industries that were not at all prominent or did not exist in 1890—automobiles, rubber goods, electrical machinery, gasoline engines, copper fixtures, and power laundries—engaged nearly 10 per cent of the work force. Between 1890 and 1914, the number of workers in foundry and machine shops, paper and pulp mills, railroad shops, and brass factories all quintupled. In furniture, hosiery and knitting, meat packing, boots and shoes, leather tanning, and dairy processing, the work forces more than doubled. They remained much the same size in agricultural implements, iron and steel milling, and men's clothing, but automation revolutionized their productivity.[15]

Equally noteworthy between 1890 and 1914 was the increasing concentration of workers in large establishments and in big cities. The average number of employees per establishment rose from thirteen to twenty-one, on the way to twenty-five just five years later. By 1920, one-quarter of the manufacturing work force labored for enterprises employing over 1,000 people, 40 per cent for those employing more than 500, and almost three-fourths for those over 100. Corporations, as opposed to partnerships or proprietorships, employed 89 per cent. Over one-third worked for companies whose products were worth more than $1 million annually; over 80 per cent, for companies producing over $100,000. Cheese factories with their average five employees and wagon shops with fourteen were anachronisms. At the forepoint of the trend were railroad shops with 257 workers each, confectioneries with 243, and tanneries with 217. Rolling mills, automobile factories, paper mills, and gasoline engine plants all averaged over 150 workers; furniture factories and agricultural implement shops, over 100. Boot and shoe factories, meat-packing plants,

---

[14] *Eleventh Census of the United States, 1890: Manufacturing Industries: Totals for States and Industries, Part 1*, pp. 628–634; *Fourteenth Census of the United States, 1920: Manufactures, Reports for States, with Statistics for Principal Cities*, 1613; *Thirteenth Census of the United States, 1910: Volume VIII, Manufactures*, 564–565; *Thirteenth Census of the United States, 1910: Abstract of the Census with Supplement for Wisconsin*, 282–287.

[15] *Fourteenth Census of the United States, 1920: Manufactures, Reports for States with Statistics for Principal Cities*, 1617–1625, 1636–1637; *ibid.*, *Manufactures, General Report and Analytical Tables, Volume VIII*, 90, 102–119; *Thirteenth Census of the United States, 1910: Abstract of the Census with Supplement for Wisconsin*, 282–292, 326–345.

knitting shops, lumber mills, and men's clothing factories all employed an average of fifty or more workers.[16]

Milwaukee's share of the state's work force held steady at one-third in 1914. The remainder concentrated in the seventeen next largest cities. Factories in these eighteen cities hired 62 per cent of manufacturing workers; Milwaukee, Racine, and Kenosha alone hired more than 40 per cent. Just over one-half concentrated in the southeast corner and in the Rock and Fox river valleys. Sheboygan had 4 per cent, and by 1919, Stevens Point, West Allis, and Waukesha combined had another 4 per cent.[17]

In thirteen of the eighteen largest cities, at least nine out of ten wage earners worked for businesses organized as corporations in 1910. In Kenosha, thirteen corporations, each of which made products worth more than $100,000 in total, employed 93 per cent of all wage-earners. More than half worked for Jeffery Automobiles, Simmons Mattress, or American Brass. In Racine, 86 per cent worked for one of forty-two similar corporations; in Milwaukee, the percentage was the same for 291 corporations. More than one Milwaukee wage-earner in five worked in seven giant plants that employed over 1,000 persons each.[18]

As in 1890, immigrants and their children continued to provide the bulk of Wisconsin's work force in 1910. However, this ethnic mixture was soon to change, as immigrants from northwestern Europe gave way to those from southern and eastern Europe. Drastic changes in the nature of work, production control, and the workplace underlaid this ethnic shift. Simply put, the high-speed "skilled" precision machinery of the new industrialism greatly diminished the need for skill in those who ran it. Unskilled workers could be trained in a matter of days or hours to perform repetitive tasks that produced more items than had ever before been dreamed of. Mechanical engineers had become the new wizards of the workplace. Their passion for efficiency, standardization, and productivity led them to devise

---

[16] *Fourteenth Census of the United States, 1920: Manufactures, Reports for States, with Statistics for Principal Cities*, 1620–1637; ibid., *Occupations*, 128–129, 169–185, 264–323; *Thirteenth Census of the United States, 1910: Abstract of the Census with Supplement for Wisconsin*, 282–292, 326–345, 368–373.

[17] *Thirteenth Census of the United States, 1910: Occupation Statistics, Volume IV*, 531–533; ibid., *Population: Reports by States, with Statistics for Counties, Cities, and other Civil Divisions*, 1075–1076.

[18] Korman, *Industrialization, Immigrants, and Americanizers*, 78–80; Richard H. Keehn, "Industry and Business," in Nicholas C. Burckel, ed., *Racine: Growth and Change in a Wisconsin County* (Racine, 1977), 177–215, 281–295; Esther F. Ethier, "Social and Economic Changes of Milwaukee, 1870–1900" (bachelor's thesis, University of Wisconsin, 1923), 11–23.

complex, single-purpose machines which reduced the human variable and could be run at high speeds for long periods to produce countless copies of a standardized product. Group drives powered by electricity or steam propelled the new machines and permitted the simultaneous operation of dozens of engines at different speeds.[19]

Owners and engineers took maximum advantage of this machinery by controlling every aspect of production and redesigning factories. They arranged machinery in close sequential order so that a product would move from start to finish along a conveyor belt or assembly line, pausing only long enough at each machine for it to perform the requisite operation with the help of someone to pull a lever or push a button. The assembly line propelled the product using non-human power, so machine tenders had neither to move nor to wait long for the next piece. "Progressive" production like this greatly increased speed and productivity, eliminated human variability, and reduced waste. To accommodate continuous-flow production, factories were redesigned on a single level, leading to sprawling buildings in industrial suburbs like West Allis, Cudahy, and South Milwaukee, where land was abundant and cheap. However, few Wisconsin factories completed this assembly-line transition before World War I. Larger ones, such as Allis-Chalmers, International Harvester, Bucyrus, J. I. Case, and Jeffery-Nash Motors, led the way.[20]

To be sure, skilled craftsmen continued to exercise significant control over production. The pace of work was modified by the "stint"—the notion during that era about how much production was "reasonable" in a given interval. Even de-skilled craftsmen continued to insist upon union work rules, the foremost of which was that workers determine output quotas. Craftsmen and mechanics continued to enforce what they regarded as a code of "manly" behavior, forging a

---

[19] *Thirteenth Census of the United States, 1910: Occupation Statistics, Volume IV,* 138–151, 531–533; *Thirteenth Census of the United States, 1910: Population, Reports by States, with Statistics for Counties, Cities, and other Civil Divisions, Volume III,* 1075–1076. Alan I. Marcus and Howard P. Segal, *Technology in America: A Brief History* (San Diego, 1989), 225–232; Stephen Meyer III, *The Five Dollar Day: Labor Managers and Social Control in the Ford Motor Company, 1908–1921* (Albany, 1981), 9–29, 42–46; Stephen Meyer, *"Stalin over Wisconsin": The Making and Unmaking of Militant Unionism, 1900–1950* (New Brunswick, New Jersey, 1984), 16–21; Daniel Nelson, *Managers and Workers: Origins of the New Factory System in the United States, 1880–1920* (Madison, 1975), 3–25; David Montgomery, *Workers' Control in America: Studies in the History of Work, Technology and Labor Struggles* (Cambridge, England, 1979), 9–12.

[20] Meyer, *Five Dollar Day,* 29–36; Marcus and Segal, *Technology in America,* 230–233; Korman, *Industrialization, Immigrants, and Americanizers,* 78–80. For a more detailed discussion of these innovations at Allis-Chalmers, see Stephen Meyer, "Technology and the Workplace: Skilled and Production Workers at Allis-Chalmers, 1900–1941," in *Technology and Culture,* 29 (October, 1988), 839–847.

united front in defense of their prerogatives and adhering to a creed that the quality of the product and the well-being of fellow workers took precedence over production quotas. Craftsmen also defended their work rules by staging slowdowns, restricting output, and conducting sympathy strikes. Economist John R. Commons of the University of Wisconsin, a fervent supporter of organized labor, admitted that in effect many workers engaged in a continuous but unorganized strike.[21]

Owners, managers, and technicians responded with a three-pronged program to control the workplace: scientific management, professional recruitment and retention of workers, and what came to be called "welfare capitalism." "Scientific management" was a catchall term for measures designed to specialize and bureaucratize work and to centralize planning and decision making. It was coined by Frederick W. Taylor (1856–1915), a former steelworker whose ideas transformed the workplace. Taylor used time-motion studies, microcosmic cost-accounting, detailed job analyses, and "micromotion" techniques to maximize productivity and efficiency. Scientific management also would allow "experts" to set the standards for the time and effort necessary for each job, and to develop pay scales based upon differing piece rates. All parts of production that involved thought or judgment—planning, inventory management, quality control and so on—were transferred to a centralized top management. The many powers previously exercised by shop foremen were parceled out to specialists responsible for a single aspect of the job: discipline, output, quality, and so on. Supervisors and record keepers proliferated, as did unskilled and semiskilled workers.[22]

Professionalizing personnel practices developed mostly after 1900. Before then, the personnel process was largely informal. Craftsmen and shop foremen possessed almost complete authority to hire and fire, with unpredictable results that dissatisfied owners and managers. They became beguiled by psychologists' claims that they could design instruments to identify specific nuances of personality or mental acuity which suited prospective workers for a particular job. They also

---

[21] Montgomery, *Workers' Control in America*, 9–31; Meyer, *Five Dollar Day*, 49–94. See also David Montgomery, *The Fall of the House of Labor: The Workplace, the State, and American Labor Activism, 1865–1925* (Cambridge, England, 1987), 17–19, and Richard Edwards, *Contested Terrain: The Transformation of the Workplace in the Twentieth Century* (New York, 1979), 18–33.

[22] Montgomery, *Workers' Control in America*, 43–53; Montgomery, *Fall of the House of Labor*, 214–256; Meyer, *Five Dollar Day*, 43–65; Nelson, *Managers and Workers*, 55–78; Korman, *Industrialization, Immigrants, and Americanizers*, 75–84; Marcus and Segal, *Technology in America*, 234–236.

became convinced that a system of education could be designed to train workers in technical skills and instill work habits and obedience. Some, such as Allis-Chalmers, favored reviving apprenticeship programs in the form of management-run "shop schools." Others favored industrial education in the public schools. In 1908, International Harvester organized a school for apprentices and four years later began an association with the University of Wisconsin's Extension Division to teach practical courses. By 1910, both approaches had gained support among employers, labor unions, educational reformers, and social workers—enough support to make Wisconsin a national leader in vocational-technical education.[23]

Welfare capitalism, also known as welfare work or industrial sociology, signified company programs like recreational and entertainment facilities, educational programs, insurance and pension plans, savings and loan operations, affordable housing, incentive pay, and industrial health, safety, and sanitation measures. Management hired specialists to consolidate these efforts, at the expense of foremen and supervisors. Critics tended to view welfare capitalism as either sheer paternalism or a method of social control.[24]

In Wisconsin, in-house welfare had its greatest impact on giant firms like Allis-Chalmers, Bucyrus, U.S. Steel's Bay View works, and especially the Milwaukee plant of Chicago-based International Harvester, a national pioneer in the movement. Professor Commons pronounced the Harvester program one of the country's most enlightened. Charles W. Price, a former businessman who had educated himself about industrial welfare by reading publications of the American Social Science Association, headed Harvester's program and so impressed Commons that Commons later appointed him to launch the welfare and safety drive of Wisconsin's Industrial Commission.

Harvester's program was the special project of the McCormick family, which owned the company and was influenced by social settlement figures such as Jane Addams and Graham Taylor, and by the University of Chicago's school of education. Price was brought in to resolve a conflict between welfare staff members who wanted a technical school for workers and managers who worried about productivity and profits. Price put the program completely under company control and satisfied both groups. In 1908, Milwaukee Harvester instituted an employee benefit association, followed by a workers' lunchroom, a social and recreational center, and a company band.[25]

[23] Nelson, *Managers and Workers*, 79–100; Korman, *Industrialization, Immigrants, and Americanizers*, 25–40, 91–109; Marcus and Segal, *Technology in America*, 238–239.
[24] Nelson, *Managers and Workers*, 101–121; Meyer, *Five Dollar Day*, 95–147.
[25] Korman, *Industrialization, Immigrants, and Americanizers*, 87–111.

[2]

Although technological innovation and systematization had their greatest impact in manufacturing, they also affected agriculture, domestic service, office work, retail sales, and the professions. In agriculture, the most important effects flowed from the transition to dairy husbandry and the increasing use of labor-saving machinery. The factory system allowed a handful of people to manage the milk of a thousand cows supplied by dozens of dairymen. Farmers became more dependent upon the systematic application of technical knowledge; the milkmaid with her pail and stool became a thing of the past.[26]

The pages of Wisconsin agricultural journals abounded with discussions of the changing nature of farm work, the importance of keeping apace in technology and knowledge, a growing crisis over hired help, and the continuing viability of agriculture as a means of climbing the social ladder. As early as 1895, a Granger from Lafayette County assured the annual convention of the Wisconsin State Agricultural Society that "we are passing from an era of muscle to an era of brain." He observed that he had begun farming in the era of "the cradle, the scythe, and the flail," realizing perhaps a few hundred dollars a year, while his sons now "cut their grass with a steel mower, reap their harvests with a twine binder, thresh their grain with a steam thresher, and if at the close of the year their accounts do not disclose a balance of one or two thousand dollars in their favor, they soundly denounce the trusts and combines of our land." If farmers did not keep pace with the advancing progress of the age, he admonished, "in the great struggle for survival of the fittest we may be left."[27]

Fifteen years later, *Hoard's Dairyman* observed that "the average dairy farmer of today in the extent of his knowledge on these questions, is a prince by the side of his brother of 25 or 30 years ago.... There was never a time in the history of the world when there was as many farmers studying hard on the problems of the farm as to-day." The editors of *Hoard's* constantly chided farmers "who really are afraid to get new ideas, lest they should become discontented with

---

[26] Eric E. Lampard, *The Rise of the Dairy Industry in Wisconsin: A Study in Agricultural Change, 1820–1920* (Madison, 1963), 91–98, 212–215, 237–293, 335–351; F. M. White, "The Tractor is Here," in *Wisconsin Country Magazine*, 10 (October, 1915), 12–16, 36; "The Automobile and the Farmer," *Hoard's Dairyman*, July 27, 1911, p. 810; Walter H. Ebling et al., *A Century of Wisconsin Agriculture, 1848–1948*, Department of Agriculture, Crop and Livestock Reporting Service, *Bulletin*, no. 290 (1948), 62, 79. See Chapter 2 for a complete discussion of this transition.

[27] T. J. Van Mater, "Milestones Along the Life of a Granger," in *Transactions of the Wisconsin State Agricultural Society*, 1895, pp. 209–210.

the old ones [and] so be compelled to change their practices and methods." The gospel of agricultural progress through technology, expertise, and systematization was also sounded by the *Wisconsin Farmer*, the university's *Wisconsin Country Magazine*, and by spokesmen for the College of Agriculture and its extension division. The majority of farm wives felt left out of this transformation. Some complained to the Country Life Commission that their work was "little changed from that of previous generations, but there is now a shortage of household help for hire and a need to feed and care for field hands, neither an improvement."[28]

Agricultural leaders also agonized over the mounting crisis in finding and keeping hired help. By 1915, one-quarter of the agricultural labor force consisted of wage workers, but gains in productivity and efficiency were already obviating the need for unskilled farm labor. Greater employment opportunities in manufacturing and service, along with the lure of urban amenities, were causing a serious shortage among younger people who in times past had regularly "hired out" for wages, with or without room and board. In 1893, a correspondent complained to *Hoard's Dairyman*, as correspondents complained perennially, that the most difficult task facing dairy farmers was "to secure competent help." The *Dairyman's* oft-repeated solution was to treat workers better, "to put up a comfortable tenant house and fence off a quarter acre of good ground," because these "various et ceteras of domestic life count a good deal more to the laborer than they do to the farmer."[29]

While the "rural drain" raised one set of concerns about agricultural labor, an increase in tenancy and mortgages raised others. Wisconsin's rate of farm tenancy was lower than it was in other north-central states, but it was already on the rise by 1914, especially in the New North. More investors and corporations, including some from out of state, were purchasing farms and hiring managers, arousing fears about a growing class of tenant farmers and agricultural wage workers who could never aspire to ownership. To combat such fates, the *Wisconsin Farmer* urged younger men to hire out for a few years and save their money until they could afford to rent a farm. The next step was "to secure as a partner an ambitious, energetic, thrifty young woman, who will make a good housekeeper, as his wife." With "no

[28] "The Progress of Dairy Thought," *Hoard's Dairyman*, February 11, 1910, p. 52 (quote); *Hoard's Dairyman*, October 27, 1893, p. 572 (quote); Kate L. Sabin, "Our Relation to the Common Schools," in the *Transactions of the Wisconsin State Agricultural Society*, 1896, p. 126; Jane B. Knowles, " 'It's Our Turn Now': Rural American Women Speak Out, 1900–1929," in Wava G. Haney and Jane B. Knowles, eds., *Women and Farming: Changing Roles, Changing Structures* (Boulder, 1988), 303–315.

[29] *Hoard's Dairyman*, February 10, 1893, p. 2848 (quote); August 18, 1893, p. 417; February 5, 1904, p. 1182 (quote).

fear of hard labor, long hours, strict attention to business, painstaking application and strict economy, a few years as a tenant farmer will suffice" for a man to buy his own farm.[30]

Domestic service and housekeeping, too, changed dramatically owing to new technologies and perspectives on homemaking. A household appliance revolution was in the making, led by the washing machine and the vacuum cleaner, which appeared in urban middle-class houses around 1900, even before schools of home economics preached efficient, productive, and systematic housework. Their instructors in "domestic science" began holding annual conventions in 1899, formed the American Home Economics Association late in 1908, and launched the *Journal of Home Economics* in 1909. Their concepts were popularized among middle- and upper-class women by such mass-circulation magazines as *Good Housekeeping* (1885) and *Everyday Housekeeping* (1894). In Wisconsin, three schools participated in this transformation in important ways: the University of Wisconsin-Stout along with the Menomonie and Dunn County school systems; the University in Madison; and Milwaukee-Downer College.[31]

Nor did sales clerks escape the effects of mechanization and systematization, for department store managers prized efficiency, productivity, and profitability as much as factory managers. Department stores went to great expense to create ambiances that convinced customers they were being pampered. They rationalized the cost of an extensive sales force on the grounds that a skilled, agreeable salesperson boosted the size of the average transaction and ensured return business.[32]

The "feminization" of the clerical labor force and the advent of scientific management went hand-in-hand. Prior to the 1890's, the typical business office was small and staffed almost entirely by men.

---

[30] Charles J. Galpin and Emily F. Hoag, *Farm Tenancy: An Analysis of the Occupancy of 500 Farms*, UW Agricultural Experiment Station, *Research Bulletin*, no. 44 (1919), 6–18; Benjamin H. Hibbard and John D. Black, *Farm Leasing Systems in Wisconsin*, UW Agricultural Experiment Station, *Bulletin*, no. 47 (1920), 1–10, 58–60; Harry L. Russell and Frank B. Morrison, *Experiments in Farming*, UW Agricultural Experiment Station, *Bulletin*, no. 319 (1920), 55; *Wisconsin Farmer*, December 29, 1898, p. 818 (quotes); *ibid.*, April 3, 1902, p. 209; *ibid.*, March 20, 1913, p. 309. Tenant farming and absentee ownership of large farms existed in Wisconsin from the territorial period forward, but were escalating in the late nineteenth and early twentieth centuries.

[31] Marcus and Segal, *Technology in America*, 202–224. For a provocative argument that the new industrialism in housework actually increased the burden on homemakers, see Ruth Schwartz Cowan, *More Work for Mother: The Ironies of Household Technology from the Open Hearth to the Microwave* (New York, 1983).

[32] Susan Porter Benson, *Counter Cultures: Saleswomen, Managers, and Customers in American Department Stores, 1890–1940* (Urbana and Chicago, 1986), 1–10, 124–296; Leslie Woodcock Tentler, *Wage-Earning Women: Industrial Work and Family Life in the United States, 1900–1930* (New York, 1979), 26–57.

Scant division of labor existed among copyists, bookkeepers, clerks, and office boys, all of whom communicated freely. Most clerks were expected to know something about how the business actually functioned. But by the 1890's the proliferation of large corporations increased the volume and complexity of office work and thereby the need for larger staffs, new procedures, and business machines. Accordingly, owners turned to scientific management to stimulate productivity and efficiency, maximize profits, and gain control over their employees. Addressographs, mimeographs, adding machines, cash registers, check makers, and, above all, typewriters mechanized office work.[33]

Office workers no longer expected to plan their own work. Their jobs, like those on the factory floor, were now broken down into their component parts, quantitatively measured, and standardized. Managers tried to see that each task was performed at the lowest cost, in the shortest time, and to suit each employee to his or her job. But they never showed individuals how their tasks fit into the total process. They redesigned offices and procedures to facilitate work flow and minimize distractions. Motivational programs rewarded workers who met standards, penalized slackers, and stressed "morale." Mostly women filled the specialized jobs created by the new machines and routinized procedures. After all, it was felt they were used to being paid less than men, being subordinated to male managers, and not coveting promotion. And women supposedly possessed a higher tolerance for boring, repetitious tasks.[34]

The professions, too, were transformed by the passion for productivity and efficiency in what has come to be called a "search for order." During the last quarter of the nineteenth century, nearly all the professions (law, medicine, public health, social work, librarianship, teaching) experienced phenomenal growth and formed national associations to represent their interests. Each group developed its own body of knowledge, methodology, code of ethics, a shorthand vocabulary largely incomprehensible to the uninitiated, standards for training, and certification by state governments. Professional schools, most of them publicly financed and closely tied to professional associations, mushroomed.[35]

---

[33] Margery W. Davies, *Woman's Place is at the Typewriter: Office Work and Office Workers, 1870–1930* (Philadelphia, 1982), 97–128; Marcus and Segal, *Technology in America*, 226–227. The typewriter was invented by Milwaukeean Christopher Latham Sholes in 1867. See Frederic Heath, "The Typewriter in Wisconsin," in *WMH*, 27 (March, 1944), 263–275.

[34] Davies, *Woman's Place*, 163–175; Alice Kessler-Harris, *Out to Work: A History of Wage-Earning Women in the United States* (New York, 1982), 148–149.

[35] Robert H. Wiebe, *The Search For Order, 1877–1920* (New York, 1967), 112–163; Burton J. Bledstein, *The Culture of Professionalism: The Middle Class and the Development of Higher Education in America* (New York, 1976), 86–128.

As their prestige rose, professionals were consulted for solutions to nearly every significant societal problem. They responded by applying their particular discipline's norms and values to a wider arena: the need for specialization, expert knowledge, and application of scientific and rational methodology; the vision of society as a meritocracy governed by impersonal rules; the ideal of disinterested public service; the efficacy of planning and predictability; and the preference for a dispassionate, objective outlook.[36]

Women benefited somewhat from the expansion of professions. It paved the way for a small percentage from upper-middle-class backgrounds to enter the work force in slightly elevated positions, but it did so only in a sporadic and limited manner. Most women remained confined to a few, female-dominated professions, chiefly teaching, nursing, librarianship, and social work. If they managed to break into male-dominated professions, they generally were treated as unequal colleagues whose merit was judged by a double standard.[37]

Professionalism and efficiency aside, most Wisconsin workers and contemporary observers were more concerned about concrete issues such as income, the length of the workday, the threat of unemployment, dangerous and unhealthful working conditions, and the expanding employment of women and children. A substantial income gap existed between and among white-collar and blue-collar workers; the skilled, semiskilled, and unskilled; men, women, and children; immigrants and native-born; and whites and blacks. Industry of course paid higher wages to a highly skilled minority of workers and lower wages to the unskilled majority, rendering industry-wide wage averages a faulty yardstick. In 1914, for example, weekly wages in the railroad industry ranged from $41.53 for passenger engineers to $9.42 for track hands, with at least a dozen gradations in between. In iron and steel, the gap between skilled and unskilled males was $19.20 to $11.20; in foundry and machine shops, skilled men averaged $14.85 and women, $6.60. "Standard" income levels were further skewed by the existence of a native-born, white, male elite. The compilers of the 1920 *Census of Manufactures* refused to calculate average earnings because of the wide range across ethnicity, gender, age, and skill levels and because the number of wage earners fluctuated monthly.[38]

---

[36] Bledstein, *Culture of Professionalism*, 248–286; Samuel Haber, *The Quest for Authority and Honor in the American Professions, 1750–1900* (Chicago, 1991), 193–205, 359–362.

[37] Penina Migdal Glazer and Miriam Slater, *Unequal Colleagues: The Entrance of Women into the Professions, 1890–1940* (New Brunswick, New Jersey, 1987), 12–33.

[38] *Fourteenth Census of the United States, 1920: Manufactures, Reports for States with Statistics for Principal Cities*, 16–17; Peter R. Shergold, *Working-Class Life: The "American Standard" in Comparative Perspective, 1899–1913* (Pittsburgh, 1982), 3–7, 224–227; Alice Kessler-Harris, *A Woman's Wage: Historical Meanings and Social Consequences* (Lexington, Kentucky, 1990), 6–22, 33–56; *Senate Documents*, 61 Cong., 2 sess., no. 747

Periodic unemployment was the common lot and the greatest fear of most workers. Those in manufacturing and mining commonly lost between one-quarter and one-third of their hours each year through illness and layoffs. This produced a whole range of economic and social evils, including lower wages, the need to supplement family income through child and women's labor and taking-in boarders, waste from the inability of families to plan budgets, the downgrading of status and exploitation of casual laborers, and consequent psychological trauma. Authorities disagreed about how much periodic unemployment occurred and about its impact on annual income, but all concurred that the effect on workers' lives was substantial.[39]

These conditions meant that many workers failed to keep pace with the rising cost of living. After the depression of 1893–1897, the economy embarked upon a period of growth which lasted until 1921, except for brief recessions in 1907, 1911, and 1914. Computations of cost-of-living increases and changes in real income vary, but all demonstrate that American-born, white, male elite workers alone kept pace. Retail food prices rose from 60 to 72 per cent between 1900 and 1912; annual food costs per family jumped from $301 to $493. The poverty line for a family of four rose from $516 to $640 between 1893 and 1909. In 1914, the amount needed for satisfactory family life hovered around $800 a year, but between 80 and 95 per cent of all male heads of household earned less than that. Few employers attempted to refute these statistics; most justified them in terms of the law of supply and demand.[40]

(serial 5865), *Abstracts of Reports of the Immigration Commission with Conclusions and Views of the Minority*; Edgar Syndenstricker, "Conditions of Labor in the Principal Industries," in U.S. Commission on Industrial Relations, *Records, 1911–1915* (15 microfilm reels), reel 9, in General Records of the Department of Labor, RG174, National Archives and Records Administration. See also *Senate Documents*, 64 Cong., 1 sess., vol. 19, no. 415 (11 vols., serials 6929–6939), *Industrial Relations: Final Report and Testimony Submitted to Congress by the Commission on Industrial Relations* (reprinted, New York, 1970), and National Industrial Conference Board, *Wages in the United States, 1914–1926* (New York, 1927), 77–122.

[39] Sydenstricker, "Conditions of Labor in the Principal Industries," in U.S. Commission on Industrial Relations, *Records*; *Senate Documents*, 64 Cong., 1 sess., vol. 19, no. 415 (11 vols., serials 6929–6939), *Industrial Relations: Final Report and Testimony Submitted to Congress by the Commission on Industrial Relations*; Paul F. Brissenden, "Earnings of Factory Workers, 1899 to 1927: An Analysis of Pay-Roll Statistics," in *Fourteenth Census of the United States, 1920: Census Monograph, No. 10* (1929), 81–129; Paul H. Douglas, *Real Wages in the United States, 1890–1926* (New York, 1930; reprinted 1966), 581–605.

[40] U.S. Bureau of the Census, *Historical Statistics of the United States: Colonial Times to 1970, Part 1*, pp. 199–214; Steven Dubnoff, "A Method for Estimating the Economic Welfare of American Families of Any Composition, 1860–1909," in *Historical Methods*, 13 (Summer, 1980), 171–77; "Retail Prices, 1890–1913," U.S. Bureau of Labor Statistics, *Bulletin*, no. 140 (1914), 11–15; Frances P. Valiant, "Trend of Wages and

Wisconsin workers were somewhat better off than the national average, but income disparities echoed national patterns along lines of occupation, gender, race, ethnicity, age, periodic unemployment, and shrinking real income. Between 1899 and 1914, average annual earnings for state workers jumped from $436 to $603; the national figures were $446 to $576. The state's per capita real income rose 2 per cent, while the nation's fell 5 per cent, raising Wisconsin from twenty-eighth to twenty-second among the states. Even so, the majority of manufacturing employees still fell below the poverty line. The median yearly wage in the state's eighteen largest cities jumped to $583 by 1914, barely above the national figure of $576. That year, only Racine, Kenosha, Ashland, Superior, Beloit, and Madison surpassed both the national average and the poverty line.[41]

Despite the fact that wealth was growing faster than population, the state's Bureau of Labor and Industrial Statistics (BLIS) reported in 1895 that "there seems to be as much misery and want as ever" and "as much complaint of low wages and bad conditions in other respects." Although acknowledging that hard times might have depressed industry-wide averages artificially, the bureau insisted that the disproportionate number of skilled laborers more than offset that circumstance. It asserted that common laborers and unskilled workers generally made $300 or less a year, and that over half Wisconsin's farm laborers had suffered declines in wages during the preceding three years.[42]

Prices, 1879–1912," and "Annual Earnings and Family Income of Adult Male Wage Earners in the Principal American Industries," in U.S. Commission on Industrial Relations, *Records, 1911–1915* (15 microfilm reels), reel 9, in General Records of the Department of Labor, RG174, National Archives and Records Administration; *Senate Documents*, 64 Cong., 1 sess., vol. 19, no. 415 (11 vols., serials 6929–6939), *Industrial Relations: Final Report and Testimony Submitted to Congress by the Commission on Industrial Relations* (reprinted, New York, 1970); Montgomery, *Workers' Control in America*, 34–40; Kessler-Harris, *A Woman's Wage*, 6–22, 33–56; Philip S. Foner, *Women and the American Labor Movement: From Colonial Times to the Eve of World War I* (New York, 1979), 459–469.

[41] Brissenden, "Earnings of Factory Workers," in *Fourteenth Census of the United States, 1920: Census Monograph No. 10* (1929), 81, 107, 140, 150; Walter H. Ebling and Emery C. Wilcox, *Wisconsin Farm Prices, Production, and Income*, Department of Agriculture, *Bulletin*, no. 249 (1944), 102–103, 110–111. According to the *Thirteenth Biennial Report* of the Bureau of Labor, Census and Industrial Statistics, average annual earnings of all individuals in Wisconsin rose from $467.66 to $518.81—11 per cent—between 1904 and 1907. See also *Eleventh Census of the United States, Manufacturing Industries, Totals for States and Industries, Part 1*, pp. 628–637; *Eleventh Census of the United States, 1890: Statistics of Cities, Part 2*, pp. 278–285, 334–335, 418–421, 478–485; Clarence D. Long, *Wages and Earnings in the United States, 1860–1890* (Princeton, 1960), 48–160; Carrie Cropley, *Kenosha: From Pioneer Village to Modern City, 1835–1935* (Kenosha, 1958), 58–59.

[42] Bureau of Labor and Industrial Statistics, *Biennial Report*, 1895–1896, pp. 288–299 (quotes); *Census of Manufactures, 1914: Volume I, Reports for States with Statistics for*

By the turn of the century, BLIS noted that the overall situation had actually deteriorated. Between 1888 and 1897, its statistics proved "a downward tendency in the course of wages," and demonstrated "a gradual decrease in the number employed at the higher rates and a corresponding increase in those employed at the lower rates." Industries with increasing proportions of women and children had grown faster than those employing skilled adult males. The more complex an industry's organization, the higher the average wage—but the greater the disparity between top and bottom.[43]

A decade later, the bureau found that Wisconsin's average annual manufacturing wage had risen from $467.66 in 1904 to $529.30 in 1909, while the daily rate in 1909 ranged from $0.33 to $2.49. The average daily wage for men in forty-seven occupations was nearly double that for women, and skilled workers at E. P. Allis earned between $2 and $5 a day, compared to $1.34 to $1.70 for the unskilled. The company's wage schedule had thirty or forty classifications, with several gradations in each category, but the average wage was low because of the high proportion of unskilled workers. Machinists and laborers in four different shops were all paid different rates.[44]

In 1908, annual earnings of native-stock male heads of household in Milwaukee averaged between $579 and $652. Immigrant heads of household made between $416 to $464; their sons, $509 to $652. Among women, native-stock workers averaged $239 a year; immigrants, $175; and their daughters, $204. Although six of ten native-born heads of household earned enough to provide sole support for their families, only three in ten immigrants did. Thirty-eight per cent of native-born males earned under $400 a year, 52 per cent of immigrants did; 42 per cent of native-born women made less than $200 per year, compared to 62 per cent of foreign-born women. Immigrant families depended more than native-born families upon child labor, boarding, and other sources of income.[45]

Principal Cities and Metropolitan Districts; Brissenden, "Earnings of Factory Workers," in *Fourteenth Census of the United States, 1920: Census Monograph No. 10*, pp. 43–53; National Industrial Conference Board, *Wages in the United States, 1914–1926* (New York, 1927), 15–49; Edgar Z. Palmer, *The Prewar Industrial Pattern of Wisconsin*, University of Wisconsin Bureau of Business Research and Service, *Wisconsin Commerce Studies*, vol. 1, no. 1 (Madison, 1947), 57–61.

[43] Bureau of Labor and Industrial Statistics, *Biennial Report*, 1899–1900, pp. xi, 231–233 (quotes), 301, 706–835.

[44] *Ibid.*, 1899–1900, pp. xi, 301, 706–835; *ibid.*, 1900–1901, pp. 853–877; *ibid.*, 1909–1910, pp. 804–818; Korman, *Industrialization, Immigrants, and Americanizers*, 28–37.

[45] *Senate Documents*, 61 Cong., 2 sess., vol. 1, no. 338 (2 vols., serials 5665 and 5666), *Immigration in Cities: Study of Selected Districts in New York, Chicago, Philadelphia, Boston, Buffalo, Cleveland, and Milwaukee* (reprinted, New York, 1970); *ibid.*, vol. 2; Louis J.

When it came to working hours, variations among workers were less striking; progress, more uniform. The six-day week remained standard, but the number of hours per day ranged from the new eight-hour to the old twelve-hour day, with more people working longer hours than shorter. The eight-hour day was the Holy Grail for labor from the 1880's through World War I—the aim of a broad coalition whose components, motives, tactics, and effectiveness varied over time. The coalition's members disagreed over private versus political action and a universal versus a piecemeal approach. The coalition's fortunes waxed and waned as public opinion fluctuated, and as employers reassessed the impact on productivity, efficiency, and profits. Although progress was slow and uneven before 1909, it accelerated rapidly during the next decade, impelled by humanitarianism, scientific management and social sciences, labor solidarity, and progressive politics.[46]

In the early 1900's, the AFL temporarily abandoned its enthusiasm for the eight-hour day because of growing mistrust of politics and government, repression by business, fear of competition from immigrants, women, and children, and the belief that it could co-operate with industry on some benefits. The AFL used collective bargaining to secure reductions in hours. It somewhat reluctantly supported legislation to protect women, children, and special classes of workers whom it had no desire to organize. After 1907, the AFL resumed its support for hours reduction as part of its "new unionism," motivated in part by competition from more radical labor organizations. Advocates of the new unionism sought more control over the workplace, the co-operation of workers across skill and industry lines, and a greater willingness to strike and engage in political action. Labor leaders of all persuasions believed that hours reduction would enhance the workingman's life by increasing leisure, raising wages, reducing the pool of unemployed, and improving working conditions.[47]

Joining organized labor in support of hours reduction were economists, sociologists, the recreation and scientific management move-

---

Swichkow and Lloyd P. Gartner, *The History of the Jews of Milwaukee* (Philadelphia, 1963), 165–166.

[46] David R. Roediger and Philip S. Foner, *Our Own Time: A History of American Labor and the Working Day* (New York, 1989), 145–193; Benjamin Kline Hunnicutt, *Work Without End: Abandoning Shorter Hours for the Right to Work* (Philadelphia, 1988), 12–36; Daniel T. Rodgers, *The Work Ethic in Industrial America, 1850–1920* (Chicago, 1978), 90–91, 156–160. Nationally, the average work week declined from 59.4 hours to 54.9 between 1896 and 1916; the average workday, from 9.90 to 9.15 hours.

[47] Roediger and Foner, *Our Own Time*, 145–193; Hunnicutt, *Work without End*, 18–23.

ments, and feminist organizations which were concerned about working women and the length of the workday. Women advocates of consumer protection and opponents of child labor together sought legislative solutions for modern industrialism's woes.

Not surprisingly, few employers evinced much enthusiasm for hours reduction before 1910. Instead, most clung to the notion that the more hours, the more work—and the fewer workers. The new unionism provoked a counteroffensive by the National Association of Manufacturers and the National Metal Trades Association. Even the National Civic Federation, dedicated to co-operation between business and labor and whose leaders included John R. Commons, Samuel Gompers, and John Mitchell, dragged its feet on the issue. Only after 1910 did the combination of labor activism, progressive labor legislation, and the arguments of scientific management become irresistible.[48]

In Wisconsin, workdays of ten to twelve hours had been the norm in the early 1890's. A survey of 152,563 employees in 1903 revealed that 90 per cent worked ten or more hours a day. By 1920, however, the Wisconsin workday was markedly shorter. Between 1903 and 1920, the percentage of those working sixty hours or more declined from 58 to 29, and the percentage of those working forty-eight hours or less increased from 9 to 46 per cent.[49]

Wisconsin's workers were even less enamored of periodic unemployment than of long hours. Nationally, unemployment fluctuated considerably between 1893 and 1915, the former a depression year and the latter a recession year. It jumped from 3 per cent in 1892 to 11.7 in 1893, peaking at 18.4 per cent in 1894. It remained between 12 and 15 per cent for the next four years, before dropping to 6.5 in 1899. With slight variations, it remained between 4 to 5 per cent until 1906, when it dropped below 2 per cent. In the recession year of 1908, unemployment jumped to 8 per cent, hovered between 5 and 7 per cent through 1913, and then jumped again to 8.5 per cent in 1915. Another 5 to 15 per cent of the work force suffered from underemployment, usually because of split shifts or abbreviated workdays. Whatever their jobs, men were about 11 per cent more likely to experience unemployment than women, although their chances of being idled for four months or longer were about even.[50]

---

[48] Roediger and Foner, *Our Own Time*, 149–193; Montgomery, *Workers' Control in America*, 91–112.

[49] *Thirteenth Census of the United States, 1910: Manufactures, Volume IX*, 1336–1338; *Fourteenth Census of the United States, 1920: Manufactures, Reports for States, with Statistics for Principal Cities*, 17, 1609, 1617–1618; Bureau of Labor and Industrial Statistics, *Biennial Report*, 1903–1904, pp. 67–68; 1909–1910, pp. 819–820; Industrial Commission, *Report on Allied Functions for the Two Years Ending June 30, 1914* (1914), 49–50.

[50] U.S. Bureau of the Census, *Historical Statistics of the United States: Colonial Times to*

According to a BLIS survey of 1,499 Wisconsin businesses and factories in 1897, employment fluctuated between 71,207 and 109,839 over the year. It was at its lowest point in January, peaked in October, and ended the year about 10 per cent higher than it began. Jobless figures varied widely in Milwaukee. During the recession year of 1913, the U.S. Commission on Industrial Relations reported that nearly 35,000 persons in Milwaukee had been unemployed at some point that year. The secretary of the Wisconsin State Federation of Labor estimated that one-quarter of all employees had been idled.

The head of a private employment bureau put the number at 10,000, of whom 4,500 were unskilled immigrants. The fledgling Wisconsin Free Employment Office in Milwaukee (a part of the state's industrial commission) claimed to have handled 15,660 people in 1913, about 40 per cent of whom were skilled, an equal number unskilled, and 3,000 of whom were described as "floaters, hoboes and tramps." The commission attributed the rise in joblessness to seasonal slumps in the building trades and to "unusual dullness" in railway shops, iron and steel mills, breweries, and other principal industries. The Milwaukee Merchants' and Manufacturers' Association also cited "dullness" as the reason unemployment was up 60 per cent in the winter and 25 per cent overall. The new industrialism and scientific management had managed to propel most businesses towards year-round operation, but those trends did little to alleviate periodic unemployment.[51]

At several times in their lives, most Wisconsin workers had to search for new jobs. A fortunate few found them through friends, relatives, fellow workers, or newspaper ads, or by making the rounds of factory gates. But most eventually relied upon the elaborate, informal network of private employment brokers. "Pool rooms, cafés, grocery stores, lodging houses, even street corners, and public parks," wrote a prominent early director of Milwaukee's Free Employment Office, "became improvised labor markets." Saloonkeepers, head-hunters, contractors and subcontractors, "padrones" and straw bosses all received money from employers and employees for their services. All too often, they bilked jobseekers. Help from immigrant aid societies, fraternal and benevolent associations, employer labor exchanges,

---

1970, Part 1, p. 135; Lebergott, *Manpower in Economic Growth*, 184–185, 408–410, 522; Isaac A. Hourwich, *Immigration and Labor* (New York, 1912; reprinted, 1969), 114–147; *Eleventh Census of the United States, 1890: Special Census Report on Occupations of the Population of the United States*, 103–108.

[51] Bureau of Labor and Industrial Statistics, *Biennial Report*, 1897–1898, pp. 567–687; 1909–1910, pp. 805–810; Korman, *Industrialization, Immigrants, and Americanizers*, 37; "Abstract of Report of J. H. Bradford, special agent, on Unemployment Situation in Milwaukee," in the U.S. Commission on Industrial Relations, *Report*, 1915; Industrial Commission, *Bulletin*, 1913, vol. 2, p. 219; Meyer, *Five Dollar Day*, 75–94.

and trade unions was more reliable, but reached few workers. Even with all these options, many still resorted to private employment agencies, some of which specialized in women or immigrants. Milwaukee's Enders' agency, run by a woman, advertised for women in 1882, while the C. W. St. John agency offered services to southern and eastern Europeans. Aided by all these agencies, E. P. Allis hired between 200 and 800 new men each year during the 1890's. Bucyrus experienced an annual turnover of between 200 and 350 per cent, meaning that it hired some only for a few hours or a few days a week. The general manager of Milwaukee's International Harvester works in 1909 said his firm had "a floating element all the time coming and going."[52]

[3]

Regardless of how long or frequently they had employment, Wisconsin's workers faced workplace conditions that were dangerous, unsanitary, and unhealthful. The same capitalist logic that led to low wages, long hours, and job insecurity also rationalized investing as little as possible in health and safety. In the 1890's in Milwaukee, unguarded machinery, poor lighting, improper ventilation, toxic fumes, and excessive dust were ubiquitous. Sanitation standards were virtually nonexistent, and workers injured on the job were unlikely to receive much compensation from their employers, no matter how benevolent their outlook.[53]

Employers could ignore elementary precautions: doors which swung outward, guards around dangerous machinery, rails on stairs and around elevator shafts. Sash and woodenware factories, sawmills, cooperages, and foundries were crammed with revolving shafts, pulleys, and belts, all capable of maiming and killing in an instant. Newspapers of the day developed a whole vocabulary of euphemisms to describe the "sudden and terrible death" of a worker whose clothing became entangled around a shaft. If the unfortunate man merely lost an arm or a hand, he could hardly count himself lucky; survivors and their families frequently were thrown upon the mercy of benevolent societies or charities. The premiums for accident insurance were beyond the means of most workers; and if they sued, the company often escaped unscathed, thanks to three common law defenses: assumed risk on the victim's part; "contributory negligence," also on his part; and placement of blame for the accident on the actions of a co-

---

[52] William M. Leiserson, *Adjusting Immigrant and Industry* (New York, 1924), 28–48 (quote); Korman, *Industrialization, Immigrants, and Americanizers*, 26–40, 111 (quote).
[53] Korman, *Industrialization, Immigrants, and Americanizers*, 28–48, 111.

worker. As a rule, employers managed to avoid either responsibility or philanthropy.[54]

A national crisis over industrial accidents came to a head between 1900 and 1920. Industrial accidents accounted for 10 per cent of deaths among people of working age from 1907 to 1912. In 1913, out of a work force of 38 million, there were 25,000 industrial fatalities and 700,000 injuries which disabled the victim for more than four weeks. In Wisconsin, industrial accidents accounted for 53 per cent of all mishaps reported in 1906—more than double the total for 1905, and almost five times greater than for 1903. The courts generally held employers unaccountable, but extensive publicity gradually fueled public outrage. In response, the courts began bestowing more frequent and more generous awards. By 1910, this about-face created what employers darkly termed "a compensation crisis."[55]

Concern over factory health and safety in Wisconsin had begun as early as 1878, when the legislature mandated fireproof ladders on factories. In 1883, the legislature established the Bureau of Labor and Industrial Statistics "to collect, assort, systematize and present . . . statistical details relating to all departments of labor in the state, especially in its relations to the commercial, industrial, social, educational and sanitary condition of the laboring classes." The law also empowered the commissioner to inspect factories and make a record of "the methods of protection from accidents and the means of escape from fire." Although an 1887 law provided more specifically for the guards and protection on various machines and in various places, inadequate staff and meager authority plagued the bureau.[56]

Over the years, the number of inspectors was increased from one to twelve, with the stipulation that one inspector be a woman. The office staff grew to the same size. However, the problems remained. The commissioner, a well-known compiler of Wisconsin history and statistics named Frank Flower, made virtually no attempt to enforce existing labor laws, much less to press for new ones. He regarded himself as "a mere gleaner of facts" and pleaded lack of funds. Most

---

[54] Glaab and Larsen, *Factories in the Valley*, 220–257.

[55] Robert Asher, "The Limits of Big Business Paternalism: Relief for Injured Workers in the Years before Workmen's Compensation," and Anthony Bale, "America's First Compensation Crisis: Conflict Over the Value and Meaning of Workplace Injuries Under the Employers' Liability System," in David Rosner and Gerald Markowitz, eds., *Dying for Work: Workers' Safety and Health in Twentieth Century America* (Urbana, 1987), 19–31 and 34–39; Bureau of Labor and Industrial Statistics, *Biennial Report*, 1903–1904, pp. 76–77; *ibid.*, 1905–1906, p. 1290; *ibid.*, 1907–1908, pp. 10–25; *ibid.*, 1909–1910, pp. 71–75.

[56] Arthur J. Altmeyer, *The Industrial Commission of Wisconsin: A Case Study in Labor Law Administration* (Madison, 1932), 9–16; *Laws of Wisconsin*, 1883, pp. 267–268 (Chapter 319).

of the bureau's work remained informational until 1911, when it was superseded by the Industrial Commission.[57]

Despite these limitations, BLIS nonetheless provided the state's most accurate, continuous record of working conditions between 1883 and 1910. In 1894, it reported 309 industrial accidents, forty-four of them fatal. In 1898, it found only sixty-two accidents with ten fatalities, expressed skepticism about employers' reporting of mishaps, and blandly observed that under laissez-faire capitalism, and lacking adequate legislation and enforcement, there could be no guarantees of health and safety. In 1902, the bureau recorded 2,043 accidents and forty-eight fatalities, again lamenting that the law did not compel employers to reveal "the number and particulars of each accident." The bureau reported 1,285 accidents in 1903 and 3,443 in 1905.[58]

In the 1907-1908 report, BLIS recorded a jump to 7,186 accidents. As for the impact of the 1905 law mandating physician reporting, the bureau matter-of-factly observed that modern industrial methods meant more accidents would occur. The bureau devoted 140 pages of its 1909-1910 report and seven pages of its subsequent one to "Industrial Accidents And Employers' Liability." It seems fair to credit those efforts with doing much to build the climate of opinion that produced Wisconsin's epochal workmen's compensation law in 1911. Armed with that law, and with broad new powers for factory inspection and enforcement, the newly created Wisconsin Industrial Commission reported 19,911 industrial accidents between September, 1911, and April, 1914, though it cautioned that only 1,386 would have been counted under the old law.[59]

Of all the work-related social and political issues in the period 1890-1920, none was more momentous than employment of children and women. The new industrialism had undermined the importance of skill and strength and worsened age and gender differentials in wages, so many employers looked to women and children as the surest way to cut labor costs. Coincidentally, the rising cost of living lowered the incomes of millions of male heads of household, forcing

---

[57] Bureau of Labor and Industrial Statistics, *Biennial Report*, 1887-1888, p. ix; 1897-1898, p. 440; 1900-1901, p. 1220. The Bureau almost certainly underestimated the number of industrial accidents. Before a 1905 mandated reporting by physicians, it relied upon notification by employers. Its successor, the Industrial Commission, claimed that thorough statistics of accidents were not available when it assumed responsibility in 1911.

[58] Bureau of Labor and Industrial Statistics, *Biennial Report*, 1893-1894, pp. 193-198; 1897-1898, pp. xii-xiii, 451-452; 1900-1901, pp. 1215-1220; 1903-1904, pp. 76-77; 1905-1906, p. 1209.

[59] *Ibid.*, 1907-1908, pp. 3-143; 1909-1910, pp. 71-142; Industrial Commission, *Report on Allied Functions for the Two Years Ending June 30, 1914* (1914).

more wives and children into the workplace. They then unintentionally provided employers with a rationale for keeping incomes low and displacing adult males. In Wisconsin, the ranks of child labor peaked in 1910 at 23,898, representing 2.7 per cent of the work force and fully 8 per cent of the population between ten and fifteen years of age. To be sure, not all these children labored in mills, foundries, or tanneries; about half were agricultural workers, and presumably they benefited from the fresh air and sunshine.[60]

Before 1900, awareness of child labor was largely limited to the working class, which displayed a mixture of self-interest and empathy. Organized labor instinctively recognized child labor as a threat to wage levels and jobs, and generally sought to abolish or curtail it. But most child laborers came from working-class families that needed the additional income, and sympathy for them led to remedies that would only ameliorate the practice and not abolish it. Improving wages, working conditions, and hours for child workers frequently seemed the best resolution, one that had some hope of success against the phalanx of employers.

Gradually, a consensus developed among middle- and upper-middle-class Americans that bolstered organized labor's position about child labor's evils. They were brought around in several ways. Muckraking investigators sensitized the comfortable classes with exposés like John Spargo's *The Bitter Cry of the Children* (1906). Sixty-nine periodical articles on child labor appeared between 1902 and 1906, compared to only four in the preceding five years. Social workers and government agencies documented the evils of child labor in chilling bureaucratic prose. Women's clubs, religious and civic organizations, and study groups relentlessly aired the issue. In 1904, a group of social workers and Social Gospel ministers formed the National Child Labor Committee, which co-ordinated investigations, publications, boycotts, and lobbying. In 1907, the committee hired photographer Lewis W. Hine, born and raised in Oshkosh, to capture the evils of child labor in pictures and words. He traversed the country for the next several years, developing ingenious methods for deceiving employers while surreptitiously taking thousands of graphic pictures. Armed with this overwhelming evidence, the committee pushed for both state and federal legislation. In response, the federal government sponsored children's conferences, established the Children's

---

[60] Walter I. Trattner, *Crusade for the Children: A History of the National Child Labor Committee and Child Labor Reform in America* (Chicago, 1970), 21–44; *Eleventh Census of the United States, 1890: Population, Progress of the Nation, Part 2*, p. 360; *Fourteenth Census of the United States, 1920: Children in Gainful Occupations*, 11–13. Wisconsin consistently ranked below national norms in the number of children employed.

Bureau in 1912, and passed a short-lived child labor law in 1916—by which time thirty-five states had enacted child labor laws of one kind or another.[61]

In Wisconsin, concern over child labor mirrored the national pattern. Prodded by the State Federation of Labor and the Social Democratic party during the 1890's, the legislature enacted fairly minor restrictions on work hours and conditions and charged the Bureau of Labor and Industrial Statistics to enforce them. Until about 1900, the bureau seemed remarkably sanguine, generally accepting data returned by employers at face value, and taking a detached, almost clinical approach.[62]

Then things began to change. An 1899 law prohibited all work by children under fourteen, restricted the hours worked by those under sixteen, and empowered the BLIS to visit, inspect, and enforce the law. Spurred to action at last, the bureau responded with a 142-page report that took a much stronger position. It acknowledged that many employers did treat child workers decently, but concluded that many others displayed "the grossest inhumanity." The reports of its factory inspectors were rife with "tales of cruel neglect and maltreatment of defenseless working children by the proprietors of workshops that would read well beside the history of the early days of English factory life." All too often, young workers were "crowded into unsafe and unwholesome rooms whose floors, in most cases, are covered with filth and uncared for refuse, whose atmosphere is one perpetual stench of sickening disease-breeding odors, to which vulgarity, blasphemy and indecency add their polluting influence, and compelled to do work too exacting and severe for their feeble strength." The bureau found 945 workers under age fourteen in an investigation of seventy-five establishments in eleven industries. It praised organized labor for its support, and castigated employers for their opposition.[63]

Despite stronger laws and enforcement, child labor persisted. In 1901, BLIS acknowledged that the prohibition against employing any one under fourteen was violated extensively, assuredly far more youngsters had been employed than the 688 who had been discovered and had been relieved of their jobs under the law. In 1903, six

[61] Trattner, *Crusade for the Children*, 21–68; Judith M. Gutman, *Lewis W. Hine and the American Social Conscience* (New York, 1967; 2nd ed., *Lewis W. Hine, 1874–1940: Two Perspectives*, London, 1974), 12–35, 68–107; Walter Rosenblum, Naomi Rosenblum, and Alan Trachtenberg, *America and Lewis Hine: Photographs, 1904–1940* (Millerton, New York, 1977), 12–14, 18–20, 33–35, 46–50, 54–55, 59, 68, 71, 84–87; Hugh C. Bailey, *Edgar Gardner Murphy: Gentle Progressive* (Coral Gables, Florida, 1968), 65–108.

[62] Bureau of Labor and Industrial Statistics, *Biennial Report*, 1897–1898, pp. 540–554.

[63] *Ibid.*, 1899–1900, pp. 266–406.

hundred more were dismissed from work and, in 1905, an additional 357. Later, the legislature tightened the law and prohibited employing anyone under sixteen in dangerous occupations, or more than fifty-five hours a week. It led BLIS to dismiss 1,174 illegal workers between November, 1906, and July, 1908; but it also issued 11,649 work permits. During the next fiscal year, the number of permits dropped to 6,345, a figure which did not include large numbers of children aged fourteen and fifteen who worked on farms, as domestics or newsboys, or in various street trades. The bureau also noted that, contrary to its own statistics, more young girls than boys were employed, legally or illegally.[64]

BLIS estimated that earnings from child labor kept 30 per cent of the 4,009 families it surveyed above a $650 annual income poverty line for a family of six in 1910. It calculated that 55 per cent of those families were distressed anyway, and charged that many of the rest resorted to child labor because they were improvident and heedless of the risks to their children's health and well-being. In its last biennial report (1910–1911), the bureau published a special study of truancy which concluded that 27 per cent of the state's children between the ages of seven and fourteen did not attend school. Another report on the newsboys of Milwaukee proposed regulating all street trading, not just selling newspapers, which were the principal sources of communication before radio appeared popularly in the 1920's and 1930's.

Charles (later Carl) Sandburg, the poet and historian who was then secretary to Milwaukee's Socialist mayor Emil Seidel, added an articulate voice to the child labor crusade in a series of articles for the Milwaukee *Social Democratic Herald* between December 16, 1909, and January 1, 1910. Sandburg expressed outrage at the number of young men "shut out from the finer chances of life, in mills and factories, running from Kenosha to Superior, and from Marinette to Madison." Encouraged by legislation enacted in 1911 and 1913, the new Industrial Commission rejoiced that "the child labor problem is no longer to any great extent concerned with the enforcement of the law regulating hours and employments, but rather with the need for aiding children to secure proper employment with fair rates of pay, and finding a remedy for the constant shifting that now is the rule of child employment."[65]

The dialogue over the changing role of women in the workplace proved to be more portentous than that over child labor. The number

---

[64] *Ibid.*, 1900–1901, pp. 1224–1230; 1903–1904, pp. 1307–1310; 1905–1906, pp. 1301–1309; 1907–1908, pp. 657–661; 1909–1910, pp. 499–574.

[65] *Ibid.*, 1910–1911, pp. 31–96; Milwaukee *Social Democratic Herald*, January 1, 1910; Industrial Commission, *Report on Allied Functions for the Year Ending June 30, 1914* (1914), 53–57.

of gainfully employed children declined by more than one-third in the 1910's. But for women, the trend was opposite. By 1914, women constituted one-fifth of the work force, and nearly one woman in four was gainfully employed. Whether or not they worked outside the home, Wisconsin women retained primary responsibility for managing households and rearing children. The introduction of household appliances and the development of domestic science eliminated much back-breaking drudgery. But appliances also raised the standards of housework dramatically, so, at a time when hired help was disappearing, the number of hours required by housework remained about the same. Even relatively affluent women, with the help of a single servant, regularly spent between fifty-six and sixty hours a week cooking, baking, straightening rooms, sewing, ordering food, caring for children, managing household accounts, scrubbing floors, laundering, beating rugs, washing windows, ironing, and more. Almost everyone equated housework with "women's work," regardless of class, and females could expect no help from males even when they worked outside the home. Their only hope of relief lay in domestic science, and in appliances that most families could not afford nor could they run, since as late as 1912, only 16 per cent of the nation's homes had been wired for electricity.[66]

With some variation, that same situation confronted Wisconsin's other large category of "invisible workers": farm women. The themes that farm women worked too long and hard, and that their husbands and fathers were loath to share the burden or pay for new household technologies, permeated agricultural publications. In a column entitled "The Farmer's Wife," *The Wisconsin Agriculturist* argued in 1903 that farm women must know the ins and outs of dairying, cooking, butchering, rug making, poultry raising, nursing, dressmaking, laundering, and finance. The *Agriculturist* sometimes blamed women for shouldering non-essentials, but it also periodically reminded male readers that their wives were equally entitled to labor-saving devices because their work was equally important and their income depended on the work of both. *Hoard's Dairyman* sounded the same refrain.[67]

But some commentators suggested that farm women should take

---

[66] *Fourteenth Census of the United States, 1920: Children in Gainful Occupations*, 12–14; Schwartz-Cowan, *More Work for Mother*, 69–172; S. J. Kleinberg, "Escalating Standards: Women, Housework and Household Technology in the Twentieth Century," in Frank J. Coppa and Richard Hammond, eds., *Technology in the Twentieth Century* (Dubuque, 1983), 1–2; Glenna Matthews, *"Just a Housewife": The Rise and Fall of Domesticity in America* (New York, 1987), 35–173.

[67] Department of Agriculture, *Annual Report*, 1911, pp. 361–362; *Wisconsin Agriculturist*, June 17, 1897, p. 12; September 23, 1903, p. 12; August 27, 1908, p. 14; *Hoard's Dairyman*, April 23, 1909, p. 398.

on additional tasks. Dean William Henry of the College of Agriculture urged women to take up buttermaking because it was easier and less confining than keeping house and less tiring than teaching. The *Agriculturist* noted with satisfaction that one farm wife had branched out into the wallpaper supply business, and suggested that others could earn extra spending money by raising poultry or canning tomatoes. For the most part, however, observers acknowledged that farm women were already overburdened, and they concentrated on offering solutions and on raising the husbands' consciousness. There exists little or no evidence that many Wisconsin farmers actually purchased vacuum cleaners or washing machines to make life easier for their wives.[68]

The position of the farmer's wife was felt to be analogous to the female worker at the mill or factory. She was regarded as a mere sojourner, temporarily outside her natural sphere, of limited usefulness, whose earnings were purely supplementary, and whose existence posed a threat to male workers' livelihoods. Indeed, working women were largely young and single, were of recent immigrant stock, and remained in the work force for a relatively brief period— five years or less. The vast majority worked in occupations overwhelmingly populated by women, were virtually unrepresented in skilled or supervisory positions, earned incomes half those of men, and almost never belonged to labor unions.[69]

In 1907, some 95 per cent of all adult women workers toiled in only forty-seven of the census bureau's 303 enumerated occupations.

---

[68] William Henry, "A New Opening," in *Wisconsin Agriculturist*, May 15, 1894; April 1, 1895, p. 10; December 9, 1897, p. 10; *Second Wisconsin Country Life Conference* (Madison, 1912), 7–10; *Wisconsin Agriculturist*, January 14, 1915, p. 18; *Wisconsin Farmer*, July 13, 1916, p. 906.

[69] *Eleventh Census of the United States, 1890: Occupations, Part 2*, pp. 337–341, 408–413; *Fourteenth Census of the United States, 1920: Occupations, Volume IV*, 797–798; *Twelfth Census of the United States, 1900: Special Report on Occupations*, 508–509; Bureau of Labor and Industrial Statistics, *Biennial Report*, 1895–1896, pp. 105–107, 392–393; 1898–1899, pp. 481, 647–656, 765; 1903–1904, p. 249; Industrial Commission, *Cost of Living of Wage Earning Women in Wisconsin* (1916), 19–20; Industrial Commission, *Report on Pea Canneries, Season of 1913: Hours of Labor of Female Employes* (1913), 17; Jean Krueger, "A Study of the Working Periods of Wage-Earning Women in Wisconsin, Based upon Statistics Gathered by the State Industrial Commission" (master's thesis, University of Wisconsin, 1917), 18–21; Ann Marie Larson, " 'Put Yourself in Her Place': The Serving Class of the Midwest, 1890–1915" (senior research paper, Cooperstown Graduate Program of the State University of New York at Oneonta, 1985, in the New York State Historical Association library, Cooperstown), 95. Such patterns were nationwide. See for example, Julie A. Matthaei, *An Economic History of Women in America: Women's Work, the Sexual Division of Labor, and the Development of Capitalism* (New York, 1982), 101–240, and Joseph A. Hill, *Women in Gainful Occupations, 1870 to 1920* (U.S. Census Monograph, 1929, reprinted, New York, 1972), 7–134.

Nearly half of Wisconsin's female work force was found in occupations almost exclusively filled by women. There were almost no women in heavy industry or in most of the skilled crafts, but they dominated the textile industry and needle trades, domestic and personal service, teaching, some semiskilled occupations, and, increasingly, department store clerking and low-level office work. But where men and women worked in the same industry or factory, the women were usually relegated to a limited number of specific, low-paid, unskilled or semiskilled jobs. As late as 1913, even unionized women earned about half the wages of organized males. Their annual earnings were about $429 a year at a time when the state calculated that $494 was the minimum on which a woman could survive on her own.[70]

Women themselves usually bore the onus for their own underrepresentation in organized labor. In 1913, a survey covering three-fourths of the state's unions reported that only twelve of seventy-two had any women members and that 80 per cent of all union members were skilled men. Only garment workers, boot and shoe, musicians, and bottling unions reported significant numbers of women. Unions typically viewed women as pawns in employers' efforts to de-skill work, undermine wage scales and worker control, and destroy the labor movement. The unions reasoned that women were transient workers with no aspirations to permanent jobs and no breadwinning responsibilities; they lacked solidarity and a desire to unionize; and they worked in jobs that unions were reluctant to organize. The unions feared that actions designed to improve wages, hours, or working conditions for women might undermine the concept of the "family wage," take jobs away from male heads of household, and vitiate unionization. Therefore, why bother with women?[71]

Despite the antipathy—or, at best, the apathy—of organized labor and the opposition of most employers, the plight of Wisconsin women workers began to receive sympathetic attention around 1900. Women's groups, mixed-gender reform organizations, and those who

---

[70] U.S. Bureau of the Census, *Statistics of Women at Work Based on Unpublished Information from the Schedules of the Twelfth Census: 1900* (1907); Bureau of Labor and Industrial Statistics, *Biennial Report*, 1905–1906, pp. 925, 990–991; Wisconsin State Federation of Labor, *Labor Conditions in Wisconsin: A Report by the Executive Board* (5 vols., Milwaukee, 1913–1917), 1913, p. 9.

[71] Kessler-Harris, *Out To Work*, 152–157, 202–204; Foner, *Women and the American Labor Movement*, 213–255; Barbara Mayer Wertheimer, *We Were There: The Story of Working Women in America* (New York, 1977), 198–376; Alice Henry, *Women and the Labor Movement* (New York, 1923), 53–106; Wisconsin State Federation of Labor, *Labor Conditions in Wisconsin*, 9–10; Bureau of Labor and Industrial Statistics, *Biennial Report*, 1907–1908, pp. 1053–1054; Alice Kessler-Harris, "Where are the Organized Women Workers?" in *Feminist Studies*, 3 (Fall, 1975), 92–110.

had campaigned against child labor started the work. Principal among them was the Federation of Women's Clubs, founded in 1896 by middle- and upper-class women, which addressed problems and promulgated solutions for many civic and cultural problems, including industrial and social conditions. The National Consumers' League, founded contemporaneously in New York with state leagues quickly following, aimed at improving working conditions for women and children through direct action by consumers and by advocating protective legislation. The league surveyed working conditions, requested reforms, boycotted businesses that refused to co-operate, and rewarded those that did with a "white label" and a place on its "white list." In Wisconsin, the two organizations began a collaboration in 1899 that continued into the 1930's.[72]

Other groups also promoted the cause of working women. The Women's Union Label League, founded in 1899, was primarily an organization of working-class women endorsed by the American Federation of Labor. It supported the eight-hour day, abolition of child labor, equal pay for women, and shop and factory reforms. The Women's Trade Union League, formed by the AFL at its 1903 convention, was a coalition of working- and middle-class women dedicated to fostering female labor organizations. The American Association for Labor Legislation, founded in Madison in 1906 by University of Wisconsin economists Richard T. Ely, John R. Commons, and John B. Andrews, influenced public opinion and lawmakers by publishing research, testifying before investigative bodies, and drafting legislation.[73]

These voluntary associations were supplemented by federal and state public bodies such as the U.S. Bureau of Labor Statistics, Wisconsin's Bureau of Labor and Industrial Statistics and later its Industrial Commission, and a 1913 joint legislative committee which investigated organized vice (often known as the Teasdale Vice Com-

---

[72] Karen J. Blair, *The Clubwoman as Feminist: True Womanhood Redefined, 1868–1914* (New York, 1980), 93–116; Louis I. Athey, "The Consumers League and Social Reform" (doctoral dissertation, University of Delaware, 1965), 109–204; Halford Erickson, "The Consumer's Influence on Production," in Bureau of Labor and Industrial Statistics, *Biennial Report*, 1900–1901, pp. 282–314; Elizabeth Anne Payne, *Reform, Labor and Feminism: Margaret Drier Robins and the Women's Trade Union League* (Urbana, 1988), 44–116; Irwin Yellowitz, *Labor and the Progressive Movement in New York State, 1897–1916* (Ithaca, 1965), 40–144; Genevieve G. McBride, *On Wisconsin Women: Working for Their Rights from Settlement to Suffrage* (Madison, 1993); Genevieve G. McBride, "Theodora Winton Youmans and the Wisconsin Woman Movement," in *WMH*, 71 (Summer, 1988), 243–275.

[73] Belva Mary Heron, "Labor Organizations among Women," in University of Illinois, *Bulletin*, no. 2 (1905), 52–58; Nancy Schrom Dye, *As Equals and As Sisters: Feminism, the Labor Movement, and the Women's Trade Union League of New York* (Columbia, Missouri, 1980), 1–7.

mittee for its chairman, Senator Howard Teasdale of Sparta). BLIS published reports on topics like "Sweating in the Garment-Making Trades," "Women Workers in Milwaukee Tanneries," and "Women Engaged in Factories," in which it matter-of-factly cataloged industry's ills and abuses. The Industrial Commission concluded that most working women actually either supported themselves or contributed substantially to the family kitty, and that they were not working merely for "pin money," as employers contended. And the legislature's "vice committee" unearthed a wealth of information on wages, hours, and working conditions in Wisconsin cities as it looked into the causes of prostitution and organized vice. Not the least shocking revelation was testimony that prostitutes in Milwaukee commonly earned ten dollars a day, after deducting their expenses—more than most female workers earned in a week.[74]

Newspapers gave these findings great exposure. Foremost among them was the Milwaukee *Leader*, the official organ of both the Social Democratic party and the Wisconsin State Federation of Labor. The plight of women workers consistently outraged the *Leader*, but the paper frequently displayed confusion over whether the solution lay in banning women, organizing them into unions, or advocating protective legislation. The paper endorsed a Socialist alderman's efforts to bar women from working in tanneries and foundries, and it agreed with Frank J. Weber, secretary of the Federated Trades Council, that "thousands of girls and young women are suffering intolerable conditions and working for starvation wages in Milwaukee's shops and factories because they refuse to organize into trade unions, hoping that some young man will come along and marry them and thus release them from their slavery." The *Leader* also urged "another attempt at organizing the women in the laundries of Milwaukee," noting that the "success that accompanied the organization of the girls in the breweries is pointed out as indicative of what can be accomplished in the laundries." It lauded the Industrial Commission for refusing to grant exemptions to the maximum hours law for women, as requested by the state's confectioners, hosiery and shoe manufacturers, and the Wisconsin Telephone Company.[75]

---

[74] Marie Obenauer, "Employment of Women in Power Laundries in Milwaukee," U.S. Bureau of Labor Statistics, *Bulletin*, no. 122 (1913), 73–79; Bureau of Labor and Industrial Statistics, *Biennial Report*, 1900–1901, pp. 177–281, 641–759; 1907–1908, pp. 1027–1173; Industrial Commission, *Cost of Living of Wage Earning Women*, 8–20; Legislature, Committee on White Slave Traffic and Kindred Subjects, *Report and Recommendations of the Wisconsin Legislative Committee to Investigate the White Slave Traffic and Kindred Subjects* (1914).

[75] Milwaukee *Leader*, December 6, 1912, January 4, October 4, 30 (quote), and December 8, 19, 1913.

In reporting state vital statistics in 1914, the *Leader* noted that "women having a gainful occupation to which they may return more readily seek divorce than those who have no gainful occupation," and also noted that the other states urged the minimum wage for girls as a preventive against the rapacity of employers." Accordingly, the *Leader* favored banning young women from certain categories of domestic employment. It acknowledged that the female strikers at a Milwaukee shoe factory picket were more militant than the men, and it endorsed laws regulating minimum wages and maximum hours. The *Leader* and organized labor never totally resolved their confusion, but by 1910 generally lent at least qualified support to protective legislation and to unionizing women generally.[76]

The fact that in Wisconsin organized labor was so heavily socialist made it more receptive to state intervention, and the eagerness of the radical Industrial Workers of the World (IWW) to organize nearly everyone into "one big union" provided additional incentive. The State Federation of Labor also relied upon the co-operation and good will of voluntary associations and state agencies in advancing its own cause. Perhaps some labor leaders believed that disclosure of the federation's evils would either generate a backlash, or ensure protective legislation that would discourage employers from opposing labor. Whatever the reasoning, organized labor in Wisconsin approached both organizing female workers and protective legislation for women and children very warily. It preferred collective bargaining for adult males and remained fearful that legislated minimums and maximums might become permanent standards.[77]

Those who wrote about the plight of Wisconsin women workers painted substantially the same deplorable picture. They found that most women remained in the work force less than five years, were occupationally segregated, and remained on the lowest rungs of the occupational and wage ladders. Nearly all women in the brass industry in 1905 were concentrated in five of fifty-five job categories; and women "owned" only ten of the sixty-nine jobs in the furniture industry. Women earned roughly half what men did, even if both were organized, worked in the same industry, and did the same job. The average annual wage of unionized workers in Wisconsin in 1913 was $712; among women it was $429. Only twelve of the state's seventy-two trade unions recruited women in 1913, and only 8 per cent of the state's unionized work force was female. The state did not appoint

---

[76] *Ibid.*, January 17, 21 (quote), February 13, July 14, and October 16, 1914.

[77] On the general attitude of organized labor towards women and children in the work force, see Irwin Yellowitz, *Industrialization and the American Labor Movement, 1850–1900* (Port Washington, New York, 1977), 3–62, 105–115.

a woman factory inspector until 1901, and not until 1916 did the Industrial Commission have a women's department.[78]

[4]

Powerless to combat these trends as individuals, American workers gradually embraced unionization. Between the Great Strike of 1877 and the Haymarket Riot of 1886, the movement was dominated by the Knights of Labor, who advocated abolition of the wage system, industrial unionism, political action, and organization of all who "gain their bread by the sweat of their brow." After 1886, momentum passed to Samuel Gompers and the American Federation of Labor, which was dedicated to "pure and simple trade unionism." The AFL was divided internally, however, and permitted affiliation by federal or central trade unions that accepted unskilled workers. It made some efforts to organize women, immigrants, and Negroes, and it pledged to work for federal laws that would benefit working people. The AFL majority still remained opposed to organizing unskilled and minority workers, to demands for radical reconstruction of the economic system, and to class-based political activity.[79]

Trade unionists affiliated with the AFL dominated the Wisconsin labor movement, but they held variant views. Milwaukee labor unions had developed largely in response to the new industrialism, so the lines between skilled and unskilled labor, and trade unionism versus political action, were often blurred. When the Milwaukee Federated Trades Council (MFTC) and the Wisconsin State Federation of Labor

[78] Krueger, "A Study of the Working Periods of Wage-Earning Women," 18–21; Bureau of Labor and Industrial Statistics, *Biennial Report*, 1885–1886, p. 295; 1895–1896, pp. 105–107, 392–393; 1899–1900, pp. 481, 647, 651, 656, 765; 1900–1901, pp. 18, 53, 670–671, 681; 1903–1904, p. 249; 1905–1906, pp. 990–991; Industrial Commission, *Cost of Living of Wage Earning Women in Wisconsin*, 19–20; Industrial Commission, *Denial of Petition of Extending Women's Hours in Candy Factories* (1913), 10; Industrial Commission, *Report on Pea Canneries, Season of 1913: Hours of Labor of Female Employes*, 6; Industrial Commission, *Report on Allied Functions, 1912–1914* (1914), 48–50; Wisconsin State Federation of Labor, *Labor Conditions in Wisconsin: A Report by the Executive Board of the Wisconsin State Federation of Labor* (Milwaukee, 1913), 9; Gordon M. Haferbecker, *Wisconsin Labor Laws* (Madison, 1958), 91–103; Gertrude Schmidt Weiss, "History of Labor Legislation in Wisconsin" (doctoral dissertation, University of Wisconsin, 1933), 235–236; *Milwaukee Leader*, July 17, 1913.

[79] Philip S. Foner, *History of the Labor Movement in the United States: From Colonial Times to the Founding of the American Federation of Labor* (New York, 1947), vol. 1, pp. 409–524; vol.2 (1955), 11–30; Joseph G. Rayback, *A History of American Labor* (New York, 1959; expanded and updated, 1966), 54–185; Norman J. Ware, *The Labor Movement in the United States, 1860–1895* (New York, 1929), 155–190; Yellowitz, *Industrialzation and American Labor*, 3–9, 37–46; Thomas W. Gavett, *Development of the Labor Movement in Milwaukee* (Madison, 1965), 27–34.

(WSFL) emerged as Milwaukee's affiliates of the AFL, Socialists led them, and Socialists' acceptance of capitalism and aversion to industrial unionism and political action were highly suspect. Then progressive Republicans intensified their bid for working-class votes by supporting labor legislation, and the Socialist-trade union alliance adapted to keep pace. The continued influx of German skilled workers predisposed the MFTC and WSFL towards revisionist Socialism, while the need to broaden their appeal to Polish and other eastern European workers inclined them to political action. On the employer side, T. A. Chapman, E. P. Allis, Valentine Blatz, and others moved towards a paternalistic stance, and thus tended to undermine business opposition to pro-labor legislation. From the 1870's on, state government had, albeit grudgingly and sporadically, enacted pro-labor measures, ranging from restrictions on child labor to regulation of apprenticeships.[80]

Before 1886, organized labor in Milwaukee was divided between the Knights of Labor and the Central Labor Union (CLU). The Knights established forty-two local assemblies with 25,000 members, about half of whom worked in Milwaukee. The CLU had 5,300 members. The two temporarily suspended their rivalry to co-operate in the Eight-Hour League, which successfully lobbied for a city ordinance that gave municipal employees the eight-hour day. This momentum led to a major recruiting drive by both unions, setting in motion events that culminated in the Bay View massacre of May, 1886.

Public reaction to Bay View temporarily crippled both organizations. Recovery began in February, 1887, when Milwaukee molders, typographers, and cigar makers formed the Milwaukee Federated Trades Council, which was quickly embraced by the national AFL. The MFTC constitution specifically banned organized political action and emphasized "unity of action and organization among working people . . . to combat the evergrowing encroachments of organized and consolidated capital." Quarrels over political action, industrial unionism, and socialism plagued the MFTC in its early years. External problems also hurt it. MFTC and the decimated Knights of Labor established competing locals in several crafts, and jurisdictional disputes and bickering weakened both. By November, 1890, there were fifty-two trade unions in Milwaukee, with memberships ranging from fifty to 700.[81]

---

[80] Gavett, *Development of the Labor Movement*, 3–10, 90–113, 202–210; Ozanne, *Labor Movement in Wisconsin*, 34–56; J. David Hoeveler, Jr., "The University and the Social Gospel: The Intellectual Origins of the 'Wisconsin Idea,' " in *WMH*, 59 (Summer, 1976), 282–298.

[81] Gavett, *Development of Labor Movement*, 5–34, 77–78 (quote); Ozanne, *Labor Movement in Wisconsin*, 3–6.

Relations with the national AFL also were strained, as local MFTC interests sometimes conflicted with national policy. More important was an internal dispute between MFTC and its member building trades unions, who wanted greater autonomy. Although the MFTC successfully co-ordinated an 1891 strike of several building trades locals, the locals formed a council that remained independent from 1897 to 1907. MFTC also failed to assist the Amalgamated Association of Street Railway Employees effectively during its month-long strike against the Milwaukee Electric Railway and Light Company in 1896, a conflict described by Samuel Gompers as "a strike without parallel in the labor world." Combining strikebreakers, great wealth, and political clout, the company crushed the fledgling union, despite public opinion in favor of the workers.[82]

The MFTC focus on trade union activity did not lead it to ignore political action. In October, 1893, its leaders organized for the municipal elections by meeting with representatives of the Populists, the Socialist Labor party, and the newly formed Social Democratic Verein (League), a group of thirty or so German-speaking "revisionist" socialists with trade-union ties. Victor Berger led the Social Democratic Verein and became editor of *Vorwärts* in 1893. He saw to it that *Vorwärts* was designated as the state's official labor newspaper. The coalition united under the banner of the Cooperative Labor Ticket. Thus, the MFTC abandoned its aversion to political action and suspicion of co-operation with non-trade unionists, adopting a declaration of principles with a decidedly Socialist-Populist bent. It endorsed federal or municipal ownership of all public utilities, the direct election of all officials, and a number of Populist monetary reforms.[83]

The Cooperative Labor Ticket received less than 8 per cent of the statewide gubernatorial vote in 1894, but the coalition continued under the label of the People's party. After much infighting, the Populist convention of 1894 endorsed both the People's party platform and the AFL's political program, a victory for the Socialists because the AFL program demanded collective ownership of all means of production and distribution. When the Populist ticket, backed by the *Vorwärts*, received 10,000 Wisconsin votes in 1894 and 1896, Berger proclaimed that he would continue the alliance, provided the members moved in the right direction. The Populist nomination of Dem-

---

[82] Gavett, *Development of the Labor Movement*, 81–88.
[83] *Ibid.*, 88–93; Theodore Mueller, "Milwaukee Labor Movement," unpublished paper at the Milwaukee County Historical Society, 17–24. For a detailed development of the internal struggle over political action, see Writings of Frank J. Weber, box 3, and Minutes of Meetings, 1900–1903, box 6, in Federated Trades Council of Milwaukee Records, 1900–1950, University of Wisconsin-Milwaukee Area Research Center.

ocrat William Jennings Bryan for president that fall generated a leftwing Socialist bolt to the Marxist Socialist Labor party (SLP).

Berger and his followers affiliated with a different Socialist party: the Social Democratic party (SDP), founded by Eugene V. Debs after the federal government had crushed his American Railway Union during the Pullman Strike in 1894. On July 7, 1897, Debs made an impassioned plea for the SDP to an enthusiastic crowd at Milwaukee's West Side Turner Hall. Two days later, Milwaukeeans organized Branch One of the Social Democratic party, and in early August the MFTC endorsed it.[84]

The euphoria of the MFTC-SDP marriage lasted only a few months. The MFTC and several other local trade unions sent delegates to the SDP's 1898 convention, which adopted a platform and ticket that appealed to them. However, the ticket received only 2,500 votes in the municipal elections, and many Socialists were convinced that trade unions had secretly aided a Populist-Democratic fusion. The MFTC and the SDP continued to work together, but the antagonism of non-Socialist unions grew more apparent. In December, 1899, by a large majority, the MFTC elected an executive committee comprised entirely of Socialists, led by Berger, who in *Vorwärts* insisted that, although trade unions were proletarian class organizations, they must function solely in the private sector and organize workers of every political affiliation. Berger did acknowledge, however, that the seventy trade unions of the MFTC "offer us a broad field for our socialistic agitation of the Social-Democratic type of Socialism."[85]

In February, 1900, the MFTC agreed to elect delegates to the city convention of the SDP. Sixty-seven of the 147 were union members, and the nominated candidates came exclusively from union ranks. The convention also urged all SDP members to join a union. The MFTC later endorsed the SDP slate, prompting about a dozen non-Socialists to walk out and nine to resign. These dissidents appealed to the executive board of the AFL, which instructed Frank Weber, MFTC's leader and the AFL state organizer, to deny their request. Completely victorious, the Socialists thereupon rewrote the MFTC constitution to include support for collective ownership, public works for the unemployed, national accident, unemployment, and retirement insurance, and international arbitration for war. They stopped short of endorsing the SDP by name, but charged all members "to actively support, with their ballots and otherwise, the political party

---

[84] Gavett, *Development of the Labor Movement*, 81–88; Roger E. Wyman, "Voting Behavior in the Progressive Era: Wisconsin as a Case Study" (doctoral dissertation, University of Wisconsin, 1970), 153–211, 526, 570–573, 836–841.

[85] Gavett, *Development of the Labor Movement*, 95–97.

whose platform is nearest to the . . . declaration of principles and the . . . demands."

Thus joined, the SDP and the MFTC in effect had an interlocking directorate with several prominent individuals in positions of power in both organizations. The MFTC contributed money to SDP campaigns and enterprises, such as the Social Democratic Printing Company and the People's Realty Company. It adopted both the *Vorwärts* and the English-language *Social Democratic Herald* (soon to become the Milwaukee *Leader*) as official newspapers. The SDP required that all members join unions, patronize only businesses displaying the union label, nominate union leaders and members for office, and function as the political arm of the MFTC.

In 1902, anti-Socialists formed the Central Trade and Labor Union (CTLU), which Samuel Gompers and the national AFL leadership at first refused to recognize. Gompers' and the AFL's growing fear of radicalism, however, eventually worked to the CTLU's advantage. In July, 1902, the MFTC alarmed the AFL by proposing an organization called the National Municipal Labor League to co-ordinate activities on the city and state levels. The AFL quickly condemned the idea because it appeared to be intended to bring about a new federation of labor. This negative reaction and a lukewarm response by central labor organizations divided the MFTC leadership, with Weber acting as peacemaker. Relations between Gompers and the Socialists worsened in the 1890's as well, each side accusing the other of sabotaging the labor movement. The MFTC consistently pressed the AFL to endorse independent action by working-class parties, accused Gompers of "throwing the labor vote to capitalist candidates in the hope of getting labor legislation out of them," and refused to join the AFL in endorsing Republican union member W. J. Cary of Milwaukee for Congress.[86]

Berger and the Socialists in the MFTC steadfastly refused to secede from the AFL, believing that such action "would be a crime against the trades unions and a fatal error in . . . Socialist propaganda." However, Berger did oppose the Industrial Workers of the World (IWW), and at first the MFTC refused to join him in denouncing that more radical group. Berger eventually prevailed, and both the MFTC and the WSFL drafted letters denouncing the IWW. A meeting in Racine between Berger and Eugene V. Debs, who founded the Social Democratic party and supported the IWW, only heated the controversy.

---

[86] *Ibid.*, 97–102. See also Frederick I. Olson, "The Socialist Party and the Union in Milwaukee, 1900–1912," in *WMH*, 44 (Winter, 1960–1961), 110–116; Marvin Wachman, *History of the Social-Democratic Party of Milwaukee, 1897–1910* (Urbana, 1945), 10–74, and Carl D. Thompson, *Labor Measures of the Social-Democrats Milwaukee Administration* (n.p., 1911).

Berger felt that the SDP could not survive without trade unions' support, so he adamantly opposed Debs's experiment in industrial unionism. Berger insisted that he harbored no illusions about the conservatism and narrow self-interest of the craft unions, and he warned Socialists against overestimating trade-union commitment to the fundamental social and economic tasks of the labor movement. He stressed his belief in a "personal union of the workers–[by] having the same persons take an active interest in both the trade-union and the political labor movement," thus forming "a giant army moving on two roads for the abolition of the capitalist system." Berger eschewed militant strikes, preferring to win concessions through labor solidarity, integrity, and steadfastness. Milwaukee unionists adopted the rhetoric and program of Socialism, but concentrated upon wage increases, better working conditions, and the enactment of labor legislation within the prevailing economic order. They viewed Socialism as what labor historian Thomas W. Gavett has called "a unifying ideology through which they could channel their drives and ambitions." Both parties to what came to be known in the labor movement as the "Milwaukee Idea" found common ground in that idea through compromise, pragmatism, and caution.[87]

For a few years after the Milwaukee Idea fell into place, the labor movement expanded dramatically. Between late 1899 and early 1904, the number of affiliated locals in the MFTC jumped from seventy to 105, membership increased from 20,000 to 23,000, and it hired a full-time business agent. But that early promise was followed by a decade of stagnation so debilitating that the MFTC actually had fewer members in 1914 than in 1904. One of the primary reasons was ethnocultural conflict between the predominantly Teutonic and Yankee leadership of the MFTC and the rank-and-file workers, who were principally southern and eastern European, especially Polish. Ethnic antagonism, disputes over which language to use in meetings, and the powerful opposition of the Catholic church to socialism had a dampening effect. Equally distracting was the amount of time and energy expended by MFTC leaders on "union welfarism" at the expense of organizing drives. In addition to agitating for health and safety improvements, member unions opened a home for sick and disabled workers, raised money for the unemployed, and lobbied the common council.[88]

More rewarding in the long run were the MFTC's lobbying efforts to transfer responsibility to the state for health and safety, unemployment and workmen's compensation, and the welfare of women

[87] Gavett, *Development of the Labor Movement*, 102–105; Milwaukee *Leader*, August 19, 21, 1913.
[88] Gavett, *Development of the Labor Movement*, 114–117.

and child workers. MFTC also tried to expand, but was handicapped by infighting with the Milwaukee Building Trades Council. After five years of separate activity, the two organizations explored a possible merger in late 1900, but efforts foundered because of the building trades group's insistence upon retaining its own charter and union card. The MFTC established its own building trades section in 1905, and the two bodies merged temporarily two years later. The trades council received a charter from the building trades department of the AFL, but the Panic of 1907 reduced membership, and both organizations continued to squabble over jurisdiction, political action, and trade autonomy.[89]

As important as these problems were, they paled into insignificance beside employer efforts to undermine unionism. Between 1904 and 1915, the National Association of Manufacturers, the National Metals Association, and the National Founders Association worked hard against unions in response to unprecedented union growth between 1897 and 1903, when membership quadrupled. Business and industry mobilized an arsenal: strikebreakers, coercion, court injunctions, open shop campaigns, Americanization programs, and company unions. Many of the larger, "enlightened" employers joined Gompers and other labor leaders, as well as "disinterested" scholars, in the National Civic Federation. The group was dedicated to preventing conflict and violence through welfare programs, to safety movements, the arbitration of disputes, and promoting acceptance of unions by management. In Milwaukee, as elsewhere, employers' attitudes ran the gamut from grudging toleration to outright hostility. The Milwaukee Foundrymen's Association (MFA) included most of the city's metalworking companies and took its lead from the parent National Founders Association, whose name varied slightly from the local group's. When the coremakers union struck in 1902 over demands for a minimum wage and a ten-hour day, the MFA proclaimed a commitment to an open shop. All relations between MFA members and the union ceased in November, 1904. The MFA and the Metal Trades Association formed the Metal Trades and Founders Bureau, dedicated to making Milwaukee an open-shop city by using strikebreakers, detectives, and blacklists. By 1905, the use of detectives and other methods of industrial spying was widespread.[90]

The Milwaukee Merchants' and Manufacturers' Association, local affiliate of the National Association of Manufacturers, established a

---

[89] Korman, *Industrialization, Immigrants, and Americanizers*, 52–53.

[90] Gavett, *Development of the Labor Movement*, 117–122; Montgomery, *Fall of the House of Labor*, 5–6; Montgomery, *Workers' Control in America*, 49–67; Ozanne, *Labor Movement in Wisconsin*, 26–28, 31–33; Darryl Holter, "Labor Spies and Union-Busting in Wisconsin, 1890–1940," in *WMH*, 68 (Summer, 1985), 243–249.

committee to lobby for legal restrictions on unionism, and established a trades school in 1906 to train non-union skilled workers. Employers also found it easier and easier to persuade courts to issue injunctions. (So many were issued against the molders union during its prolonged 1906 strike that the *Social Democratic Herald* sarcastically noted, "This injunction business is getting to be such an old story that a striker who hasn't been served with his daily 'injunct' does not feel quite right.") Milwaukee employers also frustrated the spread of real unionism by establishing company unions. It is one of the great ironies of Wisconsin's labor movement that its most important victories in legislation occurred during a period of reverses in its primary arenas of organization and collective bargaining.[91]

[5]

Although Milwaukee was the mainstream of Wisconsin's labor movement, there were important tributaries. In Racine, the first labor movement centered around the Knights of Labor, which was popular enough to attract 10,000 people to their 1886 Independence Day celebration. As the Knights organization faded in the 1890's, craft unions affiliated with the American Federation of Labor replaced it. The craft unions wanted to maintain a closed shop, increase wages, reduce hours, and enforce union rules. The most important among these were the building laborers (1888), cigar makers (1891), and molders (1897). The first two were instrumental in the city's initial Labor Day celebration in 1892 and in starting the Racine Trade and Labor Council (RTLC) in 1894, which had twenty-two unions and 2,200 members by 1901. The RTLC promoted the use of the union label by Racine businesses, campaigned (mostly for Socialists and Progressives) on behalf of candidates for public office, and lobbied for free school textbooks, an elective school board, immigration restriction, a county hospital, vocational education, and an end to the "third degree" by police. Racine's most important labor leader was William Sommers, who wanted new unions organized along industrial lines led by established craft unions. In 1915, he persuaded the RTLC to undertake organizing drives among rubber clothing workers, automobile workers, and machinists, and to support strikes by bartenders and auto workers.[92]

---

[91] Gavett, *Development of Labor Movement*, 122–125 (quote). See also Bruno Ramirez, *When Workers Fight: The Politics of Industrial Relations in the Progressive Era, 1898–1916* (Westport, Connecticut, 1978), 65–135.
[92] Joseph M. Kelly, "Growth of Organized Labor," in Nicholas C. Burckel, ed., *Racine: Growth and Change in a Wisconsin County* (Racine, 1977), 345–349; Gengo Suzuki,

Organizing activity in Kenosha came relatively late because of the city's later industrial development, the preponderance of unskilled and semiskilled workers, and the large number of southern and eastern European immigrants. Before 1902, most unions rarely lasted long enough to receive official charters. That year, locals representing the metal polishers, carpenters, machinists, musicians, retail clerks, and cigar makers formed the Kenosha Trades and Labor Council (KTLC), which was chartered by the AFL. The KTLC asserted the right to help determine wages, hours, working conditions, and health and safety towards the goal of "human betterment." It actively supported the fight against child labor and demands for safer and more sanitary housing conditions for workers. In May, 1901, about a hundred union machinists struck the city's major factories, including Simmons Mattress, T. B. Jeffery, Chicago-Rockford Hosiery, and Badger Brass, demanding a nine-hour day but not a change in the six-day week. The machinists won their point after a two-month strike, but suffered a proportionate decrease in pay. Still, by 1904, Labor Day celebrations in Kenosha involved 10,000 people.[93]

The most serious strike took place against the Allen Tannery, beginning in April, 1906, when 150 men walked out, demanding a raise to ten dollars a week. Over a four-day period, violence broke out several times. Only tireless negotiating by Mayor James Gorman and labor organizer A. E. Buckmaster prevented a pitched battle between strikers and police. Workers received a partial wage increase, but struck again in 1907 and 1909, amid even more violence. Although the Allen Tannery workers were not unionized, the KTLC enthusiastically supported their demands. More than a thousand people attended solidarity meetings, at which one prominent union official charged that the new Citizen's Alliance and Manufacturer's Association intended to "destroy the labor unions and replace well paid mechanics and union men with cheap and degraded labor." Few strikes occurred between 1909 and 1915.[94]

In Sheboygan, union activity closely resembled Milwaukee's. German immigrants—many of them skilled craftsmen imbued with democratic socialism—supplied the impetus. On May 30, 1890, representatives of the cigar makers, brewery workers, tailors, and tanners formed the Central Labor Union of Sheboygan (CLU). They were

---

"Industrial Relations in the City of Racine, Wisconsin" (master's thesis, University of Wisconsin, 1927), 48–52.

[93] John W. Bailey, "Labor's Fight for Security and Dignity," in Neuenschwander, ed., *Kenosha County*, 223–235; Cropley, *Kenosha*, 78–79; *The Vindicator* (West Superior), December 2, 1898.

[94] Bailey, Labor's Fight for Security and Dignity," in Neuenschwander, ed., *Kenosha*, 231–235.

soon joined by hod carriers, furniture and dock workers, shoemakers, and carpenters. The AFL chartered the CLU in 1892, and it organized the city's first Labor Day celebration in 1894. That same year, the CLU lent considerable financial and moral support to a tannery strike involving 4,000 workers. As in Milwaukee, the Social Democratic party and the CLU joined in financing a pro-labor, German-language paper. The CLU continued to add member unions, and, in 1903, switched to English for its meetings. It agitated for the eight-hour day and for labor and welfare legislation.[95]

The cities on the western shore of Lake Winnebago endured turmoil in labor relations. Labor unrest in Neenah-Menasha dated at least from the 1870's; most organizing efforts did not survive a single strike until very late in the century. Employers supported the ethic of individualism and treated employees paternalistically. However, frequent strikes in the 1880's and 1890's testified to worker dissatisfaction. Unionization began in the woodenware industry, then spread. In 1900, five small craft unions of skilled and semiskilled workers, totaling only about 200, formed a Central Trade Council. The paper mills remained unorganized because the unsteady nature of the work discouraged employees from complaining about long hours and low wages. Then, in 1901, discontent over Sunday night work became so widespread that the International Brotherhood of Papermakers, an AFL affiliate, attempted to organize mill workers on a platform of shortening hours, eliminating Sunday night work, and establishing union wage scales. Mill owners uniformly opposed unionization, but made limited concessions while seeking to undermine the organizers.[96]

The union's first strike, against the Kimberly-Clark Co., was moderately successful and emboldened a push to abolish Sunday night work. The mill owners formed themselves into the Northwestern Paper and Pulp Manufacturers' Association, and at first appeared to accede to union demands; they then reversed themselves, saying that the experiment had proven the financial necessity of Sunday night work. After much switching of positions by the owners, the union called a strike in June, 1904, which led to sporadic fighting between the mill workers and strikebreakers. By using strikebreakers, the companies succeeded in returning to full operation by the end of August. The union ran out of funds and supporters, and workers who had not been replaced went back to work—Sunday nights included. For the next thirty years, mill owners prevented unionization through a combination of threats, intimidation, and labor spying. The Menasha Wooden Ware Co. similarly broke the woodworkers' union with shut-

---

[95] Sheboygan *Times*, September 4, 1936.
[96] Glaab and Larsen, *Factories in the Valley*, 233–248.

downs and firings, leaving the Fox River Valley with only a handful of small craft unions which had little influence over the large manufacturers. This pattern was to be repeated time and again, in city after city, throughout Wisconsin, but nowhere so consistently as in the Fox Valley.[97]

Unionization in Oshkosh gained momentum during the depression of the 1890's, partly in response to a campaign by the *Labor Advocate*. The desire for shorter working hours, primarily through Sunday closing, animated organization of retail clerks, teamsters, barbers, machine woodworkers, and brewery employees. Oshkosh unions opened a retail co-operative store, organized educational and debating clubs, sponsored Labor Day galas, and lent support to the People's party.[98]

Then came the woodworkers' strike of the late spring and summer of 1898. Labor organizations and labor strife had been common throughout the state from the 1880's forward, especially in lumber-related industries. But the events of 1898 in Oshkosh have come to rival those in Bay View in 1886 as a quintessential Wisconsin labor struggle that gained national notoriety. More than 1,500 members of Oshkosh's Amalgamated Woodworkers struck the sash-and-door industry in a walkout which lasted fourteen weeks. Periodic layoffs and wage cuts had devastated woodworkers during the depression, and they demanded a minimum wage of $1.50 a day, abolition of woman labor, weekly payment of wages, and recognition of their union. But the seven companies affected by the strike would not negotiate. The city was divided, literally and figuratively, by the Fox River. The Polish, Bohemian Germans, and German workers on the south side were pitted against the native-born American workers, the professional and business classes, and the mill owners on the north side; but many middle-class residents did indeed support the strikers. Daily skirmishing among strikers, police, strikebreakers, and company-hired private detectives grew ever more strident. Strikers' wives marched, carrying eggs, salt, pepper, and sand to intimidate strikebreakers and police. When a sixteen-year-old worker was clubbed to death by strikebreakers during a melee on June 23, strikers staged a martyr's funeral. The mill owners persuaded Governor Scofield to mobilize the state militia, with orders to shoot to kill.[99]

---

[97] *Ibid.*, 248–256.

[98] Ozanne, *Labor Movement in Wisconsin*, 19–22; Lawrence C. Reno, "Organized Labor in Oshkosh," in Wisconsin State Federation of Labor, *Wisconsin Labor*, 1952, p. 71; *The Age of Labor* (Oshkosh), April 22, 1893; *Labor Advocate* (Oshkosh), June 10, July 14, 21, August 18, October 20, 28, November 17, and December 1, 1893, January 6, 13, and April 7, 1894, January 18, 1895, June 26, 1897.

[99] Ozanne, *Labor Movement in Wisconsin*, 22–24. Virginia Crane of the University of Wisconsin-Oshkosh generously shared her work in progress on the history of this strike.

The McMillen company where the boy was killed offered a compromise settlement, and the troops were withdrawn. But confrontations resumed in August, resulting in the arrest of a number of strikers, including nine women. Finally, the union achieved a wage compromise on August 20. It involved a return to the higher pre-depression wage levels, a pledge of no winter layoffs, and a promise not to penalize workers for union membership. The union gained neither recognition nor a contract, and women and children retained their jobs. The companies had gone on the offensive to end the strike. Nathan Paine, son of George M. Paine, president of the Paine Lumber Company, Oshkosh's largest, lodged complaints on behalf of the company against the Amalgamated Woodworkers' Chicago-based organizer and a local picket captain, charging them with conspiracy. The men were thereupon indicted and brought to trial. None other than Clarence Darrow, who later achieved permanent renown in the Scopes "Monkey" Trial, secured their acquittal; but in the wake of the strike the union disintegrated.[100]

In La Crosse, the first general labor organization was the Grand Labor Council, established in 1891 with delegations from trade unions. In 1902, most of the same unions formed the La Crosse Trades and Labor Council, chartered by the AFL. By 1910 it had grown enough to hire its first business agent and co-ordinated several important strikes: against the street railway company in 1909, breweries in 1910, and rubber plants in 1915.[101]

In Ashland and Superior, remote and isolated from urban Wisconsin and Minnesota, unionization proved even more difficult than elsewhere. Ashland already had a Central Labor Union, as well as a local of the American Railway Union by 1893. But the Pullman Strike of 1894 led to the demise of the railway union and retarded organizational efforts. The depression hit Ashland workers extremely hard; many appealed for charity or committed petty offenses that would assure them of jail time. Ashland's dockworkers struck for a wage increase from a meager 12.5 cents an hour to 15 cents, but they failed even in that, and most of the strike leaders

---

[100] *Ibid.*, 24–25.

[101] *Ibid.*, 14–16; Mary Taylor, comp., City of Eau Claire, Intensive Historic/Architectural Survey, *Final Report* (n.p., 1983), 61–62; George B. Engberg, "Collective Bargaining in the Lumber Industry of the Upper Great Lakes States," in *Agricultural History*, 24 (October, 1950), 205–211; A. R. Reynolds, *The Daniel Shaw Lumber Company: A Case Study of the Wisconsin Lumbering Frontier* (New York, 1957), 39–92; John Darling, "History of La Crosse Central Labor Bodies," and D. R. Kinney and Louis Alberts, "Let the Charter Speak," both in the Wisconsin State Federation of Labor, *Annual Labor Review and Convention Program*, August 18–23, 1941; Joan M. Rausch and Richard Zeitlin, comps., City of La Crosse Intensive Historical-Architectural Survey, *Final Report* (Milwaukee, 1984), 313.

either went to jail or fled town. On March 13, 1892, the local representing bricklayers, plasterers, stonecutters, carpenters, and trimmers formed the Superior Trades and Labor assembly. Six years later, the assembly was able to support its own newspaper, *The Vindicator*, which reported principally on organizational efforts and events. Most of the assembly unions marched with the Retail Clerks Association in support of earlier closing times for stores, and they backed strikes by longshoremen and also the Amalgamated Association of Street Railway Employees.[102]

Organizational drives elsewhere yielded warmer outcomes than those in Wisconsin's cold-weather cities. In Beloit, for example, by June of 1903, a four-year organizing effort by the International Association of Machinists and the AFL produced twenty-one unions with 2,000 members in a city of 14,000, making Beloit the most thoroughly organized city in the state. Stores displayed union cards in their windows, customers bought union-made goods from unionized clerks, and grocery stores and meat markets closed in the early evening by virtue of their contract with the retail clerks union. The Beloit *Labor Journal* circulated widely, and the city's two daily newspapers sported union labels. As for strikes, the iron molders won two successive disputes in 1902 and 1903, and secured a minimum daily wage of $3 in 1903.[103]

However, another 1903 strike, by 525 members of the machinists against the Berlin Machine Works, ignited employer reaction. The strikers demanded a nine-hour day, a minimum of 26.5 cents an hour, and a maximum of one apprentice for every five machinists. The Chicago Employers' Association, a leader in a nationwide drive for the open shop, helped Beloit employers establish a local affiliate that quickly signed up more than a thousand members. In order to encompass small businesses and non-union workers, it changed its name to the Citizens' Alliance and issued an open-shop tract written by Joseph V. Quarles of Milwaukee, a prominent attorney, judge, and U.S. senator. Within six months, union membership had dropped from 1,341 to 117, several locals had returned their charters, the *Labor Journal* collapsed, and union cards and labels disappeared.[104]

---

[102] Ashland *Appeal*, August 15, and September 15, 1894; Ashland *Commonwealth*, January 12, 1895; *The Vindicator* (West Superior), June 10, 24, July 15, August 12, 26, September 2, 16, 23, October 7, 21, November 18, and December 2, 1898, January 2, 1899; Paul R. Lusignan, comp., Superior Intensive Survey, *Report* (n.p., 1983), 121–124.

[103] Ozanne, *Labor Movement in Wisconsin*, 28–31; Beloit *Labor Journal*, July 18, August 2, and September 6, 14, 1902, January 17, February 14, and March 21, 1903; Frederick W. Job, *A Tale of Two Cities* (2nd ed., Chicago, 1904).

[104] Beloit *Labor Journal*, January 17, February 14, and March 21, 1903; Job, *A Tale of Two Cities*.

In Madison, unionization proceeded more slowly but lasted longer, owing largely to a high percentage of skilled craftsmen in the city's industries. The first major unionization drive took place in 1892, spearheaded by Frank J. Weber of Milwaukee, arguably the state's most prominent labor figure of his day. In April of 1893, several craft unions organized the Madison Federated Trades Council (MFTC). During its first several years, the MFTC backed strikes by the carpenters and printers (1893), tailors (1895), plumbers (1903), masons (1904), and streetcar workers (1907). The 1893 printers strike brought economics professor Richard T. Ely to the union's defense, even to the point of walking a picket line and writing a pamphlet—activities that culminated in Ely's rebuke by the Board of Regents on charges of radicalism. Many early strikes were unsuccessful. The MFTC had to regroup on a couple of occasions. In 1903, when it had 720 members, it was rechartered by the AFL. From that point forward, the council experienced slow but steady growth, changing its name to the Madison Federation of Labor (MFL) in 1912. Between then and 1916, its membership more than doubled, and the number of locals increased to almost one hundred. A successful strike in 1915 by machinists against several small factories on behalf of an eight-hour day signified that Madison unions had achieved a degree of permanence.[105]

Milwaukee aside, the drive of Wisconsin labor for recognition and power produced mixed results. Its most apparent successes occurred along the Lake Michigan shore and, to a lesser extent, in La Crosse, Eau Claire, Madison, and Superior. Its most dismal failures occurred in Beloit, Ashland, and the Fox River Valley, though its efforts in the Wisconsin River Valley yielded only slightly better results. The modest successes generated employer counterattacks involving strikebreakers, spies, private detectives, blacklists, yellow dog contracts, injunctions, the state militia, and all the political clout employers could muster. Bitter, protracted, and violent strikes serve as a barometer to the intensity of the conflicts. A large number took place between 1901 and 1905; most were "control strikes," meaning that they were concerned primarily with union recognition and employee enforcement of work rules. Strike activity had declined after the unrest of 1886–1887 and during the depression years 1893–1897. But it peaked between 1901 and 1904, just before employers' associations strove for the open shop. Not until 1916 did the number of strikes

---

[105] Mollenhoff, *Madison*, 190–192, 270–271, 418–419; "Madison Federated Trades," in Wisconsin State Federation of Labor, *Wisconsin Labor*, 1952, p. 123; Robert R. Alford and Harry M. Scoble, *Bureaucracy and Participation: Four Wisconsin Cities* (Chicago, 1969), 104–106; International Typographical Union of North America, Madison Local 106, *Fifty Years, 1903–1953* (Madison, 1953), 5–6; "Labor Scrapbook," in R. N. Qualey Papers, 1906–1909; *Union Labor News* (Madison), January, 1953.

equal those of 1903. Between 1881 and 1905, Wisconsin experienced 799 strikes of which 494 were called by labor organizations and 303 were spontaneous. They involved 99,224 workers, and threw another 126,400 people out of work. Most were over wages, hours, or union recognition. About one in three was completely successful; almost one in five was at least partially successful. Between 1901 and 1905, there were 243 strikes involving 834 establishments, 19,277 strikers, and 26,758 other workers. Of these strikes, 27 per cent were completely successful, and 35 per cent, partially. So, despite the risks of walking off the job, the odds allowed a degree of success.[106]

Much nineteenth-century strike activity occurred in sawmills, where workers generally succeeded in shortening the workday but failed to eliminate the company store, payment in scrip, and withholding of pay until the end of the season. Besides major strikes in Eau Claire and Oshkosh, there were others in the Menominee River Valley in 1885–1886, in Ashland and Washburn in 1890, and in the Wisconsin River Valley in 1892. The woodworkers' strike in Oshkosh in 1898 was followed by others in Chippewa Falls, Rice Lake, Marinette, and Sheboygan. Notable strikes occurred outside wood-related industries, of course. A 1901 machinists' strike in Milwaukee lasted eight weeks; it was noteworthy for being the first major strike to be ended by court injunction. Milwaukee iron molders struck in 1906 and stayed out for two years; they eventually failed, primarily because of the companies' use of detectives and strikebreakers. The Racine TLC backed a strike by city bartenders in 1914, and advocated a boycott of Welch's grape juice because the company had contributed $50,000 to the prohibition movement. A 1916 strike by the auto workers' union against the Racine Manufacturing Company produced substantial violence.[107]

Kenosha underwent strikes by machinists and ice handlers, and by workers at Simmons Mattress, Badger Brass, and the Allen Tannery in the 1900's. In Neenah-Menasha strikes occurred against Menasha Wooden Ware between 1885 and 1904, and against Neenah Boot & Shoe in 1896. The International Brotherhood of Papermakers waged almost continuous industrial warfare against the valley's paper mills before capitulating in 1904, leaving the manufacturers in an even stronger position. Only a few locals in the Fox River Valley managed

---

[106] P. K. Edwards, *Strikes in the United States, 1881–1974* (New York, 1981), 1–133; *House Documents*, 59 Cong., 2 sess., no. 822 (serial 5213), U.S. Commissioner of Labor, *Twenty-First Annual Report, 1906: Strikes and Lockouts* (1907), 480–485, 576–578; Montgomery, *Workers' Control in America*, 49–67, 91–97. The U.S. government collected no strike data between 1906 and 1914.

[107] Ozanne, *Labor Movement in Wisconsin*, 17–33, 171–201; Kelly, "Growth of Organized Labor" in Burckel, ed., *Racine*, 347–349.

to abolish Saturday night work; most such efforts were frustrated, as were those in the Wisconsin and Chippewa river valleys. Strikes on behalf of an eight-hour day in the Rhinelander paper mills in 1912, and in Marinette in 1916, were foiled by the Western Paper Manufacturers' Association. Strikes were not always effective in improving labor conditions, but—since they lacked political strength—strikes were the most potent weapon unions and workers possessed.[108]

[6]

Unionization was still young when Wisconsin established a statewide labor federation. It emanated from Milwaukee, all but guaranteeing that the fledgling Wisconsin State Federation of Labor (WSFL) bore the stamp of the "Milwaukee Idea." The Milwaukee Federated Trades Council (MFTC) was itself barely four years old when it issued invitations to a meeting to form the WSFL in June, 1893. The thirty-seven delegates included twenty-two from Milwaukee, nine from Oshkosh, two from Madison, and one each from Ashland, Marinette, Racine, and West Superior. The initial ranks also included the central labor federations of Ashland, Madison, Marinette, Milwaukee, Oshkosh, and West Superior. All told, they represented between 10 and 15 per cent of the state's unions, and about two-thirds of its municipal labor councils. WSFL's major goals were to establish a political arm and to provide mutual assistance to local unions in organizing drives, strikes, and boycotts. WSFL's membership was about 2,500, less than one-fifth of the state's unionized workers. At first, it was governed by a part-time president, an unpaid vice-president, a secretary, and three trustees. Following the MFTC pattern, the state federation abolished the office of president in 1894, replacing it with a state organizer, and electing an *ad hoc* chairman for each meeting.[109]

The new federation was primarily the brainchild of Frank J. Weber, the AFL's state organizer, a founding officer of the MFTC, and a veteran of every Milwaukee workingmen's political party. A native Milwaukeean of German immigrant parents, Weber had worked as a sailor, carpenter, and schoolteacher, and had served as an AFL organizer among West Virginia coal miners and Southern longshoremen. He held the post of state organizer for twenty-three years, re-

---

[108] Bailey, "Labor's Fight for Security and Dignity," in Neuenschwander, ed., *Kenosha County*, 225–234; Glaab and Larsen, *Factories in the Valley*, 233–254; George Engberg, "Labor in the Lake States Logging Industry, 1839–1930" (doctoral dissertation, University of Minnesota, 1949), 371–377; Robert F. Fries, *Empire in Pine: The Story of Lumbering in Wisconsin, 1830–1900* (Madison, 1951), 216–218.

[109] Gavett, *Development of the Labor Movement*, 88–89; Ozanne, *Labor Movement in Wisconsin*, 34–36.

porting to an elected executive board. From its beginning, Weber functioned as the heart and soul of the WSFL, holding every office, and chairing its legislative committee for three decades. He served several terms in the state legislature, including the legendary 1911 session, and played key roles in getting reform bills passed. Weber needed all the skills at his command to hold together the diverse factions that constituted the WSFL, and to compromise a dozen issues, each with the potential to destroy that fragile coalition.[110]

The most potentially divisive issue was the WSFL's relationship to socialism. The federation's first political platform did not advocate collective ownership, and was more Populist than Socialist. Perhaps the most significant speech given at the first WSFL convention in 1893 was that of Victor L. Berger, who spoke for two hours in German, charging delegates to "promote an enlightened strong working class, which, when the time comes, will be able to take over the reins of civilization."[111]

During the second WSFL convention in Oshkosh in 1894, the platform advocated "collective ownership for the people of all means of production and distribution," the same plank that victorious Socialists had succeeded in inserting into the AFL's 1893 platform. The convention also endorsed the People's party in the 1894 fall elections, since it had "socialized" its platform. By 1896, however, delegates from Racine and Superior opposed endorsing socialism. Outside Milwaukee, Sheboygan, and Manitowoc, union leaders generally had to seek support from Republicans and Democrats, and they were reluctant to identify with a third party. Even so, the plank advocating public ownership was adopted again, 24–11. After founding of the Socialist Party of America (SPA) in 1897, with the Milwaukee SDP as "Branch One," the issue became more urgent. At their 1898 convention in La Crosse, WSFL delegates sponsored a resolution pledging the federation to support the Social Democratic Party of America. After heated debate, the convention defeated the resolution, 16–8, and instead adopted another requiring that the WSFL avoid partisan politics at its conventions. Weber followed with a successful resolution committing the federation to "sever its connection with all political parties."[112]

During the next two years, the Socialists' strength increased. Socialists held the majority of delegates' seats at the WSFL convention in Sheboygan in 1900. Under Weber, delegates from the MFTC carried two resolutions, the first calling upon working people "to sever

---

[110] Gavett, *Development of the Labor Movement*, 88–89; Ozanne, *Labor Movement in Wisconsin*, 36–45.
[111] Ozanne, *Labor Movement in Wisconsin*, 37–39.
[112] *Ibid.*, 39.

their connection and refuse any support to the Republican and Democratic parties . . . and to vote for socialism." The second pledged to "recommend to the officers thereof [the WSFL] and to all trade unionists of the state to educate themselves along the lines of international socialism." The Socialist triumph was confirmed by the election of Frederick Brockhausen, a member of the cigar makers local of the MFTC, over Martin Jesko, a nonsocialist cigar maker from Racine. Jesko walked out of the convention, taking with him nine Oshkosh and six Racine locals, plus one each from Madison, Marinette, Green Bay, and Sheboygan, in addition to the trades and labor councils of Oshkosh, Racine, and Green Bay. Two Milwaukee building trades locals joined them.

This schism cost the federation one-fifth of its 5,000 members, but the loss was largely offset by the addition of 740 new members from Milwaukee. (Milwaukeeans constituted nearly 70 per cent of the WSFL by 1901.) The Socialist victory assured their domination of the state federation for the next thirty-five years, but Socialists retained sway by downplaying their doctrine and instead stressing organizational drives, collective bargaining, and lobbying for protective legislation, all in co-operation with non-socialists and non-unionists.[113]

For the rest of the Progressive Era, the WSFL split into three unequal factions: the majority Socialists, the Milwaukee building trades locals, and the non-Milwaukee unions, nearly all of which were indifferent or hostile to socialism. Despite this split, federation membership grew to 6,800 by 1903, with 70 per cent in the Milwaukee area.

During the 1890's, Socialist control was undermined by personal and ideological rivalry between Frank Weber and Victor Berger. Their relationship was especially strained between 1896 and 1898, when Weber seemed more intent on holding the WSFL together through compromise than in committing it to socialism. It warmed when Weber, as Wisconsin organizer of the AFL, persuaded the AFL to ignore an appeal by the building trades local about the MFTC's endorsement of Social Democratic party candidates in the 1900 spring elections. Berger and Weber were in accord about remaining in the AFL and about opposing the IWW. But Berger remained suspicious of Weber, primarily because he remained a friend and confidant of Samuel Gompers, whom Berger detested for his opposition to socialism.[114]

By 1905, WSFL membership surpassed 9,000. Then, beset by the employers' open shop counterattack, membership leveled off until 1912, when it jumped to 11,200. Three years later, it reached 16,500

---
[113] *Ibid.*, 39–40.
[114] *Ibid.*, 40–45.

when the federation persuaded some unaffiliated unions to join. Those who refused to affiliate included the railroad brotherhoods and the Milwaukee building trades—both of which objected to the WSFL's socialist orientation—and locals which did not feel that the benefits were commensurate with the dues. As late as 1901, only thirty-three of Milwaukee's sixty craft locals were WSFL members. The federation's reluctance to organize unskilled workers, like its opposition to the IWW, reflected its continuing domination by craft unions. Its failure to make headway in the metal trades and paper mills stemmed from the fact that both industries were immune to worker boycotts of their products. Brewers, on the other hand, feared the consequences of a workers' boycott, and they needed union support in their fight against temperance and prohibition. The building trades unions remained aloof from both the MFTC and the WSFL. Their members owned their own tools and regarded themselves as capable of starting their own construction enterprises in the event of a strike or lockout. These unions also functioned as fraternal lodges that provided benefits to the sick and injured, offered a social outlet, reinforced ethnic ties, and assisted social mobility. So many of their members saw no need to join a federation.[115]

From the outset, the WSFL viewed itself as the labor movement's political arm through which workers could achieve reforms at the polls. It promoted legislation favorable to organized labor and the working class through two interrelated strategies: electing Social Democrats to the state legislature, and lobbying for specific bills. By 1905, the legislature had seated one Social Democratic senator and four assemblymen, all from Milwaukee districts. The legislature of 1911, which achieved lasting fame for its passage of labor and welfare legislation, included two Social Democratic senators and twelve assemblymen. Easily the most prominent was Frank Weber, who served in the assembly from 1907 to 1911, 1915, and 1923 to 1925. Next in prominence was Frederick Brockhausen, secretary-treasurer of the WSFL, who served in the assembly from 1905 through 1911. Weber and Brockhausen sponsored labor's legislative proposals and represented it on key committees. The remaining Socialist legislators were a mixed bag: some were immigrants affiliated with Milwaukee trade unions, others were Yankees; some were trade unionists. Others were professional men, at least two of whom combined socialism with the Social Gospel. One was Senator Winfield R. Gaylord, a Mississippi-born minister and a lecturer for the national Socialist party; the other, Carl D. Thompson, also a clergyman, was the SDP's state organizer. Most legislators represented predominantly Germanic districts, but a

[115] *Ibid.*, 49–56.

few, such as Martin Gorecki, who served in 1913, exemplified WSFL efforts to attract southern and eastern Europeans.[116]

The SDP legislators mainly advocated WSFL-sponsored measures and worked to defeat those it opposed. In theory the federation formally opposed official linkage to any political party; in practice, it rarely missed an opportunity to identify with the Social Democratic party's interests. As "general organizer" (for he eschewed the title of "president"), Frank Weber worked with two appointed union officers in drafting legislation, lobbying for its enactment, and co-ordinating the activities of Socialist lawmakers. At each annual convention, the legislative committee reported on the status of dozens of bills. Its summary assessments ranged from characterizing the 1909 session as the "greatest almighty-dollar-serving legislature that was ever convened in the state," to Fred Brockhausen's praise of its 1911 counterpart as one that "has given more consideration to labor legislation than any of its predecessors" and "the first in the history of the state to have within it a noticeable element for human rights." Weber and the federation's legislative committee also worked closely with the Bureau of Labor and Industrial Statistics and with its successor, the Industrial Commission.[117]

In 1908, condemning the AFL policy of "defeat your enemy and reward your friend," Weber asserted that "both the Republican and Democratic parties, as such, are antagonistic to organized labor." In a similar vein in 1905, Brockhausen warned against believing that the middle class was friendly to labor, when its representatives "propose legislation the most harmful to labor" and "strike out blindly in all directions without practical results." On the other side, John R. Commons railed that Socialists frequently sided with the enemies of progressive reform, while Charles McCarthy and Francis McGovern preached that "the way to beat the Socialists is to beat them to it." Thus Social Democrats and Progressive Republicans frequently co-operated with the WSFL in pragmatic support of labor legislation. But each side's ideology precluded anything more permanent or broad-gauged.[118]

---

[116] Ozanne, *Labor Movement in Wisconsin*, 39–45; *Wisconsin Blue Book, 1905*, pp. 1075–1123; *1907*, pp. 1125–1178; *1909*, pp. 1093–1146; *1911*, pp. 736–786; *1913*, pp. 638–689; *1915*, pp. 488–539.

[117] Wisconsin State Federation of Labor, *Official Directory*, 1896–1897, pp. 9–17; 1899–1900, pp. 3–21; Wisconsin State Federation of Labor, Annual Convention, *Proceedings*, 1905, pp. 27–33; 1906, pp. 25–46, 72–73; 1907, pp. 21–44; 1908, pp. 28–48, 104–107; 1909, pp. 19–45; 1910, pp. 25–46, 60–61; 1911, pp. 17–33, 40–50; 1912, pp. 28–54, 89–90; 1913, pp. 3–11, 23–27, 50–92; Wisconsin State Federation of Labor, Annual Convention, *Official Report*, 1915, pp. 67–85.

[118] Wisconsin State Federation of Labor, *Proceedings*, 1905, pp. 31–32 (quote); 1907, pp. 23–24; 1908, pp. 38–39 (quote); 1910, p. 39; Herbert F. Margulies, *The Decline of*

Equally subversive of WSFL's hopes for a comprehensive legislative program were the inherent conflicts between trade unionism and socialism. The Socialists' ultimate goal of collective ownership implied government intervention. And government intervention did not square with trade unions' insistence that collective bargaining by them was preferable to protective legislation. The Socialists' claim of working on behalf of the entire working class frequently seemed incompatible as well with labor's practice of organizing into local craft unions. In 1905, the WSFL leaders acknowledged that they did not sympathize with many AFL policies and that they favored industrial unionism. But they also insisted that a reorientation towards industrial unionism could come only as a "natural result of industrial evolution, intelligently aided by continued agitation, education and organization among the rank and file of the organizations at present affiliated with the American Federation of Labor."[119]

Agriculture remained a WSFL problem. It had difficulty co-operating with farm organizations, particularly the Wisconsin Society of Equity (a successor to the Grange, founded in 1902), and that failure bedeviled WSFL's vision of working-class solidarity. By 1907, the two organizations exchanged convention delegates, and Weber declared hopefully that "the farmer is beginning to realize that his interests are identical with those of other laboring men." Two years later, however, Brockhausen admitted that attempts at co-operation between the legislative committees of the two organizations had ended in frustration, mainly because "the Equity is not an organization of farmers, but instead a mixture of such and business men and men of strong tendencies toward capitalistic politics."[120]

Even more troublesome was the WSFL's persistent ambivalence on the question of working women. At the 1907 convention, Weber conceded that "woman has invaded the industrial field, and that she is here to stay is a fact gradually forcing itself upon the public." However, he also insisted that "it is not intended by the laws of nature that woman should be a breadwinner; she was created as the keeper of home—to be healthy, strong and a happy wife, and a willing and joyful mother." Organized labor remained uneasy about women workers and child labor long after others in the reform movement had united on these issues. Protective legislation for women and chil-

---

the *Progressive Movement in Wisconsin, 1890–1920* (Madison, 1968), 152–157; Charles McCarthy, *The Wisconsin Idea* (New York, 1912), 294–300.

[119] Wisconsin State Federation of Labor, Annual Convention, *Proceedings*, 1905, pp. 58–59; 1913, pp. 27–29.

[120] *Ibid.*, 1907, pp. 33–34; 1909, p. 22.

Redefining Work 297

dren was, potentially at least, contradictory to the WSFL's ultimate goal of keeping both out of the workplace.[121]

Despite these internal contradictions, the WSFL's legislative agenda was remarkably consistent and forward-looking. Its platform continued to advocate socialist nostrums. It concentrated its energies on enacting practical legislation to improve the lot of workers within the capitalist system. As early as the mid-1890's, the federation advocated a state income tax, universal suffrage, safety and sanitation laws, government work relief for the unemployed, the payment of wages in cash, and the abolition of child labor and the company store. Its political platform consistently demanded free, compulsory education, an eight-hour day, direct legislation, sanitary inspection of workshop and home, employer liability, the abolition of contract labor and sweatshops, and the establishment of postal savings banks. Over the years, the WSFL also lobbied for repeal of the anti-boycott law, control over apprenticeship programs, the abolition of convict labor, mandatory display of the union label, and the arbitration of labor disputes. The WSFL opposed compulsory arbitration as "involuntary servitude," but it did favor "arbitration as a last resort." Suspicious of efforts by employers associations to standardize wages, hours, contract forms, and education of apprentices, unions supported a bill to establish a system of vocational schools and a state-controlled apprentice training program.[122]

The federation regarded unemployment as the greatest single problem affecting all working people, and accordingly pushed for regulation of private employment agencies and the establishment of free public ones. As early as 1894, it proposed work relief for the unemployed. In 1910, it co-operated with BLIS in a survey of the social and economic effects of unemployment, and called for direct government aid. For the most part, the state federation upheld aggressive unionization and state "welfarism" as the best solutions to unemployment.[123]

---

[121] *Ibid.*, 1907, pp. 35–38 (quote); 1909, pp. 32–33, 55, 59, 66–67; 1912, pp. 94–95; 1913, pp. 64–67, 76–77.

[122] *Ibid.*, 1905, pp. 3–4; 1911, pp. 48–49; Ozanne, *Labor Movement in Wisconsin*, 124–129; Weiss, "History of Labor Legislation," 28–86, 133–155, 379–382; Haferbecker, *Wisconsin Labor Laws*, xi, 17–182; Altmeyer, *Industrial Commission of Wisconsin*, 12–13, 16, 268–270, 284–286; Gavett, *Development of the Labor Movement*, 107–111, 134–135; Wisconsin State Federation of Labor, *Proceedings*, 1906, pp. 33–34, 39–43; *ibid.*, 1909, pp. 34–45; 1912, pp. 38–45; 1913, pp. 78–81, 90–93.

[123] Ozanne, *Labor Movement in Wisconsin*, 123, 127–130; Altmeyer, *Industrial Commission of Wisconsin*, 12; Haferbecker, *Wisconsin Labor Laws*, 86–93, 98–99, 112–117, 122; Weiss, "History of Labor Legislation," 226–240, 370–375; Wisconsin State Federation of Labor, *Proceedings*, 1909, pp. 30–31; 1913, pp. 64–68; Gavett, *Development of the Labor Movement*, 109–110.

Organized labor was among the first to demand state intervention to guarantee worker safety, health, and sanitation. It outspokenly sought more state health and safety inspectors who would have more discretion and authority. As trade unionists and as socialists, the WSFL and SDP were skeptical about giving authority over industrial relations to an appointed commission of "experts," none of whom truly represented organized labor or the working class. Indeed they tended to mistrust any plan devised by middle-class progressive Republicans. Brockhausen was deliberately restrained in his report to the WSFL convention on the 1911 legislative session, styling much of the legislation as "meritorious," and the employers' liability law as "merely a step in the right direction." He concluded by cautioning the delegates that "all legislation by the capitalistic parties only is and only can be a patchwork on our body politic."[124]

[7]

For all its visibility and influence, organized labor was but one voice among many calling for more state intervention in the new industrial society. Voluntary associations also lobbied for protective legislation, especially for women and children. The state branch of the national Consumer's League, organized in 1899 at the annual meeting of the State Federation of Women's Clubs, initially worked in the private sector and tried to convince women not to shop on Saturday afternoons, in order to give shop girls a shorter work week. In the early 1900's, the Wisconsin Child Labor Committee sought laws regulating child labor, sweatshops, and prison contract labor. The American Association for Labor Legislation (AALL) worked for protective labor legislative and social security laws at the state level, testified before legislative committees, helped draft legislation, and published the *American Labor Legislation Review*. Even after moving to New York in 1910, the AALL continued to be active in Wisconsin, owing largely to John R. Commons and his students.[125]

Both the Milwaukee Children's Betterment League and the Child Labor Committee, in concert with the Federation of Women's Clubs and the Consumer's League, lobbied to strengthen child labor laws.

---

[124] Wisconsin State Federation of Labor, *Proceedings*, 1911, pp. 6, 40–50; Altmeyer, *Industrial Commission of Wisconsin*, 10–20, 105–109; Haferbecker, *Wisconsin Labor Laws*, 15–33; Weiss, "History of Labor Legislation," 46–102.

[125] Haferbecker, *Wisconsin Labor Laws*, 12–13; Erickson, "The Consumer's Influence on Production," in the Bureau of Labor and Industrial Statistics, *Biennial Report*, 1900–1901, pp. 282–314; Weiss, "History of Labor Legislation," 28–45, 129–255.

The Child Labor Committee was composed of educators, social workers, factory inspectors, attorneys and judges, settlement house residents, women's and men's clubs, and church organizations. With the other organizations, it advocated expanding compulsory education, prohibiting employment of children under age fourteen, eliminating night work, decreasing the number of working hours, and increasing the number of inspectors. The *Catholic Citizen*, edited by Humphrey J. Desmond, an advocate of the church's teachings on social justice, pressed for similar labor and welfare reforms.[126]

Augmenting demands by organized labor and voluntary reform associations were three influential public institutions: the University of Wisconsin, the Legislative Reference Library, and the Bureau of Labor and Industrial Statistics. President John Bascom, who had left the university in 1887, had long been a vigorous defender of labor unions and of government intervention on behalf of working people. As he said, "the state like the individual has the duty to be righteous." From 1889 onward, a small but influential cadre of faculty members added their voices to the rising chorus, attacking laissez-faire capitalism and promoting state government as a force for social improvement and moral power.[127]

The Legislative Reference Library was a state agency devoted to legislative research and bill-drafting. Ostensibly it was nonpartisan. However, its director, Charles McCarthy, came from an immigrant, working-class background, was a close associate and admirer of professors Ely and Commons, had ties to organized labor and to many national reform associations, and served as research director of the U.S. Commission on Industrial Relations. McCarthy and Commons were the primary authors of the progressive labor legislation of 1911–1913. In other words, McCarthy's critics were not entirely amiss when they styled the Legislative Reference Library a "progressive bill factory."[128]

---

[126] Richard J. Orsi, "Humphrey Joseph Desmond: A Case Study in American Catholic Liberalism" (master's thesis, University of Wisconsin, 1965), *passim*.

[127] Haferbecker, *Wisconsin Labor Laws*, 6–8, 10, 14–15; Hoeveler, "The University and the Social Gospel," in *WMH*, 59: 290–298 (quote); Joseph Dorfman, *The Economic Mind in American Civilization* (5 vols., New York, 1959), 3: 161–164, 276–294; *ibid.*, 4: 211–214, 377–395; Richard T. Ely, *Ground Under Our Feet: An Autobiography* (New York, 1938), 121–164; John R. Commons, *Myself: The Autobiography of John R. Commons* (New York, 1938; reprinted, Madison, 1964), 95–165; Benjamin F. Rader, *The Academic Mind and Reform: The Influence of Richard T. Ely in American Life* (Lexington, Kentucky, 1966), 28–105; Lafayette G. Harter, Jr., *John R. Commons: His Assault on Laissez-Faire* (Corvallis, Oregon, 1962), 163–256.

[128] Charles B. Austin, "Administration of Labor Laws: Summary of Labor Laws in Force, 1909," in American Association for Labor Legislation, *Legislative Summary*,

Founded in 1883 as a data-gathering agency, the Bureau of Labor and Industrial Statistics (BLIS) gradually evolved from a position of timid neutrality into a sometime advocate of labor legislation. Its biennial report for 1903–1904 featured a 130-page article, "Workmen's Compensation for Industrial Accidents," which set forth "the principal requisites of a proper scheme of compensation." In 1909–1910, BLIS published statistics showing how the employers' liability system had failed and how compensation systems in other countries benefited them. The Industrial Commission, which came into being in 1911, was founded on the concept of continuous involvement by state government in all aspects of labor and industrial relations, including wages, hours, safety and sanitary conditions, accident compensation, child and woman labor, arbitration and conciliation, industrial education, and apprenticeship programs. Thus had government and public policy, in the space of thirty tumultuous years, evolved from unbridled laissez-faire to active regulation of labor and social welfare.[129]

Wisconsin's leading employers and farm organizations generally refused to join in the demands for labor legislation. The Milwaukee Merchants' and Manufacturers' Association worked, after 1894, to block any legislation that might improve labor's wages, hours, or bargaining position. In 1911, the Wisconsin Association of Manufacturers joined it. Together, the two associations defended the status quo in commerce and industry, opposed militant unionism, resisted state intervention or regulation, and preached the glories of untrammeled capitalism.[130]

The major farm organizations, especially the Wisconsin Dairymen's Association, were generally indifferent to the plight of industrial laborers and hostile towards most proposals to improve their lot. (After all, farmers too were employers, and were therefore conscious of rising costs and possible precedents.) Most of the labor legislation of 1911–1913 achieved passage only by exempting agricultural work-

---

no. 1 (Madison, 1909); McCarthy, *Wisconsin Idea*, 156–170; Edward A. Fitzpatrick, *McCarthy of Wisconsin* (New York, 1944), 90–126.

[129] William Dunton Kerr, "Workmen's Compensation for Industrial Accidents," in Bureau of Labor and Industrial Statistics, *Biennial Report*, 1903–1904, pp. 409–439; "Industrial Accidents in Wisconsin (Second Report)," in Bureau of Labor and Industrial Statistics, *Biennial Report*, 1909–1910, pp. 67–142.

[130] Haferbecker, *Wisconsin Labor Laws*, 11–13; Robert Asher, "The 1911 Workmen's Compensation Law: A Study in Conservative Labor Reform," in *WMH*, 57 (Winter, 1973–1974), 123–140; Robert S. Maxwell, *La Follette and the Rise of the Progressives in Wisconsin* (Madison, 1956), 153–164; W. Elliott Brownlee, Jr., *Progressivism and Economic Growth: The Wisconsin Income Tax, 1911–1929* (Port Washington, New York, 1974), 818–898; Wyman, "Voting Behavior in the Progressive Era," 306–307.

ers. Alone among agricultural groups, the Wisconsin Society of Equity, composed largely of self-employed and economically marginal farmers, perceived any benefit from labor legislation or evinced any sympathy for industrial workers. Efforts at co-operation by the Society of Equity and the WSFL failed to produce any benefits to either.[131]

As the century turned, Wisconsin's legislature was being pressed on all sides to enact corrective labor laws: by trade unions, by journalists and voluntary reform associations, by academicians and newly fledged "experts," by politicians and bureaucrats, indeed by an increasingly aroused general public. Their voices bespoke a growing consensus that state government ought to play a larger role in overseeing and regulating the modern, urban-industrial society. Contemporary analysts were contending that these issues were so fraught with socio-economic consequences, and so invested with the general welfare, that they could no longer be entrusted entirely to the workings of economic forces or private interest groups.

The reasons for seeking change, like the changes proposed, were as diverse and complex as the organizations and institutions that propounded them. Taken separately, each specific proposal was a mixture of motivations, goals, and approaches which frequently were contradictory or incompatible. Yet each seemed to make a degree of sense, and all tended in the same general direction. Indisputably, change was in the air; the question was how to achieve it in the arena of politics and government.

The nature of the American political process dictated a strategy of compromise, coalition, and consensus that would ultimately produce concrete legislation, each law embodying partial, *ad hoc* solutions to be debated and voted up or down. Whether one's ultimate goal was to remove women and children from the work force, or to enhance their positions in it, or to ensure them a minimum wage, pragmatic support for varied protective measures advanced the cause. Whether one aimed to improve conditions in the factory for the individual worker, or to promote industrial harmony, or to increase productivity and profit, the maintenance of a safe, sanitary workplace had much to recommend it. Within the span of a single generation—roughly from 1885 to 1905—the New Industrialism had so revolutionized the workplace, and the nature of work, that the majority of Wisconsinites had come to believe that state intervention was not simply desirable, not merely legitimate, but absolutely imperative. However clumsy and

---

[131] Julia A. Roberts, "Farm Organizations and Labor in Wisconsin" (master's thesis, University of Wisconsin, 1946), 59–60.

halting the first steps, however daunting the obstacles, change was about to occur. Many would call it progress.[132]

[132] On the "revolt against laissez-faire," see Rader, *Academic Mind and Reform*, 28–82; Harter, *John R. Commons*, 205–256, and James T. Kloppenberg, *Uncertain Victory: Social Democracy and Progressivism in European and American Thought, 1870–1920* (New York, 1986). On the "process of compromise, coalition and consensus" necessary to effect concrete legislation, see John D. Buenker, "The Progressive Era: A Search for a Synthesis," in *Mid-America*, 51 (July, 1969), 175–193, and John D. Buenker, John C. Burnham, and Robert M. Crunden, *Progressivism* (Cambridge, 1977), 31–70, 112–125.

7

A Passion for Newness and for System

[1]

"MY own life is not yet a long life," marveled Hamlin Garland in the 1920's, "but I have seen more of change in certain directions than all the men from Julius Caesar to Abraham Lincoln." The novelist was born on September 14, 1860, in West Salem, Wisconsin, just before Lincoln was elected president. He had, as he said, witnessed "the reaping hook develop into the combined reaper and thresher, the ox-team give way to the automobile, the telegraph to the radio, and the balloon to the flying ship." He had experienced "the installation of electric light, the coming of concrete highways, and the establishment of air mail." Television, he fearlessly prophesied, "is certain to arrive tomorrow."[1]

Indeed, technological innovation dramatically altered every facet of life in Wisconsin during the Progressive Era, from family dynamics to formal education, from recreation to religion. Central to this metamorphosis were the revolutions in transportation and communications, which compressed time and space, fostered cultural homogenization, engendered social stratification, and reaggregated much of the population into complex, impersonal structures. The economic imperative that bound workers to mass production also demanded more and more insatiable consumers. Professional men and technicians, businessmen and intellectuals, fascinated with high-speed machinery and the modern industrial corporation, sought to reorder society by "systematizing" the fabric of American life.[2]

---

[1] Hamlin Garland, *Back-Trailers from the Middle Border* (New York, 1928), 375; John W. Dodds, *Life in Twentieth Century America* (New York, 1965; revised ed., 1972), 9–11.
[2] Alan I. Marcus and Howard P. Segal, *Technology in America: A Brief History* (San Diego, 1989), 180–181; Joel Colton and Stuart Bruchey, "Introduction," and Harold G. Vatter, "Technological Innovation and Social Change in the United States, 1870–

Most of the advances in communications and transportation derived from putting either electricity or the internal combustion engine to use. Commercially generated electricity for public consumption reduced human effort per unit of production, improved living standards, and reshaped the work force. New transformers changed direct current to less expensive alternating current; new water-driven turbines generated electricity in greater volume. Electric power companies searched for household and industrial applications so generating plants could operate at full capacity, day and night. By the turn of the century, electrically-powered trolley cars and interurban railroad trains were the norm. Electricity powered high-speed presses and enabled mass-circulation newspapers, magazines, and books to proliferate. Soon it did the same for photography, motion pictures, and radio. On the eve of World War I, electricity powered the vacuum cleaners, washing machines, and refrigerators that connoted ease and affluence in middle- and upper-class homes.[3]

Wisconsin was among the nation's pioneers in electricity, but electrification occurred relatively slowly statewide, primarily because The Milwaukee Electric Railway and Light Co. concentrated on transportation to the detriment of supplying lighting and generating power. Nevertheless, electrification made steady progress, and by 1914 Wisconsin industries used about 24,000 electric motors which supplied 255,668 primary horsepower—38 per cent of the state's total power. The nation's first hydroelectric, general central station opened in Appleton in 1882, and in 1886 Appleton began the country's first successful electric trolley car system. In 1886, there were already thirty-two electrical lighting plants in the state. By 1907, there were 193, fifty-nine of which provided round-the-clock service. About one Wisconsin home in twelve was electrified; one in sixteen was blessed with full-time service. About 60 per cent of the state's total electrical capacity was used to run streetcar systems. Interurban railway systems and the desire to generate hydroelectricity from Wisconsin's abun-

---

1980," in Joel Colton and Stuart Bruchey, eds., *Technology, the Economy, and Society: The American Experience* (New York, 1987), 1–37; Robert H. Walker, *Everyday Life in Victorian America, 1865–1900* (Malabar, Florida, 1967, entitled *Life in the Age of Enterprise*; revised ed., 1994), 44–73.

[3]Vatter, "Technological Innovation and Social Change," in Colton and Bruchey, eds., *Technology, the Economy, and Society*, 33–35; Marcus and Segal, *Technology in America*, 141–158; Thomas P. Hughes, *Networks of Power: Electrification in Western Society, 1880–1930* (Baltimore, 1983), 1–46; David E. Nye, *Electrifying America: Social Meanings of a New Technology, 1880–1940* (Cambridge, 1990), ix–xi, 381–391; Harold L. Platt, *The Electric City: Energy and the Growth of the Chicago Area, 1880–1930* (Chicago, 1991), 15–21, 82–91, 279–289; George W. Hilton and John F. Due, *The Electric Interurban Railways in America* (Stanford, California, 1960), 45–90; Walker, *Everyday Life in Victorian America*, 44–48; Dodds, *Life in Twentieth Century America*, 129–137. See also Chapter 4.

dant waterpowers intensified efforts to develop the utility. Electrification was primarily an urban phenomenon; in 1917, two-thirds of the state's customers resided in its twenty largest cities.[4]

The internal combustion engine had, if anything, an even more revolutionary effect than commercial electricity. It powered the automobile, the motor truck, the diesel locomotive, and the airplane, along with their industrial applications, and it transformed the world. Together, electricity and the internal combustion engine improved the standard and quality of life, contacts among diverse peoples, the pace and volume of suburbanization, and the way the metropolis looked. Electricity especially transformed industry. Internal combustion's favorite offspring, the automobile, soon became the cheapest and most efficient agent of personal transportation ever invented. Its incredible proliferation after 1914 marked a sea change in working and living patterns, creating an "automobile culture" that was soon to be standardized and global in nature.[5]

The communications and transportation revolutions likewise worked their magic on Wisconsin life. Three communications devices had been used for decades—the telegraph, the typewriter, and the telephone—and they continued to play roles. Telegraphy, the oldest marvel, depended upon a skilled operator who understood code, fixed locations for transmission and reception, and poles and wires. The typewriter, invented by C. Latham Sholes of Milwaukee in 1865, was still regarded as a curiosity at the Philadelphia Centennial Exposition. But, by the early twentieth century, the typewriter had become an indispensable machine in the business world, one that significantly increased the speed and accuracy of written communications.[6]

---

[4] *Eleventh Census of the United States, 1890: Manufacturing Industries, Volume VI, Part I, Totals for States and Territories,* 754–759; *Fourteenth Census of the United States, 1920: Manufactures, 1919, Reports for States, with Statistics for Principal Cities,* 1626; Forrest McDonald, *Let There Be Light: The Electric Utility Industry in Wisconsin, 1881–1955* (Madison, 1957), 3–178; Joseph M. Canfield, *TM: The Milwaukee Electric Railway & Light Company* (Chicago, 1972), 1–9; Clay McShane, *Technology and Reform: Street Railways and the Growth of Milwaukee, 1887–1900* (Madison, 1974), 65–105; Hilton and Due, *Electric Interurban Railways,* 353–357; Larry A. Reed, "Domesticating Electricity in Appleton," in *WMH,* 65 (Winter 1981–1982), 120–121; Lucile M. Kane, *The Falls of St. Anthony: The Waterfall that Built Minneapolis* (St. Paul, 1987), 123.

[5] Colton and Bruchey, "Introduction," and Vatter, "Technological Innovation and Social Change" in Colton and Bruchey, eds., *Technology, the Economy, and Society,* 5–6, 33–34; John W. Oliver, *History of American Technology,* 477–483; McDonald, *Let There Be Light,* 99.

[6] Oliver, *History of American Technology,* 433–450, 457–516; Marcus and Segal, *Technology in America,* 135–165; Walker, *Everyday Life in Victorian America,* 44–73; Dodds, *Life in Twentieth Century America,* 129–154; Wayne E. Fuller, *RFD: The Changing Face of Rural America* (Bloomington, Indiana, 1964), 1–17, 287–314.

The telephone, invented in 1876, enjoyed a number of advantages over both telegraph and typewriter. Like the telegraph, it required strung wires for transmission, but unlike the telegraph, telephone senders and receivers could be placed anywhere, needed no expert operators, and required no translation into code. Between 1881 and 1900, the number of telephones installed grew between 9 and 27 per cent annually. In 1900, about 1.5 million telephones were in use in the United States; by 1918, about 10 million. The phone was primarily an urban phenomenon before 1900. Then rural telephone hookups expanded by an astounding 449 per cent between 1902 and 1907. In Wisconsin, there were 225,265 telephones by 1915, of which 118,598 were urban residential, 48,546 business, and 57,020 rural.[7]

Equally vital to the communications revolution was an explosion in mass-circulation newspapers, periodicals, and books—representing a conflation of changes in technology, organization and marketing, mass society, and literacy rates. By 1902, electrically driven presses made it possible for a newspaper to print up to 500,000 copies daily. Paper manufacturers in Wisconsin and elsewhere had learned how to mass-produce cheap newsprint which fed the nation's ravenous presses. Telegraphy led to regional and national news services and businesses created new markets by advertising their products widely and thus helping to fill newspapers' pages. Newspapers' content mixed messages from political, economic, and moral reformers with tales of scandal and violence, sensationalism, and human interest stories. Cheaper postal rates, new railway networks, and the development of trucks facilitated mass circulation. Millions of newcomers to the nation's cities looked to the newspaper as a source of information, style and opinion, and a sense of community in a universe of anonymous individuals and antagonistic groups. By 1914, the newspaper had achieved its modern format and enjoyed near monopoly status as purveyor of news and opinion. Between 1892 and 1914, daily newspapers increased in number from 1,650 to 2,250, and their average circulation doubled.[8]

---

[7] Neil H. Wasserman, *From Invention to Innovation: Long-Distance Telephone Transmission at the Turn of the Century* (Baltimore, 1985), 1–13, 119–126; John Brooks, *Telephone: The First Hundred Years* (New York, 1975), 59–155; Dodds, *Life in Twentieth Century America*, 137; Walker, *Everyday Life in Victorian America*, 53; Marcus and Segal, *Technology in America*, 158–165; Oliver, *History of American Technology*, 435–440; Railroad Commission, *Annual Report*, 1915, pp. 603–619; Railroad Commission, *Rules for Telephone Service in Force, October 12, 1914*, broadside; John L. Miller, "A History of the Telephone Industry as a Regulated Business in Wisconsin" (doctoral dissertation, University of Wisconsin, 1940), 1–57.

[8] Frank Luther Mott, *American Journalism: A History of Newspapers in the United States through 260 Years: 1690 to 1950* (New York, 1941; revised ed., 1950), 546–560, 577–592; Gunther Barth, *City People: The Rise of Modern City Culture in Nineteenth-Century America* (New York, 1980), 48–109; Bernard A. Weisberger, *The American Newspaper-*

In Wisconsin, the number of newspapers increased from 440 to 611 between 1893 and 1915. The median circulation rose from 567 to 6,457 between 1876 and 1916; the number of rural and village weeklies, from 387 to 537; urban dailies, from twenty-one to fifty-eight. City newspapers also increased in size, going from four or eight pages to sizes similar to those maintained in the last half of the twentieth century. They printed more state and national news, and developed features, including women's, sports, finance, health, and literary (chapter-a-day) sections. Editorially, some papers engaged in social criticism ("muckraking" as it became known). Successful papers thrived from subscriptions and classified, commercial, and legal advertising. The number of foreign-language newspapers remained stable, but their circulations steadily declined. Between 1884 and 1910, the combined circulation of the *Germania, Herald*, and *Seebote*, Milwaukee's three largest German dailies, dipped from 92,000 to 45,000, while the city's three biggest English-language papers more than tripled circulation to 150,000. The number of politically independent newspapers grew from seventy-eight to 174, reflecting a trend towards "objectivity" and the fear of antagonizing advertisers. The number of avowedly Republican papers grew from 184 to 297; Democratic papers dropped from 145 to 103. The state's major Republican papers became weapons in the factional war between Stalwarts and Progressives.[9]

Popular magazines joined in the communications industry's phenomenal growth. Their target audience was the middle class, whose appetite for "the American Dream" encompassed material success, "good taste," and what would later be styled "family values." Magazines such as the *Ladies' Home Journal* and the *Saturday Evening Post* abounded with true accounts of men and women who had become rich and famous through pluck, sobriety, and undaunted striving. Equally popular were fictional stories of heroes who were honest,

---

man (Chicago, 1961), 121–155; David Paul Nord, *Newspapers and New Politics: Midwestern Municipal Reform, 1890–1900* (Ann Arbor, Michigan, 1981), 11–19, 124–126; Oliver, *History of American Technology*, 444–448; Christopher P. Wilson, *The Labor of Words: Literacy Professionalism in the Progressive Era* (Athens, Georgia, 1985), 17–39; Gerald J. Baldasty, *The Commercialization of News in the Nineteenth Century* (Madison, 1992), 36–148.

[9] "The Wisconsin Press," in the *Wisconsin Blue Book, 1893*, pp. 351–361; "The Wisconsin Press," in the *Wisconsin Blue Book, 1913*, pp. 318–332; Donald E. Oehlerts, comp., *Guide to Wisconsin Newspapers, 1833–1957* (Madison, 1958); Donald L. Shaw, "Bias in the News: A Study of National Presidential Campaign Coverage in the Wisconsin English Daily Press, 1852–1916" (doctoral dissertation, University of Wisconsin, 1966), 30–33, 49, 78–90; Carl Wittke, *The German-Language Press in America* (New York, 1957), 243–244; Adolf Gerd Korman, "Wisconsin's German-American Press During the Progressive Movement" (master's thesis, University of Wisconsin, 1953), 42–55.

courageous, and hard-working, and heroines who were chaste, supportive, and self-sacrificing—the embodiment of "true womanhood."

Like newspapers, magazines engaged in circulation wars, cutting newsstand and subscription prices, offering premiums, rebates, discounts, and contests, and turning to advertising for profits. The apotheosis of successful advertising was achieved by the advertising-only mail-order catalogs of Sears, Roebuck and Montgomery Ward. By 1918, the total volume of advertising nationally was $1.5 billion.[10]

Even as the communications revolution enshrined the written word and put a premium on literacy, other technological innovations challenged the written word's hegemony. The telephone and phonograph had already established "wireless telegraphy." By 1904, the first land-based wireless systems had been established on the Atlantic Coast, and wireless stations created a sensation at the Louisiana Purchase Exposition in St. Louis. By 1914, the vacuum tube, the regenerative circuit, the superheterodyne, and the frequency modulator were giving birth to the "radio age."[11]

The radio-age generation was even more awed by the development of the motion picture. By 1896, vaudeville theaters were showing short motion pictures as "chasers" designed to clear out the house between shows. Before long, the roles were reversed, and fledgling motion-picture companies mushroomed. By 1910, "nickelodeon" (meaning the five-cent price of admission) had become a household word, and America had 10,000 motion picture theaters, plus 1,400 other entertainment establishments that showed movies as part of their fare.[12]

In 1914, the Milwaukee *Sentinel* estimated that one-eighth of Wisconsin's population could attend movies at the same time in the state's fifty-four theaters offering two to fifteen shows daily. The pop-

---

[10] Stephen Fox, *The Mirror Makers: A History of American Advertising and its Creators* (New York, 1984), 15–71; Roland Marchand, *Advertising the American Dream: Making Way for Modernity, 1920–1940* (Berkeley and Los Angeles, 1985), xvii–xxi, 24; Walker, *Everyday Life in Victorian America*, 175–206; Dodds, *Life in Twentieth Century America*, 79–108; Daniel Pope, *The Making of Modern Advertising* (New York, 1983), 61, 108–111, 180–183, 224–226; *Hoard's Dairyman*, May 8, 1914, p. 576; Theodore Peterson, *Magazines in the Twentieth Century* (2nd ed., Urbana, 1956), 1–39; James P. Wood, *Magazines in the United States* (3rd ed., New York, 1971), 93–146; Christopher P. Wilson, "The Rhetoric Of Consumption: Mass-Market Magazines and the Demise of the Gentle Reader, 1880–1920," in Richard Wightman Fox and T. J. Jackson Lears, eds., *The Culture of Consumption: Critical Essays in American History, 1880–1980* (New York, 1983), 41–64.

[11] Oliver, *History of American Technology*, 496–502; Dodds, *Life in Twentieth Century America*, 182–183; Marcus and Segal, *Technology in America*, 163–165.

[12] Oliver, *History of American Technology*, 504–516; Dodds, *Life in Twentieth Century America*, 172–182; Marcus and Segal, *Technology in America*, 212–216.

ularity of movies raised questions about the content of what was shown on the screen and prompted attempts at censorship, spearheaded by Milwaukee's reform-minded City Club, which successfully sponsored a city ordinance prohibiting display of the "nude human form, or parts thereof, between the shoulders and the knees," or of the "human form, whether nude or not, as to be suggestive of lewdness or obscenity, or that contain words, letters or characters which convey a lewd or obscene idea, or that portray murderous or criminal personal actions, encounters or assaults." Similarly, the legislature's so-called Teasdale Vice Committee disapproved of the new medium, admission to which was within "the reach of children, and classes living even in the poorest sections of great cities," and which exposed them to "a sensational and lurid exposition of life" in a crowded, darkened room. The committee recommended "a more rigid supervision of all that takes place in the moving picture theater."[13]

[2]

The transportation revolution brought improvements in old modes and the development of new ones, mostly through electrical power and the internal combustion engine. By 1914, all major forms of twentieth-century transportation had proven their potential, defining the terms of a passionate debate over whether "the masses" should be transported en masse, or in individual private conveyances. The world's largest rail network and a dazzling array of technological improvements had been accomplished between 1875 and 1900 in America. In Wisconsin, railroad mileage more than doubled, nearly all of it in the southern two-thirds of the state. The location of the rail lines and the ability of promoters to attract settlers and commercial freight were major factors in the settlement and urban patterns of the Cutover. Then, between 1900 and 1920, the Chicago, Milwaukee, and St. Paul, the Chicago and North Western, and the Wisconsin Central laid nearly 2,000 miles of track, linking the settled parts of Wisconsin with the New North's lumber and paper mills, iron mines, and Lake Superior ore ports. The railroads advertised and ran demonstration trains, luring thousands of settlers northward.[14]

---

[13] Milwaukee *Sentinel*, June 27, 1914; Harnell Hart to unnamed woman, February 17, 1914, "Public Morals" folder, box 3, in the Records of the City Club of Milwaukee, 1909–1975, University of Wisconsin-Milwaukee Area Research Center; *Milwaukee Code*, 1914, p. 449 (article 3, section 105); Legislature, *Report and Recommendations of the Wisconsin Legislative Committee to Investigate the White Slave Traffic and Kindred Subjects*, 1914, pp. 75–76.

[14] Walker, *Everyday Life in Victorian America*, 59–70; Oliver, *History of Technology*, 415–427; Robert C. Nesbit, *Wisconsin: A History* (2nd ed., by William F. Thompson, Madi-

Electric interurban railways boomed at the same time and reinforced rail's supremacy. Interurbans linked city streetcar systems and the transcontinental railroad, distinguished by their use of electric power rather than the steam used by transcontinental lines, their emphasis on passenger service rather than freight, and by equipment that was heavier and faster than streetcars. They operated on trolley tracks in cities, and adjacent to highways or on private rights-of-way in rural areas. Most were owned by local streetcar and utilities companies and ran on electricity provided by central power stations to overhead cables, with transformers generating the varied amounts of power required by the engines for city and rural travel. Passenger traffic accounted for nine-tenths of interurban business; most lines ran trains hourly between larger cities. The cars' accommodations were inferior to those of main-line railroads, but interurbans had lower fares, more frequent service, and superior accessibility. Because they were generally undercapitalized, and had to compete fiercely with railroads and automobiles, they lasted only a few decades. But for a brief time they seemed to offer the solution to the problem of cheap mass transportation in urbanized areas.[15]

Interurbans came early to Wisconsin, due to the networks of medium-sized cities along the shore of Lake Michigan, and in the Fox, Wisconsin, and Rock river valleys. About a third of Wisconsin's 383 miles of interurban trackage was built before 1900; the remainder, by 1910. More than half of Wisconsin's trackage belonged to The Milwaukee Electric Railway and Light Co. (TMERL). By 1909 it had acquired or constructed lines to Wauwatosa, Waukesha, Racine, Kenosha, Hales Corners, Muskego, Oconomowoc, Watertown, Burlington, and East Troy. At that point, TMERL's holding company, North American, was acquired by a group of investors who were skeptical of interurbans and who jettisoned projected extensions to Chicago, Madison, and Lake Geneva. The Milwaukee Northern Railway Company ran to Port Washington and Sheboygan, where it connected with the interurban line run by the Wisconsin Power and Light Company. The new line ran westward through Kohler and Sheboygan Falls to Plymouth, then on to the resort community of Elkhart Lake. For several years, Chicagoans could reach Elkhart Lake via interurbans alone. By 1903, a three-line system also ran between Fond du Lac and Green Bay, covering sixty-seven miles on the western shore of Lake

---

son, 1989), 317–327, 383–386; Arlan Helgeson, *Farms in the Cutover: Agricultural Settlement in Northern Wisconsin* (Madison, 1962), 4–5, 44–45; William F. Raney, "The Building of Wisconsin Railroads," in *WMH*, 19 (June, 1936), 387–403.

[15] Hilton and Due, *Electric Interurban Railways*, 3–148, 353–357; William D. Middleton, *The Interurban Era* (Milwaukee, 1961), 10–227; Canfield, *TM*, 104–111, 126–137, 170–180.

Winnebago and in the Fox River Valley. From 1900 until the Great Depression, communities along the Lake Michigan shoreline and in the Fox Valley boasted one of the nation's most useful interurban systems. Except for the gap between Elkhart Lake and Fond du Lac, there was a convenient link between Chicago and Green Bay that operated for a number of years.[16]

In the rest of Wisconsin, interurban systems operated between Eau Claire and Chippewa Falls from 1898 to 1926, from Wausau to Schofield between 1909 and 1934, and from Manitowoc to Two Rivers between 1902 and 1926. Madison failed to achieve an interurban connection, although merchants and promoters devised several schemes to link the capital city with La Crosse, Stevens Point, Green Bay, Milwaukee, Chicago, and Rockford.

Between the 1890's and 1910, the urban transportation revolution in Wisconsin involved the transition from horse-drawn street railways to cable cars and trolley cars. Overhead wires called "trollers" brought power to trolleys. They were made possible by transformers that adjusted the voltage and raised streetcar speeds to nearly thirty miles an hour. In 1890, the nation had 1,260 miles of electric traction lines, compared to 5,700 miles of horse-drawn railways and 500 miles of cable cars. Twelve years later, some 22,000 miles of electric trolley lines accounted for 97 per cent of America's urban mass transit.[17]

Cyclists literally paved the way for the automobile. A cycling craze in the 1890's had blossomed by the turn of the century into a $15 million industry. In 1900 the nation had 312 bicycle factories and more than 10 million bikes on the road. People wrote bicycle songs and poems and designed clothing for cycling safety and comfort. Before long they agitated for road signs, traffic signals, and better roads—all useful for motorists later on. The League of American Wheelmen and similar cycling organizations were the first to press for hard-surfaced highways.[18]

The automobile combined the bicycle's traits of independence and individual control with the power, speed, and carrying capacity of the railroad. The auto was originally made in Europe and was not distributed in the U.S. until about 1895. Then its appeal to the American fascination with technology and its promise of overcoming vast expanses of space and time all but guaranteed that the nation would

---

[16] Hilton and Due, *Electric Interurban Railways*, 353–357; Canfield, *TM*, 203–321; McDonald, *Let There Be Light*, 104–111, 126–137, 170–180.

[17] David V. Mollenhoff, *Madison: A History of the Formative Years* (Dubuque, 1982), 278–280. See also Chapter 4 for a discussion of urban transit.

[18] Dodds, *Life in Twentieth Century America*, 14–15; Walker, *Everyday Life in Victorian America*, 56–57; Marcus and Segal, *Technology in America*, 205–207; Robert A. Smith, *A Social History of the Bicycle: Its Early Life and Times in America* (New York, 1972), 17–204.

become obsessed with "automobility." The automobile gradually brought about the virtual demise of mass rail transit and profoundly affected the American way of life. It hastened the decline of localism, ethnicity, and class differences, thereby contributing to the triumph of a standardized, nationalized, middle-class culture and the rise of the modern metropolis. The automobile industry quickly became the prime mover in America's mass-production economy: the leading product of mass consumption, the chief consumer of steel, petroleum, rubber, glass, and paint products, the driving force behind related service industries and real estate booms, and the *raison d'être* for surfacing and expanding urban streets and rural highways.[19]

The automobile did not accomplish any of these marvels before 1910. The preceding two decades were spent creating an automobile consciousness through exposure and press coverage. Even though motor cars were originally playthings for the upper classes, the coverage about them in the popular press was overwhelmingly positive. Auto races and trade shows were widely attended, and regulatory laws were few and lenient. Many predicted that the car would cure social ills ranging from urban congestion to rural isolation. Horse-breeders, livery stable owners, and horse-drawn vehicle drivers' associations of course opposed autos, but the public dismissed them as self-interested. Farmers and the urban lower classes expressed an antipathy tinged with envy which virtually disappeared when affordable automobiles became commonplace. The first automobiles were costly, and remained so for several years. But their numbers grew phenomenally. Registrations in the United States rose from 8,000 in 1900 to 9.2 million in 1920, annual sales mushroomed from 4,000 to nearly 2 million, and automobile manufacturing rose from 150th in product value to third. Between 1904 and 1912, the number of trucks zoomed from 700 to 42,000. In Wisconsin, motor vehicle registrations rose from 160 in 1900 to 1,600 in 1905 and 14,200 in 1910, ranking it fifteenth, fourteenth, and tenth among the states. The national average was one car per 125 people in 1910; Wisconsin ranked sixteenth with one per 104. Four years later, Wisconsin registrations passed the 50,000 mark, representing about 8 per cent of the nation's total.[20]

---

[19] James J. Flink, *America Adopts the Automobile, 1895–1910* (Cambridge, 1970), 2–4; George E. Mowry and Blaine A. Brownell, *The Urban Nation, 1920–1980* (revised ed., New York, 1981), 14–15.

[20] Flink, *America Adopts the Automobile*, 11–291; James J. Flink, "Three Stages of American Automobile Consciousness," *American Quarterly*, 24 (October, 1972) 451–457; Richard Harmond, "Is the Love Affair Over? Americans and the Automobile," in Frank J. Coppa and Richard Harmond, eds., *Technology in the Twentieth Century* (Dubuque, 1983) 89–94; *Fourteenth Census of the United States, 1920: Manufactures, 1919, General Report and Analytical Tables*, 160–170. Many of my insights into this topic were provided by a paper by Clay McShane, "The Emergence of the Internal Combustion

A Passion for Newness and for System 313

Madison had but eight automobiles as late as 1903, but they attracted favorable notice. The *Wisconsin State Journal* editorialized that autos would reduce horse manure underfoot, improve opportunities for social life, and reduce dependence on railroads. That same year, the city council set a twelve-mile-per-hour speed limit, required adequate brakes and lights, and directed "autoists" to slow down or stop for horses. The following year, it reduced the speed limit to five miles an hour in central parts of Madison and ten miles elsewhere. In 1905, only one household in a hundred owned an automobile; in 1910, one in twenty-three; by 1915, one in eight. In Milwaukee, the automobile age began on May 18, 1899, when George L. Odenbrett became the first driver to appear on the city's streets. Scarcely three years later, the common council adopted an ordinance regulating the speed and use of automobiles and providing for a fine of one to five dollars or a jail sentence of up to ninety days. By 1906, automobile advertisements were standard fare in the city's newspapers. Within seven years, Milwaukee boasted 3,608 cars and had become, along with Kenosha and Racine, a major producer of automobiles and auto parts.[21]

The same generation that contended with the changes in practical conceptions of space and time made possible by the automobile and the electric trolley also witnessed the end of earth-bound transportation. On December 17, 1903, Wilbur Wright made his initial fifty-nine-second flight. By 1911, there were 300 airplanes in the United States and, two years later, some were reaching speeds of 300 miles per hour. Even before World War I, Americans were experimenting with commercial plane travel and air mail. It was in the winter of 1915–1916 that a native Milwaukeean, William Mitchell, took his first flying lesson. As Captain Billy Mitchell, he would later make his mark upon military aviation.[22]

[3]

This transportation and communications revolution enabled the reordering of society. The improvements nominally "brought people closer together," but they did so in a manner that reinforced and

---

Automobile: An Urban Phenomenon," delivered to the Organization of American Historians, Washington, D.C., March 25, 1990. I want to thank Professor McShane for sharing these and related notions with me. Michael L. Berger, *The Devil Wagon in God's Country: The Automobile and Social Change in America, 1893–1929* (Hamden, Connecticut, 1979), 73 (quote).

[21] Mollenhoff, *Madison*, 360–368; Bayrd Still, *Milwaukee: The History of a City* (Madison, 1948; reprinted, 1965), 391, 405, 449, 496, 553.

[22] Isaac Don Levine, *Mitchell: Pioneer of Air Power* (New York, 1943), 9–28, 86–87.

widened social divisions. Electricity, telephones, automobiles, and other marvels all tended to trickle down, from the most advantaged to the least privileged, along the old fault lines of wealth, race, ethnicity, religion, gender, age, and geographical location. The machine metaphor and the business model of organization can be used to explain the phenomenon as follows.

Those in power strove to restructure most aspects of life into large-scale, complex, impersonal systems made up of discrete, hierarchically arranged components. The new managers of society taught such values as productivity, efficiency, predictability, docility, standardization, and the perpetual consumption of goods and services. They sought to acculturate everyone into the discipline and world view of the modern urban-industrial order.[23]

Indispensable to such systematization was the rise of university-trained professionals, both in long-established disciplines like medicine, law, architecture, engineering, and military science, as well as in new areas like social work, urban planning, public health, housing, business management, and social science. All shared the belief that modern life was so complex that it could be comprehended only by breaking it down into manageable segments, each to be mastered by persons with specialized knowledge and skill. Professionals formed associations, published journals, held conferences, established schools, lobbied lawmakers, entered public service, and developed rituals and symbols. People in every endeavor sought to invest their particular specialties with an aura of professionalism, and to impose each specialty's structure, principles, and values on the rest of society, often in the name of reform. And the mass of Americans, bewildered by the complexity and pace of modern life, increasingly turned to experts who proclaimed themselves to be objective, incorruptible, and all-knowing.[24]

---

[23] Marcus and Segal, *Technology in America*, 135–215; Thomas P. Hughes, *American Genesis: A Century of Invention and Technological Enthusiasm, 1870–1970* (New York, 1989), 1–7, 184–220, 459–472; Hughes, *Networks of Power*, 1–17, 461–465; Robert H. Wiebe, *The Search for Order, 1877–1920* (New York, 1967), 133–163; Robert H. Wiebe, *The Segmented Society: An Introduction to the Meaning of America* (New York, 1975), 36–46; Richard Wightman Fox and T. J. Jackson Lears, eds., *The Culture of Consumption* (New York, 1983), x–xviii, 1–38; Loren Baritz, *The Servants of Power: A History of the Use of Social Science in American Industry* (Westport, Connecticut, 1960), 4–38; Daniel J. Boorstin, *The Americans: The Democratic Experience* (New York, 1973), 89–410; Donald MacKenzie and Judy Wajcman, eds., *The Social Shaping of Technology: How the Refrigerator Got Its Hum* (Philadelphia, 1985), 2–25; Lawrence Chenoweth, *The American Dream of Success: The Search for the Self in the Twentieth Century* (North Scituate, Massachusetts, 1974), 1–62; Olivier Zunz, *Making America Corporate, 1870–1920* (Chicago, 1990), 1–36, 199–204; Platt, *The Electric City*, 82–91.

[24] Wiebe, *The Search for Order*, 112–163; Burton J. Bledstein, *The Culture of Professionalism: The Middle Class and the Development of Higher Education in America* (New York,

The extent to which the citizens of Progressive Era Wisconsin enjoyed the benefits of technology, and were affected by systematization, depended largely upon their individual socio-economic circumstances, geographical location, and ethno-cultural background. Benefits reached the richest first, then descended in economic order. As for location, people in larger cities were better situated than those on farms or in villages. To be affluent and urban, especially in the southern half of the state, provided the most creature comforts; to be poor and rural, especially in the Cutover, provided the least. To have dark skin, or to be an immigrant from southern and eastern Europe, generally limited access to the new benefits. Native Americans, who were generally poor, rural, racially distinct, and embraced a culture that eschewed materialism and creature comforts, were the least likely to benefit from the new technology. African Americans, though generally urban, fared little better. Economies of scale dictated that providers of technology earned the greatest profits from city dwellers; but well-to-do dairy farmers and small-town businessmen generally acquired electricity, telephones, and automobiles ahead of most urban workers.

As for systematization, the rural poor and racial minorities were also the least touched, while middle-class people, especially in larger cities, were the most. The industrial working class found itself constrained by scientific management and was the main target of enforced acculturation and campaigns of social uplift. Even so, social segregation, lack of access to transportation and communications media, and vibrant Old World cultures allowed many immigrant workers to escape or evade social systematization.[25]

The most prosperous dairymen in the southeastern quadrant of the state were enmeshed in the evolving urban-industrial systems, but Wisconsinites who lived on rural, unincorporated land remained outside it for the most part, and thus did without technological benefits. Some dreamed of reaping those marvels without submitting to congestion, regimentation, and standardization; and their dream seemed attainable, particularly because of the small-town experience. People

---

1976), 46–128; Don S. Kirschner, *The Paradox of Professionalism: Reform and Public Service in Urban America, 1900–1940* (Westport, Connecticut, 1986), 1–23; Samuel Haber, *The Quest for Authority and Honor in the American Professions, 1750–1900* (Chicago, 1991), 193–205, 359–362; Marcus and Segal, *Technology in America*, 165–175; Dorothy Ross, *The Origins of American Social Science* (Cambridge, England, 1991), xiii–xvii, 471–475.

[25] Zahava Fuchs and Douglas G. Marshall, *The Socioeconomic Composition of Wisconsin's Population, 1900–1960*, UW Department of Rural Sociology, *Population Series*, no. 12 (1968), 114–119; Walter H. Ebling et al., *A Century of Wisconsin Agriculture, 1848–1948*, Department of Agriculture, Crop and Livestock Reporting Service, *Bulletin*, no. 290 (1948), 86–88; Charles J. Galpin, *Rural Life* (New York, 1922), 107–117.

who lived in villages or cities of under 1,000 were significantly more urbanized than those who lived in unincorporated hamlets. Whatever its population, the extent of a city's immersion in the urban-industrial system depended upon its geographical location. For example, because of their proximity to Milwaukee, the state's metropolis in 1910, Cudahy (3,691), Wauwatosa (3,346), West Milwaukee (1,458), and North Milwaukee (1,860) were more caught up in "the system" than larger, distant communities like Antigo (7,196), Merrill (8,689), or Beaver Dam (6,758). The same was true of Two Rivers (4,850), Sheboygan Falls (1,630), and De Pere (4,477), all of which were "twins" to larger cities—Manitowoc, Sheboygan, and Green Bay.[26]

Whatever their location or incorporation status, all of Wisconsin's villages and most smaller cities occupied a no-man's land between rural and urban. Their residents' origins and memories were almost all rooted in agriculture, and their economic health depended upon supplying goods and services to their agricultural hinterlands. However, small-towns aspirations, both individual and corporate, were often aggressively urban. For individuals, they frequently served as way stations or staging grounds where businessmen and entrepreneurs prepared to meet the challenges of a larger arena. As communities, they frequently proclaimed their ambition to increase in size, population, and wealth, reaching for the status and power of metropolis. If that goal proved beyond grasp, small-town leaders tried to acquire the amenities of the big city, hoping to rival it in style and sophistication. They were beginning to develop an uneasy awareness that the new urban-industrial system was a threat that could relegate farm, village, or small city to a subordinate, functional position. Small towns frequently manifested a love-hate relationship towards both the countryside and the big city. Small-town people might envy and attempt to emulate their big city cousins, but they still believed in their own moral and physical superiority.[27]

Critics of midwestern small-town life generally agreed that local merchants exploited farmers, while local citizens often patronized or embarrassed them. The economist Thorstein Veblen, born in Mani-

---

[26] *Thirteenth Census of the United States, 1910: Population, Volume III, Reports by States, with Statistics for Counties, Cities and Other Civil Divisions*, 1049–1071. For definitions of communities by size, see Lewis E. Atherton, *Main Street on the Middle Border* (Bloomington, Indiana, 1954; reprinted, 1984), chap. 14, and Richard R. Lingeman, *Small Town America: A Narrative History, 1620–the Present* (New York, 1980; reprinted, Boston, 1981).

[27] Lingeman, *Small Town America*, 258–337; Berger, *The Devil Wagon*, 77–102; Atherton, *Main Street*, 217–242, 330–358; Lewis E. Atherton, "The Midwestern Country Town—Myth and Reality," in *Agricultural History*, 26 (July, 1952), 73–80; Jane Marie Pederson, *Between Memory and Reality: Family and Community in Rural Wisconsin, 1870–1970* (Madison, 1992).

towoc County and raised on farms in Wisconsin and Minnesota, charged that the "country town of the great American farming-region is the perfect flower of self-help and cupidity," whose merchants treated farmers with "circumspection" or "salesmanlike pusillanimity." He accused small-town merchants of trying to monopolize the farmers' trade, of charging them exorbitant prices driven by needless duplication of overhead and personnel, and of being "aggressively and truculently" conservative. Only when farmers and townspeople joined hands to boost real estate prices did merchants hide their hostility and condescension.[28]

More dispassionately, the rural sociologist Charles Galpin argued that the village, in wanting to become more city-like, flaunted its belief in its superiority to the nearby farmers and thereby antagonized them—the same people the banker, storekeeper, and blacksmith recognized as "the goose that lays the golden egg." Village businessmen's goal was to placate the farmer and retain his business "without building him and his mind, capacities, and wishes, into the community fabric." This was accomplished by presenting the farmer with "a few donations, as privileges in order to bind him," and sometimes by "craft" rather than by "open dealing." Farmers accordingly remained spectators or aliens. To remedy this situation, Galpin urged starting comprehensive rural communities to foster what he termed "rurbanism," meaning a "mesh of interrelated social interests uniting small-city dweller and farmer." Indeed, as the century wore on, the differences between small towns and big cities began to diminish. In many respects, rural communities, like urban neighborhoods, grew ever more homogeneous. At the same time, distinctions of class, wealth, and social status multiplied and became more apparent; larger towns had correspondingly larger and more fully developed social systems.[29]

Potential profits varied with population concentration and income and therefore determined when communities got telephones, electricity, and running water. In 1903, the private electric utility in the village of Cassville in Grant County (population 979 in 1900) had only twenty-eight subscribers, all of them in the business district. When the electrical company's owner advertised for an engineer to run the plant from sunset to midnight—moonlit nights excepted—

[28] Thorstein Veblen, "The Country Town," in *The Freeman* (New York), July 11 (417–420) and July 18 (440–445), 1923; Atherton, *Main Street*, 49; Atherton, "Midwestern Country Town," in *Agricultural History*, 26: 73–74; Berger, *The Devil Wagon*, 77–80; Lingeman, *Small Town America*, 332–335.

[29] Charles J. Galpin, *The Social Anatomy of an Agricultural Community*, UW Agricultural Experiment Station, *Research Bulletin*, no. 34 (1915), 25–27, 33; John H. Kolb, *Emerging Rural Communities: Group Relations in Rural Society, a Review of Wisconsin Research in Action* (Madison, 1959), 6–11, 91–105.

for thirty dollars a month, he received no takers. Then the dynamo broke down, and it took the manufacturer several months to make the repairs.

Business districts had few embellishments. Merchants usually resisted "beautification" projects sponsored by women's groups because of their devotion to low property taxes. The concert hall in Beaver Dam (population 5,128 in 1900) was typical of small Wisconsin cities' cultural amenities. It was a ninety-foot-long room on the second floor of a building that also housed a tavern, a law office, and a newspaper. The audience sat on folding chairs, facing a stage illuminated by kerosene footlights and a curtain bearing a painted view of the Bay of Naples. Although small-town rituals and ceremonies conveyed a sense of timelessness, the towns themselves were being absorbed inexorably into the economy and culture of the new urban-industrial order.[30]

The desire to emulate larger cities characterized Neenah-Menasha, whose combined 1910 population of 11,815 made them tributary to Appleton (16,773), Green Bay (25,236), and Oshkosh (33,062), as well as to the national paper industry. Boosters still proclaimed Neenah as "the boss city of the Lower Fox" and Menasha as the "city of paper and pails," and business associations, social clubs, and fraternal organizations urged residents to buy local products, work for better public services, and "always say something good about my town." Both still lagged behind the Fox Valley's larger cities, and both were dominated by manufacturers who believed in voluntary action, limited government, and low taxes—not in planting flowers or cleaning up the streets. Municipal services in both communities improved slowly; the city councils bettered services only when community leaders told them to. There was no adequate municipal water system in Neenah-Menasha until 1905; telephone service was not fully available until a few years later. By 1900, the main streets and larger buildings had electricity, but installation in houses largely awaited World War I. Despite these relative deprivations, Neenah-Menasha's working-class population was generally passive and acquiescent, inspired by faith that the city fathers, on whom they largely relied for employment, were reasonable.[31]

---

[30] Lingeman, *Small Town America*, 258–363. Berger, *The Devil Wagon*, p. 210, presents the small rural town as a social and economic victim of urbanization of the countryside.

[31] Charles N. Glaab and Lawrence H. Larsen, *Factories in The Valley: Neenah-Menasha, 1870–1915* (Madison, 1969), 212–219; Stuart M. Blumin, *The Emergence of the Middle Class: Social Experience in the American City, 1760–1900* (Cambridge, England, 1989), 305–310.

By the early twentieth century, when nearly all small- to medium-sized cities had brick or concrete streets and sidewalks and a scattering of automobiles, Lynxville (Crawford County, population 322 in 1900), Necedah (Juneau County, 1,209), and Mazomanie (Dane County, 902) still had wooden sidewalks, dirt streets, and horses and wagons. Some towns put on airs; others seemed to smile at their pretensions. Gillett (Oconto County and unincorporated in 1900), like many other towns, was featured on postcards on which were superimposed paved sidewalks and trolley car lines—a tongue-in-cheek emulation of larger municipalities. Wisconsin Rapids (4,493), according to a fictionalized account, was "conspicuous for variety," with the bankers, cranberry growers, lumber kings, and pulp and paper mill owners on Quality Row having "all the education and culture that money can purchase." Sturgeon Bay (3,372) advertised itself as the "Fraternal City," boasting that it had one fraternal organization for every 150 citizens and claiming that the small-town banker "must be a man of parts, as versatile in accomplishment as the man who plays trap drums in the orchestra pit."[32]

Fort Atkinson (3,043 in 1900 and 3,877 in 1910) merchants were touted in the *Jefferson County Union* in 1903 as "progressive" because they believed in "being up-to-date on all subjects pertaining to their business, whether it be in the goods they dispose of or in the treatment of their employees." Ten years later the paper boasted of macadamized streets, twelve miles of cement sidewalks, two public parks, a city hall, electrical lighting, a good waterworks system, three weekly newspapers, and a variety of businesses. Its leading newspaper frequently urged citizens to "boom your home town." A few years later, in a similar vein, the *Jefferson County Union* described Fort Atkinson's growth as "solid and gradual," saying there was work for everyone, that "the city continues to improve along all lines" and was "commonly called 'the greatest little city in the world.'"[33]

While Wisconsin's villages and small cities envied the growth and technological progress they associated with large cities, life in those cities was neither of one piece nor necessarily of a higher quality. Living conditions in the larger and more industrialized cities closely paralleled the segmentation and stratification of its working conditions. Socio-economic circumstances differentiated neighborhoods,

---

[32] Sturgeon Bay Advertising Company, *Sturgeon Bay, Wisconsin* (Sturgeon Bay, 1905), unpaginated; Ellen Lenore Minahan, *End of the Corduroy* (Boston, 1947), 355. The observations about villages and small cities were gained from studying photographs in Classified File 25 in the iconographic collections of the SHSW archives.

[33] *Jefferson County Union* (Fort Atkinson), December 11, 1903, August 28, 1908, May 30, 1913, and June 6, 1913.

and ethnicity reinforced those circumstances. The same general formula apportioned the fruits of the new technology, defining the fault lines of inequality.[34]

The urban upper class generally resided in exclusive neighborhoods where large, multi-storied, single-family homes, possessing up-to-date technological amenities and a staff of live-in servants, stood on groomed lawns fronted by tree-lined sidewalks. In Milwaukee it was Yankee Hill; in Kenosha, Yankeetown; in Madison, University Heights; in Racine, the south lakefront. Most such neighborhoods were located near—but not too near—the central business district, although the trolley car and the automobile were already facilitating exclusive suburbs. The upper classes embodied what Thorstein Veblen famously called "conspicuous consumption." They commanded deference from the rest of society and exercised dominion through a complex network of commercial transactions, political alliances, professional and business associations, philanthropic agencies, cultural organizations, social clubs, church membership, and school ties.[35]

Just below them on the social pyramid stood a large and variegated middle class, made up of corporate executives, professionals, small businessmen, clerks, salaried artisans and craftsmen, and some white-collar employees. Middle-class residential sections were usually graduated completely according to the size and value of real property, the quality of urban amenities and services, the occupational status and ethnic backgrounds of their occupants, and, increasingly, the number and quality of electrical appliances and automobiles. Middle-class people were preoccupied with style and taste, material success and child-rearing, self-improvement and self-realization.[36]

The broad base of the social pyramid was "the other half": the workers whose incomes, education, occupations, and quality of life fell below the minimum requirements imposed by even the most generous definition of "middle class." The great majority were immigrants and people of color. They typically dwelled in residential zones

[34] Jacob A. Riis, *How the Other Half Lives: Studies Among the Tenements of New York* (New York, 1890), 16; Gunther Barth, *City People: The Rise of Modern City Culture in Nineteenth-Century America* (New York, 1980), 3–23; Jon C. Teaford, *The Twentieth-Century American City* (Baltimore, 1986; revised ed., 1993), 2–30.

[35] Frederic Cople Jaher, *The Urban Establishment: Upper Strata in Boston, New York, Charleston, Chicago, and Los Angeles* (Urbana, 1982), 1–15, 711–730; E. Digby Baltzell, *The Protestant Establishment: Aristocracy and Caste in America* (New York, 1964), vii–xiii; Walker, *Everyday Life in Victorian America*, 127–131.

[36] William Bruce Wheeler and Susan D. Becker, *Discovering The American Past: A Look at the Evidence* (Boston, 1990), 50–93; Loren Baritz, *The Good Life: The Meaning of Success for the American Middle Class* (New York, 1989), xii; Blumin, *The Emergence of a Middle Class*, 258–297; Walker, *Everyday Life in Victorian America*, 207–244; Dodds, *Life in Twentieth Century America*, 55–65.

characterized by high population density, low-grade housing, and close proximity to factories. Their streets were apt to be unpaved and unlighted; their houses, dilapidated and lacking telephones, electricity, and indoor toilets. Frequently these zones had inadequate sewage and garbage disposal, sporadic police and fire protection, and poor or nonexistent educational and recreational facilities. An index to their standard of living exists in statistics for infant and child mortality, infectious diseases rates, crime rates, and organized vice and gambling. Perhaps the zones' only saving grace was that similar people clustered together and pooled their resources in efforts at social betterment and maintaining ethno-cultural traditions. To the upper and middle classes, many working-class citizens constituted a "social problem," which they tried to remedy by means of isolation, repression, social control, moral uplift, and social and environmental improvement.[37]

Recreation and entertainment offered more evidence of the growing complexity and segmentation of society. Leisure, like work, was increasingly systematized—a far cry from the spontaneous "folk games" that had served for centuries. Shorter work weeks, a new middle class with sufficient time and money, the steady erosion of Puritan-Victorian values by consumerism, urbanism, and cosmopolitanism, the mobility afforded by new modes of transportation, and the potential for commercializing leisure-time activities through mass communications and advertising—all these worked to transform leisure. Some advocated sports and entertainment as a means of re-creating the individual and enhancing productivity and efficiency. Others advocated organized athletics as a means of instilling the habit of following rules and regulations, or as "rational amusements" whereby systematic observation would improve participants' well-being. Active sports like bicycling, tennis, ice skating, and swimming drew their share of active participants, but the trend was towards passive activities where spectators paid money to watch entertainers or athletes. Some leisure activities temporarily united people across

---

[37] John Bodnar, "The Transplanted: A Roundtable," in *Social Science History*, 12 (Fall, 1988), 57–84, 169–183; John D. Buenker, "Immigration and Ethnic Groups," in John A. Neuenschwander, ed., *Kenosha County in the Twentieth Century* (Kenosha, 1976), 8–16; John D. Buenker, "The Immigrant Heritage," in Nicholas C. Burckel, ed., *Racine: Growth and Change in a Wisconsin County* (Racine, 1977), 90–95; Judith W. Leavitt, *The Healthiest City: Milwaukee and the Politics of Health Reform* (Princeton, 1982; reprinted, Madison, 1996), 10–41; Walker, *Everyday Life in Victorian America*, 131–138; Still, *Milwaukee*, 384–390; Mollenhoff, *Madison*, 234–242, 419–427; Roy Rosenzweig, *Eight Hours for What We Will: Workers and Leisure in an Industrial City, 1870–1920* (Cambridge, England, 1983), 93–168; Paul Boyer, *Urban Masses and Moral Order in America, 1820–1920* (Cambridge, 1978), 162–190, 205–219, 277–292; Marc Fried, *World of the Urban Working Class* (Cambridge, 1973), 224–258. See also Chapter 4.

gender, socio-economic, ethno-cultural or geographical lines; others widened and deepened those divisions. Middle-class diversions stressed decorum, prosperity, and respectability. But there also existed a more raffish "sporting fraternity," composed of immigrants, workingmen, Negroes, displaced men, and upper-class "slummers" who patronized boxing and wrestling matches, horse races, saloons, gambling dens, burlesque, and houses of prostitution.[38]

By 1900, baseball had evolved from an informal folk game to a professional spectator sport with precise rules and statistical measurements of performance. (Industrialists endorsed employee teams, and the employees' ambivalent reaction suggested that they suspected the connection between rules on the field and off.) The baseball park was one of the few places where all segments of the population could meet in a common competitive pursuit. Milwaukee's Cream City Club joined baseball's infant National League in 1878, but dropped out when its last-place finish resulted in poor attendance. During the next two decades, Milwaukee played in the Union and Western leagues and, from 1897 to 1900, was managed by the legendary Connie Mack. In his last year, Milwaukee finished second in the inaugural season of the new American League, but Mack's move to Philadelphia, and a last-place finish in 1901, ended Milwaukee's major league status until 1953. In 1902, Milwaukee joined the American Association as a charter member and remained a bellwether of Class AAA baseball (just one step below the major leagues) for nearly half a century. It developed a national reputation as a premier baseball town where amateur and semi-professional teams regularly drew enthusiastic crowds.[39]

Collegiate football also attracted spectators nationally and rivaled professional baseball for the complexity of its rules and its grassroots appeal. College football was supposedly a game played by students, but it became "King Football" in the late 1890's and early 1900's, exhibiting some disturbing tendencies: huge expenditures, lax eligibility standards, fierce training schedules, a win-at-any-cost attitude,

---

[38] Marcus and Segal, *Technology in America*, 202–207; Foster Rhea Dulles, *A History of Recreation: America Learns to Play* (New York, 1940, as *America Learns to Play: A History of Popular Recreation, 1607–1940*; reprinted, 1965); Benjamin G. Rader, *American Sports: From the Age of Folk Games to the Age of Televised Sports* (Englewoods Cliffs, New Jersey, 1983; revised ed., 1990), 17–49; Dodds, *Life in Twentieth Century America*, 155–235; Walker, *Everyday Life in Victorian America*, 139–206; Stephanie Coontz, *The Social Origins of Private Life: A History of American Families, 1600–1900* (New York, 1988), 344–346.

[39] Rader, *American Sports*, 107–134; Donald J. Mrozek, *Sport and American Mentality, 1880–1910* (Knoxville, 1983), 166–182; Barth, *City People*, 148–191; Still, *Milwaukee*, 404–405; Mollenhoff, *Madison*, 430; Charles C. Alexander, *Our Game: An American Baseball History* (New York, 1991), 9–11; Harold Seymour, *Baseball: The Early Years* (New York, 1989), 86, 128, 159–160, 173, 255–261, 305–321.

and physical mayhem to the point of disabling injuries and death. University faculties tried to take control, and some colleges joined leagues, such as the Intercollegiate Conference of Faculty Representatives, which evolved into what became known as the Western Conference (or "Big Ten"). At the University of Wisconsin, as elsewhere, sports, and particularly football, achieved incredible popularity. The Badgers played their first intercollegiate football schedule in 1890, beginning with Whitewater, which it defeated 106–0, then losing to Minnesota, Lake Forest, and Northwestern. Within three years, it was the most popular activity on campus. The daily student paper, the *Cardinal*, rationalized Wisconsin losses, pilloried its opponents, and lionized campus heroes, some of whom were plainly hired hands, not students. Faculty efforts to regulate eligibility, expenditures, and schedules usually met with opposition by alumni, students, regents, townspeople, and some administrators. In an address to the Madison Alumni Association in January, 1906, Frederick Jackson Turner charged that football had become "a business, carried on far too often by professionals supported by levies on the public, bringing in vast gate receipts, demoralizing student ethics, and confusing the ideals of sports, manliness, and decency." A faculty committee subsequently recommended a two-year moratorium on intercollegiate athletics, leading to a compromise of a five-game football schedule in exchange for reduced emphasis on athletics. This reform movement was short-lived. The ubiquitous Charles McCarthy took the university baseball team on a Japanese tour in 1909; Turner departed for Harvard in 1910; football and other sports were restored to their former glory by 1914.[40]

Apart from baseball and football, most Progressive Era sports encouraged widespread, popular participation, but they also tended to reinforce class divisions. Basketball, invented in the 1890's, was played primarily in YMCA's, schools, and private athletic clubs. Even so, it attracted criticism because of ferocious competition, rowdy fans, and nascent professionalism. Golf and tennis were played at private clubs by elites, and more women were taking part. The U.S. Lawn Tennis Association, the Amateur Athletic Union, and the U.S. Golf Association codified rules and regulations, endorsed equipment and clothing, sponsored competitions, settled arguments, and policed against professionalism. Bicycling, even during the height of its popularity in the 1890's, remained largely a leisure-time activity of the upper

---

[40] Rader, *American Sports*, 134–144; Mrozek, *Sport and American Mentality*, 166–182; Merle Curti and Vernon Carstensen, *The University of Wisconsin: A History, 1848–1925* (2 vols., Madison, 1949), 1: 693–710, 2: 533–548 (quote); Harva Hachten, " 'On Wisconsin'—Universal Favorite," in *Wisconsin Then and Now*, 20 (September, 1973), 7–8.

and middle classes, although bicycle racing did appeal to spectators across class lines. The same was true of automobiles; it was just beginning as an amusement for the masses by 1914.

So popular were sports that newspapers covered even the amateur events. "Skating came before Thanksgiving this year, our young folks having inaugurated the season Thursday," reported the *Grant County News* in 1893, adding that some "accumulated a good deal of sport while others accumulated dampness by breaking through the ice." A decade later, the Wausau *Daily Record* pronounced ice skating by "steel shod thousands . . . the king of outdoor recreations," observing that "its votaries comprise both young and old, the rich and the poor." In May, 1909, the Eau Claire *Daily Telegram* printed a letter from the president of the Minnesota-Wisconsin baseball league requesting co-operation "in the suppression of Rowdy Ball and the using of Profane Language on the field." Less than a month later, the paper complained that the game between Winona and Eau Claire had been marred by "too much rag-chewing . . . benching and ordering off the field . . . bickering and scrapping." College football strayed from campuses to other venues, too, as at the 1895 state fair. The *Wisconsin Agriculturist* promoted the game between the University of Wisconsin and Northwestern University, promising that it would be "interesting, scientific and extremely exciting," and not "merely a game of brute force." A good football player had "good judgment, quick perception, ability to keep his temper, quickness and sand" and, the paper said, "boys brought up on a farm have more of these qualities than boys who are city bred."[41]

Entertainment, like sports, also became more commercial and thrived because of spectatorship fostered by better transportation and communications. State and county fairs changed from a place where people exhibited their wares and exchanged information to a place where people went to be entertained by professionals. Vaudeville provided live entertainment to countless audiences in small towns and big cities, then moved to movie houses for between-show acts. Chautauqua meetings offered live lectures by famous evangelists, professors, politicians, and business leaders, as well as participation in wholesome singing, dancing, and music. Local literary and scientific clubs, some along Chautauqua lines, read books, wrote and read papers, conducted debates, and held discussions and demonstrations. Richard T. Ely and Robert M. La Follette were among the mainstays of the Chautauqua circuit. A woman in Loyal (Clark County) later recalled that her father extolled La Follette's talks that "excited

[41] *Grant County News* (Lancaster), November 22, 1893; Wausau *Daily Record*, January 21, 1902; Eau Claire *Daily Telegram*, May 13, June 4, 1909; *Wisconsin Agriculturist*, August 15, 1895, p. 3.

and electrified audiences," and how, "long after the tent had gone, my father would be discussing the ideas of 'Fighting Bob.'" She remembered that "normal life was unthinkable" and that she "was feverish with excitement and prayed for no rain during this special week." At the 1904 state fair, La Follette shared billing with the pacing horse Dan Patch, the Philippines Constabulary Band, Milwaukee Mayor David Rose, and automobile, bicycle, and motorcycle races. The *Wisconsin Agriculturist* said in 1895 that "there is no occasion during the year when a farmer can do better work in the interest of his farm than by attending these great agricultural fairs." It also warned of "tricksters" at fairs, a "class of persons" who had "schemes and tricks innumerable that appear to be easy and simple," and "wheels and machines that are doctored to turn as the proprietor may wish them," not to mention "tented shows which are disgusting in coarseness and vulgarity."[42]

Parks and resorts, too, developed because of the automobile's popularity. Wisconsin's first state park, Interstate State Park at St. Croix Falls, was built in conjunction with Minnesota along the dells of the St. Croix in the 1890's. (It failed to attract many visitors until the automobile brought it within reach of Minneapolis-St. Paul.) By 1900, the Wisconsin Central Railway was extolling the healthful climate of the Fox River Valley as a place for "the lame, the halt, and the blind, and the played-out unfortunates of the big cities" to recuperate, because the area's residents "live so long that their poor relations die of despair." Another Wisconsin Central pamphlet advertised Fifield (Price County) as a great place to catch a fabled "muskallonge," "one of those cruel, leaping savages that snatches your silver spoon with all the eagerness of a nocturnal house breaker." A 1905 pamphlet praised Sturgeon Bay on Wisconsin's Door County "thumb" as an ideal resort because of its "glorious climate, the magnificent drives in all directions, its natural position where the storms that sweep the lake cannot touch it, its accessibility, its superiority as a fishing ground." Many Milwaukeeans rode the excursion boat *Bloomer Girl* to Whitefish Bay and the elegant Schlitz Park. On July 3, 1904, the Milwaukee *Sentinel* reviewed the state's tourism picture. It reported that thirty members of the Chicago Automobile club had arrived in Waukesha by way of the Pfister hotel in Milwaukee and a supper stop in Oconomowoc, where there was to be a yacht race the next day.

---

[42] Berger, *The Devil Wagon*, 107–109; Maybelle Gravitz, "Chautauqua: 'The Most American Thing in America,'" in *Wisconsin Then and Now*, 18 (June, 1972), 4–5, 8; Joseph E. Gould, *The Chautauqua Movement: An Episode in the Continuing American Revolution* (New York, 1961), 72–96; Victoria Case and Robert Ormond Case, *We Called It Culture: The Story of Chautauqua* (Garden City, New York, 1948), 192–202, 214–240; *Wisconsin Agriculturist*, August 15, 1895, p. 1, August 19, 1897, p. 8.

The holiday crowds at Delavan were "the biggest in history of the resort industry in that place" and business was also booming at Waupaca County's Chain O'Lakes, Elkhart Lake (Sheboygan County), and Lake Mills (Jefferson County). "All of the pretty little Wisconsin resorts are gathering in their guests and on the Fourth almost everyone but the small boy has planned to be out of the city."[43]

The systematization, commercialization, and professionalization of recreation and entertainment proceeded faster in urban areas than rural. Early in 1915, a Sauk County farmer took exception to the notion that the "telephone and the automobile and rural free delivery of the mail have been heralded as the great emancipators of the farmer and his family from the loneliness and seclusion of farm life." He cited his Skillet Creek Farmers' Club as proof that "old fashioned informal, back door hospitality" still persisted. While the club sometimes had "professors up from Madison to tell us something special, . . . we really seem to learn the most, and enjoy the most, the things that are prepared right here by members of the Club." The residents of various rural communities also formed old settlers' or pioneer clubs that held picnics and listened to narratives about early settlement, such as the Dane County Pioneer Association, founded in 1910, and the Fond du Lac Old Settlers' Club (1906). In small communities such as Lake Mills, organizers still invited guests to "a few games of cards, some dancing, and a little some thing to brace up with on the side." In larger cities, such as Eau Claire in 1909, an amateur minstrel show staged by the Elks competed with professional productions of *Uncle Tom's Cabin* and a lecture series under the Women's Club's aegis. Recreation in industrial Kenosha and Racine was determined by class and ethnicity: the upper and middle classes tended towards full-dress parties, teas, dances, and catered picnics; working-class ethnics and their families, towards neighborhood saloons.[44]

Madison's "Yankee-university elite," secure on the west side not far from the campus, moved in a "clam tight" circle; the workers and

---

[43] Harry D. Baker interview, January 17, 1950, transcription, SC1009; Wisconsin Central Railway, *Fond du Lac, Oshkosh, Neenah, Menasha* (n.p., 1900), p. 34, and *Concerning Fifield, Wis. on the Wisconsin Central Lines: Fishing in General and Muskallonge in Particular* (Milwaukee, 1899); *Sturgeon Bay, Wisconsin* (Sturgeon Bay, 1905), unpaginated; Bob Taylor, "From Milwaukee's Album," Milwaukee *Journal*, January 19, 1934; Milwaukee *Sentinel*, July 3, 1904.

[44] W. A. Toole to the editor, *Wisconsin Agriculturist*, February 11, 1915, p. 25 (quotes); Minutes of July 21, 1910, Meeting, Meeting and List of Members, in the Dane County Pioneer Association Records; Fond du Lac *Commonwealth*, March 24, 1906; George H. Bishop to Hoard, February 24, 1896, in the Halbert L. Hoard Papers; Eau Claire *Daily Telegram*, May 1, 7, June 4, 1909; Thomas J. Noer, "Popular Culture and Leisure Time," in Neuenschwander, ed., *Kenosha County*, 87–91; Thomas C. Reeves, "Education and Culture," in Burckel, ed., *Racine*, 431–444.

artisans of the east side frequented saloons and vaudeville theaters. All came together on Saturday afternoons, rooting for the university's athletic teams, especially football. In Milwaukee, despite the popularity of motion pictures, and the city's reputation as "the poorest theatrical city in the United States," live music and theater remained popular. According to a 1911 survey, Milwaukee had forty-five "cheap" theaters, the majority of whose seats cost less than twenty-five cents; they offered movies, burlesque, vaudeville, and melodrama. Milwaukee's elite attended balls, cotillions, and parties, joined the Curlers' Club, and gussied up for Sunday horse races. The appearance of Sarah Bernhardt at the Pabst Theater in 1906 attracted a "brilliant" audience, "composed largely of handsomely gowned women and men in evening dress, representatives of Milwaukee's best social circles." At the other end of the social scale, a notorious "stall saloon" attracted a clientele of stevedores, railroad workers, sailors, and laborers. Some large employers provided recreational opportunities for workers, including bowling, billiards, baseball, dancing, concerts, plays and picnics, because "the psychological attitude of employees toward each other and toward the firm is coming to be recognized as a practical and significant element in determining the output of factories and the sales of stores."[45]

[4]

The family and the home were not the least of the institutions transformed by systematization. The most obvious transformation was the decrease in household size, as the number of boarders and live-in servants declined drastically. Less apparent were the "privatization" of the family and the rise of what came to be called the "New Familialism." Before the industrial revolution of the late eighteenth and early nineteenth centuries, nuclear families were regarded as social building blocks engaged in reciprocal relationships with the outside world. Intervention into family operations by relatives, neighbors, clergy, and civil officials was the norm. The family was a unit of production as well as reproduction; husbands, wives, children, servants, and boarders interacted with one another, as well as with the larger society. During the industrial revolution, the separation of residence

[45] Mollenhoff, *Madison*, 234–247; 419–436; Still, *Milwaukee*, 401 (quote); Milwaukee *Sentinel*, January 15, February 19, 1893, April 1, 22, June 4, 1894, July 20, August 1, 1904, and February 11, 18, 20, 21, 22, 25, 1906; Wisconsin Conference of Charities and Corrections, *Proceedings*, October 12–15, 1911, pp. 89–96; "Recreation for Employees," press release, 1913–1914, box 4, City Club of Milwaukee Records, 1909–1975, University of Wisconsin-Milwaukee Area Research Center (quote).

and work together with increasing specialization turned family and society into distinct, almost adversarial entities. The chief breadwinner (usually a man) became the family's "ambassador to the outside world," and the home a "refuge" from the competitive, mechanistic, and impersonal universe of work. Home was the province of the wife and mother, whose role was to provide the security, warmth, and nurturing lacking in the outside world. The home came to mirror that wider world in its specialization of roles and space, a separation reinforced by Victorian notions of modesty. The sanctity of home was declared in song, verse, and fiction, and crafts objects decorated with mawkish phrases—"God Bless Our Home," "Home Is Where the Heart Is."[46]

As production of goods and services, education, and health care moved outside the home and were taken over by society in general, family members took care of one another's emotional and psychological needs, supplied the interest, excitement, and stimulation missing in the impersonal world of work, and provided companionship and emotional satisfaction. This ideal "compassionate family" relocated the axis from mother-child to husband-wife relationships, adding to the responsibilities and expectations of both spouses. Men were expected to provide a higher standard of living, participate more in child rearing, and select their wives, rather than their male cronies, as their companions of choice. In exchange, wives were expected both to combine innovations in household technology with domestic science to meet higher and higher standards of cleanliness, comfort, and nutrition, and to meet their husbands' expectations for sexual relations, companionship, and unflagging support. All of this coincided with growth in consumerism, advertising, and leisure time.[47]

---

[46] Paul C. Glick, *American Families* (New York, 1957), 175–193; Rudy Ray Seward, *The American Family: A Demographic History* (Beverly Hills, California, 1978), 111–158; John Demos, *Past, Present and Personal: The Family and the Life Course in American History* (New York, 1986), 4–30; Steven Mintz and Susan Kellogg, *Domestic Revolutions: A Social History of American Family Life* (New York, 1988), 107–109; Richard Sennett, *Families Against the City: Middle Class Homes of Industrial Chicago, 1872–1890* (Cambridge, 1970), 184–214; Coontz, *The Social Origins of Private Life*, 251–286; Thomas Bender, *Community and Social Change in America* (New Brunswick, New Jersey, 1978; 2nd ed., Baltimore, 1982), 114–135.

[47] Demos, *Past, Present and Personal*, 26–32; Coontz, *The Social Origins of Private Life*, 330–364; Mintz and Kellogg, *Domestic Revolutions*, 107–131; Robert L. Griswold, "Divorce and the Legal Redefinition of Victorian Manhood" and Margaret Marsh, "Suburban Men and Masculine Domesticity, 1870–1915," in Mark C. Carnes and Clyde Griffen, eds., *Meanings For Manhood: Constructions of Masculinity in Victorian America* (Chicago, 1990), 96–127; Mark C. Carnes, *Secret Ritual and Manhood in Victorian America* (New Haven, 1989), 11–14, 152–159; Elaine Tyler May, *Great Expectations: Marriage and Divorce in Post-Victorian America* (Chicago, 1980), 61–70; Ruth Schwartz Cowan,

Architects, home economists, and journalists crusaded for the new homes conducive to the redefined familialism. They borrowed the concepts and vocabulary of scientific management and social science. In general, specialists thought every housewife should become a household efficiency expert. They recommended replacing the rambling, cluttered Victorian dwelling with a trim, well-organized bungalow that could be cleaned and maintained by one woman without assistance, freeing the "new woman" for outside activities. Conservatives urged preservation of the traditional family by treating housewives as professionals. All lauded simplicity, cleanliness, standardization, and using labor-saving devices to lighten housewives' work and turn the home into a "unit of consumption." This required new standards and a new regimen. The same was true of nutritionists' and domestic scientists' efforts to effect a "revolution at the table."[48]

The new familialism and household administration did not penetrate very deeply into the lives of the immigrant-stock working class or the majority of Wisconsin's farmers, who clung to preindustrial family structures and conceived of themselves as home-based production units. Hired help and boarders frequently lived under the family's roof, dined at the same table, and were, in many respects, part of the family. Husbands and wives of both the working class and the farm often saw themselves as partners in a joint enterprise and not as companions or romantic partners. If they had heard of them, they generally lacked the financial resources to institute "domestic science" in their households or buy the new appliances. Settlement-house workers, night-school teachers, extension workers, and some writers exercised a little influence on workers and farm families, but economic realities and cultural traditions slowed progress and blunted the impact of new ideas.[49]

More Work for Mother: The Ironies of Household Technology from the Open Hearth to the Microwave (New York, 1983), 63–68, 99–101. According to Richard M. Bernard, in *The Melting Pot and the Altar: Marital Assimilation in Early Twentieth-Century Wisconsin* (Minneapolis, 1980), xiv, 48, and 117, Robert and Belle Case La Follette, Carl Sandburg and Lillian Steichen, and Ella Wheeler and Robert Wilcox all eliminated the word "obey" from their wedding vows.

[48] Gwendolyn Wright, *Building the Dream: A Social History of Housing in America* (New York, 1981), 155–176 (quote); Cowan, *More Work for Mother*, 71–101; Harvey A. Levenstein, *Revolution at the Table: The Transformation of the American Diet* (New York, 1988), passim; Walker, *Everyday Life in Victorian America*, 207–224; Seward, *The American Family*, 134–136.

[49] Richard J. Altenbaugh, "Urban Immigrant Families: A Comparative Study of Italians and Mexicans," in Jean E. Hunter and Paul T. Mason, eds., *The American Family: Historical Perspectives* (Pittsburgh, 1991), 125–141; Bodnar, *The Transplanted*, 57–84; John Modell and Tamara K. Hareven, "Urbanization and the Malleable Household: An Examination of Boarding and Lodging in American Families," and Tamara K. Hareven, "Family Time and Industrial Time: Family and Work in a Planned Corpo-

Many contemporaries interpreted the new familialism as a reaction to a national crisis concerning the family. They saw evidence of a crisis in an escalating divorce rate, a declining birth rate, the emergence of the New Woman, the proliferation of women in the work force, the exodus of farm children to the city, and in child labor, juvenile delinquency, and domestic abuse. Between 1890 and 1910, the number of divorces in the country rose from 33,411 to 83,045 annually. More than two-thirds were granted to women, reflecting their changing expectations of marriage, somewhat improved economic prospects, and courts' growing proclivity to grant women child custody, maintenance, and alimony. A liberalization of the legal grounds for divorce naturally led to more divorces and created a hodge-podge of laws from state to state. Ironically, this "liberalization" was essentially conservative, emphasizing that adultery, desertion, abuse, and drunkenness violated middle-class standards. Those who wanted divorce liberalized desired to protect women, not to emancipate them. The advocates included many of the same people who sought temperance and an end to organized vice. But divorce was made difficult by its expense, legal complexities, and the stigma it entailed. An increase in life expectancy kept pace with the increase in divorce, so it appeared on the surface that the family continued as a stable institution. Nonetheless, a rising divorce rate and a decline in the birthrate among native-born city dwellers together seemed to herald a crisis in societal values. President Theodore Roosevelt darkly warned Americans of several generations' standing that they were committing "race suicide" because their birth rates were declining in comparison to southern and eastern Europeans and non-whites.[50]

Domestic violence, child labor, juvenile delinquency, and orphaned and destitute children led to family-oriented remedial movements. These used several approaches—social justice, social control, and systematization—and several remedies—child labor restrictions, "mothers pension" laws, juvenile and family courts, new institutions for neglected or abused children, and the revamping of divorce laws. Some observers perceived a struggle between forces that desired to preserve the family and forces whose goals might destroy it. Feminists, socialists, and similar "radicals" generally were lumped into the

---

ration Town, 1900–1924," in Tamara K. Hareven, ed., *Family and Kin in Urban Communities, 1700–1930* (New York, 1977), 164–203; Berger, *The Devil Wagon*, 55–74; Jeanne Hunnicutt Delgado, ed., "Nellie Kedzie Jones's Advice to Farm Women: Letters from Wisconsin, 1912–1916," in *WMH*, 57 (Autumn, 1973), 3–21.

[50] Roderick Phillips, *Untying the Knot: A Short History of Divorce* (Cambridge, England, 1991), 171–185, 226–238; Roderick Phillips, *Putting Asunder: A History of Divorce in Western Society* (Cambridge, England, 1988), 439–515; William L. O'Neill, *Divorce in the Progressive Era* (New Haven, 1967), viii, 5–31, 89; Mintz and Kellogg, *Domestic Revolutions*, 108–113.

second category. Divorce reform usually aimed at standardizing the states' procedures and regulations: residency requirements, waiting periods before remarriage, and reducing the number of grounds for divorce. Some activists sought to curb domestic violence by punishing abusers (even to the point of publicly whipping them), others sought to decriminalize violence and to create special domestic tribunals. The Wisconsin Children's Home Society, established in 1892, found homes for 600 children in its first five years of operation. The Wisconsin Home and Farm School, set up outside Milwaukee in 1902, provided physical and emotional shelter. Most family reformers emphasized placing children with stable families, and on teaching parents about child rearing, birth control, prenatal care, housework, and keeping marriages together.[51]

[5]

The "New Woman" was a principal element in much Progressive Era social thought and reform. Her attitudes and activities directly challenged the separate spheres assigned to men and women by societal norms. This belief, like belief in the private family, was of recent vintage and was seldom applied. Prior to the industrial revolution, the vast majority of women spent their lives in home-centered activities. They reared and taught children, nursed other family members, made food and clothing and other necessities, thus enabling the family to subsist. Almost everyone esteemed their work. Marriage often was a working partnership, in which husband and wife toiled side by side at tasks differentiated by gender but considered equally complex, skilled, and essential. Emotional support and affection were desirable, but secondary, and they were not exclusively the province of wives.

But industrialization and urbanization had transformed the home from a unit of production into a unit of consumption. It had separated workplace and residence, turned husbands into absentee breadwinners, and stripped wives of most of their productive tasks. As the wider society assumed responsibility for education, nursing,

[51] O'Neill, *Divorce in the Progressive Era*, 26–28; Mintz and Kellogg, *Domestic Revolutions*, 108–131; Elizabeth Pleck, *Domestic Tyranny: The Making of Social Policy Against Family Violence from Colonial Times to the Present* (New York, 1987), 69–144; Susan Tiffin, *In Whose Best Interest? Child Welfare Reform in the Progressive Era* (Westport, Connecticut, 1982), 281–291; Mark H. Leff, "Consensus for Reform: The Mothers'-Pension Movement in the Progressive Era," in *The Social Service Review*, 47 (September, 1973) 397–417; Anthony M. Platt, *The Child Savers: The Invention of Delinquency* (Chicago, 1969), 3–15, 46–82, 176–181; LeRoy Ashby, *Saving the Waifs: Reformers and Dependent Children, 1890–1917* (Philadelphia, 1984), 3–37.

and social work, housewives assumed new responsibilities—especially shopping for and managing necessary goods. Mass production and distribution, the culture of consumption, and the advent of domestic science made wives responsible for the family's standard of living. This new responsibility, and the time it took, substantially offset any savings in time and mental and physical energy made possible by the new appliances that appeared during this period.[52]

The switch from home-produced to store-bought food, clothing, medicine, and other staples meant more fetching and hauling for women, despite home delivery and mail order. Automobile manufacturers quickly perceived women as a potential market, and urged them to learn how to drive. Indoor plumbing, running water, electricity, natural gas, and heating oil reorganized housewives' duties; they did not eliminate or truly lighten them. Washing machines, electric irons, and the like may have moderated the hard work and drudgery of wash day; but they also escalated the volume of laundry and redefined the notion of "clean." The new labor-saving devices in effect created more work for mother.[53]

The more the family and the home became a refuge, the greater the emotional demands on wives and mothers. Although male expectations varied by class and ethnicity and changed over time, under the new mind-set women's role became more secondary, supportive, and subordinate. A husband's long work hours thrust most of the burden of child rearing on women, including the responsibility for socializing children to succeed in a public world from which wives and mothers were increasingly excluded.[54]

The trend towards separate spheres and homes as consumption units proceeded unevenly. Urban upper- and upper-middle-class women were most affected. Their families did not require income from their work; their husbands and fathers could afford to purchase labor-saving appliances and to hire domestic help. For others, even by 1912, the lack of electricity in four out of five households limited

---

[52] Cowan, *More Work for Mother*, 63–69; Gerda Lerner, *The Majority Finds Its Past: Placing Women in History* (New York, 1979; reprinted, 1981), 129–144; Glenna Matthews, *"Just a Housewife": The Rise and Fall of Domesticity in America* (New York, 1987), 35–85, 100–171.

[53] Cowan, *More Work for Mother*, 71–98; Virginia Scharff, *Taking the Wheel: Women and the Coming of the Motor Age* (New York, 1991), 15–67; Berger, *The Devil Wagon*, 59–67; Lerner, *The Majority Finds Its Past*, 135–136.

[54] Lerner, *The Majority Finds Its Past*, 132–133; Alice Kessler-Harris, "American Women and the American Character: A Feminist Perspective," in John A. Hague, ed., *American Character and Culture in a Changing World: Some Twentieth-Century Perspectives* (Westport, Connecticut, 1979), 227–241; S. J. Kleinberg, "Escalating Standards: Women, Housework and Household Technology in the Twentieth Century," in Coppa and Harmond, eds., *Technology in the Twentieth Century*, 1–7; Matthews, *"Just a Housewife,"* 97–111; Levenstein, *Revolution at the Table*, 60–97.

the spread of appliances. And even though most middle-class women probably could afford servants, they still generally did much of their own housework, leaving themselves little leisure time. The pool of domestic workers declined precipitously, the result of expanding employment opportunities and greater promise of personal freedom and self-fulfillment in other jobs. Although increases in household productivity and efficiency were available to many working-class women through settlement houses, social workers, visiting nurses, and extension agents, they rarely benefited to the same degree as their more affluent sisters.[55]

The wives of farmers and workers had little need or opportunity to emerge from their "separate sphere." Agricultural chores generally were apportioned along gender and age lines, but on the farm there was no clear-cut segregation of residence from workplace. Husbands, wives, children, and hired hands frequently collaborated. Few farm women had the leisure time, or means of transportation, to socialize with their peers, except when the entire family was involved. Most complaints about rural isolation and the drudgery of farm labor were voiced by women, but few of them were in a position to benefit from the preachings of advice columnists, settlement workers, and academic reformers.[56]

Despite the growth in numbers of jobs for women in industry, offices, and retail sales after 1900, nearly one-quarter of female wage-earners in 1910 still worked in domestic positions, supervised by women of higher socio-economic status. Most frequently, ethnicity, religion, culture, and even race separated employee from employer, for immigrant stock and black women constituted a disproportionately large share of the domestic work force. Individual situations varied, of course, but the mistress-servant relationship was basically an exploitative one, characterized by rituals of deference and maternalism. Because of the low esteem in which housework was held, domestic workers were, in effect, "servants of servants." Mistresses frequently took out their own frustrations on the only people over whom they exercised control, by holding their servants to higher standards of cleanliness and nutrition. The opportunities for female employ-

---

[55] Cowan, *More Work for Mother*, 92–101, 145–150, 190–191; Lerner, *The Majority Finds Its Past*, 132–143; Matthews, *"Just a Housewife,"* 92–115. According to a modern observer of popular culture, Shere Hite, in *The Hite Report, Women and Love: A Cultural Revolution in Progress* (New York, 1987), working wives still did about 70 per cent of the domestic chores in the 1980's.

[56] Delgado, ed., "Nellie Kedzie Jones's Advice," in *WMH*, 57: 3–27; Jane B. Knowles, " 'It's Our Turn Now': Rural American Women Speak Out, 1900–1920," in Wava G. Haney and Jane B. Knowles, eds., *Women and Farming: Changing Roles, Changing Structures* (Boulder, 1988), 303–315; "What Farm Women Will Buy," *Wisconsin Agriculturist*, January 14, 1915, p. 18, and "Wisconsin Wives Are Happy," May 27, 1915, p. 12.

ment in other areas prompted many servants, especially those who were young and single, to seek other jobs. Some jobs were often dangerous and unhealthy, but their higher pay and greater freedom made them attractive.[57]

Initially, at least, these new kinds of jobs had little affect on the middle and upper classes. Women from those classes had more opportunity for education in the late 1800's and early 1900's, but the cult of domesticity, the definition of what constituted a "lady," and the belief that women's biological destiny could be fulfilled only in homemaking and motherhood relegated women to their preordained niche. For men, their status was measured largely by how well they provided for their families; for women, by how well they maintained the living conditions for their husbands and children. The very few women who entered the professions often found themselves treated condescendingly and viewed with suspicion, and the more so if they had eschewed the traditional roles of wife and mother. A growing number of younger women sought to resolve this dilemma by taking up traditional "female" occupations like teacher or nurse, or new ones like librarian or social worker. The public did not view employment as an educator or "civilizer" as the same threat to the established order as work in woman suffrage activities or entry into the male strongholds of business, government, law, and so forth. Normative ideas about women confined them to a few segments of public life of seemingly small consequence. A far larger proportion of middle- and upper-class women simply continued to labor, without compensation, as housewives and mothers, while seeking autonomy, sorority, and social efficacy through membership in voluntary associations and clubs.[58]

Chief among such organizations were the Wisconsin affiliates of the General Federation of Women's Clubs (GFWC), the Woman's Christian Temperance Union (WCTU), the National Consumers'

---

[57] Judith Rollins, *Between Women: Domestics and Their Employers* (Philadelphia, 1985), 155–232; Faye E. Dudden, *Serving Women: Household Service in Nineteenth-Century America* (Middletown, Connecticut, 1983), 104–242; David M. Katzman, *Seven Days a Week: Women and Domestic Service in Industrializing America* (New York, 1978), 146–183; Donna L. Von Raaphorst, *Union Maids Not Wanted: Organizing Domestic Workers, 1870–1940* (New York, 1988), 95–154; William D. Jenkins, "Housewifery and Motherhood: The Question of Role Change in the Progressive Era," in Mary Kelley, ed., *Woman's Being, Woman's Place: Female Identity and Vocation in American History* (Boston, 1979), 142–153.

[58] Karen J. Blair, *The Clubwoman as Feminist: True Womanhood Redefined, 1868–1914* (New York, 1980), 1–6; Penina Migdal Glazer and Miriam Slater, *Unequal Colleagues: The Entrance of Women into the Professions, 1890–1940* (New Brunswick, New Jersey, 1987) 3–23; LeeAnne Giannone Kryder, "Self-Assertion and Social Commitment: The Significance of Work to the Progressive Era's New Woman," in *Journal of American Culture*, 6 (Summer, 1983), 25–30.

League (NCL), and the National Women's Trade Union League (NWTUL). The GFWC was not officially founded until the early 1890's, but its origins lay in thousands of older local literary and cultural clubs around the country. The women's club movement in Wisconsin can trace its beginnings to Sparta in 1871 with the formation of Clio, a literary society. By 1893, there were thirty-two literary or cultural clubs in the state; the number more than doubled during the next three years, impelled by the depression and national GFWC activity. Plans for a statewide federation were laid in 1895. In October, 1896, delegates from sixty-three clubs held an organizational meeting in Milwaukee and formed the Wisconsin Federation of Women's Clubs (WFWC). The WFWC's first official convention met in Oshksoh on October 10–11, 1897, with over 100 delegates, representing more than fifty clubs in thirty-eight cities. By 1900, membership passed the 6,000 mark; a decade later, the WFWC had 172 local affiliates, with 7,350 members; and in 1915, 213 clubs with 10,502 members, nearly all of them professionals in their own right or the wives of influential businessmen, professionals, or political figures.[59]

The WFWC took great pains to assert the essential conservatism of its philosophy, its acceptance of a subordinate and supportive role for women, and the sanctity of home, family, and motherhood. It insisted that its forays into public life would increase women's value and contentment as wives and mothers. Even though the federation co-operated on specific issues with suffragists, socialists, and "new women," it disagreed with those who agitated for sexual equality. "We do not wish to be considered a specimen or have a career.... We want a harvest of honest citizenship, of manly boys, and modest girls, happy workingmen and women, sanitary homes, clean morals, and religious influences," said federation president Carrie Edwards in 1910. According to president Emma Crosby in 1912, the WFWC member "was to be not a *new* woman, but an *improved* woman." When Wisconsin women finally achieved the right to vote in school board elections in 1902, WFWC president Theodora Youmans felt compelled to assure them that they should not feel "that in voting on school matters you are committing yourself to any advanced suffrage

[59] Blair, *The Clubwoman as Feminist*, 93–116; Jane Cunningham Croly, *The History of the Woman's Club Movement in America* (New York, 1898; microfilm ed., New Haven: Research Publications, Inc., 1975), 1151–1170, 1184; Theodora Penny Martin, *The Sound of Our Own Voices: Women's Study Clubs, 1860–1910* (Boston, 1987), 31–182; Anne Firor Scott, *Natural Allies: Women's Associations in American History* (Urbana, 1991), 141–174; Theda Skocpal and Gretchen Ritter, "Gender and the Origins of Modern Social Policies in Britain and the United States," in *Studies in American Political Development*, 5 (Spring, 1991), 36–93; Genevieve McBride, *On Wisconsin Women: Working for Their Rights from Settlement to Suffrage* (Madison, 1993).

theories or to the vicissitudes of a political life." Voting, she said, was "simply an expression of your practical interest in the school."[60]

The 1911 annual convention at Green Bay featured a lively debate over whether the WFWC would endorse the proposed woman suffrage amendment to the Wisconsin constitution. Astonishingly, the federation refused. The national GFWC endorsed suffrage in 1914, but some leading Wisconsin federationists continued to oppose it until the adoption of the Nineteenth Amendment in 1920. Ellen C. Sabin, president of Milwaukee-Downer College, expressed her conviction, at the Federation's convention in 1902, that "it is superfluous to train a girl away from the lines she must follow." "Home is woman's place, and home-making is the most womanly of occupations. The time has gone by when girls are educated without the idea that they are to become mothers, and all women are interested in the home and in child training." In 1897, Oshkosh educator and prominent clubwoman Rose C. Swart averred that "it is not as the rivals of men but as their loyal assistants that we should undertake the public service."[61]

Nor did the WFWC completely transcend its elitist outlook. As late as 1897, three-fourths of the local clubs continued to emphasize literature; many still advocated blue laws, immigration restriction, the disfranchisement of immigrants, prohibition, and curfews. Some continued to provide charity from the safety of their own homes, obviating the necessity of personal contact with less fortunate women. The national GFWC convention met in Milwaukee in 1900 and divided on the race issue. Wisconsin delegates joined those from Massachusetts and four other states in an unsuccessful effort to seat the representative of a Negro women's club. Some WFWC members kept their focus on moral issues, not political: "indecent attractions" at state and county fairs, obscene postcards, pool halls, burlesque houses, unwholesome motion pictures, and suggestive songs and magazine articles. These same women promoted domestic science and manual training in part because of their concern over "the servant problem."[62]

---

[60] Wisconsin Federation of Women's Clubs, *Proceedings*, 1902, p. 9; 1910, pp. 8–9; 1912, p. 96; Croly, *History of the Woman's Club Movement*, 1151–1159; Wisconsin State Federation of Women's Clubs, *Directory of the Founders* (n.p., 1897); David P. Thelen, *The New Citizenship: Origins of Progressivism in Wisconsin, 1885–1900* (Columbia, Missouri, 1972), 86–89; Janice Steinschneider, *An Improved Woman: The Wisconsin Federation of Women's Clubs, 1895–1920* (Brooklyn, New York, 1994), 36, 77, 93; McBride, *On Wisconsin Women*, 169–197 (quote on p. 170).

[61] Wisconsin Federation of Women's Clubs, *Proceedings*, 1902, pp. 9, 30 (quote); 1910, pp. 8–9; 1897, p. 72 (quote); Wisconsin Federation of Women's Clubs, *Proceedings, Reports, and Directory of Clubs* (1915), p. 58.

[62] Thelen, *New Citizenship*, 87–88; Wisconsin Federation of Women's Clubs, *Proceedings*, 1897, pp. 37–40; *ibid.*, 1898, p. 36.

ABOVE: Wisconsin's second state capitol, Madison, c. 1902. Much of this structure was destroyed by fire in 1904. BELOW: The Wisconsin building at the World's Columbian Exposition of 1893, Chicago.

ABOVE: Jackson County loggers, c. 1895, as the lumbering era drew to a close. BELOW: Farmers' co-operative cheese factory near Lake Mills (Jefferson County), 1909.

ABOVE: Stump-littered pasture and woodlot in the Cutover near Glidden (Ashland County). BELOW: Florence County farm family. Both photos were taken c. 1890–1895.

ABOVE: Salesmen of Wisconsin's Cutover near Sobieski (Oconto County).
BELOW: Trying out a McCormick mower on a hayfield somewhere in the New North.

ABOVE: East Water Street, Milwaukee, c. 1911. The Flemish Renaissance city hall looms in the background. BELOW: Workers taking a break at Milwaukee's International Harvester plant, c. 1910.

Factory workers dwarfed by their machinery and its wondrous creations in the Allis-Chalmers works, West Allis (Milwaukee County), c. 1910.

ABOVE: Paving Main Street with brick, Racine, 1901. BELOW: Foot traffic and trolley tracks, Milwaukee, c. 1910.

Wisconsin Blue Book

ABOVE: The University of Wisconsin campus, Madison, c. 1890. Bascom Hall crowns the heights; Park Street runs north to south at the foot of Bascom Hill. BELOW: Lecture classroom in the UW College of Agriculture.

WHi (X3) 28791

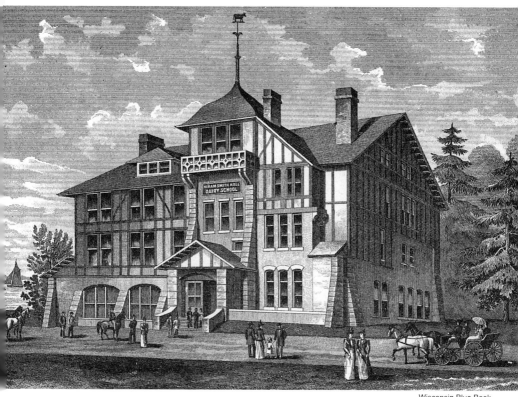

ABOVE: Hiram Smith Hall on the Ag School campus, named for the prominent dairyman and UW regent, c. 1900. BELOW: UW dairy science class, c. 1910.

William Dempster Hoard.

Richard T. Ely.

BELOW: Charles R. Van Hise, president of the University of Wisconsin from 1903 until his death in 1918, pictured in his Bascom Hall office.

John R. Commons.

Edward A. Ross.

BELOW: Charles R. McCarthy and his staff at the Legislative Reference Library, 1906.

WHi (X3) 30873

ABOVE: An old-fashioned business office with modern appurtenances, Green Bay, 1906. BELOW: Lake schooners in the harbor at Manitowoc, winter of 1893–1894.

WHi (X3) 20994

ABOVE: Main Street, Kenosha, 1898. BELOW: Wine room in a Milwaukee dance hall, photographed c. 1913 for a joint legislative vice investigation.

ABOVE The residences of Henry Mitchell (left) and Jerome I. Case, Racine, c. 1895. BELOW: Colored Odd Fellows on Madison's capitol square, 1913.

ABOVE: Gwinnet Court tenements in Madison's "Greenbush," c. 1905.
BELOW: Residential interior, Green Bay, c. 1895.

ABOVE: Urban hustle and bustle: the juncture of Grand and Water streets, Milwaukee, 1901. BELOW: The future encounters the past near Black River Falls (Jackson County), c. 1910.

ABOVE: Woman's Christian Temperance Union tent at a Chautauqua meeting, Racine, 1906. BELOW: German Singing Society outing at Wausau, 1913.

ABOVE: Ada James (center, with banner) campaigning for woman's suffrage, c. 1911. BELOW: (Left) Lizzie Black Kander. (Right) Theodora Winton Youmans.

ABOVE: Political barbecue, Menomonie (Dunn County), c. 1895.
BELOW: The Wisconsin legislative assembly, 1899.

ABOVE: (Left) Belle Case La Follette and her daughter Mary with Irvine Lenroot, Madison, 1906. (Right) Young Robert Marion La Follette during the brief period when he affected a beard. BELOW: Senator La Follette with his political associates James J. Blaine and Herman L. Ekern.

Governor La Follette on the dais at the St. Louis world's fair, 1904.

(Left) La Follette the orator on the Chautauqua circuit, 1907. (Below) "Fighting Bob" with muckraking journalist Lincoln Steffens, c. 1915.

ABOVE: (left) La Follette the senator, 1908. (Right) John T. McCutcheon depicted La Follette in the *Chicago Tribune,* December 29, 1911. BELOW: (Left) James O. Davidson, 1907. (Right) Francis E. McGovern.

ABOVE: (Left) Edward Scofield. (Right) Isaac Stephenson.
BELOW: (Left) Nils P. Haugen. (Right) John Coit Spooner.

WHi (X3) 39609 WHi(X3) 4472

ABOVE: (Left) Emil Seidel, Frederic C. Howe, and Victor L. Berger. (Right) David S. Rose. BELOW: Daniel M. Hoan in the mayor's office, Milwaukee.

Milwaukee County Historical Society

While admitting that domestic science or home economics could strengthen the family unit, Theodora Youmans of Waukesha, president of the WFWC and herself a professional journalist, expressed her concern in 1901 that girls and women "in service" would become so scarce that they might band together in "some sort of co-operative housekeeping scheme." To avoid this "dire calamity," Mrs. Youmans recommended making "household service so attractive that it will hold its own among other employments for women." For that reason, the federation endorsed a loan fund to train domestic science teachers at Milwaukee-Downer. This tone of elitism pervaded much of the federation's preaching. The Fond du Lac Women's Club, for example, supported a Saturday afternoon school for children of the poor, and motherless girls learned sewing, cooking, cleaning, and the like. The report of the first convention's educational committee in 1897 concluded that, inasmuch as "the city child in particular . . . lacks the ability to appropriate to himself, to mentally digest what he learns," schools should concentrate on industrial training for boys and household science for girls. "We [the people and women of Wisconsin] should teach more how to live and less how to know." Another 1897 convention speaker advocated reform of county asylums, because so many inmates were women, and many of those were "ladies of wealth, culture and refinement who are confined day after day in the same room or ward with the lowest element of our foreign-born population, ignorant and filthy, many of them unable to speak the English language."[63]

Notwithstanding these conservative tendencies, over time the WFWC underwent a remarkable transformation that drew its members into the public sphere, forged bonds of sisterhood across class and ethnic lines, and shifted its focus to socio-economic issues. This metamorphosis stemmed in part from women's clubs assuming leadership in the popular education movement that involved public and traveling libraries, university extension courses, church lecture series, and community discussion clubs. But persons lower on the social ladder also influenced them. Numerous correspondents advised extension director Jerome H. Raymond that local women's clubs were the best-suited groups to sponsor classes. Increased contacts between clubwomen and their less fortunate sisters also helped transform the WFWC. Superior's East End Women's Relief Corps, Madison's Benevolent Society, and Milwaukee's West Side Catholic Relief Corps actually visited the homes of the poor. The poor took matters into their own hands by seeking help from "charity" women at institutions

---

[63] Wisconsin Federation of Women's Clubs, *Proceedings*, 1901, pp. xxii, 2, 33, 37–38, 40; *ibid.*, 1908, pp. 36–37; *ibid.*, 1910, pp. xxiii; Blair, *The Clubwoman as Feminist*, 108–109; Wisconsin Federation of Women's Clubs, *Proceedings*, 1913, pp. 41–64; Steinschneider, *An Improved Woman*, 34.

like Milwaukee's Free Hospital, the House of Mercy, and the Catholic Girls Home.[64]

As early as 1895, mothers from Milwaukee's working-class south side began to urge clubwomen to reorient their educational reform work. Seventy-two Appleton working women requested that the WFWC admit their group. At least one Milwaukee club announced in 1897 that it would welcome any like-minded woman. The Kenosha Women's Club refocused on topics like women's influences and inheritance laws for women and children, while continuing to discuss literature. The Milwaukee Social Economics Club did much the same, featuring discussions of woman's work, woman's influence in municipal reform, and woman's new place in the home, business, and society. In Ashland, because there were too many clubs, one switched from weekly to biweekly meetings. The Milwaukee *Journal* and *Sentinel*, La Crosse *Press*, Superior *Leader*, and Appleton *Post* all published special editions about women's clubs activities. As the movement evolved, it served as a kind of school for conservative middle-class women, merging their familiar self-improvement and cultural programs with preparation for the wider world of political activism and policy making.[65]

This tendency had existed from the first in the WFWC. In 1897, one representative noted "a growing tendency to practical work, and that those who began life with the modest title of Reading Club or for the more ostensible purpose of studying Greek Mythology and literature have almost invariably left their lighter reading or their digging after Greek roots for some questions of living interest." Two of the five WFWC standing committees were devoted to library development and education, topics which received a great deal of discussion time at every convention. Lutie Stearns, secretary of the Wisconsin Free Library Commission, acknowledged that her agency "depends upon the women's clubs more than upon any and all other agencies combined to aid it in its work of establishing free libraries in Wisconsin." Between 1897 and 1901, women's clubs were instrumental in establishing thirty-seven public libraries—ten more than existed in the entire state in 1893. They were equally successful with traveling libraries. By 1898, Wisconsin ranked second only to New York.[66]

In 1891, several Milwaukee women's clubs formed the Wisconsin Woman's School Alliance, of which women in Fond du Lac and Port-

---

[64] Thelen, *New Citizenship*, 88–92.
[65] Steinschneider, *An Improved Woman*, 20–27; McBride, *On Wisconsin Women*, 134–168.
[66] Wisconsin Federation of Women's Clubs, *Proceedings*, 1897, pp. 17–57; 1899, pp. 33–35; 1901, p. 22.

age later established branches. The alliance at first concentrated on improving the physical environment of the city's schools, but the economic depression and the influence of members from the south side led it to focus more on the problems of students from poor neighborhoods. Club members collected and sewed clothing for schoolchildren and persuaded the city to hire a truant officer, whose primary task was to supply clothes to those students who had been unable to attend because of inadequate clothing. The alliance also pressed the school board for informal kindergartens, parent-teacher conferences, and manual training courses. Its vacation school provided weekly excursions to nearby lakes and farms and classes in manual training, art, music, and nature study to 400 of the city's neediest children. The Milwaukee *Sentinel* hailed vacation schools as "one of the most successful experiments in latter day altruism." Likewise, an 1897 emphasis on manual training that began in Madison aimed at curing the social ills suffered by the disadvantaged and working class youngsters. Similarly, practical education for the sons and daughters of farmers was a central WFWC concern.[67]

The WFWC applied a practical approach to public service as well as education. The time had come, President Ella Neville stated in 1900, "when it is not enough that woman should be alone a homemaker, she must make the world a larger home." Remarks along those lines peppered conventions annually throughout the Progressive period. Consistent with its evolving service ethic, the WFWC increased its efforts to alleviate the working and living conditions of women and children, and to improve the general civic climate. "True women," said Appleton clubwomen in 1896, would not tolerate the exploitation of their sisters and their children. Evidence of the level of exploitation varied widely. In 1890 the state Bureau of Labor and Industrial Statistics had insisted that virtually no children were employed in factories, but five years later the U.S. Labor Commission had charged that the exploitation of women and children was worse in Wisconsin than anywhere else. Such contradictions led the Milwaukee Ethical Society and the Sociological Club to conduct their own investigation of the city's factories. The movement spread to other cities and to demands that state factory inspectors enforce the law. By 1899, their persistence had turned inspectors in Milwaukee, Racine, and Sheboygan into zealots, and the labor bureau director to propose that the legislature appoint clubwomen "honorary factory inspectors" since public sentiment on behalf of laws was essential to their enforcement. Also in 1899, the Madison Woman's Club joined

---

[67] *Ibid.*, 1903, pp. 17–40; 1906, p. 65; 1908, pp. 52–60; Thelen, *New Citizenship*, 92–95 (quote); American Association of University of Women, *Wisconsin Women: A Gifted Heritage* (Madison, 1982), 60–62.

the State Federation of Labor in lobbying for a more stringent factory inspection law that required, among other provisions, seats for all working women. At its 1899 convention, the WFWC outlined its campaign against child and woman labor in a meeting that the Milwaukee *Sentinel* termed "remarkable for the frank and outspoken stand which the clubwoman took on the industrial question as it relates to women and child labor and the sweat-shop." Clubs undertook other worker-related activities as well. In Appleton, Wausau, Madison, and Ashland they co-operated with their city's labor unions to close stores at night. In 1899, the Milwaukee Social Economic Club helped organize several women's groups into a local branch of the National Consumers League which aided the Milwaukee Federated Trades Council in organizing members' wives into a Union Label League to oversee the NCL's boycott of offending establishments. Other Milwaukee women's clubs provided meeting places and sponsored free summer trips to the country for working women.[68]

Women's clubs in Ashland, Madison, and Milwaukee worked to provide special wards and matrons for women and children and a juvenile court. In Milwaukee, they established the state's first social settlement and participated in movements for home rule, municipal ownership of utilities, and creating "the city beautiful." Elsewhere in the state, they crusaded for clubhouses and playgrounds for children. The WFWC successfully pushed for female probation officers and for the appointment of women to the University of Wisconsin's Board of Regents and to the state Board of Control. The federation's work gradually drew praise and attention. In 1897, Madison's *Wisconsin State Journal* exulted that, at a meeting of the Civil Service Reform League, "the ladies were in the majority, as they always are, whenever a movement is made for the betterment of society." In 1899, the superintendent of Green Bay's schools said, "Reformatory work accomplished by woman's clubs has greatly improved social order."[69]

After 1900, the WFWC concentrated on what might be called "municipal housekeeping." By the time of its 1914 convention in Racine, thirteen of its seventeen standing committees dealt with questions of social welfare: civics, conservation, country life and rural club extension, education, political science, home economics, industrial and social conditions, legislation, a loan fund for higher education, policy, press, public health, and reference libraries. The group formulated strategy, lobbied, and monitored enforcement. Reports on critical bills at the preceding and upcoming legislative sessions became con-

[68] Wisconsin Federation of Women's Clubs, *Proceedings*, 1897, pp. 49, 66; 1899, pp. 1–2; 1900, pp. 47–50; 1903, p. 4; 1910, p. 3; Steinschneider, *An Improved Woman*, 33; McBride, *On Wisconsin Women*, 169–200; Thelen, *New Citizenship*, 95–98.
[69] Thelen, *New Citizenship*, 95–98; Steinschneider, *An Improved Woman*, 20–27.

A Passion for Newness and for System 341

vention staples. In 1907, topics included parole reform, industrial safety, objectionable medical advertisements, pure food and drugs, sanitation in bakeries, billboard regulation, marriage among the insane, feeble-minded and epileptic, tenements, maximum hours for railroad employees, state aid to rural schools, garbage collection, trade schools, playgrounds, midwife certification, sweatshops, women's working conditions, and child labor. Three years later, the legislative report concentrated on seeking "better laws regarding sanitation, pure food, and adulterated textiles," and on using federation influence to better conditions "in laundries, grocery stores, meat markets, milk wagons, restaurants and hotel kitchens." Consistently, the WFWC pressed for widespread use of school buildings and grounds as community centers and playgrounds, for municipal improvement, for campaigns against tuberculosis, and for public health measures generally.[70]

Reflecting upon the accomplishments of the landmark 1911 session of the legislature, the federation claimed partial credit for laws affecting street trades, women's reformatories, spring waterfowling, the state teachers' insurance and retirement fund, the Milwaukee teachers' pension fund, the regulation of dry goods stores, the child labor and children's bureau, vocational training, tenement regulation, and the juvenile court system. At the 1915 convention, the legislative committee proudly reported that it had learned how to lobby. "If it were possible for all of you to see our Legislature in session and to visit a few of the committees you would be able to realize how the work of this committee might be developed," the report concluded. "When there are bills up affecting the grocery business, the grocers or their paid lobbyists are there. When the bills affect the factories, their men are there.... When the bills affect the homes, why should we not be there?"[71]

Growing social and political involvement especially characterized the women's club movement in Milwaukee and Madison. By 1914, Milwaukee had seventeen clubs with 1,554 members, most of them Yankee, German, or Jewish, most of them comfortably middle-class. The largest, the College Endowment Association, had 493 members; the next largest, the Council of Jewish Women, 352 members. A few of these members focused on American art, the history of Wisconsin, South America, or the works of Dante. But most emphasized "live issues" such as the past, present, and future of women, social culture, social economics, vocational guidance, parliamentary law and social

[70] Wisconsin Federation of Women's Clubs, *Proceedings*, 1901, pp. 17–56; 1903, pp. 17–54; 1906, pp. 2–3, 42–58; 1907, pp. 5–8, 69–71; 1910, pp. 77–78.
[71] *Ibid.*, 1911, pp. 3–6; 1912, pp. 84–112; 1914, pp. 78–80, 104–107; 1915, pp. 93–97; Steinschneider, *An Improved Woman*, 36–37.

science, philanthropy, citizenship, home economics, current events, public school playgrounds and child labor, and the interests of home. In 1900, nine different women's clubs were involved in the city beautification movement, causing the head of the Milwaukee Municipal League, John A. Butler, to rhapsodize that one woman could accomplish more than four men because "women are practically free and independent [of conflicts of interests] and with them lies the creation of the right public sentiment."[72]

Typically, Milwaukee's women's clubs retained a degree of class and ethnic exclusiveness despite their efforts to benefit and uplift the less fortunate. The Council of Jewish Women members were primarily middle-class women of German ancestry who wanted principally to better the lot of eastern European immigrants. Their actions mingled altruism and snobbery. The council's most prominent leader, Lizzie Black Kander, was the wife of a prominent merchant. She earned a reputation as a "Jewish Americanizer" and founded the Milwaukee Jewish Mission, which became the Abraham Lincoln settlement house. She helped establish both a girls' trade school and several social centers and became well-known for her philanthropy and activism. But Kander's philosophy was essentially conservative; she aimed simply to raise up the ignorant, foreign-born poor to bourgeois respectability. She was also a tireless self-promoter whose good intentions did not always conceal a patronizing tone.[73]

The Woman's Club of Madison, founded in 1893, consisted almost entirely of the wives of prominent businessmen, civic and political leaders, and university professors and administrators. Nearly all were of Yankee stock. The wives of the governor, mayor, and the university president were ex officio members, and several of them played prominent roles. Always exclusive and focused on high culture, the Madison group gradually broadened its scope to include virtually every social welfare issue. Its proximity to the university enabled it to secure the services of national experts like John R. Commons from the university, Florence Kelley, a Madison native and National Consumer League president, Margaret F. Byington of the Russell Sage Foundation, and Jane Addams of Chicago's Hull House. Like many another women's group of the time, Madison's club advocated raising public consciousness about social problems, improving public education, and attacking societal problems head-on, with action rather than discussion.[74]

---

[72] Wisconsin Federation of Women's Clubs, *Proceedings*, 1914, pp. 122–125; Still, *Milwaukee*, 387–388 (quote); Thelen, *New Citizenship*, 87–98.

[73] Ann S. Waligorski, "Social Action and Women: The Experience of Lizzie Black Kander" (master's thesis, University of Wisconsin, 1970), 43–62, 82–105.

[74] Woman's Club of Madison, *Yearbook*, 1899–1900, pp. 6–14; 1908–1909, pp. 8–17;

Besides the WFWC and its local affiliates, Wisconsin women formed other "municipal housekeeping" organizations. The Wisconsin Consumers' League, for example, was founded by members of the WFWC at its 1898 convention. It had an almost immediate impact, even though the organization's leading historian included Wisconsin among the smaller and less permanent leagues. The National Consumers' League was founded in New York in 1891 and dedicated itself to improving the working conditions of women and children through direct action and the passage of protective legislation. Its motto was "Investigate, educate, legislate, enforce," and its methods included consumer boycotts and labeling products with a "white label," indicating a union-manufactured product.[75]

Another organization was the Wisconsin Branch of the American Association of University Women (AAUW), founded in Milwaukee in 1894 and in Madison in 1908. First led by Ellen C. Sabin, the association worked to interest young women in a higher education that would not compromise their femininity. Ordinarily, this meant private female colleges and seminaries, or, in public universities, courses of study that were segregated by gender. Beginning in 1866, the University of Wisconsin was "open alike" to students of both sexes, but the actual progress of co-education was slow and marred by inequalities. By 1876, women constituted one-quarter of the student body, but even when they were allowed to enroll in so-called "men's courses," they frequently had to write their examinations in separate rooms. It was not until 1885 that Belle Case La Follette became the first woman to earn a law degree. Eight years later, a woman, Kate Everest Levi, a well-known Wisconsin historian, was among the first three students to earn a doctorate from the university, and a full-time dean of women was appointed in 1896. In general, however, women were still confined to the College of Letters and Sciences programs until after 1900.[76]

Complete equality was not established until 1909, after President Charles R. Van Hise, concerned over the tendency of students of either gender to avoid courses designed primarily for the opposite sex, proposed offering separate sections for women. The resultant

---

1911–1912, pp. 9–22; 1912–1913, pp. 9–21; 1913–1914, pp. 12–22; Mollenhoff, *Madison*, 374.

[75] Nancy Schrom Dye, *As Equals and as Sisters: Feminism, the Labor Movement, and the Women's Trade Union League of New York* (Columbia, Missouri, 1980), 1–7; Louis I. Athey, "The Consumers League and Social Reform" (doctoral dissertation, University of Delaware, 1965), *passim*; Skocpol and Ritter, "Gender and the Origins of Modern Social Policies," in *Studies in American Political Development*, 5: 57–61.

[76] Kohler, *Story of Wisconsin Women*, 22–27; American Association of University Women, *Wisconsin Women*, 17–33, 50–52; Curti and Carstensen, *University of Wisconsin*, 1: 364–381, 660–661; *ibid.*, 2: 81–86.

furor, led by Helen Remington Olin, a prominent alumna, clubwoman, and wife of Madison reform leader John M. Olin, moved the Board of Regents to declare that "men and women shall be equally entitled to membership in all classes in the University," and, "There shall be no discrimination on account of sex in granting scholarships or fellowships in any of the colleges or departments of the University." For good measure, the 1909 legislature decreed that "all schools and colleges of the university shall in their respective departments and class exercises, be open without distinction to students of both sexes."[77]

The Woman's Christian Temperance Union (WCTU) had a more broadly based program than its name suggests. One historian has called it "the first mass organization of American women," one that "enabled women to move widely into public life of 1900" while retaining ties to the nineteenth-century "doctrine of spheres." Frances Willard, its noted leader, facilitated this move into the public sphere by connecting suffrage, women's rights, and other causes with opposition to strong drink. Willard was born in upstate New York, was raised on a farm near Janesville between the ages of seven and nineteen, and had attended the forerunner of Milwaukee-Downer College. She conducted her WCTU career out of Evanston, Illinois. In 1892, when the General Federation of Women's Clubs had 20,000 members nationwide and the National American Woman Suffrage Association had 13,000, the WCTU claimed 150,000. The elimination of alcoholic beverages remained its central focus, but its "do-everything" policy included universal suffrage, physical and sex education in the schools, mothers' pensions, child and woman protective labor legislation, pure food and drug laws, uniform divorce laws, and the elimination of obscenity.[78]

The Wisconsin chapter of the WCTU, which eventually grew to almost 10,000 members, made its headquarters in Milwaukee. It disseminated its message through its lecture bureau and a publication, *The Motor*. Like the WFWC, the WCTU was divided into departments, but its were devoted mostly to alcohol issues: abstinence pledges, teaching "scientific temperance" in the schools, recruiting among foreign-language speakers, working among inmates in prisons and almshouses, eliminating medication with alcohol as an ingredient or alcohol as a medicine, and enforcing Sabbath laws. It ran a home for

---

[77] Curti and Carstensen, *University of Wisconsin*, 2: 82–86; Reuben Gold Thwaites, ed., *The University of Wisconsin: Its History and Its Alumni with Historical and Descriptive Sketches of Madison* (Madison, 1899), 162.

[78] Ruth Bordin, *Woman and Temperance: The Quest for Power and Liberty, 1873–1900* (New Brunswick, New Jersey, 1990), 3–14, 95–162; Ruth Bordin, *Frances Willard: A Biography* (Chapel Hill, North Carolina, 1986), 3–13.

wayward women and recruited new members through "[ings" in private residences, churches, and fraternal h[the Wisconsin WCTU publicly blamed "industrial cor driving women into prostitution, and it denounced chil[labor. Local chapters sponsored recreational clubs for poor boys, lectures on municipal reform, segregation of women and children in jails, manual training in the schools, and child study circles. As a substitute for that venerable Wisconsin institution, the neighborhood saloon, the WCTU advocated public libraries, social centers, and temperance halls.[79]

Still, the threat to the existing order posed by the WCTU was as nothing compared to that posed by those who advocated suffrage for women. Agitation for enfranchising women antedated the Civil War, but its modern history dated from the formation of the Wisconsin Woman Suffrage Association (WWSA) in Milwaukee in 1869, at a convention attended by national leaders Susan B. Anthony and Elizabeth Cady Stanton. The members were generally upper-middle-class women of British-American origins, many of whom were professionals; all regarded suffrage primarily as a long stride towards gender equality. From 1885 to 1913, the WWSA was headed by the Reverend Olympia Brown, a Racine-based Universalist minister and feminist who believed that education, moral suasion, and legal action by elite women would eventually convert their male peers. This platform failed to attract the vast majority of women; it also antagonized large numbers of men, because it encouraged comparisons between the voting qualifications of native-stock elite females and foreign-stock, working-class males. Worse yet, Brown's further involvement with the WCTU hurt the chances of building a broad-based suffrage coalition. Her WCTU association somewhat extended the appeal of suffrage to women, but it also reinforced the belief that suffrage and prohibition were inseparable twins, virtually guaranteeing the opposition of "wets," advocates of "personal liberty," and the beer and liquor interests. Many prominent suffragists also belonged to the WFWC, the WCTU, the Consumers' League, or the Women's Trade Union League. But the WWSA generally eschewed these groups' municipal housekeeping goals until the advent of a new generation. The other organizations, in turn, generally avoided taking a stand on woman suffrage; their leaders and members divided ideologically on the question, and they feared that open advocacy of so "radical" a cause might alienate supporters of their programs.[80]

[79] Thelen, *New Citizenship*, 98–99, 114; Kohler, *Story of Wisconsin Women*, 53–58; American Association of University Women, *Wisconsin Women*, 33–39, 86–88.
[80] Lawrence L. Graves, "The Wisconsin Woman Suffrage Movement, 1846–1920" (doctoral dissertation, University of Wisconsin, 1954), 55–65, 95–100; Charles E. Neu,

After several futile efforts, the WWSA convinced the legislature in 1885 to grant woman suffrage in school elections. The argument that voting on school issues was a logical extension of a mother's traditional role as teacher in the home probably carried more weight than arguments advocating sexual equality. Because the law did not provide for separate ballots for school board elections, local officials still refused to allow women to vote in general elections. Olympia Brown challenged this refusal in 1887 when she was arrested for trying to vote in a municipal election. A Racine circuit court judge initially held that the law, by failing to provide for separate ballots, also enfranchised women in municipal elections; then the Wisconsin Supreme Court reversed his decision. In November, 1888, the court also overturned a decision by an Oconto County judge that permitted local poll watchers to receive women's ballots separately; the court agreed that it was the responsibility of the legislature to write such a provision into the suffrage law.

These two decisions undermined public confidence in the WWSA and left the organization with a debt of $2,000. The association eventually raised the money to pay off its indebtedness, but it was not easy. The treasury stood at $136.07 at the time of the annual convention in 1890.[81]

During the next two decades, the WWSA membership, treasury, and influence all suffered lean times. By 1893, membership stood at 500, only half of it active. The treasury had dwindled to $108.10. So frustrated were the WWSA leaders by the lack of grassroots support that the 1894 convention adopted a resolution stating "that the indifference of women has been a greater obstacle to the success of the cause than the selfishness of men." The following year, at the urging of Brown and Carrie Chapman Catt, a native of Ripon, WWSA delegates agreed to affiliate with the National American Woman Suffrage Association. Their action seemed something less than momentous, considering that state conventions rarely drew more than thirty delegates, and that the membership of local chapters stood at sixteen in Richland Center, seventeen in La Crosse, eighteen in Racine, and but thirty each in Milwaukee and Waukesha. In 1900, the state treasurer complained that Iowa "has two hundred and fifty live working Equal Suffrage Clubs to Wisconsin's one hundred seventy-one live paid-up individual members." Because the national body apportioned delegates to its conventions on the total of dues-paying members, Wis-

---

"Olympia Brown and the Woman's Suffrage Movement," in *WMH*, 43 (Summer, 1960), 277–287; Steinschneider, *An Improved Woman*, 33–41, 53–55, 93–95; Thelen, *New Citizenship*, 18–22.

[81] Graves, "The Wisconsin Woman Suffrage Movement," 51–80; McBride, *On Wisconsin Women*, 46–131.

consin's delegation shrank from six in 1897 to one from 1907 to 1910, and its contribution to the national body in 1910 was $13. In 1909, only $88 remained in the treasury.[82]

If there was a bright spot during those dark years, it was that the WWSA's official periodical, *The Wisconsin Citizen*, fared relatively better. It was begun in 1885 to publicize the court battles over school suffrage, and it continued bimonthly publication until World War I, even though it frequently required extra donations. It was published in several different locations, under a succession of editors, and its content varied accordingly. It dispensed state and national suffrage news to keep the Wisconsin suffrage community informed and to attract new women and men to the movement. Like the organization it served, younger members much criticized the paper for its traditionalism and drabness.[83]

In large part because of the WWSA's persisting doldrums, equal suffrage made little legislative progress before 1910. Periodically, efforts were made to extend the franchise to women in some fashion; but they rarely made it to a final vote before 1901. That year the legislature finally required the provision of separate ballots and ballot boxes for women who voted on school matters. Measures to extend the franchise to other offices were introduced in each session, but the lackluster state of affairs garnered neither much support or opposition. Despite his wife's prominence in the movement, Governor La Follette (1901–1906) failed to mention woman suffrage in a single one of his messages to the legislature. Nonetheless, an equal-suffrage bill actually passed the senate in 1909—only to be killed by the assembly on a vote of 53–34.[84]

The WWSA's feebleness was even more striking when compared to the success enjoyed by most other women's organizations, chiefly the WFWC and the WCTU. Between 1897 and 1919, the Federation of Women's Clubs nearly tripled the number of local clubs and the size of its membership; and its influence with the public, the legislature, and government agencies grew correspondingly. The WFWC successfully evaded taking a position on woman suffrage until 1912. During their 1911 convention, WFWC delegates refused to act on pro-suffrage resolutions, but did agree to make the proposed constitutional amendment on equal voting rights a priority item for the

---

[82] Graves, "The Wisconsin Woman Suffrage Movement," 80–88 (quotes); McBride, *On Wisconsin Women*, 135–199.

[83] Graves, "The Wisconsin Woman Suffrage Movement," 88–92.

[84] *Ibid.*, 100–105; Robert M. La Follette, *La Follette's Autobiography: A Personal Narrative of Political Experiences* (Madison, 1913; reprinted, 1960), 311–388; *Wisconsin Assembly Journal*, 1909, pp. 69, 629, 702, 742–745; *Wisconsin Senate Journal*, 1909, pp. 189, 484, 528, 565.

1912 meeting. At this time, local clubs began inviting suffragist speakers, and several other clubs added suffrage to their lists of discussion topics. At the WFWC meeting in 1912, Theodora Youmans, chair of the policy committee, failed to persuade the committee to endorse the suffrage referendum. Undaunted, she introduced a minority report which the convention adopted by a two-to-one margin, even though some leaders opposed it. The convention also elevated to its presidency a stanch suffragist, Sophia Strathearn of Kaukauna.

The WCTU advocated equal suffrage as early as 1875, and created the position of superintendent of "franchise" in 1883, but suffrage always occupied a lesser position on its agenda than temperance and some municipal housekeeping issues. WCTU leaders had no success in advancing woman suffrage. Even during Olympia Brown's 1907–1909 tenure as superintendent of franchise, she was unable to generate sufficient enthusiasm for it among local unions, despite regular articles in *The Motor*. Only about one-quarter of the local WCTU groups responded to her plea for signatures on the giant suffrage petition being prepared by the NAWSA. The WCTU generally allowed local temperance unions and individuals to determine their levels of involvement in suffrage. The marriage between temperance and suffrage was uneasy and barren of results.[85]

Reduced to seventy members by 1910, the Suffrage Association soon staged a remarkable comeback that involved a coalition which forced the issue to a referendum in 1912, and ultimately brought about ratification of the Nineteenth Amendment to the U.S. Constitution seven years later. The Wisconsin revival was part of a national resurgence, but it was due primarily to a new generation of women who infused the effort with a more appealing ideology and more aggressive tactics. Many of this new generation belonged to the GFWC, the WCTU, the Consumers League, the Women's Trade Union League, and similar organizations. They had witnessed at first hand how the emphasis on municipal housekeeping had won converts and allies, among both women and men. Conviction and expediency led them to urge WWSA to soft-pedal the equal rights argument, and to push harder for a range of social and economic reforms which women could help bring to fruition once they had the vote. This plan had far greater appeal to the other activists (labor unionists, socialists, social workers, intellectuals, religious leaders, and government officials), with whom they had already co-operated.[86]

---

[85] Graves, "The Wisconsin Woman Suffrage Movement," 95–100; Steinschneider, *An Improved Woman*, 37–38.

[86] Graves, "The Wisconsin Woman Suffrage Movement," 111–121; Marilyn Grant, "The 1912 Suffrage Referendum: An Exercise in Political Action," in *WMH*, 64 (Winter, 1980–1981), 107–116; McBride, *On Wisconsin Women*, 201–234.

Younger suffragists urged the WWSA to bring working women into the organization, and they expressed more concern about wages, hours, and living and working conditions than about equal rights. The newcomers also courted foreign-stock, working-class males by downplaying nativism and temperance, stressing bread-and-butter issues, and tailoring their messages to suit ethnic audiences. They believed the WWSA's traditional tactics (education, moral suasion, legal action, and nonpartisan appeals to individual legislators) were ineffectual in the new world of organization and high-speed transportation and communications. Instead they borrowed new political tactics from their more militant sisters in England and the East: holding political parties responsible for their stand on suffrage, appealing to the voters instead of merely to legislators, staging parades and mass rallies, seeking exposure in the press and on movie screens, canvassing door-to-door, and using the telephone, the automobile, and even the airplane to carry their message everywhere. In less than a year, this combination of reform ideology and activism transformed the state's dormant woman suffrage movement.[87]

Chief architects of this transformation were Mary Swain Wagner, a native of Oshkosh who returned to Wisconsin in 1910 after serving the movement in New York, and Ada James of Richland Center, the daughter of Laura Briggs James, a prominent WFWC official, and David G. James, the most active proponent of women's rights in the Wisconsin senate. Swain Wagner arranged a successful lecture tour by a militant English suffragist in the fall of 1910, and served as the WWSA's lobbyist during hearings on the suffrage bill introduced by Senator James in the 1911 legislative session. Meanwhile, Swain Wagner and others unsuccessfully sought to oust Brown and her sister officers. Failing that, they met in Milwaukee to propose a new, lively organization, the Political Equality League, to replace the "bunch of doddering old ladies" who controlled the WWSA. More charitably, Ada James referred to Brown as a "gritty old pioneer" with fine leadership qualities, but regretted that she was not "a little sweeter and sympathetic" and less jealous of her authority. Swain Wagner pushed her own candidacy as the Political Equality League (PEL) president, but the majority preferred Ada James. Her father persuaded her to take the job in April, 1911. The PEL quickly outstripped the WWSA, although James said that she could "see no reason why there can't be two or more organizations—each working in harmony along dif-

---

[87] For the national context, see Eleanor Flexner, *Century of Struggle: The Woman's Rights Movement in the United States* (Cambridge, 1959), 229–262; Aileen S. Kraditor, *The Ideas of the Woman Suffrage Movement, 1890–1920* (New York, 1965), 43–74, 123–162, 219–48; and Anne F. Scott and Andrew M. Scott, *One Half the People: The Fight for Woman Suffrage* (Philadelphia, 1975), 24–33.

ferent lines." The reputation and success of the PEL benefited a good deal from the participation of Belle Case La Follette, who brought the experience of years of campaigning with her husband. Despite the opposition of the brewing lobby, the measure calling for a suffrage referendum passed both houses of the legislature by mid-May and was signed by Governor Francis McGovern on June 2, 1911. The referendum itself occurred more than a year later, in November, 1912.[88]

An effective band of female Socialists also got on the suffrage bandwagon, serving as liaisons between the Social Democratic party and mainstream suffragists. Chief among these were Meta Berger, Victor's wife and a long-time member of the Milwaukee school board; Maud McCreery, women's editor of the Milwaukee *Leader*; Annie Gordon Whitnall, school board director and wife of city treasurer Charles P. Whitnall; Elizabeth Thomas, New York-born Quaker and school board director; and May Wood Simons, wife of Social Democratic party intellectual Algie M. Simons and a member of the Woman's National Committee of the Socialist Party of America. All but Berger were "Yankees"; the party's large Germanic contingent still held to the traditional view of woman's place: *Kinder, Kirche, Kuchen.* None of these women held high office in the SDP, and Meta Berger complained privately about being excluded from party strategy sessions held in her own home. Socialists talked about gender equality but did not always practice it.[89]

The WWSA and PEL leaders were willing to accept support from any quarter, regardless of ideology on matters other than voting rights. The SDP, fresh from a 1910 triumph in Milwaukee, was confident that enfranchising women would aid it materially. Consequently, the WWSA made Meta Berger and Emil Seidel, the socialist mayor of Milwaukee, vice-presidents of the organization, included party members as speakers on their programs, and stressed SDP endorsement in its campaign literature. For its part, the SDP strongly endorsed equal suffrage in talks and literature, and SDP lawmakers supported suffrage bills in the legislature. At a joint 1915 convention, the WWSA and PEL even offered Meta Berger the presidency, an honor she declined because she felt it would damage the suffragist cause in conservative quarters. This alliance between suffragists and Social Democrats soon came undone when Mrs. Berger affiliated with the National Woman's party, the SDP opposed American involvement

---

[88] Graves, "The Wisconsin Woman Suffrage Movement," 111–121 (quotes); Grant, "The 1912 Suffrage Referendum," in *WMH*, 64: 110–113 (quotes).

[89] John D. Buenker, "The Politics of Mutual Frustration: Socialists and Suffragists in New York and Wisconsin," in Sally M. Miller, ed., *Flawed Liberation: Socialism and Feminism* (Westport, Connecticut, 1981), 113–119, 126–133.

in World War I, and militant anti-socialists turned the Milwaukee school board elections of 1917 and 1919 into ideological battles. Socialists and suffragists of all genders and persuasions lobbied together for the Nineteenth Amendment, but they did so as temporary and wary collaborators, not as allies. Even among the party faithful, there existed a fissure between Yankee matrons and German hausfraus.[90]

During the campaign that preceded Wisconsin's referendum on a woman suffrage amendment to the Constitution in November, 1912, a broad coalition got behind it: the WWSA, the PEL, the SDP, the State Federation of Labor, the State Teachers Association, the WCTU, the Grange, and the Society of Equity. The WFWC took no official stand on the matter, but several of its most important members—among them Ada James, Theodora Youmans, Jessie Jack Hooper, and Lucy Morris—happened to be major figures in the suffrage movement.

The returns made it clear that their efforts failed; the referendum lost by almost two to one. The reasons were several. The SDP, WSFL, Equity, Grange, and other male-dominated organizations had failed to turn out their membership in favor of the referendum. What was more, the German-American Alliance, the United States Brewers Association, and various business and foreign-language associations had succeeded quite well in their antisuffrage campaign. Then, too, the WWSA and the PEL frequently had worked at cross-purposes during the campaign. Efforts to combine forces consistently failed, principally because Rev. Olympia Brown was reluctant to surrender her authority. Adding to the confusion, Swain Wagner formed a third suffrage organization, besides the WWSA and PEL. It advocated confrontation on the British model. As in many another broad-based coalition, the various groups supporting suffrage bickered over larger policy matters as well as minor issues—for example, using the automobile as a campaign vehicle.

Despite the herculean efforts of the key women (James, Youmans, La Follette, Berger, and so forth); despite automobiles, stereoscopic slide presentations, and even a movie featuring Jane Addams and NAWSA president Anna Howard Shaw; despite all the rhetoric and hard work—the referendum carried only fourteen of seventy-one counties, nearly all of them in Scandinavian or Yankee strongholds. Crystal Eastman Benedict, a national organizer for the NAWSA who moved to Milwaukee and worked for the PEL, attributed the defeat to overestimation of the support expected from Scandinavians, socialists, and progressive Republicans, underestimation of the power

---

[90] See the papers of the Wisconsin Woman Suffrage Association, 1883–1925, Meta Berger's unpublished autobiography in the Victor L. Berger Papers, 1862–1980, and the Maud McCreery Miscellany file.

of the beer and liquor interests, the general conservatism of Wisconsin voters, and the ignorance and prejudice of many males. Youmans disagreed, blaming the loss on too little general education about woman suffrage, and too little organization. The legislature authorized a similar referendum during a stormy 1913 session, but Governor McGovern vetoed it on the grounds that voter opinion could not have changed very significantly in only a year.[91]

In the months immediately following the referendum, WWSA membership fell to 300, although its paper, the *Wisconsin Citizen*, retained 1,400 subscribers. By 1915, a reconciliation between the WWSA and the PEL under the presidency of Theodora Youmans caused a modest revival, though Youmans continued to complain that women on the average feared action and responsibility. Those who were unhappy with the compromise between the PEL and the WWSA, such as Meta Berger, formed a Wisconsin branch of the National Woman's party. It appeared that the woman suffrage movement in Wisconsin was about to sink back into its pre-1910 doldrums. Not even its leaders understood how well they had planted the seeds of equal suffrage and how they would yield fruit less than five years later.[92]

[6]

Religious leaders were following a similar course to women in the late nineteenth and early twentieth centuries, invading the public sphere, urging that society and government assume greater responsibility for reform. The movement was variously called "the New Religion," "Applied Christianity," or "the Institutional Church," but most commonly it became known as "the Social Gospel." Traditionally, both clergy and laity conceived of religion primarily as a way to achieve individual salvation, within rigidly drawn sectarian boundaries. Church membership, regular attendance, prayer, strict observance of rituals and regulations, and avoidance of sin were primarily private

---

[91] Graves, "The Wisconsin Woman Suffrage Movement," 121–214; Grant, "The 1912 Suffrage Referendum," in *WMH*, 64: 111–116; Buenker, "Politics of Mutual Frustration," in Miller, ed., *Flawed Liberation*, 130–132; Crystal Eastman Benedict, "Why We Lost in Wisconsin," in the Wisconsin Woman Suffrage Association Records, 1883–1925; Theodora W. Youmans, "Historical Sketch of Woman Suffrage in Wisconsin," January, 1917, in the Wisconsin Woman Suffrage Association Records, 1883–1925; Theodora W. Youmans, "How Wisconsin Women Won the Ballot," in *WMH*, 5 (1921–1922), 15–23; James I. Clark, *Wisconsin Women Fight for Suffrage* (Madison, 1956), 8–17.

[92] Graves, "The Wisconsin Woman Suffrage Movement," 215–266; McBride, *On Wisconsin Women*, 234–293. On the struggle between the NWP and the NAWSA, see Christine A. Lunardini, *From Equal Suffrage to Equal Rights: Alice Paul and the National Woman's Party, 1910–1928* (New York, 1986), 1–83.

matters, incumbent upon each individual, whatever his or her socioeconomic status or whatever was occurring in the outside world. The chief moral issues dealt with sexuality, food and drink, entertainment, and observance of the Sabbath, and not with social or economic justice. Religious bodies generally prized charity highly, but put the burden for it on individual conscience, thereby making churches into defenders of the economic status quo. Some espoused "The Gospel of Wealth" and argued that the greater a person's material possessions, the greater his or her sanctity. For the most part, though, the only forays that churches made into the public arena (antislavery had been an exception many years before) were to defend the "correct" belief or behavior of the faithful, and to remove temptations to belief and behavior initiated by "the world" or by other denominations.[93]

In the latter years of the nineteenth century, some Protestant religious leaders began manifesting concerns about the working class, and other reformist currents, often linking them to traditional concerns about Sabbatarianism and temperance. For example, the Episcopal bishop of the Fond du Lac diocese told the Wisconsin Sabbath Association in 1895 that it was not "undemocratic" to close theaters on Sunday and thus "diminish the gain of the few in the interests of the many," not "illiberal" to ban "amusements which weary and exhaust the human frame," and not "unprogressive in desiring the saloons to be closed on Sunday which filch the poor man's wages and break up family life." The Christian Endeavor Society appealed to workingmen by publishing in 1897 a letter from Samuel Gompers, president of the American Federation of Labor, stating that it was "absolutely dangerous to all our interests and to our progress that the workers should be required to toil more than six days in the week." Mixing moralistic appeals with reform imagery in an 1896 Milwaukee address, the secretary of the National Christian Citizenship League said, "No one . . . favors the repeal of these righteous laws but blatant infidels, howling anarchists, and blind, greedy, grasping monopolies." Writing in 1895 in the magazine of the Wisconsin Congregational church, "a working man" chided readers, "The evident insincerity of some church members is one of the greatest causes keeping the working man out of church." It was, he said, "hardly any

[93] Thelen, *New Citizenship*, 99–101; Charles Howard Hopkins, *The Rise of the Social Gospel in American Protestantism, 1865–1915* (New Haven, 1940), 14–23; Irvin G. Wyllie, *The Self-Made Man in America: The Myth of Rags to Riches* (New Brunswick, New Jersey, 1954), 55–74, 116–132. On the division of American religions into those with "right belief" and those with "right behavior," see Paul Kleppner, *The Cross of Culture: A Social Analysis of Midwestern Politics, 1850–1900* (New York, 1970), 69–71, and Richard J. Jensen, *The Winning of the Midwest: Social and Political Conflict, 1888–1896* (Chicago, 1971), 58–89. The actual division is more complex, but the Kleppner-Jensen typology conveys the basic idea.

use for the minister to preach Christ, if the congregation does not practice Christ."[94]

Another correspondent to the Congregational magazine took a different tack in 1902. "Pilgrim" denounced Milwaukee socialism, said that workers' "spiritual and moral degradation" posed a worse danger than capitalists, and argued that the church "is not so much in need of the union worker as the union worker is in need of the church." Five years before, a Clintonville minister declared to the state convention of the Epworth League that the closing years of the century were bringing on "a social crisis, such as the world has not seen before." "[P]ay attention to the questions of sociology," he admonished.[95]

Even before 1893 many Wisconsin religious leaders had begun stressing the connection between spiritual well-being and socioeconomic and political conditions. Milwaukee Methodist Sabin Halsey and Madison Congregationalist Eugene G. Updike had openly sided with workers in labor disputes. In 1892, Halsey denounced any religion "that is satisfied to sit down at the feet of worldly aristocracy and minister solely to them while hundreds and thousands are crying for the bread of life." Judson Titsworth, pastor of Milwaukee's Plymouth Congregational Church, considered by some the Midwest's foremost "institutional church" leader, led a church that had a boys' club, manual training classes, and classes for adults. Richard T. Ely of the University of Wisconsin faculty was one of the earliest academic proponents of blending the Social Gospel with social science. He won few adherents, but in 1892 was invited to address both the Milwaukee Ministerial Council and the state Congregational convention. The onset of the 1893–1897 depression convinced a number of other clergymen that, in the blunt words of an Ashland minister, "a man cannot become a Christian with an empty stomach." Clergymen began articulating the idea that Protestant churches were overemphasizing "individualistic evangelization," thereby estranging most workers from their churches. They accordingly searched for a way to "break down the partitions between rich and poor in church and social life."[96]

---

[94] "The Bishop's Address to the W. S. Association," in *Diocese of Fond du Lac*, 13 ([December], 1895), 2 (quote); *Lord's Day Papers*, 26 (September, 1896), and 31 (February, 1897, quote), and 74 (n.p., 1900); National Religious Liberty Association, *American Sentinel*, January 7, 1897 (quote); A. McK., "Reaching the Masses," in *Our Church Life*, 1 (September, 1895), 157; "Labor Day," in *Wisconsin Congregational Church Life*, 18 (September, 1911), 1.

[95] Pilgrim, "Milwaukee Letter," in *Our Church Life*, 9 (December, 1902), 10; S. H. Anderson, "Report of Department on Literary Work," in Wisconsin State Epworth League of the Methodist Episcopal Church, *Proceedings*, 1895, pp. 47–49.

[96] Thelen, *New Citizenship*, 99–102.

To accomplish this, some tried discussion groups, such as the Church and Labor Social Union and the Christian Labor Union in Milwaukee, where workingmen and parishioners and clergymen could consider issues of mutual concern. Leaders of the Milwaukee Federated Trades Council co-operated with the Christian Labor Union, and the Wisconsin State Federation of Labor invited a minister to speak at its 1893 convention about the labor problem and the church. At their 1895 meeting, Congregationalists recommended that "the right aspirations and demands of labor be as often voiced in the pulpit as the errors of 'socialists and anarchists' are denounced." To put these aspirations into action, numerous churches expanded their social services to include soup kitchens, rescue missions, hospitals, and homes for dependent women and children. Others developed manual training classes, campaigned for better public schools, expanded YMCA activities to factory workers, or opened co-operative stores and factories. In 1896, clergymen organized a statewide convention to discuss more humane ways of ministering to the thousands of "tramps"—meaning men forced into transience and homelessness by the depression. By 1900, the editor of the *Wisconsin State Journal* observed, many churches were stressing the Bible somewhat less and had begun to search for spirituality "in ethical movements, in benevolence, in expressions of genuine brotherhood."[97]

Social Gospelites believed, too, that gambling, prostitution, and liquor were interwoven in the socio-economic and political fabric, and accordingly they supported corrupt practices acts, the civil service, and nonpartisan local elections. Some had a restricted sense of democracy and sought to disfranchise or neutralize the votes of the foreign-stock working class. Others more generously believed they should "study the heart of the laboring classes," then "go down where they are, win their confidence, and teach them how to use it." In the mid-1890's, Milwaukee clergymen formed several committees to "federate the moral forces of the city"; ministers mounted similar campaigns in Green Bay, Sheboygan, Racine, Madison, Ashland, Superior, and Fond du Lac. Even tiny El Paso, in Pierce County, experienced a joint Protestant-Catholic crusade in 1897.

"Municipal purging is in the air," the Congregationalist *Our Church Life* exulted in 1895, and the Milwaukee Civic Federation attracted many church members to its ranks with its pledge "to organize the public conscience." A Superior minister urged his followers to "awake to the axiom that city governments as well as individuals must give an account to God, and the path of history is strewn with wrecked, ruined cities which disregarded that truth." Individualism

[97] *Ibid.*, 102–106.

and materialistic greed came in for attack. A Milwaukee Methodist preacher scored the greedy competition fostered by the Gospel of Wealth and Social Darwinism as "a form of war, and not much more merciful than battles with gun and saber." Low wages, according to the editor of Milwaukee's *Catholic Citizen*, reinforced materialism, fostered socialism and labor unions, isolated rich and poor, and created an "earthly civilization of organized selfishness." In Appleton a Presbyterian minister predicted the evolution of a new society in which humans would cease to compete, and "co-operate with one another to make common cause, burying their mutual differences before a common foe." Some spoke of a "Christian sociology"; others of championing the "public interest."[98]

Besides Judson Titsworth of Milwaukee, Social Gospel clergymen appeared all over Wisconsin. Richard Henry Edwards, pastor of the First Congregational Church of Madison from 1906 through 1912 and chaplain to the 1,200 Congregationalist students at the University of Wisconsin, had nearly as impressive a career as Titsworth. He had graduated from the Union Theological Seminary in New York, and had YMCA experience before coming to Madison. There he formed a "social problems group" which discussed current topics and heard lectures by university and state government figures and visitors from other cities. As an instructor in the extension division, Edwards edited a series of publications on issues like alcohol, race, immigration, labor, concentrated wealth, and business ethics; as a graduate student, he took courses from John R. Commons and Edward A. Ross, collaborating with them on development of their *Studies in American Social Conditions*, which served as discussion guides for civic organizations, social settlement clubs, betterment leagues, and so forth. Edwards' wife, Anna Camp, who had studied under John Dewey at the University of Chicago and had tutored the deaf daughter of millionaire Charles Crane, ran analogous programs for women.[99]

The New Religion had its greatest impact on traditional Protestant denominations, but it also affected Catholics and Jews, especially in Milwaukee. For Catholics, the key figure was Humphrey J. Desmond, editor of the *Catholic Citizen* in Milwaukee and other Catholic newspapers in St. Paul, Memphis, and Washington, D.C. He developed a reputation as a spokesman for liberal Catholics. Desmond was influenced heavily by the social teachings of the 1891 papal encyclical *Rerum Novarum*, and he held strong convictions: that the church must

---

[98] *Ibid.*, 104–111.

[99] Richard Henry Edwards, ed., *Studies in American Social Conditions* (7 part series, Madison, 1908–1910), *passim*. These are arranged as a series of problem studies with exposition, bibliography, and proposed solutions, as well as a preface entitled "The Social Problems Group Idea."

minister to the physical needs of southern and eastern European immigrants if it was to maintain their allegiance, and that the only effective way to stem the popularity of socialism was to adopt many of its social welfare proposals. Feeling as he did, Desmond urged his readers to co-operate with Protestants and secular reformers on a wide range of ameliorative measures. He favored voluntary action by Catholic associations when possible and lent support to most protective and welfare legislation. Desmond and his fellow liberals also backed labor unions, even to the point of allowing them to act against scabs.

The *Catholic Citizen* fiercely denounced the American Protective Association and the Social Democratic party, as expected, but it not so expectedly endorsed some third parties in their 1890's campaigns against corporate power and the regular Republican and Democratic organizations. Desmond accused public utilities and the liquor interests as the chief corrupters of city government and preached that "municipal socialism is the true line of municipal reform." Archbishop Sebastian B. Messmer and the German Catholic *Central-Verein* frequently disagreed with Desmond, but they, too, advocated some social justice measures as a way to undermine socialist influence and keep the faithful in the fold. The paper had a philosophy of "solidarism" and looked forward to the ultimate establishment of a "Christian co-operative order," more humane than either doctrinaire socialism or corporate capitalism.[100]

Milwaukee's Jewish community made different adjustments under the New Religion. Principally it moved from dispensing short-term emergency aid to supporting social welfare in the long run. Performing charitable work, especially among fellow Jews, was one of the strongest Hebrew traditions. Jewish mutual aid societies and ladies' associations had begun dispensing welfare benefits from the beginning of the community's existence in the mid-nineteenth century. The founding in 1900 of the Milwaukee Jewish Settlement and in 1902 of the Federated Jewish Charities marked the opening of the new era. Several women's groups coalesced to form the settlement, patterned after social settlements in British and American cities. Its most famous resident, Lizzie Black Kander, the "Lady Bountiful" of Milwaukee Jewish philanthropy, became permanently known as the author of a culinary classic, the *Settlement House Cook*

---

[100] Aaron I. Abell, *American Catholicism and Social Action: A Search for Social Justice, 1865–1950* (Garden City, New York, 1960), 131–138, 149–155; Richard J. Orsi, "Humphrey Joseph Desmond: A Case Study in American Catholic Liberalism" (master's thesis, University of Wisconsin, 1965); Philip Gleason, *The Conservative Reformers: German-American Catholics and the Social Order* (Notre Dame, 1968), 116–13; Thelen, *New Citizenship*, 103, 153, 313.

Book. Kander and other prosperous German Jews helped thousands of immigrants make the transition to American life. The Federated Jewish Charities and its welfare agency, the Hebrew Relief Association, administered to over a thousand people a year between 1902 and 1920, providing them with everything from education to day care.[101]

The New Religion or Social Gospel was primarily an urban phenomenon, but it also wrought change in rural churches. Rural churches' three biggest problems were the rivalry between town and country parishes, absentee and unprepared ministers, and "overchurching": too many small congregations spread over a wide area. Tiny congregations required missionary funds; some were served only occasionally by ministers. By 1898, these conditions led to an interdenominational conference which discussed remedies. Reformers concentrated on three solutions: consolidation of, or cooperation among, underpopulated congregations; upgrading the qualifications and preparation of rural pastors; and establishing social centers in rural church buildings. The automobile and farm-to-city migration were already leading to consolidation. By 1913, at least twenty federations of rural churches had been accomplished in Wisconsin, involving different combinations of Baptists, Congregationalists, Methodists, and Presbyterians. Low pay and isolation frequently led to mediocre and part-time preachers, many of whom were older and resistant to urban culture and Social Gospel tenets. Reformers advocated pastoral training that included rural sociology, economics, and agricultural science; some proposed a specialized rural theological seminary. Church reform was a major focus of the Country Life Movement after 1908. The movement pushed further education and new social programs, and praised the clergymen who participated. Rural social centers were often controversial, but they proved popular with younger members of many congregations. Successful programs were instituted in Oconto, Richland, Vilas, Pierce, Grant, Langlade, Outagamie, and Marathon counties among a broad spectrum of congregations: Catholics, Lutherans, Baptists, Congregationalists, Presbyterians, Methodists, and German Reformed Christians.[102]

---

[101] Louis J. Swichkow and Lloyd P. Gartner, *The History of the Jews of Milwaukee* (Philadelphia, 1963), 215–224; Waligorski, "Social Action and Women," 43–62; Thelen, *New Citizenship*, 117–118, 127–128.

[102] Brian W. Beltman, "Rural Church Reform in Wisconsin During the Progressive Era," in *WMH*, 60 (Autumn, 1976), 3–24; Berger, *The Devil Wagon*, 127–145; H. A. Berman, "The Country Church," *Wisconsin Agriculturist*, March 4, 1915, p. 36; John Rouse to A. Frank Mann, *ibid.*, April 1, 1915, p. 9.

The participation of Social Gospel clergy and women's organizations in the generalized movement for change can be credited to the rapid, large-scale changes taking place in Wisconsin's socio-economic system. The benefits of technological innovation were being broadcast throughout the state, beginning with affluent city dwellers in the southeast and ending in the New North. As awareness of this metamorphosis spread, Wisconsinites in many walks of life united into groups of like-minded persons. They debated, resisted, moderated, and shaped the course of change, each seeking to impose an individual brand of order and system upon a seemingly inchoate process. Whatever their individual goals, the proponents of change pursued them through organized, purposeful intervention in public life. At first they operated principally through voluntary association in the private sector. Then, pragmatically, they began to form coalitions with other activist groups and with agencies of government, often seeking intervention by state government to secure changes in a wide variety of areas. Individually, these reformist streams were mere trickles; collectively, they formed a tide of unprecedented demands upon state government in number, scope, and variety. The turn of a new century coincided with the flowering of a broad, multifaceted reform impulse whose pressure on state government to impose order and system upon the fabric of Wisconsin life was to prove irresistible.

8

Education for Progress

[1]

THE same historical processes that gave rise to the New Woman and the New Religion also produced what educator-philosopher John Dewey called the "New Education." Unless children were "trained in social directions, enriched by historical interpretation, controlled and illuminated by scientific principles," Dewey said, "we certainly are in no position even to locate the source of economic evils, much less to deal with them effectively." As the only modern institution with the potential to accomplish this task, the school must develop "our impulses and tendencies to make, to do, to create, to produce, whether in the form of utility or of art." It must become "an embryonic community life, active with types of occupations that reflect the life of the larger society." Students, in Dewey's famous phrase, must "learn by doing."[1]

The New Education took shape in efforts to make education democratic, relevant, and practical—a defining and fundamental institution in American society. Dewey's disciples all spoke of "progressive education," but most of them reshaped, and frequently distorted, his vision. Occasionally the derivatives worked at cross-purposes, contravening Dewey's first principles: compulsory education, a longer school year and day, kindergartens, expanded secondary education, grouping by ability, intelligence testing, experiential learning, adult and vocational education, child-centered teaching, and "education for life."

Progressive education gradually split into three overlapping, and sometimes antagonistic, wings. The "social efficiency" wing strove to integrate public education and the labor market by training students for the workplace. The "utilitarian-democratic" wing stressed the

---

[1] John Dewey, *The School and Society*, in *The Child and the Curriculum* and *The School and Society* (Chicago, 1956, reprint of 1915 edition), 8, 24, 26, 28–29; Morton White, *Social Thought in America: The Revolt Against Formalism* (Boston, 1947; revised ed., 1957), 94–103; Lawrence A. Cremin, *The Transformation of the School: Progressivism in American Education, 1876–1957* (New York, 1961), pp. viii–x.

need for schools to adjust constantly, in order to prepare students for the rapidly changing world. The "child-centered" wing concentrated on devising teaching and curricular innovations to arouse students' curiosity and serve their interests and needs.[2]

In Wisconsin, the New Education umbrella sheltered many individuals, interest groups, and programs, making public education one of the most hotly debated topics of the Progressive Era. The debate permeated the conventions of the Wisconsin Teachers' Association, the *Wisconsin Journal of Education*, the reports of state superintendents of education, the findings of commissions and study groups, the pronouncements of university and normal school administrators and faculty, and legislative debates. Reformers of all stripes came to believe that extensive revamping of the education system was crucial to the advancement of their interests. Virtually the only professional educators who did not frame their arguments within that paradigm were associated with private and parochial schools, the University of Wisconsin faculty, and the Wisconsin Education Association (WEA).

Probably the most articulate and comprehensive advocate of the New Education was Charles McCarthy, who wanted to infuse every public school with doses of democracy, practicality, and social efficiency. "When Bob La Follette goes out to talk in this country he can say a lot of good things about this state," McCarthy wrote the county superintendent of Oneida County in 1913, "but if someone happens to pop up in the audience and say, 'How about Wisconsin's schools,' there is mighty little that he can say." Impractical and elitist educators and unprincipled politicians dominated local education, McCarthy believed. In his view, Wisconsin schools were failing to equip the majority of youngsters for the work force and citizenship, or to provide meaningful social opportunity. "Today we cannot give the worker free land or capital," he wrote, "but we can throw wide the doors of opportunity by giving them the right kind of education. . . . I am convinced that people have got to do things for themselves,—they cannot have it forced on them from above, that they have got to 'learn by doing,' and the only safety in our government and our institutions lies in providing means of education on this principle." He denounced the National Educational Association for retarding progress and preached that the new progressive education system should be taken out of it members' hands.[3]

---

[2] David Hogan, "Education, Progressive" in John D. Buenker and Edward R. Kantowicz, eds., *Historical Dictionary of the Progressive Era, 1890–1920* (New York, 1988), 128–129; Cremin, *The Transformation of the School*, 115–176.

[3] Charles McCarthy to W. C. Bagley, May 26, 1913, to F. A. Lowell, April 7, 1913 (quote), to Henry C. Campbell, May 13, 1913, to James A. Patten, October 29, 1913, to Charles R. Van Hise, November 4, 1913, to James J. Hill, January 7, 1914, to E. H.

The tenets of the New Education also permeated the 1911 report of the commission on industrial and agricultural training, of which McCarthy was secretary and chief author. Its membership included state superintendent of education Charles P. Cary, the chairman; Charles R. Van Hise, president of the University of Wisconsin; and Louis E. Reber, director of the university's extension division. "If we desire the equality of opportunity which our fathers had to continue," their report stated, "this must depend upon the brain power of the individual," gained "through education which will fit him to meet his own needs and those of this state and country."[4]

In 1901, Charles McKenny, the president of the Milwaukee Normal School, told the annual convention of the Wisconsin Teachers' Association (WTA), that "the end [goal] of education is not merely individualistic but also social," and deplored the separation of schoolchildren from "the industrial phases of life." Earlier, WTA president W. N. Parker had said that manual training would equalize opportunity for urban youngsters and guarantee that they "are being trained to be independent citizens, to have minds of their own, that will enable them to meet the new problems that every day of life's experience must of necessity bring to them." *Hoard's Dairyman* lauded the "practical" bent of the New Education when it proclaimed "educators have come to believe that there is mental development in studying the root of an alfalfa plant as well as in the study of a Latin root. . . ." To learn the functions of the various parts of a plant was quite as valuable—probably more so—than memorizing poetry. Superintendent Cary observed in 1904 that "while the student may to advantage breathe the pure air of Mt. Olympus for a portion of the day, the same student may well, for another portion of the day, come down to such practical affairs as shop work, bread making, or sewing."[5]

Miles, October 22, 1913, to John B. Lennon, March 12, 1914, to Herbert Quick, September 29, 1914, and to John D. Rockefeller, Jr., October 11, 1915 (quote), all in the Charles R. McCarthy Papers.

[4] Commission upon the Plans for the Extension of Industrial and Agricultural Training, *Report*, 1911, pp. 1–5; Michael V. O'Shea, "A Memory Gem," *Wisconsin Journal of Education*, 42 (June, 1910), 156; "The Progress of a Decade," *Wisconsin Journal of Education*, 43 (March, 1911), 59; Michael V. O'Shea, "Industrial Education," *Wisconsin Journal of Education*, 43(March, 1911), 59; Michael V. O'Shea, "A Dynamic View of the School," *Wisconsin Journal of Education*, 42 (May, 1910), 125; Michael V. O'Shea, "Learn to Do by Doing," *Wisconsin Journal of Education*, 42 (May, 1910), 127. See also O'Shea to J. H. Kellogg, June 9, 1909, and to John R. Carr, December, 12, 1912, in the O'Shea Papers.

[5] Charles McKenny, "Changes Which Would Result in Our Present Methods of Instruction and Courses of Study if We Were Governed by the Psychology of the Child," in Wisconsin Teachers' Association, *Proceedings*, 1901, pp. 121–122; W. N. Parker, "President's Address," in Wisconsin Teachers' Association, *Proceedings*, 1900,

Of all the issues facing educational reformers, none seemed more urgent or perplexing than the rural school. To this day, folkloric nostalgia surrounds the one-room rural schoolhouse. But serious problems also surrounded it at the turn of the century. Experts saw it as a major cause of rural population decline, social insecurity, and dissatisfaction with country living. To them, the revitalization of rural education seemed the best way to retard the exodus of young people to the city and to begin upgrading the quality of rural life. Perhaps the main problems with "the little red schoolhouse" were that there were so many of them—a legacy of the independent school districts established during the settlement period—and that district residents were loath to surrender their dwindling control over their schools. In 1898, more than one-quarter of Wisconsin's country schools served fewer than twenty pupils a year; 6 per cent served fewer than ten. Two years later, state superintendent Lorenzo D. Harvey reported that half the state's children were enrolled in rural schools where the children were not separated into grades ("ungraded"), where the teachers' wages were lowest, the equipment was the poorest, and the teaching the weakest. In 1904, according to Harvey's successor, there were still 6,773 one-room-school districts; in 1912, about 20 per cent of the state's 6,500 country schools had fifteen or fewer students. Besides lacking satisfactory educational resources, these schools suffered discrepancies in expenditures, length of school terms, curriculum, and quality of teaching. Some rural districts were willing to finance quality education, but it seemed plain to many reformers that many farmers devoted more thought to their cows than their children.[6]

From the 1890's onward, the consolidation of school districts and the creation of county-wide school boards assumed panacea status among reformers and educators. Bills to effect consolidation and county school boards appeared regularly in the legislature after 1898, as did bills to provide state aid to districts that merged or created "graded" schools. However, the industrial and agricultural training commission still found, in 1911: "Notwithstanding numerous enact-

---

pp. 73–74 (quote); "Teaching Agriculture," *Hoard's Dairyman*, August 2, 1907, p. 685; Department of Public Instruction, *Biennial Report*, 1902–1904, p. 104 (quote); Department of Public Instruction, *Biennial Report*, 1906–1908, pp. 7–34. See also the brief discussion of the New Education in David P. Thelen, *The New Citizenship: Origins of Progressivism in Wisconsin, 1885–1900* (Columbia, Missouri, 1972), 23, 192, 438.

[6] Brian W. Beltman, "Rural Renaissance in an Urban Age: The Country Life Movement in Wisconsin, 1895–1918" (doctoral dissertation, University of Wisconsin, 1974), 103–108; James I. Clark, "The Wisconsin State Department of Public Instruction, 1903–1921" (doctoral dissertation, University of Wisconsin, 1961), 133; Conrad E. Patzer, "The Country School System," in Charles McKenny, ed., *Educational History of Wisconsin* (Chicago, 1912), 33–64.

ments of the legislature during the past ten years, looking toward the consolidation of schools, little or nothing has yet been accomplished in this state in this direction." In 1924, Conrad E. Patzer, longtime chairman of the WTA's legislative committee and supervisor of practice teaching at the Milwaukee Normal School, headlined a section of his survey of Wisconsin education "Consolidation as Remote as Ever," primarily because the legislature had refused to make it mandatory and left it up to districts.[7]

Patzer summed up the complaints of a multitude of educational reformers about the independent school district. First was the problem of "Many Grades, Many Subjects and Many Recitations," in one- and two-room schools. These demands exhausted even the most dedicated teacher, leaving students to devise often misdirected self-activity. Next was "Irregularity of Attendance and Short School Year," which meant that nearly one-third attended less than 120 days and almost 85 per cent less than 160 days, despite a 1907 compulsory education law that required nine months attendance a year in Milwaukee, eight in other cities, and six in towns and villages. Finally, there was "The Small Administrative Unit and Inequality of Taxation," which resulted in a proliferation of local school officials—one for every 5 1/2 children in daily attendance—and in inequalities of taxation based upon variations in district size, assessed valuation, and number of children. Many rural children were virtually denied a high school education since most districts were too small to support one and high schools elsewhere charged tuition. At the turn of the century, only about one-sixth of the pupils in Wisconsin's rural schools went to high school. And of those who did attend city high schools, few returned to the farm.[8]

Teacher preparation was dismal. A 1900 report by a special WTA committee concluded that rural schools' "great, comprehensive defect is in the quality of the teaching itself. . . . Country teachers are, in most cases, young, immature, half-trained, [and] ineffective. . . ." The committee found that many were paid "at so low a rate as to

---

[7] Commission upon the Plans for the Extension of Industrial and Agricultural Training, *Report*, 1911, p. 122 (quote); Conrad E. Patzer, *Public Education in Wisconsin* (Madison, 1924), 190–206; William T. Anderson, "The Development of the Common Schools," in the *Wisconsin Blue Book, 1923*, pp. 111–114.

[8] Patzer, *Public Education in Wisconsin*, 76–78, 201–206; Patzer, "Country School System," in McKenny, ed., *Educational History*, 63; Anderson, "Development of the Common Schools," in the *Wisconsin Blue Book, 1923*, pp. 114–116; Henry S. Yonker, "Secondary Education," in McKenny, ed., *Educational History*, 84–90; Malcolm Rosholt, *Our County, Our Story: Portage County, Wisconsin* (Stevens Point, 1959), 158; Belle S. Bradford to Norman Hapgood, undated but probably November or December, 1915, in the McCarthy Papers; Edward A. Fitzpatrick, "The Educational System," in Milo Milton Quaife, ed., *Wisconsin: Its History and its People, 1634–1924* (4 vols., Chicago, 1924), 2: 254–257.

utterly preclude the securing of efficient teaching." One-third of all rural teachers dropped out each year. The state superintendent blamed this on the county superintendents, who were popularly elected and therefore subject to public pressure. The county superintendents issued teaching certificates to ill-prepared men and women, and they also lacked the time and staff to supervise teachers and inspect schools. Each new school year novice teachers poured into the country schools. The best ones succeeded in teaching their students everything from geography to Shakespeare, but most lacked training, maturity, and meaningful supervision. Like military recruits thrown prematurely into battle, they did their best, moving from school to school until they burned out.[9]

Much of the blame, according to some educators and rural leaders, lay with the University of Wisconsin and the state normal schools, both of which geared their teacher preparation courses towards urban needs. Another problem was the salary gap between rural and urban schools. The two circumstances sent the most competent teachers heading for the city at the earliest opportunity. Males who taught country schools used the experience to prepare for a more lucrative career. Young women often either married within a few years and stopped teaching, or else moved and pursued their vocations in the city. Reformers therefore pressed for counties to start their own normal schools. The first two opened in Marathon and Dunn counties in September, 1899; by 1913 there were thirty-three. Reformers pressed for state aid to high schools that gave courses in rural teaching; that program made only minimal progress. They also urged greater supervision of country teachers and county-level testing of pupils who completed eighth grade. There were also efforts to establish a statewide minimum wage and pension system for teachers, and to recruit more male teachers.[10]

---

[9] Department of Public Instruction, *Biennial Report*, 1898–1900, pp. 26–32 (quotes), 70–73; *ibid.*, 1894–1896, p. 14; Everett L. Walters, "Teacher Qualification and Certification," in Clay J. Daggett, ed., *Education in Wisconsin* (Whitewater, 1936), 240; Henry Colin Campbell, *Wisconsin in Three Centuries, 1634–1905* (4 vols., New York, 1906), 165–166; Lafayette County, *Annual Report, School Directory, and County Board Proceedings*, 1913–1914, p. 4; Janet R. Rankin, "School Service in Wisconsin," *Educational Review*, 52 (September, 1916), 114; Arthur A. Shillander, "A Study of the Rural School Situation in Wisconsin with Reference to a Minimum Salary Law" (bachelor's thesis, University of Wisconsin, 1910), 13–40; George A. Glyer, "A Report of the Condition of the Rural Schools of Douglas County, Wisconsin" (master's thesis, University of Wisconsin, 1915), 31–36; Fitzpatrick, "The Educational System," in Quaife, ed., *Wisconsin*, 2: 252; Wayne E. Fuller, *The Old Country School: The Story of Rural Education in the Middle West* (Chicago, 1982), 214–215.

[10] Fitzpatrick, "The Educational System," in Quaife, ed., *Wisconsin*, 2: 274–278; Fuller, *The Old Country School*, 214–215; Beltman, "Rural Renaissance," 125–131; Kenneth C. Acrea, Jr., "Wisconsin Progressivism: Legislative Response to Social

Putting agricultural courses into rural schools was another priority. As a speaker at the 1901 Wisconsin Farmers' Institute put it: "Rotation of crops is as inspiring as the position of the preposition; the fertilization of apples and corn as interesting as the location of cities . . . ; the economy of the horse and cow and sheep come as close to life as the duties of the President and the causes of the Revolutionary War." Speaking to the WTA in 1909, La Crosse Normal School president Fassett A. Cotton urged teachers to instruct "country reading, country arithmetic and country geography," and to infuse their curriculum with seed selection, soil testing, orchard and livestock management, cooking, sewing, and gardening. Rural schools taught "the farm boy or girl nothing that will help him or her to comprehend farm problems in after life," wrote William D. Hoard in 1909, maintaining a complaint he had iterated as early as 1901, when he said "Much of the trash that is taught in our schools could be thrown out. . . ." In 1904, State Superintendent of Public Education Charles P. Cary agreed that the time was "ripe now for making the elements of agriculture a required study in the country schools." He added, "Nothing will tend more to prevent the ill-advised rush of country boys to the city than to convince them that farming may be made scientific, and that in no occupation does the application of brains pay a better or surer dividend."[11]

These concerns solidified into two concrete proposals. The first, in 1901, called for giving counties the authority to operate schools of agriculture and domestic economy (Dunn County opened the first in the state and nation in 1902); the second, in 1905, sought to require agriculture as a class in rural district schools. Related proposals

---

Change, 1891 to 1909" (doctoral dissertation, University of Wisconsin, 1968), 299–300, 395–397; Patzer, *Public Education in Wisconsin*, 131–189; Patzer, "The Country School System," in McKenny, ed., *Educational History*, 62–65; A. A. Thompson, "County Training Schools for Teachers," in McKenny, ed., *Educational History*, 232–239; "General Educational Notes," *Wisconsin Journal of Education*, 35 (June, 1903), 110.

[11] Charles McCarthy, "To Improve Rural Education and to Aid in Rural Development," *Wisconsin Equity News* (Madison), February 10, 1913; Beltman, "Rural Renaissance," 115–122, quoting the 1901 Farmers' Institute bulletin; Fassett A. Cotton, "Country Life and Country Schools," in Wisconsin Teachers' Association, *Proceedings*, 1909, pp. 172–182; "Agricultural Teaching in the Common Schools," *Hoard's Dairyman*, February 1, 1901, p. 1016; "Teaching Agriculture," *ibid.*, August 2, 1907, p. 685; "Education in Rural Schools," *ibid.*, October 1, 1909, p. 1012; Anna M. Keppel, "Country Schools for Country Children: Backgrounds of the Reform Movement in Rural Elementary Education, 1890–1914" (doctoral dissertation, University of Wisconsin, 1960), 97; Lorenzo D. Harvey, "Some Lines of Work in the Organization and Development of our School System," 1899, typescript in the Lorenzo D. Harvey Papers; Department of Public Instruction, *Biennial Report*, 1902–1904, pp. 65–67 (quote).

sought to restore rural schools' function as neighborhood social centers as in the settlement era, which many still did in any case. These developments encouraged educational reformers such as Herbert Quick, who told a 1911 conference on social centers that "the country school of the future" would correlate teachers, textbooks and curriculum to country living to the point where "tests of soil will be made in the school laboratory." Two years later, the president of the Milwaukee school directors urged the establishment of an agricultural course and school in the city in addition to the county's agricultural school, and, in 1915, a distinguished educator, Edward A. Fitzpatrick, hailed Oconto County for developing a course of study of an "intensely practical bent" with a vision of "better schools, better farms, better homes."[12]

Between 1909 and 1915 the campaign to reform Wisconsin's rural schools culminated in struggles over reorganizing country schools and teacher certification. Country and city superintendents, principals of schools that trained rural teachers, presidents of the state normal schools, and Charles McCarthy and progressive politicians lobbied for change. They asked for county boards of education which would have the power to consolidate individual rural districts, fix supervisors' salaries, and appoint assistant supervisors and diploma examiners. Opponents branded the measure undemocratic; it received only half-hearted support from the state department of public instruction, and accordingly it failed. The legislature then appointed a special committee, headed by Senator James H. Stout of Menomonie, the person most responsible for the Stout Training School and other educational reforms in Dunn County and across the state. The committee held hearings in several locations and reported overwhelming support for county boards of education. Governor Francis E. McGovern (1911–1915), a former rural teacher, principal, and school superintendent, threw his support behind it, arguing that county-wide boards would "remedy the weaknesses and evils of the country school system." In 1913, the measure was endorsed widely by groups like the Stout committee, the Committee of Fifteen appointed by Cary, the presidents and regents of the state normal schools, and the Wisconsin Teachers' Association. It passed after four

---

[12] Patzer, *Public Education in Wisconsin*, 71; Clark, "The Wisconsin State Department of Public Instruction," 26–31; Acrea, "Wisconsin Progressivism," 394–395; Carl Quickert, ed., *Washington County, Wisconsin: Past and Present* (2 vols., Chicago, 1912), 1: 155–156; Samuel A. Connell, "President's Annual Address," in Milwaukee Board of School Directors, *Reports*, 1913, pp. 7–18; Edward A. Fitzpatrick, "The Second Balcony of Education," *Educational Review*, 48 (June, 1914), 50–60; John M. Ware, ed., *A Standard History of Waupaca County, Wisconsin* (2 vols., Chicago, 1917), 174–175.

months of debate and negotiation, but was repealed only two years later on the recommendation of Governor Emanuel L. Philipp (1915–1921), who was influenced by county boards. Town boards resumed control of rural schools, and a newly created state department of education focused on urban schools.

Efforts to standardize the certification of state teachers were somewhat more successful, but still they accomplished less than reformers desired. The state normal schools and other activists worked to define a course of study for certification, and to require certification examinations. Laws adopted in 1901 and 1909 were strengthened in 1913 by requiring teachers to complete a standard common school course and two years of instruction and training, including one year of professional-level education courses.[13]

[2]

Rural education aroused more controversy during the Progressive Era than urban, but in the long run the debate over urban schools was more significant. Most of the educational reformers' ideas about schooling for life, work, and citizenship were framed within urban, industrial, multi-ethnic contexts. They hoped such schooling would meet the needs of both the individual and the community. Society, as it grew more complex and more wedded to technology, demanded more formal education of citizens; and the nation's commitment to equal opportunity required expansion and diffusion of educational opportunity. Both considerations demanded longer school years, raising the age requirement for compulsory attendance, centralizing, standardizing, and professionalizing instruction and administration, and improving access to schooling at all levels. In short they meant making the curriculum more practical and useful.[14]

Wisconsin responded in part by moving to establish "continuation" or vocational schools—an effort which can be seen as a micro-

---

[13] Patzer, *Public Education in Wisconsin*, 123–130, 193–197 (quote); Charles McCarthy to George A. Bossford, March 7, 1913, to R. Fulton Cutting, April 24, 1914, and to A. C. Monohan, October 12, 1915, all in the McCarthy Papers; Clifford S. Liddle, "The Development of the Common School District in the Towns of La Grange, Linn, and Sugar Creek, Walworth County, Wisconsin" (doctoral dissertation, University of Wisconsin, 1942), 40–41.

[14] Cremin, *The Transformation of the School*, 23–57; Marvin Lazerson, *Origins of the Urban School: Public Education in Massachusetts, 1870–1915* (Cambridge, 1971), pp. xi–xviii, 241–257; David Nasaw, *Schooled to Order: A Social History of Public Schooling in the United States* (New York, 1979), 87–157; Paul C. Violas, *The Training of the Urban Working Class: A History of Twentieth Century American Education* (Chicago, 1978), 229–236.

cosm of the conflict in the state's cities over the New Education. Working-class children, whose ranks were being swelled by urbanization and immigration, served as a focus of conflict. The compulsory education laws of 1891 and 1901 mandated eight months' schooling each year for children through age fourteen. After that, most city children faced a lifetime of unskilled factory labor, with little or no chance for occupational advancement or cultural enrichment. The obvious solution was further education. But many families needed their children's income; high schools were few in number, and they geared curricula to preparing students for college. This meant adding vocational education to existing high school curricula, or else providing instruction in academic subjects in the factory, either during or after the work day.[15]

Two assumptions—later muddled as events unfolded—were paramount. First, vocational education was to provide an alternative to normative education as a way of achieving a fulfilling, responsible, and prosperous life. Second, it was not to be narrowly technical, but rather was to develop the whole person. Students should learn not simply how to perform tasks, but also why the tasks were done in certain ways and where they fit into the larger scheme. It was felt as well that vocational education should equip students either to negotiate for better conditions within their occupational and class orbit, or else to pursue social mobility. The model urged by the industrial and agricultural training commission in 1911 was a modified version of the German "continuation school," which was much admired by Wisconsin's educational reformers.[16]

Many of those directly affected by the continuation school proposal viewed it differently. Some working-class parents opposed any further education that was not job-related; others viewed vocational schooling as a thinly disguised two-track system, designed to relegate their children to a lifetime of poorly paid, dead-end labor. Some professional educators regarded all vocational education as a dilution of the school's primary intellectual function; others objected to public

---

[15] Commission upon the Plans for the Extension of Industrial and Agricultural Training, *Report*, 1911, pp. 14–71; Charles McCarthy to Herbert A. Miles, April 2, 1913, to Secretary, National Child Labor Committee, April 7, 1913, to Senator Charles S. Page, June 12, 1913, to E. F. Du Brul, December 16, 1913, to Mrs. S. Quackenbush, October 6, 1915, all in the McCarthy Papers; Cremin, *The Transformation of the School*, 20–34.

[16] Patzer, *Public Education in Wisconsin*, 65–68; Herbert E. Miles, *Wisconsin Legislation Governing Industrial and Continuation Education*, Wisconsin State Board of Industrial Education, *Bulletin*, no. 2 (1912), 5–6; Derek S. Linton, "American Responses to German Continuation Schools During the Progressive Era," unpublished conference paper, 1990, in the author's files.

educational enterprises not under their direct supervision. Industrialists tended to favor simple trade schools which taught only specific job skills and "desirable" work habits.[17]

Prior to 1910, trade unionists were ambivalent at best about vocational education. Some saw it as a good apprenticeship system; others, as a way to train future strikebreakers. By 1908, however, the state convention of the American Federation of Labor adopted a resolution endorsing industrial education as the right of all children under public auspices. In 1909, using the newly formed Milwaukee School of Trades (part of the public schools) as one of its models, a special AFL committee endorsed three kinds of trade schools: public continuation schools for those already employed, union-sponsored supplemental trade schools, and public trade schools which would balance general education and shop instruction.[18]

The result was a 1911 law that was essentially a compromise among management, labor, the "new educators," and the state's department of public instruction. The new continuation school measure also received support from the state's leading farm organizations, because of its provisions for agricultural education, as well as from the Wisconsin Teachers' Association and the Madison-based American Association for Labor Legislation. The law reflected these points of view in its management structure. It required every city of over 5,000 persons (cities and villages with smaller populations were authorized to follow suit if they wished) to establish schools that would instruct students in trades, industry, commerce, and the household arts, as well as in English, citizenship, physical education, sanitation, hygiene, safety, and whatever other subjects each local board of industrial education might deem appropriate. Each board had to consist of two employers, two employees, and either the city superintendent or a local high school principal; curricula had to be approved by the superintendent of public instruction. The superintendent also was authorized to appoint a supervisor of industrial education, subject to approval by the State Board of Industrial Education. It, too, was broadly based, consisting of three employers, three employees, the state superintendent, and the deans of the University of Wisconsin's College of Engineering and Extension Division. Every child fourteen and over was required to attend a continuation school, unless en-

---

[17] Cremin, *The Transformation of the School*, 34–41; Charles McCarthy, *The Wisconsin Idea* (New York, 1912), 141–151; Patzer, *Public Education in Wisconsin*, 207–208; Clark, "The Wisconsin Department of Public Instruction," 255–292; Edward A. Fitzpatrick, *McCarthy of Wisconsin* (New York, 1944), 260–276.

[18] Arthur M. Evans, *Vocational Education in Wisconsin* (Chicago, 1913), 2–29; Frank Joseph Woerdehoff, "Dr. Charles McCarthy: His Educational Views and Influence upon Adult Education in Wisconsin" (doctoral dissertation, University of Wisconsin, 1954), 104–132.

rolled in another school. State aid and city property taxes supported the system.[19]

[3]

Less publicized, but of equal importance to advocates of the New Education, was the expansion of secondary education. Between 1890 and 1906, the number of high schools in Wisconsin increased from 169 to 288; the enrollment, from 11,449 to 27,768; and the number of teachers, from 376 to 1,334. Between 1895 and 1910, the number of schools offering a three-year diploma jumped from 128 to 286, the pupil-teacher ratio declined by one-third, and the number of subjects a teacher was required to teach was reduced. The state had only 939 high school graduates in 1890; in 1910 there were 4,154. The state superintendent estimated in 1908 that more than half the 271 high schools had either been built or wholly rebuilt since 1900.[20]

The dropout rate was more than 65 per cent at the beginning of the century. To curb it, officials added courses in agriculture, manual training, and domestic science, and they redesigned other courses to meet pupils' needs, making high school more meaningful and useful. This plan worked. Ten years later, the dropout rate had been reduced to 57 per cent, and most dropouts occurred during the first two years. School officials attributed the change to manual training, domestic science, agriculture, and commercial courses in which half the state's eligible students enrolled. Another tactic in some high schools awarded academic credit for work done outside the classroom, emulating the university's "extension" concept. High school was indeed becoming the "people's college," where social classes mingled and learned democracy firsthand.[21]

The expansion of kindergartens also reflected the advance of the New Education. Nearly a hundred cities added kindergartens to their schools between 1890 and 1912. Under Wisconsin law, free public

---

[19] Cremin, *The Transformation of the School*, 41–51; Patzer, *Public Education in Wisconsin*, 208–210; Commission upon the Plans for the Extension of Industrial and Agricultural Training, *Report*, 1911, pp. 26–28.

[20] Cremin, *The Transformation of the School*, 140; Patzer, *Public Education in Wisconsin*, 79–100; Charles McKenny, "The Elementary School of City Systems," in McKenny, ed., *Educational History*, 69–70; Yonker, "Secondary Education," in McKenny, ed., *Educational History*, 84–117.

[21] Lazerson, *Origins of the Urban School*, 241–257; Nasaw, *Schooled to Order*, 87–157; Greer, *The Great School Legend*; and Violas, *Training of Urban Working Class*, all stress the contrary view that vocational education was planned to relegate working-class children to a life of drudgery and poverty. For a partial corrective, see Diane Ravitch, *The Revisionists Revised: A Critique of the Radical Attack on the Schools* (New York, 1977), 116–174.

education theoretically was available to everyone between the ages of four and twenty. But the state's first tax-supported kindergarten did not open until 1873 in Manitowoc, and it was 1887 before the legislature empowered local school districts to establish kindergartens. Progressive to the core, kindergarten substituted "happy activity" for rote learning and the three R's. In 1907 and in 1909, kindergarten supporters beat back legislative proposals that would have prohibited spending public money on educating children under six.[22]

Of all the educational innovations of the period, none was more quintessentially "progressive" than the use of public school buildings as community social centers. The social center movement was pioneered by Edward J. Ward, a Social Gospel minister and college professor who established a social center network in Rochester, New York, in 1907. Ward's notion was to bypass the existing political structure by using public school buildings, after hours, as a home for a civic movement based on the example of the direct democracy of the New England town meeting. He envisioned citizens assembling in public buildings to discuss, debate, and educate themselves on a broad range of topics affecting public policy. In 1910, the university's Extension Division hired Ward as an advisor on social and civic center development. The following year, the legislature authorized school boards to establish, at public expense, "evening schools, vacation schools, reading rooms, library stations, debating clubs, gymnasiums, public playgrounds, public baths and similar activities," while allowing the free use of school buildings to "citizens organized into a nonpartisan, nonsectarian, nonexclusive association" for discussing public issues. In the state, about 300 districts had begun the program by 1914, and Ward gained national recognition through his 1913 book *The Social Center*. Seventy-one cities in twenty-one states eventually emulated Wisconsin's laws.[23]

Where they were successful, the social centers stimulated grassroots discussion of public issues and concrete proposals for remedies. In Fond du Lac, the Lincoln social center, which met at a local factory, exemplified the "good live organizations or clubs of working men" that Ward advocated. But, by 1914, even Ward admitted that many of the three hundred districts began to "languish after a time, and in many cases, ... the community civic assembling has been abandoned." He argued the need for a salaried professional to support

---

[22] Nina C. Vandewalker, "The Kindergarten in Wisconsin," in McKenney, ed., *Educational History*, 211–217; Patzer, *Public Education in Wisconsin*, 72, 377.

[23] Edward J. Ward, ed., *The Social Center* (New York, 1913), 1–174, 324–339; Edward W. Stevens, Jr., "Social Centers, Politics and Social Efficiency in the Progressive Era," *History of Education Quarterly* (Spring, 1972), 16–33; *Laws of Wisconsin*, 1911, pp. 619–621, 627–629 (Chapters 509 and 514).

the work in each school district. However, some Extension Division district representatives disliked Ward and criticized him for his arrogant manner, authoritarian philosophy, and inefficient administration. A different director might have made a difference for Wisconsin social centers, but despite their shortcomings they did represent a sincere effort to institutionalize life-long, participatory education.[24]

Educational reform took hold in most of Wisconsin's major cities. Milwaukee steadily increased services and courses for students who were destined for the industrial workplace rather than higher education. School expenditures grew twice as fast as the city's population between 1870 and 1910; it provided free textbooks after 1897 and school lunches after 1904; and its School of Trades taught mechanical drawing, machine design, plumbing, and industrial pattern making. As early as 1895, the president of the Milwaukee school board argued for a curriculum that would blend vocational and standard education. A decade later, the city superintendent of schools, Carroll G. Pearse, said he believed, "The course of study in the high schools of any city ought to be shaped to meet the needs of that particular community." Milwaukee school officials pressed for vacation schools for poorer children and acquiesced in immigrant parents' demands for teaching German, Polish, and Italian languages in the schools.

School officials throughout the state sang the virtues of "practical" education, and some ventured beyond mere curricular reform. Many schools began to require vaccination, introduced health and hygiene into the curriculum, and waged campaigns against alcohol and tobacco. Three years later Pearse added that, although he agreed with the prevailing view that "the high school is the poor man's college," he also believed that schools should not deprive working-class children of the opportunity to enjoy knowledge for its own sake. They were places "where the sons and daughters of rich and poor must meet upon a common footing, enjoy common privileges and learn to know and respect each other for what they are and for what they can do."[25]

---

[24] Edward J. Ward, "Definite Remuneration of District Secretarial Service Necessary for Systematic and Continuous Social Center Development," June 1, 1914; Mr. Neville, "The Bureau of Civic and Social Center Development, and How It Has Functioned in the Life of the People of the Oshkosh District," p. 3, n.d.; "Report of Mr. O'Connor, District Representative, Fourth District," n.d., 7–8; "Report from the Secretary of the Lecture Department upon Mr. Ward's Work," June 4, 1914, all in box 39, folder 616, Charles R. Van Hise Papers, University of Wisconsin Archives.

[25] For evidence of widespread educational reform in cities, see Madison Public Schools, *Annual Reports*, 1896–1897, pp. 33–35, 1904–1905, pp. 30 and 61, and 1910–1911, p. 62; La Crosse Public Schools, *Reports*, 1912–1913 and 1913–1914, pp. 41–50; W. H. Schulz, "Public Schools of Eau Claire," in William F. Bailey, ed., *History of Eau Claire, Wisconsin* (Chicago, 1914), 415–509; Beloit *Daily News*, *The Book of Beloit* (Beloit, 1936), 5; Ashland Board of Education, *Rules and Regulations, Course of Study*,

[4]

As formal schooling became more respected and widespread, the demand for trained teachers grew, too. The University of Wisconsin had operated a teacher training department at various times during the nineteenth century, but the burden fell primarily on the state normal schools, which emphasized teacher education. The first opened in Platteville in 1866, and by 1891 there were four more: in Whitewater, Oshkosh, River Falls, and Milwaukee. All offered both two-year and four-year courses. Two-year courses prepared elementary school teachers; the four-year course also groomed students for specialized institutions of higher learning. In the 1890's, normal schools were established in Stevens Point, Superior, and La Crosse, and new courses of study were adopted. In addition, the university reopened its teacher training department, county normal schools were established, high schools were authorized to prepare teachers, and in 1911 the Stout Institute at Menomonie became a state-operated training school for instructors in manual training and domestic science. By 1897, Wisconsin's normal schools had one student for every 690 people, and had a national reputation for teacher training.[26]

Several of these schools were anxious to become fully accredited four-year schools which could train high school teachers. The university, however, felt that they should offer only the first two years of training, preparing students for matriculation at Madison. Normal school regent Theodore Kronshage defended his school's position on the grounds that an upper-division university course "comparing Aristotle's educational theories with those of Plato . . . gives about as much potential force to a course designed to train teachers for our secondary schools as the perfume of a hot house violet gives to the constellations." An alliance between the university and the state's private colleges also hampered the normal schools' four-year hopes. Normal schools were criticized for their reluctance to train teachers

---

and *Report of the Public Schools*, 1898, p. 5; Superior Board of Education, *Reports*, 1902–1903 and 1903–1904, p. 33; Racine Board of Education, *Annual Report*, 1913, pp. 19–20; Baraboo Board of Education, *Annual Report*, 1897, pp. 25–28; John P. Mann, " 'Readin', 'Ritin', and 'Rithmetic," in Gordon A. Bubolz et al., eds., *Land of the Fox: Saga of Outagamie County* (Appleton, 1949), 191; Jennie L. Webster, comp., *Eau Claire County History* (n.p., 1949), 3. On Milwaukee, see Bayrd Still, *Milwaukee: The History of a City* (Madison, 1948), 272, 360, 415–418; Milwaukee Board of School Directors, *Annual Report*, 1895, pp. 31–37, 1909, pp. 26–41 and 104–105, and 1913, pp. 82, 101.

[26] Patzer, *Public Education in Wisconsin*, 131–177; Albert Salisbury, "The State Normal Schools," in John William Stearns, ed., *The Columbian History of Education in Wisconsin* (Milwaukee, 1893), 281–282; Albert Salisbury, *The Normal Schools of Wisconsin* (Milwaukee, 1897), 3; Charles McCarthy to Theodore Kronshage, Jr., December 9, 1913, in the McCarthy Papers.

in agriculture, the manual arts, and domestic science, as well as for their failure to attract male students. Kronshage pronounced the latter goal as "the greatest present need of our school system." As for women teachers in the normal schools, he denounced a movement to give them equal pay as "absolutely fundamentally wrong, sociologically wrong and economically wrong."[27]

In 1914 the normal schools' campaign for collegiate status suffered a blow from a survey authorized by the State Board of Public Affairs. The report contended, "While a great deal of the teaching in the normal schools is of the highest order, much is at best mediocre, and at least half is inexcusably poor." Moreover, "The presence of the college course tends strongly to create an aristocracy both among members of the faculty teaching in these courses and among the students taking them," leading to the widespread assumption that "the teacher training courses, the real work of the normal school, are of lesser dignity and minor importance."[28]

[5]

Nowhere in Wisconsin did the New Education generate more controversy than within the university. The Madison campus experienced enormous growth, emerging as perhaps the foremost public university in the nation by 1914. During the quarter-century following the resignation of President John Bascom in 1887, the university evolved from a tight-knit, homogenous community of just over 500 students, nearly 70 per cent of whom were in the College of Letters and Science, to a complex amalgam of nearly 5,000 students, 43 per cent of whom were enrolled in the more "practical" schools—agriculture, engineering, law, and medicine. During the same span, the faculty grew from thirty-five full-time members to nearly 700, many of whom had national reputations. The university's budget swelled from $218,867 during the 1887–1888 academic year to just over $3 million

---

[27] Theodore Kronshage, Jr., "The Service Rendered by the Normal Schools of Wisconsin," *Normal School Bulletin*, 1 (December, 1914), 74 (quote); Kronshage to A. N. Farmer, December 7, 1914 (quote); Kronshage to John A. H. Keith, December 2, 1915, in the Kronshage Papers; Richard P. Bailey, "The Wisconsin State Colleges, 1875–1955, with Respect to the Function of Preparing Secondary School Teachers" (doctoral dissertation, University of Wisconsin, 1959), 101–102, 132; Walker D. Wyman, " 'Breathtaking Development'—1866–1968," in Walker D. Wyman, ed., *History of the Wisconsin State Universities* (River Falls, 1968), 1–16; Richard D. Gamble, *From Academy to University 1866–1966: A History of Wisconsin State University-Platteville, Wisconsin* (Platteville, 1966), 154–156.

[28] State Board of Public Affairs, A. N. Farmer, comp., *Conditions and Needs of Wisconsin's Normal Schools: Report of Cooperative Survey*, 1914, pp. 26–27 (quotes), 101, 320 (quote).

during 1913–1914. Under presidents Thomas C. Chamberlin (1887–1892) and Charles Kendall Adams (1892–1902), buildings were erected for the law and engineering schools, the College of Agriculture, physical education and military training, the university library, and the state historical society. During the tenure of president Charles R. Van Hise (1903–1918), the university lands were doubled in acreage and about $3 million worth of new buildings were constructed. The departmental structure and curriculum of the university were restructured and revised on several occasions, mainly to reflect newly professionalized disciplines such as pharmacy, education, commerce, political economy, public administration, home economics, journalism, and librarianship.[29]

Emphasis on professionalization, specialization, research, and public service was mirrored in the expansion of the College of Agriculture, Extension Division work, establishment of a Graduate School and summer session, and the role played by some faculty members in state government. Many faculty members, among them Richard T. Ely, Frederick Jackson Turner, John R. Commons, Edward A. Ross, and Van Hise himself, achieved national reputations, and many of their colleagues enjoyed localized academic celebrity. In the process of taking to heart the needs and outlook of the state and its people, the university came to buttress many persons—"the progressives," broadly defined—who sought political and societal reforms. The University of Wisconsin thus became a force for change.[30]

New Education advocates were prominent and vocal at the university. The most outspoken champion, Charles McCarthy, regularly flayed academe for its elitism and impracticality, while demanding education that was democratic, practical, and imbued with a social agenda. "Show me the president or the faculty capable of keeping up with the spirit of the times," he complained in 1915, "unless urged and whipped on by outside impulses." In *The Wisconsin Idea*, he rejoiced that the university was known "not only for its philosophy of service to the state . . . but for the practical courses which deal with every factor in the life of the state." He singled out the College of Agriculture and the Extension Division for proving that the university "should be an institution for all the people within the state and not merely for the few who could send their sons and daughters to Madison." Similarly, Richard T. Ely said that his School of Economics, Political Science and History, founded in 1892, "aims to train for intelligent citizenship, and aspires to do a work for civic life which may be compared to that of West Point for military life." His distin-

---

[29] Merle Curti and Vernon Carstensen, *The University of Wisconsin: A History, 1848–1925* (2 vols., Madison, 1949), 1: 501–579, 608–659, 711–739.
[30] *Ibid.*, 2: 3–43.

guished colleague Frederick Jackson Turner observed that "the steady pressure of democracy upon its universities to adapt them to the requirements of all the people" was healthy and praiseworthy, for it meant "the breaking down of the traditional required curriculum; the union of vocational and college work in the same institution; the development of agricultural and engineering colleges and business courses; the training of lawyers, administrators, public men, and journalists. . . ." William H. Lighty, director of the Extension Division, argued that "modern society has been rapidly growing more democratic and with this movement has sprung forth . . . an effort to make our educational agencies conform more nearly to the needs of life." These views were echoed by many lesser-known advocates of change within the university community, expressing satisfaction that the university was taking its resources into every corner of the state.[31]

But the most influential voices on the New Education and the university were those of its presidents, and they were not of one mind. In the 1887–1888 university catalog, Thomas Chrowder Chamberlin included among the university's primary objectives the provision of "trustworthy technical training in the leading professions," and contributing "directly to the higher education of the people." Chamberlin encouraged faculty research and graduate studies, hired established scholars, championed the undergraduate seminar, and fostered development of the colleges of agriculture and engineering. As he said in 1900: "Scholarship for the sake of the scholar simply is refined selfishness. Scholarship for the sake of the state and the people is refined patriotism." He established the summer session in 1887 and the Extension Division in 1891 in order to widen the university's impact on the state. In the words of a later historian, Chamberlin's administration "marked the crossing from a college to a university."[32]

So oriented was the campus towards outreach and practical education by 1893 that John Johnston, a regent from Milwaukee, said at the inauguration of Chamberlin's successor, "there is not a county in Wisconsin which is not richer because of the university." In response, incoming president Charles Kendall Adams, a historian, expressed his conviction that the university was the "creation and the possession of the people." He endorsed the new School of Economics, Political Science and History, and pledged to expand the Exten-

---

[31] McCarthy to Michael Cleary, May 3, 1915, in the McCarthy Papers (quote); McCarthy, *Wisconsin Idea*, 124–41, 184–193; Richard T. Ely, "The School of Economics, Political Science and History," in Reuben Gold Thwaites, ed., *The University of Wisconsin: Its History and its Alumni with Historical and Descriptive Sketches of Madison* (Madison, 1899), 222; William H. Lighty, "Carrying the University to the Work and the Worker," typescript, in box 99, Lighty Papers.

[32] Curti and Carstensen, *University of Wisconsin*, 1: 542, 560.

sion Division, because "There are thousands, yea, tens of thousands, who desire to avail themselves of such instruction, but cannot leave their homes to go to the university."

These endorsements aside, Adams highly qualified his commitment to Chamberlin's blueprint for growth. As Chamberlin's successor, he persuaded the legislature to appropriate money for research, expanded the publication of research bulletins, and sympathized with the faculty's academic aspirations. But Adams also believed that the university's primary obligation was to teach undergraduates, and, despite his rhetorical support of extension, he let it slide nearly to extinction. Adams was a devotee of the Gospel of Wealth, and he encouraged matriculation by children of affluent parents, to the point where the Board of Visitors was requested to investigate whether he propagated "aristocratic tendencies." (He was cleared.) He established a school of commerce, and though he failed to revive classical studies, he did succeed in founding the School of Music. Adams was immensely popular with students, faculty, regents, and legislators, and his popularity translated into generous appropriations for the university.[33]

Adams resigned for reasons of health in 1900, and Edward A. Birge, dean of Letters and Science, served nearly three years as acting president. Birge, a zoologist, was too conscious of his interim status to mount assaults on the New Education, but he made no secret of his opposition to many of its tenets. He preached that the "school system is not merely a means of affording a 'practical education', but it is also an expression of that intellectual life which was once peculiar to universities and seemed limited to them." He contended that universities existed "rather to advance knowledge than to diminish ignorance," and argued that they also should furnish "a broad and well marked way into the intellectual life as well as ways out into affairs."[34]

Thus somewhat stalled during the Adams and Birge administrations, the New Education found its most powerful champion in Charles R. Van Hise (1903–1918). He was the first University of Wisconsin alumnus to become its president, and the first person to receive a doctorate from the university. He was a nationally recognized geologist who believed in research, applied science, university outreach, and public service, and, importantly, he was a classmate and friend of Governor Robert M. La Follette. John Bascom, Frederick Jackson Turner, and La Follette had all mentored Van Hise, who was

---

[33] *Ibid.*, 561–579 (quotes); Charles Forster Smith, *Charles Kendall Adams: A Life-Sketch* (Madison, 1924), 47, 118.

[34] Edward A. Birge, "The University in Retrospect," typescript of 1915 University of Wisconsin baccalaureate address, in box 17, Birge Papers.

a utilitarian by upbringing and professional training. He possessed a keen sense of social justice, of the economic basis of politics, and of the potential for using politics as an instrument of social change.[35]

In his inaugural address in 1903, Van Hise left little doubt about his commitment to the course laid out by Chamberlin, even where that meant resuscitating initiatives that had foundered under Adams and Birge. Like many in his day, he used the relationship between the German university and the state as a model. He said that "if the University of Wisconsin is to do for the state what it has a right to expect, it must develop, expand, strengthen creative work at whatever cost." He defined service to the state along two major lines: by having faculty members share their expert knowledge with government agencies of all kinds, and by reinvigorating and expanding the Extension Division. As he said in 1905, "I shall never be content until the beneficent influence of the University reaches every family in the state."[36]

After ten years as president, Van Hise evaluated progress towards that ideal in an address to a visiting delegation from the Philadelphia City Club. He took as his text Lord Bryce's dictum that "a university should reflect the spirit of the times, without yielding to it." Van Hise assured the visitors that the university did indeed reflect the spirit of the times. It did so by recognizing that "science and applied science should be taught in the university alongside the traditional subjects and with equal privileges," that engineering, domestic science, agriculture, and commerce were just as surely "learned professions" as were law, medicine and the ministry. The university also recognized that people "must continue their education throughout life," and, through the Extension Division and other departments, it willingly undertook "any line of educational work for which it is the best fitted instrument, without regard to the preconceived notions of anybody, anywhere, concerning the scope of the university." Its aim was to enable every qualified boy and girl in Wisconsin "to obtain an education broad and complete, fitted to the demands of the present time. . . ."[37]

---

[35] Charles R. Van Hise, "Inaugural Address," in University of Wisconsin, *The Jubilee of the University of Wisconsin* (Madison, 1905), 123–128. See also Charles R. Van Hise, *The Conservation of Natural Resources in the United States* (New York, 1910), and *Concentration and Control: A Solution of the Trust Problem in the United States* (New York, 1912).

[36] Curti and Carstensen, *University of Wisconsin*, 2: 87–90. Van Hise, like many of his colleagues, used the relationship between the German university and the state as a model.

[37] *Ibid.*, 2: 295–301; Charles R. Van Hise, "An Address to the Philadelphia City Club's Expedition, at the Golf Club, Madison, May 23, 1913," reprinted, *ibid.*, 2: 611–624 (quotes on pp. 615–617, 619, and 621); Maurice M. Vance, *Charles Richard Van Hise: Scientist Progressive* (Madison, 1960).

The University of Wisconsin, Van Hise said, had committed itself to providing both people and ideas to the state's "government by experts." He denied that the university was "in politics," as many critics charged. "If, however," he continued boldly, "it is meant that the University is attempting to lead in the advancement of the people; if it is meant that problems which relate to water powers, to forests, to marketing, to the public utilities, to labor, are legitimate fields of university inquiry and teaching, then the university is in politics, and will remain there so long as it is a virile institution worthy of the support of the people of this state." In this address, delivered at the floodtide of progressive reform in state and nation, Van Hise inextricably linked the New Education with the Wisconsin Idea.

Besides supporting applied knowledge, graduate and professional education, and extension, Van Hise saw liberal arts and undergraduate education as central to education. In his view, conflict need not occur among teaching, research, and service interests, nor between pure and applied research; all were facets of the scholarly profession and of a vibrant university. Distinguished scholars should teach introductory courses so that undergraduates would benefit; specialized researchers would in turn be required to confront universals and generalities. The best way to produce such a faculty, Van Hise believed, was "for each member of the staff to resolve that he will become a recognized scholar in his field and begin at once some productive work."[38]

Van Hise's desire to effect broad-gauged education for all students was expressed in a practical way in a 1903 curriculum revision. It sought to provide students with freedom of choice while avoiding overspecialization and fragmentation. Except for pharmacy, music, and education, students in Letters and Science were required to take English and two foreign languages, and to choose two fields from among science, mathematics, and history during their freshman and sophomore years. Juniors and seniors were to concentrate on their major subjects; about one-half their total credits were required and one-half elective. Those with technical or professional goals took one-sixth of their courses in other colleges. The upshot of the new curriculum was that the humanities expanded, emphasizing modern languages, journalism, philosophy, and psychology; the English department became more specialized and "scientific"; and the social science faculty, already distinguished in history and economics, worked to strengthen sociology and political science, both of which straddled the supposed line between pure and applied study.[39]

---

[38] Curti and Carstensen, *University of Wisconsin*, 2: 295–301; Van Hise, "Inaugural Address," in *Jubilee*, 106–107, 123.

[39] Curti and Carstensen, *University of Wisconsin*, 2: 315–344.

The mathematics and physics departments similarly achieved national eminence by marrying pure and applied science, and the departments worked closely with the College of Engineering and the Geological Survey. Chemistry, pharmacy, astronomy, and geology all flourished. The music, library, and teacher training programs began later, but were firmly established by 1914. Consistent with the greater emphasis on faculty research, the hodgepodge of departmental graduate programs evolved by 1905 into the graduate school, with 148 students. That year, the university awarded ten doctorates and thirty-four master's degrees; by 1910, eighteen and 110, respectively. Most graduate degrees were earned by students in traditional liberal arts subjects; fewer, but an ever-growing number, were earned in agriculture, engineering, and the professional fields of medicine and law.[40]

Led by several prominent social scientists on its faculty, the university was emerging in the late nineteenth and early twentieth centuries as one of the leading seats of "progressive" thought. Van Hise's books on conservation and business trusts, like Charles McCarthy's *Wisconsin Idea*, became vital texts for reformers throughout the country. Richard T. Ely was celebrated as a founder of both the New Economics and the American Economic Association, even before he came to Wisconsin in 1892. Ely blended Christian socialism and the social sciences, thereby reorienting the study of political economy. He inspired two generations of scholars and activists, even after he himself turned towards conservativism.[41]

Ely's erstwhile pupil, John R. Commons, eventually surpassed his mentor as an opponent of laissez-faire capitalism. He pioneered the fields of institutional economics and labor history, and directed the preparation of two monumental studies: *A Documentary History of American Industrial Society* (1910–1911) and *The History of Labour in the United States* (1918–1935). He was a virtual prototype of the ideal university professor, as defined by Van Hise: eminent scholar in a "practical" field, beloved teacher, and public servant who drafted major pieces of legislation, advised officeholders, and served on government agencies at all levels.

The sociologist Edward A. Ross was another protégé of Ely's. He provided intellectual underpinnings for a wide range of reforms, including factory safety, abolition of child labor, limitation of working

---

[40] *Ibid.*, 344–373.
[41] *Ibid.*, 334–344; Benjamin G. Rader, *The Academic Mind and Reform: The Influence of Richard T. Ely in American Life* (Lexington, Kentucky, 1966), 28–160; Robert J. Gough, "Richard T. Ely and the Development of the Wisconsin Cutover," in *WMH*, 75 (Autumn, 1991), 3–6.

hours, a minimum wage for women, and—less edifyingly—eugenics and immigration restriction.[42]

The historian Frederick Jackson Turner reoriented the study of United States history away from European origins towards a consideration of the influence of the American frontier. His emphasis on geography and environmental factors, and on socio-economic development and democratic institutions, reinforced the reformist temper of the times and absorbed U.S. historians for nearly half a century.

The philosopher Max Otto, author of *Things and Ideals* (1924) and *The Human Enterprise* (1940), was one of the country's leading interpreters of humanism and instrumentalism and a legendary teacher. He presented philosophy as a method students could use to deal with the problems of their own lives, rather than with problems posed by scholars.[43]

Another galaxy of academic stars existed in the College of Agriculture, also representative of the New Education and the Wisconsin Idea. Deans William A. Henry and Harry L. Russell succeeded in establishing agricultural science as a legitimate academic discipline and in striking an acceptable balance between broad scientific courses and specialized ones. The college's Experiment Station managed to find an equilibrium between pure and applied science, thus satisfying both academics and the state's farmers. Its discoveries in livestock breeding and feeding, milk-fat testing, cheese curing, and tuberculosis control won over many doubters. Its innovations in agricultural education, engineering, economics, and journalism, and in rural sociology achieved national recognition. Its outreach activities enhanced the university's status in every region of Wisconsin. The college's growth alarmed some faculty members in Letters and Science, and generated rivalries for resources, but the College of Agriculture succeeded, as the university's historians put it later, in "breaking down rigid barriers between related fields of knowledge and in bridging so remarkably the stubborn, traditional gulf between discovery and application."[44]

The emergence of the Extension Division was more problematic. Its prototypes—the agricultural short course and the farmers' institutes—had been established in 1888, and proved very successful. Ur-

---

[42] Lafayette G. Harter, Jr., *John R. Commons: His Assault on Laissez-Faire* (Corvallis, Oregon, 1962), 69–239.

[43] Julius Weinberg, *Edward Alsworth Ross and the Sociology of Progressivism* (Madison, 1972), 56–176; Richard Hofstadter, *The Progressive Historians: Turner, Beard, Parrington* (New York, 1968), 47–164.

[44] *Wisconsin Blue Book, 1927*, pp. 369–370; Curti and Carstensen, *University of Wisconsin*, 2: 374–424 (quote, 424); Wilbur H. Glover, *Farm and College: The College of Agriculture of the University of Wisconsin, a History* (Madison, 1952), 112–286. For a more detailed discussion of the development of the College of Agriculture, see Chapter 2.

ban outreach also succeeded. Community-sponsored lecture courses in Madison and Milwaukee were well-received, and President Chamberlin persuaded the regents to fund ten more such courses for 1891–1892. Each course cost sixty dollars, consisted of six lectures, and earned participants a certificate of credit equivalent to one semester hour, provided that they completed the required reading and passed an examination. The subjects included American history, English and Scandinavian literature, economics, antiquities of India and Iran, bacteriology, plant physiology, electricity, and landscape geology. All told, 8,500 people attended and 4,500 completed the exercises, leading the university to affiliate with the Chicago Society for University Extension, the Chautauqua movement, and the American Society for the Extension of University Teaching. Although Chamberlin left Madison for the University of Chicago the following year, the new division expanded offerings to thirty-two lecture courses and received requests for forty-eight.[45]

Using the English educational system and the American Chautauqua movement as models, Chamberlin's successor Charles Kendall Adams sought a separate staff to co-ordinate outreach. Under Adams, the Extension Division hired a full-time secretary, established correspondence courses, and launched a news service. In 1895–1896, extension offered fifty-seven courses in forty-three locations, including northern Illinois. Adams reported in 1896 that extension had stimulated thousands of Wisconsinites intellectually, attracted new students to the campus, improved citizenship, initiated local reforms, and generated good feelings towards the university. However, Madison students began to complain that professors spent too much time off campus; faculty members withdrew from extension work because it reduced research time; and communities deplored the cost and the use of younger, less renowned teachers. Then extension enrollments and revenues began to decline, and secretary Jerome H. Raymond resigned and was not replaced. The program was turned over to the new School of Education, which attempted to run it with only six or eight people—none of them among the university's stars. Nationally, extension work declined even more than at Wisconsin, where lectures and correspondence courses were moribund for a dozen years. But overall, the popularity of the extension concept was borne out in Wisconsin by the continued expansion of farmers' institutes and the short course, and by the conversion of the summer school for teachers into a full summer session in 1899.[46]

A resurgence in extension work began under Acting President Ed-

---

[45] Curti and Carstensen, *University of Wisconsin*, 1: 710–719, 722–726.
[46] *Ibid.*, 1: 726–731. For an example of early extension activity in Milwaukee, see Milwaukee *Sentinel*, October 25, 1893.

ward A. Birge and Governor La Follette in his first term, both in 1901. Birge asked for a new extension secretary, and La Follette declared in his message to the legislature that the state owed it to the people of Wisconsin to find the means for every young person to attain an education at the University of Wisconsin in any course desired. But a struggle developed over extension during the Van Hise administration. The staff of the Free Library Commission, led by Charles McCarthy, Frank A. Hutchins, and Henry E. Legler, importuned Van Hise to resuscitate extension, but he was less than enthusiastic. Finally, in late 1905, Van Hise conceded that "a state university should not be above meeting the needs of the people, however elementary the instruction necessary to accomplish this." Six months later, he asked, and received from, the regents $2,500 to revivify extension; but he remained reluctant to do so on a grand scale.[47]

Meanwhile, McCarthy and Legler escalated their campaign. McCarthy discovered that 35,000 Wisconsinites paid out about $800,000 a year for private correspondence courses, and most of them expressed support for a public extension program. Soon William H. Lighty, another Ely protégé, was appointed director of the correspondence program and immediately began pressing faculty members to take part in a revived general program. In 1906 a joint committee of the faculty and the Free Library Commission recommended resuming extension programs, and President Van Hise, at last committing himself to the extension ideal, requested $7,500 for it.

Thus converted, Van Hise persuaded the 1907 legislature to authorize extension and correspondence work, separate from that managed by the College of Agriculture, and to appropriate $20,000 for the work. After considerable debate and negotiation, he appointed Louis E. Reber as the Extension Division's first director. Reber stayed for twenty years and built extension into a powerful organization that combined Van Hise's service ideal with the social reformist aspirations of McCarthy, Hutchins, Legler, and Lighty. His ideal was an extension division that "endeavors to interpret the phraseology of the expert and offers the benefits of research to the household and the workshop, as well as to municipalities and state." Reber divided the work into four departments: correspondence study, instruction by lecture, debating and public discussion, and general information and welfare. Of these, only correspondence study carried college credit. Thirty-five academic departments developed more than 200 courses, but more than half of all enrollments during the first term were in non-credit "vocational" or "utilitarian" courses.

[47] Curti and Carstensen, *University of Wisconsin*, 2: 549–558.

To establish a separate identity for extension, Reber demanded and received a special staff, set up a network of administrators and teachers throughout the state, used itinerant instructors, and produced a textbook for every correspondence course. The lectures department functioned primarily as a speakers' bureau for informational purposes, though lecturers were to entertain somewhat as well. The department of debating and public discussion sought to generate intelligent and active interest among a wide spectrum of Wisconsin citizens on a wide variety of issues. The department allied itself with the Free Library Commission and operated a lending library on the most compelling issues of the day. The department of general information and welfare used bulletins and institutes "to act as a medium between the great federal and state departments, national societies and state universities, on the one hand, and the people of the state on the other, in the dissemination of results of investigation and research."[48]

So well received was Reber's handiwork that extension's budget soared from $20,000 to $225,000 between 1907 and 1914—twice that of any other extension program in the country. By 1914, Reber had established field districts in Milwaukee, Oshkosh, La Crosse, Superior, Wausau, and Eau Claire, and the number of students enrolled in correspondence courses had reached 15,000 (4,000 of whom were first-time participants). Observers attributed the growth to effective use of publicity, the persuasive powers of field representatives, willingness to prepare any course for which there was a demand, and focus upon practical courses. Other universities adopted Wisconsin's extension textbooks, and the royalties helped support expansion. Between 1910 and 1915 the number of library packages distributed by the debating and public discussion department increased from 2,000 to 5,000, making it a showpiece (some said "the darling") of Wisconsin's reformers.[49]

The lecture department organized a summer Chautauqua and various lyceum courses, and the department of general information and welfare multiplied its functions at a bewildering pace. Its informational bulletins ran the gamut from *The Prevention and Cure of Tuberculosis* to *Frosts in Wisconsin*. Its institutes and reference bureaus were

---

[48] *Ibid.*, 2: 549–571 (quotes); Charles A. Wedemeyer, "University Extension—A Lively Mechanism for the Wisconsin Idea," *A Resourceful University: The University of Wisconsin-Madison in Its 125th Year* (Madison, 1975), 69–76; Ruth H. Olcott, "An Analysis of Changing Times and an Expanding Nation upon Five Selected Institutions of Higher Learning from 1869 to 1917" (doctoral dissertation, University of Houston, 1954), 161–178.

[49] Curti and Carstensen, *University of Wisconsin*, 2: 571–575.

equally varied, including a bureau of visual instruction that collected motion pictures and assumed responsibility for the University Press Bureau in 1913.[50]

Dearer to Van Hise's heart than extension, and even more controversial, was the notion that university faculty members should serve state government directly as advisers, consultants, commission members, and drafters of legislation. He had all but ignored extension work in his 1903 inaugural address, but he had praised Germany's practice of using scholars as government officials and predicted the trend would be adopted in the United States and in Wisconsin. Governor La Follette had already begun to seek faculty experts for service on various state boards and commissions, and by 1912, forty-six university professors and administrators were members of one state agency or another. Activists celebrated their contributions, but conservatives, including a few of the participants themselves, regarded them with more skepticism. Van Hise was leery of opponents' charges and of claims by the university's "friends" that Wisconsin was "a university that rules a state." University professors, he demurred in 1913, "carefully refrain from offering advice or assistance except as they are called upon to do so," and he cautioned that such advice was technical and apolitical. Whatever the reality, the perception that faculty members played a key role in legislation and administration became a hallmark of the Wisconsin Idea, for critics and advocates alike.[51]

By 1914, the University of Wisconsin had unquestionably emerged as a prestigious institution by purely academic standards. But its fame nationwide also depended on its threefold "extramural activities": government service, agricultural outreach, and university extension. In 1903, Britain's Mosely Education Commission ranked it second only to the University of Michigan among state universities. One commissioner termed it "the wholesome product of a commonwealth of three millions of people; sane, democratic, industrial and progressive; with ideals and unafraid of ideas." In 1909 Lincoln Steffens exulted that "the state university is coming to be a part of the citizen's own mind, just as the state is becoming a part of his will." In his capacity as assistant editor of *Outlook*, Theodore Roosevelt asserted that "in no other state in the union has any university done the same

---

[50] *Ibid.*, 2: 575–577.

[51] Van Hise, "Inaugural Address," in *Jubilee*, 120–121; Curti and Carstensen, *University of Wisconsin*, 2: 87–90, 549–552, 621–622 (quote); McCarthy, *Wisconsin Idea*, 313–317; John R. Commons, *Myself: The Autobiography of John R. Commons* (New York, 1938; reprinted, Madison, 1964), 110–111; Howard J. McMurray, "Some Influences of the University of Wisconsin on the State Government of Wisconsin" (doctoral dissertation, University of Wisconsin, 1940), 40–49.

work for the community that has been done in Wisconsin by the University of Wisconsin." And so it went, the praise and encomia heaped ever higher upon the Madison campus.[52]

Impressive though all this was, it was offset by several ominous considerations. One was the fact that the university had gradually developed its own propaganda machine, exemplified by the *University Press Bulletin*, and its own legislative lobby, which often exaggerated accomplishments and glossed over conflicts and controversies. The College of Agriculture and the Extension Division were especially adroit at publicizing successes, and at cultivating an influential constituency that pressured the legislature for funding. They ably convinced special interest groups of the value to the public of various programs and projects—advice that could and would be turned against those who used it.[53]

This effusive national praise also obscured the fact that the role of the University of Wisconsin in the New Education and the Wisconsin Idea was the subject of serious dispute, even among its own faculty. As John R. Commons observed in his autobiography, a university was not a single, unified entity but rather a collection of individuals whose opinions differed quite as widely as the opinions held by the public at large. Within the university, arguments raged over the relative importance of research, over teaching and governmental service, over pure versus applied research, over liberal arts versus professional training, and, above all, over the legitimacy of extension work and public service. Frustrated by faculty insistence upon having a scholar head extension, Charles McCarthy complained to President Van Hise, "the professors in the University have, as a body, opposed this whole work and a man who would be acceptable to them would in my opinion be of no value to this movement." English professor James F. A. Pyre gave extension work short shrift in his 1920 history of the university, despite his own participation in it, observing pointedly that true outreach to the public should concern itself with presenting "some just impression of a value in art or morals or an elusive concept of gravitation, rather than toward providing . . . [the public] with cheaper electricity or subtilizing his philosophy of municipal sewage."[54]

Nor did the university's activist orientation always find favor with the Board of Regents, the legislature, or other public officials. Indeed, since regents were appointed by governors, usually for partisan purposes, and often lacked a university education themselves, the

---

[52] Curti and Carstensen, *University of Wisconsin*, 2: 107–111, 587–592.
[53] *Ibid.*, 2: 559–567.
[54] Commons, *Myself*, 110–111; Curti and Carstensen, *University of Wisconsin*, 2: 559, 564–565.

remarkable thing was their pattern of support, both for the institution, its traditions and prerogatives, and for its sometimes "radical" departures. Much of the university's success in cultivating regent support was due to its policy of justifying research, teaching, public service, and extension activities for what they contributed to the state's economy. Added to this were Van Hise's skill and patience with board members—and their consequent view of themselves as insiders and their pride in the university's national celebrity.[55]

These considerations notwithstanding, conflicts over academic freedom were frequent and serious enough to belie any claims of universal harmony among conservatives and progressives on the board and on the faculty. In 1894, a clash between Richard T. Ely and ex-officio Regent Oliver E. Wells, the state superintendent of public instruction, achieved national notoriety. The regents eventually censured Wells and adopted the famous dictum that the University of Wisconsin "should ever encourage that continual and fearless sifting and winnowing by which alone the truth can be found." Although widely hailed in state and nation as a milestone in the struggle for academic freedom and faculty autonomy, the "sifting and winnowing" pledge was to be tested severely during the next two decades.[56]

In July, 1909, an article in *Collier's*, then an influential opinion magazine, charged that leading regents had interfered with the running of the economics department and were conspiring to depose Van Hise partly because of some economics professors' outspoken views on the conservation of natural resources. The Milwaukee *Journal* claimed that some regents actively opposed faculty research about corporate wealth and related issues. These accusations were given greater credence when in 1910 Frederick Jackson Turner accepted an appointment at Harvard, partly in protest against the regents' alleged interference in academic affairs. Faculty representatives charged that the board adjusted departments' recommendations on salaries, promotion, and tenure, manipulated teaching loads and schedules, and belittled research that was either not clearly practical or that threatened the socio-economic status quo. After an intense meeting, the regents acknowledged that "it was agreed by all that there was a great deal of dissatisfaction, uneasiness, and apprehension in the minds of the members of the faculty . . . due to various actions of the regents which had led the faculty to distrust the motives and purposes of the regents." Regents concurred that they had "no intention of interfering with the customary methods of educational administration by the faculty."[57]

---

[55] Edward A. Birge, "The University of Wisconsin: A Reply," *Educational Review*, 50 (November, 1915), 418.
[56] Curti and Carstensen, *University of Wisconsin*, 1: 508–527.
[57] *Ibid.*, 2: 53–66.

A continuing conflict about the university and academic freedom is testified to by several other events: the regents' censure in 1910 of Edward A. Ross for allowing an unauthorized progressive educator to speak to his class, a passionate defense by Van Hise of academic freedom in his 1912 commencement address, and the board's reluctance to accept, as a gift from the class of 1910, a plaque bearing the "sifting and winnowing" declaration. Although the plaque was finally affixed to Bascom Hall in 1915, and Van Hise proclaimed it as a guarantee that "from that day [of the resolution's adoption] to this, no responsible party or no responsible authority has ever succeeded in restricting freedom of research and teaching within these walls," the record clearly reflected differences about the university's autonomy.[58]

Also troubling were the university's relationships with a succession of governors and legislatures, although the long-term outcome generally benefited the university. The principal battleground was usually the budget, since the portion met by legislative appropriation always far outweighed other sources: land grant endowments, federal aid, gifts and bequests, tuition and fees. Over time, the university succeeded in augmenting the appropriation, but it did so at the expense of some of its autonomy, yielding to demands that government assume more authority over its internal operations. Prior to 1899, the university received designated portions of the mill tax, and its income soared despite the economic depression. Even the most conservative governors supported the university, emboldening President Adams to fatten his requests. This led the 1897 legislature to investigate the university's finances and to propose closer supervision. In 1899 the legislature substituted a biennial appropriation. Other proposals would have excluded the university president from the board of regents, and required the regents to report directly to the legislature.[59]

Pro-university forces proposed restoring the mill tax and reducing specific appropriations made by the legislature. They met short-lived success in 1905, when Van Hise and La Follette persuaded lawmakers to finance the university with a tax of two-sevenths of a mill for each dollar of assessed value, giving the regents the authority to allocate the revenue as they saw fit. In 1906 there was another legislative investigation that produced 2,055 typewritten pages of testimony by 154 witnesses on many subjects. One critic stigmatized Van Hise as "The Champion Wanter" another observed that the university's lobbyists "are the slickest and the smoothest that ever came down the pike." Although none of the committee's harsher recommendations was enacted, the pattern had been solidly established. Thereafter, the university would request an increase in the mill tax in the "confident

[58] *Ibid.*, 2: 66–72.
[59] *Ibid.*, 1: 580–607.

belief that every dollar will be returned many fold to the state, even if the material point of view alone be considered," and the legislature would in turn intrude more in university governance.[60]

By 1910, five cents of every Wisconsin tax dollar supported the university. The 1911 legislature, the most progressive in the state's history, raised the university's share of the mill tax to three-eighths and provided money for new buildings as well. The 1913 legislature was even more generous, appropriating over a million dollars for construction, but it reinstituted the practice of specifying how the money was to be spent—an authority that more conservative legislatures would later wield with relish. Ironically, progressive Republicans contributed to the university's woes by enacting socio-economic programs, by introducing more precise accounting methods, by triggering taxpayer reaction against extravagance, and by launching their own investigation of the campus. Gleeful conservatives seized the opportunity to punish the university for its progressive policies. Later, Governor Francis McGovern reversed himself and rejected the investigation's indictment of the university's alleged inefficiency. The normal schools and the state department of public instruction joined in the chorus of university criticism, accusing it of empire building. The normal schools had their own board of regents, buttressed by public and political support in the areas where the schools were situated. They aspired to be full-fledged institutions of higher learning, to gain a monopoly over teacher preparation, and to achieve parity in funding. Led by normal school regent Theodore Kronshage, Governor McGovern's law partner, they lobbied as effectively as their university counterparts.[61]

Then as now, university faculty and administration tended to look down their noses at the normal schools. They alternated among attempts to convert the normal schools into preparatory "feeders" for the university, to turn them into trade schools, or to abolish them altogether. Graduates of the two-year normal school course were allowed to enter the university with the rank of junior beginning in 1890, but in 1896 a two-track system went into place, one track leading to a bachelor of philosophy in pedagogy with two additional years' work, the other to a "regular" university degree with three additional years' work. In 1907, the normal schools failed to persuade the legislature to allow them to confer bachelor degrees, and Van Hise countered with a proposal that they train only elementary school teachers and serve as junior colleges for prospective secondary school teachers who would then complete their studies in Madison. Van Hise and the university regents, in coalition with several private colleges, placated

[60] *Ibid.*, 2: 159–190.
[61] *Ibid.*, 2: 267–283.

the normal schools in 1909 by liberalizing their policies on transfer credits. Then in 1911 a new law stipulated that the university would apply towards a bachelor of arts degree the full sixty credits earned by normal school graduates, and it provided that the two-year normal schools could not expand their existing courses of study without legislative approval. In practice, however, many University of Wisconsin departments refused to comply in individual cases. This incensed the normal schools, and they continued, albeit unsuccessfully, their push to become four-year institutions. Thus the Madison campus held the normal schools at arm's length, giving the appearance of being elitist and self-serving, and, quite unnecessarily, dividing the state's higher education ranks for many decades, to their mutual detriment.[62]

The university's relations with the state's public schools were even more contentious than its relations to normal schools. The presence of the state superintendent of public instruction on the university's Board of Regents made for a volatile situation, as in the struggle over high school accreditation between the department of public instruction and the university. To upgrade the quality of its incoming students, the university insisted upon the inspection and accreditation of preparatory secondary schools. It had certified 138 by 1895 and 315 by 1910. However, the state superintendent had the statutory authority to recommend curriculum, set the requirements for teacher certification, supervise some high school work, and stipulate which schools were entitled to state funds.[63]

This double-headed system of inspection worked with little overt friction before 1906. Then the Wisconsin Teachers' Association and its journal, the *Wisconsin Journal of Education*, began complaining that university inspection forced many secondary schools to neglect the needs of students not planning to attend the university in Madison. Superintendent of Public Instruction Charles P. Cary charged that university inspection had caused some schools to ignore "local needs, local conditions, and local limitations" and created "in the high schools nervous strain and in the public mind jealousy and contention." In 1907, Cary and then Dean Birge of the university tried, but failed, to reach agreement on a system of joint inspection. Two years later, Cary clashed bitterly with President Van Hise over a legislative bill that would have required the university to accept any graduate of a high school approved by the department of public instruction and to abandon its own inspection system. Frustrated, Cary introduced a similar resolution to the Board of Regents. Debate and maneuvering consumed eight months before the board rejected it.[64]

[62] *Ibid.*, 2: 96, 259–266.
[63] *Ibid.*, 2: 234–242.
[64] *Ibid.*, 2: 242–246.

The election campaign of 1912 was tumultuous generally, and was made more so by Cary. He provided Stalwart Republicans (who opposed the progressive laws adopted in 1911) with one of their most effective arguments: by denouncing Wisconsin as the "university state." Cary charged that "the capitol is an annex to the University to be used for experimental and laboratory purposes." During his own re-election campaign the following year, he promised voters "freedom from domination by higher institutions of learning." Cary's crusade against university inspection of high schools did not succeed during his tenure, but even so he did manage to undermine public confidence in university inspection and helped galvanize opposition to both the New Education and the Wisconsin Idea.[65]

This internecine warfare among the university, the normal schools, and the department of public instruction inevitably strengthened sentiment in favor of a central board of education. Some advocates of the New Education believed that a central board would be the most effective agency for guaranteeing that every Wisconsinite, regardless of location or socio-economic circumstances, would have equal access to a quality education. For them and for others who thought of themselves as "progressives," a central board stemmed logically from their conviction that a nonpartisan commission of experts was the most efficient body for planning and administering every aspect of modern life. But the notion of a central board also appealed to many who abhorred the New Education and the Wisconsin Idea. They saw it as a mechanism for removing the university from the political arena, for preventing professors from teaching and researching "socialism" and "radicalism," for curtailing duplication and spending, and for reducing the "university state" to a "state university."[66]

Van Hise, the university's regents, and Cary all opposed a central board. Cary regarded it as a threat to his hegemony. But such a board came along in 1915, and lasted eight years. It was called the State Board of Education and got its boost from Stalwart Republicans, especially from Governor Emanuel L. Philipp, who had scored the university for extravagance, radicalism, and inefficiency in the 1914 gubernatorial campaign. But lobbying by the university, the normal schools, and Cary reduced functions of the State Board of Education to a pale shadow of Philipp's concept of a single central body with central control over all educational matters. Van Hise later regretted having opposed the central board concept, and even offered to serve as the university's representative.[67]

---

[65] *Ibid.*, 2: 246–259; Patzer, *Public Education in Wisconsin*, 90–95.
[66] Curti and Carstensen, *University of Wisconsin*, 1: 72–75; 2: 267–273; Patzer, *Public Education in Wisconsin*, 222–223.
[67] Curti and Carstensen, *University of Wisconsin*, 2: 96, 259–266, 273–294.

The university's student body grew commensurately with the physical plant, nearly quintupling in size between 1893 and 1915. Growth, however, did not change its character. Students did not complain about the faculty's increased concentration on research, service, and extension. Student involvement in politics arose only whenever La Follette was a candidate, but that was because of his celebrity as the university's most prominent alumnus, not because of his political ideology. Students focused mostly on the usual campus concerns: housing arrangements, fraternities and sororities, entertainment and recreation, and athletics. The development of an effective student government, newspapers, yearbook, and other extracurricular activities stimulated more responsibility within the student body. But irresponsible behavior attracted more concern among faculty members and administrators. Hazing, cheating, drinking, and vandalism surfaced periodically; then as ever, such conduct caused many Wisconsinites to fuss about student morals. In fact, as in every era, most students were law-abiding, many were churchgoing; but the image of Madison's university students as social butterflies, transient athletes, unintelligent, rich, immoral, and irresponsible enjoyed currency throughout the period. A riot in October, 1914, in which at least a thousand students battled police and town gangs in the city streets, did little to enhance the reputation of the university's student body or to strengthen the hand of its supporters.[68]

[6]

The free public library movement was another aspect of the New Education's emphasis on democratic and practical learning. Promoters styled libraries "the people's university," and preached that disseminating reading material was essential to the success of university extension, correspondence courses, social centers, and continuation schools. Between 1880 and 1900, the popular concept of libraries as private preserves for an educated, affluent elite was gradually displaced by the concept that libraries, like churches and schools, could be transformed into powerful engines that could help reconstruct society. Public libraries, it was felt, might become crucial agencies for acculturating the masses who were separated from the mainstream by class or ethnicity. As with other reforms, a bewildering complex of people and ideas was involved, many of them inherently incompatible and contradictory, ranging from social justice to social control. Frank A. Hutchins—generally regarded as the father of Wisconsin's free library movement—asserted in 1893, "The thought that a library, supported by the public, should, first of all, be an educator of the

[68] *Ibid.*, 1: 659–692; 2: 497–532.

masses . . . making its treasures free and accessible to the poor and ignorant . . . has been too often lost under a mass of traditions relating to the necessity of rigid rules for its conduct." His female counterpart, Lutie E. Stearns, preached that community librarians should not remain hidden in their offices, but should go out among the people and respond to their needs and desires.[69]

The essence of the free public library movement was to bring the benefits of formal education to those who were unable to achieve one, especially members of the urban working class and persons isolated in rural Wisconsin, particularly residents of the New North. The public library was society's chief instrument for self-education. Through it, enterprising individuals could climb the socio-economic ladder, enrich their lives, and become enlightened citizens. No one believed this more firmly than Andrew Carnegie, who donated millions of dollars to communities around the country, including Wisconsin, for constructing or purchasing library buildings. As Carnegie said in 1897, the free public library principally benefited "the great mass of people, the wage-earners, the laborers, the manual toilers."[70]

Many Wisconsinites concurred. "What the people need, the common people, the laboring people, the mechanics, the masses, the people who have not much extra time in life," wrote an Eau Claire librarian in the *Bulletin* in 1913, "is a library system that has a strongly democratic organization." The Free Library Commission stated in 1912 that the "library helps workers to do their work," "the library builds up good morals," and "the library is more democratic than any other institution in the city." On a less exalted plane, many touted the public library, the church, and the social center as positive alternatives to the saloon, the pool hall, and the movie house. Advocates viewed libraries as agencies of Americanization where immigrants could study English and imbibe American culture and values. But the commission also served old-country interests, providing "Norwegian books for the Norwegian, Swedish books for the Swede, Polish books for the Polock, and Yiddish books for the good citizen who can read no other language."[71]

---

[69] David I. Macleod, *Carnegie Libraries in Wisconsin* (Madison, 1968), 6–20, 64–103; Free Library Commission, *Biennial Report*, 1913–1914, pp. 7–9; Lutie E. Stearns, "The Library and the Community," *Wisconsin Library Bulletin*, 7 (July–October, 1911), 99; Frank A. Hutchins, "Free City Libraries," in Stearns, ed., *Columbian History of Education*, 413 (quote); Earl Tannenbaum, "The Library Career of Lutie Eugenia Stearns," in *WMH*, 39 (Spring, 1956), 164; Paul H. Neystrom, "How to Reach the Workingman," *Wisconsin Library Bulletin*, 7 (November–December, 1911), 168 (quote); "The Function of the Library," *ibid.*, 9 (February, 1913), 2–3.

[70] Macleod, *Carnegie Libraries*, 4–18.

[71] William H. Dixon, "A Discussion of the Public Library," *Wisconsin Library Bulletin*, 9 (October 1913), 163–165 (quote); "Opportunity Talks," *ibid.*, 11 (April, 1915), 96;

Despite their positive rhetoric, few reformers truly believed that working people, especially men, would patronize libraries without a great deal of urging and socialization by librarians and working-class groups alike. In an article entitled "How to Reach the Workingman," University of Wisconsin economist Paul H. Neystrom acknowledged that libraries were losing potential working-class patrons to saloons and pool halls. Libraries could learn from them, he said, and advertise themselves more effectively. In contrast to the library, he argued, the saloon welcomed the working man, made him "warm and comfortable," allowed him to smoke and spit if he wanted, and did not close at nine o'clock. A saloon made him "feel that the place is for him, and not that he is but an accident to be tolerated, if noticed at all, as in some libraries." Neystrom proposed reaching the working man through his interests, especially sports, hobbies, and politics, in a comfortable environment. As the *Wisconsin Library Bulletin* put it, a man "goes to the saloon not so much because of his thirst for drink, as because of a thirst for unrestrained social opportunity." Libraries, the *Bulletin* said over and over again, had to do the same. Unfortunately, they mostly failed.[72]

Despite its general failure to reach the working class, the free library movement enjoyed success. The number of libraries grew from twenty-eight in 1895 to 126 in 1904 and to 211 in 1922. Credit goes to co-operation between state government and hundreds of local agencies, both private and public, with a modest assist from Andrew Carnegie.

Of the sixty Wisconsin communities in which Carnegie funded buildings, all but four—Barron, Elroy, Hudson, and Ladysmith—already had tax-supported public libraries. Eleven municipalities actually rejected Carnegie's offer, though six later reversed themselves. Serious controversies arose in other cases. In practice, Carnegie libraries were supported by businessmen and professionals far more than they were by workingmen. Arguments in favor of accepting a Carnegie gift frequently ran along "chamber of commerce" lines,

---

Free Library Commission, *Biennial Report*, 1911–1912, pp. 5 (quote), 9–11 (quote); Clarence B. Lester, "The Library Movement in Wisconsin," in Quaife, ed., *Wisconsin*, 2: 411–432; Kathryn Saucerman, "A Study of the Wisconsin Library Movement, 1850–1900" (master's thesis, University of Wisconsin, 1944), 30–41.

[72] Neystrom, "How to Reach the Workingman," *Wisconsin Library Bulletin*, 7 (November–December, 1911), 168–171; "Library Atmosphere," *ibid.*, 9 (February, 1913), 2. Other articles that make the same points include J. R. Bloom, F. H. Denison, and Molly Catlin, "The Library as a Civic Force and Factor," *ibid.*, 5 (December, 1909), 92–93; Lutie E. Stearns, "The Problem of Public Leisure," *ibid.*, 9 (October, 1913), 163; Maud van Buren, "Some Publicity Methods," *ibid.*, 9 (August, 1913), 129. Macleod, *Carnegie Libraries*, 35–41 and 87–88, describes the indifference or opposition of the working class to public libraries.

exemplified by a Wausau enthusiast who envisioned "a building of magnificent proportions . . . wrought in Marathon County granite, which will stand like the pyramids of Egypt. . . ."[73]

Women often started local agitation for libraries, particularly through women's clubs or the WCTU, groups interested in literary studies and social uplift. Church groups, educators, newspaper editors, businessmen, and civic boosters frequently joined the crusade. Most libraries owed their existence to local elites and respectable reformers. Many began as private collections which were gradually opened to the public, then were turned over to municipalities which had been empowered by statute to establish libraries.[74]

In 1895, responding to pressure from local groups and the Wisconsin Library Association (headed by Lutie Stearns), the legislature established the Wisconsin Free Library Commission (WFLC), an advisory body. Originally its members were unpaid and were appointed by the governor. The commission's first appropriation was only $500, so Senator James H. Stout of Menomonie, a wealthy lumberman who had introduced and shepherded the bill through the legislature, provided additional funding. This allowed Frank Hutchins, who had drafted the legislation, to function as full-time chairman, to inaugurate a nationally innovative system of traveling libraries in Stout's home county, Dunn County, and to establish a summer library school in Madison. So impressive were their efforts that the legislature swelled the commission's appropriation to $4,000 in 1897, enough to sustain Hutchins as a full-time, salaried secretary. By the time Hutchins left the commission in 1904, it had helped establish almost a hundred local libraries and 350 traveling ones; had trained 119 librarians and assistants; and had founded the Legislative Reference Library. Traveling libraries were housed in farmhouses, post offices, country stores, and railway stations, with collections that were gradually adjusted to local needs and tastes. In Hutchins' view, traveling libraries were needed especially in hamlets in the New North, where the bulk of the residents were either young men who worked in the woods and mills and spent the off-season loafing in saloons, or else were immigrants who spoke and read little or no English.[75]

---

[73] Macleod, *Carnegie Libraries*, 21–42, 87–88.

[74] *Ibid.*, 25–28, 66–88; Saucerman, "A Study of Wisconsin Library Movement," 30–41, 66–69; Lester, "Library Movement," in Quaife, ed., *Wisconsin*, 417–424.

[75] Alan E. Kent, "Frank Avery Hutchins: Pioneer of the Book," *Wisconsin Library Bulletin*, 51 (September–October, 1955), 3–5; Frank A. Hutchins, "City Libraries in Wisconsin," in Stearns, ed., *Columbian History of Education*, 413–419; Frank A. Hutchins, *Free Traveling Libraries in Wisconsin* (Madison, 1896), 5–15; Marjorie Perham, "History of the Wisconsin Library Association," *Wisconsin Library Bulletin*, 51 (September–October, 1955), 22–24. Stout was instrumental in all manner of educational legislation statewide.

The WFLC claimed it performed more functions than any other library commission in the country. Besides running the traveling library network, it supplied speakers and publicity, and did everything it could, including mobilizing citizens, to explain how libraries help communities. Once a town arrived at a favorable decision, the commission offered advice, furnished lists of books with instructions about how to buy them, helped catalog them, and organized the library. If a town wanted a new library building, the commission offered planning suggestions and advised the local library board on how to secure funding. As the need for expert librarians increased, the WFLC, in conjunction with the University of Wisconsin, expanded its summer program into a full-fledged library school in 1907, emphasizing practical over theoretical instruction. In its first year, the new school produced twenty-two librarians; by 1912 it had graduated 141, mostly women, 118 of whom held library positions, though only thirty-four of them in Wisconsin.[76]

The WFLC promoted new traveling libraries at fairs, at summer normal school courses and farmers' institutes, through letters to country school teachers, advertisements in agricultural weeklies and newspapers, and automobile tours. In conjunction with University Extension, the commission helped start the Department of Debating and Public Discussion, providing it with lending packages of readings about contested issues of the day. The commission also sent reading materials to logging camps, which had virtually nothing to read, not even newspapers. By 1915, the commission found that, according to ten large libraries statewide, more people were reading books and "a larger percentage of the books read are of an informative and educational character rather than purely recreational."[77]

The WFLC also helped create the Legislative Reference Library (LRL), which, under Charles McCarthy's direction, grew to become a vital force for the Wisconsin Idea and served as a prototype for dozens of other states. A 1901 statute authorized the commission to maintain "a small working library, as complete as may be, of the several public documents of this and other states," and to stock the library with reference works. The same statute also "directed" cooperation between the LRL and the state historical society in providing reference books to legislators. The LRL's purpose, in McCarthy's

---

[76] Free Library Commission, *Biennial Report*, 1911–1912, pp. 4–25; Free Library Commission, *ibid.*, 1913–1914, p. 7.

[77] Martin P. Anderson, "The Loan Package Library: A Tool for Implementing Adult Education in a Democracy," *The Library Quarterly*, 20 (April, 1950), 119–123; Mary Burchard Orvis, "Wisconsin's Package Libraries," *Independent*, August 22, 1912, p. 436; "Are People Reading More or Less?" *Wisconsin Library Bulletin*, 11 (December, 1915), 345 (quote).

view, was to serve members of the legislature and state government in a practical way in order that "all legislation may be made better and be placed upon a more scientific basis," providing them with as much information as feasible on subjects of proposed legislation. That information was to be carefully gathered and digested by expert lawyers, statisticians, engineers, and what he termed "scientific men." By 1905, the LRL had begun drafting bills for legislators who requested them, with the stipulation that the work was "merely clerical and technical."[78]

[7]

The State Historical Society of Wisconsin and its expansion between 1887 and 1913 under Reuben Gold Thwaites also reflected the New Education. Thwaites opened the library to everyone, saying it was "no longer an academic sanctum into which the select few alone may enter," but rather "an institution for the people, and an important factor in the system of popular education." At the same time he pledged to expand the library as "a great workshop for scholars," including both faculty and students at the university. He allowed graduate students to publish in the *Wisconsin Historical Collections*, promoted lectures by renowned scholars, and raised the standards for books and papers issued under the Society's imprint. He tirelessly courted a wide range of constituencies throughout the state by means of historic tours (he called them "pilgrimages"), markers, field conventions, and school projects, thus enlarging the Society's reputation across the state and nation, gaining the support of groups like the Federation of Women's Clubs, the Sons and Daughters of the American Revolution, educators, librarians, and local historical societies. By 1907, Thwaites had succeeded in tripling, since 1887, the library's holdings to 364,649 titles, increasing its endowment by 385 per cent, raising its annual state appropriation from $5,000 to $70,948, assembling a thoroughly professional staff, establishing a state archives, and pushing membership close to the 1,000 mark. Emblematic of the Society's alliance with the University of Wisconsin was the grand classical structure at the west end of Madison's State Street, dedicated in 1900 and housing the joint collections of the two institutions.[79]

By the turn of the century, it was plain not only to pundits and

---

[78] Free Library Commission, *Legislative Reference Department* 1911, pp. 4–16; Fitzpatrick, *McCarthy of Wisconsin*, 41–53; McCarthy, *Wisconsin Idea*, 224 (quote); Marion Casey, *Charles McCarthy: Librarianship and Reform* (Chicago, 1981), 25–45.

[79] Clifford L. Lord and Carl Ubbelodde, *Clio's Servant: The State Historical Society of Wisconsin, 1846–1954* (Madison, 1967), 87–196.

academics in Madison but also to the plumber and housewife in Kenosha that Wisconsin, like the rest of the nation, was in the grip of epochal change. One era was drawing to a close; a new era, still shrouded in mist, was dawning. A full-scale technological revolution had given rise to new industries, new systems of production, indeed a new way of working. Cities large and small had expanded dramatically, creating new modes of transportation and communication, transforming neighborhoods, altering the fabric of everyday life. Opportunity and prosperity loomed at every turn—as did social and economic problems that multiplied and grew ever more complex and thorny. All at once the values and norms of the Gilded Age appeared quaint, outmoded, somehow trite.

Wisconsin's little red schoolhouse was one casualty of this revolution. Clearly, the days of classical curriculum, local autonomy, the short school year, and the termination of formal education at puberty were numbered. The new urban-industrial society demanded universal literacy and formal education. Inspired by the tenets of "progressive education," a variety of constituencies had developed a lengthy agenda of educational reforms designed to make schooling at all levels practical, democratic, and socially useful. Although they were frequently at odds with one another over goals and methods, most educational reformers came to realize that implementation demanded a statewide approach, mandated by the state legislature and overseen by the state department of public instruction. This emerging consensus embroiled educational reformers in politics and government at all levels. In the process, formal education emerged as both a vital component and an indispensable product of what came to be called the Wisconsin Idea.

9

On the Eve of Reform

[1]

IN 1893, Wisconsin's system of government and politics—its polity—was ill-equipped to respond to the public's growing demand for state intervention in social and economic affairs. Judged by the standards of the late twentieth century, the 1893 state government in Madison was minuscule, inexpensive, and uninvolved. Not counting elected officials, the entire governing apparatus employed fewer than 450 persons, most of whom were clerks, stenographers, messengers, maintenance workers, guards, and inspectors. More than a third worked for the legislature. The two agencies with the largest number of employees were the Department of Public Property, with thirty-three, mostly blue-collar, and the office of the State Supervisor of Inspectors of Illuminating Oils, with its fifty investigators statewide. The entire Treasury Department had only nine employees; the Bureau of Labor, Census and Industrial Statistics, six; the Dairy and Food Commission, four. State governmental general expenditures (not including university and school support expenses) for the 1891–1892 biennium were not quite $3 million; twenty years later they were about $14 million.[1]

In common with its sister states, Wisconsin government in 1893 consisted primarily of political parties and the courts. Both had evolved to fill a void in governance left by the U.S. Constitution and to adjudicate conflicts between political democracy and socio-economic oligarchy. The major function of government was to allocate benefits and resources to the party faithful, including individuals, groups, and organizations. Its highest aim was to act as a catalyst for entrepreneurs, both individual and corporate, to convert the state's natural resources into liquid capital. Given contemporary society's faith in private property and free enterprise, in the sanctity of contracts and franchises, and in the stimulating effects of economic com-

---

[1] "The State Finances," in the *Wisconsin Blue Book, 1893*, pp. 329–332, "State Government," *ibid.*, 560–573; "State Finances, General Statement," *ibid.*, *1913*, pp. 314–317.

petition, few persons objected to this system. Fewer yet petitioned for government ownership, regulation, or planning. An ethno-cultural partisan politics rationalized this narrow governmental focus—a politics that guaranteed massive voter participation, parochial loyalties and conflicts, and a focus on issues that largely ignored socio-economic and demographic dislocations.[2]

To a great extent, Gilded Age Wisconsin government was of, by, and for the two major political parties. Both Republicans and Democrats existed as intricately constructed and tightly disciplined "machines," welding together voters, party officials, and officeholders at all levels in the continuous pursuit, exercise, and defense of governmental power and its perquisites. Widespread electoral support (absolutely vital in an age of universal male suffrage, frequent and closely contested elections, and substantial voter turnout) percolated up from towns, wards, and precincts. In exchange, benefits trickled down from Madison to strategic locales and people. Political parties also supplied a degree of co-ordination among the various branches of state government and within the maze of overlapping agencies of federal, state, county, municipal, and town governments. Parties were notably reluctant to provide their constituents with clear policy options, except in matters involving ethno-cultural conflict or partisan advantage. Legislative apportionment, the mechanics of patronage, electoral and legislative procedures, and similar matters of political leverage were always spelled out in the clearest possible (and one-sided) terms. At every turn, officeholders were enjoined, by appeals to partisan loyalty and personal self-interest, to place party concerns ahead of the day-to-day operations of government.[3]

Even though neither the constitution nor the statutes explicitly sanctioned political parties, the Republican and Democratic organizations exercised pervasive power throughout the electoral and governmental systems. They assumed responsibility for voter registration and turnout, and for the naturalization as citizens of potential voters. Through an elaborate, and completely intramural, system of caucuses and conventions, they arranged for and supplied candidates for every

---

[2] See especially, Stephen Skowronek, *Building a New American State: The Expansion of National Administrative Capacities, 1877–1920* (Cambridge, England, 1982), 39–46; Morton Keller, *Affairs of State: Public Life in Late Nineteenth Century America* (Cambridge, 1977), 289–342; Richard L. McCormick, *The Party Period and Public Policy: American Politics from the Age of Jackson to the Progressive Era* (New York, 1986), 197–227; and James Willard Hurst, *Law and the Conditions of Freedom in the Nineteenth-Century United States* (Madison, 1956), 3–32.

[3] Ballard C. Campbell, *Representative Democracy: Public Policy and Midwestern Legislatures in the Late Nineteenth Century* (Cambridge, 1980), esp. 12–24, 80–96, 175–202; Skowronek, *Building a New American State*, 39–41; Keller, *Affairs of State*, 526–543; McCormick, *The Party Period and Public Policy*, 143–181.

office, from justice of the peace to governor. They drafted party platforms for maximum appeal to the electorate; they orchestrated campaigns that were part religious ritual, part mass entertainment; they edited candidates' speeches, printed and distributed ballots, mobilized voters, and catered election-night bashes. They aimed to limit candidates to a chosen few and to turn out a maximum number of voters on election day.[4]

In Madison, the two major party organizations exerted influence through their legislative caucuses and in face-to-face negotiations with partisans in state government. On extraordinary occasions, for example in 1891 and 1893, party leaders such as Democratic state chairman Edward C. Wall even directed matters from a post on the floor of the state assembly, though he was not an elected official. On most occasions, however, parties exerted influence more circumspectly, in caucus and committee rooms, hotels and restaurants, offices and private residences. Parties mostly concerned themselves with the legislature's organization and operations, the creation and distribution of patronage, and the allocation of resources and benefits to the party's advantage. Party officials were usually involved in selecting presiding officers and other legislative leaders, and in the appointment of chairmen and members to key committees.[5]

Their role in the legislative process was much more complex and problematical. Both party organizations exercised discipline over matters of vital political significance, such as legislative apportionment, election procedures, creation of new offices, patronage, the designation of official state printers and newspapers, and the banks in which the state treasurer deposited public funds. Next on the list was the parties' involvement in the ethno-cultural measures that mattered to their constituents. Of the six unanimous Democratic votes in the assembly during the 1891 session, five came over the repeal of the infamous Bennett Law, the issue on which the party had mobilized its winning coalition of foreign-language-speaking groups. Beyond partisan and ethno-cultural issues, the ability or desire of party leaders to impose strict discipline varied enormously. The majority of bills were designated "private" or "local," dealing with corporate and county and municipal issues. The "you scratch my back and I'll scratch yours" formula saw them through the legislature. Republicans were predisposed to favor a slightly more activist state government; Democrats were somewhat more sympathetic to labor, debtors, and renters; but both parties were hostile towards government inter-

---

[4] Keller, *Affairs of State*, 534–543; Campbell, *Representative Democracy*, 9–31.

[5] Campbell, *Representative Democracy*, 31–53, 173–193. Wall assumed personal command because so few of the newly elected Democrats had any previous legislative experience.

vention. Republicans believed that a "harmony of interests" kept the socio-economic order intact. Democrats espoused "personal liberty." Both translated into an operational consensus that limited state government to promoting what legal scholar J. Willard Hurst has termed a "release of energy" in the private economic sector.[6]

Self-interested lobbyists seeking particular benefits or exemptions continually reinforced this bipartisan consensus. Except for those who pled the cause of the Wisconsin Dairymen's Association, nearly all Gilded Age lobbyists represented the state's major corporations, chiefly railroads, public utilities, lumbering companies, and manufacturers. Often officials and officeholders of both parties doubled as lobbyists for one or more major concerns. Democratic state chairman Wall represented street railway and electric utilities, brewers, and oleomargine manufacturers in both Madison and Washington. His Republican counterpart, Henry Clay Payne, was an executive of The Milwaukee Electric Railway and Light Co., the Wisconsin Telephone Company, and the Milwaukee and Northern Railroad. Politicians' and business lobbyists' goals were not necessarily identical, or even compatible. The politician primarily sought to carry a precinct or win an election; the businessman sought to meet a payroll and show a profit. So long as business interests monopolized lobbying, politicians and officeholders experienced little conflict. But in the 1890's the rise of newly organized interest groups and more broadly interventionist ideologies forced many politicians to "broker" socio-economic interests in much the same way they brokered ethno-cultural and geographical interests. Politicians on the make found it harder and harder to resist the temptation to meld their ambitions with the causes of new interest groups and ideologies.[7]

The state's judicial system was equally instrumental in filling the governance void and in reinforcing the anti-interventionist consensus. As for the state's citizens, they were constitutionally hostile to the exercise of executive power, and suspicious of legislative authority. Tales of lobbyists' influence peddling and lawmakers' fiscal irresponsibility circulated widely; not all were true, but the perception of chicanery led many citizens to look to the judiciary as their only possible champion. The popular argument suggested that because judges were better safeguarded from both special interests and demagogues,

---

[6] Campbell, *Representative Democracy*, 90–97; Hurst, *Law and the Conditions of Freedom*, 9–11. See also James Willard Hurst, *Law and Economic Growth: The Legal History of the Lumber History in Wisconsin, 1836–1915* (Cambridge, 1964; reprinted, Madison, 1984), 9–59.

[7] Campbell, *Representative Democracy*, 191–193; McCormick, *The Party Period and Public Policy*, 311–342; David J. Rothman, *Politics and Power: The United States Senate, 1869–1901* (Cambridge, 1966), 37–38.

they were more capable than legislators of giving expression to the public will, and to acting on the public's behalf. In practice, of course, most judges remained immune to the reform rhetoric and instead defended private property and the sanctity of contracts, charters, and franchises. In the nineteenth century, entrepreneurs quite literally had friends at court. The result was a formidable body of "judge-made law" that sanctioned government's promotion of private enterprise and hamstrung measures aimed at regulation, taxation, redistribution, or protection of the disadvantaged.[8]

Reaction against this judge-made law began to build in the 1890's and reached its zenith during the Progressive Era. In Wisconsin, it was a frequent refrain of Robert M. La Follette, Charles McCarthy, John R. Commons, and similar reformers who viewed the judicial system as little better than a conspiracy of the privileged classes against regulatory, tax, labor, welfare, or environmental legislation. Reformers' convictions manifested themselves in proposals for the election and recall of judges, the establishment of the Legislative Reference Library to guarantee "judge-proof" laws, the expansion of the executive-administrative branch of government, and the construction of a regulatory, social-service state. It revealed itself in calls for what came to be called "sociological jurisprudence," by which laws were tailored to suit the economic and social conditions prevailing in each individual community, and in which judicial decisions were rooted in systematic study of socio-economic data and comparative law and institutions.[9]

Constrained by parties and courts, Gilded Age government in Wisconsin revolved primarily around the legislature. The framers of the constitution regarded legislatures as bulwarks of representative government and champions of "the people" against "the interests." But legislatures' reputations declined precipitously during the last quarter of the nineteenth century. The criticism that led to this decline

---

[8] Skowronek, *Building a New American State*, 41–45; Keller, *Affairs of State*, 362–370; Hurst, *Law and the Conditions of Freedom*, 8–30; Charles McCarthy, *The Wisconsin Idea* (New York, 1912), 233–241; Albert H. Sanford, *The Government of Wisconsin* (New York, 1912), 74–89; James Alva Wilgus, *The Government of the People of the State of Wisconsin* (Philadelphia, 1897), 89–98.

[9] McCarthy, *Wisconsin Idea*, 242–253; LaFayette G. Harter, Jr., *John R. Commons: His Assault on Laissez-Faire* (Corvallis, Oregon, 1962), 89–130. See also Morton White, *Social Thought in America: The Revolt Against Formalism* (Boston, 1947; revised ed., 1957); James Willard Hurst, *The Growth of American Law: The Law Makers* (Boston, 1950); Eric F. Goldman, *Rendezvous With Destiny: A History of Modern American Reform* (New York, 1952), 134–140; Oscar Kraines, *The World and Ideas of Ernst Freund: The Search for General Principles of Legislation and Administrative Law* (Tuscaloosa, Alabama, 1974), 4–63; Philippa Strum, *Louis D. Brandeis: Justice for the People* (Cambridge, 1984), 114–158, 335–339, 413–416; Roscoe Pound, *The Spirit of the Common Law* (Boston, 1921); and Oliver Wendell Holmes, Jr., *The Common Law* (Boston, 1881).

combined two potentially contradictory, but uniformly negative, lines of argument. One portrayed the legislature as a tightly organized and disciplined hierarchy whose leadership efficiently marshaled majorities for the benefit of special interests. The other characterized legislatures' operations as haphazard and chaotic, leaving individual lawmakers and lobbyists free to wheel and deal. Before the state established the Legislative Reference Library, bills were engrossed in longhand, and legislators frequently passed scraps of scribbled-on paper as bills to the speaker's desk. Nuisance bills were often drafted by attorneys, at the request of "a country member," in order to extort money or favors from corporations. Even honest and conscientious lawmakers were rendered ineffectual by the lack of any method for organizing and disseminating relevant information, and by the lack of informed assistance in bill drafting. No mechanism existed for checking the accuracy of bills, for weeding out overlapping, repetitive, or contradictory measures, or for informing members about committee hearings. In such a world the lobbyist reigned supreme, holding forth in saloons and hotels and in legislative halls. Party bosses and lobbyists manipulating hapless lawmakers: it was a stereotypical view, widely held—and fundamentally accurate.[10]

Charges of outright legislative corruption were, for the most part, exaggerated, emanating from a combination of partisanship, personal ambition, reformer frustration, and righteous indignation. Bribery and corruption sometimes occurred, and some key roll-call votes seem to admit of no other explanation. But the bulk of legislative policy-making flowed from less sinister, if not always admirable or desirable, causes. For all their faults and limitations, Wisconsin's lawmakers generally made a sincere effort to balance concerns and pressures, and even, on occasion, to transcend them.[11]

The two hallmarks of the Wisconsin legislature of the 1890's were long-term loyalty to a party and ethnic voting. Republicans normally succeeded other Republicans, and Democrats usually begat more Democrats. Even so, only one in four legislators returned for a second term. Less than 4 per cent served three consecutive terms. Lawmaking was, after all, a part-time occupation. Continuity depended primarily upon the cadre of multiple-term legislators, the canon of formal and informal rules and procedures, and, above all, party dis-

---

[10] Campbell, *Representative Democracy*, 2, 31–53; McCarthy, *Wisconsin Idea*, 194–195; Sanford, *Government of Wisconsin*, 37–51; Wilgus, *Government of the People*, 58–75; Robert M. La Follette, *La Follette's Autobiography: A Personal Narrative of Political Experiences* (Madison, 1913; reprinted, 1960), 77–137.

[11] Campbell, *Representative Democracy*, 194–201; Robert C. Nesbit, *The History of Wisconsin. Volume III: Urbanization and Industrialization, 1873–1893* (Madison, 1985), 633–643.

cipline and partisan succession. Biennial sessions lasted approximately a hundred days, of which only about two-thirds were actual workdays. Frequent temporary adjournments, long weekends abetted by free railroad passes, and seemingly interminable roll-call votes consumed large blocks of time, often forcing a last-minute scramble to complete business. Despite these difficulties, the public complained that the legislature was in session for too long, passed too many laws, and cost too much money.[12]

The typical legislator of the 1890's was a middle-aged, middle-class white male serving his first term. Within those parameters, however, diversity reigned. The legislature's ethnic and religious makeup frequently mirrored that of the state, although Yankees and Irish Catholics tended to be overrepresented, Germans and Scandinavians underrepresented. Lawmakers came from a fairly wide range of occupations. Roughly one-third were farmers; another one-third were businessmen; and 10 per cent each were lawyers, professionals, or men engaged in sales, service, or skilled labor. Ethnicity and religion, for both individual lawmakers and their constituents, were far better predictors of party affiliation than were either occupation or geography. Most legislators resembled the ethnic and religious complexion of their constituents.

Compared to other institutions of the 1890's, membership in the Wisconsin legislature was reasonably open, at least to middle-class males. Clearly subject to party discipline, legislators seldom cited party affiliation as a rationale for their voting record; instead, they cited the welfare and desires of their constituents. In fact, lawmakers expended great time and effort trying to discern the electorate's wishes. They returned home frequently, traveled around their districts, digested newspaper editorials and letters to the editor, and read constituent letters and petitions. The demands of party loyalty and constituent opinion sometimes conflicted; a legislator slighted either at his peril.[13]

By the end of the century, pressure groups were rapidly becoming a vital third element in the legislative equation after party loyalty and constituent opinion. Because lobbyists did most of their work behind the scenes, their influence can only be inferred by trying to match reports of their alleged activity with patterns of roll-call voting. Few "smoking guns" have come to light. Interest groups on either side

---

[12] Campbell, *Representative Democracy*, 24–26, 40–53; Nesbit, *History of Wisconsin. Volume III*, 624–626; Kenneth C. Acrea, Jr., "Wisconsin Progressivism: Legislative Response to Social Change, 1891–1909" (doctoral dissertation, University of Wisconsin, 1968), 204.

[13] Campbell, *Representative Democracy*, 31–45; Nesbit, *History of Wisconsin, Volume III*, 643–647; Acrea, "Wisconsin Progressivism," 187–195.

of contentious ethno-cultural issues were extremely visible and vocal, but they enjoyed little success. Lobbyists on governmental or electoral issues—bar associations, civic organizations, taxpayer groups, or city and town officials—also stood little chance, unless their interests coincided with the partisan and personal advantage of the legislator. On the other hand, lobbyists representing business interests or occupational groups (such as brewers or printers) on well-defined issues often wielded substantial power. Only the large railroads, lumber companies, and organizations like the Merchants' and Manufacturers' Association of Milwaukee employed full-time lobbyists in Madison. Most businesses, occupational groups, and trade or civic associations delegated this job to part-time committees, or made sporadic efforts to exert pressure whenever salient legislation arose. The roster of lobbyists resident in Madison generally fluctuated with the legislative calendar. Most interest groups focused so narrowly that conflict between establishments in the same industry, or among groups from functionally different economic sectors (shippers and manufacturers versus railroads, for example) were commonplace. Lawmakers frequently encouraged competing interest groups to hammer out compromises—in effect delegating legislative power to private enterprise. Their influence as the "third house" of the legislature was sporadic rather than pervasive, however, and is hard to gauge because the legislature passed most bills without a formal roll-call vote. The great majority of votes seem to have been controlled by the complex partisan and ethno-cultural strands that bound together lawmakers and constituents, not by special-interest lobbyists.[14]

More often than not, the executive and administrative branches of state government were merely tangential to the hustle and bustle of the legislative arena. Wisconsin's constitution vested executive power in a governor, a lieutenant-governor (elected independently), a secretary of state, a treasurer, an attorney general, and a superintendent of public instruction. Not all necessarily belonged to the same party, and the lines of authority connected them to the legislature, not to the governor. Governors were limited to two-year terms; only seven of eighteen governors in the nineteenth century served more than a single term. As late as 1893, the entire "executive branch" consisted of the governor, lieutenant-governor, a private secretary, an executive

---

[14] Campbell, *Representative Democracy*, 56–78, 100–102, 150–153, 176–177; Albert O. Barton, *La Follette's Winning of Wisconsin (1894–1904)* (Madison, 1922), 94–95; Allen F. Lovejoy, *La Follette and the Establishment of the Direct Primary in Wisconsin, 1890–1904* (New Haven, 1941), 5–21; Nesbit, *History of Wisconsin, Volume III*, 645–647; Acrea, "Wisconsin Progressivism," 1–12. For an enlightening discussion of the diversity of interests among various business, see Robert H. Wiebe, *Businessmen and Reform: A Study of the Progressive Movement* (Cambridge, 1962).

clerk, a messenger, and a janitor. Writing in 1905, political scientist James D. Barnett of the University of Wisconsin observed that it was the prevalent opinion of the constitution makers that "the Governor would have, and should have, very few duties to perform." Apart from his duties as commander-in-chief of the Wisconsin militia and court of last resort for pardons, the governor was enjoined to execute the laws faithfully, periodically communicate the condition of the state, make recommendations to the legislature, and transact all necessary business with other government offices. Even his chief policy-making weapon, the veto, was circumscribed by provision for a legislative override. Over the years, some governors had been able to exert influence through their power to appoint and remove public officials at all levels of government. Even that authority, however, was subject to legislative tinkering. So was the governor's leverage as an ex officio member of more and more state boards and agencies. A few governors managed to increase executive authority modestly. But the hegemony of the legislative branch was still largely intact in the early 1890's.[15]

Nor did any of the three men who occupied the governor's chair during that turbulent decade show much determination to alter the power relationships. George W. Peck, a former mayor of Milwaukee and the author of *Peck's Bad Boy* and other humorous writings, was the only Democratic governor (1891–1895) between 1876 and 1933. He was elected almost entirely because of his party's pledge to repeal the anti-immigrant Bennett Law. In his 1891 message to the legislature, Peck urged fiscal austerity, denied the need for additional legislation, and advocated early adjournment. A dedicated partisan, he concerned himself with legislative reapportionment, prosecution of previous Republican treasurers for malfeasance, and promotion of the Democratic party's credos: "personal liberty" and "limited government." Even during the depression years of 1893 and 1894, Peck generally maintained that local government and private charity bore responsibility for relief and welfare. Rather than calling for state government intervention, he used the prestige of his office to solicit private donations of food and clothing for the unemployed.[16]

Peck's successor, William Upham (1895–1897), a wealthy lumber-

---

[15] *Wisconsin Blue Book, 1893*, pp. 560–563; Sanford, *Government of Wisconsin*, 52–60; James D. Barnett, "The History of the Office of Governor in Wisconsin," in the *Iowa Journal of History and Politics*, 3 (April, 1905), 226–255; Nesbit, *History of Wisconsin, Volume III*, 627–637; Wilgus, *Government of the People*, 75–78.

[16] David P. Thelen, *The New Citizenship: Origins of Progressivism in Wisconsin, 1885–1900* (Columbia, Missouri, 1972), 59; Herbert F. Margulies, *The Decline of the Progressive Movement in Wisconsin, 1890–1920* (Madison, 1968), 29; Milwaukee *Sentinel*, November 27, 1893; Nesbit, *History of Wisconsin, Volume III*, 626–637; "Wisconsin's Former Governors, 1848–1859," in the *Wisconsin Blue Book, 1960*, pp. 136–138.

man from Marshfield, doomed himself to a single term when he discontinued the suits against former treasurers, thereby saving their principal bondsmen, Republican leaders Philetus Sawyer of Oshkosh and Charles F. Pfister of Milwaukee, a considerable sum. Upham personally opposed the act but eventually signed it, at the cost of his political career. The episode was a graphic illustration of the governor's subordinate position to party and legislature, though Upham did manage to exert some reciprocal influence on the legislature through his support of a bill which established a Board of Arbitration and Conciliation and a civil service system for Milwaukee.

Upham's successor, Edward Scofield of Oconto (1897–1901), another wealthy lumberman, was the candidate of the regular Republican organization. He, too, had to deal with escalating demands for reform within his own party. Widely portrayed as a machine stooge, Scofield's major claim to fame was the issue he handed Bob La Follette and the other reformers by utilizing a free railroad frank to ship his household goods (including a cow) from Oconto to Madison. In fact Scofield was not as villainous as his enemies declared, although he was indifferent or even hostile towards the aims of legislative reformers. Scofield generally left reformers free to define their own agendas, and he employed his veto power judiciously. Among his vetoes was an 1897 bill designed to impose an *ad valorem* tax on sleeping cars, freight lines, and railroad equipment companies. Apart from this veto, Scofield actively supported general overhaul of the state taxation system. He signed bills providing for a temporary tax commission in 1897 and a permanent one in 1899. Also in 1899, he chose not to veto a bill abolishing free railroad passes. He was more interested in administration than legislation, and accordingly introduced the first gubernatorial budget and also struggled to construct a central accounting system. Compared to La Follette and his successors, Peck, Upham, and Scofield appear remarkably passive governors. But judged by the standards of the 1890's, they were about as active as prevailing wisdom and custom allowed.[17]

The constitutional establishment of a separate administrative branch, consisting of the departments of state, treasury, law, and education, contributed to the relative powerlessness of Wisconsin governors. Department heads were elected independently; the legislature determined their authority and duties explicitly. In addition, by

---

[17] Thelen, *New Citizenship*, 80–81, 163, 207–210, 306; Margulies, *The Decline of the Progressive Movement*, 29–48; Robert C. Nesbit, *Wisconsin: A History* (2nd ed., by William F. Thompson, Madison, 1989), 406–410; *Wisconsin Blue Book, 1960*, pp. 140–146; Edward Scofield, *Governor's Message*, doc. 1, pp. 1–12, in *Wisconsin Public Documents*, 1897–1898, vol. 1; Edward Scofield, *Governor's Message*, doc. 1, pp. 3–40, in *Wisconsin Public Documents*, 1899–1900, vol. 1.

1893 the legislature had created eight additional departments and eleven more state boards, commissions, and agencies to deal with such diverse subjects as labor, census and industrial statistics, public property, pensions, charitable and correctional institutions, health and vital statistics, fish and game, and dairy and food inspection. Even so, the entire administrative branch consisted of less than 300 persons. For better or for worse, the entire state bureaucracy of 1893 could easily have fit into a modern-day lecture hall on the University of Wisconsin campus.[18]

[2]

The primary conduit between the state's limited government and its politically inclined electorate was a deeply ingrained system of ethnocultural partisan politics. The vast majority of voters (all of whom were male) identified passionately and persistently with one of the major parties, dismissing independents. Voters typically inherited partisan allegiance from their fathers, practiced it assiduously throughout their adult lives, and bequeathed it to their sons. For most voters, the important thing about a candidate was his partisan affiliation; they unswervingly voted for "the party," not "the man." Campaigns and ballots were designed to produce impressive voter turnouts and straight-ticket voting. Politics was important, and people voted. Nearly as many Wisconsinites voted for assembly candidates as for president in 1884, 1888, and 1892, and in almost the same partisan proportions. The same held true for gubernatorial elections. There was little difference between the votes cast for governor and those cast for assembly candidates in all elections between 1884 and 1894, and the drop in total votes during off-year, non-presidential contests was usually less than 10 per cent. In races for the state senate between 1867 and 1894, voters returned the candidate of the incumbent party 80 per cent of the time.[19]

[18] *Wisconsin Blue Book, 1893*, pp. 481–499, 563–573; McCarthy, *Wisconsin Idea*, 172–193; Sanford, *Government of Wisconsin*, 61–73; Wilgus, *Government of the People*, 79–88; Hollis W. Barber, "Development of some of the Administrative Departments of the Government of Wisconsin from 1850–1930" (doctoral dissertation, University of Wisconsin, 1935).
[19] Roger E. Wyman, "Voting Behavior in the Progressive Era: Wisconsin as a Case Study" (doctoral dissertation, University of Wisconsin, 1970), 6–7; Campbell, *Representative Democracy*, 9–30; Keller, *Affairs of State*, 522–565; Richard J. Jensen, *The Winning of the Midwest: Social and Political Conflict, 1888–1896* (Chicago, 1971), xii–xiii, 6–16, 45–46; and three books by Paul Kleppner: *The Cross of Culture: A Social Analysis of Midwestern Politics, 1850–1900* (New York, 1970), 35–129; *The Third Electoral System, 1853–1892: Parties, Voters and Political Cultures* (Chapel Hill, 1979), 3–47; *Who Voted? The Dynamics of Electoral Turnout, 1870–1980* (New York, 1982), 1–54.

Such results were not accidental. They derived from politicking by members of elaborate party organizations which nurtured voter loyalty and participation. Each party's overall welfare was entrusted to a state central committee, consisting of representatives from every congressional district. Each district had its own central committee, whose members were delegates from senatorial and assembly districts. This structure was replicated all the way down to the precinct and town level. Individual committeemen were responsible to the hierarchy for generating the maximum number of votes at each election, by whatever means necessary. Although technically they held part-time, unpaid positions, committeemen generally devoted substantial time and effort to their avocation, reaping rewards in unofficial (and frequently extralegal) benefits: contracts, franchises, patronage, and insider business deals. Their success depended largely upon cultivating voters personally.[20]

An effective party operative had to be "one of the boys" when it came to where and how he lived, recreational and entertainment preferences, and public demeanor. He had to befriend constituents seeking work, food, or rent money, as well as those in trouble with the law or officialdom. He had to be "one of their own," both in class and ethnic origin and in his actual sympathies. The pyramidal party structure served as an information network, too. Tactical tidbits and petitions for aid percolated up; marching orders and benefits filtered down. Local politicians constantly sounded out potential voters and informed their superiors about grass-roots concerns. Party committees enlivened everyday tedium with picnics, excursions, parties, and rallies where inspirational rhetoric was mixed with food, drink, and fun. And, in an age when most Americans were forced to rely upon voluntary associations during hard times, parties also supplied much of the glue that held families and society together.[21]

Wisconsin's party politics were strongly ethno-cultural. Each voter's party affiliation usually reflected his ethnic and religious identities. In general, the questions that were the most socially divisive, generated the most heat, and produced the greatest voter turnout were those that plumbed Wisconsinites' psyches most deeply: religion, language, and cultural values and practices. Ethnicity, religion, and political affiliation were virtually inherited. A threat to any one of the three was apt to provoke a strong reaction.

The interplay between ethnicity and religion, on the one hand,

---

[20] Campbell, *Representative Democracy*, 9–31; Keller, *Affairs of State*, 522–565.
[21] Clifton K. Yearley, *The Money Machines: The Breakdown and Reform of Governmental and Party Finance in the North, 1860–1920* (Albany, 1970), 121–135; Jensen, *Winning of the Midwest*, 2–11; Kleppner, *Who Voted?*, 13–27; Kleppner, *Third Electoral System*, 9–15.

and political affiliation, on the other, was complex, sometimes mysterious, and variable over time. Among Irish and Polish voters, Catholicism and Democratic party affiliation were standard. Among Norwegians and Swedes, it was evangelical Lutheranism and the Republican party. Within most ethnic groups, however, intramural religious differences with significant political consequences were the rule, not the exception. This was especially true for Wisconsin's large German population, which was divided both religiously and politically. For those of Dutch ancestry, Catholicism almost always equaled Democratic politics; Protestantism usually equaled Republicanism. Among Belgians, Republican affiliation was universal, regardless of religious differences.

Early in state history, ethnicity determined political alignments; gradually, this tendency gave way to religion as a determinant. That evolution led to the Democratic party's emergence as a coalition of "liturgical" or "ritualistic" communicants, principally Catholic, while the Republican party solidified as an alliance of "pietistic" or "evangelical" groups. Both parties steadily assumed the character of "political churches," as pietism increasingly translated itself into government activism about ethno-cultural matters. The Democratic party's insistence upon personal liberty became more and more the first line of defense for ritualists.[22]

Ethno-cultural politics in Wisconsin stemmed chiefly from the way nineteenth-century immigration unfolded, and from the divergence between Republican governmental activism and the Democrats' emphasis on personal liberty. The Republican party was founded during the 1850's, a decade marked by cultural and political divisions over both slavery and immigration, particularly the flood of Catholic and Lutheran newcomers. The Republican party reflected the convictions of its Yankee, pietistic Protestant core constituency. It advocated governmental intervention at all levels to halt the spread of slavery, promote economic development, and socialize immigrants through prohibition, Sunday "blue laws," compulsory public education, mandatory use of English, and limitations on voting and officeholding. The conflicts that arose guaranteed that the first decade following statehood would be a watershed in Wisconsin's history: the political alignments forged then persisted, in the main, throughout the rest of the century.

This process accelerated during the Civil War decade, which focused opinion on divisive issues. The Democrats, already designated

---

[22] Wyman, "Voting Behavior in the Progressive Era," 8–29; Campbell, *Representative Democracy*, 9–31; Jensen, *Winning of the Midwest*, 58–88; Kleppner, *Cross of Culture*, 5–91. See also Edgar Litt, *Beyond Pluralism: Ethnic Politics in America* (Glenview, Illinois, 1970), 1–75.

as a coalition of outsiders and marginal people, had to bear the additional burden of being stigmatized as the party of secession and treason throughout the Civil War and Reconstruction, roughly 1861 to 1875. Titanic conflicts over prohibition in the 1870's, and over Bible reading and compulsory English in the schools during the late 1880's and early 1890's, solidified the existing political alignments. The Republican party came to rely upon Yankees, Scandinavians, British, Protestant Dutch, Belgians, and a growing percentage of German Protestants. The Democrats' voting strength was just as firmly rooted in the Catholic Irish, Poles, Czechs, Dutch, and Germans, who coexisted uneasily with roughly half the German Protestant population (especially Lutherans) and a minority of influential Yankees.[23]

Both parties practiced ethno-cultural politics in order to reinforce the proclivities of their loyalists, and to woo fence-sitters. Both parties tried to appeal to specific ethno-cultural groups; they usually selected their candidates with ethno-culturalism in mind. Both parties regularly polled and made note of the language skills of potential voters, and they printed tracts in foreign languages. The parties were not averse to capitalizing on ethno-cultural rivalries, and they dispensed patronage and constructed "balanced" tickets with ethno-cultural considerations at the fore. These tactics paid dividends on election day, frequently producing a legislature that was a microcosm of the electorate. In the 1893 assembly, four-fifths of its Irish Catholics, all of its German Catholics, three-fourths of its German Lutherans, and two-thirds of all its Protestants from continental Europe were Democrats. They constituted over two-thirds of the Democrats' assembly delegation. As for assembly Republicans, two-thirds were either Yankees, Britons, or Scandinavian Lutherans, and three-fourths of assemblymen who had those ethno-cultural backgrounds were Republicans.[24]

The economic depression of the next four years and other disruptive developments skewed ethno-cultural distinctions among the major parties, but those distinctions endured. In 1894 and 1896, voters tended to blame incumbent Democrats for the depression, and Republicans gained among almost every ethno-cultural group. But the impact of those defections was far less drastic when viewed in the context of the entire decade. By 1900, the majority of German, Irish, Polish, and Bohemian defectors had made their way back into the Democratic party. Over the entire decade, the correlation between Catholicism and Democratic voting significantly outweighed any

[23] Wyman, "Voting Behavior in the Progressive Era," 29–69; Kleppner, *Cross of Culture*, 35–91; Jensen, *Winning of the Midwest*, 58–88.

[24] Campbell, *Representative Democracy*, 9–31, 122–149, 191–193; Litt, *Beyond Pluralism*, 42–74.

other. A sizable number of Scandinavian voters cast Populist party ballots in 1896, then returned to the fold by the end of the decade. The Republican party's greatest and most lasting gains during the 1890's occurred among German Protestants, who had been strongly Democratic since territorial days.[25]

Both parties avoided controversial socio-economic issues that might upset the existing political order. They also agreed that state government should limit economic intervention to the promotion of growth and development, and they eschewed regulation, taxation, or any measures designed to redistribute wealth or power. This strategy worked because so few organized socio-economic interests made any demands on state government prior to the mid-1890's; there were almost no countervailing economic forces to placate. Dissenters, whether they were Grangers, Populists, or Socialists, had to rely upon third-party vehicles, which rarely got very far.[26]

Despite the constraints imposed by ethno-cultural partisan politics and limited government, Wisconsinites gradually began to respond to dissenters' demands for change by means of new laws. Groups which challenged the alliance between big business and the two major parties made the most insistent demand. The depression of 1893–1897 helped their cause and brought about some political realignments at the local level. So did the scandals that afflicted politics and business, such as the Republican treasurer cases and Democratic attempts to gerrymander legislative districts. And so did the growing ethno-cultural conflicts, exemplified by the rise of the anti-Catholic American Protective Association and a controversy over the statue honoring Father Jacques Marquette in the United States capitol.

In Wisconsin, as in the rest of the nation, a sense of impending crisis permeated the 1890's, a mood implied in Frederick Jackson Turner's assertion in 1893 that "the frontier has gone, and with its going has closed the first period of American history." Even as he spoke, the depression was spreading across the land like an iron-cold fog. The transformation from a rural, agrarian society to an urban, industrial one moved rapidly in the nineties, hurtling ill-prepared Wisconsinites into an unknown world. The uneven nature of these changes widened existing fault lines in the structure of society and opened new fissures. (Later, historians would speak of "the crisis of the nineties.") The severity of these dislocations drove the discon-

---

[25] Wyman, "Voting Behavior in the Progressive Era," 70–235; Campbell, *Representative Democracy*, 24–30; Kleppner, *Third Electoral System*, 16–47; Kleppner, *Cross of Culture*, 369–376; David L. Brye, *Wisconsin Voting Patterns in the Twentieth Century, 1900–1950* (New York, 1979), 163–210.

[26] Campbell, *Representative Democracy*, 150–174; Kleppner, *Cross of Culture*, 5–34; Keller, *Affairs of State*, 522–564.

tented and disadvantaged to mount angry challenges to the politics of equilibrium that had long confined socio-economic differences within the two-party system.

In 1892 the nascent People's party, bristling with demands for economic and political reforms, captured almost 9 per cent of the nation's popular vote and twenty-two electoral votes in the presidential election. Even more importantly, around the country the Populists also elected an impressive array of congressmen, state legislators, and other government officials. In 1896, with much of the impetus for reform siphoned off by William Jennings Bryan's candidacy on the Democratic ticket, the presidential election was the most polarizing and realigning contest in decades. It energized the lower social orders and genuinely frightened America's middle and upper classes. It was as if an alarm bell had rung somewhere down the hall. The formation in 1897 of the Social Democracy of America, with its Milwaukee contingent proudly designated "Branch One," administered a further shock. Within a short time, politicians of both mainstream parties—and the corporate interests that backed them—began reevaluating their ideological orientations, if only to stem the tide of radicalism.

Impressed by these developments, Robert M. La Follette and others within the Republican party settled upon a reform agenda that soon became vital in their campaign to wrest power from the old guard. Once in command, La Follette-led insurgents elaborated the reform agenda in an effort to consolidate their power and discredit the old guard elements within the party. As this process unfolded, the distinctions between reformers and insurgents blurred more and more, and their effort greatly expanded the size, scope, and impact of state government. They also challenged traditional ethno-cultural politics with a new, issue-oriented, candidate-centered style of politics.[27]

[3]

Far and away the most dedicated and effective reformer in the Wisconsin legislature was Albert R. Hall, five-term Republican assemblyman from rural Dunn County. Hall was a nephew of Oliver Hazard

---

[27] Thelen, *New Citizenship*, 290–312; Robert S. Maxwell, *La Follette and the Rise of the Progressives in Wisconsin* (Madison, 1956), 10–26; Lovejoy, *La Follette and the Establishment of the Direct Primary*, 23–54; Margulies, *The Decline of the Progressive Movement*, 3–50; Carroll P. Lahman, "Robert Marion La Follette as Public Speaker and Political Leader, 1855–1905" (doctoral dissertation, University of Wisconsin, 1940), 314–476; Barton, *La Follette's Winning of Wisconsin*, 42–164.

Kelly, founder of the Patrons of Husbandry. He embodied Kelly's Granger philosophy of having state government regulate various businesses in the interest of farmers and consumers. Hall had been born in Vermont, was raised in Massachusetts and Minnesota, and served with distinction in the Civil War. A farmer, manufacturer, and public servant, he had served seven consecutive terms in the lower house of the Minnesota legislature, including three as speaker, before moving to Knapp, Wisconsin, in 1880. Eccentric, zealous, and self-effacing, Hall formed a powerful coalition during the 1890's on behalf of three measures that became hallmarks of the progressive agenda: the abolition of free railroad passes for legislators, the *ad valorem* taxation of railroads, and the creation of an independent and expert railroad commission. According to a contemporary of his, the journalist Albert O. Barton, Hall was "the statesman of the hour immediately preceding the La Follette movement, the strongest and most influential individual force in the state in preparing the public mind for the revolution to come." Even La Follette, who was not usually quick to share credit, praised Hall as "one of the pioneers of the Wisconsin movement" and said he "never knew a better man." Alone among Wisconsin's legislators, Hall is memorialized with a bronze tablet in the state assembly chamber.[28]

Hall's district was largely peopled by the less prosperous farmers of northern and western Wisconsin, a constituency that would later give La Follette overwhelming support. Many were Scandinavians and most were true-blue Republicans; but nearly all had become uneasy about the party's connections with railroads, lumber companies, public utilities, and other business interests. As these misgivings grew, Hall and several colleagues emerged as leaders of a regional faction within the party. Another was James O. "Yim" Davidson, a Norwegian-born three-term assemblyman from Crawford County between 1893 and 1897, and later state treasurer, lieutenant-governor, and La Follette's successor in the executive mansion in 1906. Another was William O'Neill of Bayfield County, whose voting record was virtually identical to Hall's in 1893 and 1895. Yet another was George E. Bryant of Dane County, a colonel in the Civil War, longtime Republican committeeman, and La Follette's political mentor, who was elected to the

---

[28] Barton, *La Follette's Winning of Wisconsin*, 93–101; La Follette, *Autobiography*, 92–94, 100–104; *Wisconsin Blue Book, 1899*, pp. 769–770; Maxwell, *La Follette and the Rise of the Progressives*, 13, 17, 27, 35–37; Margulies, *The Decline of the Progressive Movement*, 39, 94; Thelen, *New Citizenship*, 169–170, 234, 246, 268–269. For a laudatory view of Hall's influence on La Follette, see Lincoln Steffens, "Enemies of the Republic. Wisconsin: A State Where the People Have Restored Representative Government—The Story of Governor La Follette," in *McClure's Magazine*, October, 1904, pp. 563–579.

assembly in 1898. Joining Bryant in the assembly that year were Philo A. Orton of Lafayette County, an advocate of insurance regulation, and Andrew H. Dahl, a Norwegian American from Vernon County who became a force in several progressive Republican administrations. Spanning the entire decade, as assemblyman from 1891 to 1895 and senator thereafter, James J. McGillivray of Jackson County made his mark as a proponent of antitrust legislation. Although he was a wealthy lumberman, state senator James H. Stout of Menomonie represented much the same constituency as Albert Hall. He urged state responsibility for education and welfare. Joining these others in the senate in 1899 was lumberman William H. Hatton, representing Portage and Waupaca counties, who became significant in several legislatures.[29]

Reformist representatives from the urban-industrial quarter of the state appeared in the legislature about the same time. Milwaukee's Municipal League and the League of Wisconsin Municipalities intensified their lobbying for economic and political reforms, including home rule, caucus reform, civil service, tax relief, and utilities regulation. The Wisconsin State Federation of Labor and its ally the Social Democratic party heightened their demands for government recognition of collective bargaining, employer liability, industrial health and safety regulations, and the curtailment of child labor. In 1898, prominent political and civic activists formed the Republican Club of Milwaukee County, which pledged its opposition to the "encroachments of the political machine in its control of the great political parties of this state." It urged the legislature to promote property tax equity, primary elections by Australian ballot, the abolition of free railroad passes and other franking privileges, and antitrust legislation. In the 1898 caucuses and convention, the Republican Club backed La Follette against Governor Scofield, who won his second term. Milwaukee-based reformers experienced difficulty in getting their progressive legislative candidates elected during the 1890's; they frequently had to rely on other lawmakers for support. The outstanding exception to this pattern was six-term state senator Julius E. Roehr, who won consecutively from 1896 through 1906, and who worked with the Milwaukee Municipal League on behalf of corrupt

---

[29] *Wisconsin Blue Book, 1895*, pp. 673–674, 676, 695; *ibid., 1897*, pp. 661, 662, 668, 674; *ibid., 1899*, pp. 760, 761, 766–767, 775, 788; Thelen, *New Citizenship*, 169–170, 173, 193, 210, 269; Margulies, *The Decline of the Progressive Movement*, 19–50; Barton, *La Follette's Winning of Wisconsin*, 456–469; Evening Wisconsin Company, *The Law Makers of Wisconsin, 1899–1901* (Milwaukee, 1899), 16, 33, 34, 35, 48, 67, 77; David P. Thelen, "Social Tensions and the Origins of Progressivism," in *Journal of American History*, 106 (September, 1969), 333–334; Fred Greenbaum, "The Social Origins of Wisconsin Progressives," *OCC Scholar*, 11 (December, 1968), 35–43.

practices legislation, tax reform, lobbyist registration, and utility regulation.[30]

Throughout the 1890's, reformist lawmakers increased in numbers and influence. By 1900, they had compiled a creditable and incremental record in a variety of legislative areas: education, tax revision, railroad regulation, labor protection, and election reform. These men differed from their Progressive Era successors more in degree than in kind. They set many precedents, and they paved the way for the more dramatic departures that followed in the next decade and a half.

The Wisconsin legislatures of 1891 through 1895 have been characterized by historian Kenneth Acrea as largely "unresponsive." Supposedly, their chief duty was to adjust or tinker with the workings of county and local government; half the bills introduced in each session addressed these areas. The 1891 and 1893 legislatures were destined to be the last with Democratic majorities for forty years. They were elected because of the Bennett Law and its fallout, during a time of prosperity. Both parties manifested fairly consistent factionalism along "progressive" and "conservative" lines, but reformers exerted far more influence within the Republican party. Democratic lawmakers spent a disproportionate amount of time and energy on matters of little long-term significance. Foremost was the repeal of the Bennett Law, the issue that had swept the party into power in 1890, and whose political potential they hoped to exploit for as long as possible. The Republicans obliged by resisting its repeal and by backing a substitute bill retaining the English-language mandate. Keeping that issue uppermost in the minds of voters, especially German Lutherans, was the key campaign strategy orchestrated by Democratic state chairman Edward Wall.[31]

A discernible bipartisan reformist coalition gradually took shape in the legislature around issues like antitrust legislation, the appraisal of railroad property, and railroad passes for legislators. Never disciplined, stable, or in a majority position, this coalition has been characterized as a loosely organized group of legislators "who saw a bit beyond the moment at hand and considered state affairs with a slightly larger viewpoint than did most of their colleagues." Its effec-

---

[30] Barton, *La Follette's Winning of Wisconsin*, 102–132 (quote); Thelen, *New Citizenship*, 173, 269, 276, 288; Margulies, *The Decline of Progressive Movement*, 42–43; *Wisconsin Blue Book, 1899*, p. 754; Evening Wisconsin Company, *The Law Makers of Wisconsin*, 32; Alexander M. Thomson, *A Political History of Wisconsin* (Milwaukee, 1902), 373–374.

[31] Acrea, "Wisconsin Progressivism," 143–147; Campbell, *Representative Democracy*, 28–29, 54–62, 92, 114–116, 192; Laurence J. Younce, "The Political Conditions in Wisconsin from 1890 to 1900" (master's thesis, Marquette University, 1929), 29–30. For an interesting account by a longtime Republican activist, see Ralph G. Plumb, *Badger Politics, 1836–1930* (Manitowoc, 1930), 96–121.

tiveness was severely constrained by two insurmountable realities: conservatives controlled most of the key legislative committees, and the state senate wielded almost absolute power over legislation emanating from the more popularly attuned assembly. Equally inhibiting, perhaps, was the lack of any dynamic, charismatic leadership to build and sustain an effective reform movement.[32]

These limitations notwithstanding, the 1893 legislature managed to enact several substantive education measures. It established new normal schools, expanded the University of Wisconsin's extension department, and systematized teacher certification. It made little progress towards either greater state regulation or professionalization of education, generally deferring to local and school officials' opposition. It made some timid forays into conservation, regulating the sale of wild game to commercial distributors and granting drainage districts the right of eminent domain. Despite a flurry of bills and debate over child labor, employer liability, wages and hours, a state board of arbitration, the prohibition of private police and labor spies, and a free employment office, no significant labor legislation was enacted in 1891 or 1893. The senate killed most of this proposed legislation— if indeed it managed to pass the assembly. Efforts to stipulate state authority over hard-surface roads, and to inspect and regulate mines, steam boilers, and banks, all failed, due primarily to a narrow definition of public responsibility. More than a hundred bills to regulate businesses and professions were introduced in both 1891 and 1893; few of any consequence were enacted. A general law defining trusts and condemning "conspiracies of trade" did pass, but substantive measures considered at the behest of consumers or other "hostile" petitioners all failed.[33]

The same fate befell a number of measures aimed at resolving the state's taxation and revenue problems. Most of the measures sought to equalize local property taxes, to increase revenue from taxes on license fees, and to enact more productive and equitable levies. Wisconsin had inaugurated license-fee taxes in 1854. They permitted railroads, telephone and telegraph, life insurance, sleeping car, and express companies to pay a fixed percentage of their gross receipts in lieu of other taxes. With the onset of the depression in 1893, the taxes on these major corporations declined in proportion to the decline in their gross income, while other Wisconsinites continued to pay on the perpetually growing value of their property. As citizens

---

[32] Acrea, "Wisconsin Progressivism," 182–211; Thelen, *New Citizenship*, 119–121; Plumb, *Badger Politics*, 96–106; Alfred S. Harvey, "The Background of the Progressive Movement in Wisconsin" (master's thesis, University of Wisconsin, 1933), 55–76.

[33] Acrea, "Wisconsin Progressivism," 150–159; Thelen, *New Citizenship*, 33–34, 77, 97, 119–121; Campbell, *Representative Democracy*, 54–78, 150–174.

became aware of this inequity, interest rose in the subject of taxation, particularly in the state assembly. At Albert Hall's urging, the lower house enacted bills to institute an inheritance tax and a temporary state tax commission; the senate, however, rejected them. The assembly itself rejected sixteen bills for new taxes or the revision of existing ones, mostly sponsored by Hall, O'Neill, and McGillivray.[34]

The legislatures of 1891 and 1893 also made a substantial effort to restructure the state's political system, particularly about the way parties nominated candidates. The nomination process had long consisted of a complex system of party caucuses and conventions which gave control to officeholders and professional politicians. In order to prevent large attendance and participation, party leaders often resorted to snap caucuses. A growing number of reformers came to agree with the Superior *Evening Telegram* that snap caucuses were "the drawbridge which must first be scaled before the castle of corruption and bad government can be captured." Many critics favored instituting nonpartisan elections; still others endorsed the concept of "regulated partisanship," meaning state supervision of caucuses and conventions to ensure compliance with Wisconsin's secret ballot act. Some reformers began to press for popular selection of candidates, a process generally referred to as the "direct primary." Many direct primary advocates also wanted a civil service program as an alternative to patronage, corrupt practices legislation, and the registration of lobbyists. (A smaller but vocal segment sought the vote for women, at least in some local elections.) The 1891 legislature enacted a direct primary law limited to Milwaukee and to city and county officials. It was repealed in 1893, to be replaced by a statute providing for popular election of delegates from Milwaukee County to both parties' conventions. Democratic politicians were principally responsible for both laws, a result of their having been hard-pressed to manipulate caucuses and conventions in highly populous areas. The laws were soon embraced by urban reform groups like Milwaukee's Municipal League, which by then were becoming disenchanted with the efficacy of nonpartisanship. But other election reforms had less success. Bills to permit limited woman suffrage and to petition Congress for a constitutional amendment for the direct election of U.S. senators both failed in 1893.[35]

---

[34] Acrea, "Wisconsin Progressivism," 161–176; Thelen, *New Citizenship*, 208–210, 295, 302–303; Campbell, *Representative Democracy*, 70–71.

[35] Acrea, "Wisconsin Progressivism," 178–179; Thelen, *New Citizenship*, 192–194, 215–218 (quoting the *Evening Telegram*), 307–308; Waldo Schumacher, "The Direct Primary in Wisconsin" (doctoral dissertation, University of Wisconsin, 1923), 10–11; Walter E. Spahr, "The Wisconsin Primary Election Law" (master's thesis, University of Wisconsin, 1917), 1–21; Lovejoy, *La Follette and the Establishment of the Direct Primary*, 23–54.

The fall elections of 1894 dealt a severe blow to the Democrats, reducing their numbers from 56 to 32 in the assembly (of 100 seats) and from 24 to 13 in the senate. The entire Republican state ticket swept to victory by more than 50,000 votes, and the GOP regained control of Wisconsin's delegation in Congress. The 1894 election heralded a major party realignment that made Republican control of state government an institution until the 1930's. Part of the reason for this electoral upheaval was the modest success in 1894 of the People's party in temporarily wooing away a substantial number of normally Democratic voters, especially in the state's industrial cities. Just over half the party's total vote of 25,604 in the gubernatorial race was cast in the cities of Milwaukee, Sheboygan, Racine, and La Crosse; some 35 per cent of it was in Milwaukee, where nearly one-fifth of the voters cast People's ballots for governor. Worse than the People's party for the Democrats was their strategy of substituting the anti-Catholic American Protective Association for the Bennett Law, which had brought German Catholics and Protestants together in 1890 and 1892. This gambit held most Catholics in line, but not German Lutherans, who feared the Catholic church more than they did the APA. Most important of all to the Democratic loss was the success of Republicans in blaming both the national and state Democratic administrations for the depression, and for the timidity and ineffectiveness of the administrations' efforts to provide relief and recovery.[36]

Almost equally portentous for Republicans was a political coup involving railroad passes pulled off by Hall during the 1895 spring elections. Initially he failed to convince his party of the wisdom of conducting a referendum on railroad passes, so he took matters into his own hands. Hall paid for the printing of referendum ballots, distributed them at caucuses around the state, then lobbied for the measure. When the votes were counted, more than 50,000 favored abolition of the passes, with less than 1,000 opposed. This ploy greatly enhanced Hall's reputation and demonstrated the overwhelming grass-roots support for this key measure on his agenda. Nevertheless, it took three more legislative sessions before the proposal was enacted.[37]

The legislature produced by the 1894 Republican landslide bore out the adage that the more things change, the more they remain

---

[36] Wyman, "Voting Behavior in the Progressive Era," 117–202; Jensen, *Winning of the Midwest*, 209–237; Kleppner, *Cross of Culture*, 179–368; Brye, *Wisconsin Voting Patterns*, 174–181; James R. Donoghue, *How Wisconsin Voted, 1848–1960* (Madison, 1962), 49–50, 71–73.

[37] Barton, *La Follette's Winning of Wisconsin*, 99–101; Thelen, *New Citizenship*, 234; Acrea, "Wisconsin Progressivism," 167–168, 252–256; Younce, "The Political Conditions in Wisconsin," 315–323. The ratings are Acrea's.

the same. The depletion of Democratic ranks spelled an end to the bipartisan coalition of 1893. The remaining Democrats represented primarily German areas in the eastern third of Wisconsin and in Marathon County; only two members of the Democrats' assembly contingent could reasonably be considered "progressive," as rated by Kenneth Acrea in his study. The new Republican majority was markedly more reform-minded than its predecessor, in the sense that it favored an active response to demands for social change. Acrea also finds that the assemblymen from Grant, Crawford, Vernon, La Crosse, Dunn, and Chippewa counties were "strongly progressive," while those from Wood, Portage, Adams, Waukesha, and Marquette counties were "slightly progressive." There were also four new Republicans of Scandinavian descent, all of whom were reformers from the western part of the state.

On the other hand, most of the newcomers lacked legislative experience, while the party's conservative war horses still controlled the major committees of both houses. As a result, the 1895 legislature passed a few more reform measures than its predecessors, but most dealt with "soft" progressive issues such as increased state support for education and charitable institutions and a revival of the state board of immigration. On "hard" progressive issues such as tax reform, railroad regulation, and labor protection, there were not nearly enough militant reformers to carry the day. Even many of those who voted with the Republican reformers two-thirds of the time regularly helped to block more drastic measures that struck at the heart of the conservative alliance with big business.[38]

Led by Senator James H. Stout, the 1895 legislature mandated a study of the state school code, gave the state superintendent authority to set standards for manual education and to overhaul educational requirements for county superintendents, authorized construction of a joint library for the university and the state historical society, and created a fund for county teachers' institutes. It rejected, however, efforts to expand normal school programs, to establish agricultural experiment stations in northwestern Wisconsin, and to start campus-based institutes for the scientific study of socio-economic programs. It also acted on environmental issues, appointing a commission to study the feasibility of state parks and charging state wardens with the responsibility of preventing forest fires. But it failed to take any action against the sawdust pollution of rivers by lumber companies. In response to urging by Governor Upham, the legislature established the State Board of Arbitration and Conciliation to handle labor disputes. (Its inadequacy was quickly revealed during the protracted

---

[38] Acrea, "Wisconsin Progressivism," 195–211.

1896 strike against The Milwaukee Electric Railway and Light Co., when the corporation refused arbitration.) Pushed by Theodore Prochnow, a German immigrant Republican assemblyman (and former People's party figure) from Milwaukee, the legislature also enacted laws prohibiting the blacklisting of strikers, mandating weekly payment of wages, and requiring a full train crew on all runs.[39]

The 1895 legislature also demonstrated a not especially productive interest in state public service. It passed a weakened bill to regulate public grain elevators, provided funds to the State Board of Health for cholera control, authorized the distribution of UW Dean of Agriculture William A. Henry's handbook for settlers in the Cutover, and established the office of bank examiner. It failed to take positive action on good roads, certification of water sources, vaccination of children, boiler inspection, a geological and natural history survey, a commissioner of state medical examiners, a waterways commission, and a measure to permit the state insurance commissioner to issue building insurance to private citizens. In the area of business regulation, the legislature banned filled cheese, dairy products adulterated by antiseptics, and colored oleomargarine; but it failed to outlaw lumber company stores or fix railroad passenger rates. It also refused to enact any railroad measures, although support for them increased somewhat. While providing for the care of drunkards and drug addicts as sick people, and establishing a state home for mentally defective persons, the legislature also insisted that all recipients of state aid must work if they were able. In general, most legislators exhibited more concern for the maintenance of welfare facilities than for the condition of their inmates.[40]

The most controversial measures considered by the 1895 legislature involved tax and election reform. The assembly refused to pass a bill sponsored by Albert Hall to increase railroad license fees and to conduct a systematic evaluation of railroad property. Although the assembly concurred with his proposals to establish a temporary state tax commission and levy a tax on express companies, the senate adamantly continued to hold the line against tax revision. Lobbyists for the state's street railway and electric lighting utilities pulled off a coup in 1895. They succeeded in adding utilities to the list of those paying relatively innocuous state license fees, thus exempting their clients from paying local taxes. This led progressive Republicans and the Milwaukee Municipal League to collaborate in efforts to repeal the license-fee tax and to tax utilities on the value of their property. The legislature in 1895 was under pressure to open up the nomination and electoral processes, and accordingly granted women the right to

---

[39] *Ibid.*, 153–161; Thelen, *New Citizenship*, 80–81, 263–265.
[40] Acrea, "Wisconsin Progressivism," 161–164.

vote in school board elections and reestablished the system of caucuses and conventions in Milwaukee County, requiring preliminary meetings of electors to nominate delegates and candidates who were then voted upon at the caucus. It also passed a civil service law for Milwaukee city employees, which electric railway executive Henry Clay Payne felt obliged to support in order to avoid greater challenges. And the legislature enacted a compromise corrupt-practices law that provided no enforcement machinery and divided the measure's staunchest supporters. Tougher bills about voter participation in the nomination process and certain corrupt election practices were tabled in the senate. Finally, the legislature enacted a very general statute forbidding racial discrimination in publications. On balance, the 1895 legislative session was one of reasonably substantive achievements, and one that held much promise for the future.[41]

[4]

Few elections in Wisconsin history rival that of 1896, either in immediate impact or long-term consequences. It climaxed the Republican trend launched in 1894 and inaugurated forty years of Republican supremacy. The party's presidential and gubernatorial candidates, William McKinley and Edward Scofield, each received 60 per cent of Wisconsin's total vote, an improvement of almost 12 per cent over 1888, the last pre-Bennett Law election. The Republican margin in the assembly mushroomed to 91–8; in the senate, to 29–4. Unlike earlier realignments, that of 1896 affected every significant ethno-cultural, socio-economic, and geographical segment of the population, and moreover it proved much more enduring. For the Democratic coalition, the presidential candidacy of William Jennings Bryan was a disaster.[42]

Equally momentous was the shift in the logic of voting and political affiliation that came about in 1896—a shift that continued to grow over the next two decades. The previous balance of ethno-cultural politics was significantly upset by the continuing depression which cut across ethnic boundaries. Although the partisan alignment established in 1896 continued to be ethnic and religious in nature, it grew less so as time wore on. The 1896 election marked the start of an

---

[41] *Ibid.*, 164–181; Thelen, *New Citizenship*, 192–194, 215–218; Schumacher, "Direct Primary in Wisconsin," 12–13; Lovejoy, *La Follette and the Direct Primary*, 23–31; Spahr, "Wisconsin Primary Election Law," 21–31.

[42] Wyman, "Voting Behavior in the Progressive Era," 117–212; Kleppner, *Cross of Culture*, 179–368; Jensen, *Winning of the Midwest*, 269–308; Brye, *Wisconsin Voting Patterns*, 181–210; Donoghue, *How Wisconsin Voted*, 50–51, 72–74.

inexorable erosion of traditional ethno-cultural politics and marked the first halting steps towards a politics based more upon ideology and class and socio-economic divisions. This journey would not end until well after the Progressive Era, but its first stages significantly improved the chances of reformist candidates, besides advancing socio-economic and ideological issues.[43]

With Democrats virtually absent from the 1897 legislature, factionalism inevitably flowered within the majority Republican ranks. The reform faction had already attained sufficient strength to guarantee that bringing up its agenda for consideration would constitute the session's most important business. Reformers, however, were in the minority, especially on controversial economic and political proposals, and party regulars maintained their hold on the most important committees and positions. As in previous sessions, conflicts over taxation, expansion of state public services, business regulation, and election reform were the most momentous. Greater consideration of broader, statewide measures continued apace. Led by James H. Stout, chairman of the senate education committee, the legislature increased financial support for the university, the normal schools, the historical society, and the joint library project. It expanded aid to traveling and school libraries, and approved a university summer course in library science. It authorized counties to establish normal schools for training rural school teachers and it expanded state aid and authorized accreditation for high school programs in manual training and agricultural education. Some education efforts failed—especially those to establish a teachers' pension fund and to create a state board of supervisors to replace the county superintendents of education. In the area of conservation, the 1897 legislature established the Geological and Natural History Survey and a commission to plan for a state forestry department. A renewed attempt to codify the fish and game laws resulted in gains for statewide uniformity.[44]

Despite increased pressure from organized labor and its allies, the legislature tabled a wide range of labor bills, including one which would have regulated child and women's labor, prohibited "yellow dog" contracts, put ceilings on work hours, and dealt with working conditions in factories. A single modest gain granted the new arbitration board the power to initiate its own investigations. Except for the passage of a couple of minor good roads bills and the establishment of a semi-official state agriculture board, legislation to expand public services got short shrift.

---

[43] Wyman, "Voting Behavior in the Progressive Era," 202–232; Kleppner, *Cross of Culture*, 369–376; Jensen, *Winning of the Midwest*, 269–308; Kleppner, *Third Electoral System*, 357–382; Plumb, *Badger Politics*, 110–114.
[44] Acrea, "Wisconsin Progressivism," 296–302.

Measures dealing with business regulation, too, had a rough road, with Governor Scofield generally wielding his influence and veto power in opposition to the progressives' agenda. However, the legislature did extend state regulatory authority over physicians, pharmacists, and other providers of health care; prevent mergers by noncompetitive railroads; enforce the payment of claims against life and fire insurance companies; revise the 1895 banking code; and draft a similar code for building and loan associations. Albert Hall got his proposal to appoint a commission to investigate railroad finances through the legislature, but only in weakened form. His pet railroad commission and anti-pass bills were tabled, after spirited debate, but Hall managed to achieve a limit of three cents per mile on passenger fares charged by the larger railroads. Hall's bill to enact an inheritance tax also failed to pass. The governor vetoed a proposal to regulate the hours and cleanliness of bakeries, as well as an attempt to strengthen the antitrust law; eventually he signed a watered-down version of the antitrust bill. The railroad committee quashed measures to raise the license-fee tax on street railways and to prevent freight rate discrimination by railroads.[45]

As state revenues declined, efforts to reform the tax system grew more intense. The results were mixed. The legislature levied minor taxes on gasworks, electric light and power companies, life insurance companies' surpluses gained on fixed premiums, and mortgages. It permitted local governments to levy small taxes on businesses and authorized an emergency state assessment to avoid dependence upon the early payment of corporate taxes. But none of these did much to resolve the state's revenue crisis, or to satisfy demands for tax equity. The legislature's most presaging action was the creation of a temporary state commission charged with recommending revisions in the tax system. Even though reformers failed to achieve repeal of the 1895 law allowing utilities to get by with license-fee taxes, they succeeded in tripling the tax. They also prevented the state's water companies from taking refuge under the license-fee tax, insisting upon taxing corporate property in the same manner as private property. Led by Jim Davidson, progressive Republicans won restoration of *ad valorem* taxation to sleeping car, freight line, and railway equipment companies; but Governor Scofield then vetoed the bill. An uproar arose, forcing Republicans to pledge reenactment of the Davidson bill in their 1898 platform.[46]

---

[45] *Ibid.*, 302–310; Thelen, *New Citizenship*, 33–34, 77, 97, 119–121; Campbell, *Representative Democracy*, 91–94, 163–166.

[46] Acrea, "Wisconsin Progressivism," 311–314; Thelen, *New Citizenship*, 40, 204–208, 276–307; Campbell, *Representative Democracy*, 70–71. To understand the wider context involved in the taxation conflicts of the 1890's, see W. Elliot Brownlee, Jr.,

Pressure for electoral reform, too, yielded gains in the 1897 legislature. Many of the organizations that had previously advocated nonpartisan elections converted to advocating regulated partisanship, while the La Follette faction announced its support for direct primaries. The result was the passage of the Mills Law, which required state regulation of caucuses outside Milwaukee County and guaranteed voters protection by means of a secret ballot. The law was essentially a compromise between insurgent "Half-Breeds" and conservative "Stalwarts" in the Republican fold. (Cynics called it a "masterpiece of obfuscation," for it left the selection of candidates largely to party leaders.) The same could fairly be said of the legislature's corrupt practices act, which was characterized by one contemporary national expert as "relatively rudimentary." Its major provision called for the reporting of campaign receipts and expenditures. A related attempt to require the registration of lobbyists, headed by George Bryant, went down to defeat. Solidly backed by the Milwaukee Municipal League, reformers did succeed in extending civil service coverage to police and fire departments outside Milwaukee.[47]

The elections of 1898 accelerated both Republican hegemony and internal party factionalism. Angered by Scofield's liberal use of the veto, and by the intransigence of the regular Republican leadership, three groups of Half-Breeds formed a loose coalition during the Republican caucuses and conventions. The first consisted of reformist legislators, led by Albert Hall and others from the western half of the state, whose agenda had defined the legislative battles of the decade. The second consisted mostly of the members of the Republican Club of Milwaukee County, whose platform of electoral reform, tax revision, and business regulation largely complemented the agrarian reformers' platform. The third consisted of the followers of Robert M. La Follette, who were determined to take control of the GOP from the business-oriented triumvirate of Philetus Sawyer, John Coit Spooner, and Henry Clay Payne. They had only lately embraced some of the key issues, such as the direct primary and the abolition of railroad passes, that had achieved prominence through the efforts of Hall and his allies. These three factions formed a loose coalition around La Follette, who had begun his campaign to wrest the gubernatorial nomination from Scofield. The governor's problems multiplied when

---

Progressivism and Economic Growth: The Wisconsin Income Tax, 1911–1929 (Port Washington, New York, 1974), and John O. Stark, "The Establishment of Wisconsin's Income Tax," in *WMH*, 71 (Autumn, 1987), 27–45.

[47]Acrea, "Wisconsin Progressivism," 316–318; Thelen, *New Citizenship*, 192–194, 215–218, 307–308; Schumacher, "Direct Primary in Wisconsin," 13; Plumb, *Badger Politics*, 114–115.

Hall revealed that Scofield had used his railroad franking privileges to ship personal effects from his home in Oconto during 1897— including "one cow (crated)." The governor's abuse of this privilege made the crated-cow phrase a rallying cry to unify the three factions behind La Follette. However, the old guard held fast. After a brief and bitter campaign, Scofield secured the Republican renomination for governor, though only by endorsing several progressive planks which were unsavory to him, and by accepting some running mates favored by the insurgents.[48]

Outwardly, the 1898 election had all the hallmarks of a Republican landslide, since the entire state ticket was swept into office. In the legislature, Republicans won an 81–19 advantage in the assembly and an incredible 31–2 edge in the senate. But there were indications of change afoot. Scofield's total vote had declined by over 90,000 from 1896, and his share of the vote fell by more than 7 per cent. Moreover, he ran about 7,000 votes behind the rest of the state ticket, and his greatest losses occurred in counties where progressive sentiment was strongest. Scofield lost 1,000 votes in Milwaukee County, 600 in La Follette's Dane County, and several hundred each in Adams and Vernon counties. In five of the state's most heavily Norwegian towns, the gap between Scofield and the rest of the Republican ticket exceeded 15 per cent. Since Norwegians were both the most loyal Republican ethnics in the state and the core ethnic group in La Follette's coalition, their defections speak volumes about what happened in 1898— and about what was to occur in the near future.[49]

Given this background, it is hardly surprising that the 1899 legislature quickly became an internecine battlefield between Stalwart and Half-Breed Republicans. The session served as a preview of the next three decades. The Half-Breeds won their share of victories, enacting several key pieces of legislation which foreshadowed the Progressive Era. Despite this, La Follette's law partner Gilbert Roe dismissed the 1899 legislature as no different from any other. Its actual nature, however, was far more complicated and ambiguous. In retrospect, it seems plausible to view the Wisconsin legislature of 1899 as the first of the Progressive Era, rather than the last of the Gilded Age.

As seen from the legislative floor, there was far more difference between 1899 and 1893 than there would be between 1899 and 1901. Most of the major issues that would energize and polarize the legislatures of 1901–1905 had already been vigorously contested during several previous sessions; these same issues constituted the agenda

---

[48] Wyman, "Political Behavior," 242–247; Plumb, *Badger Politics*, 116; "The Jersey and the Law," in *Wisconsin Then and Now*, 1 (September, 1954), 6–7.

[49] Wyman, "Political Behavior," 247–249; Brye, *Wisconsin Voting Patterns*, 181–210; Donoghue, *How Wisconsin Voted*, 50–52, 72–74.

for the Stalwart-versus-Half-Breed conflict of 1899. Perhaps more importantly, by the end of the decade, the trend towards direct intervention by state government had gained irresistible momentum. Most of the debates between party regulars and Half-Breeds in 1899 were over the scope and character of government involvement, not over its necessity or desirability. To be sure, government intervention had not yet attained the status of a panacea; but it had established itself in the collective legislative psyche as an almost indispensable ingredient of any viable policy.[50]

By far the two greatest areas of controversy in 1899 were tax reform and electoral revision. The temporary tax commission appointed in 1897 presented its recommendations early in the session. It proposed a permanent commission with comprehensive investigatory power to study the merits of *ad valorem* taxation of railroads; temporarily raising, and eventually abolishing, the railroad license-fee levy; taxation of corporations and individuals at the same rates; and enactment of an inheritance tax. Of the legislature's responses, the most positive was at last to pass Hall's inheritance tax bill—only to have the state supreme court invalidate it. The legislature also agreed to extend the life of the temporary tax commission, partly because its modest recommendations had assuaged most of the fears of both moderates and conservatives. The legislature enacted a new license-fee system for taxing insurance companies, as well as measures to remove express, sleeping car, freight line, and railroad equipment companies from the license-fee tax shelter. The new fees were too modest to arouse much opposition—or to raise any substantial revenue.

The bill to increase the license-fee tax paid by the insurance companies was introduced by Assemblyman Philo Orton of Darlington, who accused the insurance industry's lobbyists of being "as smooth as razors dipped in oil and as sharp." The major effect of the measure was to raise the tax bill of the state's largest insurance company, the Northwestern Life Insurance Company of Milwaukee, from $35,000 to $224,000—an amount comparable to the University of Wisconsin budget. The railroad tax package, known as the Whitehead bill after senate tax committee chairman John Whitehead of Janesville, was part of a design by business-oriented conservatives to stave off the *ad valorem* taxation of railroads, public utilities, and other industries. In exchange, the Stalwarts succeeded in tabling proposals to raise railroad license fees and to tax the stock of guaranty, trust, and annuity corporations, while accepting somewhat broader applications of the license-fee tax on street railway and electric lighting utilities.

Overall, the 1890's taxation crusade established important prece-

---

[50] Acrea, "Wisconsin Progressivism," 328–333; Plumb, *Badger Politics*, 117–118.

dents. It forced some affluent individuals and corporations to pay delinquent taxes, initiated *ad valorem* taxation of sleeping car and express companies, increased taxes on other non-railroad public utilities and insurance companies, enacted a short-lived inheritance tax, and established a state commission with significant potential for effecting a real tax revolution.[51]

Moves towards the adoption of the direct primary did not fare as well. La Follette and the Republican Club of Milwaukee County had joined Hall and his coalition in pressing for the direct primary, but they failed, pointing up the fact that the opponents of electoral reform still controlled much of the legislative process. Still, the legislative reformers of the 1890's could draw some satisfaction from their enactment of civil service laws, the regulation of party caucuses, and their partial success in making it more difficult for corporate lobbyists to control caucuses and conventions.[52]

There is little doubt that the substantive issues, techniques, and rhetoric of the 1897 and 1899 legislatures were similar in many respects to those that followed. This was especially true in labor legislation. New laws limited child labor, required safety devices on certain machinery, increased employer liability for railroad workers, required weekly or semi-weekly payment of wages in cash, regulated employment bureaus, established a board of arbitration, prohibited the blacklisting of union members and the hiring of private armies by employers, and legitimized the union label—all in all, establishing a trend that would continue throughout the Progressive Era.

However, the relatively modest amount of actual reform legislation, even though it framed the key elements of later reform agendas, also demonstrated the limits imposed by the prevailing political order. Lacking the leadership of a dynamic and powerful chief executive, a man who could effectively advance himself as the champion of substantial reform, there was no one who could generate sufficient popular pressure or mobilize and discipline a critical mass of legislators. The small achievements, the promises, even the frustrations of the 1899 legislature, taken altogether, greatly enhanced the appeal of a new, issue-oriented, candidate-centered politics capable of producing such a leader, and of providing him with a clear mandate.[53]

---

[51] Acrea, "Wisconsin Progressivism," 315–316; Thelen, *New Citizenship*, 204–210 (Orton quote), 276, 307. In Acrea's opinion, the 1899 tax reform measures had only "symbolic value."

[52] Acrea, "Wisconsin Progressivism," 316–320; Thelen, *New Citizenship*, 215–218, 307–308; Schumacher, "Direct Primary in Wisconsin," 13. Acrea (p. 334) concludes, correctly, that "the promise of the future was fulfilled with the methods of the past, and the line of continuity was not broken between the two."

[53] Acrea, "Wisconsin Progressivism," 328–334; Thelen, *New Citizenship*, 119–120, 307–308.

10

The Advent of La Follette

[1]

THE emergence of Robert M. La Follette as the recognized leader of a progressive Republican movement to which he was a conspicuously late convert was the product of a complex process of adaptation and growth. In his autobiography, written in 1913 at the zenith of the Progressive Era, La Follette insists that he had been a progressive from the time "when I was boy" who read "a dog-eared copy of one of Henry George's early books." Even on the family farm during the 1870's, he contends, "I heard and felt this movement of the Grangers swirling about me; and I felt the indignation which it expressed in such a way that I suppose I have never fully lost the effect of that early impression."

Supposedly, these early convictions were reinforced by the speeches of Edward G. Ryan, chief justice of the Wisconsin Supreme Court and author of the decision upholding the Potter railroad regulation law, and by a celebration of human freedom uttered by the brilliant agnostic orator Robert G. Ingersoll. La Follette's liberal outlook was broadened and deepened by his education at the University of Wisconsin during the presidency of John Bascom, whom La Follette hails as "the guiding spirit of my time, and the man to whom Wisconsin owes a debt greater than it can ever pay." It was from Bascom that La Follette claims to have derived his lifelong appreciation for the social forces that were transforming state and nation in the late nineteenth century, and for the spirit of social responsibility and public service that soon was to form the essence of "the Wisconsin Idea."[1]

---

[1] Robert M. La Follette, *La Follette's Autobiography: A Personal Narrative of Political Experiences* (Madison, 1913; reprinted, 1960), 3–16. The story of La Follette's rise to the governorship has been told so many times that the major people and events are well-known. Until the 1960's, it was told largely by people close to or strongly sym-

By the same token, La Follette asserts in his autobiography that he distinguished himself as an opponent of machine politics as early as 1881, when he revolted against the Republican "boss" of Dane County, Elisha W. Keyes. In discussing his three terms in the House of Representatives (1885–1891), La Follette presents himself as a champion of Native Americans and a forthright opponent of "pork barrel" legislation, even when it might have benefited his own district. He avows that he never "derived benefit from the two sources of power by which machine politics chiefly thrives—I mean patronage, the control of appointments to office, and the use of large sums of money in organization." And he glories in his claim that he "never used railroad passes while . . . a member of Congress, nor at any other time while I held a public office." In summing up his congressional career, which he views as a continuous crusade against private economic interests that sought to control the legislative process, La Follette proclaims that "in several instances, and in a limited way, I tried to fight against them—singly." His decade-long campaign to gain the Republican nomination for governor was a time in which he built upon his already well-established and carefully nurtured progressivism. It was then that he founded a movement of "the people" against "the interests" and "the machine." To an astonishing degree, his own interests coincided with the public good. Unabashedly, he counts every personal gain in that quest as a victory for popular and just government, every setback as the result of fraud and bribery perpe-

---

pathetic towards La Follette and his movement: his own *Autobiography*; the biography written by his wife and daughter (Belle Case La Follette and Fola La Follette), *Robert M. La Follette* (2 vols., New York, 1953); Albert O. Barton, *La Follette's Winning of Wisconsin* (Madison, 1922); the various articles written by Lincoln Steffens, chiefly his chapter on Wisconsin in his *The Struggle For Self-Government* (New York, 1906) and his article, "Enemies of the Republic: Wisconsin: A State Where the People Have Restored Representative Government—The Story of Governor La Follette," in *McClure's Magazine*, October, 1904, pp. 564–579. Only a few political opponents, most notably Stalwart Republican Emanuel L. Philipp, challenged La Follette's account as self-serving or contrived, but their writings had little apparent influence on scholarly or popular interpretations. Most writers seem to have accepted the account in the *Autobiography*. Not until the early 1960's did professional historians begin to subject that version to analysis and criticism: David P. Thelen, *The Early Life of Robert M. La Follette, 1855–1884* (Chicago, 1966) and *The New Citizenship: Origins of Progressivism in Wisconsin, 1885–1900* (Columbia, Missouri, 1972); Herbert F. Margulies, *The Decline of the Progressive Movement in Wisconsin* (Madison, 1968); Stanley P. Caine, *The Myth of a Progressive Reform: Railroad Regulation in Wisconsin, 1903–1910* (Madison, 1970); Roger E. Wyman, "Voting Behavior in the Progressive Era: Wisconsin as a Case Study" (doctoral dissertation, University of Wisconsin, 1970); and Kenneth C. Acrea, Jr., "Wisconsin Progressivism: Legislative Response to Social Change, 1891 to 1909" (doctoral dissertation, University of Wisconsin, 1968). I have tried in this chapter to reconcile and synthesize these disparate accounts in a manner consistent with the public record.

trated by a powerful cabal of business tycoons and stalwart Republican politicians.[2]

With the exception of brief discussions of Albert Hall's contributions, La Follette makes no mention in his autobiography of the important role played by reformist legislators during the 1890's. He frankly acknowledges that he had never heard of the direct primary before 1897, but he credits no particular individual or group for educating him about that issue to which he owed so much of his later success and celebrity. Beyond naming a few men who became integral members of his organization, he pays homage to only a few anonymous, generic categories of supporters: university men, officeholders, bureaucrats, journalists, and "progressives." Although he concludes the discussion of his pre-gubernatorial career with the injunction that "*we* entered upon the campaign of 1900 . . . in which *we* were destined to be finally victorious, with great enthusiasm," the chosen pronoun seems more imperial than plural.[3]

In fact, La Follette's political odyssey was far more complex and instructive than he admits. "Fighting Bob" may have been a consistent progressive from the onset of his political consciousness, but there is precious little evidence of this in the public record prior to 1897. By the time he began to profess a few concrete measures of the reformist agenda, such as the direct primary and *ad valorem* taxation of railroads, he had already exhibited a multifaceted persona, composed of several elements that often coexisted uneasily.

Born on June 14, 1855, on a farm in the Town of Primrose in Dane County, twenty-five miles southwest of Madison, Robert Marion La Follette was the youngest of five children. His parents had arrived in Wisconsin in 1850 by way of Indiana. (Their son was destined to become the state's first Wisconsin-born governor.) Although his father died when he was only eight months old, young Robert imbibed generously of the political and civic activism of his paternal French Huguenot relatives, as well as of the dedication to formal education modeled by his mother's Scottish family. As a young boy, he was outgoing and exuberant, mixing easily with the children of his predominantly Norwegian neighbors and readily adapting to their culture and folkways. Growing up as he did during the Civil War, he nurtured a fierce allegiance to the Republican party as the savior of the Union, as well as a passionate hostility towards Democrats, whom he knew as "copperheads" and "traitors."[4]

---

[2] La Follette, *Autobiography*, 17–97 (quotes on 31, 39).
[3] *Ibid.*, 77–97 (quote on 97; emphasis added).
[4] Thelen, *Early Life of La Follette*, 4–12; Thelen, *New Citizenship*, 292–296; La Follette and La Follette, *La Follette*, 1–12. For an interpretation of La Follette as a "political prophet" who combined moralism with political skill and savvy, see John Milton Coo-

His mother remarried in 1862. Her new husband was a strict disciplinarian and religious fundamentalist twenty-five years her senior. Her youngest son, strong-willed and extroverted, grew increasingly rebellious. He learned to harbor a powerful aversion towards older authority figures who wielded their power arbitrarily, which inclined the young boy away from organized religion, especially since his stepfather frequently insisted that his idealized biological father was roasting in hell for his agnosticism. This aversion also engendered in him a strong moralistic streak that colored his perception of people who opposed him and of ideas that opposed his own. He was deeply devoted to his mother and his siblings, and he committed himself to the ideal of a close-knit family protecting its members against a hostile world outside, a dream that he later strove to actualize with his own wife and children. Although the La Follette farm was relatively prosperous (and therefore atypical of those worked by Grangers and Populists), young Robert reveled in hard work to support himself, while pursuing formal education to better himself. He burned hot and bright. Throughout his adult life, La Follette's predisposition towards excessive exertion in pursuit of his ambitions would periodically drive him to exhaustion, necessitating a substantial period of recuperation.

In the fall of 1873, nurturing her son's ambition, Bob's mother moved to Madison, took in student boarders, then sold some of her land in 1875 to help him enroll in his first class at the University of Wisconsin that fall. The twenty-year-old freshman was imbued with a strong appetite for work and a keen dedication to upward mobility, leavened with a "natural sociability." But La Follette was not a great success as a student. Indeed, his undergraduate academic record was so undistinguished that he received his bachelor of science degree in 1879 only because President Bascom cast a tie-breaking vote to end a spirited debate during the June faculty meeting where all faculty members voted to award degrees. Apparently the charismatic president felt that the young man's natural intelligence, ambition, popularity, and extracurricular activities outweighed his mediocre academic record. The admiration was mutual, although it seems likely that the student was as much attracted by Bascom's moralistic rhetoric as by his admonitions in favor of social justice and civic responsibility. La Follette was much less taken by the university's most progressive-minded faculty member, the classicist and historian William Francis Allen.[5]

---

per, Jr., "Robert M. La Follette: Political Prophet," in *WMH*, 69 (Winter, 1985–1986), 91–105.

[5] Thelen, *Early Life of La Follette*, 12–20; Thelen, *New Citizenship*, 292–296; Bernard A. Weisberger, *The La Follettes of Wisconsin: Love and Politics in Progressive America* (Madison, 1994), 3–23; Carroll P. Lahman, "Robert Marion La Follette as Public Speaker

La Follette's real major was not the scientific curriculum he opted for, but extracurricular activities, especially oratory, dramatics, and journalism. One classmate later remembered him as "chairman of the undergraduate greeters." His greatest achievement occurred in his senior year, when, after a strenuous campaign to represent the University of Wisconsin, he won a six-state oratorical contest at the University of Iowa. Carried around the city on the shoulders of an ecstatic student body, the young orator experienced a foretaste of political celebrity. It was a heady moment.

La Follette was enterprising almost to a fault in those days. He borrowed money to become publisher of the privately run student newspaper, the *University Press*, where he excelled at soliciting advertising and earned enough money to help support his mother while putting himself through school. The paper's editorial policies were strictly mainstream, and its pages contained paeans to self-made men, middle-class virtues, and, of course, the Republican party. As editor and student leader, La Follette assisted moderately in the battle to curb the influence of fraternities in campus politics—one of the few instances early in his adult life where he clearly identified himself with "the people" against "special interests." On the other hand, he was particularly vitriolic in diatribes against the "tramps" produced by the depression of 1873–1877. In short, La Follette was energetic, prominent, and successful in the student milieu, but he was far from being a radical. According to the most careful student of La Follette's early life, David P. Thelen, his college experiences "may have had a latent effect," but it seems more probable that they "became 'progressive' to him only after he discovered progressive ideas fifteen years later."[6]

Admitted to the bar in 1880, after studying law for less than a year, La Follette that fall secured his first public office: district attorney of Dane County. He subsequently portrayed his election and conduct in office as the first of many triumphs over machine politics, but the reality was far less clear-cut. There is little contemporary evidence to support La Follette's later claim that "Boss" Keyes made any serious effort to prevent his election and re-election. Moreover, the political faction that eventually overthrew Keyes's so-called "Madison Regency" was led by John C. Spooner, Philetus Sawyer, and other promi-

---

and Political Leader, 1855–1905" (doctoral dissertation, University of Wisconsin, 1939), 1–43. La Follette's mother had five children: Ellen, William, Marion (who died young), Josephine, and Robert. She was married and widowed twice by early 1856. Thelen describes the mix of faculty, curriculum, and pedagogy on the Madison campus as intended to "incubate a progressive."

[6]La Follette, *Autobiography*, 12–15; Thelen, *Early Life of La Follette*, 21–50 (quotes on 50, 292); Thelen, *New Citizenship*, 292–293; La Follette and La Follette, *La Follette*, 13–45; Lahman, "Robert Marion La Follette," 44–140.

nent business-oriented Republicans who felt that the Madison postmaster was not energetic enough in promoting the interests of the state's railroads, lumber companies, and manufacturers. Finally, Keyes's successor in Dane County, and La Follette's political mentor, was George E. Bryant, a well-to-do landowner and cattle-breeder whose later conversion to "progressivism" coincided with La Follette's. As district attorney, La Follette honed his skills as a moralistic orator, ruthlessly prosecuting drunks and vagrants and seldom missing an opportunity to use the office as a partisan weapon against Democratic wrongdoers.[7]

As representative from Wisconsin's Second Congressional District between 1885 and 1891, La Follette conceded himself to be "no other than a party regular." He consistently proved himself to be "the steadfast friend of every interest in his district," especially dairymen and tobacco farmers. He championed the cause of the state's dairy farmers against meat packers by supporting a federal ban on the sale of oleomargarine. On the major national issues of the day, such as the tariff, currency, and civil rights, La Follette was, as David Thelen puts it, "like his district, a northern Republican partisan who represented his constituents' views." His discussion of the tariff battles of the 1880's in his autobiography reflects far more La Follette's crucial role in the Payne-Aldrich Tariff battle of 1909 than details about his earlier stance. He developed a personal relationship with Congressman William McKinley of Ohio, who in 1896 became the presidential standard-bearer of regular Republicanism against Populism and Bryanism. However, La Follette also manifested an uncommon sensitivity to the opinions of his constituents, and a corresponding willingness to oppose Republican leadership and orthodoxy if the popular mandate were clear enough. For example, he voted for the Interstate Commerce Act, said that the Sherman Antitrust Act was "one of the most important acts ever conceived," and denounced such pork-barrel legislation as appropriations for rivers and harbors. He also frustrated efforts by Wisconsin lumber barons and railroads to cut timber on Indian lands—an action that could hardly have endeared him to Philetus Sawyer and Henry Clay Payne.[8]

It was during his congressional career that La Follette fused his oratorical and dramatic skills, his sensitivity to popular opinion, and his proclivity for converting economic and political issues into moral ones. Thus he assured his dairy constituents that oleomargarine was

---

[7] Thelen, *Early Life of La Follette*, 51–100; La Follette, *Autobiography*, 17–21; La Follette and La Follette, *La Follette*, 46–52; Lahman, "Robert Marion La Follette," 141–179.

[8] La Follette, *Autobiography*, 41–59; Thelen, *New Citizenship*, 293–294; Weisberger, *La Follettes of Wisconsin*, 23–27.

a "monstrous product of greed and hypocrisy," and gained notoriety for an attack on Democratic Speaker of the House John G. Carlisle during a debate over the protective tariff. La Follette was capable of mercilessly flaying other politicians in public, then greeting them amiably afterward. His blend of oratory, moralistic imagery, and popular appeal was so potent that opponents stigmatized him as a demagogue, a charge that would grow throughout his career. The truth or falsity of that characterization was the major issue of La Follette's re-election campaign in 1888.[9]

As congressman, La Follette says he "worked out a complete plan for keeping my constituents informed on public issues and the record of my services in Congress; it is the system I have used in constantly widening circles ever since." He and his operatives developed "a complete descriptive poll list of my district," and he sent constituents copies of legislation and "hundreds of thousands of speeches, my own and others." Still the consummate undergraduate greeter, he enjoyed working crowds at caucuses, conventions, and county fairs, and seemingly transformed himself when addressing an audience, whether in a courtroom, on a stage or platform, or on the floor of the House of Representatives. Even those in his own party who mistrusted his tendencies to pander to popular sentiment and occasionally to take an independent course valued him for his spellbinding oratory and his ability to draw and hold a crowd—and moreover to mobilize it to political action.[10]

Clearly it is impossible to guess what might have been the course of La Follette's political odyssey had he not been a victim of the Democratic landslide of 1890. His *Autobiography* conveys the distinct impression that he was in the vanguard of those congressmen who had already comprehended the problems associated with the consolidation of wealth and who were turning their attention to the plight of workers and farmers. He cites his support of several key regulatory measures in Congress as evidence that the congressman of the 1880's was the ideological ancestor of the insurgent senator of 1909 and after. However, La Follette also devotes considerable space to demonstrating the significance of his decade-long struggle against the regular Republican organization in Wisconsin from 1894 to 1904, a battle that might never have occurred had he remained in Congress. In particular, he titles the chapter describing the beginning years of that decade as "The Crucial Period of My Public Life," and he treats

---

[9] La Follette, *Autobiography*, 41–59; David P. Thelen, *Robert M. La Follette and the Insurgent Spirit* (Boston, 1976), 1–15 (quote); La Follette and La Follette, *La Follette*, 61–89; Lahman, "Robert Marion La Follette," 180–281.

[10] Thelen, *New Citizenship*, 293–295; La Follette, *Autobiography*, 29–30 (quotes), 41–59; La Follette and La Follette, *La Follette*, 66–67, 81–84.

his response to Philetus Sawyer's alleged bribery attempt in the Republican treasurers' cases as a kind of progressive epiphany. According to La Follette, Sawyer met with him in the parlor of a Milwaukee hotel on September 17, 1891, and offered him money to use his influence with his brother-in-law, Robert G. Siebecker, the presiding judge. As one of the major bail bondsmen in these actions, Sawyer stood to lose a good deal of money, to say nothing of suffering political embarrassment.[11]

La Follette indignantly rejected the offer as an attempted bribe, but Sawyer forever afterward insisted that La Follette misunderstood his intent. La Follette informed Judge Siebecker, who promptly withdrew. When Sawyer, in a newspaper interview, claimed that he had been unaware of La Follette's relationship with Siebecker, and that his offer to retain him as an attorney had been genuine and innocent, La Follette broadcast the facts as he saw them.

The resulting firestorm rendered La Follette persona non grata to all but a few friends, plunging him into a depression from which it took months to recover. He regarded the incident as a turning point in his career, even though he believed that "sooner or later, I probably would have done what I did in Wisconsin." The incident "shocked me into a complete realization of the extreme to which this power that Sawyer represented would go to secure the results it was after." It also forced him to comprehend the sinister pattern and purpose that explained the legislative orientation of the regular Republicans during his congressional career. Thus enlightened, La Follette set himself upon a path to break the power of corrupt influence and to advance representative government.[12]

Despite La Follette's heroic efforts to reconcile his epiphany of 1891 with his claims of life-long progressivism, the result still smacks of rationalization after the fact. If La Follette had indeed always been aware of the corrupt alliance between big business and the Republican machine, it is hard to see why he was so shocked by Sawyer's relatively minor exercise in influence peddling. If that incident really constituted a defining moment for him, finally revealing the breathtaking extent of the alliance, it is difficult to understand why La Fol-

---

[11] Barton, *La Follette's Winning of Wisconsin*, 52–53; La Follette, *Autobiography*, 58–65; La Follette and La Follette, *La Follette*, 95–100; Thelen, *Insurgent Spirit*, 18–19; Lahman, "Robert Marion La Follette," 282–313. For Sawyer's perspective, see Richard N. Current, *Pine Logs and Politics: A Life of Philetus Sawyer, 1816–1900* (Madison, 1950), 255–275, and Ellis Evans, "Philetus Sawyer: A Business Man in Politics" (master's thesis, University of Wisconsin, 1939), 98–115.

[12] La Follette, *Autobiography*, 65–72 (quote on 70); Margulies, *The Decline of the Progressive Movement*, 16–19; Barton, *La Follette's Winning of Wisconsin*, 49–50; Allen F. Lovejoy, *La Follette and the Establishment of the Direct Primary in Wisconsin, 1890–1904* (New Haven, 1941), 23–25; Weisberger, *La Follettes of Wisconsin*, 27–32.

lette waited almost six more years before publicly embracing the reforms supposedly designed to dismantle it. Instead, he pursued the traditional strategy of capturing the organization from the inside, by forging a coalition of discontented Republicans, courting them with promises of recognition, patronage, and other benefits.

Disparities and an abundance of leaders plagued this emerging faction. The state central committee did not even solicit his oratorical services during the 1892 campaign, but La Follette persuaded it otherwise, making numerous speeches on behalf of a state ticket headed by John C. Spooner and masterminded by his sworn enemies Philetus Sawyer and Henry Clay Payne. (He rationalized by insisting that he was only stumping for the national Republican slate headed by President Benjamin Harrison.) What was more, La Follette refused to discuss the Sawyer incident, dismissing demands that he do so as a Democratic ploy. He also made no public outcry when the organization replaced him as Dane County Republican chairman with Spooner's brother. Outwardly calm, outwardly loyal, La Follette played the role of the steadfast party wheelhorse, storing up his resentments for the future.[13]

During what he terms his ensuing "six years struggle with the Wisconsin bosses," La Follette proved himself a veritable genius at traditional politics and coalition building. He crafted an assortment of political outsiders into the most efficient and effective electoral apparatus in the state's history, beginning with a loyal inner circle: his wife Belle, his law partners Sam Harper, Gilbert Roe, and Albert Zimmerman, and his mentor, George E. Bryant. Next came fellow university alumni and students, many of whom became fanatic supporters and some of whom had hopes a victorious La Follette would appoint them to office. Many faculty members joined alumni, especially younger, more socially aware ones, who were impressed by La Follette's concern for their institution and respect for their knowledge. From its inception, the La Follette faction appealed partly along generational lines, enlisting a disproportionate number of youthful, better-educated "men on the make." By 1900, noted Elisha Keyes a bit sourly, "new faces appeared in greater number at the state Republican convention than ever before." He saw them as "young men whose enthusiasm has taken the place of experience." Some of these new faces doubtless shared La Follette's commitment to the Christian-based, socially involved philosophy of university President John Bascom; but his opponents insisted that they were also imbued with less lofty motives. According to the stalwart John Whitehead, La

---

[13] Margulies, *The Decline of the Progressive Movement*, 18–19; La Follette, *Autobiography*, 72–76; Barton, *La Follette's Winning of Wisconsin*, 49–50; La Follette and La Follette, *La Follette*, 104–105; Acrea, "Wisconsin Progressivism," 232–235.

Follette "successfully appealed to these young men on the ground of self-interest, all the while, of course, putting up a show of very great seriousness and solemnity." He encouraged them to seek local offices and promised that, together, "they would break up the old ring and have a chance at the political crib themselves."[14]

Even more interest-based were La Follette's overtures to politicians disgruntled over their treatment by the regular Republican organization. He cultivated the good will of anyone who felt ill-treated or frustrated by Sawyer's, Spooner's, or Payne's decisions about recognition, promotion, or preference. He usually implied that factional leaders might achieve higher office, and that followers might reap some patronage. La Follette's use of clerks, oil and factory inspectors, fair guards and ticket sellers, and game wardens as political operatives soon become legendary. As early as 1894, he boasted to a friend, "[Y]ou ought to take a look at the procession that files up to my office eight o'clock in the morning with petitions and prayers and papers and applications and recommendations." (He hastily added that they were "all right good fellows deserving the best in the shop.")[15]

La Follette's two greatest coups among disaffected Republicans were the dairyman and former governor William Dempster Hoard and Isaac "Uncle Ike" Stephenson, a Marinette lumberman who aspired to the United States Senate. His alliance with Hoard extended back into the 1880's, when La Follette had pressed for federal taxation of oleomargarine and had lent Hoard his poll lists and key advisers for Hoard's gubernatorial campaign. Their mutual antipathy towards Henry Clay Payne strengthened the alliance. Payne had openly lobbied against the oleo tax on behalf of Milwaukee meat packers, and he blamed Hoard's defense of the Bennett Law for the ensuing Republican disaster at the polls. By 1892, La Follette and Hoard were the two most prominent outsiders among the Republican elite. The La Follette-Stephenson collaboration did not come about until 1899, when the ruling triumvirate denied the seventy-year-old

---

[14] La Follette, *Autobiography*, 77–97 (quote on 77); Barton, *La Follette's Winning of Wisconsin*, 19–21, 51–64; Margulies, *The Decline of the Progressive Movement*, 17–22 (quotes); La Follette and La Follette, *La Follette*, 90–95; Thelen, *New Citizenship*, 299–301; Lahman, "Robert Marion La Follette," 314–494. See also David P. Thelen, "Robert La Follette's Leadership, 1891–1896," in *Pacific Northwest Quarterly*, 62 (July, 1971), 97–109; Kenneth Acrea, "Wisconsin's Reform Coalition, 1892–1900: La Follette's Rise to Power," in *WMH*, 57 (Winter, 1973–1974), 123–140; Edward N. Doan, *The La Follettes and the Wisconsin Idea* (New York, 1947), 20–35; and Ralph G. Plumb, *Badger Politics, 1836–1930* (Manitowoc, 1930), 96–121.

[15] Margulies, *The Decline of the Progressive Movement*, 21–23 (quotes), 40–41; Barton, *La Follette's Winning of Wisconsin*, 55–64; Thelen, *New Citizenship*, 299–301; Acrea, "Wisconsin Progressivism," 221–233.

millionaire his elevation to the Senate and instead backed Milwaukee corporate attorney Joseph V. Quarles. Stephenson vowed revenge and the realization of his goal, no matter what the cost. His conversion not only improved the Half-Breed faction's political base but also provided it with an estimated $400,000 in campaign funds over the next decade. Stephenson also purchased the Milwaukee *Evening Wisconsin*, giving the faction an editorial organ in the state's largest metropolitan area.[16]

Hoard's dairying and agricultural connections (he owned and edited *Hoard's Dairyman*) provided La Follette with access to tens of thousands of disciplined voters on Wisconsin farms. So close had their relationship become by 1896 that one reformist editor protested that "Hoard and his man for governor, Mr. La Follette" ought to learn that "there are more momentous issues involved in the present campaign than the dairy cow." Indeed La Follette never allowed anyone to forget that he had grown up a farm boy. He frequently adverted to his rural roots, and he was most comfortable and effective mixing with, or speaking to, farmers at county fairs and College of Agriculture institutes. He traversed rural Wisconsin by horse and carriage, talking to farmers in fields and farmhouses, chatting about the weather and the price of milk, and incidentally soliciting votes and adding names and addresses to his mailing list. His toil paid dividends. By 1896, the Wisconsin Dairymen's Association, *Hoard's Dairyman*, and the *Wisconsin Farmer* all endorsed La Follette as a "friend of the farmer."

In his inaugural message as governor in 1901, La Follette sounded much like William Jennings Bryan when he proclaimed, "Wisconsin is an agricultural State. With comparatively few exceptions her cities are only centers of farm prosperity." From the outset, La Follette depended heavily upon rural voters for electoral support, and they represented the core of his political base during most of his career.[17]

Equally crucial was La Follette's cultivation of Scandinavian, especially Norwegian, politicians and voters. For nearly half a century, Scandinavians had constituted the GOP's most reliable ethnic voting bloc; but as the turn of the century drew nearer, they were growing more discontented with their share of offices and benefits. The dom-

---

[16] Margulies, *The Decline of the Progressive Movement*, 24–25, 31–34, 45–46, 84–95; Barton, *La Follette's Winning of Wisconsin*, 145, 185, 244; La Follette, *Autobiography*, 57, 63, 74, 83, 87–88, 95–99; Thelen, *New Citizenship*, 299–300; Isaac Stephenson, *Recollections of a Long Life, 1829–1915* (Chicago, 1915), 212–222.

[17] Margulies, *The Decline of the Progressive Movement*, 25–26; Thelen, *New Citizenship*, 299–304 (quote); Eric E. Lampard, *The Rise of the Dairy Industry in Wisconsin: A Study in Agricultural Change, 1820–1920* (Madison, 1963), 333–351, 405, 425–428; Governor (1901–1906), Robert La Follette, *Governor's Message*, doc. 1, p. 25, in *Wisconsin Public Documents*, 1899–1900, vol. 1.

inant Yankees had reserved most of the plums for themselves, and tended to take the Scandinavian vote for granted. As a result of the Bennett Law debacle, the leaders of the regular Republicans had become almost obsessed with wooing German Protestant voters away from the Democrats, while ignoring the Scandinavian faithful. The Scandinavians, who viewed Democrats as their mortal enemies, could only pray for a champion who would lead them into power within the existing organization.

Bob La Follette seemed to them a savior. After all, he had been raised among Norwegians and even spoke their language with some fluency. He seemed to be aware that Norwegians dominated or nearly dominated several western counties. In his *Autobiography*, La Follette stresses their strong commitment to democracy and progressive reform even in the old country, a claim for which the evidence is decidedly mixed. It seems more likely that the Scandinavians' mutual status as outsiders, combined with their shared determination to reform or reclaim the Republican party, drew them and La Follette together, at least initially. Whatever the attraction, La Follette consciously promoted his Scandinavian alliance through patronage, by grooming his young law clerk John M. Nelson for future office, and by cementing relations with Nils Haugen, Herman Ekern, "Yim" Davidson, Irvine Lenroot, and other Scandinavian politicians. The bulk of Scandinavians were less affluent farmers in the northwestern quadrant of the state, a factor which further reinforced La Follette's dependence upon rural support.[18]

By 1894, according to Albert O. Barton, La Follette's set himself the goal of taking the governorship out of the hands of the machine. That aim was reinforced by the fact that the Democratic reapportionment of 1891–1893 had virtually dismantled La Follette's former congressional district. He realized that the party leaders would never give him the gubernatorial nomination in 1894, so La Follette persuaded his former congressional colleague, Haugen, the only Republican member of Congress from Wisconsin to survive the 1890 Democratic landslide, to make the race. Haugen's candidacy had potential for melding the two largest segments of La Follette's evolving coalition. As he said, Scandinavian voters "felt a certain national pride in Congressman Haugen's prominence and success, and I counted on their giving him very strong support." What was more, he confided

---

[18] Margulies, *The Decline of the Progressive Movement*, 26–28; Barton, *La Follette's Winning of Wisconsin*, 55–59; Wyman, "Voting Behavior in the Progressive Era," 592–671; La Follette, *Autobiography*, 77–80; Jorgen Wiebull, "The Wisconsin Progressives, 1900–1914," in *Mid-America*, 47(Summer, 1965), 191–221; David L. Brye, "Wisconsin Scandinavians and Progressivism, 1900–1950," in *Norwegian-American Studies*, 27 (1977), 163–193; Thelen, *New Citizenship*, 300–301.

The Advent of La Follette

to Belle, Haugen was bound to be the dairy industry's choice, especially since Hoard distributed 62,500 circulars to WDA members. When Haugen expressed reluctance to leave his House seat, La Follette sent some 1,200 letters to friends and political acquaintances around the state, asking them to urge Haugen to run. The response proved positive, and La Follette finally prevailed by telling Haugen that even though he might lose his congressional seat and at the convention, the cause merited the sacrifice.[19]

La Follette assumed full responsibility for managing Haugen's campaign. He avoided substantive issues and instead used anti-machine rhetoric and ethnic appeals. He achieved a substantial coup by convincing two Norwegian-language newspapers widely read in Wisconsin, the Chicago *Skandinaven* and the Minneapolis *Tidende*, to endorse Haugen. Several prominent legislative progressives, including Hall, Stout, McGillivray, Sanborn, and Dahl also backed Haugen. However, the campaign suffered a setback when Horace A. Taylor, editor of Madison's *Wisconsin State Journal* and La Follette's bitter enemy, announced his candidacy for the Republican nomination. Haugen's earlier support of the Bennett Law and reports that he was sympathetic to the anti-Catholic American Protective Association also hurt him.

After battles in various Republican caucuses, the Haugen forces mustered only about one-third of the votes they needed for the state party convention. Support from Scandinavian regions and rural areas in the northwest was not sufficient. On the sixth ballot, Haugen lost the nomination to William H. Upham, a Marshfield businessman.

Despite the outcome, La Follette professed to be "tremendously enthused and stimulated for the work ahead." His ambition and optimism remained keen, and his skills as a political organizer were growing apace. The nascent progressive faction had learned that antipathy between La Follette and the Stalwart leadership was deep and abiding, that ethno-cultural issues had to be buried, and that the Half-Breeds needed a larger, more solid organization.[20]

---

[19] Barton, *La Follette's Winning of Wisconsin*, 64–67; Margulies, *The Decline of the Progressive Movement*, 28–29; La Follette, *Autobiography*, 77–81; La Follette and La Follette, *La Follette*, 102–109; Evans, "Philetus Sawyer," 115–121. For Haugen's viewpoint, see Nils P. Haugen, *Pioneer and Political Reminiscences* (Evansville, Wisconsin, 1930); Nils P. Haugen, "Pioneer and Political Reminiscences" (Part 6), in *WMH*, 12 (March, 1929), 271–293; and Stuart D. Brandes, "Nils P. Haugen and the Wisconsin Progressive Movement" (master's thesis, University of Wisconsin, 1965).

[20] Barton, *La Follette's Winning of Wisconsin*, 67–68; Margulies, *The Decline of the Progressive Movement*, 29–30; La Follette, *Autobiography*, 77–82 (quote); La Follette and La Follette, *La Follette*, 112–115; Lovejoy, *La Follette and the Direct Primary*, 25–27; Weisberger, *La Follettes of Wisconsin*, 33–34; Acrea, "Wisconsin Progressivism," 234–266; Thelen, "Robert La Follette's Leadership," 101–109; Acrea, "Wisconsin's Reform Coalition," in *WMH*, 57: 135–144.

By 1896, La Follette was ready to make the governor's race in his own right. In 1895, the legislature discontinued the treasurer cases, thus making his charges of the pernicious influence of the corrupt Republican machine more believable and aiding his candidacy. The Stalwarts had come to regard Governor Upham as a political liability, and preferred Edward Scofield instead. Meanwhile, La Follette demonstrated his Republican bona fides by giving a seconding speech for William McKinley at the national convention in St. Louis. Back in Wisconsin, he campaigned successfully enough on his own behalf to arrive at the state party convention in Milwaukee with a plurality of delegate votes. On the first day, La Follette was the leading vote-getter against five other candidates. The next day, quite suddenly, he was defeated by Scofield.

What had transpired during the intervening evening rivaled the Sawyer incident as a lesson in sinister machine politics. According to La Follette, the switch in delegate votes had been accomplished by outright bribery—or so loyalists (who said they had refused bribes) told him, Harper, Bryant, and others. Shortly after midnight, La Follette claimed, Milwaukee GOP boss Charles F. Pfister visited him privately and said that "we've got you skinned," recommended that he "behave" himself and go along with the outcome, and promised that "we will take care of you when the time comes" if he did. Refusing, La Follette went down to defeat as had Haugen, on the sixth ballot. Privately, Sawyer admitted, "I never want to go through so hard a fight again."[21]

Supporters pleaded with him, La Follette said, to run as an independent. Instead he opted to make twenty-five speeches on behalf of McKinley and the Republican ticket and to defend the party's monetary and tariff record against the "radicalism" of William Jennings Bryan. When McKinley, with Spooner's approval, offered him a federal position as comptroller of the currency, La Follette publicly refused, implying that he was spurning yet another Stalwart attempt to buy him off. (Indeed, Belle later wrote, his "refusal of a $6,000 job probably made a more profound impression on Wisconsin citizens than happenings of much greater importance.") While the complete truth of the 1896 convention and of La Follette's refusal of the federal post remain matters of dispute, there is no gainsaying his astuteness

---

[21] Barton, *La Follette's Winning of Wisconsin*, 68–70; Margulies, *The Decline of the Progressive Movement*, 30–32; La Follette, *Autobiography*, 82–85 (quote); Acrea, "Wisconsin Progressivism," 266–275; Current, *Pine Logs and Politics*, 286–292 (quote); Thelen, "Robert La Follette's Leadership," 104–109; Acrea, "Wisconsin's Reform Coalition," in *WMH*, 57: 144–147.

at turning both incidents to his advantage, and weaving them into the folklore of progressive politics.[22]

Behind the scenes, of course, La Follette continued to demonstrate his own skill at the very machine politics he was denouncing in public. Using his friendship with McKinley and his speeches on behalf of the Republican ticket as leverage, La Follette made several trips to Ohio in an attempt to persuade the president-elect to give him a slice of federal patronage. Such a coup would have enabled La Follette to reward many of his followers and expand his power and reputation. But McKinley refused to deviate from the tradition of allowing senators and congressmen to dispense patronage. However, La Follette did succeed in frustrating Payne's ambitions to be appointed postmaster general. La Follette, Haugen, and Hoard countered efforts for Payne by launching a counter-initiative to make Hoard secretary of agriculture. This ploy forced McKinley to reject both Payne and Hoard, thereby enabling La Follette to undercut Payne's stature while gaining Hoard's increased support.[23]

In both 1894 and 1896, the Half-Breeds had avoided taking issue with Republicans' substantive policies. Save for an occasional nod in the direction of Hall's anti-railroad agenda, they had not openly advocated any pathbreaking reforms. They had consciously promulgated such traditional American values as democracy, fair play, and honesty, and railed against the abuse of power by a self-perpetuating, moneyed elite. By La Follette's own account, he had never even heard of the direct primary at the time of his 1896 convention defeat. It was not until he was preparing an address entitled "The Menace of the Machine," to be delivered at the University of Chicago on Washington's birthday in 1897, that he came to understand the advantage of subsuming his personal ambition in favor of a substantive reform agenda with a potential for popular appeal.

In that momentous speech, La Follette described the existing system of caucuses and conventions as tools of a corrupt organization. Only by abolishing the caucus and the convention could the nation

---

[22] La Follette, *Autobiography*, 84–85; Barton, *La Follette's Winning of Wisconsin*, 70–74; Margulies, *The Decline of the Progressive Movement*, 30–32; La Follette and La Follette, *La Follette*, 116–121 (quote); Lovejoy, *La Follette and the Direct Primary*, 27–29; Weisberger, *La Follettes of Wisconsin*, 34.

[23] Margulies, *The Decline of the Progressive Movement*, 33–36; Barton, *La Follette's Winning of Wisconsin*, 79–80; Acrea, "Wisconsin's Reform Coalition," in *WMH*, 57: 145–147; Alfred S. Harvey, "Background of the Progressive Movement in Wisconsin" (master's thesis, University of Wisconsin, 1933), 80–90. For a detailed discussion of Payne's bid for a cabinet position, see Dorothy Ganfield Fowler, "The Federal Influence of Wisconsin, 1880–1907" (doctoral dissertation, University of Wisconsin, 1928), 75–126.

"go back to the first principles of democracy, go back to the people." Only then would every citizen "share equally in the nomination of the candidates of his party and attend primary elections, as a privilege as well as a duty." Only the direct primary, held under the provisions of the general election law, would guarantee that "intelligent, well-considered judgment will be substituted for unthinking enthusiasm."

In the direct primary, La Follette had hit upon the ideal reform issue, an issue that ostensibly elevated his quest for power above the realm of partisanship and ambition, while at the same time providing a mechanism to reward thousands of followers who were denied office by the regular organization. It provided the perfect answer to supporters, especially younger men who were not part of the machine but who wanted a chance for office.[24]

La Follette and his inner circle set out to exploit the direct primary issue, both in the legislature and with the public. He induced Assemblyman William T. Lewis of Racine to introduce a primary election bill in the 1897 legislature. (He later claimed that he realized the bill had no chance of passage, but advocated it as the start of "a long educational campaign to prepare the way for its adoption.") For the public, he and Sam Harper prepared a pamphlet containing his University of Chicago speech, excerpts from positive newspaper reaction, and a summary of Lewis' direct primary bill. They distributed the package throughout the state, as free supplements offered to the editors of local newspapers, obeying Harper's dictum that the pamphlet be touted as nonpartisan so that a paper's political orientation would not predispose editors for or against it. In the late summer of 1897 La Follette also hit the county fair circuit—"following-the-ponies," as he called it—popularizing the direct primary through his oratory.[25]

His speeches rang throughout Wisconsin like a tocsin for change. A Milwaukee *Journal* reporter exclaimed that his "words bite like coals of fire. . . . [A]ll the passions of man, he paints in strong words

---

[24] Ellen Torelle, Albert O. Barton, and Fred L. Holmes, comps., *The Political Philosophy of Robert M. La Follette as Revealed in His Speeches and Writings* (Madison, 1920), 27–29, 53–57 (quote); Barton, *La Follette's Winning of Wisconsin*, 76–92; Margulies, *The Decline of the Progressive Movement*, 36–37; Thelen, *New Citizenship*, 302–309, and *Insurgent Spirit*, 26–29; La Follette and La Follette, *La Follette*, 120; La Follette, *Autobiography*, 85–86; Weisberger, *La Follettes of Wisconsin*, 35; Lahman, "Robert Marion La Follette," appendix, 56–77; Acrea, "Wisconsin Progressivism," 346–348.

[25] Lovejoy, *La Follette and the Establishment of the Direct Primary*, 31–42; Barton, *La Follette's Winning of Wisconsin*, 80–89; Margulies, *The Decline of the Progressive Movement*, 36–37; Thelen, *New Citizenship*, 291–295, 302–307. According to Emanuel L. Philipp, *Political Reform in Wisconsin: A Historical Review of the Subjects of Primary Election, Taxation, and Railway Regulation*, eds., Stanley P. Caine and Roger E. Wyman (Madison, 1973), 16–19, La Follette was indifferent to Lewis' bill, but La Follette "should be given whatever credit is due for the ultimate adoption of the primary system in Wisconsin."

and still stronger gestures. . . . He never wearies and he will not allow his audience to weary." A *Chicago Times-Herald* journalist, writing in September, 1897, attributed La Follette's spellbinding oratory to the fact that he was "essentially democratic in his tastes" and "looks men straight in the eyes and talks to them slowly, deliberately, earnestly. His intense individuality compels magnetic response." B. J. Daly, an Oshkosh Democrat who heard him speak at the Winnebago County fair, was so impressed with La Follette's attack on the Republican party that he said it "convinced me of the man's perfect honesty. . . . Surely, if he is not honest he dissembles well."[26]

At a conclave of Sauk County Republican clubs in Fern Dell (near Mirror Lake) on August 20, 1897, La Follette widened his critique of the political system by exposing the role state corporations played in it. Charging that the corporation had "invaded all departments of business, all activities of life," he stigmatized it as "a machine for making money, demanding of its employees only obedience and service, reducing men to the status of privates in the regular army." Corporate interests were not satisfied with mere economic hegemony; they had captured the Republican party. He demanded a condemnation of "the men who betray it and of the methods by which they control, only to prostitute it to base and selfish ends." He blamed sinister corporate influence during the 1897 legislative session for the defeat of several reform measures, including Jim Davidson's proposal for a tax on corporations, the corrupt campaign practices bill, and Albert Hall's anti-railroad-pass measure. Linking corporate influence directly to machine politics, he insisted that the substitution of the direct primary for the caucus-convention system would destroy both heads of the beast, and "place the nominations directly in the hands of the people." The furious tone of his 1897 oratory provides powerful evidence for Barton's contention that it was during this period that La Follette "discovered himself and developed the master passion to which he was later so unreservedly to give himself."[27]

To persuade those outside the reach of his voice, La Follette engineered the purchase of a Madison newspaper called the *Old Dane* in the fall of 1897. He raised funds through letters to supporters in

---

[26] Barton, *La Follette's Winning of Wisconsin*, 82–92 (quotes); Margulies, *The Decline of the Progressive Movement*, 37–38; La Follette and La Follette, *La Follette*, 122–124; La Follette, *Autobiography*, 86–89; Thelen, *New Citizenship*, 302–307; Lovejoy, *La Follette and the Establishment of the Direct Primary*, 38–41; Lahman, "Robert Marion La Follette," 78–94; Acrea, "Wisconsin Progressivism," 348–355.

[27] Torelle, Barton, and Holmes, comps., *Political Philosophy of La Follette*, 118–119; Barton, *La Follette's Winning of Wisconsin*, 77, 80–81 (quotes); Margulies, *The Decline of the Progressive Movement*, 39–40; La Follette, *Autobiography*, 89–90; Acrea, "Wisconsin's Reform Coalition," in *WMH*, 57: 147–149; Harvey, "Background of the Progressive Movement," 90–109.

five key counties, threatening to withdraw from politics unless they contributed. He changed the name of the paper to *The State* and appointed future Congressman John M. Nelson as its editor. On its masthead, La Follette and Nelson printed their platform, a curious combination of orthodox Republicanism and reformism. They extolled tariff protection, adequate revenues, sound money, economical administration, and character and competency as the criteria for appointing public officials. They also advocated reciprocal trade agreements, equal and just taxation of individuals and corporations, the direct primary, the regulation of legislative lobbyists, and the prohibition of corrupt practices in campaigns and elections.[28]

On July 15, 1898, defying yet another political convention, La Follette announced his intention to run for the governorship, challenging Scofield's bid for a second term. He proclaimed his candidacy in an address which he mailed to hundreds of thousands of eligible voters. He pledged to work for his masthead agenda and took pains to expose Scofield's abuse of the public trust in shipping his cow and other belongings to Madison, making the cow a household joke throughout the campaign.[29]

Another famous address helped La Follette's 1898 campaign, and the direct primary cause. It was a March 12, 1898, speech before the Good Government Club of the University of Michigan in Ann Arbor. In it he described the typical political convention as a mixture of spectacle and conspiracy, and he used sarcasm and hyperbole to make his points. Delegates rushed about in frenzied pursuit of votes and favors and reveled in the carefully orchestrated hoopla, he charged, while party leaders quietly and efficiently made "the deals, and bargains, and trades, and pledges, and promises of appointment . . . that will settle all the business of the convention at the appointed time." When the delegates had completed their scripted roles, the "minority from their quiet corner in the hotel have ruled the great majority of the plain citizens of the state," and the subservient delegates have rushed to the "loaded wagon" for their personal spoils. The only solution, he concluded in a now familiar refrain, was the direct primary, where voter and candidate "must be brought within reaching distance of each other, must stand face to face."

La Follette's elation at the favorable reception accorded his Ann

---

[28] La Follette, *Autobiography*, 90–92; Barton, *La Follette's Winning of Wisconsin*, 111–114; Margulies, *The Decline of the Progressive Movement*, 42; La Follette and La Follette, *La Follette*, 125–125; Lovejoy, *La Follette and the Establishment of the Direct Primary*, 41–42; Acrea, "Wisconsin Progressivism," 356–359.

[29] La Follette, *Autobiography*, 93–94; Robert S. Maxwell, *La Follette and the Rise of the Progressives in Wisconsin* (Madison, 1956), 36; Edward Scofield, *Governor's Message*, doc. 1, p. 10, in *Wisconsin Public Documents*, 1897–1898, vol. 1.

Arbor speech was cut short by the untimely death on March 19 of his law partner, chief adviser, and closest friend, Samuel A. Harper. La Follette remained at Harper's bedside for four days and nights while his friend struggled with pneumonia. "No man," he later wrote, "has ever been so completely a part of my own life." He frequently marked subsequent triumphs by saying, "If Sam could only have lived to see this!"[30]

La Follette declared his candidacy on July 15 and touched off a propaganda war between his maverick organization and the regular Republicans. Both factions set up correspondence bureaus that flooded voters with literature and letters. La Follette's dealt largely with his qualifications and with reforms designed to destroy the alliance between the Stalwarts and the corporations; Scofield's largely defended his administration's record. The Stalwarts' chief newspaper, the *Wisconsin State Journal*, charged that "more money is being spent in behalf of Mr. La Follette than was ever expended on behalf of any man seeking a nomination in the state." The paper wondered where the money came from for *The State*, the speaking tours, the conferences, and the "army of typewriters and clerks ... employed in writing letters and addressing circulars and newspapers." The La Follette forces countered by making public, a week before the state Republican convention, the practice of allowing state employees to draw their pay in advance, with the transactions recorded in an unofficial "doodle-book." The Scofield administration lamely explained that the practice was "customary," but promised to stop it, while charging La Follette with siphoning off state money for his campaign.[31]

La Follette's candidacy received a major boost on July 27, when the newly founded Republican Club of Milwaukee County endorsed him. The organization was composed primarily of prominent Milwaukeeans who opposed Henry Clay Payne and The Milwaukee Electric Railway & Light Company, and who supported the municipal ownership mayoral campaign of Henry J. Baumgaertner. The club backed tax equity, the direct primary, and both anti-pass and antitrust legislation. And it endorsed La Follette. Its members quickly formed local organizations in most of the city's wards, and they mailed out tens of

---

[30] Torelle, Barton, and Holmes, comps., *Political Philosophy of La Follette*, 30–31; Barton, *La Follette's Winning of Wisconsin*, 105–110 (quotes); Margulies, *The Decline of the Progressive Movement*, 60; La Follette, *Autobiography*, 95 (quote); La Follette and La Follette, *La Follette*, 125; Lovejoy, *La Follette and the Establishment of the Direct Primary*, 44–46; Lahman, "Robert Marion La Follette," 98–101; Acrea, "Wisconsin Progressivism," 356–359.

[31] Barton, *La Follette's Winning of Wisconsin*, 110–115 (quote); Margulies, *The Decline of the Progressive Movement*, 44–45; La Follette, *Autobiography*, 95–98; La Follette and La Follette, *La Follette*, 125–129; Acrea, "Wisconsin's Reform Coalition," in *WMH*, 57: 149–153.

thousands of pieces of literature, much of it in German or Polish. At the August 12 primary election, Republican Club delegates won half Milwaukee County's places at the state convention. For the first time, La Follette had significant support in the state's metropolis, led by such seasoned and influential political activists as Baumgaertner, Francis and John McGovern, Theodore Kronshage, and Charles F. P. Pullen.[32]

In some ways, the 1898 state Republican convention in Milwaukee was a reprise of 1896. A few key Stalwarts, such as Congressman Joseph Babcock, wanted to dump Scofield, but the organization decided to honor the two-term tradition. Party leaders then pulled out all the stops to secure Scofield's renomination, triggering charges of delegate bribery from the La Follette forces. La Follette claimed that the Stalwarts had distributed $8,300 among the delegates the night before the balloting to ensure Scofield's renomination. Whether or not this was so, the convention did indeed swing to Scofield, who won renomination on the first ballot, 620 1/2 votes to 436 1/2, with only eight votes going to others. The Republican old guard still held sway, but the gap was narrowing.

This time the Half-Breeds won their share as well. Led by La Follette's law partner, Gilbert Roe, the committee on resolutions drafted a platform supporting the *ad valorem* taxation of railroads, Hall's anti-pass bill, and legislation to regulate lobbyists. Although Roe failed to obtain endorsement of the direct primary, he did succeed in including a plank that recognized the defects of the caucus-convention system and favored "such legislation as will secure to every citizen the freest expression of his choice in the selection of candidates." In the spirit of compromise, the platform also included a favorable reference to the first Scofield administration. By skillful maneuver, Bryant got the platform adopted before delegates balloted for the gubernatorial nomination; he justified this sequence because Scofield had refused to be bound by the 1896 platform's endorsement of anti-pass legislation. In addition, the La Follette faction was generally pleased by the nominations of James O. Davidson for state treasurer, Jesse Stone for lieutenant-governor, and Emmett R. Hicks for attorney general.[33]

Despite these accommodations, the Half-Breed and Stalwart split

---

[32] Barton, *La Follette's Winning of Wisconsin*, 116–132; Margulies, *The Decline of the Progressive Movement*, 42–43; Acrea, "Wisconsin Progressivism," 361–362.

[33] Barton, *La Follette's Winning of Wisconsin*, 133–137; Margulies, *The Decline of the Progressive Movement*, 43–45; La Follette, *Autobiography*, 95–97; Lovejoy, *La Follette and the Establishment of the Direct Primary*, 46–50; Acrea, "Wisconsin Progressivism," 363–368; Philipp, *Political Reform in Wisconsin*, 18–19; Current, *Pine Logs and Politics*, 301–302.

continued unabated. La Follette did not campaign for the ticket because of exhaustion and illness, a failure that widened the gulf. He took ill in Madison, and for several weeks could barely digest simple foods like malted milk. His doctor, Philip Fox, recommended a long convalescence in San Diego, and Bob and Belle did not return to Wisconsin until April, 1899. In the meantime, his supporters enthusiastically accepted the patronage positions distributed by Scofield administration allies. After his recovery, feisty as ever, La Follette gave the 1899 legislature a mixed review. He granted it some merit for finally passing a modified form of Hall's anti-pass bill, for enacting Whitehead's tax law, and for making the tax commission permanent. But he strongly criticized its defeat of a direct primary measure and of Hall's proposals to tax and regulate railroads. These three issues left him with a powerful agenda for 1900.[34]

La Follette was astute enough to realize that a strategy of "harmony" would prevail in 1900, partly because most of the Stalwart leaders who had so bitterly opposed his nomination were no longer on the scene. Philetus Sawyer died in March of that year at age eighty-three; John C. Spooner was immersed in national politics and foreign affairs; Henry Clay Payne was in ill health and was seeking a national cabinet post, an ambition he realized during Theodore Roosevelt's presidency. The new titular head of Wisconsin's Republican party, Charles Pfister, was plodding and unimaginative. (His potential rival, Whitehead, regarded him as "something of a booby.") At the same time, several other erstwhile Stalwarts sniffed the changing political winds and defected to the La Follette camp. The biggest prize was Ike Stephenson, who brought along his organization, his senatorial ambitions, and his checkbook. Second was Joseph Babcock, dean of the Wisconsin delegation in Congress and a shrewd campaign strategist, who was also smarting from blighted senatorial ambitions. Babcock did such a yeoman job in the campaign that some opposition newspapers criticized the "Bob-Bab" alliance. A third defector was Emanuel Philipp, another wealthy Wisconsin businessman, who hoped to assume the powerful role of broker between the fading Stalwarts and the ascendant Half-Breeds.[35]

---

[34] Barton, *La Follette's Winning of Wisconsin*, 137–138; Margulies, *The Decline of the Progressive Movement*, 44–45; La Follette, *Autobiography*, 93–97; Thelen, *Robert M. La Follette*, 29–30; La Follette and La Follette, *La Follette*, 129; Weisberger, *La Follettes of Wisconsin*, 35–36; Harvey, "Background of the Progressive Movement," 110–118.

[35] Barton, *La Follette's Winning of Wisconsin*, 139–145; Margulies, *The Decline of the Progressive Movement*, 45–47; La Follette, *Autobiography*, 98–104; La Follette and La Follette, *La Follette*, 130; Lovejoy, *La Follette and the Establishment of the Direct Primary*, 49–50. Stephenson, *Recollections*, 212–222, contends that La Follette was reluctant to run in 1900 until one of his emissaries outlined the harmony campaign strategy and handed La Follette a $2,500 contribution. On Babcock, see John D. Hercher, "The

Taking his counsel from Stephenson, Babcock, and Philipp, La Follette decided to mend his fences with the state's railroads and other corporations. He met in Chicago with Milwaukee business leaders and with the president of the Chicago and North Western Railway, assuring them that he was not anti-business, that he sought only fairness in railroad and corporate taxation, and that he opposed prohibition. In a letter to Thomas H. Gill, an attorney for the Wisconsin Central and a personal friend, La Follette maintained that, in crafting a law providing for the *ad valorem* taxation of railroads, he "would favor equal and exact justice to each individual and to every interest, yielding to neither clamor on the one hand, nor being swerved from the straight course by any interest upon the other." Seemingly reassured, the railroad lobby agreed not to oppose La Follette's nomination; and, according to Whitehead, the St. Paul's management even pledged financial support. (They and the Stalwarts later claimed that La Follette had promised, in exchange for their support or neutrality, to give special preference to the railroads.)[36]

La Follette formally announced his candidacy for governor on May 16, 1900. Five other Republicans had already tossed their hats into the ring. Initial press response ranged from hostile to lukewarm, but it gradually improved. To accelerate that improvement, La Follette issued public declarations that he would not block Spooner's re-election to the Senate, even assuring the Milwaukee *Sentinel* that it was "the faithful observance of the pledges then given [1898] which entitles Governor Scofield's administration, at this time, to public approval, in which I heartily join." Two years later, the *Sentinel* published letters exchanged between La Follette supporter H. G. Kress of Manitowoc and Payne in May of 1900, discussing a possible rapprochement. Although Payne allegedly refused to sign an agreement that would allow La Follette to be governor, in exchange for no gubernatorial opposition to Payne as national committeeman or to Spooner's re-election to the Senate, hostilities between the two subsided. Many Stalwarts became obliging to La Follette. One La Follette supporter later said that Stalwarts voluntarily appeared in the headquarters to help. Privately, La Follette confided to Gilbert Roe, "I have been engaging in the mollifying business to a large extent." He instructed James Stone to "do the best you can to harmonize things

---

Political Campaigns of Joseph W. Babcock'' (master's thesis, University of Wisconsin, 1932), 47–58.

[36] Barton, *La Follette's Winning of Wisconsin*, 144–145 (quote); Margulies, *The Decline of the Progressive Movement*, 47–48; La Follette, *Autobiography*, 100–103; Steffens, "Enemies of the Republic," in *McClure's Magazine*, October, 1904, pp. 563–579; La Follette and La Follette, *La Follette*, 130–131.

as much as possible between our old friends so as to work with our new friends with as little friction as possible."[37]

So irresistible was the momentum of La Follette's campaign by early summer that on one memorable day he even carried the Republican caucuses in Scofield's home county of Oconto and in Waukesha, the stronghold of state senator A. M. "Long" Jones, another declared candidate. One of the few discordant notes in this "harmony campaign" was sounded by Scofield, who charged that La Follette had secretly knifed him in the 1898 election. Since La Follette won the Oconto caucus the very next day, the impact of Scofield's blast was negligible. Nor was a pilgrimage by Whitehead and several cohorts to Spooner and Scofield of any more moment; Spooner responded by issuing a long public announcement declaring that he would not seek re-election in 1903. Between June 30 and July 24, Long and the other four candidates all withdrew, virtually assuring La Follette of the nomination by acclamation. Last-minute efforts by a few Stalwarts to field another challenger came to naught. On the eve of the state convention in Milwaukee, Whitehead and three of the withdrawn candidates came to La Follette's hotel room "for the purpose of striking our colors and surrendering to you." Next day he was nominated by Bryant in a convention chaired by Congressman Henry C. Adams, another ally. La Follette was chosen by acclamation and entered the hall to a standing ovation so prolonged it delayed his acceptance speech by several minutes.[38]

The fall campaign was a whirlwind of activity devoid of substantive issues. La Follette covered an estimated 6,433 miles, visited sixty-one of the state's seventy counties, and gave some 208 speeches to almost 200,000 people—an average of more than ten speeches a day, six days a weeks, for seven weeks. During the last three weeks, he traveled on a rented Wisconsin Central train, speaking anywhere from twenty minutes to two hours, ten or more times a day. On a single day, October 23, he traveled 150 miles, made fifteen speeches lasting over seven hours, and met crowds totaling 11,000 people. The rallies were rousing and boisterous, featuring brass bands, uniformed marchers,

---

[37] Barton, *La Follette's Winning of Wisconsin*, 141–142 (quotes), 150–156; Margulies, *The Decline of the Progressive Movement*, 48–49; 103–105; Lovejoy, *La Follette and the Direct Primary*, 50–51; Acrea, "Wisconsin Progressivism," 369–379 (quotes); Acrea, "Wisconsin Reform Coalition," in *WMH*, 57: 155.

[38] Barton, *La Follette's Winning of Wisconsin*, 156–158 (quote); Margulies, *The Decline of the Progressive Movement*, 48–49; La Follette, *Autobiography*, 103–105; Lovejoy, *La Follette and the Establishment of the Direct Primary*, 51–54; Lahman, "Robert Marion La Follette," 98–101; Philipp, *Political Reform*, 19–26. See also Robert C. Twombly, "The Reformer as Politician: Robert M. La Follette in the Election of 1900" (master's thesis, University of Wisconsin, 1964), 57–120.

parades, and the occasional booming cannon. But La Follette's speeches were almost entirely devoid of the rhetoric and ideology of progressive reform. Even loyal Albert Barton acknowledges that, in the typical 1900 speech, La Follette "devoted about one-tenth of his time to a discussion of primary elections, largely academic, but raised no other state issues." There was little in them to recall the candidate of 1898 or harken the governor who was to be. Mostly, the candidate extolled the successes achieved by the national Republican party at promoting prosperity and extending America's overseas empire in the Pacific and the Caribbean. He tied himself inseparably to the fortunes of William McKinley and his running mate Teddy Roosevelt, and he uncharacteristically gloried in occupying third place on the ticket of "Mac and Teddy and Bob."[39]

La Follette's third-place position in that campaign slogan proved prophetic; he rode to victory largely on the coattails of the McKinley-Roosevelt ticket. Even though he became the first Wisconsin governor to enjoy a plurality of more than 100,000 votes, and garnered almost 60 per cent of the total cast, La Follette still ran 1,400 votes behind the national slate. His was clearly a partisan triumph, a straight-ticket production. The vote was certainly no mandate for any of the reform issues that had characterized La Follette's 1898 challenge, and that was so largely because the candidate himself had chosen to ignore them. Harmony had been an ingenious campaign strategy, and clearly harmony had worked. But soon it would prove to be incompatible, both with La Follette's nature and with the momentum of reform.[40]

[39] Barton, *La Follette's Winning of Wisconsin*, 159–164; Margulies, *The Decline of the Progressive Movement*, 49–50; La Follette, *Autobiography*, 103–105; Thelen, *Robert M. La Follette*, 30–31; La Follette and La Follette, *La Follette*, 131–135; Lahman, "Robert Marion La Follette," 102–141; Twombly, "Reformer as Politician," 1–56; Harvey, "Background of the Progressive Movement," 118–124.

[40] Barton, *La Follette's Winning of Wisconsin*, 164; Margulies, *The Decline of the Progressive Movement*, 50; Lovejoy, *La Follette and the Establishment of the Direct Primary*, 54; Weisberger, *La Follettes of Wisconsin*, 35–36; David L. Brye, *Wisconsin Voting Patterns in the Twentieth Century, 1900 to 1950* (New York, 1979), 225–258; James R. Donoghue, *How Wisconsin Voted, 1848–1972* (Madison, 1962; reprinted, 1974), 50–52, 73–74; Plumb, *Badger Politics*, 118–121; Twombly, "Reformer as Politician," 1–56.

11

Reform Ascendant

[1]

GOVERNOR La Follette quickly served notice that a new age of executive leadership and governmental activism was dawning in Madison. For years, legislative clerks had droned governors' inaugural addresses to the legislature. Not so with La Follette. He broke precedent by forcefully delivering his own message on January 10, 1901, thus underscoring the aura of newness that permeated his ascension to the governorship: he was the first Wisconsin-born chief executive, the first to be a graduate of the University of Wisconsin, the first governor in a new century, and the recipient of the largest plurality by which a governor had been elected. His decision to address the legislature in person stirred such anticipation that "not a sound was heard in the assembly chamber except the governor's clear and distinct voice," an amazing occurrence considering that the message took two hours to read and filled almost forty-three pages in the official record. It was generally polite and professional in tone, but the governor's occasional references to "the political machine," to "tax-dodgers" and "lobbyists" hinted strongly that he was launching an assault on politics as usual.[1]

He particularly grabbed attention with his matter-of-fact assertion that Wisconsin owed over $300,000 for excess appropriations by the previous legislature, and had a net balance of only $4,125.94 in the general fund. He recommended cost-cutting measures and consolidation in various areas to help remedy this problem, of course, but he left little doubt that he believed the fiscal solution lay in revenue enhancement, not in retrenchment. He voiced appropriate concern over the 50 per cent increase in state spending over the past decade,

---

[1] Robert M. La Follette, *Governor's Message*, doc. 1, pp. 1–43, in *Wisconsin Public Documents*, 1899–1900, vol. 1; Milwaukee *Sentinel*, January 11, 1901 (quote); Albert O. Barton, *La Follette's Winning of Wisconsin, 1894–1904* (Madison, 1922), 165–168; Herbert F. Margulies, *The Decline of the Progressive Movement in Wisconsin* (Madison, 1968), 51; Robert S. Maxwell, *La Follette and the Rise of the Progressives in Wisconsin* (Madison, 1956), 27–28.

but he also defended it: "there is abundant evidence of expanding usefulness and of unquestioned public benefits derived from most of the new expenditures incurred by the State." Pointedly, he devoted almost one-third of his address to methods for revamping the tax system to increase the revenue it yielded, and he made only passing references to possible savings. Although La Follette stopped short of presenting tax reform as the most effective remedy for the state's fiscal malaise, his linking of the two topics made a powerful unconscious impression, even upon those who favored retrenchment.[2]

Over the course of his address, La Follette touched on over two dozen topics for potential legislation. He advocated more state aid to local schools, especially for "practical" education, funding guarantees for normal schools, and more funding for the university. He supported more effective supervision of the state's charitable, penal, and reformatory institutions, and better equipment, organization, and training for the state militia. He urged the legislature to enact more severe penalties for businesses guilty of price fixing or market allocation, and to tighten restrictions on lobbying. In the area of cost-cutting, he proposed stricter supervision of inspectors of illuminating oils and of state highway funds, and reorganization of several administrative departments. He acknowledged the growing influence of women in public life by suggesting their appointment to numerous state boards. He also suggested self-insurance of state property and urged the requisite second passage of the resolution providing for a constitutional amendment to prohibit free railway passes for legislators—the culmination of Albert R. Hall's tireless crusade. He advocated stronger banking laws, caution in approving general incorporation charters for cities, augmented factory inspection powers for the Bureau of Labor Statistics, closer supervision of veterinary medicine, and more authority for the dairy and food commissioner. Finally, he praised the work of the Free Library Commission, headed by James H. Stout, in founding free circulating libraries; and he hinted strongly at the desirability of civil service reform for state employees. Closing with a reference to the recent "harmony campaign" that seemed almost nostalgic, Governor La Follette prayed that his administration and the legislature would strive to "preserve that comity of relation which will aid in accomplishing the largest measure of good to the great Commonwealth which has honored us with its confidence and invested us with its authority."[3]

---

[2] La Follette, *Governor's Message*, 1901, pp. 1–18 (quote on p. 6); Milwaukee *Journal*, January 11, 1901; Milwaukee *Sentinel*, January 11, 1901; *Wisconsin State Journal*, January 12, 1901; Barton, *La Follette's Winning of Wisconsin*, 166–167.

[3] La Follette, *Governor's Message*, 25–43.

Despite his range of subjects, La Follette devoted nearly half his message to two familiar issues: tax reform and the primary election law. They had faded into the background, and their resurrection would quickly shatter that facade of calm. Comprehensive tax reform was called for partly in response to the fiscal imperative, but mostly (as he said) to ensure that "the excess of burden which has so long rested upon certain classes of our citizens would be transferred to those who have carried less than a proportionate share in the past." To accomplish that transfer, La Follette recommended that the temporary tax commission established in 1899 be either disbanded after four years or converted into a permanent body with extensive functions and enforcement authority. "In no case, however, should assessment be left to the taxpayer, whether corporation or individual, without some check or safeguard for the State," La Follette said. He stopped short of endorsing the *ad valorem* taxation of railroads and other transportation and communication corporations, but he did favor substantial increases in their tax bills, through means recommended by the temporary tax commission. He said that "with no other class of property is there presented so flagrant an example of open disregard of the law as in the case of bonds, mortgages, securities, and the average amount of money in possession and on deposit." He dismissed the objection that higher taxation would place a "premium on perjury," increase the interest rate, and drive money and business out of Wisconsin, and instead said he would accept either *ad valorem* taxation or increased assessments based upon gross earnings calculated by an official state agency. Either way, he made it absolutely clear that railroads and other corporations would soon be paying higher taxes. Cutting an even wider swath, he warned that it was "not unlikely that a complete revision of tax legislation may result in reconstructing the system upon radically different lines."[4]

As for a direct primary election law, La Follette declared his election a clear mandate for a measure that would "enable every voter to express his personal choice by direct vote for the candidate of his party." He refuted arguments that primaries would inordinately benefit urban politicians and encourage unqualified candidates. He countered that popular nomination would inspire "men of the highest talent and especial fitness for public life" to run. He also downplayed fears that primaries could result in nominees who had a minority of voter support with a plan for a "second choice" option that would virtually guarantee the winning candidate a majority of first- and second-choice votes combined. Any primary system should be

---

[4] *Ibid.*, 6–18 (quotes on pp. 7, 15, 18).

"plain and simple," La Follette said, and promised lawmakers that they, not he, would decide the details, knowing that they would "faithfully execute the command of the people."[5]

Intentionally or not, La Follette drew the battle lines over tax reform and the direct primary that would dominate the next two legislative sessions, and destroy the apparent comity within Republican ranks. By focusing so exclusively on these two issues, he also frustrated one of the ambitions of Albert R. Hall, a principal ally. Having finally won his anti-free-pass crusade, Hall turned to a tough railroad regulation measure which he had introduced during each of the three previous sessions. He regularly bombarded his legislative colleagues with comparative rate data for comparable distances in Wisconsin and neighboring states, demonstrating that Wisconsin shippers were being systematically overcharged. His allies in this struggle in the 1890's were several Milwaukee-based reformers, especially grain merchants Edward P. Bacon and Robert Eliot, and the Milwaukee Chamber of Commerce. Because working out an accommodation with the railroads had become less and less possible in the 1890's, the Milwaukee group began to work more closely with Hall and agrarian organizations for creation of a state regulatory commission. In 1899, the Milwaukeeans vainly backed the "Taylor Bill," a near carbon copy of the Interstate Commerce Act.[6]

During the 1900 campaign, La Follette convinced Hall to withdraw his proposal for a railroad regulation plank in the Republican platform "as a matter of tactics." La Follette claimed that railroad regulation "had an important place in my plans for a comprehensive state program," but "I did not consider it wise to bring it forward for immediate and serious consideration." Nor did he want the convention "to go on record against a thing we were all in favor of." La Follette further rationalized that it was "important to keep the field of discussion narrowed to the subjects which could be adequately treated in a single address," and that the railroad commission was to be the superstructure of his entire program, which could be built only after an education campaign had prepared a foundation for that structure. La Follette's harmony campaign entered into his decision as well, since it aimed to defuse railroad's opposition by downplaying both taxation and regulation. Convinced against his will, Hall was persuaded by the Milwaukee grain merchants led by Bacon to intro-

---

[5] *Ibid.*, 18–25.
[6] Stanley P. Caine, *The Myth of a Progressive Reform: Railroad Regulation in Wisconsin, 1903–1910* (Madison, 1970), 6–20; W. L. Burton, "The First Wisconsin Railroad Commission: Reform or Political Expediency?" (master's thesis, University of Wisconsin, 1952).

duce in 1901 a less drastic regulatory measure that deleted the provision which would have allowed the commission to establish initial rates for intrastate rail traffic. La Follette pointedly ignored the measure throughout the session. He replied to an inquiry that he was "not informed with regard to it or its prospect for favorable consideration." In fact, the bill was strikingly similar to the one on which he later based much of his reform reputation. Nevertheless, in 1901 La Follette rejected it as "not such a measure as I should have been willing to make a fight for as a law covering the subject." Whatever Hall's personal feelings about La Follette's behavior, outwardly he remained a loyal soldier. Meanwhile, both he and the Bacon forces stepped up the pressure for railroad regulation.[7]

Legislative and newspaper reaction to La Follette's message was both positive and restrained. Hall styled the message a "strong one" that "will give the legislature plenty of work," pledged himself to tax reform and the direct primary, and made no mention of railroad regulation. Senator John Whitehead, a Stalwart leader, said the governor's review was "fearless and comprehensive," and endorsed his analysis of tax reform. The president *pro tem* of the state senate, which would pass a resolution of censure against La Follette before the end of the session, called the message "comprehensive" and his position on taxation "fearless and conservative." Editorial opinion was somewhat more mixed, depending on a paper's ideological bent, but it was still generally positive. The more conservative newspapers mostly regarded it as an able message and more conservative than anticipated; the more progressive, like the Antigo *Item*, pointed out that La Follette would have a "hard row to hoe, as there appears to be a strong combination against him in the legislature."

Nearly all of the newspapers surveyed by the *Wisconsin State Journal* credited the new chief executive with sincerity, integrity, and a determination to see his legislative program through to fruition. One of the few openly skeptical notes was sounded by the Oshkosh *Times*, which asked whether La Follette had discovered that "the reformer 'stunt' was not a popular or profitable one" and wondered, "Has the 'reformer' merged into the 'machine politician?' " The Democratic Milwaukee *Journal*, a consistent La Follette critic, scoffed at his moderate stance on railroad taxation: "We expected to see a blast of just

---

[7] Caine, *The Myth of a Progressive Reform*, 18–20 (quotes); Robert M. La Follette, *La Follette's Autobiography: A Personal Narrative of Political Experiences* (Madison, 1913; reprinted, 1960), 101–105 (quotes); Emanuel L. Philipp, *Political Reform in Wisconsin: A Historical Review of the Subjects of Primary Election, Taxation, and Railway Regulation,* abridged and edited by Stanley P. Caine and Roger E. Wyman (Madison, 1973), 169–173; Barton, *La Follette's Winning of Wisconsin,* 178.

indignation which would take off their tax dodging heads and here is the breath of a lamb."[8]

[2]

Beneath this placid surface, however, lurked a volcano whose eruption split both the legislature and the Republican party into two contentious factions. Each side blamed the other for firing the first shot. The La Follette forces dated the conflict from a meeting held by "the machine element of the party," now calling themselves "Stalwarts." On the opening day of the session, its leaders and legislative contingent consolidated their control of the state senate and pledged to defeat La Follette's bills. Among their number were most of the old guard politicians who had blocked La Follette's rise to power in the 1890's, and who were highly skeptical of his harmony campaign. Most looked to the party's federal officeholders, such as Spooner, Babcock, and Payne, for leadership. Most had class ties to local political machines and to newspapers which opposed La Follette and adhered to the caucus-convention system. Nearly all sympathized with the interests of the railroads, lumber companies, manufacturers, and public utility companies, sharing their commitment to minimal taxation and regulation. According to the "Half-Breeds," the old guard was willing to use any means (including bribery, political blackmail, liquor, and prostitutes) to ensnare wavering lawmakers and to protect the business-political nexus. The Stalwarts stoutly opposed La Follette and his works during the 1901 session, in the hope of regaining control of party and government in 1902.[9]

For their part, the Stalwarts placed the blame squarely upon La Follette and his inner circle, charging them with machine tactics, ideological warfare, and authoritarianism. Their most able spokesman, Emanuel Philipp, synthesized the Stalwart indictment in *Political Reform in Wisconsin*, published a few years later in the politically charged atmosphere of 1910. According to Philipp and his group, the chief culprits were La Follette and his two private secretaries, Jerre Murphy and John J. Hannan, who limited access and privilege to those with progressive orientations. Never in the state's history, Philipp contended, had any politician built and maintained such an

---

[8] Milwaukee *Sentinel*, January 11, 12, 1901; *Wisconsin State Journal*, January 12, 14 (quotes), 1901; Milwaukee *Journal*, January 11, 12, 1901.
[9] La Follette, *Autobiography*, 106–115; Barton, *La Follette's Winning of Wisconsin*, 168–170; Maxwell, *La Follette and the Rise of the Progressives*, 30–33, 40–43; Margulies, *Decline of the Progressive Movement*, 51–61. See also William J. Goldschmidt, "The Legislative Lobby in Wisconsin, Since 1901" (bachelor's thesis, University of Wisconsin, 1912).

effective machine, rewarding his followers with patronage and punishing his enemies with threats. La Follette's reputation and accomplishments were based upon "a record of passion and prejudice . . . of persecution and reprisal . . . of wrong and retaliation . . . of broken friendships and the birth of lasting enmity . . . of malice, hatred and all uncharitableness."[10]

As with most things, the reality of the situation was more complex and nuanced. Even so devoted an admirer of La Follette as Albert O. Barton acknowledged that there was "no great exaggeration" in Philipp's version of the split, and that "many stalwarts were more honest and better patriots than many in the camp of reform." Much of the opposition to the Half-Breeds was rooted in a misunderstanding or personal dislike of La Follette, loyalty to ethno-cultural partisan politics and the Republican party, and fear or weariness of socio-economic and ideological conflict. At the same time, however, Barton believed that the "active and interested opposition came . . . from the big corporations who saw in La Follette's ascendancy a menace to the continuation of their privileges, and from the old wheel horses of the party, the governmental agents of these interests who also foresaw their tenures of office and privileges in jeopardy." In the final analysis, the bitter Progressive-Stalwart conflict was a volatile mixture of ideology, of contending socio-economic interests, and of two partisan forces fighting for supremacy in the state party.[11]

[3]

The issues that ignited the explosion were the direct primary and the *ad valorem* taxation of railroads. The battle over the primary was joined on January 28, 1901, when the administration bill was introduced in both the assembly and the senate. During the February hearings before the committee on elections, the administration and the Stalwarts both hauled out their big guns to testify; the Stalwarts relied heavily upon federal officeholders. The opponents generally argued that primary elections would lead to minority rule, favor cities, cost too much to operate, and inhibit ethnically and geographically balanced tickets. According to La Follette, Philipp surreptitiously informed him that he controlled enough votes in the senate to enact the primary bill—provided the governor would agree to

---

[10] Philipp, *Political Reform in Wisconsin*, 16–26, 37–38; Barton, *La Follette's Winning of Wisconsin*, 169–171; Margulies, *Decline of the Progressive Movement*, 56–60; Maxwell, *La Follette and the Rise of the Progressives*, 31–32, 40–43.

[11] Barton, *La Follette's Winning of Wisconsin*, 170, 196; Margulies, *Decline of the Progressive Movement*, 53–60; Maxwell, *La Follette and the Rise of the Progressives*, 30–32.

drop his fight for *ad valorem* taxation. This incident, in which Philipp supposedly boasted that he "owned" several senators, caused a permanent rift between the two. On February 19, Philipp's cohort, Charles Pfister, bought the state's most important Republican newspaper, the Milwaukee *Sentinel*. The paper's new editor, Lansing Warren, who died later that year, came to Madison to consult with La Follette. Depending upon whose version of their meeting one believes, La Follette rejected all suggestions for modifying or dropping the bill, causing Warren to warn that "the *Sentinel* will begin skinning you tomorrow." Pleased with the paper's reorientation, Elisha Keyes wrote to Senator Spooner that the *Sentinel* was "our paper." The *Sentinel* accordingly claimed that the original version of the Republican platform had merely recommended, rather than demanded, primary elections. The progressive Republicans denounced that assertion as a lie or subterfuge.[12]

The first real test of strength in this intraparty warfare came during an all-night session of the assembly on March 19 as it debated advancing a substitute primary election bill to a third hearing. Twice the speaker was compelled to remove Stalwart lobbyists and managers from the floor. The sergeant-at-arms searched the city for missing members, while some of those on the floor passed the time in "song and jest and the circulating liquor bottle." Not until the last assemblyman rose from a sickbed to arrive at 7:00 the following morning was the measure finally advanced. Two days later, the amended bill narrowly passed, 51–48. Sixteen of the assembly's eighteen Democrats combined with thirty-two Republicans in opposition, while forty-nine Republicans joined the two remaining Democrats in support. Some who were later accounted Stalwarts voted for the measure.[13]

When the Senate primary bill finally cleared the elections committee in early April, the Stalwarts were fully in charge. On April 11, the senate defeated the original bill, as well as several compromise measures, nearly all of which were introduced by administration supporters. Instead, the senate, by a vote of 20–13, adopted a substitute,

---

[12] La Follette, *Autobiography*, 104–114 (quote); Barton, *La Follette's Winning of Wisconsin*, 169–173; Philipp, *Political Reform in Wisconsin*, 27–47; Maxwell, *La Follette and the Rise of the Progressives*, 28–32 (quote); Margulies, *Decline of the Progressive Movement*, 51–59; Allen Fraser Lovejoy, *La Follette and the Establishment of the Direct Primary in Wisconsin, 1890–1904* (New Haven, 1941), 56–58; Waldo Schumacher, "The Direct Primary in Wisconsin" (doctoral dissertation, University of Wisconsin, 1923), 17–19; Walter E. Spahr, "The Wisconsin Primary Election Law" (master's thesis, University of Wisconsin, 1917), 24–31.

[13] Barton, *La Follette's Winning of Wisconsin*, 170–173 (quote); Philipp, *Political Reform in Wisconsin*, 32–43; La Follette, *Autobiography*, 107–111; Maxwell, *La Follette and the Rise of the Progressives*, 33–34; Margulies, *Decline of the Progressive Movement*, 51–59; *Wisconsin Assembly Journal*, 1901, pp. 626–627; Milwaukee *Sentinel*, March 22, 1901.

drafted by Henry Hagemeister of Green Bay, that would have confined primary elections to county and village offices. The Hagemeister bill, considered even by Emanuel Philipp as "a crudely drawn, brief measure that could not have been made effective had it been enacted into law," was modified slightly to require a referendum on the measure at the next general election. Neither side was willing to agree on conceivable compromises; the Stalwarts' intransigence played right into La Follette's hands. The assembly sought to amend the senate bill by including cities and some state offices, but the upper house refused to concur. Forced to choose between the Hagemeister bill with a referendum clause or nothing, the lower house narrowly approved it, 48–46, with some loyal supporters of the primary declaring themselves in the negative. Their actions conformed closely to La Follette's assertion that "*no bread* is often better than *half a loaf*," and that each piece of reform legislation must be a "*full step*" forward.[14]

The governor vetoed the Hagemeister primary bill and issued a blistering message that Barton said was of "rare lucidity, literary finish, and argumentative power." (Philipp derided it as "an insult in the form of a message," a "stump speech" in which the governor dared to "scold like a fishwife.") The message denounced the bill as a subterfuge and a betrayal of the party platform. La Follette attacked its sponsors as tools of corporations, political machines, and federal officeholders. He left no doubt that he would make the primary a major election issue and intended to enact a comprehensive primary law in 1903. In response, Senator Julius Roehr of Milwaukee introduced a resolution of official protest against the governor. The resolution charged that La Follette's allegations "transcend all bounds of official propriety and constitutional right," and protested "against the aspersions cast upon our official acts, upon our personal motives, and upon our private characters." More than half the Republican members of both houses voted in favor of Roehr's resolution.[15]

---

[14] La Follette, *Autobiography*, 115–116; Barton, *La Follette's Winning of Wisconsin*, 173–175; Philipp, *Political Reform in Wisconsin*, 43–48; *Wisconsin Senate Journal*, 1901, pp. 830, 1026–1035, 1061–1063; *Wisconsin Assembly Journal*, 1901, pp. 1022, 1116–1118; Milwaukee *Sentinel*, April 12, 15, 26, May 3, 4, 11, 1901; Kenneth C. Acrea, Jr., "Wisconsin Progressivism: Legislative Response to Social Change, 1891 to 1909" (doctoral dissertation, University of Wisconsin, 1968), 413–415; Carroll P. Lahman, "Robert Marion La Follette as Public Speaker and Political Leader, 1855–1905" (doctoral dissertation, University of Wisconsin, 1939), 531–587; Herbert F. Margulies, *Senator Lenroot of Wisconsin: A Political Biography, 1900–1929* (Columbia, Missouri, 1977), 20–27.

[15] Barton, *La Follette's Winning of Wisconsin*, 173–176; La Follette, *Autobiography*, 107–118; Philipp, *Political Reform in Wisconsin*, 43–47 (quote); Maxwell, *La Follette and the Rise of the Progressives*, 34–35; Margulies, *Decline of the Progressive Movement*, 51–59. According to Gerd Korman, "Political Loyalties, Immigrant Traditions, and Reform:

Equally divisive, to both party and polity, was the struggle over tax revision. The Republican platform of 1900 had pledged to revamp the system so that every individual and corporation would bear a "justly proportionate" share of the tax burden. La Follette's legislative message had given little hint of his stance about railroad and corporation taxation; he advised the legislature to wait until the temporary tax commission had reported. Its report concluded that railroads were paying only half as much in taxes on their property per dollar of valuation as the average individual paid. It recommended one of two remedies. Either raise the license tax fee to produce $600,000 more revenue each year, or assess the railroads on an *ad valorem* basis, the actual value of their property to be determined by a careful investigation. In light of La Follette's statements prior to the harmony campaign, it is not surprising that he quickly backed a bill to evaluate railroad property, with an eye towards taxing it at the same rate as homes, farms, and other businesses were taxed. The administration buttressed its case with substantially similar data to that of the tax commissioner from the Bureau of Labor and Industrial Statistics. Concurrently, Senator John Whitehead introduced a measure to raise the railroad license fee tax from 4 to 5.5 per cent of gross earnings. Railroad attorneys lobbied furiously against both bills. The Pfister-owned *Sentinel* issued daily diatribes against *ad valorem* taxation, stigmatizing it as radical and anti-business. The chief lobbyist for the Wisconsin Central Railroad convinced chairman Hall to withhold his committee's report until early April, a decision reinforced by Hall's being seriously ill.[16]

On April 10, in a 4–3 split, the committee on assessment and collection of taxes recommended indefinite postponement of the bill to raise the license fee tax, with Hall among the minority. After considerable debate, the assembly voted on April 23 for indefinite postponement, 50–39, with several tax reform advocates joining the opposition because they preferred the *ad valorem* measure. Then on May 2, the assembly dispatched the *ad valorem* bill, 51–45, with the Republicans split along lines remarkably similar to the direct primary vote. The *ad valorem* defeat came on the same day the governor be-

---

The Wisconsin German-American Press and Progressivism, 1909–1912," in *WMH*, 40 (Spring, 1957), 161–168, La Follette's veto cost him the support of *Die Germania*, the state's leading German-language newspaper.

[16] *Wisconsin Blue Book, 1901*, pp. 690–691; La Follette, *Governor's Message*, 1901, pp. 6–18; La Follette, *Autobiography*, 105–110; Ellen Torelle, Albert O. Barton, and Fred L. Holmes, comps., *The Political Philosophy of Robert M. La Follette as Revealed in His Speeches and Writings* (Madison, 1920), 64–68; Philipp, *Political Reform in Wisconsin*, 97–129; Maxwell, *La Follette and the Rise of the Progressives*, 34–37, 87–91; Margulies, *Decline of the Progressive Movement*, 51–55; Barton, *La Follette's Winning of Wisconsin*, 174–180; Margulies, *Senator Lenroot*, 25–27.

rated the legislature in what came to be called his "dog tax veto" message. That bill was an obscure levy upon dogs that would require their owners to pay a license fee tax of one to three dollars. La Follette seized upon what he called the "humorous absurdity" of the "attempt to raise a few hundred dollars in taxes upon dogs owned by a class of people already overburdened with taxes, while the corporations of the state were paying hundreds of thousands of dollars less than their just share." So he used the opportunity to castigate the legislature in no uncertain terms, charging that even opponents of tax reform had accepted the discrepancies in tax burden found by the state's tax commission and the bureau of statistics. He blamed the legislature's failure to equalize taxation on the same sinister forces that had defeated the direct primary and chided lawmakers for wanting to adjourn without acting on meaningful tax reform. "I am very certain that the people of this state are more anxious for an approximately equitable distribution of the tax burden, even if the session should be protracted thereby," he admonished them. But, in the end, the 1901 legislature contented itself with minor enlargements of the scope and duties of the tax commission, establishment of county supervisors of assessments, and the taxation of mortgages and mortgaged real estate.[17]

Despite the defeat of the direct primary and *ad valorem* taxation in 1901, La Follette and the "progressive" Republicans (as they came to be known) made significant strides in shifting the political momentum in their direction. By publicizing the tactics of the Stalwarts and their corporate allies, they convinced a segment of the electorate that machine politics and government by special economic interests were realities that needed to be dealt with. La Follette's opponents' wounds were primarily self-inflicted, the result of their arrogance and hubris. Despite his hyperbole, by refusing to compromise and forcing the legislature to go on record concerning the primary and tax reform, the governor had constructed an unambiguous test for differentiating supporters from opponents and induced individual lawmakers to choose sides. He had achieved election through his mastery of an old politics that sought to blur divisive economic and political issues. Now he strove to govern by a new politics that would focus on such issues, reorienting partisanship and political discourse

---

[17] La Follette, *Autobiography*, 118 (quotes); Barton, *La Follette's Winning of Wisconsin*, 174–180; Philipp, *Political Reform in Wisconsin*, 128–139; Maxwell, *La Follette and the Rise of the Progressives*, 37–38, 90–91; Margulies, *Decline of the Progressive Movement*, 55–59; *Wisconsin Assembly Journal*, 1901, pp. 1080–1084 (quotes); Milwaukee *Sentinel*, April 11, 24, May 3, 1901; *Wisconsin State Journal*, April 10, 23, May 2, 1901; Acrea, "Wisconsin Progressivism," 411–412; Lahman, "Robert Marion La Follette," 587–603.

along socio-economic and ideological bases. Above all, La Follette succeeded in persuading a growing number of politicians and voters that progressive reform and membership in his political organization were synonymous. Although Philipp, a perceptive and candid Stalwart, despised La Follette's tactics and methods, he admitted that the governor's handling of the primary issue was "the most astute political move that had ever been attempted in Wisconsin." Such tactics, he said, could hardly fail "to excite the wondering admiration of the ordinary citizen who lacks genius in political manipulation but who approves of success at any cost and by any methods."[18]

[4]

Long before the November, 1902, election, it was obvious it would differ from the harmony campaign of 1900 as night differs from day. On August 18, 1901, fifty-nine Republican legislators signed a manifesto opposing La Follette's renomination and heralding the formation of the Wisconsin Republican League. Popularly called "The Eleventh Story League" because it occupied the entire eleventh floor of Milwaukee's Hermann building, the league enlisted nearly all of Wisconsin's federal officeholders, such prominent Stalwart leaders as Philipp, Pfister, Payne, and Keyes, and several industrialists and financiers. The league sought to flood the state with anti-La Follette literature, and to pack Republican caucuses and conventions.

La Follette, who was seriously ill for several weeks, finally entered the fray in the early spring of 1902 with a characteristic speaking tour at fairs and popular gatherings, concentrating almost completely upon the primary and *ad valorem* taxation. He usually praised or damned local area legislators for their stance on those two key issues. The 1901 sessions had provided proof that La Follette needed a compatible legislature, therefore leading him to exert his influence in legislative races. The two issues captured the attention of the citizenry and state newspapers, and served as debate topics in high schools. So successfully had La Follette identified his own course with those two questions, however, that the candidate himself was becoming the issue for many.[19]

---

[18] Philipp, *Political Reform in Wisconsin*, 44–46 (quotes); La Follette, *Autobiography*, 118–119; Barton, *La Follette's Winning of Wisconsin*, 184–186; Maxwell, *La Follette and the Rise of the Progressives*, 39; Margulies, *Decline of the Progressive Movement*, 66–67.

[19] Barton, *La Follette's Winning of Wisconsin*, 181–201; Roger E. Wyman, "Voting Behavior in the Progressive Era: Wisconsin as a Case Study" (doctoral dissertation, University of Wisconsin, 1975), 254–255; Maxwell, *La Follette and the Rise of the Progressives*, 43–44; Margulies, *Decline of the Progressive Movement*, 60–64; Margulies, *Senator Lenroot*, 28–38.

The 1902 campaign inaugurated a period of factional bitterness within the Republican party nearly equal to the antipathy between Republicans and Democrats during the Civil War era. To combat the Stalwart *Sentinel*, the La Follette forces persuaded Ike Stephenson to back the purchase of the Milwaukee *Free Press*. A furious and caustic propaganda battle ensued. The La Follette camp produced a 144-page booklet entitled the *Voters' Hand-Book* to set forth its version of what happened during the 1901 legislative session. The *Free Press* printed it and distributed it to every Republican household in the state—some 125,000 copies. The *Free Press* created a sensation by charging that the Stalwarts had "purchased" the editors of hundreds of newspapers and, in effect, paid them to run syndicated editorials about the issues. Expanding its earlier efforts, the La Follette group assembled an extensive library of poll lists that facilitated personal contact with hundreds of thousands of voters. At the same time, it engaged in what historian Roger Wyman has called "the most blatant personal use of patronage the state has ever seen." Some state employees revised poll lists, circulated literature, and gathered information on the activities of Stalwarts; others mailed literature and canvassed potential voters. These overtly political activities contributed to a threefold increase in the cost of running the affected offices during La Follette's five years in office, and they were the butt of jokes and stories in the Stalwart press.[20]

On the stump, La Follette hammered at the primary and taxation issues, incorporating them into a wider conceptual framework of "the people versus the interests," and recasting his program and organization as "the progressive movement." Rejecting the pejorative "Half-Breed" label, La Follette and his allies now styled themselves "Progressives." During the summer of 1902, they maneuvered for position in nearly every Republican caucus in the state, seeking compatible legislative candidates and convention delegates. Aided by Bryant as chairman of the state control committee, they succeeded in transferring the Republican convention from Milwaukee, where the Stalwarts and the Eleventh Story League largely held sway, to Madison, where administration forces were in control.

This coup was facilitated by a changing of the guard among Stalwarts following Philetus Sawyer's death and Theodore Roosevelt's ascension to the presidency following the assassination of President William McKinley. Spooner, Payne, and Babcock were turning their

---

[20] Barton, *La Follette's Winning of Wisconsin*, 201–208; *Voters' Hand-Book: The Truth About the Governor, the Legislature, Taxation, and Primary Elections* (Milwaukee, 1902); Wyman, "Voting Behavior in the Progressive Era," 254–255; Maxwell, *La Follette and the Rise of the Progressives*, 47–48; Margulies, *Decline of the Progressive Movement*, 64–65; *Wisconsin Blue Book, 1903*, p. 1042.

attention to national politics, spending an increasing amount of time in Washington. Payne was appointed postmaster general in 1902. Spooner and La Follette negotiated a working compromise whereby Spooner agreed not to interfere in state and local political affairs; the governor agreed not to oppose Spooner's re-election to the U.S. Senate in 1903, "unless necessary to protect the success of the platform." La Follette publicly praised Spooner's record and pledged his support, albeit ambiguously. That mutually beneficial arrangement assured Spooner's re-election, and strengthened the chances of La Follette's legislative program. It also left Charles Pfister as the nominal leader of the Stalwarts, a situation which the Progressives gleefully exploited, for even many Stalwarts expressed reservations about Pfister's abilities.[21]

Thus advantaged, La Follette easily secured renomination over John M. Whitehead, whom Lincoln Steffens dubbed the "flower" of the Stalwarts. La Follette also engineered a slate of compatible running mates and a platform that was a virtual panegyric to him. It reaffirmed the 1900 platform principles and endorsed the La Follette administration as "conspicuously able, honest, impartial, and ever mindful of public interests." It proclaimed the direct primary and the equal and uniform taxation of all property as "issues of supreme importance in the ensuing state campaign," and effusively praised the tax commission. The party regretted "the failure of the last legislature" to pass those laws and condemned the "pernicious activity of federal officials in this state . . . in assisting professional lobbyists before the Legislature and elsewhere in the work of defeating legislation in repudiation of party pledges." Even its endorsement of Senator Spooner for re-election was contingent upon his support of the platform and his willingness to work to elect a compatible legislature. In both his acceptance speech and on the campaign trail, La Follette railed against the 1901 legislature and the party's federal officeholders for unethically blocking popular progressive measures. The Democrats witlessly played into La Follette's hands by nominating Milwaukee's favorite, but corrupt, mayor, David S. Rose, whose administration would soon be intensively investigated by the Milwaukee County district attorney, Francis E. McGovern. Rose's reputation made him the perfect foil for the progressive Republicans' anti-corruption, anti-special-interest crusade.[22]

---

[21] Wyman, "Voting Behavior in the Progressive Era," 255–256; Barton, *La Follette's Winning of Wisconsin*, 190–201; Maxwell, *La Follette and the Rise of the Progressives*, 45–46 (quote); Margulies, *Decline of the Progressive Movement*, 31–32, 46–47, 64–65.

[22] *Wisconsin Blue Book, 1903*, pp. 1032–1034 (quotes), 1042–1043; Barton, *La Follette's Winning of Wisconsin*, 209–229; Maxwell, *La Follette and the Rise of the Progressives*,

The Democrats, aided surreptitiously by some prominent Stalwarts, attempted to make La Follette the major issue, accusing him of using dictatorial methods, usurping power, making false charges against the legislature, and of being a radical and a populist. The Milwaukee *Journal* campaigned against "La Folletteism," which it defined as an "infection" whose victims demonstrated symptoms of an "impudent assertion of their own infallibility, an ignoring of their own devious ways and the instant imputation of dishonesty or corruption to any who dare differ with them. . . ." Attempting to turn La Follette's anti-corruption theme against him, the Stalwarts released a series of letters exchanged by H. G. Kress of Manitowoc and Henry Payne, which purported to give evidence of a secret deal La Follette made with Payne and the railroads during the 1900 campaign. Taken more seriously were charges that several textbook companies had made campaign contributions, in exchange for replacing Lorenzo Harvey with Charles P. Cary as superintendent of public instruction. But none of these charges damaged La Follette.

Both La Follette and Rose campaigned along traditional, ethnocultural, partisan lines. They also implicitly acknowledged that a new trend was emerging—one that crossed party lines and emphasized ideology. Rose openly urged discontented Stalwarts to bolt; La Follette wooed "fair-minded" Democrats. His team mobilized some of the latter for local Republican caucuses, angering Whitehead. Whitehead ascribed La Follette's bipartisan deal to the fact that the leaders of both groups were University of Wisconsin graduates, who shared "a kind of freemasonry." Two-time Democratic presidential candidate William Jennings Bryan openly urged progressive Democrats to support La Follette over Rose.[23]

Superficially, La Follette and his forces won a sweeping victory. He carried all but ten counties and bested Rose 193,417 to 145,818. His faction's involvement in legislative elections resulted in effective progressive Republican control of the assembly and parity with the Stalwarts in the state senate. However, La Follette ran almost 10,000 votes behind the rest of his ticket, and the total Republican vote was off some 70,000 from 1900. On the Democrats' side, Rose outpolled others on his slate by close to 10,000 votes, while the total Democratic vote declined by around 15,000. An estimated 30,000 Democrats

---

45–46; Wyman, "Voting Behavior in the Progressive Era," 258–259; Margulies, *Decline of the Progressive Movement*, 65–66.

[23] Milwaukee *Journal*, May 1, 1902; Maxwell, *La Follette and the Rise of the Progressives*, 46–47; Margulies, *Decline of the Progressive Movement*, 66–67 (quote); Barton, *La Follette's Winning of Wisconsin*, 141–142, 202–208; Wyman, "Voting Behavior in the Progressive Era," 259.

crossed over to vote for La Follette; even more Stalwarts either supported Rose or stayed home. It also seems clear that La Follette received many Social Democratic votes in Milwaukee County, where Emil Seidel, the socialist gubernatorial candidate, ran well behind his ticket, receiving only 10,824 votes to La Follette's 26,754. Socialist leader Victor Berger was not impressed. He regarded La Follette as a "half-baked reformer" who in winning had merely gained the "mistaken sympathy of the working man."[24]

[5]

La Follette's annual message clearly outlined his 1903 legislative agenda, especially immediate enactment of a strong primary law as enunciated in the platform. His principal argument for switching to primary elections held that the "menace of the machine" had been supplanted by the menace of special interest groups that wanted control of officeholders. His message placed the primary election more squarely within the framework of socio-economic democracy than before. He now saw it as an indispensable remedy for the control that business interests, especially public service corporations, had assumed over caucuses and conventions. The Republican party, he said, was constructed upon "certain deep-seated ideas which lay hold of the convictions of men . . . its promise to perform." The voter enters into a "covenant" with the party, and "the party's bound to keep its pledged word." La Follette reviewed the history of tax reform legislation and the recommendations of the temporary tax commission, and discoursed over more than thirty pages about comparative freight rates. He demanded comprehensive reform that included *ad valorem* taxation of railroads, systematic valuation of their property, and a permanent railroad commission with real regulatory authority. The last proposal had not appeared in the party platform and had received little or no attention during the campaign. La Follette later stated that he introduced the measure in 1903 in the hope of educating the public and legislature for its eventual passage in 1905. He also claimed that its introduction forced the railroad lobby and the Stalwarts to expend some of their energy and resources in yet another

---

[24] *Wisconsin Blue Book, 1903*, pp. 447, 1077, 1087; Wyman, "Voting Behavior in the Progressive Era," 259; Margulies, *Decline of the Progressive Movement*, 66–67; Barton, *La Follette's Winning of Wisconsin*, 213, 230; Maxwell, *La Follette and the Rise of the Progressives*, 47–48; Marvin Wachman, *History of the Social Democratic Party of Milwaukee, 1897–1910* (Urbana, 1945), 11, 45 (quote); Edwin E. Witte, "Labor in Wisconsin History," in *WMH*, 35 (Winter, 1951), 83–86, 137–142; Frederick I. Olson, "The Socialist Party and the Unions in Milwaukee," in *WMH*, 44 (Winter, 1960–1961), 110– 116.

field, and, ultimately, to accept *ad valorem* taxation in order to prevent the establishment of a railroad commission.[25]

The tax commission's 1903 report unequivocally recommended *ad valorem* taxation of railroads, and estimated that the tax would produce nearly a million dollars more in annual revenue than the old gross earnings method of calculation. However, it also proposed retaining the license-fee system of taxation for the time being, so that the state would continue to receive annual revenues during the valuation process. Once the process was completed, the report argued, the state could demand supplementary payments or issue refunds, depending upon the nature of the discrepancy. Even if the railroads challenged the new system in the courts, as they almost certainly would, the state would continue to collect revenues under the prevailing arrangement. The commission also urged the exemption of mortgages from taxation, proposing technical changes designed to eliminate the objections raised by La Follette in his 1901 veto message. More importantly, it endorsed the reinstatement of the inheritance tax that the state supreme court had ruled unconstitutional in 1899, with suggestions for appropriate restructuring. The report also recommended abolishing the ex-officio board of assessment which evaluated the property of freight lines and sleeping car and railroad equipment companies; the commission would assume the board's duties. In essence, the commission proposed that all property taxes, including those levied upon corporations, be made *ad valorem*, and that the commission should undertake the task of valuation.[26]

[6]

The legislative battle over the primary resumed on January 30, 1903, with the introduction in the assembly of a measure strikingly similar to the 1901 bill. A few Stalwarts vainly tried to slow down the administration juggernaut by proposing amendments or prolonging debate, but a slightly revised version passed the assembly 70–19 just one week later. Alarmed, the Stalwarts persuaded Congressman Joseph

---

[25] Robert M. La Follette, *Governor's Message*, doc. 1, pp. 25–57, 63 (quote), in *Wisconsin Public Documents*, 1901–1902, vol. 1; Barton, *La Follette's Winning of Wisconsin*, 235; Caine, *Myth of a Progressive Reform*, 29; Maxwell, *La Follette and the Rise of Progressivism*, 48–49; Margulies, *Decline of the Progressive Movement*, 68; La Follette, *Autobiography*, 120–124; Torelle, Barton, and Holmes, comps., *Political Philosophy of La Follette*, 72–76, 88–90.

[26] Tax Commission, *Biennial Report*, 1903, pp. 150–217; Maxwell, *La Follette and the Rise of Progressivism*, 92–98; Philipp, *Political Reform in Wisconsin*, 139–145; Barton, *La Follette's Winning of Wisconsin*, 231–237.

Babcock, a La Follette ally during the harmony campaign, to direct the anti-primary battle in Madison.

In the senate, Andrew L. Kreutzer of Wausau introduced amendments designed to reduce the political impact of primary elections. Some members supported them out of conviction; others, in the hope of delaying or killing the measure. On March 5, Senator Whitehead, the Stalwart's gubernatorial candidate in 1902, succeeded in postponing consideration of the assembly bill for three weeks, by which time Babcock presumably would have taken charge. To the disappointment of many Stalwarts and at the behest of President Theodore Roosevelt (who wished to avoid a Wisconsin Republican split over a proposal so universally favored by progressive reformers across the country), Babcock, Spooner, and other federal officeholders decided to permit its passage with a referendum provision attached. This strategy allowed the Stalwarts to evade responsibility for defeating the measure, while giving them a chance to convince the voters to vote no on the referendum. Even so, Kreutzer, Whitehead, and other Stalwart senators sponsored several unsuccessful amendments to limit primary elections' scope and impact.[27]

Then the senate finally adopted an amendment, introduced by John C. Gaveney of Trempealeau County, the stepson-in-law of Elisha Keyes, stipulating primaries for county and municipal offices but requiring a popular referendum on how to select candidates for state, legislative, and congressional positions. When the assembly refused to concur, a month-long conflict ensued, with the Progressives accusing their opponents of violating their campaign pledges and the Stalwarts charging that the administration forces were afraid to let the voters decide for themselves. Resolution occurred when both sides agreed that the entire primary bill be submitted to a referendum vote in the 1904 election. Except for the omission of a second-choice provision and stringent corrupt-practices code, the final measure was everything that the La Follette forces had urged.[28]

The battle over railroad taxation proceeded similarly. The administration and the tax commission agreed on most aspects of *ad valorem*

---

[27] Lovejoy, *La Follette and the Establishment of the Direct Primary*, 76–79; Maxwell, *La Follette and the Rise of Progressivism*, 48–49; Philipp, *Political Reform in Wisconsin*, 59–60; Barton, *La Follette's Winning of Wisconsin*, 237–239; Schumacher, "The Direct Primary in Wisconsin," 20–21; Spahr, "The Wisconsin Primary Election Law," 32–38; Acrea, "Wisconsin Progressivism," 415–416; Margulies, *Senator Lenroot*, 38–41, 45.

[28] *Wisconsin Assembly Journal*, 1903, pp. 204–211, 1375; *Wisconsin Senate Journal*, 1903, pp. 610–614; Milwaukee *Sentinel*, April 19, 1903; *Wisconsin State Journal*, June 3, 1903; Lovejoy, *La Follette and the Establishment of the Direct Primary*, 79–83; Maxwell, *La Follette and the Rise of Progressivism*, 49–50; Philipp, *Political Reform in Wisconsin*, 60–61, 70; Barton, *La Follette's Winning of Wisconsin*, 239–240; Lahman, "Robert Marion La Follette," 744–754; Acrea, "Wisconsin Progressivism," 415–416.

taxation, and the measure sailed relatively smoothly. Even the state's leading railroad officials had acknowledged the popular groundswell favoring a tax revolution, so they concentrated on minimizing its impact. Public hearings began on February 11, 1903. During their run, the presidents of the Chicago and North Western, the Wisconsin Central, the Chicago, Milwaukee and St. Paul, and the Chicago, Burlington and Quincy lines downplayed the significance of the proposed law and conveniently ignored the comparative figures presented by the tax commission. They seem to have viewed the bill as the lesser of two evils, compared to the railroad commission version. A bill based upon the tax commission's recommendations passed the assembly on March 6 with almost no overt opposition, 87–0. The senate bickered more lengthily and contentiously. The committee on taxation husbanded its bill until it was forced to deal with the assembly version in mid-March. The senate then amended the assembly measure to exempt railroad bonds from taxation and to postpone its effective date for one year. A conference committee deadlocked until senate members agreed to tax railroad bonds, and assembly members consented to postpone implementation. The state would continue to collect revenue under the license fee system until the tax commission could complete its evaluation of railroad property and assessment of the *ad valorem* tax. In its first full year as the state board of assessment, the tax commission more than doubled local property assessments and more than tripled state assessments from their 1899 estimates. A few smaller railroads actually received refunds based on the commission's 1904 new *ad valorem* assessments. The major lines were less fortunate. Their tax bills rose as much as 30 per cent over the old license fee system. (The North Western's went from $628,753 to $817,985.) The legislature also enacted a court-proofed inheritance tax and allowed mortgages to be taxed as an interest in real estate, in the hope that creditors would in that way share in the tax burden. The final tax reform measure was a proposed constitutional amendment to pave the way for a state income tax. However, a technical error later invalidated the law.[29]

Railroad freight-rate regulation did not fare as well as railroad tax reform and primary elections during the 1903 legislative session. La Follette had deliberately omitted regulation from the 1902 campaign,

[29] *Wisconsin Assembly Journal*, 1903, pp. 479, 900; *Wisconsin Senate Journal*, 1903, pp. 105, 818; Milwaukee *Sentinel*, February 11, March 7, 1903; *Wisconsin State Journal*, May 20, 1903; Maxwell, *La Follette and the Rise of Progressivism*, 50–52, 93–100; Margulies, *Decline of the Progressive Movement*, 68; Philipp, *Political Reform in Wisconsin*, 143–151; Barton, *La Follette's Winning of Wisconsin*, 241–245; Torelle, Barton, and Holmes, comps., *Political Philosophy of La Follette*, 62–64, 68–70; La Follette, *Autobiography*, 120–124; Acrea, "Wisconsin Progressivism," 411–412; Lahman, "Robert Marion La Follette," 813–846; Margulies, *Senator Lenroot*, 41–45.

but regularly conferred with its two chief advocates—Albert Hall and the Milwaukee merchants led by Edward P. Bacon and Robert Eliot, and George H. D. Johnson. These merchants helped provide data to the Milwaukee *Free Press*, which mounted an attack on the state's railroads in hopes of achieving regulation. La Follette believed the public was behind both new rates and regulation, so he arranged for the gathering of the data he later cited in his 1903 message. Then he enlisted legislators to lead the fight, as suggested by Hall, assemblyman James A. Frear of Hudson, and the Milwaukee group: Irvine Lenroot of Superior, Frank A. Cady of Grand Rapids, and Lieutenant-governor James O. Davidson. In his January 15 message, La Follette proposed two possible remedies to Wisconsin's railroad rate problems: allowing the legislature to make the changes or appointing an expert commission to study the matter and determine a reasonable rate structure. La Follette advocated the latter.[30]

The railroads and the large manufacturers who benefited from rebates and subsidies given them by the railroads together devised a defensive campaign. A few days before La Follette delivered his message, representatives of seventy large manufacturing concerns from twenty-six municipalities gathered at the Pfister Hotel in Milwaukee "for the purpose of 'protecting and furthering the interests of every branch of manufacturing in the state.'" They established the Wisconsin Manufacturers' Association (WMA), and swore to defeat any attempt to increase railroad taxes or to regulate freight rates. "It may be that the session of 1903 will resemble . . . the session of 1874," confided Elisha Keyes to a La Crosse businessman, "as the public mind seems to be under the impression that the railroads need overhauling." La Follette delayed until March 6 before permitting the assembly committee on railroads to propose a bill modeled on Hall's defeated 1901 compromise proposal. Debate revolved around three substantive issues: Should the commission be elected or appointed? Should it have the power to set rates or merely to review them? And should there be provision for "special rates" that benefited large shippers? These questions led to modifications to the bill.[31]

The committee hearings on the bill consumed much of March and April and dwelled largely on La Follette's statistical tables which had been prepared by Halford Erickson of the Bureau of Labor and In-

---

[30] Caine, *Myth of a Progressive Reform*, 27–34; Milwaukee *Free Press*, July 31, 1903; Philipp, *Political Reform in Wisconsin*, 172–174; Maxwell, *La Follette and the Rise of Progressivism*, 52–53; La Follette, *Autobiography*, 146–155; Barton, *La Follette's Winning of Wisconsin*, 244–245; Acrea, "Wisconsin Progressivism," 404–405; Torelle, Barton, and Holmes, comps., *Political Philosophy of La Follette*, 72–76, 88–90.

[31] Caine, *Myth of a Progressive Reform*, 29–37 (quotes); Philipp, *Political Reform in Wisconsin*, 175–176; Maxwell, *La Follette and the Rise of Progressivism*, 53; Lahman, "Robert Marion La Follette," 847–869.

dustrial Statistics. The anti-regulation coalition countered with their own data, compiled mostly by Burton Hanson, general solicitor for the Chicago, Milwaukee and St. Paul Railway, who told the assembly committee that one table in La Follette's message contained "637 distinct errors, nearly all of which are against the railroad companies." The confrontations grew so contentious that Thomas C. Richmond, a Madison lawyer and Irish-born progressive Democrat, almost came to blows with Hanson. Using Hanson's data as his point of departure, Emanuel Philipp issued a pamphlet entitled *The Truth About Wisconsin Freight Rates* that purported to demolish the reformers' case. La Follette eventually became convinced that a regulatory commission itself should exercise rate-making power, and he startled the measure's opponents on April 24 by issuing a special message to the assembly. In it he asked the legislature to empower the state bank examiner to audit the railroads' books to determine if they were evading license fee taxes by rebating some earnings to major shippers. The governor followed that with a second message on April 28 in which he castigated the "railroad lobbyists" and demanded the creation of a regulatory commission with the authority to set rates. The very next day, representatives of 151 state manufacturers and shippers gathered in the senate chamber and issued a protest to the assembly against the railway commission bill."[32]

The assembly did just that on April 30, by a 43–50 count, making it apparent that the railroads and the manufacturers had won the lobbying battle. The pro-regulation forces suffered even more convincing defeats on motions to conduct a railroad regulation referendum during the 1904 election and to adopt a less stringent substitute measure. La Follette later insisted that he had not really expected to win the regulatory fight in 1903 and that he had pursued it so that "the railroad lobby could not spend any time in resisting . . . railroad taxation" and because "the contest stirred the people of the state as they had never been stirred before, and laid the foundations for an irresistible campaign in 1904."

Future events clearly lent themselves to La Follette's retrospective rationalization. But there is also substantial evidence that he had carried the day on tax reform well over a month before the final vote on railroad regulation. Why, if the regulatory measure was only a trap to ensure tax reform, had La Follette given it more time than necessary? Had he not deceived regulation advocates as much as regulation opponents? If the 1903 fight for regulation was an earnest struggle to the bitter end, La Follette himself surely deserves much

[32] Caine, *Myth of a Progressive Reform*, 37–46; Philipp, *Political Reform in Wisconsin*, 175–178 (quote); La Follette, *Autobiography*, 125; Acrea, "Wisconsin Progressivism," 404–406; Margulies, *Senator Lenroot*, 42–44.

of the blame for its having been a struggle, since he had failed to articulate the issue during the 1902 campaign and had not effectively countered the onslaught of the railroad lobby with his renowned oratorical and organizational skills. Regardless of the reasons for railroad regulation's defeat in 1903, its opponents celebrated their victory in the barroom at Madison's Park Hotel, where Philipp himself led the group in singing "In the Good Old Summertime."[33]

[7]

The 1904 election became a landmark in Wisconsin's political history. It turned out to be the last in which the candidates were chosen by the caucus-convention method, since voters ratified the direct primary in the referendum that year. Most importantly, the 1904 election proved to be the one that catapulted the Progressives into hegemony over both party and state, leaving the Stalwarts to wander in the political wilderness for most of the next decade. For political sound and fury, the 1904 election set a standard that may never be equaled. It stirred public interest and political involvement to a fever pitch.

Both the Progressives and the Stalwarts were eager to transfer their conflict from the floor of the legislature to the hustings. As historian Dorothy Ganfield Fowler observes, "Each group was determined to annihilate the other and neither was scrupulous about the methods used." By this juncture, La Follette had developed his organization and tactics to perfection, beginning with one of the most comprehensive lists of possible voters assembled in the pre-computer age. At the top were some 1,500 loyal wheel horses who would organize support or raise contributions. Just below them were 10,000 voters of unquestioned allegiance who would influence others by their example. At the base were roughly 100,000 other electors who would respond to reasonable requests for help. All were indexed according to residence, age, nationality, party and factional ties or sympathies. The organization regularly revised and updated this directory. It enabled distribution of campaign literature (La Follette headquarters delivered over 1.6 million pieces during the 1904 campaign), and the mobilization of caucus delegates and voters. Each electoral district had at least one full-time organizer, often a state employee or paid worker. When he visited caucuses throughout the state, La Follette "read the roll call," pointing out to audiences how their assembly-

[33] Caine, *Myth of a Progressive Reform*, 46; Philipp, *Political Reform in Wisconsin*, 178–179; La Follette, *Autobiography*, 123–124 (quote); Barton, *La Follette's Winning of Wisconsin*, 244–245.

men and senators had voted on the key issues. He thus established ideological orientation and loyalty to his organization as requirements for re-election, deliberately polarizing the electorate. Even some steadfast progressives squirmed at La Follette's public excoriation of Republicans who were otherwise trusted and respected public servants. La Follette, however, refused to let them off the hook. As he said, "the fight is between the railroads and the people."[34]

For their part, the Stalwarts sought to blunt La Follette's ideological and socio-economic appeals by stigmatizing him as a radical advocate of class warfare and a megalomaniac who was destroying the Republican party to build a personal political machine. They flagrantly used federal officeholders and business employees as political operatives, dictated editorial positions to many of the state's newspapers, and courted contributions by special interest groups—tactics which contributed to the campaign's apocalyptic atmosphere. The North Western and the Milwaukee Road alone contributed over $50,000 to defeat La Follette—part of an estimated $500,000 spent by the state's businesses. James J. Hill of St. Paul, who headed the Great Northern Railway, reportedly dispatched sixty men to Wisconsin to fight La Follette. Congressman Babcock devised Stalwart strategy, producing an even bigger fiasco than that of Charles Pfister's 1902 campaign. Babcock decided to oppose La Follette's renomination bid by supporting two alternate candidates who were widely respected and not overtly associated with the Stalwart wing: Judge Emil Baensch of Manitowoc and former Congressman Samuel A. Cook, a lumberman and Civil War veteran from Neenah. The plan was to consolidate Stalwart support behind the man who demonstrated the most viability. The Stalwarts also prepared to challenge the La Follette forces for control of the party convention and rented Madison's largest theater, the Fuller Opera House, as the site for a possible alternative convention. Throughout the caucus season, they kept up a steady drumbeat of charges that the progressives had "stolen" several caucuses, even using the votes of known Democrats and Social Democrats. Both sides resorted to assembling "snap caucuses" to steal a march on their opponents. In Appleton, where Stalwarts won, the *Post* observed that never "in the history of Outagamie county have the people become so thoroughly agitated over politics; and Appleton last night saw the fiercest fight for delegate supremacy ever known at the city cau-

---

[34] Dorothy Ganfield Fowler, *John Coit Spooner: Defender of Presidents* (New York, 1961), 301; Margulies, *Decline of the Progressive Movement*, 69–71 (quote); Barton, *La Follette's Winning of Wisconsin*, 287–312; Maxwell, *La Follette and the Rise of Progressivism*, 66–67; Wyman, "Voting Behavior in the Progressive Era," 261–264; La Follette, *Autobiography*, 137–138; Ruth F. Robinson, "The Control of the Republican Party in Wisconsin, 1904" (master's thesis, University of Wisconsin, 1970), 1–22.

cuses." Despite several disputed caucus outcomes involving 108 delegate seats, both sides predicted victory when the convention gathered in Madison on May 18, 1904.[35]

The "Red Gym Convention" of 1904 quickly became Wisconsin legend. (The gymnasium in question was a red-brick, fortress-like structure on the Lake Mendota shore of the University of Wisconsin campus.) Preliminaries began on May 17, when the Republican state central committee, which the pro-La Follette forces controlled, decided the disputed delegate cases in La Follette's favor, 59 1/2 to 43 1/2. That same evening, Stalwart delegates met at the Fuller Opera House and demanded that the convention respect the rights of all delegates equally.

The main event began at noon on May 18, amid rumors of possible violence and in an atmosphere crackling with excitement. An hour before, the anti-La Follette delegates and their supporters met at the Fuller Opera House and marched to the Red Gym four abreast behind a pair of American flags. Upon arriving, they and all the delegates found that the gym had been fortified against them, "not unlike a penal institution," as La Follette backer Albert O. Barton wrote. The delegates were forced to enter the gymnasium single file through a side entrance at the end of a barbed-wire runway patrolled by members of a small army of burly university football players, wrestlers, and fraternity brothers, supplemented by some tough-looking characters recently resident in the Madison city jail. Once inside, delegates found themselves separated from spectators by an eight-foot-high wire fence. Most prominent among the security forces were Evan "Strangler" Lewis, a champion wrestler, and "Norsky" Larson, a Badger football star. (La Follette disingenuously described these gentlemen as "fine, clean, upright fellows who were physically able to meet any emergency.") To enter, the delegates had to provide tickets countersigned by the state central committee. Since each side accused the other of counterfeiting the ducats, delegates frequently had to submit to harassment and outright manhandling by security guards attempting to verify their credentials.[36]

Amidst this atmosphere bristling with all manner of hostile emo-

---

[35] Barton, *La Follette's Winning of Wisconsin*, 312–316; Margulies, *Decline of the Progressive Movement*, 70–73; Lovejoy, *La Follette and the Establishment of the Direct Primary*, 84–85; Robinson, "Control of the Republican Party," 10–22; Wyman, "Voting Behavior in the Progressive Era," 263–265 (quote); Lahman, "Robert Marion La Follette," 852–877; Margulies, *Senator Lenroot*, 48–53.

[36] Barton, *La Follette's Winning of Wisconsin*, 340–361 (quotes on pp. 348, 359); Margulies, *Decline of the Progressive Movement*, 73–75; Lovejoy, *La Follette and the Establishment of the Direct Primary*, 85–87; Robinson, "Control of the Republican Party," 22–38; La Follette, *Autobiography*, 138–140 (quote); Philipp, *Political Reform in Wisconsin*, 68–69; Margulies, *Senator Lenroot*, 53–56.

tions, the delegates accepted the report of the state central committee regarding the seating of the Ashland County delegation, 575 5/6 to 485 1/6. They then turned down the minority report, 485 1/6 to 526 5/6. Both votes demonstrated that the La Follette forces were in charge. By almost identical margins, the convention accepted the majority ruling on the other disputed county delegations, and as Barton put it, "the steam roller went remorsely on to the end." At that point, the delegates supporting Baensch for governor began to file out of the gym, led by their floor leader, Janesville's M. G. Jeffris, who departed shouting, "I protest that this convention is not legally organized." The delegates pledged to Cook, however, remained in the hall and participated in the remainder of the convention's business— the ultimate triumph of La Follette, his slate of running mates, and his platform. Their decision inadvertently supplied the convention with enough delegates to legitimate its deliberations and to invalidate later Stalwart attempts to undo its handiwork.[37]

To complicate matters further, Baensch announced his withdrawal as a gubernatorial candidate, leaving only Cook, who was badly compromised by the Red Gym developments, as a Stalwart challenger to La Follette. Declaring itself to be the "legitimate" Republican party convention, the group at the Fuller Opera House constituted itself as the "National Republican Party," nominated Cook, adopted a conservative platform, and elected Spooner, Quarles, Babcock, and Baensch delegates to the national Republican convention. Although Elisha Keyes exulted that the opera house gathering "was a great success" and "stood out in most favorable contrast with the game wardens carnival" in the Red Gym, results soon proved otherwise. The Stalwarts won an apparent victory in advance of the Republican national convention, when the national credentials committee decided to seat the delegates selected at the opera house. A progressive delegation tried without avail to enlist the backing of Theodore Roosevelt for the slate of Red Gym delegates (La Follette, Stephenson, Stout, and William D. Connor), possibly sowing some of the seeds of the hostility between Roosevelt and La Follette that were to erupt in 1912. However, Stalwart elation was short-lived. Both Wisconsin Secretary of State Walter L. Houser, a progressive, and the state supreme court ruled that the Red Gym proceedings were legitimate.[38]

---

[37] Barton, *La Follette's Winning of Wisconsin*, 359 (quote), 367–378; Margulies, *Decline of the Progressive Movement*, 75–77; Lahman, "Robert Marion La Follette," 877–893.

[38] Barton, *La Follette's Winning of Wisconsin*, 362–366, 379–415; Margulies, *Decline of the Progressive Movement*, 77–78 (quotes); Robinson, "Control of the Republican Party," 30–38; La Follette, *Autobiography*, 140–141; Wyman, "Voting Behavior in the Progressive Era," 266–268; Lahman, "Robert Marion La Follette," 893–906; Herbert W. Chynoweth, *Argument of H. W. Chynoweth: Filed with Republican National Committee*

Disheartened, Cook withdrew and was hastily replaced by Edward Scofield, the former governor, whose prospects less than thrilled Stalwarts generally. Many resolved to vote for another ghost of the 1890's, Democratic candidate George W. Peck, whose political philosophy was scarcely distinguishable from that of conservative Republicans. The Democrats' 1904 platform was slightly more progressive than their reactionary 1902 platform. Members of the emerging progressive faction among the Democrats were denounced as "La Follette servitors" when they tried for positive platform stands about primary elections, railroad regulation, and other reforms. La Follette accordingly made obvious appeals to "fair-minded Democrats." He raced around the state in a new automobile (unusual in that day), subsisting on cheese sandwiches and milk supplied by farmers along his route. He concentrated on questionable legislative districts and openly endorsed Democrats who passed the progressive test. He went so far as to endorse the progressive Democratic candidate who unsuccessfully tried to unseat Congressman Babcock.

La Follette received an unexpected boost when Lincoln Steffens published an article in the October, 1904, issue of *McClure's Magazine* entitled "Wisconsin: A State Where The People Have Restored Representative Government—The Story of Governor La Follette." In it, Steffens asserted that he had come to Wisconsin determined to expose La Follette as an egomaniac, charlatan, and demagogue, but had discovered that his subject was a sincere and effective reformer, a champion of the people against the special interests. The issue appeared in the last week of September, and was sold out by October 2.

In a final campaign masterstroke, the governor issued a statement on the eve of the election remitting all state taxes for the coming year, on the grounds that his administration's careful husbandry of public funds had produced a huge surplus. The announcement took the edge off Stalwart charges of extravagance and ingratiated La Follette with taxpayers. (In reality, however, most of the surplus resulted from an unexpected refund on a Civil War debt. La Follette's manipulation of this happenstance was a classic example of both his political savvy and his *chutzpah*.)[39]

---

in Behalf of Isaac Stephenson, Robert M. La Follette, James H. Stout and W. D. Connor (Milwaukee[?], 1904).

[39] *Wisconsin Blue Book, 1905*, pp. 1018–1021, 1026–1029, 1036–1038; Lincoln Steffens, "Enemies of the Republic. Wisconsin: A State Where the People Have Restored Representative Government—The Story of Governor La Follette," *McClure's Magazine*, October, 1904, pp. 564, 579; Barton, *La Follette's Winning of Wisconsin*, 416–430; Margulies, *Decline of the Progressive Movement*, 79–81; Torelle, Barton, and Holmes, comps., *Political Philosophy of La Follette*, 76–82, 90–92; Wyman, "Political Behavior in the Progressive Era," 268.

The Stalwarts and the Democrats virtually ignored the substantive issues and endeavored to make La Follette and his machine the focus of the campaign. They branded him a dictator who was trying to perpetuate himself by running for a third term, and as a radical seeking to stir up class hatreds and drive industry from the state. They accused him of gross corruption, and revived and expanded upon some of the scandals of 1902. To undercut his last-minute tax remission coup, his opponents charged him with looting funds given Wisconsin by the federal government. Stalwart leaders purchased the *Wisconsin State Journal* and turned loose their political cartoonists, who caricatured La Follette savagely. In Milwaukee, Mayor Rose removed from office all election officials suspected of pro-La Follette leanings or bipartisan trade-offs. Only Emanuel Philipp, who published a *Red Book* of railroad rates for the campaign, made any effort to focus on substantive issues, and even he cast La Follette as a villain whenever he could.[40]

The results of the 1904 election fully justified the claim of a later historian, Roger Wyman, that it was "one of the most momentous in Wisconsin history." President Theodore Roosevelt swept the state with 63.2 per cent of the popular vote, more than 3 per cent better than he had won as William McKinley's running mate in 1900. The Roosevelt landslide aided La Follette's re-election, since the governor's margin was only 50.5 per cent, down more than 9 percentage points from 1900. Moreover, La Follette finished almost 20,000 votes behind the rest of the Republican state ticket, whose median vote approached 56 per cent. Since Scofield, running on the National Republican ticket, captured less than 3 per cent, it was obvious that a sizable number of Stalwarts had switched to Peck after casting their presidential ballots for Roosevelt. The Democratic gubernatorial candidate ran some 25,000 votes ahead of the rest of his party's slate, and almost 3 per cent better than had his predecessor in 1900. Even with the increased support provided by "fair-minded" Democrats and Social Democrats, La Follette had lost more than 37,000 votes compared to 1900.

Most voters clung to ethno-cultural, partisan moorings in 1904, but their ticket-splitting increased along the lines of ideology and personality. Scandinavians remained the bedrock among La Follette voters; Catholics of various ethnic backgrounds remained loyal to the Democrats. Native-stock Yankees and British-American Protestants remained heavily Republican in 1904, but there were defectors from

---

[40] Barton, *La Follette's Winning of Wisconsin*, 431–442; Margulies, *Decline of the Progressive Movement*, 81–82; Philipp, *Political Reform in Wisconsin*, 178–179; Lovejoy, *La Follette and the Establishment of the Direct Primary*, 88–89; Margulies, *Senator Lenroot*, 56–58.

La Follette. The huge German vote, as usual, remained complex, with Catholics strongly Democratic, Protestants predominantly Republican, and Lutherans evidencing some negative reaction to La Follette. German urban workers, on the other hand, displayed a corresponding attraction for La Follette, even while voting for Democrats or Social Democrats on the local level.[41]

La Follette's campaign tactic of polarizing the legislature along ideological and personal lines paid significant dividends, at least in the short run. Republicans controlled the assembly with eighty-five members to eleven Democrats and four Social Democrats. They controlled the senate 28-4-1. More importantly for backers of the reform agenda, progressive majorities were elected in both houses, owing in part to La Follette's "calling the roll" on the campaign trail. The door was now open wide for the selection of a progressive Republican for U.S. senator to replace Joseph V. Quarles, whose term was expiring. Equally heartening for the La Follette group was the referendum vote, which overwhelmingly favored the direct primary, 130,699 to 80,192. Only 47 per cent of gubernatorial voters participated in the referendum, so the measure clearly did not have majority support among all voters; far more people chose to express their objections or concerns by abstention than by voting nay. The direct primary was most popular among Scandinavians, least so among Germans. Many German voters reportedly saw primaries as a threat to personal liberty, especially their freedom of assembly. This, to them, was every bit as dangerous as prohibition or compulsory English laws. The prospect of a direct primary also caused consternation in Yankee and British districts, which had disproportionately benefited under the caucus-convention system. And the direct primary was considerably less popular among Catholics than Protestants. Adding to Stalwart woes were the death of Henry Clay Payne in October, 1904, the virtual abandonment of state politics by John C. Spooner, and the discrediting of Charles Pfister and Joseph Babcock. It would take Emanuel Philipp the better part of a decade to pick up the pieces and rebuild the Stalwart machine.[42]

By relentlessly hammering away at issues of economic and political power, the La Follette forces produced the highest voter turnout recorded in Progressive Era Wisconsin. In the process, they effectively

---

[41] *Wisconsin Blue Book, 1905*, pp. 302–548; Wyman, "Voting Behavior in the Progressive Era," 268–269; David L. Brye, *Wisconsin Voting Patterns in the Twentieth Century, 1900 to 1950* (New York, 1979), 225–244; Lovejoy, *La Follette and the Establishment of the Direct Primary*, 90–95.

[42] Wyman, "Voting Behavior in the Progressive Era," 269–270; Brye, *Wisconsin Voting Patterns*, 227–244; Barton, *La Follette's Winning of Wisconsin*, 443–451; Margulies, *Decline of the Progressive Movement*, 81–82; Lovejoy, *La Follette and the Establishment of the Direct Primary*, 94–95; Schumacher, "Direct Primary in Wisconsin," 21–24.

transformed the politics of faction into the politics of ideology and put progressives in control of state government. Prior to 1904, they had been pejoratively called Half-Breeds, friends of the governor, or even "Bobolettes." Afterwards, they were firmly established as "Progressives." From that day forward, their opponents were saddled with the burden of being "conservatives" or "reactionaries," whatever the more complex reality. So stigmatized, the Stalwarts and their conservative Democratic counterparts were condemned to be cast as perpetual villains.

By embracing ideology over faction, the Progressives had infused politics with a brand of socio-economic realism which most mainstream politicians had previously avoided. By identifying himself so completely with those issues, La Follette had also accelerated the new tendency towards elevating the candidate above the party. These changes produced animosity, suspicion, and strife, alienating many politicians and voters. This atmosphere would later be turned against the Progressives by their adversaries. "In the intensity of the passions aroused," Barton later wrote of 1904, "in desperate, relentless, dramatic warfare no other campaign in the state's history approximates this one."[43]

[8]

Before the 1905 legislature could deal with substantive issues, it first had to select a successor to Senator Quarles, a task that proved distracting and divisive. The two announced candidates were Isaac Stephenson, La Follette's financial angel, and William D. Connor, a wealthy Marshfield lumberman, chairman of the Republican state central committee and a member of the La Follette slate of delegates to the 1904 national convention. A recent convert to the progressive cause, Connor professed to be appalled by the railroad lobby's tactics, and presented himself as a liaison between reformers and businessmen. La Follette declared his support for Stephenson. While he was in St. Louis at the Louisiana Purchase Exposition, however, the governor received two disturbing reports: Connor was seeking support from legislators for his election; and many legislators were refusing to vote for Stephenson, and some wanted La Follette himself to accept the senatorship—or else they might try to re-elect Quarles. In any case, an open fight between Connor and Stephenson might prevent enactment of further reform legislation and also damage the

---

[43] Barton, *La Follette's Winning of Wisconsin*, 287 (quote), 450–451; Wyman, "Voting Behavior in the Progressive Era," 270–451; Margulies, *Decline of the Progressive Movement*, 81–82; Brye, *Wisconsin Voting Patterns*, 230–244.

progressive coalition. La Follette and Connor met privately, and Connor reportedly challenged La Follette by asking if he were "aware that the man who can control twelve votes cannot only control the senatorship but can defeat your legislation?" Never one to back down in the face of threat, La Follette responded angrily, and the two men parted in mutual antagonism.[44]

La Follette pondered his options and apparently decided that the only way to prevent a fissure and to ensure passage of his legislative program was to present himself as a senatorial candidate. Clearly he had national political aspirations, even for the presidency, but he was willing to postpone those until "all the pledges which we had made to the people were redeemed in letter and spirit." Inaugurated on January 5, 1905, he resolved to remain as governor "until our legislation had been enacted and its efficiency proven," even calling a special session the following December. Not until January, 1906, did La Follette resign his governorship and depart for the U.S. Senate.

His decision helped pass reform legislation during the 1905 sessions. He was less successful in mollifying either Connor or Stephenson. The latter was driven to break with La Follette. Outwardly, at least, Stephenson continued to be a dependable ally and fount of financial largess. Inwardly, he grew more wary of La Follette's ambitions and resolved to accept nothing less than La Follette's full support in his final senatorial quest, now postponed until 1909.[45]

La Follette devoted one-third of his three-hour speech to the 1905 legislature to railroad regulation. He modified his 1903 stance and demanded a new commission empowered to enact absolute, as opposed to maximum, rates; but he also urged that the commission determine rates for specific types of goods, "as from time to time their importance may demand consideration." Such a "conservative" course, he said, would mediate between "the pressing needs of shippers" and the "rights of the transportation companies." La Follette sought a middle course between those advisers who favored an even stronger commission and those who wanted to mollify opposition. His caution was due in part to a legislative caucus of December 10, 1904, that revealed that only fifteen of thirty-three senators solidly supported a strong commission. Besides, La Follette was a lame duck governor waiting to go to the U.S. Senate, a fact which compromised

---

[44] Margulies, *Decline of the Progressive Movement*, 84–85; Edward N. Doan, *The La Follettes and the Wisconsin Idea* (New York, 1947), 41; Bernard Weisberger, *The La Follettes of Wisconsin: Love and Politics in Progressive America* (Madison, 1994), 43; Barton, *La Follette's Winning of Wisconsin*, 332–333 (quote); Belle Case La Follette and Fola La Follette, *Robert M. La Follette* (2 vols., New York, 1953), 1: 130–131.

[45] Margulies, *Decline of the Progressive Movement*, 85; La Follette, *Autobiography*, 159 (quote); Caine, *Myth of a Progressive Reform*, 74–75; Maxwell, *La Follette and the Rise of the Progressives*, 82–83; Margulies, *Senator Lenroot*, 58–61.

his command of the legislature and virtually forced him to accept whatever regulatory measure legislators adopted.[46]

Railroads and the Stalwarts proposed a regulatory commission with the power only to change freight and passenger rates on complaints from shippers, rather than to set rates afresh. The Milwaukee *Sentinel* termed this plan "just and fair" and La Follette's scheme "confiscation." The railroad-Stalwart campaign was orchestrated by Philipp, Burton Hanson of the Chicago and North Western, and Frank K. Bull, president of the Wisconsin Manufacturers' Association, who was converted from a position of outright opposition to any state regulation. The administration measure was introduced on February 10; the Stalwart version, in the state senate on March 2. At this point, the pro-La Follette forces began to fragment, with some endorsing the Stalwart bill and others drafting their own variations. Foremost among the defectors was Senator William H. Hatton of New London, chair of the railroad committee and La Follette's choice to champion his bill. Hatton was a wealthy lumberman with extensive real estate holdings in Chicago, and he feared a Potter Law-like debacle and the loss of shipping rebates to the timber industry. Responsibility for the administration bill therefore passed to Senator James A. Frear, who believed in the strongest possible railroad commission; but it soon became clear that Frear could not fashion a majority. As support grew for a weakened commission, the administration, uncharacteristically, began to dissemble.[47]

On March 30, pro-administration legislators on the assembly railroad committee introduced a compromise bill. It limited the proposed commission to the investigation and revision of rates upon complaint. It also specifically guaranteed the continuation of some rebates to big shippers. Less than three weeks later, this watered-down version passed the assembly by a wide margin.

The ensuing battle in the senate revolved around two issues: the appellate power of the courts to review commission decisions, and the method of choosing commission members. Administration forces actually won a slight victory on the court issue, successfully circumscribing the judiciary's power to issue injunctions or stays of execution of commission orders. The Stalwarts and the railroads favored election of commissioners, largely to deprive La Follette of the ap-

---

[46] Robert M. La Follette, *Governor's Message*, doc. 1, pp. 48–49 (quotes), in *Wisconsin Public Documents*, 1903–1904, vol. 1; Caine, *Myth of a Progressive Reform*, 74–77 (quotes); Maxwell, *La Follette and the Rise of the Progressives*, 75–76; La Follette, *Autobiography*, 145–147; Doan, *La Follettes and the Wisconsin Idea*, 40–41; Milwaukee *Free Press*, January 13, 1905.

[47] Caine, *Myth of a Progressive Reform*, 75–84; Margulies, *Senator Lenroot*, 61–65; Philipp, *Political Reform in Wisconsin*, 178–183; Maxwell, *La Follette and the Rise of Progressives*, 75–78.

pointive power. A handful of Progressives agreed, seeing election as ideologically consistent with the direct primary and popular election. The final version stipulated gubernatorial appointment of commissioners, with the advice and consent of the senate. (Fourteen years later, these ideological positions would be completely inverted, as progressive lawmakers fought for an elected commission because Governor Emanuel Philipp had packed the commission with pro-railroad people.) In a panic, La Follette even appealed to William Jennings Bryan to exert his influence over the four Democrats in the Wisconsin senate, and issued another of his patented messages to the legislature just before it debated final passage on May 18.[48]

During an intense seven-hour debate before a standing-room-only gallery, supporters of the compromise bill beat down every administration amendment. In the subsequent conference committee, assembly members meekly acquiesced in the senate version. La Follette signed the bill on June 13, after much consultation, and later called it "a very strong regulatory bill," adding that "it was more sweeping than any legislation enacted by any state up to that time." Philipp pronounced the finished product "a good, wholesome measure, one that could have been improved in some respects, it is true, but for all that a bill that could be described as sane, safe, and calculated to accomplish the purposes for which it was designed." The ever-loyal Hall, fearless champion of railroad regulation, acknowledged that while the reform was "not all that the friends of state control would like, it's a tremendous stride in the right direction." James Frear predicted "the merit of the legislation will largely lie with the manner of its enforcement." Indeed that proved to be the case.[49]

La Follette desired a strong commission chairman who would stand up to the railroads, but the statutes constrained him by requiring the advice and consent of the senate. He decided against the candidate of the hard-core Milwaukee reformers led by Bacon and Robert Eliot. Instead, he proposed Nils Haugen, former congressman and gubernatorial candidate, former state railroad commissioner, and scourge of the railroads when he served as chairman of the tax commission that proposed and implemented *ad valorem* taxation. He was as suspicious of railroad management as the governor. For the other two commissioners, the governor nominated Halford Erickson, head of the Bureau of Labor and Industrial Statistics, and economist and railroad expert Balthazar H. Meyer of the University of Wisconsin. The

---

[48] Caine, *Myth of a Progressive Reform*, 85–95; Philipp, *Political Reform in Wisconsin*, 183–184; Acrea, "Wisconsin Progressivism," 406–408.

[49] La Follette, *Autobiography*, 146 (quote), 150–155; Caine, *Myth of a Progressive Reform*, 96–123 (quotes on pp. 110, 122, 123); Philipp, *Political Reform in Wisconsin*, 183 (quote), 185–194.

senate approved both Erickson and Meyer, but rejected Haugen, 16–11. Outraged, Haugen blamed the railroad aristocracy's belief that "the first rights of our American corporation, that to choose the Jury before which it will be tried, has been sorely violated." La Follette then settled on John Barnes of Rhinelander, a Democratic attorney who had represented the railroads against regulation and taxation attempts. The senate quickly approved him, prompting the *Sentinel* to comment, "Governor La Follette has, intentionally or not, atoned in a measure for his original blunder." Leadership of the commission quickly passed to Meyer, whose knowledge of railroad law and national experience with regulation placed him head and shoulders above his colleagues. He believed in business-government co-operation and steered the commission along that course, pleasing industry spokesmen and frustrating hard-line advocates of regulation.[50]

By La Follette's own reckoning, the railroad commission was the capstone of his reform program and a model deserving wide emulation. In his *Autobiography*, he devotes six pages to a discussion of the commission's procedures, philosophy, and value to the people of Wisconsin. La Follette claims that the commission reduced transportation charges by over $2,000,000 a year, eliminated free passes and rebates, increased railroad activity and revenue, and that "railroad taxation in Wisconsin has been increased by the progressive legislation in six years nearly twice as much as the increase for all of the United States." He attributes the fact that "there has never been an appeal taken in any railroad rate case decided by the Railroad Commission" to a universal recognition that it consistently proceeded "honestly, capably, and scientifically." He concludes by promising benefits to shippers when "the other states of the country and the federal government make rates as we do in Wisconsin."

To a remarkable degree, La Follette's self-interested paean to the railroad commission went largely unchallenged until the 1960's, when a new generation of revisionist historians subjected Progressive Era business regulation to critical scrutiny. In their view, Wisconsin emerges more as a follower than a leader in railroad regulation. (Indeed, even La Follette acknowledged that his measure owed much to the advice of reformers in Texas, Iowa, and Minnesota and to Interstate Commerce Commissioner Charles A. Prouty.) Historian Stanley P. Caine convincingly argues that La Follette's politically motivated acceptance of "half a loaf" of regulation legislation, coupled with his decision not to press for Nils Haugen or some equally strong chairman of the commission, transformed a body "with the potential

---

[50] La Follette, *Autobiography*, 149; Caine, *Myth of a Political Reform*, 122–136 (quotes on pp. 127, 129); Philipp, *Political Reform in Wisconsin*, 185–186. In his *Autobiography*, La Follette does not even mention his nomination of Haugen.

for remaking the state's rate structure [into] a complaint-oriented administrative body which operated principally for the benefit of those vocal interests in the state which sought limited rate corrections." La Follette clearly promised more than he delivered—and claimed more for his achievement than it deserved. Still, given the enormous wealth and political influence opposing railroad regulation, perhaps little more was possible.[51]

[9]

Although railroad regulation occupied center stage during the entire 1905 legislative session, other solid achievements occurred, too. The legislature made the tax commission a permanent state agency, greatly expanding its powers and duties. The commission received the authority to assess the property of telephone companies, street railways, and all electric light, heat, and power companies owned by street railways, and to levy taxes according to the *ad valorem* formula calculated for railroads. The commission now also appointed a review board to hear appeals in certain local assessment cases. The legislature also rectified the error on the proposed 1903 constitutional amendment to permit an income tax. With the assistance of Charles McCarthy and John R. Commons, it enacted a comprehensive civil service law and established another three-man commission to administer civil service. La Follette was enthusiastic about the law, partly because it was a response to criticism of his patronage tactics, and partly because it gave him an opportunity to protect many of his appointees with permanent status. On the positive side, the law assured competing socio-economic interests that state officials would be relatively impartial and incorruptible. Of the 387 government employees who took the first civil service test, only seventeen, mostly game wardens, failed to pass.[52]

The 1905 legislature also recodified the state bank examination system; La Follette later claimed the new code virtually eliminated bank failures. It passed a stringent anti-lobby law which required lobbyists to register with the secretary of state, to keep all communications with legislators public and formal, and to publish the details of all arguments or agreements. La Follette's interest in the conserva-

[51] La Follette, *Autobiography*, 149–155 (quotes); Maxwell, *La Follette and the Rise of the Progressives*, 76–77; Margulies, *Decline of the Progressive Movement*, 84, 94; Caine, *Myth of a Progressive Reform*, 186–203.
[52] La Follette, *Autobiography*, 155–157; Maxwell, *La Follette and the Rise of the Progressives*, 75, 80–82; Margulies, *Senator Lenroot*, 66–67; Acrea, "Wisconsin Progressivism," 411–417.

tion of natural resources was instrumental in the legislature's establishing a state department of forestry, empowered to purchase land for a forest reserve. It was also the legislative session responsible for the steps that led to construction of a new capitol building. The building burned on February 27, 1904, just a few months after La Follette had canceled the insurance policy in favor of self-insurance by the state. (The 1905 legislature met in temporary quarters on the university campus.) Necessity impelled the legislature to reorganize and enlarge the State Capitol Commission it had created in 1903, and to set financial and planning guidelines for the commission to follow. The current neoclassical structure was dedicated in 1917. Total construction costs ran to $8 million, "without graft."[53]

Those who expected La Follette to resign the governorship and head off to Washington when he returned to Madison in the fall of 1905 were sorely disappointed. He surprised almost everyone by calling the legislature into special session, ostensibly to append a second-choice provision to the direct primary law. In fact La Follette and his advisers wanted to prevent the possibility of a Stalwart candidate's winning with a plurality in a primary contest that featured two or more Progressives. The effort failed, largely because of opposition organized by William D. Connor, who was alienated by La Follette's handling of the senatorial election during the 1905 regular session. Undaunted, the governor revealed his plan to investigate and then regulate the state's insurance companies. The legislature acquiesced by appointing a joint committee headed by Senator Frear and Assemblyman Herman L. Ekern. It was asked to examine the companies' lobbying, campaign contributions, methods of soliciting business and paying commissions to agents, investments, securities, other assets, and methods of safeguarding them. Deliberations began in January, 1906, just about the time La Follette finally resigned to take his seat in the U.S. Senate.[54]

[10]

From early January, 1906, until his death on June 18, 1925, Robert M. La Follette used the United States Senate as a forum to repeat nationally what he had done with the Republican party in Wisconsin. Originally standing alone in the Senate, La Follette soon became the

---

[53] La Follette, *Autobiography*, 155–157; Maxwell, *La Follette and the Rise of the Progressives*, 75, 80–82, 165; Doan, *La Follettes and the Wisconsin Idea*, 41–42; Acrea, "Wisconsin Progressivism," 404–407, 415–416.

[54] Maxwell, *La Follette and the Rise of the Progressives*, 74–75, 111–113; Acrea, "Wisconsin Progressivism," 404–407.

unofficial leader of a group of midwestern and western "insurgents" who challenged the party's pro-business eastern establishment on a wide range of issues. In his maiden speech, he advocated strengthening the proposed Hepburn railroad rate act. In 1911, he was instrumental in the formation of the National Progressive Republican League, organized to promote the candidacy of a progressive instead of renominating President William Howard Taft, who had sided with the Stalwarts on most issues. The following year, La Follette emerged as a full-blown presidential candidate, only to be undone by Taft and Theodore Roosevelt in a battle reminiscent of the 1904 Republican convention in Madison. La Follette was the highest-ranking federal officeholder to oppose U.S. intervention in World War I. Increasingly he identified himself with underdogs and "radical" causes. By the time he ran for president on the Progressive party ticket in 1924, he was endorsed by several labor and radical organizations. He received nearly 5 million popular votes, but carried only Wisconsin and North Dakota. Throughout his senatorial career, he greatly enhanced Wisconsin's national reputation for progressive government and politics. No matter how involved he was in national affairs over the last two decades of his life, La Follette continued to exert a powerful influence on the politics of his home state, though with decidedly mixed results.[55]

Evaluating Robert La Follette's three terms as governor is a daunting task. Nearly seventy-five years after his death, "Fighting Bob" remains the most celebrated figure in Wisconsin history. The legend, which La Follette himself did much to develop and perpetuate, has resisted most attempts to reduce it to historical reality. This is all the more true because most historians are highly sympathetic to La Follette's professed goals. (Historians are inclined to love him for the enemies he made, even if for nothing else.) The harder one tries to separate the man from the movement and its accomplishments, the more one appreciates La Follette's unparalleled success at weaving those elements into a seamless web. It is true that the legislative achievements of the La Follette years were, in large measure, the culmination of struggles begun in the 1890's by reformers who continued to be the greatest supporters of progressivism in the new century. But it is true, also, that it is difficult to see how those efforts could have come to fruition without a charismatic chief executive intent upon identifying his own political fortunes with their agenda. He provided the crucial ingredient, and it is impossible to imagine any of his contemporaries playing that critical role as effectively. While "Fighting Bob" was not sufficient cause for the triumph of

---

[55] La Follette, *Autobiography*, 159–210; Doan, *La Follettes and the Wisconsin Idea*, 43–137; Margulies, *Decline of the Progressive Movement*, 84–100, 106–123, 149–150, 160–163; Weisberger, *La Follettes of Wisconsin*, 44–76, 132–178.

reform in turn-of-the-century Wisconsin, he was certainly necessary and probably indispensable.

The most important and lasting achievement of the La Follette years was the revamping of the tax structure, an achievement that placed Wisconsin in the vanguard of states promoting the Progressive Era's "revolution in taxation." The equalization of property taxes, the establishment of a permanent tax commission, the enactment of an inheritance tax, and the launching of a proposed constitutional amendment that would ultimately result in the adoption of the nation's first successful state income tax made Wisconsin a prototype of the principles advocated by the National Tax Association and similar reform organizations. In addition to going a long way towards tax equity, Wisconsin's new tax structure also provided the potential for raising the amount of revenue necessary to finance a modern state government and a new service state.

The La Follette administration's impact on the political system was equally profound, but more ambiguous. The direct primary, civil service, anti-lobbying legislation, and the inauguration of issue-oriented, candidate-centered campaigning did much to remedy the evils of ethno-cultural, partisan politics and to force politicians and voters to focus more squarely on "real" questions—meaning socio-economic ones. But it did so at a great price, because it severely undermined the party infrastructure and the "mystic chords of memory" that connected large numbers of Wisconsinites to politics and government. Paradoxically, the more "pure" and "rational" politics and government became, the less invested Wisconsinites felt. A viable civil service and reliance upon appointive, independent, expert commissions made government more honest, efficient, economical, and rational; but they also removed government ever further from the political control and the purview of the average Wisconsinite. Since most of these negative trends were long-term and gradual, at the time they did little to detract from La Follette's claim that he had restored government and politics to the people. The establishment of the state railroad commission, flawed and compromised though it was, was a giant step in the direction of constructing a regulatory state, with all the strengths and weaknesses that historians have detected therein. La Follette's successors incrementally expanded it into a full-scale public service commission, with jurisdiction over all the state's public utilities, and used it as a model to set up other, similar commissions that were central to what became "the Wisconsin Idea." The achievements of the La Follette administration were not nearly so innovative, positive, or monumental as "Old Bob" widely proclaimed, but they were certainly seminal and irreversible.[56]

---

[56] The fullest discussion of "the revolution in taxation" is Clifton K. Yearley, *The Money Machines: The Breakdown and Reform of Governmental and Party Finance in the North,*

[11]

Besides reacting to initiatives from the executive office, the legislatures of 1901, 1903, and 1905 also continued to build upon the laws and programs adopted in the 1890's. Each successive legislature demonstrated a greater proclivity for expanding governmental authority and responsibility, frequently proceeding farther and faster than La Follette and his circle led them. The senate continued to act as a check upon the more activist assembly, and conservatives continued to hold the key positions. Nevertheless, the legislative branch overall grew steadily more "progressive," meaning that it more willingly advocated governmental intervention on behalf of the economically disadvantaged. Representatives from Oconto, Lincoln, Dunn, Adams, Marquette, and Grant counties were in the vanguard, frequently assisted by "mildly progressive" lawmakers from Bayfield, Sawyer, and Washburn counties. In 1901, legislators from the timber counties and the urban-industrial southeastern quadrant remained largely indifferent or hostile towards reform measures; by 1905, their orientation was changing as divisions along socio-economic lines grew more pronounced and calls for government intervention became more insistent. Legislators from both north and southeast tended towards greater activism and radicalism in 1905, prodded by the five Social Democratic legislators from Milwaukee. Their enthusiasm for reform hardened the resistance of "softer" progressives from the more developed and prosperous dairy-farming areas of the state. By the conclusion of the 1905 special session, William D. Hoard and the Wisconsin Dairymen's Association had all but openly split from the progressive reform coalition, partly because they resented La Follette's "dictatorial" tactics, but largely because the evolving conception of a social-service state was incompatible with their own ideas. Instead they envisioned what might be termed a "night-watchman state." Gradually, their fear of "doctrinaire radicals" overcame their antipathy towards "wealthy malefactors." Many other soft progressives shared these feelings by 1906.[57]

1860–1920 (Albany, 1970). See also John D. Buenker, *The Income Tax and The Progressive Era* (New York, 1985), 1–56. The most balanced and thorough analysis of Progressive Era business regulation is Thomas K. McCraw, ed., *Regulation in Perspective: Historical Essays* (Cambridge, 1981). See also his *Prophets of Regulation: Charles Francis Adams, Louis D. Brandeis, James M. Landis, Alfred E. Kahn* (Cambridge, 1984). On the ambiguous impact of Progressive Era political reforms, see Arnold Bennett Hall, "The Direct Primary and Party Responsibility in Wisconsin," in the *Annals of the Academy of Political and Social Science*, 106 (March, 1923), 40–54; Walter Dean Burnham, *Critical Elections and the Mainsprings of American Politics* (New York, 1970); and Acrea, "Wisconsin Progressivism," 411–412.

[57] Acrea, "Wisconsin Progressivism," 393–394, 417–442; Eric E. Lampard, *The Rise*

Nowhere was the course heading towards the social-service state more apparent than in the legislature's public education initiatives. In the main, they aimed at broadening educational opportunities for a wide range of children and adults, increasing state financial support, and augmenting the supervisory authority of the office of the state superintendent of public instruction. They also manifested a growing commitment towards "practical" education, especially vocational schooling and citizenship training. The legislatures of 1901 through 1905 raised the compulsory education age to fourteen (a try for sixteen failed in 1905); increased state financial aid to the University of Wisconsin, the normal schools, and county schools of agricultural and domestic science; mandated uniform textbooks for ungraded rural schools; provided for rural school inspection; required high schools to admit students from districts without secondary educational facilities; and allowed school districts to provide free evening lectures for working people. Private commercial schools were brought under state supervision. The legislature also established new agricultural experiment stations and empowered the Free Library Commission to provide a catalogue of state publications, expand its traveling libraries, and authorize traveling and permanent libraries for counties. In a move of far-reaching implications, the 1901 legislature authorized the library commission to establish what soon evolved into the Legislative Reference Library.[58]

Progress in conservation was less visible, save for the establishment of a state department of forestry; but the trend towards greater state responsibility continued. La Follette-era legislatures enacted a weak water pollution bill, established fish hatcheries and state parks, suspended the sale of public lands, continued and expanded the geological and natural history surveys, and consolidated local drainage districts. But they also turned down several other conservation proposals and used an unsystematic, hit-and-miss approach. Efforts to expand public services were slightly more productive. In 1901, the legislature increased the power of the State Board of Health to investigate sweatshops and established the Live Stock Sanitary Board. In 1903, it permitted counties to levy taxes for road construction and regulated the hours of maternity hospitals. In 1905, it created a hygiene laboratory, founded a grain and warehouse commission, and began regulating automobile drivers.

However, those same legislatures defeated proposals to aid highway construction, establish tuberculosis sanitariums and a state liquor

---

of the Dairy Industry in Wisconsin: A Study in Agricultural Change, 1820–1920 (Madison, 1963), 344–351. See also Chapter 2.

[58] Acrea, "Wisconsin Progressivism," 394–398; Conrad E. Patzer, *Public Education in Wisconsin* (Madison, 1924), 470–472.

commission, and extend the board of health's authority to logging camps. They generally increased aid to existing charitable and penal institutions, but established no new ones. Several measures aimed at business regulation and antitrust activity also failed, though they pointed towards future action.[59]

In labor legislation, especially, the legislature outran the La Follette administration. La Follette asserted the importance of the labor vote to his success in his *Autobiography,* implying that he merited this vote because of his efforts on behalf of labor legislation. In truth, however, there is little to suggest that labor legislation occupied a prominent place on his agenda, and there is much to indicate instead that legislators from districts where organized labor was beginning to flex political muscle deserve the credit. They were urged on by social workers, intellectuals, women's clubs, reform organizations, and the Bureau of Labor and Industrial Statistics. In 1901, their efforts succeeded in banning children under fourteen from employment where liquor was sold, requiring safe scaffolding on construction projects, establishing a free employment office in Milwaukee, and empowering state inspectors to enforce modest anti-sweatshop regulations. The following year, they tightened the state's railroad employer liability law, established three new free employment offices, and added state inspection of tenements. From 1905 on, the number of labor bills rose significantly, driven by Social Democratic lawmakers from Milwaukee. Many were introduced by Assemblyman Frederick Brockhausen, a Danish-born and German-trained cigar maker from Milwaukee and secretary-treasurer of the Wisconsin State Federation of Labor.

At Brockhausen's urging, the 1905 legislature enacted additional safety rules for railroads, machinery, and construction projects, and succeeded in removing the "assumed risk" defense in employer liability cases. However, the assembly tabled bills mandating one day's rest in seven, requiring proof of notice before garnisheeing wages, and abolishing the "contributory negligence" defense in employer liability cases. At the same time, the senate, influenced by the state's employers, defeated or tabled measures mandating an eight-hour day on construction projects run by local government, limiting the use of injunctions, broadening the rights of railroad employees, requiring employer registration of industrial accidents, demanding that railroads use safe braking and coupling equipment, and insisting upon three days' notice of dismissal for most employees. Those small achievements in 1905 made it clear that labor legislation was a main

---

[59] Acrea, "Wisconsin Progressivism," 398–410; Maxwell, *La Follette and the Rise of the Progressives,* 164–165; Caine, *Myth of a Progressive Reform,* 137–151.

order of business for the future and that progressive politicians had better assign it higher priority.[60]

By the time Bob La Follette left for the U.S. Senate in January, 1906, his progressive coalition was beginning to self-destruct. The internecine battles over the senatorship and the railroad commission had alienated Stephenson, Connor, Hoard, and a host of lesser lights. La Follette then exacerbated the situation by committing what historian Roger Wyman has judged as "probably the greatest single political blunder of [his] long career": he tried to replace his lieutenant-governor, James O. Davidson, as a potential gubernatorial candidate in 1906. Events began to unfold in the summer of 1905, when La Follette, his law partner Alfred T. Rogers, Herman L. Ekern, and James A. Stone decided that Davidson was too uneducated and uncommitted to lead the progressive Republican cause. La Follette believed Davidson was apt to conciliate Republicans of all ideological persuasions, and was incapable of understanding the reform program complexities. He and his advisers feared that under Davidson the Stalwarts would regain control and undo much of what had been accomplished. As Rogers noted, special interests "will first attempt to elect men who are unaggressive or unable to carry forward the progressive work. The discouraged and apathetic public sentiment which will surely follow readily lends itself to the election of public officials who are subservient tools of special interests."[61]

Events quickly demonstrated that the strategy to dump Davidson was fraught with pitfalls. Affable and approachable, Davidson enjoyed enormous personal popularity with people at nearly every point on the political spectrum, especially among his fellow Norwegian Americans. He was sworn in as governor, quickly instituting an open-door policy that was the complete antithesis of La Follette's ideological screening process. Davidson also had "paid his political dues" through service at the local level, in the legislature, and as state treasurer and lieutenant-governor. By the prevailing political rules, he had earned the governor's mansion. A charter member of Albert Hall's bipartisan reform coalition in the 1890's, he continued to proclaim his loyalty to the cause. He personified the self-made man and successful immigrant, having been a penniless newcomer who had risen from laborer to store owner, and from township official to gov-

---

[60] La Follette, *Autobiography*, 131–134; *Wisconsin Blue Book, 1905*, p. 1109; Acrea, "Wisconsin Progressivism," 410–415; Maxwell, *La Follette and the Rise of the Progressives*, 154; Gertrude Schmidt Weiss, "History of Labor Legislation in Wisconsin" (doctoral dissertation, University of Wisconsin, 1933), 1–52; Gordon M. Haferbecker, *Wisconsin Labor Laws* (Madison, 1958), 5–15. See also Chapter 6.

[61] Margulies, *Decline of the Progressive Movement*, 85–88 (quote); Wyman, "Voting Behavior in the Progressive Era," 277–278; Acrea, "Wisconsin Progressivism," 413–417; Isaac Stephenson, *Recollections of a Long Life, 1829–1915* (Chicago, 1915), 227–230.

ernor. He was the only Norwegian-born politician to become governor, and he was the most prolific vote getter among Wisconsin's Norwegians, who had consistently and heavily supported progressives at the polls. To make matters even worse for La Follette, who prided himself on his sensitivity to Norwegian sensibilities, he proposed to replace Davidson with a Swedish American, at a time when the two countries were on the brink of war and when Norwegian voters outnumbered all other Scandinavians in Wisconsin by more than two to one.[62]

La Follette's choice to replace Davidson, Irvine Lenroot, was a thirty-seven-year-old attorney from Superior. He had served three terms in the assembly, avidly supported progressive legislation, ably drafted legislation, and built effective legislative coalitions. As assembly speaker during the 1905 session, he was instrumental in the railroad commission battle and in managing other key administration undertakings. Despite his proven abilities, however, Lenroot seemed cold and distant compared to Davidson. Rumors that he was a closet "dry" undermined his appeal to many ethnic groups. Despite La Follette's blessing of Lenroot, more than 200 progressive Republican leaders, including La Follette's mentors Hoard and Bryant, signed a petition supporting Davidson's nomination and re-election. Stephenson ordered the *Free Press* to remain editorially neutral, damaging Lenroot's prospects in Milwaukee. Connor, already at war with La Follette, offered his financial and electoral support to Davidson, signing on as his running mate for lieutenant-governor. Haugen pointedly reminded La Follette that Davidson was owed the nomination since he had earlier consented to be lieutenant-governor only because La Follette had lured him with the bait of succession.

Many progressive Republicans failed to discern any substantive difference between Lenroot and Davidson. Many moderate progressives indeed welcomed Governor Davidson as someone who could heal the wounds inflicted by more than a decade of factional quarreling. While many Stalwarts viewed the Davidson-Lenroot contest as a fortuitous opportunity to drive a major wedge into the ranks of their adversaries, they agreed with Elisha Keyes that Davidson was "a peaceable man, . . . not belligerent or aggressive. He is the kind of man

---

[62] Wyman, "Voting Behavior in the Progressive Era," 276–277; Margulies, *Decline of the Progressive Movement*, 86–87; Maxwell, *La Follette and the Rise of the Progressives*, 84–85. According to Philip La Follette, his father was shocked when Davidson announced his candidacy, believing Davidson had intended only to serve out La Follette's third term. See Donald Young, ed., *Adventure in Politics: The Memoirs of Philip La Follette* (New York, 1970), 15. To the contrary, Haugen asserts that Davidson only agreed to be lieutenant-governor on the understanding that he would eventually assume the higher office. See Nils Haugen, "Pioneer and Political Reminiscences" (Part 6) in *WMH*, 12 (March, 1929), 275.

the party needs in this state...." Both Stalwarts and moderate progressives joined in denouncing La Follette as a vindictive overlord. They saw his attempt to control the outcome of the state's first primary election as a cynical betrayal of the very reform to which he owed much of his reputation as a champion of democracy.[63]

Unlike the general elections of 1902 and 1904, Wisconsin's first gubernatorial primary did not hinge on the ideological split between Stalwarts and Progressives. To the extent that it did, hard-core Progressives generally found themselves on the receiving end of charges about bossism, machine politics, and special interests. The 1906 gubernatorial primary campaign was essentially a hybrid that crossed the emerging politics of personality with traditional ethno-cultural politics. On the personality side, the public viewed Lenroot as a stand-in for La Follette. It was a contest between the acerbic, confrontational style of one progressive Republican leader and the accommodating, easy-going style of another. On the ethno-cultural side, the primary was a classic intraparty struggle between two of the state's most fiercely Republican ethnic groups: 155,122 Norwegians versus 48,812 Swedes. La Follette, Lenroot, and their Norwegian allies fervently wooed Norwegian voters, but they could not overcome Norwegians' ethnic pride in Davidson nor their hostility towards the Swedes who had ruled their homeland for nearly a century. The most widely read Norwegian-language newspaper, *Skandinaven* of Chicago, strongly endorsed Davidson and published scores of letters from Wisconsin-bred Norwegians supporting him. Norwegian voters left little doubt that they were Norwegians first, Republicans second, Progressives third, and La Follette supporters a distant fourth.

In the end, "Yim" Davidson smashed Lenroot, 105,593 votes to 61,178 and sixty-eight counties to three. Moreover, Connor received the lieutenant-governor's nomination, making the La Follette forces more anxious still. Francis McGovern lost re-election as Milwaukee County's district attorney, to a more conservative Republican; Babcock defeated a progressive Republican in the Third Congressional District. Primary victories of Gustav Kuestermann in the Ninth Congressional District and William J. Cary in the Fourth provided some solace for the Progressives. Some expressed hope that the primary results would end factionalism. But events proved otherwise. The damage incurred by the defections of Davidson, Connor, Stephenson, Hoard, and their followers would never be repaired.[64]

---

[63] Wyman, "Voting Behavior in the Progressive Era," 277–280; Margulies, *Decline of the Progressive Movement*, 87–88, 95–98 (quotes); Maxwell, *La Follette and the Rise of the Progressives*, 84; Acrea, "Wisconsin Progressivism," 452; Margulies, *Senator Lenroot*, 20–67.

[64] Wyman, "Voting Behavior in the Progressive Era," 280–282; Margulies, *Decline of*

Undeterred by their primary defeat, the La Follette-Lenroot faction fought to oust Connor as state chairman and to challenge Davidson's control of the Republican state central committee. They failed in both efforts. Temporarily stymied, they resignedly gave at least the appearance of backing the Davidson-Connor ticket, helping the governor poll 57.5 per cent of the vote, the highest Republican total since the harmony campaign of 1900. Babcock lost in the Third, causing some progressives to celebrate, but his Democratic successor offered them little long-term comfort. And in what some judged a further affront to the spirit of direct democracy and primary elections, McGovern, as an independent candidate with La Follette's reluctant backing, won re-election in a close four-man race in which his closest rival was a Social Democrat. The Republicans retained their customary stronghold on both houses of the legislature, but factional squabbling raised doubts about passing further reform legislation.[65]

[12]

Before dealing with substantive issues, the 1907 legislature had to cope with selecting another U.S. senator. Spooner resigned effective April 30, 1907, and five at least nominally progressive Republicans quickly declared their candidacies: Lenroot, Stephenson, state senator William Hatton, and Congressmen Henry Allen Cooper of Racine and John J. Esch of La Crosse. Cooper and Lenroot, seemingly at La Follette's urging, eventually withdrew, but the other three battled on for several weeks in the Republican legislative caucus. La Follette made little effort to intervene until mid-May, when he telegraphed assembly speaker Herman Ekern: "Stephenson must win. Fight hard." In the end, Stephenson emerged victorious with backing from La Follette, who apparently was satisfied that "Uncle Ike" would serve only the remaining two years of Spooner's term as his reward for service to the state, the party, and progressive reform. Highly skeptical, Stephenson later attributed La Follette's dilatory tactics to a "sudden delicacy of feeling" that "forbade any zealous attempt to influence the action or mold convictions of these men whom the

---

the *Progressive Movement*, 88–97, and *Senator Lenroot*, 67–69; Maxwell, *La Follette and the Rise of the Progressives*, 84–85. For the view of Lenroot's campaign manager, see Albert Erlebacher, "Herman L. Ekern: The Quiet Progressive" (doctoral dissertation, University of Wisconsin, 1965), 62–70.

[65] Wyman, "Voting Behavior in the Progressive Era," 282–283, 425–430; Margulies, *Decline of the Progressive Movement*, 98–99; Maxwell, *La Follette and the Rise of the Progressives*, 85.

outer world had erroneously regarded as parts of a well organized political machine."

Hatton and McGovern announced their senatorial candidacies in 1909, along with Samuel Cook, the Stalwarts' original gubernatorial candidate in 1904, apparently believing that Stephenson meant to serve only two years. To their dismay, Stephenson decided to seek reelection, motivated by his resentment at La Follette's lukewarm support in 1907 and seeming condescension. La Follette remained publicly neutral in the 1908 senatorial primary, but his closest supporters backed Hatton, after failing to convince McGovern to withdraw. Stephenson spent more than $100,000 in a newspaper campaign that carried the day, winning in thirty-nine counties though with only 32 per cent of the total vote. The other two "progressive" candidates polled 42 per cent between them. The results clearly demonstrated the continuing factionalism among progressive Republicans, and set the stage for another clash during the 1909 legislative session.[66]

The schism grew wider during the election year of 1908. The Davidson-Connor alliance had become so strained that the governor chose former senator John Strange as his running mate in the primary. The new team had no intraparty opposition, but the La Follette-Lenroot faction increased its leverage when Lenroot won the primary over an incumbent Stalwart in the Eleventh Congressional District. In 1908, La Follette was making his first, and futile, attempt to gain the Republican presidential nomination, and he disrupted the state party convention, first by trying to incorporate his planks about the second-choice primary and tariff revision into the platform, then by trying to gain control of the central committee. In both cases, he suffered stunning defeats at the hands of the combined forces of Davidson and Stephenson. Still, La Follette maintained a facade of friendship and co-operation with Davidson's wing of the party, largely because Davidson in the main supported progressive reform. But La Follette soon stirred up another hornets' nest by refusing to abide by the results of the very primary process which was his proudest gubernatorial achievement. His protégé Herman Ekern, the assembly speaker, lost in the primary to Albert Twesme, a Stalwart, and La Follette then encouraged Ekern to run as an independent. The campaign became heated as Davidson campaigned for Twesme. Twesme won narrowly, worsening the breach between governor and senator.[67]

Having already alienated Stephenson and McGovern by backing

---

[66] Wyman, "Voting Behavior in the Progressive Era," 282–284; Margulies, *Decline of the Progressive Movement*, 99–101 (quotes); Acrea, "Wisconsin Progressivism," 476–477; Stephenson, *Recollections of a Long Life*, 230–250.

[67] Wyman, "Voting Behavior in the Progressive Era," 284–285; Margulies, *Decline of the Progressive Movement*, 102–104.

Hatton in the senatorial preference primary of 1908, La Follette inflicted further damage by refusing to abide by the decision of the Republican electorate, which chose Stephenson. He acted through another protégé, John J. Blaine, a state senator from Grant County, and challenged Stephenson's victory, charging that the junior senator had bought the primary election by outspending the other three candidates combined. A legislative investigation headed by Blaine failed to produce any solid evidence of illegal activity, and Stephenson was re-elected in the general election despite La Follette's opposition. Still refusing to concede, La Follette orchestrated an unsuccessful effort to have Congress void Stephenson's election. By the time Stephenson was finally exonerated in 1912, any hope of reconciliation between the two Wisconsin senators had evaporated.[68]

[13]

The achievements of James O. Davidson's administration (1906–1911) usually receive short shrift from historians, sandwiched as they were between the mountain peaks of progressive reform represented by the La Follette years (1901–1906) and the even more illustrious years of the McGovern administration (1911–1915). A comparison of points of view helps create a different perspective.

Viewed from the perspective of the early 1890's, the Davidson legislative sessions of 1907 and 1909 constituted "the flood-tide of progressivism," a culmination "in which middle-class views of social and economic harmony received their fullest expression," according to historian Kenneth Acrea. Viewed from the vantage of 1912, however, the accomplishments of those years laid groundwork needed for the more thoroughgoing socio-economic reforms adopted in 1911—reforms that recognized the inherent inequality of society, provided direct aid to the disadvantaged, and marshaled state power in the service of hitherto ignored segments of society. Viewed from the 1990's, the Davidson years stand as a transition or conduit between two visions of Wisconsin society and polity that manifested both striking continuities and dramatic departures.

Assessing James O. Davidson's personal contribution to this metamorphosis is an even more protean task. Davidson was the temperamental antithesis of La Follette, and he was far less enamored of executive activism and ideological politics. A self-conscious progressive Republican, strongly supportive of the reform legislation of the

---

[68]Wyman, "Voting Behavior in the Progressive Era," 285; Margulies, *Decline of the Progressive Movement*, 105; Stephenson, *Recollection of a Long Life*, 250–255; Erlebacher, "Herman L. Ekern," 74–81.

previous five years, Davidson nevertheless confided to several allies that it was time for a respite from turmoil and agitation, for consolidation and refinement of what had already been accomplished, and for "a business administration." In June, 1906, he informed Connor that "a very good proportion at least of the people, are willing to have a rest from the turbulence that has been with us in the past, but none are willing to sacrifice a single principle that we have contended for." Accordingly, the new governor proved reluctant to exercise dynamic leadership, was inclined to yield initiative to the legislature, supported additions and refinements to existing programs, and was cautious about stepping on unfamiliar ground.[69]

Less constrained by executive initiative, the legislatures of 1907 and 1909 were themselves in a period of transition. Lawmakers from the urban industrial southeast and from the less affluent border counties of the western uplands spurred their colleagues to continue the decade-long trend towards greater attention to lower-middle-class and blue-collar Wisconsinites. Enthusiasm among representatives from more prosperous dairy areas and lumbering regions continued to wane. The small contingent of Democratic legislators became more activist; the dominant Republican contingent suffered a decline among hard-core progressives, some of whom drifted towards moderation, social harmony, and rationalized economic policy. The tiny cohort of Social Democrats, by contrast, grew ever more militant and more influential. Conservatives or mild progressives continued to dominate most of the important committees, so many of the more radical socio-economic initiatives were watered down through amendments or else were sidetracked. Bills dealing with economic matters increased dramatically in number. (There were so many bills, and the legislature deliberated so long over them, that Emanuel Philipp sarcastically referred to the 1907 legislature as "the Long Parliament.") In the end, the legislatures of the Davidson years kept the momentum of progressive reform going and sowed many seeds for the harvest of 1911.[70]

They excelled in the area of business regulation, particularly in expanding the jurisdiction and powers of the Railroad Commission.

---

[69] Acrea, "Wisconsin Progressivism," 455 (quote), 478–494; Margulies, *Decline of the Progressive Movement*, 91–99 (quote). Spooner characterized Davidson as being "limp as a wet rag" and "spineless if it was not for the influence of his wife." See Fowler, *John Coit Spooner*, 324. McCarthy, according to Marion Casey, *Charles McCarthy: Librarianship and Reform* (Chicago, 1981), 56–57, regarded Davidson as "medieval," both in the conservative nature of his ideology and in his falling between the administrations of La Follette and McGovern.

[70] Acrea, "Wisconsin Progressivism," 466–470; Caine, *Myth of a Progressive Reform*, 178–185; Edward A. Fitzpatrick, *McCarthy of Wisconsin* (New York, 1944), 118–120; Philipp, *Political Reform in Wisconsin*, 186.

The 1907 legislature extended the commission's scope to include supervision of the state's street railways and telegraph and express companies. It also brought a variety of public utility companies under the commission's oversight. Building on that new base, the 1907 legislature enacted a two-cents-a-mile limit on railroad passenger fares, and empowered the Railroad Commission to review charges of excessive rates brought against street railway companies. Finally, it empowered the commission to monitor the issuance of stocks and bonds and other paper securities, a function later embellished by the addition of a "blue sky" law in the 1913 legislature. When the Railroad Commission became the Public Service Commission in 1931, it had already been functioning in that capacity for nearly two decades, thanks largely to the work of the 1907 legislature.[71]

Wisconsin also became a national model for the regulation of insurance corporations in the same legislature. A joint committee established during the 1905 special session called by Governor La Follette began an investigation of life insurance companies in response to a national scandal. It scrutinized three disparate carriers: Northwestern Mutual of Milwaukee, the state's largest company; Union Central Life Insurance Company of Cincinnati, a medium-sized stock company with numerous Wisconsin policyholders; and the Wisconsin Life Insurance Company of Madison, a small company doing most of its business within the state. It found all three guilty of questionable internal management practices requiring "efficient, comprehensive, conservative, remedial legislation." The committee proposed reforms; bills were drafted even before the legislature convened in January of 1907. Eventually, over seventy-five separate insurance reform bills were introduced during that session. With James A. Frear as secretary of state, Herman Ekern as assembly speaker, and Julius Roehr chairman of the joint committee on banking and insurance, the success of insurance regulation was virtually guaranteed.[72]

Several of the bills generated little or no opposition. But proposals to regulate the election of company directors, limit allowable ex-

---

[71] Wyman, "Voting Behavior in the Progressive Era," 289–290; Maxwell, *La Follette and the Rise of the Progressives*, 96–97; Caine, *Myth of a Progressive Reform*, 186–203; Philipp, *Political Reform in Wisconsin*, 185–193; David Nord, "The Experts Versus the Experts: Conflicting Philosophies of Municipal Utility Regulation in the Progressive Era," in *WMH*, 58 (Spring, 1975), 219–236.

[72] Maxwell, *La Follette and the Rise of the Progressives*, 105–127 (quote on p. 113); Acrea, "Wisconsin Progressivism," 467–469; Harold F. Williamson and Orange A. Smalley, *Northwestern Mutual Life: A Century of Trusteeship* (Evanston, Illinois, 1957), 133–138; Morton Keller, *The Life Insurance Enterprise, 1885–1910: A Study in the Limits of Corporate Power* (Cambridge, 1963), 13–15, 71–72, 255–262; H. Roger Grant, *Insurance Reform: Consumer Action in the Progressive Era* (Ames, Iowa, 1979), 12–60; Albert Erlebacher, "The Wisconsin Life Insurance Reform of 1907," in *WMH*, 55 (Spring, 1972), 213–230, and his "Herman L. Ekern," 82–136.

penses, and stipulate the amount of those expenses that could be "loaded" into the premium payment set off battles. Proponents moderated their original bills to achieve their passage. The major insurance companies worked energetically against them. Miles M. Dawson, a nationally renowned insurance expert who had served as an actuary to the Wisconsin insurance investigation committee, urged Davidson to veto the "Ekern legislation" regarding expense and premium limitations, saying the state otherwise would turn into an "insurance wilderness." Prudential, Metropolitan, Travelers, and others threatened to retire from the state. The Milwaukee *Sentinel* denounced the proposed laws as "socialistic" and predicted both defections by out-of-state companies and retaliatory legislation elsewhere against Wisconsin-based insurers. Despite all such protests, Davidson signed every insurance reform bill that the legislature placed before him. And despite the wrangling and dire predictions, the new laws did not bring on economic ruin. Twenty-four non-Wisconsin companies ultimately withdrew in protest; several larger national firms rapidly adjusted. Northwestern Mutual, New York Life, Metropolitan, and Prudential experienced increases in revenue. Tax receipts from insurance companies in the first five years after 1907 more than doubled those of 1901–1906. Inspired by such results, subsequent legislatures strengthened the state's regulatory authority.[73]

Davidson-era legislatures extended the state's regulatory arm into several other industries. A 1907 law ordered the banking commissioner to develop a uniform system of accounting for building and loan associations; a 1909 law prohibited branch banking and limited each bank to only one deposit station. Also in 1909, the office of the Dairy and Food Commissioner was empowered to supervise sanitary conditions in food preparation and handling, but was granted almost no discretion in establishing standards. The 1909 legislature modified the building code for Milwaukee apartments and tenements after the courts had invalidated a 1907 measure, but it failed to extend similar regulations to other cities. The 1907 legislature also defeated attempts by John Whitehead, a Stalwart senator, to reduce railroads' liability for property damage and to reduce the lines' compensation to injured employees. Most of these actions either defended or slightly augmented existing regulatory legislation, and most provided inadequate enforcement machinery.[74]

---

[73] Maxwell, *La Follette and the Rise of the Progressives*, 116–123; Acrea, "Wisconsin Progressivism," 467–469; Williamson and Smalley, *Northwestern Mutual Life*, 138–146; Grant, *Life Insurance Enterprise*, 61–63, 71–77, 93–98, 124–131; Erlebacher, "Wisconsin Life Insurance Reform," in *WMH*, 55: 217–228, and "Herman L. Ekern," 111–136; Keller, *Life Insurance Enterprise*, 262–275.

[74] Acrea, "Wisconsin Progressivism," 468–469.

However, the same legislatures proved reluctant to expand state regulation into other fields. In 1907, measures to license electrical and civil engineers, to empower city governments to control smoke and air pollution, and to regulate butcher shops were all tabled. In 1909, the same thing happened to bills to allow cities to grant utility franchises of indeterminate length and to direct the attorney general to file suits against former insurance commissioners who accepted fees or other compensation from the companies that they were supposed to regulate. The 1909 legislature also defeated a package of utility regulation bills sponsored by a Milwaukee Social Democratic senator, Winfield R. Gaylord, to require utility companies to recognize employee unions, pay into a fund to finance possible municipal ownership, and shape their service to the needs of the public. Wisconsin took significant steps towards becoming a regulatory state in 1907 and 1909, but it did so cautiously.[75]

The same could be said of the Davidson legislatures' approach to public service: they demonstrated more than usual interest, but with mixed results. They established the office of state fire marshal, consolidated the Milwaukee free employment office with that of the state factory inspector, founded an internal waterways commission, and directed the tax commission to oversee the issuance of stocks and bonds. As required, they successfully shepherded through both legislatures a proposed constitutional amendment allowing the use of state funds for highway construction; and they authorized the geological survey to experiment with different methods of highway construction depending upon topography and soil. They also expanded the scope and powers of the state board of immigration, and provided for a scientific study of the merits of state-run insurance programs, which would later bear fruit. Although the legislature approved a teachers' employment office in the Bureau of Labor and Industrial Statistics, Davidson vetoed it on the grounds that it was demeaning to suggest that teachers could not find positions without state help. The legislature itself shrank from enacting Senator Gaylord's bill to establish a state board of public works to supervise timber, mineral, and water rights, create state-owned industries utilizing these resources, and sell products on the open market. By rejecting such an overtly socialist approach to public works, the legislature demonstrated its concept of the state as a "broker" or "adjuster" whose power was limited to mediating disputes and providing data to the private sector, rather than as a competitor or superior.[76]

Nor were the Davidson legislatures especially anxious for the state to assume more responsibility for those unable or unwilling to care

[75] *Ibid.*, 469–470.
[76] *Ibid.*, 463–466.

for themselves. The 1907 legislature made provision for educational aids and services to blind Wisconsinites, with the aim of making them self-supporting, while the 1909 legislature established a facility at Oshkosh to house the criminally insane, with little attention to treatment. The state prison at Waupun was authorized to operate a binding-twine plant with inmate labor, then to sell the twine at cheap prices to area farmers. The 1909 legislature added a woman member to the Board of Control as a roving inspector of penal and charitable institutions, concerning herself primarily with the welfare of female inmates. Efforts to create a pardons board and parole agents failed in 1909, although the Board of Control was authorized to issue pardons and paroles. Both legislatures rejected measures for the mandatory sterilization of the "unfit" and those suffering from epilepsy, idiocy, and imbecility.[77]

While relatively uninterested in the unfortunate, these legislatures were quite interested in making state government a guarantor of public morality, although most such attempts came to little or naught. Numerous bills to regulate or eliminate prostitution, pornography, gambling, and tobacco products were introduced, but most died in committees. Alcohol control was more successful. The 1907 legislature banned liquor licenses within one mile of the state university and tightened the rules and machinery for prosecution of offenders in dry areas. However, the assembly defeated a measure to permit counties the option of voting to ban liquor. The 1909 legislature prohibited people under twenty-one years of age from entering a bar or saloon unless accompanied by a parent, increased the penalties for selling liquor to those already intoxicated, and absolutely prohibited liquor sales to those under eighteen. It also enacted a law forbidding the sale of alcoholic beverages to American Indians or "mixed bloods." However, that same legislature also tabled numerous bills designed to tighten restrictions on the liquor traffic.[78]

By 1909, the liquor question had come to the fore and the divisive specter of prohibition was threatening the unity of the progressive Republican coalition. Many members of that faction regarded alcoholic beverages as a major cause of social ills, ranging from industrial accidents to poverty; they regarded prohibition as the only feasible solution. Others in the progressive wing, chiefly the McGovern contingent, viewed prohibition as an attempt to force Yankee Protestant mores down the throats of unwilling Wisconsinites. To La Follette and most of his followers, prohibition was a carry-over from ethno-cultural, partisan politics that distracted voters and politicians from the real socio-economic issues. The threat of prohibition drove a

[77] *Ibid.*, 470–472. See also Chapters 5 and 8 above.
[78] *Ibid.*, 472–473.

wedge between the two largest ethno-cultural blocs in the state, Germans and Scandinavians, virtually destroying any chance for their collaboration on other questions. What many progressive Republicans regarded as a legitimate and necessary extension of state power, others saw as either an egregious affront to personal liberty and ethno-cultural sensibilities or as a highly effective lever with which conservatives in both parties could split their ranks and regain power. Some idea of the potential divisiveness of prohibition may be gained from the 1910 Republican primary. La Follette received 144,056 votes in the senatorial preference vote, but McGovern received only 82,265 votes for governor, primarily because 40,879 presumably progressive voters cast their ballots for William M. Lewis, a Racine manufacturer running as an independent "dry" progressive. La Follette successfully sidestepped the explosive liquor issue during his entire career, while McGovern was openly "wet." So it seems fair to attribute the difference largely to a deep-seated division over prohibition within progressive Republican ranks. Progressives' views on most other issues were virtually identical.[79]

It was during the Davidson years that the legislature took significant steps towards enhancing state authority over the environment and natural resources. The State Board of Forestry, led by Edward M. Griffith, who had been appointed by La Follette, began with 40,000 acres of state forest reserves in 1903 and expanded them to 340,000 acres by 1910, with a goal of 2 million acres. The legislature created the State Park Board in 1907. It commissioned a 1909 plan by landscape architect John Nolen, resulting in Peninsula State Park in Door County (1910), Devil's Lake State Park in Sauk County (1911), and Wyalusing State Park in Grant County (1917). In addition, the 1907 legislature prohibited the sale of Indian lands to private purchasers and reserved the mineral rights to the state. It also defeated an attempt to weaken the fish and game code and tightened requirements and procedures for selecting fish and game wardens. The most important conservation action of the Davidson years was the establishment in 1909 of a joint committee on water powers, forestry, and drainage, chaired by state senator Harlan P. Bird. The Bird committee conducted extensive investigations in northern Wisconsin, gathering data, interviewing residents, and gaining firsthand knowledge of the area and its resources. Its final report later formed the basis for the comprehensive conservation program inaugurated by the landmark legislature of 1911.[80]

---

[79] *Idem*; Wyman, "Voting Behavior in the Progressive Era," 335–337; Margulies, *Decline of the Progressive Movement*, 80, 98, 106, 129, 166; Jeffrey Lucker, "The Politics of Prohibition in Wisconsin, 1917–1933" (master's thesis, University of Wisconsin, 1968), 1–20; Milwaukee *Journal*, September 6–8, 1910.

[80] Acrea, "Wisconsin Progressivism," 459–461; Maxwell, *La Follette and the Rise of the*

Nowhere was the piecemeal, incremental approach of the Davidson-era legislatures in extending state government's authority and responsibility more evident than in public education. All told, the 1907 legislature considered 122 separate bills relating to education. To begin with, it increased state aid to local grade schools by 50 per cent and raised to eight months the length of the school year necessary to qualify for aid. Other measures required transporting of children from districts with ungraded schools to those with graded schools; authorized the state superintendent to set standards for school equipment; provided for manual training in high schools and increased from four to eight the number of county schools of agriculture and domestic science eligible for state financial support; authorized local school districts to establish technical schools; broadened the scope of both farm institutes and adult education; founded a school of mining at Platteville; increased the number of normal schools eligible for state aid; approved a medical school for the University of Wisconsin; and abolished in-state tuition at its law school. Finally, the 1907 legislature authorized $20,000 to the university, in conjunction with the Free Library Commission and local school and library boards, to revive and expand the extension program.[81]

The 1909 legislature concentrated on augmenting the higher education system. It established a normal school at Eau Claire, increased the number of accredited county teacher training schools, and raised state aid to them by 50 per cent if they remained open year round. The legislature also designated the College of Agriculture as technical adviser to county schools of agriculture; approved physical plant expansions on several normal school campuses; prohibited the University of Wisconsin regents from stipulating gender requirements for admission; and encouraged consolidation and upgraded standards for the state's 6,500 rural elementary schools. Not all such measures succeeded. The assembly, for example, tabled an attempt to allow the Milwaukee school district to use its buildings as after-hours social and recreation centers, and Governor Davidson vetoed a bill to create a teachers' retirement fund, believing that it infringed upon individual independence.

Predictably, this *ad hoc* approach to improving public education produced mix results. The legislature left the task of school consoli-

---

Progressives, 165–166; A. Allan Schmid, "Water and the Law in Wisconsin," in *WMH*, 45 (Spring, 1962), 203–215; Dennis East II, "Water Power and Forestry in Wisconsin: Issues of Conservation, 1890–1915" (doctoral dissertation, University of Wisconsin, 1971); John Nolen, *State Parks for Wisconsin*, State Park Board, 1909; State Forester, *Report*, 1909 and 1910, p. 5.

[81] Acrea, "Wisconsin Progressivism," 454–458; Patzer, *Public Education in Wisconsin*, 472–474; Casey, *Charles McCarthy*, 58–62; Fitzpatrick, *McCarthy of Wisconsin*, 260–276; Merle Curti and Vernon Carstensen, *The University of Wisconsin: A History, 1848–1925* (2 vols., Madison, 1949), 2: 549–594. See also Chapter 8.

dation largely to rural school districts themselves, merely dangling the carrot of state aid as incentive. It also provided few programs for the benefit of poorly educated young adults, and no aid whatsoever to the northern two-thirds of the state. Constructing a universal educational system adequate for an industrializing and urbanizing state out of a hodgepodge of local, largely rural school districts was daunting. Legislators worked haltingly and pragmatically at the task, guided by what they knew of the past rather than by some exalted vision of the future.[82]

Even so, the 1909 legislature did seminal work in one educational area: agricultural and vocational education. It set the stage for significant accomplishment in 1911 by forming a distinguished interim commission on the subject: McCarthy, Van Hise, Superintendent of Public Instruction Cary, University Extension Director William Lighty, and the superintendent of the Milwaukee public schools. The commission's charge was to provide schooling for the "educationally disinherited" or "forgotten groups," meaning those who had dropped out of school at a young age to enter the work force. McCarthy undertook a fact-gathering expedition, out of his own pocket, and visited cities in Germany, Great Britain, France, and Belgium, as well as New York, Boston, Pittsburgh, and Lowell, Massachusetts. Dean Harry Russell of the College of Agriculture headed a subcommittee on agricultural education. The result was a report which was submitted to the 1911 legislature and which formed the basis for Wisconsin's pathbreaking vocational-technical education legislation of that session.[83]

This step-by-step approach of the Wisconsin legislature during the Davidson era was vital to developing the social service state, particularly in labor legislation. Pressure for labor laws came from many organizations and individuals, including the State Federation of Labor and its offshoots; the Bureau of Labor and Industrial Statistics; Charles McCarthy and the Legislative Reference Bureau; the American Association for Labor Legislation founded by John R. Commons and his protégé John B. Andrews; the Wisconsin Federation of Women's Clubs; and the Milwaukee affiliates of the National Child Labor Committee and the Women's Trade Union League. Their

---

[82] Acrea, "Wisconsin Progressivism," 456–459; Curti and Carstensen, *University of Wisconsin*, 2: 159–190; Patzer, *Public Education in Wisconsin*, 474–476. See also the essays in Charles McKenny, ed., *Educational History of Wisconsin: Growth and Progress of Education in the State from Its Foundation to the Present Time* (Chicago, 1912), and Chapter 8.

[83] Fitzpatrick, *McCarthy of Wisconsin*, 236–259; Casey, *Charles McCarthy*, 63–65; Curti and Carstensen, *University of Wisconsin*, 2: 87–122; Patzer, *Public Education in Wisconsin*, 207–210, 476; Commission Upon the Plans for the Extension of Industrial and Agricultural Training, *Report*, 1911.

ideas and the resulting bills were sponsored primarily by Social Democratic legislators and by their Republican and Democratic colleagues from the state's urban, industrial centers. In the 1907 session they achieved few successes; hostile amendments and exemptions sought by the major industrial organizations weakened most bills. They did manage to enact laws that struck at the common law defense of contributory negligence in railroad employer liability cases, regulated numbers of crew members, and limited railroad workers to sixteen hours of work in twenty-four. Pro-labor legislators also prohibited the removal of safety devices from industrial machinery and banned the employment of children under sixteen from several occupations.[84]

It was the 1909 legislature that laid the groundwork for the epochal labor legislation of 1911, even though most of its proposals failed at the time. It succeeded in requiring an eight-hour day on state-run construction projects (though only after exempting cities, towns, municipal corporations, and school districts). It also tightened child labor laws. The houses together created a future legislative agenda by defeating a variety of measures: making election day a legal holiday, allowing unions to solicit help from other workers during trade disputes, requiring the weekly payment of wages in cash, stipulating an eight-hour day in numerous occupations, mandating one day's rest in each week, making railroads pay union-scale wages, limiting working hours in bakeries to sixty per week, establishing an industrial commission, and providing for workmen's compensation in industrial accidents.[85]

As it turned out, this defeat of so many pro-labor measures in the 1909 session proved to be a last ditch stand by the Stalwarts, and it served mainly to increase the pressure for their later passage. Moreover, a key pro-labor victory in 1909 was the creation of a special committee to investigate the feasibility of insurance for industrial accidents. A progressive Republican senator, Albert W. Sanborn of Ashland, headed it and received expert advice from a staff headed by John R. Commons and Charles McCarthy. The committee conducted

---

[84] Acrea, "Wisconsin Progressivism," 461–463; *Wisconsin Blue Book, 1907*, pp. 1127, 1160–1164; *ibid., 1909*, pp. 1095, 1130–1133; Maxwell, *La Follette and the Rise of the Progressives*, 153–157; Arthur J. Altmeyer, *The Industrial Commission of Wisconsin: A Case Study in Labor Law Administration* (Madison, 1932), 9–16; Robert Asher, "The 1911 Workmen's Compensation Law: A Study in Conservative Labor Reform," in *WMH*, 57 (Winter, 1973–1974), 123–127; Weiss, "History of Labor Legislation," 1–45; Haferbecker, *Wisconsin Labor Laws*, 5–14.

[85] Acrea, "Wisconsin Progressivism," 462–463; Maxwell, *La Follette and the Rise of the Progressives*, 157; Altmeyer, *Industrial Commission of Wisconsin*, 9–16, 25–27; Asher, "The 1911 Wisconsin Workmen's Compensation Law," 127–135; Weiss, "History of Labor Legislation," 46–61; Haferbecker, *Wisconsin Labor Laws*, 17–20, 34–42.

extensive investigations of worker compensation programs in several states and European nations. McCarthy provided invaluable assistance on how to draft a bill that would meet any constitutional challenge in state or federal courts. Commons and other scholars on the Madison campus provided their detailed analyses of social legislation, while the State Federation of Labor and the Merchants' and Manufacturers' Association of Milwaukee both provided advice during public hearings. After extensive deliberations, the committee decided to make employers' participation in the compensation program voluntary, but provided them with an incentive to sign up by recommending abolition of their common law defenses of assumed risk and contributory negligence. The result was to be a system in which injured employees would receive automatic compensation, unless the damage had been inflicted through willful misconduct. Employees could opt out of the state-operated system only by purchasing private insurance, or through self-insurance. To administer the system, the committee proposed a three-man board. In this manner, the scene was set for 1911.[86]

When it came to taxes, the two Davidson legislatures' activity was largely defensive, complementary, or preparatory. In 1907, the legislature frustrated attempts to exempt from taxation real estate owned by telephone companies or banks, trust and guaranty bank receipts, and credits and stocks. On the positive side, it provided a thirty-year tax exemption for those who planted 1,500 or more trees per acre, and gave its all but unanimous approval, for the second time, to a proposed constitutional amendment permitting a graduated income tax. Nils Haugen and the state tax commission strongly supported an income tax, arguing that it would be far easier to administer and much harder to evade than a personal property tax, and that it would fall most heavily on those with the ability to pay. The need for more sources of revenue to run an expanding state government also encouraged adoption of an income tax. As the state constitution required, the issue was put before the public in 1908, which overwhelmingly endorsed it, 85,696 to 37,729. The income tax amendment carried every county save Manitowoc.[87]

Despite this impressive support, the legislature failed to enact an

---

[86] Maxwell, *La Follette and the Rise of the Progressives*, 157–158; Casey, *Charles McCarthy*, 78–79; Altmeyer, *Industrial Commission of Wisconsin*, 16–25; Weiss, "History of Labor Legislation," 50–69; Haferbecker, *Wisconsin Labor Laws*, 15–17, 184–187.

[87] Acrea, "Wisconsin Progressivism," 473–474; Maxwell, *La Follette and the Rise of the Progressives*, 96–99, 103; John O. Stark, "The Establishment of Wisconsin's Income Tax," in *WMH*, 71 (Autumn, 1987), 27–45; Fitzpatrick, *McCarthy of Wisconsin*, 120–124; Casey, *Charles McCarthy*, 79; Stuart D. Brandes, "Nils P. Haugen and the Wisconsin Progressive Movement" (master's thesis, University of Wisconsin, 1965), 110–151; Wyman, "Voting Behavior in the Progressive Era," 452–454.

income tax in 1909. Davidson strongly endorsed it in his inaugural message, and his lieutenants in the assembly, headed by C. A. Ingram of Durand, quickly introduced a bill so full of technical defects that even its advocates allowed it to expire in committee. Determined to enact a law that would survive a court test, the legislature appointed a special interim committee to draft a solid bill. It was headed by Senator John C. Kleczka, a Polish-American attorney from Milwaukee with degrees from both Marquette University and the Catholic University of America, and it accomplished its mission in advance of the 1911 legislative session. The 1909 legislature also acted to prevent avoidance of the state inheritance tax through prior distribution of estates, appointed a committee to confer with railroad companies on collection of their unpaid license fees, levied an *ad valorem* tax on telephone companies, and defeated Stalwart proposals not only to reduce the tax on bank stock but also to abolish the state tax commission.[88]

Opening yet another avenue of fiscal reform, the legislature in 1908 authorized the tax commission to investigate the structure and operations of the state's financial machinery. The commission recommended consolidation of all active disbursement funds, uniform classification of expenditures, a centralized audit system for all state boards and commissions, and the creation of a budget agency responsible for drafting appropriation bills and for retiring the state debt. This position squared nicely with that of the legislature's joint finance committee, and after holding several public hearings, the legislative committee made similar recommendations and prepared model schedules for all governmental agencies. The combined labors of the two investigative bodies thus prepared the ground for the major administrative and fiscal reforms of 1911.[89]

The only electoral reform issue of any substance considered in 1907 and 1909 was woman suffrage—and that eventually ran into a stone wall. A 1901 law had provided for separate female ballot boxes, making woman suffrage in school board elections practicable. But subsequent legislatures expended a great deal of heat and shed little light on the issue. The 1903 legislature defeated three separate suffrage bills, one of them memorializing Congress to propose an amendment to the U.S. Constitution. In 1905, a proposal to allow

---

[88] Acrea, "Wisconsin Progressivism," 474; Maxwell, *La Follette and the Rise of the Progressives*, 99–101; *Wisconsin Blue Book, 1909*, p. 558; Brandes, "Nils P. Haugen," 152–182; Stark, "Establishment of Wisconsin's Income Tax," in *WMH*, 71: 27–31. For a revisionist view of the origins of the tax, see W. Elliott Brownlee, Jr., *Progressivism and Economic Growth: The Wisconsin Income Tax, 1911–1929* (Port Washington, New York, 1974), 41–59.

[89] Maxwell, *La Follette and the Rise of the Progressives*, 97–98; Acrea, "Wisconsin Progressivism," 473–474;

women to vote on municipal and town matters was defeated on a 43–34 vote. Two years later, both houses killed measures to amend the statutes of 1898 in order to enfranchise women, with the senate barely putting down a motion to reconsider, 15–14. Although the 1909 assembly killed a similar bill through the device of indefinite postponement, the senate passed a nearly identical measure and sent it back to the lower house for concurrence. By a vote of 53–34, the assembly refused to concur; but the closeness of the votes in 1907 and 1909 helped to build the momentum that would bring success in 1911, at least for a brief time. The 1907 legislature took a negative step by proposing a successful constitutional amendment designed to end the constitutionally guaranteed practice of voting by alien males who had taken out their "first papers." It was adopted in November, 1908, following its passage in a statewide referendum, 85,677 to 37,719. It went into effect December 1, 1912.[90]

[14]

Despite Bob La Follette's doubts regarding Jim Davidson's ideology and capacity to lead, his administration continued to build the momentum of progressive reform. Similarly, the factional bickering that had rent the Republican party during La Follette's tenure continued to erupt periodically in the legislature, but it failed to prevent a majority of lawmakers from working to extend the achievements of the La Follette era and from laying the groundwork necessary for the grand accomplishments yet to come, during the administration of Francis E. McGovern. Wisconsin had gained national recognition for transforming its state railroad commission into a virtual public utilities commission, and for enacting a new code for the regulation of insurance companies. The many legislative initiatives undertaken in education and conservation, though sporadic and piecemeal, contributed to the public's growing desire for state intervention and responsibility. The legislatures of 1907 and 1909 failed to enact any major labor laws, but generated interest and controversy in several bills which became major issues in ensuing elections and legislative sessions. The same could be said for the legislature's handling of the

[90] Acrea, "Wisconsin Progressivism," 474–477; Lawrence L. Graves, "The Wisconsin Woman Suffrage Movement, 1846–1920" (doctoral dissertation, University of Wisconsin, 1954), 102–105; Genevieve G. McBride, *On Wisconsin Women: Working for Their Rights from Settlement to Suffrage* (Madison, 1993), 193–200; *Wisconsin Blue Book, 1909*, pp. 24, 558. See also Chapter 7. The constitutional amendment also extended the franchise to "persons of Indian blood" who had been declared citizens by Congress and to "civilized persons of Indian descent and not members of any tribe," while gradually disfranchising resident aliens.

woman suffrage question. The 1907 legislature alone proposed four constitutional amendments that were approved almost 3–1 by the state's voters: state aid for highway construction, an income tax, stronger gubernatorial veto power, and significant alterations in the requirement for suffrage. Perhaps most importantly, the Davidson-era legislatures created several investigative bodies whose findings paved the way for later landmark legislation. Harlan Bird's committee outlined an ambitious program for the conservation of natural resources. The interim committee on industrial and agricultural education, thanks largely to Charles McCarthy's extraordinary efforts, generated a report that would eventually make the state a model in those fields. John Kleczka's committee meticulously constructed a "judge-proof" state income tax, and the joint committee on industrial accidents not only produced the essential outlines of workmen's compensation but also laid the groundwork for a comprehensive industrial code to be administered by an effective quasi-independent commission. By 1910, thanks to the combined efforts of the state tax commission and the legislative joint finance committee, the outlines of an integrated fiscal and budgetary system had been sketched in.

All of these initiatives, even those that withered or fell short of accomplishment, kept in motion the dynamics of the La Follette era and paved the way for much of what followed. Without the continuity provided by Davidson and his allies in the legislature—to say nothing of his allies in academe and in the ranks of organized labor—the pace and momentum of the Progressive impulse might well have slackened. Robert M. La Follette, tireless and charismatic, was sui generis, and no amount of scholarly nitpicking can materially diminish his accomplishments or his singular importance in Wisconsin history. Francis E. McGovern, the inheritor, embodied much of the best of the Progressive ideal and brought La Follette's program to fruition. But it was James O. Davidson, big-hearted and affable, who provided the crucial bridge between the two. Had it not been for Davidson, the Progressive upsurge begun in La Follette's term might well have lost momentum and continuity, and the McGovern administration might well have foundered for lack of solid footings and the impetus necessary to achieve success.

Reviewing the events of the first decade of the new century, most Wisconsinites must have recognized that their state had undergone a metamorphosis. Regardless of whether they welcomed change or decried it, few could ignore or deny the reality of the transformation. The reforms of the La Follette and Davidson years had almost totally reconfigured the state's tax system along more equitable and productive lines, and had set in motion the demands for a comprehensive fiscal and budgetary system. The two governors and their cohorts in the legislature had overhauled the electoral process in order to curb the power of political bosses and machines, and had introduced a new brand of issue-oriented, candidate-centered, independent politics. Intentionally or not, they had also created a new type of political machine that synthesized the most effective elements of old and new. They had brought the railroads, utilities, and other businesses that impinged on "the public interest" under the scrutiny and regulation of state government. To a degree unimaginable in 1890, they had involved state government in public education at all levels, as well as in the conservation and development of the state's natural resources. They had made the first meaningful forays into the complex and controversial thicket of labor and welfare legislation, preparing the way for the outpouring of such measures soon to come. Mirroring these reforms was a tremendous growth in the size, scope, cost, authority, responsibility, and efficacy of state government in general, and of the executive and legislative branches in particular.[91]

By 1910 Wisconsin had staked its claim to being the most progressive state in the Union. The footings and foundation were in place. The speed with which the rest of the structure was erected would amaze all who observed it during the next five years.

[91] Acrea, "Wisconsin Progressivism," 497–530; Maxwell, *La Follette and the Rise of the Progressives*, 195–204; Margulies, *Decline of the Progressive Movement*, 80–104.

12

The Most Progressive State

[1]

THE elections of 1910 proved to be a major watershed in the history of the Progressive Era, not only in Wisconsin but throughout most of the United States. The electorate's growing perception that regular Republican policies aggrandized the rich and powerful prompted voters that year to shift decisively towards candidates who advocated government intervention on behalf of other segments of society. Those candidates were largely insurgent Republicans, progressive Democrats, and revisionist Socialists.

So sweeping was the electoral upheaval of 1910 in the Northeast that the New York *Times* called it a "political revolution." The Republicans lost nearly a quarter of their congressional seats in New England and the Middle Atlantic States, while the Democrats gained twelve seats in New York, eight in Ohio, five in Illinois, and four each in Pennsylvania, Missouri, New Jersey, and West Virginia. Observers attributed the revolt mostly to voter dissatisfaction with the high cost of living, which they ascribed to conservative Republicans' tariff and tax policies. Numerous state legislatures began their 1911 sessions with progressive majorities, whether Democratic, insurgent Republican, or some combination of both.[1]

In one of the most significant turnabouts in the annals of Congress, the Democratic party gained fifty-six seats in the House of Representatives, achieving a solid majority of 228 to 161. The midwestern and western insurgents in Congress who were revolting against the old guard Republican leadership also gained way. Led by Senator La Follette, many insurgents joined the National Progressive Republican

---

[1] New York *Times*, November 8, 1910; David Sarasohn, *The Party of Reform: Democrats in the Progressive Era* (Jackson, Mississippi, 1989), 59–154; John D. Buenker, *Urban Liberalism and Progressive Reform* (New York, 1973), 222–224; Samuel P. Hays, *The Response to Industrialism, 1885–1914* (Chicago, 1957), 149–150.

League, dedicated to overthrowing both party leaders and their policies. Their strategy produced the Progressive (or "Bull Moose") party in 1912, a Congress controlled by Democrats and progressive Republicans, and a Democratic president, Woodrow Wilson, whose administration in effect became the capstone of progressivism.[2]

Socialist candidates' strength also indicated that the electorate's mood was changing, especially at the local level. Nationally, party membership jumped from 10,000 to 118,000 between 1902 and 1912, and the number of Socialist periodicals rose to more than 300. By 1912, more than 12,000 Socialists held office in 340 municipalities, including seventy-nine mayors in twenty-four states. Around the country, the number of Socialist state legislators reached twenty in 1912, and a high of thirty-three in fourteen states by 1914. In the 1912 presidential election, labor leader Eugene V. Debs polled 6 per cent of the popular vote—an all-time high. Small wonder that some informed observers regarded socialism as the wave of the future![3]

In Wisconsin, Republican insurgence, Democratic resurgence, and Socialist emergence interacted with social and intellectual currents to produce a swing to the left. Progressives remained in apparent control of the state Republican party, but their strength had been undermined by the alienation of moderate leaders like Jim Davidson, William D. Hoard, Ike Stephenson, and William Connor. If these moderates effected a truce with the Stalwarts, who were on the mend, they could mount a formidable challenge to the Progressives. Indeed, they might block an ambitious agenda that included the election of a truly progressive governor, the enactment of a comprehensive legislative program for which the groundwork had already been laid, and the re-election of Robert M. La Follette to the U.S. Senate. At the very least, the alienated moderates were likely to cut into the Progressives' core constituency—rural, small-town, and middle-class voters. Political expediency therefore dictated that they campaign for new voters among urban, working-class citizens—the same direction in which the Progressives' ideological odyssey was inexorably tending.[4]

---

[2] *Congressional Quarterly's Guide to U.S. Elections* (2nd. ed., 1985), 1116; Ken W. Hechler, *Insurgency: Personalities and Politics of the Taft Era* (New York, 1964), 11–177; Laurence James Holt, *Congressional Insurgents and the Party System, 1909–1916* (Cambridge, 1967); George E. Mowry, *The Era of Theodore Roosevelt* (New York, 1958), 226–273; David P. Thelen, *Robert M. La Follette and the Insurgent Spirit* (Boston, 1976), 52–78; Roger E. Wyman, "Insurgency and the Elections of 1910 in the Middle West" (master's thesis, University of Wisconsin, 1964); Herbert F. Margulies, *Senator Lenroot of Wisconsin: A Political Biography, 1900–1929* (Columbia, Missouri, 1977), 69–108.

[3] James Weinstein, *The Decline of Socialism in America, 1912–1925* (New York, 1967; reprinted, New Brunswick, 1984), 1–26, 93–118.

[4] Herbert F. Margulies, *The Decline of the Progressive Movement in Wisconsin, 1890–*

Unfortunately for the Progressives, many urban, working-class voters remained loyal to either the Democrats or the Socialists. Their emotionally charged political affiliations had resistant roots. To make matters worse for the Progressives, both Democrats and Socialists were intensifying their efforts, successfully, to retain or attract those same voters. Progressive Democrats were led by outspoken liberals such as Paul Husting, John Aylward, Joseph E. Davies, Adolph J. Schmitz, and William Wolfe. They strove to revise their party's Bourbon policies and to purge its leadership of what Aylward dubbed "the old railroad crowd," aligning themselves nationally with the presidential aspirations of progressive Democrat Woodrow Wilson. By reorienting their party's ideology, they managed to improve its competitive position during a political season in which conservatism, whether real or perceived, seemed the path to oblivion. The Democrats' day was coming, but not quite yet.[5]

Far more portentous in 1910 was the ascent of the Social Democrats (SDP) in Milwaukee and other industrial centers. The party had been founded in 1898 as a political vehicle for the Milwaukee Federated Trades Council and the State Federation of Labor, and its core constituents were primarily skilled workers of German ancestry. Party leaders built on that foundation and self-consciously broadened their appeal to include white-collar workers, small businessmen, unskilled laborers, and southern and eastern European immigrants. Between 1898 and 1910, the SDP's share of Milwaukee's mayoral vote jumped from 5 to 47 per cent, catapulting Emil Seidel and the entire party ticket into city-wide office in 1910 and making Milwaukee the largest Socialist-administered municipality in the nation. In addition, SDP candidates captured twenty-three of thirty aldermanic seats, one-quarter of the school board membership, and a majority on the county board of supervisors. Victor Berger that year became the first Socialist ever elected to the House of Representatives. Outside Milwaukee, the SDP made short-lived inroads in central and southeastern Wisconsin and won mayors' seats in Manitowoc and West Salem. By 1911, the party counted 117 locals beyond Milwaukee County borders, and there was talk about forming county organizations statewide. Both Berger and Seidel tried hard to build ideological and organizational bridges between the urban, working-class-oriented SDP and the state's less affluent farmers. The state party board engaged Oscar Ameringer, an Oklahoma socialist, to investigate the pos-

---

1920 (Madison, 1968), 99–104; Roger E. Wyman, "Voting Behavior in the Progressive Era: Wisconsin as a Case Study" (doctoral dissertation, University of Wisconsin, 1970), 284–288.

[5] Sarasohn, *Party of Reform*, 112–118; Margulies, *Decline of the Progressive Movement*, 126–127 (quote), 137, 149.

sibility of organizing them. These indications of Socialist momentum had a powerful effect on progressive Republicans. Charles McCarthy, Francis McGovern, and other strategists conceded frankly that "the only way to beat the Socialists 'is to beat them to it.' "[6]

Lobbying groups, too, were propelling progressive Republicans towards the left. Lobbyists were recent arrivals on the political scene, but were growing in strength and influence. Some directly promoted the philosophy of intervention by state government into many areas as the sine qua non of reform. Others did so merely by implication. Two of the former groups were the State Federation of Labor and the Wisconsin Society of Equity. Each was working-class in membership and orientation. The Federation of Labor was the socio-economic arm of the SDP; the Society of Equity represented less affluent, more militant farmers in northern and western Wisconsin. The latter kinds of groups were broadly middle-class in composition and outlook, and were motivated by a complex mixture of ideology, altruism, fear, and class. Among them were the Consumer's League, the Child Labor Committee, the Women's Trade Union League, the Wisconsin Conference of Charities and Corrections, the Wisconsin Federation of Women's Clubs, the American Association for Labor Legislation, the Municipal League of Milwaukee, and the League of Wisconsin Municipalities, to name only the most active and visible. These diverse organizations had widely varying political agendas. Even so, most of their proposals required government involvement, allegedly, at least, on behalf of the less affluent and less powerful. [7]

Two groups of state public servants also were adding their voices to this budding consensus. The first consisted of the directors and staff members of state agencies, commissions, and bureaus: the Bureau of Labor and Industrial Statistics, the Department of Public Instruction, the Free Library Commission, the Board of Control, the Tax Commission, the Railroad Commission, the Dairy and Food Commission, the State Historical Society, the Insurance Commission,

---

[6] Bernard E. Fuller, "Voting Patterns in Milwaukee, 1896–1920: A Study with Special Emphasis on the Working Class of the City" (master's thesis, University of Wisconsin-Milwaukee, 1973), 20–78; Joseph A. Gasperetti, "The 1910 Social-Democrat Mayoral Campaign in Milwaukee" (doctoral dissertation, University of Wisconsin-Milwaukee, 1970), *passim*; Weinstein, *Decline of Socialism*, 107, 116–118; James J. Lorence, " 'Dynamite for the Brain': The Growth and Decline of Socialism in Central and Lakeshore Wisconsin," in *WMH*, 66 (Summer, 1983), 251–254; Charles McCarthy, *The Wisconsin Idea* (New York, 1912), 294–300 (quote); Sally M. Miller, *Victor Berger and the Promise of Constructive Socialism, 1910–1920* (Westport, Connecticut, 1973), 37–71.

[7] For more detailed discussions of these interest groups, see Chapters 2, 4, 6, 7, and 8. See also David P. Thelen, *The New Citizenship: Origins of Progressivism in Wisconsin, 1885–1900* (Columbia, Missouri, 1972), 55–289, and volume 2, *The Industrial Era*, of Charles A. Beard and Mary R. Beard, *The Rise of American Civilization* (2 vols., New York, 1927).

the Board of Health, the Board of Agriculture, and others. Progressive Republican governors had appointed most of the directors and staff members, who shared the governors' activist, expansionist philosophy of state government. At the University of Wisconsin end of Madison's State Street, calls for even more radical departures in government intervention emanated from President Charles R. Van Hise and from many of the most distinguished faculty and staff members, especially in the social sciences, humanities, agricultural extension, and engineering. Many were charter members of La Follette's Saturday Lunch Club and advised or worked for state agencies.[8]

Standing with a foot in each of these camps, and serving as chief liaison between them and the progressive Republican political establishment, was Charles R. McCarthy, director of the Legislative Reference Library. An adjunct member of the university's political science faculty, a salaried public servant, valued adviser to the executive branch, and chief bill drafter of the legislature, McCarthy was a human conduit for progressive ideas and actions and perhaps the most influential person in state government by 1910. While forever asserting the apolitical, technical nature of his role in legislation and administration, McCarthy was of course a progressive activist and strategist who passionately, and intentionally, steered the Republican party on a leftward course. He discoursed candidly about his areas of agreement and disagreement with Socialists and other radicals; he openly embraced the State Federation of Labor and the Wisconsin Society of Equity. Moreover he possessed the political savvy to translate the convictions of civil servants and academics into law and public policy.[9]

[2]

In both major parties, the 1910 primary elections were fought largely along ideological lines, and generally ended in victories for progressive candidates. Even though the vote for United States senator was technically "only preferential," the contest for the Republican nom-

---

[8] Merle Curti and Vernon Carstensen, *The University of Wisconsin: A History, 1848–1925* (2 vols., Madison, 1949), 2: 19–33, 87–111; McCarthy, *Wisconsin Idea*, 20–33, 313–317; J. David Hoeveler, Jr., "The University and the Social Gospel: The Intellectual Origins of the 'Wisconsin Idea,' " in *WMH*, 59 (Summer, 1976), 282–298; Howard J. McMurray, "Some Influences of the University of Wisconsin on the State Government of Wisconsin" (doctoral dissertation, University of Wisconsin, 1940). See also Chapter 8.

[9] McCarthy, *Wisconsin Idea*, 194–232; Marion Casey, *Charles McCarthy: Librarianship and Reform* (Chicago, 1981), 25–101; Edward A. Fitzpatrick, *McCarthy of Wisconsin* (New York, 1944), 41–139.

ination attracted national attention because it involved Bob La Follette, the leading congressional insurgent and thorn in the side of President William Howard Taft. Removing La Follette from the Senate and preventing him from challenging for the Republican presidential nomination in 1912 were the chief orders of business for Taft and the Republican old guard. For insurgents and reformers, enhancing La Follette's national prestige and paving the way for an avalanche of progressive reform in state and nation were equally high priorities. Led by Emanuel Philipp, Isaac Stephenson, William D. Connor, and Charles Pfister, Wisconsin's Stalwarts filled their campaign chest with a reported $114,000 (an enormous sum in those days) and held a "Taft Republican" convention in Milwaukee to launch their ticket, which pitted against him Samuel A. Cook of Neenah, who was briefly La Follette's Stalwart opponent in the 1904 governor's race. The Stalwart convention also nominated conservative state senator Edward T. Fairchild of Milwaukee for governor, as well as a full slate for the other statewide and legislative offices. The Taft Republican convention was given its charge by Vice-president James S. Sherman, representative of the Taft administration and of regular Republicans nationally.[10]

The Progressives countered with a speaking tour by nationally recognized insurgent leaders including U.S. Senators William Borah, Joseph Bristow, Moses Clapp, and Albert Cummins, Congressman George Norris, and Gifford Pinchot, chief forester of the United States and a confidant of former President Theodore Roosevelt. The Rough Rider himself refrained from any endorsements during the primary campaign, but he indirectly aided the Progressives with his own speaking tour of the Midwest, where he plumped for many of the reform measures that would, in 1912, become an integral part of his "New Nationalism." Both Roosevelt and La Follette had shifted noticeably to the left during the preceding few years, and both men skillfully blended the traditional "people versus the interests" theme with a growing public concern over economic inequities. Wisconsin newspapers supportive of La Follette and the Progressive slate stressed that litany. They blasted Stalwart hopefuls as reactionaries, "Tories," and tools of the cabal headed by state Republican chairman Connor, Philipp, Stephenson, and Pfister. Because the final decision on the senatorship lay with the state legislature, the La Follette forces realized that a victory in the preferential primary had to be matched

---

[10] Margulies, *Decline of the Progressive Movement*, 105–106; Wyman, "Voting Behavior in the Progressive Era," 288–294; Milwaukee *Journal*, September, 2, 3, 5, 1910; Robert S. Maxwell, *Emanuel L. Philipp: Wisconsin Stalwart* (Madison, 1959), 58–71; Milwaukee *Sentinel*, September, 3, 4, 6, 1910.

by a progressive Republican majority in both houses and a strong progressive governor. These facts dictated nomination of a monolithically progressive ticket capable of augmenting La Follette's strength where it had always been weakest: the lakeshore counties.[11]

The gubernatorial candidate who best fit those needs was Francis E. McGovern, former Milwaukee County district attorney, unsuccessful senatorial candidate in 1908, and leader of the influential and progressive Republican Club of Milwaukee County. McGovern practiced a brand of urban progressivism with a socio-economic emphasis, owing largely to his collaboration with intellectuals, activists, social workers, and labor leaders, and to his experience at trying to best the Socialists at their own game. McGovern's candidacy, however, had some major drawbacks. The La Follette and McGovern factions were mutually wary of the other's ambitions, each seeing the other as a potential rival, not a partner. Privately, La Follette intimates expressed suspicions of "the Milwaukee crowd," while the Milwaukeeans feared that La Follette often sacrificed reform for political expediency and personal ambition. Their mutual wariness sometimes prevented effective collaboration on elections and legislation. Over the longer run, it put at risk the continued success of the progressive Republican coalition.[12]

McGovern's openly "wet" stance towards alcohol was even more threatening, especially among Scandinavians and Yankees. La Follette himself had always managed to sidestep the issue, but many of his cohorts were determined to interject it into the campaign on moral grounds. They backed the candidacy of Racine County manufacturer and legislator William T. Lewis, a longtime La Follette follower who supported county option prohibition. Lewis' candidacy confused the clear ideological alignment the Progressives desired, and it benefited Fairchild. But the damage seriously affected only the governor's race. The progressive Republicans' other statewide candidates faced only a single Stalwart opponent. La Follette's organization worked tirelessly to hold its supporters in line for McGovern. Even ex-Governor James O. Davidson, an avowed prohibitionist, re-

---

[11] Margulies, *Decline of the Progressive Movement*, 112–116; Wyman, "Voting Behavior in the Progressive Era," 291–294; Milwaukee *Journal*, September 9, 10, 1910; Milwaukee *Sentinel*, September 9–11, 1910.

[12] Albert O. Barton, *La Follette's Winning of Wisconsin, 1894–1904* (Madison, 1922), 30, 118–120, 181–186; Margulies, *Decline of the Progressive Movement*, 109–115; Thelen, *New Citizenship*, 272–273; Bayrd Still, *Milwaukee: The History of a City* (Madison, 1948; reprinted, 1965), 299–320; David G. Ondercin, "Corruption, Conspiracy, and Reform in Milwaukee, 1901–1909," in *Historical Messenger*, 26 (Spring, 1966), 112–117; Duane Mowry, "The Reign of Graft in Milwaukee," *Arena*, December, 1905, pp. 589–593. See also Chapter 4.

mained on the sidelines, largely because he disliked Connor more than he did La Follette.[13]

This strategic jockeying in the 1910 Republican primary resulted in a landslide victory for La Follette and the entire Progressive slate. He swamped his Stalwart opponent, with an astounding 77.7 per cent of the vote, carrying all but one of seventy-one counties. La Follette won so unequivocally that even several "tory" newspapers conceded that he deserved re-election. Teddy Roosevelt, visiting Milwaukee, declared that every Republican legislator had a duty to cast his ballot for Wisconsin's controversial senator. The La Follette landslide transferred itself to the entire progressive Republican ticket, although in significantly different proportions. Hounded by prohibitionists who supported Lewis, McGovern received only 82,265 votes (compared to La Follette's 144,056), or about 46 per cent to the senator's 77.7 per cent. Even had McGovern received all of the 40,879 votes taken by Lewis, he still would have fallen nearly 22,000 votes shy of La Follette. Fairchild received over 14,000 more votes than Cook, suggesting that La Follette's national celebrity made sizable inroads among Stalwarts.[14]

McGovern managed to carry fifty-two counties, but he polled a majority in only sixteen of those, nearly all in the east and central regions of the state. In the traditional progressive strongholds of the north and northwest, McGovern ran far behind La Follette, doing well only where La Follette's margin exceeded 85 per cent. In many of those counties, Lewis cut deeply into the normal progressive vote, winning a majority in Jackson County and pluralities in Barron, Pepin, Richland, and Crawford counties. His support was predictably greatest among temperance-leaning Scandinavians and Yankees. Fairchild found the bulk of his support in Stalwart northern counties, such as Iron, Florence, and Sawyer. In normally progressive Rusk County, Fairchild managed to win a plurality of 34 per cent, as McGovern and Lewis supporters canceled each other out. The remainder of the Progressives' statewide ticket ran somewhere between La Follette's high and McGovern's low, since they were neither buoyed by national notoriety nor stigmatized by wetness.[15]

---

[13] Margulies, *Decline of the Progressive Movement*, 105–106, 116; Wyman, "Voting Behavior in the Progressive Era," 293–294; Milwaukee *Journal*, September, 5–7, 1910; Milwaukee *Sentinel*, September 5–7, 1910; Wyman, "Insurgency and the Elections of 1910," 226–233.

[14] Milwaukee *Journal*, September 7–9, 1910; Margulies, *Decline of the Progressive Movement*, 106–107; Wyman, "Voting Behavior in the Progressive Era," 294–295; Milwaukee *Sentinel*, September 7–9, 1910; Wyman, "Insurgency and the Elections of 1910," 226–233.

[15] Milwaukee *Journal*, September 7–9, 1910; Margulies, *Decline of the Progressive Movement*, 106–107; Wyman, "Voting Behavior in the Progressive Era," 430–432; Milwau-

The primary results on the Democratic side were almost as decisive for the cause of reform, except in the preferential primary for U.S. senator, in which conservative Charles H. Weisse defeated progressive Burt Williams. Beyond that, all the Democratic progressives seeking statewide office, headed by gubernatorial candidate Adolph J. Schmitz, carried the day. The party, however, was struggling. In Milwaukee County, its ticket failed to receive the 20 per cent of the total primary vote necessary to earn a place on the general election ballot. Democratic crossovers to vote in the Republican primary, combined with the impressive strength of the Socialists, had reduced the party to an "also ran" in Milwaukee County. Statewide, where the Socialists posed no serious threat, Democrats polled only about one-third of the total primary vote.[16]

In drafting their platforms for the 1910 general election campaign, all three parties tried to outdo one another in professing their progressivism. The Republicans praised La Follette effusively as "the pioneer" of the national progressive movement and pledged that their legislators would vote for him. Their platform commended the state's progressive Republicans for their many contributions to the statutes: "Experience has abundantly demonstrated the wisdom of all these laws." And it condemned the Taft administration and the Republican regulars in Congress for failures in tariff reform, antitrust enforcement, conservation, and corrupt practices reform. The platform hailed the party as the champion of the people against all special interests, pledging ratification of the federal income tax amendment; direct election of U.S. senators; a second-choice primary; initiative, referendum, and recall; a law guaranteeing open political meetings; home rule for cities; state aid for highway construction; and a state income tax. It supported conservation legislation, public health measures, investigation of ways to combat the rising cost of living, employer liability and workmen's compensation laws, maximum work hours of labor for women and children, and improved health and safety legislation. It praised the University of Wisconsin as "the people's servant, carrying knowledge and assistance to the homes and farms and workshops." And it favored extending *ad valorem* taxation to all public service corporations.[17]

The Social Democratic party's platform made twenty-one specific legislative proposals on both the state and national level, many of which resembled the Republican agenda: labor and factory legisla-

---

kee *Sentinel*, September 1–2, 3, 5, 6–10, 1910; Wyman, "Insurgency and the Elections of 1910," 226–233.

[16] Milwaukee *Journal*, September 7–9, 1910; Milwaukee *Sentinel*, September 7–9, 1910; Wyman, "Insurgency and the Elections of 1910," 226–233.

[17] *Wisconsin Blue Book, 1911*, pp. 670–676.

tion, conservation measures, home rule, recall, state and federal income and inheritance taxes, and agricultural education. But it also went beyond the Republicans by calling for nationalization of all trusts and public utilities, abolition of the U.S. Senate, restriction of "Asiatic coolie labor," municipal ownership of local public utilities, free textbooks and equipment for schoolchildren, and a public referendum on all state and federal laws. Both major parties stood "for capitalism and the present economic system," the SDP platform said, proclaiming itself to be "the American political expression of the international movement of the modern working class for better food, better houses, sufficient sleep, more leisure, more education and more culture."

The Democratic platform read more like a pale imitation of the Republicans'. It condemned nearly all things and all persons Republican, making no distinction between Progressives and Stalwarts. The Democrats echoed the Republicans on income taxation, direct election of senators, conservation legislation, corrupt practices legislation, industrial insurance, good roads, home rule, and initiative, referendum, and recall. They joined the Socialists in opposing prohibition—an issue on which the Republican platform was deliberately silent. The Democrats were especially critical of the progressive Republicans for fiscal extravagance and for passage of the 20 per cent laws that had undone the Democrats in Milwaukee County. An objective reader of the three 1910 party platforms would be hard pressed to see the Democrats as little else than a "me-too" party.[18]

In the face of a progressive monolith, stalwart Republicans and conservative Democrats had but three options: hastily assemble an independent slate, organize a boycott of the general election, or support the primary victors in a show of party loyalty that might pay future dividends. Both groups quickly rejected the first as unrealistic, and fluctuated between the last two. Some Stalwarts ineffectually urged a boycott of the statewide Republican ticket, then wavered when a state supreme court ruling designated Stalwart Levi Bancroft as the official Republican candidate for attorney-general after the Progressive candidate, Frank Tucker, drowned before the primary. The ruling galled La Follette because Bancroft was one of his most vitriolic critics and had dubbed him "the mad mullah of Wisconsin." In reaction, the La Follette forces ran their campaign manager, Charles Crownhart, as an independent candidate for attorney-general, leaving the Stalwarts to cast themselves as defenders of party loyalty, in order to salvage at least one statewide office. The Stalwart press, headed by the Milwaukee *Sentinel*, stigmatized the progressive

---

[18] *Ibid.*, 684–689, 694–698.

Republican platform as virtual socialism, but nevertheless urged voters to cast their ballots for the entire party ticket—in order to keep the state's congressional delegation Republican and to advance President Taft's prospects for re-election in 1912.[19]

Evidence of an organized voter boycott against the statewide ticket surfaced only in Marathon and one or two other counties. Voter turnout was lower than it had been since 1890, but only about 700 below what it had been in 1906, the last previous non-presidential election year. Still, the Republican vote for governor slipped by over 20,000 votes between 1906 and 1910; the Democratic vote increased by over 7,000; and the Social Democratic, by more than 15,000. Running at the head of the statewide Republican ticket, Francis McGovern captured 52 per cent of the vote and won by a plurality of 50,000 votes over Adolph Schmitz, his Democratic opponent, who won 35 per cent. Underscoring his party's growing strength statewide, Social Democrat William A. Jacobs won the balance, 13 per cent.[20]

Those general proportions prevailed in all statewide contests except attorney-general; Bancroft captured only 37.4 per cent and defeated his Democratic opponent by a mere three percentage points. Crownhart won only 15.8 per cent, but cut deeply into the normal Republican vote, especially where La Follette typically ran strongest. The independent Progressive candidate carried Pierce County with almost 60 per cent, and forged a plurality in seven other counties, mostly in the northwest. Five of those eight counties were among the dozen most Scandinavian in the state; the other seven most Scandinavian counties voted a straight Republican ticket, regardless of ideological distinctions among individual candidates. Nor did Crownhart woo many "fair-minded" Democrats, a failure experienced by the entire Republican ticket. Probably this resulted from the progressive character of the Democratic slate. Bancroft's strongest showing came in northern lumbering and mining counties which the Stalwarts had successfully defended against La Follette and other Progressives in the past. Collectively, Bancroft and Crownhart merely split the normal Republican vote.[21]

---

[19] Margulies, *Decline of the Progressive Movement*, 106, 128–129; Wyman, "Voting Behavior in the Progressive Era," 295–296 (quote), 430–432; Wyman, "Insurgency and the Elections of 1910," 234–256; Milwaukee *Sentinel*, September 29, 1910; Milwaukee *Journal*, September 30, 1910; Maxwell, *Emanuel L. Philipp*, 68–69.

[20] *Wisconsin Blue Book, 1909*, pp. 408–412; *ibid., 1911*, pp. 189–276; Wyman, "Voting Behavior in the Progressive Era," 295–296; Margulies, *Senator Lenroot*, 105–108.

[21] *Wisconsin Blue Book, 1911*, pp. 277–282; Milwaukee *Sentinel*, November 1–9, 1910; Milwaukee *Journal*, November 1–9, 1910; Wyman, "Voting Behavior in the Progressive Era," 295–296, 430–432; Wyman, "Insurgency and the Election of 1910," 234–256; Margulies, *Decline of the Progressive Movement*, 128–129; James R. Donoghue, *How Wisconsin Voted, 1848–1972* (Madison, 1962; revised ed., 1974), 75.

Stalwart Republicans were reluctant to vent their spleen against their party's statewide ticket, but had few qualms about retaliating against congressional and legislative candidates. That tendency was especially strong in the Fifth Congressional District, where a nearly 30 per cent drop in the Republican vote of 1908 in Waukesha County was the key to Victor Berger's narrow victory. In the Sixth Congressional District, both major party candidates suffered a decline in voter support from 1908, allowing Democrat Michael E. Burke of Beaver Dam to retain his party's only seat in the House of Representatives. In the Ninth District, Democrat Thomas F. Konop of Kewaunee was able to nose out Republican Congressman Gustav Küstermann by a mere five votes. In the Ninth, the total Republican vote declined by over a third from 1908, and the Democratic vote fell by 20 per cent. The Republican candidates in the state's other eight congressional districts also received far fewer voters than in 1908. Nevertheless, they all won relatively easy victories.[22]

Losses in assembly races augured even more ill for progressive Republicans. A shift of one state senate seat to the Social Democrats still left the McGovern administration with twenty-seven votes out of a possible thirty-three, and most of those leaned towards progressivism. In the assembly, however, the Republican delegation declined from seventy-six to fifty-nine, while the Democrats' delegation jumped from nineteen to twenty-nine and the Social Democrats' from five to twelve. The Republicans still had nearly 60 per cent of the potential assembly votes, but it remained to be seen how many of those Republicans would consistently support McGovern's highly progressive legislative agenda. The ideological split in the party's ranks might require substantial Republican co-operation with both the Social Democrats and urban progressive Democrats, especially on path-breaking socio-economic and labor legislation.[23]

[3]

If the new governor was troubled by such possibilities, he gave no hint of it when, on January 12, 1911, he delivered what remains even today one of the most remarkable inaugural messages ever delivered to an American legislature. At forty-four, Francis Edward McGovern was at the height of his mental and physical powers. His large, piercing eyes testified to his intelligence, determination, strength of char-

---

[22] *Wisconsin Blue Book, 1911*, pp. 288–334; Milwaukee *Sentinel*, November 7–9, 1910; Milwaukee *Journal*, November 8–10, 1910; Wyman, "Voting Behavior in the Progressive Era," 431.
[23] *Wisconsin Blue Book, 1909*, pp. 1093, 1151; *ibid., 1911*, pp. 736–786.

acter, passion for social justice, and fierce ambition. Unmarried, completely devoted to politics and public service, he rivaled La Follette in his tendency to equate improvement of the general welfare with his personal political advancement. Born in 1866 to Irish American parents on a farm near Elkhart Lake in Sheboygan County just after the Civil War, young Francis began teaching in a rural school at age seventeen. He then entered the University of Wisconsin where he distinguished himself as a debater, orator, and scholar, before graduating with honors in 1890. While serving as a high school teacher and principal, he studied law and was admitted to the bar at Milwaukee in June, 1897. Shortly afterward, he became one of the founders of the Republican Club of Milwaukee County, which gradually evolved into a statewide political organization devoted to McGovern. As assistant, then full-fledged, district attorney of Milwaukee County from 1901 to 1909, he received national recognition for the graft trials against the corrupt administration of mayor David S. Rose. Despite occasional self-righteous moralism, McGovern developed into a canny politician attuned to the ethno-cultural sensibilities of Milwaukee's polyglot population, one who advocated government help for the disadvantaged. His ethnic origins, his continuing interaction with the progressive thinkers at the university, the realities of practical politics in a working-class city, and the challenge posed by the Social Democrats all combined to produce in McGovern a dynamic urban progressivism akin to his Socialist rivals'. His campaign for the U.S. Senate in 1908, while unsuccessful, had given him statewide visibility and convinced the La Follette forces that an alliance between their organization and McGovern's was the best hope for success in 1910 and beyond.[24]

The theme of McGovern's inaugural address was the need for strong government action as the only counterweight against corporations and other special interests. "Few legislatures," he challenged the lawmakers at the outset, "have convened in Wisconsin with equal opportunity for doing good," even though "from the first our state has been a leader in the Progressive movement and in carrying forward the work of constructive reform legislation." He acknowledged that the new giant corporations had produced some social benefits, but said they had all too frequently "put arbitrary power in the hands of a few who have used this power to oppress the people and debauch

---

[24] *Ibid., 1911*, pp. 731–732; Margulies, *Decline of the Progressive Movement*, 108–116, 131–134; David G. Ondercin, "The Early Years of Francis Edward McGovern, 1866–1910" (master's thesis, University of Wisconsin-Milwaukee, 1967), *passim*; Cyril C. Cavanaugh, "Francis E. McGovern and the 1911 Wisconsin Legislature" (master's thesis, University of Wisconsin, 1961), 6–11. See also Francis E. McGovern, "What Is The Remedy?", in *La Follette's Weekly Magazine*, November 5, 1910, pp. 1–2.

their government." As a remedy, government "must be made representative of all the people, and economic forces must be so regulated as to secure a fair chance for all in every walk of life." Protecting property, rewarding industry, encouraging thrift, and stimulating enterprise were important, he said, but were justified only if pursuing them would "afford to the weak, the unselfish and the defenseless, as well as to the man of average ability and means a fair start and an equal chance in the race of life." McGovern minced no words in warning the legislators that the people of Wisconsin demanded action and results "without unnecessary delay."[25]

His proposals began with suggested reforms in the primary election and corrupt practices laws. He saw the principal weakness in the primary law as a loophole that let "nominations . . . be made by the vote of a mere plurality." So he called for the addition of the "second choice" provision that La Follette had long suggested to strengthen the statute. "Many good citizens now vote for men rather than for parties, and are more deeply interested in political ideas and legislative programs than in party organizations or partisan candidates," he said; the second-choice ballot would guarantee that "a compact, cohesive and well drilled minority" could not carry the day because a multiplicity of progressive candidates divided the majority vote. He denounced the influence of campaign contributions as "sinister," and called for the tax-supported publication of candidate qualifications, limits on campaign spending, cost accounting of all expenditures, and prohibition of all political activity on election days. To compel compliance, he proposed penalties including imprisonment and disqualification for public office. "The influence of money in political campaigns in Wisconsin must be removed," he said, a poignant remark in light of the continuing debate at the close of the twentieth century.[26]

"To make and keep the government really representative of the people," he proposed enacting that great triad of political reforms that mark the Progressive Era: initiative, referendum, and recall. Of the three, McGovern regarded the initiative as the most important because it enabled the electorate to propose legislation directly. The referendum, he said, "is negative in its operation," acting only "as a check or brake upon unwise or corrupt legislative action." The recall

---

[25] Francis E. McGovern, *Governor's Message*, doc. 1, pp. 3–5, in *Wisconsin Public Documents*, 1909–1910, vol. 1. In what was probably an unwitting prophecy of McGovern's 1912 support for Theodore Roosevelt, at the expense of his relationship with La Follette, the governor also asserted that "the newly awakened public conscience demands a *square deal*." [Emphasis added.] See also Cavanaugh, "McGovern and the 1911 Wisconsin Legislature," 54–55.

[26] McGovern, *Governor's Message*, 1911, pp. 5–8.

McGovern judged "more drastic in its effects," and he then ommended that a higher percentage of voters be required t a petition for recalling a public official from office than to ward a referendum. Of course he urged the legislature to b process of amending the constitution to enable initiative, ~.erendum, and recall "to bring the government closer to the people." Following the same reasoning, McGovern endorsed home rule for the state's largest cities on matters of "purely local affairs," stressed the need for increased co-operation between state and local governments, and urged the legislature to heed a recent constitutional amendment by providing state aid for road construction.[27]

Not only should the legislature make state government representative of all the people, it should also give Wisconsinites control over the economic conditions under which they earned their living, McGovern said. Political reforms and representative government were vital because they paved "the way for laws, social adjustments and civil institutions which are calculated to secure and maintain desirable conditions in the daily life and occupations of men." In brief, political democracy was desirable because it was essential to instituting economic democracy. This philosophy distinguished McGovern's brand of urban progressivism from that of such moderates as Stephenson, Davidson, and Hoard, and even from that of La Follette as governor, although as senator La Follette had moved a considerable distance in McGovern's direction. This philosophy also differentiated McGovern and his cohorts from socialism, because it accepted the essentials of the private-property and the profit-and-wage systems, and held that a just government could and should represent all socioeconomic classes.[28]

His vision of economic democracy embraced "a more enlightened and humane system of compensating workmen injured in the course of their employment." The existing employer liability system produced perpetual and expensive litigation that benefited neither employee nor employer. McGovern wanted it replaced by "a system of just, prompt and certain compensation." Germany had an ideal cumpulsory system, McGovern said, but the state constitution required that Wisconsin's system be optional and elective. Running a workmen's compensation system would require another administrative agency, so McGovern proposed bringing together all state bodies that dealt with labor into one department, "with power to employ subordinates and to designate their duties." McGovern forthrightly ac-

[27] *Ibid.*, 25–29.
[28] *Ibid.*, 9; Margulies, *Decline of the Progressive Movement*, 108–116, 131–133; Wyman, "Voting Behavior in the Progressive Era," 298–300; Thelen, *La Follette and the Insurgent Spirit*, 52–124.

knowledged that this move would increase expenses and expand the scope of state authority over the workplace, but he argued that the gains in efficiency, economy, and social justice would more than justify the changes.[29]

Promoting public health was also one of the state's most important responsibilities, the governor said, and he recommended expanding the boards of health and hygiene and of public libraries in order to improve sanitation and prevent disease. He requested an appropriation of $15,000 to initiate a state program to care for indigent and handicapped children. As for railroads, he said that a recent state supreme court decision had limited the ability of the Railroad Commission to enforce the 1907 law concerning stocks and bonds. McGovern called for amendments to broaden the commission's investigative and enforcement powers over securities issued by public service companies so as to curb stock-watering.

Turning to education, which he characterized as a social investment that had already paid Wisconsin substantial dividends, McGovern outlined a broad program involving consolidation of country schools, a minimum wage law for teachers, and elected county boards of education to improve the quality of instruction, and especially an ambitious program of industrial, agricultural, and continuing education. McGovern pointed to Germany as the ideal model for using education to improve industrial efficiency, as had Charles McCarthy in a 1911 report.[30]

The state's natural resources, "a question of vital public interest," received attention, too. Specifically, he advocated state intervention in forest fire prevention; reforestation, especially of lands at the headwaters of principal rivers and streams; the designation of waterpowers as public utilities subject to regulation by the Railroad Commission; the continuation of the ongoing soil survey; and the eradication of noxious weeds. McGovern's tax plan was also farsighted. He praised the income tax as "theoretically . . . the most just and equitable of all taxes" because it was based upon the "ability to pay," and he called for both the ratification of the proposed Sixteenth Amendment to the U.S. Constitution and the enactment of a graduated state income tax. To raise additional revenue, as well as to increase the scope of state regulation, McGovern asked for a license fee tax on automobiles, a levy on mineral extraction, and the *ad valorem* taxation of telephone companies.[31]

In four brief pages, he outlined the boldest strategy for government economic planning ever envisioned in any state of the Union to date. He grounded his plan firmly in such basic American values

[29] McGovern, *Governor's Message*, 1911, pp. 9–13, 34–35.
[30] *Ibid.*, 30–34, 40–46.
[31] *Ibid.*, 13–25.

as private ownership of property, representative government, democracy, equality of opportunity, and faith in progress. Wisconsin producers and consumers were at the mercy of "those who wastefully or selfishly dominate the markets," he said. He challenged the legislature to establish an ex officio commission of public officials, and representatives of labor, industry, and agriculture to "co-ordinate the statistical and economic investigations of the state in all of its departments" and to recommend legislation in the public interest. This board, he believed, would improve the efficiency and economy of state agencies, investigate the recent increase in the cost of living, and study methods for marketing farm products co-operatively. It would also investigate ways to foster settlement of the state's uncultivated lands and to reduce the rising tide of farm tenancy. The board's work, McGovern said, would ultimately benefit the whole state—farmers, workers, consumers, and manufacturers.[32]

Perhaps to defuse the inevitable charges of radicalism, McGovern concluded by pointing out that most of his key proposals had already received popular approval, either through referendum votes or in the recommendations of commissions. They were "made in response to a strong, insistent demand which comes to us from the people as a whole, rather than from any party or faction." That demand was "for an increasingly enlightened appreciation of the rights of the average man," and for a "return to the ideal of equality before the law in both business and politics." His proposals, McGovern declared, "have the single end in view of securing homely justice among men in the material activities of life." Representative government and industrial democracy were interdependent and were under attack "by the arrogance of wealth." He was not extreme, McGovern said, because the great challenge for modern government was to "make legislation keep pace with rapidly developing social and commercial conditions. . . . In other years, and largely by other hands, the ground was broken and the grain planted from which has sprung the abundant legislative harvest which now waits to be garnered by you." The men of 1911, McGovern concluded dramatically, were "indeed fortunate in our opportunities; may we be fortunate also in the use we make of them."[33]

[4]

Other progressive spokesmen shared the new governor's optimism and vision. On January 2, Alfred T. Rogers wired McGovern that he had "greater opportunity than any Governor in the state's history to

[32] *Ibid.*, 35–39.
[33] *Ibid.*, 47–49.

do big things." Commenting on McGovern's inaugural address, *La Follette's Weekly Magazine* exulted that "no message thus far submitted to a 1911 state legislature expresses the will of the people more vigorously, more clearly, more intelligently or more fearlessly than the message of Governor Francis E. McGovern of Wisconsin." It reported that Republican leaders were determined to enact into law the Republican platform, McGovern's message, and commission reports on everything from industrial accidents to vocational education, conservation to taxation. Waxing ecstatic, Charles McCarthy announced on January 16 that the Legislative Reference Library had already drafted over a hundred administration-backed bills, and that the final total might reach as high as 1,500. To a remarkable degree, the 1911 legislature did indeed sustain its energy and fulfill its promise over six long months. Its 185 working days fell just three days short of the record established by the "Long Parliament" of 1907.[34]

The composition of the 1911 legislature was remarkable on several counts. For one thing, 43 per cent of its members had at least some college education—an impressive number in an age when a high school education was just becoming the norm. That fact alone meant legislators were attuned to the progressive mindset and proposals, and it made them more likely to defer to university experts and political leaders. For another thing, the legislature of 1911 represented a polar shift in behavior from the legislature of the 1890's. Rodney A. Elward, a UW graduate and onetime Milwaukee journalist as well as former secretary to Congressman Dahle, substantiated the transformation in a June, 1910, article in *La Follette's Weekly Magazine*, written after a ten-year absence from Madison. He marveled at the "unreal appearance" of Wisconsin legislative politics, which he attributed to the "incredible" and "almost impossible" revolution wrought by "the political sanitary measures adopted . . . during the past decade." Gone, he exclaimed, were such staples of the 1890's as free bars, the "corpulent, suave, and domineering lobbyists," and the "artificial blondes from Chicago, Minneapolis, and other distant cities" who haunted legislative corridors, "occupying places on the payroll, and whose work was performed by other, and competent, clerks." The legislature of those days had been composed of "men of limited knowledge of public affairs, often astonishingly ignorant," and managed by political bosses and lobbyists, the present membership seemed to consist of "bright, intellectually active, and apparently independent men, largely graduates of the University."

---

[34]Alfred T. Rogers to McGovern, January 2, 1911, McGovern Papers; Margulies, *Decline of the Progressive Movement*, 134; Milwaukee *Journal*, January 3, 11–12, 16, July 15, 1911; Milwaukee *Sentinel*, January 4, 11, 17, 20, 1911; *La Follette's Weekly Magazine*, January 14, 1911.

For a final thing, the numbers, too, were promising. Assembly Republicans had suffered a loss of thirteen seats from the previous legislature, but several of the losers had been Stalwarts who were replaced by either progressive Democrats or Socialists. The prospects for collaboration among progressives were bright.[35]

Determining the probable boundaries for such an inter-party coalition, however, was a complex problem. Geography, socio-economic interests, ethnic and cultural proclivities all constituted potential fault lines within the two major parties. Rural progressives often hesitated to support advanced labor and welfare measures; the prohibition issue continued to threaten progressive solidarity, especially among Republicans. Only the Social Democrats—Milwaukee-based, labor-union-affiliated, heavily German, and "dripping wet"—were largely immune to internal fracturing. On virtually every issue involving advantage-seeking among the parties—such as legislative apportionment, home rule, voting qualifications, and election mechanics—party loyalty overwhelmed ideological conviction. The same was generally true of ethno-cultural issues. Progressive Republicans and Democrats and Socialists frequently co-operated, but rarely on matters that were either too "socialistic" or too obviously in the self-interest of labor unions. To provide the best forum for tripartisan progressive collaboration, Senator Albert W. Sanborn of Ashland and assembly speaker Charles A. Ingram of Durand, both Republican leaders, agreed that all major legislative proposals should first be considered by joint committees of the whole in each house. At the conclusion of each joint committee hearing, the bills would be referred to the proper committees of each house, together with suggestions for amendment and recommendations for action. Administration forces also defeated a resolution to have the assembly members make committee assignments instead of the speaker. These actions did much to keep the progressive Republicans in control. Nonetheless, other factions of all three parties were able to exert influence, especially on matters of political reform. Fourteen Socialist members often managed to play the two major parties against one another.[36]

The 1911 legislature started in high gear in mid-January, as all

---

[35] *Wisconsin Blue Book, 1911*, pp. 736–786; Rodney A. Elward, "Ten Years Ago and Today," *La Follette's Weekly Magazine*, June 25, 1910, p.7; Cavanaugh, "McGovern and the 1911 Wisconsin Legislature," 54–55, 113–123; William M. Leiserson, "The Wisconsin Legislation of 1911," *The Survey*, October 14, 1911, pp. 1000–1003; Margulies, *Decline of the Progressive Movement*, 131–134; McMurray, "Some Influences of the University," 34; Casey, *Charles McCarthy*, 75–77.

[36] Cavanaugh, "McGovern and the 1911 Wisconsin Legislature," 54–55, 86–102; Leiserson, "Wisconsin Legislation of 1911," *The Survey*, October 14, 1911, pp. 1000–1003; *Wisconsin Blue Book, 1911*, pp. 736–786; Milwaukee *Journal*, January 15–17, 1911; Milwaukee *Sentinel*, January 15–17, 1911.

three parties introduced a flurry of legislation. The progressive Republicans sponsored bills for home rule, nonpartisan local elections, a state highway commission, an industrial accident law, corrupt practices legislation, and a limit on hours women could work. The Milwaukee Social Democrats sponsored a plethora of public ownership and pro-labor measures. (Frank J. Weber even introduced a resolution calling for a state constitutional convention.) Democrats less ambitiously sponsored measures designed to protect their party's second-place status. By mid-February, the Stalwart Milwaukee *Sentinel* announced that over 900 bills already had been introduced in the assembly and 375 in the senate. The paper complained that the lower house had handled 400 measures on Valentine's Day alone, and that Charles McCarthy's "bill factory" had drafted over a thousand bills, with more to come. On March 28, the *Sentinel* revealed that, of the legislature's 133 members, only three had failed to introduce at least one bill. By April 6, the assembly passed the one thousand mark in bills proposed. Efforts to set a deadline for introducing new bills occasioned prolonged and frequently acrimonious debate.[37]

Not surprisingly, all this proposed legislation beleaguered legislative clerks, who were frequently unable to keep pace. Several times in February and March, the legislature marked time while waiting for the state printer to return sufficient copies of proposed bills. On April 6, the *Sentinel* crowed that not a single one of the progressive Republicans' twenty-four major platform pledges had yet been enacted, and that, with two exceptions, "all are in the embryonic stage." Only the resolution ratifying the federal income tax amendment had been adopted; workmen's compensation and the good roads bill had passed the senate, and the assembly was on the verge of passing the corrupt practices and second-choice primary measures. The remaining bills were still bottled up in committee. Some legislative leaders pushed for night sessions since committee hearings took up daytime hours. Progressives were frustrated over this state of affairs, to the *Sentinel*'s joy. It attributed much of the delay to legislators' retaliating against the leadership plan to postpone consideration of "unimportant" special-interest bills "until planting time." Predictably, the assembly and the senate blamed one another, as did each of the three party contingents. When the Social Democrats announced their intention to force a roll-call vote on every single one of their measures reported unfavorably in committee, the *Sentinel* observed that "the legislature may spend the summer in Madison."[38]

---

[37] Milwaukee *Journal*, January 17–20, 1911; Milwaukee *Sentinel*, January 17–20, February 14–15, March 28, April 6, 1911. The three who had failed to introduce bills were Speaker C. A. Ingram of Durand, Assemblyman Henry J. Janssen of De Pere, and Assemblyman Nicholas Schmidt of Marathon in Marathon County.

[38] Milwaukee *Sentinel*, January 28, February 15, March 24, 27, April 6 (quotes), 1911.

The Most Progressive State 535

As late as April 11, the Milwaukee *Journal*, which was progressively Democratic, lamented that the legislature was running significantly behind the 1909 pace of measures passed and signed by the governor. From that point forward, however, the legislature gained momentum. From mid-May to early July, a flood of bills were enacted. By May 23, the leadership appointed a joint committee to explore an adjournment date. The next day, assembly members celebrated the passage of a compromise apportionment bill by marching to the senate chamber, singing "Tramp, Tramp, Tramp." Turned back at the door by the sergeant at arms, the assemblymen marched back to their chamber and let off steam by singing songs popular thirty years before. By then, the senate had virtually completed its calendar and took to recessing from day to day, while waiting for the assembly to catch up. On June 29, the *Journal* ran a political cartoon in which an older woman ("Wisconsin") and a younger one ("Progressive Legislature of 1911") exchanged mutual thanks and congratulations. At noon on July 14, the 1911 legislature at last adjourned, sine die.[39]

[5]

Summarizing and evaluating the achievements of the most productive and progressive legislature in Wisconsin history is a prodigious task. Probably the most useful strategy is to sort its major accomplishments into several categories—for example political and governmental restructuring, labor and welfare measures, conservation, education, tax reform, and economic regulation and planning—in order to discern and assess patterns of change and continuity over two decades of reform.

Perhaps ironically, some of the most hotly contested battles of the session were fought over political issues, at least some of which had little to do with progressivism and almost everything to do with partisan advantage, even though the combatants were usually anxious to cloak their efforts in the mantle of reform. The opening partisan shot was fired on January 12, immediately after McGovern delivered his high-minded inaugural message. Administration Republicans introduced bills for home rule, nonpartisan local elections, and 20 per cent minimum ballot qualification—all of which would have favored Milwaukee Republicans against both Democrats and Socialists. The Democrats reacted by trying to remove the power to appoint committees from progressive Republican speaker Ingram. Social Democrats combined with most Republicans to defeat this maneuver, but three Republican measures introduced by Senator Henry H. Boden-

---

[39] *Ibid.*, April 11, May 24–25, June 23, 29, July 15, 1911; Milwaukee *Journal*, June 29, 1911.

stab continued to fuel partisan warfare for the rest of the session, reapportionment of the legislative and congressional seats being the most bitterly fought. State supreme court guidelines specified that legislative districts must be "compact, contiguous and reasonably convenient," giving progressive Republicans, Stalwarts, Socialists, and Democrats room to jockey shamelessly for advantage, drawing and redrawing lines almost daily to effect a politically viable compromise. A coalition of Socialists, Stalwarts, and Democrats apparently succeeded in passing a reapportionment bill on June 23, but progressive Republicans called upon McGovern to veto it, threatening a court challenge. The governor did in fact veto the bill on July 8, calling it unfair and unconstitutional. Pleased, progressive Republicans agreed to cooperate with the Socialists on a compromise plan. Finally, on July 13, the two groups settled on a bill which passed the assembly 58–7. The senate concurred the following day, and McGovern quickly signed the new law, avoiding the possibility of a special session.[40]

Scarcely less partisan was the contest over the percentage of primary votes necessary for a party to qualify for the general election in Milwaukee County. The Socialists' strong showing in 1910 had left the Democrats with less than the exacting 20 per cent requirement; and Socialist legislators quickly moved to protect their position by lowering the necessary percentage. Milwaukee Republicans supported the 20 per cent requirement, hoping that a sizable majority of normally Democratic voters would prefer Republicans over Socialists. To persuade Democratic legislators to vote for their pet second-choice primary bill, many Republicans eventually agreed to lower the figure to 10 per cent. Democrats vainly attempted to abolish the percentage requirement altogether, then succeeded with an amendment that dropped the minimum to 5 per cent. For their part, the Socialists favored any plan that would keep the Democrats on the ballot, in order to prevent the two major parties from combining against them in general elections.[41]

To the Socialists' ultimate detriment, the Republicans and the Democrats discovered more effective and outwardly "progressive" measures for achieving an alliance, devices that married partisan self-interest and anti-Socialist passions to progressive convictions about democracy and local autonomy. They worked especially for a law to require a majority, rather than a plurality, for victory in nonpartisan local elections. The National Municipal League's model city charter contained such a feature, which was widely favored by "good govern-

[40] Milwaukee *Journal*, January 12–15, 1911; Milwaukee *Sentinel*, January 13–19, May 9, 24, 26, June 2, 6, 22, 24, July 3, 5–8, 11, 15, 1911.
[41] Milwaukee *Sentinel*, January 13, 19, June 2, 6, 1911; Milwaukee *Journal*, January 19, 1911.

ment" reformers as a weapon against machine politics. These reformers contended that local governments essentially kept house and did not make policy, and they were convinced that local government nonpartisan elections would eliminate patronage, corruption, and escalating expenditures and taxes. In Wisconsin, such sentiments were given tremendous impetus by the success of the Social Democrats in 1910, because nonpartisan elections would facilitate the fusion of both major parties behind a single, non-socialist candidate. Progressives waffled, however. McGovern and La Follette especially held concerns that such a course might undermine the Republicans' partisan advantage in state and national elections. At best, they remained highly skeptical.[42]

Mindful of these realities, advocates of nonpartisan local elections adopted a two-part strategy: mandate them for judicial and school board contests in time for the spring elections in Milwaukee, and delay action on a more comprehensive measure until later. Spearheaded by Milwaukee progressive Republicans Henry H. Bodenstab in the senate and Erich C. Stern in the assembly, the judiciary and school board election bills sailed through both houses over Socialist and some progressive opposition. The Stern bill provided for nonpartisan judicial elections in Milwaukee County and passed the assembly 55–35, despite Speaker Ingram's unexpectedly joining the Socialists against it. In the senate, John J. Blaine, a close La Follette ally, joined with the two Milwaukee Socialist senators in trying to defeat it. Even after passage, Winfield R. Gaylord continued to twit progressive Republicans regarding the "unprogressive" nature of nonpartisan elections. Stern's proposal for nonpartisan school board elections in Milwaukee cleared the assembly, in a closer 45–31 vote, and had no trouble in the senate. McGovern signed both measures into law on March 3, in time for the spring primary elections.[43]

An across-the-board nonpartisan election proposal introduced by Stern, Bodenstab, and progressive Republican Thomas Mahon of Shawano County, however, encountered far longer delays and greater opposition. It passed the senate on April 11, with only Blaine and the two Milwaukee Socialists providing the opposition. Then it ran into serious problems in the assembly. There, a coalition of administration Republicans and Social Democrats succeeded in defeating it, 52–21.

---

[42] Milwaukee *Sentinel*, April 11, 1910; Still, *Milwaukee*, 319; Melvin G. Holli, "Urban Reform in the Progressive Era," in Lewis L. Gould, ed., *The Progressive Era* (Syracuse, 1974), 133–151; Samuel P. Hays, "The Politics of Reform in Municipal Government in the Progressive Era," *Pacific Northwest Quarterly*, 55 (October, 1964), 157–169.

[43] Milwaukee *Journal*, January 17–20, 1911; Milwaukee *Sentinel*, January 13, 17–20, February 10, 15, 17, 28, March 3, 1911; Still, *Milwaukee*, 516–527; Cavanaugh, "McGovern and the 1911 Wisconsin Legislature," 85–91.

But pressure for nonpartisan elections continued to build outside the legislature. The Milwaukee City Club and other good government organizations escalated their campaigns, while the self-styled nonpartisan and progressive Milwaukee *Journal* pointed to the success of similar experiments in Pittsburgh, Boston, and other cities. When Milwaukee Republicans and Democrats united behind the mayoral candidacy of Gerhard A. Bading in the 1912 spring elections to oust most of the Socialist administration, the measure gathered irresistible momentum. A special session of the legislature enacted it, and it was signed by a still-reluctant McGovern on May 6, 1912.[44]

Much the same mixture of ideology and partisanship infused, and confused, the battle over municipal home rule. Populists, Social Democrats, and progressives of both major parties had been demanding some form of self-government for Milwaukee since the 1890's. In 1907, the legislature had responded to those demands by allowing "cities of the first class" (meaning only Milwaukee) to hold a convention in order to draft a comprehensive home rule charter for submission to the next legislature. Over the resistance of Democratic Mayor David S. Rose and the chamber of commerce, progressive Republican and Social Democratic delegates drafted a charter which the state senate approved, but the more Stalwart-influenced assembly did not. Thus the problem was bequeathed to the 1911 legislature. Again progressive Republicans Bodenstab and Stern, aided by Social Democrat Winfield Gaylord, headed pro-home-rule forces with another two-step strategy: first, a new statute; second, a constitutional amendment. The statute permitted cities to interpret liberally the general welfare clause of the 1898 law about city charters, especially where tax rates and bonded indebtedness for public improvements were concerned. The amendment permitted municipalities to amend their charters and to adopt new ones.

Despite the widespread consensus among Socialists and progressives of both major parties, partisan and ideological conflict jeopardized these measures. A compromise worked out by Stern and Gaylord added the phrase "subject to the constitution and general laws of the state," thus guaranteeing the success of the amendment in late June. But some Milwaukee Republicans, led by Stern and Bodenstab, hurt the chances of changing the city charter law by insisting upon nonpartisan elections with a mandatory majority vote. Disagreements over the applicability of home rule to smaller cities, and over its effect on existing utility franchises, also occasioned debate and parliamentary maneuvering. Still, the law passed by the end of June. (The 1913

---

[44] Milwaukee *Journal*, January 12, 17, April 8, 12, 1911; Milwaukee *Sentinel*, January 12, 17–19, April 11, 13, 20–21, June 6, 1911; Cavanaugh, "McGovern and the 1911 Wisconsin Legislature," 91–92.

legislature later endorsed the home rule constitutional amendment for the second time, as required by the constitution, but voters defeated it in 1914, as part of a general reaction against progressivism.)[45]

Somewhat less convoluted in motive and maneuvering were the 1911 session's other major political reforms, such as a stringent corrupt election practices act. The Republicans' 1910 platform pledged they would seek a law to restrict campaign expenditures, keeping them to a stipulated amount and to specified purposes, while providing "rigorous penalties" for violations, including imprisonment and disqualification of candidates. The progressive Republican team of Bodenstab and Stern introduced appropriate bills, supported by progressives of both parties, and by the Social Democrats. Debate revolved around the effectiveness of the proposed enforcement machinery. On July 12, McGovern signed the act, which provided for imprisonment of up to three years and fines of up to $1,000, as well as disqualification from holding office.[46]

To facilitate the future elections of progressive Republican candidates, the 1911 legislature adopted what La Follette had long held to be the most serious omission of the 1903 primary law—the second-choice provision. It would allow voters to pick both their first and second choices, thus supposedly preventing a Stalwart candidate's being chosen by a plurality if several Progressive candidates split the majority vote. Stalwarts derided it as the "Mary Ann law" (a metaphor from the story of the girl who never was asked to the prom, except in desperation). But it passed the assembly in early April and the senate in early May without serious opposition, probably because the Stalwarts realized that the law's procedures would be too complicated to attract the great majority of voters. That prognosis proved correct during the law's short life. Republican voters did indeed virtually ignore the second-choice option in the 1914 primary, and Emanuel Philipp therefore became the realization of La Follette's worst fears by being nominated by a plurality in a primary election in which several progressive candidates split the majority vote. Adding insult to injury, Governor Philipp then recommended repealing the "Mary Ann law," and met little opposition, even among disgruntled pro-

---

[45] Still, *Milwaukee*, 258, 306, 316–318, 377–378, 521, 536, 558–559; Milwaukee *Sentinel*, January 13, 17, 19, 21, April 13, 17, 20, 26, 27, May 4, June 2, 22–23, 27, 29, 1911; Frederic C. Howe, *Wisconsin: An Experiment in Democracy* (New York, 1912), 62–66; *Wisconsin Statutes, 1913*, pp. 32, 535–616; Cavanaugh, "Mc Govern and the 1911 Wisconsin Legislature," 92–102.

[46] Milwaukee *Journal*, January 12–13, 17–19, 1911; Milwaukee *Sentinel*, January 18, March 30, May 11–12, June 2, 6, 29, July 12, 1911; Cavanaugh, "McGovern and the 1911 Wisconsin Legislature," 66–71; *Wisconsin Statutes, 1913*, pp. 84–93; McCarthy, *Wisconsin Idea*, 102–116; Howe, *Wisconsin*, 54–56; Lorian P. Jefferson, "Corrupt Practice Laws: Wisconsin," *American Political Science Review*, 5 (November, 1911), 577–579.

gressive Republicans, by 1914. Despite, or perhaps because of, its short, unhappy life, the enactment of the second-choice primary was powerful testimony to how irresistible the tide of Wisconsin progressive reform appeared to be running in 1911.[47]

Direct popular election of U.S. senators, replacing legislative elections, also came into law in 1911. This movement shortly swept the entire nation in the form of the Seventeenth Amendment to the Constitution, a measure sponsored by a coalition of insurgent Republicans, headed by La Follette, and resurgent Democrats. It had a particular urgency for La Follette and Wisconsin progressives, because a disinclined Wisconsin legislature might have endangered his own re-election, and because direct election was widely held to be a remedy for the conditions under which Ike Stephenson had become the state's junior senator. In addition, two of the staunchest proponents of direct election—Governor McGovern and Democratic state senator Paul Husting—aspired to be the senatorial candidates in 1914. Openly, at least, the debate over direct election occurred between supporters of a bill submitted by Husting to make a preferential vote for senator binding upon the legislators, and those who argued for waiting until Congress submitted the expected amendment for ratification by the states. Both houses of the legislature passed versions of Husting's measure, but they disagreed over the method of selection, thereby necessitating a conference committee. The committee agreed to achieve the goal of direct election by having individual legislators pledge themselves to a specific candidate, but the assembly narrowly refused, 35–39, to adopt this report. In the final debate, John E. McConnell of La Crosse, who was nominally the leader of the assembly's progressive Republicans, argued in favor of waiting until Congress proposed an amendment. Speaker Ingram called this chancy, because the issue was still "in the air" in Congress. Leading the Stalwart attack was Assemblyman Ove H. Berg of Ashland, who contended that the bill subverted the intent of the state constitution by denying legislators free choice. Most Social Democrats joined the Stalwarts in opposition, simply because they wanted to abolish the U.S. Senate. As events unfolded, the eventual winners were those who favored waiting for Congress to propose the Seventeenth Amendment.[48]

---

[47] Milwaukee *Journal*, January 17, 1911; Milwaukee *Sentinel*, January 18, April 6, May 12, June 2, 6, 1911; Cavanaugh, "McGovern and the 1911 Wisconsin Legislature," 71–73; *Wisconsin Statues, 1913*, pp. 22–34; Maxwell, *La Follette and the Rise of the Progressives*, 219; Margulies, *Decline of the Progressive Movement*, 129, 134, 145, 152, 157, 178–179, 184–185, 187, 233–234, 284; Howe, *Wisconsin*, 53–54.

[48] Milwaukee *Journal*, January 26–27, 1911; Milwaukee *Sentinel*, January 26–27, April 21, May 10, 23, 26, June 2, 8, 29, 1911.

Similarly complicated by "unprogressive" side issues were attempts to adopt one of the signal innovations of the Progressive Era: the triad of initiative, referendum, and recall. The entire package had been included in the platforms of all three parties; and on January 19 Husting proposed it as a constitutional amendment. All three elements were generally anathema to conservatives, but recall drew the greatest fire, at least in public. In an effort to enhance the chances of initiative and referendum, progressive Republican assemblymen Chauncey W. Yockey of Milwaukee and Lewis E. Gettle of Edgerton (Rock County) introduced separate measures providing for initiative and referendum. The issue generated serious differences of editorial opinion among Milwaukee's non-socialist newspapers, with the progressive *Free Press* and *Journal* endorsing the measures in principle, while the Stalwart *Sentinel* and *Evening Wisconsin* attacked them as "radical" and "infantile." All four papers agreed, however, that the voting percentages required to initiate and approve legislation should be set high enough to prevent the Social Democrats and extreme progressives from forcing radical socio-economic policies on the state. To counter the opposition, Charles McCarthy prepared a detailed exposition of all three measures and their nationwide popularity, released on April 8. Still the wheels continued to grind slowly. It was not until early June that the proposed constitutional amendments for initiative and referendum passed both houses, and not until June 29 that both houses concurred in the report of the conference committee.[49]

In the meantime, the proposed constitutional amendment for recall, introduced by Husting, experienced an equally rocky course. His original resolution included all officials, including judges, but on April 19 that provision sparked a hot debate over the possibility that the Social Democrats might use recall to remove antilabor judges in Milwaukee. After an exchange of mutual recriminations, the senate, by a 15–12 vote, accepted a substitute resolution submitted by its judiciary committee exempting judges. The amended resolution then passed 20–7, with only Stalwarts and two conservative Democrats voting against it. For good measure, the senate memorialized Congress in favor of initiative, referendum, and recall amendments

---

[49] Milwaukee *Journal*, January 19–20, April 8, 1911; Milwaukee *Sentinel*, January 20, March 30, April 8, 15, 19, 27, May 8, 11, 16, 19, June 2, 8, 29, 1911; Milwaukee *Evening Wisconsin*, February 14, April 25, May 5, 1911; Milwaukee *Free Press*, May 9, 23, 1911; Cavanaugh, "McGovern and the 1911 Wisconsin Legislature," 111–112; McCarthy, *Wisconsin Idea*, 116–123, 309–313; *Wisconsin Statutes, 1913*, pp. 30–33; Wyman, "Voting Behavior in the Progressive Era," 455; McCarthy to Frederic C. Howe, April 12, 17, 1911, McCarthy to La Follette, April 17, 1911, and Howe to McCarthy, April 19, 1911, all in the McCarthy Papers; S. Gail Lowrie, "Initiative and Referendum," *American Political Science Review*, 5 (November, 1911), 590–592.

to the U.S. Constitution. On May 16, the amended recall resolution cleared the assembly, 64–1. Thus all three "direct democracy" measures passed their first hurdle on the rocky road to becoming amendments to the Wisconsin constitution. (The 1911 legislature also mandated separate ballots for national, state, and local elections and instituted a presidential preference primary.)[50]

Completing the progressive agenda of political reform, the 1911 legislature enacted four other measures that were generally not so infused with partisan and anti-socialist motives. By far the most idealistic was the prohibition of legislative logrolling and vote trading introduced by progressive Republican assemblyman Merlin Hull of Black River Falls. It passed the assembly on March 28 and the senate on April 27, with little committed opposition. More substantive was a proposed constitutional amendment to streamline the amendment process by eliminating the requirement that each proposal be approved by two consecutive legislatures before it could be submitted to the people for a referendum. Proponents, such as McCarthy, argued that the change would make it possible to amend the state constitution in six months instead of two years. This outraged Stalwarts and conservative Democrats, but a coalition of Progressives and Socialists had little difficulty in achieving passage. Ironically, the very process that the measure was designed to supplant delayed its ultimate test until 1914, at which time it suffered the fate of nearly all things progressive.

A more immediate backlash occurred with the administration proposal to make the post of insurance commissioner appointive instead of elective. Even some Progressives attacked it as a blatant device for freezing La Follette loyalist Herman Ekern into office; others derided it for the apparent contradiction it posed to the progressive doctrine of popular control over government. The Progressives countered by citing another of their cardinal principles: administration by apolitical "experts," a category into which Ekern fit somewhat ambiguously. After signing the bill, Governor McGovern quickly appointed Ekern to a four-year term—a move he would later come to regret.[51]

As its final foray into political reform, the 1911 legislature made an ambivalent move in the direction of woman suffrage. The bill was introduced by Senator David G. James of Richland Center, father of prominent feminist Ada L. James, who was the first president of the Political Equality League. It passed the senate on March 31, but ran

---

[50] Milwaukee *Sentinel*, April 19, May 16, 1911; McCarthy, *Wisconsin Idea*, 255–256; *Wisconsin Statutes, 1913*, p. 33; Howe, *Wisconsin*, 55–59.

[51] Milwaukee *Sentinel*, March 28, April 27, May 3, 10, June 27, 1911; *Wisconsin Statutes, 1913*, p. 32; Maxwell, *La Follette and the Rise of the Progressives*, 123; Margulies, *Decline of the Progressive Movement*, 121, 139.

into problems in the assembly. Its sponsors saved the day by accepting an amendment to submit the measure to a popular referendum during the next general election. Thus revised, the bill passed the lower house, 49–18, on May 16. The senate concurred on May 26. The bill was signed by a reluctant McGovern in early June, and suffragists celebrated by launching a statewide "Votes For Women" campaign in Racine the same day. The measure's overwhelming defeat in a statewide referendum of November, 1912, graphically demonstrated the fact that much of the support uttered on behalf of woman suffrage was largely for public consumption, and that many legislators used the referendum strategy as a ploy to avoid going on record against a bill with so much support. McGovern's refusal to back another woman suffrage bill in 1913 soon provided further proof of the ambivalence, if not the outright duplicity, of many otherwise progressive lawmakers. For many such men, the hour for woman suffrage had not yet struck.[52]

[6]

Far more important in the grand scheme of things was the flood of socio-economic legislation that poured forth in 1911, headed by several key labor and welfare measures. The State Federation of Labor-Social Democratic coalition advocated most of these. Indeed, Social Democratic lawmakers had earlier introduced a barrage of labor and welfare bills, ranging from the regulation of wages and hours of labor to prohibition against using private detectives and strikebreakers. Most of them failed of enactment. On the major bills in the 1911 session, however, the WSFL-SDP partnership conceded the initiative to progressive Republican leaders, because they professed compatible views, controlled the legislative machinery, and would therefore receive the blame in the event of failure. Most progressive Republicans followed their leaders on these issues, but some from rural areas, especially northwestern Wisconsin, expressed serious reservations

---

[52] Milwaukee *Sentinel*, March 31, April 26–27, May 16–17, 26, 1911; Lawrence L. Graves, "The Wisconsin Woman Suffrage Movement, 1846–1920" (doctoral dissertation, University of Wisconsin, 1954), 111–214; Genevieve G. McBride, *On Wisconsin Women: Working For Their Rights from Settlement to Suffrage* (Madison, 1993), 201–234; Kenneth W. Duckett, "Suffragettes on the Stump: Letter from the Political Equality League of Wisconsin, 1912," in *WMH*, 38 (Autumn, 1954), 31–34; Marilyn Grant, "The 1912 Suffrage Referendum: An Exercise in Political Action," in *WMH*, 64 (Winter, 1980–1981), 107–116; Wyman, "Voting Behavior in the Progressive Era," 454–455; Marie Anne Laberge, "Working Together or Working Apart: Socialist Women in the Wisconsin Suffrage Movement, 1910–1920" (master's thesis, University of Wisconsin, 1986).

about them. Progressives, therefore, needed Socialist and urban Democratic support. The problem was somewhat offset, however, by the partial conversion on labor and welfare issues of many of the state's most powerful industrialists, collectively represented by the Merchants' and Manufacturers' Association of Milwaukee and the Wisconsin Manufacturers' Association. These industrialists stoutly opposed any measures that would enhance the position of organized labor, facilitate worker control of the workplace, or establish government-mandated standards for wages, hours, and conditions of labor. They had converted to the extent that they had come to comprehend the necessity—and the possible benefits—of voluntary, co-operative programs that might lower labor costs and increase worker efficiency and morale. Particularly on questions of industrial health and safety they had come to realize that the high cost of accidents, in terms of lost productivity and litigation, dictated their acceptance of some government involvement.[53]

Industrialists' receptiveness improved especially after 1905, when state courts began to return a higher percentage of verdicts in favor of workers in employer liability suits. This change made more appealing a system of workmen's compensation that would eliminate most tort litigation. Even though the courts still dismissed almost two-thirds of worker suits, many employers regularly complained that lawyers and judges were trying to put them out of business. More thoughtful manufacturers probably agreed with Wisconsin Chief Justice Roujet D. Marshall that the existing system "is all wrong in its basic features . . . [and] illogical and wholly unadaptable to our complex industrial life." Reinforcing this growing consensus was the evidence gathered and analyzed by experts from Wisconsin associated with the Legislative Reference Library, the American Association for Labor Legislation, and the Bureau of Labor and Industrial Statistics. The statistical evidence revealed countless flaws in the existing employer liability system, and the superiority of workmen's compensation programs in other countries.[54]

---

[53] Robert Asher, "The 1911 Workmen's Compensation Law: A Study in Conservative Labor Reform," in *WMH* 57 (Winter, 1973–1974), 123–129; Donald J. Berthrong, "Social Legislation in Wisconsin, 1836–1900" (doctoral dissertation, University of Wisconsin, 1951), 321–336; Donald W. Rogers, "From Common Law to Factory Laws: The Transformation of Workplace Safety Law in Wisconsin Before Progressivism," *American Journal of Legal History*, 39 (April, 1995), 177–213; Gertrude Schmidt Weiss, "History of Labor Legislation in Wisconsin" (doctoral dissertation, University of Wisconsin, 1933), 1–61; Gordon M. Haferbecker, *Wisconsin Labor Laws* (Madison, 1958), 34–40; Irene Osgood, Review of Labor Legislation of 1909, (New York, 1910), 14–15. See also Jennie W. M. Turner, comp., *Workmen's Compensation in Wisconsin, 1905–1913: Planks in Party Platform and History of Bills, with Votes* (Madison, 1916).

[54] Asher, "The 1911 Wisconsin Workmen's Compensation Law," in *WMH*, 57: 126–129 (quote); McCarthy, *Wisconsin Idea*, 156–163; Haferbecker, *Wisconsin Labor Laws*,

Responding to this changing climate, the 1909 legislature had created the Industrial Insurance Committee, headed by progressive Republican Senators Albert W. Sanborn of Ashland and John J. Blaine of Boscobel, and including Senator Edward T. Fairchild of Milwaukee (who would emerge as McGovern's Stalwart opponent during the 1910 Republican gubernatorial primary) and four moderately progressive assemblymen. Chief among these was Wallace Ingalls of Racine, a serious student of European systems of workmen's compensation and a self-proclaimed spokesman for his district's "enlightened" industrialists. Ingalls argued that workmen's compensation would lessen the "natural antagonism between the interests of the employer and employees" and improve workers' "devotion to their work." During the committee's hearings, representatives of International Harvester, Allis-Chalmers, the Pabst Brewing Company, and the vice-president for Wisconsin of the National Association of Manufacturers, among others, testified generally in favor of the principle of payments to injured workers regardless of liability. (They differed among themselves over the best system.) Throughout, the committee was advised closely by Charles McCarthy and his staff, who were, in turn, in frequent touch with John R. Commons and his group. Chairman Sanborn pronounced the existing system "absolutely intolerable," and predicted that the committee would produce a system based upon the "hearty cooperation of both the laboring man and the employer." He also cautioned that "haste should be made slowly."[55]

The WSFL-SDP partnership had long advocated compulsory workmen's compensation, but the committee never seriously entertained such a scheme, because of the adamant opposition of employers and of the courts. On the advice of McCarthy, Sanborn, and the attorney for the WSFL, the committee also considered and rejected the idea of worker contributions to help fund the system. The committee agreed on a plan that would pay injured workers 65 per cent of their wages for the duration of their incapacity, up to a maximum equal to a death benefit of $3,000. Determined upon establishing a voluntary program, the committee declared its abhorrence of insurance by existing casualty companies because of their "excessive rate" and

---

38–40; Weiss, "History of Labor Legislation," 62–71; Arthur J. Altmeyer, *The Industrial Commission of Wisconsin: A Case Study in Labor Law Administration* (Madison, 1932), 9–16.

[55] Asher, "The 1911 Wisconsin Workmen's Compensation Law," in *WMH*, 57: 129–132 (quotes); Haferbecker, *Wisconsin Labor Laws*, 41–42; Weiss, "History of Labor Legislation," 65–72; Altmeyer, *Industrial Commission of Wisconsin*, 9–16; Maxwell, *La Follette and the Rise of the Progressives*, 156–157. For a brief, perceptive summary of 1911 labor legislation, see Thomas W. Gavett, *Development of the Labor Movement in Milwaukee* (Madison, 1965), 107–111.

because, in the words of one employer, such companies used "every subterfuge to withhold the payment of just compensation." Instead, the majority of the committee favored insurance by employer mutual associations, under the supervision of a newly created industrial accident board, because, as Sanborn observed, such quasi-independent, expert public bodies were "the ones the laboring man has to depend upon for a square deal." To persuade employers to "elect" such a course, the committee recommended removing nearly all of the existing common-law defenses in liability cases for those companies that refused to join. Despite employer protests, the committee stipulated that owners explicitly had to elect to join in order to participate in the program. And despite the argument of the WSFL that workers should be able to choose between litigation and fixed compensation *after* an industrial accident, the committee decided that every employee would be covered automatically by the insurance, unless he or she specifically declined it, in writing, at the time of initial employment. Such was the essence of the final report that the Industrial Insurance Committee delivered to the legislature and the governor on January 10, 1911.[56]

The very next day, Sanborn successfully moved for the creation of a joint legislative committee on industrial insurance. The day after, Governor McGovern strongly endorsed the Industrial Insurance Committee's recommendations in his inaugural message and called for swift enactment of the forthcoming bill, which Sanborn introduced on January 17. Despite this momentum, disagreement over specifics delayed passage for more than three months. On January 27, several Democratic legislators announced their opposition, largely because of the expense and centralization of authority involved in establishing the Industrial Accident Board. Employers' organizations generally favored passage in order to achieve social peace, industrial efficiency, and cost-cutting, but they also attempted to restore the three common-law defenses for those companies that elected not to provide workmen's compensation. The WSFL-SDP group lobbied for the right of workers to choose between litigation and mandated compensation *after* being injured. When on March 23 the New York state court of appeals declared a compulsory workmen's compensation law unconstitutional, Daniel Hoan, Milwaukee's city

---

[56] Asher, "The 1911 Wisconsin Workmen's Compensation Law," in *WMH*, 57: 132–138 (quote); Cavanaugh, "McGovern and the 1911 Wisconsin Legislature," 55–58; Weiss, "History of Labor Legislation," 72–101; Milwaukee *Sentinel*, January 5, 10, 1911; Milwaukee *Journal*, January 10–11, 1911; Wisconsin State Federation of Labor, *Employee's Compensation Bill Supported and Advocated by the Wisconsin State Federation of Labor* (Milwaukee, [1911?]); Haferbecker, *Wisconsin Labor Laws*, 41–42; Casey, *Charles McCarthy*, 78–79.

attorney, a Social Democrat and former counsel to the WSFL, unsuccessfully petitioned the Wisconsin legislature to adopt the elective provision favored by organized labor. The senate denied Hoan's proposal, and restored the three common-law defenses for employers who did not choose to participate. (The monthly magazine of the MMAM rejoiced that "the measure in its new form will not work injustice to Wisconsin employers and employes.") Progressive Republicans also had to contend with desertions in their ranks. Several rural members fought to exempt farmers and small agricultural processors from the law. Sanborn cajoled and compromised, achieving adoption by the senate on March 30 by a vote of 22-3.[57]

A coalition of progressive Republicans and Social Democrats was upset by the senate's restoration of the common-law defenses and was concerned about the New York court decision. The group worked successfully to separate the defenses section of the bill from the rest so that the courts could approve the law itself even if they objected to the provisions governing employer participation. The MMAM voiced objections to the possible loss of the fellow-servant and assumed-risk defenses inherent in the coalition's strategy, but it eventually gave in. The assembly rejected a series of proposed amendments and on April 21 voted 69-13 in favor of passage. Twelve Democrats who objected to the $5,000 salaries to be paid the commissioners formed the only organized opposition. The senate thereupon concurred. On May 4, 1911, fulfilling a major platform pledge, Governor McGovern signed Wisconsin's epochal workmen's compensation law—the first in the nation to be found constitutional. The following day, he appointed John R. Commons, Joseph D. Beck, and Charles H. Crownhart as the three principal members of the Industrial Accident Board.[58]

In its final form, the measure allowed most employers only three options. They could choose to stay out of the system, and take their chances on a "contributory negligence" defense in the courts; or they could establish their own systems of "self-insurance"; or they could form "mutual companies" to share risks and costs. Any com-

---

[57] Asher, "The 1911 Wisconsin Workmen's Compensation Law," in *WMH*, 57: 138–140 (quote); Cavanaugh, "McGovern and the 1911 Wisconsin Legislature," 56–59; Milwaukee *Journal*, January 11–12, 27, 28, March 23–24, 30, 31, 1911; Milwaukee *Sentinel*, January 11–12, 18–19, 27, March 23–24, 30–31, 1911; McGovern, *Governor's Message*, 1911, pp. 9–13; Robert F. Wesser, "Conflict and Compromise: The Workmen's Compensation Movement in New York, 1890's–1913," *Labor History* 12 (Summer, 1971), 345–372.

[58] Asher, "The 1911 Wisconsin Workmen's Compensation Law," in *WMH*, 57: 138–140; Cavanaugh, "McGovern and the 1911 Wisconsin Legislature," 59–61; Milwaukee *Journal*, April 12–13, 21–22, May 4–6, 1911; Milwaukee *Sentinel*, April 12–13, 21–22, May 4–6, 1911; Howe, *Wisconsin*, 86–103.

pany with over four employees, farmers excluded, was required to elect either the self-insurance or mutual-company options, or else remain exposed to litigation with reduced defense. The Industrial Accident Board was empowered to administer the entire system and to rule upon individual settlements. When they took a job, workers at companies covered by either compensation alternative had to agree, in writing, whether or not to participate. Despite the basically voluntary nature of the program and the negative consequences of refusal, the great majority of Wisconsin employers chose not to participate during the first two years. On May 12, the MMAM announced its intention to file a friendly test case in the state courts, supposedly to establish the law's constitutionality. Whatever the association's intention, a large number of employers, especially those with relatively few employees, decided to wait until the court ruled and meanwhile take their chances in court. In the end, the Wisconsin Supreme Court affirmed the law's legality, giving the state and the 1911 legislature the prize in the effort to put a successful workmen's compensation law into place.[59]

The 1911 legislature also used precedent laws to require substantial improvements in the conditions for children and women in industry. In late February, Republican assemblyman Clinton B. Ballard of Appleton introduced legislation to strengthen child labor laws by requiring the Bureau of Labor and Industrial Statistics to issue a work permit before anyone under age sixteen could be employed, prohibiting the hiring of children between the ages of fourteen and sixteen in a number of dangerous occupations, and mandating an eight-hour day and a forty-eight-hour work week for males under sixteen and females under eighteen. The assembly committee on the welfare of women and children favored passing the bill as written, but the assembly itself amended it to exempt agricultural occupations and to allow municipal, county, and juvenile court judges, as well as factory inspectors, to issue work permits. The assembly approved the

---

[59] Asher, "The 1911 Wisconsin Workmen's Compensation Law," in *WMH*, 57: 138–140; Cavanaugh, "McGovern and the 1911 Wisconsin Legislature," 59–61; Weiss, "History of Labor Legislation in Wisconsin," 80–102; Haferbecker, *Wisconsin Labor Laws*, 42–43; Altmeyer, *Industrial Commission of Wisconsin*, 26–104; McCarthy, *Wisconsin Idea*, 156–163; *Wisconsin Statutes, 1913*, pp. 1617–1627; Milwaukee *Sentinel*, May 12, 1911; Philemon Tecumseh Sherman, *The Progressive Cost of Workmen's Compensation: An Opinion by P. Tecumseh Sherman* (New York, 1914), *passim*; George H. Russell, *Facts About Workmen's Compensation and Liability Insurance* (Milwaukee, 1911), 3–14; Gray (Fred L.) Co., *Workmen's Compensation in Wisconsin: Its Scope and Cost* (Minneapolis?, 1911?), *passim*; William A. Fricke, *The Value and Need of Co-operation Under the Workmen's Compensation Act: An Address* (Wausau, 1913?), 1–24, and *Workmen's Compensation: Scope and Application of the Wisconsin Law* (Wausau, 1911), 3–23; Leiserson, "Wisconsin Legislation of 1911," *The Survey*, October 14, 1911, p. 1001.

amended bill in early June, and the senate concurred with only minor changes on June 20. Eight days later, McGovern added his signature.[60]

Women's turn came in mid-May, when the chairman of the assembly committee on the welfare of women and children, Republican S. Clayton Goff of Elkhorn, introduced a bill to limit working women to a ten-hour work day and a fifty-five-hour work week. It also restricted their nighttime employment to eight and forty-eight hours respectively. A week later, a coalition of progressive Republicans and Social Democrats beat back attempts to exempt specific industries, while more conservative members rejected, 49–34, an amendment proposed by Milwaukee Socialist Frank B. Metcalfe to limit female employment to an eight-hour day and fifty-hour week. Progressives and Socialists then combined to defeat a motion to kill the entire bill, 47–42. Early the next month, the assembly approved the original Goff bill, 44–28. In the senate, however, Henry Krumrey of Plymouth led a movement to exempt industries in cities with populations under 10,000 (cities of the fourth class). The senate first approved Krumrey's amendment, then acceded to the assembly and agreed to drop the exemption. McGovern signed the bill on July 3, to the applause of organized labor, women's groups, and social reformers. [61]

Establishment of the Industrial Commission capped the 1911 achievements in labor and welfare legislation. Its creation met surprisingly little opposition and fulfilled yet another platform pledge. Progressive Republican assemblyman Thomas J. Mahon of Eland (Shawano County) introduced the bill which many Stalwarts and conservative Democrats appreciated because of its potential benefits of economy and efficiency The legislation put the state's many (and increasing) labor and welfare programs under the single administra-

[60] Cavanaugh, "McGovern and the 1911 Wisconsin Legislature," 63–64; Maxwell, *La Follette and the Rise of the Progressives*, 158, 163; Berthrong, "Social Legislation in Wisconsin," 336–347; Weiss, "History of Labor Legislation in Wisconsin," 129–225; Altmeyer, *Industrial Commission of Wisconsin*, 9–10, 181–185, 268–283; Haferbecker, *Wisconsin Labor Laws*, 69–85; *Wisconsin Statutes, 1913*, pp. 1233–1247; Milwaukee *Journal*, February 28, June 20–21, 30, 1911; Milwaukee *Sentinel*, February 28, June 20–21, 30, 1911; Laura Scott, *Summary of Laws in Force 1910: Child Labor* (American Association for Labor Legislation, *Legislative Review* no. 5, New York, 1910), 58–59, 74–75, 128–131; Leiserson, "Wisconsin Legislation of 1911," *The Survey*, October 14, 1911, p. 1002.

[61] Cavanaugh, "McGovern and the 1911 Wisconsin Legislature," 63–66; Maxwell, *La Follette and the Rise of the Progressives*, 158–159; *Wisconsin Statutes, 1913*, pp. 1233–1247; Berthrong, "Social Legislation in Wisconsin," 389–396; Weiss, "History of Labor Legislation," 308–332; Altmeyer, *Industrial Commission of Wisconsin*, 9–10, 181–185; Haferbecker, *Wisconsin Labor Laws*, 86–98; Milwaukee *Journal*, May 24, June 6, July 3–4, 1911; Milwaukee *Sentinel*, May 24, June 6, July 3–4, 1911; Maud Swett, *Summary of Labor Laws in Force 1909: Woman's Work* (American Association for Labor Legislation, *Legislative Review* no. 4, Madison, 1909), 14–15; Leiserson, "Wisconsin Legislation of 1911," *The Survey*, October 14, 1911, pp. 1001–1002.

tion of a quasi-independent commission of experts appointed by the governor. Astute employers may also have comprehended the advantage of focusing their lobbying efforts on a single board. For progressive Republicans, Democrats, and Socialists, Mahon's proposal represented the culmination of efforts to consolidate administration of all the pieces of specific labor and welfare legislation for which they had struggled for twenty years. It would also establish a government agency that would function as a permanent, and powerful, advocate for the working people of Wisconsin, becoming, in John Commons' view, a fourth branch of government.[62]

The commission would administer all such programs, including the new workmen's compensation and child and women's labor laws. It would enforce their provisions, conduct investigations, compel the attendance of witnesses at hearings, and levy penalties for violations of the state's labor laws. It would subsume all existing labor and welfare agencies, including the Board of Arbitration, the Bureau of Labor and Industrial Statistics, and the new Industrial Accident Board.[63]

On June 27, the assembly passed the Industrial Commission bill, 53–13. The senate quickly concurred, 17–8. The governor signed the bill on the last day of June, and immediately appointed the three members of the now subordinate Industrial Accident Board (Commons, Beck, and Crownhart) to the new Industrial Commission of Wisconsin.

The genius of the new law lay in its simplicity and clarity. Instead of trying to enumerate, in easily circumvented detail, the machines, devices, and specifications involved, the law established just two absolute standards. The first made it every employer's duty to provide employees and "frequenters" of his establishment with a safe work place and conditions of labor, and to "do every other thing reasonably necessary to protect the[ir] life, health, safety, and welfare." The second vested the commission with whatever powers and jurisdiction "as may be necessary adequately to enforce and administer all laws and all lawful orders." Such a generic approach was intended to avoid endless nit-picking over details, and to place absolute responsibility for safety and health squarely upon employers and the commission. Credit for this inspired line of reasoning was due largely to Commons

---

[62] Cavanaugh, "McGovern and the 1911 Wisconsin Legislature," 61–62; Francis H. Bird, "The Proposed Wisconsin Industrial Commission," *The Survey*, 26 (April 22, 1911), 151–152; Maxwell, *La Follette and the Rise of the Progressives*, 159–163; Milwaukee *Journal*, June 27, 28, 30, 1911; Milwaukee *Sentinel*, June 27, 28, 30, 1911.

[63] Cavanaugh, "McGovern and the 1911 Wisconsin Legislature," 62–63; Thomas J. Mahon, "Conserving Human Life," *La Follette's Weekly Magazine*, June 3, 1911, p.7; Haferbecker, *Wisconsin Labor Laws*, 17–33; Altmeyer, *Industrial Commission of Wisconsin*, 16–24; Howe, *Wisconsin*, 104–117; Casey, *Charles McCarthy*, 78.

and McCarthy. Their ideals and steadfastness were to pay enormous dividends over the next several decades.[64]

[7]

Turning to taxation, the 1911 legislature produced another socioeconomic landmark: the first successful state income tax in the nation's history. Its enactment culminated events set in motion by the abortive proposal of an income tax amendment to the state constitution in the 1903 legislative session. The electorate finally approved the amendment in 1908. The next legislature (1909) charged a committee, headed by Milwaukee Republican senator John Kleczka, with drafting an income tax bill for consideration in 1911. Meanwhile, in 1909, a coalition of insurgent Republicans and Democrats, of which Robert M. La Follette was the most influential leader, shepherded through Congress an income tax amendment to the U.S. Constitution—thereby guaranteeing that the 1911 Wisconsin legislature would have to deliberate both measures. Opponents of the income tax in several states tried to use the impending federal tax as a threat to defeat a proposed state income tax, or vice versa, but this did not occur in Wisconsin. The assembly unanimously ratified the eventual Sixteenth Amendment to the U.S. Constitution on February 9; the senate followed, also unanimously, on May 26.[65]

The bill prepared by the interim tax committee was drafted largely by tax commissioner Nils Haugen, a longtime advocate of income taxation, as a substitute for the ineffective and inequitable personal property tax. However, chairman Kleczka was dissatisfied with both Haugen's technical knowledge and his attitude. Accord-

[64] Cavanaugh, "McGovern and the 1911 Wisconsin Legislature," 62–63; McCarthy, *Wisconsin Idea*, 163–170; *Wisconsin Statutes, 1913*, pp. 1617–1637 (quotes on 1630); John R. Commons, "How the Wisconsin Industrial Commission Works," *American Labor Legislation Review*, 3 (February, 1913), 9–14, and "Constructive Investigation and the Industrial Commission of Wisconsin," *The Survey*, January 4, 1913, pp. 440–442; Altmeyer, *Industrial Commission of Wisconsin*, 26–298; Milwaukee *Journal*, June 27–30, 1911; Milwaukee *Sentinel*, June 27–30, 1911; Leiserson, "Wisconsin Legislation of 1911," *The Survey*, October 14, 1911, p. 1001. In his autobiography *Myself* (New York, 1938), 154–156, Commons credited the original idea to Francis H. Bird of the Legislative Reference Library staff.

[65] John O. Stark, "The Establishment of Wisconsin's Income Tax," in *WMH*, 71 (Autumn, 1987), 27–30; John D. Buenker, *The Income Tax and the Progressive Era* (New York, 1985), 295–337; *Senate Miscellaneous Documents*, 71 Cong., 3 sess., no. 240 (serial 9346), *Ratification of the Constitution and Amendments by the States* (1931), 10–11; *Wisconsin Assembly Journal*, 1911, pp. 193–194; *Wisconsin Senate Journal*, 1911 p. 713; Milwaukee *Journal*, February 10, May 27, 1911.

ingly, Kleczka invited Charles McCarthy to draft a substitute measure. McCarthy in turn obtained the services of Delos R. Kinsman, a professor of economics at the Whitewater Normal School and an authority on income taxation. In 1903, in the published version of his doctoral dissertation, entitled *The Income Tax in the Commonwealths of the United States,* Kinsman had all but concluded that the difficulties of administering an income tax would be so great that they would render one impractical. McCarthy's enthusiasm and storehouse of information converted Kinsman, however, and he took a three-month leave of absence from Whitewater to draft a law that would be effective, equitable, and immune to judicial veto, and would raise sufficient revenue. Opponents of the tax generated a storm of controversy. Haugen and economist Thomas S. Adams, future chair of the Tax Commission, denounced Kinsman's bill as "impracticable, unworkable and in violation of justice," even though they supported Kinsman's general goals. After receiving Adams' advice on the bill, McCarthy replied that the economist's suggestions were "critical rather than constructive and at present probably will have the effect of killing the whole matter." Such disputes over details among advocates of the income tax played into the hands of those who opposed it.[66]

Under Kinsman's guidance, pro-tax legislators avoided several pitfalls that had doomed similar ventures to failure or revocation. By putting administration of the income tax in the hands of the state Tax Commission, they protected it from the caprices of local assessors. By providing for a formula that returned 70 per cent of the revenue to cities, villages, and towns, and 20 per cent to counties, they deflected claims that state government would bleed local jurisdictions dry. By allowing people to use their personal property tax payments as an offset against their income tax, they capitalized on the unpopularity of the property tax and reinforced their commitment to equity. By treating individuals and corporations substantially alike, they minimized the impact of claims that the income tax represented an anti-business vendetta. By creating a graduated scale based upon "the ability to pay" and by granting relatively high personal exemptions, they remained true to the progressive credo of economic democracy.[67]

---

[66] Stark, "Establishment of Wisconsin's Income Tax," in *WMH*, 71: 30–32; "Genesis of Wisconsin's Income Tax Law: An Interview with D. O. Kinsman," in *WMH*, 21 (September, 1937), 3–4; Fitzpatrick, *McCarthy of Wisconsin*, 120–124; Stuart D. Brandes, "Nils P. Haugen and the Wisconsin Progressive Movement" (masters' thesis, University of Wisconsin, 1965), 152–187.

[67] Stark, "Establishment of Wisconsin's Income Tax," in *WMH*, 71: 33–43; "Genesis of Wisconsin's Income Tax Law," in *WMH*, 21: 5–8; Howe, *Wisconsin*, 133–139; Casey, *Charles McCarthy*, 79–80.

Even so, the bill encountered strong opposition in both houses, especially from those legislators, mostly Democrats, who were particularly attuned to the arguments of the state and Milwaukee manufacturers' associations, and similar lobbies. Wealthy industrialists and merchants of the lakeshore counties and the Fox Valley clearly had the greatest stake in preventing income taxation, since their personal property was largely untouched by the existing personal property tax system. They sought to recruit allies among those who feared even slightly higher taxes, such as wage earners and small businessmen. They stigmatized proposed state tax investigators as "ferrets," and tried to raise the limit on the dollar amount they could make in payments to others for services rendered, thereby making it difficult to discover real income. Led by Republican senator Howard Teasdale of Sparta, they unsuccessfully attempted to push the effective date ahead to 1912, probably in the hope of mounting a later legal challenge. Most importantly, they backed Teasdale's amendment providing for a referendum on the tax, despite the overwhelming support in the 1908 referendum. It is difficult to discern consistent partisan, socio-economic, or geographical patterns in the several votes taken on proposed amendments, but there can be little doubt that the most consistent proponents were those Republicans most closely associated with La Follette or McGovern, solidly aided by Social Democrats. Nor can there be much doubt that the proponents' primary motives were the desire for equitable taxation and increased revenue for the social service state.[68]

The legislative history of the 1911 income tax, from its introduction on January 27 to its signing by Governor McGovern on July 14, is too complex to rehearse here. Suffice it to say that even pro-tax experts frequently disagreed on the effect and wisdom of the various amendments, and that the assembly was consistently more enthusiastic than the senate about producing a comprehensive and effective law. The senate significantly weakened the proposed enforcement machinery, postponed the effective date of the tax, and agreed to submit the final product to another referendum, but it passed the bill, 20–6. In the assembly, the senate's weakened sections were strengthened, and the measure passed, 58–25. By then the assembly Democrats constituted the only organized opposition. The senate finally concurred in the assembly version, but only after more sharp debate. The final margin was 15–14. Even before Mc-

---

[68] Stark, "Establishment of Wisconsin's Income Tax Law," in *WMH*, 71: 33–43; "Genesis of Wisconsin's Income Tax Law," in *WMH*, 21: 8–12; Brandes, "Haugen," 181–188; McCarthy, *Wisconsin Idea*, 83–87; Maxwell, *La Follette and the Rise of the Progressives*, 100–102; Cavanaugh, "McGovern and the 1911 Wisconsin Legislature," 104–111.

Govern signed the measure, both the Wisconsin and Milwaukee manufacturers' associations announced their intention of testing the law in court.[69]

In its final form, Wisconsin's pioneer income tax levied a 1 per cent rate on incomes of over $1,000 a year, thereby exempting the vast majority of working people. It further advantaged lower-income persons by providing for exemptions of $800 for single individuals and $1,200 for married couples. It was graduated to a high of 6 per cent on incomes of over $12,000 a year, but the personal property tax offset moderated the impact of the tax on high-income people who had considerable investment income. Although it raised the tax bill of anyone who was already paying taxes, it generally did so equitably. Overall, the new tax improved significantly upon the deeply flawed personal property tax, while substantially increasing government revenues at all levels. On average, farmers, merchants, and clerks were probably the biggest beneficiaries; the greatest losers were generally persons with relatively high incomes derived primarily from wages, salaries, or fees (as distinct from investment income).

The new tax was subjected to brutal attacks even before it went into effect, but it survived all tests in court. By 1917 it was a model for four other states, and for another nineteen states by 1933. Despite its unquestionable success, the income tax law nonetheless became a major weapon in the arsenal of Stalwarts and conservative Democrats, and a major cause of the eventual downfall of the progressive Republicans.[70]

---

[69] Stark, "Establishment of Wisconsin's Income Tax Law" in *WMH*, 71: 33–43; "Genesis of Wisconsin's Income Tax Law," in *WMH*, 21: 13–15; Cavanaugh, "McGovern and the 1911 Wisconsin Legislature," 104–111; Milwaukee *Journal,* January 27, February 8, 10, March 7, May 1, 4, 11, 13, 23, 26, 27, June 2, 22, 24, July 6, 14, 1911; Milwaukee *Sentinel,* January 27, February 8, 10, March 7, May 1, 4, 11, 13, 23, 26, 27, June 2, 22, 24, July 6, 14, 1911.

[70] Stark, "Establishment of Wisconsin's Income Tax," in *WMH,* 71: 33–43; "Genesis of Wisconsin's Income Tax," in *WMH,* 21: 10–14; Maxwell, *La Follette and the Rise of the Progressives,* 100–104; *Wisconsin Statutes,* 1913, pp. 767–774. For a view that the income tax was designed to benefit farmers at the expense of manufacturers and therefore adversely affected Wisconsin's industrial development, see W. Elliot Brownlee, Jr., *Progressivism and Economic Growth: The Wisconsin Income Tax, 1911–1929* (Port Washington, New York, 1974), and "Income Taxation and the Political Economy of Wisconsin, 1890–1930" in *WMH,* 59 (Summer, 1976), 299–324. For views stressing the equity and favorable impact of the income tax, see John O. Stark, "Harold M. Groves and Wisconsin Taxes," in *WMH,* 74 (Spring, 1991), 196–214; and Kossuth Kent Kennan, "The Wisconsin Income Tax," *Quarterly Journal of Economics,* 26 (November, 1911), 172.

[8]

In the field of conservation, the 1911 legislature's pioneering achievements proved short-lived, due largely to self-interested opponents. Even so, the laws laid the groundwork for what would later emerge as one of the nation's most stringent and comprehensive programs for the conservation of natural resources. Once again, the starting point for legislative deliberations was the report of an interim body created in 1909 to examine waterpower, forestry, and drainage, chaired by Senator Harlan P. Bird. The committee held hearings in eleven cities, compiled 3,000 pages of testimony, and submitted an 800-page report, including drafts of proposed legislation. However, the two most ardent advocates of conservation on the committee, Senators Paul Husting and Henry Krumrey, filed a sixty-page minority report that took sharp issue with their colleagues' views on waterpower and also proposed minor alternatives on forestry. At nearly the same juncture, the temporary, and largely ex officio, state Conservation Commission produced a report that agreed substantially with Krumrey and Husting. The commission was headed by university president Charles Van Hise, a nationally recognized expert on conservation, and it largely reflected the views of state forester Edward M. Griffith, who had been appointed by Governor La Follette. In the main, both the Krumrey-Husting and Conservation Commission reports urged government intervention to preserve the state's water and forest resources. Voters, too, supported stringent conservation, having approved in 1910 by a vote of 62,406 to 45,847 a constitutional amendment empowering state government to raise funds for developing waterpowers and forests. In his inaugural message, McGovern strongly endorsed the general outlines of the Krumrey-Husting and Conservation Commission reports. Thus the legislature seemed prepared to enact another path-breaking program.[71]

Ominously, however, two commission members, paper manufacturer George A. Whiting of Neenah and lumberman William Irvine of Chippewa Falls, filed their own minority report, which mostly agreed with the Bird interim committee's majority report, particularly about waterpowers. They saw water rights as inherently private, bluntly writing, "the only way to conserve water power is to use it." Virtually everyone agreed that the state should issue indeterminate

---

[71] Maxwell, *La Follette and the Rise of the Progressives*, 164–169; Vernon R. Carstensen, *Farms or Forests: Evolution of a State Land Policy for Northern Wisconsin, 1850–1932* (Madison, 1958), 27–43; Dennis East II, "Water Power and Forestry in Wisconsin: Issues of Conservation, 1890–1915" (doctoral dissertation, University of Wisconsin, 1971), 205–213; McGovern, *Governor's Message*, 1911, pp. 13–19.

franchises for using waterpowers, and that the franchise income should finance conservation work. But the Krumrey-Husting and Conservation Commission plans went further. They declared that the use of water in navigable streams was a public trust, and that the state should regulate all energy derived from that water for the general welfare. McGovern developed a similar theme in his message to the 1911 legislature. He recommended authorizing the Railroad Commission to regulate their use in the interest of consumers, with the cost to be defrayed by a new franchise tax.[72]

Responsibility for drafting the actual legislation was entrusted to a special senate committee on waterpowers, forestry, and drainage, whose members were progressive Republicans Krumrey, Otto Bosshard, and John J. Blaine; Paul Husting, a Democrat; and Social Democrat Winfield Gaylord. The committee sponsored a bill that declared that the issuance of a franchise by the state to an individual or organization was equivalent to establishing a public utility for any other purpose, making the energy derived subject to government regulation and taxation. It stipulated that waterpower franchise holders must conduct their business in the public interest, and it gave the Railroad Commission the power to issue twenty-year franchises subject to both a fee and a yearly rental. It also gave the state the authority to terminate the contract at any time, should the franchise holder violate the letter or spirit of the act, or if the government decided to enter the public power field directly. Despite numerous objections voiced during the hearings on the bill, the legislature finally passed it on June 22.[73]

Opponents of the measure, chiefly paper manufacturers and hydroelectric companies, wasted no time in taking their case to court. In January, 1912, the Wisconsin Supreme Court declared the act unconstitutional because it deprived franchise holders of their private riparian rights and property without due process of law or just compensation. Aroused by the court's sweeping decision, McGovern called a special legislative session in the spring of 1912 and instructed McCarthy to draft a new bill which would pass judicial inspection. McCarthy responded with a measure that accepted the notion of private ownership of riparian lands and waters, charged the Railroad Commission with issuing indeterminate franchises to private owners

---

[72] Maxwell, *La Follette and the Rise of the Progressives*, 165–169 (quote); East, "Water Power and Forestry," 209–213; Carstensen, *Farms or Forests*, 38–40. See also Paul H. Hass, "The Suppression of John F. Dietz: An Episode in the Progressive Era in Wisconsin," in *WMH*, 57 (Summer, 1974), 255–309.

[73] East, "Water Power and Forestry," 209–213; Carstensen, *Farms or Forests*, 38–40; Cavanaugh, "McGovern and the 1911 Wisconsin Legislature," 112; Milwaukee *Journal*, January 20, March 2, May 13, 23, 27, June 9, 22, July 11, 1911; Milwaukee *Sentinel*, January 20, March 2, May 13, 23, 27, June 9, 22, July 11, 1911.

and public utilities, and limited state regulation to overseeing dam construction specifications and issuing certificates to public utilities allowing them to overflow private lands. Husting, as chair of the senate conservation committee, protested that he had not been consulted and that the McCarthy bill "promotes and legalizes the monopolization of the water power sources of the state." McGovern then waffled on his 1911 position, perhaps concerned over his prospects for re-election in 1912, and certainly fearful that Husting would emerge as a threat to his plans for elevation to the U.S. Senate in 1914. With both Republican and Democratic progressives at odds with each other, the special session failed to produce any waterpower legislation whatsoever.[74]

Similar problems plagued efforts to expand the reforestation program. Both the interim committee and the Conservation Commission had backed Griffith's forestry program, which envisioned a forest reserve of at least 2 million acres "to protect the headwaters of our most important rivers; to aid in retaining our wood-using industries within the state by supplying them with timber . . . and to protect the beauty of our wonderful northern lake region that should annually bring millions of dollars into the state through tourists, campers, hunters and fishermen." Accordingly, Griffith proposed creating a conservation commission, an adequate forest patrol system, prohibition of slash burning, and co-operation with neighboring states and the federal government. He estimated the state could raise $600,000 a year to pay for the programs by imposing a tax of two-tenths a mill for every thousand dollars of assessed valuation. McGovern responded with a recommendation that the legislature immediately develop a plan for fire protection and reforestation; he carefully excluded agricultural land from forest reserves. The public hearings and floor debates revealed serious pockets of opposition to the proposals. Many Stalwarts and conservative Democrats attacked reforestation's costliness, thus prefiguring the "extravagance" theme of their 1912 and 1914 campaigns. Proponents of peopling and farming the Cutover also opposed the bills, arguing that the state's resources would be better served by clearing stumplands and promoting agricultural resettlement. Their argument appealed to railroad, lumber, and land companies, which owned vast tracts of cutover land and yearned to sell it to homesteaders.[75]

Unable to kill the forestry measure outright, its opponents in the senate succeeded in reducing the appropriation from $600,000 to

[74] East, "Water Power and Forestry," 217–226 (quote); A. Allan Schmid, "Water and the Law in Wisconsin," in *WMH* 45 (Spring, 1962), 203–215.

[75] East, "Water Power and Forestry," 276–296; Carstensen, *Farms or Forests*, 39–43; State Forester, *Report*, 1909–1910, p. 5.

$200,000 and the time limit to ten years. (Indeed, proponents had to muster their forces to prevent a further cutback to $100,000.) The senate finally passed the revised measure, 20–7, on June 12. In the assembly, Speaker Ingram led the attack against reforestation. He charged that it was a plot to allow the lumber companies to sell their worthless land to the state at a premium. As a result, the assembly slashed the appropriation to $50,000 and the time limit to five years. Thus emasculated, the bill passed the assembly on June 22 and was signed by the governor on June 30. Its most enthusiastic proponents could derive some small comfort from the fact that the Conservation Commission was established as a permanent body, part ex officio and part appointive, with the power to enforce the new laws and formulate new proposals. But an annual appropriation of only $1,000 severely constricted it. The end came three years later, when the state supreme court struck down the reforestation law on the grounds that the expenditures served no "public purposes," and that reforestation did not constitute "works of internal improvement within the meaning of the constitution." These two court decisions effectively demolished the conservation work of the McGovern administration and the 1911 legislature, although their efforts provided inspiration and precedent for later successes.[76]

[9]

The field of public education profited much more immediately than conservation during the 1911 session. Charles McCarthy, in *The Wisconsin Idea*, boasted that "over fifty laws relating to the betterment of Wisconsin schools were passed at the session of 1911," but in fact only a few of those proved of lasting importance. Of these, the most significant was clearly the establishment of what evolved into Wisconsin's system of locally based vocational, technical, and adult education schools. Perhaps more than any other single measure passed in 1911, this was McCarthy's brainchild. He was determined to transplant to Wisconsin the German system of "continuation" schools, which emphasized the latest in vocational and technical training for those not pursuing higher education. They put this training within a wider context that included ongoing instruction in selected academic subjects and responsible citizenship, so as to produce technically proficient, well-rounded, thinking human beings and involved citizens. McCar-

---

[76] Cavanaugh, "McGovern and the 1911 Wisconsin Legislature," 112; East, "Water Power, and Forestry," 296–300 (quotes); McCarthy, *Wisconsin Idea*, 153–155, 273; Carstensen, *Farms or Forests*, 40–43; Milwaukee *Journal*, January 20, May 27, June 22, July 11, 1911; Milwaukee *Sentinel*, January 20, May 27, June 22, July 11, 1911.

thy believed that industrial training "must be judged by its effect upon the life of the people and upon human happiness and a varying number of our great problems, social and economic and moral."[77]

In many ways, the continuation schools, in particular, and vocational and technical education, in general, logically complemented the celebrated University Extension program that McCarthy had helped to develop earlier. In 1910, he outlined his ideas on vocational education in a six-page letter to President Van Hise, in which he spelled it out as all of one piece with both Extension and the College of Agriculture extension programs. He told Van Hise that he envisioned a plan by which local school districts, University Extension, and the University of Wisconsin's teacher-training program would combine to develop schools most appropriate to the economic character of each community. McCarthy's appointment to the commission on industrial and agricultural training created by the 1909 legislature gave him a chance to put forward his ideas as the chief author of its final report. In the process, he assembled an unlikely coalition of supporters that included the brewery lobby, the State Federation of Labor, the Wisconsin Manufacturers' Association, and several prominent educators and politicians. To prepare, McCarthy studied at first hand the industrial education systems of Germany, Great Britain, Ireland, and Belgium, as well as those in New York, Pittsburgh, Boston, and Lowell, Massachusetts. He turned over preparation of the agricultural section of the report to a committee of non-commission members headed by College of Agriculture Dean Harry L. Russell.[78]

The final report itself, as presented to McGovern on January 10, 1911, consisted of three unequal parts: a twelve-page introduction and summary, a 100-page discussion of industrial education, and a twenty-one-page section on agricultural education. The evaluation of the German continuation schools praised their local orientation but rejected their "army drill-like plan." To achieve schooling of the greatest number at the least cost, the report proposed that an independent board, dominated by employers and laborers, administer the system with the Superintendent of Public Instruction, the dean

---

[77] Fitzpatrick, *McCarthy of Wisconsin*, 260–266; McCarthy, *Wisconsin Idea*, 141–152; Conrad E. Patzer, *Public Education in Wisconsin* (Madison, 1924), 207–210; Maxwell, *La Follette and the Rise of the Progressives*, 163; Casey, *Charles McCarthy*, 80–84.

[78] Fitzpatrick, *McCarthy of Wisconsin*, 261–266; Cavanaugh, "McGovern and the 1911 Wisconsin Legislature," 83–84. In the McCarthy Papers, see McCarthy to Edward T. Devine, December 16, 1909; to Jane Addams, December 16, 1909; to Edward C. Elliott, January 27, 1910; to Arthur D. Dean, February 4, 1910; to John D. Rockefeller, Jr., April 16, 1910; to Norman Hapgood, October 6, 1910; to James F. Trottman, March 16, 1911; Addams to McCarthy, December 23, 1909; Elliott to McCarthy, January 31, 1910; Dean to McCarthy, February 5, 1910; and the undated draft plan and draft legislation in box 22.

of University Extension, and the dean of the College of Engineering as ex officio members. (This reflected McCarthy's conviction that most university faculty and public school teachers and administrators were not well suited to providing the type of instruction needed, leading later to friction between the Industrial Education Board and the Department of Public Instruction.) Both labor and management accepted the report's recommendations. Milwaukee Republican assemblyman Charles B. Perry introduced the bill, which moved through the legislature with little objection and was signed by the governor on July 7. Racine became the first city to comply with the new law, with local manufacturer Herbert E. Miles as first president of the state board, and Manitowoc organized an evening continuation school during the 1911–1912 school year. By the end of 1912, more than twenty cities had established continuation schools, and the number continued to grow.[79]

As companion legislation to vocational and continuing education in 1911, lawmakers enacted an apprenticeship law overseen by the newly created Industrial Commission. Contracts of indenture were to be standardized and all aspects of apprenticeship were subject to review by the commission. The legislature also inaugurated a pension plan for some public school teachers, although it remained extremely limited until 1921. Building upon legislation first passed in 1901 and upon the recommendations of the commission on industrial and agricultural training, the legislature also provided incentives for using county school buildings as social centers.[80]

Government solicitude for the University of Wisconsin also reached a zenith in 1911 in many respects, with Van Hise in the president's seat, McGovern in the governor's mansion, McCarthy and Commons at the height of their careers, and the legislature itself populated heavily by university alumni. In his biennial report, Van Hise requested an increase in the mill tax awarded to the university, an increase in faculty salaries, some new departments, and a building program that ran to nearly $3 million. He argued that the outlay would pay rich dividends to the state. McGovern echoed these sentiments in his legislative message. For the most part, the legislature

---

[79] Fitzpatrick, *McCarthy of Wisconsin*, 265–276; *Wisconsin Statutes*, 1913, pp. 320–324; Milwaukee *Journal*, February 9, June 23, 1911; Milwaukee *Sentinel*, February 9, June 23, 1911; Kathleen A. Paris, "Education for Employment: 70 years of Vocational, Technical and Adult Education in Wisconsin," *Wisconsin Blue Book, 1981–1982*, pp. 99–117; Patzer, *Public Education in Wisconsin*, 208–209. See also Chapter 8.

[80] Maxwell, *La Follette and the Rise of the Progressives*, 163; *Wisconsin Statutes*, 1913, pp. 314–317; William F. Raney, *Wisconsin: A Story of Progress* (Appleton, 1963), 423–438; Edward J. Ward, *The Social Center* (New York, 1913), 302–338; Caroline L. Hunt, "Public Schools as Social Centers," *La Follette's Weekly Magazine*, June 12, 1909, pp. 8–9; Milwaukee *Journal*, May 27, 1910.

responded positively, even though some senators tried to substitute a fixed cash appropriation for the mill tax and to raise tuition for out-of-state students. Because 1911 was the first time that the legislature drafted an appropriation bill that lumped the university together with other state agencies, it was easier for some legislators to make comparisons invidious to the university. In the end, the legislature continued its generosity to the Extension Division and the College of Agriculture; and it agreed to increase the mill tax from 2/7 to 3/8, and the campus construction budget by 50 per cent.[81]

But Van Hise and the regents did not get all they asked for. The legislature provided only a fraction of the president's request for new dormitories. It specifically excluded faculty members from serving on the newly established Board of Public Affairs, despite the expertise of several. The legislature also debated bills that would have abolished farmers' institutes, probed the university's purchasing system, and restricted the sale and consumption of alcoholic beverages on and near the campus. More ominously, perhaps, the legislature toyed with the notion of fixing admissions requirements and even with replacing the Board of Regents with a statewide board of education. None of these bills passed, but the legislature gave some evidence that the honeymoon between the campus and state government was winding down. In the near future, the university administrators would have cause to look back on 1911 as a golden year.[82]

[10]

Comprehensive regulation and planning of the economy also gave rise to legislative departures. High on the list was the inauguration of a system of modern state highways. The Wisconsin Geological and Natural History Survey had tested road materials, constructed model highways, and begun educating the public in 1897, the year it was created. Led by its director from 1909 to 1925, William Hotchkiss, the agency pled the cause of a state-financed highway system before audiences of auto clubs, rural mail carriers, municipal organizations, "good roads" associations, and farmers. Frugal and skeptical of government, Wisconsin's large rural population initially opposed highway expansion and improvement. But gradually farmers and small-town residents were persuaded of the benefits of better highways, and

---

[81] Curti and Carstensen, *University of Wisconsin*, 2: 184–186; *Wisconsin Assembly Journal*, 1911, pp. 63–64, 308; *Wisconsin Senate Journal*, 1911, pp. 953–956, 1116.

[82] Curti and Carstensen, *University of Wisconsin*, 2: 185–186; *Wisconsin Assembly Journal*, 1911, pp. 131, 141, 159, 212, 252, 283, 499, 581, 641, 673–674, 741–744, 878, 1412, 1433, 1446, 1487; *Wisconsin Senate Journal*, 1911, pp. 565–567, 788, 816.

of their vital role in a modernizing agricultural economy. So well did Hotchkiss and his colleagues do their work that by 1908 Wisconsin's voters overwhelmingly approved (116,107 to 46,762) a constitutional amendment authorizing the legislature to establish such a program. The 1909 legislature failed to enact a highway law because of disagreements over the scope of authority to be granted to the proposed state highway commission. Thereupon the legislature created a special joint committee on highways, chaired by Republican assemblyman John R. Jones of Leon (Monroe County), the chief opponent of highway centralization.[83]

The committee's majority report, written by Jones, argued that the state's diversity in local finances, population base, and road conditions required a law that would leave control almost entirely in the hands of local governments. In a minority report, Republican senator John S. Donald of Mount Horeb, a La Follette loyalist, proposed instead a strong state commission and financial controls. His plan was favored by Hotchkiss, the state's county highway commissioners' association, and Governor McGovern. Donald wrote a bill that encompassed the gist of the minority report, but emphasized the majority view. It passed the senate with relative ease, but encountered vociferous opposition in the assembly, mainly concerning local prerogatives. Eventually, however, the assembly concurred and McGovern signed the measure on June 14. It created a five-man State Highway Commission that included the state geologist and the dean of the university's College of Engineering as ex-officio members. The assembly vote revealed strong opposition to a centralized program of highway construction: fully 40 per cent of those who voted cast ballots in the negative. Most of the dissenters were Democrats, and most came either from the more established eastern counties where their constituents feared being taxed for the benefit of less-developed areas, or from regions where topography would entail higher construction costs.[84]

The state aid road law of 1911 enjoined county boards to submit to the State Highway Commission a design for interconnected systems of prospective state highways, beyond the limits of municipalities. It also provided that county boards elect highway commissioners from a list supplied by the state commission. If completed roads met

[83] Ballard Campbell, "The Good Roads Movement in Wisconsin, 1890–1911," in *WMH*, 49 (Summer, 1966), 273–293; Maxwell, *La Follette and the Rise of the Progressives*, 171; William O. Hotchkiss, *The Highway Work of the Geological Survey* (Madison, 1908), 1–7.

[84] Campbell, "The Good Roads Movement in Wisconsin," 289–293; Legislature, Special Joint Committee on Highways, *Report of the Special Joint Committee on Highways . . . 1909*, pp. 7–19; Milwaukee *Journal,* January 12, March 5, 29, June 2, 6, 8, 14, 1911; Milwaukee *Sentinel*, January 12, March 4, 29, June 2, 6, 8, 14, 1911.

standards to be developed by the state commission, towns and counties could petition the state for reimbursement of up to one-third the cost of construction. However, the legislature appropriated only $350,000 for these reimbursements—an action full of portent for the future.[85]

The 1911 legislature also promoted agricultural prosperity, especially in the underdeveloped regions of the north and northwest. Members of the Wisconsin Society of Equity championed the cause. They were generally less affluent farmers working marginal lands in those areas of the state, who were joined in some instances by the state's railroad and lumbering interests which were seeking to entice farmers to resettle in the Cutover. In theory, some agricultural resettlement efforts conflicted with the conservation programs espoused by the progressive Republicans. In fact, many legislators apparently believed that there was room for both in the northern half of the state, if the state planned and managed things properly. The Society of Equity and the Grange sought exemption of marketing co-operatives from the restrictions imposed by state and federal anti-trust laws as a way to help promote agricultural prosperity in the Cutover. Many members of the two groups were farmers of Finnish, Czech, Scandinavian, or German ancestry who looked to their countries of origin for models. So did such agricultural reformers as Charles McCarthy and his close confidant, Sir Horace Plunkett, an esteemed Irish land reformer. Together, they were instrumental in laying plans for an organization of American agricultural societies, whose purposes were to introduce economy and efficiency in producing and distributing farm products, and to promote farm co-operatives. With only agricultural processors, wholesalers, and similar middlemen voicing serious opposition, the 1911 legislature exempted marketing co-operatives from the antitrust laws and gave the new Board of Public Affairs the task of investigating agricultural marketing.[86]

Other agricultural legislation in 1911 empowered counties to lend money to farmers for improving their lands, and authorized counties to borrow money and issue and sell bonds to establish schools of agriculture and domestic economy. The Society of Equity was espe-

---

[85] Campbell, "The Good Roads Movement in Wisconsin," 289–293; *Wisconsin Statutes*, 1913, pp. 883–895.

[86] Fitzpatrick, *McCarthy of Wisconsin*, 180–187; Maxwell, *La Follette and the Rise of the Progressives*, 170–171; *Wisconsin Statutes*, 1911, pp. 1314–1319; Rudolph K. Froker and Joseph G. Knapp, *Farmers Purchasing Associations in Wisconsin*, Farm Credit Administration, *Bulletin*, no. 20 (1937), 11–17; Writers' Program, Wisconsin, *Wisconsin: A Guide to the Badger State*, compiled by Workers of the Writers' Program of the Works Projects Administration in the State of Wisconsin (New York, 1941), 105–112; George F. Comings, "Co-operation," in State Board of Agriculture, *Annual Report*, 1912, pp. 3–7.

cially pleased with a law that arranged to complete a state-operated binder-twine plant, whose "employees" were in fact prison inmates.[87]

Other new regulating and planning laws tackled municipal and economic instutions. One strengthened municipalities' hands in dealing with street railway companies, by permitting local governments to issue franchises of indeterminate length, and to revoke them if traction utilities failed to serve the public interest. Another established a modest system of bank deposit guarantees protecting depositors, at least minimally. Another, building upon the state's landmark insurance code, completed the dismemberment of assessment life insurance companies by ordering their final valuation and the distribution of credits among their members.

Far more radical was the establishment of the State Life Insurance Fund, which built upon a program enacted during the La Follette administration of 1903. The capitol fire of 1904 had generated intense criticism because it forced the government to borrow money from general revenue funds, but the program survived despite all. It was eventually expanded to include local governments, school districts, and library boards. Support for state expansion into life insurance originated with the Social Democrats, but was greatly augmented by the findings of both a 1906 joint committee on life insurance and of an interim committee investigating workmen's compensation. The 1911 legislature established the State Life Fund, which could issue policies to Wisconsin residents between the ages of twenty and fifty, in increments of $500, to a maximum of $3,000. The law demanded medical examinations for purchasers of insurance, established the loan and surrender values of policies, and permitted annuity policies. This program became controversial nationally. Private insurance companies expressed both amazement and amusement, while progressive periodicals like *Outlook* hailed it as a model. Relatively few Wisconsinites actually availed themselves of the State Life Fund. Even so, it served as a yardstick against which to measure (and regulate) the services and costs of private insurance companies.[88]

In the realm of economic regulation and planning, by far the most ambitious venture of the 1911 legislature was the creation of the Board of Public Affairs. Not until the New Deal, when Congress enacted national industrial recovery and agricultural adjustment acts

---

[87] Margulies, *Decline of the Progressive Movement*, 134–135; *Wisconsin Statutes*, 1913, pp. 314–317, 1014–1060, 2191–2193; Theodore Saloutos, "The Wisconsin Society of Equity," *Agricultural History*, 14 (April, 1940), 88–90; Milwaukee *Journal*, January 27, May 23, June 28, 1911; Milwaukee *Sentinel*, January 27, May 23, June 28, 1911.

[88] Maxwell, *La Follette and the Rise of the Progressives*, 123–127; *Wisconsin Statutes*, 1913, pp. 1401–1407, 1413–1504; Howe, *Wisconsin*, 71–85, 118–125; Milwaukee *Journal*, June 24, July 6, 1911; Milwaukee *Sentinel*, June 24, July 6, 1911.

during the Great Depression, would any American governmental entity depart so dramatically from American tradition. La Follette, as governor, reportedly discussed a similar idea, but the actual model was the Milwaukee Social Democrats' Bureau of Economy and Efficiency, on which John R. Commons had served as chief adviser for eighteen months. At Commons' invitation, Charles McCarthy evaluated the bureau's staff and accomplishments, finding them useful in suggestive, though not constructive, ways. This was enough to get things rolling. Commons proposed the concept of a state board to Governor McGovern, who convened a group of sympathetic people to talk over the idea. He then directed McCarthy to draft the necessary legislation for the 1911 session. From these collective efforts, the proposed bureau evolved from an agency designed to promote economy and efficiency in government to one that also would conduct "fundamental studies about Wisconsin's human and social welfare." Here was state planning on a new plane.[89]

The Board of Public Affairs bill was introduced in the assembly on March 31 by Lewis Gettle and made its way through two committees before passing 61–3. The senate amended it and passed it on June 28 by a vote of 16–7. McGovern signed it into law on July 6. The new statute made the governor the board's chairman, and the board itself consisted of a mix of appointive and ex-officio members. As its chief of staff, McCarthy generated most ideas for investigation—and he never ran short of ideas.[90]

In a seventeen-page memorandum dedicated to planning "betterment," McCarthy committed the Board of Public Affairs to devising constructive legislation and educating an informed citizenry. In its four years of existence, the board completed nearly twenty surveys, some controversial, of Wisconsin government and society, including agricultural conditions, public finance, land tenure and farm tenancy, immigration, prison labor, and education. The investigation of the University of Wisconsin, conducted by New York efficiency expert William Allen, aroused suspicion between the two pillars of the Wisconsin Idea at opposite ends of State Street. Still, as a result of the survey, the board claimed to have saved the taxpayers half a million dollars, in part by squeezing $100,000 out of the normal schools' budget and another $200,000 out of the university's. Its 1912 report

---

[89] Maxwell, *La Follette and the Rise of the Progressives*, 169–170; Fitzpatrick, *McCarthy of Wisconsin*, 141–142; McCarthy, *Wisconsin Idea*, 202, 253, 292; Cavanaugh, "McGovern and the 1911 Wisconsin Legislature," 102–104; Casey, *Charles McCarthy*, 77–78.

[90] Fitzpatrick, *McCarthy of Wisconsin*, 141–145; Howe, *Wisconsin*, 126–132; McCarthy to John R. Commons, September 18, 1911; McCarthy to Francis E. McGovern, December 20, 1912; and McCarthy to "members of the Public Affairs Commission," July, 1911, all in the McCarthy Papers.

on agricultural marketing and co-operation provided the basis for a controversial marketing commission act sponsored by the McGovern administration in 1913. It was to have been the agricultural equivalent of the Industrial Commission, but the proposed agency kindled bitter conflict and played a major role in the disintegration of the Progressive movement itself. The Board of Public Affairs was short-lived, and its achievements fell short of its expectations. Even so, the fact of its establishment in 1911 proved the strength of the Progressive movement's power and the scope and nature of its vision of Wisconsin's future. As the heat of midsummer closed in on Madison and the members of the 1911 legislature completed their work, progressives throughout the United States looked on—astonished, enheartened, moved almost to euphoria. The Wisconsin Idea was in full flower; the "service state" was at hand.[91]

[11]

From every quarter came praise for the accomplishments of Wisconsin's lawmakers, and for their leaders both in and out of public office. From Harvard, Frederick Jackson Turner congratulated his friend McCarthy on Wisconsin's "great step forward," proclaiming that "her sons in other sections ought to be proud of her initiative in tackling such fundamental problems." Gifford Pinchot, friend and confidant of presidents, wrote that his "admiration for the work in Wisconsin grows steadily stronger." Efficiency expert William H. Allen of New York's municipal research bureau applauded McCarthy for what he called his "winter of conquest." The progressive ferment lured Theodore Roosevelt to Madison and inspired him to write several laudatory articles in *Outlook*, of which he was assistant editor. Frederic C. Howe, scholar and progressive activist, adviser to Woodrow Wilson, and a close observer of the 1911 legislative session, was soon to write of Wisconsin: "It is an experiment station in politics, in social and industrial legislation, in the democratization of science and higher education. It is a state-wide laboratory in which popular government is being tested in its reaction on people, on the distribution of wealth, and on social well-being."[92]

---

[91] Fitzpatrick, *McCarthy of Wisconsin*, 143–155; Maxwell, *La Follette and the Rise of the Progressives*, 169–170; *Wisconsin Statutes*, 1913, pp. 720–722; Milwaukee *Journal*, June 21, 24, July 6, 1911; Milwaukee *Sentinel*, June 21, 24, July 6, 1911; Curti and Carstensen, *University of Wisconsin*, 2: 269–293.
[92] Casey, *Charles McCarthy*, 75–87; Howe, *Wisconsin*, vii–xii, 183–192. The most important of Roosevelt's *Outlook* articles was entitled "Wisconsin: An Object Lesson for the Rest of the Nation," May 27, 1911, pp. 143–145; the others appeared July 29, September 23, and December 23, 1911.

Never ones to hide their lights under a basket, both Bob La Follette and Charles McCarthy soon put pen to paper and sang the praises of Wisconsin's progressive achievements. In La Follette's case, political ambition stirred him to write. He was determined to wrest the Republican presidential nomination from his nemesis William Howard Taft and to set his party, and the nation, on the same progressive course that he and his followers and successors had so gloriously sailed in Wisconsin. The result was the first edition of *La Follette's Autobiography* (1912), which, while primarily a personal campaign tract, nevertheless succeeded in conflating the achievements of 1906–1911 with those of his own administration (1901–1906).

In McCarthy's case, ambition for the progressive cause itself produced *The Wisconsin Idea* (also 1912). As the momentous election of 1912 drew closer, he envisioned the realization of a national progressive utopia modeled on the one that he had worked to create in Wisconsin. It mattered little to him which progressive candidate or faction succeeded; what mattered was the triumph of the ideas, the legislation, and the programs.

The reviews of *The Wisconsin Idea* made it apparent that many politically sophisticated people took at face value much of what La Follette and McCarthy wrote about the triumph of progressivism in Wisconsin. Some were unkind enough to point out, correctly, that McCarthy's book showed signs of having been hastily slapped together, that its author was often more panegyrist than analyst, and that many of the measures which he praised so lavishly had yet to be tested in day-to-day operation. In the *Political Science Quarterly*, for example, Edward M. Sait quipped that "Wisconsin in the language of Chesterton is glowing in the memory of tomorrow afternoon." Such skepticism, however, was rare. More typical was the review in the *Annals* of the American Academy of Political and Social Science, which said, "Wisconsin has done something unique in making a living place for her citizens." The reviewer for the New York *Mail Express* wrote, "Wisconsin is a state that is teaching the whole country." His counterpart on the Chicago *Record-Herald* wrote that "no well-informed person could seriously question that Wisconsin leads in social legislation." The Chicago *Continent* declared, "Wisconsin is the first commonwealth to make good as a commonwealth in fact as well as in name." The socialist New York *Call* concluded that "whatever has been done in Oregon and elsewhere toward securing the rule of the people, it is in Wisconsin more than anywhere else that progressivism has worked itself out in a manner to give us a definite idea of what it represents and what results it can secure."[93]

---

[93] Edward M. Sait, reviews of *The Wisconsin Idea* and of "Wisconsin: An Experiment in Democracy," in *Political Science Quarterly*, 28 (March, 1913), 160–163; George Willis

But perhaps the most noteworthy praise for Wisconsin's progressivism came from another great Progressive, a man who would soon proclaim "the New Nationalism" and stand for president as the candidate of a new Progressive party: Theodore Roosevelt. (His praise was also the most ironic, because Roosevelt would run, at least partly, at the expense of La Follette's own political and ideological aspirations, and in a manner guaranteed to fracture Wisconsin's progressive movement.) Wisconsin, the former president wrote in his foreword to McCarthy's *Wisconsin Idea*, had "become literally a laboratory for wise experimental legislation aiming to secure the social and political betterment of the people as a whole." Other states had made important theoretical and legislative contributions to reform, but "in Wisconsin there has been a successful effort to redeem the promises by performance, and to reduce theories into practice." Throughout the Union, Roosevelt concluded, "we need to learn the Wisconsin lesson of scientific popular self-help, and of patient care in radical legislation."[94]

Cooke, "Wisconsin and Progressivism," New York *Call*, September 29, 1912; David Y. Thomas, "The 'New Idea' in State Government," *The Dial*, September 1, 1912, p. 134. Other reviews appeared in *The Nation*, May 9, 1912, p. 474; New York *Times*, April 31, 1912; *Annals of the American Academy of Political and Social Sciences*, 42 (July 12, 1912), 347; *Review of Reviews*, 45 (May, 1912), 639; *Journal of Political Economy*, 20 (July, 1912), 762; New York *Mail Express*, April 6, 1912; Chicago *Record-Herald*, June 20, 1912; and Chicago *Continent*, July 4, 1912.

[94] Theodore Roosevelt, "Preface," in McCarthy, *Wisconsin Idea*, vii–xi.

13

Wisconsin Ideas

[1]

OVER the last eighty years, the term "the Wisconsin Idea" has achieved such an exalted status that to invoke it seldom elicits a request for definition or elucidation. The very words resound with righteousness, enlightenment, and justice for all. By the same token, "the Idea" has been used to justify a wide and bewildering variety of actions and programs, many of them mutually contradictory, and at least some of which would have been vehemently denounced by the giants of the Wisconsin Progressive movement. This paradox should come as no surprise. Even during the Progressive Era, "the Wisconsin Idea" was never the product of a single mind or entity, any more than it was the platform of an organization or political party. The Wisconsin Idea was, and remains, a broad, emotive descriptor for a general attitude or approach to public policy—not a set of carefully enunciated precepts.

Fittingly, its most comprehensive and ambitious exposition, Charles McCarthy's book *The Wisconsin Idea*, published in 1912, also lacks integration. Only in the introductory chapters and in a relatively brief conclusion does McCarthy seriously attempt integration and analysis, and the results are largely superficial and skewed. The body of the book is a series of discrete chapters on business regulation, electoral and governmental transformation, education, labor, health and public welfare, administration, the legislature, and "the law and economic progress." McCarthy, by his own admission, cut and pasted the book together in a fortnight using materials from his famous scrapbooks. He intended it to advance the candidacies of progressives during a crucial election year, so it could hardly have turned out otherwise.[1]

---

[1] Charles McCarthy, *The Wisconsin Idea* (New York, 1912), xiii–xiv, 1–33, 273–306. In a letter to Albert W. Sanborn on April 2, 1912, McCarthy admitted that he had "not read the entire book through since the time I wrote it myself and hardly know what is in it." Writing to Sir Horace Plunkett on February 27 and April 2, 1913,

Almost from its inception, then, participants and scholars alike have differed sharply over the origins, nature, and evolution of "the Wisconsin Idea." In fact, the debate dates from the differences in perspective reflected by McCarthy in his book and by Robert M. La Follette in his autobiography, both written as 1912 campaign tracts. True to form, La Follette never dealt with progressive reform in Wisconsin except as an extension of his own personality and of the political movement he headed. He does give appropriate credit to populist Judge Edward G. Ryan, to university presidents John Bascom and Charles R. Van Hise, to agrarian reformers, law partners, Norwegian voters, and members of his Saturday Lunch Club. But La Follette focuses clearly on the contribution that each made to Fighting Bob's personal triumphs. Appropriately, his discussion of Wisconsin's developments ends with his election to the U.S. Senate. The rest of his autobiography focuses squarely on national developments. In contrast, McCarthy concentrates on what happened in the state after La Follette's move to Washington, and especially on the achievements of the legislative session of 1911 under the direction of Francis McGovern, who by 1912 was one of La Follette's most bitter political enemies.[2]

In "The Soil," easily the strangest chapter in an often strange book, McCarthy sought and found the "roots" of the Wisconsin Idea in the ethno-cultural character of the state's population and in the coming of Richard Ely to the University of Wisconsin in 1892, a man who preached "a curious new doctrine." McCarthy pays lip service to the contributions of Wisconsin's New England and Scandinavian strains, but the state is so progressive because it "is fundamentally a German state." "The doctrine that the state should have more to do with economic welfare had spread throughout the entire country," he writes, "but in no place had it found better soil nor had greater results than in the German state of Wisconsin." He acknowledges that the spirit of service had animated the University of Wisconsin since the presidency of John Bascom (1874–1887), but insists that the service ideal had only come to fruition in German states on either side of the ocean. "If Wisconsin is a prosperous state to-day," McCarthy concludes, "there is no doubt that it is largely because of German ideas and ideals, early instituted in the state." These values were instilled in Wisconsin primarily by German activist-intellectuals "of the Carl Schurz type" and by American scholars trained in Germany, chiefly Ely. Here was "another singular coincidence. The pupil of

---

McCarthy called the book "a pretty poor piece of work" which he had penned only "because Colonel Roosevelt asked." The letters are in the McCarthy Papers.

[2] Robert M. La Follette, Sr., *La Follette's Autobiography: A Personal Narrative of Political Experiences* (Madison, 1913; reprinted, 1960), 3–158.

Knies and Wagner, coming from Germany with his German political ideals, succeeded Bascom as a teacher of political economy in the German university of the German state of Wisconsin. A curious condition surely!" McCarthy leaves little doubt that he viewed Richard T. Ely as the primary source of what became the Wisconsin Idea.[3]

It is scarcely to be wondered that McCarthy attributed so much influence to Ely, since what little analysis appears in *The Wisconsin Idea* derives from Ely's works. McCarthy was himself a trained political economist, and Ely's ideas formed much of the core of the progressive branch of that discipline. Moreover, McCarthy had been educated largely by scholars trained in German universities, and he kept abreast with German affairs and academic life through reading, correspondence, and personal contacts. For his part, Ely did not claim authorship of the Wisconsin Idea. In his autobiography, he writes that "the source of good government in the final analysis must be its citizens," but in language very similar to McCarthy's, he goes on to say, "The success of the University of Wisconsin [and of good government] has been, in large part, due to the character of Wisconsin's population, which consists largely of those of German and Norwegian ancestry.... I think most of the credit is due the German strain in the population, for they were men of high ideals and they brought with them some of the best things from Germany. They had the idea of service to the state and they were firm believers in education."[4]

Still, Ely concedes, "leadership was needed to rally these forces and this was furnished by the senior La Follette." In a ten-page discussion, Ely gives Fighting Bob primary credit for turning Wisconsin into "a political laboratory for advanced measures." La Follette "backed every progressive movement in Wisconsin, and although it is not necessary to endorse everything that La Follette said and did, we must admit that he fought a good fight and that he often won out." Ely sadly recounts his break with La Follette over World War I, but acknowledges that, fourteen years later, he was inclined to wish that La Follette had been elected president in 1924.[5]

Ely was ambivalent about the role played by the university in Wisconsin reform. On the one hand, he accords Charles R. Van Hise status second only to La Follette among progressives. He relished his membership in the Saturday Lunch Club and praised his colleagues John R. Commons, Balthazar H. Meyer, Edward A. Ross, and Fred-

---

[3] McCarthy, *Wisconsin Idea*, 19–33; Benjamin G. Rader, *The Academic Mind and Reform: The Influence of Richard T. Ely in American Life* (Lexington, Kentucky, 1966), 110–118.

[4] Richard T. Ely, *Ground Under Our Feet: An Autobiography* (New York, 1938), 208; Rader, *Academic Mind and Reform*, 28–105.

[5] Ely, *Ground Under Our Feet*, 210–218; Rader, *Academic Mind and Reform*, 179–188.

erick Jackson Turner for their contributions. On the other hand, Ely stresses that the university's involvement had been exaggerated and misunderstood, that it politicized the campus to its eventual detriment, and that his own department of political economy was one of the most conservative in the nation. Indeed his entire career may be viewed as a transit from left to right.[6]

Ely's skepticism about the centrality of the university to the Wisconsin Idea was shared by John R. Commons, who wrote in his autobiography, *Myself*, that "perhaps nine-tenths" of the university faculty had always been "on the conservative or reactionary side." He denies that Wisconsin was ever "a university that governs a state," and writes, "I was never called in except by Progressives, and only when they wanted me. I never initiated anything. I came only on request of legislators, of executives, or committees.... The same was true of many other members of the faculty. A university is not a government, it is a collection of individuals."[7]

For all the credit he gave the faculty in *The Wisconsin Idea*, Charles McCarthy also criticized most of them for their timidity and unwillingness to lend themselves to public service. He backed the 1914 investigation of the university undertaken by William Harvey Allen of New York's Bureau of Municipal Research at the behest of the Board of Public Affairs. Even before it was finished, Allen's report was known to be negative. It greatly perplexed McCarthy because Emanuel Philipp and the Stalwart Republicans used it to castigate "the university state" and "the bill factory" in the 1914 campaign. Philipp removed several professors from state service and intimidated others into voluntary resignation—the opposite of McCarthy's intent.[8]

For his part, Commons generally agreed with Ely in giving La Follette and his movement primary credit for the achievements of Wisconsin progressivism, but he took specific issue with the Ely-McCarthy notion of its Germanic roots. "I sometimes have heard from people of other states that the Wisconsin pioneer success in administering progressive legislation must have come from the large German element in the state who brought with them the traditions of the effi-

---

[6] Ely, *Ground Under Our Feet*, 179–207; Richard T. Ely, "The University as a Commercial Asset of Wisconsin," *Wisconsin State Journal*, February 19, 1915; Rader, *Academic Mind and Reform*, 172–181.

[7] John R. Commons, *Myself: The Autobiography of John R. Commons* (New York, 1938; reprinted, Madison, 1964), 110; Lafayette G. Harter, Jr., *John R. Commons: His Assault on Laissez-Faire* (Corvallis, Oregon, 1962), 69–130.

[8] Marion Casey, *Charles McCarthy: Librarianship and Reform* (Chicago, 1981), 96; Edward A. Fitzpatrick, *McCarthy of Wisconsin* (New York, 1944), 147–156; Merle Curti and Vernon Carstensen, *The University of Wisconsin: A History, 1848–1925* (2 vols., Madison, 1949), 2: 267–283.

cient government of Germany," Commons avers, "but the Germans in Wisconsin, although exceeding in numbers any other of its many nationalities, have been the least active, politically, of all." Ironically, Commons praises McCarthy as being "as distinct a personality and pioneer as were La Follette and [Victor] Berger in the political field." Commons confesses that he "came to depend on him for everything I tried to do in the state of Wisconsin. He seemed to know everybody in the legislature and in the local politics of the state, and knew just who were leaders and how they would react." He praises the Legislative Reference Library as "telegraphic" because "McCarthy wired to civil service organizations, to state governments, to individuals, for statutes, bills before legislatures, clippings, and comments." McCarthy had, or could get immediately, "almost everything one might need on all sides of every debatable issue before the public, or the legislature, or Congress." McCarthy, he said, played the key role in drafting every major piece of legislation associated with the Wisconsin Idea.[9]

[2]

Comparing the views of La Follette, McCarthy, Ely, and Commons on the origins of Wisconsin progressivism yields some interesting differences of interpretation. La Follette focuses on his own career. He ignores the ethnic factor almost entirely, mentions Ely and Commons only in passing, and devotes only a few paragraphs out of 342 pages to McCarthy and the Legislative Reference Library. Of the four, only La Follette pays any serious attention to the possible rural origins of the Wisconsin Idea, and even he focuses largely upon Madison and Milwaukee.

McCarthy eulogizes Ely and the state's German Americans, while avoiding nearly all mention of La Follette or Commons, despite the fact that Commons bore much responsibility in drafting most of the labor legislation of which McCarthy was so proud.

Ely glorifies the Germanic origins of his ideas and gives La Follette principal credit. He mentions Commons infrequently, and only in passing. Of McCarthy, he says only that "he had all the political gifts of the Irish, and he did a great piece of work as a backer and coworker with La Follette." Ely was skeptical of the importance of the university.

Commons openly disputes with Ely and McCarthy concerning the German connection, downplays the contribution of the university,

---

[9] Commons, *Myself*, 106–111; Harter, *John R. Commons*, 55–59, 94–95, 108, 138–143, 268–272.

and lauds La Follette, Berger, and McCarthy. He gives Ely his due as a mentor and as the man who was instrumental in bringing him to Madison, but he says nothing of Ely as a source of progressive thought.[10]

Several decades of subsequent scholarship have not done much to clarify the origins of the Wisconsin Idea. Even though he wrote in the immediate afterglow of 1911, progressive thinker and activist Frederic C. Howe gives La Follette almost the entire credit for Wisconsin's prominence, although he also stresses the role of the university. As for individuals, Howe virtually ignores Van Hise, Commons, McCarthy, and McGovern, and he does not even mention Ely. So La Follette-centered is Edward N. Doan's *The La Follettes and the Wisconsin Idea* (1947) that McCarthy and Van Hise are absent altogether and McGovern appears only as La Follette's enemy in 1912 and after.

In *La Follette and the Rise of the Progressives in Wisconsin* (1956), Robert S. Maxwell borrowed from McCarthy by entitling his brief introductory chapter "The Soil of Progressivism," but his treatment is much more cogent and analytical than McCarthy's. He styles Wisconsin reform "a volatile and many-sided movement," with "agrarian and industrial elements . . . drawn together and cemented by intellectual leadership into the powerful force that became progressivism." Wisconsin reform, he writes, "was distinguished from the reforms of other states chiefly in that it was more comprehensive and far-reaching rather than more radical." Maxwell focuses tightly on political progressivism, and incorporates La Follette's perspective for the years before 1910, when he switches to the urban-labor perspective of McGovern and the "service state." He discusses the contributions of the University of Wisconsin and the Legislative Reference Library with admirable objectivity and catalogs La Follette's faults and failures, but he concludes that "after credit has been duly apportioned the student of the rise of the progressive movement in Wisconsin must return to Robert M. La Follette."[11]

Herbert F. Margulies stresses the heterogeneity of the Progressive movement more than Maxwell, and concentrates more on the reasons for its decline than for its success. But he too makes La Follette and his political faction the moving force in his book, *The Decline of the Progressive Movement in Wisconsin, 1890–1920* (1968). Margulies

---

[10] La Follette, *Autobiography*, 15, 31–32; McCarthy, *Wisconsin Idea*, 27–33; Ely, *Ground Under Our Feet*, 208–216; Commons, *Myself*, 103–131; Casey, *Charles McCarthy*, 85; Fitzpatrick, *McCarthy of Wisconsin*, 109–110.

[11] Frederic C. Howe, *Wisconsin: An Experiment in Democracy* (New York, 1912), *passim*; Edward N. Doan, *The La Follettes and the Wisconsin Idea* (New York, 1947), 3–73; Robert S. Maxwell, *La Follette and the Rise of the Progressives in Wisconsin* (Madison, 1956), 3–9, 195–206.

postulates that the roots of La Follette's movement are rural and Scandinavian, as opposed to German, and states that the later discord arose from the fragility of the alliance between those forces and the Milwaukee-based faction led by McGovern. Margulies defines the Wisconsin Idea very precisely as the mutually beneficial relationship that existed between the state university and La Follette and his lieutenants. He singles out Ely as "influential and representative" in the way he applied German economic thought to the role government should take in socio-economic matters. Margulies stresses the inherent conflict that existed between La Follette's vision of the Wisconsin Idea as a concept that opposed special interests, and promoted both direct democracy and limited government, as well as the welfare state concept that increasingly animated McCarthy, McGovern, Van Hise, Commons, and Ely.[12]

In contrast to both Maxwell and Margulies, Vernon Carstensen in a 1956 article trains the spotlight on the University of Wisconsin. He acknowledges the importance of La Follette, McCarthy, and Van Hise, and of the geographical propinquity between the Capitol and the campus. Then he goes on to state that "probably more important in the origin and early development of attitude and practices that comprised the Wisconsin Idea was the way in which the University had developed." He traces the evolution of the service ideal from the university's founding and concludes that "the large program of legislative reform, the expert work of the professors, the work of the Legislative Reference Library, the vigorous extension work of the University, and the staunch devotion of the University to the principle that the professors should be untrammeled in their pursuit of truth, were part of the Wisconsin Idea."[13]

Eric E. Lampard, in *The Rise of the Dairy Industry in Wisconsin* (1963), takes a different tack. He portrays the university and the political establishment primarily as reactors to the initiatives of the Wisconsin Dairymen's Association, and suggests that "the Wisconsin Idea of Dairying" was a prototype and inspiration for the later, more comprehensive version. Together, the WDA, the College of Agriculture, and state government erected what Lampard terms a "great edifice of dairy education" and regulation which "anticipated the more comprehensive 'Wisconsin Idea' of the Progressive period." Lampard is particularly critical of McCarthy's book as a "progressive's

---

[12] Herbert F. Margulies, *The Decline of the Progressive Movement in Wisconsin, 1890–1920* (Madison, 1968), 3–50, 283–290.

[13] Vernon Carstensen, "The Origin and Early Development of the Wisconsin Idea," in *WMH*, 39 (Spring, 1956), 181–188; J. David Hoeveler, Jr., "The University and the Social Gospel: The Intellectual Origins of the 'Wisconsin Idea,'" in *WMH*, 59 (Summer, 1976), 282–298.

political tract" intended to woo the German vote, which had been divided among the Democrats, Socialists, and Stalwart Republicans. He calls McCarthy's version "a political gambit in which [William D.] Hoard and the dairy leaders were sacrificed." However, Lampard also points out that by 1910 the Wisconsin Idea had evolved into something significantly different than the original version. As new interest groups, including less affluent farmers, made unprecedented demands on the university and state government for more services, the WDA leaders began to find themselves in the ranks of those who criticized the progressives for their supposed radicalism, statism, and extravagance.[14]

The scholarly trend away from identifying La Follette and Madison as the incubators of the Wisconsin Idea reached its zenith in the early 1970's with the publication of David P. Thelen's revisionist books, *The New Citizenship: Origins of Progressivism in Wisconsin, 1885–1900* (1970) and *Robert M. La Follette and the Insurgent Spirit* (1976). In the former, Thelen asserts that Wisconsin "insurgency" originated in the grass-roots response of thousands of ordinary citizens in Milwaukee and other cities to the crises associated with the depression of 1893–1897. So devastating were the effects of the depression, Thelen argues, that people formerly divided along ethno-cultural, socio-economic, locational, and ideological lines were forced to unite in common cause as taxpayers, consumers, and citizens, and to displace the negative "mugwumpery" of good government reformers with the "social progressivism" later characteristic of the Wisconsin Idea. Beginning with private, voluntary associations, they pioneered a "new politics" that forced politicians to deal with "real" issues, such as equitable taxation, direct democracy, and utility regulation. Thelen believes that La Follette began promoting progressive causes only in 1897, and that until after his inauguration in 1901 he ignored earlier progressives' work in the legislature. He credits voters and earlier reformers for converting La Follette to progressivism, who had achieved office by appealing to their concerns over issues and frustrations over their political ineffectiveness. Once in office, he adjusted to the demands of farmers and workers for improvements in their workplaces. In this way, La Follette gradually altered the meaning of the Wisconsin Idea from grass-roots insurgency against special privilege to the social service state administered by quasi-independent expert commissions.[15]

---

[14] Eric E. Lampard, *The Rise of the Dairy Industry in Wisconsin: A Study in Agricultural Change, 1820–1920* (Madison, 1963), ix–xii, 333–351.

[15] David P. Thelen, *The New Citizenship: Origins of Progressivism in Wisconsin, 1885–1900* (Columbia, Missouri, 1970), 290–308, and *Robert M. La Follette and the Insurgent Spirit* (Boston, 1976), 16–78. See also Thelen's *The Early Life of Robert M. La Follette,*

Even more broad-based in its focus on the origins and evolution of Progressive Era reform in Wisconsin was Kenneth C. Acrea's doctoral dissertation, "Wisconsin Progressivism: Legislative Response to Social Change, 1891 to 1909" (completed on the Madison campus, appropriately enough, in the turbulent year of 1968). Like Thelen, Acrea believes the reformist impulse arose from the reaction by large numbers of citizens to the traumatic socio-economic changes that transformed the state at the end of the nineteenth century. Unlike Thelen, however, he assigns the primary role to reform-minded legislators, epitomized by Albert R. Hall, who expanded their area of influence during successive legislatures between 1891 and 1909. They developed, widened, and enacted an agenda of progressive reform, based primarily upon the notions of governmental responsibility for those whom socio-economic change had hurt and of making government accessible to everyone, instead of merely to a small clique of special interests. Acrea stresses the evolutionary nature of the Wisconsin Idea, its diverse origins, and the continuity of reform efforts over two decades. He sees Bob La Follette as a relative latecomer, motivated at least as much by personal ambition as by conviction, and as a man who provided the executive leadership lacking prior to 1900. Acrea focuses on the legislatures of the La Follette and Davidson administrations, plainly contradicting "Fighting Bob's" claims for the revolutionary nature of his reform program and also enhancing the accomplishments and significance of the Davidson years. Unfortunately, Acrea did not continue his story into the McGovern years.[16]

Further complicating the search for the Wisconsin Idea is the fact that the Progressive Era was a nationwide phenomenon with which Wisconsin enjoyed a synergistic relationship. What happened in Wisconsin occurred, in different guises and to different degrees, in other American states, and on the national level. Indeed, many of Wisconsin's signature laws, programs, and agencies had analogs not only elsewhere in the United States, but also in Europe, Australia, New Zealand, and Japan. Paralleling the Wisconsin Idea, at least in some of its most important aspects, were the "Iowa Idea" of Albert B. Cummins, the "New Idea" of New Jersey's George L. Record and Woodrow Wilson, the "Oregon System" of William S. U'Ren, and several others. The 1912 presidential campaign also produced the "New Freedom" of Woodrow Wilson and the "New Nationalism" of Theodore Roosevelt.

1855–1884 (Chicago, 1966) and Margulies, *Decline of the Progressive Movement*, 104–105, 135.

[16] Kenneth C. Acrea, Jr., "Wisconsin Progressivism: Legislative Response to Social Change, 1891 to 1909" (doctoral dissertation, University of Wisconsin, 1968), *passim*.

Like the Wisconsin Idea, each was designed to respond to two interrelated developments. The first was the rise of the "trusts"—upon which blame was put for most of the country's economic ills, including the high cost of living, shoddy or dangerous products, environmental damage, inequitable taxation, the exploitation of workers and consumers, and the decline in economic opportunity and competition. The second was the widespread acknowledgment that business corrupts politics—that trusts and other special interests employed bribery and other devises to gain privileges and benefits at every level of government: lucrative contracts, tax breaks, suppression of organized labor, and freedom from government regulation.[17]

Mostly to combat these twin menaces, reformers constructed the "ideas" or "systems," which generally involved two related strategies. The first was to expand the size, scope, and authority of government at all levels, so that it might intervene in the socio-economic order on behalf of those who were demanding protection against corporate excesses. The second was the reconstruction and purification of politics and government, in order to curb the pernicious influence of "special interests" by granting "power to the people" and promoting honest, cost-effective government by apolitical experts. The measures to bring about these sometimes paradoxical ends were devised and adapted by an informal network of intellectuals, social activists, and politicians, whose range was national, and even international. According to historian Daniel T. Rodgers, these individuals and organizations communicated with one another in three interrelated "social languages" or "clusters of ideas" that were full of potential contradictions, that varied in importance and intensity over time, and from which participants drew to meet their immediate needs, all of this without a great deal of concern for philosophical cohesion. In the kaleidoscopic world of American society and culture, this was as close as the nation could possibly come to constructing a cohesive progressive movement or a coherent ideology worthy of the designation "progressivism."[18]

---

[17] On the scope of progressive reform in the United States, see esp. John D. Buenker and Nicholas C. Burckel, eds., *Progressive Reform: A Guide to Information Sources* (Detroit, 1980); John D. Buenker, John C. Burnham, and Robert M. Crunden, *Progressivism* (Cambridge, 1977); Daniel T. Rodgers, "In Search of Progressivism," *Reviews in American History*, 10 (December, 1982), 113–132; and Arthur S. Link and Richard L. McCormick, *Progressivism* (Arlington Heights, Illinois, 1983). On the international nature of progressive reform, see esp. James T. Kloppenberg, *Uncertain Victory: Social Democracy in European and American Thought, 1870–1920* (New York, 1986); Ross Evans Paulson, *Women's Suffrage and Prohibition: A Comparative Study of Equality and Social Control* (Glenview, Illinois, 1973); and Peter J. Coleman, *Progressivism and the World of Reform: New Zealand and the Origins of the American Welfare State* (Lawrence, Kansas, 1987).

[18] Buenker, Burnham, and Crunden, *Progressivism*, 31–70; Rodgers, "In Search of

The first such cluster of ideas was the language of "antimonopolism," a traditional American concept that gained new currency in the 1890's, when many mainstream people, at least temporarily, began to see things through Socialist and Populist lenses. Suddenly, the inequities, and the iniquity, of the system were apparent to one and all. (In 1905, Kansas progressive journalist William Allen White, an erstwhile foe of the Populists, wryly observed that "it is funny how fast we have all found the octopus.") In Wisconsin, antimonopolism was most frequently translated as opposition to "the special interests," meaning railroads, lumber barons, public utilities, and manufacturers in the industrial southeast. But the meaning was substantially the same everywhere.

The second was the language of "social bonds," a dialect readily spoken by Social Gospel ministers, social scientists, and settlement house residents, and a conscious repudiation of classical economics, limited government, and rugged individualism. Permeating progressive economic, social, political, and educational thought, this language provided an intellectual justification for the conservation of human and natural resources, the New Education, the whole range of labor and welfare legislation, and the regulation of economic activity.

Finally, there was the language of "social efficiency," a marriage of social science expertise to industrial scientific management. In its undiluted form, social efficiency, with its emphasis on impersonal, quantitative measurements and non-judgmental, rational analysis, seemed to be in direct conflict with the language of social bonds, with its concern for morality, humanistic values, empathy, and compassion. Reduced to its darker side as social control or coercion, the language of social efficiency was used to justify repressive measures aimed at the socialization or segregation of the lower social orders, such as prohibition, immigration restriction, blue laws, disfranchisement, and eugenics. Expressed in more positive environmentalist terms, social efficiency manifested itself in attempts to improve disadvantaged people by ameliorating the conditions under which they lived and worked. Many progressive thinkers, including most of those in Wisconsin, were able to profess both social bonds and social efficiency simultaneously, especially if they conceived of society as an organism instead of a machine, if they substituted the public interest and the general welfare for the yardsticks employed by industrial engineers and cost accountants, and if they stressed the importance of the environment over heredity.[19]

Progressivism," *Reviews in American History*, 10: 121–123; Richard L. McCormick, *The Party Period and Public Policy: American Politics from the Age of Jackson to the Progressive Era* (New York, 1986), 311–356.

[19] Rodgers, "In Search of Progressivism," *Reviews in American History*, 10: 123–127.

The evidence in the public record and in their personal correspondence leaves no doubt that those who played the leading roles in the evolution of what became known as the Wisconsin Idea were firmly connected to the institutional and intellectual networks that defined progressive thought within a national and international context. They were simultaneously the receptors, generators, and conduits of reformist ideas, laws, and institutions. Chief among those individuals were La Follette, McCarthy, Commons, McGovern, Ely, Van Hise, and a number of other scholars and politicians. Preeminent among the state's institutions were the university, the Legislative Reference Library, the various quasi-independent, expert commissions, and the progressive wings of the state's major political parties.

[3]

For almost thirty years, Wisconsin, progressivism, and Robert M. La Follette were virtually synonymous in the American mind. Fighting Bob had cultivated this synonism during the 1890's, and he adroitly reinforced and exploited it until his death in 1925. Then and now, it was almost impossible for writers to mention the Badger State without referring to its progressive reputation, and equally difficult to discuss either without La Follette occupying center stage. Anything that enhanced Wisconsin's progressive reputation almost inevitably advanced La Follette's national celebrity; he rarely failed to extol the achievements of his native state while he advertised his credentials for political office. The skills he nurtured as a collegiate orator and actor, and honed on the stump and at county fairs and Chautauquas, guaranteed him an attentive, usually appreciative audience throughout his career.

La Follette also proved astute at advertising himself and his native state by way of the printed word, whether in newspapers or *La Follette's Weekly Magazine*. His confrontational style, graphic vocabulary, and carefully cultivated image as a champion of the people against special

---

See also Paul Boyer, *Urban Masses and Moral Order in America, 1820–1920* (Cambridge, 1978), 189–283; Edward A. Ross, *Social Control: A Survey of the Foundations of Order* (New York, 1924; reprinted, Cleveland, 1969), esp. pp. vii–lvi; Charles Horton Cooley, *Human Nature and the Social Order* (New York, 1902; reprinted, 1964), esp. pp. ix–xxxviii; William G. Staples, *Castles of Our Conscience: Social Control and the American State, 1800–1985* (New Brunswick, New Jersey, 1991), 17–78; David W. Noble, *The Progressive Mind, 1890–1917* (Chicago, 1970), 37–80, 137–179; Robert H. Wiebe, *The Search for Order, 1877–1920* (New York, 1967), 11–223; Roy Lubove, *The Professional Altruist: The Emergence of Social Work as a Career, 1880–1930* (Cambridge, 1965; reprinted, New York, 1969), 1–117; and Gerald M. McFarland, "Social Control," in John D. Buenker and Edward R. Kantowicz, *Historical Dictionary of the Progressive Era, 1890–1920* (New York, 1988), 436–437.

interests rendered him and Wisconsin reform a favorite subject for articles by muckraking journalists. His leadership of the congressional insurgents, his founding of the National Progressive Republican League, and his acrimonious public clashes with other high-profile politicians, including presidents Roosevelt, Taft, and Wilson, gained national press coverage for himself and his home state. In the U.S. Senate, La Follette rarely failed to cite Wisconsin precedents for his ideas and actions, regularly introduced legislation patterned after that of his native state, and frequently proclaimed that it was his mission to do with the Republican party nationally what he had done with it in Wisconsin. Although his *Autobiography* was fundamentally an advertisement for himself, it clearly asserted the proposition that only under the administration of President La Follette could the United States hope to become as progressive as Wisconsin.[20]

With the exception of La Follette, the man who did the most to enhance Wisconsin's progressive reputation, and to personify the symbiotic relationship between Wisconsin reformers and those elsewhere, was Charles McCarthy. Seriously flawed though it was, his book *The Wisconsin Idea* received scores of favorable reviews and had a wide impact throughout the country. Perhaps its most lasting contribution to our understanding of Progressive Era Wisconsin is its documentation of the breadth of the reformers' vision, and the intensity, enthusiasm, and optimism with which they approached their task. McCarthy and his staff found much of the information they used by studying statutes and reports issued by the governments of other states and nations, by visiting other locales periodically, by corresponding with counterparts elsewhere, and by digesting myriad popular and scholarly works of the day. McCarthy served on, or acted as frequent consultant to, many of the most renowned reform organizations, including the National Municipal League, the National Civic Federation, the National Popular Government League, the Bureau of Municipal Research, the National Society for the Promotion of Industrial Education, and the Agricultural Organization Society. He helped several states, the Philippine Islands, and the Progressive party to establish their own legislative reference libraries and, at the request of La Follette and Wisconsin Congressman John M. Nelson, he drafted plans for a similar service for the U.S. Congress. He played an important role in writing the platforms of both the national and Illinois Progressive parties in 1912, and served as an adviser to their executive committees. He frequently provided Theodore Roosevelt with advice, both solicited and otherwise; and he responded to requests for advice from both progressive Republican governors

---

[20] La Follette, *Autobiography*, 159–321; Thelen, *La Follette and the Insurgent Spirit*, 52–124.

(Hiram Johnson of California and Walter Stubbs of Kansas) and progressive Democratic governors (Edward F. Dunne of Illinois, David I. Walsh of Massachusetts, James M. Cox of Ohio, and Martin Glynn of New York).[21] An intellectual, a social and political activist, and a civil servant in the best sense of the word, Charles McCarthy was uniquely qualified to distill progressive ideas from the ferment of reform thought and transform them into legislation and public policy.[22]

Equally integral to the synergistic relationship between Wisconsin and national progressivism were key members of the University of Wisconsin faculty, with John R. Commons and Charles R. Van Hise leading the way. Their involvement in national and international scholarly networks and organizations facilitated the reciprocal exchange of information, hypotheses, and research sources and methodologies. Their writings and speeches were analyzed and critiqued by scholars and students, politicians, public servants, and activists. Only the University of Chicago rivaled the Madison campus for recognition as the seat of progressive thought. Several Madison faculty members served on commissions at both the state and national level, often simultaneously. The university trained hundreds of students who later occupied important positions in government, public service, and education. They carried the essentials of the Wisconsin Idea to other locales, where they adapted them to existing conditions and culture. In these veins, Van Hise wrote the influential *Concentration and Control* and *The Conservation of Natural Resources*, advised President Roosevelt on business regulation and conservation, helped draft the legislation establishing the Federal Trade Commission, advised the U.S. Chamber of Commerce on regulatory legislation, was a member of Roosevelt's Country Life Commission, served on the utilities bureau of the U.S. Conference of Mayors, and participated in the Institute for Government Research. In 1912, President Taft appointed him chairman of the arbitration board that settled a strike of the railroad brotherhoods against the eastern railways.

Commons was almost certainly the university's most service-oriented and nationally recognized faculty member. His American Association for Labor Legislation was the most respected and effective organization of its kind in the entire country, judging from the frequency with which Commons and his cohorts testified about these matters before legislative bodies and aided them in drafting legislation, much of it modeled on Wisconsin precedents. He served with Charles McCarthy on the U.S. Commission on Industrial Relations

---

[21] Fitzpatrick, *McCarthy of Wisconsin*, 12–280; Casey, *Charles McCarthy*, 13–145, and numerous items in the McCarthy Papers.
[22] McCarthy, *Wisconsin Idea*, xii–xiv; Fitzpatrick, *McCarthy of Wisconsin*, 62–71; Casey, *Charles McCarthy*, 46–74.

and consulted several other boards and commissions, including the National Civic Federation and the National Civil Service Reform League. Another key university figure was Richard T. Ely. By the time the Progressive Era was underway, he was already becoming less activist and more conservative, but he nevertheless exerted persisting influence through his merging of the Social Gospel with institutional economics and through his role in establishing the activist American Economic Association. Between them, Commons and Richard T. Ely trained a legion of economists who served on countless university faculties and in government service at all levels. Several other Wisconsin-based economists, such as Kossuth Kent Kennan, Delos R. Kinsman, Thomas S. Adams, and Balthazar H. Meyer, were employed regularly as national experts on taxation and business regulation. Sociologist Edward A. Ross and historian Frederick Jackson Turner also traveled in national progressive circles. Dozens of Wisconsin's most prominent activists moved in the national and international circles of progressive thought and organization, and functioned as major links and conduits in the symbiotic relationship between state and nation.[23]

This evidence obviously casts doubt on the contention of La Follette, McCarthy, Howe, and others that the Wisconsin Idea was sui generis, and that Wisconsin was *the* premier model and laboratory for progressive reform throughout the country. The documentation cited for that contention is impressive, as far as it goes. Twenty-seven other states adopted some form of a legislative reference library by 1950; nine states established county schools of agriculture and domestic economy, based at least partly on the Wisconsin model; several others borrowed from its industrial education and university extension systems. According to the American Association for Labor Legislation, five other states quickly copied the essentials of Wisconsin's system of workmen's compensation, while others borrowed liberally from the state's Industrial Commission. Wisconsin pioneered the first successful state income tax, despite the failures of several other states, as well as the first comprehensive program of direct primary elections in the country. North Carolina boasts of being "the Wisconsin of the South," and Austin, Texas, is proud of being compared to Madison. Even allowing for hyperbole, there was plainly some truth in McGovern's 1914 boast that "the Republicans of Minnesota, the Progressives

---

[23] Curti and Carstensen, *University of Wisconsin*, 2: 87–122; Commons, *Myself*, 95–182; Harter, *John R. Commons*, 69–204; Ely, *Ground Under Our Feet*, 121–164, 251–281, 296–299; Rader, *Academic Mind and Reform*, 28–105; Maurice M. Vance, *Charles Richard Van Hise: Scientist Progressive* (Madison, 1960), 148–176; Julius Weinberg, *Edward Alsworth Ross and the Sociology of Progressivism* (Madison, 1972), 56–176; Richard Hofstadter, *The Progressive Historians: Turner, Beard, Parrington* (New York, 1968), 47–164.

of Pennsylvania, and the Democrats of Ohio, all have recognized the leadership of Wisconsin among the commonwealths of the country and have sent delegations here to learn from us."[24]

Even so, it is equally important to recognize that Progressive Era Wisconsin was strategically situated in a much broader information system from which it borrowed as much as it contributed. Moreover, it must be emphasized that no state or country can or should slavishly copy another, even if what they are taking has been wildly successful in its place of origin. Every state, including Wisconsin, drew its ideas and models from several sources, then synthesized and adapted them to accommodate its own unique circumstances and traditions.

Perhaps the clearest picture of this continuous, reciprocal process appears in the celebrated exchange between Wisconsin and Pennsylvania in 1913. In May of that year, a delegation of 121 Pennsylvanians, whom the *Wisconsin State Journal* called "pilgrims," spent several days in Madison studying the university's extension division. They also listened to lectures by McGovern about the Board of Public Affairs, by Thomas S. Adams about the Tax Commission, by Halford Erickson about the Railroad Commission, by Commons about the Industrial Commission, and by McCarthy about the LRL. Returning to Pennsylvania, they devised a similar outreach system that was modified to meet their specifications. The following November, McCarthy, Van Hise, and university deans Louis Reber and Lois Kimball Matthews returned the visit, going to Philadelphia to inspect how Frederick W. Taylor's industrial efficiency system operated. Such networking and sharing helped make the Progressive Era progressive.[25]

[4]

Given the disagreements among participants and historians alike about the Wisconsin idea, the only hope of coming to a minimal understanding of it lies in the inductive, rather than the deductive, method. The Wisconsin Idea's tenets must be adduced from an anal-

---

[24] Francis E. McGovern, *Francis E. McGovern on Campaign Issues, 1914* (Milwaukee, 1914), 5; John D. Buenker, "Wisconsin as Maverick, Model, and Microcosm," in James H. Madison, ed., *Heartland: Comparative Histories of the Midwestern States* (Bloomington, Indiana, 1988), 81–83; Richard Nelson Current, *Wisconsin: A Bicentennial History* (New York, 1977), 194–198; Chester C. Platt, *What La Follette's State Is Doing: Some Battles Waged for More Freedom* (Batavia, New York, 1924), 268–278.

[25] *Wisconsin State Journal*, May 22–25, 1913; Casey, *Charles McCarthy*, 44, 108; Curti and Carstensen, *University of Wisconsin*, 2: 591, 611–624. See also "About That Visit to the Wisconsin University," *Chamber of Commerce News* (Boston), June 30, 1913, in the McCarthy Papers; Green Bay *Gazette*, May 22, 1913; Fond du Lac *Daily Commonwealth*, May 26, 1913; and James S. Hiatt, "The Philadelphia Pilgrimage and the Wisconsin Idea," *American School Board Journal*, 47 (July, 1913), 26–29, 33.

ysis of the sources already discussed, as well as from political party platforms, speeches and writings of other politicians and intellectuals, from governors' messages, court decisions, the reports of expert commissions, and contemporary newspapers and periodicals. What emerges from this exercise is a loose set of principles and assumptions that coexist uneasily, at best, and that are, at worst, fraught with paradox and contradiction. They were concepts that evolved and changed over time; concepts that were, in their most advanced and elaborated forms, too radical for a great number of Wisconsinites to accept.

Despite these shortcomings, the Wisconsin Idea of 1912 was about as coherent and comprehensive an ideology as American politics ever permits. At least three generations of historians have failed in their quest to identify a unified and unifying ideology of "progressivism." They have produced only lists of general, ambiguous, and even contradictory ideas, leading to the conclusion that members of a cohesive movement could not have held them simultaneously. This realization led Daniel Rodgers to propose that historians abandon the concept of a coherent progressive ideology, and replace it with his three social languages or clusters of ideas, all of which were present, in various combinations and permutations, in the Wisconsin Idea of 1912.[26]

The best starting point for attempting to reconstruct the Wisconsin Idea lies in the recognition that virtually all Wisconsin progressives conceived of society and polity in Rodgers' language of social bonds—variously expressed as a "commonwealth," "the public interest," "the general welfare," or "a public trust." This view extended past Wisconsin to the world in general. It posits that there exists a definable, collective good that is greater than the sum of individual or private interests, that transcends all of these particular concerns, and that can best be achieved through enlightened cooperation fostered by public institutions. Rodgers astutely observes that, for Progressives, this commonwealth conception represented a fundamental intellectual revolt "against a particular set of formal fictions traceable to [Adam] Smith, [John] Locke, and [John Stuart] Mill—the autonomous economic man, the autonomous possessor of property rights, the autonomous man of character."

In Rodgers' commonwealth or civic society model, citizens and officeholders alike regard politics as a public activity animated by a shared commitment to advance the common good. Good government is therefore measured by the extent to which it promotes the

---

[26] Rodgers, "In Search of Progressivism," *Reviews in American History*, 10: 111–123; John D. Buenker, "The Progressive Era: A Search for a Synthesis," *Mid-America*, 51 (July, 1969), 175–193; Peter G. Filene, "An Obituary for 'The Progressive Movement,'" *American Quarterly*, 22 (Spring, 1970), 20–34.

general welfare, and in terms of the honesty, altruism, and devotion to the public interest of those who govern, rather than by how well they respond to constituent requests. The commonwealth model can perhaps best be understood by contrasting it with what has been called the "marketplace" model, which had manifested itself in Wisconsin and elsewhere during the pre-Progressive Era. In the marketplace way of seeing the world, society and polity are perceived of as competitive arenas, where socio-economic, ethno-cultural, and similar interest groups compete for power, wealth, status, and recognition. The public interest, therefore, becomes nothing more than the sum of competing private interests. Politicians act as brokers, not policy makers. They mediate disputes among warring competitors and distribute benefits according to the power of the contestants; government exists solely to facilitate the private pursuit of particularistic goals, and to enhance the opportunities available to competitors.[27]

Wisconsin's Yankee settlers first established the commonwealth notion, which arose out of their strong sense of community as citizens; they saw themselves as living in the "city upon a hill" and performing an "errand into the wilderness." The commonwealth notion was rooted in conceptions of the organic state which American scholars had imbibed from German-trained teachers. According to Richard T. Ely's intellectual biographer, he rejected the view of John Locke and the eighteenth-century Enlightenment philosophers that the state was an "artificial creation of rational men to protect their natural rights." In its place, he substituted a view instilled by his German professors that "the state was the most important instrument of the social organism." Ely himself wrote that the nation, in its economic life, "is an organism, of which individuals, families, groups . . . etc., in their economic life form parts." Especially in an urban, industrial environment, he said, these "numberless parts are in an infinite variety of manner interdependent. Infinite interrelations! Infinite interdependencies!" In such a setting, the state was teacher and ethicist; it was essential to human progress. Ely described the goal of industrial reform as the realization of "social solidarity," and the state as the only agency capable of coercing philanthropy. This view squared, at least in general terms, with Catholic and Lutheran con-

---

[27] Rodgers, "In Search of Progressivism," *Reviews in American History*, 10: 123–126; Harter, *John R. Commons*, 205–256; Daniel J. Elazar, "Political Culture on the Plains," *Western Historical Quarterly*, 11 (July, 1980), 260–283; Sidney Fine, *Laissez Faire and the General-Welfare State: A Study of Conflict in American Thought, 1865–1901* (Ann Arbor, 1956; reprinted, 1964), 167–372. Harter calls Commons' brand of progressivism a "revolt against laissez-faire."

ceptions of an organic society, and with the sense of a co-operative commonwealth desired by Social Democrats.[28]

At first glance, the commonwealth conception might seem to be at odds with "the people versus the interests" belief that resulted in so much progressive rhetoric and action, especially during the La Follette years. That belief would seem to be rooted in permanent socio-economic conflict against what a 1915 writer in *The Nation* called the "dragon of the interests." Over time, attitudes moved away from the notion of ongoing conflict towards an emerging harmony of interests. If government action could eliminate the unfair advantage of the "interests" and promote equality of opportunity, then harmony and stability would prevail. Even La Follette, the virtual inventor of "interest-bashing," could assure the readers of his *Autobiography* that "progressive government produces business prosperity." The object of progressive legislation, he said, "was not to 'smash' corporations, but to drive them out of politics, and then to treat them exactly the same as other people are treated. Equality under the law was our guiding star." Regulation of utilities and railroads had benefited consumers and stockholders alike, and thus all of Wisconsin.

Similarly, John R. Commons talked of "class partnership," arguing that workmen's compensation and the establishment of an industrial commission to regulate wages, hours, and health and safety conditions in factories worked to the mutual advantage of workers, owners, and consumers. The "notions of utilitarian idealism, constructive research, class partnership and administrative efficiency" permeated his book on labor and administration (1913). Frederick Jackson Turner likewise expressed his confidence that the university, as the guardian of the public weal, could harmonize the apparently conflicting interests of labor and capital.[29]

This belief in the eventual harmony of interests, especially between

---

[28] Barry Alan Shain, *The Myth of American Individualism: The Protestant Origins of American Political Thought* (Princeton, 1994), 23–47, 320–328; Alice E. Smith, *The History of Wisconsin. Volume I: From Exploration to Statehood* (Madison, 1973), 546–647; Current, *Wisconsin: A Bicentennial History*, 34–66, 174–216; Rader, *Academic Mind and Reform*, 48–53 (quotes); Ely, *Ground Under Our Feet*, 149–164.

[29] Stuart Morris, "The Wisconsin Idea and Business Progressivism," *Journal of American Studies*, 4 (July, 1970), 50; La Follette, *Autobiography*, 137, 150–155; Commons, *Myself*, 69–92; Harter, *John R. Commons*, 25–44; Rader, *Academic Mind and Reform*, 54–82; John Milton Cooper, Jr., "Frederick Jackson Turner and the Wisconsin Idea: A Recently Discovered Letter," in *WMH*, 57 (Summer, 1974), 310–312; Curti and Carstensen, *University of Wisconsin*, 1: 630–643; John R. Commons, *Labor and Administration* (New York, 1913), 51–84; "Human Happiness a Business Asset," *La Follette's Weekly Magazine*, November 23, 1912, p. 1. According to Herbert F. Margulies, *Senator Lenroot of Wisconsin: A Political Biography, 1900–1929* (Columbia, Missouri, 1977), 48, Lenroot saw himself as a mediator between capital and labor.

capital and labor, was the tenet that most separated progressive Republicans from the Social Democratic party, at least theoretically. Still, Wisconsin Socialists were hardly revolutionaries; they were committed to the eventual establishment of a co-operative commonwealth through education, moral suasion, union activity, and democratic politics within the existing system. Once they had achieved that goal, a similar harmony of interests presumably would prevail. In the meantime, the SDP believed in co-operating with progressives and reformers on labor, welfare legislation, and on measures to democratize the political system. McCarthy, McGovern, and their followers candidly acknowledged that the only way to prevent the SDP from gaining strength was to enact many of its platform pledges. Consequently, SDP legislators voted for the McGovern administration's socio-economic legislation in 1911, but remained organizationally distinct. The Milwaukee *Leader*, the SDP newspaper run by Victor Berger, criticized the progressive Republicans for openly wanting to steal the SDP's thunder. SDP leaders even contended that much of the 1911 legislation was a capitalist sop to frustrate socialism's ultimate triumph. In the practical political realm, however, the SDP moderated both its rhetoric and its program to win votes. As a result, the SDP and the progressive Republicans gave voters little to choose between. Ironically, progressive Republicans gained little or nothing politically from SDP supporters, while the similarity of their programs left the Progressives vulnerable to Stalwarts who charged that they were merely Socialists in disguise.[30]

Closely related to the commonwealth concept were the notions of "social investment" and what Ely and McCarthy called "the new individualism." Social investment was the belief that society as a whole needed to invest money and effort in endeavors like education, agricultural research, industrial and vocational schools, rural betterment, and resettlement of the Cutover. Even though the immediate beneficiaries might be individuals or private groups or organizations, the benefits eventually would redound to the public welfare. The university illustrates the point. Charles McCarthy explained its philosophy as the notion that the state profits from investments in bettering human beings and protecting human welfare. More specifically, he believed that business and human welfare could grow side by side. McCarthy concluded *The Wisconsin Idea* by asking a putative

---

[30] Sally M. Miller, *Victor Berger and the Promise of Constructive Socialism, 1910–1920* (Westport, Connecticut, 1973), 30–31; McCarthy, *Wisconsin Idea*, 294–300; Milwaukee *Leader*, August 11, 1913; Ely, *Ground Under Our Feet*, 87–91. For charges that the Wisconsin Idea was "socialism in disguise," see the reviews in Milwaukee *Sentinel*, August 28, 1912; Rochester, New York *Post-Express*, April 10, 1912; and the Brooklyn *Eagle*, April 13, 1912, clippings in the McCarthy Papers.

"Mr. Business Man" if he did not believe that it would "pay well to make a heavy investment in hope, health, happiness and justice," and whether there was not "something worth while, something which will pay in the strong ideal of this *New Individualism* of Wisconsin?" Indeed, the university compiled data to prove the point. La Follette in 1912 asked Van Hise for reports detailing the contributions to the state in concrete economic terms. Van Hise sent a bundle. Eric Lampard, historian of Wisconsin's dairy industry, notes in several places that what he calls the Wisconsin Idea in Dairying was justified because it brought a great financial return to both dairymen and the state economy. Bluntly put, it reinforced the slogan of the Wisconsin Dairymen's Association: "What is good for the dairy is good for Wisconsin".[31]

Under the Wisconsin Idea, the government was to generate and invest the required social capital, build the necessary infrastructure, establish and monitor the operational guidelines, guarantee equitable distribution of the benefits, provide for the welfare of the poor, and protect the public interest from exploitation. The state university was to supply the necessary technical and theoretical knowledge. Together, the government and the university were to provide the social investment for the program's many endeavors, whose beneficiaries were private citizens and groups, but which would ultimately enhance the general quality of life. Government, education, and the private citizenry together would create an environment conducive to the realization of individual potential, and to the pursuit of all legitimate goals. As McCarthy said, "State activity means investment and all the advanced states of the world make heavy investments."[32]

Employing government and public education to help individuals realize their own potential, thus ultimately benefiting the commonwealth, was the essence of Ely and McCarthy's "new individualism." McCarthy credited Ely with "a curious new doctrine, a 'new individualism,' that men deserved the right of opportunity and benefited by it; that it was the duty of the state to preserve to them opportunities; that the state was a necessary good and not a necessary evil;

---

[31] McCarthy, *Wisconsin Idea*, 273–303; Rader, *Academic Mind and Reform*, 48–53, 83–105; Ely, *Ground Under Our Feet*, 152–153, 221; Lampard, *Rise of the Dairy Industry*, 333–351; Milwaukee *Sentinel*, March 8, 1910; Van Hise to La Follette, October 2, 1912, in the La Follette Papers.

[32] McCarthy, *Wisconsin Idea*, 156–303 (quote, p. 290); James A. Frear, "The Cost of Progressive Government," *La Follette's Weekly Magazine*, August 17, 1912, p. 8; Robert M. La Follette, "The Wisconsin Way Brings Business Security," *La Follette's Weekly Magazine*, November 2, 1912, p. 4; "Human Happiness a Business Asset," *La Follette's Weekly Magazine*, November 23, 1912, p. 1. See also the Republican party platforms in the *Blue Books* for 1911 (pp. 670–676) and 1913, (pp. 571–575), and McGovern's 1911 and 1913 messages to the legislature.

that the great institution of private property was good, and furthermore existed for public good, but that if any particular part of it did not exist for the public good, it should be *made* to do so." Ely saw the state as the only force powerful enough to counteract "the unrestricted tyranny of the strong" that characterized modern industrial capitalism. To Ely, true liberty meant "the expression of positive powers of the individual." Benjamin Rader explains that Ely believed the state's task was to "promote positive liberty by regulating the conditions of contract between a large corporation and the individual, or even by setting up a public school system."[33]

The Wisconsin Idea also included the conviction that a modern urban-industrial state could be governed only by applying professionals to tasks and making them answerable to a well-educated citizenry. These two interrelated beliefs pervaded the writings of La Follette, McGovern, McCarthy, Van Hise, and their supporters, so much so that they almost constitute a litmus test for separating progressives from conservatives. In his inaugural address as university president, Van Hise said that "the college-trained man, and especially the university-trained man, is directly or indirectly, to control the destinies of the nation." La Follette explained that railroad and utility regulation could profit both stockholders and the public "simply because the regulation is scientific." In his instructive chapter on administration, McCarthy stated flatly that the state could not, for example, regulate utilities without "a thorough understanding of the intricate systems of cost accounting and efficiency used by these great economic units," by which he meant business corporations. To protect the public interest, he went on, scientific rules and regulations must take the place of "miscellaneous law." These rules and regulations "must be made by trained workers; . . . they must be made upon tests, measurements, and close observation. This is as much of a science, as great a work and demands as high an education, as any work now known in human endeavor." To McCarthy's conviction, Ely added that the conflict between the corporations and the public could be equalized only by having state government use professional experts: "Apart from the question of the simple difference in economic strength as between the contesting parties, we have the question of skill on the two sides." Expert administration, said John R. Commons, was the "instrument which society must gradually forge and improve for using social knowledge in the interest of valid social purposes." Wisconsin reformers' faith in the almost mystical power of professionals echoed the sentiments of such nationally renowned progressive intellectuals as Louis D. Brandeis, Walter Lippmann, Herbert

---

[33] McCarthy, *Wisconsin Idea*, 16–18, 27–33 (quote), 273–305; Rader, *Academic Mind and Reform*, 50–53 (quotes); Ely, *Ground Under Our Feet*, 279–282.

Croly, Simon Patten, and Herman Metz, all of whom saw the disinterested, apolitical "expert" as the vital conduit between government and the electorate. The expert, and only the expert, could translate the inchoate demands of the mass of voters into concrete legislation and agencies; only the expert could be entrusted with the responsibility of day-to-day operations.[34]

An indispensable corollary to this belief in professionals' expertise was that good government must be efficient and economical. Turn-of-the-century intellectuals and reformers were caught up in what historian Samuel Haber calls "the efficiency craze," inspired by gains in industrial productivity attributed to the "scientific management" theories of Frederick W. Taylor and his disciples. Most progressives rejected the movement's tendency to make workers mere appendages of machines and systems. Still, many embraced the notion of "social efficiency," which promised the eventual achievement of social harmony and equity through the leadership of the "competent."

Taken one way, social efficiency justified the imposition of conformity upon the lower social orders through prohibition, blue laws, language requirements, and compulsory education in public schools. Taken another way, social efficiency sounded very much like the "new individualism" and "social investment" concepts of the Wisconsin Idea, and whose goal was the full-blown social service state. McCarthy digested the works of leading efficiency theorists—Taylor, Croly, Lippmann, Brandeis, Frederick A. Cleveland, Morris L. Cooke, and William Harvey Allen of the New York Bureau of Municipal Research. He carried on a serious correspondence with all of these men and secured Allen's services as a consultant and investigator for the Board of Public Affairs. In *The Wisconsin Idea*, McCarthy praised Cleveland as "probably the first man to apply their idea [of business efficiency] to the administration of governmental institutions," and asked rhetorically why state government should not be the chief efficiency expert for the people. Commons, who helped McCarthy draft the legislation that established the Board of Public Affairs, used as his model the Milwaukee Bureau of Economy and Efficiency (on which he had served) established by the Social Democratic administration of Mayor

---

[34] McCarthy, *Wisconsin Idea*, 45–87, 192 (quote); Charles R. Van Hise, "Inaugural Address," in University of Wisconsin, *The Jubilee of the University of Wisconsin* (Madison, 1905), 98–128 (quote 121); Fitzpatrick, *McCarthy of Wisconsin*, 131–134; Casey, *Charles McCarthy*, 25–45; Commons, *Labor and Administration*, 195; Ely, *Ground Under Our Feet*, 121–163; Rader, *Academic Mind and Reform*, 83–105; Curti and Carstensen, *University of Wisconsin*, 2: 87–90; Morris, "Wisconsin Idea and Business Progressivism," *Journal of American Studies*, 4: 42–45; Charles R. Van Hise, "The Wisconsin Idea," *La Follette's Weekly Magazine*, June 14, 1913, p. 15; Samuel Haber, *Efficiency and Uplift: Scientific Management in the Progressive Era, 1890–1920* (Chicago, 1964), 99–116; Herbert D. Croly, *Progressive Democracy* (New York, 1914), 350–369.

Emil Seidel. For the most part, Wisconsin progressives eschewed the social-control and industrial-regime aspects of the efficiency craze, and embraced its social-service or general-welfare components, tempered with humanism and compassion. They aimed at delivering the best social services to the largest number of people on a continuous basis.[35]

As McCarthy's frequent references to cost accounting demonstrate, the architects of the Wisconsin Idea desired economical government, not merely expert and efficient government. The Wisconsin constitution encouraged economy, since it prohibited incurring long-term indebtedness to finance public projects. Besides, Wisconsin was not an especially wealthy state, and its citizens prized frugality. The new state inheritance and income taxes significantly increased revenue by the high point of the Progressive Era, but unprecedented growth in expenditures to implement the new social programs offset these new taxes. Progressives in general realized that they could achieve a full service state only if they convinced voters that they exercised the utmost frugality in management and finances, and if expenditures and taxes did not rise precipitously. They also sought to place the university and several key commissions on continuing appropriations, in order to make them immune from shifts in public opinion and enable them to engage in long-range planning. Such considerations also underlay the progressives' desire to create a budget system, and to give the Board of Public Affairs responsibility for supervising the entire fiscal system.

McCarthy tried to undercut the economy argument by asserting that experts and quality services were expensive, as well as by urging voters and taxpayers to view them as social investments with future dividends. He also realized that the progressive Republicans could not exceed the average taxpayer's tolerance. He had no real choice but to present cost effectiveness as one of the virtues of the Wisconsin Idea. Perhaps more than any other single cause, the progressives' failure to convince the majority of voters of the truth of that claim led to their downfall in 1914.[36]

[35] McCarthy, *Wisconsin Idea*, 191–193; Fitzpatrick, *McCarthy of Wisconsin*, 35–38; Casey, *Charles McCarthy*, 45–74; Curti and Carstensen, *University of Wisconsin*, 2: 611–624; Morris, "Wisconsin Idea and Business Progressivism," *Journal of American Studies*, 4: 42–45; Haber, *Efficiency and Uplift*, ix–xii, 58–74; Croly, *Progressive Democracy*, 32–39. In his 1913 message to the legislature, pp. 52–53, McGovern defined "governmental efficiency."

[36] McCarthy, *Wisconsin Idea*, 201–205, 290–294; Maxwell, *La Follette and the Rise of the Progressives*, 101–104; Curti and Carstensen, *University of Wisconsin*, 2: 159–190; Margulies, *Decline of the Progressive Movement in Wisconsin*, 136–151; Roger E. Wyman, "Voting Behavior in the Progressive Era: Wisconsin as a Case Study" (doctoral dissertation, University of Wisconsin, 1970), 307–311.

To realize this ideal urban-industrial state, the Wisconsin Idea's proponents emphasized education. Above all, it had to be democratic and practical. Democracy meant that educational opportunities from kindergarten through graduate or professional schools should be accessible to all, in terms of geographical location, cost, and admissions requirements. Practicality meant blending the theoretical and the practical to erase all arbitrary or elitist distinctions between academic education and vocational-technical training. McCarthy and his followers sought to infuse vocational-technical training with the spirit of the German continuation school which combined "on the job" manual training with exposure to each job's wider technical, scientific, social, and political context. The progressives also tried to persuade university faculty members to abandon a purely theoretical approach to their research and instruction and to emphasize practical applications wherever feasible.[37]

The twin principles of democracy and practicality pervaded every educational issue during the Progressive Era in Wisconsin: upgrading of rural schools, creation of continuation schools and the Board of Industrial Education, development of county schools of agriculture and domestic economy, expansion of state and county normal schools, state supervision of the apprenticeship program, expansion of extension programs, the abortive effort to create a State Board of Education to integrate instruction at all levels, and the founding of social centers in the public schools to provide enrichment and civic education to adults. These ideas and programs were at the heart of the slogans "A university that runs a state" and "The boundaries of the campus are the boundaries of the state." They found their ultimate expression in McCarthy's efforts to create a separate school to train public servants in conjunction with the American Political Science Association, the Progressive party, the Bureau of Municipal Research, and Columbia University.[38]

Woven together, the commonwealth model and the concepts of social investment, the new individualism, professional expertise, humanistic efficiency, fiscal economy, and practical, democratic public education constituted the intellectual framework on which to erect Wisconsin's service state—a variant of what historian Sidney Fine has

---

[37] McCarthy, *Wisconsin Idea*, 141–152; Fitzpatrick, *McCarthy of Wisconsin*, 260–276; Casey, *Charles McCarthy*, 80–83. See also Robert H. Foss, "Theodore Kronshage, Jr.," in *WMH*, 26 (June, 1943), 414–425.

[38] McCarthy, *Wisconsin Idea*, 247–255; Fitzpatrick, *McCarthy of Wisconsin*, 131–134; Casey, *Charles McCarthy*, 69–71; McCarthy to Robert C. Brooks, January 6, 1914, to James A. Patterson, October 29, 1913, to Charles R. Van Hise, October 31 and November 4, 1913, to Richard T. Ely, November 1, 1913, to Charles R. Crane, November 6, 1914, to Theodore Kronshage, December 9, 1913, and to Edward A Fitzpatrick, October 27, 1913, all in the McCarthy Papers.

characterized as the "general welfare state." Another historian, Richard L. McCormick, has demonstrated that the Progressive Era throughout the entire country was marked by a transition of state government focus. At the beginning, government was a distributor of benefits and resources apportioned on the basis of political power and influence. At the conclusion, it was a positive interventionist force responsible for the administration, regulation, and planning of nearly every aspect of modern life. This metamorphosis implies that progressives viewed the state, at least potentially, as the embodiment of the public interest and guardian of the public trust. The Wisconsin service state, writes Kenneth Acrea, was based upon the convictions that "an active government, charged with regulating the life processes of the state, might compensate for the changes and dislocations which were part of a maturing society," and that "such a maturing society could no longer afford the luxury of wasted resources, either material or human." This mutually held belief in the service state permeated the writings of Ely, Commons, Van Hise, McCarthy, and Ross, as well as the reports of the commissions and *ad hoc* committees on taxation, insurance, continuing education, and the like. The kernel of it appeared in La Follette's gubernatorial messages and speeches, and the mature philosophy became even more central in his *Autobiography*. It was the explicit theme of the Republican and Social Democratic platforms of 1910 and 1912 and of McGovern's messages to the legislatures of 1911 and 1913. Most obviously, it was the foundation stone on which stood the three pillars of the Wisconsin Idea: the Legislative Reference Library, the University of Wisconsin, and the quasi-independent commissions of experts.[39]

[4]

The first pillar of the Wisconsin Idea, the Legislative Reference Library, as constructed by Charles McCarthy and his staff, was the very model of efficiency and expertise in organization, operation, and outcome. It reflected his determination to transform Wisconsin into the state whose laws were better than any other state's because the scientific method had been applied to them. McCarthy created the library from scratch, without the aid of earlier examples. Bob La Follette rarely lavished praise on his associates, but he did acknowledge that "the bureau of investigation and research established as a leg-

---

[39] Maxwell, *La Follette and the Rise of the Progressives*, 153–172; Fine, *Laissez Faire and the General-Welfare State*, 373–402; McCormick, *Party Period and Public Policy*, 197–227; Morris, "Wisconsin Idea and Business Progressivism," *Journal of American Studies*, 4: 39–45; Acrea, "Wisconsin Progressivism," 521–522.

islative reference library conducted by Charles McCarthy, a man of marked originality and power, has proved of the greatest assistance to the legislature in furnishing the latest and best thought of the advanced students of government in this and other countries." It was, La Follette said, "a model which the Federal Government and ultimately every state in the Union will follow."[40]

McCarthy devised a set of principles that he later recommended as guidelines to those who wanted to establish similar libraries: the library should be conveniently located for use by the legislature; material should be accessible and compact; all past bills should be indexed; records of vetoes and platforms should be kept in a handy place, along with digests of every law before the legislature; and the agency must be completely nonpartisan. The director should be "well trained, original, not stiff, 'one who can meet an emergency with tact,' " and learned in both economics and political science. Likewise staff members and bill draftsmen should be well-trained, willing ask the legislators directly what they wanted, and determined to gather information well ahead of the time it might be needed.[41]

McCarthy divided the LRL into two separate and independent departments—one for research, the other for drafting bills. McCarthy ran the former personally. He continually wired or wrote to sources of information in the United States and abroad for letters, newspapers, periodicals, pamphlets, leaflets, bills, veto messages, judicial briefs and decisions, party platforms, books, articles, and miscellaneous publications from home and abroad. Such were his collecting habits that a Dallas newspaper once observed of him that he gathered everything "from the cost of digging sewers in Kamchatka to whether women in Honolulu really wanted suffrage [sic]."[42] McCarthy also traveled far and wide to observe matters firsthand, consulting with experts and gathering materials to be shipped to Madison: "We want to know what the dearly bought experience of other places is."

McCarthy personally supervised processing and cataloging materials besides collecting them. Armed with his trademark blue pencil, he checked off every item he wanted clipped and mounted in one of the library's topical scrapbooks. McCarthy conceded that much of the scrapbook material was indeed "scrappy" and that his biggest problem was to keep the "dead stuff out and the live stuff in." He regularly summarized the scrapbooks, so that legislators and scholars

---

[40] Fitzpatrick, *McCarthy of Wisconsin*, 41–49; Casey, *Charles McCarthy*, 25–32; Commons, *Myself*, 107–110; La Follette, *Autobiography*, 15; McCarthy, *Wisconsin Idea*, 16–18, 28–33, 286–303.

[41] Fitzpatrick, *McCarthy of Wisconsin*, 51–61; Casey, *Charles McCarthy*, 38–39 (quote).

[42] Casey, *Charles McCarthy*, 32–34 (quote); Fitzpatrick, *McCarthy of Wisconsin*, 62–71; Commons, *Myself*, 107–111.

would not have to wade unguided through reams of source material. He believed the scrapbook format was of great value to legislators.[43]

While the LRL research department was a beehive, buzzing with discussion among staffers, legislators, university faculty members and students, and out-of-town researchers, the LRL bill-drafting department was a quiet haven where legislators worked in isolation from outside influences. Five commandments governed it, displayed prominently on the wall: no bill drafting in the reference room; no bills or amendments drafted without specific, detailed, written instructions from legislators; no suggestions made about the contents of any bill; no liability accepted for the legality or constitutionality of any bill; and no responsibility accepted for making the bills conform to the rules and numbering system of a particular legislative session. McCarthy insisted that the work of the bill drafting department was clerical and technical, not ideological or partisan, but Stalwarts and other critics frequently charged he ran a "progressive bill factory" infused with his own ideology. (Privately, McCarthy and other progressives acknowledged his and the LRL's contribution to the content of key reform legislation.)[44]

The university's status as the second pillar of the Wisconsin Idea was, and remains, probably its most widely celebrated aspect. Frederic Howe called the university "the brain of the commonwealth." Faculty members and administrators helped draft bills, formally advised governors, state officials, and legislators, and served on numerous commissions. The Extension Division and colleges of agriculture and engineering preached the gospel of efficiency, economy, and expertise everywhere in the state. The Madison campus was grouped with other state universities in California, Iowa, Illinois, Kentucky, and North Carolina as a "guarantor of continued equality of opportunity" and a "vehicle of upward mobility," both practical and democratic.[45] Professor Ely stressed his beliefs that the state university could and should blend academic and practical experience and that it should adhere to President Van Hise's dictum that "the strength of the state university lies in its close relation to the State." For Van Hise, historians Merle Curti and Vernon Carstensen later concluded, accommodation

---

[43] Casey, *Charles McCarthy*, 34–35 (quote); Fitzpatrick, *McCarthy of Wisconsin*, 61–65; McCarthy, *Wisconsin Idea*, 217–218.

[44] Casey, *Charles McCarthy*, 36–38; Fitzpatrick, *McCarthy of Wisconsin*, 49–50; McCarthy, *Wisconsin Idea*, 196–200; Margulies, *Decline of the Progressive Movement*, 148–151.

[45] Morris, "Wisconsin Idea and Business Progressivism," 40–43; William E. Walling, *Progressivism—And After* (New York, 1914), 120; McCarthy, *Wisconsin Idea*, 124–141, 313–317; Curti and Carstensen, *University of Wisconsin*, 2: 611–626; Allan Nevins, *The State Universities and Democracy* (Urbana, 1962), 53–54; Howe, *Wisconsin*, 151–182. For a discussion of several of the articles written about the university, see Curti and Carstensen, *University of Wisconsin*, 2: 588–591.

of the campus to the practical needs of the state and its people constituted "both a justification and a goal."[46]

In their grander vision, Van Hise, McCarthy, and many faculty members viewed the relationship between the university and state government as too episodic, informal, and ineffectual. Commons implied that view in his oft-quoted observation that he functioned only at the pleasure of state officials. McCarthy's detailing of faculty service to state government in the appendix of *The Wisconsin Idea* may, in fact, be considered somewhat hyperbolic. Elsewhere, more candidly, McCarthy flayed the faculty for its general lack of participation in public affairs, just as he criticized politicians for their frequent refusal to cultivate expert advice. McCarthy and other progressive intellectuals ardently desired to replace the *ad hoc* brain trust and Saturday luncheon groups with a permanent system of trained, apolitical, civil-service experts, somewhat along German lines. Ely left Johns Hopkins for Madison for reasons along those lines. He wanted to establish "a civil academy to do somewhat for the civil service that which West Point and Annapolis do for the military and naval services." In the same vein, speaking at commencement at Indiana University in 1910, Frederick Jackson Turner argued that the university could help reconcile the conflict between capital and labor by providing training in science, law, politics, and history for a cadre of "administrators, legislators, judges, and experts for commissions who shall disinterestedly and intelligently mediate between contending interests." Van Hise, McCarthy, Commons, Ely and others all wanted such a school on the university campus; McCarthy, who liked to think big, even dreamed of creating a national school for public servants. In the long run, neither the sporadic university-government arrangement encompassed by the Wisconsin Idea, nor the state's new civil service system, was considered adequate to the task.[47]

---

[46] Morris, "Wisconsin Idea and Business Progressivism," *Journal of American Studies*, 4: 41–44; Ely, *Ground Under Our Feet*, 181; Charles R. Van Hise, "Commencement Address, 1910," in Ellwood P. Cubberley, *Readings in Public Education in the United States* (New York, 1934), 480 (quote); Curti and Carstensen, *University of Wisconsin*, 2: 549 (quote); Vance, *Charles Richard Van Hise*, 83–90, 108–122; Rader, *Academic Mind and Reform*, 175–181; Carstensen, "Origin and Early Development of the Wisconsin Idea," in *WMH*, 39: 182, 188; Hoeveler, "The University and the Social Gospel," in *WMH*, 59: 294–298; Van Hise to La Follette, October 2, 1912, in the La Follette Papers.

[47] Morris, "Wisconsin Idea and Business Progressivism," *Journal of American Studies*, 4: 44–53; Commons, *Myself*, 101–107; McCarthy, *Wisconsin Idea*, 247–255; Ely, *Ground Under Our Feet*, 181; Rader, *Academic Mind and Reform*, 110–112; Frederick Jackson Turner, "Pioneer Ideals and the State University," in Frederick Jackson Turner, *The Frontier in American History* (New York, 1921; reprinted, Tucson, 1986), 285–286; Fitzpatrick, *McCarthy of Wisconsin*, 131–134; Casey, *Charles McCarthy*, 69–71; Vance, *Charles Richard Van Hise*, 171–172.

The third pillar of the Wisconsin Idea consisted of several quasi-independent expert commissions established between 1899 and 1914. "If any praise was due the state's various governmental experiments," McCarthy said, "it is probably because of the appointive commissions, the non-partisan spirit, the expert and the effective civil service law." McCarthy was not entirely sanguine about the possible dangers of centralizing so much authority in bodies largely immune to direct popular influence. Nevertheless he argued that "commission government seems to be the best method to extend the legislative power scientifically, and the only way also of using judicial determination in great economic questions confronting the people." In an increasingly complex world, "legislation for the future on great economic questions will be based upon a broad determination of policies by a legislative body, the carrying out of which will be entrusted to efficient servants and experts, responsible in every manner to the representatives of the people and the people in general." He deemed this approach "essential in the Wisconsin Idea." McCarthy's enthusiasm for the appointive expert commission was shared, for the most part, by Commons, Van Hise, La Follette, McGovern, and the other prominent Wisconsin progressives.[48]

No single pattern existed for establishing these appointive expert commissions. A number evolved over several legislative sessions as experiments with *ad hoc*, piecemeal remedies for specific problems. Lawmakers concluded that so many of the measures were interrelated that they justified a more comprehensive and continuous approach. Sometimes that process operated in reverse, as legislators cumulatively assigned additional related duties and powers to commissions originally intended to have jurisdiction over a single, precise area. Occasionally, a single commissioner and his staff would be transformed into a full-scale regulatory commission. In any case, commission structure clearly moved from the specific to the general, from the particular to the comprehensive, and from diffused authority to centralized.[49]

---

[48] Hollis W. Barber, "Development of Some of the Administrative Departments of the Government of Wisconsin from 1850–1930" (doctoral dissertation, University of Wisconsin, 1935), 8–153; McCarthy, *Wisconsin Idea*, 45–47, 172–188 (quote); La Follette, *Autobiography*, 149–157; Commons, *Myself*,153–162; Vance, *Charles Richard Van Hise*, 112–113; Maxwell, *La Follette and the Rise of the Progressives*, 196–199; Acrea, "Wisconsin Progressivism," 496–527; Wyman, "Voting Behavior in the Progressive Era," 289–299. In his 1913 message to the legislature, McGovern said that "centralization of authority and responsibility is the one indispensable condition of efficiency in administration. Hence our expert commissions and boards."

[49] Barber, "Development of Some of the Administrative Departments," 8–31; Maxwell, *La Follette and the Rise of the Progressives*,153–172; Acrea, "Wisconsin Progressivism," 496–527; "State Government by Commissions," *La Follette's Weekly Magazine*,

The gradual metamorphosis between 1883 and 1911 of the Bureau of Labor and Industrial Statistics into the Industrial Commission illustrates this evolutionary phenomenon. The bureau was founded initially as a data-collecting agency with minimal inspection duties. Its staff grew from two to seven by 1899 and the scope of its inspection and enforcement duties expanded commensurately. The legislature regularly increased its staff, budget, and duties between 1900 and 1911, culminating with the enactment of the workmen's compensation and industrial apprenticeship laws. At that point, the legislature consolidated supervision of all of the state's welfare and labor programs in the new Industrial Commission, concluding the evolutionary process.

The cumulative form of metamorphosis occurred with the Railroad Commission over the course of more than twenty years. It was established in 1905 and was granted authority over the rates and service of the state's railway companies. Succeeding legislatures entrusted the commission with regulating urban trolley-car systems and most other public utilities, as well as with supervising sales of stocks and bonds. Although it did not officially become the Public Service Commission until 1931, the Railroad Commission had achieved that status in all but name by the end of the Progressive Era.[50]

Lying somewhere between the industrial and the railroad commissions in its development was the Tax Commission. It was formed as a temporary data-gathering body in the mid-1890's, and was made permanent in 1899. It had responsibility for equalizing property taxes and collecting the new inheritance tax. Over the next decade, the legislature gave it authority over license fees and the *ad valorem* taxation of railroads and several public utilities. In 1911, it was charged with enforcing the new state income tax. Similar histories involved the Insurance Commissioner, the Conservation Commission, the Board of Industrial Education, and the Board of Agriculture.[51]

Probably the most ambitious foray into regulation, administration, and planning by commission was the short-lived Board of Public Af-

---

June 28, 1913, p. 15; Walter C. Owens, "The Progressive and Government," *La Follette's Weekly Magazine*, August 24, 1912, p. 8.

[50] Barber, "Development of Some of the Administrative Departments," 32–110, 250–261, 280–291; *Wisconsin Blue Book, 1986*, pp. 414–416, 462–473; Maxwell, *La Follette and the Rise of the Progressives*, 74–79; Howe, *Wisconsin*, 67–117; Acrea, "Wisconsin Progressivism," 505–507; Wallace Mendelson, "The Public Service Commission of Wisconsin: A Study in Administrative Procedure" (doctoral dissertation, University of Wisconsin, 1940), 3–7.

[51] Barber, "Development of Some of the Administrative Departments," 161–169, 170–181, 195–206, 221–222, 243–247, 298–301; *Wisconsin Blue Book, 1968*, pp. 402–406, 412–414, 445–450; Howe, *Wisconsin*, 118–125, 133–139; Acrea, "Wisconsin Progressivism," 504–509.

fairs, established by the legislature in 1911. Its members were nearly all elected public officials subject to electoral sanctions, though the board functioned largely at the direction of McCarthy and other appointed staff members. It engaged professional experts from outside Wisconsin—for example the New York Bureau of Municipal Research—to conduct investigations and make recommendations. In its brief history, the Board of Public Affairs conducted nearly twenty investigations or surveys of such areas as agricultural conditions, public finance, education, prison labor, and the university. It significantly reformed state budgetary practices, reduced waste and inefficiency in spending, and fostered development of the co-operative movement. Even though the board was reduced to a far less powerful position under the conservative governorship of Emanuel Philipp (1915–1921), its very existence tends to bolster the validity of Kenneth Acrea's conclusion that "one measure of a true [Wisconsin] progressive was his faith in the quasi-public State commissions."[52]

[5]

The successful operation of an efficient, economical service state managed by expert professionals required strong guarantees of popular sovereignty. McCarthy frankly acknowledged this problem in the *Wisconsin Idea*. His chapter on administration attempts to convince readers that the Wisconsin system had more than adequate safeguards. He admitted that "it may seem strange" that civil service, appointive officers, and commissions predominated in a state "where there is so much confidence in democracy and where the direct primary election is in favor." He explained away the contradiction by pointing to the fact that primary elections applied only to "executive offices and to those who legislate and formulate policies." Wisconsinites, he was certain, were sophisticated enough to distinguish between "those who determine a policy and those who are chosen for administrative or technical skill—as servants merely to carry out the will of the people as expressed in the law." To be efficient required that commissions possess "liberal doses" of power, but the public interest was safeguarded by "the addition of the non-partisan spirit and an efficient civil service." Therefore, he concluded, "the appointive commission is an aid to democracy."[53]

---

[52] Fitzpatrick, *McCarthy of Wisconsin*, 140–156; Maxwell, *La Follette and the Rise of the Progressives*, 169–172; Acrea, "Wisconsin Progressivism," 506–507; Howe, *Wisconsin*, 126–132; Casey, *Charles McCarthy*, 77–78; "Making Public Business Really Businesslike," *La Follette's Weekly Magazine*, November 2, 1912, p. 3.

[53] McCarthy, *Wisconsin Idea*, 172–176; Ely, *Ground Under Our Feet*, 214–217; Commons, *Myself*, 150–159.

McCarthy suggested three other measures for supervising commissions: the glare of constant publicity; the payment of sufficiently high salaries to attract expert people of integrity; and what he termed "the checks and spurs which sustain the integrity of the whole system," especially the accountability of civil servants, commissioners, and appointed officials to a legislature that was, in turn, answerable to the voters. Tentatively, McCarthy suggested devising some means "whereby commissions may be called before the legislature in the same manner in which members of the English cabinet are subjected to questions or interpellation in the British parliament." Without such a mechanism, he said, the best guarantee was a fearless, honest, and capable legislature and a "half-dozen concrete, vital elements— the accountant, the statistician, the actuary, the chemist, red blood and a big stick."[54]

Potential tension between expert government and democratic accountability demanded a high degree of popular control of the state's elective offices. This meant designing an electoral system that gave the individual voter maximum leverage over nominations, elections, and legislation, that was insulated from the corrupting influence of politicians and their corporate allies, and that forced candidates to deal directly with issues of state and local concern, rather than resorting to partisan or ethno-cultural appeals, or to national questions. The open primary, electoral corrupt practices legislation, lobbyist registration laws, and the initiative, referendum, and recall would give weight and force to these principles. At the local level, they resulted in nonpartisan local elections, the separation of local elections from state and national ones, and the option of adopting the commission form of municipal government. Over time, these structural alterations produced the transition from the ethno-cultural, party-ordered politics of the nineteenth century to the issue-oriented, candidate-centered politics of the more recent past. Coincidentally, they earned for Wisconsin a lasting reputation for democratic politics, clean government, a sophisticated electorate, and a broadly humane ideology—in short, "a progressive state."[55]

Proponents of the Wisconsin Idea sought to extend the principle of popular control to the judiciary as well. Like progressives across the nation, they were upset by the frequency with which conservative judges struck down reform legislation. They were also upset by the

[54] McCarthy, *Wisconsin Idea*, 77–193 (quotes on pp. 177, 181, 193).

[55] *Ibid.*, 33–123; Howe, *Wisconsin*, 25–37, 51–66; Leon D. Epstein, *Politics in Wisconsin* (Madison, 1958), 22–44; Neal R. Peirce and John Keefe, *The Great Lakes States of America: People, Politics, and Power in the Five Great Lakes States* (New York, 1980), 108–162; John H. Fenton, *Midwest Politics* (New York, 1966), 44–74; "Making Voting Easier," *La Follette's Weekly Magazine*, February 1, 1913, p. 3; "News Worth Remembering," *La Follette's Weekly Magazine*, May 11, 1912, p. 13; "State Government by Commissions," *La Follette's Weekly Magazine*, June 28, 1913, p. 15.

reasons why, since the judges engaged in legalistic interpretations of either common law or constitutions, when their real motives were transparently ideological. McCarthy criticized judges for relying upon precedent rather than his preference of "sociological jurisprudence" that commissioners used. He charged that judge-made law ignored the larger socio-economic issues. And he castigated "the ridiculous assumption of fatherhood and protectorship which some American judges, in their pomposity, have attained." Their obstinacy had been "the means of retarding the march of progress in legislation and of establishing into the body of our government certain fallacies which have been a real and potential danger to the whole fabric of the state." McCarthy had an answer: make economics, sociology, political science, and history a part of law school curricula and create a reference library for jurists similar to that available to legislators; make amendment of state and federal constitutions far easier, so that the public could negate unpopular decisions; and make judges more responsive to voters through fairly frequent elections and the introduction of judicial recall.[56] A functional democratic partnership between state and local government was also a goal of the Wisconsin Idea. Yankee settlers brought with them a vision of grass-roots, town-meeting democracy. The state constitution reflected this commitment in the number of functions it allocated to town, county, and municipal governments. Legislators from rural and village districts guarded these local prerogatives throughout the nineteenth century, while at the same time they sought to extend state authority over Wisconsin's cities. Many progressive reforms in fact required more centralization of power in Madison, so their designers frequently took pains to involve local governments in the administration and division of benefits. For example, more than one-third of all revenues derived from the activities of the state tax commission, including 90 per cent of income tax revenues, were returned to local governments. Similarly, the highway commission funneled state aid to local governments, which did much of the actual construction and maintenance. Local-state co-operation permeated the university's extension system and the outlying two-year university centers, where local governments supplied the physical plants and apparatus.

County and local governments were leery of centralized control from Madison, just as they were of cities and city governments whose power and influence increased dramatically between 1890 and 1920. A proposed constitutional amendment to grant home rule to municipalities failed in the 1914 reaction against progressivism—even

[56] McCarthy, *Wisconsin Idea*, 233–272 (quotes on p. 240); Ellen Torelle, Albert O. Barton, and Fred L. Holmes, comps., *The Political Philosophy of Robert M. La Follette As Revealed in His Speeches and Writings* (Madison, 1920), 177–181.

though, ironically, local control became an issue in that election. Not even limited municipal home rule was achieved until 1924.[57]

In theory, the Wisconsin Idea involved the establishment of an efficient, economical, and honest general welfare state managed by apolitical experts who were subject to control by sophisticated voters who were sensitive to local governments. In practice, of course, things never worked that consistently or coherently. The reform program of the La Follette administration never achieved the multi-faceted service state of the McGovern years. Politics is rarely static for long, and the volatile politics of the Progressive Era ensured that no program, no ideology, no slogan would long endure. Even though La Follette himself largely evolved along with the Wisconsin Idea, many of his original backers found the concept's later metamorphosis too profound and sweeping. The fully evolved Wisconsin Idea appealed most strongly to social scientists, public servants, labor unionists, Social Democrats, urban dwellers, and proponents of Teddy Roosevelt's New Nationalism. By 1912, it was beset by internal tensions and contradictions that proved difficult to ignore or reconcile.

Perhaps the worst inconsistency was the universal progressive conundrum between efficiency, expertise, and economy on the one hand, and "power to the people" on the other. Quasi-independent commissions, the proliferation of appointive offices, and the extension of civil service were logically at odds with making government more accessible and responsive to the ordinary citizen. Efforts to distinguish between those who made policy and those who merely applied policy to everyday operations usually proved impossible to sustain. The structures designed to make bureaucrats immune from special interests just as readily isolated them from the people they were supposed to serve. The Railroad Commission illustrates graphically how commissions could sometimes become the servants of the very special interests they were established to combat. In the end, the safeguards against such an eventuality proved unconvincing, and sometimes unavailing, to many. The very fact that progressives spent so much time trying to rationalize the apparent contradiction proved

---

[57] McCarthy, *Wisconsin Idea*, 66–73; Epstein, *Politics in Wisconsin*, 57–76; Current, *Wisconsin: A Bicentennial History*, 214–215; Charles D. Rosa, "Wisconsin Public Revenues," in the *Wisconsin Blue Book, 1935*, pp. 29–44; Harold M. Groves, "The Wisconsin State Income Tax," *Wisconsin Blue Book, 1933*, pp. 51–67; J. Roy Blough, "The Wisconsin System of Taxation," *Wisconsin Blue Book, 1931*, pp. 49–69; Ballard Campbell, "The Good Roads Movement in Wisconsin, 1890–1911," in *WMH*, 49 (Summer, 1966), 273–293; John O. Stark, "The Establishment of Wisconsin's Income Tax," in *WMH*, 71 (Autumn, 1987), 27–45; M. W. Torkelson, "Wisconsin Highways," *Wisconsin Blue Book, 1931*, pp. 9–29; Harold L. Henderson, "Public Education in Wisconsin," *Wisconsin Blue Book, 1931*, pp. 71–98; Conrad E. Patzer, *Public Education in Wisconsin* (Madison, 1924), 116–123, 404–412.

that the contradiction did exist and was important. Their failure to devise a solution to this dilemma was the bane of progressives throughout the United States and Europe. Indeed, it has continued to plague their successors to the present.[58] Efforts to infuse the basically mechanistic and profit-driven notion of efficiency with transforming humanistic and socially organic values also were failures, as Stuart Morris has argued. World War I and the booming prosperity of the 1920's enabled businessmen to recapture their old position as "agents of progress." Productivity and profit were restored as the benchmarks against which to measure "social efficiency." Government, hailed by the progressives as the "efficiency expert" promoting the general welfare, was presently transformed into either a barrier to economic progress or the handmaiden of business and industry. The progressive dream that public service would displace business as the most desired vocation of young Americans proved illusory; soon the universities were producing far more would-be capitalists than would-be public servants. By 1914, even a prominent progressive like Herbert Croly—author of *The Promise of American Life* and founder of *The New Republic*—would say that public administration and corporate management were "coming to meet on the same plane of scientific method and social responsibility." Of course, not all progressives acquiesced so easily in the proposition that "the business of America is business." But it was not until the onset of the Great Depression in 1930 that liberal thinkers regained the attention, and the confidence, of the majority of Americans.[59]

Several related problems compounded the progressives' dilemma of how to reconcile professional administration with popular government. First there was the difficulty of squaring the centralization of power in Madison with insistence upon local autonomy. To their credit, Wisconsin progressives devised a formula to do just that. Their plans for revenue sharing, industrial and agricultural education, and home rule were aimed at maintaining a realistic balance between state and local control. However, the reaction against the income tax and home rule in 1914 demonstrated that many Wisconsinites regarded such balancing efforts as inadequate against the momentum of centralization.

---

[58] Kloppenberg, *Uncertain Victory*, 267–277, 381–394; Haber, *Efficiency and Uplift*, 99–116; Morris, "Wisconsin Idea and Business Progressivism," *Journal of American Studies*, 4: 43–49; George Brown, "Sovereignty and Democracy in Wisconsin Elections," in the *Wisconsin Blue Book, 1935*, pp. 71–93; McCarthy to Frederick Cleveland, April 9, 1912, in the McCarthy Papers.

[59] Morris, "Wisconsin Idea and Business Progressivism," *Journal of American Studies*, 4: 49–60; Paul W. Glad, "Progressives and the Business Culture of the 1920s," *Journal of American History*, 53 (June, 1966), 75–89; Croly, *Progressive Democracy*, 399–400; Haber, *Efficiency and Uplift*, 117–168.

What was more, the progressives' self-conscious efforts to justify every expansion of state responsibility and authority with a cost-benefit analysis betrayed their frustration. On the one hand, failing to meet the cost-benefit test would disqualify otherwise worthwhile programs. On the other hand, the cost-benefit test limited the realization of the reformist impulse. McCarthy tried forthrightly to get voters to look at both sides of the revenue ledger, at both the money and at the services and benefits; the sway of the "extravagance" issue in 1914 suggests that he fell short. Finally, the means Wisconsin progressives chose to achieve popular participation in politics—the open primary and nonpartisan local elections—in the end frustrated their purpose. The reforms actually eroded the grass-roots infrastructure of the political party system, causing a decline in voter participation and making government at all levels less accessible to citizens. As the role of political parties in elections and governance shrank, organized interest groups benefited—the same special interests the progressives were determined to curtail.[60]

Two other lines of argument backfired against the men who forged the Wisconsin Idea. The first was their stress on the Germanic roots and composition of their movement, by which they hoped to attract theretofore antagonistic German voters. Assigning credit to German thinkers risked alienating other ethnic groups whose contributions had been at least as important. The Great War of 1914–1918, and the anti-German hysteria that swept Wisconsin, proved this strategy lethal. Equally destructive were the progressives' persistent attempts to justify so much labor and welfare legislation because it would theoretically undercut the Social Democrats. This tactic did little to woo Socialist support; indeed, it likely made co-operation more difficult. It also lent credence to the conservatives' claims that progressive Republicans were wild-eyed radicals, at least as dangerous as the Socialists; and it provided the Stalwarts with ammunition against the socioeconomic measures that the progressives and the Socialists worked so hard to enact. The fact that Milwaukee's Socialists were overwhelmingly Germanic, and that they opposed American involvement in the Great War on both ethnic and ideological grounds, delivered a double-barreled blast to Wisconsin progressivism.[61]

---

[60] Epstein, *Politics in Wisconsin*, 57–70; Bayrd Still, *Milwaukee: The History of a City* (Madison, 1948; reprinted, 1965), 316–318, 377–378, 521, 536, 558–559; Wyman, "Voting Behavior in the Progressive Era," 322–327; Frederick N. McMillin, "City Government in Wisconsin," in the *Wisconsin Blue Book, 1931*, pp. 395–400; John L. Flokstra, "The Legal Basis of School Organization and Administration in Wisconsin" (doctoral dissertation, University of Chicago, 1944), *passim*.

[61] Margulies, *Decline of the Progressive Movement*, 152–157; Wyman, "Voting Behavior in the Progressive Era," 937–961; Morris, "Wisconsin Idea and Business Progressivism," *Journal of American Studies*, 4: 54–56.

Of less political significance, but of greater long-term consequence, was the anomalous role assigned the University of Wisconsin by proponents of the Wisconsin Idea. The Madison campus was the proudest boast of the state by 1912. It enjoyed a reputation for involvement in public service that persists three-quarters of a century later. However, its celebrity held potential for backlash. The close association of the state university with the progressive wing of the Republican party produced resentment among conservatives in both major parties; attacks on the progressives became attacks on the university, and vice versa. In a broader sense, the immersion of the campus in politics, of whatever ideological or partisan stamp, undermined its claim to being a universal institution above the *Sturm und Drang* of politics. Once the university proclaimed public service as its reason for existence, then justified its ever-growing budget requests on those grounds, and boasted of its economic value to the state, it could not escape retaliation by those who had different agendas or different accounting methods. The more faculty members and administrators became involved in partisan politics, the harder it was for them to take refuge behind the shields of academic freedom and tenure. Like much else in the Wisconsin Idea, the role of the university as public servant was fraught with paradox.[62]

Of at least equal consequence in the criticism of the Wisconsin Idea is the fact that it appeared to ignore substantial groups, among them women, African Americans and Native Americans, immigrants of southern and eastern European stock, and the lower socio-economic orders in general. Like progressive reform elsewhere, the Wisconsin brand pretty much ignored elements of society that had no effective organization or political significance. Tens of thousands of Wisconsin women, most of them from the upper and middle classes, belonged to important women's, consumers, and child welfare organizations, and they played a vital role in the passage of most of the major legislation that distinguished Wisconsin progressivism. But they lacked the right to vote, and therefore could neither punish nor reward officeholders. In the original edition of his *Autobiography*, La Follette devotes only three pages out of 700-some to women and public service. He writes that he had always "been much impressed with the fact that women were as keenly interested as men . . . in the whole Progressive program" and had always felt that "women should play a larger part than they do in the greater housekeeping of the state." He praises his wife Belle for her "grasp of the great problems, socio-

---

[62] Morris, "Wisconsin Idea and Business Progressivism," *Journal of American Studies*, 4: 50–55; Curti and Carstensen, *University of Wisconsin*, 2: 267–283; Sallee McNamara, "The Record Re-examined: The Stalwarts, the Progressives; Education and Public Welfare in Wisconsin" (master's thesis, University of Wisconsin, 1965), 4–48.

logical and economic," points with pride to his record of "using the peculiar executive abilities of women in the state service," and says he "cannot remember a time when I did not believe in woman suffrage." He concludes his brief paean to "co-suffrage" by announcing his intention to campaign for woman suffrage in the 1912 referendum. But it was not to be. Even though all three major political parties openly endorsed it, woman suffrage was defeated by better than two to one.[63]

The other architects of the Wisconsin Idea expressed less concern than La Follette about the status of women. They were interested in female welfare, in the work force and in the home, but they expressed themselves as if women were a dependent class in need of protection—somewhat comparable to the children for whom women had primary responsibility. Wisconsin's progressive men seemed to share the opinion of most male labor unionists, socialists, and conservatives that women needed protection in the workplace; they all felt that everyone would be better off if women were able to stay home. They freely acknowledged the achievements of individual women and the contributions of women's organizations towards reforms, but their acknowledgement betrayed a mind-set in which women were limited to kinds of "housekeeping." Progressives' speeches, writings, and legislative programs demonstrate neither vision of, nor commitment to, gender equality. It is hard to believe that Wisconsin progressives could not have enacted woman suffrage if they had regarded it as a high-priority issue, since they enacted so many other reforms. After the defeat of the 1912 referendum, the McGovern administration all but abandoned woman suffrage. It did not surface again, for all practical purposes, until the proposal of the Nineteenth Amendment in 1919 forced the issue.[64]

---

[63] La Follette, *Autobiography*, 134–136; Genevieve G. McBride, *On Wisconsin Women: Working for Their Rights from Settlement to Suffrage* (Madison, 1993), 164–200; Janice Sternschneider, *An Improved Woman: The Wisconsin Federation of Women's Clubs, 1895–1920* (Brooklyn, New York, 1994), 17–58; Thelen, *La Follette and the Insurgent Spirit*, 86–95, 100, 166; Bernard A. Weisberger, *The La Follettes Of Wisconsin: Love and Politics in Progressive Wisconsin* (Madison, 1994), 154–156; Ann S. Waligorski, "Social Action and Women: The Experience of Lizzie Black Kander" (master's thesis, University of Wisconsin, 1970), *passim*.

[64] McBride, *On Wisconsin Women*, 201–293; Lawrence L. Graves, "The Wisconsin Woman Suffrage Movement, 1846–1920" (doctoral dissertation, University of Wisconsin, 1954), 121–214; Theodora W. Youmans, "How Wisconsin Women Won the Ballot," in *WMH*, 51 (1921–1922), 15–23; Robert M. La Follette, "Suffrage Veto," *La Follette's Weekly Magazine*, June 7, 1913, p. 1; Marilyn Grant, "The 1912 Suffrage Referendum: An Exercise in Political Action," in WMH, 64 (Winter, 1980–1981), 107–116; John D. Buenker, "The Politics of Mutual Frustration: Socialists and Suffragists in New York and Wisconsin," in Sally M. Miller, ed., *Flawed Liberation: Socialism and Feminism* (Westport, Connecticut, 1981), 113–133.

Of even less interest to the architects of the Wisconsin Idea was the status of Negroes and the new immigrants. Wisconsin's black population was very small and had little or no political clout, so it is not surprising that they were ignored. In their attitude towards Negroes, Wisconsin progressives were probably no worse or no better than other white reformers of the period. Numerous scholars have since demonstrated that most progressive reformers regarded Negroes as inferior, and looked the other way at disfranchisement and segregation, if they did not actually advocate such measures themselves as a means of "purifying" the political system. Even the socialists had difficulty extending "the universal brotherhood of workers" to people of color.

As for southern and eastern European immigrants, several Wisconsin progressives, especially professors Ross and Commons, were among the nation's loudest advocates of immigration restriction. Ross based his position on popular social theories of the day, which he helped to perpetuate. Commons stressed the negative economic consequences of unrestricted immigration, especially on industrial workers. The state's labor unions, and Victor Berger and the Social Democrats, held much the same view. Wisconsin progressives were sympathetic to welfare laws that benefited southern and eastern Europeans. Some even advocated measures for social control. For example, Progressive-dominated legislatures experimented with eugenics laws and eliminated voting by aliens. In the eyes of La Follette and McCarthy, the European groups most in need of political recognition and government help were Germans and Scandinavians, both of whom had achieved sufficient numbers, organization, and sophistication to count.[65]

Nor did Wisconsin's progressives take much notice of the state's Native Americans. They left Indian policy to the federal government, even though those policies sometimes clashed with state or local regulations. La Follette earned a well-deserved reputation as a champion of Native American rights during his tenure in the House of Representatives, and following his elevation to the U.S. Senate he was appointed to the Committee on Indian Affairs, where he worked to protect tribes' coal and timber lands from exploitation by extractive industries. As a rule, however, the tenets of the Wisconsin Idea were

---

[65] Joe William Trotter, Jr., *Black Milwaukee: The Making of an Industrial Proletariat, 1915–1945* (Urbana, 1985), 3–33; Rader, *Academic Mind and Reform*, 235; Harter, *John R. Commons*, 15, 38, 168–169, 188, 228, 233; John R. Commons, *Races and Immigrants in America* (New York, 1907; reprinted, 1967), *passim*; Weinberg, *Edward Alsworth Ross*, 149–176; Edward A. Ross, *The Old World in the New: The Significance of Past and Present Immigration to the American People* (New York, 1914), *passim*; Miller, *Victor Berger*, 20–22, 38, 52, 81–82, 229. See also Chapter 5.

almost exclusively of, by, and for white males of northwestern European ancestry.[66]

To be fair, it must be acknowledged that the practitioners of the Wisconsin Idea were far more inclined towards positive, environmentalist interpretations of social efficiency and the more inclusive, organic language of social bonds than they were towards the mechanistic, coercive aspects of social engineering and social control. Even when professing the latter, they usually went out of their way to emphasize the superiority of the former. That was especially true of McCarthy and Ely, and was generally the case even with Ross and Commons, who, of the progressives, expressed the greatest disdain for immigrants and Negroes. By the standards of the 1990's, Wisconsin progressives fall far short in their attitudes and actions towards women and the ethnic and racial minorities. On the other hand, by the standards of their own day, they appear more enlightened than most of their contemporaries. Even so, as Daniel Rodgers argues persuasively, the language of social efficiency emerged fairly late in Progressive Era thought, and eventually came to dominate rhetoric about antimonopolism and social bonds. By the 1910's, indications were that the same process was underway in Wisconsin. Sentiment in favor of sterilizing "defectives," of restricting immigration, suppressing vice, prohibiting alcoholic beverages, tightening voting requirements for immigrants, and similar measures of social control built steadily and came to the fore. Blatant intolerance and discrimination against Catholics and people of German ancestry dominated discourse from 1914 until the end of the Great War. Ironically, most of these developments, at one and the same time, were justified in the name of progressivism and the Wisconsin Idea, even as they were contributing mightily to progressivism's demise.[67]

In spite of all their inadequacies and internal inconsistencies, the tenets of the Wisconsin Idea performed several vital functions. For one, certain aspects of the Idea served as rallying points for elements of the unstable coalition that dominated state politics during the Pro-

[66] La Follette, *Autobiography*, 71–73, 376–378, 383; Thelen, *La Follette and the Insurgent Spirit*, 9, 55; David R. Wrone, "Indian Treaties and the Democratic Idea," in *WMH*, 70 (Winter, 1986–1987), 83–101; John F. Berens, "Old Campaigners, New Realities: Indian Policy Reform in the Progressive Era, 1900–1912," *Mid-America*, 59 (January, 1977), 51–64. See also Frederick E. Hoxie, *A Final Promise: The Campaign to Assimilate the Indian, 1880–1920* (Lincoln, Nebraska, 1984).

[67] Rudolph J. Vecoli, "Sterilization: A Progressive Measure?" in *WMH*, 43 (Spring, 1960), 190–202; Peter R. Weisensel, "The Wisconsin Temperance Crusade to 1919" (master's thesis, University of Wisconsin, 1965); Herbert F. Margulies, "Anti-Catholicism in Wisconsin Politics, 1914–1920," *Mid-America*, 44 (January, 1962), 51–56, and "The Decline of Wisconsin Progressivism, 1911–1914," *Mid-America*, 39 (July, 1957), 131–155; Paul Glad, *The History of Wisconsin. Volume V: War, a New Era, and Depression, 1914–1940* (Madison, 1990), 3–54.

gressive Era. For another, the Idea supplied that coalition with a necessary (though often minimal) conceptual framework and a sense of direction for a vast outpouring of legislation. Finally, it provided one of the most geographically and economically diverse states in the nation with a unifying and enduring public culture. It conferred order and meaning upon Wisconsin's social and political processes, articulated the assumptions and rules that governed behavior, and set the standards by which its constituent groups were defined and legitimized. As historians Neal Peirce and John Keefe have put it, succeeding generations of Wisconsinites continued to experience the Wisconsin Idea as "an amalgam of strong political traditions and self-perpetuating political myths, of high government expectations and high taxes to prove it, of economic diversity in the extreme (cows to heavy machinery) and a distinctive quality of life found in few of its sister states." It is true that Wisconsinites seldom agreed about what, exactly, the Wisconsin Idea was; but they were, and seemingly remain, adamantly convinced of its existence, it uniqueness, and its importance.[68]

[68] Peirce and Keefe, *Great Lakes States*, 108.

14

Disintegration and Legacy

[1]

EVEN as progressive Republicans basked in the afterglow of the achievements of the 1911 legislature, factionalism and political backlash were gnawing away at their triumphant movement. The Progressives had failed to lure many Democrats or Socialists into their coalition, while the "radical" tinge of their achievements had further alienated most moderate and stalwart Republicans. Moreover, the clash between Senator La Follette's presidential ambitions and Francis McGovern's senatorial aspirations was a disaster waiting to happen, one that would destroy the tenuous alliance between them and transform them into antagonists, seemingly more interested in thwarting one another than in championing further reforms. Emanuel Philipp and the resurgent Stalwarts exploited these cracks in the progressive structure and mounted an effective propaganda campaign accusing progressivism of a multitude of sins. As if that were not enough, the ideological political axis that the Progressives had labored so hard to impose was skewed by the resurgence of ethnocultural divisions. Despite all the progressive rhetoric and a shift towards "the issues" (especially economic issues), ethnicity and religion continued to determine voters' party allegiance and voting behavior.[1]

From its inception, Wisconsin progressivism was more an idea, a complex and ever-changing system of alliances, than it was a political party. To a large degree its success depended on the personalities and resources of individuals, on the ethnic origins, religion, and aspirations of various blocs of voters, and on quirks of geography and economics. The "Progressive Movement" was not even a movement in the normally understood sense of the term; its membership varied

[1] Herbert F. Margulies, *The Decline of the Progressive Movement in Wisconsin, 1890–1920* (Madison, 1968), 124–163; Roger E. Wyman, "Voting Behavior in the Progressive Era: Wisconsin as a Case Study" (doctoral dissertation, University of Wisconsin, 1970), 236–327, 937; Robert S. Maxwell, *La Follette and the Rise of the Progressives in Wisconsin* (Madison, 1956), 173–193.

from election to election and from one legislative session to the next, and its putative leaders often fought among themselves over goals, strategy, and tactics, pragmatically shifting ground to gain advantage over their adversaries—and sometimes their friends. With the introduction of the direct, open primary in 1906, these factional feuds turned into institutions, and soon spread to the entire electorate.[2]

The original coalition that elected La Follette in 1902 and 1904 and provided him legislative majorities was itself a volatile mix. It included many elements for whom the progressives' achievements seemed to signal the arrival of the millennium. Many farmers, shippers, and lumbermen, for example, were satisfied once their chief adversaries, the railroads, had been partially restrained through *ad valorem* taxation and the creation of the Railroad Commission. Ambitious young men and ethnic politicians were also satisfied once their support of La Follette led to preferment the Stalwarts denied them. The Dairymen's Association was by 1910 reasonably happy with the new "night watchman state," but it had little desire to work towards a social service state focused on Wisconsin's industrial cities and the marginal farmers in the Cutover. Not all progressives were ideologues; not all of them wanted to continue in the crusade. As Isaac Stephenson put it in his autobiography, once "the old railroad-corporation crowd, the inner ring which controlled party affairs to the exclusion of all others, had been fairly routed and some good laws were placed on the statute books . . . there the task ended for me." Similarly with James O. Davidson, who admitted in 1906 that "a very good portion of the people, at least, are willing to have a rest from the turbulence that has been with us in the past." And La Follette's most powerful political ally, William D. Hoard, told a colleague in 1911 that he had never seen "so malign and selfish a spirit as La Follette has infused his followers with."[3]

---

[2] Margulies, *Decline of the Progressive Movement*, 91–93; Wyman, "Voting Behavior in the Progressive Era," 270–300, 914–917; Maxwell, *La Follette and the Rise of the Progressives*, 56–73. Stuart D. Brandes, "Nils P. Haugen and the Wisconsin Progressive Movement" (master's thesis, University of Wisconsin, 1965), p. 3, argues that progressive reform in Wisconsin was "a play in three acts—1901–1904, 1904–1909, and 1910–1914." Kenneth C. Acrea, Jr., "Wisconsin Progressivism: Legislative Response to Social Change, 1891 to 1909" (doctoral dissertation, University of Wisconsin, 1968), provides ample evidence to conclude that there was an earlier, fourth phase from 1893 to 1901, in which legislative reformers like Albert R. Hall took the initiative.

[3] Margulies, *Decline of the Progressive Movement*, 84–92, 95–96 (quotes); Wyman, "Voting Behavior in the Progressive Era," 259–275; Eric E. Lampard, *The Rise of the Dairy Industry in Wisconsin: A Study in Agricultural Change, 1820–1920* (Madison, 1963), 341–351; Maxwell, *La Follette and the Rise of the Progressives*, 173–174; Isaac Stephenson, *Recollections of a Long Life, 1829–1915* (Chicago, 1915), 233–240; Padraic M. Kennedy, "Lenroot, La Follette, and the Campaign of 1906," in *WMH*, 42 (Spring, 1959), 163–174.

The defection of these earlier moderate progressives probably began with La Follette's decision to seek the U.S. Senate seat that Stephenson desired and for which he had contributed so generously to the progressive cause. La Follette's ill-advised attempt to block Davidson's renomination for governor in 1906 in favor of Irvine Lenroot exacerbated the problem. In addition to alienating many Norwegians who had consistently backed La Follette, Lenroot's candidacy in the Republican primary unintentionally revived the prohibition issue, which had the potential to shatter the progressive coalition beyond repair. Already unhappy, Stephenson and his Milwaukee *Free Press* refused to aid La Follette for the first time since their collaboration had begun in the late 1890's. The following year, La Follette widened the rift by waiting until the last minute to instruct his followers in the legislature to back Stephenson's bid for Wisconsin's other Senate seat. Although "Uncle Ike" eventually was elected to the remaining two years of that term, his antipathy towards La Follette grew apace. During the 1908 senatorial preference primary, La Follette maintained strict public neutrality in the Republican race among Stephenson, William Hatton, and Francis McGovern, all progressives of varying degree. Stephenson captured the nomination, and La Follette's closest followers led the crusade against him during the 1909 legislative session on the grounds that he had "bought" the primary. For most moderate progressives, the La Follette-McGovern alliance, the leftward surge of the 1910 platform and campaign, and the "radical" nature of many of the laws passed by the 1911 legislature were the last straws that propelled them into the Stalwarts' ranks.[4]

These defections coincided with and aided the Stalwart revival under the leadership of Emanuel Philipp. Skillfully aligning his movement with the administration of William Howard Taft in 1909, Philipp gained a powerful ally in Taft, achieved great influence over federal patronage in Wisconsin, and established himself as the state's foremost Republican loyalist. Taft and Philipp agreed on ideology and shared a hatred of La Follette and his National Progressive Republican League, founded in 1911, which they feared might be a vehicle for La Follette to win the Republican presidential nomination in 1912. The Taft administration did everything it could to aid Philipp, including sending Vice-president James Sherman to Wisconsin in 1910 to address the "Stalwart Convention." Philipp, in turn, remained loyal to the Taft administration in its trials, even after it became obvious that Taft was going to suffer the worst electoral rebuke ever dealt a sitting president. Philipp also cultivated every defecting

---

[4] Margulies, *Decline of the Progressive Movement*, 92–107; Wyman, "Voting Behavior in the Progressive Era," 275–288; Stephenson, *Recollections of a Long Life*, 233–240; Maxwell, *La Follette and the Rise of the Progressives*, 177–180.

moderate progressive, stressing the antipathy they shared towards La Follette and McGovern, as well as common grievances about the legislation of 1911: fiscal extravagance, ideological radicalism, excessive state intervention, and the elitist attitude supposedly manifested by the La Follette and McGovern organizations towards other Republicans. Mixing these ingredients, Philipp hit upon the recipe for unseating the progressive Republicans in 1914.[5]

Further complicating the progressives' hold on office was the desertion of many "fair-minded Democrats" from the progressive coalition. The emergence of a substantial progressive movement within the state and national Democratic parties was making it possible for many Wisconsin Democrats to reconcile their ideological and partisan loyalties. The state Democratic party, for example, nominated progressives John A. Aylward and Adolph J. Schmitz for governor in the elections of 1906, 1908, and 1910, and, more importantly, the national party nominated Woodrow Wilson for president in 1912. True, many Democratic legislators helped to form the core of conservative opposition in the 1911 legislature. But others, most notably Paul Husting, emerged among the session's most consistent, outspoken, and effective advocates of progressive legislation. In 1912, though, they were divided ideologically. Wisconsin's Democrats united politically behind the progressive Wilson, on the national level, and the ultra-reactionary John C. Karel in the gubernatorial race. The party's platform compromised contortedly between the two positions. It pilloried McGovern for extravagance and the proliferation of undemocratic, expensive commissions, but it stopped short of calling for repeal of any major 1911 legislation. Unfortunately for progressive Republicans, most progressive Democrats voted for Schmidt over Karel in an intensely fought primary. That contest was almost equally unfortunate for Stalwarts because conservative Democrats declared for Karel. During the general election campaign, the two Democratic factions behaved according to a tacit compromise, agreeing to vote a straight party ticket that included both Wilson and Karel. La Follette himself emitted strong signals in favor of Wilson's candidacy, reinforcing the Democrats' compromise. La Follette was the most outspoken critic of the Taft administration and the prime mover in the effort to unseat him prior to Roosevelt's entry into the lists. La Follette bitterly attacked Roosevelt in his autobiography, and the editorial slant of *La Follette's Weekly Magazine* during the 1912 cam-

---

[5] Robert S. Maxwell, *Emanuel L. Philipp: Wisconsin Stalwart* (Madison, 1959), 58–59; Margulies, *Decline of the Progressive Movement*, 128–129; Wyman, "Voting Behavior in the Progressive Era," 292–301.

paign was plainly pro-Wilson. There was clearly little incentive for Democrats to cross party lines that year.[6]

Adding to progressive Republican woes was the almost total failure to loosen Social Democratic voters from their moorings. Both La Follette and McGovern had received appreciable Socialist support in previous campaigns, but the growing strength of the SDP and its stunning victory of 1910 in Milwaukee obviated the need for continuing support. Even after 1911, Victor Berger and other leaders of the SDP and Wisconsin State Federation of Labor continued to regard the progressive Republicans as false friends who wanted to steal the SDP constituency and frustrate the eventual triumph of socialism. For their part, McGovern and the other Milwaukee progressive Republicans had painstakingly crafted their own identity and organization. They welcomed Socialist legislative support and craved Socialists' votes, but only if the progressive Republicans remained in charge — a conviction reinforced by Berger's defeat of McGovern's ally Henry Cochems for Congress in 1910. Many Milwaukee progressive Republicans allied with Democrats and Stalwarts in a fusion movement designed to oust the Socialists, and they endorsed the nonpartisan local election law that facilitated this strategy. But McGovern resisted, largely because he feared fusion would dilute the party's position on the state and national levels. In the end, however, McGovern reluctantly signed the nonpartisan local election law on May 6, 1912. The Socialists regarded his capitulation as a virtual declaration of war against their party.[7]

With the Stalwarts absorbing so many moderate Republicans under Philipp's leadership, with most Democrats returning to the party fold, and with the Social Democrats maintaining their independence, the progressive Republicans were guaranteed to have been in serious trouble by 1912, even if the shaky alliance between La Follette and

---

[6] Margulies, *Decline of the Progressive Movement*, 136–138; Wyman, "Voting Behavior in the Progressive Era," 300–306; Robert M. La Follette, *La Follette's Autobiography: A Personal Narrative of Political Experiences* (Madison, 1913; reprinted, 1960), 204–321; David P. Thelen, *Robert M. La Follette and the Insurgent Spirit* (Boston, 1976), 6; Bernard A. Weisberger, *The La Follettes of Wisconsin: Love and Politics in Progressive America* (Madison, 1994), 143–144; *La Follette's Weekly Magazine*, June 29, July 20, July 27, October 26, 1912; Maxwell, *La Follette and the Rise of the Progressives*, 190.

[7] Margulies, *Decline of the Progressive Movement*, 109–157; Wyman, "Voting Behavior in the Progressive Era," 299–308; Sally M. Miller, *Victor Berger and the Promise of Constructive Socialism, 1910–1920* (Westport, Connecticut, 1973), 17–44, 69–86; Marvin Wachman, *History of the Social-Democratic Party of Milwaukee, 1897–1910* (Urbana, 1945), 67–76; Frederick I. Olson, "The Milwaukee Socialists, 1897–1941" (doctoral dissertation, Harvard University, 1952), 129–150; Bernard E. Fuller, "Voting Patterns in Milwaukee, 1896–1920: A Study with Special Emphasis on the Working Class of the City" (master's thesis, University of Wisconsin-Milwaukee, 1973), 83–143.

McGovern had held together. It was one of the most bizarre ironies in Wisconsin's unique political history, as historian Roger Wyman observes, that "the chief political harvest of the immense accomplishments of the 1911 legislature, a landmark of the entire progressive movement in the United States, was a net loss of political support."[8]

These developments soon paled into insignificance beside the destructive struggle between Robert M. La Follette and Francis E. McGovern. There can be no doubt that, by 1910 if not before, McGovern saw himself as La Follette's equal and his legitimate successor as leader of the Wisconsin progressive Republican movement. Only their general agreement on ideology, combined with their finely honed sense of political reality, restrained them from engaging in all-out combat, even before 1912. As early as the 1906 primary, when McGovern refused to back Lenroot in La Follette's scheme to unseat Davidson, La Follette instinctively agreed with Lenroot's assertion that "if the McGovern crowd try to make any trouble he would find that he isn't as big a man as he thinks when it gets down to a question between you and him." In 1908, McGovern virtually ignored La Follette's first presidential boom, while La Follette tried and failed to get McGovern to withdraw from the senatorial preference primary in favor of Hatton. McGovern's refusal resulted in a victory for Stephenson, who soon completed his drift back to the Stalwart camp.[9]

In 1910, despite the obvious advantages of a La Follette-McGovern alliance, the former attempted to persuade the latter to withdraw from the Republican gubernatorial primary in favor of Thomas Morris. Extended three-way negotiations ensued, and La Follette finally agreed to a ticket with McGovern for governor and Morris for lieutenant-governor. La Follette openly and honestly applauded McGovern's 1911 achievements, but McGovern's obvious efforts to build his own patronage organization, stressing progressive Republicans from the eastern part of the state, alarmed La Follette. A La Crosse Republican leader warned in 1911 that McGovern "is building up a little machine all his own. All the appointments he has made thus far have been made without consulting any of the leaders in this part of the state, and a fine new insurrection is well under way." McGovern campaigned almost exclusively for legislative candidates loyal to him in both 1910 and 1912—a tactic not apt to go unnoticed by La Follette, the man who had perfected the technique of calling the legislative roll. It was no secret that McGovern's ultimate ambition was to join

---

[8] Wyman, "Voting Behavior in the Progressive Era," 270–288.
[9] Maxwell, *Emanuel L. Philipp*, 101–115; Margulies, *Decline of the Progressive Movement*, 42–43; Herbert F. Margulies, *Senator Lenroot of Wisconsin: A Political Biography, 1900–1929* (Columbia, Missouri, 1977), 67–68; Ralph G. Plumb, *Badger Politics, 1836–1930* (Manitowoc, 1930), 155–164.

La Follette in the Senate, a prospect abhorrent to La Follette and anathema to most conservative Republicans. During the 1910 Republican primary campaign, Walter Goodland, editor of the progressive Racine *Times* and a supporter of William M. Lewis for the gubernatorial nomination, proclaimed that "those who are close to La Follette know that he does not have the highest opinion of the qualities of Mr. McGovern," whom La Follette and thousands of Wisconsin voters considered "self-centered, selfish and cares nothing for anything or anybody that stands in the way of his own personal ambitions." In January, 1911, regular Republican strategist William Anderson told President Taft, "McGovern is nearly as vain and ambitious as La Follette, though he is far from being as selfish; and I think they are sure to clash when a successor to Sen. Stephenson is to be chosen, if not before."[10]

The fragile La Follette-McGovern coalition did not survive the Senator's second bid for the presidency in 1912. He was backed by his newly formed National Progressive Republican League, and was the early front runner, carrying the banner of the congressional Insurgents and other party dissidents to deny Taft renomination. McGovern and his followers dutifully enlisted in the cause, even though few national observers gave La Follette much of a chance. Once Theodore Roosevelt entered the fray, La Follette's supporters deserted to him. In the dozen presidential preference primaries held in early 1912, Roosevelt received a substantial majority of the popular vote and convention delegates; La Follette won delegates only from North and South Dakota and Wisconsin. La Follette's precipitous slide was greatly accelerated by his "flunk" before a gathering of the Periodical Publishers' Association of America in Philadelphia on February 2, 1912. On the brink of exhaustion, worried about his daughter Mary, who faced tricky surgery the next day, and suffering from acute indigestion, La Follette foolishly tossed down a large shot of whiskey before embarking on a two-and-a-half-hour, convoluted speech that droned on until 1:30 in the morning. The speech deteriorated into a diatribe against newspapers for their collusion with big business and conservative politicians. Many in the audience left in protest; others heckled the speaker. Afterward, La Follette collapsed into his chair and buried his head in his hands, leaving the toastmaster, the publisher of the *New York World*, to apologize to the newspaper world for the "wicked, foolish and untruthful attack that has just been made upon it." Even his closest advisers in the audience could see that the Senator had self-destructed. On the back of his invitation, Congress-

---

[10] Margulies, *Decline of the Progressive Movement*, 115–119; Wyman, "Voting Behavior in the Progressive Era," 293–296; Racine *Times*, August 23, 1910; Margulies, *Senator Lenroot*, 67, 107, 135, 140–141.

man Henry Allen Cooper scribbled hasty notes of the disaster, concluding that "it ends him for the Presidency."[11]

Within a few short weeks, many of La Follette's remaining supporters joined the movement to Roosevelt. Amidst rumors that he was about to withdraw from the race, Lenroot and Wisconsin Secretary of State Walter Houser drafted a withdrawal statement, but La Follette refused to sign. La Follette doggedly hiked the campaign trail throughout the primary season, even though everyone but himself and a handful of associates knew that the Republican nomination would be a contest between Taft and Roosevelt. Francis McGovern clearly recognized the situation. His primary concern was his own re-election in 1912. He believed that he could retain office only by running on a united party ticket headed by a dynamic, effective progressive candidate for president; and he felt Teddy Roosevelt was the only man who met those qualifications.[12]

In early June, Roosevelt's representatives approached McGovern and offered to support him for the temporary chairmanship of the Republican convention later that month. In that job, McGovern would have a large say in deciding delegate disputes between Taft and Roosevelt. McGovern had gained progressive support by calling the regular candidate for chairman, New York Senator Elihu Root, a "standpat tory" whose election would guarantee Taft's renomination and Republican defeat in November. The Roosevelt people regarded McGovern as a distinguished progressive, and as a close ally of La Follette whose election would solidify a Roosevelt-La Follette coalition to stop Taft from winning a first ballot victory. McGovern, in turn, had already assured the former president of his support, though only if La Follette's chances were hopeless. That seemed to be the case. Around June 12, McGovern informed Roosevelt that he was available. When the convention opened on June 18, Taft delegates were in apparent control. McGovern's name was placed in nomination by a close friend, progressive wheelhorse Henry F. Cochems of Milwaukee, and seconded by a North Dakota delegate. At that moment, Walter Houser—La Follette's campaign manager and a Wisconsin delegate—stunned the Insurgents by taking the floor and

---

[11] Weisberger, *La Follettes of Wisconsin*, 132–141; Thelen, *La Follette and the Insurgent Spirit*, 90–92; La Follette, *Autobiography*, 256–261, 322–342; Maxwell, *La Follette and the Rise of the Progressives*, 182–184 (quote); Margulies, *Senator Lenroot*, 121–135; Albert Erlebacher, "Herman L. Ekern: The Quiet Progressive" (doctoral dissertation, University of Wisconsin, 1965), 194–197.

[12] Weisberger, *La Follettes of Wisconsin*, 139–142; Thelen, *La Follette and the Insurgent Spirit*, 261–284; La Follette, *Autobiography*, 261–284; Maxwell, *La Follette and the Rise of the Progressives*, 180–186; Herbert F. Margulies, "The Background of the La Follette-McGovern Schism," in *WMH*, 40 (Autumn, 1956), 21–29; Erlebacher, "Herman L. Ekern," 197–200.

Disintegration and Legacy 619

shouting that this arrangement had been made without La Follette's knowledge or consent. "We make no deals with Roosevelt," he concluded. "We make no deals with Taft. . . . Let no man think that Bob La Follette has traded. . . . We make no trades."[13]

Houser's outburst stopped the progressive revolt dead in its tracks and set in motion the events that would eventually elect Woodrow Wilson president. Taft was nominated on the first ballot, with 561 delegate votes to 107 for Roosevelt and 41 for La Follette. However, 344 Roosevelt delegates refused to participate. A few weeks later, most of them joined with other progressives to form the Progressive party as a vehicle for Roosevelt's presidential campaign and for one of the most advanced political agendas ever espoused by a mainstream party. With Taft and Roosevelt vying for the normal Republican vote, Wilson piled up 435 out of 531 electoral votes, even though he received just over 40 per cent of the popular vote.[14]

In Wisconsin, the La Follette-McGovern split was likewise disastrous, even though it took somewhat longer for the drama to unfold. McGovern received about an equal number of letters and telegrams praising as condemning his actions in Chicago, but La Follette's loyalists shunned him. McGovern countered by saying publicly that he believed he had acted in the best interest of the Wisconsin progressive movement, the Republican party, and La Follette's political future. He averred that his course was the only way the Wisconsin delegation could remain neutral; any other action would have doomed the progressive cause, left the regulars in complete control, and brought certain defeat in November. Many of the governor's closest advisers urged him to endorse Roosevelt openly and to seek re-election at the head of a Wisconsin Progressive party ticket. Others warned McGovern against this plan because it would alienate La Follette even more. McGovern maintained a noncommittal silence until late summer. Then he finally announced that he would support the "Progressive candidate for President and not the reactionary one."[15]

For his part, La Follette in his weekly magazine denounced Mc-

---

[13] Margulies, *Senator Lenroot*, 138–141; Margulies, *Decline of the Progressive Movement*, 108, 119–123; Maxwell, *La Follette and the Rise of the Progressives*, 187–188; Wyman, "Voting Behavior in the Progressive Era," 301–303.

[14] Maxwell, *La Follette and the Rise of the Progressives*, 190–191; Margulies, *Decline of the Progressive Movement*, 136–142; Margulies, *Senator Lenroot*, 140–143; Wyman, "Voting Behavior in the Progressive Era," 303; Victor Rosewater, *Back Stage in 1912: The Inside Story of the Split Republican Convention* (Philadelphia, 1932); John D. Buenker, "The Election of 1912," in John D. Buenker and Edward R. Kantowicz, eds., *Historical Dictionary of the Progressive Era, 1890–1920* (New York, 1988), 136–137.

[15] Margulies, *Decline of the Progressive Movement*, 120–121; Maxwell, *La Follette and the Rise of the Progressives*, 190; Wyman, "Voting Behavior in the Progressive Era," 303–305; Milwaukee *Journal*, September 3, 4, 5, 1912. See also Francis E. McGovern, *Nationalize the Wisconsin Idea: Statement of Governor Francis E. McGovern* (Chicago, 1912).

Govern as a turncoat who had "plunged bodily into the Roosevelt tar barrel," an act that " 'musses him up' shockingly as a Progressive Republican candidate for Governor of Wisconsin." He admitted a "deep and lasting resentment" towards McGovern for his actions at the convention, but reluctantly urged the governor's re-election as "a vote for the progressive movement." He also grudgingly acknowledged that McGovern's actions at the convention were outweighed by "his record in the Governor's office—a record of earnest and faithful co-operation with the legislature in carrying to fulfillment every pledge made in 1910." Realistically, La Follette had little choice. The alternatives were the reactionary Democrat John C. Karel or the Social Democrat Carl D. Thompson. An independent progressive candidacy was not an option because it would have guaranteed Karel's election.

La Follette pressured local progressive Republicans to choose between himself and McGovern. He pointedly renamed their grassroots organizations "La Follette Progressive Clubs" and strengthened his grip on the progressive Republican apparatus. According to McGovern loyalists, La Follette wanted to purge the party organization of those who might back McGovern's anticipated bid for the U.S. Senate in 1914. The Milwaukee *Free Press*, reflecting Isaac Stephenson's viewpoint, proclaimed that La Follette "cannot brook divided leadership" and that he had become "an embittered, raging and solitary figure, on a St. Helena of his own creation. . . ." As for his presidential preference, La Follette remained more sphinxlike than McGovern. He refused to express his choice publicly, but he published articles in *La Follette's Magazine* lauding Wilson and William Jennings Bryan for their progressive beliefs. One, by California Senator John D. Works, urged all true progressives to vote for Wilson. Publicly, La Follette warned Republican voters not to be fooled by the Progressive party's liberal facade and enjoined them: "Don't bolt."[16]

Whatever their actions, McGovern and La Follette did manage, for a while, to spare Wisconsin's Republican party the disaster that befell the party nationally, and to postpone the disintegration of the Wis-

---

[16] Margulies, *Decline of the Progressive Movement*, 120–121; Maxwell, *La Follette and the Rise of the Progressives*, 180–191; Wyman, "Voting Behavior in the Progressive Era," 304–306; Milwaukee *Free Press*, September 28, November 4, 1912; Milwaukee *Daily News*, September 19, 1912; Milwaukee *Evening Wisconsin*, September 27–28, 1912; Milwaukee *Sentinel*, November 3, 1912; Milwaukee *Journal*, September 28, 1912. See also the coverage and opinion pieces in *La Follette's Weekly Magazine* for August 31, September 28, October 5, 12, 19, 26, 1912, and La Follette to Rudolph Spreckels, August 21, 1912, and to Charles Crane, August 21, 1912, in B-107, La Follette Papers, Library of Congress, in which he explains why he backed McGovern in 1912 despite his actions at the convention.

consin progressive movement. The key to this short-lived success was the prevention of the creation of a state-level Progressive party with a full slate of candidates. Wisconsin Republican voters had to resolve the Taft-Roosevelt dilemma at the polls; the rest of the ballot presented no problems since it featured traditional Republican-Democrat-Socialist contests. In nearly every state where a full-fledged Progressive party slate emerged, the fissure at the top among Republican voters spread all the way to the bottom of the ballot, producing successful Democratic candidates at all levels. Wilson captured only 41 per cent of Wisconsin's presidential vote, besting Taft by 33,634 votes and Roosevelt by 101,782. The Social Democratic candidate, Eugene V. Debs, improved his percentage slightly, from 6.1 to 8.4, over 1908. Roosevelt's relatively poor showing was sweet revenge for La Follette, all the more so since McGovern's endorsement of Roosevelt appeared to carry less weight than La Follette's admonition against bolting the Republican party. Roosevelt's problems in Wisconsin were perhaps symbolized during his visit to Milwaukee on October 14, when he was struck by a would-be assassin's bullet. (Characteristically, he refused to allow the incident to deter him from making a scheduled speech.) In November, Woodrow Wilson became the first Democrat to carry Wisconsin in twenty years, and the last for another twenty.[17]

[2]

The McGovern ticket's campaign pitted Progressives against Stalwarts, head-to-head, with no separate Progressive party candidates to distract or confuse the voters. The entire statewide Republican ticket achieved election, despite the division between McGovern and La Follette loyalists. The principals on the ticket had sensibly agreed to campaign strictly on state-level issues and to remain silent on the presidential contest. On the stump, McGovern praised the 1911 legislature and pledged more of the same. He defended the income tax and effectively countered charges of extravagance with statistical evidence. Karel, he charged, was the candidate of Stalwart Republicans and reactionary Democrats, and he hammered hard on the theme of the public welfare versus special interests. Karel campaigned openly as an ardent foe of all things progressive, especially the state income tax and increased government spending for the service state.

[17] *Wisconsin Blue Book, 1913*, pp. 171–283; Wyman, "Voting Behavior in the Progressive Era," 304–308; Maxwell, *La Follette and the Rise of the Progressives*, 190–141; Milwaukee *Journal*, November 6–10, 1912; Stan Gores, "The Attempted Assassination of Teddy Roosevelt," in *WMH*, 53 (Summer, 1970), 269–277.

He charged that the progressive Republicans were guilty of "ruthless extravagance" and promised a substantial reduction in taxes and a complete house cleaning of state government.[18]

The Democratic attack on the income tax and related issues was led by the party's candidate for lieutenant-governor, Harry Bolens, a Port Washington manufacturer and publisher who had organized the campaign of the Wisconsin Manufacturers' Association against the tax in 1911. Bolens linked resentment against increased taxation to concerns about increased government expenditures, the proliferation of appointive commissions, and bureaucratic intrusion into personal finances. Speeches and editorials condemning the new system began in Rock County and spread to other parts of the state. As early as April, Lenroot had reported "very general opposition to the income tax." In June, Attorney General Levi Bancroft, the lone Stalwart holding state office, had charged that the tax drove away capital, fostered dishonesty, and degraded taxpayers. Bolens' case was bolstered in July when the Tax Commission's first assessments required most taxpayers to pay more than before. Karel pronounced the tax "obnoxious and inquisitorial" and "the most pernicious law that was ever put on the statute books of Wisconsin."[19]

Resentment against the income tax and higher government expenditures ran so high that progressive Republicans felt the need to defend and justify both. Governor McGovern, Nils Haugen, state Republican chairman and state senator George E. Scott, the *Wisconsin State Journal*, and the Superior *Telegram* all issued defenses of the income tax, emphasizing its advantages over the personal property tax and its equity. McGovern declared that opposition came primarily from vested interests bent upon preserving their tax shelters and upon destroying the reform structure enacted by the progressives over the past two decades. Others issued statistical defenses against the charges of extravagance. The *Wisconsin State Journal* argued that the Industrial Commission, for one, had actually reduced expenditures by eliminating the costs of litigation. In general, progressive Republicans presented the contest as yet another case of "the people versus the interests" and invoked the doctrines of social investment, the new individualism, and the need for government by commission.[20]

---

[18] *Wisconsin Blue Book, 1913*, pp. 584–585; Milwaukee *Journal*, July 8, August 15–17, November 6–10, 1912; Milwaukee *Daily News*, July 11, 1912; Wyman, "Voting Behavior in the Progressive Era," 303–304; Maxwell, *La Follette and the Rise of the Progressives*, 190–191; Margulies, *Decline of the Progressive Movement*, 136–142.

[19] Margulies, *Decline of the Progressive Movement*, 136–138; Milwaukee *Free Press*, June 17, October 30, 1912; Milwaukee *Sentinel*, July 4, October 26, 1912; Janesville *Gazette*, July 12, October 1, 10, 16, 1912; Racine *Times*, November 5, 1912.

[20] Margulies, *Decline of the Progressive Movement*, 139–142; Racine *Times*, October 23,

Unabashedly, many Stalwarts worked openly for Karel's election. To ensure Karel's nomination over Adolph Schmitz and the rest of the Democrats' progressive slate, some Stalwarts even voted in the Democratic primary. Styling themselves (as they often did) as "regular" Republicans, many Stalwarts sought to read McGovern out of the party for collaborating with Roosevelt. The Milwaukee *Sentinel* proclaimed that the governor's race lacked a "real Republican candidate" who could be trusted to "puncture this monstrous and sanctimonious humbug that has been sucking the veins of the taxpayers of Wisconsin, like a vampire for the last ten years." William Connor and other Stalwart leaders composed campaign literature for Karel, assaulting the income tax and the progressive machine. They courted the fiscally conservative German Republicans, focusing on the income tax. They lobbied hard for Karel among rural Republicans, who had formed the core of progressive support since 1894. Suspicious of the labor legislation of 1911, and distrustful of big government by commission, many farmers had come to regard the income tax as the last straw. They had previously supported the 1908 constitutional amendment and the 1911 statute, but many developed second thoughts after their first income tax bills arrived in 1912. The direct nature of the assessment made many farmers and workers painfully aware that they were being taxed on the fruits of their labor more than before. In the end, the taxation-extravagance argument proved relatively ineffective in 1912. Nevertheless, it had demonstrated its potential and became the strongest anti-progressive issue for 1914.[21]

Besieged on all sides, McGovern and the state Republican ticket managed a somewhat ambiguous victory. On the positive side, McGovern received almost 18,000 more votes than he had in 1910, an outcome that could be read as an endorsement of his record with the 1911 legislature. The Social Democratic gubernatorial votes, both from 1910 and from Debs's 1912 total, declined modestly, so McGovern's numbers suggested that the leftward strategy of the previous two years had borne some fruit. Moreover, McGovern's percentage of the total gubernatorial vote had remained about the same, while the hotly contested state campaign, combined with one of the most titanic presidential elections in the nation's history, had increased voter turnout by 35,000 over 1910. There was a negative side, how-

---

1912; *Wisconsin State Journal*, October 1, 2, 5, 13, 18–19, 22, 1912; Green Bay *Semi-Weekly Gazette*, October 26, 30, 1912; Superior *Telegram*, October 24, 1912; La Crosse *Tribune*, October 11, 21, 1912.

[21] Milwaukee *Sentinel*, October 12, 1912; Wyman, "Voting Behavior in the Progressive Era," 304–305; Maxwell, *La Follette and the Rise of the Progressives*, 190–191; Margulies, *Decline of the Progressive Movement*, 140–142; *Milwaukee Journal*, June 24, July 8, August 15–16, September 12, 17, 1912; Milwaukee *Evening Wisconsin*, October 26, 1912.

ever. McGovern's total vote was 14,000 less than that of Taft and Roosevelt combined, while Karel ran 3,000 votes ahead of Wilson—a sure sign of Republican defections in the gubernatorial race. More significantly, McGovern's plurality over his Democratic opponent shrank from over 51,000 in 1910 to just over 12,000 in 1912: the smallest Republican plurality since 1892 and the lowest GOP victory margin since 1881. A small group of La Follette supporters had "cut the head off the state ticket," and a significant number of Stalwarts had voted for Karel. But those crossovers were somewhat offset by several thousand Wilson backers who split their ballots for McGovern. Nearly all of the Roosevelt voters had cast a straight Republican ballot on the state level. Reflecting the bias and confusion of the time, *La Follette's Magazine* said that McGovern's reduced plurality was a "rebuke" for his flirtation with Roosevelt and the Bull Moose ticket, while the Milwaukee *Free Press* rejoiced that the incumbent governor had received the largest number of votes of any candidate in the 1912 election. The Milwaukee *Journal* acknowledged that McGovern was a "thoroughly Progressive" and "unusually efficient" governor, but said he had failed as a political leader. The paper noted the irony of his "extremely narrow re-election victory" since in 1911 it had seemed that he was "certain of winning any public office that he wished, excepting, of course, the seat of Senator La Follette himself."[22]

More ominous for the future of progressive reform were the results in the legislative elections. Wilson's coattails were long enough to have increased the Democrats' seats in the state assembly from twenty-nine to thirty-four, though factionalism between Karel's "tories" and the progressive wing weakened the contingent. The Republican bloc in the assembly rose by one to sixty members, almost evenly divided between La Follette and McGovern partisans. Democrats also captured eleven of the nineteen Milwaukee County seats, defeating such prominent progressive Republicans as Erich Stern and Charles Perry, and dealt a severe blow to Socialist candidates at the city, county, and state levels. Milwaukee's Social Democratic contingent, which had been instrumental in passing the historic 1911 progressive legislation, was reduced from twelve to five members. In short, the election undermined McGovern's Milwaukee support in the assembly. In the senate, twenty-five Republicans were opposed by only seven Democrats and one Socialist; but the Republican ranks

---

[22] *Wisconsin Blue Book, 1913*, pp. 214, 260; Milwaukee *Journal*, November 6 (quotes), 7–10, 1912, January 10, 1913; Maxwell, *La Follette and the Rise of the Progressives*, 191; Margulies, *Decline of the Progressive Movement*, 142; Wyman, "Voting Behavior in the Progressive Era," 305–308; *La Follette's Weekly Magazine*, November 15, 1912; Milwaukee *Free Press*, November 18, 1912.

were loaded with La Follette men, a situation that would bedevil McGovern throughout a stormy 1913 session.[23]

The uneasy La Follette-McGovern truce imploded almost as soon as the returns were declared official. The catalyst was La Follette lieutenant Herman Ekern, whom McGovern had appointed state insurance commissioner. As the Republican caucus approached in early January, McGovern forces lobbied for him to select Merlin Hull of Black River Falls, a staunch advocate of co-operative marketing and state aids to marginal farmers, as assembly speaker. Acting independently, Ekern sent letters to various assemblymen and newspaper editors endorsing his ally Lewis L. Johnson of Door County, who wanted to strengthen the state's fire insurance laws. He also rented an office in Madison to serve as Johnson's campaign headquarters. Incensed, McGovern and Tax Commissioner Nils Haugen decided to replace Ekern with the Insurance Commission's actuary: fellow Norwegian Lewis A. Anderson of Madison. Since McGovern's power to remove executive officers like Ekern expired at noon on January 8, he quickly scheduled a hearing to decide his fate. Five minutes before the hearing was to begin on January 6, the governor's office served Ekern with a complaint based upon charges by McGovern's executive clerk Harry C. Wilbur, who accused Ekern of "official misconduct, neglect of duty," and violating the conditions of his appointive office by electioneering for Johnson.[24]

A tense hearing ensued during which McGovern refused to allow Ekern's attorneys to cross-examine witnesses, so they filed written objections to the entire proceeding. Ekern admitted that he had campaigned for Johnson—just as he had for La Follette and the entire state ticket during the recent election—and he warned the governor that "we have in this state a law prohibiting the proposition that a candidate for public office may be coerced into compliance with the executive will, under penalty of forfeiture of high official station by his friends." To no one's surprise, Ekern was dismissed. The state's leading politicians reacted to his dismissal largely along factional and partisan lines, while most observers agreed the contretemps was a continuation of the La Follette-McGovern feud of 1912. Everyone predicted that the schism would only grow wider and more intense,

---

[23] *Wisconsin Blue Book, 1913*, pp. 638–690; Milwaukee *Journal*, September 3–5, November 7–10, 1913. For an analysis of why Polish-Americans, despite their enthusiasm for progressive Republican programs, continued to vote Democratic or Socialist, see Michael Kruzka to McGovern, December 30, 1912, box 9, McGovern Papers.

[24] Erlebacher, "Herman L. Ekern," 201–202; Milwaukee *Journal*, January 3, 8, 1913; Maxwell, *La Follette and the Rise of the Progressives*, 191.

and that the two men "are certain to engage in a life and death struggle."[25]

La Follette used the pages of his magazine to denounce Ekern's firing, linking it to the same sinister forces that he claimed were behind Roosevelt's candidacy and the formation of the Progressive party. He saw a connection through George W. Perkins, a partner of J. Pierpont Morgan, a director of both U.S. Steel and International Harvester, and one of the prime movers behind Roosevelt. Since Ekern had established himself as a scourge of the "insurance trust," La Follette reasoned, his removal from office was a high-priority item for Perkins and his Wall Street cronies, a plot in which McGovern knowingly or unknowingly participated.[26]

McGovern then appointed Lewis Anderson as insurance commissioner, with Anderson accepting on the assumption that the office was vacant. However, Ekern informed Anderson that his appointment was only "pretended" and asked him to turn it down. Anderson accepted anyway, and Ekern suspended him for five days, vowing a fight in court. On January 21, Anderson and William L. Essmann, the superintendent of the capitol, went to Ekern's office to ask him to turn over department records and vacate the premises. Ekern refused and barricaded himself in his office. Essmann fetched five policemen, who broke the glass on Ekern's office door but were still unable to gain entry. At that point, one of Ekern's attorneys appeared bearing a temporary injunction prohibiting any interference with Ekern as commissioner, and Ekern appealed to the state supreme court. On January 29, La Follette supporters in the senate succeeded in passing a resolution for an investigation.[27]

During the subsequent tense and angry hearing, Wilbur reiterated his charges, while Ekern submitted a lengthy deposition detailing his relationship to Johnson's speakership campaign. In the deposition, Ekern also claimed that McGovern had been "rather curt and noncommittal" when Ekern had attempted to discuss proposed insurance legislation with him. Ultimately Ekern prevailed. The committee's final report exonerated him, nullified McGovern's dismissal, refused to consent to Anderson's appointment, and recommended future legislation. On May 30, the state supreme court, in a split decision, concurred with the senate's findings, 5–2. The majority opinion, written by Roujet D. Marshall, declared that McGovern had denied Ekern due process and the opportunity to prepare a defense. It also ruled that Ekern's involvement in the speakership contest had

---

[25] Erlebacher, "Herman L. Ekern," 202–203 (quote); Milwaukee *Journal*, January 8–10, 13 (quote), 1913; Milwaukee *Evening Wisconsin*, January 18, 1913.
[26] Milwaukee *Journal*, January 17, 1913.
[27] *Ibid.*, January 21–24, 1913; Erlebacher, "Herman L. Ekern," 205–208.

not violated the provisions of the statute under which he was appointed because that restriction only applied to regular political campaigns. (The two dissenters argued that removal of an administrative official from office was an executive power, and that the majority opinion prevented the governor from carrying out his constitutional and statutory duties.) The state was ordered to pay Ekern's legal fees of $2,000 on the grounds that he had been protecting his legitimate prerogatives. Afterward, in a particularly petty act of reprisal, Ekern's father was fired from his job as a capitol janitor.[28]

Ekern's victory ("a hollow one," according to his biographer) did little to end the acrimony, or to heal the La Follette-McGovern split. In May, McGovern legislators fiercely attacked a package of fire insurance bills prepared by Ekern's office. In the senate, lawmakers who favored the measures and were led by a La Follette ally, eked out a victory over McGovern. In the assembly, however, a coalition of McGovernites, Stalwarts, and Democrats sent the bills down to defeat. The same combination also frustrated efforts to consolidate the offices of insurance commissioner and state fire marshal. The senate passed the bill 21–9 on May 14, but it died in the assembly the previous day. Efforts to revive it proved unavailing and quickly became entangled with McGovern's proposal to appoint Clement P. Host of Milwaukee as state fire marshal. For a moment, on May 14, it seemed that Host's appointment had been confirmed in the senate by a single vote, only to have Lieutenant-governor Thomas Morris, another La Follette progressive, overturn the final tally by ruling from the chair that the vote of Willard T. Stevens of Rhinelander had erroneously been recorded in the affirmative. Continuing their guerila warfare over the insurance commissioner's office, the two factions clashed on May 23 over a bill to make the office elective again. On July 5, the La Follette forces continued the assault on McGovern's removal power by enacting a bill requiring senate approval for removals.[29]

There was also a fight over concurrence in Thomas Mahon's appointment to the Industrial Commission as a replacement for John R. Commons, who had resigned to become a member of the U.S. Commission on Industrial Relations. (Mahon, from Shawano County, was McGovern's floor leader in the assembly.) To frustrate McGovern and Mahon, pro-La Follette legislators backed Lewis L. Johnson,

---

[28] Erlebacher, "Herman L. Ekern," 205–208 (quote); Milwaukee *Journal*, February 5–7, May 30–31, 1913.

[29] Erlebacher, "Herman L. Ekern," 208–209; Milwaukee *Journal*, May 7, 14–15, 18, 20–21, 31, June 3, 5, 30, August 8–9, 1913; Wyman, "Voting Behavior in the Progressive Era," 308; *Wisconsin State Journal*, May 21, 1913; Green Bay *Gazette*, May 21, 22, 1913; *Wisconsin Assembly Journal*, 1913, pp. 949–950, 968–969, 1047, 1088–1109, 1112–1114, 1155–1168, 1212–1213.

whose candidacy for speaker had precipitated the Ekern-McGovern feud. Several legislators threatened to force a special session to deal with the governor over the appointment. An ensuing stalemate forced the governor to withdraw Mahon's name in favor of Fred M. Wilcox of Appleton, who was not closely identified with either faction. He was confirmed and served on the commission until 1934.[30]

The La Follette-McGovern feud escalated throughout the 1913 session. So many invitations to gubernatorial functions were returned marked "decline with regrets" by La Follette supporters that McGovern suspected an organized boycott. Asked by a reporter if he had been consulted by La Follette about a certain federal appointment, McGovern retorted that he had "no influence or communication with La Follette." One of the major blowups occurred in early May, when the governor refused to attend a major party rally in Madison on May 14, organized by Madison banker Sol Levitan, a solid La Follette backer who later became state treasurer. McGovern announced that he had not been properly invited and that since the gathering would be more of a "factional rally" than a party function, Levitan and his associates "would have to play the political game they were in without me." Levitan responded that McGovern "got his fingers in the tar" during the last election and that real Republicans "wanted to see if he had gotten the tar off." Neither the governor nor many of his supporters attended the rally, where Lieutenant-governor Morris proclaimed La Follette the only leader of the progressive Republicans and Congressman James Frear praised the Senator and the Wisconsin Idea as "the hope of the nation."[31]

Another public flare-up between the La Follette and McGovern camps occurred less than two weeks later, when McGovern vetoed a bill requiring another referendum on woman suffrage in 1914. In his veto message, the governor argued that not enough time had elapsed since the earlier referendum for enough voters to have changed their minds, and that woman suffrage, once adopted, would be difficult to rescind if the experiment proved unsuccessful. McGovern's floor leaders in the assembly and senate, Thomas J. Mahon and Edward F. Kileen, voted against the measure, even though both had voted for woman suffrage in 1912. The margins of 17–15 in the senate and 47–26 in the assembly were deemed too narrow to sustain a possible override of his veto, especially in the upper house. McGovern ignored a last-minute directive from Theodore Roosevelt, sent through *Wis-*

---

[30] Milwaukee *Journal*, July 30, August 8–9, 1913; "News Worth Remembering," *La Follette's Weekly Magazine*, August 16, 1913, p. 11.

[31] Milwaukee *Journal*, May 7–10, 16, 1913; "News Worth Remembering," *La Follette's Weekly Magazine*, May 24, 1913, p. 10; Albert W. Sanborn to McGovern, May 6, 1913, McGovern Papers.

consin State Journal editor Richard Lloyd Jones, calling upon all progressive lawmakers to vote for the referendum bill. La Follette dismissed McGovern's reasoning as "trivial," and called upon the legislature to override the veto instead of waiting for another two years.[32]

A third McGovern-La Follette eruption occurred during a Progressive Club banquet in Milwaukee on June 6. The chief instigators were McGovern allies Medill McCormick and Henry Cochems, both of whom made fiery anti-La Follette speeches. McCormick, scion of the Chicago *Tribune* family and later a congressman and senator from Illinois, delivered the major address in which he accused the Wisconsin senator of sacrificing principle to personal ambition and of misrepresenting many of the facts of the 1912 election in his autobiography. Cochems, who was especially popular among German voters, echoed McCormick and added an indictment on the grounds of "perfidy." Outraged, La Follette coldly responded, "I will pay no more attention to Medill McCormick than I would pay to a cur in the street."[33]

Coming on the heels of the supreme court's decision in the Ekern case, both the woman suffrage veto and the June 6 attack on La Follette unleashed a barrage of editorial flak at McGovern. The *Wisconsin State Journal* charged that the governor "proposes to make Wisconsin his by killing the tried and true La Follette kind of Progressivism and substituting therefor the Rooseveltian kind. . . ." The Fond du Lac *Reporter*, a Stalwart paper, denounced the governor as a "man of disappointed hopes" who had received "many hard knocks during the past several months." After completing a tour of the state in early June, the Milwaukee *Journal*'s Madison correspondent reported a "strong feeling against Governor McGovern—a determination, in fact, not to support him for any office in the future." He also detected a "cordial feeling and understanding between Tory Democrats and Tory Republicans, casting doubt on the future for progressive Republicans."[34]

Factional strife among progressive Republicans also manifested itself in efforts on the La Follette side to adjourn the session or to

---

[32] Milwaukee *Journal*, May 7, 13, June 7, 1913; Green Bay *Gazette*, May 28, 1913; Waupaca *Republican Post*, June 5, 1913; Robert M. La Follette, "Suffrage Veto," *La Follette's Weekly Magazine*, June 7, 1913, p. 1. McGovern's veto of suffrage drew criticism from Lincoln Steffens, Theodora Youmans, and Emaline Pankhurst of England. See *Wisconsin State Journal*, November 5, 9, 13, 1913.

[33] Milwaukee *Journal*, June 7, 1913. For a relatively objective view of the McGovern-La Follette split see Nell R. (Mrs. John R.) Commons to La Follette, February 18, May 30, June 7, 1913, in B-73, La Follette Papers, Library of Congress.

[34] William T. Evjue, *A Fighting Editor* (Madison, 1968), 204 (quote); Milwaukee *Journal*, 6–7, 1913; Fond du Lac *Reporter*, June 11, 1913; Green Bay *Gazette*, May 31, 1913.

recess until January, 1914, a date which would have stymied McGovern's chance to achieve an impressive legislative record in 1913, and would have impeded a campaign for the U.S. Senate in 1914. The adjournment and recess question were intertwined with a Republican bill to reorganize the legislature by reducing the number of committees from forty to eleven, and to shorten sessions by establishing a joint committee on revision to review all bills prior to their formal introduction. The assembly defeated the bill finally on May 28, 44–36. Then the senate passed a recess resolution on the same day, and McGovern retorted with a blistering message to the legislature denouncing the idea. "Your predecessors . . . never subordinated the duty of enacting important legislation to the allurements of fishing, farming or factional politics; and you should not think of setting the example now," he said. "That this resolution was introduced . . . after much secret conference but without open consultation reveals something as to the motives back of it." He also criticized the legislature for failing to pass several important measures and charged it to remain in session until it completed this work. A few days later, the assembly defeated the recess resolution, 57–26, with co-operation between most Democrats and McGovern Republicans. It also set June 28 as the adjournment date, and June 13 as the last day to introduce new business. Angered, Senator George Scott drafted a resolution, which passed 22–8, blasting McGovern for interference in the assembly vote and defending the legislature's productivity. Scott also argued that several important measures required more deliberation than was possible, unless the session lasted into the late summer. Despite this resolution, the McGovern administration managed to keep the legislature in session until August 9.[35]

By the time the 1913 legislature finally adjourned, the session had lasted 214 days, surpassing by twenty-five days the previous record—the so-called Long Parliament of 1907. The legislators had long since exhausted the limits of their $500 salaries, and had to draw on their private resources. (A move the following year to increase legislators' salaries to $600 and add travel expenses was defeated in a 1914 referendum, a victim of public reaction against extravagance and "big government.")[36]

To keep the pot boiling, Democratic legislators maneuvered to play McGovernites against La Follette supporters, partly because that was the only strategy on which they could agree. The assembly Democrats

---

[35] Milwaukee *Journal*, January 8, May 30, 1913; Maxwell, *La Follette and the Rise of the Progressives*, 192; Green Bay *Gazette*, May 24, 1913; Fond du Lac *Commonwealth*, May 28–29, June 4, 1913 (quote); *Wisconsin Assembly Journal*, 1913, pp. 1234–1238, 1257–1258.

[36] *Wisconsin Blue Book, 1915*, p. 319; Milwaukee *Journal*, August 9–10, 1913.

divided into two factions in their pre-session caucus in a dispute over seating the Milwaukee delegation, whose members had been elected in anti-Socialist fusion campaigns. On the recommendation of its credentials committee, the Democratic caucus voted 15–9 to unseat the Milwaukee assemblymen, and elected progressive Edward J. Kneen of La Crosse as its candidate for speaker, with Charles F. Viebahn of Watertown as caucus chair. Throughout the session, the Democrats remained divided into "Tory" and "Progressive" camps, but they voted together whenever the outcome would push the two progressive Republican factions farther down the path to mutual destruction. On May 30, the Milwaukee *Journal* observed that "passage or failure of legislation this session is more largely the work of the Democratic minority than in any previous session." Democrats had "swung first to one side and then to the other, defeating measures to which they have objected, practically at will."[37]

Outside the legislature, conflict festered between conservative and progressive Democrats. The Wilson administration had inadvertently weakened the progressive cause by appointing its most effective leaders to positions in Washington. By late May, according to the Milwaukee *Journal*, conservative Democrats were already plotting their strategy for wresting the party's gubernatorial nomination away from the "Wilson men," because the "all-Progressive distribution of plums has not made them any happier." Summing up the role of the Democratic minority at the end of the session, the *Journal* concluded that Democrats had "contributed to the failure of the two Republican factions to win decisive victories." On the one hand, Democrats had voted with McGovernites to defeat the recess resolution, and a package of insurance bills; on the other, they had voted with the La Follette camp to defeat McGovern bills to establish a marketing commission and to reorganize the legislature, and also had voted with it to enact mothers' pension and court administration measures. Since Paul Husting, a progressive Democratic senator, was expected to run against McGovern for the U.S. Senate in 1914, progressive Democrats had an ulterior motive in keeping the governor's record of legislative achievement minimal. Right-wing Democrats, of course, took pleasure in tormenting both McGovern and La Follette.[38]

With both major parties suffering from factionalism and both keeping their eyes on the 1914 elections, it was hardly surprising that the 1913 legislature fell significantly short of its immediate predecessors in passing progressive legislation. Still, it was a sorry outcome, con-

---

[37] Milwaukee *Journal*, May 22, 30, August 10, 1913; McCarthy to Louis Brandeis, January 21, 1913, and to Frank Walsh, March 6, 1914, McCarthy Papers.
[38] Milwaukee *Journal*, May 22, 30, August 10, 1913; McCarthy to Frank Walsh, March 6, 1914, and to Joseph Davies, January 7, 1914, McCarthy Papers.

sidering that all three major party platforms had pledged to expand upon the achievements of the previous decade. The Republican platform congratulated Wisconsin for pioneering "the great onward movement," which it attributed to "the leadership of our foremost public man, Senator Robert M. LaFollette." However, it also proclaimed that "no greater progress has ever been made in any commonwealth in the same time than during the administration of Governor Francis E. McGovern. . . ." The party promised, among other things, to enact measures to improve rural education, defend the income tax against reactionary special interests, strengthen the Industrial Commission, give state financial aid to "mothers duly adjudged worthy by competent courts," and to work for the abolition of contract prison labor. Portentously, the platform made no reference to the agricultural marketing bill and other state aids to marginal farmers that were to be among the chief goals of the McGovern administration.[39]

The Democratic platform denounced the "reckless and unjustifiable expenditure of public moneys" by the Republican administration and endorsed the establishment of a state budget system. It condemned the state income tax and demanded that it be submitted to a popular referendum in April, 1913; but it urged adoption of the federal income tax proposed by the Wilson administration.

The Social Democrats advocated home rule for cities, municipal ownership of public utilities and all natural resources, judicial recall, woman suffrage, and the abolition of prostitution. In addition to proposing an industrial program to expand upon the legislation of 1911, the Socialists also pledged to enact a broad agricultural program. They condemned the "hypocrisy" of the main political parties "who still pretend that they differ in principle," and they stood for "every radical change that will bring more wealth, more culture and more security to the masses of the people," even though they considered such measures "mere palliatives, capable of being carried out even under the present conditions."[40]

If anything, McGovern's message to the legislature of January 9, 1913, was more ambitiously progressive than any of the party platforms. He lavishly praised the accomplishments of the 1911 legislature, and he enjoined the 1913 legislature to "strengthen and perfect by amendment the principal measures enacted two years ago wherever experience may have shown that improvement is possible." Along those lines he proposed minor adjustments in the workmen's compensation and Industrial Commission statutes. Then the governor asked for a minimum wage law for women, compensation for

[39] *Wisconsin Blue Book, 1913*, pp. 571–575.
[40] *Ibid.*, 584–585, 600–604.

those stricken with industrial diseases, and abolition of prison contract labor. He defended the implementation of the state income tax and speculated on the eventual abolition of the personal property tax. He proposed some adjustments in the statutes providing for state aid in highway and bridge construction and maintenance. In brief, matter-of-fact references, McGovern asked for a "blue sky law" to protect stock market investors; the adoption of the initiative, referendum, and recall amendments to the state constitution first approved by the 1911 legislature; the establishment of county school boards for rural districts; and additional appropriations for the new continuation schools. He endorsed the work of the special committee investigating the fire insurance industry, defended the role of the state university in setting standards for public schools, and advocated an "anti-price discrimination" statute similar to those in Iowa, Massachusetts, the Dakotas, and elsewhere. Turning to governmental efficiency and economy, the governor outlined a system for comprehensive accounting and budgeting, and recommended making the State Board of Public Affairs a permanent body.[41]

McGovern's major goals for 1913 lay in conserving the state's natural resources and providing state aid to less affluent farmers. In particular, he called for the "regulation of water powers" to replace the measure invalidated by the state supreme court, and he proposed a permanent fund to finance reforestation. He also urged higher state taxation of mineral deposits, the destruction of noxious weeds, the reclamation of wetlands, and the prevention of soil erosion. He put particular emphasis on his conviction that "so far as hydraulic energy is required for public purposes the state should reserve the right to compel the maximum development of the water powers for which franchises are granted."

Turning to agriculture, McGovern boldly proposed that state government and the university should co-operate in a comprehensive program to aid settlers in the Cutover, from the selection of land and the credit with which to purchase it right down to improved roads. Even more ambitious was his proposal to create a marketing commission that would facilitate and supervise the formation and operation of agricultural marketing co-operatives. He also recommended co-operative agricultural credit associations and similar agencies that would be empowered to lend money to farmers. Taken altogether, these recommendations amounted virtually to the creation of an agricultural service state, similar to that established for industrial workers in 1911.[42]

[41] Francis E. McGovern, *Governor's Message*, doc. 1, pp. 3–15, 22–28, 32–38, 44–51, in *Wisconsin Public Documents*, 1911–1912, vol 1.
[42] *Ibid.*, 15–21, 28–32, 38–43.

In a conclusion designed to motivate the legislature to even greater heights of reform, McGovern said that Wisconsin had never been more prosperous nor more revered for its progressive leadership. The secret of that exalted status, he said, was not "the result of chance or magic" but rather the product of "three relatively simple things: popular rule, scientific methods of legislation, and centralized administration." These three "harmonize the divergent political philosophies of Hamilton and Jefferson, rejecting the error in each, and holding fast to that which is good in both." Thanks largely to Wisconsin's leadership, he concluded, "everywhere special privilege and boss control are going the way of despotism in China and tyranny in the Balkan peninsula."[43]

Rhetoric aside, in practice the La Follette-McGovern feud confounded the entire 1913 session, as La Follette loyalists consistently undermined the governor's legislative agenda, to the point of seeking to block or weaken legislation with which they were in basic agreement. Senator George E. Scott, a prominent La Follette supporter from Prairie Farm (Dunn County), confided to McCarthy that he would continue to support progressive legislation only when it emanated "from a source that is not objectionable to a majority of the men who have fought the hard fights for right legislation in Wisconsin." Alarmed by such blatant admissions, and angered by what he interpreted as corroborating evidence in legislative voting patterns, Charles McCarthy wrote La Follette a reproving letter on April 25 in which he maintained that La Follette's name was being used "by little and ambitious men to foment a war between factions in this state which nobody can profit by except the force of evil in the long run." Putting the matter as bluntly as possible, he said that certain legislators were prepared to vote down good bills "in order that he [McGovern] may not gain in any way by the passage of such legislation." When La Follette did not reply, McCarthy wrote again on May 5, stating that several men were out to emasculate the Board of Public Affairs and that they were "masquerading under your name but . . . are not really friendly to you or to the things which you represent." In both letters, he urged La Follette to intervene.[44]

La Follette finally replied on May 31, pleading that his work in the Senate made it difficult to keep up on legislative details in Wisconsin. He admitted that occasional efforts misrepresented his "attitude" on legislation, but denied that he had ever "attempted to run the affairs of Wisconsin from Washington." He added that, during a recent visit to Madison, he had found the "same earnestness and enthusiasm for

---

[43] *Ibid.*, 51–53.
[44] George E. Scott to McCarthy, August 7, 1914, McCarthy to La Follette, April 25, May 5, 1913, McCarthy Papers; Fitzpatrick, *McCarthy of Wisconsin*, 114.

advanced constructive work which prevailed in the old days when I was in the executive office." He also flatly refuted any notion that his friends in either house would be influenced in their attitude towards legislation and chastised McCarthy for assuming that McGovern's judgment on any piece of legislation was superior to that of the legislature. He closed by reaffirming his faith in the men "upon whom I have always relied upon for counsel," a cohort that obviously did not include McCarthy.

Exasperated, McCarthy responded that La Follette did not understand the real situation in Madison and that "I see that you absolutely misunderstand me and that you give me very little credit for the hard work and toil of this session." Angrily, he declared that the progressive cause was more important than factional politics or personal conflicts.[45]

That spring, McCarthy complained to the editor of the *Review of Reviews* that "no important legislation of any consequence has passed the legislature yet, and we can not tell till about the 15th of June exactly where we are." McCarthy said there were at least ten different parties in the assembly, and that the situation was exacerbated greatly by "the personal row between La Follette and McGovern," which permitted "a bunch of reactionaries" to play off the factions one against another, thus preventing the enactment of progressive legislation. McGovern, too, was upset. He confided in June to a young supporter that all of his present troubles were due to his Bull Moose declaration of the previous fall and that "my progressive friends must have patience until the battle is fought out to the end." Like McCarthy, the governor said that La Follette "has assumed the role of dictator here; and until the question of whether we are political serfs or free men is finally settled here in Wisconsin, no other issue can receive much consideration."[46]

Compounding McGovern's problems was an unexpected rise in state expenditures during 1913. The chief culprit, ironically, was a favorable response for state aid provided by the highway legislation of 1911. The legislature had only budgeted $350,000; the requests from local highway commissions reached $800,000 by early summer. Anticipating even greater demands, the legislature appropriated an additional $450,000 to cover 1913 and budgeted $1,200,000 annually for future years. While the public's enthusiasm for roads validated the wisdom of the good roads program, its high cost added to the

---

[45] La Follette to McCarthy, May 31, 1913, McCarthy to La Follette, June 6–7, 1913, McCarthy Papers; Albert O. Barton to La Follette, February 18, 1913, in B-73, La Follette Papers, Library of Congress.

[46] McCarthy to W. B. Shaw, May 26, 1913, McCarthy to Roosevelt, March 18, 1913, McCarthy Papers; Maxwell, *La Follette and the Rise of the Progressives*, 191–192 (quote).

growing chorus that accused the administration, and progressive reform in general, with extravagance. To make matters worse, the university's appropriation rose from $1,500,000 in 1911–1912 to $2,000,000 for 1913–1914, a figure nearly seven times larger than the university's cost during La Follette's first term. In addition, new buildings on the Madison campus, at several normal schools, and at the state's charitable and penal institutions, also cost a good deal. Finally, the adoption of a new budget system recommended by the Board of Public Affairs resulted in omnibus appropriation bills submitted late in the session, thereby hampering the governor's veto authority. Faced with such fiscal pressures, McGovern reluctantly announced a $1,500,000 general purpose tax levy at the end of October. To the average citizen, this indeed must have seemed like extravagance.[47]

[3]

In spite of factionalism and reaction, the 1913 legislature managed to cobble together a modest record of progressive achievements. For one, it succeeded in advancing to the next level the ten constitutional amendments proposed by the 1911 legislature, making them eligible for popular referendum in 1914. Except for two amendments intended to expand the state's role in providing insurance to its citizens, the remainder dealt with further alterations in politics and government: initiative, referendum, and recall; simplified procedures for amending the state constitution; the reorganization of circuit courts; an increase in legislative compensation; urban charter reform; and clarifications in procedures for acquiring private property by eminent domain. The course of the resolution ratifying the proposed Seventeenth Amendment to the Constitution, mandating the direct election of U.S. senators, was relatively smooth. La Follette had done much to popularize this measure, which resonated strongly with Wisconsinites because of the machinations surrounding the election of Isaac Stephenson that year. It was also of great importance to McGovern, who preferred to trust his chances for election to the Senate in 1914 to the electorate, as opposed to the legislature. The ratification resolution sailed through the Wisconsin senate 28–0 on February 13 and through the assembly 89–1 just five days later.[48]

---

[47] Margulies, *Decline of the Progressive Movement*, 142–143; Milwaukee *Journal*, July 30, August 6, 8, 1913. For McGovern's explanation of the appropriations bills, see Francis E. McGovern, *Francis E. McGovern On Campaign Issues, 1914* (Milwaukee, 1914), 21–32.

[48] Milwaukee *Journal*, January 15–16, February 13–14, 18–19, May 5, 7, 14, 16, 22, June 3, 6, 27, July 1, 31, August 1, 1913; *Wisconsin Statutes*, 1913, pp. 30–33; *Senate Miscellaneous Documents*, 71 Cong., 3 sess., no. 240 (serial 9346), *Ratification of the*

The legislature also made some significant adjustments to the landmark labor legislation of 1911. The vast majority of businesses had chosen not to participate in workmen's compensation, since the act had allowed employers to retain the common law defense of "worker's contributory negligence" and required that they file an explicit affidavit of participation in the system. Consequently, the 1913 legislature abolished the contributory negligence defense and reversed the logic of the original law by stating that employers were automatically included in the system unless they filed an affidavit to the contrary. As a result, the number of cases adjudicated under workmen's compensation rose from 846 in 1912 to 8,496 in 1914, while the amount of the awards increased from $60,000 to $851,000. By 1914, the system was covering an estimated 90 per cent of all industrial accidents in the state. To high acclaim, the legislature also placed all women workers under the protection of the Industrial Commission, which was authorized to formulate and enforce a code of maximum hours and minimum wages that would ensure their health, safety, and welfare. And it prohibited anyone from employing female workers more than ten hours a day or fifty-five hours a week, or more than eight hours per night in a forty-eight-hour week. Visiting Madison that October, the muckraking journalist Ida M. Tarbell said Wisconsin was considered in the East as "the Germany of the United States, in the sense that it has blazed the trail for many of the labor laws which are now being taken up nationally." The 1913 legislature also managed to agree on changes in the employment of convict labor, all of which aimed at compensating prisoners for working in prison industries or on public roadways, or for continued good behavior behind bars, provided that the inmate not attempt to escape or violate discipline.[49]

On the other hand, a number of labor bills fell victim to the 1913 infighting. One of these was a McCarthy-inspired plan for "compulsory sickness insurance," similar to a German scheme adopted during the late nineteenth century. McCarthy wanted to link sickness insurance to workmen's compensation, on humanitarian, economic, and social efficiency grounds. Many progressives remained skeptical, and when the legislature finally agreed to appoint a study committee, McGovern vetoed the necessary appropriation, forcing McCarthy to scramble for funds and information. In the end, the movement for sickness insurance proceeded no further, falling victim to the general

---

Constitution and Amendments by the States (1931), 12–13; *Wisconsin Assembly Journal,* 1913, p. 194; *Wisconsin Senate Journal,* 1913, p. 194.

[49] *Wisconsin Statues,* 1913, pp. 1234–1247, 1617–1637, 2191–2197; Maxwell, *La Follette and the Rise of the Progressives,* 158; Milwaukee *Journal,* October 27, 1913 (quote); *Wisconsin Assembly Journal,* 1913, pp. 926–929, 1114–1115, 1186–1186.

reaction against progressivism. Similarly, a measure mandating one day's rest in seven for industrial workers passed the lower house on June 6, but only after a stormy debate concerning its impact on manufacturers. It later died in the senate. Efforts to establish a minimum wage for teachers also encountered opposition in both houses, and McGovern vetoed a compromise act.[50]

Turning to social welfare, the 1913 legislature placed Wisconsin in the vanguard of states that enacted so-called "mothers' pension laws," which provided financial support to widows caring for dependent children. A broad-based coalition, including women's organizations, labor unions, moral reformers, settlement house residents, and most progressive organizations and politicians, supported mothers' pension laws, which had been boosted in 1909 by a White House conference called by President Roosevelt. Prevailing thought of the time held that the purpose of the pensions was to keep children out of public institutions and to keep homes intact despite poverty; only inefficiency or immorality were sufficient reasons to break up a home. During 1913, Wisconsin and seventeen other states joined Illinois, Missouri, and Colorado, which had enacted laws earlier, in the "wildfire spread of widow's pensions." The Republican party platform and Senator La Follette endorsed the concept. Debate focused on how the program would be administered and financed. On May 22, the assembly agreed to a compromise that involved concurrent supervision by local juvenile court judges and the State Board of Control, and joint financing by state and county governments. In two letters written to La Follette shortly afterward, John Commons' wife Nell attacked the compromise version as "vicious" and "evil," charging that it had been introduced to prevent passage of the "wise one" proposed by the McGovern administration. The amended bill finally passed the senate, 18–3. The final version authorized the Board of Control to study the operation of the system and to make recommendations for change by March 1, 1915.[51]

---

[50] Milwaukee *Journal*, May 24, June 6, July 9, August 1, 1913; McCarthy to Henry V. Schwalbach, July 3, 1912, to Matthew S. Dudgeon, March 10, 1914, McCarthy Papers. On the national movement, see Ronald L. Numbers, *Almost Persuaded: American Physicians and Compulsory Health Insurance, 1912–1920* (Baltimore, 1978). Highly favorable assessments of Wisconsin's labor legislation appear in *La Follette's Weekly Magazine*, January 10, March 18, and June 6, 1914.

[51] *Wisconsin Statutes*, 1913, pp. 348–350; Milwaukee *Journal*, May 22, June 3, 13, 26, July 11, 1913; *Wisconsin State Journal*, January 10, 1913; Nell D. Commons to La Follette, May 30, June 7, 1913, box 73, in B-73, La Follette Papers, Library of Congress; Mark H. Leff, "Consensus for Reform: The Mothers' Pension Movement in the Progressive Era," *Social Service Review*, 47 (September, 1973), 397–417; Theda Skocpol, *Protecting Soldiers and Mothers: The Political Origins of Social Policy in the United States* (Cambridge, 1992), 424–479; "Profit by Experience," *La Follette's Weekly Magazine*, June 7, 1913, p. 3.

Focusing on another segment of the female population, miscreants between sixteen and thirty, the legislature established the Industrial Home for Women at Taycheedah, intended for first-time offenders. The goal was to separate them from more hardened criminals and to teach them a productive trade. The legislature also adopted more stringent measures for preventing tuberculosis and other communicable diseases. The new regulations required physicians and public officials to report these diseases and they set standards for care. Another measure allowed municipalities to hire nurses, mandated disposable drinking cups on trains, specified procedures for disinfecting living quarters, and provided public funds for treating indigents. The legislature also spelled out in greater detail the procedures required to prevent blindness in newborn infants, and enjoined physicians and midwives to consult with the State Board of Health about proper treatment.[52]

Turning to regulatory measures, an area in which Wisconsin had a firm foundation, the 1913 legislature enacted after extensive debate what was called a "blue sky law" for the supervision of stock transfers. It required stock brokers and dealers to obtain a license from the Railroad Commission, to report all transactions to the commission, and to comply with any orders issued by the commission. The law gave the commission authority to conduct investigations of securities companies, and to insist that they refrain from further transactions during the investigation period. Companies and their officers found guilty of violations, or which refused to comply with commission directives, were liable to fines or prison terms. The new statute was applied explicitly as well to the stock offered by public utilities.[53]

Other regulatory measures were more moderate. The legislature brought plumbers, hotels, and restaurants under stricter supervision by the State Board of Health, enacted a comprehensive code for the registration, licensing, and regulation of motor vehicles, and appropriated $40,000 for the Board of Public Affairs and extended its life for three years, thus reinforcing the state's commitment to planning and regulation.[54]

Like most of its Progressive Era predecessors, the 1913 legislature dealt with proposals to fine-tune the political system. But when the smoke had cleared, almost nothing of substance had been accom-

---

[52] *Wisconsin Statutes*, 1913, pp. 960–961, 974–979, 2198–2202; Milwaukee *Journal*, May 24, June 13, 22, July 2, 31, 1913; *Wisconsin Assembly Journal*, 1913, p. 1220.

[53] *Wisconsin Statutes*, 1913, pp. 1514–1522; Milwaukee *Journal*, August 2, 1913.

[54] *Wisconsin Statutes*, 1913, pp. 720–722, 1144–1149, 1503–1504, 1514–1522, 1600–1602; Milwaukee *Journal*, June 6–7, 18, July 9–10, 31, August 2, 4, 1913; *Wisconsin Assembly Journal*, 1913, pp. 988–989, 1028–1029, 1079, 1129–1130, 1134–1135, 1297–1298.

plished. McGovern's veto on May 13 of a joint resolution calling for another referendum on woman suffrage precipitated a storm of reaction that widened the rift between La Follette and McGovern partisans. A proposed constitutional amendment providing for the recall of all public officials except judges was approved, but statutes to establish procedures failed to pass. The only recall bill enacted into law in 1913 was one to reduce the number of petition signatures necessary to require Milwaukee officials to face a recall election. The legislature also approved the home rule amendment proposed by its immediate predecessor, but voters rejected it in 1914. The same fate befell the proposed constitutional amendment to establish procedures for direct legislation through initiative and referendum.[55]

Some political measures generated more heat. Progressive Republicans of all stripes banded together to frustrate an attempt by Democratic assemblyman O. F. Roessler of Jefferson to repeal the second-choice primary election law. During the assembly debate, Democrat Judson Hall of Waukesha said that he had consulted with fifty-two county clerks since the 1912 election and that "in every case they urged that I do what I could to kill off the Mary Ann law." Calling it "the biggest nuisance that ever happened" and "a system of nominating by elimination," Hall urged the committee on education to recommend approval of the Roessler bill. Perhaps anticipating a wide-open primary fight for the Republican gubernatorial nomination in 1914, progressive lawmakers in both major parties thwarted the effort to kill one of their favorite schemes for "democratizing" the electoral process: fusion candidates. Socialists moved to repeal the nonpartisan primary election law that had allowed several fusion candidates in Milwaukee to triumph over Socialist or McGovernite opponents. The bill, introduced by Social Democrat Gabriel Zophy of West Allis, was ignored as an "innocent affair" until Democratic assemblyman Thomas A. Manning of Milwaukee finally asked Zophy point-blank if the effect of his cleverly worded bill would be to repeal the nonpartisan primary. Zophy replied, "I guess that would be about the result," conceding that "some of these things slip through just like an eel." This failed to impress fusion advocates, who quickly killed the bill.[56]

Democrats sponsored a bill to facilitate the process by which "Bull Moose" candidates could get their names on the ballot. It barely made it through the assembly, and failed in the senate. The senate

---

[55] Milwaukee *Journal*, May 7, 13–14, 22, June 3, 6, 13, July 1, 31, August 1, 1913; *Wisconsin State Journal*, May 21, 1913; *Wisconsin Assembly Journal*, 1913, p. 1143.

[56] *Wisconsin Statutes*, 1913, pp. 30–33; Milwaukee *Journal*, May 14, June 6, 1913; *Wisconsin State Journal*, May 22, 1913; Green Bay *Gazette*, May 22, 1913; *Wisconsin Assembly Journal*, 1913, pp. 1155–1168.

also killed a measure, sponsored by the Milwaukee City Club with Socialist backing, to place most city administrative officials under civil service. Completing its frustrated efforts at political reform, the 1913 legislature also made short work of a proposal favored by McCarthy, Commons, and other progressives to transfer much of the legislature's work to a legislative commission. Thus, for all the flurry of activity and expenditure of energy by the legislatures of 1911 and 1913—and thanks to the voter reaction against the several proposed constitutional amendments in November of 1914—Wisconsin's political system remained almost exactly the same.[57]

Nor did the 1913 legislature break much new ground in educational reform. It succeeded in increasing the number of industrial schools in the state to forty-five and appropriated $10,000 to start and maintain a program that hired agricultural specialists to aid farmers in counties that lacked schools of agriculture and domestic economy. It increased the amount of state aid to high schools, especially for vocational courses of study, and appropriated $10 million to fund the entire state educational system. Despite the fact that the university continued to receive most of that appropriation, there were indications of an impending backlash. University supporters had to work hard to fend off the creation of a state board of education that would subsume the regents and the campus under its aegis, thereby greatly enhancing the power of the superintendent of public instruction, an outspoken critic of the university. They also had to strain to prevent introduction of a four-year college course in some of the normal schools. Adding to the university's sense of being under siege was a survey commissioned by William Harvey Allen. The Allen Survey branded the university as "inefficient," which proved a godsend to conservatives, a serious embarrassment to the university and the state, and a source of division among leading progressives, some of whom felt hoist by their own petard. In a desperate attempt to control the damage, the Board of Public Affairs conducted and published its own report in 1914, softening Allen's criticisms and relegating his original report to an appendix. Incensed, Allen issued a defense of his findings in a periodical entitled *Everybody's Business*, published by his Wisconsin Efficiency Bureau. He later sided with the plan of Governor Philipp and State Superintendent of Public Instruction Charles P. Cary to place the university under a comprehensive state board of education.[58]

---

[57] Milwaukee *Journal*, June 13, 25, August 8, 1913.
[58] *Ibid.*, January 16, May 24, July 2, 9, 12, 30, 31, August 8, 1913; Merle Curti and Vernon Carstensen, *The University of Wisconsin: A History, 1848–1925* (2 vols., Madison, 1949), 2: 267–294; *Wisconsin Assembly Journal*, 1913, pp. 994, 1038–1039, 1050–1051, 1073, 1095, 1132–1133, 1144–1149, 1467–1469, 1494–1496.

Among the measures enacted in 1913 were at least two that smacked of the "social control" or "coerced efficiency" strain of Progressive Era thought. Legislators introduced a record number of bills in 1913 to regulate public morals, many proposing "impracticable remedies." The causes included liquor control, curtailment of prostitution, and regulation of marriage. One of those adopted was a bill introduced by Republican senator Victor Linley of Superior for a temporary commission to investigate prostitution and related vices. Fellow Republican senator Howard Teasdale of Sparta, who was later to serve as chairman of the commission, strongly supported the bill, which passed the assembly, 67–13, on May 8, after heated debate. Its advocates included Milwaukee Socialist Carl Minkley, who said that low wages were the main underlying cause of prostitution, and Republican Newcomb Spoor of Berlin (Green Lake County), who predicted that the investigation would drive the "white slave trade" out of the state.[59]

More reflective of the growing social efficiency strain within Wisconsin progressive thought was the enactment of a bill introduced by Republican senator and physician George E. Hoyt of Menomonee Falls to permit the involuntary sterilization of "criminal, insane, feeble-minded and epileptic persons" confined in state and county institutions. The eugenics movement resonated positively with many progressives who stressed considerations of efficiency, productivity, and rationalism over personal liberty or mere humanity. In Wisconsin, the program eventually gained the backing of important individuals and organizations such as Edward A. Ross, Charles R. Van Hise, and the State Medical Society. Its principal opponents were oddly paired: the Catholic church and the Social Democratic party.[60]

First introduced in the Wisconsin legislature in 1907, the sterilization measure cleared the assembly that year, 36–24, but died in the senate after opponents succeeded in removing the provision to compensate the board of examiners. A similar fate befell bills in 1909 and 1911. Proponents gathered strength, employing a somewhat unsettling slogan: "Sterilization or racial disaster." The superintendent of the State Hospital for the Insane, Dr. Charles Gorst, urged Wisconsin lawmakers to "wake up and be equally as progressive" as the eleven states that had already enacted laws for sterilizing "defectives." The bill passed the senate 22–3 on July 9, with only Democrats Paul Husting and William Bichler and Republican Timothy Burke of Green

[59] Milwaukee *Journal*, January 15, May 9, 20, June 11, 13, August 2, 1913; *Wisconsin Assembly Journal*, 1913, pp. 977–978.
[60] *Wisconsin Statutes*, 1913, pp. 333–334; Rudolph J. Vecoli, "Sterilization: A Progressive Measure?" in *WMH*, 43 (Spring, 1960), 191–198.

Bay voting in opposition. It had more trouble in the assembly, where it finally squeaked through, 39–37.[61]

Nowhere did the twin corrosives of factionalism and reaction do more damage than on conservation and agricultural measures, the two areas in which McGovern hoped to establish a reputation in 1913. Both were crucial to the governor's strategy of augmenting his support in the northwestern counties, a region where his urban, labor-oriented brand of progressivism had not attracted substantial numbers of voters. McGovern proposed a law almost identical to his waterpowers bill that was defeated during the 1912 special session. Following the same script, Senator Husting countered with the bill that he had sponsored in 1912, one that refused to acknowledge private riparian rights to ownership and use of waterpower. Husting's proposal prompted opposition from over fifty waterpower owners, leading McGovernites to believe the Husting bill was doomed. They were in error. Although Husting's original bill was weakened by amendments, it was eventually enacted and signed by McGovern. Despite their success in weakening the final bill, waterpower owners immediately began laying plans to seek repeal or changes in it during the next session.[62]

Attempts to expand the forest reserve were even less productive. McGovern recommended continuing the policy of buying up forest land and instituting a specific long-term policy. To satisfy timber owners, he also proposed moderating forest land taxes. Nevertheless, lumbermen campaigned against the program. They persuaded assemblyman William J. Whiteside of Hurley and state senator Willard T. Stevens of Rhinelander to introduce a bill providing a temporary halt in land purchases, as well as the appointment of a committee to investigate forest reserve operations. This offered the legislature a clear choice between Progressivism and Toryism, and Toryism prevailed. The Stevens-Whiteside bill passed both houses. State Forester Edward M. Griffith and the forestry board headed by Van Hise urged the governor to veto the bill because curtailing purchases until July 1, 1915, would cripple forestry work in the state. Unmoved, McGov-

---

[61] Vecoli, "Sterilization" in *WMH*, 43: 196–202; *Wisconsin Statutes*, 1913, pp. 333–334; Milwaukee *Journal*, June 13, July 9, 26–27, 31; *Wisconsin Senate Journal*, 1913, p. 1113; *Wisconsin Assembly Journal*, 1913, p. 1634.

[62] McGovern, *Governor's Message*, 1913, pp. 15–21; Dennis East II, "Water Power and Forestry in Wisconsin: Issues of Conservation, 1890–1915" (doctoral dissertation, University of Wisconsin, 1971), 226–257, 343–346; Milwaukee *Journal*, May 2, 7, June 18, 21, 24, 27, July 5, 10, 11, August 4, 1913; *Wisconsin Statutes*, 1913, pp. 1115–1123; McCarthy to Gifford Pinchot, July 12, 21, 1913, and Granville D. Jones to McCarthy, May 2, 1913, McCarthy Papers; A. Allan Schmid, "Water and the Law in Wisconsin," in *WMH*, 45 (Spring, 1962), 203–215; *Wisconsin Assembly Journal*, 1913, pp. 993–994.

ern declined to exercise his veto power, explaining that the setback was only temporary. Compounding this apparent desertion of the conservation cause, the governor appointed George O'Connor of Eagle River, an outspoken opponent of the forest reserve, to the forestry board. McGovern professed ignorance of O'Connor's views, but his hometown Milwaukee *Journal* denounced the new appointee as "a known, paid, anti-forestry lobbyist." McGovern's explanation for both actions was that he favored persuasion over coercion to gain northerners' compliance. Others, however, accused him of courting conservative support against Paul Husting for their looming senatorial contest.[63]

McGovern's ambitious agricultural program, which was designed to assist and empower the farmers of the New North, also ended badly for him. His agenda included state-guaranteed loans to farmers, the fostering of rural co-operative credit societies and co-operative land colonies, and, above all, the establishment of a marketing commission, analogous to the Industrial Commission, to facilitate the co-operative marketing of agricultural products. These measures received strong endorsements from the Wisconsin Society of Equity and the National Farmers Union. The more affluent members of the Wisconsin Dairymen's Association and most Stalwarts and conservative Democrats felt that the plan smacked of state paternalism, if not outright socialism. McGovern's measures posed a dilemma for La Follette supporters in the legislature because they generally sympathized with their principles but were loath to let McGovern profit politically from their enactment, especially in the northwestern part of the state where he previously had been weak.[64]

The major impetus for an agricultural service state clearly came from Charles McCarthy, who corresponded regularly with agricultural reformers in the United States and Europe. In 1912, with the support of the Board of Public Affairs, McCarthy had sent a member of his staff, John Sinclair, to Europe to study the situation in Denmark, Germany, and Great Britain. McCarthy then outlined to McGovern five priorities for investigation: agricultural co-operation, co-operative credit, marketing of agricultural products, co-operative

---

[63] McGovern, *Governor's Message*, 1913, pp. 18–21; East, "Water Power and Forestry in Wisconsin," 276–339, 386–391; Vernon R. Carstensen, *Farms or Forests: Evolution of a State Land Policy for Northern Wisconsin, 1850–1932* (Madison, 1958), 48–74; Milwaukee *Journal*, May 22, June 18, 25, August 8, 1913; *Wisconsin Statutes*, 1913, pp. 1050–1056.

[64] McGovern, *Governor's Message*, 1913, pp. 38–44; *Wisconsin Farmer*, March 6, July 9, August 13, 1914; *Wisconsin Equity News*, September 10, 1913; A. W. Sanborn, *Cooperation Among Farmers Especially in Marketing*, State Board of Agriculture, *Bulletin*, no. 2 (1913), 14–15; *Wisconsin Agriculturist*, September 3, 1914; Milwaukee *Daily News*, February 13, 1914.

retail stores, and related miscellaneous matters. He also recommended that the College of Agriculture and rural public schools teach courses on co-operative marketing and that the board publish a magazine for and about co-operatives. Together with Gifford Pinchot and Sir Horace Plunkett, McCarthy also worked behind the scenes to found and promote the National Agricultural Organization Society, worked closely with the Society of Equity on behalf of his agricultural agenda, lobbied the secretary of agriculture in Washington, and put pressure on a reluctant Harry Russell, dean of the College of Agriculture, to get involved in his program.[65]

McGovern believed that the average farmer had been denied the credit advantages granted to merchants and manufacturers, largely because he was a single individual. He therefore proposed that Wisconsin study the German system of rural banks and co-operative credit associations. He also endorsed the idea developed by the Board of Public Affairs for co-operative land colonies that were permitted to purchase at low rates cutover tracts on which the original owners had allowed the taxes to lapse, sell them to individual members of the association at a profit, and use these profits to establish co-operative creameries, cheese factories, and warehouses, to finance road construction, and to purchase farm machinery too expensive to be acquired by individuals. The governor also recommended an "antiprice discrimination" law, as existed in nine other states, to prevent large corporations from using their national leverage to undersell small businesses and co-operatives in one area, and to charge high prices elsewhere. McGovern also proposed forming marketing co-operatives, to be supervised by a state commission, as a means of narrowing the gap between the low food prices paid to primary producers and the high retail cost of food to consumers. As a whole, McGovern's agenda would have radically restructured what he condemned as "our present wasteful system of distribution" that "levies a heavy toll" on both producers and consumers.[66]

The 1913 legislature responded to McGovern with two important steps to deal with the credit disadvantages suffered by marginal farmers: co-operative credit associations and land mortgage associations. Co-operative credit associations could receive money from their members as deposits or in payment for shares in the organization,

---

[65] McCarthy to McGovern, July 5, 1912, to Sir Horace Plunkett, January 4, 22, 1913, to David F. Houston, July 14, 1913, to Gifford Pinchot, March 5, 1913, to Wallace Buttrick, June 5, 1913, to Colonel Edward M. House, October 28, 1913, Plunkett to McCarthy, September 11, 1912, January 7, 1913, Gifford Pinchot to McCarthy, July 14, 1913, Charles R. Van Hise to McCarthy, July 3, 1913, Leonard G. Robinson to McCarthy, August 11, 1913, all in the McCarthy Papers.

[66] McGovern, *Governor's Message*, 1913, pp. 38–44.

and they could either lend their assets to association members or invest them in anticipation of financial returns. These associations were also authorized to pay dividends to their members, and their capital stock was exempt from taxes. Land mortgage associations were to be formed by fifteen or more resident property owners in an area. The associations would make loans using the agricultural lands, forests, and dwellings of the state as security. The associations could lend up to 65 per cent of value in exchange for a first mortgage on the applicant's land, house, or forest. The resulting statute spelled out in detail the organization, operation, restrictions, supervision, and tax liability of land mortgage associations.[67]

Despite these successes with agricultural credit, McGovern failed to achieve the capstone of his farm program: direct co-operative marketing under the supervision of a state commission. This defeat imparted an aura of failure to the entire legislative session of 1913, adding weight to the charges that La Follette legislators blocked important legislation in order to deny McGovern credit. The measure had the strong endorsement of the Board of Public Affairs and was compatible with the traditions of the Wisconsin Idea and the service state. In a special message to the legislature, McGovern specifically linked the marketing bill to the Railroad Commission's regulation of the relations between shippers and carriers and to the Industrial Commission's supervision of relations between employers and workers. The marketing bill, he said, dealt with the "still more intimate and comprehensive relation of producer and consumer," an area that was "of broader import and significance than either of the others" but was also "in perfect harmony with the political philosophy that underlies both." La Follette and McGovern lawmakers quickly turned the marketing issue into a political football. They introduced competing versions of the bill, differing primarily over the question of whether to establish a separate marketing commission or to make the Industrial Commission responsible for supervision. Writing to La Follette on April 25, McCarthy cautioned that leading legislators were attempting to undermine McGovern's entire program, especially the marketing bill. He assured La Follette that the administration's version was sound and implored him to exert his influence on its behalf. La Follette replied that McCarthy was "quite in error in supposing that my friends in either house are influenced upon this or any other matter of legislation by their personal feelings toward any individual," and said that his supporters might possibly "resent having legislation 'doped out' to them by any one." He told McCarthy he would continue to rely upon his supporters for counsel, and that they and

---

[67] *Wisconsin Statutes*, 1913, pp. 1314–1319, 1545–1550; Milwaukee *Journal*, May 14, 28, June 13, August 1, 2, 1913.

he disagreed with McCarthy and McGovern only on the question of how to enact a "workable measure."[68]

On May 6, the assembly passed Merlin Hull's marketing bill; the senate concurred a few weeks later, over the objections of McGovernites. The governor vetoed the measure on May 27, calling it insufficient and unconstitutional, despite its general similarity to the administration version. The following day, the assembly defeated the administration marketing bill and, on June 4, La Follette lawmakers led the fight to frustrate an attempt to resuscitate it by attaching a provision to submit it to a referendum vote in 1914. McCarthy tried to break the political impasse by enlisting Albert Sanborn and William Hatton, both former senators, to prepare a compromise measure that the senate committee on state affairs endorsed on June 9. Despite furious efforts by McCarthy, McGovern, and supporters of the administration, the Sanborn-Hatton compromise bill died.

On June 19, M. Wes. Tubbs, secretary-treasurer of the Wisconsin branch of the American Society of Equity, wrote the governor that "the sentiment generally prevails that the Legislature of 1913 has not measured up to its possibilities," and warned that legislators who stood in the way of a marketing commission would suffer at the next election. Consumers would "not be satisfied with fragmentary, ineffective and unworkable legislation when the 'real thing' is within reach," he said. He sent the same message to every legislator, but it failed to have the desired effect. Although both houses passed versions of the compromise bill, a conference committee had severely weakened McGovern's original idea by reducing the proposed commission's power and providing marketing co-operatives with little protection from antitrust laws. On August 8, thoroughly dissatisfied, McGovern vetoed the measure. More than any other single event, the defeat of the marketing commission bill saddled both the 1913 legislature and the second McGovern administration with a reputation for ineptitude and failure. Despite widespread support for co-operative marketing in Wisconsin progressive circles, it was not to be realized for eight more years.[69]

From the vantage point of the 1990's, the legislative session of 1913

---

[68] McCarthy to La Follette, April 25, 1913, and to W. B. Shaw, May 26, 1913, La Follette to McCarthy, May 31, 1913, all in the McCarthy Papers; McGovern to C. A. Albert, July 15, 1913, to D. O. Mahoney, July 11, 1913, to John R. Commons, June 10, 1913, Albert W. Sanborn to McGovern, July 6, 1913, all in box 21, McGovern Papers.

[69] Milwaukee *Journal*, May 6, 7, 14, 27, 28, June 4, 10, 20, 24, July 2, August 1, 9, 1913; McCarthy to La Follette, May 10, June 3, 6, 7, 1913, Gifford Pinchot to McCarthy, June 20, 1913, McCarthy to Pinchot, June 20, 30, 1913, all in the McCarthy Papers; M. Wes. Tubbs to McGovern, June 19, 1913, box 21, McGovern Papers; Fond du Lac *Commonwealth*, June 1913; *Wisconsin Assembly Journal*, 1913, pp. 936, 1176–1188, 1198–1201, 1209–1210, 1260–1265.

is best described as a mixed bag. Despite pervasive and bitter factionalism, it somehow managed to ratify the Seventeenth Amendment, endorse the ten proposed amendments to the state constitution initiated by its illustrious predecessor in 1911, enact mothers' pension, minimum wage, and anti-price discrimination legislation, improve rural education, and establish land mortgage associations and rural credit societies. On the other hand, it failed to approve another woman suffrage referendum, enact sickness insurance, develop a comprehensive fire insurance code, or strengthen the industrial education system. More ominously, it retreated from the high ground on waterpowers and forest reserve legislation, waffled in support of higher education, made concessions to the protest movements against higher taxes and public expenditure, and above all failed to enact a co-operative marketing program on which most progressives agreed in principle. It clearly fell significantly short of the record of its immediate predecessors, as well as of the promises made in the Republican party's 1912 platform and in McGovern's inaugural message. Both La Follette and McGovern progressives agreed that factionalism within the progressive Republican ranks was the chief culprit for the legislature's spotty record, each group blaming the other. Even while recognizing the tremendous opportunity that their continued feuding would afford Stalwarts and conservative Democrats in 1914, they proved unwilling or unable to close ranks as they had done two years earlier. The reactionaries in both parties were determined to exploit the opening—their first in more than a decade—to its fullest.[70]

McGovern's quest for a U.S. Senate seat, and progressivism in general, faced another formidable obstacle as the 1913 session wound down: a comprehensive budget bill. This legislature was the first to tackle the job under the new statute, and lawmakers waited until late in the session before presenting the governor with omnibus appropriation bills. In addition, they called for record expenditures. Both the nature and timing of such bills angered McGovern. He recognized the negative political ramifications of a substantial increase in expenditures, but nevertheless felt he had no alternative but to accept all or nothing. Then tax projections made it apparent that revenues would fall significantly short of appropriations, and McGovern authorized a supplementary levy of $1,500,000. He was of course fully aware that there would be political fallout. Criticism of his administration's "extravagance" began the moment he signed the bills. It peaked by January, 1914, orchestrated by conservative newspaper editors. Typical was the comment of a Janesville *Gazette* columnist: "Mc-

---

[70] For a balanced assessment of the 1913 legislature's work, see Wyman, "Voting Behavior in the Progressive Era," 308–309.

Govern has got to answer for this high tax proposition and there is the whole trouble in a nut shell. Taxes, taxes, taxes." Even one of McGovern's most loyal supporters was moved to write that "it seems that the people quite generally are of the opinion that the last legislature was too extravagant."[71]

The debate over the governor's decision not to veto the appropriations bill forced an unusual confrontation between McGovern and McCarthy. Frustrated, McGovern proposed that he be given the equivalent of a line item veto (as it would be termed in the 1990's) over specific sections of budget bills. McCarthy bluntly wrote to McGovern, on April 1, 1914, that "you are making a mistake if you stand for the veto of appropriation items." He reminded the governor that he had always opposed the old budget system because it meant each department had to justify its expenditures every two years, and that he favored "continuing appropriations which can be only overturned by the majority of both houses and the governor." McCarthy also gave a newspaper interview along these lines. Several days later, McGovern responded, taking umbrage at McCarthy's public statements and observing that "there was enough discord in the Capitol and enough evidence of want of harmony in the Progressive camp without any further proof of insurgency." Their clash, though it did not result in a permanent break, well illustrates the intensity of the conflict that permeated Wisconsin's progressive movement by 1914.[72]

[4]

The anti-tax movement steadily gained momentum early in 1914, aided by conservative newspaper comment. In mid-February, attorneys Charles Pierce of Janesville and Thomas C. Richmond of Madison organized two meetings of businessmen and farmers from three southern counties, forming the supposedly "nonpartisan" Home Rule and Taxpayers League, which quickly gained control of the anti-tax campaign. In a letter to the reactionary Madison *Democrat*, Richmond charged that real democracy in Wisconsin had been replaced by bureaucracy. The Home Rule and Taxpayers League soon forged an alliance with Emanuel Philipp, the Milwaukee businessman and

---

[71] Margulies, *Decline of the Progressive Movement*, 144; Wyman, "Voting Behavior in the Progressive Era," 309; Janesville *Gazette*, January 31, 1914; George Thompson to Harry Wilbur, February 27, 1914, box 46, McGovern Papers; Milwaukee *Sentinel*, March 3, 1914. On August 7, 1913, McGovern sent a special message to the legislature explaining his reasons for not vetoing the appropriation bills. See *Wisconsin Assembly Journal*, 1913, pp. 1688–1692.

[72] McCarthy to McGovern, April 1, 1914; McGovern to McCarthy, April 6, 1914, box 15, McGovern Papers.

architect of the Stalwart renaissance who was determined to use antiprogressive reaction as his springboard into the governor's mansion. The league met in Madison in May, endorsed Philipp's candidacy, and decided to call a pre-primary convention in Madison on June 22. Philipp agreed to foot the bill. The convention descended on the city like a whirlwind. In a powerful opening address, Pierce damned fourteen years of progressive rule, blaming its proponents for excessive spending and for politicizing the university. The delegates liked what they heard, drafted a reactionary platform, endorsed Philipp for governor and Levi Bancroft, fellow Stalwart and former attorney general, for the U.S. Senate, and adjourned—all within three hours.[73]

In his kickoff campaign speech in July, Philipp hit the extravagance issue hard, arguing that state expenditures had risen from $4 million to $13 million between 1900 and 1913 largely because of increases in the university budget and the creation of so many commissions. Throughout the campaign, he skillfully blended that theme with the claim that he was engaged in "a fight for constitutional representative government, as opposed to the delegated powers which build up a dangerous bureaucracy." (The Taxpayers League put it succinctly in one of its campaign slogans: "Do you want a democracy or a bureaucracy?") As historian Herbert F. Margulies has demonstrated, the anti-progressive coalition conflated its two main arguments into an all-purpose indictment: undemocratic government by commission was the cause of exorbitant spending and oppressive taxes. For good measure, the coalition implicated the other two pillars of the service state: the university and the Legislative Reference Library. (Another effective slogan was coined by Charles P. Cary, state superintendent of public instruction, who had long been annoyed by the university: "Do we want a State University or a University State?") Philipp accused the university of hogging money needed for rural schools, and of being a nursery for bureaucrats, experts, and socialists. As a remedy, he proposed placing the university under a comprehensive state board that would divide state funds among all public educational institutions. Phillip branded the LRL a "progressive bill factory," and he vowed to abolish it.[74]

Conservative Democrats, led by John C. Karel, echoed Phillip and the Stalwarts. They succeeded in putting through an entire slate of reactionary candidates at the party's primary convention in July, outflanking pro-Wilson Democrats. That group quickly assembled its own slate, headed by John Aylward for governor and Paul Husting

---

[73] Margulies, *Decline of the Progressive Movement*, 144–145; Wyman, "Voting Behavior in the Progressive Era," 310–311; Janesville *Gazette*, February 17, 1914.
[74] Margulies, *Decline of the Progressive Movement*, 147–148; Wyman, "Voting Behavior in the Progressive Era," 310–311; Milwaukee *Sentinel*, April, 24, 1914.

for the U.S. Senate. Despite his progressive background, however, Aylward adopted a platform that was scarcely less reactionary than those of Philipp and Karel. Aylward vowed to repeal the income tax, reduce the number of state commissions by two-thirds, cut the state payroll by $1 million, depoliticize the university and reduce its appropriations, rein in the LRL, and remove the state from the insurance field. Against the advice of President Wilson, conservative Democrats backed Thomas Kearney of Racine against Husting in the senatorial primary.[75]

McGovern also had to contend with the apparent collaboration of Senator La Follette and his followers in the campaign to denounce his administration's "extravagance." To thwart McGovern's election, La Follette loyalists met in Madison at the end of March and announced their intention to petition McGovern to call a special session of the legislature for the purpose of cutting costs. In early June, Secretary of State John S. Donald warned Lieutenant-governor Thomas Morris, a third candidate in the Republican primary, not to criticize the Stalwarts in his campaign. Donald said that the old ideological divisions were no longer important. The pro-La Follette *Wisconsin State Journal* backed Morris against McGovern because, it said, he had tried to control spending, backed the call for the special session, and favored a high tariff. On July 25, an editorial in *La Follette's Weekly Magazine* blasted McGovern for "waste and looseness in administration" and blamed him for failing to reduce highway appropriations with a veto. McGovern responded angrily that the fault lay with a La Follette man, senate floor leader and Republican state chairman George E. Scott. Scott of course denied that he was acting on orders from La Follette in Washington and reiterated that the governor was the real culprit.[76]

With their ranks splintered, progressive Republicans were unable to agree even on a gubernatorial candidate. The first to enter the fray was former state senator William Hatton, principal sponsor of the act that had created the Railroad Commission and a La Follette loyalist of long standing. Many other La Follette loyalists, however, felt Hatton had become tainted by his association with McGovern on the Board of Public Affairs. Another progressive, former state treasurer and assemblyman Andrew Dahl of Westby (Vernon County), announced in late June as "the La Follette candidate." He did so

---

[75] Wyman, "Voting Behavior in the Progressive Era," 313–314; Margulies, *Decline of the Progressive Movement*, 148–149.

[76] Margulies, *Decline of the Progressive Movement*, 149–150; Wyman, "Voting Behavior in the Progressive Era," 313–314; Robert M. La Follette, "Exclusive Responsibility," *La Follette's Weekly Magazine*, July 25, 1914, p. 1, and "Fixing the Responsibility," *ibid.*, August 8, 1914, p. 11.

over the opposition of Walter Houser, who denounced this move as one that would help elect Emanuel Philipp. Despite Houser, Senator La Follette gave Dahl's candidacy his blessing. For his part, Dahl professed his long service "in the fight with La Follette against Philipp and the interests." But Dahl also promised to reduce spending on the university, the normal schools, and highways, and to abolish the Board of Public Affairs—a stand intended to link Hatton and McGovern in the public consciousness. His supporters touted him as "a candidate who believes in progress without extravagance."[77]

Dahl's candidacy irked Charles McCarthy because he was endorsed by La Follette and yet joined with Philipp and William D. Hoard in attacking the LRL and pledging to abolish the bill-drafting department. McCarthy countered with a pamphlet ironically entitled *The Bill Factory*, in which he defended the bill-drafting department's value and reasserted its apolitical nature. McCarthy was particularly annoyed at La Follette because at that very moment the Senator was leading the movement to establish a similar bill-drafting department for Congress.[78]

Joining Philipp, Hatton, and Dahl in the crowd of Republican gubernatorial hopefuls was Speaker Merlin Hull of the assembly, who had feuded with McGovern over the marketing commission. His entry brought the number of serious progressive Republican candidates to three, all of whom proclaimed their impeccable progressive credentials and simultaneously denounced the movement's supposed sins. Two relative unknowns hewed to the same general strategy. These five men on the more-or-less progressive side virtually guaranteed Philipp's victory by plurality, and they also lent a conservative aura to the entire primary campaign.[79]

If anything, the Republican senatorial primary was even more complicated than the gubernatorial, since it combined party factionalism with religious conflict. Morris had shattered any hope of a clear Progressive-Stalwart face-off between McGovern and Levi Bancroft, since he was the La Follette candidate. Bancroft's support was diluted by

---

[77] Wyman, "Voting Behavior in the Progressive Era," 311–314; Erlebacher, "Herman Ekern," 210–212; Margulies, *Decline of the Progressive Movement*, 150–152; Andrew H. Dahl, "Fifteen Years of Fighting," *La Follette's Weekly Magazine*, August 22, 1914, p. 5. The Milwaukee *Free Press*, September 11, 1914, *Daily News*, July 7, 1914, and *Journal*, June 12, 15, September 11, 1914, all denounced Dahl's candidacy as an anti-Hatton move by La Follette.

[78] Casey, "Charles McCarthy," 88–96; McCarthy to Fred MacKenzie, August 5, 1914, to Andrew Dahl, June 23, 25, 1914, to Mark Sullivan, June 25, 30, 1914, to Nellie Dunn, July 3, 1914, to John Nelson, July 8, 1914, and to William H. Hatton, June 29, 1914, all in the McCarthy Papers; Commons to La Follette, July 17, 1914, La Follette Papers, Library of Congress.

[79] Wyman, "Voting Behavior in the Progressive Era," 311–312; Margulies, *Decline of the Progressive Movement*, 151–154.

the entry of three moderate to conservative candidates: John Strange of Neenah, who had been lieutenant-governor during the Davidson administration; senator Timothy Burke of Green Bay; and assemblyman Charles Estabrook of Milwaukee. Adding to the confusion, Davidson endorsed McGovern as "in every respect La Follette's equal" and as having the "decided advantage that he can work with other people, something La Follette never will learn." In addition to splitting the progressive vote, Morris' candidacy touched off a virulent anti-Catholic diatribe, comparable to that which had manifested itself among Wisconsinites in the American Protective Association in the 1890's and would flare up anew with the Ku Klux Klan in the 1920's. This bigotry found its greatest support among largely Lutheran Norwegians, who had long been the electoral mainstay of La Follette and progressivism.

The appearance of anti-Catholicism was first detected by Herman Ekern in April, 1914, when he read an unsigned letter to the editor in *Skandinaven*, the most influential Norwegian-language newspaper in the Midwest and published in Chicago, that asked rhetorically whether "Scandinavians and Protestant citizens of Wisconsin" could vote for a Roman Catholic, given that the "history and record of the Catholic power is black, blood stained and rotten, and cannot bear the light of day. . . ." On the same day, Ekern received a letter from a voter in Waushara County inquiring whether McGovern or Charles P. Cary, the state school superintendent, were Catholics or members of the Knights of Columbus. Ekern thereupon solicited reports from informants in various parts of the state and tried to dissuade the editor of *Skandinaven* from opposing Morris. Instead, the newspaper, apparently bowing to subscriber pressure, endorsed McGovern in early August; moreover, it subsequently attacked Morris' Catholicism. The religious issue was also given impetus by the nation's leading anti-Catholic newspaper, *The Menace*, published in Missouri, but widely read in Wisconsin, and by such organizations as the Knights of Luther and the Guardians of Liberty.[80]

Religious bigotry is never edifying, and the ensuing primary campaign was not one to make Wisconsinites proud. McGovern's secretary and political strategist Harry Wilbur worked to use Morris' Catholicism to his boss's advantage. In late May, Wilbur received a letter

---

[80] Herbert F. Margulies, "Anti-Catholicism in Wisconsin Politics, 1914–1920," *Mid-America*, 44 (January, 1962), 51–54; John D. Buenker, *Urban Liberalism and Progressive Reform* (New York, 1973), 152; Milwaukee *Free Press*, June 1, August 25, 1914 (quote). To La Follette and his inner circle, the real issue in the primary was "McGovern's treachery." See Walter L. Houser, "A Betrayal of Wisconsin Voters," p. 5, "The Chronology of F. E. McGovern," p. 3, and Robert M. La Follette, "Morris," p. 1, all in *La Follette's Weekly Magazine*, August 29, 1914.

from a loyalist in the western part of the state informing him that many Scandinavian voters were hostile to Morris because of his religion, and that Ekern had retaliated by charging that McGovern was "an apostate" and "at heart a Catholic." Wilbur immediately responded, acknowledging that he understood "the opposition to Morris and the ground on which it is based," adding "that particular feature is going to play a large part in the campaign, though, of course, all the work along that line will be done quietly." Morris lost in the primary, but it is impossible to calculate the effect the anti-Catholic campaign had on the vote. It is clear that McGovern fared better among Scandinavian voters in the western part of the state than he ever had in any previous primary. Moreover, the progressive nominee for secretary of state, John S. Donald, informed La Follette that the unexpectedly narrow margin of his victory was due to the mistaken perception that he was an Irish Catholic. The Catholic issue did not play much of a role in the general election, and it did not surface prominently again until the 1920 Republican primary.[81]

Apart from the religious issue, the primary elections of September, 1914, principally demonstrated the pernicious effects of factionalism mixed with reaction. McGovern received only 32.2 per cent of the Republican senatorial vote, besting Morris and Bancroft each by 11,000 votes. Combined, the two overtly Progressive candidates had swamped the Stalwart candidate by 63 to 26 per cent. The other three entrants divided 11 per cent of the total vote that might otherwise have gone to Bancroft. In the gubernatorial primary, Emanuel Philipp benefited from this competition among the progressive candidates and received a plurality of 35 per cent. Had William Hatton and Andrew Dahl been able to combine forces, one of them undoubtedly would have received nearly 7,000 votes more than Philipp. That strategy would have produced a progressive ticket from top to bottom, since the other successful statewide candidates were all progressives. The election was tailor-made for the "Mary Ann" second-choice option, but it proved a dismal failure because very few voters chose to exercise that prerogative. La Follette's ingeniously constructed defense mechanism had failed to prevent his ultimate nightmare: the triumph of a minority Stalwart candidate in a field of Progressives.[82]

Nor did progressive Republican candidates realize any benefit

---

[81] Margulies, "Anti-Catholicism in American Politics," *Mid-America*, 44: 53–56; Margulies, *Decline of the Progressive Movement*, 159–162; Erlebacher, "Herman Ekern," 211.

[82] Wyman, "Voting Behavior in the Progressive Era," 313–315; Margulies, *Decline of the Progressive Movement*, 152, 160–162; Milwaukee *Journal*, September 1–3, 1914; *Wisconsin Blue Book, 1915*, pp. 233–245; *La Follette's Weekly Magazine*, July 18, August 22, 1914; Maxwell, *La Follette and the Rise of the Progressives*, 193.

from another of La Follette's strategies: crossover votes in an open primary. The ideological division between Democratic "progressives" Paul Husting and John Aylward and "tories" John Karel and Thomas Kearney forced most Democrats to vote for a Democratic candidate, whether left or right. So closely matched were the two factions that Husting captured the senatorial nomination and Karel the gubernatorial. Ironically, the primaries produced Democratic and Republican tickets that were mirror images, pitting progressives McGovern and Husting against one another for the U.S. Senate and conservatives Philipp and Karel against one another for the governorship.[83]

Social Democratic voters also declined to cross party lines to support progressive Republicans. Notwithstanding the McGovern administration's outstanding record on labor legislation, the Milwaukee Federated Trades Council, the State Federation of Labor, and the party's leaders all admonished Socialists to vote for their own in the primary, despite a lack of contests. However much they co-operated on specific legislation, the Socialists were well aware that progressive Republicans rejected their ultimate goal of collective ownership of the means of production, and that Progressives openly worked to defeat Socialists by stealing their thunder on ameliorative legislation. Many progressive Republicans in Milwaukee had voted in 1912 for the nonpartisan local election law. They had also participated in the anti-Socialist fusion campaigns of 1912 and 1914, which had cut deeply into Socialist power in Milwaukee. With some justice, the Social Democratic party sneered at what it termed "the hypocrisy of the capitalist political parties" and declined to participate in "a mad scramble for public office and plutocratic favors." As Herbert Margulies observes, the Socialists "had every reason to protect their identity and independence by remaining aloof from the factional politics and statewide competition of the major parties."[84]

The Republicans' platform had to accommodate Emanuel Philipp at the head of an otherwise progressive statewide ticket, so they shrewdly crafted one designed to be all things to all factions. It praised the achievements of past progressive administrations and affirmed the principle of government regulation of the economy in the public interest. It also pledged economy in higher education and highway construction, the elimination of "non-essential" commissions, and stricter local control over highway construction. It affirmed its pride in the university, but vowed to limit costs and raise out-of-state tuition. On waterpowers and reforestation legislation, the plat-

---

[83] Wyman, "Voting Behavior in the Progressive Era," 313–315; Margulies, *Decline of the Progressive Movement*, 148–149; Milwaukee *Journal*, September 1–3, 1914.

[84] Margulies, *Decline of the Progressive Movement*, 152–157; *Wisconsin Blue Book, 1915*, p. 455.

form favored a middle course between development and conservation. It concluded with the usual peroration about attaining all good things through unified Republican action. Unwilling to content himself with this ambivalent message, McGovern boldly sought to make his candidacy a referendum on progressivism itself, a movement he termed a broad-gauged experiment on "how to perfect the government and bring it nearer to the people, how to make it really representative of them, and then how to use its vast powers to improve the condition and promote the happiness of every member of the human family, however humble or lowly he might be."[85]

The Democratic platform was if anything even more schizoid. It praised the Wilson administration and promised to roll back much of what the progressive Republicans had accomplished. It pledged to eliminate many state offices, pare expenses, rein in the LRL, and make the university "subservient to the people who support it." On several specific issues, the Democrats endorsed the principles of progressive Republican programs while condemning their administration. Only the Social Democrats ran on an uncompromisingly progressive program, with no concessions to "extravagance" or anti-government rhetoric.[86]

With their gubernatorial candidates plainly inclined towards reaction, the progressive leaders of both parties faced a crisis of conscience. The Wilson administration and the Democratic National Committee pressured liberals to project unity and harmony, so Husting and his associates embraced Karel and his associates. Husting depended upon the national party for financial and organizational backing and accordingly linked his entire ticket to the substantial progressive achievements of the Wilson administration—a strategy also calculated to lure La Follette Republicans into his column against McGovern. Truly it was a season for trimming and truckling. McGovern, hoping to offset possible losses due to the defection of La Follette loyalists, made a bid for Stalwart support by casting himself as a "regular" Republican who endorsed the entire party ticket, including Philipp. (He defended his actions by arguing that Philipp had been nominated under the very system designed by the progressives and that voters wanted only the laws already enacted, not a new and more radical platform.) For his part, Philipp made a conscious effort to moderate his anti-progressive rhetoric, a move that cynics hailed as a "supposed eleventh hour conversion."[87]

---

[85] McGovern, *McGovern on Campaign Issues, 1914* (Milwaukee, 1914), 3–4.
[86] *Wisconsin Blue Book, 1915*, pp. 452–460.
[87] Margulies, *Decline of the Progressive Movement*, 158–163; Wyman, "Voting Behavior in the Progressive Era," 314–319; Maxwell, *La Follette and the Rise of the Progressives*,

Unable to swallow Emanuel Philipp, many other progressive Republicans hastily assembled behind the independent candidacy of La Follette loyalist John J. Blaine, a former state senator from Boscobel. (Despite a statement that Philipp's election could result in "*the end of progressive* Wisconsin for a *decade*," La Follette rejected entreaties that he resign his Senate seat to oppose both of the reactionary candidates as an independent candidate for governor.) Blaine entered the fray as an unabashed progressive, advocating the initiative, referendum, and recall. He viewed the race as the same as those ten years earlier—between Stalwarts and Half-Breeds. By the time La Follette arrived in the state to campaign for Blaine, it was too late. Blaine failed to attract significant liberal Democratic support, despite his endorsement of Wilson two years before. Husting all but ignored the statewide races and openly courted votes from La Follette Republicans.[88]

In 1914, after fourteen victorious years, the progressive Republicans finally tasted defeat. Yet the election hardly constituted a decisive repudiation of the movement and its works. Philipp's winning total of 140,787 votes was the lowest received by any Republican gubernatorial candidate since William D. Hoard in 1890. (His 43 per cent share was even lower than Hoard's; indeed, it was the lowest ever awarded a Republican gubernatorial candidate in the state's history.) Blaine won only 10 per cent of the gubernatorial vote, but he received the votes of over 32,000 progressive Republicans who would not vote for Philipp. Without Woodrow Wilson at the head of the Democratic ticket, Karel's share declined by nearly 50,000, from 48 per cent to 37 per cent. Most of the remaining gubernatorial votes were captured by Social Democrat Oscar Ameringer, whose 8 per cent represented the standard SDP fraction. Philipp ran significantly behind the Republican party's other statewide candidates by anywhere from 14,000 to 17,000 votes. All of his running mates—Lieutenant-governor Edward F. Dithmar, Secretary of State John S. Donald, Treasurer Henry Johnson, and Attorney General Walter C. Owen—were regarded as progressives. So were the great majority of the twenty-one Republican senators and the sixty-two Republican assemblymen who controlled the legislature.[89]

192–193; *Wisconsin State Journal*, September 17, October 28, 1914; Milwaukee *Free Press*, September 24, 1914; Milwaukee *Sentinel*, September 28, 1914 (quote); *La Follette's Weekly Magazine*, August 8, October 17, 24, 1914; McGovern to C. J. Sumner, September 12, 1914, and to A. K. James, September 21, 1914 in the McGovern Papers.

[88] Margulies, *Decline of the Progressive Movement*, 159; Wyman, "Voting Behavior in the Progressive Era," 314–316; Erlebacher, "Herman Ekern," 212–213; Milwaukee *Journal*, November 24, 1914; Milwaukee *Sentinel*, October 6–7, 1914.

[89] *Wisconsin Blue Book, 1915*, pp. 222–227; Milwaukee *Journal*, November 4–6, 1914;

Nor did Francis McGovern's defeat by Paul Husting in the Senate race necessarily constitute a repudiation of progressivism. The election was so close that it took several days to determine that McGovern had fallen short by a mere 966 votes, mostly because he had failed to lure Socialist voters away from Emil Seidel—a consequence of the failure of the progressives' leftward strategy of 1910–1911. Moreover, Husting was a strong progressive in his own right, particularly about natural resources and direct democracy. His tough stance on waterpowers had gained him a national reputation; the Wilson administration, having engineered the most productive congressional session of the Progressive Era, worked hard for his election. There is little doubt that Husting's margin of victory was provided by La Follette progressive Republicans who vented their wrath on McGovern by voting for probably the most progressive Democrat in Wisconsin. The vote totals are suggestive: Husting ran 15,000 votes ahead of Karel, while McGovern trailed Philipp by about 7,000. What was more, the total votes cast in the senatorial race numbered 17,500 fewer than for the governorship.[90]

Years of factionalism and intraparty bickering, of name-calling and backbiting, had undoubtedly soured many Wisconsinites on politics—right, left, and center. But perhaps the biggest indicator that the electorate had grown weary of "La Follette ideas" was the overwhelming defeat of the ten proposed constitutional amendments that were also on the 1914 ballot. These had been proposed by the progressive legislature of 1911 and had survived the partisan bloodletting of its successor in 1913. Except for the measures designed to raise legislative salaries and to reorganize the circuit court system, the proposals were mostly logical extensions of clearly established progressive policies: the initiative, referendum, and recall; elaboration of the state insurance program; increasing municipal powers of charter revision and eminent domain; and simplifying the process for amending the constitution. Responsibility for mobilizing voter support during the fall of 1914 was entrusted to Charles A. Rosa, a trusted La Follette-oriented former jurist and assemblyman from Beloit.

Rosa never had a chance. Not one of the ten proposals received so much as 40 per cent of the votes cast. The two amendments to expand the state's public insurance program received less than one-quarter

---

Margulies, *Decline of the Progressive Movement*, 159–163; Wyman, "Voting Behavior in the Progressive Era," 316–318; Maxwell, *La Follette and the Rise of the Progressives*, 192–193.

[90] *Wisconsin Blue Book, 1915*, pp. 222–228; Milwaukee *Journal*, November 4–6, 1914; Margulies, *Decline of the Progressive Movement*, 159–163; Wyman, "Voting Behavior in the Progressive Era," 318–319.

approval from those who bothered to vote on them. Tens of thousands of voters ignored the constitutional referenda altogether.[91]

Although it is clear in retrospect that the election of November, 1914, marked the end of the Progressive Era in Wisconsin, contemporaries were far from agreement on what, exactly, had ended and what would continue. On November 4, for example, Emanuel Philipp exalted that his election was "a complete repudiation of the much heralded Wisconsin idea" and proof that "our people have had enough of experimental legislation." In the Madison *Democrat*, Ellis B. Usher wrote that the results "could scarcely be more conclusive of the general revolt against so-called 'progressive' policies" and that the state "was determined to repudiate the 'Wisconsin Idea.' " To no one's surprise, Senator La Follette placed the blame squarely on McGovern and the 1913 legislature, and attempted to convey the impression that Wisconsin progressivism would be fine now that his nemesis had been removed. Focusing more narrowly, the Milwaukee *Sentinel* rejoiced in the destruction of La Follette's political machine and the discrediting of its creator: "Never has there been a greater fall in the history of politics of the state than is shown by the results of the late election...." More soberly, the Milwaukee *Journal* observed that talk of "repudiating anything is silly," pointing out that Philipp had won the Republican primary only by a plurality and that he was not a reactionary, indeed was not nearly conservative enough to please "the old gang [of] Stalwart Republicans"—the ones who had voted for Karel. The *Journal* predicted that Philipp would "go forward until he stands among the most liberal-minded Republicans of the state, for he has grown wonderfully in this direction." Indeed, a few days after the election, the governor-elect said that the voters had selected him because he had promised "to give them an efficient, economical and sanely progressive administration of their public affairs."[92]

Of all the 1914 races, the bitterest loss was probably Francis McGovern's. As if to demonstrate anew how complex and ephemeral was the politics of coalition and faction in Progressive Era Wisconsin, McGovern blamed his defeat primarily on the unlikely triumvirate of Henry Cochems, Theodore Roosevelt, and Robert M. La Follette. In

---

[91] *Wisconsin Statutes*, 1913, pp. 30–33; Wyman, "Voting Behavior in the Progressive Era," 318; Maxwell, *La Follette and the Rise of the Progressives*, 192–194; Margulies, *Decline of the Progressive Movement*, 162–163; Milwaukee *Journal*, November 4–6, 1914.

[92] Milwaukee *Journal*, November 4, 1914; Milwaukee *Free Press*, November 8, 1914; Ellis B. Usher, " 'Wisconsin Idea' Given Rebuke by Badger Electors," Madison *Democrat*, November 8, 1914; George P. Mathes, "La Follette Fallen Idol in Wisconsin," Milwaukee *Sentinel*, November 4, 1914; Robert M. La Follette, "Nothing Vital Lost," *La Follette's Weekly Magazine*, November 5, 1914, pp. 1–2.

his scenario, Cochems—his erstwhile friend and ally—had secured Roosevelt's endorsement of John G. Blaine, thereby uniting the three against Emanuel Philipp's candidacy, which McGovern had embraced. Even more incredibly, he continued, Cochems' long association with McGovern had convinced thousands of Philipp supporters that McGovern was working behind the scenes for Blaine. As a result, McGovern said, he had lost support among both Blaine and Philipp supporters, though for totally contradictory reasons. Musing over the irony of having Cochems, Roosevelt, and La Follette united in their opposition to him because of his loyalty to the Republican ticket, McGovern sighed that "verily the whirligig of time brings many changes and politics makes strange bed fellows." To another correspondent, he identified the real villain: "the La Follette outfit made the most secret, insidious and effective assault I have ever known in my political experience." The lost election marked a watershed in his career. Although he was only forty-eight years old, Francis E. McGovern never again held elective office.[93]

[5]

In the longer view, the election of 1914 marked the end of what historian Robert S. Maxwell calls "the first chapter of the history of the state's progressivism." But those later chapters were separated from the first by interludes of conservatism or reaction, and were often characterized by as many discontinuities as continuities. The succeeding chapters' persistent elements were provided by two interrelated phenomena: Wisconsinites' memories and personal recollections of the original Progressive Era, and their enduring attraction to politicians named La Follette. However much the participants and content of the various progressive chapters changed over time, they remained variations on the themes enunciated in the Wisconsin Idea and that old battle cry, "the people against the interests." The more that factionalism and cross-cutting issues muddied the political waters, the more the majority of Wisconsin voters were inclined to view the La Follettes as an island—the only island—in a sea of change. That phenomenon helped re-elect "Fighting Bob" to the U.S. Senate by overwhelming majorities in 1916 and 1922, and to give him almost 55 per cent of the state's presidential vote in 1924. It made the "Cubs

---

[93] McCarthy to John S. Murdock, November 17, 1914, McCarthy Papers; McGovern to Edythe L. Tate, November 19, 1914, to Edward Randolph Wood, December 4, 1914, to Pierre De Pew, December 9, 1914, to William Tanquery, December 11, 1914, all in box 18, McGovern Papers.

of the Old Lion," Philip and Robert, Jr., a three-term governor of Wisconsin and a U.S. senator respectively.[94]

To the frustration of a great many conservatives and progressives alike, Emanuel Philipp's three terms as governor (1915–1921) were characterized far more by moderation than by reaction. As historian Robert C. Nesbit has quipped, "The promised dismantling of the progressive ark turned into a minor shifting of ballast...." The main targets of Philipp's campaign fusillade managed to survive those six years almost intact, in part because of their essential conservatism. The University of Wisconsin responded to the governor's threat to subsume it under a central board of education by doing all in its power to demonstrate that it did not "run the state" and that its contributions to private enterprise were far more tangible and noteworthy than its occasional forays into radicalism. Charles McCarthy brilliantly defended the Legislative Reference Library (the "progressive bill factory"), saving it from Philipp's ax and eventually becoming almost as trusted an adviser to him as he had been to his progressive predecessors.

Nor did Philipp dismantle any of the major quasi-independent commissions, though he did reduce the Board of Public Affairs, the Tax Commission, and others to mere administrative agencies. In Nesbit's words, "Everywhere that he looked for evidences of radicalism or an officious bureaucracy discharging useless functions he seemed to discover well-qualified civil servants performing socially or economically useful services." The Philipp administration did kill off the second-choice primary and prevented the adoption of the initiative, referendum, recall, and similar experiments in direct democracy. But it left virtually undisturbed the rest of the political structure designed by La Follette. By defending the civil liberties of antiwar critics in a time of patriotic hysteria, Philipp inadvertently moved closer to La Follette and the Social Democrats. He did indeed cut the budget and sacked many progressive officials who were unprotected by the civil service, but he rationalized these actions as providing more efficient and economical administration of a progressive service state.[95]

Impressed by Philipp's apparent mellowing, an increasing number of progressives came to view him as a fundamentally honest and open-

---

[94] Maxwell, *La Follette and the Rise of the Progressives*, 203; Paul W. Glad, *History of Wisconsin. Volume V: War, a New Era, and Depression, 1914–1940* (Madison, 1990), 20–21, 50–53; Harold F. Gosnell and Morris H. Cohen, "American Government and Politics," *The American Political Science Review*, 35 (October, 1941), 920–921; La Follette, *Autobiography*, 134–135.

[95] Robert C. Nesbit, *Wisconsin: A History* (2nd ed., by William F. Thompson, Madison, 1989), 436–440; Margulies, *Decline of the Progressive Movement*, 164–172; Fitzpatrick, *McCarthy of Wisconsin*, 72–89; Glad, *History of Wisconsin. Volume V*, 398–558.

minded leader who was capable of ideological growth in their direction. This conviction was reinforced by the governor's apparent rejection of Charles Pfister's counsel, his independence in matters of patronage and legislation, and his opposition to measures sponsored by the railroad and liquor industries which he had served as a lobbyist. To Socialists and ultra-progressives, this apparent rapprochement between Philipp and other moderate Stalwarts on the one hand, and Progressives seeking to disprove charges of extravagance, radicalism, and bureaucratic inefficiency on the other, was proof positive that the Wisconsin Idea had always been more about expert, efficient administration of socio-economic change than about equity and social justice. Moreover, a new generation of would-be officeholders and power brokers found this deradicalized brand of progressive Republicanism to be an intellectual compromise that enabled them to rationalize their pursuits. They looked upon the long-entrenched progressive "Madison ring" in much the same way as young Bob La Follette viewed the Stalwart bosses of the 1890's. These new-style conservatives billed themselves as "champions of the people" against the "special interests" represented by the progressives. Paradoxically, this strategy led them to accept most of what the progressives had wrought during the preceding fourteen years—provided it could be managed and kept under control by the new regime.[96]

These semantical gymnastics infuriated La Follette and his cohorts, who wrote the second chapter of Wisconsin progressivism during the height of the Great War. They portrayed the war in the familiar context of a conspiracy against the people by war profiteers, superpatriots, and other special interests, thereby bringing together a coalition of labor unionists, farm organizations, consumers, oppressed German-Americans, and antiwar liberals. The glue that bound them was resentment at economic disparities exacerbated by wartime inflation, and the perceived sacrifice of the interests of working-class Americans to those of financiers, industrialists, and international elites. The alliance excluded Social Democrats, who shared a similar perspective and had suffered similar persecution; but neither they nor the La Follette progressives were willing to risk a partnership. Aided by factional infighting among the Stalwarts, and a resurgence of anti-Catholicism, the new progressive coalition managed to elect John J. Blaine governor for three terms (1921–1927) during the era of Warren Harding and Calvin Coolidge—the high season of reaction nationally. Blaine produced no noteworthy reform legislation, although he kept Wisconsin's progressive reputation intact and pro-

---

[96] Margulies, *Decline of the Progressive Movement*, 164–172; Nesbit, *Wisconsin: A History*, 436–440.

vided Bob La Follette with solid support for his re-election to the Senate in 1922 and his run for the presidency in 1924. La Follette's unsuccessful presidential candidacy established him as the foremost progressive in the land and strongly reinforced the perception of Wisconsin as "the most progressive state."[97]

This second chapter of Wisconsin progressivism effectively ended with the death of Fighting Bob on June 18, 1925. But the subsequent conservative resurgence lasted less than five years. Then, galvanized by the devastating impact of the Great Depression, the younger generation of La Follettes would write a third chapter and once more thrust Wisconsin into the national spotlight as a bulwark of progressivism.

[97] Margulies, *Decline of the Progressive Movement*, 170–192; Thelen, *La Follette and the Insurgent Spirit*, 99–194; Weisberger, *La Follettes of Wisconsin*, 179–276; Chester C. Platt, *What La Follette's State Is Doing: Some Battles Waged for More Freedom* (Batavia, New York, 1924), 18–32, 66–85, 114–143; Margulies, *Senator Lenroot*, 310–379; Edward N. Doan, *The La Follettes and the Wisconsin Idea* (New York, 1947), 84–131.

APPENDIX

THE GOVERNORS OF WISCONSIN, 1893–1914

Name	Birthplace	Party	Term in Office	Birth/Death
WILLIAM H. UPHAM	Massachusetts	Rep.	Jan. 7, 1895–Jan. 3, 1897	1841–1924
EDWARD SCOFIELD	Pennsylvania	Rep.	Jan. 4, 1895–Jan. 6, 1901	1842–1925
ROBERT M. LA FOLLETTE	Wisconsin	Rep.	Jan. 7, 1901–Dec. 31, 1906	1855–1925
JAMES O. DAVIDSON	Norway	Rep.	Jan. 1, 1906–Jan. 1, 1911	1854–1922
FRANCIS E. MCGOVERN	Wisconsin	Rep.	Jan. 2, 1911–Jan. 3, 1915	1866–1946
EMANUEL L. PHILIPP	Wisconsin	Rep.	Jan. 4, 1915–Jan. 2, 1921	1861–1925

APPENDIX

ESSAY ON SOURCES

THE VOLUME of primary and secondary source material available for the study of the history of the Progressive Era in Wisconsin is so extensive and richly textured that a truly comprehensive bibliographical essay could easily evolve into a mini-book, and, if appended to the preceding text, would result in a volume whose bulk would defy binding between two covers. Moreover, the bibliographical information and commentary would bury the reader under an avalanche of detail.

I have chosen, therefore, to highlight in three sections those primary and secondary sources that I believe are indispensable to anyone seeking a working knowledge of the history of the Progressive Era in Wisconsin. The first section consists of a simple bibliographical listing of the most significant manuscript collections, government documents, organizational records, autobiographies and memoirs, newspapers and periodicals, dissertations and theses, journal articles, and published books, arranged in alphabetical order within those generic categories. The second section evaluates the utility of several of the items included on that list. The final section consists of an even more subjective attempt to introduce the reader to those sources I believe to be the most worthwhile for placing the Wisconsin experience within the wider context of the entire Progressive Era.

SELECTED BIBLIOGRAPHY
See Note on Citations for abbreviations.

MANUSCRIPT COLLECTIONS   (All in the archives of the State Historical Society of Wisconsin, Madison.)

John J. Blaine Papers.
John Rogers Commons Papers.
James O. Davidson Papers.
Herman L. Ekern Papers.
William Dempster Hoard Papers.
Theodore Kronshage Papers.
Robert M. La Follette Papers.
Charles McCarthy Papers.
Francis E. McGovern Papers.

Michael V. O'Shea Papers.
Emanuel Lorenz Philipp Papers.
Charles Rosa Papers.
Charles Richard Van Hise Papers.
Board of World's Fair Managers, "Final Report" (2 vols.), in Secretary of State, Chicago World's Fair, 1893, Records, 1891–1894, box 3, Series 282, Wisconsin State Archives.

GOVERNMENT DOCUMENTS

UNITED STATES

Eleventh Census of the United States, 1890.
Twelfth Census of the United States, 1900.
Thirteenth Census of the United States, 1910.
Fourteenth Census of the United States, 1920.
U.S. Commissioner of Indian Affairs, *Annual Reports*, 1893–1915.
U.S. Commission on Industrial Relations, *Final Report*, 1915.
U.S. Commission on Immigration, *Final Report*, 1911.

WISCONSIN

Wisconsin Blue Book, 1893–1915.
Bureau of Labor and Industrial Statistics, *Biennial Reports*, 1893–1911.
Industrial Commission, *Biennial Reports*, 1912–1916.
Secretary of State, *Tabular Statements of the Census Enumeration*, 1895, 1905.
Wisconsin Assembly Journal, 1891–1913.
Wisconsin Senate Journal, 1891–1913.
Laws of Wisconsin, 1893–1913.
Wisconsin Statutes, 1889, 1898, 1911, 1913.
Wisconsin Public Documents, 1890–1892, 1913–1914.

NEWSPAPERS AND PERIODICALS

Oehlerts, Donald E., comp. *Guide to Wisconsin Newspapers, 1833–1957*. Madison: SHSW, 1958.
Hoard's Dairyman (Fort Atkinson), 1893–1914.
La Follette's Weekly Magazine (Madison), 1909–1914.
Wisconsin Farmer (Madison), 1893–1914.
Wisconsin Journal of Education (Madison), 1893–1914.
Wisconsin State Journal (Madison), 1900–1914.
The Catholic Citizen (Milwaukee), 1893–1899.
Milwaukee *Journal*, 1893–1914.
Milwaukee *Leader*, 1911–1914.
Milwaukee *Sentinel*, 1893–1914.
Wisconsin Patriot (Milwaukee), 1894–1898.
Wisconsin Agriculturist (Racine), 1893–1914.
Wisconsin Blue Book, 1911, pp. 383–397. ("The Wisconsin Press.")

Autobiographies and Memoirs

Baker, Ray Stannard. *American Chronicle: The Autobiography of Ray Stannard Baker*. New York: C. Scribner's Sons, 1945.
Commons, John R. *Myself: The Autobiography of John R. Commons*. New York: Macmillan, 1938; reprinted, Madison: UW Press, 1964.
Ely, Richard T. *Ground Under Our Feet: An Autobiography*. New York: Macmillan, 1938.
Frear, James A. *Forty Years of Progressive Public Service: Reasonably Filled with Thorns and Flowers*. Washington: Associated Writers, 1937.
Haugen, Nils P. *Pioneer and Political Reminiscences*. Evansville, Wisconsin: Antes Press, C. 1930.
La Follette, Robert M. *La Follette's Autobiography: A Personal Narrative of Political Experiences*. Madison: La Follette Co., 1913; reprinted, Madison: UW Press, 1960.
Stephenson, Isaac. *Recollections of a Long Life, 1829–1915*. Chicago, private, 1915.

Organizational Records

American Association for Labor Legislation Records, 1908, 1910–1911.
Wisconsin Federation of Women's Clubs. *Proceedings*, 1897–1915.
Wisconsin State Federation of Labor, Annual Convention. *Proceedings*, 1893–1915.
Wisconsin Woman Suffrage Association Records, 1893–1914.
Woman's Club of Madison. *Yearbook*, 1899–1915.

Theses and Dissertations

Acrea, Kenneth C., Jr. "Wisconsin Progressivism: Legislative Response to Social Change, 1891 to 1909." Doctoral dissertation, University of Wisconsin, 1968.
Bell, Velma F. "The Negro in Beloit and Madison, Wisconsin." Master's thesis, University of Wisconsin, 1933.
Beltman, Brian W. "Rural Renaissance in an Urban Age: The Country Life Movement in Wisconsin, 1895–1918." Doctoral dissertation, University of Wisconsin, 1974.
Berthrong, Donald J. "Social Legislation in Wisconsin, 1836–1900." Doctoral dissertation, University of Wisconsin, 1951.
Botts, Howard A. "Commercial Structure and Ethnic Residential Patterns in the Shaping of Milwaukee: 1800–1900." Doctoral dissertation, University of Wisconsin, 1985.
Brandes, Stuart D. "Nils P. Haugen and the Wisconsin Progressive Movement." Master's thesis, University of Wisconsin, 1965.
Bremer, Gail D. "The Wisconsin Idea and the Public Health Movement, 1890–1915." Master's thesis, University of Wisconsin, 1963.
Buchanan, Thomas R. "Black Milwaukee, 1890–1915." Master's thesis, University of Wisconsin-Milwaukee, 1973.
Burton, Thomas R. "The First Wisconsin Railroad Commission: Reform or Political Expediency?" Master's thesis, University of Wisconsin, 1952.

Casey, Marion. "Charles McCarthy: Policy Maker for an Era." Doctoral dissertation, University of Wisconsin, 1971.

Cavanaugh, Cyril C. "Francis E. McGovern and the 1911 Wisconsin Legislature." Master's thesis, University of Wisconsin, 1961.

Cavanaugh, James A. "Dane and Milwaukee Counties and the Campaign of 1912." Master's thesis, University of Wisconsin, 1969.

Clark, James I. "The Wisconsin State Department of Public Instruction, 1903–1921." Doctoral dissertation, University of Wisconsin, 1961.

East, Dennis II. "Water Power and Forestry in Wisconsin: Issues of Conservation, 1890–1915." Doctoral dissertation, University of Wisconsin, 1971.

Fuller, Bernard E. "Voting Patterns in Milwaukee, 1896–1920: A Study with Special Emphasis on the Working Class of the City." Master's thesis, University of Wisconsin-Milwaukee, 1973.

Galford, Justin B. "The Foreign Born and Urban Growth in the Great Lakes, 1850–1950: A Study of Chicago, Cleveland, Detroit, and Milwaukee." Doctoral dissertation, New York University, 1957.

Gasperetti, Joseph A. "The 1910 Social-Democratic Mayoral Campaign in Milwaukee." Doctoral dissertation, University of Wisconsin-Milwaukee, 1970.

Graves, Lawrence L. "The Wisconsin Woman Suffrage Movement, 1846–1920." Doctoral dissertation, University of Wisconsin, 1954.

Harvey, Alfred S. "Background of the Progressive Movement in Wisconsin." Master's thesis, University of Wisconsin, 1933.

Hercher, John D. "The Political Campaigns of Joseph W. Babcock." Master's thesis, University of Wisconsin, 1932.

Hilton, Robert T. "Men of Metal: A History of the Foundry Industry in Wisconsin." Master's thesis, University of Wisconsin, 1952.

Knapp, Hugh H. "The Social Gospel in Wisconsin, 1890–1912." Master's thesis, University of Wisconsin, 1968.

Lahman, Carrol P. "Robert Marion La Follette as Public Speaker and Political Leader, 1855–1905." Doctoral dissertation, University of Wisconsin, 1939.

Lewthwaite, Gordon R. "The Regionalization of Butter and Cheese Production in Wisconsin." Doctoral dissertation, University of Wisconsin, 1956.

Linnevold, Benjamin O. J. "The Wisconsin Cheese Industry and Government." Doctoral dissertation, University of Wisconsin, 1949.

McMurray, Howard J. "Some Influences of the University of Wisconsin on the State Government of Wisconsin." Doctoral dissertation, University of Wisconsin, 1940.

McNally, Charles J. "The History of Public Utility Legislation in Wisconsin." Master's thesis, Marquette University, 1935.

McNamara, Sallee. "The Record Re-examined: The Stalwarts, the Progressives; Education and Public Welfare in Wisconsin." Master's thesis, University of Wisconsin, 1965.

Olcott, Ruth H. "An Analysis of the Changing Times and an Expanding Nation upon Five Selected Institutions of Higher Learning from 1869 to 1917." Doctoral dissertation, University of Houston, 1954.

Olson, Frederick I. "The Milwaukee Socialists, 1897–1941." Doctoral dissertation, Harvard University, 1952.

Ondercin, David G. "The Early Years of Francis Edward McGovern, 1866–1910." Master's thesis, University of Wisconsin-Milwaukee, 1967.

Rice, Robert M. "The Populist Party in Milwaukee." Master's thesis, University of Wisconsin-Milwaukee, 1967.
Robinson, Ruth F. "The Control of the Republican Party in Wisconsin, 1904." Master's thesis, University of Wisconsin, 1930.
Saucerman, Kathryn. "A Study of the Wisconsin Library Movement, 1850–1900." Master's thesis, University of Wisconsin, 1944.
Schaars, Marvin A. "The Butter Industry of Wisconsin." Doctoral dissertation, University of Wisconsin, 1932.
Schefft, Charles E. "The Tanning Industry in Wisconsin: A History of Its Frontier Origins and Its Development." Master's thesis, University of Wisconsin, 1938.
Schumacher, Waldo. "The Direct Primary in Wisconsin." Doctoral dissertation, University of Wisconsin, 1923.
Simon, Roger D. "The Expansion of an Industrial City: Milwaukee, 1880–1910." Doctoral dissertation, University of Wisconsin, 1971.
Twombly, Robert C. "The Reformer as Politician: Robert M. La Follette in the Election of 1900." Master's thesis, University of Wisconsin, 1964.
Wan, Chien Chung. "Consolidated Balance Sheet and Income Statement of Wisconsin Agriculture Since 1910." Doctoral dissertation, University of Wisconsin, 1950.
Weisenel, Peter R. "The Wisconsin Temperance Crusade to 1919." Master's thesis, University of Wisconsin, 1965.
Weiss, Gertrude Schmidt. "History of Labor Legislation in Wisconsin." Doctoral dissertation, University of Wisconsin, 1933.
Woerdehoff, Frank J. "Dr. Charles McCarthy: His Educational Views and Influence upon Adult Education in Wisconsin." Doctoral dissertation, University of Wisconsin, 1954.
Wyman, Roger E. "Voting Behavior in the Progressive Era: Wisconsin as a Case Study." Doctoral dissertation, University of Wisconsin, 1970.
Younce, Laurence J. "The Political Conditions in Wisconsin from 1890–1900." Master's thesis, Marquette University, 1929.

ARTICLES

Acrea, Kenneth. "The Wisconsin Reform Coalition, 1892–1900: La Follette's Rise to Power." *WMH*, 52 (Winter, 1968–1969), 132–157.
Asher, Robert. "The 1911 Wisconsin Workmen's Compensation Law: A Study in Conservative Labor Reform." *WMH*, 57 (Winter, 1973–1974), 123–140.
Beltman, Brian W. "Rural Church Reform in Wisconsin During the Progressive Era." *WMH*, 60 (Autumn, 1976), 3–24.
Bird, Francis H. "The Proposed Wisconsin Industrial Commission." *The Survey*, April 22, 1911, pp. 151–152.
Booth, Douglas E. "Municipal Socialists and City Government Reform: The Milwaukee Experience, 1910–1940." *Journal of Urban History*, 12 (November, 1985), 51–74.
Campbell, Ballard. "The Good Roads Movement in Wisconsin, 1890–1911." *WMH*, 49 (Summer, 1966), 273–293.
Cassell Frank A., and Marguerite E. Cassell. "Wisconsin at the World's Columbian Exposition of 1893." *WMH*, 67 (Summer, 1984), 243–262.

Carstensen, Vernon. "The Origin and Early Development of the Wisconsin Idea." *WMH*, 39 (Spring, 1956), 181–188.
Commons, John R. "How the Wisconsin Industrial Commission Works." *American Labor Legislation Review*, February, 1913, pp. 9–14.
———. "How Wisconsin Regulates Her Public Utilities." *American Review of Reviews*, August, 1910, pp. 215–217.
———. "The Wisconsin Public Utilities Law." *American Review of Reviews*, August, 1907, pp. 221–224.
Cooper, John Milton, Jr. "Robert M. La Follette: Political Prophet." *WMH*, 69 (Winter, 1985–1985), 91–105.
Cronon, E. David. "Father Marquette Goes to Washington: The Marquette Statue Controversy." *WMH*, 56 (Summer, 1973), 266–283.
Durand, Loyal, Jr. "The Cheese Manufacturing Regions of Wisconsin, 1850–1950." *Transactions of the Wisconsin Academy of Sciences, Arts and Letters*, 42 (1953), 109–130.
Erlebacher, Albert. "The Wisconsin Life Insurance Reform of 1907." *WMH*, 55 (Spring, 1972), 213–230.
Fleischmann, Arnold. "The Territorial Expansion of Milwaukee: Historical Lessons for Contemporary Urban Policy and Research." *Journal of Urban History*, 14 (February, 1988), 147–177.
Friedman, Lawrence M., and Michael J. Spector. "Tenement House Legislation in Wisconsin: Reform and Reaction." *American Journal of Legal History*, 9 (January, 1965), 41–63.
Gores, Stan. "The Attempted Assassination of Teddy Roosevelt." *WMH*, 53 (Summer, 1970), 269–277.
Gough, Robert J. "Richard T. Ely and the Development of the Wisconsin Cutover." *WMH*, 75 (Autumn, 1991), 3–38.
Grant, Marilyn. "The 1912 Suffrage Referendum: An Exercise in Political Action." *WMH*, 64 (Winter, 1980–1981), 107–118.
Greenbaum, Fred. "The Social Origins of Wisconsin Progressives." *OCC Scholar*, 11 (December, 1968), 35–43.
Hass, Paul H. "The Suppression of John F. Dietz: An Episode of the Progressive Era in Wisconsin." *WMH*, 57 (Summer, 1974), 255–309.
Hall, Arnold Bennett. "The Direct Primary and Party Responsibility in Wisconsin." *Annals of the American Academy of Political and Social Science*, 106 (March, 1923), 40–54.
Hoeveler, J. David. "The University and the Social Gospel: The Intellectual Origins of the 'Wisconsin Idea.'" *WMH*, 59 (Summer, 1976), 282–298.
Holter, Darryl. "Labor Spies and Union-Busting in Wisconsin, 1890–1940." *WMH*, 68 (Summer, 1985), 243–265.
Kane, Lucile. "Selling Cut-Over Lands in Wisconsin." *Business History Review*, 28 (September, 1954), 236–247.
———. "Settling the Wisconsin Cutovers." *WMH*, 40 (Winter, 1956–1957), 91–98.
Kennan, Kossuth Kent. "The Wisconsin Income Tax." *Quarterly Journal of Economics*, 26 (November, 1911), 169–178.
Kennedy, Padraic M. "Lenroot, La Follette, and the Campaign of 1906." *WMH*, 42 (Spring, 1959), 163–174.

Larsen, Lawrence H. "Urban Services in Gilded Age Wisconsin." *WMH*, 71 (Winter, 1987–1988), 83–117.
Lorence, James J. "'Dynamite for the Brain': The Growth and Decline of Socialism in Central and Lakeshore Wisconsin, 1910–1920." *WMH*, 66 (Summer, 1983), 251–273.
Lurie, Nancy O. "Wisconsin: A Natural Laboratory for North American Indian Studies." *WMH*, 53 (Autumn, 1969), 3–20.
McDonald, Forrest. "Street Cars and Politics in Milwaukee, 1896–1901." Part I. *WMH*, 39 (Spring, 1956), 166–170.
Margulies, Herbert F. "Anti-Catholicism in Wisconsin Politics, 1914–1920." *Mid-America*, 44 (January, 1962), 51–56.
―――. "The Decline of Wisconsin Progressivism, 1911–1914." *Mid-America*, 39 (July, 1957), 131–155.
Marsden, K. Gerald. "Patriotic Societies and American Labor: The American Protective Association in Wisconsin." *WMH*, 41 (Summer, 1958), 287–294.
Morris, Stuart. "The Wisconsin Idea and Business Progressivism." *Journal of American Studies*, 4 (July, 1970), 39–60.
Mowry, Duane. "The Reign of Graft in Milwaukee." *Arena*, December, 1905, pp. 589–592.
Myers, R. David. "The Wisconsin Idea: Its National and International Significance." *Wisconsin Academy Review*, 37 (Fall, 1991), 4–7.
Nord, David. "The Experts Versus the Experts: Conflicting Philosophies of Municipal Utility Regulation in the Progressive Era." *WMH*, 58 (Spring, 1975), 219–236.
Olson, Frederick I. "The Socialist Party and the Union in Milwaukee, 1900–1912." *WMH*, 44 (Winter, 1960–1961), 110–116.
Ondercin, David G. "Corruption, Conspiracy, and Reform in Milwaukee, 1901–1909." In Milwaukee County Historical Society, *Historical Messenger*, 26 (December, 1970), 112–122.
Reed, Larry A. "Domesticating Electricity in Appleton." *WMH*, 65 (Winter, 1981–1982), 120–121.
Sait, Edward M. Review of *The Wisconsin Idea* and *Wisconsin: An Experiment in Democracy*. *Political Science Quarterly*, 28 (March, 1913), 160–163.
Simon, Roger D. "Housing and Services in an Immigrant Neighborhood: Milwaukee's Ward 14." *Journal of Urban History*, 2 (August, 1976), 435–458.
Smith, Guy-Harold. "The Settlement and the Distribution of the Population of Wisconsin." *Transactions of the Wisconsin Academy of Sciences, Arts and Letters*, 24 (1929), 53–107.
Steffens, Lincoln. "Enemies of the Republic. Wisconsin: A State Where the People Have Restored Representative Government—The Story of Governor La Follette." *McClure's Magazine*, October, 1904, pp. 563–579.
Thelen, David P. "Robert La Follette's Leadership, 1891–1896." *Pacific Northwest Quarterly*, 62 (July, 1971), 97–109.
―――. "Social Tensions and the Origins of Progressivism." *Journal of American History*, 56 (September, 1969), 323–341.
Weibull, Jörgen. "The Wisconsin Progressives, 1900–1914." *Mid-America*, 47 (Summer, 1965), 191–221.
Wrone, David R. "Indian Treaties and the Democratic Idea." *WMH*, 70 (Winter 1986–1987), 83–106.

BOOKS

Aderman, Ralph M., ed. *Trading Post to Metropolis: Milwaukee County's First 150 Years*. Milwaukee: Milwaukee County Historical Society, 1987.

Altmeyer, Arthur J. *The Industrial Commission of Wisconsin: A Case Study in Labor Law Administration*. Madison: UW, 1932.

Andersen, Theodore A. *A Century of Banking in Wisconsin*. Madison: SHSW, 1954.

Barton, Albert O. *La Follette's Winning of Wisconsin, 1894–1904*. Madison: A. O. Barton, 1922.

Bernard, Richard M. *The Melting Pot and the Altar: Marital Assimilation in Early Twentieth-Century Wisconsin*. Minneapolis: University of Minnesota Press, 1980.

Bieder, Robert E. *Native American Communities in Wisconsin, 1600–1960: A Study of Tradition and Change*. Madison: UW Press, 1995.

Brownlee, W. Elliot, Jr., *Progressivism and Economic Growth: The Wisconsin Income Tax, 1911–1929*. Port Washington, New York: Kennikat Press, 1974.

Brye, David L. *Wisconsin Voting Patterns in the Twentieth Century, 1900 to 1950*. New York: Garland, 1979.

Burckel, Nicholas C., ed. *Racine: Growth and Change in a Wisconsin County*. Racine: County Board of Supervisors, 1977.

Caine, Stanley P. *The Myth of a Progressive Reform: Railroad Regulation in Wisconsin, 1903–1910*. Madison: SHSW, 1970.

Campbell, Ballard C. *Representative Democracy: Public Policy and Midwestern Legislatures in the Late Nineteenth Century*. Cambridge: Harvard University Press, 1980.

Canfield, Joseph M. *TM: The Milwaukee Electric Railway & Light Company*. Chicago: Central Electric Railfans Association, 1972.

Carstensen, Vernon R. *Farms or Forests: Evolution of a State Land Policy for Northern Wisconsin, 1850–1932*. Madison: UW, 1958.

Casey, Marion. *Charles McCarthy: Librarianship and Reform*. Chicago: American Library Association, 1981.

Clark, James I. *Farming the Cutover: The Settlement of Northern Wisconsin*. Madison: SHSW, 1956.

Commons, John R. *Labor and Administration*. New York: Macmillan, 1913; reprinted, New York: A. M. Kelley, 1964.

Conzen, Michael P. *Frontier Farming in an Urban Shadow: The Influence of Madison's Proximity on the Agricultural Development of Blooming Grove, Wisconsin*. Madison: SHSW for UW Department of History, 1971.

Current, Richard N. *Pine Logs and Politics: A Life of Philetus Sawyer, 1816–1900*. Madison: SHSW, 1950.

Curti, Merle, and Vernon Carstensen, *The University of Wisconsin: A History, 1848–1925*. 2 vols. Madison: UW Press, 1949.

Derleth, August. *Still Small Voice: The Biography of Zona Gale*. New York: Appleton-Century Company, 1940.

Doan, Edward N. *The La Follettes and the Wisconsin Idea*. New York: Rinehart, 1947.

Donoghue, James R. *How Wisconsin Voted, 1848–1972*. Madison: UW, Bureau of Government, 1962; revised ed., Madison: UW Institute of Governmental Affairs, 1974.

Ebling, Walter H., comp. *Wisconsin Agriculture in Mid-Century*. Madison: UW, De-

partment of Agriculture, Crop and Livestock Reporting Service. *Bulletin*, no. 325 (1954).
Ebling, Walter H., et al. *A Century of Wisconsin Agriculture, 1848–1948*. Madison: UW, Department of Agriculture, Crop and Livestock Reporting Service. *Bulletin*, no. 290 (1948).
Epstein, Leon D. *Politics In Wisconsin*. Madison: UW Press, 1958.
Ettenheim, Sarah C. *How Milwaukee Voted, 1848–1968*. Milwaukee: Milwaukee Institute of Governmental Affairs, UW Extension, 1970.
Fitzpatrick, Edward A. *McCarthy of Wisconsin*. New York: Columbia University Press, 1944.
Fries, Robert F. *Empire in Pine: The Story of Lumbering in Wisconsin, 1830–1900*. Madison: SHSW, 1951.
Galpin, Charles J. *Rural Life*. New York: Century Co., 1922.
Garber, Randy, ed. *Built in Milwaukee: An Architectural View of the City*. Milwaukee: Milwaukee, Department of Development, 1981.
Gavett, Thomas W. *Development of the Labor Movement in Milwaukee*. Madison: UW Press, 1965.
Glaab, Charles N., and Lawrence H. Larsen. *Factories in the Valley: Neenah-Menasha, 1870–1915*. Madison: SHSW, 1969.
Glover, Wilbur H. *Farm and College: The College of Agriculture of the University of Wisconsin, a History*. Madison: UW Press, 1952.
Haferbecker, Gordon M. *Wisconsin Labor Laws*. Madison: UW Press, 1958.
Harter, Lafayette G., Jr. *John R. Commons: His Assault on Laissez-Faire*. Corvallis, Oregon: Oregon State University Press, 1962.
Helgeson, Arlan. *Farms in the Cutover: Agricultural Settlement in Northern Wisconsin*. Madison: SHSW for UW Department of History, 1962.
Henry, William A. *Northern Wisconsin: A Hand-Book for the Homeseeker*. Madison: Democrat Printing Company, 1896.
Holmes, Fred L. *Old World Wisconsin: Around Europe in the Badger State*. Eau Claire: E. M. Hale, 1944.
Holmes, Michael S. *J. I. Case: The First 150 Years*. Racine: Case Corp., 1992.
Howe, Frederic C. *Wisconsin: An Experiment in Democracy*. New York: C. Scribner's Sons, 1912.
Hunt, Robert S. *Law and Locomotives: The Impact of the Railroad on Wisconsin Law in the Nineteenth Century*. Madison: SHSW, 1958.
Hurst, James Willard. *Law and Economic Growth: The Legal History of the Lumber Industry in Wisconsin, 1836–1915*. Cambridge: Belknap Press of Harvard University Press, 1964; reprinted, Madison: UW Press, 1984.
Klueter, Howard R., and James J. Lorence. *Woodlot and Ballot Box: Marathon County in the Twentieth Century*. Wausau: Marathon County Historical Society, 1977.
Kohler, Ruth De Young. *The Story of Wisconsin Women*. Kohler: Committee on Wisconsin Women for the 1948 Wisconsin Centennial, 1948.
Korman, Gerd. *Industrialization, Immigrants, and Americanizers: The View from Milwaukee, 1866–1921*. Madison: SHSW, 1967.
La Follette, Belle Case, and Fola La Follette. *Robert M. La Follette*. New York: Macmillan, 1953.
Lampard, Eric E. *The Rise of the Dairy Industry in Wisconsin: A Study in Agricultural Change, 1820–1920*. Madison: SHSW, 1963.

Lampman, Robert J., ed. *Economists at Wisconsin, 1892–1992*. Madison: Board of Regents, UW System, 1993.
Larson, Laurence M. *A Financial and Administrative History of Milwaukee*. Madison: UW, *Bulletin*, no. 242. Economics and Political Science Series, vol. 4, no. 2 (1908).
Leavitt, Judith W. *The Healthiest City: Milwaukee and the Politics of Health Reform*. Princeton: Princeton University Press, 1982; reprinted, Madison: UW Press, 1996.
Lord, Clifford L., and Carl Ubbelohde, *Clio's Servant: The State Historical Society of Wisconsin, 1846–1954*. Madison: SHSW, 1967.
Lovejoy, Allen Fraser. *La Follette and the Establishment of the Direct Primary in Wisconsin, 1890–1904*. New Haven: Yale University Press, 1941.
Lurie, Nancy O. *Wisconsin Indians*. Madison: SHSW, 1980; reprinted, 1987.
McBride, Genevieve G. *On Wisconsin Women: Working for Their Rights from Settlement to Suffrage*. Madison: UW Press, 1993.
McCarthy, Charles. *The Wisconsin Idea*. New York: Macmillan, 1912.
McGovern, Francis E. *Nationalize the Wisconsin Idea*. Chicago: National Committee Progressive Party, 1912.
McKenny, Charles, ed. *Educational History of Wisconsin*. Chicago: Delmont, 1912.
Macleod, David I. *Carnegie Libraries in Wisconsin*. Madison: SHSW for UW Dept. of History, 1968.
McShane, Clay. *Technology and Reform: Street Railways and the Growth of Milwaukee, 1887–1900*. Madison: SHSW for UW Dept. of History, 1974.
Margulies, Herbert F. *The Decline of the Progressive Movement in Wisconsin, 1890–1920*. Madison: SHSW, 1968.
———. *Senator Lenroot of Wisconsin: A Political Biography, 1900–1929*. Columbia, Missouri: University of Missouri Press, 1977.
Martin, Roy L. *History of the Wisconsin Central*. Boston: Railway and Locomotive Historical Society, 1941.
Maxwell, Robert S. *Emanuel L. Philipp: Wisconsin Stalwart*. Madison: SHSW, 1959.
———. *La Follette and the Rise of the Progressives in Wisconsin*. Madison: SHSW, 1956.
Miller, Sally M. *Victor Berger and the Promise of Constructive Socialism, 1910–1920*. Westport, Connecticut: Greenwoods, 1973.
Mollenhoff, David V. *Madison: A History of the Formative Years*. Dubuque: Kendall/Hunt Pub. Co., 1982.
Neuenschwander, John A., ed. *Kenosha County in the Twentieth Century: A Topical History*. Kenosha: Kenosha County Bicentennial Commission, 1976.
Ozanne, Robert W. *The Labor Movement in Wisconsin: A History*. Madison: SHSW, 1984.
Palmer, Edgar Z. *The Prewar Industrial Pattern of Wisconsin*. University of Wisconsin, Bureau of Business Research and Service. *Wisconsin Commerce Studies*, vol. 1, no. 1 (1947).
Patzer, Conrad E. *Public Education in Wisconsin*. Madison: Wisconsin, Department of Public Instruction, 1924.
Pederson, Jane Marie. *Between Memory and Reality: Family and Community in Rural Wisconsin, 1870–1970*. Madison: UW Press, 1992.
Peterson, Walter F. *An Industrial Heritage: Allis-Chalmers Corporation*. Milwaukee: Milwaukee County Historical Society, 1978.

Philipp, Emanuel L. *Political Reform in Wisconsin: A Historical Review of the Subjects of Primary Election, Taxation, and Railway Regulation*, abridged and edited by Stanley P. Caine and Roger E. Wyman. Madison: SHSW, 1973.

Platt, Chester C. *What La Follette's State Is Doing: Some Battles Waged for More Freedom.* Batavia, New York: Batavia Times Press, 1924.

Plumb, Ralph G. *Badger Politics, 1836–1930.* Manitowoc: Brandt Printing and Binding Co., 1930.

Rader, Benjamin G. *The Academic Mind and Reform: The Influence of Richard T. Ely in American Life.* Lexington, Kentucky: University of Kentucky Press, 1966.

Rankin, George William. *William Dempster Hoard.* Fort Atkinson: W. D. Hoard & Sons Co., 1925.

Rippley, La Vern J. *The Immigrant Experience in Wisconsin.* Boston: Twayne, 1985.

Ross, Edward A. *The Old World in the New: The Significance of Past and Present Immigration to the American People.* New York: Century Co., 1914.

Roth, Filibert. *On the Forestry Conditions of Northern Wisconsin.* Madison: Wisconsin, Geological and Natural History Survey. *Bulletin*, no. 1, Economic Series, no. 1 (1898).

Sanford, Albert H. *The Government of Wisconsin.* New York: C. Scribner's Sons, 1912.

Schafer, Joseph M. *Four Wisconsin Counties: Prairie and Forest.* Madison: SHSW, 1927.

———. *The Winnebago-Horicon Basin: A Type Study in Western History.* Madison: SHSW, 1937.

Steinschneider, Janice. *An Improved Woman: The Wisconsin Federation of Women's Clubs, 1895–1920.* Brooklyn, New York: Carls Pub., 1994.

Still, Bayrd. *Milwaukee: The History of a City.* Madison: SHSW, 1948; reprinted, 1965.

Swichkow, Louis J. and Lloyd P. Gartner. *The History of the Jews of Milwaukee.* Philadelphia: Jewish Publication Society of America, 1963.

Stevens, Michael E., ed. *The Family Letters of Victor and Meta Berger, 1894–1929.* Madison: SHSW, 1995.

Thelen, David P. *The Early Life of Robert M. La Follette, 1855–1884.* Chicago: Loyola University Press, 1966.

———. *The New Citizenship: Origins of Progressivism in Wisconsin, 1885–1900.* Columbia, Missouri: University of Missouri Press, 1972.

———. *Robert M. La Follette and the Insurgent Spirit.* Boston: Little Brown, 1976.

Torelle, Ellen, Albert O. Barton and Fred L. Holmes, comps. *The Political Philosophy of Robert M. La Follette as Revealed in His Speeches and Writings.* Madison: Robert M. La Follette Co., 1920.

Trotter, Joe William, Jr. *Black Milwaukee: The Making of an Industrial Proletariat, 1915–1945.* Urbana: University of Illinois Press, 1985.

Turner, Jennie W. M., comp. *Workmen's Compensation in Wisconsin, 1905–1913: Planks in Party Platform and History of Bills, with Votes.* Madison: compiler's carbon in SHSW, 1916; also microfiched.

Vance, Maurice M. *Charles Richard Van Hise: Scientist Progressive.* Madison: SHSW, 1960.

Wachman, Marvin. *History of the Social-Democratic Party of Milwaukee, 1897–1910.* Urbana: University of Illinois Press, 1945.

Ward, Edward J., ed. *The Social Center.* New York: D. Appleton and Co., 1913.

Weisberger, Bernard A. *The La Follettes of Wisconsin: Love and Politics in Progressive America.* Madison: UW Press, 1994.
Whitbeck, Ray H. *The Geography and Economic Development of Southeastern Wisconsin.* Madison: Wisconsin, Geological Natural History Survey. *Bulletin*, no. 58 (1921).
Williamson, Harold F., and Kenneth H. Myers II. *Designed for Digging: The First 75 Years of Bucyrus-Erie Company.* Evanston, Illinois: Northwestern University Press, 1955.
Williamson, Harold F., and Orange A. Smalley. *Northwestern Mutual Life: A Century of Trusteeship.* Evanston, Illinois: Northwestern University Press, 1957.
Wisconsin Women: A Gifted Heritage. Project directors Jeannine Goggin and Patricia Alland Manske; eds. Andrea Bletzinger and Anne Short for Wisconsin State Division, American Association of University Women. Amherst, Wisconsin: Palmer Publication, 1982.

*　　*　　*

The bulk of the most significant secondary literature on Progressive Era Wisconsin focuses on the period after 1900, and on political developments, as opposed to economic, social, demographic, and ethno-cultural developments. Much of the non-political picture must be painstakingly sketched from the data contained in government publications, chiefly the censuses of the United States and Wisconsin and the reports by agencies of Wisconsin state government. Easily the most useful sources are the U.S. decennial census volumes on population, which contain a bonanza of demographic data for computation, analysis, and comparison for 1890 to 1920. These provided much of the raw material for the chapters on urbanization and ethnicity, as well as for observations concerning the changing age, gender, and nativity of the state's people. The census volumes on agriculture are vital to an understanding of the metamorphosis that recast Wisconsin farming during these years, since they include extensive data on the number, size, and value of farms, acreage under cultivation, and amount and value of farm products. The censuses of manufactures document changing patterns of investment, establishment size, power sources, product value, and value added by manufacturing. The censuses of occupation are indispensable for comprehending the rapidly changing nature of work, the workplace, and the work force, since they provide detail about skill levels, the age and gender of workers, and the size, location, and nature of the industries. The information gleaned from the federal censuses should be supplemented by the published reports of the Wisconsin state censuses of 1895 and 1905. The biennial reports of the Bureau of Labor and Industrial Statistics, and of its successor, the Industrial Commission, contain a number of highly useful studies of child and women's labor, industrial accidents and illnesses, housing, public health, and other socially important topics. Unfortunately, their reliability, especially in earlier volumes, is suspect because of the bureau's practice of relying upon the voluntary co-operation of employers in gathering data. Careful analysis of these government documents is vital.

A number of descriptive and interpretive works provide valuable insights into the generic forces that transformed Wisconsin into a modern, urban, industrial, multi-ethnic state between 1890 and 1920. In the literature of economic development, Eric E. Lampard's *The Rise of the Dairy Industry in Wisconsin: A Study in*

Agricultural Change, 1820–1920 (1963) stands as a classic. His rich discussion of the causes and nature of the transition from cereal grain agriculture to dairy husbandry, and of the "industrial revolution in dairying" engineered by the Wisconsin Dairymen's Association, leaves almost no questions unexamined or unanswered. Lampard's well-documented contention that the co-operation between the WDA, the UW College of Agriculture, and state government was both precedent and prototype for the more comprehensive Wisconsin Idea is the most plausible of all the explanations offered for the origins of that august concept. The role of the College of Agriculture in that collaboration is examined in equally rich detail by Wilbur H. Glover in *Farm and College: The College of Agriculture of the University of Wisconsin, a History* (1952). Read in conjunction, these two works provide an incredibly complete picture of the process that made Wisconsin "America's Dairyland" by 1914.

That the state was anything but a dairy monolith, however, is convincingly demonstrated by two works produced by agricultural statistician Walter H. Ebling and his associates: *A Century of Wisconsin Agriculture, 1848–1948* (1948) and *Wisconsin Agriculture in Mid-Century* (1954). Digesting a mountain of data gleaned from U.S. and Wisconsin state censuses, as well as from countless reports of the College of Agriculture and the Wisconsin Department of Agriculture, Ebling deftly sketches the evolution of the state's agricultural diversity. The complexity and controversial nature of the era's agricultural metamorphosis is evident from a sustained reading of contemporary periodicals such as *Hoard's Dairyman*, *Wisconsin Agriculturist*, and *Wisconsin Farmer*. In his doctoral dissertation "Rural Renaissance in an Urban Age: The Country Life Movement in Wisconsin, 1895–1918," Brian W. Beltman examines the important role played by Wisconsin in the nationwide movement to revitalize rural life during a period of bewildering technological, socio-economic, and demographic change. Much of that work was carried on by the department of rural sociology of the College of Agriculture, and is reflected in the publications of sociologist Charles Galpin and his colleagues.

Closely intertwined with the transformation of agriculture was the debate over the future of the vast Cutover region. Robert F. Fries's *Empire in Pine: The Story of Lumbering in Wisconsin, 1830–1900* (1951) is the definitive history of the state's lumbering industry. The bulletin of the state Geological and Natural History Survey prepared by state forester Filibert Roth in 1898, entitled *On the Forestry Conditions of Northern Wisconsin*, captures the urgency of the crisis and the need for immediate and drastic action. The tremendous difficulties involved in the agricultural settlement of the Cutover are illuminated by Arlan Helgeson's careful analysis in *Farms in the Cutover: Agricultural Settlement in Northern Wisconsin* (1958), which explains the evolution of "Wisconsin's Appalachia." The frequently bitter controversy between conservationists and advocates of agricultural settlement of the Cutover is spelled out in Vernon Carstensen's *Farms or Forests: Evolution of a State Land Policy for Northern Wisconsin, 1850–1932*. The formidable opposition to reforestation and other forms of conservation is documented by Dennis East II in his 1971 doctoral dissertation at the University of Wisconsin, "Water Power and Forestry in Wisconsin: Issues of Conservation, 1890–1915."

Related to these issues is the question of how the Cutover region dealt with the void created by the virtual disappearance of the lumbering and flour-milling industries after 1890. The most comprehensive and accurate picture of the post-lumbering economy of northern Wisconsin emerges from two case studies: *Factories in the Valley: Neenah-Menasha, 1870–1915* (1969), by Charles N. Glaab and Lawrence W. Larsen, which documents the conversion of those twin industrial cities, and by extension much of the Fox River Valley, from an almost complete reliance upon flour milling to an emphasis on papermaking and other wood-related industries; and *Woodlot and Ballot Box: Marathon County in the Twentieth Century* (1977), by Howard R. Klueter and James J. Lorence, which analyzes the process that allowed the Wisconsin River Valley to survive the loss of the lumbering industry and to build a thriving economy based upon papermaking, wood processing, and many small industries.

Unfortunately, there are no comparable case studies to illuminate the impact of the "neotechnic revolution" and the "new industrialism" on the southeastern section of the state. Some idea can be derived from the studies of Milwaukee, Racine, Kenosha, Madison, and Beloit mentioned below. Some, too, can be gleaned from the studies of specific industries and of particular manufacturing companies cited in the relevant footnotes. The most comprehensive picture emerges from two publications written by contemporary economic geographer Ray H. Whitbeck: *The Geography and Industries of Wisconsin* (1913), which includes a significant amount of information on the rest of the state, but concentrates most directly on the southeast quarter; and *The Geography and Economic Development of Southeastern Wisconsin* (1921), which provides a detailed, county-by-county analysis of industrial development that focuses especially on the evolution of metals-related and other heavy industries. Placing those developments within a longer chronological framework is Edgar Z. Palmer's *The Prewar Industrial Pattern of Wisconsin* (1947), and two articles that appeared in the *Wisconsin Blue Book* during the 1920's: "Geography and Industries of Wisconsin" (1925), 39–60, by W. O. Hotchkiss, and "A Short Industrial History of Wisconsin" (1929), 1–49, by Joseph H. H. Alexander.

The best introduction to the rise of the "new urbanism" of the period can be found in the relevant chapters of studies of specific cities. David V. Mollenhoff's *Madison: A History of the Formative Years* (1982) is a marvelous example of the "new urban history" that weaves together technological, socio-economic, ethnocultural, and political developments. Although it is now over a half-century old, Bayrd Still's *Milwaukee: The History of a City* (1948) remains a classic urban biography and the most comprehensive study of the Cream City ever written. Focusing more tightly on the evolution of the cityscape itself are two highly detailed doctoral dissertations: Roger D. Simon's "The Expansion of an Industrial City: Milwaukee, 1880–1910" (1971) and Howard A. Botts's "Commercial Structure and Ethnic residential Patterns in the Shaping of Milwaukee, 1880–1900" (1985). Together, these two studies convey a well articulated sense of how and why economic considerations stood at the heart of urban development in the state's largest city. That point is the central theme of a perceptive article by Arnold Fleischmann in the *Journal of Urban History* (February, 1988) entitled "The Territorial Expansion of Milwaukee: Historical Lessons for Contemporary Urban Policy and Research."

The importance of co-operation between volunteer civic groups and municipal government in urban reform movements during the Progressive Era is illustrated by two monographs on Milwaukee. Clay McShane's *Technology and Reform: Street Railways and the Growth of Milwaukee, 1887–1900* (1974) examines the economic and political problems generated by the adoption of electric-powered mass transit. Judith W. Leavitt's *The Healthiest City: Milwaukee and the Politics of Health Reform* (1996) shows how a coalition of public health professionals, civic organizations, and political leaders overcame ignorance, fear, and vested economic interests in their successful campaign for a healthy environment. The need for greater municipal responsibility providing generation of urban services is illustrated by Lawrence H. Larsen in "Urban Services in Gilded Age Wisconsin," in *WMH*, 71 (Winter, 1987–1988), 83–117. John A. Neuenschwander, ed., *Kenosha County in the Twentieth Century: A Topical History* (1976) and Nicholas C. Burckel, ed., *Racine: Growth and Change in a Wisconsin County* (1977) both provide insight into the impact of urbanization in southwest Wisconsin.

The best single source for understanding the situation of the Native American tribes in Wisconsin during this period are the annual reports, 1893–1915, of the U.S. Commissioner of Indian Affairs. They include the yearly evaluations sent to the U.S. Department of the Interior from the persons who ran the U.S. Indian agencies, which oversaw government relations with the tribes. Robert Bieder's *Native American Communities in Wisconsin, 1600–1960: A Study of Tradition and Change* (1995) cogently summarizes the impact of changing federal policy on Wisconsin Indians during this period. David R. Wrone's "Indian Treaties and the Democratic Idea," in *WMH*, 70 (Winter, 1986–1987), 83–106, places the new policy of "forced assimilation" embodied in the Dawes Act within the historical context of 200 years of ambivalence and contradictory attitudes on the part of mainstream America. What little work exists on African Americans in the state during the Progressive Era focuses on Milwaukee and a few other cities. Thomas R. Buchanan's master's thesis, "Black Milwaukee, 1890–1915" (1973), examines patterns of residential and occupational discrimination. Joe William Trotter's *Black Milwaukee: The Making of an Industrial Proletariat, 1915–1945* (1985) concentrates on the post-World War I era, but its introductory chapter analyzes the evolution of Milwaukee's African-American community over the previous several decades. Although clearly dated in its outlook, "The Negro in Beloit and Madison," a 1933 master's thesis by Velma Bell is useful for comparing African Americans' experience in those two smaller cities with the Milwaukee experience.

No comprehensive study exists about the statewide import of specific immigrant groups from southern and eastern Europe (the "New Immigration"), although there are studies concerning particular locales. *The Immigrant Experience in Wisconsin* (1985) by La Vern J. Rippley is largely descriptive, but it provides historical context in which to interpret immigration from southern and eastern Europe. Fred L. Holmes's *Old World Wisconsin: Around Europe in the Badger State* (1944) is both popular and episodic, but it also conveys how several southern and eastern European groups contributed to the state's celebrated ethno-cultural diversity. Even allowing for its considerable bias in methodology and intent, the report of the United States Commission on Immigration (Dillingham Commission) contains worthwhile data on the residential and occupational patterns of these newcomers to Milwaukee. Patterns of intricate social interaction among ethnic groups are delineated by Richard Bernard in *The Melting Pot and the Altar: Marital Assimilation in Early Twentieth Century Wisconsin* (1980), which includes as well Bernard's astute observations about the impact of the "new" immigration on the "old." *Races and Immigrants in America* (1908) by John R. Commons and

The Old World in the New: The Significance of Past and Present Immigration to the American People (1914) by Edward A. Ross reveal the racist assumptions held by at least two of Wisconsin's most illustrious progressive intellectuals and bear eloquent testimony to the ambivalence with which such influential thinkers viewed the plight of the immigrant working class.

As already noted, the best primary sources for a study of the changing nature of the workplace and the work force, and of the efforts of workers to cope with ever-growing harsh realities, are the biennial reports of the Bureau of Labor and Industrial Statistics and the Industrial Commission, the U.S. censuses of occupations, and the proceedings of the annual conventions of the Wisconsin State Federation of Labor. Although it does not focus specifically on Wisconsin, *Industrial Relations: Final Report and Testimony Submitted to Congress by the Commission on Industrial Relations* (1916) contains a great deal of relevant information, largely because Charles McCarthy and John R. Commons were two of the commission's most influential members. Robert Ozanne, *The Labor Movement in Wisconsin: A History* (1984), discusses labor strife in the wood-products industries and the activities of the Wisconsin State Federation of Labor. Thomas Gavett's *Development of the Labor Movement in Milwaukee* (1965) presents a much more detailed account of the evolution of the Milwaukee Federated Trades Council and the Wisconsin State Federation of Labor, stressing the interlocking directorate between those two organizations and the Social Democratic Party. Gerd Korman's *Industrialization, Immigrants, and Americanizers: The View from Milwaukee, 1866-1921* (1967) analyzes the impact of the "new industrialism," "scientific management," and "welfare capitalism" upon workers. The growing influence of organized labor on Wisconsin politics, and of state government on the workplace, are amply documented in three durable works: Arthur J. Altmeyer, *The Industrial Commission of Wisconsin: A Case Study in Labor Law Administration* (1932); Gertrude Schmidt, "History of Labor Legislation in Wisconsin" (doctoral dissertation, University of Wisconsin, 1933); and Gordon M. Haferbecker, *Wisconsin Labor Laws* (1958).

Much of the material regarding the changing status of women and their growing influence in public life must be gleaned from such primary sources as the proceedings of the Wisconsin Federation of Women's Clubs, the Wisconsin Woman Suffrage Association Records, 1883-1925, and the yearbooks of the Woman's Club of Madison. The federation's proceedings were the key source for Janice Steinschneider's *An Improved Woman: The Wisconsin Federation of Women's Clubs, 1895-1920* (1994), which confirms the social conservatism of most members. The papers of the Wisconsin Woman Suffrage Association and the organization's various publications inform much of Lawrence L. Graves's 1954 doctoral dissertation "The Wisconsin Woman Suffrage Movement, 1846-1920." Valuable information regarding individuals and organizations can be gathered from two other publications: *The Story of Wisconsin Women* by Ruth De Young Kohler (1948), and *Wisconsin Women: A Gifted Heritage* (1982), produced by the Wisconsin chapter of the American Association of University Women. The single most important work published thus far on the women's movement is Genevieve McBride, *On Wisconsin Women: Working for Their Rights from Settlement to Suffrage* (1993), emphasizing the years from 1890 to 1920.

The impact of the Social Gospel or the "new religion" on Progressive Era Wisconsin can be determined primarily from Hugh H. Knapp's 1968 master's thesis, "The Social Gospel in Wisconsin, 1890-1912." It focuses on Protestant denominations and their influence on public life. Analyses of the effect of the Social Gospel on Catholics is contained in Richard J. Orsi's 1965 master's thesis, "Humphrey Joseph Desmond: A Case Study in Catholic Liberalism," and on Jews in Louis J. Swichkow and Lloyd P. Gartner, *The History of the Jews of Milwaukee* (1963).

The impact of the "new education" is best apprehended through the biennial reports of the Wisconsin Department of Public Instruction, the proceedings of the Wisconsin Teachers' Association, and the *Wisconsin Journal of Education*. Much can also be gleaned from two older topical histories of education: Conrad E. Patzer, *Public Education in Wisconsin* (1924) and Charles McKenny, ed., *Educational History of Wisconsin* (1912). Useful for an understanding of the rise of vocational education are Arthur M. Evans, *Vocational Education in Wisconsin* (1913), and Frank J. Woerdehoff, "Dr. Charles McCarthy: His Educational Views and Influence upon Adult Education in Wisconsin" (doctoral dissertation, University of Wisconsin, 1954).

The critical role of the University of Wisconsin during the Progressive Era has produced a substantial body of literature. The two-volume *The University of Wisconsin: A History, 1848–1925* (1949), written by Merle Curti and Vernon Carstensen, remains a classic study, chiefly because it delineates the synergistic relationship between the people of the state and their flagship institution. Maurice Vance's *Charles Richard Van Hise: Scientist Progressive* (1960) demonstrates the mutual influences on each of institution and its president. The memoirs of Richard T. Ely (*Ground Under Our Feet: An Autobiography*) and of John R. Commons (*Myself: The Autobiography of John R. Commons*), together with Benjamin Rader's *The Academic Mind and Reform: The Influence of Richard T. Ely in American Life* and Lafayette Harter's *John R. Commons: His Assault on Laissez-Faire*, examine the ideas of two of the University's most important faculty members. Three articles—Vernon Carstensen, "The Origin and Early Development of the Wisconsin Idea"; J. David Hoeveler, Jr., "The University and the Social Gospel: The Intellectual Origins of the Wisconsin Idea"; and Stuart Morris, "The Wisconsin Idea and Business Progressivism"—present significantly different interpretations of the role of the University in progressive reform. Two doctoral dissertations—Howard J. McMurray, "Some Influences of the University of Wisconsin on the State Government of Wisconsin" (University of Wisconsin, 1940), and Ruth H. Olcott, "An Analysis of the Impact of Changing Times and an Expanding Nation upon Five Selected Institutions of Higher Learning from 1869 to 1917" (University of Houston, 1954)—also present different perspectives.

Closely related to the University of Wisconsin in the spread of progressive ideas were the Free Library Commission, parent of the Legislative Reference Library; traveling libraries and local public libraries; and the State Historical Society of Wisconsin. Marion Casey's 1971 dissertation, "Charles McCarthy: Policy Maker for an Era," and her subsequent book, *Charles McCarthy: Librarianship and Reform* (1981), provide numerous insights into both the WFLC and the LRL, as does Edward Fitzpatrick's less objective *McCarthy of Wisconsin*. Kathryn Saucerman's 1944 master's thesis, "A Study of the Wisconsin Library Movement, 1850–1900," details the evolution of the WFLC. David Macleod, *Carnegie Libraries in Wisconsin*, stresses the interaction among local groups, the WFLC, and the Carnegie fund in the founding of public libraries. *Clio's Servant: The State Historical Society of Wisconsin, 1846–1954* by Clifford L. Lord and Carl Ubbelohde describes the efforts of Reuben Gold Thwaites to transform the Society into a resource for all the people of the state.

Anyone who endeavors to study Wisconsin politics and government in the Progressive Era confronts an embarrassment of riches. Seemingly every figure of significance has left a collection of private papers, nearly all of which are housed in the State Historical Society of Wisconsin. The biggest single trove, and the most readily accessible, is *The Wisconsin Progressives*, a microfilm version of the papers of Ely, Ross, McCarthy, Van Hise, and Commons, edited by Harry Miller (1985). The series consists of 350 reels of microfilm, and includes a finding aid for each collection. The records themselves consist primarily of correspondence, drafts of speeches and writings, diaries, newspaper files, and scrapbooks.

The Charles McCarthy papers are invaluable because he was the primary conduit between progressive ideas and reform legislation as well as the most astute and blunt analyst of the period's political machinations. His voluminous correspondence documents the synergistic relationship between reform activities in Wisconsin and those in other states, at the national level, and even in the international arena.

The John R. Commons papers are especially useful for information about such reforms as civil service, workmen's compensation, utility regulation, and the Industrial Commission. They also give occasional hints regarding Commons' frustration over the feud between La Follette and McGovern and its debilitating effect on the progressive movement. Unfortunately, much of Commons' correspondence and other documentation have not survived, though most of his speeches and articles have. The Charles R. Van Hise papers deal mostly with university administration, but there also is a significant amount of information about his personal role, and that of the university, in political and legislative struggles. The Richard T. Ely papers help us understand the evolution of the commonwealth concept, the new individualism and social investment, and other building blocks of "the Wisconsin Idea." They also demonstrate Ely's role as the mentor of many of the Progressive Era's leading intellectuals. The Edward A. Ross papers also deal primarily with his significant contribution to the formation of progressivism and the Wisconsin Idea. Together with the Ely and Van Hise papers, they shed a good deal of light on the university's fight to maintain academic freedom and integrity while being involved in ideological and partisan politics. All five collections richly document the symbiotic relationship that existed between Wisconsin progressivism and progressivism in the rest of the nation.

Of relatively less value are the papers of the three progressive governors—La Follette, Davidson, and McGovern—and of other political figures, such as Henry Cullen Adams, John J. Blaine, Herman L. Ekern, Isaac Stephenson, Charles D. Rosa, John Mandt Nelson, and Harry Curran Wilbur. In the main, they tend to focus on the "nitty-gritty" of politics and on such unlofty subjects as patronage, personal feuds, fund raising, and logrolling. They do serve as a reminder that personal ambition and partisan advantage often better explain the actions of acknowledged progressives than do ideological convictions. Most of these collections contain surprisingly little about the origins and evolution of the era's landmark accomplishments, suggesting strongly that leading politicians defined progressivism largely in terms of loyalty to a particular individual or faction.

The La Follette papers are divided between the State Historical Society of

Wisconsin and the Library of Congress; the Society holds those prior to his elevation to the United States Senate in 1905. The contents are largely political and document La Follette's credentials as a master political organizer and strategist who orchestrated events and people in the most minute detail. They also show him to be a man who totally conflated the progressive movement and the state's welfare with his personal political ambition, and who was capable of being both magnanimous and generous to his political allies and vindictive towards those who crossed him.

Particularly disappointing are the forty-seven manuscript boxes of the McGovern papers, which contain almost no material about the inside story of the legislatures of 1911 and 1913, which epitomized the apex and nadir of progressive reform in the state. They provide few clues to the governor's practical role in shepherding progressive legislation through the legislative process. Instead, they focus largely on the efforts of McGovern and his followers to gain or retain control of the progressive movement and the Republican party, especially after the 1912 national convention. In responding to inquiries regarding his personal position on a variety of reform matters, McGovern always took a progressive stance, except on woman suffrage. The most informative segment deals with the marketing commission campaign of 1913-1914 (box 21). Correspondence with McCarthy, Van Hise, and Commons also is revealing.

Insights into Progressive Era Wisconsin, documenting the state's importance nationally, are found unexpectedly in the papers of the era's three presidents, all available on microfilm from the Library of Congress. The Theodore Roosevelt papers include correspondence between Roosevelt and La Follette, McGovern, McCarthy, and other Wisconsin notables. The letters shed a different light upon the events and alignments of 1911-1914. They subtly document Roosevelt's growing distaste for La Follette and for the effects of factional fighting in a state that should have been one of his political strongholds. Much of Roosevelt's correspondence is also available in two published collections: Elting E. Morison, ed., *The Letters of Theodore Roosevelt*, (8 vols., Cambridge, 1951-1954) and Hermann Hagedorn, ed., *The Works of Theodore Roosevelt* (24 vols., New York, 1923-1926). The William Howard Taft papers demonstrate his growing antagonism towards the activities of the Republican Insurgents in Congress between 1909 and 1912, an animosity directed especially at La Follette as their leader and Taft's most outspoken critic. They also show how Taft tried to undermine La Follette's presidential aspirations in 1912 and to support the resurgent stalwart movement in Wisconsin led by Emanuel Philipp. The Woodrow Wilson papers contain correspondence with McCarthy regarding the Democratic platform and about McCarthy's concerns regarding the administration's patronage policies and its role in the 1914 election. They also contain correspondence with Joseph E. Davies, John Aylward, John Karel, and other Wisconsin Democrats on similar subjects. Many of these appear in Arthur S. Link et al., eds., *The Papers of Woodrow Wilson* (60 vols., Princeton, 1966-). Another relevant and useful collection in the Library of Congress is the papers of the National Progressive Republican League, founded by La Follette and his fellow Insurgents to unseat Taft and the standpatters in 1911.

In reconstructing the process through which progressive legislation was ultimately enacted, the two indispensable government documents are the journals of the Wisconsin assembly and senate which are published biennially after each legislative session ends. The journals enable the tracing of each piece of reform legislation from introduction through final passage, and enable analysis of roll call votes. Scholars also should consult the compilations of Wisconsin statutes and their annotations, which assist with tracing new laws and of amendments and additions to existing statutes. The legislative journals contain only actions, not debates and testimony. For those, one must consult newspapers, such as the Milwaukee *Sentinel* and *Journal* or the *Wisconsin State Journal*, which sometimes covered hearings and floor debates.

Newspapers of the period were unabashedly partisan and ideological, so it is important to be aware of the orientation of each and to read them comparatively. For example, the coverage given workmen's compensation by the stalwart Republican Milwauke *Sentinel*, the progressive independent Democratic Milwaukee *Journal*, and the Socialist Milwaukee *Leader* differs markedly and requires a sophisticated comparison. The governors' addresses and messages to the legislature also are valuable for tracing the evolution of progressive legislation, as are the reports of the *ad hoc* legislative committees formed to study such subjects as workmen's compensation, insurance regulation, conservation, and industrial education.

The most productive strategy for gaining some measure of intellectual control over the vast published literature on the political aspects of Progressive Era Wisconsin is to divide it roughly into three fairly distinct chronological periods peopled by three different generations of writers. The first generation consists of those authors who themselves participated in the events that they chronicled. The starting points here are of course *La Follette's Autobiography* and McCarthy's *The Wisconsin Idea*. Although each book is seriously flawed in different ways, they are indispensable for gaining a historical sense of the movement at its two periods of zenith, and for capturing the mood of exuberance and optimism that animated it. Read comparatively, they provide a reasonably clear picture of the similarities and differences, the continuities and changes that characterized progressive reform over a decade and a half. Reinforcement for McCarthy's interpretation permeates McGovern's succinct campaign tract *Nationalize the Wisconsin Idea*. Lincoln Steffens' pieces written during the first decade of the century present an unabashedly La Follette-centered interpretation. Published in that fateful year of 1912, Frederic Howe's *Wisconsin: An Experiment in Democracy* looks at developments from a more detached, nationwide perspective, and conveys a powerful sense of Wisconsin's reputation as "the most progressive state." Taken together, La Follette and Steffens personify the older, anti-special-interest, democratic strain of progressivism. McCarthy, McGovern, and Howe exemplify the New Nationalism brand that contains many of the seeds of the New Deal and of twentieth-century liberalism.

Despite its author's close connection to its protagonist and its limited chronological range, Albert Barton's *La Follette's Winning of Wisconsin, 1894–1904* is absolutely must reading. The book is rich in detail and alive with astute insights into personal motivations and political machinations. Barton essentially celebrates La Follette's triumph as a victory for good government and in the best interests of the people of Wisconsin. But in many instances he is surprisingly objective, analytical, and even critical. Less valuable, but essential to an understanding of the intellectual and political milieu of progressivism in Wisconsin and the nation, are the autobiographies of Richard T. Ely and John R. Commons.

Commons' is especially useful for its discussion of the legislative process, while Ely focuses on the ideological underpinnings provided by the "New Social Science" and the "New Religion." They both also provide insights into the personalities of La Follette, McCarthy, and others.

Two other books convey a powerful sense of what might be called the "cult of La Follette" that enjoyed currency during the inter-war years. The two-volume biography begun by Belle Case La Follette and completed by their daughter Fola supplies intimate perceptions of public events and hints strongly at the influential role that Belle played in her husband's career. Despite its "Bob-centric" perspective, the book becomes more objective about his later career, especially in the sections written by Fola. Published at the time of La Follette's 1924 presidential run, Chester Platt's *What La Follette's State Is Doing: Some Battles Waged for More Freedom* attributes every single progressive achievement to his protagonist. The value of the book lies in Platt's discussion of Wisconsin's impact on progressive developments in other states—an impressive legacy, even if read circumspectly.

Critics and dissenters fortunately provide the necessary antidote to these assessments. Heading that list is Emanuel Philipp's *Political Reform in Wisconsin: A Historical Review of the Subjects of Primary Election, Taxation, and Railway Regulation* (1910). An unremittingly stalwart world-view skews the book, which is nonetheless remarkably prescient in its discussion of the effects of the direct primary. It also identifies many of the flaws inherent in the structure and operation of the Railroad Commission. Philipp infuses the book with an ironic sense of humor and skepticism regarding the perfectibility of human nature, and he effectively challenges many articles of faith in the progressive credo. Isaac Stephenson takes a position somewhere in the middle of the progressive-stalwart spectrum in his *Recollections of a Long Life, 1829–1915*. He demonstrates the growing disillusionment of moderates with progressivism's turn to the left, as well as their unwillingness to acknowledge La Follette as the unquestioned leader of the movement and of the Republican party. The book also documents Stephenson's absolutely vital role as La Follette's financial angel. In his *Pioneer and Political Reminiscences* (1930), Nils Haugen is even more devastating than Stephenson in his critique of La Follette. Haugen portrays him as an unscrupulous politician who used the progressive movement as a vehicle for rationalizing his personal ambitions. He differs from Stephenson mostly in that La Follette rather than progressivism disillusioned him. Ralph Plumb reduces the struggle between progressives and stalwarts to a factional fight within the dominant Republican party in *Badger Politics, 1836–1930* (1930). He downplays both ideological differences and progressive reform while attempting to locate the Progressive Era within the longer context of a century of Wisconsin political development.

The second generation of historians of Progressive Era Wisconsin emerged just after World War II, about two decades subsequent to the elder La Follette's death and just after his two sons, Phil and Bob, Jr., had presided over their version of its sequel. Less emotionally involved, and having the benefit of chronological distance and historical perspective, the second generation historians usually painted a portrait that was more nuanced and that stressed impersonal forces more than personalities. The two chief figures in this generation are Robert S. Maxwell and Herbert F. Margulies. Despite the title *La Follette and the Rise of the Progressives in Wisconsin* (1956), Maxwell defines the progressive movement as a "union of soil, shop, and seminar," and emphasizes the multiplicity of people and forces that combined to make Wisconsin the pre-eminent progressive state in the nation by 1912. In *Emanuel L. Philipp: Wisconsin Stalwart* (1959), Maxwell presents Philipp as a worthy antagonist with real concerns about the direction in which the progressives were taking the state. In *The Decline of the Progressive Movement in Wisconsin* (1968), Margulies stresses the tenuous coalition that characterized the state's progressive movement from the outset, objectively analyzes the strengths and weaknesses of its leaders, and concludes that the movement imploded because of factionalism and because it had failed to prepare the electorate adequately for the sweeping reforms enacted in 1911. He also demonstrates the importance of such extraneous factors as a resurgence of anti-Catholicism and the outbreak of World War I. In *Senator Lenroot of Wisconsin* (1977), Margulies limns a rich portrait of a staunch progressive and La Follette protégé who was eventually alienated by party factionalism and La Follette's opposition to World War I. Equally important in this second-generation revisionism is Eric Lampard's *The Rise of the Dairy Industry in Wisconsin*, especially its concluding chapter entitled "The Wisconsin Idea in Dairying."

Several lesser revisionist works belong in this generation of scholarship. In *La Follette and the Establishment of the Direct Primary in Wisconsin, 1890–1904* (1941), Allen Fraser Lovejoy traces the evolution of sentiment for that crucial reform in state and nation, emphasizing La Follette's pragmatism and late conversion to the movement, as well as his waffling on the provisions of the final measure. In his 1964 master's thesis "The Reformer as Politician: Robert M. La Follette in the election of 1900," Robert C. Twombly examines the compromises and ambiguous understandings that characterized the "harmony campaign" that made La Follette governor. Vernon Carstensen's article "The Origin and Early Development of the Wisconsin Idea" attributes the concept to the ideal of public service by the University as preached by President John Bascom long before La Follette, McCarthy, and the rest appeared on the public scene. Although frequently an exercise in hero worship, Edward Fitzpatrick's *McCarthy of Wisconsin* (1944) describes the crucial behind-the-scenes role played by the Legislative Reference Library and McCarthy in many of the Progressive Era's foremost achievements. Finally, Edward N. Doan's *The La Follettes and the Wisconsin Idea* (1947) stresses the continuity in Wisconsin politics during the first three decades of the twentieth century.

Revising the revisionists is a coterie of scholars who did their graduate work on the Madison campus during the tumultuous decade of the 1960's, where they learned to question all verities—eternal and otherwise. Leery of big government and of crusades, they subject the period's reforms to intense scrutiny and are at pains to point out the compromises and political deals that undermined their outward purposes. These scholars were imbued with the new social history, and place the impetus for reform in grass-roots movements and in the persistent labors of activists who rarely gained celebrity. David P. Thelen takes the lead in this group with three interrelated books: *The Early Life of Robert M. La Follette, 1855–1884* (1966); *The New Citizenship: Origins of Progressivism in Wisconsin, 1885–1990* (1972); and *Robert M. La Follette and the Insurgent Spirit* (1976). In the first, Thelen challenges La Follette's self-portrait of his pre-congressional years, portraying him more as a pragmatic young man on the make than as a lifelong champion of progressive causes. In the second, he locates the origins of progressivism in the response to economic depression of the 1890's undertaken by numerous grass-roots organizations of consumers, taxpayers, and citizens; he presents La Follette as a man who belatedly embraced the cause of reform in order to revive his stagnating political career. In the third, Thelen interprets La Follette as a lifelong political opportunist who co-opted a nationwide insurgent movement of consumers and distorted it into a "producer-oriented" one that promised government largess in exchange for votes.

Complementing Thelen, Stanley P. Caine and Roger E. Wyman inaugurated their revisionist work in 1973 by editing and revising Emanuel Philipp's *Political Reform in Wisconsin*. In their introduction, they acknowledge their agreement with much of Philipp's critique of La Follette, the direct primary, and railroad regulation. In *The Myth of a Progressive Reform: Railroad Regulation in Wisconsin, 1903–1910* (1970), Caine further takes La Follette to task for his blatant manipulation of the railroad regulation and taxation issues, his courting of railroad support during the harmony campaign, and for serious undermining of the Railroad Commission bill in the interest of gaining election to the U.S. Senate. In his massive dissertation "Voting Behavior in the Progressive Era: Wisconsin as a Case Study," Wyman presents a mountain of statistical evidence to demonstrate his contention that ethno-cultural, partisan voting continued to dominate Wisconsin politics during the period, and that the progressives owed much of their electoral success to their ability to practice the "old politics" while professing the new.

Kenneth C. Acrea also applies the grass-roots approach, but to progressive legislation, rather than to politicians and elections. His doctoral dissertation, "Wisconsin Progressivism: Legislative Response to Social Change, 1891 to 1909" (1968), documents the evolution of a reform coalition within the legislature over time, largely in response to ever-building constituent pressure for government intervention. In Acrea's story, La Follette is more reactor than actor, while reform occurs outside his initiatives. Acrea's hero, if there is one, is Albert R. Hall, the populist-oriented assemblyman from northwestern Wisconsin who persuaded his colleagues and La Follette that the time for reform had come.

These same revisionist themes are evident in several other works of the 1960's and '70's. In his article, "The Experts Versus the Experts: Conflicting Philosophies of Municipal Utility Regulation in the Progressive era," in *WMH*, 58 (Spring, 1975), David Nord interprets the regulation of public utilities by state government, in Wisconsin and elsewhere, as an industry-supported effort to evade stricter regulation, or even municipal ownership, at the local level. Stuart D. Brandes, in his master's thesis "Nils P. Haugen and the Wisconsin Progressive Movement" (1965), elaborates on Haugen's critique of La Follette, while Marion T. Casey, in her dissertation "Charles McCarthy: Policy Maker for An Era" and her book *Charles McCarthy: Librarianship and Reform* (1981), places McCarthy center stage. W. Elliot Brownlee, in his *Progressivism and Economic Growth: The Wisconsin Income Tax, 1911–1929*, interprets the tax as an effort by progressives to win back their shrinking rural support by providing the revenue to finance an agricultural service state. Brownlee contends that the tax reduced the state's manufacturing base, thereby retarding its economic growth. Continuing the trend of revising the revisionists, John O. Stark, "The Establishment of Wisconsin's Income Tax," *WMH*, 71 (Autumn, 1987), strongly refutes Brownlee's interpretation and presents the tax as part of a nationwide revolution in taxation dedicated to the principle of apportioning taxes on the basis of the ability to pay.

To comprehend fully the nature and significance of the Progressive Era in Wisconsin, it is necessary to compare Wisconsin with other states during the same period, and to place Wisconsin developments within the broader context of the entire Progressive Era. This is relatively easy, since there are several outstanding studies of the Progressive Era in individual states. The prototype is George E. Mowry's *The California Progressives* (1951), which credits reform there to the Republican party and attributes it largely to the efforts of activists who were middle-class, economically comfortable, college-educated, and "touched by the long religious hand of New England." The most recent entry, Thomas R. Pegram's *Partisans and Progressives: Private Interest and Public Policy in Illinois, 1870–1922* (1992) is an incisive analysis of the rise and fall of the reformist impulse in a state geographically contiguous to Wisconsin but light years away in its public and political cultures. Pegram demonstrates how fragile coalitions of intellectuals, settlement house workers, and civic club leaders stirred great public support for a variety of reforms, only to be ultimately frustrated by the state's complex social and ethnic divisions, as well as by their own inability to resolve the dilemma between efficiency and expertise, on the one hand, and popular participation and control, on the other. Focusing on another Wisconsin neighbor with characteristics far more similar, Carl H. Chrislock's *The Progressive Era in Minnesota, 1899–1918* (1971) portrays the progressive movement there as bipartisan, with deep roots in the agrarian radicalism of the late nineteenth century. He also examines the connections between progressivism and the Nonpartisan League and Farmer-Labor Party. Hoyt Landon Warner's *Progressivism in Ohio, 1897–1917* (1964) stresses the urban origins of Ohio's progressive reform, while Robert S. La Forte's *Leaders of Reform: Progressive Republicans in Kansas, 1900–1916* (1974) argues that reformers from the western two-thirds of the state were too moderate, and too devoted to prohibition, to gain much support among the urban working classes in the eastern one-third. Robert W. Cherny's *Populism, Progressivism, and the Transformation of Nebraska Politics, 1885–1915* (1981) examines how such prominent national leaders as insurgent Republican George W. Norris, a La Follette ally, and populist Democrat William Jennings Bryan, who frequently aided the cause of Wisconsin progressivism, arose out of Nebraska.

The most comprehensive study of the Progressive Era in a New England state is Richard M. Abrams, *Conservatism in a Progressive Era: Massachusetts Politics, 1900–1912* (1964), which finds that by 1900 the commonwealth had already achieved many of the goals of progressive reform sought by other states, and that "progressives" expended much of their time and energy defending their accomplishments and positions against more radical labor legislators and urban Democrats, both of whom represented immigrant-stock, working-class voters. As detailed by James E. Wright, *The Progressive Yankees: Republican Reformers in New Hampshire, 1906–1916* (1987), and Winston A. Flint, *The Progressive Movement in Vermont* (1941), reform in those two rock-ribbed Republican states never moved beyond the good-government, anti-special-interest stage that characterized the La Follette administrations. *From Realignment to Reform: Political Change in New York State, 1893–1910* (1981), by Richard L. McCormick, focuses on the efforts of patrician reformers, personified by Charles Evans Hughes, to prevent business organizations and political machines from corrupting the electoral, legislative, and administrative processes. In terms of legislative accomplishments, New York was one of the few states to rival Wisconsin. Ransom E. Noble, *New Jersey Progressivism Before Wilson* (1946), examines the evolution of the "New Idea" that concentrated on railroad and utility regulation, labor legislation, and political reform. Noble contends that the Wilson administration of 1910–1912 simply amplified earlier accomplishments.

Racism seriously compromised progressive reform everywhere in the Old South. Nevertheless, several states still prided themselves on their "progressivism." Sheldon Hackney, *Populism to Progressivism in Alabama* (1969), centers the reformist influence there in "a loose federation of the leadership and membership of different associations and informed groups interested in short-term reform." Their common denominator, Hackney writes, was a shared opposition to the forces of modernization in state and nation. In *Old Virginia Restored: An Interpretation of the Progressive Impulse, 1870–1930* (1968), Raymond H. Pulley examines the ambiguous nature of reform in Virginia, while Dewey W. Grantham, *Hoke Smith and the Politics of the New South* (1958), equates progressivism in Georgia with the drive to modernize, urbanize, and industrialize the region. Lewis L. Gould's *Progressives and Prohibitionists: Texas Democrats in the Wilson Era* (1973) stresses the disruptive influence exerted by moralistic reformers on the efforts of pro-Wilson Democrats to ally the state with the reformist trend in the national Democratic party.

Locating the Wisconsin experience within the broader context of the entire Progressive Era is a far more protean task, because both the primary source material and the historical literature are vast and varied. Besides the mountain of primary source material housed in the State Historical Society of Wisconsin and the Library of Congress, much is also available in the Southern Historical Collection of the University of North Carolina at Chapel Hill, the Bancroft Library of the University of California at Berkeley, and various other local, state, and regional repositories.

Perhaps the best place to begin the search for historical literature is John D. Buenker and Nicholas C. Burckel, eds., *Progressive Reform: A Guide to Information Sources* (1980), which contains information on 1,656 books, articles, and dissertations arranged into topical chapters: general accounts; origins and nature; autobiography and biography; progressive thought; urban, state, regional, and national reform; cultural and moral, political and economic, and social welfare issues; non-mainstream efforts; foreign policy; and decline, persistence, and legacy. In addition, it includes detailed indexes to authors and subjects to aid searches for linked materials. Today it can be supplemented easily by using electronic searching devices. Equally valuable as an initial source is John D. Buenker and Edward R. Kantowicz, eds., *Historical Dictionary of the Progressive Era, 1890–1920* (1988). It contains over 800 relatively brief entries providing basic facts about the most significant people, events, organizations, legislation, and concepts of the period, along with a brief assessment by each entry's author of the topic's historical importance in the Progressive Era. Two hundred Progressive Era scholars wrote the entries, and each is accompanied by a brief bibliography.

The pioneering effort at encompassing all of the period's facets within a single interpretive framework was by Benjamin Parke DeWitt, in *The Progressive Movement: A Non-Partisan, Comprehensive Discussion of Current Tendencies in American*

Politics (1915). Over the next several decades, progressive reform generally was viewed as the logical extension of the agrarian radicalism personified by the Populists during the 1890's. The most influential work in that regard was John D. Hicks's *The Populist Revolt: A History of the Farmers' Alliance and the People's Party* (1931). The switch to a more urban, middle-class focus was led by Richard Hofstadter in *The Age of Reform: From Bryan to F.D.R.* (1955), which posited a "status revolution" among the nation's traditional elites, who embraced reform in order to regain their former influence in a changing universe. A decade later, Robert H. Wiebe's *The Search for Order, 1877–1920* (1967) assigned the pivotal role to a rising new elite of managers, technicians, professionals, and intellectuals striving to impose their vision and values on the rest of society. In between, Samuel P. Hays, *The Response to Industrialism: 1885–1914* (1957), found the reform influence in the growing tendency of large groups of Americans to organize and intervene purposefully in the socio-economic and political orders.

Over the last three decades, a cohort of historians has revised and reinterpreted those earlier explanations of the furious activity that characterized the Progressive Era. The essence of that debate and its various resolutions can be found in five important journal articles: David P. Thelen, "Social Tensions and the Origins of Progressivism," *Journal of American History*, 56 (September, 1969), 323–341; John D. Buenker, "The Progressive Era: A Search for a Synthesis," *Mid-America*, 51 (July, 1969), 175–193; Peter G. Filene, "An Obituary for 'The Progressive Movement,'" *American Quarterly*, 22 (Spring, 1970), 20–34; Daniel T. Rodgers, "In Search of Progressivism," *Reviews in American History*, 10 (December, 1982), 113–132; and Richard L. McCormick, "The Discovery That Business Corrupts Politics: A Reappraisal of the Origins of Progressivism," *American Historical Review*, 66 (April, 1981), 247–274.

Readers seeking longer, more detailed analyses should consult any of the following books: Lewis L. Gould, ed., *The Progressive Era* (1974); John D. Buenker, John C. Burnham, and Robert M. Crunden, *Progressivism* (1977); John Whiteclay Chambers II, *The Tyranny of Change: America in the Progressive Era, 1900–1917* (1980); and Arthur S. Link and Richard L. McCormick, *Progressivism* (1983). Those who prefer their history without such a heavy dose of interpretive controversy should read any of the following books: William L. O'Neill, *The Progressive Years: America Comes of Age* (1975); Irwin Unger and Debi Unger, *The Vulnerable Years: The United States, 1896–1917* (1978); and John Milton Cooper, *Pivotal Decades: The United States, 1900–1920* (1990).

Because historians have just begun to examine the phenomenon of progressive reform in an international context, there are only a few book-length studies from that perspective. Ross Evans Paulson, *Women's Suffrage and Prohibition: A Comparative Study of Equality and Social Control* (1973), explores the similarities and differences among those two reform movements in the United States, Great Britain, and Australia. James T. Kloppenberg, *Uncertain Victory: Social Democracy and Progressivism in European and American Thought, 1870–1920* (1986), posits the existence of a "transatlantic community" of intellectuals and activists who sought to find a middle path between revolutionary socialism and laissez-faire capitalism. Peter J. Coleman, *Progressivism and the World of Reform: New Zealand and the Origins of the American Welfare State* (1987), examines the similarities and differences in the way that these two English-speaking countries approached the problem of social security in an urban, industrial environment.

Essay on Sources

As with every aspect of the Progressive Era, the nature of its legacy to future generations is the subject of intense controversy. The question of whether the ensuing decade of the 1920's represented a continuation or a complete break with the Progressive Era is thoughtfully explored by Arthur S. Link, "What Happened to the Progressive Movement in the 1920's?" in the *American Historical Review*, 64 (July, 1959), 833–851, and by Paul W. Glad, "Progressives and the Business Culture of the 1920's," in the *Journal of American History*, 53 (June, 1966), 75–89. Conflicting views of the relationship of progressivism to the New Deal of the 1930's are presented by Otis L. Graham, *An Encore for Reform: The Old Progressives and the New Deal* (1967), and Andrew M. Scott, "The Progressive Era in Perspective," in the *Journal of Politics*, 21 (November, 1959), 685–701. Finally, for two opposing perspectives on the overall legacy of the Progressive Era, see Richard Abrams, "The Failure of Progressivism," in Richard Abrams and Lawrence Levine, eds., *The Shaping of Twentieth-Century America* (1971), 207–224, and Thomas McCraw, "The Legacy of the Progressive Era," in Lewis L. Gould, ed., *The Progressive Era* (1974), 181–202.

INDEX

Acrea, Kenneth: assesses Progressive era, 418, 422, 500, 577, 594, 600
Adams, Charles Kendall: speaks to UW graduates, 19–20; as UW president, 376; and "new education," 377; and Gospel of Wealth, 378; and UW Extension Division, 383; and legislature, 389
Adams, Henry C.: 57, 67, 68, 70, 453
Adams, Thomas S.: 552, 583, 584
Adams County: 428; agriculture, 26–27, 44; and Progressivism, 422, 492
Addams, Jane: 252, 342, 351
Africa: 116
African Methodist Episcopal Church Literary Society: 202
Afro-American League: 199
Afro-American Review: 201
Agricultural College Extension. *See* University of Wisconsin Extension Division
Agricultural Experiment Station. *See* University Experiment Station
Agricultural Organization Society: 78, 581
Agriculture: and World's Columbian Exposition, 3, 4, 7; and depression of 1893-1897, 13; "golden age" of, 25–31, 80; Wisconsin as "America's Dairyland," 25–31, 40–42, 46–56; transition from logging to dairying, 26–27; parity, 28; specialization of, 30; tariff protection, 30; as way of life, 35–36, 38; conversion from wheat to dairying, 38–39, 42; feed crops, 42–43; silo storage, 43; cash crops, 43–46; specialty crops, 46; mechanization, 55, 138; and College of Agriculture, 56–66; resettlement of Cutover, 72, 74, 86, 563; farm co-operatives, 76–77; implement manufacturing, 80, 103–104, 244, 248; migration from farms to cities, 137–139; and labor, 216, 244–246; and technological innovation, 253–254; and child labor, 267; and WSFL, 296. *See also* Farms and farming
Airplanes: 313
Albanians: 223
Allen, William Francis: 434
Allen, William Harvey: 565, 572, 591, 641
Allen Tannery, 105, 114, 284, 290
Allis, E. P.: 104, 277
Allis, E. P., Company: at World's Columbian Exposition, 4; and depression of 1893-1897, 11–12; and "new industrialism," 109; Reynolds-Corliss engine, 109; amalgamation of, 121; workers, 217, 260, 264
Allis-Chalmers: agricultural implement manufacturing, 104, 108; builds "Manhattan" Corliss engine, 109; weakened by infighting, 110; rivaled by Fairbanks, Morse and Company, 116; horizontal integration, 120; formed, 121; assembly-line production, 250; in-house welfare, 252; and workmen's compensation, 545
Allis Reliance Works: 107
Aluminum Company of America (Alcoa): 87
Aluminum Goods Manufacturing Company (Mirro): 87
Aluminum Sign Company of Two Rivers: 87
Amalgamated Association of Street Railway Employees: 278, 288
Amalgamated Street Railway Employees: 154
Amalgamated Woodworkers: 286–287
Amateur Athletic Union: 323
American Association for Labor Legislation (AALL): and John R. Commons, 8, 233, 582; and working women, 273; accomplishments, 298; supports continuing education, 370; and labor laws, 508–509; lobbies for government intervention, 518; and labor statistics, 544, 583

American Association of University Women (AAUW): 343
American Brass Company: 249
American Co-operative Association: 77
American Economic Association: 381, 583
American Federation of Labor (AFL): formed, 235; and work hours, 261; and Women's Union Label League, 273; goals, 276, 278, 292; and MFTC, 276–280, 282, 293; and socialists, 276–280; and CTLU, 280; charter organizations, 282–285, 287–289; and Frank Weber, 291, 295; and WSFL, 293, 295–296; and industrial education, 370
American Federation of Voters: 239
American Foundrymen's Association (AFA): 102, 121
American Hide and Leather Company: 105
American Home Economics Association: 255
American Immigration Company: 72
American Labor Legislation Review: 298
American Political Science Association: 593
American Protective Association (APA): 184–185, 239, 357, 414, 421, 443
American Railway Union: 279, 287
American Social Science Association: 252
American Society for Testing Materials: 121
American Society for the Extension of University Teaching: 383
American Society of Equity. *See* Society of Equity
American Steel Barge Company: 117–118
American Tobacco: 111
Amerika (newspaper): 227
Ameringer, Oscar: 517–518, 657
Anderson, Lewis A.: 625–626
Anderson, William: 618
Andrews, John B.: 273
Anheuser-Busch: 8
Annals of the American Academy of Political and Social Science: 567
Anthony, Susan B.: 345
Anti-Catholicism: in Milwaukee, 164; and Lutherans, 183; and APA, 184–185, 239; in 1914 elections, 653–654
Antigo: 316
Antigo Item: 459
Anti-Semitism: 214, 215, 231
Apples: 45
Appleton: canning industry, 88; manufacturing, 90; first Wisconsin groundwood mill opens, 92; and Kimberly, Clark & Company, 93; Institute of Paper Chemistry, 94; automobile industry, 99–100; urbanization, 127, 129; and industrialization, 136; population and demography, 136, 318; MML chapter in, 174; naturalization rates, 219; electric plant, 304; and WFWC, 338; and women's societies, 339; and labor reform, 340
Appleton *Post:* 338, 477–478
Arcadia: 206
Argentina: 114
Arizona: 84
Armenian Apostolicism: 223
Armenians: immigrants, 204, 208, 210–212; workers, 213, 216; and religion, 225
Arnold, William A.: 168
Arnold, Joseph: 128n
Arts: at World's Columbian Exposition, 5; supported by lumber barons, 84; and Sunday blue laws, 185; and ethnic societies, 228, 230–232
Ashland: foundries, 103; industrial growth, 117; population and demography, 143, 208; public utilities, 152; and municipal reform, 160; MML chapter in, 174; immigrant labor, 217; naturalization rates, 219; Polish Catholics in, 224; wages, 259; labor, 287–288, 290–291, 340; and women's societies, 338; and reform, 340, 355
Ashland County: and Northern Wisconsin Farmers Association, 73; industrial growth, 117; and Chippewa Tribe, 191; southern and eastern Europeans in, 208; and Catholics, 224
Asia: 116
Associated Charities: 157, 217
Association for the Advancement of Milwaukee: 135
Assyrians: 148–149
Atlantic Equipment Company: 121
Australia: 117, 577
Austrian Galicia: 203
Austrians: immigrants, 139, 181, 204, 208–210, 212; population and demography, 206; workers, 215; and religion, 223
Automobile industry: and internal combustion engine, 99–100; in Racine, 113–114; vertical integration, 120; impact on cities, 134; and labor, 248; development of culture, 305; and American life, 311–312, 324; regulation of, 313
Aylward, John: 517, 614, 650–651, 655

Babcock, Joseph: and Edward Scofield, 450; and La Follette, 450–451; and Stalwart Republicans, 460, 477; and national politics, 467–468; and direct primary legis-

Index

lation, 471–472; elected delegate by "National Republican party," 479; discredited, 482; and 1906 elections, 497–498
Babcock, Stephen M.: 50, 62, 63
Bacon, Edward P.: 458–459, 474
Badger Brass: 284, 290
Badger State Banner (newspaper): 14
Bading, Gerhard: 171–172, 538
"Bad Lands" (Milwaukee neighborhood): 197
Bad River Reservation: 191, 192
Baensch, Emil: 477, 479
Bain Wagon Company: 13, 114
Baker, Ray Stannard: 22–23
Ballard, Clinton B.: 549
Bancroft, Levi: 524–525, 622, 650, 652, 654
Banks: failures, 10–11, 13, 16–17; and depression of 1893-1897, 12; proposed regulation of, 17
Baptists: immigrants, 182–183; and immigrants, 185, 224; blacks and, 200–201; churches, 225; rural, 358. *See also* Protestants
Bardon, Thomas: 160
Barley: 13, 29, 43
Barnes, John: 487
Barnett, James D.: 408
Barron: 395
Barron County: agriculture, 26, 44; cheese production, 54; and Chippewa Tribe, 191; southern and eastern Europeans in, 206–208; Russians in, 209; and 1910 elections, 522
Barton, Albert O.: on Albert R. Hall, 416; on La Follette, 442, 447, 454, 463; on Republican party split, 461; on "Red Gym Convention," 478
Bascom, John: supports labor, 299; and Charles R. Van Hise, 378; La Follette and, 431, 434, 570
Baseball: 185, 322
Basketball: 323
Baumgaertner, Henry J.: 167, 449, 450
Bayfield County: fruit production, 45; and Northern Wisconsin Farmers Association, 73; and Chippewa Tribe, 191; southern and eastern Europeans in, 206, 208; and Orthodox churches, 224; Progressive representatives from, 492
Bay View: in depression of 1893-1897, 12; iron and steel plants, 101, 120; Allis Reliance Works, 107; breweries, 107; industrialization, 132; 1886 massacre, 164, 277
Bay View Iron Works: 107
Beaver Dam: foundries, 103; industrialization, 115, 117; social systematization, 316; entertainment, 318
Beaver Dam Malleable Iron Company: 117
Beck, Joseph D.: 547, 550
Becker, Sherburn M.: 168
Beer, 4, 8. *See also* Brewing industry
Beffel, J. M.: 169
Beggs, John I.: 154
Belgians: 181, 412–413
Belgium: 508, 559
Belle City Malleable Iron Company: 103
Beloit: and depression of 1893-1897, 12, 14; annexes farmland, 27; milk production, 53; papermaking, 91; foundries, 103; industrialization, 115–116; and AFA, 121; urbanization, 126–127; population and demography, 136–137, 210; MML chapter in, 174; blacks in, 195–198, 201–202; societies in, 202; naturalization rates, 218–219; wages, 259; labor unions, 288
Beloit Iron Works: 116
Beloit *Labor Journal:* 288
Benedict, Crystal Eastman: 351
Benevolent Society (Madison): 337
Bennett Law: enrages German Catholics and Lutherans, 183–184; and immigrants, 225; and Jews, 226; and Slavs, 236–237; Democrats and, 402, 408, 418, 421; and Henry Clay Payne, 440; causes Republican defeats, 442
Berg, Ove H.: 540
Berger, Meta: 350, 352
Berger, Victor: and socialism, 21–22, 165, 169; and David S. Rose, 146; 1904 mayoral election, 168; elected to Congress, 169, 517, 526, 615; leads Social-Democratic Verein, 278; and labor, 279–281, 292; and Frank J. Weber, 293; and La Follette, 470; and immigration restriction, 608
Berlin: 44–45, 155
Berlin Iron Works: 116
Berlin Machine Works: 288
Bernhardt, Sarah: 327
Bible: 184, 225–226
Bichler, William: 642
Bicycling. *See* Cycling
Big Ten. *See* Intercollegiate Conference of Faculty Representatives
The Bill Factory (by Charles McCarthy): 652
Bird, Harlan P.: 506, 513, 555
Birge, Edward A.: 378, 383–384, 391
The Bitter Cry of the Children (by John Spargo): 267
Black River: 85
Black River Falls: 14

Blacks: and housing, 149, 196–197; population and demography, 182, 194–196; migrants, 185–186; discrimination against, 194, 196–199; employment, 197–198; churches, 200–201; societies, 201–202; and labor, 202, 235, 246; and politics, 202, 236; and Prohibition, 237; and new technology, 315; and GFWC, 336; ignored by reformers, 608

Blaine, John J.: La Follette protégé, 500; and 1911 legislative session, 537; and Industrial Insurance Committee, 545; and waterpower franchises, 556; gubernatorial candidate, 657, 660; as governor, 662–663

Blatz, Valentine: 277

Bloomer Girl (excursion boat): 325

Board of Agriculture: as State Agricultural Society, 31, 69; assesses Wisconsin agriculture, 31–32; on dairy farming, 41; on specialty crops, 46; assumes WDA's regulatory work, 71; and government intervention, 519; and Wisconsin Idea, 599

Board of Arbitration: 409, 422–423, 425, 550

Board of Commerce (Madison): 135–136

Board of Control: 340, 505, 518, 638

Board of Education: 392

Board of Forestry: 506

Board of Health: 423, 493, 519, 639

Board of Immigration: 27

Board of Industrial Education: 370, 599

Board of Public Affairs: 584; investigates UW, 58–59, 565, 572, 641; on normal schools, 375; established, 561, 564–565; investigates agricultural marketing, 563; and Milwaukee Bureau of Economy and Efficiency, 591; and Wisconsin Idea, 599–600; and Progressive factionalism, 634; and new budget system, 636; and co-operative marketing, 645–646; proposed abolition of, 652; and Emanuel Philipp, 661

Board of Regents (UW): and Hiram Smith, 46, 57; praises William A. Henry, 57; and Theodore Kronshage, 66; rebukes Richard T. Ely, 289; and gender discrimination legislation, 340, 507; and WFWC, 340; and academic freedom, 387–389; censures Oliver E. Wells, 388; and public school inspections, 391; superintendent of DPI on, 391; legislature considers replacing, 561

Board of Visitors: 378

Boden Corporation: 112

Bodenstab, Henry H.: 535–539

Bohemians: 181, 236, 244–245, 413

Bolens, Harry: 622

Book Lovers Club: 202

Borah, William: 520

Borden, Gail: 53

Bosshard, Otto: 556

Boston: 105, 508, 538, 559

"Branch One" (SDP): 165, 415

Brandeis, Louis D.: 590–591

Brazil: 114

Brewing industry: product value, 82; market grows, 88, 105–106; and subsidiary industries, 105; technological innovations, 105; in Milwaukee, 112; labor, 214–215, 244; unemployment, 263; and working women, 274; and woman suffrage, 350–351; lobbyists for, 407; in vocational education coalition, 559. *See also* Beer

Briggs and Stratton Corporation: 100

Bristow, Joseph: 520

British: immigrants, 181, 237; workers, 216, 244–245; and Republican party, 236; political affiliations, 413, 481; and direct primary, 482

Brockhausen, Frederick: 293, 294–296, 298, 494

Brown, Olympia: 345, 346, 349, 351

Brown County: cabbage production, 45; butter zones, 55; papermaking, 93; population and demography, 137; and Oneida Tribe, 190–191; southern and eastern Europeans in, 206

Bryan, William Jennings: 415, 424; and La Follette, 444, 469, 486

Bryant, George E.: in Republican faction, 416–417; and lobbyist registration, 427; and La Follette, 439, 453; and 1896 state Republican convention, 444; and 1898 Republican platform, 450; and James O. Davidson, 496

Bryce, Lord: 379

Buckmaster, A. E.: 284

Buckwheat: 13, 29

Bucyrus Company. *See* Bucyrus Steam Shovel and Dredge Company

Bucyrus-Erie Company: 104

Bucyrus Steam Shovel and Dredge Company: relocates from Ohio, 108; bankruptcy and reorganization of, 111, 121; assembly-line production, 250; in-house welfare, 252; workers, 264

Buffalo: population, 127

Buffalo (N.Y.): 49, 97, 107, 117

Bulgarians: 208, 215, 223

Bull, Frank K.: 485
Bureau of Indian Affairs (BIA): supervises Indian logging, 188–189; agricultural fairs, 190; and Green Bay Agency, 191; and health and medicine, 192–193; and acculturation of Indians, 193
Bureau of Labor and Industrial Statistics (BLIS): 400, 544; on depression of 1893-1897, 11, 13, 16; and state regulation of labor, 22; on farm labor, 138–139; on housing, 147–148, 149; made state watchdog, 177; on manufacturing wages, 259–260; on seasonal employment fluctuation, 263; and labor laws, 265–266, 299–300; on industrial accidents, 266; and child labor, 268–269, 339, 548; and working women, 273–274; and Frank J. Weber, 295; and unemployment, 297; investigates tax burden, 464; on railroads, 474–475; urges labor legislation, 494, 508–509; teachers' employment office proposal vetoed, 504; calls for government intervention, 518; subsumed by Industrial Commission, 550; and Wisconsin Idea, 599. *See also* Industrial Commission
Bureau of Municipal Research: 581, 593
Burke, Michael E.: 526
Burke, Timothy: 642–643, 653
Burlington: 310
Burnett County: 34, 191, 208
Burnham, Daniel H.: 2
Business: and profit sharing, 7; University of Wisconsin Extension Division and, 65; growth of professions, 256–257; modernization of offices, 257; and 1897 legislature, 426
Butler, John A.: 342
Butter: production, 30, 41, 52; and associated dairying, 49; and oleomargarine threat, 51, 56, 68–69; shift from cheese production, 67; labeling law, 68
Butter zones: 55
Byington, Margaret F.: 342

Cady, Frank A.: 474
Caine, Stanley P.: assesses Progressive era, 487–488
Calabrians: 230
Calumet County: 137, 237
Calvary Baptist Church (Milwaukee): 200
Camp, Anna: 356
Campbell, Helen: 21
Campbellsport: 207
Camp Douglas: 128

Canada: 75, 111, 114; immigrants from, 181–182, 209, 244
Canadian Anthracite Coal Company: 84
Canning industry: 45–46, 87–88
Capitol: burns, 489
Carlisle, John G.: 437
Carnegie, Andrew: 394–396
Carstensen, Vernon: assesses Progressive era, 575
Cary, Charles P.: and industrial and agricultural training commission, 362; and public education, 366–367; and UW public school inspections, 391–392; opposes State Board of Education, 392; and Kress-Payne correspondence, 469; and 1906 elections, 497; on agricultural and vocational education commission, 508; and William Harvey Allen, 641; and UW's relationship to state, 650; and anti-Catholicism, 653
Cary, W. J.: 280
Case, J. I., Company: at World's Columbian Exposition, 4; and automobile industry, 100; agricultural implement manufacturing, 103–104; diversifies, 113–114; opens South Works, 114; and mass transit, 133; Italian workers, 211, 216; Danish workers, 217; assembly-line production, 250
Cassville: 317–318
Catholic Citizen (newspaper): 183–184, 237, 299, 356, 357
Catholic Girls Home: 338
Catholics: and Social Democratic party, 165, 169; and David S. Rose, 167–168; and ethno-cultural disputes, 181–183; and Bennett Law, 183–184; and anti-Catholicism, 184–185, 239, 421; schools, and Indians, 191; ethnic discord, 223; immigrants, 223–224; churches, 223–225; in Milwaukee, 225; and parochial schools, 225–226; societies, 229–230; and Democratic party, 236; and Prohibition, 237; and Social Gospel, 356–358; and rural social centers, 358; political affiliations, 412, 481–482; and direct primary, 482; oppose eugenics, 642
Catt, Carrie Chapman: 346
Cattle: 29, 42
Central Association (Racine): 157
Central Labor Union (CLU): and Polish laborers, 235; and Eight-Hour League, 277; in Sheboygan, 284–285; in Ashland, 287
Central Trade and Labor Union (CTLU): 280
Central Trade Council: 285

Central-Verein: 357
Chain migration: 217, 222
Chamberlin, Thomas C.: 376–377, 383
Chapman, T. A.: 277
Chautauqua movement: 324, 383, 385
Cheese: production, 30, 41; and associated dairying, 49, 51; filled cheese scandal, 51, 56, 67–68; processed, 51; cold-curing process, 62; labeling law, 68; factories in Middle and New North, 88; factory labor, 244
Cherries: 45
Cheyenne Valley: 195
Chicago: 49, 97, 107; World's Columbian Exposition in, 2–9; market for pork, 42; meat-packers and oleomargarine, 68; investors in Wisconsin papermaking, 92; and railroads, 97–98, 122; Pabst beer promoted in, 112; and Rock River Valley, 115; and interurban railways, 310–311
Chicago, Burlington and Quincy Railway: 473
Chicago, Milwaukee and St. Paul Railway: and depression of 1893-1897, 12; work force, 107; increases mileage, 309; and *ad valorem* taxation legislation, 473; and regulation, 475
Chicago and North Western Railway: 177; and Racine, 141; increases mileage, 309; La Follette and, 452; and *ad valorem* taxation legislation, 473; supports Stalwart position, 485
Chicago Automobile Club: 325
Chicago Brass Company: 13, 114
Chicago *Continent:* 567
Chicago Employers' Association: 288. *See also* Citizens' Alliance
Chicago *News Record:* 22
Chicago *Record-Herald:* 567
Chicago-Rockford Hosiery: 284
Chicago *Skandinaven:* 443
Chicago Society for University Extension: 383
Chicago Times-Herald: 447
Chickens. *See* Poultry
Child Labor Committee: 298–299, 518
Children: immigrants' health and medicine, 149–150; and Wisconsin Conference of Charities and Corrections, 177; Indians' health and medicine, 192; and labor, 218, 262, 266–269; and WSFL, 296–297; and Wisconsin Child Labor Committee, 298–299; and BLIS, 340, 548–549; and U.S. Labor Commission, 340; and WFWC, 340

Children's Bureau: 267–268
Chile: 114
Chippewa County: 224, 244, 422
Chippewa Falls: bank failures, 10–11; lumber mill closes, 85; canning industry, 88; sash, door, and blind factories, 90; strikes, 290; interurban railways, 311
Chippewa Lumber and Boom Company: 83
Chippewa River Valley: 34, 83–85, 92–96, 291
Chippewa Tribe: cedes land to U.S.: 179; and allotment, 187; and logging, 189; and farming, 190; population, 191; religion, 194
Christian Endeavor Society: 185, 353
Christian Labor Union: 355
Church and Labor Social Union: 355
Churches: and poor relief, 157; and Indians, 190–191; blacks and, 200–201; as ethnic nuclei, 222–223; immigrant discord, 223–224; in Milwaukee, 225; immigrant organizations, 228; rural congregations, 358. *See also* Religion
Churchill, Josie: 36
Cities: topography, 126–128; demography, 136–137, 140–143; immigrants settle in, 139–142, 206; municipal services, 143–144, 145–46; and "privatism," 145; machine politics, 145–146; political graft, 146–147, 167–168; utilities, 151–155, 176; and consumer co-operatives, 155–156; poor relief, 157; housing reform, 158; public health, 159–160; and tax redistribution, 175–176; attract southern and eastern Europeans, 210; increasing concentration of workers in, 248; beautification projects, 318; socio-economic stratification, 319–321
Citizens' Alliance: 288
Citizen's Alliance and Manufacturer's Association: 284
Citizens' Business League (Milwaukee): 135
City Club (Milwaukee): 158
Civic Federation (Ashland): 160
Civic Federation (Superior): 160
Civic Union (Madison): 147
Civil rights: 199–200, 236
Civil Service Reform League: 340
Clapp, Moses: 520
Clark County: increase in farm acreage, 26; 1910 land values, 34; milk condensery in, 53; and Winnebago Tribe, 192; southern and eastern Europeans in, 206–208; Russians in, 209; politics, 237
Clayton: 224

Cleveland, Frederick A.: 591
Cleveland (Ohio): 97, 107–108
Clintonville: 100
Clio (literary society): 335
Coal: 81, 118
Cochems, Henry: 615, 618, 629, 659–660
Coleman: 207
College Endowment Association: 341
College of Agriculture (UW): and Cutover, 27, 74, 86; awards prizes for best farm homes, 33; and WDA, 39, 56; and cattle disease, 48; publications of, 55; founded, 56–57; extension service, 57–58, 65–66; growth of, 57–66; controls farmers' institutes, 60; and Ransom A. Moore, 60; agricultural short course, 60–61; teaching vs. research in, 61–62; and agricultural economics department, 63–64; usurps WDA's teaching function, 71; and Wisconsin Society of Equity, 77; and tuberculosis, 177; and agricultural progress, 254; expands, 376, 382; publicity, 387; and county schools of agriculture, 507; funding, 561; and Charles McCarthy, 645
College of Engineering (UW): 370, 381, 560
College of Letters and Science (UW): 382
Collier's (magazine): 388
Colored Helping Hand Intelligence Office: 201
Columbia County: 44, 55
Columbian History of Education in Wisconsin: 2, 5
Columbia University: 593
Columbus: 88
Combined Locks: 93
Commercial Association: 95
Committee of Fifteen: 367
Committee of Forty-Five: 160
Committee on Indian Affairs: 608
Commons, John R.: 342, 571, 584; at World's Congress Auxiliary, 6–7; and Progressivism, 8–9, 573–575; and Social Gospel, 20; and Emil Seidel administration, 170; and immigrants, 220, 223–224, 608; and trade unionism, 235, 251; on International Harvester welfare program, 252; and National Civic Foundation, 262; and AALL, 273, 298; and socialism, 295; and Woman's Club of Madison, 342; and laissez-faire capitalism, 381; on universities, 387; opposes "judge-made" law, 404; and tax commission, 488; on Industrial Insurance Committee, 509–510; and workmen's compensation, 545; on Industrial Accident Board, 547; on Industrial Commission, 550; and Wisconsin Idea, 572–573, 582–583; and commonwealth model, 587; and professional expertise, 590; and social efficiency, 591; and service state, 594; and UW's relationship to state, 597; and expert committees, 598
Commons, Nell, 638
Communications: telegraph, 305; typewriter, 305; telephone, 306; mass-circulation magazines, 306–307; "radio age," 308; movies, 308–309; censorship, 309
Communist party: 232
Concentration and Control (by Charles R. Van Hise): 582
Condenseries: 49, 52–54
Congregationalists: 182–183, 224, 355, 358
Congress (U.S.): 84, 124, 188, 515, 517
Connor, William D.: "Red Gym Convention" delegate, 479; runs for U.S. Senate, 483–484; opposes direct primary, 489; alienated by Progressives, 495–497, 516; chairman of Republican state central committee, 498; and 1910 elections, 520; and John C. Karel, 623
Conservation: legislation regarding, 419, 422, 425, 488, 493, 506; waterpower, 555–557; reforestation, 557–558
Conservation Commission: 555, 557–558, 599
The Conservation of Natural Resources (by Charles R. Van Hise): 582
Cook, Samuel A.: 477, 479, 499, 520, 522
Cooke, Morris L.: 591
Coolidge, Calvin: 662
Coombes, John: 33–34
Cooper, Henry Allen: 498, 618
Cooperative Labor Ticket. *See* People's party
Co-operatives: 63, 76–78, 155–156, 645–646
Coptic Catholicism: 223
Corcoran, Cornelius: 146
Corn: 13, 29–30, 40, 43
Cornucopia: 224
Cornwall: 180
Corporations: growth during neotechnic revolution, 118–121; vertical and horizontal integration, 119–120; super-corporations, 120; rise of, 247–249; and farms, 254
Corrupt Practices Act: 161
Cosmopolitan (magazine): 229
Cotton, Fassett A.: 366
Council of Jewish Women: 341–342
Country Life Movement: seeks to improve quality of rural life, 35–36, 38, 65; Coun-

try Life Conference, 70; and Charles McCarthy, 78; stems rural population drain, 139; Country Life Commission, 254, 582; and church reform, 358
Cox, James M.: 582
Coxey's Army: 23
Cranberries: 43–45
Crane, M. Oveda: 33
Crawford County: agriculture, 44; apple production, 45; southern and eastern Europeans in, 207; and Progressivism, 422; politics, 522
Cream City Club: 322
Cream City Social and Literary Society: 202
Creameries: 49, 54–55, 88, 244
Crivitz (Polish settlement): 206
Croatian Catholic Union: 230
Croatian Fraternal Union: 230
Croatians: 203–204, 207, 214, 223, 225, 230
Croly, Herbert: 590–591, 604
Cromwell, William N.: 154
Crosby, Emma: 335
Crownhart, Charles: 524–525, 547, 550
Cudahy, Patrick: 215
Cudahy: company town, 108; industrialization, 133; southern and eastern Europeans in, 206; factories, 250; and social systematization, 316
Cudahy Company: 106–107, 112, 217
Cumberland: 207
Cummins, Albert: 520, 577
Curlers' Club: 327
Curti, Merle: 596–597
Curtis, Dexter: 162
Cutover: and depression of 1893-1897, 16; and dairy farming, 55; and farmers' institutes, 60; land speculation in, 71–76; and immigrants, 72–74, 139, 206–208, 213, 217; and College of Agriculture, 74; reclamation and resettlement, 75, 557, 563; and American Society of Equity, 76; and lumber barons, 84; agriculture *vs.* reforestation, 86; pulp and paper industry, 90–92; migration to, 137–138; and railroads, 309
Cycling: 311, 321, 322–323
Czech Roman Catholic Union: 230
Czechs: immigrants, 139, 203, 207, 209–210, 212; language, 204–205; population and demography, 206; workers, 213, 217–218; religion, 223, 225; and schools, 226; societies, 230; politics, 236–237; and Prohibition, 237; farmers, 563
Czech-Slavic Benevolent Society: 230

Dahl, Andrew: 417, 443, 651–652, 654
Daily Cardinal (UW newspaper): 323
Dairy and Food Commission: and pasteurization, 53; dairy commissioner created, 67; assumes WDA's regulatory work, 71; size, 400; powers increase, 503; calls for government intervention, 518
Dairy industry: 2; at World's Columbian Exposition, 4, 7, 49; regulation of, 21; Wisconsin Idea in, 25; conversion from wheat farming to, 38–39, 42; suitability of Wisconsin for, 40; growth of, 40–42, 46–47; and "balanced dairy ration," 47; improvement of breeds, 47–48; and associated dairying, 49–50; unsanitary conditions, 50–51; filled cheese scandal, 51, 56; oleomargarine threat, 51, 56, 68–69, 436–437; cheese production, 51–52, 54, 56, 67–68; butter production, 52, 54–55, 67–69; fluid milk production, 52–53, 54; and Dairy and Food Commission, 53; and Medical Milk Commission, 53; and pasteurization, 53, 62; industrialization and, 54–56; Babcock test, 62; bovine tuberculosis, 62–63; co-operative herd improvement associations, 63; and roads, 70; product value, 82; mechanization of, 138, 253; and labor, 248; La Follette supports, 436; role in promulgating Wisconsin Idea, 575–576
Dakotas: 29, 83
Daly, B. J.: 447
Dane County: and farm mortgages, 29; agriculture, 44, 116; butter zones, 55; and railroads, 97–98; population and demography, 137; and Norwegian immigrants, 181; southern and eastern Europeans in, 207, 209; Russians in, 209; franchise requirements, 237; in 1898 election, 428
Dane County Pioneer Association: 326
Danes: immigrants, 181–182; workers, 217, 245; Lutherans, 224; folk schools, 226; societies, 228
Danish language: 227
Dan Patch: 325
Darrow, Clarence: 287
Davidson, James O.: and *ad valorem* taxation, 416; member of Republican faction, 416; and La Follette, 442, 613, 616; proposes corporation tax, 447; nominated for state treasurer, 450; and railroad regulation, 474; 1906 gubernatorial race, 495–498; 1908 elections, 499–500; as governor, 500–512; political legacy, 512–

514; alienated by Progressives, 516; 1910 elections, 521–522; Kenneth C. Acrea comments on, 577; loses Progressive drive, 612; endorses Francis McGovern, 653
Davidson Theater: 199
Davies, Joseph E.: 517
Dawes General Allotment Act: 187
Dawson, Miles M.: 503
Day, Frederick T.: 17
Debs, Eugene: 165, 279, 280–281, 516
The Decline of the Progressive Movement in Wisconsin (by Herbert F. Margulies): 574–575
Delavan: 326
Dells Paper & Pulp Company: 95
Democratic National Committee: 656
Democratic party: and depression of 1893-1897, 18–19; and public utilities, 153, 161; in Madison, 162; in Milwaukee, 163–169, 171; and Bennett Law, 183, 418; religious ritualists unite under, 183; blacks and, 202; immigrants and, 236–237; and Prohibition, 238; and WSFL, 292–293, 295; and partisanship in state government, 401–403, 412–414; opposes government intervention, 402–403; and party loyalty, 405; and Civil War, 412–413; 1894 elections, 418, 421–422; 1904 platform, 480; supports La Follette, 481; in 1907 and 1909 legislative sessions, 501; and labor legislation, 509; Progressive Democrats, 515, 517; 1910 elections, 523–526; and 1911 legislative session, 533–566; and commonwealth model, 588; progressive wing emerges, 614; benefits from La Follette-McGovern discord, 630–631; 1913 platform, 632; 1914 elections, 656
Denmark: 644
Department of Agriculture (state): 74, 205
Department of Debating and Public Discussion Extension (UW): 397
Department of Public Instruction: 518, 559
Department of Public Property: 400
Department of the Interior (U.S.): 189
De Pere: 93, 316
Depression of 1893-1897: bank failures, 10–11, 13, 16–17; unemployment, 11–13; tramps, 14; and Cutover, 16; class conflict during, 17–18; and politics, 19; devastates Milwaukee, 107; and public utilities, 152; Republicans blame Democrats for, 421

Desmond, Humphrey J.: 183–184, 299, 356–357
Detroit: 97, 107–108, 108
Devil's Lake State Park: 506
Dewey, George: 112
Dewey, John: 360
Dietrich, Hervey: 161
Discrimination: housing, 134, 141; against Indians, 189, 189, 194, 194; against blacks, 194, 196–199; against immigrants, 219–220; against women, 343–344
Dithmar, Edward F.: 657
Division of Immigration: 205
Dixon, Thomas: 199
Doan, Edward N.: 574
A Documentary History of American Industrial Society: 381
Dodge County: decline in farm acreage, 27; cheese production, 51, 54; iron ore, 82, 98; black settlements in, 195; southern and eastern Europeans in, 208
Domestic science: 255
Donald, John S.: 562, 651, 654, 657
Door County: agriculture, 43; fruit production, 45; lumbering, 82n, 91; canning industry, 88; Peninsula State Park, 506
Douglas County: and Northern Wisconsin Farmers Association, 73; industrial growth, 117; population and demography, 127, 137; southern and eastern Europeans in, 206, 208; Russians in, 209; and Catholics, 224; labor force, 244
Duluth (Minnesota): 97
Dumore Company: 113
Dunn County: cheese production, 54; Southern and eastern Europeans in, 208; domestic science in schools, 255; normal school, 365; opens agricultural school, 366; educational reforms, 367; traveling libraries, 396; and Progressivism, 422, 492
Dunne, Edward F.: 582
Dutch: 181–182, 412–413
Dziennik Ludowy (newspaper): 236

Eagle River: 94, 205
East End Women's Relief Corps: 337
Eastern Orthodox Christianity: 223
East Troy: 310
Eau Claire: milk production, 53; Empire Lumber Company closes, 85; breweries, 88; canning industry, 88; manufacturing, 88, 90; diversifies manufacturing base, 95–96; population and demography, 136,

142; housing, 148–149; poor relief, 157; municipal services, 173; strikes in, 290; and interurban railways, 311; football, 324; recreation in, 326; extension field district in, 385; normal school, 507
Eau Claire County: population and demography, 127, 137; southern and eastern Europeans in, 208; and Catholics, 224; labor force, 244
Eau Claire *Daily Telegram:* 324
Eau Claire National Bank: 84
Eau Claire Pulp and Paper Company: 92
Ebling, Walter H.: 25
Economy: depression of 1893-1897, 9–23; and immigration, 232–234; wages, 256–260; cost of living, 258–259; unemployment, 262–264
Edgerton: 184, 225–226
Education: 2; at World's Columbian Exposition, 5, 8; and depression of 1893-1897, 19; proposed state intervention in, 21; in Milwaukee, 130, 156, 172; blacks and, 198–199; of immigrants, 225–226; agricultural, 366–367; curriculum reform, 368–369, 373, 380; vocational, 368–371; central board of education established, 392; legislation affecting, 419, 422, 425, 493, 507–508, 641; vocational schools, 558–560; and Wisconsin Idea, 593. *See also* "New education"; Schools; University of Wisconsin; University of Wisconsin Extension
Education Society: 226
Edwards, Carrie: 335
Edwards, Richard Henry: 356
Eight-Hour League: 277
Eisendrath Tannery: 105
Ekern, Herman: and La Follette, 442; and state insurance regulation, 489, 502–503; and James O. Davidson, 495–496; and Isaac Stephenson, 498; 1908 elections, 499; as insurance commissioner, 542, 625–627; investigates anti-Catholicism, 653–654
Electricity: and "neotechnic revolution," 81, 98; and laundry industry, 99; and manufacturing of electrical machinery, 99; and Racine companies, 113; and railroads, 123; machinery workers, 248; and technological innovations, 304–305; and interurban railways, 310. *See also* Public utilities
Eleventh Story League. *See* Wisconsin Republican League

Elgin (Ill.): 49
Eliot, Robert: 458, 474
Elkhart Lake: 310–311, 326
Elks (club): 202, 326
El Paso: 355
Elroy: 395
Elward, Rodney A.: 532
Ely, Richard T.: and Social Gospel, 6, 20, 354; and Progressivism, 8, 9, 573–575; and University of Wisconsin Extension Division, 21; on demography, 126; and AALL, 273; and Madison Federated Trades Council, 289; on Chautauqua circuit, 324; achieves national reputation, 376; and political economics, 381; and Oliver E. Wells, 388; publishes *The Soil,* 570–571; and the Wisconsin Idea, 570–573, 583; and commonwealth model, 586–587; and new individualism, 588–590; and professional expertise, 590; and service state, 594; on UW's relationship to state, 596–597
Emery, John Q.: 41, 50–51, 68, 69
Empire Lumber Company: 84, 85, 95
Employers Mutual Liability Insurance Company: 95
Enders' Agency: 264
English language: 183–184, 190–191
Episcopalians: and ethno-cultural disputes, 181–183; and Indian education, 191; blacks and, 201; and Sunday blue laws, 353
Epworth League: 185, 354
Equal Suffrage Clubs: 346
Equity Home Market: 77
Erickson, Halford: 474, 486–487, 584
Esch, John J.: 498
Essmann, William L.: 626
Estabrook, Charles: 653
Estonians: 204, 224
Eugenics: 239–240, 642
Everett, C. M.: 160
Everitt, James A.: 76
Everybody's Business (by William Harvey Allen): 641
Everyday Housekeeping (magazine): 255
Extension, University of Wisconsin. *See* University of Wisconsin Extension

Fairbanks, Morse and Company: 115–116, 197
Fairchild, Edward T.: 520–522, 545
Falcons (club): 228–229

Index

Falk, Herman: 110
Falk, Otto H.: 110
Falk Corporation: 110
Families: immigrant, 221–222; changing dynamics, 327–328, 331; "New familialism," 327–330; and divorce, 330–331; and domestic violence, 330–331
Farm Bureau *News:* 55
Farmers' institutes: 60, 65, 190, 397
Farms and farming: mortgages, 28–29; contrast between northern and southern Wisconsin, 32–34; modernization of, 35–36; isolation and drudgery, 36–37, 138; and medicine, 37; migration of young to cities, 37, 65, 137–139; mortality rates, 37; horses, 42; women on, 138, 270–271, 333; on reservations, 187, 190; laborers, 247; tenant, 254–255; and villages, 316–317; and "New familialism," 329. *See also* Agriculture
Favill, Stephen: 46, 48
Federal Steel: 120–121
Federal Trade Commission: 582
Federated Jewish Charities: 231, 357
Federated Trades Council (Milwaukee): 165
Federation of Women's Clubs: 273, 347, 398
Fern Dell: 447
Fifield: 325
Filer & Stowell Company: 110
Fine, Sidney: 593–594
Finnish language: 204, 227
Finnish Temperance Hall: 232
Finns: immigrants, 181, 203–204, 208–211; population and demography, 206; and labor, 217, 236; and religion, 223–224; and schools, 226; societies, 231–232; farmers, 563. *See also* Scandinavians
First Bohemian Catholic Central Union: 230
Fish Brothers Wagon Works: 113
Fisheries: 3, 4
Fitzpatrick, Edward A.: 367
Flax: 29, 40
Florence County: 207, 522
Florida: 84
Flour: 81, 82–83, 88, 97, 117–118, 244; collapse of wheat farming, 91
Flower, Frank: 265
Folkets Avis (newspaper): 227
Fond du Lac: furniture manufacturing, 90; diversifies manufacturing, 96; tanning industry, 105; municipal services, 129; population and demography, 136; public utilities, 152; consumer co-operatives, 155; and interurban railways, 310–311; women's societies, 338–339; moral reform, 355; Lincoln social center, 372
Fond du Lac County: cheese production, 54; population and demography, 137; southern and eastern Europeans in, 207–208; Russians in, 209; labor force in, 244
Fond du Lac Old Settler's Club: 326
Fond du Lac *Reporter:* 629
Fond du Lac Women's Club: 337
Football: 322–324, 327
Foreign languages: 224, 411. *See also specific languages*
Forest County: 137, 191–192
Forests: 85–86
Fort Atkinson: 31, 115
Fort Howard. *See* Green Bay
Forty Thousand Club (Madison): 135
Foundries and machine shops: compared to logging industry, 82; foundrymen's associations, 102; growth, 103; in Racine, 113; labor, 214–217, 244, 248; wages, 257; workplace conditions, 264; women and, 274
Four Wheel Drive Auto Company: 100
Fowler, Dorothy Ganfield: 476
Fox, Philip: 451
Fox Lake: 195
Fox River Valley: and depression of 1893-1897, 12; apple production, 45; milling, 83; woodenware factories, 89; papermaking, 91–94; industrialization, 136; manufacturing work force, 249; and labor unions, 285–286, 290–291; and interurban railways, 310–311; promoted by Wisconsin Central Railway, 325; industrialists oppose income tax, 553
France: 111, 114, 181, 508
Fraternal organizations. *See* Societies
Frear, James: and railroad regulation, 474, 485–486; and state insurance regulation, 489, 502; praises La Follette and Wisconsin Idea, 628
Free African Methodist Church: 201
Free Hospital (Milwaukee): 338
Free Library Commission: 493, 507, 518
Freethinkers: 181–183
French-Canadians: 179–180
Frontier Thesis: 6, 382, 414
Frosts in Wisconsin (Chautauqua bulletin): 385
Fuller and Johnson: 12, 116–117
Fuller Opera House (Madison): 477–479

706

THE HISTORY OF WISCONSIN

Gale, Zona: 228
Galesville: 45
Galpin, Charles: 32, 36, 37, 65, 317
Gambling: 146–147, 156–157, 322
Garland, Hamlin: 6, 7, 138n, 303
Gary, Elbert Henry: 111
Gasoline engine: 98, 99–100, 113, 248
Gates, James L. "Stumpland": 72
Gaveney, John C.: 472
Gavett, Thomas W.: assesses Milwaukee unionists, 281
Gaylord, Winfield R.: 294, 504, 537–538, 556
General Federation of Women's Clubs (GFWC): refuses to admit blacks, 200; founded, 334–335; endorses suffrage, 336; membership, 344; and new generation of women, 348
General Paper Company: 94
"The Genius of Wisconsin" (statue): 5
Geological and Natural History Survey: 425
Geological Survey: 381
George, Henry: 431
German-American Alliance: 351
Germania (newspaper): 307
Germania Association: 228
German language: Cutover propaganda in, 72–73; taught in public schools, 226, 373; newspapers, 227
German Reformed Christians, 358
Germans: immigrants, 40, 102, 139, 181–182, 209–211; in Eau Claire, 142; and Milwaukee Anti-Vaccination Society, 151; oppose efficiency politics, 162; and Milwaukee politics, 163; and Social Democratic party, 165, 165n; Teutonic *vs.* Yankee ways of life, 180–181; population, 186; workers, 213–216, 244–245; stereotypes, 214; and naturalization, 219; and intermarriage, 221; in Milwaukee, 222; and religion, 223, 224; and parochial schools, 225–226; societies, 228; and unions, 235–236; political affiliations, 236, 412–413, 482; and Prohibition, 237, 506; and women's societies, 341; in legislature, 406; and APA, 421; and direct primary, 482; farmers, 563; and Progressive reform, 570–573, 575, 605
Germany: 111, 508, 559, 530, 644
Gettle, Lewis E.: 541, 565
Gill, Thomas H.: 452
Gillett: 319
Gimbel Brothers Department Store: 77, 197–198

Gisholt Machine Company: 12, 116, 117
Glynn, Martin: 582
Goff, Guy: 168
Goff, S. Clayton: 549
Golf: 323
Gompers, Samuel: 262, 276, 278, 280, 282, 293, 353
Good Government Club (Superior): 160
Good Government Club (University of Michigan): 448
Good Housekeeping (magazine): 255
Goodland, Walter: 617
Good Roads Movement: 36
Gorecki, Martin: 295
Gorman, James: 284
Gorst, Charles, Dr.: 642
Gospel of Wealth: 15, 378
Government, state: size, 400; functions, 400–401; function of party politics, 401–402, 410–412; and political interest groups, 403; judicial system, 403–404; power structure, 407; governor, 407–409; and reformers, 415–420, 425, 427
Grain Exchange: 122
Grand Labor Council: 287
Grand Rapids (Wis.). *See* Wisconsin Rapids
The Grange: on extension courses, 21; and dairy advocates, 47; and road improvement, 70; supports woman suffrage, 351; seeks anti-trust law exemptions, 563
Grant County: black settlements in, 195; southern and eastern Europeans in, 207; and Catholics, 224; and electricity, 317–318; rural social center, 358; and Progressivism, 422, 492; Wyalusing State Park, 506
Grant County News: 324
Great Britain: 48, 139, 181–182, 508, 559, 644
"Great White City." *See* World's Columbian Exposition
Greek language: 204–205, 226
Greeks: immigrants, 139, 181, 204, 208, 210–212; and housing, 196; population and demography, 206; stereotypes, 214; workers, 214–216; and religion, 223, 225; societies, 230
Green Bay: agriculture near, 39; milk production, 53; pea canning, 87; manufacturing, 90, 96, 103; papermaking, 93; population and demography, 127, 136, 142, 316, 318; unsanitary conditions, 150; municipal services, 173; Polish Catholics in, 224; and WSFL, 293; and interurban

Index 707

railways, 310–311; WFWC convention in, 336; women's societies, 340; moral reform, 355
Green Bay Agency: 191
Greenbush (Madison neighborhood): 149, 196, 212
Green Lake County: 27, 116
Griffith, Edward M.: 506, 555, 557, 643
Guardians of Liberty: 239, 653
Gueder, William: 167

Haber, Samuel: 591
Hagemeister, Henry: 463
Hales Corners: 310
Hall, Albert R.: pre-Wisconsin activities, 415–416; and Progressive agenda, 416; and tax reform, 420; and railroad regulation, 421, 423, 447, 450–451, 456, 458–459, 464, 474, 486; and railroad finance investigations, 426; leads Half-Breeds, 427–428; and inheritance tax bill, 429; supports direct primary, 430; in La Follette's autobiography, 433; and Nils Haugen, 443; assessed by Kenneth C. Acrea, 577
Hall, Judson: 640
Halsey, Sabin: 354
Hamilton Beach: 113
Hannan, John J.: 460–461
Hanson, Burton: 475, 485
Harding, Warren: 662
Harley-Davidson Motor Company: 100
Harper, Samuel A.: 439, 444, 446, 449
Hart, Charles W.: 104n
Harvey, Lorenzo: 363, 469
Hatton, William H.: as state senator, 417; withdraws support from railroad regulation legislation, 485; runs for Senate, 498–500, 613; and La Follette, 616; runs for governor, 651–652; 1914 primary election, 654
Haugen, Nils: and La Follette, 442–443, 486–487; and secretary of agriculture position, 445; and James O. Davidson, 496; and income tax legislation, 510, 551–552, 622; and Herman Ekern, 625
Hay: 29, 43
Haymarket Riot: 276
Health, public. *See* Public health
Heath, Frederic: 165
Hebrew Free Loan Association: 231
Hebrew language: 204–205
Hebrew Relief Association: 231, 358

Henry, William A.: dean of College of Agriculture, 56, 57–58; publishes *Northern Wisconsin: A Hand-book for the Homeseeker,* 73–74, 423; on farm women, 271; establishes agricultural science as academic discipline, 382
Hepburn railroad rate act: 490
Hermann building (Milwaukee): 466
Hero (Finnish society): 231–232
Hicks, Emmett R.: 450
Hill, James J.: 117, 477
Hine, Lewis W.: 267
The History of Labour in the United States: 381
Hoan, Daniel: 170, 171, 172, 546–547
Hoard, William Dempster: on alfalfa, 43; spokesman for dairy interests, 46–47; advocates silage, 47; publishes *Dairy Temperament of Cows,* 48; and Star Union Company of Chicago, 48; on dairymen, 50; and College of Agriculture, 57; and agricultural economics, 65; elected governor, 67; and National Dairy Union, 67; and Wisconsin Society of Equity, 77–78; on rural schools, 366; and La Follette, 440, 612; and secretary of agriculture position, 445; alienated by Progressives, 492, 495–497, 516; role assessed, 575–576; and Andrew Dahl, 652
Hoard's Dairyman (magazine): on dairy farm prosperity, 31; on farmers' low self-esteem, 37–38; and William D. Hoard, 47; on Babcock test, 50, 62; on value of Dairy School, 60; and tuberculosis test, 63; and educational reform, 70; and Interstate Commerce Commission, 70; on agriculture in Cutover, 72; on dairying technology, 253–254; and shortage of hired help on farms, 254; on farm women, 270; on "new education," 362; endorses La Follette, 441
Hofa Park (Polish settlement): 206
Hogs: 29, 40, 42, 106
Home for the Aged (Milwaukee): 231
Home Rule and Taxpayers League: 649–650
Hooper, Jessie Jack: 351
Hope of Our Fathers: 231–232
Horlick, William: 53
Horlick Malted Milk: 113
Horn and Blum Company: 88
Host, Clement P.: 627
Hotchkiss, William, 561–562
House of Mercy: 338
Houser, Walter: 479, 618–619, 652

Housing: discrimination, 134, 141, 196–197; BLIS statistics on, 147–149; unsanitary conditions, 148–149, 197; reform, 158, 176–177; for blacks, 196–197; immigrant, 210–211; and "New Familialism," 329
Howe, Frederic C.: 77, 566, 574, 596
Hoyt, George E.: 642
Hudson: 395
Hull, Merlin: 541, 625, 647, 652
The Human Enterprise (by Max Otto): 382
Hungarians: immigrants, 139, 203–204, 207–208, 210, 211–212; and housing, 148; population and demography, 206; stereotypes, 214; workers, 214–216; and religion, 223, 225
Hunger Point (La Crosse neighborhood): 212
Hunner, John: 10
Huron: 224
Hurst, J. Willard: 402–403
Husting, Paul O.: leads Progressive Democrats, 517; and direct elections, 540; and initiative, referendum, recall, 541–542; and conservation legislation, 555–557; and 1911 legislative session, 614; 1914 senate race, 631, 650–651, 655–657; opposes sterilization, 642; proposes waterpowers bill, 643; defeats Francis McGovern, 658
Hutchins, Frank A.: 384
Hygeia Mineral Springs Company: 3

Icelanders: 181, 224
Illinois: 29, 73, 104, 195, 383, 515
Illinois Steel: 120
Imatra societies: 232
Immigrants and immigration: opposition to, 18; in urban and industrialized areas, 139–142, 210; northwestern Europeans, 180–182; Americanization of, 185; southern and eastern Europeans, 185–186, 203–214, 233–235; recruitment of, 205–206; chain migration, 210; and housing, 210–211; and U.S. Immigration Commission, 213–214; and labor, 215–218, 235, 244–246, 249; and child labor, 218, 260; and citizenship, 218; and education, 219, 225–226; and Old World institutions, 220; and family, 221–222; and societies, 227–230, 232; restriction of, 233–234; and wages, 260; and unemployment agencies, 264; and social systematization, 315; and Wisconsin Idea, 608

The Income Tax in the Commonwealths of the United States (by Delos R. Kinsman): 552
Independence: 206
Indiana: 29, 195
Indians: and French-Canadians, 179–180; population and demography, 182, 191–193; acculturation of, 185–188, 190–194; and Dawes General Allotment Act, 187; and logging, 188–189; discrimination against, 189, 194; Indian agents, 189; and farming, 190; schools, 190–191; health and medicine, 192; alcohol, 192–193, 238, 505; and religion, 193–194; and new technology, 315; La Follette and, 432, 436; suffrage, 512n; ignored by reformers, 608
Industrial Accident Board: 547–548, 550
Industrial Commission: Charles W. Price and, 252; supersedes BLIS, 266; on child labor, 269; on working women, 273–274, 276; and Frank J. Weber, 295; goals, 300; established, 549–550; and apprenticeships, 560; John R. Commons lectures on, 584; and BLIS, 599; and Thomas Mahon, 627–628; and co-operative marketing, 646
Industrial Co-operative Union: 77
Industrial Home for Women: 639
Industrial Insurance Committee: 545–546
Industrialization: roots of, 80–81; decline of flour milling and lumbering, 81; "neotechnic revolution," 81, 118–121; and residential dispersion, 130–131; and unskilled labor, 246–247; effect on family, 331
Industrial Workers of the World (IWW): Finnish activists, 217, 236; and workingmen's associations, 232; alarms SDP, 235; and women, 275; opposition to, 280, 293–294
Ingalls, Wallace: 545
Ingersoll, Robert G.: 431
Ingram, C. A.: 511, 533, 540, 558
Ingram, Orrin H.: 84
Institute for Government Research: 582
Institute of Paper Chemistry: 94
Insurance: reform legislation, 502–503; state commission, 518, 599, 625
Intercollegiate Conference of Faculty Representatives: 323
Internal combustion engine: 81, 305
International Association of Machinists: 288
International Brotherhood of Papermakers: 285, 290
International Harvester Company of Amer-

ica: 111; horizontal integration, 120; formed, 121; and labor, 215, 264; assembly-line production, 250; in-house welfare, 252; and workmen's compensation, 545
Interstate Commerce Act: 436
Interstate Commerce Commission: 70, 122
Interstate State Park: 325
Iowa: 55, 73, 346
Ireland: 181–182, 559
Irish: workers, 216, 244–245; Catholics and parochial schools, 226; societies, 228; political affiliations, 236, 412–413; and Prohibition, 237; in legislature, 406
Iron County: 73, 191, 206–208, 522
Iron industry: and "neotechnic revolution," 81–82; manufacturing in southeastern Wisconsin, 97; Lake Superior and, 98, 101; Milwaukee foundries, 103; and Racine companies, 113; on Mesabi Range, 117; labor, 215, 217, 244, 248; wages, 257; and unemployment, 263; and railroads, 309
Irvine, William: 555
Italian language: 204–205, 226, 373
Italians: immigrants, 139, 181, 203–204, 207, 210–212; and housing, 148–149, 158, 196; population and demography, 206; and labor, 213–216, 218n, 236, 244; stereotypes, 214; and religion, 223–225; societies, 230–231

Jackson County: 26, 45, 192, 522
Jacobs, William A.: 525
James, Ada: 349, 351
James, David G.: 349, 542
James, Laura Briggs: 349
Janesville: annexes farmland, 27; milling, 83; box manufacturing, 90; foundries, 103; industrialization, 115–116; urbanization, 126–127; municipal services, 129, 173; population and demography, 136–137; public utilities, 155; poor relief, 157; John M. Nolen and, 163; labor force in, 245; Frances Willard and, 344
Janesville *Gazette:* 648–649
Janesville *Recorder:* 18
Janssen, John T.: 156
Japan: 577
Jefferson County: agriculture, 30, 33, 44; and railroads, 97–98; and tourism, 326
Jefferson County Union: 47, 319
Jeffery, Thomas B.: 33, 100

Jeffery Company: 100, 115, 249, 284. *See also* Nash Corporation
Jeffery-Nash Motors: 250
Jeffris, M. G.: 479
Jesko, Martin: 292–294
Jewish Children's Home: 231
Jewish Community Center: 231
Jews: immigrants, 139, 204, 208, 211–212; and housing, 148–149, 158, 196; and ethno-cultural disputes, 181–183, 223; population and demography, 206; workers, 213–216; stereotypes, 214; anti-Semitism, 214, 215, 231; in Milwaukee, 216n, 225; Orthodox, 223, 225; in Kenosha, 225; Sabbath Schools, 226; societies, 231, 341–342; Council of Jewish Women, 341–342; and Social Gospel, 357–358
Johnson, George H. D.: 474
Johnson, Henry: 657
Johnson, Hiram: 582
Johnson, Lewis L.: 625, 627–628
Johnson's Wax: 113
Johnston, John: 22, 377
Joliet Steel: 120
Jonas, Karel: 237
Jones, A. M. "Long": 453
Jones, John R.: 562
Jones, Nellie Kedzie: 36, 37
Jones, Richard Lloyd: 629
Jones Island (Milwaukee neighborhood): 212
Journal of Home Economics: 255
Judiciary: 404, 601–602
Juneau County: 26, 27, 192

Kaiser, John H., Lumber Company, 95
Kallen, Horace M.: 234
Kander, Elizabeth Black: 231, 342, 357–358
Kansas: 29
Karel, John C.: and 1912 gubernatorial race, 614, 620–624; and anti-Progressive coalition, 650; 1914 elections, 655–658
Kaukauna: 93
Kearney, Thomas: 651, 655
Keefe, John: 610
Kelley, Florence: 342
Kelly, Oliver Hazard: 415–416
Kennan, Kossuth Kent: 583
Kennedy, W. B., Lodge (Masons): 202
Kenosha: and depression of 1893-1897, 13; annexes farmland, 27; bedding manufacturing, 90; automobile industry, 100, 313; foundries, 103; tanning industry, 105; industrial growth, 113, 114–115, 136, 249,

259; corporate growth, 119; urbanization, 127; population and demography, 128, 136–137, 210; mass transit, 133; and TMERL, 154; John M. Nolen and, 163; municipal services, 173; blacks in, 195–199, 202; crime in, 199; societies in, 202, 229–230; southern and eastern Europeans in, 207–208, 224, 229; Russians in, 209; housing, 210, 211; contagious diseases, 213; and labor, 216–217, 284, 290; naturalization rates, 218–219; churches and parishes in, 225; ; and interurban railways, 310; recreation in, 326
Kenosha County: cabbage production, 45; population and demography, 137, 210; southern and eastern Europeans in, 206–208; Russians in, 209; labor force, 244
Kenosha *Telegraph-Courier:* 19
Kenosha Trades and Labor Council (KTLC): 284
Kenosha Women's Club: 338
Kentucky: 195
Kewaunee: 88
Kewaunee County: 27, 54, 137, 207
Keyes, Elisha W. "Boss": and La Follette, 432, 435; on youth at Republican convention, 439; on Milwaukee *Sentinel,* 462; and Wisconsin Republican League, 466; and John C. Gaveney, 472; on railroad regulation, 474; on Fuller Opera House convention, 479
Kickapoo River Valley: 45
Kileen, Edward F.: 628
Kimberly: 93
Kimberly, Clark & Company: 93, 285
King, Charles: 229
Kinnickinnic River Valley: 108
Kinsman, Delos R.: 552, 583
Kleczka, John C.: 511, 513, 551–552
Knapp, Stout & Co. Lumber Company: 83
Kneen, Edward J.: 631
Knights of Columbus: 653
Knights of Labor: 235, 276, 277
Knights of Luther: 653
Knights of Pythias: 201
Koenig, Joseph: 87
Koetting, John B.: 17
Kohler: 88, 103, 310
Kohler Company: 88
Konop, Thomas F.: 526
Krakow (Polish settlement): 206
Kress, H. G.: 452, 469
Kreutzer, Andrew L.: 472
Kronshage, Theodore: 66, 374–375, 390, 450

Krumrey, Henry: 78, 549, 555–556
Kruszka, Michael: 229
Kuryer Polski (newspaper): 227, 229, 237
Küstermann, Gustav: 526

Labor: and depression of 1893-1897, 18; skilled, 110n; unskilled, 138–139, 247, 249–250; and Amalgamated Street Railway Employees, 154; Bay View massacre, 164, 235; child, 177, 218, 262, 266–269, 548–549; wages, 189, 256–260; blacks and, 197–198, 202; and unions, 202, 235, 261–262, 276–298; immigrant, 213–218; "basketeering," 217; Finnish activists, 217; "head hunters," 217, 263; and poor conditions, 218; composition of work force, 242–247; rise in clerical occupations, 246–247, 255–256; salaried *vs.* waged employees, 247; personnel practices, 251–252; welfare capitalism, 252; professions, 256–257; unemployment, 257, 262–264, 297; and rising cost of living, 258–259; working hours, 261, 262; workplace conditions, 264–266; industrial accidents, 265–266; workmen's compensation, 266, 544–548; and women, 266–276, 549; support for, 298–299, 299–300; legislature and, 299–302; and legislation, 422, 425, 494–495, 508–510, 637–638; and State Board of Arbitration and Conciliation, 422–423; and Industrial Commission, 549–551
Lac Court Oreilles Reservation: 191
Lac du Flambeau Reservation: 189, 191
La Crosse: bank failures, 11; unemployment, 12; milling, 83; breweries, 88; manufacturing, 90, 96, 103; population and demography, 127, 136, 142; municipal services, 129, 173; housing, 148–149; and Wisconsin Telephone Company, 152; poor relief, 157; John M. Nolen and, 163; MML chapter in, 174; and labor unions, 287; and suffrage societies, 346; normal schools, 374; extension field district in, 385; and Populists, 421
La Crosse County: strawberry production, 45; milk condensery in, 53; population and demography, 127, 137; and Winnebago Tribe, 192; southern and eastern Europeans in, 207; and Polish Catholics, 224; labor force, 244; and Progressivism, 422
La Crosse *Press:* 338
La Crosse Trades and Labor Council: 287

Ladies' Home Journal (magzine): 307
Ladysmith: 395
La Follette, Belle Case: 343, 350, 439, 444
La Follette, Philip F.: 661
La Follette, Robert M.: quoted on Progressive movement, xii; and Richard T. Ely, 8; and Frederick Jackson Turner, 9; tours Chautauqua circuit, 324–325; on woman suffrage, 347; and Charles McCarthy, 361, 570, 634–635, 646–647; and Charles R. Van Hise, 378; and extension service, 384; and University of Wisconsin, 386, 389; affects student involvement in politics, 393; opposes "judge-made" law, 404; and Edward Scofield, 409, 417; and reform agenda, 415; and Albert R. Hall, 416; and direct primary, 427, 430, 433, 445–446, 447–451; influences on, 431; Progressive origins self-described, 431, 432–433, 437–438; and Indians, 432, 436, 608; early life, 433–435; publishes *University Press,* 435; as Dane County district attorney, 435–436; in Congress, 436, 437; Philetus Sawyer allegedly bribes, 438; replaced as Dane County Republican chairman, 439; use of patronage, 439–440, 467; and Isaac Stephenson, 440–441; and William Dempster Hoard, 440–441, 443; and Scandinavian voters, 441–442; and Nils Haugen, 442–443; 1896 Republican state convention, 444–445; 1898 Republican state convention, 448–450; 1900 gubernatorial campaign, 451–454; and railroads, 452, 458–459, 472–476, 484–488; inaugural addresses, 455–458, 470–471; as governor, 458–466, 471–476, 483–489; and *ad valorem* railroad taxation, 461–462, 464–465, 470–472; and direct primary, 461–463, 471–472, 482; 1902 campaign, 466–470; 1904 campaign, 476–483; "Red Gym" convention of 1904, 478–479; resigns governorship, 489; in U.S. Senate, 489–490; political legacy, 490–491; and labor, 494; 1906 election, 495–498; and insurance reform, 502; and Prohibition, 506; and National Progressive Republican League, 515–516; 1910 election, 520–521; and nonpartisan elections, 537; and Seventeenth Amendment, 540; and U.S. income tax amendment, 551; publishes *La Follette's Autobiography,* 567; and Wisconsin Idea, 570–573, 580–581; on origins of Wisconsin Progressivism, 573–577; and commonwealth model, 587; and professional expertise, 590; and service state, 594; on Legislative Reference Library, 594–595; and expert committees, 598; and Progressive factionalism, 611–613; criticizes Taft administration, 614; and Francis E. McGovern, 616–620, 625–631, 634–635, 651–652, 659; self-destructs during 1912 speech, 617–618; denounces Herman Ekern's firing, 626; and 1913 Republican party platform, 632; and John S. Donald, 654; dies, 663

La Follette, Robert M., Jr.: 661

La Follette's Autobiography: Progressive origins, 431–433, 437–438; Norwegian influence, 442; Railroad Commission, 487; labor, 494; and Charles McCarthy, 570; Progressive legislation, 587; service state, 594; women and public service, 606

La Follette's Weekly Magazine: on Francis E. McGovern, 532, 624, 651; Rodney A. Elward writes in, 532; La Follette advertises himself in, 580–581; editorials favor Woodrow Wilson, 614–615, 620; praises William Jennings Bryan, 620

Lake Forest: 323
Lake Mills: 326
Lakeside Malleable Company: 103
Lake Superior Agricultural, Industrial, and Fine Arts Society: 118
Lampard, Eric E.: assesses Progressive era, 54, 575–576, 589
Land and River Improvement Company: 17
Landreth, Albert: 87
Lange Canning Company: 95
Langlade County: 44, 55, 209, 358
Lappen, Frank A.: 10, 16–17
Lappen, Frank A., Furniture Company: 10, 16–17
Larsen, William: 87–88
Larson, "Norsky": 478
Latin Quarter (Madison neighborhood): 149
Latvians: 224
Lawrence University: 94
Lawson, Publius V., Jr.: 89
Layton Corporation: 106, 112
League of American Wheelmen: 311
League of Wisconsin Municipalities: and public utilities, 156; as statewide information clearinghouse, 174; and direct primary elections, 175; and economic and political reforms, 417; and government intervention, 518
Legislative Reference Library: Charles McCarthy and, 9, 76, 532, 584, 661; supports

712   THE HISTORY OF WISCONSIN

labor, 299; and WFLC, 396–397; and State Historical Society, 397–398; guarantees "judge-proof" laws, 404; and library commission, 493; and labor laws, 508–509; and labor statistics, 544; John Commons and, 573; and Progressivism, 574; and Wisconsin Idea, 575, 580, 594–596; and service state, 594; principles, 595; research department, 595–596; bill drafting department, 596; and anti-Progressive coalition, 650–651, 661

Legislature (Wisconsin): and *Northern Wisconsin: A Hand-book for the Homeseeker,* 73; control of municipal affairs, 144; and public utilities, 156; compulsory school attendance and Indians, 191; and civil rights, 199; and UW, 389–390, 560–561; and lobbyists, 403–404, 406–407, 488–489, 518; reputation declines, 404–405; and ethnic voting, 405; and nuisance bills, 405; and party loyalty, 405; inefficiency in, 405–406; during 1890's, 406, 425–430; ethno-cultural composition, 413; and bipartisan legislation, 418–419; conservation legislation, 419, 422, 493, 643–644; educational legislation, 419, 422, 493, 507–508, 558–560, 641; tax reform, 419–420, 429–430; direct primary legislation, 420, 430, 445–446, 461–463, 466, 471–472, 482; establishes State Board of Arbitration and Conciliation, 422–423; business legislation, 423; public service legislation, 423, 493, 501–502, 504; *ad valorem* taxation of railroads, 426, 450, 461–462, 464–465, 470–473; Mills Law, 427; railroad regulation legislation, 458–459, 472–476, 484–488; tax commission, 488; labor legislation, 494–495, 508–510, 543–551, 637–638; insurance legislation, 502–503, 542, 564; penal institution reform, 505; liquor legislation, 505–506; and State Board of Forestry, 506; and income tax, 510–511, 551–554; and fiscal reform, 511; and woman suffrage, 511–512, 542–543; in 1911, 532–533, 533–566; reapportionment of, 536; election legislation, 536–538; municipal home rule, 538–539; second-choice provision, 539–540, 640; direct election, 540; initiative, referendum, and recall, 541–542; constitutional amendment streamlines, 542; prohibition of legislative logrolling and vote trading, 542; and Industrial Commission, 549–550; waterpower legislation, 555–557; reforestation legislation, 557–558; and roads, 561–563; and agriculture, 563–564; and Board of Public Affairs, 564–566; 1912 elections, 624–625; 1913 adjournment question, 629–630; 1913 session assessed, 631–632; La Follette-McGovern feud confounds, 634–636, 648; legislation affecting politics, 636, 640–641; welfare legislation, 638; public health legislation, 639; moral legislation, 642; agricultural legislation, 644–646; marketing commission bill defeated, 647; comprehensive budget bill, 648–649

Legler, Henry E.: 384

Lenroot, Irvine: and La Follette, 442, 613, 616, 618; and railroad regulation, 474; 1906 gubernatorial race, 496–497; runs for U.S. Senate, 498; 1908 elections, 499; and income tax, 622

Levi, Kate Everest: 343

Levitan, Sol: 628

Lewis, Evan "Strangler": 478

Lewis, William M.: 617

Lewis, William T.: 446, 506, 521–522

Lewis Motor Car Company: 113

Leyse Aluminum Corporation. *See* Aluminum Sign Company of Two Rivers

Liberal Club (Milwaukee): 22

Life (Finnish society): 231–232

Light (Finnish society): 231–232

Lighty, William H.: 376, 384, 508

Lincoln, Abraham, Settlement House: 231, 342

Lincoln County: agriculture, 27; social stratification, 32; population and demography, 127; Russians in, 209; and Progressivism, 492

Lincoln Civic League: 202

Linley, Victor: 642

Lippmann, Walter: 590–591

Lithuanian language: 204–205

Lithuanians: immigrants, 139, 203–204, 209–211; population and demography, 206; workers, 214, 216; and religion, 223–225

Little Chute: 93

Live Stock Sanitary Board: 493

Logan, Ben: 35

Logging and lumbering: Wisconsin leads nation, 2; at World's Columbian Exposition, 4–5; and depression of 1893-1897, 12; transition to agriculture, 26–27; in Cutover, 27; resettlement in logged-over areas, 71–72; and manufacturing, 81; production, 82; state's leading industry,

82; lumber barons, 83–84, 124; 1898 forest survey, 85; decline of, 85–86, 89; forest fires, 86; wasteful techniques, 86; sash, door, and blind factories, 90; paper mills, 94; amalgamation of industry, 121; and railroads, 124, 309; and Indians, 188–189, 436; and labor, 217–218, 244–246, 248–249; lobbyists for, 403, 407; sawdust pollution, 422; and reforestation, 557; and forest preserve legislation, 643–644
London: 88
Lord's Day Papers: 185
Louisiana Purchase Exposition: 49, 308
Lowell (Mass.): 508, 559
Loyal: 324–325
Lublin: 224
Lush, Charles K.: 140
Lutherans: and Milwaukee politics, 163; and ethno-cultural disputes, 181–183; and Bennett Law, 183–184; hostility towards, 185; and Indians, 191; immigrants, 223–224; churches, 225; and parochial schools, 225–226; and societies, 230; and politics, 236; and rural social centers, 358; and political affiliations, 412, 482; and anti-Catholicism, 421, 653–654. *See also* Protestants
Luxembourg: 181
Lynxville: 319

Mack, Connie: 322
Madison: and depression of 1893-1897, 12; and lumber barons, 83, 124; foundries, 103; industrialization, 115–117, 135–136, 142; "Madison Compromise," 116–117, 135–136, 142; and AFA, 121; population and demography, 128, 136–137, 141–142, 210; municipal services, 129, 144–145, 161–163; mass transit, 132, 134; automobiles, 134, 313; political graft, 147; housing, 149; public health, 150, 151, 159; public utilities, 153, 155; poor relief, 157; and Civic Center movement, 161–162; John M. Nolen and, 163; interventionist Progressive government of, 173; MML chapter in, 174; blacks in, 195–198, 201–202; southern and eastern Europeans in, 207; labor in, 216, 246, 288, 340; manufacturing wages, 259; and WSFL, 291, 293; recreation, 326–327; and women's societies, 337, 341–342; and manual training, 339; and AAUW, 343; and moral reform, 355; lecture courses in, 383; library school in, 396; and state government, 400–410; lobbyists, 407; La Follettes move to, 434; Republican convention moved to, 467; Ida M. Tarbell visits, 637; Home Rule and Taxpayers League meets in, 650
Madison Alumni Association: 323
Madison *Democrat:* 649, 659
Madison Federated Trades Council: 289
Madison Federation of Labor (MFL): 289
Madison Gas, Light and Coke Company: 153
Madison Literary Club: 159
Madison Park and Pleasure Drive Association: 162–163
Madison Temperance Board: 147
Magazines: 307–308
Magyar language: 204–205
Mahon, Thomas: 537, 549, 627–628
Mahoney, D. O.: 78
Malleable Iron Range Company: 117
Manitowoc: bank failures, 10; pea canning, 87; shipbuilding, 88; foundries, 103; manufacturing, 115; population and demography, 136; naturalization rates, 218–219; interurban railways, 311; social systematization, 316; state's first kindergarten, 372; and Social Democratic party, 517; continuation school in, 560
Manitowoc County: decline in farm acreage, 27; cheese production, 54; population and demography, 137; southern and eastern Europeans in, 207; Russians in, 209; and voting privileges, 237
Manitowoc Aluminum: 87
Manning, Thomas A.: 640
Manufacturers', Shippers', and Jobbers' Association: 118
Manufacturing: and World's Columbian Exposition, 3, 4, 7–8; effect of 1893-1897 depression on, 11; aluminum production, 87; woodenware, 89; in southeastern Wisconsin, 97; electricity and, 98–99; internal combustion engine and, 99–100; basic metals processing, 101; foundries, 101–103; of agricultural implements, 103–104, 110–111; tanning, 105, 111–112; brewing, 105–106, 112; meat-packing, 106, 112; vertical and horizontal integration, 120; and labor, 213–218; increase in jobs, 246; and women, 247; small shops superseded, 248; and mechanical engineers, 249–250; and Progressive production, 250; unemployment, 258; workplace conditions, 264; industrial accidents, 265; child labor, 268

Marathon County: increase in farm acreage, 26; resettlement of, 75; papermaking, 93; non-wood enterprises, 95; and Stockbridge-Munsee Tribe, 191; southern and eastern Europeans in, 206, 208; and Catholics, 224; and voting privileges, 237; labor force in, 244; rural social center in, 358; normal school, 365; 1910 elections, 525
Marathon Electric Manufacturing Company: 95
Marathon Paper Mills Company: 94–95
Margulies, Herbert F.: assesses Progressive era, 574–575, 650, 655
Marinette: manufacturing, 90, 115; naturalization rates, 219; labor strikes, 290–291; and WSFL, 291, 293
Marinette County: and Potawatomi Tribe, 191–192; Southern and eastern Europeans in, 206–208; Russians in, 209; labor force in, 244
Marketing Commission: 644
Marquette, Father Jacques: 184, 414
Marquette County: 44, 422, 492
Marshall, Roujet D.: 544, 626
Marshfield: 90, 155
Marxist Socialist Labor party: 279
Masons (fraternal order): 202
Massachusetts: 45, 336
Matthews, Lois Kimball: 584
Maxwell, Robert S.: assesses Progressive era, 574, 660
Mazomanie: 319
McCarthy, Charles: and Legislative Reference Library, 9, 76, 594–596, 661; and Social Gospel, 20; and Harry L. Russell, 58; and agricultural economics, 65; agricultural activist, 78–79, 563, 644–645; and socialism, 295, 518; and labor, 299, 508–509; and college baseball, 323; advocates "new education," 361–362, 376; and school reform, 367; publishes *The Wisconsin Idea*, 376, 558, 567, 569, 572, 581; and Free Library Commission, 384; and UW faculty, 387; opposes "judge-made" law, 404; and tax legislation, 488, 552; on James O. Davidson, 501n; and agricultural and vocational education commission, 508, 513; and Industrial Insurance Committee, 509–510; and 1911 legislature, 519, 542; and initiative, referendum, and recall, 541; and workmen's compensation, 545; drafts waterpower bill, 556–557; and continuation/vocational schools, 558–560, 593; and Board of Public Affairs, 565; publishes *The Soil*, 570–571; and Wisconsin Idea, 570–573, 581–582; on origins of Wisconsin Progressivism, 573–577; addresses Pennsylvania visitors, 584; and new individualism, 588–589; and professional expertise, 590; and social efficiency, 591; and cost effectiveness, 592, 605; and service state, 594; and UW, 597; and expert committees, 598; and appointive commissions, 600–601; on judiciary, 602; quarrels with La Follette, 634–635, 646–647; and 1913 appropriations bill, 649
McClure's Magazine: 480
McConnell, John E.: 540
McCormick, Medill: 629
McCormick, Richard L.: 594
McCormick and Deering: 111
McCormick family: 252
McCreery, Maud: 350
McGillivray, James J.: 417, 420, 443
McGovern, Francis E.: and Harry L. Russell, 58; and Charles McCarthy, 78; and co-operative marketing, 78; as Milwaukee district attorney, 146; and Republican Club of Milwaukee County, 164; and David S. Rose, 167–168, 468, 527; runs for governor, 169; and nonpartisan election law, 171; and socialism, 295, 518; and woman suffrage, 350, 352; supports county-wide school boards, 367; and UW investigation, 390; relations with La Follette, 450, 616–620, 625–631, 634–635, 651–652, 659–660; 1906 elections, 497–498; 1908 senatorial candidate, 499; and Prohibition, 506; 1910 elections, 521–522, 525; 1911 inaugural address, 526–531; early life, 527; 1911 term, 531–568; boasts of Wisconsin national leadership, 583–584; addresses Pennsylvania visitors, 584; and professional expertise, 590; and service state, 594; and expert committees, 598; and Progressive factionalism, 611; pilloried by Democrats, 614; and Theodore Roosevelt, 618; 1912 elections, 621–624; defends income tax, 622; and Herman Ekern, 625–627; and 1913 legislative session, 636–649; marketing commission bill, 646–647; comprehensive budget bill, 648–649; and anti-Catholicism, 653; 1914 elections, 654–657; defeated, 658–660
McGovern, John: 450
McKenny, Charles: 362
McKinley, William: 424, 467; and La Follette, 436, 444–445, 454

McMillen Company: 287
Mears, Nellie: 5
Meat-packing: 106, 112, 120, 215, 248
Medical Milk Commission: 53
The Menace (anti-Catholic newspaper): 653
Menasha: milling, 83; breweries, 88; woolen mill, 88; woodenware factories, 89; Kimberly, Clark & Company, 93; industrialization, 136; municipal services, 173, 318; labor, 245, 285–286, 290
Menasha Wooden Ware Company: 89, 285–286
Menasha Wood Split Pulley Company: 89
Menominee County: 255
Menominee River Valley: 290
Menominee Tribe: and farmers' institutes, 60; cedes land to U.S., 179; and allotment, 188; and logging, 188–189; population, 191; and religion, 194
Menomonee River Valley: 107, 108, 132
Menomonie: 374
Merchants' and Manufacturers' Association: of Milwaukee, 122–123, 135, 167; lobbyists for, 407; advises Industrial Insurance Committee, 510; opposes labor legislation, 544; and workman's compensation, 547–548
Merrill: 155, 316
Mesabi Range: 117
Messmer, Sebastian B.: 357
Metal Trades and Founders Bureau: 282
Metal Trades Association: 282
Metcalfe, Frank B.: 549
Methodists: immigrants, 182–183; and Epworth League, 185; blacks and, 200; and Prohibition, 239; rural, 358. *See also* Protestants
Metropolitan Insurance: 503
Metz, Herman: 591
Mexico: 114
Meyer, Balthazar H.: 486–487, 571, 583
Michigan: 98, 99, 195
Midwestern Wooden Ware Association: 94
Miles, Herbert E.: 560
Miles, John J.: 199
Milk: condensed and evaporated, 41; fluid, 52–53, 54; contaminated, 150–151; State Medical Society lobbies for inspection of, 177. *See also* Dairy industry
Mills Law: 427
Milwaukee: and depression of 1893-1897, 10, 11–12, 16, 17, 19, 107; partisan politics in, 19; socialism in, 21–22, 165–172, 492, 517; market for pork, 42; dairy products win awards in, 49; milling, 83; manufacturing, 90; papermaking, 91–92; Great Lakes metal and machinery belt, 97; shipping, 97; automobile industry, 99–100, 134, 313; and AFA, 102, 121; foundries and machine shops, 102, 103, 108; tanning industry, 105; meat-packing, 106; industrialization, 106–112, 107n, 132, 135; assembly-line production, 108; manufacturers pushed to suburbs, 108–109; growth of corporations, 119; amalgamation of steel works, 120; railroad shipping rates, 122; population and demography, 127, 128, 133, 136–137, 140, 210; municipal services, 129–130, 144, 163–171; education, 130, 156, 172; mass transit, 131–134; political graft, 146–147; housing, 147–148, 158; public health, 149–150, 159; public utilities, 152–156; poor relief, 157; John M. Nolen and, 163; and municipal home rule, 174–175, 538–539; and BLIS, 177; and APA, 184; blacks in, 195–202; societies in, 201–202, 228–231; Southern and eastern Europeans in, 203–204, 206–208; Russians in, 209; immigrants in, 212, 213, 215, 217–218; Jews in, 215–216; naturalization rates, 218–219; religion in, 224–226; Poles in, 229, 233; Fourteenth Ward, 233; and WSFL, 235–236, 291–294; labor in, 245, 249, 276–277, 281–283, 290–294, 340; and corporations, 249; wages, 260; unemployment, 263; workplace conditions, 264; and working women, 274; Eugene Debs and, 279; social systematization, 316; baseball, 322; recreation, 327; WFWC and, 335, 338; GFWC convention in, 336; women's societies, 337–38, 341–342; factory reform, 339; AAUW and, 343; WCTU and, 344; suffrage societies, 345, 346; PEL and, 349; education in, 350–351, 367, 373–374; lecture courses in, 383; extension field district in, 385; civil service system established, 409, 424; and direct primary law, 420; and Populists, 421; Republican convention moved from, 467; David S. Rose purges officeholders, 481; and Progressivism, 492; free employment office established in, 494; and building codes, 503; Theodore Roosevelt wounded in, 621
Milwaukee and Northern Railroad: 403
Milwaukee Anti-Vaccination Society: 151
Milwaukee Building Trades Council: 282
Milwaukee Bureau of Economy and Efficiency: 565, 591

Milwaukee Chamber of Commerce: 122, 135, 458
Milwaukee Children's Betterment League: 298
Milwaukee City Club: 309, 538, 640
Milwaukee Civic Federation: 355
Milwaukee County: and depression of 1893-1897, 12; creation of industrial suburbs, 27; decline in farm acreage, 27; agricultural production, 45; manufacturing, 109; population and demography, 127, 137, 210; southern and eastern Europeans in, 208; Austrians in, 209; Russians in, 209; labor force in, 244; and election reform, 420; and caucus system, 424; 1898 elections, 428; 1902 elections, 470; 1910 elections, 523; Francis E. McGovern district attorney in, 527
Milwaukee County House of Correction: 167-168
Milwaukee-Downer College: 255, 336, 337
The Milwaukee Electric Railway and Light Company (TMERL): and mass transit, 133; consumer dissatisfaction with, 152-155; and MML, 164; and David S. Rose, 167; and state regulation, 173; and Amalgamated Association of Street Railway Employees strike, 278; concentrates on transportation, 304; and interurban railways, 310; and Henry Clay Payne, 403; and State Board of Arbitration and Conciliation, 423; opposed by Republican Club of Milwaukee County, 449
Milwaukee Ethical Society: 165, 339
Milwaukee *Evening Wisconsin:* 150, 227 441, 541
Milwaukee Federated Trades Council (MFTC): blacks and, 202; trade unions and, 235, 277-278; and Polish workers, 235-236; socialists and, 276-277, 517; and politics, 278-281; and IWW, 280; ethnic conflict, 281; and Milwaukee Building Trades Council, 282; and WSFL, 291, 293-294; and Union Label League, 340; and 1914 elections, 655
Milwaukee Federation of Civic Societies: 174-175
Milwaukee Foremen's Association: 102
Milwaukee Foundrymen's Association (MFA): 282
Milwaukee *Free Press:* 467, 474, 496, 541, 620, 624
Milwaukee Harvester: 4, 8, 104, 110, 11-1, 121

Milwaukee *Herald:* 307
"Milwaukee Idea": 281, 291
Milwaukee Jewish Mission: 342
Milwaukee Jewish Settlement: 231, 357
Milwaukee *Journal:* on World's Columbian Exposition, 10; on mass transit, 131; on nonpartisanship, 171, 538; on immigrant labor, 215; circulation, 227; on women's societies, 338; on UW Board of Regents, 388; on La Follette, 446-447, 459-460; campaigns against "La Folletteism," 469; on backlog in 1911 legislative session, 535; on initiative, referendum, and recall, 541; on Francis E. McGovern, 624, 629; on 1913 legislative session, 631; on George O'Connor, 644; on 1914 election results, 659
Milwaukee *Leader:* and Social Democratic party, 165; on Gerhard Bading, 171; on working women, 274-275; and Maud McCreery, 350; criticizes Progressive Republicans, 588
Milwaukee Merchants' and Manufacturers' Association: 263, 282-283, 300
Milwaukee Ministerial Council: 354
Milwaukee Municipal League (MML): and public utilities, 155-156; and middle-class reformers, 164, 166; and civil service, 167; and tax redistribution, 175-176; and John A. Butler, 342; and economic and political reforms, 417; and Julius E. Roehr, 417-418; and economic and political reforms, 420; and license fee tax, 423; and 1897 legislature, 427; lobbies for government intervention, 518
Milwaukee Normal School: 362
Milwaukee Northern Railway Company: 310
Milwaukee River: 107
Milwaukee Road Railway: 123, 477
Milwaukee School of Trades: 370, 373
Milwaukee *Sentinel:* on 1892 economic boom, 1; on World's Columbian Exposition, 7; on depression of 1893-1897, 10, 12, 16; opposes bank regulation, 17; on unemployed, 18; on Sherman Act, 19; on need for government regulation, 22; on mass transit, 132; sued by Henry Clay Payne, 167; circulation, 227; on movies, 308; on tourism, 325; on women's societies, 338; on vacation schools, 339; on WFWC, 340; on La Follette, 452; Charles Pfister buys, 462; on *ad valorem* taxation, 464; on railroad regulation, 485, 487; on

insurance reform, 503; on Progressive Republican platform, 524–525; on 1911 legislative session, 534; on initiative, referendum, and recall, 541; on 1912 gubernatorial race, 623; hails destruction of La Follette's political machine, 659
Milwaukee Social Economics Club: 338, 340
Milwaukee *Sunday Telegraph:* 220
Miner, Jean: 5
Mining: 4, 12, 180, 217, 258
Minkley, Carl: 642
Minneapolis, 83, 112, 117, 122. *See also* Twin Cities
Minneapolis *Tidende:* 443
Minnesota: 29, 55, 73, 83, 325
Mississippi River: 39, 82
Mississippi River Logging Company: 84, 85
Mississippi Valley Lumbermen's Association: 84
Missouri: 29, 180, 195, 515
Mitchell, John: 60, 163, 262
Mitchell, William: 313
Mitchell & Lewis Wagon Works: 100, 113
Mitchell Wagon Works: 217, 245
Modine Manufacturing: 113
Mole Lake Band (Chippewa): 191
Monroe: 53
Monroe County: 45, 192
Montgomery, Richard B.: 197, 200–201
Montgomery Ward catalog: 308
Moore, Ransom A.: 60
Moore Manufacturing and Foundry Company: 110
Morgan, J. P.: 111, 120, 626
Morris, Lucy: 351
Morris, Stuart: 604
Morris, Thomas: 239; and La Follette, 616; and Clement P. Host, 627; at Sol Levitan rally, 628; 1912 elections, 651–652; faces anti-Catholicism, 653–654; 1914 primary results, 654
Mosely Education Commission: 386
Mosinee: 94
The Motor (WCTU magazine): 344, 348
Mount Sinai Hospital: 231
Movies: 308–309
Mt. Pleasant: 141
Municipality (magazine): 174
Municipal services, 129; in Milwaukee, 130, 144, 163–164, 166–172; improvements in, 143–144; in Madison, 144–145; provided by private entrepreneurs, 145–146; in Superior, 160–161; incorporation of, 173–175

Municipal Voters League (Madison): 162
Murphy, Jerre: 460–461
Muskego: 310
Myself (by John R. Commons): 572

Naprzod (newspaper): 165
Narragansett Electric Light Company of Providence: 109
Nash, Charles W.: 115
Nash Corporation: 115, 133. *See also* Jeffery Company
The Nation: 587
National Advocate: 201. *See also Wisconsin Weekly Advocate*
National Agricultural Organization: 645
National American Woman Suffrage Association: 344, 346, 348
National Association of Manufacturers: 262, 282–283, 545
National Child Labor Committee: 267, 508–509
National Christian Citizenship League: 353
National Civic Federation: 262, 282, 581, 583
National Civil Service Reform League: 583
National Conference of Charities and Corrections: 157
National Consumers' League (NCL): 273, 334–335, 340, 343
National Dairy Union (NDU): 69
National Education Association: 361
National Farmers Union: 644
National Founders Association: 282
National Metal Trades Association: 121, 262, 282
National Municipal Labor League: 280
National Municipal League: 174, 536, 581
National Popular Government League: 581
National Progressive Republican League: 490, 515–516, 613, 616
"National Republican party": 479
National Society for the Promotion of Industrial Education: 581
National Tax Association: 491
National Woman's party: 350, 352
National Women's Trade Union League (NWTUL): 335
Nebraska: 29
Necedah: 128, 319
Neenah: milling, 83; boot-and-shoe factories, 88; foundry and machine tool industry, 88; and Kimberly, Clark & Company, 93; industrialization, 136; public

utilities, 152; municipal services, 173, 318; labor, 245, 285–286, 290
Neenah and Menasha Water Power Company: 93
Neenah Boot & Shoe Company: 290
Negroes: use of term, 149n. *See also* Blacks
Neighborhood House (Madison): 162
Nelson, John M.: 442
Neopit: 188
Nesbit, Robert C.: assesses Progressive era, 661
Neville, Ella: 339
The New Citizenship: Origins of Progressivism in Wisconsin (by David P. Thelen): 576
"New education": John Dewey and, 360; Charles McCarthy and, 361; tenets of, 362; and secondary education, 371; and vocational schools, 371; and kindergartens, 371–372; schools as community social centers, 372–373; UW and, 375–380; and Wisconsin Idea, 380; Charles P. Cary opposes, 392; and public libraries, 393–397; and State Historical Society, 398; benefits to society, 579
New England: 40, 180
New Hampshire: 46
New Holstein: 88
New Jersey: 45, 87, 515
New North: agriculture in, 34; resettlement of, 75; foreign-born population, 209; immigrant labor, 217; societies, 232; public libraries, 394
New Orleans: 49
Newspapers: controlled by lumber barons, 124; promote industrialization, 136; black press, 201; foreign-language, 205, 226–227, 307; recruit workers, 217; on workplace conditions, 264; exposés on child labor, 267; growth of, 306–307; and sports, 324; La Follette and, 459. *See also specific newspapers*
New York: 40, 46, 49, 105, 109, 112, 508, 515; and workmen's compensation law, 546–547
New York Call: 567
New York City Railway Company: 109
New York *Evening Post:* 66
New York Life Insurance: 503
New York *Mail Express:* 567
New York's Bureau of Municipal Research: 572, 600
New York *Times:* 515
New York World: 617
New Zealand: 577
Neystrom, Paul H.: 395

Nineteenth Amendment: 336, 348, 351
Nolen, John: 163, 506
Non-Partisan Act: 161
Norris, George: 520
North, Sterling: 36
North American Company: 310
North Chicago Rolling Mill Company: 120
North Dakota: 617
Northern Pacific Railroad: 117
Northern Wisconsin Farmers Association: 72, 73
Northern Wisconsin Immigration and Improvement Association. *See* Commercial Association
North Milwaukee: 109, 133, 316
North Side Civic League (Milwaukee): 158
North Western and Omaha Railway: 123
Northwestern Life Insurance Company of Milwaukee: 429
Northwestern Lumber Company: 83
Northwestern Mutual of Milwaukee: 502–503
Northwestern Paper and Pulp Manufacturers' Association: 94, 285
Northwestern Steel & Iron Works: 95
Northwestern University: 323–324
Norwegian language: 72–73, 227, 394
Norwegians: immigrants, 40, 181–182, 209; and agriculture, 44; homesteaders, 72; in Eau Claire, 142; workers, 217; and religion, 224; societies, 228; political affiliations, 412; Edward Scofield and, 428; James O. Davidson and, 495–496; and Swedes, 496–497; and anti-Catholicism, 653–654. *See also* Scandinavians
Nowiny Polski (newspaper): 227

Oats: 13, 29, 43
O'Connor, George: 644
Oconomowoc: agriculture, 33; public utilities, 155; and interurban railways, 310; and tourism, 325
Oconto: 188
Oconto County: southern and eastern Europeans in, 206; Polish Catholics in, 224; labor force, 244; and woman suffrage, 346; rural social center in, 358; and education, 367; La Follette carries in 1900 caucus, 453; and Progressivism, 492
Odenbrett, George L.: 313
Ohio: 29, 99, 108, 180, 195, 515
Old Abe: 7
Old Dane: 447, 448. *See also The State*
Old North: 75

Index 719

The Old World in the New (by Edward A. Ross): 234
Olin, Helen Remington: 344
Olin, John M.: 162–163, 344
Olmsted, Frederick Law, Jr.: 2
Oneida County: 66, 191
Oneida Tribe: 187, 190, 191
O'Neill, William: 416, 520
Order of the Sons of Italy: 231
Orthodox Christians: 225, 226
Orthodox Judaism. *See* Jews
Orton, Philo A.: 417, 529
Oshkosh: and depression of 1893-1897, 19; milk production, 53; clothing industry, 88; manufacturing, 90, 96; automobile industry, 99–100; foundries, 103; population and demography, 127, 136, 142, 318; urbanization, 127; municipal services, 129; housing, 148–149; public utilities, 152–153; and logging, 188; labor, 236, 245, 286–287, 290; and WSFL, 291, 293; WFWC convention in, 335; normal schools, 374; extension field district in, 385; asylum in, 505
Oshkosh Electric Light and Power Company: 152–153
Oshkosh *Labor Advocate*: 286
Oshkosh *Times*: 459
Ottawa Tribe: 179
Otto, Max: 382
Our Church Life: 355
Outagamie County: cabbage production, 45; papermaking, 93; population and demography, 137; and Oneida Tribe, 190–191; and voting privileges, 237; labor force, 244; rural social center in, 358
Outlook: 386–387, 564, 566
Owen, Walter C.: 657
Ozaukee County: decline in farm acreage, 27; apple production, 45; lumbering, 82n, 91; foreign-born population, 209; and voting privileges, 237

Pabst Brewing Company: at World's Columbian Exposition, 4, 8; in Bay View, 107; slogan battle with Schlitz, 112; and immigrant labor, 215; and workmen's compensation, 545
Pabst Theater (Milwaukee): 327
Paine, Nathan: 287
Paine Lumber Company: 96, 287
Palestinians: 204
Palmer, Lucien H.: 202
Pan-American Exposition: 49

Papermaking: rise of, 90–96; reliance on waterpower, 91; steam turbine in, 91; kraft process, 92; Neenah and Menasha Water Power Company organized, 93; trade associations, 93–94; in southeastern Wisconsin, 97; amalgamation of industry, 121; and labor, 244, 248; and railroads, 244, 248, 309; manufacturers oppose waterpower legislation, 556
Paris World's Fair (1900): 117
Parker, James R.: 199n
Parker, W. N.: 362
Parker Fountain Pen Company: 116
Park Hotel (Madison): 476
Parr, Charles H.: 104n
Patronage: 401–402, 439–440, 451, 460–461, 467, 476
Patrons of Husbandry: 416
Patten, Simon: 591
Pattison, Martin: 160–161
Patzer, Conrad E.: 364
Pawling and Harnischfeger Company: 109
Payne, Henry Clay: and Milwaukee public utilities, 154; and municipal reform, 163, 167; as corporate executive, 403; supports civil service law, 424; controls Republican party, 427; and La Follette, 436, 440, 445, 452; and 1892 campaign, 439; Republican Club of Milwaukee County opposes, 449; pursues national politics, 451, 467–468; and H. G. Kress, 452, 469; and Stalwart Republicans, 460; and Wisconsin Republican League, 466; dies, 482
Payne-Aldrich Tariff: 436
Pearse, Carroll G.: 373
Peary, Robert E.: 112
Peck, George W.: and Plankinton Bank failure, 17; gubernatorial term, 408; 1904 elections, 481
Peck's Bad Boy (by George W. Peck): 408
Peirce, Neal: 610
Peninsula State Park: 506
Pennsylvania: 105, 180, 515
People's party. *See* Populists
People's Realty Company: 280
Pepin County: 208, 522
Periodical Publishers' Association of America: 617
Perkins, George W.: 626
Perry, Charles: 560, 624
Personal Liberty League: 185
Pfister, Charles: indicted, 146, 168; and municipal reform, 163; and William Upham, 409; and 1896 state Republican convention, 444; and Republican party, 451, 468;

buys Milwaukee *Sentinel,* 462; and Wisconsin Republican League, 466; discredited, 482; and 1910 elections, 520; Emanuel Philipp rejects counsel, 662
Pfister and Vogel: 105, 111–112
Pfister Hotel (Milwaukee): 325, 474
Philadelphia: 105, 617
Philadelphia Centennial Exposition: 305
Philadelphia City Club: 379
Philipp, Emanuel: and University of Wisconsin, 59; and county-wide school boards, 368; supports State Board of Education, 392; and La Follette, 451; publishes *Political Reform in Wisconsin,* 460; and direct primary, 461–462, 466; on Hagemeister bill, 463; and Wisconsin Republican League, 466; publishes *The Truth about Wisconsin Freight Rates,* 475; celebrates victory over railroad regulation, 476; publishes *Red Book* of railroad rates, 481; and Stalwarts, 482, 613–614; and railroad-Stalwart campaign, 485–486; on 1907 legislature, 501; and 1910 elections, 520; and second-choice provision, 539–540; and UW, 572; exploits cracks in Progressive party, 611; and William Harvey Allen, 641; and Home Rule and Taxpayers League, 649–650; 1914 gubernatorial race, 650–652; and Andrew Dahl, 652; 1914 elections, 654, 656–657; hails defeat of Wisconsin Idea, 659; as governor, 661–662
Philippines Constabulary Band: 325
Phillis Wheatley (Civic) Club: 201–202
Pierce, Charles: 649–650
Pierce County: 358, 525
Pierce-Racine Company: 113
Pinchot, Gifford: 78, 520, 566, 645
Pittsburgh: 87, 108, 508, 538, 559
Plains Indians: 193–194
Plankinton, John: 112
Plankinton, William: 10, 17
Plankinton Bank of Milwaukee: 10, 16, 17
Plankinton Corporation: 106–107, 112
Plankinton House: 197–198
Platteville: 374, 507
Pleasant Ridge: 195
Plunkett, Sir Horace: 78, 563, 645
Plymouth: 90, 155, 310
Plymouth Congregational Church: 354
Poles: homesteaders, 72; immigrants, 139, 181, 203–204, 206, 208–212; and housing, 148–149, 158; and Milwaukee Anti-Vaccination Society, 151; and Social Democratic party, 165, 169; population and demography, 206; workers, 213–217, 244–245; stereotypes, 214; and intermarriage, 221; in Milwaukee, 222; and religion, 223–226; societies, 229; and labor unions, 235–236; and politics, 236–237, 412–413; and Prohibition, 237
Polish Educational Society: 229
Polish Industrial Union: 206
Polish language: 72, 226, 373, 394
Polish National Alliance (PNA): 229
Polish National Catholic Church: 225
Polish Organization of America: 229
Polish Roman Catholic Union (PRCU): 229
Political Equality League (PEL): formed, 349; and WWSA, 349–352; Belle Case La Follette and, 350; and legislature, 351
Political Science Quarterly: 567
Politics: and depression of 1893-1897, 18–19; corruption and graft, 146–147, 167–169, 414, 438, 450; blacks and, 202; immigrants and, 236–238; Prohibition and, 238–239; anti-Catholicism and, 239; unions and, 278–298; ethno-cultural party system, 401–402, 405–406, 410–414; voting trends, 410; committeemen, 411; dissenters challenge two-party dominance, 414–415; and depression of 1893-1897, 415; and direct primary election, 420, 427, 457–458, 461–463, 471–472, 482; and corrupt practices act, 427; La Follette's use of patronage, 439–440, 467; 1912 elections, 621–624; legislation regarding, 636, 640–641
Polk County: cheese production, 54; and Chippewa Tribe, 191; southern and eastern Europeans in, 208; and Orthodox churches, 224
Polonia Hall (Kenosha): 229
Population: urban growth, 127; in 1890's, 127–128; demography, 128, 130–131, 137, 139–143, 182; by 1920, 136; "natural increase," 137; rural drain, 139, 254; Indians, 182, 191–192; and interstate migration, 186; native-born, 186; blacks, 194–196; birth rate declines, 330
Populist party. *See* Populists
Populists: in Milwaukee, 22, 165–167; and dairy advocates, 47; and municipal reform, 161, 166; and 1894 convention, 278; and MFTC, 278; and William Jennings Bryan, 278–279; and Scandinavians, 414; and 1892 elections, 415; and Democratic voters, 421
Portage: 10–11, 338–339
Portage County: agriculture, 44; butter

Index

zones, 55; and Poles, 205; southern and eastern Europeans in, 206; and Catholics, 224; and Progressivism, 422
Port Edwards: 94
Port Washington: 10–11, 310
Posen (German province): 203
Potatoes: 13, 29, 43–44
Potawatomi Tribe: 179, 188, 191
Poultry: 42
Pound: 207
Presbyterians: 182–183, 358. *See also* Protestants
Prescott: 10–11, 17
The Prevention and Cure of Tuberculosis: 385
Price, Charles W.: 252
Price, William Thompson: 124–125
Price County: 137, 206, 208
Primrose, Town of: 433
Prince Hall Masonic Lodge: 201, 202
Probert, A. C.: 17
Prochnow, Theodore: 423
Progress: Wisconsin's sense of, 1–2; World's Columbian Exposition and, 2–8; conceptions of, 14–15, 23–24
Progressive (Bull Moose) party: 307, 516, 593
Progressivism: overview, vii–xii; World's Columbian Exposition and, 8–9; farm prosperity in, 32; interstate migration in, 186; Robert M. La Follette and, 431–433, 437–438, 573–577, 611–613; complexity and variety of, 611–612; historical legacy, 660–663
Prohibition: David S. Rose opposes, 147; in Madison, 162; ethno-cultural conflicts over, 238–239; and women's societies, 336; WCTU and, 344–345; and politics, 413; debated in 1909 legislative session, 505–506
Prostitution: 146–147, 156–157, 274, 322
Protestants: and APA, 184–185, 421; and Republican party, 236; and Prohibition, 237; and Social Gospel, 352–356, 358; and political affiliations, 412–413, 481–482; and direct primary, 482. *See also* Religion; specific denominations
Prouty, Charles A.: 487
Prudential Insurance: 503
Public health: state intervention proposed, 21; and contagious diseases, 129, 149–150, 192–193; in Milwaukee, 130, 159, 169; unsanitary housing, 149–150; contaminated water, 150; improvements in sanitation, 151; and typhoid fever, 153; in Madison, 159; reform, 159, 169, 177; and Indians, 192; and safety in workplace, 264–265; and schools, 373
Public Service Commission: 502, 599
Public utilities: public ownership of, 7; municipal *vs.* private ownership of, 152–155; consumer dissatisfaction with, 152–155; transportation-electric power monopolies, 154; and consumer co-operatives, 155–156; state legislature and, 156; taxation of, 175–176; regulation of, 176; and lobbyists, 403; and state license fees, 423
Pulaski (Polish settlement): 206
Pullen, Charles F.P.: 450
Pullman Strike: 279
Pyre, James F.A.: 387

Quarles, Joseph V.: 288, 441, 479
Quick, Herbert: 367

Racine: and depression of 1893-1897, 12–13, 14, 19; annexation of farmland, 27; automobiles in, 99–100, 313; tanning industry, 105; industrial growth, 113–114, 136; corporations, 119; and AFA, 121; urbanization, 127; population and demography, 127–128, 136–137, 140–141, 210; municipal services, 129, 173; mass transit, 133; segregation, 141; housing, 148–149; public utilities, 152; and TMERL, 154; poor relief, 157; MML chapter in, 174; blacks in, 195–196, 198, 200–201; societies, 202; southern and eastern Europeans in, 207–208; immigrants in, 211, 216–217; labor, 217, 244, 283, 290; naturalization rates, 218–219; Poles, 224, 229; churches and parishes, 225; societies, 229–230; and corporations, 249; manufacturing in, 249, 259; and WSFL, 291–293; and interurban railways, 310; recreation in, 326; and factory reform, 339; WFWC convention in, 340; and woman suffrage, 346, 543; and moral reform, 355; and Populists, 421; continuation school in, 560
Racine Auto: 114
Racine County: cabbage production, 45; milk condensery in, 53; population and demography, 127, 137, 210; black settlements, 195; southern and eastern Europeans in, 206–208; Russians in, 209; labor force, 244
Racine *Daily Journal*: 13
Racine Electric: 113

Racine *Labor Advocate:* 218
Racine Manufacturing Company: 113–114, 290
Racine Relief Association: 19
Racine Rubber Company: 114
Racine *Times:* 617
Racine Trade and Labor Council (RTLC): 283, 290
Racine Wagon & Carriage Company: 113
Rader, Benjamin: 590
Railroad Commission: 501–502, 584; calls for government intervention, 518; and waterpower franchises, 556–557; and Wisconsin Idea, 599; and securities regulation, 639; and co-operative marketing, 646
Railroads: and depression of 1893-1897, 12; in Cutover, 27; and state immigration board, 71; push resettlement in logged-over areas, 71–72; and logging industry, 83, 124; and Case Specials, 114; consolidation of, 123–124; and industrialization, 130; taxation of, 175–176; labor, 214–215, 217–218, 244, 247–248; wages, 257; unemployment, 263; mileage increases, 309; interurban, 310–311; lobbyists for, 403, 407; and *ad valorem* taxation, 416, 450, 461–462, 464–465, 470–472; and Progressive agenda, 416; and 1897 legislature, 426; and La Follette, 452; regulation of, 458–459, 472–476, 484–488, 501–502; oppose reforestation, 557
Rauschenberger, William J.: 144, 166
Raymond, Jerome H.: 337, 383
Rebecca Chapter of the Eastern Star: 202
Reber, Louis E.: 362, 384–385, 584
Record, George L.: 577
Recreation and leisure: increase in activities, 321–322; sports, 321–324; professional entertainment, 324; fairs, 324–325; parks and resorts, 325–326; in rural areas, 326; in Madison, 326–327; in Milwaukee, 327
Red Cliff Reservation: 191
"Red Gym Convention" (1904): 478–479
Reedsburg: 88
Reform: women and, 337–340, 342; labor, 339–340; social, 353–354; moral, 355; church, 358; educational, 361, 367–369, 373, 380; social, 381–382; achievements of 1911 legislature, 535–568
Relief Association (Racine): 157
Religion: ethno-cultural disputes, 180–183; and political affiliations, 183; and Bennett Law, 183–184; and Edgerton Bible Case, 184; and APA, 184–185; and Sunday blue laws and temperance laws, 185; blacks and, 200–201; immigrants and, 223–225; and politics, 236–237; and Social Gospel, 352–358; and voting trends, 411–412. *See also* Churches; specific denominations
Republican Club of Milwaukee County: Voters League helps form, 164; and reform, 417; and Half-Breed coalition, 427; and direct primary, 430; and La Follette, 449–450; Francis E. McGovern leads, 521, 527
Republican party: and depression of 1893-1897, 18–19; and public utilities, 153, 160–161; in Madison, 162; in Milwaukee, 163–169, 171, 171, 174; and housing, 177; and Bennett Law, 183; religious pietists unite under, 183; disavows APA, 185; blacks and, 202; and immigrants, 236–237; and Prohibition, 238–239; and labor unions, 277; and WSFL, 292–293, 295, 298; Progressive-Stalwart split, 307, 460–466, 483–489; and woman suffrage, 351; and UW, 390; and partisanship in state government, 401–403, 412–414; opposes government intervention, 402–403; and party loyalty, 405; ethnic and religious affiliations, 412; factionalism within, 416, 611, 613–614; and reform, 418; 1894 elections, 421–422; and license fee tax, 423; 1896 elections, 424–425; and Davidson bill, 426; and 1898 elections, 427–428; and Half-Breeds, 427–429, 441, 445, 450–451, 467; and *University Press,* 435; 1902 elections, 466–470; and direct primary, 471–472; and railroads, 472–476; 1904 elections, 476–483; 1904 "Red Gym Convention," 478–479; 1906 elections, 495–498; first gubernatorial primary, 497; 1908 elections, 499; and 1907 and 1909 legislative sessions, 501–512; and labor legislation, 509; and urban voters, 516–517; 1910 elections, 519–526; and 1911 legislative session, 533–566; and commonwealth model, 588; Progressive faction loses votes to SDP, 615; 1913 platform, 632; 1914 elections, 656
Reservations: 187, 188–189
Retail Clerks Association: 288
Review of Reviews: 635
Reynolds Preserving Company: 87
Rhinelander: 291
Rib Mountain: 95
Rice Lake: 290

Index

Richland Center: 90, 346
Richland County: 207, 358, 522
Richmond, Thomas C.: 475, 649
The Rise of the Dairy Industry in Wisconsin (by Eric E. Lampard): 575–576
River Falls: 155, 374
River Street (Milwaukee): 147
Roads: 561–563, 635–636
Robert M. La Follette and the Insurgent Spirit (by David P. Thelen): 576
Rock County: and *Plowing On Sunday*, 36; agriculture, 44, 116; butter zones, 55; and railroads, 97–98; population and demography, 137; Southern and eastern Europeans in, 207–209; labor force, 244
Rockefeller, John D.: 111, 117, 118
Rockford (Ill.): 97–98, 115
Rock River Valley: and railroads, 97–98; and new industrialism, 115–116; manufacturing work force in, 249; and interurban railways, 310
Rodgers, Daniel T.: assesses Progressive era, 578, 585, 609
Roe, Gilbert: 428, 439, 450, 452
Roehr, Julius E.: 417, 463, 502
Roessler, O. F.: 640
Rogers, Alfred T.: 495–496, 531–532
Rogers, William H.: 173–174
Roosevelt, Theodore: and Schlitz ad campaign, 112; on declining birth rates, 330; on UW, 386–387; La Follette and, 454, 490, 522, 581; and changing of Republican guard, 467; and direct primary legislation, 472; and "Red Gym Convention" delegates, 479; sweeps Wisconsin in 1904, 481; speaking tour of Midwest, 520; visits Madison, 566; praises Wisconsin's progress, 568; and "New Nationalism," 577; and Charles McCarthy, 581; La Follette supporters defect to, 617–618; and Francis E. McGovern, 618, 628, 659; wounded in Milwaukee, 621; and 1912 Wisconsin election returns, 621, 624; Stalwarts collaborate with, 623
Root, Elihu: 618
Root, John W.: 2
Rosa, Charles A.: 658
Rose, David S.: and political graft, 146–147, 167–168; and public health, 159; and MML, 164; and Francis E. McGovern, 167, 468, 527; and municipal home rule, 175, 538; at state fair, 325; runs for governor, 468–470; removes pro-La Follette officeholders, 481
Ross, Edward A.: and Social Gospel, 20; and immigrants, 220, 234; and eugenics, 239–240, 642; and Richard Henry Edwards, 356; achieves national reputation, 376; and social reform, 381–382; censured by Board of Regents, 389; Richard T. Ely praises, 571; and Wisconsin Idea, 583; and service state, 594; and immigration restriction, 608
Roth, Filibert: 85
Rothschild: 94
Rubber industry: 248
Rublee, Horace: 22
Rueping Tannery: 105
Rumanians: 204, 206, 208–209, 223
Rural free delivery: 36
Rural Life (magazine): 65
Rusk, Jeremiah: 72
Rusk County: and farm mortgages, 29; name changed from Gates, 72; southern and eastern Europeans in, 206; and politics, 237; and 1910 elections, 522
Russell, Harry: on consolidation of dairy industry, 52; dean of College of Agriculture, 57–58; 1915 annual report, 61–62; and cold-curing of cheese, 62; improves silage quality, 63; and University of Wisconsin Extension Division, 65; and Cutover, 74; and Wisconsin Society of Equity, 78; establishes agricultural science as academic discipline, 382; subcommittee on agricultural education, 508; and continuation/vocational schools, 559; and Charles McCarthy, 645
Russia: 111, 114, 203
Russian language: 204–205
Russians: immigrants, 139, 181, 203–204, 208, 210–211; population and demography, 206; workers, 214, 216; and intermarriage, 221; and religion, 223, 225
Ryan, Edward G.: 431, 570
Rye: 29, 43

Sabin, Ellen C.: 336, 343
St. Benedict the Moor Mission: 200
St. Croix Band (Chippewa): 191
St. Croix County: 54, 208, 244
St. Croix Falls: 325
St. Croix River: 85
St. Gall's Catholic Church: 200
St. John, C. W., Agency, 264
St. Louis: 49, 83, 84, 308
St. Mark's African Methodist Episcopal Church: 200
St. Stanislaus: 224, 226

Sait, Edward M.: 567
Saloons: 105, 146–147, 185, 192, 214, 322
Sanborn, Albert: and Nils Haugen, 443; Industrial Insurance Committee, 509, 545–547; and joint legislative committees, 533; Sanborn-Hattan Compromise bill, 647
Sandburg, Carl: 269
San Francisco: 112
Saturday Evening Post: 307
Saturday Lunch Club: 9, 519, 570–571
Sauk County: 82, 98, 447, 506
Sawyer, Philetus: lumber baron, 84; and William Upham, 409; controls Republican party, 427; overthrows "Boss" Keyes, 435–436; and La Follette, 436, 438, 440; and 1892 campaign, 439; and 1896 state Republican convention, 444; dies, 451, 467
Sawyer: 88
Sawyer County: rural population, 137; and Chippewa Tribe, 191; southern and eastern Europeans in, 206; Progressive representatives from, 492; and 1910 elections, 522
Scandinavians: immigrants, 139, 181–182; population, 186; and naturalization, 219; and religion, 224; and Republican party, 236; and Prohibition, 237, 506; and anti-Catholicism, 239; workers, 244–245; and woman suffrage referendum, 351; in legislature, 406; and political affiliations, 413–414, 481; La Follette and, 441–442; and direct primary, 482; and 1910 elections, 525. *See also* Finns; Norwegians; Swedes
Schlitz Brewing Company: 4, 107, 112
Schlitz Palm Garden (Milwaukee): 199
Schlitz Park: 325
Schloemer, Gottfried: 99
Schmitz, Adolph J.: 517, 523, 525, 614, 623
Schoenecker, Vincenz J.: 169
Schofield: 311
School of Economics, Political Science and History (UW): 376
School of Education (UW): 383
School of Music (UW): 378
School of the Capuchin Order: 200
Schools: University of Wisconsin Extension Division and, 65; services increase, 156; and Civic Center movement, 161–162; and Bennett Law, 183–184; Indian, 190–191; and immigrants, 219, 225; parochial, 225; ethnic, 226; and truancy, 269; and women's societies, 339; county-wide school boards, 363, 367–368; consolidation of, 363–364; rural, 363–368; teacher certification, 364–365, 367–368, 419; normal, 365, 374–375, 390–391, 419; secondary, 371; kindergartens, 371–372; foreign languages taught in, 373; and woman suffrage, 537. *See also* Education; "New education"; University of Wisconsin
Schulz, F. M.: 159
Scofield, Edward: on depression of 1893-1897, 16; and government regulation, 22; and Amalgamated Woodworkers strike, 286; as governor, 409; runs against La Follette, 417, 449–450; 1896 elections, 424, 444; and 1897 legislature, 426; and Republican party, 427–428; and patronage, 451; and 1900 Republican state convention, 453; replaces Samuel A. Cook as Stalwart candidate, 480–481
Scots: 102, 181, 215, 228, 245
Scott, George E.: 622, 630, 634, 651
Seaman, William H.: 167
Seaman Body Corporation: 100
Sears, Roebuck and Company: 36, 87, 308
Secor, Martin M.: 217–218
Seebote (newspaper): 307
Segregation. *See* Discrimination
Seidel, Emil: and vice in Milwaukee, 157; 1908 mayoral election, 168–169; and social reforms, 170; and partisanship, 171–172; and Carl Sandburg, 269; and WWSA, 350; 1910 elections, 517; and Milwaukee Bureau of Economy and Efficiency, 591–592
Serbians: immigrants, 139, 203, 207, 211; and religion, 223, 225; societies, 230
Serbo-American Defense League: 230
Serbo-Croatian language: 203, 205
Settlement House Cook Book (by Elizabeth Black Kander): 231
Settlement houses: 217, 231, 342, 357
Seventeenth Amendment: 540, 636, 648
Seventh Day Adventists: 191
Shaw, Anna Howard: 351
Shaw, Daniel, Lumber Company: 85
Shawano County: butter zones, 55; resettlement of, 75; and Stockbridge-Munsee Tribe, 191; Polish Catholics in, 224; and politics, 237; and voting privileges, 237
Sheboygan: and depression of 1893-1897, 12; attitudes towards tariffs, 19; pea canning, 87; breweries, 88; plumbing supplies, 88; manufacturing, 89–90, 115, 249; foundries, 103; municipal services,

Index

129; population and demography, 136, 210; housing, 147; unsanitary conditions, 150; public utilities, 152, 155; poor relief, 157; naturalization rates, 218–219; and societies, 230; labor, 284–285, 290; and WSFL, 292–293; and interurban railways, 310; social systematization, 316; and factory reform, 339; and moral reform, 355; Populists and, 421
Sheboygan County: canning industry, 54; cheese production, 88; population and demography, 127, 137, 137; southern and eastern Europeans in, 207–208; Russians in, 209; and voting privileges, 237; labor force, 244; and tourism, 326
Sheboygan Falls: 48, 90, 310, 316
Sheep: 29, 39
Shell Lake: 10–11, 17
Sherman, James: 520, 613
Sherman Antitrust Act: 19, 436
Sholes, C. Latham: 305
Sicilians: 204, 207, 230
Siebecker, Robert G.: 438
"The Significance of the Frontier in American History" (by Frederick Jackson Turner): 6
Silver Leaf Charity Club: 201
Simmons Mattress Company: 114, 249, 284, 290
Simons, Algie M.: 350
Simons, May Wood: 350
Sixteenth Amendment: 551
Skandinaven (newspaper): 497, 653
Skating: 321, 324
Skillet Creek Farmers' Club: 326
Slavs: immigrants, 102, 107; population, 206, 210
Slovak language: 204–205
Slovaks: immigrants, 139, 203–204, 207; population and demography, 206; immigrants, 211–212; workers, 214, 216; and religion, 223–225
Slovanska Lipa (newspaper): 230
Slovenian Catholic Union: 230
Slovenian language: 205
Slovenians: immigrants, 203–204, 207, 211; and religion, 223, 225; societies, 230
Smith, George H., Steel Casting Company: 110
Smith, Henry: 17, 165
Smith, Hiram: 46, 57
Smith-Lever Act: 66, 70
Sobieski: 206
The Social Center (by Edward J. Ward): 372
Social Darwinism: 15

Social Democracy of America: 415
Social Democratic Herald: 164–165, 269, 280, 283. *See also* Milwaukee *Leader*
Social Democratic party (SDP): founding of, 21; Victor Berger and, 22; and Wisconsin Society of Equity, 77; in Milwaukee, 157, 165–171, 174, 492; and public health, 159; and municipal reform, 169–171; and BLIS, 177; and trade unions, 235; and Prohibition, 237; and child labor, 268; and MFTC, 279–281; and CLU, 285; and WSFL, 292–295, 298; and woman suffrage, 350–351; denounced by *Catholic Citizen*, 357; and labor reform, 417, 494, 509; and La Follette, 470, 481; in 1907 and 1909 legislative sessions, 501; membership, 516–517; and 1910 elections, 523–526; and 1911 legislative session, 533–566; mistrusts Progressives, 615; gubernatorial vote declines in 1912, 623; 1913 platform, 632; opposes eugenics, 642; and 1914 elections, 655
Social-Democratic Printing Company: 280
Social-Democratic Verein: 278
Social Gospel: Richard T. Ely and, 6, 20, 583; in Milwaukee, 22; and child labor, 267; legislature and, 294; and religion, 352–358
Socialist Labor party: 278
Socialist Party of America: 350
Socialists: Milwaukee debate over merits of, 21–22; and American Society of Equity, 76; and public utilities, 155; and housing reform, 158; blacks and, 202; Finnish activists, 217; and workingmen's associations, 232; and labor unions, 276–281; and WSFL, 292–296; and woman suffrage, 350
Societies: blacks and, 201–202; immigrant, 227–230, 232; unemployed and, 263; women and, 334–345; GFWC, 334–346; and suffrage, 335–336, 345–352; WFWC, 335–341, 347–349; and welfare, 337–338; and libraries, 338; and education, 339; and reform, 339–340; AAUW, 343; WCTU, 344–345; WWSA, 345–352; PEL, 349–352
Society of Equity: and Harry L. Russell, 58; and agricultural economics, 65; and Cutover, 76; and mechanization of agriculture, 138; and woman suffrage, 351. *See also* Wisconsin Society of Equity
Sociological Club (Milwaukee): 339
"The Soil" (by Charles McCarthy): 570–571
Sokols (club): 228, 230

Somers, Peter J.: 17n
Sommers, William: 283
Sons and Daughters of the American Revolution: 398
Sons of Norway: 228
Soo Line: 123
South America: 117
South Dakota: 617
South Milwaukee: and Bucyrus-Erie Company, 104; and Bucyrus Steam Shovel and Dredge Company, 108; industrialization, 133; public utilities, 152; southern and eastern Europeans in, 206; factories, 250
South Side Savings Bank (Milwaukee): 17
South Side Women's Club (Milwaukee): 158
South Slavic Benevolent Union: 230
Spargo, John: 267
Sparling, Samuel: 159
Sparta: 10-11, 335
Spooner, John C.: racial views, 199n; and Republican party, 427; overthrows "Boss" Keyes, 435-436; heads state Republican ticket, 439; and La Follette, 440, 452; pursues national politics, 451, 467-468, 482; and 1900 Republican state convention, 453; and Republican party, 460, 479; and direct primary legislation, 472; resigns U.S. Senate seat, 498; on James O. Davidson, 501n
Spoor, Newcomb: 642
The Sporting and Club House Guide to Milwaukee: 147
Sports: tennis, 321, 323; and increase in leisure time, 321-322; baseball, 322; football, 322-324, 327; golf, 323; reinforce class divisions, 323-324; newspapers and, 324
Stadt Theatre (Milwaukee): 228
Standard Oil: 111, 117
Stanton, Elizabeth Cady: 345
Starkweather, Charles S.: 160-161
Star Union Company of Chicago: 48
The State (newspaper): 448
State Agricultural Society. *See* State Board of Agriculture
State Board of World's Fair Managers: 3, 4
State Capitol Commission: 489
State Federation of Labor (WSFL): founded, 21; and Wisconsin Society of Equity, 77, 301; and Social Democratic party, 165; blacks and, 202; and immigrants, 235-236; on employment, 263; and working women and children, 268, 275, 296-297; and socialists, 276-277, 292, 296, 298, 517-518; and IWW, 280; goals, 291, 297; Frank J. Weber and, 291-296; and Populists, 292; schism in, 293; and state legislature, 294-295; and AFL, 296; and agriculture, 296; and unemployment, 297; lobbies for factory inspection law, 340; and woman suffrage, 351; and labor reform, 417, 508-509; Frederick Brockhausen and, 494; advises Industrial Insurance Committee, 510; Charles McCarthy and, 519; in vocational education coalition, 559; and Progressives, 615; and 1914 elections, 655
State Federation of Labor-Social Democratic Coalition: 543, 545-546
State Federation of Women's Clubs: 21, 298
State Highway Commission: 562
State Historical Society of Wisconsin: 5, 397-398, 518
State immigration board: 73-74
State Life Fund: 564
State Medical Society: 177, 240, 642
State Park Board: 506
State Supervisor of Inspectors of Illuminating Oils: 400
State Teachers Association: 351
State v. Meyer and Nowack: 69
Stearns, Lutie E.: 338, 394, 396
Steel: and "neotechnic revolution," 81; and canning industry, 87; Bessemer process, 100-101; open hearth process, 101; foundries and machine shops, 101-103; and Racine companies, 113; amalgamation of industry, 120-121; and railroads, 123; and labor, 214, 244, 248; wages, 257; unemployment, 263
Steffens, Lincoln: 386, 468, 480
Stephenson, Isaac "Ike": lumber baron, 84; holds public office, 124; and La Follette, 440-441, 451; and Milwaukee *Free Press,* 467; "Red Gym Convention" delegate, 479; runs for U.S. Senate, 483-484; alienated by Progressives, 495, 497, 516; replaces John Coit Spooner in Senate, 498; and 1908 elections, 499-500; and 1910 elections, 520; and Progressivism, 612, 613, 616
Stern, Erich: 537-539, 624
Stevens, Willard T.: 627, 643
Stevens Point: and depression of 1893-1897, 13; breweries, 88; manufacturing, 90, 96; foundries, 103; population and demography, 136, 210; public utilities, 152; Polish Catholics in, 224; manufacturing, 249; normal schools, 374

Stine, Oscar C.: 65n
Stockbridge-Munsee Tribe: 187, 191
Stone, James: 452–453, 495–496
Stone, Jesse: 450
Stout, James H.: role in educational reform, 367, 422, 425; funds libraries, 396; as state senator, 417; and Nils Haugen, 443; at "Red Gym Convention," 479
Stout Institute: 367, 374
Stowell, John M.: 110
Strange, John: 499, 653
Strathearn, Sophia: 348
Strawberries: 45
Strikes: 18, 220, 276, 278–279, 283–291
Stubbs, Walter: 582
Studies in American Social Conditions (by John R. Commons *et al.*): 356
Sturgeon Bay: 87, 319, 325
Suffrage: immigrants and, 238; women's societies and, 335–336; WWSA and, 345–352; woman suffrage in political arena, 346, 351, 511–512, 542–543; WFWC and, 347–349; WCTU and, 348; PEL and, 349–352; socialists and, 350–351; Francis McGovern vetoes woman suffrage bill, 628
Sullivan, Louis H.: 7
Superior: and depression of 1893-1897, 11, 16, 19; milling, 83, 117–118; breweries, 88; foundry and machine tool industry, 88, 103; shipping, 88; Great Lakes metal and machinery belt, 97; industrial growth, 117–118; population and demography, 136–137, 143, 210; housing, 147–148; public utilities, 152–153; poor relief, 157; municipal reform, 160–161; MML chapter in, 174; southern and eastern Europeans in, 207–208; immigrants in, 217; labor 217, 287–288; Polish Catholics in, 224; manufacturing, 259; and WSFL, 292; and women's relief societies, 337; and moral reform, 355; normal schools, 374; extension field district in, 385
Superior *Evening Telegram:* 16, 420, 622
Superior *Leader:* 338
Superior Light and Power Company: 160
Superior Trades and Labor Assembly: 288
Supreme Court (U.S.): 189
Supreme Court (Wisconsin): and oleomargarine, 69; and TMERL, 155; outlaws Bible reading in public schools, 184; and woman suffrage, 346; rules in favor of "Red Gym Convention" proceedings, 479; declares waterpower franchise law unconstitutional, 556; rules on McGovern-Ekern insurance commissioner dispute, 626–627
Swain Wagner, Mary: 349, 351
Swanton, Milo: 42
Swart, Rose C.: 336
Sweden: 111, 181–182, 208–209
Swedes: workers, 215, 217; and religion, 223; Lutherans, 224; and political affiliations, 412; political hostility to Norwegians, 496–497. *See also* Scandinavians
Swedish language: 227, 394
Switzerland: 40, 181–182
Syrians: 204, 208, 223

Taft, William Howard, 490; and La Follette, 520, 581; and Charles Van Hise, 582; becomes ally of Emanuel Philipp, 613; and William Anderson, 617; and 1912 election, 621, 624
Tanning industry: product value, 82; in Milwaukee, 105, 112; in Racine, 113; and labor, 214, 217, 244, 248; and working women, 274
Tarbell, Ida M.: 637
Tariffs: 19
Tax Commission: 584; calls for government intervention, 518; and Wisconsin Idea, 599; first assessments of, 622; and Emanuel Philipp, 661
Taxes: and farming, 31; and relief programs, 157; and redistribution, 175–176; to support UW, 389–390; Edward Scofield and, 409; reform legislation, 419–420, 471, 473, 510–511; 1897 legislature and, 426, 426n; 1899 legislature and, 429–430; and *ad valorem* railroad legislation, 450, 461–462, 464–465, 470–473; and tax commission, 471, 488; state income tax, 510–511, 551–554, 554n
Taxpayers' League (Superior): 160
Taycheedah: 639
Taylor, Frederick W.: 251, 584, 591
Taylor, Graham: 252
Taylor, Henry C.: 63–64
Taylor, Horace A.: 443
Taylor County: 206, 209, 224
Taylor bill: 458
Teasdale, Howard: 273–274, 553, 642
Teasdale Vice Committee: 273–274, 309
Technology: and socio-economic class divisions, 314–315; and social systematization, 314–316; and small towns, 316–317
Tennessee: 195

Tennis: 321, 323
Texas: 84
Theaters: 185, 324, 326–327
Thelen, David P.: assesses Progressive era, 435–436, 576
Things and Ideals (by Max Otto): 382
Thomas, Elizabeth: 350
Thomas, Peter: 202
Thompson, Carl D.: 294, 620
Thwaites, Reuben Gold: 398
Tidende (newspaper): 227
Titsworth, Judson: 354
Tobacco: as alternative to wheat, 40; and dairy farming, 40; as cash crop, 43; legislation to improve quality, 44; and Norwegian-American farmers, 44; and Janesville cigar and cigarette companies, 116; and labor, 248; La Follette supports farmers, 436
Toepler, Frank: 99
Tomah: 10–11
Tramps: 13–14
Transportation: mass transit, 130–135; automobiles, 134; buses, 134; transportation-electric power monopolies, 154; and labor, 247; cycling, 311, 321, 322–323; trolleys, 311; airplanes, 313. *See also* Automobile industry; Railroads
Travelers Insurance: 503
Treasury Department (Wisconsin): 400
Trempealeau County: social stratification, 32; rural life, 35; apple production, 45; southern and eastern Europeans in, 206; religion in, 224
Trolleys: and commuting distance, 131; in Milwaukee, 132–133; service expands, 133; electrification of, 154; in Madison, 155; and Social Democratic party, 170; track mileage, 311
Trumpff, Gustave C.: 17
Tubbs, M. Wes: 647
Tucker, Frank: 524
Turks: 204
Turner, Frederick Jackson: "The Significance of the Frontier in American History," 6; and Progressivism, 9; and Social Gospel, 20; and University of Wisconsin Extension Division, 21; and Henry C. Taylor, 64–65; on college football, 323; achieves national reputation, 376–377; and Charles R. Van Hise, 378; and frontier history, 382, 414; leaves for Harvard, 388; praises Wisconsin's progress, 566; praised by Richard T. Ely, 571–572; and Wisconsin Idea, 583; and commonwealth model, 587; speaks at Indiana University, 597
Turner, John: 201
Turners: 228
Twesme, Albert: 499
Twin Cities: 83, 97. *See also* Minneapolis
Twin Disc Clutch: 113
Two Rivers: aluminum production, 87; shipbuilding, 88; manufacturing, 115; and interurban railways, 311; and social systematization, 316
Tyomies-Eteenpain (newspaper): 227

Ukrainians: 204, 223, 225
Uncle Tom's Cabin (by Harriet Beecher Stowe): 326
Unemployment: 11–13, 23, 128. *See also* Labor
Uniform Municipal Accounting Act: 161
Union Central Life Insurance Company of Cincinnati: 502
Union Label League: 340
Unions: and child labor, 267; Knights of Labor, 276–277, 283; AFL, 276–280, 282–285, 293, 295–296; MFTC, 276–282, 293–294; and politics, 278–281, 292–298; CTLU, 280; IWW, 280–281, 293–294; opposition to, 282–283; in Racine, 283; strikes, 283–291; in Kenosha, 284; in Sheboygan, 284–285; in Neenah-Menasha, 285; Amalgamated Woodworkers Strike, 286–287; in La Crosse, 287; in Ashland and Superior, 287–288; in Madison, 289; WSFL, 291–298; and vocational education, 370. *See also* Socialists
Unitarians: 182–183. *See also* Protestants
United Order of Odd Fellows: 201–202
United States Brewers Association: 351
United States Bureau of Labor Statistics: 273
United States Census Bureau: 40–41, 203
United States Chamber of Commerce: 582
United States Commission on Industrial Relations: 8–9, 233, 263, 299, 582
United States Conference of Mayors: 582
United States Country Life Commission: 32
United States Department of Agriculture, 30, 62, 85
United States Golf Association: 323
United States Immigration Commission: 213
United States Labor Commission: 339
United States Lawn Tennis Association: 323
United States Leather Company: 105

Index 729

United States Steel: 111, 120, 121, 252
University Experiment Station, 33; and migration of young from farms to cities, 37; and canning industry, 46; and Farmers' Institute, 60, 65; established, 60–61; and extension service, 65; and oleomargarine, 69; balances pure and applied science, 382
University Heights (Madison neighborhood): 320
University of Chicago: 252, 445–446, 582
University of Michigan: 386
University of Minnesota: 323
University of Wisconsin (UW): at World's Columbian Exposition, 5, 8; and social reform, 8; Charles Kendall Adams speaks to graduates, 19–20; and regulation of dairy industry, 21; and Stephen M. Babcock, 50; establishes College of Agriculture, 56–59; investigated by Board of Public Affairs, 58–59, 565; unveils first successful gasoline traction engine, 104; students exploited by landlords, 149; and public health, 159; and Edward A. Ross, 220; short courses and folk schools, 226; and domestic science, 255; and labor, 299; and sports, 323–324, 327; and co-education, 343–344; and education reform, 361; and teacher preparation, 365, 374; and normal schools, 374–375, 390–391; Madison campus grows, 375–376; under Charles R. Van Hise, 376, 378–381, 384–387; Graduate School, 376, 381; School of Economics, Political Science and History, 376–377; under Thomas C. Chamberlin, 376–377, 383; under Charles Kendall Adams, 376–378, 383; under Edward A. Birge, 378, 383–384; School of Music, 378; curriculum, 380; College of Letters and Science, 382; and legislature, 386, 389–390, 560–561; and publicity, 387; and academic freedom, 387–389; and public schools, 389–390; and WFLC establish library school, 397; Robert M. La Follette and, 431, 434–435; medical school, 507; calls for increased government intervention, 519; Francis E. McGovern attends, 527; and Progressive reform, 571–574; and Wisconsin Idea, 575, 580, 582–583, 596–597; and social investment, 589; and service state, 594; drawbacks of politicizing, 606; funding grows, 636; Allen survey brands as inefficient, 641; Emanuel Philipp and, 650, 661. *See also* College of Agriculture; College of Engineering; University of Wisconsin Extension Division
University of Wisconsin Extension Division: founded, 21; and College of Agriculture, 57–58, 65–66; and country agent program, 65–66; stems rural population drain, 139; and Wisconsin Conference of Charities and Corrections, 177; and Indians, 190; and International Harvester, 252; and women's societies, 337; Richard Henry Edwards and, 356; and public continuation schools, 370; and social and civic center development, 372; expands, 376, 419; Charles Kendall Adams and, 378, 383; and "new education," 379; Thomas C. Chamberlin and, 382–383; Charles R. Van Hise and, 384; Edward A. Birge and, 384; Louis E. Reber and, 384–385; and publicity, 387; and WFLC start Department of Debating and Public Discussion, 397; and State Historical Society, 398; and vocational schools, 559–560; funding, 561
University Press Bulletin: 387, 435
University Press Bureau: 386
Updike, Eugene G.: 354
Upham, William: 1895 message to legislature, 16; and depression of 1893-1897, 19; and government regulation, 22; and state immigration board, 73; promotes settlement in Cutover, 205; as governor, 408–409, 443; and State Board of Arbitration and Conciliation, 422; becomes political liability, 444
Urbanization: 126–127, 316–318
U'Ren, William S.: 577
Usher, Ellis B.: 180, 659

Van Hise, Charles R.: and William A. Henry, 57; and Charles McCarthy, 78, 387, 559; and co-operative marketing, 78; and eugenics, 240, 642; and women and education, 343; and industrial and agricultural training commission, 362; achieves national reputation, 376; as UW president, 376, 378–379; and "new education," 379–380; books on conservation and business trusts, 381; and UW Extension Division, 384; urges faculty involvement in state government, 386; and Board of Regents, 388; in *Collier's*, 388; defends academic freedom, 389; and UW finances, 389; and normal schools, 390–391; and Charles P. Cary, 391; and State Board of

Education, 392; on agricultural and vocational education commission, 508; on government intervention, 519; heads Conservation Commission, 555; requests additional funding from legislature, 560–561; and La Follette, 570; inspects Philadelphia's efficiency system, 571, 575, 582; and Wisconsin Idea, 571, 575, 582; and professional expertise, 590; and service state, 594; and UW's relationship to state, 597; and expert commissions, 598

Van Mater, T. J.: 253n

Vaudeville: 324, 327

Veblen, Thorstein: 316–317, 320

Vegetables: 40, 43–45

Vermont: 46

Vernon County: agriculture, 44; black settlements in, 195; southern and eastern Europeans in, 207; and Progressivism, 422; 1898 election, 428

Viebahn, Charles F.: 631

Vilas County: resettlement of, 75; and proposed interurban electric railway, 94; and Chippewa Tribe, 191; and Poles, 205; southern and eastern Europeans in, 208; rural social center in, 358

The Vindicator (newspaper): 288

Virginia: 195

Vorwärts (newspaper): 165–166, 278, 279, 280

Voters' Hand-Book: 467

Voters League (Milwaukee): 164, 168

Vulcan Steam Shovel Company: 121

Wales: 180, 181

Walker Manufacturing: 113

Wall, Edward C.: 154, 163, 402, 418

Walsh, David I.: 582

Walworth County: 1910 land values, 34; studied by Charles J. Galpin, 65; and railroads, 97–98; black settlements in, 195; foreign-born population, 209

Ward, Edward J.: 161–162, 372–373

Warner, Sam Bass, Jr.: 132n, 145n

Warren, Lansing: 462

Washburn: 10–11, 17, 290

Washburn County: 207, 209, 492

Washington, Booker T.: 200

Washington County: 83, 209

Water: piped from Waukesha to World's Columbian Exposition, 3, 4; power displaced by "neotechnic revolution," 81; contaminated in cities, 150–151, 153. See also Public utilities

Watertown: 48, 115, 310

Waukesha: population and demography, 136, 210; public utilities, 152; and TMERL, 154; naturalization rates, 218–219; manufacturing work force, 249; and interurban railways, 310; and tourism, 325; and suffrage societies, 346; La Follette carries in 1900 caucus, 453

Waukesha County: pipes water to World's Columbian Exposition, 3, 4; agriculture, 27, 33, 44; southern and eastern Europeans in, 207–208; foreign-born population, 209; and Progressivism, 422; and 1910 elections, 526

Waupaca County: 44, 55, 100, 326

Waupun: 505

Wausau: breweries, 88; foundry and machine tool industry, 88; manufacturing, 88, 90; population and demography, 136; consumer co-operatives, 155; public utilities, 155; naturalization rates, 219; and interurban railways, 311; and labor reform, 340; extension field district in, 385

Wausau Abrasive Company: 95

Wausau *Daily Record:* 324

Wausau Group: 94–95

Wausau Paper Mills: 94

Wausau Sulphate Fibre Company: 94

Waushara County: 33–34

Wauwatosa: 310, 316

Webb, William Walter: 185

Weber, Frank J.: on working women, 274; and MFTC, 280; and Madison unions, 289; and WSFL, 291–292, 296; and Victor Berger, 293; in legislature, 294–295; calls for state constitutional convention, 534

Weekly Advocate (newspaper): 200

Weeks, Francis H.: 17

Weisse, Charles H.: 523

Welfare: proposed state intervention in social work, 21; poor relief, 157; corporate in-house programs, 252; and women's societies, 337–338; legislation, 638

Wells, Oliver E.: 388

Welsh: 228, 245

West Allis: and Allis-Chalmers, 104, 108; industrialization, 133; southern and eastern Europeans in, 206, 210; and immigrant labor, 217; naturalization rates, 218–219; manufacturing in, 249–250

West Bend Aluminum Company: 87

Western Conference. *See* Intercollegiate Conference of Faculty Representatives

Western Foundrymen's Association: 102

Index

Western Paper Manufacturers' Association: 291
Western Publishing Company: 113
West Hotel (Superior): 148
West Milwaukee: 109, 133, 316
West Prussia: 203
West Salem: 517
West Side Catholic Relief Corps: 337
West Superior: 17, 291
West Superior Iron & Steel Company: 17, 117–118
West Virginia: 515
Weyerhaeuser, Frederick: 84
Wheat: and depression of 1893-1897, 13; Wisconsin exceeds national average in production, 29; and conversion to dairy farming, 38–39, 42; as cash crop, 43; James A. Everitt and, 76; collapse of farming, 91. *See also* Flour
Whitbeck, Ray Hughes: 101n, 119
White, William Allen: 579
Whitefish Bay: 325
Whitehead, John: promulgates railroad legislation, 429, 464, 503; on La Follette, 439–440, 459, 468–469; and 1900 Republican state convention, 453; and direct primary, 472
Whitehead bill: 429, 451
Whiteside, William J.: 643
Whitewater: 155, 323, 374
Whitewater Normal School: 552
Whiting, George A.: 555
Whitnall, Annie Gordon: 350
Whitnall, Charles P.: 350
Wilbur, Harry C.: 625–626, 653–654
Wilcox, Fred M.: 628
Wild Rose: 34
Willard, Frances: 5, 344
Williams, Burt: 523
Wilson, Woodrow: 516, 577, 581; Wisconsin Democrats unite behind, 614; assisted by Walter Houser's outburst, 619; and 1912 Wisconsin election, 621, 624; weakens Progressive cause, 631
Winnebago County: and depression of 1893-1897, 14; land values, 34; papermaking, 93; population and demography, 127, 137; southern and eastern Europeans in, 206–208; Russians in, 209; labor force, 244; La Follette speaks at fair, 447
Winnebago, Lake: 39, 43, 55, 82n
Winnebago Tribe: cedes land to U.S., 179; use of term, 180n; and allotment, 187–188; livelihood, 190; population, 191–192

Winneconne: 88
Winona (Minn.): 84, 324
Winterbotham, Ruth: 5
Wisconsin Advancement Association: 72
Wisconsin Afro-American: 197, 201
Wisconsin Agricultural Experiment Station. *See* University Experiment Station
Wisconsin Agriculturist: 270–271, 324, 325
Wisconsin Association of Manufacturers: 300
Wisconsin Bankers' Association (WBA): 122
Wisconsin Baptist Convention: 200
Wisconsin Canners Association: 88
Wisconsin Central Railway: 205, 309, 325, 464, 473
Wisconsin Chamber of Commerce: 174–175
Wisconsin Cheese Makers Association: 51, 67
Wisconsin Children's Home Society: 331
The Wisconsin Citizen (newspaper): 347
Wisconsin Colonization Company: 72
Wisconsin Conference of Charities and Corrections: 177, 518
Wisconsin Consumer's League: 298, 343, 345, 348, 518
Wisconsin Conservation Commission. *See* Conservation Commission
Wisconsin Country Life Conference. *See* Country Life Movement
Wisconsin Country Magazine: 61, 254
Wisconsin Cranberry Sales Company: 45
Wisconsin Dairymen's Association (WDA): and conversion from wheat to dairying, 39; and improvement of dairy breeds, 47–48; as embodiment of dairy revolution, 47–49; and cattle disease, 48; and boards of trade, 48–49; and industrial revolution, 49; as parent of College of Agriculture, 56; promotes dairy education and regulation, 56; and agricultural economics, 64–65; and government funding and regulation, 67, 70–71; and butter labeling law, 68; and oleomargarine, 68–69; lobbies for State Department of Agriculture, 69–70; and educational reform, 70; and pure food and drug laws, 70; and road improvement, 70; hegemony erodes, 71; and Wisconsin Society of Equity, 77, 138; and mechanization of agriculture, 138; opposes labor legislation, 300; lobbyists for, 403; endorses La Follette, 441; splits from Progressive reform coalition, 492; and Wisconsin Idea,

575–576, 589; and agricultural legislation, 644
Wisconsin Day (World's Columbian Exposition): 3, 7
Wisconsin Development Association: 72
Wisconsin Education Association (WEA): 361
Wisconsin Efficiency Bureau: 641
Wisconsin Equity News: 76, 77
Wisconsin Farmer: on mortgages, 28; assesses 1898, 31; praises College of Agriculture, 66; and gospel of agricultural progress, 254; on tenant farms, 254; endorses La Follette, 441
Wisconsin Federation of Women's Clubs (WFWC): formed, 335; philosophy of, 335–336; relief efforts, 337; and libraries, 338; and education, 339; and reform measures, 339–340; and "municipal housekeeping," 340–341; and suffrage, 347–349; and labor laws, 508–509; lobbies for government intervention, 518
Wisconsin Free Employment Office: 263
Wisconsin Free Library Commission (WFLC): 338, 384–385, 394, 396–397
Wisconsin Gas and Electric Company: 133
Wisconsin Geological and Natural History Survey: 561
Wisconsin Historical Collections: 398
Wisconsin Home and Farm School: 331
Wisconsin Idea: Richard T. Ely and, 8; in dairying, 25; Charles McCarthy and, 376; Charles R. Van Hise and, 380; and UW, 386, 596–597; Charles P. Cary and, 392; Legislative Reference Library and, 397, 594–596; origins, 574–577; prototypes, 577–578; and antimonopolism, 579; and social bonds, 579, 585; and social efficiency, 579, 591–592; leaders of, 580–583; as model, 583–584; and commonwealth model, 585–588; and social investment, 588–589; and new individualism, 589–590; and professional expertise, 590–591; and economy in government, 592; and education, 593; and service state, 593–594; and expert commissions, 598; and BLIS, 599; and Railroad Commission, 599; and Tax Commission, 599; and Board of Public Affairs, 599–600; and appointive commissions, 600–601; and popular control, 601–602; and state-local government partnership, 602–603; inconsistencies and errors, 603–607; and women, 606–607; and blacks, 608; and immigrants, 608; and Indians, 608

The Wisconsin Idea (by Charles McCarthy): and education, 558; compilation, 569; publication, 569–570; and Richard T. Ely's works, 571; UW criticized in, 572; receives favorable reviews, 581; and new individualism, 588–589; praises Frederick A. Cleveland, 591; and UW's relationship to state, 597; on administration, 600
Wisconsin Immigration and Development Association: 73, 205
Wisconsin Industrial Commission. *See* Industrial Commission
Wisconsin Journal of Education: 361, 391
Wisconsin Library Association: 396
Wisconsin Library Bulletin: 394, 395
Wisconsin Life Insurance Company of Madison: 502
Wisconsin Manufacturers' Association (WMA): 121–122; on railroad regulation, 474, 485; opposes labor legislation, 544; opposes income tax, 554; in vocational education coalition, 559
Wisconsin Marine and Fire Insurance Company Bank: 10
Wisconsin Medical Journal: 177
Wisconsin Paper Manufacturers Association: 93–94
Wisconsin Patriot (APA newspaper): 184, 239
Wisconsin Pea Packers' Association: 88
Wisconsin Power and Light Company: 310
Wisconsin Rapids: and depression of 1893-1897, 13; attitude towards tariffs, 19; agriculture, 45; papermaking, 92; public utilities, 152; consumer co-operatives in, 155; portrayed in novel, 319
Wisconsin Republican League: 466–467
Wisconsin River Valley: and depression of 1893-1897, 12; agriculture, 34, 44–45; and lumber barons, 83; papermaking, 92–95; Wausau Group builds dam, 94; industrialization, 136; and labor unions, 290–291; and interurban railways, 310
Wisconsin Sabbath Association: 353
Wisconsin State Federation of Labor. *See* State Federation of Labor (WSFL)
Wisconsin Society of Equity: and *Wisconsin Equity News,* 76; and co-operatives, 76–78; and WSFL, 296; supports labor legislation, 301; represents farmers, 518; Charles McCarthy and, 519; promotes agricultural prosperity, 563; and agricultural legislation, 644–645
Wisconsin State Journal (Madison): on industrialization, 135; on David S. Rose, 167n; on automobiles, 313; on women's socie-

ties, 340; on churches and Social Gospel, 355; and La Follette, 449, 459; Stalwarts purchase, 481; on 1913 Pennsylvania delegation, 584; defends income tax, 622; on Francis E. McGovern, 629; on Thomas Morris, 651
Wisconsin Sunday Rest Day Association: 185
Wisconsin Teachers' Association (WTA): and "new education," 361; Charles McKenny addresses, 362; on rural teachers, 364; Fassett A. Cotton addresses, 366; supports county-wide school boards, 367; supports public continuation schools, 370; and UW public school inspections, 391
Wisconsin Telephone Company: 152, 173, 274, 403
Wisconsin, University of. *See* University of Wisconsin (UW)
Wisconsin Valley Advancement Association: 94, 136
Wisconsin Valley Lumbermen's Association: 84
Wisconsin Valley Plan: 156
Wisconsin Weekly Advocate: 197, 201
Wisconsin Weekly Defender: 201
Wisconsin Woman's School Alliance: 338
Wisconsin Woman Suffrage Association (WWSA): platform, 345, 348–349; and legislature, 346, 351; membership, 346–348; and *Wisconsin Citizen,* 347, 352; and equal rights argument, 348; and PEL, 349–352; and socialists, 350–351
Wolfe, William: 517
Woman suffrage. *See* Suffrage
Woman's Christian Temperance Union (WCTU): 334; goals, 344–345; Olympia Brown and, 345; and suffrage, 348; and legislature, 351; and public libraries, 396
Woman's Club of Madison: 339–340, 342
Woman's Improvement Club: 201
Woman's National Committee (Socialist Party of America): 350
Women: and World's Columbian Exposition, 5, 8; and social reform, 21; employment and education of blacks, 197–199; societies, 201–202; immigrants, 219; jobs available to, 243, 271–272, 334; rise in women workers, 246; in manufacturing, 247–248; feminization of clerical work force, 255–256; in the professions, 257; wages, 260, 375; and employment agencies, 264; and domestic science, 270; on farms, 270–271, 333; and unions, 272–276; and WSFL, 296–297; changing family dynamics, 327–328; professional housewives, 329; and divorce, 330–331; and industrialization, 331–333; in domestic service, 333; WFWC, 334–336; and reform, 337–340, 549; and education, 339, 343–344; AAUW, 343; WCTU, 344–345, 351; and suffrage, 345–352, 511–512, 542–543, 628; WWSA, 345–352; PEL, 349–352; and socialism, 350–351; Wisconsin Idea ignores, 606–607
Women's Club (Madison): 159, 163
Women's Trade Union League (WTUL): and working women, 273; and suffrage, 345; and labor laws, 508–509; lobbies for government intervention, 518
Women's Union Label League: 273
Wood County: proposed interurban electric railway, 94; and Winnebago Tribe, 192; Catholics in, 224; labor force in, 244; and Progressivism, 422
Wood County Reporter: 13
Woods, Jesse: 201
Woodward, Frank A.: 160
Working class: 17–18, 329
Works, John D.: 620
World's Columbian Exposition: 2–9, 22–23; and economic benefits, 3; and "Waukesha Water," 3, 4; Wisconsin Day, 3, 7; Wisconsin exhibits, 3, 5; attendance, 3n; Wisconsin artists at, 5; women at, 5; Frederick Jackson Turner delivers paper, 6; awards won by Wisconsin, 7–8; and dairy farming, 49; Joseph Koenig inspired by German exhibit, 87; E. P. Allis and Company's Reynolds-Corliss engine, 109
World's Congress Auxiliary: 2, 6–7
World's Fair. *See* World's Columbian Exposition
World War I: and European boundary shifts, 204; ends German cultural hegemony, 228; and airplanes, 313; La Follette opposes U.S. intervention, 490
Wright, Frank Lloyd: 7, 9
Wright, Wilbur: 313
Wyalusing State Park: 506
Wyman, Roger: assesses Progressive era, 467, 481, 495, 616

Yankee Hill (Milwaukee neighborhood): 320
Yankees: in Racine, 141; seize control of Wisconsin's socio-economic engine, 180; conflict with Germanic ways of life, 180–181; values and immigrants, 186; and Republican party, 236; and Prohibition, 237;

and women's societies, 341; and woman suffrage referendum, 351; in legislature, 406; political affiliations, 412, 481; and direct primary, 482
Yankeetown (Kenosha neighborhood): 320
Yiddish language: 204–205, 394
Yockey, Chauncey W.: 541

Youmans, Theodora: 335–337, 348, 351–352
Young Men's Christian Association (YMCA): 217, 323

Zimmerman, Albert: 439
Zophy, Gabriel: 640

Index prepared by
JENNIFER MADER

ABOUT THE AUTHOR

JOHN D. BUENKER spent the first twenty-two years of his life in Dubuque, Iowa, gazing across the Mississippi at southwestern Wisconsin. He has spent the last twenty-seven years observing the state from its southernmost corner while teaching United States history at the University of Wisconsin–Parkside in Kenosha. In between, he earned his Ph.D. at Georgetown University and taught at state universities in Maryland and Illinois. He regularly offers courses in the history of Wisconsin and of the Progressive Era, as well as in urban and ethnic history. He is the author of five other books and of dozens of articles on the Progressive period.

ABOUT THE BOOK

THE text was composed in Baskerville by Impressions Book and Journal Services, Inc., of Madison. The book was printed by offset lithography on long-lived paper called Fraser Glacier Opaque. It was bound in Joanna Western Arrestox.

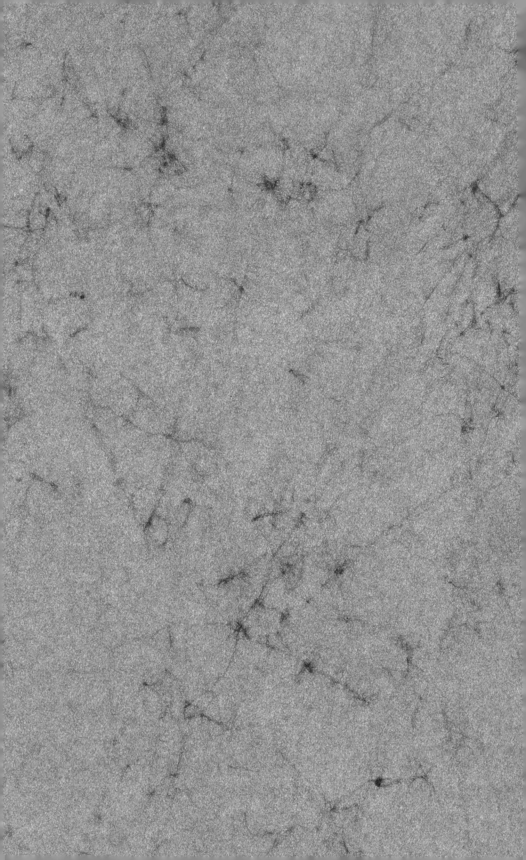